Financial & Managerial Accounting

2005e

Seventh Edition

Belverd E. Needles, Jr., Ph.D., C.P.A., C.M.A.
DePaul University

Marian Powers, Ph.D.
Northwestern University

Susan V. Crosson, M.S. Accounting, C.P.A.
Santa Fe Community College, Florida

Houghton Mifflin Company   Boston   New York

To Professor Reginald R. Rushing, Texas Tech University (Deceased)
To Professor Joseph Goodman, Chicago State University
For my accounting professors at Texas Tech University and Southern Methodist University

Senior Sponsoring Editor: Bonnie Binkert
Senior Development Editor: Margaret M. Kearney
Project Editor: Claudine Bellanton
Editorial Assistants: Lisa Goodman and Rachel Zanders
Senior Production/Design Coordinator: Sarah L. Ambrose
Senior Manufacturing Coordinator: Priscilla J. Bailey
Marketing Manager: Todd Berman

Cover Illustration © James Yang/SIS

PHOTO CREDITS: page 3, ©Edward Holub/CORBIS; page 5, Courtesy of Intel Corporation; page 115, ©DigitalVision/PictureQuest; page 157, ©Getty Images; page 197, © AP/Wide World Photos; page 247, ©Mark Richards/PhotoEdit; page 295, ©Getty Images; page 297, Courtesy of Claire's Stores, Inc.; page 341, ©Jose Luis Pelaez, Inc./CORBIS; page 383, ©BananaStock/Picturequest; page 385, Courtesy of J.C. Penney Company, Inc.; page 421, ©Getty Images; page 453, ©Ed Young/CORBIS; page 455, Courtesy of Fermi National Accelerator Laboratory; page 499, ©Getty Images; page 539, ©AP/Wide World Photos; page 575, ©Todd Gipstein/CORBIS; page 611, ©DigitalVision/PictureQuest; page 613, Courtesy of Goodyear Tire & Rubber Company; page 657, © AFP/Getty Images; page 699, © Scott Olson/Getty Images; page 747, ©Don Smetzer/Getty Images; page 783, ©Gilles Mingasson/Getty Images; page 815, Courtesy of England, Inc.; page 855, ©Steve Kagan/Getty Images; page 893, ©Stephen Marks/Getty Images; page 895, Courtesy of Enterprise Rent-A-Car; page 939, ©Sergio Piumatti; page 981, ©Ken Redding/CORBIS; page 983, Courtesy of Harley Davidson, Inc. page 1019, © David Young-Wolff/ Getty Images; page 1053, ©Larry Williams/CORBIS; page 1055, Courtesy of Nokia Corporation; page 1095, © Air Products and Chemicals, Inc., page 1127, ©AP/Wide World Photos, page 1161, ©AP/Wide World Photos.

The Toys "R" Us Annual Report (excerpts and complete) for the year ended February 1, 2003, which appears at the end of Chapter 1, pages 59–94, is reprinted by permission.

The 2003 Annual Report from Walgreens, which appears at the end of Chapter 1, pages 95–113, is reprinted with permission of Walgreen Co.

This book is written to provide accurate and authoritative information concerning the covered topics. It is not meant to take the place of professional advice.

Copyright © 2005 by Houghton Mifflin Company. All rights reserved.

No part of this work may be reproduced or transmitted in any form or by any means, electronic or mechanical, including photocopying and recording, or by any information storage or retrieval system without the prior written permission of Houghton Mifflin Company unless such copying is expressly permitted by federal copyright law. Address inquiries to College Permissions, 222 Berkeley Street, Boston, MA 02116-3764.

Printed in the U.S.A.
Library of Congress Control Number: 2003115630
Instructor's exam copy ISBN 0-618-49652-1
For orders use student text ISBN 0-618-39362-5

123456789-VH-08 07 06 05 04

the Integration of Technology in the Classroom

Online Tutoring from SmarThinking In partnership with SmarThinking, we offer personalized, online tutoring during typical homework hours. Every new text comes with a one-semester passkey that will allow access to three types of services:

- **Live help** provides access to 20 hours a week of real-time, one-on-one instruction. With Internet access, students may interact live online with an experienced SmarThinking "e-structor" (online tutor) between 9 AM and 1 AM EST, every Sunday through Thursday.
- **Questions anytime** enables students to submit questions 24 hours a day, 7 days a week, for response by an e-structor within 24 hours. Students can even submit spreadsheets for personalized feedback within 24 hours.
- **Independent Study Resources** are available around the clock and provide access to additional educational services, ranging from interactive web sites to Frequently Asked Questions posed to SmarThinking e-structors.

NEW! Introduction to Financial Accounting An interactive multi-media product that provides practical, intuitive instruction on fundamental accounting concepts. This CD-ROM combines video, audio, and text in an interactive simulation. The user learns accounting by recording a series of business transactions for a real-world company. Each transaction is described and recorded in everyday business language and reconciled to financial statements prepared in accordance with Generally Accepted Accounting Principles ("GAAP"). An accounting coach tutors students as they proceed through the program. They are not able to move ahead without correctly completing each transaction, and they receive a performance evaluation at the end of the program. This program is designed to help students:

- Understand fundamental accounting terminology
- Become intelligent readers of financial statements
- Value, record, and classify business transactions
- Assess how business decisions affect profits and liquidity

The Needles Accounting Resource Center at http://accounting.college.hmco.com

For Students
- **NEW! ACE,** an online self-quizzing program, with over 1,000 new questions, that allows students to check their mastery of the topics covered in each chapter
- **Research Activities** based on the material covered in each chapter
- **Toys "R" Us Annual Report Activities** that make use of the latest Toys "R" Us financial statements
- **Links** to the web sites of over 200 real companies and annual reports referenced in the book
- **A List of Business Readings** from leading periodicals
- **Check Figures** for end-of-chapter problems

For Instructors
- **NEW!** A brand new set of **PowerPoint Slides** that will enhance classroom presentation of text material; the new slides are concise, contain lots of examples of transactions, and explain the accounting process in clear, easy-to-follow steps
- **Text previews,** which highlight new features and provide demonstrations of supplements
- **Sample syllabi** from other first-year accounting faculty
- *Accounting Instructors' Report* newsletter, which explores a wide range of contemporary teaching issues
- **Electronic Solutions,** fully functioning Excel spreadsheets for all text exercises, problems, and cases from the printed Instructor's Solutions Manual

Teaching Accounting Online This online training course from Faculty Development Programs provides suggestions for integrating new technologies into accounting education. Available within Blackboard.com, the course includes the following modules: Designing Course Basics; Be the Student; Common Online Tools; Designing Teaching Strategies; Designing Learning Activities; Designing Outcomes Assessment; and Delivering a Course. For more information, contact your Houghton Mifflin sales representative or our Faculty Services Center at (800) 733-1717.

Brief Contents

1 Uses of Accounting Information and the Financial Statements 2

Supplement to Chapter 1 How to Read an Annual Report 49

2 Measuring Business Transactions 114

3 Measuring Business Income 156

4 Accounting Information Systems 196

5 Financial Reporting and Analysis 246

6 Merchandising Operations and Internal Control 294

7 Short-Term Financial Assets 340

8 Inventories 382

9 Current Liabilities 420

10 Long-Term Assets 452

11 Long-Term Liabilities 498

12 Contributed Capital 538

13 The Corporate Income Statement and the Statement of Stockholders' Equity 574

14 The Statement of Cash Flows 610

15 The Changing Business Environment: A Manager's Perspective 656

16 Cost Concepts and Cost Allocation 698

17 Costing Systems: Job Order Costing 746

18 Costing Systems: Process Costing 782

19 Activity-Based Systems: ABM and JIT 814

20 Cost Behavior Analysis 854

21 The Budgeting Process 892

22 Standard Costing and Variance Analysis 938

23 Performance Management and Evaluation 980

24 Short-Run Decision Analysis 1018

25 Pricing Decisions, Including Target Costing and Transfer Pricing 1052

26 Capital Investment Analysis 1094

27 Quality Management and Measurement 1126

28 Financial Performance Evaluation 1160

Appendix A The Merchandising Work Sheet and Closing Entries 1205

Appendix B Special-Purpose Journals 1213

Appendix C Accounting for Unincorporated Businesses 1227

Appendix D International Accounting 1237

Appendix E Long-Term Investments 1244

Appendix F The Time Value of Money 1251

Appendix G Future Value and Present Value Tables 1264

Contents

Preface xxi
To the Student xxxiii
About the Authors xxxviii
Check Figures xxxix

1 Uses of Accounting Information and the Financial Statements 2

■ DECISION POINT Walgreen Co. 2

ACCOUNTING AS AN INFORMATION SYSTEM 4

Business Goals, Activities, and Performance Measures 4

■ VIDEO CASE Intel Corporation 5

■ FOCUS ON BUSINESS PRACTICE
How Do Performance Measures Relate to Executive Bonuses? 7

Financial and Management Accounting 7

Processing Accounting Information 7

■ FOCUS ON BUSINESS PRACTICE
What Does Walgreens Have to Say about Itself? 7

■ FOCUS ON BUSINESS PRACTICE
How Did Accounting Develop? 8

DECISION MAKERS: THE USERS OF ACCOUNTING INFORMATION 8

Management 9

Users with a Direct Financial Interest 9

■ FOCUS ON BUSINESS PRACTICE
What Does the CFO Do? 10

Users with an Indirect Financial Interest 10

Governmental and Not-for-Profit Organizations 10

ACCOUNTING MEASUREMENT 11

What Is Measured? 11

Business Transactions as the Object of Measurement 11

Money Measure 11

The Concept of Separate Entity 12

THE CORPORATION AS A SEPARATE ENTITY 12

Corporations Differentiated from Sole Proprietorships and Partnerships 12

■ FOCUS ON BUSINESS PRACTICE
Are Most Corporations Big or Small Businesses? 13

Formation of a Corporation 14

Organization of a Corporation 14

FINANCIAL POSITION AND THE ACCOUNTING EQUATION 15

Assets 15

Liabilities 15

Owners' Equity 16

Some Illustrative Transactions 17

COMMUNICATION THROUGH FINANCIAL STATEMENTS 22

The Income Statement 22

The Statement of Retained Earnings 22

The Balance Sheet 22

The Statement of Cash Flows 24

Financial Statements of Walgreen Co. 25

GENERALLY ACCEPTED ACCOUNTING PRINCIPLES 28

Financial Statements, GAAP, and the Independent CPA's Report 28

Organizations That Influence Current Practice 29

PROFESSIONAL ETHICS AND THE ACCOUNTING PROFESSION 30

■ FOCUS ON BUSINESS ETHICS
Good Ethics = Good Business! 30

Chapter Review 31   Review of Learning Objectives 31
Review of Concepts and Terminology 32   Review Problem 34
Answer to Review Problem 35

Chapter Assignments 36   Questions 36   Short Exercises 36
Exercises 38   Problems 41   Alternate Problems 43

Skills Development Cases 44

Financial Reporting and Analysis Cases 46

Supplement to Chapter 1 How to Read an Annual Report 49

THE COMPONENTS OF AN ANNUAL REPORT 49

Letter to the Stockholders 49

Financial Highlights 50

Description of the Company 50

Management's Discussion and Analysis 50

Financial Statements 50

Notes to Financial Statements 52
Report of Management's Responsibilities 53
Report of Certified Public Accountants 53

Supplementary Information Notes 54

THE ANNUAL REPORT PROJECT 56

2 Measuring Business Transactions 114

■ DECISION POINT Continental Airlines, Inc. & The Boeing Co. 114

MEASUREMENT ISSUES 116

The Recognition Issue 116

■ FOCUS ON BUSINESS PRACTICE
Accounting Policies: Where Do You Find Them? 116

The Valuation Issue 117

■ FOCUS ON INTERNATIONAL BUSINESS
No Dollar Amount: How Can That Be? 117

■ FOCUS ON BUSINESS PRACTICE
Is It Always Cost? 118

The Classification Issue 118

ACCOUNTS AND THE CHART OF ACCOUNTS 118

Stockholders' Equity Accounts 120
Account Titles 120

THE DOUBLE-ENTRY SYSTEM: THE BASIC METHOD OF ACCOUNTING 121

The T Account 121
The T Account Illustrated 122

Analyzing and Processing Transactions 122

TRANSACTION ANALYSIS ILLUSTRATED 124

■ FOCUS ON BUSINESS ETHICS
Are Financial Statements Always Truthful? 126

THE TRIAL BALANCE 131

■ FOCUS ON BUSINESS TECHNOLOGY
Are All Trial Balances Created Equal? 132

RECORDING AND POSTING TRANSACTIONS 133

The General Journal 133
The General Ledger 134
Some Notes on Presentation 136

Chapter Review 136   Review of Learning Objectives 136
Review of Concepts and Terminology 137   Review Problem 138   Answer to Review Problem 139

Chapter Assignments 140   Questions 140   Short Exercises 141   Exercises 143   Problems 146   Alternate Problems 149

Skills Development Cases 152

Financial Reporting and Analysis Cases 153

3 Measuring Business Income 156

■ DECISION POINT Kelly Services 156

PROFITABILITY MEASUREMENT: THE ROLE OF BUSINESS INCOME 158

Net Income 158
Revenues 158
Expenses 158

INCOME MEASUREMENT ISSUES 159

The Accounting Period Issue 159

■ FOCUS ON BUSINESS PRACTICE
Fiscal Year-Ends Vary. 159

The Continuity Issue 159
The Matching Issue 160

ACCRUAL ACCOUNTING 160

Recognizing Revenues When Earned 160
Recognizing Expenses When Incurred 161
Adjusting the Accounts 161

■ FOCUS ON BUSINESS ETHICS
Aggressive Accounting or Deception? You Judge. 161

Accrual Accounting and Performance Measures 162

THE ADJUSTMENT PROCESS 163

Type 1: Allocating Recorded Costs Between Two or More Accounting Periods (Deferred Expenses) 163

■ FOCUS ON INTERNATIONAL BUSINESS
Who Needs Accounting Knowledge? 167

Type 2: Recognizing Unrecorded Expenses (Accrued Expenses) 168

Type 3: Allocating Recorded Unearned Revenues Between Two or More Accounting Periods (Deferred Revenues) 170

Type 4: Recognizing Unrecorded Revenues (Accrued Revenues) 171

■ FOCUS ON BUSINESS TECHNOLOGY
Ecommerce: What's Its Impact? 172

A Note About Journal Entries 172

USING THE ADJUSTED TRIAL BALANCE TO PREPARE FINANCIAL STATEMENTS 172

■ FOCUS ON BUSINESS TECHNOLOGY
Entering Adjustments With the Touch of a Button 175

CASH FLOWS FROM ACCRUAL-BASED INFORMATION 175

Contents **vii**

Chapter Review 176 Review of Learning Objectives 176 Review of Concepts and Terminology 177 Review Problem 178 Answer to Review Problem 179

Chapter Assignments 182 Questions 182 Short Exercises 182 Exercises 183 Problems 186 Alternate Problems 190

Skills Development Cases 192

Financial Reporting and Analysis Cases 193

4 Accounting Information Systems 196

■ DECISION POINT Hershey Foods Corp. 196

ACCOUNTING INFORMATION SYSTEMS: PRINCIPLES OF DESIGN 198

Cost-Benefit Principle 198

Control Principle 198

■ FOCUS ON BUSINESS PRACTICE
How Much Is a Used Computerized Accounting System Worth? 199

Compatibility Principle 199

Flexibility Principle 199

OVERVIEW OF THE ACCOUNTING CYCLE 199

COMPUTERIZED ACCOUNTING SYSTEMS 201

Spreadsheet Software 201

General Ledger Systems 201

■ FOCUS ON BUSINESS TECHNOLOGY
Networking: How to Get It Done 201

Structure of General Ledger Systems 203

ACCOUNTANTS, BUSINESSES, AND THE INTERNET 204

■ FOCUS ON BUSINESS PRACTICE
B to B and EDI: How Much Can They Save? 205

CLOSING ENTRIES 205

■ FOCUS ON BUSINESS TECHNOLOGY
E2K: How Much Time Can It Save? 205

Required Closing Entries 206

The Accounts After Closing 210

■ FOCUS ON INTERNATIONAL BUSINESS
Closing Doesn't Have to Be Such a Headache. 213

THE POST-CLOSING TRIAL BALANCE 213

REVERSING ENTRIES: THE OPTIONAL FIRST STEP IN THE NEXT ACCOUNTING PERIOD 214

THE WORK SHEET: AN ACCOUNTANT'S TOOL 215

Preparing the Work Sheet 216

Using the Work Sheet 222

Chapter Review 225 Review of Learning Objectives 225 Review of Concepts and Terminology 226 Review Problem 228 Answer to Review Problem 229

Chapter Assignments 229 Questions 229 Short Exercises 230 Exercises 232 Problems 236 Alternate Problems 240

Skills Development Cases 242

Financial Reporting and Analysis Cases 243

5 Financial Reporting and Analysis 246

■ DECISION POINT General Mills, Inc. 246

OBJECTIVES OF FINANCIAL INFORMATION 248

QUALITATIVE CHARACTERISTICS OF ACCOUNTING INFORMATION 248

CONVENTIONS THAT HELP IN THE INTERPRETATION OF FINANCIAL INFORMATION 250

Comparability and Consistency 250

■ FOCUS ON BUSINESS PRACTICE
How Much Is Material? It's Not Only a Matter of Numbers. 251

Materiality 251

Conservatism 251

■ FOCUS ON BUSINESS PRACTICE
When Is "Full Disclosure" Too Much? It's a Matter of Cost and Benefits. 252

Full Disclosure 252

Cost-Benefit 252

MANAGEMENT'S RESPONSIBILITY FOR ETHICAL REPORTING 253

■ FOCUS ON BUSINESS ETHICS
Questionable Accounting Practices Are Under Scrutiny. 253

CLASSIFIED BALANCE SHEET 254

Assets 254

Liabilities 256

Stockholders' Equity 257

Other Forms of Business Organization 257

Reading and Graphing Real Company Balance Sheets 258

FORMS OF THE INCOME STATEMENT 260

Multistep Income Statement 260

Reading and Graphing Real Company Income Statements 263

Single-Step Income Statement 264

USING CLASSIFIED FINANCIAL STATEMENTS 266

viii Contents

Evaluation of Liquidity 267
- FOCUS ON BUSINESS PRACTICE
  Who is Right: The Credit-Worthiness Analyst or the Profitability Analyst? 268

Evaluation of Profitability 268
- FOCUS ON BUSINESS PRACTICE
  To What Level of Profitability Should a Company Aspire? 271

Chapter Review 273 Review of Learning Objectives 273 Review of Concepts and Terminology 274 Review Problem 276 Answer to Review Problem 276

Chapter Assignments 277 Questions 277 Short Exercises 278 Exercises 280 Problems 283 Alternate Problems 285

Skills Development Cases 287

Financial Reporting and Analysis Cases 289

6 Merchandising Operations and Internal Control 294

- DECISION POINT Target Stores 294

MANAGEMENT ISSUES IN MERCHANDISING BUSINESSES 296

Cash Flow Management 296
- VIDEO CASE Claire's Stores, Inc. 297

Profitability Management 298

Choice of Inventory System 298
- FOCUS ON BUSINESS TECHNOLOGY
  Bar Codes—How Have They Influenced Choice of Inventory Systems? 299

Control of Merchandising Operations 300

TERMS OF SALE 301
- FOCUS ON BUSINESS TECHNOLOGY
  How Are Web Sales Doing? 301

APPLYING THE PERPETUAL INVENTORY SYSTEM 302

Transactions Related to Purchases of Merchandise 302

Transactions Related to Sales of Merchandise 304
- FOCUS ON BUSINESS PRACTICE
  Are Sales Returns Worth Accounting For? 305

APPLYING THE PERIODIC INVENTORY SYSTEM 306

Transactions Related to Purchases of Merchandise 307

Transactions Related to Sales of Merchandise 308

INTERNAL CONTROL: BASIC COMPONENTS AND CONTROL ACTIVITIES 309

Management's Responsibility for Internal Control 309

Components of Internal Control 310

Control Activities 310
- FOCUS ON BUSINESS ETHICS
  Which Frauds Are Most Common? 311

Limitations of Internal Control 311

INTERNAL CONTROL OVER MERCHANDISING TRANSACTIONS 312

Internal Control and Management Goals 312

Control of Cash Sales Receipts 313

Control of Purchases and Cash Disbursements 314
- FOCUS ON BUSINESS TECHNOLOGY
  How Do Computers Influence Internal Controls? 314

ACCOUNTING FOR DISCOUNTS 318

Sales Discounts 318

Purchases Discounts 318

Chapter Review 319 Review of Learning Objectives 319 Review of Concepts and Terminology 320 Review Problem 322 Answer to Review Problem 322

Chapter Assignments 324 Questions 324 Short Exercises 325 Exercises 326 Problems 330 Alternate Problems 333

Skills Development Cases 335

Financial Reporting and Analysis Cases 337

7 Short-Term Financial Assets 340

- DECISION POINT Pioneer Corporation 340

MANAGEMENT ISSUES RELATED TO SHORT-TERM FINANCIAL ASSETS 342

Managing Cash Needs During Seasonal Cycles 342
- FOCUS ON BUSINESS PRACTICE
  What a Difference a Year Makes! 343

Setting Credit Policies 343
- FOCUS ON BUSINESS PRACTICE
  Why Powerful Buyers Can Cause Headaches for Small Businesses 343

Financing Receivables 345

CASH AND CASH EQUIVALENTS 346

- FOCUS ON BUSINESS ETHICS
  What About the Unlawful Use of EFT? 347

SHORT-TERM INVESTMENTS 347

Held-to-Maturity Securities 348

Trading Securities 348

Available-for-Sale Securities 350

Dividend and Interest Income 350

ACCOUNTS RECEIVABLE 351

Uncollectible Accounts and the Direct Charge-Off Method 351

Uncollectible Accounts and the Allowance Method 352

- FOCUS ON BUSINESS PRACTICE
  Selling Goods and Services is Only Half the Problem. 353

Estimating Uncollectible Accounts Expense 353

- FOCUS ON INTERNATIONAL BUSINESS
  Why Companies in Emerging Economies Must Adapt Accounting Practices 354

Writing Off an Uncollectible Account 357

Recovery of Accounts Receivable Written Off 357

NOTES RECEIVABLE 358

Computations for Promissory Notes 358

- FOCUS ON BUSINESS PRACTICE
  How Long Is a Year? It Depends. 359

Accounting Entries for Promissory Notes 360

PREPARING A BANK RECONCILIATION 362

Chapter Review 364 Review of Learning Objectives 364 Review of Concepts and Terminology 365 Review Problem 367 Answer to Review Problem 368

Chapter Assignments 368 Questions 368 Short Exercises 369 Exercises 370 Problems 373 Alternate Problems 375

Skills Development Cases 378

Financial Reporting and Analysis Cases 380

8 Inventories 382

- DECISION POINT J.C. Penney Company, Inc. 382

MANAGEMENT ISSUES ASSOCIATED WITH ACCOUNTING FOR INVENTORIES 384

Applying the Matching Rule to Inventories 384

- VIDEO CASE J.C. Penney Company, Inc. 385

Assessing the Impact of Inventory Decisions 385

Evaluating the Level of Inventory 386

- FOCUS ON BUSINESS TECHNOLOGY
  Dell's Inventory Turnover Can Make Your Head Spin. 386

- FOCUS ON BUSINESS PRACTICE
  What a Headache! 388

INVENTORY COST AND GOODS FLOW 388

Merchandise in Transit 388

Merchandise on Hand Not Included in Inventory 389

Goods Flow Versus Cost Flow 389

METHODS OF PRICING INVENTORY AT COST UNDER THE PERIODIC INVENTORY SYSTEM 389

Specific Identification Method 390

Average-Cost Method 390

First-In, First-Out (FIFO) Method 391

Last-In, First-Out (LIFO) Method 391

- FOCUS ON BUSINESS PRACTICE
  What's a "Category Killer?" 392

PRICING INVENTORY UNDER THE PERPETUAL INVENTORY SYSTEM 393

- FOCUS ON BUSINESS TECHNOLOGY
  More Companies Enjoy LIFO! 394

COMPARISON AND IMPACT OF INVENTORY DECISIONS AND MISSTATEMENTS 395

Effects on the Financial Statements 396

Effects on Income Taxes 396

- FOCUS ON BUSINESS PRACTICE
  Does a Company's Accounting Method Affect Management's Operating Decisions? 397

Effects of Misstatements in Inventory Measurement 397

- FOCUS ON BUSINESS ETHICS
  The Temptation to Overstate Inventories 398

Inventory Measurement and Cash Flows 399

VALUING INVENTORY AT THE LOWER OF COST OR MARKET (LCM) 399

- FOCUS ON BUSINESS PRACTICE
  How Bad Can It Get? 400

Item-by-Item Method 400

Major Category Method 400

VALUING INVENTORY BY ESTIMATION 401

Retail Method of Inventory Estimation 401

Gross Profit Method of Inventory Estimation 402

Chapter Review 403 Review of Learning Objectives 403 Review of Concepts and Terminology 404 Review Problem 405 Answer to Review Problem 405

Chapter Assignments 408 Questions 408 Short Exercises 409 Exercises 410 Problems 413 Alternate Problems 414

Skills Development Cases 415

Financial Reporting and Analysis Cases 417

9 Current Liabilities 420

- DECISION POINT US Airways, Inc. 420

MANAGEMENT ISSUES RELATED TO ACCOUNTING FOR CURRENT LIABILITIES 422

Managing Liquidity and Cash Flows 422

- FOCUS ON BUSINESS PRACTICE
  Debt Problems Can Plague Even Well-Known Companies. 424

Recognition of Liabilities 424

Valuation of Liabilities 424

Classification of Liabilities 424

Disclosure of Liabilities 425

COMMON CATEGORIES OF CURRENT LIABILITIES 425

Definitely Determinable Liabilities 425

- FOCUS ON BUSINESS PRACTICE
  Small Businesses Offer Benefits, Too. 428

Estimated Liabilities 431

- FOCUS ON BUSINESS PRACTICE
  Those Little Coupons Can Add Up. 432

- FOCUS ON BUSINESS PRACTICE
  Are Frequent-Flier Miles a Liability or a Revenue? 433

CONTINGENT LIABILITIES AND COMMITMENTS 434

PAYROLL ACCOUNTING ILLUSTRATED 434

Computation of an Employee's Take-Home Pay 434

Payroll Register 436

Recording the Payroll 437

Employee Earnings Record 437

- FOCUS ON BUSINESS ETHICS
  Why Is Payroll Fraud Common? 438

Recording Payroll Taxes 438

Payment of Payroll and Payroll Taxes 438

Chapter Review 439 Review of Learning Objectives 439
Review of Concepts and Terminology 439   Review
Problem 440   Answer to Review Problem 440

Chapter Assignments 441 Questions 441   Short
Exercises 442   Exercises 443   Problems 445   Alternate
Problems 447

Skills Development Cases 448

Financial Reporting and Analysis Cases 450

10 Long-Term Assets 452

- DECISION POINT H. J. Heinz Company 452

MANAGEMENT ISSUES RELATED TO ACCOUNTING FOR LONG-TERM ASSETS 454

- VIDEO CASE Fermi National Accelerator Laboratory 455

Deciding to Acquire Long-Term Assets 455

Financing Long-Term Assets 457

Applying the Matching Rule to Long-Term Assets 458

ACQUISITION COST OF PROPERTY, PLANT, AND EQUIPMENT 459

The Importance of Classifying Expenditures Correctly 459

General Approach to Acquisition Costs 459

- FOCUS ON BUSINESS ETHICS
  Is It an Asset or Expense? The Answer Matters. 461

ACCOUNTING FOR DEPRECIATION 461

Factors That Affect the Computation of Depreciation 462

- FOCUS ON BUSINESS PRACTICE
  The Useful Life of an Aircraft Is How Long? 462

Methods of Computing Depreciation 463

- FOCUS ON BUSINESS PRACTICE
  Accelerated Methods Save Money! 466

DISPOSAL OF DEPRECIABLE ASSETS 466

Discard or Sale of Plant Assets 466

Exchanges of Plant Assets 468

ACCOUNTING FOR NATURAL RESOURCES 470

Depletion 470

Depreciation of Closely Related Plant Assets 471

Development and Exploration Costs in the Oil and Gas Industry 471

ACCOUNTING FOR INTANGIBLE ASSETS 472

- FOCUS ON BUSINESS PRACTICE
  Take a Closer Look at Subscriber Lists! 474

Research and Development Costs 474

- FOCUS ON INTERNATIONAL BUSINESS
  Lack of Comparability Is a Real Problem! 474

Computer Software Costs 475

Leasehold Improvements 475

Goodwill 475

- FOCUS ON BUSINESS PRACTICE
  Wake up, Goodwill Is Growing! 476

SPECIAL PROBLEMS OF DEPRECIATING PLANT ASSETS 476

Depreciation for Partial Years 476

Revision of Depreciation Rates 477

Group Depreciation 478

Special Types of Capital Expenditures 478

Cost Recovery for Federal Income Tax Purposes 479

Chapter Review 479 Review of Learning Objectives 479
Review of Concepts and Terminology 480   Review
Problem 482   Answer to Review Problem 483

Chapter Assignments 484 Questions 484   Short
Exercises 485   Exercises 486   Problems 488   Alternate
Problems 490

Skills Development Cases 492

Financial Reporting and Analysis Cases 494

11 Long-Term Liabilities 498

- DECISION POINT AT&T Corporation 498

MANAGEMENT ISSUES RELATED TO ISSUING LONG-TERM DEBT 500

The Decision to Issue Long-Term Debt 500

- FOCUS ON INTERNATIONAL BUSINESS
  Pushed to the Brink of Failure 501

How Much Debt to Carry 501
Types of Long-Term Debt 502
Timing of Long-Term Debt Repayment 502

THE NATURE OF BONDS 503

Secured or Unsecured Bonds 503
Term or Serial Bonds 503
Registered or Coupon Bonds 503

- FOCUS ON INTERNATIONAL BUSINESS
  Choice of Bank Debt Cripples Japanese Firms. 504

ACCOUNTING FOR BONDS PAYABLE 504

Balance Sheet Disclosure of Bonds 504
Bonds Issued at Face Value 504
Face Interest Rate and Market Interest Rate 505

- FOCUS ON BUSINESS PRACTICE
  Check Out Those Bond Prices! 505

Bonds Issued at a Discount 506
Bonds Issued at a Premium 506

- FOCUS ON BUSINESS PRACTICE
  100-Year Bonds Are Not for Everyone. 507

Bond Issue Costs 507

USING PRESENT VALUE TO VALUE A BOND 507

AMORTIZATION OF BOND DISCOUNTS AND PREMIUMS 508

Amortizing a Bond Discount 508
Amortizing a Bond Premium 512

- FOCUS ON BUSINESS TECHNOLOGY
  Speed Up the Calculations! 514

OTHER BONDS PAYABLE ISSUES 515

Sale of Bonds Between Interest Dates 515
Year-End Accrual of Bond Interest Expense 516

RETIREMENT OF BONDS 518

Callable Bonds 518
Convertible Bonds 519

OTHER LONG-TERM LIABILITIES 520

Mortgages Payable 520
Long-Term Leases 520
Pensions 522
Other Postretirement Benefits 523

Chapter Review 523   Review of Learning Objectives 523
Review of Concepts and Terminology 525   Review
Problem 526   Answer to Review Problem 527

Chapter Assignments 528   Questions 528   Short
Exercises 528   Exercises 529   Problems 531   Alternate
Problems 533

Skills Development Cases 534

Financial Reporting and Analysis Cases 535

12 Contributed Capital 538

- DECISION POINT Cisco Systems, Inc. 538

MANAGEMENT ISSUES RELATED TO CONTRIBUTED CAPITAL 540

Forming a Corporation 540
Managing Under the Corporate Form of Business 541
Using Equity Financing 543
Determining Dividend Policies 544
Evaluating Performance Using Return on Equity 545
Using Stock Options as Compensation 546

- FOCUS ON BUSINESS PRACTICE
  When Are Stock Options Worthless? Apparently Never! 547

COMPONENTS OF STOCKHOLDERS' EQUITY 547

- FOCUS ON INTERNATIONAL BUSINESS
  Hot New European Stock Markets Have Cooled! 547

DIVIDENDS 548

THE CHARACTERISTICS OF PREFERRED STOCK 549

Preference as to Dividends 549

- FOCUS ON BUSINESS PRACTICE
  Why Did Microsoft Issue Preferred Stock? 550

Preference as to Assets 551

Convertible Preferred Stock 551
Callable Preferred Stock 552

ACCOUNTING FOR STOCK ISSUANCE 552

Par Value Stock 553
No-Par Stock 554
Issuance of Stock for Noncash Assets 554

ACCOUNTING FOR TREASURY STOCK 555

Purchase of Treasury Stock 556
Sale of Treasury Stock 556

- FOCUS ON BUSINESS PRACTICE
  When Are Share Buybacks a Bad Idea? 557

Retirement of Treasury Stock 557

Chapter Review 558   Review of Learning Objectives 558
Review of Concepts and Terminology 559   Review
Problem 561   Answer to Review Problem 561

Chapter Assignments 563   Questions 563   Short
Exercises 564   Exercises 565   Problems 567   Alternate
Problems 568

Skills Development Cases 569

Financial Reporting and Analysis Cases 571

13 The Corporate Income Statement and the Statement of Stockholders' Equity 574

- DECISION POINT AMR Corporation 574

PERFORMANCE MEASUREMENT: QUALITY OF EARNINGS ISSUES 576

The Corporate Income Statement 576

- FOCUS ON BUSINESS PRACTICE
  Why Do Investors Study Quality of Earnings? 576

Choice of Accounting Methods and Estimates 577

Gains and Losses 579

Write-Downs and Restructurings 579

Nature of Nonoperating Items 579

- FOCUS ON BUSINESS ETHICS Whistle-Blowing 580

Effect of Quality of Earnings on Cash Flows and Performance Measures 580

INCOME TAXES EXPENSE 581

Deferred Income Taxes 582

Net of Taxes 583

NONOPERATING ITEMS 584

Discontinued Operations 584

Extraordinary Items 584

Accounting Changes 585

- FOCUS ON INTERNATIONAL BUSINESS
  Were Preussag's Year-End Results Really "Remarkable"? 585

EARNINGS PER SHARE 586

THE STATEMENT OF STOCKHOLDERS' EQUITY 588

Retained Earnings 588

- FOCUS ON INTERNATIONAL BUSINESS
  Why Are Reserves Common in Other Countries? 590

Restriction on Retained Earnings 590

ACCOUNTING FOR STOCK DIVIDENDS AND STOCK SPLITS 590

Stock Dividends 590

Stock Splits 593

- FOCUS ON BUSINESS PRACTICE
  Do Stock Splits Help Increase a Company's Market Price? 593

BOOK VALUE 594

Chapter Review 595   Review of Learning Objectives 595   Review of Concepts and Terminology 597   Review Problem 598   Answer to Review Problem 598

Chapter Assignments 600   Questions 600   Short Exercises 601   Exercises 602   Problems 604   Alternate Problems 607

Skills Development Cases 608

Financial Reporting and Analysis Cases 610

14 The Statement of Cash Flows 610

- DECISION POINT Marriott International, Inc. 610
- VIDEO CASE Goodyear Tire & Rubber Company 613

OVERVIEW OF THE STATEMENT OF CASH FLOWS 613

Purposes of the Statement of Cash Flows 614

Internal and External Uses of the Statement of Cash Flows 614

Classification of Cash Flows 614

- FOCUS ON INTERNATIONAL BUSINESS
  How Universal Is the Statement of Cash Flows? 616

Format of the Statement of Cash Flows 616

ANALYZING THE STATEMENT OF CASH FLOWS 616

Cash-Generating Efficiency 616

Free Cash Flow 617

- FOCUS ON BUSINESS PRACTICE
  What Do You Mean, "Free Cash Flow"? 618
- FOCUS ON BUSINESS PRACTICE
  Cash Flows Tell All. 618

PREPARING THE STATEMENT OF CASH FLOWS: OPERATING ACTIVITIES 619

Depreciation 622

Gains and Losses 622

Changes in Current Assets 623

Changes in Current Liabilities 623

- FOCUS ON BUSINESS PRACTICE
  What's Your "Burn Rate"? 624

Schedule of Cash Flows from Operating Activities 624

PREPARING THE STATEMENT OF CASH FLOWS: INVESTING ACTIVITIES 624

Investments 625

Plant Assets 626

PREPARING THE STATEMENT OF CASH FLOWS: FINANCING ACTIVITIES 627

Bonds Payable 627

Common Stock 628

Retained Earnings 628

Treasury Stock 628

Chapter Review 630   Review of Learning Objectives 630   Review of Concepts and Terminology 630   Review Problem 631   Answer to Review Problem 633

Chapter Assignments 634 Questions 634 Short Exercises 635 Exercises 636 Problems 639 Alternate Problems 642

Skills Development Cases 645

Financial Reporting and Analysis Cases 648

15 The Changing Business Environment: A Manager's Perspective 656

- DECISION POINT Honda Motor Company 656

THE ROLE OF MANAGEMENT ACCOUNTING 658

Management Accounting and Financial Accounting: A Comparison 658

- FOCUS ON BUSINESS PRACTICE
  Why Is Management Accounting Vitally Important to Excellent Companies? 658

Management Accounting and the Management Cycle 660

VALUE CHAIN ANALYSIS 664

Primary Processes and Support Services 665

Advantages of Value Chain Analysis 666

Management Accounting's Support of Value Chain Analysis 666

- FOCUS ON BUSINESS TECHNOLOGY
  How Can the Internet Be Used to Support the Value Chain? 666

MEETING THE DEMANDS OF GLOBAL COMPETITION 668

Management Tools for Continuous Improvement 668

Achieving Continuous Improvement 670

- FOCUS ON INTERNATIONAL BUSINESS
  How Has Ecommerce Changed the Nature of Business? 671

PERFORMANCE MEASURES: A KEY TO ACHIEVING ORGANIZATIONAL OBJECTIVES 671

Use of Performance Measures in the Management Cycle 671

The Balanced Scorecard 672

- FOCUS ON BUSINESS PRACTICE
  Do Many Companies Use the Balanced Scorecard? 672

Benchmarking 673

ANALYSIS OF NONFINANCIAL DATA IN A SERVICE ORGANIZATION 674

STANDARDS OF ETHICAL CONDUCT 674

- FOCUS ON BUSINESS ETHICS
  What Is Management's Responsibility for the Financial Statements? 676

Chapter Review 678 Review of Learning Objectives 678 Review of Concepts and Terminology 679 Review Problem 680 Answer to Review Problem 681

Chapter Assignments 682 Questions 682 Short Exercises 682 Exercises 684 Problems 688 Alternate Problems 691

Skills Development Cases 693

Managerial Reporting and Analysis Cases 696

16 Cost Concepts and Cost Allocation 698

- DECISION POINT Southwest Airlines 698

COST INFORMATION AND THE MANAGEMENT CYCLE 700

Use of Cost Information in the Management Cycle 700

Cost Information and Organizations 701

COST CLASSIFICATIONS AND THEIR USES 701

Cost Traceability 702

- FOCUS ON BUSINESS PRACTICE
  How Does an Airline Manage Its Fixed Costs? 703

Cost Behavior 703

Value-Adding Versus Nonvalue-Adding Costs 703

Cost Classifications for Financial Reporting 703

ELEMENTS OF PRODUCT COSTS 704

- FOCUS ON BUSINESS TECHNOLOGY
  Has Technology Shifted the Elements of Product Costs? 705

Computing Product Unit Cost 705

Prime Costs and Conversion Costs 707

INVENTORY ACCOUNTS IN MANUFACTURING ORGANIZATIONS 707

Document Flows and Cost Flows Through the Inventory Accounts 708

The Manufacturing Cost Flow 710

FINANCIAL STATEMENTS AND THE REPORTING OF COSTS 711

Statement of Cost of Goods Manufactured 711

Cost of Goods Sold and a Manufacturing Organization's Income Statement 713

Cost Reporting and Accounting for Inventories in Service, Retail, and Manufacturing Organizations 713

- FOCUS ON BUSINESS PRACTICE
  What Candy Company Has the Sweetest Share of the U.S. Market? 713

COST ALLOCATION 715

Allocating the Costs of Manufacturing Overhead 716

The Importance of Good Estimates 718

ALLOCATING MANUFACTURING OVERHEAD: THE TRADITIONAL APPROACH 718

ALLOCATING MANUFACTURING OVERHEAD: THE ABC APPROACH 720

■ FOCUS ON BUSINESS ETHICS
What Can a Company Do to Be Resource-Responsible? 721

Planning Overhead Rates 721

Applying the Overhead Rates 722

■ FOCUS ON BUSINESS PRACTICE
How Costly Is Television Talent? 724

COST ALLOCATION IN SERVICE ORGANIZATIONS 724

Chapter Review 725 Review of Learning Objectives 725 Review of Concepts and Terminology 727 Review Problem 728 Answer to Review Problem 729

Chapter Assignments 730 Questions 730 Short Exercises 730 Exercises 732 Problems 735 Alternate Problems 738

Skills Development Cases 740

Managerial Reporting and Analysis Cases 742

17 Costing Systems: Job Order Costing 746

■ DECISION POINT John H. Daniel Company 746

PRODUCT COST INFORMATION AND THE MANAGEMENT CYCLE 748

Planning 748

Executing 748

Reviewing 748

Reporting 748

JOB ORDER VERSUS PROCESS COSTING 749

■ FOCUS ON INTERNATIONAL BUSINESS
Why Does Toyota Use a Hybrid Product Costing System? 751

JOB ORDER COSTING IN A MANUFACTURING COMPANY 751

Materials 754

Labor 754

Manufacturing Overhead 754

■ FOCUS ON BUSINESS PRACTICE
How Long Does Production Take? 755

Completed Units 755

Sold Units 755

Reconciliation of Manufacturing Overhead Costs 756

A MANUFACTURER'S JOB ORDER COST CARD AND THE COMPUTATION OF PRODUCT UNIT COST 756

■ FOCUS ON BUSINESS ETHICS
Does a Product's Unit Cost Tell the Whole Story? 756

JOB ORDER COSTING IN A SERVICE ORGANIZATION 757

JOB ORDER COSTING VERSUS PROJECT COSTING 758

■ FOCUS ON BUSINESS TECHNOLOGY
Who Uses Project Costing? 759

Chapter Review 759 Review of Learning Objectives 759 Review of Concepts and Terminology 760 Review Problem 761 Answer to Review Problem 762

Chapter Assignments 763 Questions 763 Short Exercises 764 Exercises 766 Problems 771 Alternate Problems 774

Skills Development Cases 777

Managerial Reporting and Analysis Cases 779

18 Costing Systems: Process Costing 782

■ DECISION POINT Intel Corporation 782

THE PROCESS COSTING SYSTEM 784

■ FOCUS ON BUSINESS PRACTICE
What Kinds of Companies Use Process Costing? 785

PATTERNS OF PRODUCT FLOWS AND COST FLOW METHODS 785

COSTS FLOWS THROUGH THE WORK IN PROCESS INVENTORY ACCOUNTS 787

■ FOCUS ON BUSINESS ETHICS
How Hard Is It to Detect Fraud? 787

COMPUTING EQUIVALENT PRODUCTION 787

Equivalent Production for Direct Materials 788

Equivalent Production for Conversion Costs 789

PREPARING A PROCESS COST REPORT USING THE FIFO COSTING METHOD 789

Accounting for Units 789

Accounting for Costs 791

Assigning Costs 792

■ FOCUS ON INTERNATIONAL BUSINESS
How Do Businesses Today Handle the Costs of Scrap and Rework? 792

■ FOCUS ON BUSINESS TECHNOLOGY
Does Technology Make a Difference? 793

Process Costing for Two or More Production Departments 793

PREPARING A PROCESS COST REPORT USING THE AVERAGE COSTING METHOD 794

Accounting for Units 794

Accounting for Costs 794

Assigning Costs 796

USING INFORMATION ABOUT PRODUCT COST TO EVALUATE PERFORMANCE 797

Chapter Review 797 Review of Learning Objectives 797
Review of Concepts and Terminology 799 Review
Problem 799 Answer to Review Problem 800

Chapter Assignments 802 Questions 802 Short
Exercises 803 Exercises 804 Problems 806 Alternate
Problems 808

Skills Development Cases 809

Managerial Reporting and Analysis Cases 811

19 Activity-Based Systems: ABM and JIT 814

■ DECISION POINT England, Inc. 814

ACTIVITY-BASED SYSTEMS AND MANAGEMENT 816

Activity-Based Systems 816

Using Activity-Based Cost Information in the Management Cycle 817

ACTIVITY-BASED MANAGEMENT 818

■ FOCUS ON BUSINESS PRACTICE
How Do Traditional and ABC Reports Differ? 819

Value Chains and Supply Chains 819

■ FOCUS ON BUSINESS PRACTICE
How Can a Changing Business Economy Cause Strategy Shifts in a Company's Value Chain? 819

ABM in a Service Organization 820

VALUE-ADDING AND NONVALUE-ADDING ACTIVITIES AND PROCESS VALUE ANALYSIS 822

Value-Adding and Nonvalue-Adding Activities in a Service Organization 822

■ FOCUS ON BUSINESS PRACTICE
What Is VBM? 823

Process Value Analysis 823

ACTIVITY-BASED COSTING 824

The Cost Hierarchy and the Bill of Activities 824

Activity-Based Costing for Selling and Administrative Activities 827

THE NEW MANUFACTURING ENVIRONMENT AND JIT OPERATIONS 828

Minimum Inventory Levels 829

Pull-Through Production 829

Quick Setup and Flexible Work Cells 829

■ FOCUS ON INTERNATIONAL BUSINESS
Is JIT Right for Every Business? 830

A Multiskilled Work Force 830

High Levels of Product Quality 830

Effective Preventive Maintenance 830

Continuous Improvement of the Work Environment 831

ACCOUNTING FOR PRODUCT COSTS IN THE NEW MANUFACTURING ENVIRONMENT 831

Classifying Costs 831

Assigning Costs 831

BACKFLUSH COSTING 832

COMPARISON OF ABM AND JIT 835

Chapter Review 836 Review of Learning Objectives 836
Review of Concepts and Terminology 837 Review
Problem 839 Answer to Review Problem 839

Chapter Assignments 841 Questions 841 Short
Exercises 841 Exercises 842 Problems 846 Alternate
Problems 848

Skills Development Cases 850

Managerial Reporting and Analysis Cases 851

20 Cost Behavior Analysis 854

■ DECISION POINT Kraft Foods 854

COST BEHAVIOR AND THE MANAGEMENT CYCLE 856

Planning 856

Executing 856

Reviewing and Reporting 856

■ FOCUS ON BUSINESS ETHICS
Core Values Guide Kraft Foods. 856

THE BEHAVIOR OF COSTS 857

Variable Costs 858

Fixed Costs 861

Mixed Costs 862

■ FOCUS ON BUSINESS TECHNOLOGY
High-Priced vs. Low-Priced Seats 863

COST-VOLUME-PROFIT ANALYSIS 865

■ FOCUS ON INTERNATIONAL BUSINESS
C-V-P Analysis in Grams and Liters 866

BREAKEVEN ANALYSIS 866

Using Contribution Margin to Determine the Breakeven Point 868

■ FOCUS ON BUSINESS PRACTICE
Supersizing Value Meals 868

The Breakeven Point for Multiple Products 869

Using C-V-P Analysis to Plan Future Sales, Costs, and Profits 870

Applying C-V-P to a Manufacturing Business 870
Applying C-V-P Analysis to a Service Business 874

Chapter Review 876 Review of Learning Objectives 876 Review of Concepts and Terminology 877 Review Problem 877 Answer to Review Problem 878

Chapter Assignments 879 Questions 879 Short Exercises 879 Exercises 880 Problems 884 Alternate Problems 886

Skills Development Cases 887

Managerial Reporting and Analysis Cases 889

21 The Budgeting Process 892

■ DECISION POINT Johnson & Johnson 892

The Budgeting Process 894

Budgeting and Goals 894

■ FOCUS ON BUSINESS PRACTICE
What Can Cause the Planning Process to Fail? 894

■ VIDEO CASE Enterprise Rent-A-Car 895

■ FOCUS ON INTERNATIONAL BUSINESS
Budget Revision Practices in the United Kingdom 896

The Importance of Participation 896

Budgeting and the Management Cycle 896

The Master Budget 898

■ FOCUS ON BUSINESS TECHNOLOGY
Rolling Budgets Never End. 898

Operating Budgets 901

The Sales Budget 901
The Production Budget 902
The Direct Materials Purchases Budget 904
The Direct Labor Budget 904

The Manufacturing Overhead Budget 905
The Selling and Administrative Expense Budget 907
The Cost of Goods Manufactured Budget 908

Financial Budgets 908

The Budgeted Income Statement 908
The Capital Expenditures Budget 909
The Cash Budget 910

■ FOCUS ON BUSINESS ETHICS
Does Budgeting Lead to a Breakdown in Corporate Ethics? 912

The Budgeted Balance Sheet 912

Budget Implementation 915

Chapter Review 915 Review of Learning Objectives 915 Review of Concepts and Terminology 916 Review Problem 917 Answer to Review Problem 918

Chapter Assignments 919 Questions 919 Short Exercises 920 Exercises 921 Problems 925 Alternate Problems 931

Skills Development Cases 932

Managerial Reporting and Analysis Cases 936

22 Standard Costing and Variance Analysis 938

■ DECISION POINT Coach, Inc. 938

Standard Costing 940

Standard Costs and the Management Cycle 940

■ FOCUS ON BUSINESS PRACTICE
Why Go on a Factory Tour? 940

The Relevance of Standard Costing in Today's Business Environment 941

Computing Standard Costs 942

Standard Direct Materials Cost 942
Standard Direct Labor Cost 942
Standard Manufacturing Overhead Cost 943
Total Standard Unit Cost 943

Variance Analysis 944

The Role of Flexible Budgets in Variance Analysis 944

■ FOCUS ON BUSINESS TECHNOLOGY
Why Complicate the Flexible Budget? 945

Using Variance Analysis to Control Costs 946

Computing and Analyzing Direct Materials Variances 948

Computing Direct Materials Variances 948
Analyzing and Correcting Direct Materials Variances 949

Computing and Analyzing Direct Labor Variances 950

Computing Direct Labor Variances 950
Analyzing and Correcting Direct Labor Variances 951

Computing and Analyzing Manufacturing Overhead Variances 952

Using a Flexible Budget to Analyze Manufacturing Overhead Variances 953
Computing Manufacturing Overhead Variances 954
Analyzing and Correcting Manufacturing Overhead Variances 958

- FOCUS ON INTERNATIONAL BUSINESS
  Have You Bought Gold Medal Sneakers Yet? 958

USING COST VARIANCES TO EVALUATE MANAGERS' PERFORMANCE 959

- FOCUS ON BUSINESS ETHICS Ethics = Profits 959

Chapter Review 961 Review of Learning Objectives 961 Review of Concepts and Terminology 962 Review Problem 963 Answer to Review Problem 964

Chapter Assignments 967 Questions 967 Short Exercises 968 Exercises 969 Problems 971 Alternate Problems 973

Skills Development Cases 974

Managerial Reporting and Analysis Cases 976

23 Performance Management and Evaluation   980

- DECISION POINT Vail Resorts 980

ORGANIZATIONAL GOALS AND THE BALANCED SCORECARD 982

The Balanced Scorecard and the Management Cycle 982

- VIDEO CASE Harley-Davidson, Inc. 983
- FOCUS ON BUSINESS PRACTICE
  How Many Stakeholder Groups Has Harley Identified? 983

PERFORMANCE MEASUREMENT 986

What to Measure, How to Measure 986

Other Measurement Issues 986

- FOCUS ON INTERNATIONAL BUSINESS
  "Old" Doesn't Mean "Out-of-Date." 986

RESPONSIBILITY ACCOUNTING 987

Types of Responsibility Centers 987

Organizational Structure and Performance Management 988

- FOCUS ON BUSINESS TECHNOLOGY
  Keep It Simple! 988

PERFORMANCE EVALUATION OF COST CENTERS AND PROFIT CENTERS 990

Evaluating Cost Center Performance Using Flexible Budgeting 990

Evaluating Profit Center Performance Using Variable Costing 991

- FOCUS ON BUSINESS ETHICS
  Soundproofing with Blue Jeans 993

PERFORMANCE EVALUATION OF INVESTMENT CENTERS 993

Return on Investment 993

Residual Income 994

Economic Value Added 996

The Importance of Multiple Performance Measures 998

PERFORMANCE INCENTIVES AND GOALS 998

Linking Goals, Performance Objectives, Measures, and Performance Targets 998

Performance-Based Pay 998

The Coordination of Goals 999

Chapter Review 1000 Review of Learning Objectives 1000 Review of Concepts and Terminology 1001 Review Problem 1002 Answer to Review Problem 1003

Chapter Assignments 1004 Questions 1004 Short Exercises 1005 Exercises 1007 Problems 1010 Alternate Problems 1012

Skills Development Cases 1013

Managerial Reporting and Analysis Cases 1015

24 Short-Run Decision Analysis   1018

- DECISION POINT Bank of America 1018

SHORT-RUN DECISION ANALYSIS AND THE MANAGEMENT CYCLE 1020

Planning 1020

Executing 1020

Reviewing 1021

- FOCUS ON BUSINESS ETHICS
  Have Financial Scandals Affected CFOs' Workloads? 1022

Reporting 1022

INCREMENTAL ANALYSIS FOR SHORT-RUN DECISIONS 1022

Irrelevant Costs and Revenues 1022

- FOCUS ON BUSINESS TECHNOLOGY
  How Much Does It Cost to Process a Check? 1024

Opportunity Costs 1024

INCREMENTAL ANALYSIS FOR OUTSOURCING DECISIONS 1024

INCREMENTAL ANALYSIS FOR SPECIAL ORDER DECISIONS 1026

INCREMENTAL ANALYSIS FOR SEGMENT PROFITABILITY DECISIONS 1028

- FOCUS ON BUSINESS PRACTICE
  To Drop or Not to Drop a Segment? 1029
- FOCUS ON INTERNATIONAL BUSINESS
  Why Banks Prefer Ebanking 1030

INCREMENTAL ANALYSIS FOR SALES MIX DECISIONS 1030

INCREMENTAL ANALYSIS FOR SELL OR PROCESS-FURTHER DECISIONS 1032

Chapter Review 1034   Review of Learning Objectivces 1034   Review of Concepts and Terminology 1035   Review Problem 1035   Answer to Review Problem 1036

Chapter Assignments 1037   Questions 1037   Short Exercises 1038   Exercises 1039   Problems 1044   Alternate Problems 1046

Skills Development Cases 1048

Managerial Reporting and Analysis Cases 1049

25 Pricing Decisions, Including Target Costing and Transfer Pricing 1052

■ DECISION POINT Palm, Inc. 1052

THE PRICING DECISION AND THE MANAGER 1054

The Objectives of a Pricing Policy 1054

■ VIDEO CASE Nokia Corporation 1055

Pricing and the Management Cycle 1056

ECONOMIC PRICING CONCEPTS 1058

Total Revenue and Total Cost Curves 1058

Marginal Revenue and Marginal Cost Curves 1058

■ FOCUS ON BUSINESS TECHNOLOGY
  What's It Worth to Shop Online? 1060

Auction-Based Pricing 1060

■ FOCUS ON BUSINESS ETHICS
  How Big a Problem Is Fraud on the Internet? 1060

COST-BASED PRICING METHODS 1061

Gross Margin Pricing 1061

Return on Assets Pricing 1062

Summary of Cost-Based Pricing Methods 1063

Pricing Services 1063

■ FOCUS ON BUSINESS PRACTICE
  Pricing a Six-Pack 1064

Final Notes on Cost-Based Pricing Methods 1065

PRICING BASED ON TARGET COSTING 1065

Illustrative Problem: Target Costing 1068

■ FOCUS ON INTERNATIONAL BUSINESS
  What Is *Kaizen* Costing? 1070

PRICING FOR INTERNAL PROVIDERS OF GOODS AND SERVICES 1070

Transfer Pricing 1070

Developing a Transfer Price 1071

Using Transfer Prices to Measure Performance 1073

Transfer Pricing in Retail and Service Companies 1073

Chapter Review 1075   Review of Learning Objectives 1075   Review of Concepts and Terminology 1076   Review Problem 1077   Answer to Review Problem 1078

Chapter Assignments 1079   Questions 1079   Short Exercises 1079   Exercises 1080   Problems 1084   Alternate Problems 1086

Skills Development Cases 1088

Managerial Reporting and Analysis Cases 1090

26 Capital Investment Analysis 1094

■ DECISION POINT Air Products and Chemicals Inc. 1094

THE CAPITAL INVESTMENT PROCESS 1096

Capital Investment Analysis 1096

Capital Investment Analysis in the Management Cycle 1097

THE MINIMUM RATE OF RETURN ON INVESTMENT 1100

Cost of Capital 1100

■ FOCUS ON INTERNATIONAL BUSINESS
  Why Look Beyond the Cost of a Capital Investment? 1101

Other Cutoff Measures 1101

Ranking Capital Investment Proposals 1101

MEASURES USED IN CAPITAL INVESTMENT ANALYSIS 1102

Net Income and Net Cash Inflows 1102

Equal Versus Unequal Cash Flows 1102

Carrying Value of Assets 1102

■ FOCUS ON BUSINESS TECHNOLOGY
  Counting Your Pennies a New Way 1102

Depreciation Expense and Income Taxes 1102

Disposal or Residual Values 1103

THE TIME VALUE OF MONEY 1103

Interest 1104

Present Value 1104

Present Value of a Single Sum Due in the Future 1105

Present Value of an Ordinary Annuity 1105

■ FOCUS ON BUSINESS PRACTICE
  How Would You Decide Whether to Buy Rare Dinosaur Bones? 1106

THE NET PRESENT VALUE METHOD 1107

Advantages of the Net Present Value Method 1107

The Net Present Value Method Illustrated 1107

■ FOCUS ON BUSINESS ETHICS
  Why Are Luxury-Car Makers Interested in Used Cars? 1108

Contents xix

OTHER METHODS OF CAPITAL INVESTMENT ANALYSIS 1109

The Payback Period Method 1109

The Accounting Rate-of-Return Method 1110

Chapter Review 1111 Review of Learning Objectives 1111 Review of Concepts and Terminology 1112 Review Problem 1112 Answer to Review Problem 1113

Chapter Assignments 1114 Questions 1114 Short Exercises 1115 Exercises 1116 Problems 1118 Alternate Problems 1120

Skills Development Cases 1121

Managerial Reporting and Analysis Cases 1122

27 Quality Management and Measurement 1126

■ DECISION POINT Amazon.com 1126

THE ROLE OF MANAGEMENT INFORMATION SYSTEMS IN QUALITY MANAGEMENT 1128

Enterprise Resource Planning Systems 1128

■ FOCUS ON BUSINESS TECHNOLOGY
Use Prepackaged Software or Build Your Own? 1128

Using MIS in the Management Cycle 1129

FINANCIAL AND NONFINANCIAL MEASURES OF QUALITY 1130

Financial Measures of Quality 1130

■ FOCUS ON BUSINESS PRACTICE
SDWT Managers Have to "Walk the Walk" 1132

Nonfinancial Measures of Quality 1132

Measuring Service Quality 1134

■ FOCUS ON INTERNATIONAL BUSINESS
"Don't Judge Me on a Good Speech" 1134

ILLUSTRATIVE PROBLEM: MEASURING QUALITY 1135

Evaluating the Costs of Quality 1135

Evaluating Nonfinancial Measures of Quality 1139

THE EVOLVING CONCEPT OF QUALITY 1141

■ FOCUS ON BUSINESS PRACTICE
TQM Does Make a Difference 1141

RECOGNITION OF QUALITY 1141

Chapter Review 1142 Review of Learning Objectives 1142 Review of Concepts and Terminology 1143 Review Problem 1144 Answer to Review Problem 1145

Chapter Assignments 1146 Questions 1146 Short Exercises 1146 Exercises 1147 Problems 1151 Alternate Problems 1153

Skills Development Cases 1155

Managerial Reporting and Analysis Cases 1156

28 Financial Performance Evaluation 1160

■ DECISION POINT Sun Microsystems 1160

FINANCIAL PERFORMANCE EVALUATION BY INTERNAL AND EXTERNAL USERS 1162

Financial Performance Evaluation and the Management Cycle 1162

Financial Performance Evaluation by External Users 1163

Financial Reporting Under the Sarbanes-Oxley Act 1164

STANDARDS FOR FINANCIAL STATEMENT ANALYSIS 1165

Rule-of-Thumb Measures 1165

Past Performance of the Company 1165

Industry Norms 1165

■ FOCUS ON BUSINESS ETHICS
Take the Numbers with a Grain of Salt. 1167

SOURCES OF INFORMATION 1167

Reports Published by the Company 1167

■ FOCUS ON BUSINESS TECHNOLOGY
Find It on the Internet. 1168

SEC Reports 1168

Business Periodicals and Credit and Investment Advisory Services 1168

TOOLS AND TECHNIQUES OF FINANCIAL ANALYSIS 1170

Horizontal Analysis 1170

Trend Analysis 1171

Vertical Analysis 1173

Ratio Analysis 1176

COMPREHENSIVE ILLUSTRATION OF RATIO ANALYSIS 1176

Evaluating Liquidity 1177

■ FOCUS ON BUSINESS PRACTICE
There's More Than One Way to Measure Profitability. 1179

Evaluating Profitability 1179

Evaluating Long-Term Solvency 1180

Evaluating Cash Flow Adequacy 1181

Evaluating Market Strength 1181

Summary of the Financial Analysis of Sun Microsystems, Inc. 1183

Chapter Review 1183   Review of Learning Objectives 1183   Review of Concepts and Terminology 1184   Review Problem 1185   Answer to Review Problem 1187

Chapter Assignments 1189   Questions 1189   Short Exercises 1189   Exercises 1191   Problems 1194   Alternate Problems 1198

Skills Development Cases 1200

Managerial Reporting and Analysis Cases   1201

Appendix A The Merchandising Work Sheet and Closing Entries 1205

Appendix B Special-Purpose Journals 1213

Appendix C Accounting for Unincorporated Businesses 1227

Appendix D International Accounting 1237

Appendix E Long-Term Investments 1244

Appendix F The Time Value of Money 1251

Appendix G Future Value and Present Value Tables 1264

Endnotes 1271
Company Name Index 1277
Subject Index 1280

Preface

Recent business and accounting events underscore the fact that accounting matters. Now, more than ever before, accounting students need to learn how to create, analyze, and use financial statements if they are going to be successful managers in the future. They also need to understand how a company's accounting information system works. *Financial & Managerial Accounting*, 2005e (7th edition) does just that. It continues a long tradition of teaching students that a company's financial statements and the accounting information system that provides the supporting data are key to guiding a company's prosperity.

We believe that in order to read and interpret financial statements, students have to learn how to think critically. That is why in *Financial & Managerial Accounting* we continue to seek ways to help students think critically about what they are reading, how they might make a financial or managerial decision, and what roles they might play as future users of financial accounting information systems. Students also have to learn how to analyze and interpret data—where did the numbers come from? What is the significance of the numbers? What do the numbers reveal about the financial health of the company? Again, we stress the importance of critical analysis in *Financial & Managerial Accounting*, 2005e.

Financial & Managerial Accounting continues to be the leading text for students—both business and accounting majors—with no previous training in accounting or business. It is part of a well-integrated text and technology program that includes an array of print and electronic support materials for students and professors. The text consists of 28 chapters; the first 14 cover financial accounting, and the remaining 14 chapters focus on managerial accounting.

Financial & Managerial Accounting was revised with these major objectives in mind:

- To support new instructional technologies in today's business environment
- To provide a framework for making successful and ethical business decisions
- To present real-world events and relevant business practices
- To develop skills and abilities critical to life-long learning

NEW INSTRUCTIONAL TECHNOLOGIES IN TODAY'S BUSINESS ENVIRONMENT

New technologies are a driving force behind business growth and accounting education today. We have therefore developed an integrated text and technology program dedicated to helping instructors take advantage of the opportunities created by new instructional technologies. Our goal with the new 2005 edition is to expand and seamlessly integrate the technology package so users can gain experience with technology tools basic to business. Whether an instructor wants to present a user or procedural orientation, incorporate new instructional strategies, develop students' core skills and competencies, or integrate technology into the classroom, the new 2005e text provides a total solution, making it the leading choice among instructors of first-year financial and managerial accounting courses.

Technology Supplements on the Web

NEW! ***Eduspace®*** Eduspace powered by Blackboard™ is Houghton Mifflin's online homework system. The system enables students to complete homework assignments online. After students complete the assignment, they submit it electronically and immediately receive feedback on their answers. Eduspace offers a wealth of other student and instructor resources, including HMTesting (our computerized test bank), brand new PowerPoint slide presentations, and a complete course manual.

SmarThinking Houghton Mifflin and SmarThinking have partnered to provide state-of-the-art, live, online tutoring. Tutors can assist students with all examples, exercises, problems, and cases found in the text and related student supplements. An interactive interface allows tutors and students to share, annotate, and manipulate resources in real time to help illustrate concepts. A SmarThinking password is available for free and can be packaged with every new copy of the textbook.

The Needles Accounting Resource Center Web Site The Needles Accounting Resource Center Web Site (http://accounting.college.hmco.com) provides a wealth of free resources for instructors and students. For example, students can access ACE, the very popular online self-testing program that allows them to take sample quizzes and check their mastery of the chapter material. Over 1,200 new questions have been added to the ACE quizzes. An ACE icon at the end of each learning objective section reminds students to check out the ACE online review quizzes. Other resources include

- links to the web sites of over 200 real companies.
- a list of relevant readings from leading business and accounting periodicals (such as *BusinessWeek*, *Forbes*, *The Wall Street Journal*, and *The Journal of Accountancy*), which examine current business issues, the accounting profession, and career options in a broad context.
- research activities, which present extended investigations of text topics.
- Toys "R" Us annual report activities, which make use of the latest Toys "R" Us financial statements.

For instructors, the Needles Accounting Resource Center Web Site offers:

- a completely revised set of PowerPoint slides, which contain classroom presentation materials, discussion questions, and figures from the text.
- electronic solutions, available both on the web site and on a CD-ROM, which are fully functioning Excel spreadsheets for exercises, problems, and selected cases in the text.
- sample syllabi, demonstrating how other instructors organize and teach the introductory course.
- the *Accounting Instructors' Report* newsletter, which explores a wide range of contemporary teaching issues.
- Faculty Development Programs' online training, which provides suggestions for integrating new technologies into the classroom or teaching online.

NEW!* Wall Street Journal *Subscription Students whose instructors have adopted the WSJ version of *Financial & Managerial Accounting* will receive, packaged with their book, a registration card for a 10-week print and online subscription to the *Wall Street Journal*. Students fill out and return the registration card to initiate subscription privileges. The text package also includes a copy of the *Wall Street Journal Student Subscriber Handbook*, which explains how to use both print and online versions of the newspaper.

Technology Supplements on CD-ROMs

NEW!* HMAccounting *Tutor This new student tutorial CD-ROM, specifically developed for use with *Financial & Managerial Accounting*, 2005e, reinforces understanding of accounting concepts covered in the text. Organized by chapter and learning objective, this software program enables students to study more efficiently and learn interactively. The program includes

- demonstration problems with voice-over narration that illustrate important concepts.
- interactive tutorials that allow students to cover text concepts at their own pace.
- Internet cases taken directly from the 2005 text, which contain a link to a portal page for information the student needs to complete the cases.
- an interactive quizzing function to reinforce learning.
- a built-in glossary with on-screen pop-up definitions.

NEW! Mastering the Accounting Cycle: A Bridge Tutorial This new, stand-alone tutorial CD-ROM emphasizes accounting transactions, presents a review of the debit and credit mechanism, and provides a foundation for the preparation and use of financial statements. The CD contains four demonstration problems that show the connection between the balance sheet, income statement, and cash flow statement. It also has an interactive quizzing function and a built-in glossary.

HMClassPrep with HMTesting CD-ROM This instructor CD contains the computerized version of the test bank as well as other useful instructor aids.

The ***computerized test bank*** allows instructors to select, edit, and add questions, or generate randomly selected questions to produce a test master for easy duplication. Test questions are organized by learning objective and can be compiled using key words from the text. Online Testing and Gradebook functions allow instructors to administer tests via their school's network or over the Web, set up classes, record grades from tests or assignments, analyze grades, and compile class and individual statistics. This program can be used on both PCs and Macintosh computers. (A printed version of the test bank is also available upon request.)

Other Instructor Aids on HMClassPrep include

- the complete ***Course Manual*** (course planning matrix, time/difficulty chart, chapter-by-chapter instructional materials, and review quizzes).
- the ***Solutions Manual*** (a complete set of solutions to all exercises, problems, and selected cases in the text; also available in print).
- ***PowerPoint Slides*** (brand new PowerPoint slide presentations for every chapter)
- five-minute ***video cases*** tied to the in-text cases, highlighting real companies.
- ***check figures*** for end-of-chapter problems.
- ***web links*** to the Needles Accounting Resource Center Web Site at (http://accounting.college.hmco.com).

NEW! Windows General Ledger Software on the Student CD-ROM Completely updated for *Financial & Managerial Accounting*, 2005e, Houghton Mifflin's Windows General Ledger software offers coverage of accounting concepts and procedures in an extremely simple and user-friendly computerized environment. Most of the text problems in Chapters 1-14 can be solved using this program. The new GLS has an updated interface and expanded features—such as the ability to export files to Peachtree. The GLS software is included on the Student CD, which comes free with new texts purchased from Houghton Mifflin.

Also on the Student CD are check figures for the text problems, the video cases that accompany *Financial & Managerial Accounting*, and a full glossary.

Fingraph Financial Analyst CD-ROM This CD contains the educational version of a patented software program used by financial analysts and certified public accountants to analyze and summarize the financial performance of companies. The financial data reported by over 20 well-known companies have been summarized and loaded into Microsoft Excel spreadsheets that can be accessed through the Needles Accounting Resource Center Web Site at http://accounting.college.hmco.com. Students can also enter data obtained from the annual report of any company. The Fingraph software enables students to prepare financial analyses of real companies in a very short time. The software accommodates a variety of learning styles; analyses are presented in tabular, graphic, and written formats. Most of the financial chapters of *Financial & Managerial Accounting*, 2005e contain a case designed to be worked in conjunction with the CD-ROM database, in which students analyze balance sheets, income statements, and statements of cash flows of real companies.

Introduction to Financial Accounting: The Language of Business CD-ROM Bel Needles and Marian Powers developed this competency-based, interactive CD in partnership with Learning Insights. The software is designed to teach accounting to people who have little or no financial background, especially business majors and nonfinancial managers who need to learn the financial impact of operating decisions.

Electronic Working Papers CD-ROM This CD is an electronic version of the printed Working Papers for exercises, problems, and selected cases in the text. By working on these Excel-based templates, students not only learn accounting but also the basic skills required for spreadsheet applications.

A FRAMEWORK FOR SUCCESSFUL AND ETHICAL DECISION MAKING

We know that most instructors want to place more emphasis on critical analysis and on how managers use accounting information to make decisions. We also know that ethical decision making is an important topic in light of the new focus on corporate governance. We are proud to continue our long tradition of emphasizing ethical decision making. At the end of each chapter we present at least one short case, based on real public companies, in which students must address an authentic, work-related, ethical dilemma directly related to the chapter content. The cases reveal how managers must account for their business decisions. Also, we have added within the text several new Focus on Business Ethics boxes that feature examples of how real companies have faced ethical issues.

Comparative Financial Analysis

We have expanded the use of financial information in performance evaluation and measurement by introducing a new comparison case at the end of most of the financial chapters. Students compare Walgreens and Toys "R" Us, using both companies' financial statements, which are bound into the text at the end of Chapter 1. The comparison cases require students to compute ratios, make assumptions, report on the effect of seasonal sales, and describe each company's inventory management system, to name a few tasks. Again, *Financial & Managerial Accounting* continues to stress the important role of financial statements in revealing useful information about companies.

Cash Flow

We emphasize the effect of business activities on cash flow throughout the financial chapters. Beginning in Chapter 1, we introduce the statement of cash flows, and we point out the difference between income measurement and cash flow in various chapters, reinforcing it through assignments. An icon in the margin calls attention to cash flow discussions.

Key Ratios

Starting in Chapter 5, we examine financial analysis ratios and integrate them in subsequent financial chapters at appropriate points. We bring all the ratios together in a comprehensive financial analysis of Sun Microsystems, Inc., in Chapter 28. An icon % in the margin calls attention to key ratio presentations.

Management Accounting Coverage

Co-author Susan Crosson has heavily revised most of the managerial chapters (Chapters 15-28). Her efforts were directed at helping students gain confidence in their ability to understand and apply accounting concepts once they leave the classroom and enter the workplace. For example, rather than focusing on the technical details of cost accounting, the managerial chapters emphasize the management cycle critical to operating a successful business. The managerial chapters also emphasize the approaches learned from the most progressive companies, such as how to manage supply chains, analyze value chains, operate in a just-in-time environment, utilize activity-based management, apply the theory of constraints, and focus on quality.

Today, management's use of information goes far beyond computing the cost of products and services. This book explores the full range of innovative managerial systems in a value-centered economy in which managers must make critical decisions concerning product quality, customer service, and long-term relationships. The text discusses the latest in management models and technology, plus it emphasizes that performance measurement, evaluation, and compensation are essential to a manager's success in today's competitive environment. Service businesses, where many students will ultimately work, receive expanded emphasis within the text discussion and the chapter assignments.

REAL-WORLD EVENTS AND BUSINESS PRACTICES

Working toward our goal of reflecting current business practice in a context that is relevant and exciting to students, we have incorporated the following real-world elements of the text.

Actual Financial Statements

To enhance students' appreciation for the usefulness and relevance of accounting information, we include excerpts from annual reports of real companies and articles about them in business journals. In total, we cite more than 200 publicly held companies in the text so that students can apply the concepts to real companies. These companies are identified by a URL in the margin of the text or by a URL within the end-of-chapter case text.

The complete annual report of Toys "R" Us and the financial statements and notes of Walgreen Company appear at the end of Chapter 1. Chapter 5 presents the financial statements of Dell Computer Corporation in graphical form using the Fingraph Financial Analysis CD-ROM software. Chapter 28 features the financial statements of Sun Microsystems, Inc. to illustrate comprehensive financial analysis. Several of the Financial Reporting and Analysis Cases ask students to select real companies and access their financial statements on the Internet or through the Needles Accounting Resource Center Web Site at http://accounting.college.hmco.com to research the information needed to answer the questions.

Updated Decision Points

Every chapter begins with a Decision Point based on excerpts from a real company's annual report or from articles in the business press. In addition to introducing the concepts to be covered in the chapter, the Decision Point presents a situation that requires a decision by management and then demonstrates how the decision can be made using accounting information. The 2005 edition features several new Decision Points, among them Walgreens, Kelly Services, Cisco, Kraft, Coach, Palm, and Amazon.com. All of the other Decision Points have been revised and updated with the most recent financial information available.

New Focus on Business Boxes

Always a popular feature in the Needles accounting series, the Focus on Business boxes have been redesigned and over a third of them have been replaced with newsworthy feature stories. These boxes contain short summaries of items that show the relevance of accounting in four areas:

- Focus on Business Practice
- Focus on International Business
- Focus on Business Technology
- Focus on Business Ethics

Real-World Graphic Illustrations

We present graphs and tables illustrating how actual business practices relate to chapter topics. Many of these illustrations are based on data from studies of 600 annual reports published in *Accounting Trends and Techniques*. Beginning with Chapter 5, most chapters display a graphic that shows selected ratios for selected industries based on Dun & Bradstreet data. Service industry examples include advertising agencies and interstate trucking companies. Merchandising industry examples include auto and home supply companies and grocery stores. Manufacturing industry examples include machinery and computer companies. All graphs and tables have been updated with the most recent data available.

International Accounting

Recognizing the global economy in which all businesses operate today, we incorporate international accounting examples throughout the text. Each chapter includes a Financial Reporting and Analysis Case or a Managerial Reporting and Analysis Case that features an international company. Some examples include Harrods (British), Heineken (Dutch), Pioneer Corporation (Japan), and Roche (Swiss).

Video Cases

Two new 5-minute video vignettes (Claire's Boutiques and J. C. Penney) have been added to the series of video cases. Each video highlights a real company and is accompanied by an in-text case, which serves as an introduction to the chapter in which it is found. The videos work equally well as individual or group assignments, and all include a critical-thinking component and a writing assignment. The following video cases are included in the 2005 edition.

Intel Corporation (Chapter 1) examines the business goals of liquidity and profitability and the business activities of financing, investing, and operating.

Claire's Stores, Inc. (Chapter 6) describes a merchandising operation that has to regulate its inventories and generate a satisfactory gross margin in order to achieve profitability.

J.C. Penney Company, Inc. (Chapter 8) focuses on the management issues associated with accounting for inventories.

Acknowledgments

The success we have enjoyed over the years with *Financial & Managerial Accounting* is due in no small way to the countless comments and suggestions we have received from colleagues, attendees of our annual Conference on Accounting Education, and students who have used our book. While there are too many of you to name individually, we do wish to recognize those who have made special contributions to the 2005 edition of *Financial & Managerial Accounting*. We therefore thank Edward H. Julius (California Lutheran University) for his meticulous work on the Study Guide and Test Bank; Gayle Richardson (Bakersfield College) for her contribution to the Test Bank; Gail Mestas for creating the PowerPoint slides; Cathy Larson for her accuracy review of the text and solutions; Jacquie Commanday for her assistance with the Course Manual; and Sarah Evans for her developmental editing of the text and Course Manual and page layout.

We also recognize the constant support we have received over the years and particularly for this edition from senior sponsoring editor, Bonnie Binkert; senior development editor, Margaret Kearney; project editor, Claudine Bellanton; and editorial associate, Jim Dimock.

Others who have been supportive and have had an impact on this book through their reviews, suggestions, and class testing are:

Daneen Adams   *Santa Fe Community College*
Gregory D. Barnes   *Clarion University*
Mohamed E. Bayou   *The University of Michigan—Dearborn*
Charles M. Betts   *Delaware Technical and Community College*
Michael C. Blue   *Bloomsburg University*
Gary R. Bower   *Community College of Rhode Island*
Lee Cannell   *El Paso Community College*
John D. Cunha   *University of California—Berkeley*
Mark W. Dawson   *Duquesne University*
Patricia A. Doherty   *Boston University*
Lizabeth England   *American Language Academy*
David Fetyko   *Kent State University*
Sue Garr   *Wayne State University*
Roxanne Gooch   *Cameron University*
Christine Uber Grosse   *The American Graduate School of International Management*
Dennis A. Gutting   *Orange County Community College*
John Hancock   *University of California—Davis Graduate School of Management*
Yvonne Hatami   *Borough of Manhattan Community College*
Harry Hooper   *Santa Fe Community College*
Marianne James   *California State University, Los Angeles*
Edward H. Julius   *California Lutheran University*
Howard A. Kanter   *DePaul University*
Debbie Luna   *El Paso Community College*
Kevin McClure   *ESL Language Center*
George McGowan
Gail A. Mestas
Jenine Moscove
Beth Brooks Patel   *University of California—Berkeley*
LaVonda Ramey   *Schoolcraft College*
Roberta Rettner   *American Ways*
Gayle Richardson   *Bakersfield College*
James B. Rosa   *Queensborough Community College*
Donald Shannon   *DePaul Univeristy*

S. Murray Simons   *Northeastern University*
Marion Taube   *University of Pittsburgh*
Kathleen Villani   *Queensborough Community College*
Vicki Vorell   *Cuyahoga Community College*
John Weber   *DeVry Institute*
Kay Westerfield   *University of Oregon*
Andy Williams   *Edmunds Community College*

Finally, we want to identify and thank the facilitators for the last five years of COAE (Conference on Accounting Education) and congratulate our recent Technology Award winners:

2003 COAE Facilitators
Charlene Abendroth, California State University
Daneen Adams, Santa Fe Community College
Richard Fern, Eastern Kentucky University
Terry Grant, Mississippi College
Yvonne Hatami, Borough of Manhattan Community College
Rodger Holland, Columbus State University

2002 COAE Facilitators
Sharon Bell, University of North Carolina—Pembroke
Mark Henry, the Victoria College
Harry Hooper, Santa Fe Community College
Richard Irvine, Pensacola Junior College
Nancy Kelly, Middlesex Community College
Paul Mihalek, University of Hartford
Paul Weitzel, Eastern Shore Community College

2001 COAE Facilitators
Salvador Aceves, University of San Francisco
Betty Habershon, Prince George's Community College
Jim Mazza, Heald College
Roselyn Morris, Southwest Texas State University
Ginger Parker, Creighton University
David Rogers, Mesa State College
Jeanne Yamamura, University of Nevada—Reno

2000 COAE Facilitators
Mary Falkey, Prince Georges Community College
Kathy Otero, University of Texas—El Paso
Hubert Gill, University of North Florida
Rick Turpin, University of Tennessee
Lyle Hicks, Danville Area Community College
John Weber, DeVry University

1999 COAE Facilitators
Sidney Askew, Borough of Manhattan Community College
Dahli Gray, Morgan State University
Clarence Coleman, Jr., Francis Marion College
Karen Novey, Robert Morris College
James Dougher, DeVry Institute
Miriam Keller-Perkins, Berkeley College
Suzanne Wright, Penn State University

COAE Technology Award Winners
2003 - Elizabeth Murphy, DePaul University
2002 - Vicki Vorell, Cuyahoga Community College
2001 - Roselyn E. Morris, Southwest Texas State University

—B.N., M.P., and S.C.

TO THE STUDENT

HOW TO STUDY ACCOUNTING SUCCESSFULLY

The introductory accounting course is fundamental to the business curriculum and to success in the business world beyond college. Whether you are majoring in accounting or in another business discipline, it is one of the most important classes you will take. The course has multiple purposes because its students have diverse interests, backgrounds, and reasons for taking it. What are your goals in studying accounting? Being clear about your goals can contribute to your success in this course.

Success in this class also depends on your desire to learn and your willingness to work hard. It depends on your understanding of how the text complements the way your instructor teaches and the way you learn. A familiarity with how this text is structured will help you to study more efficiently, make better use of classroom time, and improve your performance on examinations and other assignments.

To be successful in the business world after you graduate, you will need a broad set of skills, which may be summarized as follows:

Technical/Analytical Skills   A major objective of your accounting course is to give you a firm grasp of the essential business and accounting terminology and techniques that you will need to succeed in a business environment. With this foundation, you then can begin to develop the higher-level perception skills that will help you acquire further knowledge on your own.

An even more crucial objective of this course is to help you develop analytical skills that will allow you to evaluate data. An important aspect of analytical skills is the ability to use technology effectively in making analyses. Well-developed analytical and decision-making skills are among the professional skills most highly valued by employers and will serve you well throughout your academic and professional careers.

Communication Skills   Another skill highly prized by employers is the ability to express oneself in a manner that others correctly understand. This can include writing skills, speaking skills, and presentation skills. Communication skills are developed through particular tasks and assignments and are improved through constructive criticism. Reading skills and listening skills support the direct communication skills.

Interpersonal Skills   Effective interaction between two people requires a solid foundation of interpersonal skills. The success of such interaction depends on empathy, or the ability to identify with and understand the problems, concerns, and motives of others. Leadership, supervision, and interviewing skills also facilitate a professional's interaction with others.

Personal/Self Skills   Personal/self skills form the foundation for growth in the use of all other skills. To succeed, a professional must take initiative, possess self-confidence, show independence, and be ethical in all areas of life. Personal/self skills can be enhanced significantly by the formal learning process and by peers and mentors who provide models upon which one can build. Accounting is just one course in your entire curriculum, but it can play an important role in your skill development. Your instructor is interested in helping you gain both a knowledge of accounting and the more general skills you will need to succeed in the business world. The following sections describe how you can get the most out of this course.

The Teaching/Learning Cycle™

Both teaching and learning have natural, parallel, and mutually compatible cycles. This teaching/learning cycle, as shown in Figure 1, interacts with the basic structure of learning objectives in this text.

The Teaching Cycle The inner (tan) circle in Figure 1 shows the steps an instructor takes in teaching a chapter. Your teacher *assigns* material, *presents* the subject in lecture, *explains* by going over assignments and answering questions, *reviews* the subject prior to an exam, and *assesses* your knowledge and understanding using examinations and other means of evaluation.

The Learning Cycle Moving outward, the next circle (green) in Figure 1 shows the steps you should take in studying a chapter. You should *preview* the material, *read* the chapter, *apply* your understanding by working the assignments, *review* the chapter, and *recall* and *demonstrate* your knowledge and understanding of the material in examinations and other assessments.

Integrated Learning Objectives Your textbook supports the teaching/learning cycle through the use of integrated learning objectives. Learning objectives are simply statements of what you should be able to do after you have completed a chapter. In Figure 1, the outside (blue) circle shows how learning objectives are integrated into your text and other study aids and how they interact with the teaching/learning cycle.

1. Learning objectives listed at the beginning of each chapter aid your teacher in making assignments and help you preview the chapter.
2. Each learning objective is referenced in the margin of the text at the point where that subject is covered. A list of related text assignments below each learning objective identifies the end-of-chapter exercises, problems, and cases that relate to that objective.
3. Every exercise, problem, and case in the end-of-chapter assignments shows the applicable learning objective(s) so you can refer to the text if you need help.
4. A summary of the key points for each learning objective, a list of new concepts and terms referenced by learning objectives, and a review problem covering key learning objectives assist you in reviewing each chapter. The Study Guide, also organized by learning objectives, provides additional review.

Why Students Succeed Students succeed in their accounting course when they coordinate their personal learning cycle with their instructor's cycle. Students who do a good job of previewing their assignments, reading the chapters before the instructor is ready to present them, preparing homework assignments before they are discussed in class, and reviewing carefully will ultimately achieve their potential on exams. To ensure that your learning cycle is synchronized with your instructor's teaching cycle, check your study habits against the following suggestions.

Previewing the Chapter

1. Read the learning objectives at the beginning of the chapter. These learning objectives specifically describe what you should be able to do after completing the chapter.
2. Study your syllabus. Know where you are in the course and where you are going. Know the rules of the course.
3. Realize that in an accounting course, each assignment builds on previous ones. If you do poorly in Chapter 1, you may have difficulty in Chapter 2 and be lost in Chapter 3.

FIGURE 1
The Teaching/Learning Cycle™ with integrated Learning Objectives

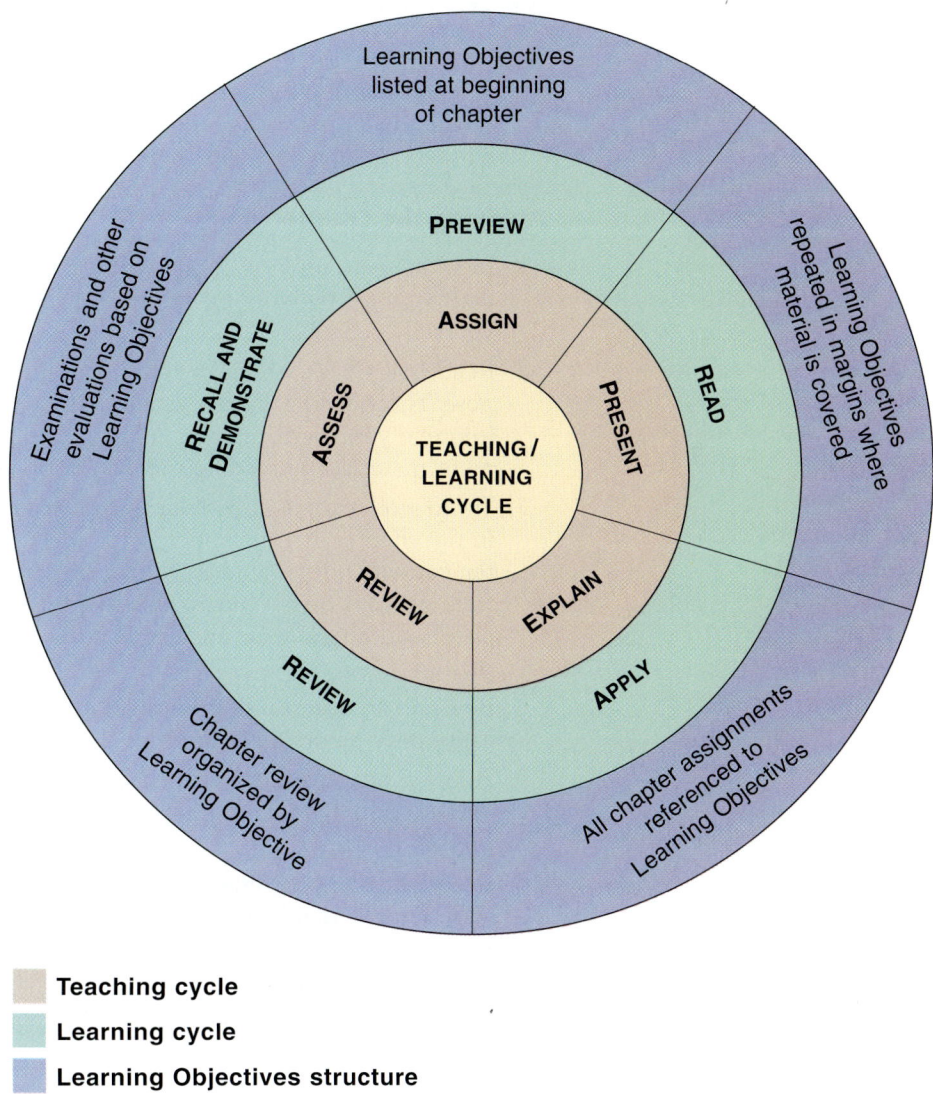

Reading the Chapter

1. As you read each chapter, be aware of the learning objectives in the margins. They will tell you why the material is relevant.
2. Allow yourself plenty of time to read the text. Accounting is a technical subject. Accounting books are so full of information that almost every sentence is important.
3. Strive to understand not only how each procedure is done, but also why it is done. Accounting is logical and requires reasoning. If you understand why something is done in accounting, there is little need to memorize.
4. Relate each new topic to its learning objective and be able to explain it in your own words.
5. Be aware of colors as you read. They are designed to help you understand the text. (For handy reference, the use of color is also explained on the back cover of the book.)
   Orange: All source documents and inputs are in orange.
   Green: All accounting forms, working papers, and accounting processes are shown in green.

Blue: All financial statements, the output or final product of the accounting process, are shown in blue.

6. If there is something you do not understand, prepare specific questions for your instructor. Pinpoint the topic or concept that confuses you. Some students keep a notebook of points with which they have difficulty.

Applying the Chapter

1. In addition to understanding why each procedure is done, you must be able to do it yourself by working exercises, problems, and cases. Accounting is a "do-it-yourself" course.
2. Read assignments and instructions carefully. Each assignment has a specific purpose. The wording is precise, and a clear understanding of it will save time and improve your performance. Acquaint yourself with the end-of-chapter assignment materials by reading the description of them in the Preface.
3. Try to work exercises, problems, and cases without referring to their discussions in the chapter. If you cannot work an assignment without looking in the chapter, you will not be able to work a similar problem on an exam. After you have tried on your own, refer to the chapter (based on the learning objective reference) and check your answer. Try to understand any mistakes you may have made.
4. Be neat and orderly. Sloppy calculations, messy papers, and general carelessness cause most errors on accounting assignments.
5. Allow plenty of time to work the chapter assignments. You will find that assignments seem harder and that you make more errors when you are feeling pressed for time.
6. Keep up with your class. Check your work against the solutions presented in class. Find your mistakes. Be sure you understand the correct solutions.
7. Note the part of each exercise, problem, or case that causes you difficulty so you can ask for help.
8. Attend class. Most instructors design classes to help you and to answer your questions. Absence from even one class can hurt your performance.

Reviewing the Chapter

1. Read the summary of learning objectives in the chapter review. Be sure you know the definitions of all the words in the review of concepts and terminology.
2. Review all assigned exercises, problems, and cases. Know them cold. Be sure you can work the assignments without the aid of the book.
3. Determine the learning objectives for which most of the problems were assigned. They refer to topics that your instructor is most likely to emphasize on an exam. Scan the text for such learning objectives and pay particular attention to the examples and illustrations.
4. Look for and scan other similar assignments that cover the same learning objectives. They may be helpful on an exam.
5. Review quizzes. Similar material will often appear on longer exams.
6. Attend any labs or visit any tutors your school provides, or see your instructor during office hours to get assistance. Be sure to have specific questions ready.

Taking Examinations

1. Arrive at class early so you can get the feel of the room and make a last-minute review of your notes.

2. Have plenty of sharp pencils and your calculator (if allowed) ready.
3. Review the exam quickly when it is handed out to get an overview of your task. Start with a part you know. It will give you confidence and save time.
4. Allocate your time to the various parts of the exam, and stick to your schedule. Every exam has time constraints. You need to move ahead and make sure you attempt all parts of the exam.
5. Read the questions carefully. Some may not be exactly like your homework assignments. They may approach the material from a slightly different angle to test your understanding and ability to reason, rather than your ability to memorize.
6. To avoid unnecessary errors, be neat, use good form, and show calculations.
7. Relax. If you have followed the above guidelines, your effort will be rewarded.

Preparing Other Assignments

1. Understand the assignment. Written assignments, term papers, computer projects, oral presentations, case studies, group activities, individual field trips, video critiques, and other activities are designed to enhance skills beyond your technical knowledge. It is essential to know exactly what your instructor expects. Know the purpose, audience, scope, and expected end product.
2. Allow plenty of time. "Murphy's Law" applies to such assignments: If anything can go wrong, it will.
3. Prepare an outline of each report, paper, or presentation. A project that is done well always has a logical structure.
4. Write a rough draft of each paper and report, and practice each presentation. Professionals always try out their ideas in advance and thoroughly rehearse their presentations. Good results are not accomplished by accident.
5. Make sure that each paper, report, or presentation is of professional quality. Instructors appreciate attention to detail and polish. A good rule of thumb is to ask yourself: Would I give this work to my boss?

About the Authors

Central to the success of any accounting text is the expertise of its author team. This team brings a wealth of classroom teaching experience, relevant business insight, and pedagogical expertise, as well as first-hand knowledge of today's students.

Belverd E. Needles, Jr., PhD, CPA, CMA
DePaul University

During his more than 30 years of teaching beginning accounting students, Belverd Needles has been an acknowledged innovator in accounting education. He has won teaching and education awards from DePaul University, the American Accounting Association, the Illinois CPA Society, the American Institute of CPAs, and the national honorary society, Beta Alpha Psi. The Conference on Accounting Education, started by Dr. Needles and sponsored by Houghton Mifflin, is in its 20th year; it has helped more than 2,000 beginning accounting instructors improve their teaching. Dr. Needles is editor of the *Accounting Instructors' Report*, in its 19th year, a newsletter that thousands of accounting teacher's rely on for new ideas in accounting education.

Marian Powers, PhD
Northwestern University

With more than 25 years of teaching experience, Marian Powers has taught beginning accounting at every level, from large lecture halls of 250 students to small classes of graduate students. She is a dynamic teacher who incorporates a variety of instructional strategies designed to broaden students' skills and experiences in critical thinking, group interaction, and communication. Consistently, Dr. Powers receives the highest ratings from students. She also brings practical experience to her students, including examples of how managers in all levels of business use and evaluate financial information. In recent years, Dr. Powers has concentrated on executive education. She has taught thousands of executives from leading companies around the world how to read and analyze the financial statements of their own companies and those of their competitors.

Susan Crosson, MS, CPA
Santa Fe Community College (Florida)

Susan Crosson, with more than 25 years of teaching at the college and university level, is recognized for her pedagogical expertise in teaching managerial accounting. Currently at Santa Fe Community College in Florida, Professor Crosson has a reputation for being able to engage university students in very large course sections and for encouraging community college students to master accounting. She believes in integrating technology into accounting education and actively uses the Internet to teach online, blended, and on-campus courses. Professor Crosson continues to promote the improvement of accounting education by serving the American Accounting Association and the Florida Institute of CPAs on a variety of committees, task forces, and sections. She is a past recipient of an IMA Faculty Development Grant to blend technology into the classroom, the Florida Association of Community Colleges Professor of the Year Award for Instructional Excellence, and the University of Oklahoma's Halliburton Education Award for Excellence.

Check Figures

Chapter 1 Problems
P 1. Total assets: $10,820
P 2. Total assets: $70,600
P 3. Total assets: $15,920
P 4. Total assets: $71,900
P 5. Total assets: $5,120
P 6. Total assets: $9,150
P 7. Total assets: $143,800
P 8. Total assets: $48,750

Chapter 2 Problems
P 1. No check figure
P 2. Trial balance: $16,450
P 3. Trial balance: $7,400
P 4. Trial balance: $11,550
P 5. Trial balance: $23,515
P 6. No check figure
P 7. Trial balance: $10,540
P 8. Trial balance: $30,710

Chapter 3 Problems
P 1. No check figure
P 2. No check figure
P 3. Adjusted Trial Balance: $125,792
P 4. Adjusted Trial Balance: $31,578
P 5. Adjusted Trial Balance: $654,209
P 6. No check figure
P 7. No check figure
P 8. Adjusted Trial Balance: $109,167

Chapter 4 Problems
P 1. Total assets: $627,800
P 2. Total assets: $113,616
P 3. May Adjusted Trial Balance: $10,338; Total assets: $9,024; Post-Closing Trial Balance: $9,094; June. Adjusted Trial Balance: $10,908; Total assets: $9,204; Post-Closing Trial Balance: $9,344
P 4. Total assets: $701,736
P 5. Total assets: $123,574
P 6. Total assets: $193,858
P 7. Total assets: $6,943
P 8. Total assets: $29,691

Chapter 5 Problems
P 1. No check figure
P 2. Net income for 20x4: $48,626
P 3. Total assets: $397,143
P 4. No check figure
P 5. Net income: $72,260; Total assets: $1,083,800
P 6. No check figure
P 7. Net income for 20x5: $22,140
P 8. No check figure

Chapter 6 Problems
P 1. Net income: $2,761
P 2. No check figure
P 3. Net income: $56,823

P 4. No check figure
P 5. No check figure
P 6. No check figure
P 7. Net income: $26,870
P 8. No check figure
P 9. Net income: $2,435
P 10. No check figure

Chapter 7 Problems
P 1. Short-term investments (at market): $354,000
P 2. No check figure
P 3. Amount of adjustment: $73,413
P 4. No check figure
P 5. Adjusted book balance: $149,473.28
P 6. Short-term investments (at market): $903,875
P 7. No check figure
P 8. Amount of adjustment: $9,533
P 9. No check figure
P 10. Adjusted book balance: $54,485.60

Chapter 8 Problems
P 1. 1. Cost of goods available for sale: $157,980
P 2. 1. Cost of goods sold for March: $4,578; for April: $15,457
P 3. 1. Cost of goods sold for March: $4,560; for April: $15,424
P 4. Estimated inventory shortage at cost: $6,052; at retail: $8,900
P 5. Estimated loss of inventory in fire: $653,027
P 6. Cost of goods available for sale: $10,560,000
P 7. 1. Cost of goods sold for April: $9,660; for May: $22,119
P 8. 1. Cost of goods sold for April: $9,580; for May: $21,991

Chapter 9 Problems
P 1. No check figure
P 2. No check figure
P 3. 1.b. Estimated Product Warranty Liability: $20,160
P 4. 3. Payroll Taxes Expense: $44,221.38
P 5. Net Pay, total: $8,176.32
P 6. No check figure
P 7. 1.b. Estimated Product Warranty Liability: $10,800
P 8. 3. Payroll Taxes Expense: $31,938.70

Chapter 10 Problems
P 1. Total cost: Land: $361,950; Land Improvements: $71,000; Building: $691,800; Furniture and Equipment: $105,400
P 2. 1. Depreciation, Year 3: a. $165,000; b. $132,000; c. $90,000
P 3. Total Depreciation Expense: 20x5: $13,280; 20x6: $18,760; 20x7: $15,728
P 4. a. Gain on Sale of Road Grader: $1,800; b. Loss on Sale of Road Grader: $2,200; c. Gain on Exchange of Road Grader: $1,800; d. Loss on Exchange of Road Grader: $2,200; e. No gain recognized

P 5. Part A. c. Amortization Expense: $492,000; d. Loss on Exclusive License: $1,476,000; Part B. d. Leasehold Amortization Expense: $1,575; e. Leasehold Improvements Amortization Expense: $2,500
P 6. Totals: Land: $852,424; Land Improvements: $333,120; Buildings: $1,667,880; Machinery: $2,525,280; Expense: $36,240
P 7. 1. Depreciation, Year 3: a. $54,250; b. $81,375; c. $53,407
P 8. Total Depreciation Expense: 20x4: $71,820; 20x5: $103,092; 20x6: $84,072

Chapter 11 Problems
P 1. 2. Bond Interest Expense: Nov. 30, $1,597,500; Dec. 31, $266,250
P 2. 1. Bond Interest Expense: Sept. 1, $754,400; Nov. 30, $377,071
P 3. Bond Interest Expense: June 30, 20x4, $144,666; Sept. 1, 20x4, $93,290
P 4. 2. Loss on early retirement: $2,261,293
P 5. Bond Interest Expense: Jan. 31, 20x4, $2,400,000; June 30, 20x4, $2,000,000
P 6. 2. Bond Interest Expense: Sept. 1, $192,800; Nov. 30, $96,400
P 7. 1. Bond Interest Expense: Nov. 30, $520,150; Dec. 31, $86,651
P 8. Bond Interest Expense: June 30, 20x3, $46,598; Sept. 30, 20x3, $96,900

Chapter 12 Problems
P 1. 2. Total stockholders' equity: $175,700
P 2. 1. 20x5 Total dividends: Preferred, $60,000; Common, $34,000
P 3. No check figure
P 4. 2. Total stockholders' equity: $950,080
P 5. 2. Total stockholders' equity: $330,375
P 6. 2. Total stockholders' equity: $1,488,000
P 7. 1. 20x3 Total dividends: Preferred, $420,000; Common, $380,000
P 8. 2. Total stockholders' equity: $475,040

Chapter 13 Problems
P 1. 2. Difference in net income: $48,800
P 2. 1. Income before extraordinary items and cumulative effect of accounting change: $108,000
P 3. 1. Income from continuing operations, December 31, 20x3: $551,250
P 4. 2. Total stockholders' equity, December 31, 20x3: $1,157,000
P 5. 2. Retained earnings: $231,500; Total stockholders' equity: $1,321,500
P 6. 1. Income before extraordinary items and cumulative effect of accounting change: $205,000
P 7. 2. Total stockholders' equity, December 31, 20x5: $2,964,000
P 8. 2. Retained earnings: $207,500; Total stockholders' equity: $1,257,500

Chapter 14 Problems
P 1. No check figure
P 2. 1. Net cash flows from: operating activities, $126,600; investing activities, ($25,800); financing activities, $14,000
P 3. 1. Net cash flows from: operating activities, ($32,600); investing activities, ($7,200); financing activities, $51,000
P 4. 1. Net cash flows from: operating activities, ($106,000); investing activities, $34,000; financing activities, $24,000
P 5. No check figure
P 6. 1. Net Cash flows from: operating activities, $274,000; investing activities, $3,000; financing activities, ($130,000)
P 7. 1. Net cash flows from: operating activities, $46,800; investing activities: ($14,400); financing activities, $87,000

Chapter 15 Problems
P 1. No check figure
P 2. Projected Cost per Unit: $22.25
P 3. No check figure
P 4. No check figure
P 5. Total traffic flow goal, 24,184
P 6. No check figure
P 7. 2. Decrease in number of rejects: 202
P 8. Average output, week eight: 92,899

Chapter 16 Problems
P 1. 2. Total unit cost: $13.72
P 2. Cost of goods manufactured: $10,163,200
P 3. 2a. Gross Margin: $191,800; 2d. Cost of Goods Manufactured: $312,100
P 4. 2. Overhead applied to Job 2214: $29,717
P 5. 2. Total costs assigned to the Grater order, activity-based costing method: $69,280.40
P 6. 1. Predetermined overhead rate for 20x6: $5.014 per machine hour
P 7. 2. Total costs assigned to the Kent order, activity-based costing method: $41,805.60
P 8. 1c. Rigger II: $11,665; BioScout: $14,940

Chapter 17 Problems
P 1. b. $66,500; i. $57,800
P 2. Manufacturing overhead applied, January 15: $108,073
P 3. 2. $185,073
P 4. 1. Audit revenue, Rainy Day Bakeries: $37,163
P 5. Contract revenue, Job Order No. P-12: $28,990
P 6. Manufacturing overhead applied, September 15: $75,480
P 7. 3. $89,647
P 8. No check figure

Chapter 18 Problems
P 1. 1. Cost per equivalent unit: $6.05; ending inventory: $7,225
P 2. 1. Cost per equivalent unit: $2.00; ending inventory: $5,372
P 3. 1. Cost per equivalent unit: $$7.00; ending inventory: $37,200

P 4. 1. Cost per equivalent unit: $3.78; ending inventory: $9,455
P 5. 1. Cost per equivalent unit: $4.70; ending inventory: $39,180
P 6. 1. Cost per equivalent unit: $0.59; ending inventory: $1,494
P 7. 1. Cost per equivalent unit: $1.25; ending inventory: $6,572
P 8. 1. Cost per equivalent unit: $213.40; ending inventory: $220,475

Chapter 19 Problems
P 1. No check figure
P 2. 1. Product unit cost: $270.00; 4. Product unit cost: $280.47
P 3. 1a. Total materials handling cost rate: 30% per dollar of direct materials
P 4. 3. Total direct cost, toy car work cell: $17,000
P 5. 3. Cost of goods sold: $564,400
P 6. 1. Product unit cost: $878.25
P 7. 3. Product unit cost: $10.43
P 8. 3. Cost of goods sold: $391,520

Chapter 20 Problems
P 1. 4. Cost per Job: $81.56
P 2. 1. 7,500 Billable Hours
P 3. 1.a. 3,500 Units
P 4. 2. 190,000 Units
P 5. 3. $806.60 per job
P 6. 1. 740 Systems
P 7. 1.a. 7,900 Units
P 8. 2. 418 Loans

Chapter 21 Problems
P 1. 1. Total manufacturing costs budgeted, November: $1,157,000
P 2. 8. Income from operations: $3,086
P 3. 1. Ending cash balance, August: $1,800
P 4. 1. Projected net income: $101,812
P 5. Ending cash balance, February, $19,555
P 6. 1. Net income: $1,860,830
P 7. 1. Ending cash balance, February: ($2,900)
P 8. 1. Net income: $52,404

Chapter 22 Problems
P 1. Total standard unit cost of front entrance: $8,510
P 2. 2. Flexible budget formula: Total Budgeted Costs = ($.35 x Units Produced) + $10,500
P 3. 1. Direct materials price variance—Metal: $832 (F); 2. Direct labor rate variance—Molding: $510 (F)
P 4. 1.b. Direct materials quantity variance: $3,720 (U); 1.h. Fixed overhead volume variance: $320 (F)
P 5. c. Actual variable overhead: $42,500
P 6. 1. Total standard direct materials cost per unit: $167.52
P 7. 1. Direct materials price variance—Liquid Plastic: $386 (F); 2. Direct labor rate variance—Trimming/Packing: $56 (U)
P 8. 1.a. Direct materials price variance—Chemicals: $12,200 (F); 1.e. Variable overhead spending variance: $100 (U)

Chapter 23 Problems
P 1. 1. Flexible Budget, Total Cost: $7,248,000
P 2. 2. Operating Income: $194,782
P 3. 1. Flexible Budge, Contribution margin: $88,200
P 4. 3. Economic value added for 20x8: $21,850
P 5. 1. Residual income: ($2,500)
P 6. 2. Operating Income: $418,555
P 7. 3a. Actual Return on Investment: 6.3%
P 8. 3. Economic value added: $126,000

Chapter 24 Problems
P 1. 1. Cost to make: $1,200,000
P 2. 1. Contribution margin: $6,420
P 3. 1. Operating loss if Baseball line is dropped: ($50,000)
P 4. 2. Contribution margin per machine hour for AZ1: $2.40
P 5. 1. Contribution margin per hour for phone calls: $130
P 6. 3. Operating income from further processing, bagel sandwiches with cheese: $.50
P 7. 1. Segment margin for Book X: $223,560
P 8. 2. $68.20

Chapter 25 Problems
P 1. 2. $23.04
P 2. 2. Tone Book: $23.39
P 3. Total billing: $14,812.71
P 4. 1. Speed-Calc 4: $78.40; 2. Speed-Calc 5: $84.84
P 5. 1. $19.20
P 6. $27.68
P 7. 1. Product Y14: $520.00; 2. Product Z33: $623.40
P 8. 1. $34.08

Chapter 26 Problems
P 1. 1. 10.15%
P 2. 1. $99,672
P 3. Positive net present value: $35,540
P 4. 1. HZT Machine: 13.4%; 2. XJS Machine: 5.5 years
P 5. Negative net present value: ($26,895)
P 6. 1. $92,536.50
P 7. Negative net present value: ($7,080)
P 8. 1. ETZ Machine: ($32,379); 2. ETZ Machine: 20.7%; 3. ETZ Machine: 5.4 years

Chapter 27 Problems
P 1. 1. Aspen, total costs of quality as a percentage of sales: 7.28%; Frisco, ratio of costs of conformance to costs of quality: 28.10%
P 2. 1. Carbondale Company, total costs of conformance: $533,600; 2. Carbondale Company, total costs of nonconformance: 10.30%
P 3. 1. Springs Division is first; Glenwood Division is last
P 4. 1. Delivery cycle time, weekly average: 73.43
P 5. 1. Partnership Portal, total costs of conformance as a percentage of sales: .58%; 2. Small Business Portal, ratio of costs of nonconformance to costs of quality: 45.03%

P 6. 1. East Division, total costs of conformance: $348,500; 2. East Division, total costs of nonconformance: 9.5% of sales
P 7. Delivery cycle time, weekly average: 58.04 hours

Chapter 28 Problems
P 1. No check figure
P 2. Increase: d, h, i
P 3. 1.c. Receivable turnover, 20x5: 13.9 times; 20x4: 15.6 times; 1.e. Inventory turnover, 20x5: 3.9 times; 20x4: 3.8 times
P 4. 1.b. Quick ratio, Reynard: 0.4 times; Bouche: 1.0 times; 2.d. Return on equity, Reynard: 11.8%; Bouche: 8.8%
P 5. Increase: a, b, e, f, l, m
P 6. 1.a. Current ratio, 20x6: 1.9 times; 20x5: 1.0 times; 2.c. Return on assets, 20x6: 8.4%; 20x5: 6.6%

Financial & Managerial Accounting

1

Chapter 1 explores the nature and environment of accounting, with special emphasis on the users and uses of accounting information.

Uses of Accounting Information and the Financial Statements

LEARNING OBJECTIVES

LO1 Define *accounting*, identify business goals and activities, and describe the role of accounting in making informed decisions.

LO2 Identify the many users of accounting information in society.

LO3 Explain the importance of business transactions, money measure, and separate entity to accounting measurement.

LO4 Describe the corporate form of business organization.

LO5 Define *financial position*, state the accounting equation, and show how they are affected by simple transactions.

LO6 Identify the four financial statements.

LO7 State the relationship of generally accepted accounting principles (GAAP) to financial statements and the independent CPA's report, and identify the organizations that influence GAAP.

LO8 Define *ethics* and describe the ethical responsibilities of accountants.

Look to the learning objectives (LOs) as a guide to help you master the material. You will see many references to LOs throughout each chapter.

Look in the margin for reminders of key concepts or ideas.

KEY POINT: Management must have a good understanding of accounting to set financial goals and to make financial decisions. Management not only must understand how accounting information is compiled and processed but also must realize that accounting information is imperfect and should be interpreted with caution.

DECISION POINT
A USER'S FOCUS

Walgreen Co. <www.walgreens.com>, a nationwide chain of more than 3,800 drugstores and pharmacies, has been a retailing success story, with 28 years of record sales and earnings. During the past five years, Walgreens has opened or remodeled 2,094 stores and by 2010 plans to operate more than 7,000 stores. In fiscal 2002, sales in stores open more than a year rose 10.5 percent.

Why is Walgreens considered successful? Customers appreciate the quality of the products that the company sells and the large selection and good service that its stores offer. Investment companies and others with a financial stake in Walgreens evaluate the success of the company and its management in financial terms, such as those contained in the Financial Highlights from the company's annual report, shown on the opposite page.[1]

Net sales, net earnings, total assets, and stockholders' equity are common financial measures of all companies, large or small. These measures are used to evaluate a company's management and to compare the company to other companies. It is easy to see the large increases at Walgreens over the years in these measures, but what do the terms mean? What financial knowledge do Walgreens' managers need to measure progress toward their financial goals? What financial knowledge does anyone who is evaluating Walgreens in relation to other companies need to understand these measures?

Walgreens' managers must have a thorough knowledge of accounting to understand how the operations for which they are responsible contribute

What kind of information do the people with a financial stake in Walgreens need to have?

to the firm's overall financial health. People with a financial stake in the company, such as owners, investors, creditors, employees, attorneys, and governmental regulators, must also know accounting to evaluate the financial performance of a business. Anyone who aspires to any of these roles in a business requires mastery of accounting terminology and concepts, the process of producing financial information, and how that information is interpreted and analyzed. The purpose of this course and this textbook is to assist you in acquiring that mastery.

← A Decision Point at the start of each chapter shows how leading businesses use the accounting information presented in their annual reports to make business decisions.

Walgreens' Financial Highlights
(In millions)

	2002	2001	2000	1999	1998
Net sales	$28,681	$24,623	$21,207	$17,839	$15,307
Net earnings	1,019	886	777	624	511
Total assets	9,879	8,834	7,104	5,907	4,902
Stockholders' equity	6,230	5,207	4,234	3,484	2,849

Accounting as an Information System

LO1 Define *accounting*, identify business goals and activities, and describe the role of accounting in making informed decisions.

RELATED TEXT ASSIGNMENTS
Q: 1, 2, 3, 4
E: 1
P: 4, 7
SD: 1, 5
FRA: 2, 4, 6, 7, 8

Each LO is stated in the margin to introduce the related text material. The list of Related Text Assignments will guide you to the appropriate questions, exercises, problems, and cases for that LO.

Today's accountant focuses on the ultimate needs of decision makers who use accounting information, whether those decision makers are inside or outside the business. **Accounting** "is not an end in itself,"[2] but *an information system that measures, processes, and communicates financial information about an identifiable economic entity.* An economic entity is a unit that exists independently—a business, a hospital, or a governmental body. The central focus of this book is on business entities and business activities, although other economic units, such as hospitals and governmental units, are mentioned at appropriate points in the text and assignment material.

Accounting provides a vital service by supplying the information that decision makers need to make "reasoned choices among alternative uses of scarce resources in the conduct of business and economic activities."[3] As shown in Figure 1, accounting is a link between business activities and decision makers. First, accounting measures business activities by recording data about them for future use. Second, the data are stored until needed and then processed to become useful information. Third, the information is communicated, through reports, to decision makers. We might say that data about business activities are the input to the accounting system and that useful information for decision makers is the output.

Business Goals, Activities, and Performance Measures

Key terms are highlighted in blue and are followed by their definition.

A **business** is an economic unit that aims to sell goods and services to customers at prices that will provide an adequate return to its owners. The list on the opposite page contains the names of some very well-known businesses and the principal goods or services that they sell.

FIGURE 1
Accounting as an Information System

Figures illustrate relationships between concepts and/or processes.

● **Stop and Think!**
What makes accounting a valuable discipline?

The primary purpose of accounting is to provide decision makers with the financial information they need to make intelligent decisions. It is a valuable discipline because of the usefulness of the information it generates. ■

STOP AND THINK! questions enhance your critical thinking skills by challenging you to pause and reflect on the implications of the concepts and techniques presented in the text. The answers appear below each question.

Video Case

Intel Corporation <www.intel.com>

Objectives

- To examine the principal activities of a business enterprise: financing, investing, and operating.
- To explore the principal performance goals of a business enterprise: liquidity and profitability.
- To relate these activities and goals to the financial statements.

Background for the Case

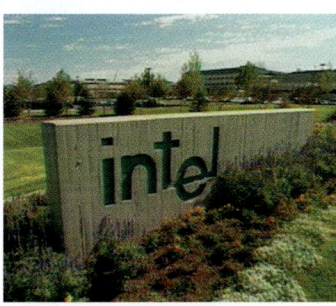

Intel Corporation is one of the most successful companies in the world. In 1971, Intel introduced the world's first microprocessor, which made the personal computer (PC) possible. Today, Intel supplies the computing industry with chips, boards, systems, and software. Its principal products include:

- **Microprocessors.** Also called central processing units (CPUs), these are frequently described as the "brains" of a computer because they act as the central control for the processing of data in PCs. This category includes the famous Pentium® processor.
- **Networking and Communications Products.** These products enhance the capabilities and ease of use of PC systems by allowing users to talk to each other and to share information.
- **Semiconductor Products.** Semiconductors facilitate flash memory, making possible easily reprogrammable memory for computers, mobile phones, and many other products. Included in this category are embedded control chips that are programmed to regulate specific functions in such products as automobile engines, laser printers, disk drives, and home appliances.

In addition to PC users, Intel's customers include manufacturers of computers and computer systems, automobiles, and a wide range of industrial and telecommunications equipment.

For more information about Intel Corporation, visit the company's web site directly or access it through the Needles Accounting Resource Center Web Site at **http://accounting.college.hmco.com/students**.

Required

View the video on Intel Corporation that accompanies this book. As you are watching the video, take notes related to the following:

1. All businesses engage in three basic activities—financing, investing, and operating—but how they engage in them differs from company to company. Describe in your own words the nature of each of these activities and give as many examples as you can of how Intel engages in each activity.
2. To be successful, all businesses must achieve two performance objectives—liquidity and profitability. Describe in your own words the nature of each of these goals and describe how each applies to Intel.
3. Four financial statements apply to business enterprises. Which statements are most closely associated with the goal of liquidity? Which statement is most closely associated with the goal of profitability? Which statement shows the financial position of the company?

> Video cases introduce key concepts and techniques presented in the chapter in the context of a real company.

www.generalmills.com	General Mills, Inc.	Food products
www.reebok.com	Reebok International Ltd.	Athletic footwear and clothing
www.sony.com	Sony Corp.	Consumer electronics
www.wendys.com	Wendy's International Inc.	Food service
www.hilton.com	Hilton Hotels Corp.	Hotels and resorts service
www.southwest.com	Southwest Airlines Co.	Passenger airline service

Icons are visual guides to key features of text and supporting study aids.

www.toyota.com

Despite their differences, all these businesses have similar goals and engage in similar activities, as shown in Figure 2. Each must take in enough money from customers to pay all the costs of doing business, with enough left over as profit for the owners to want to stay in the business. This need to earn enough income to attract and hold investment capital is the goal of **profitability**. In addition, businesses must meet the goal of liquidity. **Liquidity** means having enough cash available to pay debts when they are due. For example, Toyota may meet the goal of profitability by selling many cars at a price that earns a profit, but if its customers do not pay for their cars quickly enough to enable Toyota to pay its suppliers and employees, the

FIGURE 2
Business Goals and Activities

KEY POINT: Multiple financial goals signal that more than one measure of performance is of interest to users of accounting information. For example, lenders are concerned primarily with cash flow, and owners are concerned with earnings and dividends.

The cash flow icon highlights discussion of cash as a measure of liquidity.

The key ratio icon highlights discussion of a measure used to evaluate a company's performance.

company may fail to meet the goal of liquidity. Both goals must be met if a company is to survive and be successful.

All businesses pursue their goals by engaging in similar activities. First, each business must engage in **financing activities** to obtain adequate funds, or capital, to begin and to continue operating. Financing activities include obtaining capital from owners and from creditors, such as banks and suppliers. They also include repaying creditors and paying a return to the owners. Second, each business must engage in **investing activities** to spend the capital it receives in ways that are productive and will help the business achieve its objectives. Investing activities include buying land, buildings, equipment, and other resources that are needed in the operation of the business, and selling these resources when they are no longer needed. Third, each business must engage in **operating activities**. In addition to the selling of goods and services to customers, operating activities include such actions as employing managers and workers, buying and producing goods and services, and paying taxes to the government.

An important function of accounting is to provide **performance measures**, which indicate whether managers are achieving their business goals and whether the business activities are well managed. It is important that these performance measures align with the goals of the business. For example, earned income is a measure of profitability, and cash flow is a measure of liquidity. Ratios of accounting measures are also used as performance measures. For instance, one performance measure for operating activities might be the ratio of expenses to the revenue of the business. A performance measure for financing activities might be the ratio of money owed by the business to total resources controlled by the company. Because managers are usually evaluated on whether targeted levels of specific performance measures are achieved, they must have a knowledge of accounting to understand

Focus on Business Practice

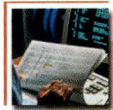

How Do Performance Measures Relate to Executive Bonuses?

A study of chief executive officers' bonus contracts shows that almost all companies use financial performance measures for determining annual bonuses. The most frequent measures are earnings per share, net income, operating income, return on equity, and cash flow. About one-third of the companies studied also use nonfinancial performance measures to determine bonuses. Examples of nonfinancial measures are customer satisfaction, product or service quality, nonfinancial strategic objectives, efficiency or productivity, and employee safety.[4]

www.gap.com

www.walgreens.com

Notations like these indicate that a direct link to the company's web site is available on the Needles Accounting Resource Center Web Site at http://accounting.college.hmco.com/students.

Focus on Business boxes highlight the relevance of accounting in four different areas: business practice, business technology, business ethics, and international business.

how they are evaluated and how they can improve their performance. Further, because managers will act to achieve the targeted performance measures, these measures must be crafted in such a way as to motivate managers to take actions that are in the best interests of the owners of the business.

FINANCIAL AND MANAGEMENT ACCOUNTING

Accounting's role of assisting decision makers by measuring, processing, and communicating information is usually divided into the categories of management accounting and financial accounting. Although there is considerable overlap in the functions of management accounting and financial accounting, the two can be distinguished by who the principal users of their information will be. **Management accounting** provides internal decision makers who are charged with achieving the goals of profitability and liquidity with information about financing, investing, and operating activities. Managers and employees who conduct the activities of the business need information that tells them how they have done in the past and what they can expect in the future. For example, The Gap, a retail clothing business, needs an operating report on each mall outlet that tells how much was sold at that outlet and what costs were incurred, and it needs a budget for each outlet that projects the sales and costs for the next year. **Financial accounting** generates reports and communicates them to external decision makers so that they can evaluate how well the business has achieved its goals. These reports to external users are called **financial statements**. Walgreens, whose stock is traded on the New York Stock Exchange, sends its financial statements to its owners (called *stockholders*), its banks and other creditors, and government regulators. Financial statements report directly on the goals of profitability and liquidity and are used extensively both inside and outside a business to evaluate the business's success. It is important for every person involved with a business to understand financial statements. They are a central feature of accounting and are the primary focus of this book.

PROCESSING ACCOUNTING INFORMATION

To avoid misunderstandings, it is important to distinguish accounting itself from the ways in which accounting information is processed by bookkeeping, computers, and management information systems.

Focus on Business Practice

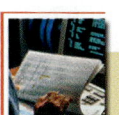

What Does Walgreens Have to Say about Itself?

Walgreens <www.walgreens.com> reports its performance in meeting the major business objectives in its annual report.[5]

Liquidity: "A chunk of our positive cash position is due to a big improvement in inventory levels.... Short-term borrowings of $441 million were completely repaid during the year. For my money, the beauty of our 2002 balance sheet rivals Monet, showing a positive cash swing from borrowing to investing of nearly $900 million."

Profitability: "We completed our 28th consecutive record year—and first billion-dollar earnings year—while opening 471 stores...."

Walgreens' main business activities are shown at the right.

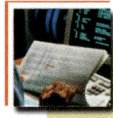

FOCUS ON BUSINESS PRACTICE

How Did Accounting Develop?
Accounting is a very old discipline. Forms of it have been essential to commerce for more than five thousand years. Accounting, in a version close to what we know today, gained widespread use in the 1400s, especially in Italy, where it was instrumental in the development of shipping, trade, construction, and other forms of commerce. This system of double-entry bookkeeping was documented by the famous Italian mathematician, scholar, and philosopher Fra Luca Pacioli. In 1494, Pacioli published his most important work, *Summa de Arithmetica, Geometrica, Proportioni et Proportionalita*, which contained a detailed description of accounting as practiced in that age. This book became the most widely read book on mathematics in Italy and firmly established Pacioli as the "Father of Accounting."

KEY POINT: Computerized accounting information is only as reliable and useful as the data that go into the system. The accountant must have a thorough understanding of the concepts that underlie accounting to ensure the data's reliability and usefulness.

People often fail to understand the difference between accounting and bookkeeping. **Bookkeeping** is the process of recording financial transactions and keeping financial records. Mechanical and repetitive, bookkeeping is only a small—but important—part of accounting. Accounting, on the other hand, includes the design of an information system that meets the user's needs. The major goals of accounting are the analysis, interpretation, and use of information.

The **computer** is an electronic tool used to collect, organize, and communicate vast amounts of information with great speed. Accountants were among the earliest and most enthusiastic users of computers, and today they use microcomputers in all aspects of their work. It may appear that the computer is doing the accountant's job; in fact, it is only a tool that is instructed to do routine bookkeeping and to perform complex calculations.

With the widespread use of the computer today, a business's many information needs are organized into what is called a **management information system (MIS)**. A management information system consists of the interconnected subsystems that provide the information needed to run a business. The accounting information system is the most important subsystem because it plays the key role of managing the flow of economic data to all parts of a business and to interested parties outside the business.

 Check out ACE for a Review Quiz at http://accounting.college.hmco.com/students.

DECISION MAKERS: THE USERS OF ACCOUNTING INFORMATION

LO2 Identify the many users of accounting information in society.
RELATED TEXT ASSIGNMENTS
Q: 5, 6, 7, 8, 9
E: 1, 2
SD: 1, 2, 5

As shown in Figure 3, the people who use accounting information to make decisions fall into three categories: (1) those who manage a business; (2) those outside a business enterprise who have a direct financial interest in the business; and (3) those people, organizations, and agencies that have an indirect financial interest in the business. These categories apply to governmental and not-for-profit organizations as well as to profit-oriented ventures.

FIGURE 3
The Users of Accounting Information

Management

Management refers to the people who have overall responsibility for operating a business and for meeting its profitability and liquidity goals. In a small business, management may consist solely of the owners. In a large business, management more often consists of people who have been hired to do the job. Managers must decide what to do, how to do it, and whether the results match their original plans. Successful managers consistently make the right decisions based on timely and valid information. To make good decisions, managers need answers to such questions as: What was the company's net income during the past quarter? Is the rate of return to the owners adequate? Does the company have enough cash? Which products are most profitable? What is the cost of manufacturing each product? Because so many key decisions are based on accounting data, management is one of the most important users of accounting information.

> **KEY POINT:** Managers are internal users of accounting information.

In carrying out its decision-making process, management performs a set of functions that are essential to the operation of the business. Although large businesses have more elaborate operations than small ones, the same basic functions must be accomplished in all cases, and each requires accounting information for decision making. The basic management functions are:

Financing the business. Financial management obtains financial resources so that the company can begin and continue operating.

Investing the resources of the business. Asset management invests the financial resources of the business in productive assets that support the company's goals.

Producing goods and services. Operations and production management develops and produces goods and services.

Marketing goods and services. Marketing management sells, advertises, and distributes goods and services.

Managing employees. Human resource management encompasses the hiring, evaluation, and compensation of employees.

Providing information to decision makers. Information systems management captures data about all aspects of the company's operations, organizes the data into usable information, and provides reports to internal managers and appropriate outside parties. Accounting plays a key role in this function.

Users with a Direct Financial Interest

Another group of decision makers who need accounting information are those with a direct financial interest in a business. They depend on accounting to measure and report information about how a business has performed. Most businesses periodically publish a set of general-purpose financial statements that report their success in meeting the goals of profitability and liquidity. These statements show what has happened in the past, and they are important indicators of what will happen in the future. Many people outside the company carefully study these financial reports. The two most important outside groups are investors and creditors.

> **KEY POINT:** The primary external users of accounting information are investors and creditors.

■ **Investors** Those who invest or may invest in a business and acquire a part ownership are interested in its past success and its potential earnings. A thorough study of a company's financial statements helps potential investors judge the prospects for a profitable investment. After investing, they must continually review their commitment, again by examining the company's financial statements.

■ **Creditors** Most companies borrow money for both long- and short-term operating needs. Creditors, those who lend money or deliver goods and services before being paid, are interested mainly in whether a company will have the cash to pay interest charges and to repay debt at the appropriate time. They study a

FOCUS ON BUSINESS PRACTICE

What Does the CFO Do?
John Connors, chief financial officer (CFO) of Microsoft <www.microsoft.com>, emphasizes that providing information to decision makers is an important accounting function:

> The way I look at it, the [chief financial officer's] principal job is providing information that the business needs to make good decisions. . . . The real purpose is getting the information that managers need to do their jobs better, whether it is in sales and marketing, research and development, in the support groups, or operations.[6]

company's liquidity and cash flow as well as its profitability. Banks, finance companies, mortgage companies, securities firms, insurance firms, suppliers, and other lenders must analyze a company's financial position before they make a loan.

USERS WITH AN INDIRECT FINANCIAL INTEREST

In recent years, society as a whole, through governmental and public groups, has become one of the largest and most important users of accounting information. Users who need accounting information to make decisions on public issues include tax authorities, regulatory agencies, and various other groups.

■ **TAX AUTHORITIES** Government at every level is financed through the collection of taxes. Under federal, state, and local laws, companies and individuals pay many kinds of taxes, including federal, state, and city income taxes; social security and other payroll taxes; excise taxes; and sales taxes. Each tax requires special tax returns and often a complex set of records as well. Proper reporting is generally a matter of law and can be very complicated. The Internal Revenue Code, for instance, contains thousands of rules governing the preparation of the accounting information used in computing federal income taxes.

www.sec.gov

■ **REGULATORY AGENCIES** Most companies must report periodically to one or more regulatory agencies at the federal, state, and local levels. For example, all public corporations must report periodically to the **Securities and Exchange Commission (SEC)**. This body, set up by Congress to protect the public, regulates the issuing, buying, and selling of stocks in the United States. Companies listed on a stock exchange also must meet the special reporting requirements of their exchange.

■ **OTHER GROUPS** Labor unions study the financial statements of corporations as part of preparing for contract negotiations; a company's income and costs often play an important role in these negotiations. Those who advise investors and creditors—financial analysts, brokers, underwriters, lawyers, economists, and the financial press—also have an indirect interest in the financial performance and prospects of a business. Consumer groups, customers, and the general public have become more concerned about the financing and earnings of corporations as well as the effects that corporations have on inflation, the environment, social problems, and the quality of life. And economic planners, among them the President's Council of Economic Advisers and the Federal Reserve Board, use aggregated accounting information to set and evaluate economic policies and programs.

● Stop and Think!
Why do managers in governmental and not-for-profit organizations need to understand financial information as much as managers in profit-seeking businesses?

Like managers of profit-seeking businesses, managers of governmental and not-for-profit organizations must report to those who fund them, and they must operate their organizations in a financially prudent way. ■

GOVERNMENTAL AND NOT-FOR-PROFIT ORGANIZATIONS

More than 30 percent of the U.S. economy is generated by governmental and not-for-profit organizations (hospitals, universities, professional organizations, and charities). The managers of these diverse entities need to understand and to use accounting information to perform the same functions as managers in businesses. They need to raise funds from investors, creditors, taxpayers, and donors, and to deploy scarce resources. They need to plan to pay for operations and to repay creditors on a timely basis. Moreover, they have an obligation to report their financial performance to legislators, boards, and donors, as well as to deal with tax authorities, regulators, and labor unions. Although most of the examples throughout this text focus on business enterprises, the same basic principles apply to governmental and not-for-profit organizations.

 Check out ACE for a Review Quiz at http://accounting.college.hmco.com/students.

Accounting Measurement

LO3 Explain the importance of business transactions, money measure, and separate entity to accounting measurement.

RELATED TEXT ASSIGNMENTS
Q: 10
SE: 1
E: 3, 4, 5
SD: 3

TERMINOLOGY NOTE:
Measurement means the analysis of transactions in terms of recognition, valuation, and classification. That is, it answers the question: How is this transaction best represented in the accounting records?

Terminology notes define terms used in the text.

Accounting is an information system that measures, processes, and communicates financial information. In this section, you begin the study of the measurement aspects of accounting. Here you learn what accounting actually measures and how certain transactions affect a company's financial position.

To make an accounting measurement, the accountant must answer four basic questions:

1. What is measured? (STRAIGHT FORWARD)
2. When should the measurement be made? (TRICKY)
3. What value should be placed on what is measured? (STRAIGHT FORWARD)
4. How should what is measured be classified? (TRICKY)

All these questions deal with basic assumptions and accepted accounting practice, and their answers establish what accounting is and what it is not. Accountants in industry, professional associations, public accounting, government, and academic circles debate the answers to these questions constantly, and the answers change as new knowledge and practice require. But the basis of today's accounting practice rests on a number of widely accepted concepts and conventions, which are described in this book. We begin by focusing on the first question: What is measured?

What Is Measured?

The world contains an unlimited number of things to measure and ways to measure them. Consider a machine that makes bottle caps. How many measurements of this machine could you make? You might start with size and then go on to location, weight, cost, and many other units of measurement. Some of these measurements are relevant to accounting; some are not. Every system must define what it measures, and accounting is no exception. Basically, financial accounting uses money measures to gauge the impact of business transactions on separate business entities. The concepts of business transactions, money measure, and separate entity are discussed in the next sections.

● **Stop and Think!**
Are all economic events business transactions?
No, because not all economic events involve exchanges of value between a business and someone else. For example, when a customer places an order, it is an economic event, but until the order is fulfilled, no exchange of value has taken place. ■

www.acehardware.com

Business Transactions as the Object of Measurement

Business transactions are economic events that affect the financial position of a business entity. Business entities can have hundreds or even thousands of transactions every day. These transactions are the raw material of accounting reports.

A transaction can be an exchange of value (a purchase, sale, payment, collection, or loan) between two or more independent parties. A transaction also can be an economic event that has the same effect as an exchange transaction but does not involve an exchange. Some examples of "nonexchange" transactions are losses from fire, flood, explosion, and theft; physical wear and tear on machinery and equipment; and the day-by-day accumulation of interest.

To be recorded, a transaction must relate directly to a business entity. Suppose a customer buys a shovel from Ace Hardware but has to buy a hoe from a competing store because Ace is out of hoes. The transaction in which the shovel was sold is entered in Ace's records. However, the purchase of the hoe from the competitor is not entered in Ace's records because even though it indirectly affects Ace economically, it does not involve a direct exchange of value between Ace and the customer.

Money Measure

All business transactions are recorded in terms of money. This concept is termed **money measure**. Of course, information of a nonfinancial nature may be recorded, but it is through the recording of monetary amounts that the diverse transactions

Tables give factual information referred to in the text.

TABLE 1. Examples of Foreign Exchange Rates

Country	Price in $ U.S.	Country	Price in $ U.S.
Australia (dollar)	0.631	Hong Kong (dollar)	0.128
Brazil (real)	0.34	Japan (yen)	0.008
Britain (pound)	1.61	Mexico (peso)	0.10
Canada (dollar)	0.704	Russia (ruble)	0.032
Europe (euro)	1.12	Singapore (dollar)	0.565

Source: *The Wall Street Journal,* May 5, 2003.

and activities of a business are measured. Money is the only factor common to all business transactions, and thus it is the only practical unit of measure that can produce financial data that are alike and can be compared.

The monetary unit a business uses depends on the country in which the business resides. For example, in the United States, the basic unit of money is the dollar. In Japan, it is the yen; in Europe, the euro; and in the United Kingdom, the pound. In international transactions, exchange rates must be used to translate from one currency to another. An **exchange rate** is the value of one currency in terms of another. For example, a British person purchasing goods from a U.S. company and paying in U.S. dollars must exchange British pounds for U.S. dollars before making payment. In effect, the currencies are goods that can be bought and sold. Table 1 illustrates the exchange rates for several currencies in dollars. It shows the exchange rate for British pounds as $1.61 per pound on a particular date. Like the prices of most goods, these prices change daily according to supply and demand for the currencies. For example, a year earlier the exchange rate for British pounds was $1.43. Although our discussion in this book focuses on dollars, selected examples and certain assignments will be in foreign currencies.

KEY POINT: The common unit of measurement in the United States for financial reporting purposes is the dollar.

THE CONCEPT OF SEPARATE ENTITY

Study notes provide useful tips on ways to avoid common pitfalls.

STUDY NOTE: For accounting purposes, a business is *always* separate and distinct from its owners, creditors, and customers. Note, however, that there is a difference between separate economic entity and separate legal entity.

For accounting purposes, a business is a **separate entity**, distinct not only from its creditors and customers but also from its owner or owners. It should have a completely separate set of records, and its financial records and reports should refer only to its own financial affairs. For example, the Jones Florist Company should have a bank account separate from the account of Kay Jones, the owner. Kay Jones may own a home, a car, and other property, and she may have personal debts, but these are not the Jones Florist Company's resources or debts. Kay Jones also may own another business, say a stationery shop. If she does, she should have a completely separate set of records for each business.

 Check out ACE for a Review Quiz at http://accounting.college.hmco.com/students.

THE CORPORATION AS A SEPARATE ENTITY

LO4 Describe the corporate form of business organization.

RELATED TEXT ASSIGNMENTS
Q: 11, 12
SE: 2
E: 2

There are three basic forms of business enterprise: the sole proprietorship form, the partnership form, and the corporate form. Regardless of its form, a business should be viewed for accounting purposes as a separate entity, and all its records and reports should be developed separately and kept apart from those of its owners.

CORPORATIONS DIFFERENTIATED FROM SOLE PROPRIETORSHIPS AND PARTNERSHIPS

A **sole proprietorship** is a business owned by one person. The individual receives all profits or losses and is liable for all obligations of the business. Sole proprietor-

FOCUS ON BUSINESS PRACTICE

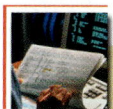

Are Most Corporations Big or Small Businesses?

Most people think of corporations as large national or global companies whose shares of stock are held by thousands of people and institutions. Indeed, corporations can be huge and have many stockholders. However, of the approximately 4 million corporations in the United States, only about 15,000 have stock that is publicly bought and sold. The vast majority of corporations are small businesses privately held by a few stockholders. Illinois alone has more than 250,000 corporations. Thus, the study of corporations is just as relevant to small businesses as it is to large ones.

STOP AND THINK!

Sole proprietorships, partnerships, and corporations differ legally; how and why does accounting treat them alike?

Accounting treats these business forms as entities separate from their owners because the financial performance of each must be measured and reported. ■

KEY POINT: A key disadvantage of a partnership is the unlimited liability of its owners. Unlimited liability can be avoided by organizing the business as a corporation.

ships represent the largest number of businesses in the United States, but typically they are the smallest in size. A **partnership** is like a sole proprietorship in most ways, but it has two or more owners. The partners share the profits and losses of the partnership according to an agreed-upon formula. Generally, any partner can obligate the partnership to another party, and the personal resources of each partner can be called on to pay obligations of the partnership. A partnership must be dissolved if the ownership changes, as when a partner leaves or dies. If the business is to continue as a partnership after this occurs, a new partnership must be formed. Both the sole proprietorship and the partnership are convenient ways of separating the business owners' commercial activities from their personal activities. But legally there is no economic separation between the owners and the businesses. (Accounting for sole proprietorships and partnerships is discussed in an appendix to this book.)

A **corporation**, on the other hand, is a business unit chartered by the state and legally separate from its owners (the stockholders). The stockholders, whose ownership is represented by shares of stock, do not directly control the corporation's operations. Instead, they elect a board of directors to run the corporation for their benefit. In exchange for their limited involvement in the corporation's actual operations, stockholders enjoy limited liability; that is, their risk of loss is limited to the amount they paid for their shares. Thus, stockholders are often willing to invest in risky, but potentially profitable, activities. Also, because stockholders can sell their shares without dissolving the corporation, the life of a corporation is unlimited and not subject to the whims or health of a proprietor or a partner.

The characteristics of corporations make them very efficient in amassing capital, which enables them to grow extremely large. As Figure 4 shows, even though corporations are fewer in number than sole proprietorships and partnerships, they

FIGURE 4
Number and Receipts of U.S. Proprietorships, Partnerships, and Corporations, 2000

Source: U.S. Treasury Department, Internal Revenue Service, *Statistics of Income Bulletin,* Spring 2001.

FIGURE 5
The Corporate Form of Business

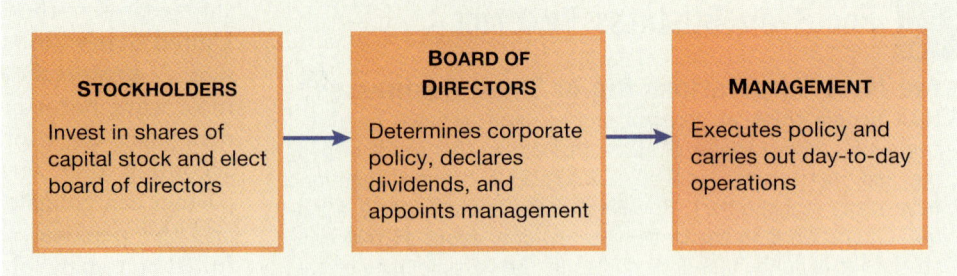

www.exxonmobil.com

contribute much more to the U.S. economy in monetary terms. For example, in 1999, ExxonMobil generated more revenues than all but 30 of the world's countries. Because of the economic significance of corporations, this book emphasizes accounting for the corporate form of business.

FORMATION OF A CORPORATION

To form a corporation, most states require individuals, called incorporators, to sign an application and file it with the proper state official. This application contains the **articles of incorporation**. If approved by the state, these articles, or company charter, become a contract between the state and the incorporators. The company is then authorized to do business.

ORGANIZATION OF A CORPORATION

The authority to manage the corporation is delegated by the stockholders to the board of directors and by the board of directors to the corporate officers (see Figure 5). That is, the stockholders elect the board of directors, which sets company policies and chooses the corporate officers, who in turn carry out the corporate policies by managing the business.

■ **STOCKHOLDERS** A unit of ownership in a corporation is called a **share of stock**. The articles of incorporation state the maximum number of shares of stock that the corporation is authorized to issue. The number of shares held by stockholders is the outstanding capital stock; this may be less than the number authorized in the articles of incorporation. To invest in a corporation, a stockholder transfers cash or other resources to the corporation. In return, the stockholder receives shares of stock representing a proportionate share of ownership in the corporation. Afterward, the stockholder may transfer the shares at will. Corporations may have more than one kind of capital stock but the first part of this book will refer only to common stock—the most universal form of capital stock.

■ **BOARD OF DIRECTORS** As noted, the stockholders elect the board of directors, which in turn decides on the major business policies of the corporation. Among the specific duties of the board are authorizing contracts, setting executive salaries, and arranging major loans with banks. The declaration of dividends is also an important function of the board of directors. Only the board has the authority to declare dividends. Dividends are distributions of resources, generally in the form of cash, to the stockholders. Paying dividends is one way of rewarding stockholders for their investment when the corporation has been successful in earning a profit. (The other way is through a rise in the market value of the stock.) Although there is usually a delay of two or three weeks between the time the board declares a dividend and the date of the actual payment, we shall assume in the early chapters of this book that declaration and payment are made on the same day.

The composition of the board of directors varies from company to company, but in most cases it includes several officers of the corporation and several outsiders. Today, the formation of an **audit committee** with several outside directors is encouraged in order to ensure that the board will be objective in evaluating management's performance. One function of the audit committee is to engage the company's independent auditors and review their work. Another is to make sure that proper systems exist to safeguard the company's resources and that reliable accounting records are kept.

■ **MANAGEMENT** The board of directors appoints managers to carry out the corporation's policies and run day-to-day operations. The management consists of the operating officers, who are generally the president, vice presidents, controller, treasurer, and secretary. Besides being responsible for running the business, management has the duty of reporting the financial results of its administration to the board of directors and the stockholders. Though management must, at a minimum, make a comprehensive annual report, it generally reports more often. The annual reports of large public corporations are available to the public. Excerpts from many of them are used throughout this book.

 Check out ACE for a Review Quiz at http://accounting.college.hmco.com/students.

FINANCIAL POSITION AND THE ACCOUNTING EQUATION

LO5 Define *financial position*, state the accounting equation, and show how they are affected by simple transactions.

RELATED TEXT ASSIGNMENTS
Q: 13, 14, 15, 16
SE: 3, 4, 5, 6, 7, 8, 9
E: 6, 7, 8, 9, 10, 11
P: 1, 2, 3, 5, 6, 8
SD: 6
FRA: 6, 8

Financial position refers to the economic resources that belong to a company and the claims against those resources at a point in time. Another term for claims is *equities*. Therefore, a company can be viewed as economic resources and equities:

Economic Resources = Equities

Every company has two types of equities, creditors' equities and owners' equity:

Economic Resources = Creditors' Equities + Owners' Equity

In accounting terminology, economic resources are called *assets* and creditors' equities are called *liabilities*. So the equation can be written like this:

Assets = Liabilities + Owners' Equity

This equation is known as the **accounting equation**. The two sides of the equation must always be equal, or "in balance." To evaluate the financial effects of business activities, it is important to understand their effects on this equation.

ASSETS

KEY POINT: Assets are resources of a business, the essence of which is expected future benefits.

Assets are economic resources owned by a business that are expected to benefit future operations. Certain kinds of assets—for example, cash and money owed to the company by customers (called *accounts receivable*)—are monetary items. Other assets—inventories (goods held for sale), land, buildings, and equipment—are nonmonetary, physical items. Still other assets—the rights granted by patents, trademarks, or copyrights—are nonphysical.

LIABILITIES

KEY POINT: A liability is a debt or obligation that is satisfied with the payment of cash or the performance of a service.

Liabilities are present obligations of a business to pay cash, transfer assets, or provide services to other entities in the future. Among these obligations are debts of the business, amounts owed to suppliers for goods or services bought on credit (called *accounts payable*), borrowed money (for example, money owed on loans payable to banks), salaries and wages owed to employees, taxes owed to the government, and services to be performed.

As debts, liabilities are claims recognized by law. That is, the law gives creditors the right to force the sale of a company's assets if the company fails to pay its debts. Creditors have rights over owners and must be paid in full before the owners receive anything, even if payment of a debt uses up all the assets of a business.

Owners' Equity

Owners' equity represents the claims by the owners of a business to the assets of the business. It equals the residual interest, or *residual equity*, in the assets of an entity that remains after deducting the entity's liabilities. Theoretically, it is what would be left over if all the liabilities were paid, and it is sometimes said to equal **net assets**. By rearranging the accounting equation, we can define owners' equity this way:

$$\text{Owners' Equity} = \text{Assets} - \text{Liabilities}$$

The owners' equity of a corporation is called **stockholders' equity**, or *shareholders' equity*. Thus the accounting equation becomes

$$\text{Assets} = \text{Liabilities} + \text{Stockholders' Equity}$$

Stockholders' equity has two parts, contributed capital and retained earnings:

$$\text{Stockholders' Equity} = \text{Contributed Capital} + \text{Retained Earnings}$$

www.tru.com

Contributed capital is the amount that stockholders invest in the business. Their ownership in the business is represented by shares of capital stock. Figure 6 is a Toys "R" Us stock certificate, which represents such ownership.

Typically, contributed capital is divided between par value and additional paid-in capital. Par value is an amount per share that is entered in the corporation's capital stock account and is the minimum amount that can be reported as contributed capital. When the value received is greater than par value, the amount over par value is called additional paid-in capital. In the initial chapters of this book, contributed capital will be shown as common stock that has been issued at par value.

Retained earnings represent the equity of the stockholders generated from the income-producing activities of the business and kept for use in the business. As you

FIGURE 6
A Toys "R" Us Stock Certificate

Source: Reprinted courtesy of Toys "R" Us.

FIGURE 7
Three Types of Transactions That Affect Retained Earnings

● **STOP AND THINK!**
How are expenses and dividends similar, and how are they different?

Expenses and dividends are the same in that they both reduce the retained earnings component of stockholders' equity. They are different in that expenses are also a component of net income, whereas dividends are a distribution of assets to stockholders resulting from net income. ∎

can see in Figure 7, retained earnings are affected by three kinds of transactions: revenues, expenses, and dividends.

Simply stated, **revenues** and **expenses** are the increases and decreases in stockholders' equity that result from operating a business. For example, the amount a customer pays (or agrees to pay in the future) to a company in return for a service provided by the company is a revenue to the company. The assets (cash or accounts receivable) of the company increase, and the stockholders' equity in those assets also increases. On the other hand, the amount a company pays out (or agrees to pay in the future) in the process of providing a service is an expense. In this case, the assets (cash) decrease or the liabilities (accounts payable) increase, and the stockholders' equity decreases. Generally speaking, a company is successful if its revenues exceed its expenses. When revenues exceed expenses, the difference is called **net income**; when expenses exceed revenues, the difference is called **net loss**. **Dividends** are distributions to stockholders of assets (usually cash) generated by past earnings. It is important not to confuse expenses and dividends, both of which reduce retained earnings. In summary, retained earnings is the accumulated net income (revenues − expenses) less dividends over the life of the business.

SOME ILLUSTRATIVE TRANSACTIONS

Let us now examine the effect of some of the most common business transactions on the accounting equation. Suppose that James and Jessica Shannon open a real estate agency called Shannon Realty, Inc., on December 1. During December, their business engages in the transactions described in the following paragraphs.

■ **OWNERS' INVESTMENTS** James and Jessica Shannon file articles of incorporation with the state and receive their charter. To begin their new business, they invest $50,000 in Shannon Realty, Inc., in exchange for 5,000 shares of $10 par value stock. The first balance sheet of the new company would show the asset Cash and the contributed capital (Common Stock) of the owners:

Assets	=	Stockholders' Equity (SE)	
Cash		Common Stock	Type of SE Transaction
1. $50,000		$50,000	Stockholders' Investments

At this point, the company has no liabilities, and assets equal stockholders' equity. The labels Cash and Common Stock are called **accounts**. These are used by accountants to accumulate amounts that result from similar transactions. Transactions that affect stockholders' equity are identified by type so that similar types may later be grouped together on accounting reports.

■ **PURCHASE OF ASSETS WITH CASH** After a good location is found, the company pays cash to purchase a lot for $10,000 and a small building on the lot for $25,000.

This transaction does not change Shannon Realty's total assets, liabilities, or stockholders' equity, but it does change the composition of the assets—it decreases Cash and increases Land and Building:

		Assets			=	Stockholders' Equity	
		Cash	Land	Building		Common Stock	Type of SE Transaction
bal.		$50,000				$50,000	
2.		−35,000	+$10,000	+$25,000			
bal.		$15,000	$10,000	$25,000		$50,000	

$50,000

KEY POINT: The purchase of an asset does not affect stockholders' equity.

KEY POINT: Assets purchased on credit are recorded for the full amount at the time of purchase.

■ **PURCHASE OF ASSETS BY INCURRING A LIABILITY** Assets do not always have to be purchased with cash. They may also be purchased on credit, that is, on the basis of an agreement to pay for them later. Suppose the company buys some office supplies for $500 on credit. This transaction increases the assets (Supplies) and increases the liabilities of Shannon Realty. This liability is designated by an account called Accounts Payable:

	Assets				=	Liabilities	+	Stockholders' Equity	
	Cash	Supplies	Land	Building		Accounts Payable		Common Stock	Type of SE Transaction
bal.	$15,000		$10,000	$25,000				$50,000	
3.		+$500				+$500			
bal.	$15,000	$500	$10,000	$25,000		$500		$50,000	

$50,500 $50,500

Notice that this transaction increases both sides of the accounting equation to $50,500.

KEY POINT: Payment of a liability does not affect stockholders' equity or the asset purchased on credit.

■ **PAYMENT OF A LIABILITY** If Shannon Realty later pays $200 of the $500 owed for the supplies, both assets (Cash) and liabilities (Accounts Payable) decrease, but Supplies is unaffected:

	Assets				=	Liabilities	+	Stockholders' Equity	
	Cash	Supplies	Land	Building		Accounts Payable		Common Stock	Type of SE Transaction
bal.	$15,000	$500	$10,000	$25,000		$500		$50,000	
4.	−200					−200			
bal.	$14,800	$500	$10,000	$25,000		$300		$50,000	

$50,300 $50,300

Notice that both sides of the accounting equation are still equal, although now at a total of $50,300.

KEY POINT: Revenues equal the price charged for the sale of goods or services.

■ **REVENUES** Shannon Realty earns revenues in the form of commissions by selling houses for clients. Sometimes these commissions are paid to Shannon Realty immediately in the form of cash, and sometimes the client agrees to pay the commission later. In either case, the commission is recorded when it is earned and Shannon Realty has a right to a current or future receipt of cash. First, assume that Shannon Realty sells a house and receives a commission of $1,500 in cash. This transaction increases both assets (Cash) and stockholders' equity (Retained Earnings):

	Assets				=	Liabilities	+	Stockholders' Equity		
	Cash	Supplies	Land	Building		Accounts Payable		Common Stock	Retained Earnings	Type of SE Transaction
bal.	$14,800	$500	$10,000	$25,000		$300		$50,000		
5.	+1,500								+$1,500	Commissions Earned
bal.	$16,300	$500	$10,000	$25,000		$300		$50,000	$1,500	
		$51,800						$51,800		

KEY POINT: Revenues are recorded when they are earned, not necessarily when payments are received.

Now assume that Shannon Realty sells a house, in the process earning a commission of $2,000, and agrees to wait for payment of the commission. Because the commission has been earned now, a bill or invoice is sent to the client, and the transaction is recorded now. This revenue transaction increases both assets and stockholders' equity as before, but a new asset account, Accounts Receivable, shows that Shannon Realty is awaiting receipt of the commission:

	Assets					=	Liabilities	+	Stockholders' Equity		
	Cash	Accounts Receivable	Supplies	Land	Building		Accounts Payable		Common Stock	Retained Earnings	Type of SE Transaction
bal.	$16,300		$500	$10,000	$25,000		$300		$50,000	$1,500	
6.		+$2,000								+2,000	Commissions Earned
bal.	$16,300	$2,000	$500	$10,000	$25,000		$300		$50,000	$3,500	
			$53,800						$53,800		

As you progress in your study of accounting, you will be shown the use of separate accounts for revenues, like Commissions Earned.

■ **COLLECTION OF ACCOUNTS RECEIVABLE** Let us assume that a few days later Shannon Realty receives $1,000 from the client in transaction 6. At that time, the asset Cash increases and the asset Accounts Receivable decreases:

	Assets					=	Liabilities	+	Stockholders' Equity		
	Cash	Accounts Receivable	Supplies	Land	Building		Accounts Payable		Common Stock	Retained Earnings	Type of SE Transaction
bal.	$16,300	$2,000	$500	$10,000	$25,000		$300		$50,000	$3,500	
7.	+1,000	−1,000									
bal.	$17,300	$1,000	$500	$10,000	$25,000		$300		$50,000	$3,500	
			$53,800						$53,800		

Notice that this transaction does not affect stockholders' equity because the commission revenue was already recorded in transaction **6**. Also, notice that the balance of Accounts Receivable is $1,000, indicating that $1,000 is still to be collected.

■ **EXPENSES** Just as revenues are recorded when they are earned, expenses are recorded when they are incurred. Expenses can be paid in cash when they occur, or they can be paid later. If payment is going to be made later, a liability—for example, Accounts Payable or Wages Payable—increases. In both cases, stockholders' equity decreases. Assume that Shannon Realty pays $1,000 to rent some equipment for the office and $400 in wages to a part-time helper. These transactions reduce assets (Cash) and stockholders' equity (Retained Earnings):

	Assets					=	Liabilities	+	Stockholders' Equity		
	Cash	Accounts Receivable	Supplies	Land	Building		Accounts Payable		Common Stock	Retained Earnings	Type of SE Transaction
bal.	$17,300	$1,000	$500	$10,000	$25,000		$300		$50,000	$3,500	
8.	−1,000									−1,000	Equipment Rental Expense
9.	−400									−400	Wages Expense
bal.	$15,900	$1,000	$500	$10,000	$25,000		$300		$50,000	$2,100	

$52,400 = $52,400

Now assume that Shannon Realty has not paid a $300 bill for utilities expense incurred for December. In this case, the effect on stockholders' equity is the same as when the expense is paid in cash, but instead of a reduction in assets, there is an increase in liabilities (Accounts Payable):

	Assets					=	Liabilities	+	Stockholders' Equity		
	Cash	Accounts Receivable	Supplies	Land	Building		Accounts Payable		Common Stock	Retained Earnings	Type of SE Transaction
bal.	$15,900	$1,000	$500	$10,000	$25,000		$300		$50,000	$2,100	
10.							+300			−300	Utilities Expense
bal.	$15,900	$1,000	$500	$10,000	$25,000		$600		$50,000	$1,800	

$52,400 = $52,400

As you progress in your study of accounting, you will be shown the use of separate accounts for expenses, like Equipment Rental Expense, Wages Expense, and Utilities Expense.

STUDY NOTE: Dividends do not qualify as expenses because they do not generate revenue; they are simply distributions to stockholders.

■ **DIVIDENDS** A dividend of $600 is declared, and it is paid by taking $600 out of the company's bank account and paying it to the stockholders for deposit in their personal bank accounts. The payment of dividends reduces assets (Cash) and stockholders' equity (Retained Earnings). Note that even though these dividends reduce retained earnings in the same way as the expenses in transactions **8, 9,** and **10,** they perform a different function. They are distributions of assets (Cash) to the stockholders, whereas the function of the expenses is to pay for services that helped produce the revenues in transactions **5** and **6.**

	Assets					=	Liabilities	+	Stockholders' Equity		
	Cash	Accounts Receivable	Supplies	Land	Building		Accounts Payable		Common Stock	Retained Earnings	Type of SE Transaction
bal.	$15,900	$1,000	$500	$10,000	$25,000		$600		$50,000	$1,800	
11.	−600									−600	Dividends
bal.	$15,300	$1,000	$500	$10,000	$25,000		$600		$50,000	$1,200	

$51,800 = $51,800

■ **SUMMARY** Exhibit 1 summarizes these 11 illustrative transactions.

✓ Check out ACE for a Review Quiz at http://accounting.college.hmco.com/students.

Exhibit 1
Summary of Effects of Illustrative Transactions on Financial Position

Exhibits illustrate financial information.

	Assets					=	Liabilities	+	Stockholders' Equity		
	Cash	Accounts Receivable	Supplies	Land	Building		Accounts Payable		Common Stock	Retained Earnings	Type of Stockholders' Equity Transaction
1.	$50,000								$50,000		Stockholders' Investments
2.	−35,000			+$10,000	+$25,000						
bal.	$15,000			$10,000	$25,000				$50,000		
3.			+$500				+$500				
bal.	$15,000		$500	$10,000	$25,000		$500		$50,000		
4.	−200						−200				
bal.	$14,800		$500	$10,000	$25,000		$300		$50,000		
5.	+1,500									+$1,500	Commissions Earned
bal.	$16,300		$500	$10,000	$25,000		$300		$50,000	$1,500	
6.		+$2,000								+2,000	Commissions Earned
bal.	$16,300	$2,000	$500	$10,000	$25,000		$300		$50,000	$3,500	
7.	+1,000	−1,000									
bal.	$17,300	$1,000	$500	$10,000	$25,000		$300		$50,000	$3,500	
8.	−1,000									−1,000	Equipment Rental Expense
9.	−400									−400	Wages Expense
bal.	$15,900	$1,000	$500	$10,000	$25,000		$300		$50,000	$2,100	
10.							+300			−300	Utilities Expense
bal.	$15,900	$1,000	$500	$10,000	$25,000		$600		$50,000	$1,800	
11.	−600									−600	Dividends
bal.	$15,300	$1,000	$500	$10,000	$25,000		$600		$50,000	$1,200	

$51,800 = $51,800

COMMUNICATION THROUGH FINANCIAL STATEMENTS

LO6 Identify the four financial statements.
RELATED TEXT ASSIGNMENTS
Q: 17, 18, 19, 20, 21
SE: 10
E: 11, 12, 13, 14, 15
P: 4, 5, 7, 8
SD: 6
FRA: 3, 5, 7

KEY POINT: Businesses communicate financial information to decision makers in the form of four major financial statements.

Financial statements are the primary means of communicating important accounting information about a business to those who have an interest in the business. It is helpful to think of these statements as models of the business enterprise because they show the business in financial terms. As is true of all models, however, financial statements are not perfect pictures of the real thing. Rather, they are the accountant's best effort to represent what is real. Four major financial statements communicate accounting information about a business: the income statement, the statement of retained earnings, the balance sheet, and the statement of cash flows.

Exhibit 2 illustrates the relationship among the four financial statements by showing how they would appear for Shannon Realty, Inc., after the eleven sample transactions shown in Exhibit 1. The time period covered is the month of December 20xx. Notice that each statement is headed in a similar way. Each heading identifies the company and the kind of statement. The income statement, the statement of retained earnings, and the statement of cash flows give the time period to which they apply; the balance sheet gives the specific date to which it applies. Much of this book deals with developing, using, and interpreting more complete versions of these basic statements.

THE INCOME STATEMENT

TERMINOLOGY NOTE:
The income statement is also called the *statement of earnings,* the *statement of operations,* or the *profit and loss statement.* Its purpose is to measure a company's performance over an accounting period.

The **income statement** summarizes the revenues earned and expenses incurred by a business over a period of time. Many people consider it the most important financial report because it shows whether or not a business achieved its profitability goal of earning an acceptable income. In Exhibit 2, Shannon Realty had revenues in the form of commissions earned of $3,500 ($2,000 of revenue earned on credit and $1,500 of cash). From this amount, total expenses of $1,700 were deducted (equipment rental expense of $1,000, wages expense of $400, and utilities expense of $300), to arrive at a net income of $1,800. To show that it applies to a period of time, the statement is dated "For the Month Ended December 31, 20xx."

THE STATEMENT OF RETAINED EARNINGS

The **statement of retained earnings** shows the changes in retained earnings over a period of time. In Exhibit 2, the beginning retained earnings is zero because the company was started in this accounting period. During the month, the company earned an income (as shown on the income statement) of $1,800. Deducted from this amount are the dividends for the month of $600, leaving an ending balance of $1,200 of earnings retained in the business.

Many companies use the **statement of stockholders' equity,** or shareholders' equity, in place of the statement of retained earnings. The statement of stockholders' equity is a more comprehensive statement that not only incorporates the components of the retained earnings statement but also includes the changes in all the stockholders' equity accounts. The statement of stockholders' equity will be explained in greater detail in a later chapter.

THE BALANCE SHEET

TERMINOLOGY NOTE:
The balance sheet is also called the *statement of financial position.* It represents two different views of a business: The left side shows the resources of the business; the right side shows who provided those resources (the creditors and the owners).

The purpose of a **balance sheet** is to show the financial position of a business on a certain date, usually the end of the month or year. For this reason, it often is called the *statement of financial position* and is dated as of a certain date. The balance sheet presents a view of the business as the holder of resources, or assets, that are equal to the claims against those assets. The claims consist of the company's liabilities and the stockholders' equity in the company. In Exhibit 2, Shannon Realty, Inc., has several categories of assets, which total $51,800. These assets equal the total liabilities of $600 (Accounts Payable) plus the ending balance of stockholders' equity of

EXHIBIT 2
Income Statement, Statement of Retained Earnings, Balance Sheet, and Statement of Cash Flows for Shannon Realty, Inc.

Shannon Realty, Inc.
Income Statement
For the Month Ended December 31, 20xx

Revenues		
Commissions earned		$3,500
Expenses		
Equipment rental expense	$1,000	
Wages expense	400	
Utilities expense	300	
Total expenses		1,700
Net income		**$1,800**

Shannon Realty, Inc.
Statement of Retained Earnings
For the Month Ended December 31, 20xx

Retained earnings, December 1, 20xx	$ 0
Net income for the month	1,800
Subtotal	$1,800
Less dividends	600
Retained earnings, December 31, 20xx	$1,200

Shannon Realty, Inc.
Statement of Cash Flows
For the Month Ended December 31, 20xx

Cash flows from operating activities		
Net income		$ 1,800
Adjustments to reconcile net income to net cash flows from operating activities		
Increase in accounts receivable	($ 1,000)*	
Increase in supplies	(500)	
Increase in accounts payable	600	(900)
Net cash flows from operating activities		$ 900
Cash flows from investing activities		
Purchase of land	($10,000)	
Purchase of building	(25,000)	
Net cash flows from investing activities		(35,000)
Cash flows from financing activities		
Investments by stockholders	$50,000	
Dividends	(600)	
Net cash flows from financing activities		49,400
Net increase (decrease) in cash		$15,300
Cash at beginning of month		0
Cash at end of month		$15,300

Shannon Realty, Inc.
Balance Sheet
December 31, 20xx

Assets		Liabilities	
Cash	$15,300	Accounts payable	$ 600
Accounts receivable	1,000		
Supplies	500	**Stockholders' Equity**	
Land	10,000	Common stock	$50,000
Building	25,000	Retained earnings	1,200
		Total stockholders' equity	51,200
Total assets	$51,800	Total liabilities and stockholders' equity	$51,800

KEY POINT: Notice the sequence in which these financial statements must be prepared. The statement of retained earnings is a link between the income statement and the balance sheet, and the statement of cash flows is prepared last.

*Parentheses indicate a negative amount.

EXHIBIT 3
Walgreen Co.'s Income Statements

> Many excerpts from the annual reports of leading businesses illustrate key concepts.

> The word *consolidated* means all companies owned by Walgreens are combined.

Consolidated Statements of Earnings*
Walgreen Co. and Subsidiaries
For the Years Ended August 31, 2002, 2001 and 2000
(Dollars in Millions, except per share data)

> Walgreens' fiscal year ends on August 31.

	Earnings	2002	2001	2000
Net Sales	Net Sales	$28,681.1	$24,623.0	$21,206.9
Costs and Deductions	Cost of sales	21,076.1	18,048.9	15,465.9
	Selling, occupancy and administration	5,980.8	5,175.8	4,516.9
		27,056.9	23,224.7	19,982.8
Other (Income) Expense	Interest income	(6.9)	(5.4)	(6.1)
	Interest expense	—	3.1	.4
	Other income	(6.2)	(22.1)	(33.5)
		(13.1)	(24.4)	(39.2)
Earnings	Earnings before income tax provision	1,637.3	1,422.7	1,263.3
	Income tax provision	618.1	537.1	486.4
	Net Earnings	$ 1,019.2	$ 885.6	$ 776.9
Net Earnings per Common Share	Basic	$ 1.00	$ .87	$ .77
	Diluted	$ .99	$ .86	$ .76
	Average shares outstanding	1,022,554,460	1,016,197,785	1,007,393,572
	Dilutive effect of stock options	9,716,486	12,748,828	12,495,236
	Average shares outstanding assuming dilution	1,032,270,946	1,028,946,613	1,019,888,808

> Income taxes (Income Tax Provision) are shown separately.

> Net earnings figure moves to statements of stockholders' equity.

Source: Walgreen Co., *Annual Report,* 2002 (year ended August 31, 2002).
*Note that in Walgreen Co.'s actual annual report, the consolidated statements of earnings are combined with the consolidated statements of shareholders' equity.

$51,200. Notice that the Retained Earnings account on the balance sheet comes from the ending balance on the statement of retained earnings.

THE STATEMENT OF CASH FLOWS

Whereas the income statement focuses on a company's profitability goal, the **statement of cash flows** is directed toward the company's liquidity goal. **Cash flows** are the inflows and outflows of cash into and out of a business. Net cash flows are the difference between the inflows and outflows. The statement of cash flows shows the cash produced by operating a business as well as important investing and financing transactions that take place during an accounting period. Notice in Exhibit 2 that the statement of cash flows for Shannon Realty explains how the Cash account changed during the period. Cash increased by $15,300. Operating activities pro-

EXHIBIT 4
Walgreen Co.'s Statements of Stockholders' Equity

Consolidated Statements of Shareholders' Equity*
Walgreen Co. and Subsidiaries
For the Years Ended August 31, 2002, 2001 and 2000
(Dollars in Millions, except per share data)

Each stockholders' equity account has a column that explains the change from year to year.

Shareholders' Equity	Common Stock Shares	Common Stock Amount	Paid-in Capital	Retained Earnings
Balance, August 31, 1999	1,004,022,258	$78.4	$258.9	$3,147.0
Net earnings	—	—	—	776.9
Cash dividends declared ($.135 per share)	—	—	—	(136.1)
Employee stock purchase and option plans	6,796,632	.6	108.3	—
Balance, August 31, 2000	1,010,818,890	79.0	367.2	3,787.8
Net earnings	—	—	—	885.6
Cash dividends declared ($.14 per share)	—	—	—	(142.5)
Employee stock purchase and option plans	8,606,162	.6	229.5	—
Balance, August 31, 2001	1,019,425,052	79.6	596.7	4,530.9
Net earnings	—	—	—	1,019.2
Cash dividends declared ($.145 per share)	—	—	—	(148.4)
Employee stock purchase and option plans	5,483,224	.5	151.7	—
Balance, August 31, 2002	1,024,908,276	$80.1	$748.4	$5,401.7

Net earnings (loss) from Income Statement

Source: Walgreen Co., *Annual Report,* 2002 (year ended August 31, 2002).

The accompanying Statement of Major Accounting Policies and the Notes to Consolidated Financial Statements are integral parts of these statements.

*Note that in Walgreen Co.'s actual annual report, the consolidated statements of earnings are combined with the consolidated statements of shareholders' equity.

KEY POINT: The purpose of the statement of cash flows is to explain the change in cash in terms of operating, investing, and financing activities over an accounting period. It provides valuable information that cannot be determined in an examination of the other three financial statements.

www.walgreens.com

duced net cash flows of $900, and financing activities produced net cash flows of $49,400. Investing activities used cash flows of $35,000.

This statement is related directly to the other three statements. Notice that net income comes from the income statement and that dividends come from the statement of retained earnings. The other items in the statement represent changes in the balance sheet accounts: Accounts Receivable, Supplies, Accounts Payable, Land, Building, and Common Stock. Here we focus on the importance and overall structure of the statement. Its construction and use are discussed in a later chapter.

FINANCIAL STATEMENTS OF WALGREEN CO.

The financial statements of Shannon Realty, Inc., are relatively simple and easy to understand. While significantly more complex, the financial statements of a large corporation like Walgreen Co. are based on the same concepts and structure. The financial statements for Walgreens are shown in Exhibits 3 through 6. Although you will not yet understand some of the terms in these statements, you can comprehend the structure and interrelationships of the statements.

These statements present data for either two or three years. They are called *comparative financial statements* because they enable the reader to compare

EXHIBIT 5
Walgreen Co.'s Balance Sheets

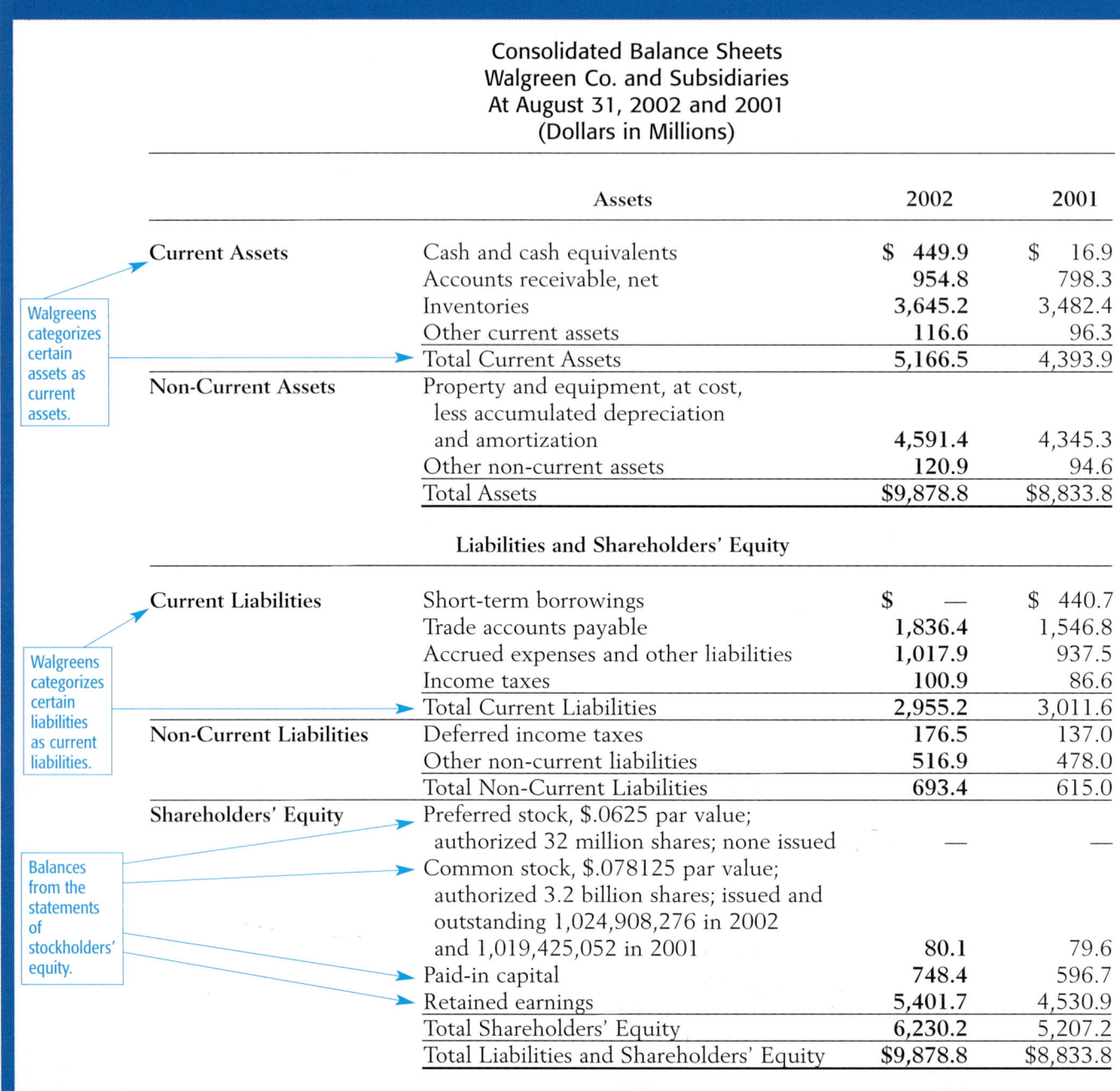

Source: Walgreen Co., *Annual Report,* 2002 (year ended August 31, 2002).
The accompanying Statement of Major Accounting Policies and the Notes to Consolidated Financial Statements are integral parts of these statements.

🛑 **STOP AND THINK!**
How are Walgreens and Toys "R" Us comparable?
Although their merchandise differs, they sell closely related products efficiently at reasonable prices in large buildings in many different locations. Thus, from an operating standpoint, they are very comparable. ■

Walgreens' performance from year to year. Also note that the year-end date of Walgreens' business, or the fiscal year, in these financial statements is August 31. A company usually may end its business year on any day it likes as long as it is consistent from year to year. Finally, note that the data are given in millions, so that net sales for 2002, shown as $28,681.1, are actually $28,681,100,000. For readability, the last five digits of the numbers are omitted.

The income statements for Walgreens, which are shown in Exhibit 3, are called *consolidated statements of earnings.* "Earnings before income tax provision" is computed before deducting "income tax provision" to arrive at "net earnings" (rather

EXHIBIT 6
Walgreen Co.'s Statements of Cash Flows

Consolidated Statements of Cash Flows
Walgreen Co. and Subsidiaries
For the Years Ended August 31, 2002, 2001 and 2000
(In Millions)

Fiscal Year		2002	2001	2000
Cash Flows from Operating Activities	Net earnings	$ 1,019.2	$ 885.6	$ 776.9
	Adjustments to reconcile net earnings to net cash provided by operating activities—			
	Depreciation and amortization	307.3	269.2	230.1
	Deferred income taxes	22.9	46.9	21.0
	Income tax savings from employee stock plans	56.8	67.3	38.5
	Other	(8.6)	2.1	13.6
	Changes in operating assets and liabilities—			
	Inventories	(162.8)	(651.6)	(368.2)
	Trade accounts payable	289.6	182.8	233.7
	Accounts receivable, net	(170.6)	(177.3)	(135.4)
	Accrued expenses and other liabilities	75.0	82.2	101.2
	Income taxes	14.3	(5.4)	28.6
	Other	30.7	17.4	31.7
	Net cash provided by operating activities	1,473.8	719.2	971.7
Cash Flows from Investing Activities	Additions to property and equipment	(934.4)	(1,237.0)	(1,119.1)
	Disposition of property and equipment	368.1	43.5	22.9
	Net proceeds from corporate-owned life insurance	14.4	59.0	58.8
	Net cash used for investing activities	(551.9)	(1,134.5)	(1,037.4)
Cash Flows from Financing Activities	Proceeds from short-term borrowings	(440.7)	440.7	—
	Cash dividends paid	(147.0)	(140.9)	(134.6)
	Proceeds from employee stock plans	111.1	126.1	79.2
	Other	(12.3)	(6.5)	(7.9)
	Net cash provided by (used for) financing activities	(488.9)	419.4	(63.3)
Changes in Cash and Cash Equivalents	Net increase (decrease) in cash and cash equivalents	433.0	4.1	(129.0)
	Cash and cash equivalents at beginning of year	16.9	12.8	141.8
	Cash and cash equivalents at end of year	$ 449.9	$ 16.9	$ 12.8

Cash flows are shown for operating activities, investing activities, and financing activities.

Cash and cash equivalents to Balance Sheets

Source: Walgreen Co., *Annual Report,* 2002 (year ended August 31, 2002).
The accompanying Statement of Major Accounting Policies and the Notes to Consolidated Financial Statements are integral parts of these statements.

than arriving at net income in one step, as was done in Shannon Realty's income statement). Because the company is a corporation, a provision is made for income taxes that Walgreens must pay. The statements show net earnings per common share, the net earnings divided by the weighted-average shares outstanding.

The consolidated statements of stockholders' equity for Walgreens in Exhibit 4 differ from Shannon Realty's statement of retained earnings in that they explain the changes in all the stockholders' equity accounts, including retained earnings.

In Exhibit 5, the ending balances of stockholders' equity accounts, including retained earnings, carry over to the stockholders' equity section of Walgreen Co.'s balance sheets. Walgreens' balance sheets present two years of data and are structured similarly to Shannon Realty's balance sheet. The only difference is that some assets are categorized as current assets and some liabilities as current liabilities. Generally speaking, current assets are assets that will be realized as cash or used up in the next year, as opposed to property, plant, and equipment and other assets, which will benefit the company for a longer time. Similarly, current liabilities are obligations that generally must be fulfilled within the next year, whereas noncurrent liabilities represent obligations to be paid more than one year from the balance sheet date. Walgreens has deferred income taxes and other noncurrent liabilities that the company will have to pay in future years, which is explained in the notes to the financial statements. From Walgreens' 2002 balance sheet, the equality of the accounting equation may be proven:

$$\text{Assets} = \text{Liabilities} + \text{Stockholders' Equity}$$
$$\$9{,}878{,}800{,}000 = \$3{,}648{,}600{,}000 + \$6{,}230{,}200{,}000$$

Finally, Walgreens' cash flow statements, shown in Exhibit 6, like that of Shannon Realty, Inc., show the changes in cash. These statements are very similar to that of Shannon Realty except that here "cash" is called "cash and cash equivalents," which means that it includes certain accounts or securities that are very similar to cash. The totals of cash and cash equivalents carry over to the balance sheet.

Check out ACE for a Review Quiz at http://accounting.college.hmco.com/students.

GENERALLY ACCEPTED ACCOUNTING PRINCIPLES

LO7 State the relationship of generally accepted accounting principles (GAAP) to financial statements and the independent CPA's report, and identify the organizations that influence GAAP.

RELATED TEXT ASSIGNMENTS
Q: 22, 23, 24
E: 1, 16
SD: 2
FRA: 1, 6

● **STOP AND THINK!**
How do generally accepted accounting principles (GAAP) differ from the laws of science?
GAAP differ from the laws of science in that they are not unchanging but rather are constantly evolving. They may change as business conditions change or as improved methods are introduced. ■

To ensure that financial statements will be understandable to their users, a set of practices, called **generally accepted accounting principles (GAAP)**, has been developed to provide guidelines for financial accounting. Although the term has several meanings in the literature of accounting, perhaps this is the best definition: "Generally accepted accounting principles encompass the conventions, rules, and procedures necessary to define accepted accounting practice at a particular time."[7] In other words, GAAP arise from wide agreement on the theory and practice of accounting at a particular time. These "principles" are not like the unchangeable laws of nature found in chemistry or physics. They are developed by accountants and businesses to serve the needs of decision makers, and they can alter as better methods evolve or as circumstances change.

In this book, we present accounting practice, or GAAP, as it is today. We also try to explain the reasons or theory on which the practice is based. Both theory and practice are important to the study of accounting. However, you should realize that accounting is a discipline that is always growing, changing, and improving. Just as years of research are necessary before a new surgical method or lifesaving drug can be introduced, it may take years for new accounting discoveries to be implemented. As a result, you may encounter practices that seem contradictory. In some cases, we point out new directions in accounting. Your instructor also may mention certain weaknesses in current theory or practice.

FINANCIAL STATEMENTS, GAAP, AND THE INDEPENDENT CPA'S REPORT

Because financial statements are prepared by the management of a company and could be falsified for personal gain, all companies that sell ownership to the public and many companies that apply for sizable loans have their financial statements audited by an independent certified public accountant. **Certified public accountants (CPAs)** are licensed by all states for the same reason that lawyers and doctors are—to protect the public by ensuring the quality of professional service. One

TABLE 2. Large International Certified Public Accounting Firms			
Firm	Home Office	Some Major Clients
Deloitte & Touche	New York	General Motors, Procter & Gamble, Sears
Ernst & Young	New York	Coca-Cola, McDonald's
KPMG	New York	General Electric, Xerox
PricewaterhouseCoopers	New York	Du Pont, ExxonMobil, IBM, Ford

KEY POINT: The purpose of an audit is to lend credibility to a set of financial statements. The auditor does *not* attest to the absolute accuracy of the published information or to the value of the company as an investment. All he or she renders is an opinion, based on appropriate testing, about the fairness of the presentation of the financial information.

ETHICAL CONSIDERATION: To lend credibility to the work of the independent auditor, the profession has developed the AICPA Code of Professional Ethics, a set of guidelines that dictate appropriate professional behavior. LO 8 covers the topic of ethics in detail.

important attribute of CPAs is independence: They have no financial or other compromising ties with the companies they audit. This gives the public confidence in their work. The firms listed in Table 2 employ about 25 percent of all CPAs.

An independent CPA performs an audit, which is an examination of a company's financial statements and the accounting systems, controls, and records that produced them. The purpose of the audit is to ascertain that the financial statements have been prepared in accordance with generally accepted accounting principles. If the independent accountant is satisfied that this standard has been met, his or her report contains the following language:

> In our opinion, the financial statements . . . present fairly, in all material respects . . . in conformity with generally accepted accounting principles.

This wording emphasizes the fact that accounting and auditing are not exact sciences. Because the framework of GAAP provides room for interpretation and the application of GAAP necessitates the making of estimates, the auditor can render an opinion or judgment only that the financial statements *present fairly* or conform *in all material respects* to GAAP. The accountant's report does not preclude minor or immaterial errors in the financial statements. However, it does imply that on the whole, investors and creditors can rely on those statements. Historically, auditors have enjoyed a strong reputation for competence and independence. As a result, banks, investors, and creditors are willing to rely on an auditor's opinion when deciding to invest in a company or to make loans to a company. The independent audit is an important factor in the worldwide growth of financial markets.

ORGANIZATIONS THAT INFLUENCE CURRENT PRACTICE

KEY POINT: The FASB is the primary source of GAAP.

KEY POINT: The AICPA is considered the primary organization of certified public accountants.

Many organizations directly or indirectly influence GAAP and so influence much of what is in this book. The **Financial Accounting Standards Board (FASB)** is the most important body for developing and issuing rules on accounting practice. This independent body issues *Statements of Financial Accounting Standards.* The **American Institute of Certified Public Accountants (AICPA)** is the professional association of certified public accountants and influences accounting practice through the activities of its senior technical committees. The Securities and Exchange Commission (SEC) is an agency of the federal government that has the legal power to set and enforce accounting practices for companies whose securities are offered for sale to the general public. As such, it has enormous influence on accounting practice. The **Governmental Accounting Standards Board (GASB)**, which was established in 1984 under the same governing body as the Financial Accounting Standards Board, is responsible for issuing accounting standards for state and local governments.

With the growth of financial markets throughout the world, worldwide cooperation in the development of accounting principles has become a priority. The **International Accounting Standards Board (IASB)** has approved more than 30 international standards.

U.S. tax laws that govern the assessment and collection of revenue for operating the federal government also influence accounting practice. Because a major source of the government's revenue is the income tax, the tax laws specify the rules for determining taxable income. These rules are interpreted and enforced by the **Internal Revenue Service (IRS)**. In some cases, the rules conflict with good accounting practice, but they still are an important influence on that practice. Businesses use certain accounting practices simply because they are required by the tax laws. Sometimes companies follow an accounting practice specified in the tax laws to take advantage of rules that can help them financially. Cases in which the tax laws affect accounting practice are noted throughout this book.

 Check out ACE for a Review Quiz at http://accounting.college.hmco.com/students.

PROFESSIONAL ETHICS AND THE ACCOUNTING PROFESSION

LO8 Define *ethics* and describe the ethical responsibilities of accountants.

RELATED TEXT ASSIGNMENTS
Q: 25
SD: 4

Ethical issues are discussed in each chapter; they relate to real business situations that require ethical judgments.

● **STOP AND THINK!**
What are some unethical ways in which a business may do its accounting or prepare its financial statements?

Unethical ways of accounting include recording business transactions that did not occur or being dishonest in recording those that did occur. Financial statements are unethically prepared when they misrepresent a company's financial situation or contain false information. ■

Ethics is a code of conduct that applies to everyday life. It addresses the question of whether actions are right or wrong. Ethical actions are the product of individual decisions. You are faced with many situations involving ethical issues every day. Some may be potentially illegal—the temptation to take office supplies from your employer to use when you do homework, for example. Others are not illegal but are equally unethical—for example, deciding not to tell a fellow student who missed class that a test has been announced for the next class meeting. When an organization is said to act ethically or unethically, it means that individuals within the organization have made a decision to act ethically or unethically. When a company uses false advertising, cheats customers, pollutes the environment, treats employees poorly, or misleads investors by presenting false financial statements, members of management and other employees have made a conscious decision to act unethically. In the same way, ethical behavior within a company is a direct result of the actions and decisions of the company's employees.

Professional ethics is a code of conduct that applies to the practice of a profession. Like the ethical conduct of a company, the ethical actions of a profession are a collection of individual actions. As members of a profession, accountants have a responsibility, not only to their employers and clients but to society as a whole, to uphold the highest ethical standards. Historically, accountants have been held in high regard. For example, a survey of over one thousand prominent people in business, education, and government ranked the accounting profession second only to the clergy as having the highest ethical standards.[8] It is the responsibility of every person who becomes an accountant to uphold the high standards of the profession.

To ensure that its members understand the responsibilities of being professional accountants, the AICPA and each state have adopted codes of professional conduct that certified public accountants must follow. Fundamental to these codes is responsibility to the public, including clients, creditors, investors, and anyone else who relies on the work of the certified public accountant. In resolving conflicts among these groups, the accountant must act with integrity. **Integrity** means that the accountant is honest and candid and subordinates personal gain to service and the public trust. The accountant must also be objective. **Objectivity** means that he or she is impartial and intellectually honest. Furthermore, the accountant must be independent. **Independence** means avoiding all relationships that impair or even appear to impair the accountant's objectivity.

One way in which the auditor of a company maintains independence is by having no direct financial interest in the company and by not being an employee of the company. The accountant must exer-

FOCUS ON BUSINESS ETHICS

Good Ethics = Good Business!
Ethics is good business. Many companies, especially those that engage in international trade, adopt codes of ethics. Management sees such self-regulation as a way of avoiding fraud and litigation. A recent survey of 124 companies in 22 countries found that 78 percent of boards of directors had established ethics standards, a fourfold increase over a ten-year period. The study also found that codes of ethics help promote tolerance of diverse practices abroad. In addition, research has shown that over time, companies with codes of ethics tend to do much better in the stock market than those that have not adopted such codes.[9] The recent Enron bankruptcy is an example of the tragic results that can occur when a company's ethical system breaks down.

cise **due care** in all activities, carrying out professional responsibilities with competence and diligence. For example, an accountant must not accept a job for which he or she is not qualified, even at the risk of losing a client to another firm, and careless work is not acceptable. These broad principles are supported by more specific rules that public accountants must follow. (For instance, with certain exceptions, client information must be kept strictly confidential.) Accountants who violate the rules can be disciplined or even suspended from practice.

A professional association, the **Institute of Management Accountants (IMA)**, has adopted the Code of Professional Conduct for Management Accountants. This ethical code emphasizes that management accountants have a responsibility to be competent in their jobs, to keep information confidential except when authorized or legally required to disclose it, to maintain integrity and avoid conflicts of interest, and to communicate information objectively and without bias.[10]

 Check out ACE for a Review Quiz at http://accounting.college.hmco.com/students.

Chapter Review

The Chapter Review restates each learning objective and its main ideas.

REVIEW OF LEARNING OBJECTIVES

LO1 Define *accounting,* identify business goals and activities, and describe the role of accounting in making informed decisions.

Accounting is an information system that measures, processes, and communicates financial information about an identifiable entity for the purpose of making economic decisions. An important type of entity is the business which engages in operating, investing, and financing activities for the purpose of achieving the goals of profitability and liquidity. Management accounting focuses on the preparation of information primarily for internal use by management. Financial accounting is concerned with the development and use of accounting reports that are communicated to those outside the business as well as to management. Accounting is a tool that provides the information necessary to make reasoned choices among alternative uses of scarce resources in the conduct of business and economic activities.

LO2 Identify the many users of accounting information in society.

Accounting plays a significant role in society by providing information to managers of all institutions and to individuals with a direct financial interest in those institutions, including present or potential investors or creditors. Accounting information is also important to those with an indirect financial interest in the business—for example, tax authorities, regulatory agencies, and economic planners.

LO3 Explain the importance of business transactions, money measure, and separate entity to accounting measurement.

To make an accounting measurement, the accountant must determine what is measured, when the measurement should be made, what value should be placed on what is measured, and how what is measured should be classified. The objects of accounting measurement are business transactions that are measured in terms of money and are for separate entities. Relating these concepts, financial accounting uses money measure to gauge the impact of business transactions on a separate business entity.

LO4 Describe the corporate form of business organization.

Corporations, whose ownership is represented by shares of stock, are separate entities for both legal and accounting purposes. The stockholders own the corporation and elect the board of directors, whose duty it is to determine corporate policy. The corporate officers or management of the corporation are appointed by the board of directors and are responsible for the operation of the business in accordance with the board's policies.

LO5 Define *financial position,* state the accounting equation, and show how they are affected by simple transactions.

Financial position refers to the economic resources that belong to a company and the claims against those resources at a point in time. The accounting equation shows financial position as Assets = Liabilities + Owners' Equity. For a corporation, the accounting equation is Assets = Liabilities + Stockholders' Equity. Business transactions affect financial position by decreasing or increasing assets, liabilities, or stockholders' equity in such a way that the accounting equation is always in balance.

LO6 Identify the four financial statements.		The four financial statements are the income statement, the statement of retained earnings, the balance sheet, and the statement of cash flows. They are the means by which accountants communicate the financial condition and activities of a business to those who have an interest in the business.
LO7 State the relationship of generally accepted accounting principles (GAAP) to financial statements and the independent CPA's report, and identify the organizations that influence GAAP.		Acceptable accounting practice consists of the conventions, rules, and procedures that make up generally accepted accounting principles at a particular time. GAAP are essential to the preparation and interpretation of financial statements and the independent CPA's report. Organizations that influence the formulation of GAAP are the Financial Accounting Standards Board, the American Institute of Certified Public Accountants, the Securities and Exchange Commission, and the Internal Revenue Service.
LO8 Define *ethics* and describe the ethical responsibilities of accountants.		All accountants are required to follow a code of professional ethics, the foundation of which is responsibility to the public. Accountants must act with integrity, objectivity, and independence, and they must exercise due care in all their activities.

Want more review? The student *Study Guide* provides a thorough review of each learning objective, a detailed outline, true/false and multiple-choice questions, and exercises. Answers are included. Ask for it at your bookstore.

REVIEW OF CONCEPTS AND TERMINOLOGY

The following concepts and terms were introduced in this chapter:

Each chapter has a glossary of the key concepts and terms defined in the chapter. The LO next to each term indicates the section in which it is discussed.

LO1 **Accounting:** An information system that measures, processes, and communicates financial information about an identifiable economic entity.

LO5 **Accounting equation:** Assets = Liabilities + Owners' Equity or, for corporations, Assets = Liabilities + Stockholders' Equity.

LO5 **Accounts:** The labels used by accountants to accumulate the amounts produced from similar transactions.

LO7 **American Institute of Certified Public Accountants (AICPA):** The professional association of certified public accountants.

LO4 **Articles of incorporation:** An official document filed with and approved by a state that authorizes the incorporators to do business as a corporation.

LO5 **Assets:** Economic resources owned by a business that are expected to benefit future operations.

LO7 **Audit:** An examination of a company's financial statements in order to render an independent professional opinion that they have been presented fairly, in all material respects, in conformity with generally accepted accounting principles.

LO4 **Audit committee:** A subgroup of the board of directors of a corporation that is charged with ensuring that the board will be objective in reviewing management's performance; it engages the company's independent auditors and reviews their work.

LO6 **Balance sheet:** The financial statement that shows the assets, liabilities, and stockholders' equity of a business at a point in time. Also called a *statement of financial position*.

LO1 **Bookkeeping:** The process of recording financial transactions and keeping financial records.

LO1 **Business:** An economic unit that aims to sell goods and services to customers at prices that will provide an adequate return to its owners.

LO3 **Business transactions:** Economic events that affect the financial position of a business entity.

LO6 **Cash flows:** The inflows and outflows of cash into and out of a business.

LO7 **Certified public accountants (CPAs):** Public accountants who have met the stringent state licensing requirements.

LO1 **Computer:** An electronic tool for the rapid collection, organization, and communication of large amounts of information.

LO5 **Contributed capital:** The part of stockholders' equity that represents the amount invested in the business by the owners (stockholders).

LO4 **Corporation:** A business unit granted a state charter recognizing it as a separate legal entity having its own rights, privileges, and liabilities distinct from those of its owners.

LO5 **Dividends:** Distributions to stockholders of assets (usually cash) generated by past earnings.

LO8 **Due care:** Competence and diligence in carrying out professional responsibilities.

LO8 **Ethics:** A code of conduct that addresses whether everyday actions are right or wrong.

LO3 **Exchange rate:** The value of one currency in terms of another.

LO5 **Expenses:** Decreases in stockholders' equity that result from operating a business.

LO1 **Financial accounting:** The process of generating and communicating accounting information in the form of financial statements to those outside the organization.

LO7 **Financial Accounting Standards Board (FASB):** The most important body for developing and issuing rules on accounting practice, called *Statements of Financial Accounting Standards*.

LO5 **Financial position:** The economic resources that belong to a company and the claims (equities) against those resources at a point in time.

LO1 **Financial statements:** The primary means of communicating important accounting information to users. They include the income statement, statement of retained earnings, balance sheet, and statement of cash flows.

LO1 **Financing activities:** Activities undertaken by management to obtain adequate funds to begin and to continue operating a business.

LO7 **Generally accepted accounting principles (GAAP):** The conventions, rules, and procedures that define accepted accounting practice at a particular time.

LO7 **Governmental Accounting Standards Board (GASB):** The board responsible for issuing accounting standards for state and local governments.

LO6 **Income statement:** The financial statement that summarizes the revenues earned and expenses incurred by a business over a period of time.

LO8 **Independence:** The avoidance of all relationships that impair or appear to impair an accountant's objectivity.

LO8 **Institute of Management Accountants (IMA):** A professional organization made up primarily of management accountants.

LO8 **Integrity:** Honesty, candidness, and the subordination of personal gain to service and the public trust.

LO7 **Internal Revenue Service (IRS):** The federal agency that interprets and enforces the tax laws governing the assessment and collection of revenue for operating the national government.

LO7 **International Accounting Standards Board (IASB):** The organization that encourages worldwide cooperation in the development of accounting principles; it has approved more than 30 international standards of accounting.

LO1 **Investing activities:** Activities undertaken by management to spend capital in ways that are productive and will help a business achieve its objectives.

LO5 **Liabilities:** Present obligations of a business to pay cash, transfer assets, or provide services to other entities in the future.

LO1 **Liquidity:** Having enough cash available to pay debts when they are due.

LO2 **Management:** The people who have overall responsibility for operating a business and meeting its goals.

LO1 **Management accounting:** The process of producing accounting information for the internal use of a company's management.

LO1 **Management information system (MIS):** The interconnected subsystems that provide the information needed to run a business.

LO3 **Money measure:** The recording of all business transactions in terms of money.

LO5 **Net assets:** Assets minus liabilities; owners' equity or stockholders' equity.

LO5 **Net income:** The difference between revenues and expenses when revenues exceed expenses.

LO5 **Net loss:** The difference between expenses and revenues when expenses exceed revenues.

LO8 **Objectivity:** Impartiality and intellectual honesty.

LO1 **Operating activities:** Activities undertaken by management in the course of running the business.

LO5 **Owners' equity:** The residual interest in the assets of a business entity that remains after deducting the entity's liabilities. Also called *residual equity* or, for corporations, *stockholders' equity*.

LO4 **Partnership:** A business that is owned by two or more people and is not incorporated.

LO1 **Performance measures:** Indicators of whether managers are achieving business goals and whether the business activities are well managed.

LO8 **Professional ethics:** A code of conduct that applies to the practice of a profession.

LO1 **Profitability:** The ability to earn enough income to attract and hold investment capital.

LO5 **Retained earnings:** The equity of the stockholders generated from the income-producing activities of the business and kept for use in the business.

LO5 **Revenues:** Increases in stockholders' equity that result from operating a business.

LO2 **Securities and Exchange Commission (SEC):** An agency of the U.S. government set up by Congress to protect the public by regulating the issuing, buying, and selling of stocks. It has the legal power to set and enforce accounting practices for firms whose securities are sold to the general public.

LO3 **Separate entity:** A business that is treated as distinct from its creditors, customers, and owners.

LO4 **Share of stock:** A unit of ownership in a corporation.

LO4 **Sole proprietorship:** A business that is owned by one person and is not incorporated.

LO6 **Statement of cash flows:** The financial statement that shows the inflows and outflows of cash from operating activities, investing activities, and financing activities over a period of time.

LO6 **Statement of retained earnings:** The financial statement that shows the changes in retained earnings over a period of time.

LO6 **Statement of stockholders' equity:** A financial statement that summarizes changes in the components of stockholders' equity. Also called *statement of shareholders' equity*.

LO5 **Stockholders' equity:** The owners' equity of a corporation, consisting of contributed capital and retained earnings.

REVIEW PROBLEM

> Not sure you understood the techniques and calculations, or want to check if you are ready for a chapter test? The Review Problem models main computations or analysis presented in the chapter and other problem assignments. The answer is provided for immediate feedback.

The Effect of Transactions on the Accounting Equation

LO5 Charlene Rudek finished law school in June and immediately set up her own law practice. During the first month of operation, she completed the following transactions:

a. Began the law practice by exchanging $2,000 for 1,000 shares of $2 par value common stock of the corporation.

b. Purchased a law library for $900 cash.
c. Purchased office supplies for $400 on credit.
d. Accepted $500 in cash for completing a contract.
e. Billed clients $1,950 for services rendered during the month.
f. Paid $200 of the amount owed for office supplies.
g. Received $1,250 in cash from one client who had been billed previously for services rendered.
h. Paid rent expense for the month in the amount of $1,200.
i. Declared and paid a dividend of $400.

REQUIRED
1. Show the effect of each of these transactions on the accounting equation by completing a table similar to Exhibit 1. Identify each stockholders' equity transaction.
2. Contrast the effects on cash flows of transactions **c** and **f** with transaction **b** and of transactions **e** and **g** with transaction **d**.

ANSWER TO REVIEW PROBLEM

1. Table of effects of transactions on the accounting equation

	Assets				= Liabilities +		Stockholders' Equity		
	Cash	Accounts Receivable	Office Supplies	Law Library	Accounts Payable	Common Stock	Retained Earnings	Type of SE Transaction
a.	$2,000					$2,000		Stockholders' Investment
b.	−900			+$900				
bal.	$1,100			$900		$2,000		
c.			+$400		+$400			
bal.	$1,100		$400	$900	$400	$2,000		
d.	+500						+$ 500	Legal Fees Earned
bal.	$1,600		$400	$900	$400	$2,000	$ 500	
e.		+$1,950					+1,950	Legal Fees Earned
bal.	$1,600	$1,950	$400	$900	$400	$2,000	$2,450	
f.	−200				−200			
bal.	$1,400	$1,950	$400	$900	$200	$2,000	$2,450	
g.	+1,250	−1,250						
bal.	$2,650	$ 700	$400	$900	$200	$2,000	$2,450	
h.	−1,200						−1,200	Rent Expense
bal.	$1,450	$ 700	$400	$900	$200	$2,000	$1,250	
i.	−400						−400	Dividends
bal.	$1,050	$ 700	$400	$900	$200	$2,000	$ 850	
	$3,050				$3,050			

2. Transaction **c**, a purchase on credit, enables the company to use the asset immediately and defer payment of cash until later. Cash is expended to partially pay for the asset in transaction **f**. The remainder is to be paid subsequently. This series of transactions contrasts with transaction **b**, in which cash is expended immediately for the asset. In each case, an asset is purchased, but the effects on cash flows are different.

Transaction **e**, a sale on credit, allows the customer to pay later for services provided. This payment is partially received in transaction **g**, and the remainder is to be received later. These transactions contrast with transaction **d**, in which payment is received immediately for the services performed. In each case, the revenue is earned initially, but the effect on cash flows is different.

Chapter Assignments

BUILDING YOUR KNOWLEDGE FOUNDATION

Questions review key concepts, terminology, and topics of the chapter.

QUESTIONS

1. Why is accounting considered an information system?
2. What is the role of accounting in the decision-making process, and what broad business goals and activities does it help management achieve and manage?
3. Distinguish between management accounting and financial accounting.
4. Distinguish among these terms: *accounting*, *bookkeeping*, and *management information systems*.
5. Which decision makers use accounting information?
6. A business is an economic unit whose goal is to sell goods and services to customers at prices that will provide an adequate return to the business's owners. What functions must management perform to achieve that goal?
7. Why are investors and creditors interested in reviewing the financial statements of a company?
8. Among those who use accounting information are people and organizations that have an indirect interest in the business entity. Briefly describe these people and organizations.
9. Why has society as a whole become one of the largest users of accounting information?
10. Use the terms *business transactions*, *money measure*, and *separate entity* in a single sentence that demonstrates their relevance to financial accounting.
11. How do sole proprietorships, partnerships, and corporations differ?
12. In a corporation, what are the functions of stockholders, the board of directors, and management?
13. Define *assets*, *liabilities*, and *stockholders' equity*.
14. Arnold Smith's corporation has assets of $22,000 and liabilities of $10,000. What is the amount of the stockholders' equity?
15. What three elements affect retained earnings? How?
16. Give examples of the types of transactions that (a) increase assets and (b) increase liabilities.
17. What is the function of the statement of retained earnings?
18. Why is the balance sheet sometimes called the statement of financial position?
19. Contrast the purpose of the balance sheet with that of the income statement.
20. A statement for an accounting period that ends in June can be headed "June 30, 20xx" or "For the Year Ended June 30, 20xx." Which heading is appropriate for (a) a balance sheet and (b) an income statement?
21. How does the income statement differ from the statement of cash flows?
22. What are GAAP? Why are they important to the readers of financial statements?
23. What do auditors mean by the phrase *in all material respects* when they state that financial statements "present fairly, in all material respects . . . in conformity with generally accepted accounting principles"?
24. What organization has the most influence on GAAP?
25. Discuss the importance of professional ethics in the accounting profession.

Short exercises are simple applications of chapter material for a single learning objective. If you need help locating the related text discussions, refer to the LO numbers in the margin.

SHORT EXERCISES

SE 1. Tell whether each of the following words or phrases relates most closely to (a) a business transaction, (b) a separate entity, or (c) a money measure:

LO3 Accounting Concepts

1. Partnership
2. U.S. dollar
3. Payment of an expense
4. Corporation
5. Sale of an asset

SE 2.
LO4 Forms of Business Enterprises

Match the descriptions on the left with the forms of business enterprise on the right:

___ 1. Most numerous

___ 2. Commands most revenues

___ 3. Two or more co-owners

___ 4. Has stockholders

___ 5. Owned by one person

___ 6. Has a board of directors

a. Sole proprietorship
b. Partnership
c. Corporation

SE 3.
LO5 The Accounting Equation

Determine the amount missing from each accounting equation below.

	Assets	=	Liabilities	+	Stockholders' Equity
1.	?		$25,000		$35,000
2.	$ 78,000		$42,000		?
3.	$146,000		?		$96,000

SE 4.
LO5 The Accounting Equation

Use the accounting equation to answer each question below.
1. The assets of Sully Company are $480,000, and the liabilities are $360,000. What is the amount of the stockholders' equity?
2. The liabilities of Eva Company equal one-fifth of the total assets. The stockholders' equity is $80,000. What is the amount of the liabilities?

SE 5.
LO5 The Accounting Equation

Use the accounting equation to answer each question below.
1. At the beginning of the year, Lanier Company's assets were $180,000, and its stockholders' equity was $100,000. During the year, assets increased by $60,000 and liabilities increased by $10,000. What was the stockholders' equity at the end of the year?
2. At the beginning of the year, Fanto Company had liabilities of $50,000 and stockholders' equity of $48,000. If assets increased by $20,000 and liabilities decreased by $15,000, what was the stockholders' equity at the end of the year?

SE 6.
LO5 The Accounting Equation and Net Income

Use the following information and the accounting equation to determine the net income for the year for each alternative below.

	Assets	Liabilities
Beginning of the year	$ 70,000	$30,000
End of the year	100,000	50,000

1. No investments were made in the business, and no dividends were paid during the year.
2. Investments of $10,000 were made in the business, but no dividends were paid during the year.
3. No investments were made in the business, but dividends of $2,000 were paid during the year.

SE 7.
LO5 The Accounting Equation and Net Income

Meader Company had assets of $140,000 and liabilities of $60,000 at the beginning of the year, and assets of $200,000 and liabilities of $70,000 at the end of the year. During the year, there was an investment of $20,000 in the business, and dividends of $24,000 were paid. What amount of net income was earned during the year?

SE 8.
LO5 Effect of Transactions on the Accounting Equation

On a sheet of paper, list the numbers 1 through 6, with columns labeled Assets, Liabilities, and Stockholders' Equity. In the columns, indicate whether each transaction that follows caused an increase (+), a decrease (−), or no change (NC) in assets, liabilities, and stockholders' equity.

1. Purchased equipment on credit.
2. Purchased equipment for cash.
3. Billed customers for services performed.
4. Received and immediately paid a utility bill.
5. Received payment from a previously billed customer.
6. Received an additional investment from a stockholder.

LO5 SE 9. Effect of Transactions on the Accounting Equation

On a sheet of paper, list the numbers **1** through **6,** with columns labeled Assets, Liabilities, and Stockholders' Equity. In the columns, indicate whether each transaction below caused an increase (+), a decrease (−), or no change (NC) in assets, liabilities, and stockholders' equity.

1. Purchased supplies on credit.
2. Paid for previously purchased supplies.
3. Paid employee's weekly wages.
4. Paid a dividend to stockholders.
5. Purchased a truck with cash.
6. Received a telephone bill to be paid next month.

LO6 SE 10. Preparation and Completion of a Balance Sheet

Use the following accounts and balances to prepare a balance sheet for Anatole Company at June 30, 20x1, using Exhibit 2 as a model:

Accounts Receivable	$ 800
Wages Payable	250
Retained Earnings	1,750
Common Stock	12,000
Building	10,000
Cash	?

Exercises are richer applications of all chapter material referenced by LOs. ➤ **EXERCISES**

LO1 E 1. The Nature of Accounting
LO2
LO7

Match the terms on the left with the descriptions on the right:

_____ 1. Bookkeeping
_____ 2. Creditors
_____ 3. Measurement
_____ 4. Financial Accounting Standards Board (FASB)
_____ 5. Tax authorities
_____ 6. Computer
_____ 7. Communication
_____ 8. Securities and Exchange Commission (SEC)
_____ 9. Investors
_____ 10. Processing
_____ 11. Management
_____ 12. Management information system

a. Function of accounting
b. Often confused with accounting
c. User(s) of accounting information
d. Organization that influences current practice
e. Tool that facilitates the practice of accounting

LO2 E 2. Users of Accounting Information and Forms of Business Enterprise
LO4

Vylex Pharmaceuticals has recently been formed to develop a new type of drug treatment for cancer. Previously a partnership, Vylex has now become a corporation. Identify the various groups that will have an interest in the financial statements of Vylex. What is the difference between a partnership and a corporation, and what advantages does the corporate form have over the partnership?

LO3 E 3. Business Transactions

Edgar owns and operates a minimart. State which of the actions below are business transactions. Explain why any other actions are not regarded as transactions.

1. Edgar reduces the price of a gallon of milk in order to match the price offered by a competitor.
2. Edgar pays a teenager cash for cleaning up the driveway behind the market.
3. Edgar fills his son's car with gasoline in payment for restocking the vending machines and the snack food shelves.
4. Edgar pays interest to himself on a loan he made to the business three years ago.

LO3 E 4. Accounting Concepts

Financial accounting uses money measures to gauge the impact of business transactions on a separate business entity. Tell whether each of the following words or phrases relates most closely to (a) a business transaction, (b) a separate entity, or (c) a money measure:

1. Corporation
2. Euro
3. Sales of products
4. Receipt of cash
5. Sole proprietorship
6. U.S. dollar
7. Partnership
8. Stockholders' investments
9. Japanese yen
10. Purchase of supplies

LO3 Money Measure

E 5. You have been asked to compare the sales and assets of four companies that make computer chips and to determine which company is the largest in each category. You have gathered the following data, but they cannot be used for direct comparison because each company's sales and assets are in its own currency:

Company (Currency)	Sales	Assets
Inchip (U.S. dollar)	20,000,000	13,000,000
Wong (Hong Kong dollar)	80,000,000	24,000,000
Mitzu (Japanese yen)	3,500,000,000	2,500,000,000
Works (Euro)	35,000,000	49,000,000

Assuming that the exchange rates in Table 1 are current and appropriate, convert all the figures to U.S. dollars and determine which company is the largest in sales and which is the largest in assets.

LO5 The Accounting Equation

E 6. Use the accounting equation to answer each question that follows. Show any calculations you make.

1. The assets of Caton Corporation are $800,000, and the stockholders' equity is $310,000. What is the amount of the liabilities?
2. The liabilities and stockholders' equity of Sung Corporation are $72,000 and $53,000, respectively. What is the amount of the assets?
3. The liabilities of Plumb Corp. equal one-third of the total assets, and stockholders' equity is $240,000. What is the amount of the liabilities?
4. At the beginning of the year, Wilde Corporation's assets were $220,000 and its stockholders' equity was $120,000. During the year, assets increased $60,000, and liabilities decreased $18,000. What is the stockholders' equity at the end of the year?

LO5 Stockholders' Equity Transactions

E 7. Identify the following transactions by marking each as a stockholders' investment (I), dividend (D), revenue (R), expense (E), or not a stockholders' equity transaction (NSE):

a. Received cash for providing a service.
b. Took assets out of the business for personal use.
c. Received cash from a customer previously billed for a service.
d. Transferred assets to the business from a personal account.
e. Paid a service station for gasoline for a business vehicle.
f. Performed a service and received a promise of payment.
g. Paid cash to purchase equipment.
h. Paid cash to an employee for services performed.

LO5 Effect of Transactions on the Accounting Equation

E 8. During the month of April, Cosmos Corporation had the following transactions:

a. Paid salaries for April, $1,800.
b. Purchased equipment on credit, $3,000.
c. Purchased supplies with cash, $100.
d. Additional investment by stockholders, $4,000.
e. Received payment for services performed, $600.
f. Made partial payment on equipment purchased in transaction b, $1,000.
g. Billed customers for services performed, $1,600.
h. Received payment from customers billed in transaction g, $300.
i. Received utility bill, $70.
j. Declared and paid dividends of $1,500.

On a sheet of paper, list the letters **a** through **j**, with columns labeled Assets, Liabilities, and Stockholders' Equity. In the columns, indicate whether each transaction caused an increase (+), a decrease (−), or no change (NC) in assets, liabilities, and stockholders' equity.

LO5 Examples of Transactions

E 9. For each of the categories below, describe a transaction that would have the required effect on the elements of the accounting equation.

1. Increase one asset and decrease another asset.
2. Decrease an asset and decrease a liability.
3. Increase an asset and increase a liability.

4. Increase an asset and increase stockholders' equity.
5. Decrease an asset and decrease stockholders' equity.

LO5 Effect of Transactions on the Accounting Equation

E 10. The total assets and liabilities at the beginning and end of the year for Flag Company are listed below.

	Assets	Liabilities
Beginning of the year	$140,000	$ 55,000
End of the year	220,000	130,000

Determine Flag Company's net income or loss for the year under each of the following alternatives:

1. The stockholders made no investments in the business, and no dividends were paid during the year.
2. The stockholders made no investments in the business, but dividends of $22,000 were paid during the year.
3. The stockholders invested $13,000 in the business, but no dividends were paid during the year.
4. The stockholders invested $10,000 in the business, and dividends of $22,000 were paid during the year.

LO5 LO6 Identification of Accounts

E 11. 1. Indicate whether each of the following accounts is an asset (A), a liability (L), or a part of stockholders' equity (SE):

a. Cash
b. Salaries Payable
c. Accounts Receivable
d. Common Stock
e. Land
f. Accounts Payable
g. Supplies

2. Indicate whether each account below would be shown on the income statement (IS), the statement of retained earnings (RE), or the balance sheet (BS).

a. Repair Revenue
b. Automobile
c. Fuel Expense
d. Cash
e. Rent Expense
f. Accounts Payable
g. Dividends

LO6 Preparation of a Balance Sheet

E 12. Listed in random order below are the balance sheet figures for the Solos Company as of December 31, 20xx.

Accounts Payable	$ 40,000	Accounts Receivable	$50,000
Building	90,000	Cash	20,000
Common Stock	100,000	Equipment	40,000
Supplies	10,000	Retained Earnings	70,000

Sort the balances and prepare a balance sheet similar to the one in Exhibit 2.

LO6 Completion of Financial Statements

E 13. Complete the following independent sets of financial statements by determining the amounts that correspond to the letters. (Assume no new investments by the stockholders.)

Income Statement	Set A	Set B	Set C
Revenues	$ 550	$ g	$120
Expenses	a	2,600	m
Net income	$ b	$ h	$ 40
Statement of Retained Earnings			
Beginning balance	$1,450	$ 7,700	$100
Net income	c	800	n
Less dividends	100	i	o
Ending balance	$1,500	$ j	$ p
Balance Sheet			
Total assets	$ d	$15,500	$ q
Liabilities	$ 800	$ 2,500	$ r
Stockholders' equity			
Common stock	1,000	5,000	50
Retained earnings	e	k	140
Total liabilities and stockholders' equity	$ f	$ l	$290

Chapter Assignments

LO6 Preparation of Financial Statements

E 14. Ridge Corporation engaged in the following activities during the year: Service Revenue, $26,400; Rent Expense, $2,400; Wages Expense, $16,540; Advertising Expense, $2,700; Utilities Expense, $1,800; and Dividends, $1,400. In addition, the year-end balances of selected accounts were as follows: Cash, $3,100; Accounts Receivable, $1,500; Supplies, $200; Land, $2,000; Accounts Payable, $900; and Common Stock, $2,000.

In proper format, prepare the income statement, statement of retained earnings, and balance sheet for Ridge Corporation (assume the year ends on December 31, 20x5). (**Hint:** You must solve for the beginning and ending balances of retained earnings for 20x5.)

LO6 Statement of Cash Flows

E 15. Waters Corporation began the year 20x4 with cash of $43,000. In addition to earning a net income of $25,000 and paying a cash dividend of $15,000, Waters borrowed $60,000 from the bank and purchased equipment for $90,000 with cash. Also, Accounts Receivable increased by $6,000, and Accounts Payable increased by $9,000.

Determine the amount of cash on hand at December 31, 20x4, by preparing a statement of cash flows similar to the one in Exhibit 2.

LO7 Accounting Abbreviations

E 16. Identify the accounting meaning of each of the following abbreviations: AICPA, SEC, GAAP, FASB, IRS, GASB, IASB, IMA, and CPA.

Problems are comprehensive applications of chapter material, often covering multiple learning objectives.

PROBLEMS

LO5 Effect of Transactions on the Accounting Equation

P 1. After receiving her degree in computer science, Carmen Vega started her own business, Custom Systems Corporation. The company completed the following transactions:

a. Invested $9,000 in cash and a systems library valued at $920 in exchange for 992 shares of $10 par value common stock in the corporation.
b. Paid current month's rent on an office, $360.
c. Purchased a minicomputer for cash, $7,000.
d. Purchased computer supplies on credit, $600.
e. Received payment from a client for programming done, $800.
f. Billed a client on completion of a short programming project, $710.
g. Paid expenses, $400.
h. Received a partial payment from the client billed in transaction **f**, $80.
i. Made a partial payment on the computer supplies purchased in transaction **d**, $200.
j. Declared and paid dividends of $250.

REQUIRED

Curious if you got the right answer? Look at the Check Figures section that precedes Chapter 1.

1. Arrange the asset, liability, and stockholders' equity accounts in an equation similar to that in Exhibit 1, using the following account titles: Cash, Accounts Receivable, Computer Supplies, Equipment, Systems Library, Accounts Payable, Common Stock, and Retained Earnings.
2. Show by addition and subtraction, as in Exhibit 1, the effects of the transactions on the accounting equation. Show new balances after each transaction, and identify each stockholders' equity transaction by type.
3. Contrast the effects on cash flows of transactions **d** and **i** with transaction **c** and of transactions **f** and **h** with transaction **e**.

LO5 Effect of Transactions on the Accounting Equation

P 2. On June 1, Henry Redmond started a new business, the Redmond Transport Corporation. During the month of June, the firm completed the following transactions:

a. Invested $66,000 in cash in exchange for 6,600 shares of $10 par value common stock of the corporation.
b. Purchased a truck for cash, $43,000.
c. Purchased equipment on credit, $9,000.
d. Billed a customer for hauling goods, $1,200.
e. Received cash for hauling goods, $2,300.
f. Received cash payment from the customer billed in transaction **d**, $600.
g. Made a payment on the equipment purchased in transaction **c**, $5,000.
h. Paid wages expense in cash, $1,700.
i. Declared and paid dividends of $1,200.

REQUIRED

1. Arrange the asset, liability, and stockholders' equity accounts in an equation similar to that in Exhibit 1, using the following account titles: Cash, Accounts Receivable, Trucks, Equipment, Accounts Payable, Common Stock, and Retained Earnings.

2. Show by addition and subtraction, as in Exhibit 1, the effects of the transactions on the accounting equation. Show new balances after each transaction, and identify each stockholders' equity transaction by type.

P 3.
LO5 Effect of Transactions on the Accounting Equation

After completing his M.B.A., Sol Lindberg set up a consulting practice. At the end of his first month of operation, he had the following account balances: Cash, $4,760; Accounts Receivable, $2,800; Office Supplies, $540; Office Equipment, $8,400; Accounts Payable, $3,800; Common Stock, $11,000; and Retained Earnings, $1,700. Soon thereafter, the following transactions were completed:

a. Paid current month's rent, $700.
b. Made payment toward accounts payable, $900.
c. Billed clients for services performed, $1,600.
d. Received payment from clients billed last month, $2,000.
e. Purchased office supplies for cash, $160.
f. Paid secretary's salary, $1,700.
g. Paid utilities expense, $180.
h. Paid telephone expense, $100.
i. Purchased additional office equipment for cash, $800.
j. Received cash from clients for services performed, $2,400.
k. Declared and paid dividends of $1,000.

REQUIRED
1. Arrange the following asset, liability, and stockholders' equity accounts in an equation similar to that in Exhibit 1: Cash, Accounts Receivable, Office Supplies, Office Equipment, Accounts Payable, Common Stock, and Retained Earnings.
2. Enter the beginning balances of the assets, liabilities, and stockholders' equity.
3. Show by addition and subtraction, as in Exhibit 1, the effects of the transactions on the accounting equation. Show new balances after each transaction, and identify each stockholders' equity transaction by type.

P 4.
LO1 Preparation of Financial
LO6 Statements

General Ledger icons indicate that the problem can be solved using Houghton Mifflin General Ledger Software for Windows, with an updated interface and available on the Student CD.

At the end of October 20xx, the Common Stock account of Sunnydale Riding Club, Inc., had a balance of $30,000, and Retained Earnings had a balance of $7,300. After operating during November, the club had the following account balances:

Cash	$ 8,700	Building	$30,000
Accounts Receivable	1,200	Horses	10,000
Supplies	1,000	Accounts Payable	17,800
Land	21,000		

In addition, the following transactions affected stockholders' equity during November:

Stockholders' investment in common stock	$16,000
Riding lesson revenue	6,200
Locker rental revenue	1,700
Salaries expense	2,300
Feed expense	1,000
Utilities expense	600
Dividends	3,200

REQUIRED
1. Using Exhibit 2 as a model, prepare an income statement, a statement of retained earnings, and a balance sheet for Sunnydale Riding Club, Inc. (**Hint:** The final total of Stockholders' Equity is $54,100.)
2. Identify the links among the financial statements in requirement 1.
3. Which of these statements are most closely associated with the goals of profitability and liquidity? Explain your answer. What other financial statement is helpful in evaluating liquidity?

P 5.
LO5 Effect of Transactions
LO6 on the Accounting Equation and Preparation of Financial Statements

Royal Copying Service, Inc., began operations and engaged in the following transactions during July 20xx:

a. Linda Friedman deposited $5,000 in cash in the name of the corporation in exchange for 500 shares of $10 par value common stock of the corporation.
b. Paid current month's rent, $450.
c. Purchased copier for cash, $2,500.
d. Paid cash for paper and other copier supplies, $190.
e. Copying job payments received in cash, $890.
f. Copying job billed to major customer, $680.
g. Paid wages to part-time employees, $280.
h. Purchased additional copier supplies on credit, $140.

i. Received partial payment from customer in transaction f, $300.
j. Paid current month's utilities bill, $90.
k. Made partial payment on supplies purchased in transaction h, $70.
l. Declared and paid dividends of $700.

REQUIRED
1. Arrange the asset, liability, and stockholders' equity accounts in an equation similar to that in Exhibit 1, using these account titles: Cash, Accounts Receivable, Supplies, Copier, Accounts Payable, Common Stock, and Retained Earnings.
2. Show by addition and subtraction, as in Exhibit 1, the effects of the transactions on the accounting equation. Show new balances after each transaction, and identify each stockholders' equity transaction by type.
3. Using Exhibit 2 as a guide, prepare an income statement, a statement of retained earnings, and a balance sheet for Royal Copying Service, Inc. (Optional: Also prepare a statement of cash flows.)

Looking for more practice? Alternate problems have the same format and learning objectives as problems that appear earlier in the chapter.

ALTERNATE PROBLEMS

P 6.
LO5 Effect of Transactions on the Accounting Equation

Brenda Kuzma started Frame-It Center, Inc., in a small shopping center. In the first weeks of operation, the firm completed the following transactions:

a. Deposited $7,000 in an account in the name of the corporation, in exchange for 700 shares of $10 par value common stock of the corporation.
b. Paid the current month's rent, $500.
c. Purchased store equipment on credit, $3,600.
d. Purchased framing supplies for cash, $1,700.
e. Received framing revenue, $800.
f. Billed customers for services, $700.
g. Paid utilities expense, $250.
h. Received payment from customers in transaction f, $200.
i. Made payment on store equipment purchased in transaction c, $1,800.
j. Declared and paid dividends of $400.

REQUIRED
1. Arrange the following asset, liability, and stockholders' equity accounts in an equation similar to that in Exhibit 1: Cash, Accounts Receivable, Framing Supplies, Store Equipment, Accounts Payable, Common Stock, and Retained Earnings.
2. Show by addition and subtraction, as in Exhibit 1, the effects of the transactions on the accounting equation. Show new balances after each transaction, and identify each stockholders' equity transaction by type.
3. Contrast the effects on cash flows of transactions c and i with transaction d and of transactions f and h with transaction e.

P 7.
LO1 Preparation of Financial
LO6 Statements

At the end of October 20xx, the Common Stock account of the Sioux City Landscaping Service, Inc., had a balance of $60,000, and Retained Earnings had a balance of $14,600. After operating during November, the company had the following account balances:

Cash	$17,400	Building	$60,000
Accounts Receivable	2,400	Lawn Equipment	20,000
Supplies	2,000	Accounts Payable	35,600
Land	42,000		

In addition, the following transactions affected stockholders' equity during November:

Stockholders' investment in common stock	$32,000
Lawn care revenue	12,400
Spraying revenue	3,400
Salaries expense	4,600
Supplies expense	2,000
Utilities expense	1,200
Dividends	6,400

REQUIRED
1. Using Exhibit 2 as a model, prepare an income statement, a statement of retained earnings, and a balance sheet for Sioux City Landscaping Service, Inc. (**Hint:** The final total of Stockholders' Equity is $108,200.)
2. Identify the links among the financial statements in **1**.
3. Which financial statement is most closely associated with the goal of liquidity? Which with the goal of profitability? Explain your answers. What other statement is helpful in evaluating liquidity?

P 8.

LO5 Effect of Transactions
LO6 on the Accounting Equation and Preparation of Financial Statements

On April 1, 20xx, Dependable Taxi Service, Inc., began operation. The company engaged in the following transactions during April:

a. Madeline Curry deposited $42,000 in a bank account in the name of the corporation in exchange for 4,200 shares of $10 par value stock in the corporation.
b. Purchased taxi for cash, $19,000.
c. Purchased auto supplies on credit, $400.
d. Received taxi fares in cash, $3,200.
e. Paid wages to part-time drivers, $500.
f. Purchased gasoline during month for cash, $800.
g. Purchased car washes during month on credit, $120.
h. Owner made a further investment in 500 shares, $5,000.
i. Paid part of amount owed for auto supplies purchased in transaction c, $200.
j. Billed major client for fares, $900.
k. Paid for automobile repairs, $250.
l. Declared and paid dividends of $1,000.

REQUIRED

1. Arrange the asset, liability, and stockholders' equity accounts in an equation similar to that in Exhibit 1, using the following account titles: Cash, Accounts Receivable, Auto Supplies, Taxi, Accounts Payable, Common Stock, and Retained Earnings.
2. Show by addition and subtraction, as in Exhibit 1, the effects of the transactions on the accounting equation. Show new balances after each transaction, and identify each stockholders' equity transaction by type.
3. Using Exhibit 2 as a guide, prepare an income statement, a statement of retained earnings, and a balance sheet for Dependable Taxi Service, Inc. (Optional: Also prepare a statement of cash flows.)

SKILLS DEVELOPMENT CASES

Conceptual Analysis ← These cases focus on conceptual accounting issues encountered in the real business world.

SD 1.

LO1 Business Activities and
LO2 Management Functions

Communication icons identify cases that focus on understanding and communicating accounting information successfully.

J.C. Penney Company, Inc., <www.jcpenney.com> is America's largest department store company. According to its letter to stockholders, financial results didn't meet company expectations.

> J.C. Penney is implementing a number of strategic initiatives to ensure our competitiveness, to meet our growth objectives, and to provide a strong return on our stockholders' investment. These initiatives include: accelerated growth in our top 10 markets; expand our women's apparel and accessories business; speed merchandise to market; reduce our cost structure and enhance customer service.[11]

To achieve its strategy, J.C. Penney must organize its management into functions that relate to the principal activities of a business. Discuss the three basic activities J.C. Penney will engage in to achieve its goals, and suggest some examples of each. What is the role of J.C. Penney's management, and what functions must its management perform to accomplish these activities?

SD 2.

LO2 Users of Accounting
LO7 Information

Critical Thinking icons identify cases that reinforce critical thinking skills.

Public companies report quarterly and annually on their success or failure in making a net income. The following item appeared in *The Wall Street Journal:* "Coca-Cola Co.'s <www.coca-cola.com> fourth-quarter net income plunged 27%, a dismal end to a disappointing year, as economic weakness in several overseas markets hurt sales of soft drinks."[12] Discuss why each of the following individuals or groups might be interested in seeing the accounting reports that support this statement:

1. The management of Coca-Cola
2. The stockholders of Coca-Cola
3. The creditors of Coca-Cola
4. Potential stockholders of Coca-Cola
5. The Internal Revenue Service
6. The Securities and Exchange Commission
7. The Teamsters' union
8. A consumers' group called Public Cause
9. An economic adviser to the president of the United States

LO3 Concept of an Asset

Ethical dilemmas provide practice in dealing with the tough choices people often face.

LO8 Professional Ethics

Ethics icons identify cases that address ethical issues.

You are asked to gather information from the Internet or business publications and apply it to the accounting concepts in the chapter.

LO1 Need for Knowledge
LO2 of Accounting

What are the relevant numbers, and what do they mean? Practice making business decisions based on accounting information.

LO5 Effect of Transactions
LO6 on the Balance Sheet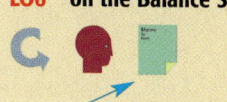

Memo icons identify cases that require short business memorandums.

The financial statements of Coca-Cola are audited by a CPA firm. Why is the report of these independent auditors important to the users of Coca-Cola's financial statements?

Group Activity: Assign each of these users to a different group. Ask each group to discuss and present why its user needs accounting information.

SD 3. Southwest Airlines Co. <www.southwest.com> is one of the most successful airlines in the United States. Its annual report contains this statement: "We are a company of People, not Planes. That is what distinguishes us from other airlines and other companies. At Southwest Airlines, People are our most important asset."[13] Are employees considered assets in the financial statements? Discuss in what sense Southwest considers its employees to be assets.

Ethical Dilemma

SD 4. Discuss the ethical choices in the situations below. In each instance, describe the ethical dilemma, determine the alternative courses of action, and tell what you would do.

1. You are the payroll accountant for a small business. A friend asks you how much another employee is paid per hour.
2. As an accountant for the branch office of a wholesale supplier, you discover that several of the receipts the branch manager has submitted for reimbursement as selling expense actually stem from nights out with his spouse.
3. You are an accountant in the purchasing department of a construction company. When you arrive home from work on December 22, you find a large ham in a box marked "Happy Holidays—It's a pleasure to work with you." The gift is from a supplier who has bid on a contract your employer plans to award next week.
4. As an auditor with one year's experience at a local CPA firm, you are expected to complete a certain part of an audit in 20 hours. Because of your lack of experience, you know you cannot finish the job within that time. Rather than admit this, you are thinking about working late to finish the job and not telling anyone.
5. You are a tax accountant at a local CPA firm. You help your neighbor fill out her tax return, and she pays you $200 in cash. Because there is no record of this transaction, you are considering not reporting it on your tax return.
6. The accounting firm for which you work as a CPA has just won a new client, a firm in which you own 200 shares of stock that you inherited from your grandmother. Because it is only a small number of shares and you think the company will be very successful, you are considering not disclosing the investment.

Group Activity. Assign each case to a different group to resolve and report.

Research Activity

SD 5. Locate an article about a company from one of the following sources: the business section of your local paper or a nearby metropolitan daily, *The Wall Street Journal, Business Week, Forbes,* or the Needles Accounting Resource Center Web Site at http://accounting.college.hmco.com/students. List all the financial and accounting terms used in the article. Bring the article to class and be prepared to discuss how a knowledge of accounting would help a reader understand the content of the article.

Decision-Making Practice

SD 6. Instead of hunting for a summer job after finishing her junior year in college, Beth Murphy started a lawn service business in her neighborhood. On June 1, she deposited $2,700 in a new bank account in the name of her corporation. The $2,700 consisted of a $1,000 loan from her father and $1,700 of her own money. In return for her investment, Murphy issued 1,700 shares of $1 par value common stock to herself.

Using the money in this checking account, Murphy rented lawn equipment, purchased supplies, and hired local teenagers to mow and trim the lawns of neighbors who had agreed to pay her for the service. At the end of each month, she mailed bills to her customers. On August 31, Murphy was ready to dissolve her business and go back to school for the fall term. Because she had been so busy, she had not kept any records other than her checkbook and a list of amounts owed by customers.

Her checkbook had a balance of $3,520, and her customers owed her $875. She expected these customers to pay her during September. She planned to return unused supplies to the Lawn Care Center for a full credit of $50. When she brought back the rented lawn equipment, the Lawn Care Center also would return a deposit of $200 she had made in June. She owed the Lawn Care Center $525 for equipment rentals and supplies. In addition, she owed the students who had worked for her $100, and she still owed her father $700. Although Murphy feels she did quite well, she is not sure just how successful she was. You have agreed to help her find out.

1. Prepare one balance sheet dated June 1 and another dated August 31 for Murphy Lawn Services, Inc.
2. Using information that can be inferred from comparing the balance sheets, write a memorandum to Murphy commenting on her company's performance in achieving profitability and liquidity. (Assume that she used none of the company's assets for personal purposes.) Also, mention the other two financial statements that would be helpful to her in evaluating these business goals.

FINANCIAL REPORTING AND ANALYSIS CASES

Using excerpts from business articles or annual reports of well-known companies, these cases ask you to extract relevant data, make computations, and interpret your results.

Interpreting Financial Reports

LO7 Generally Accepted Accounting Principles

FRA 1. J. P. Morgan Investment Management Inc. <www.jpmorgan.com> is the investment advisory service of the well-known investment bank J.P. Morgan Chase & Company. It makes investments worth billions of dollars in companies listed on the New York Stock Exchange and other stock markets. Generally accepted accounting principles (GAAP) are very important for J.P. Morgan's investment analysts. What are generally accepted accounting principles? Why are financial statements that have been prepared in accordance with GAAP and audited by an independent CPA useful for J.P. Morgan's investment analysts? What organizations influence GAAP? Explain how they do so.

LO1 Operating Goals

FRA 2. In May 2001, unable to get credit from enough of its lenders, housewares retailer Lechters, Inc., filed for Chapter 11 bankruptcy. It then secured new bank financing in the amount of $86 million. Suppliers, however, remained concerned about Lechters' ability to meet future obligations. Many retracted their terms of sale, or the number of days the company had to pay for its merchandise, and asked for cash in advance or on delivery. Smaller home-furnishing retailers like Lechters struggle against big rivals, such as Bed Bath & Beyond, which are more valuable to suppliers and thus can demand better terms and pricing. In spite of these problems and an annual net loss of $101.8 million on sales of $405 million, management believed the company could eventually succeed with its strategy under the bankruptcy.[14] Which is more critical to the short-term survival of a company faced with Lechters' problems: liquidity or profitability? Which is more important in the long term? Explain your answers.

LO6 Nature of Cash, Assets, and Net Income

FRA 3. Charles Schwab Corporation <www.schwab.com> is a well-known financial services firm. Information for 2001 and 2000 from the company's annual report is presented at the top of the next page.[15] (All numbers are in millions.) Three students who were looking at Charles Schwab's annual report were overheard to make the following comments:

> *Student A:* What a great year Charles Schwab had in 2001! The company earned net income of $2,310,000,000 because its total assets increased from $38,154,000,000 to $40,464,000,000.
>
> *Student B:* But the change in total assets isn't the same as net income! The company had a net loss of $469,000,000 because cash decreased from $4,876,000,000 to $4,407,000,000.
>
> *Student C:* I see from the annual report that Charles Schwab paid cash dividends of $61,000,000 in 2001. Don't you have to take that into consideration when analyzing the company's performance?

1. Comment on the interpretations of Students A and B, and then answer Student C's question.

Charles Schwab Corporation
Condensed Balance Sheets
December 31, 2001 and 2000
(In millions)

	2001	2000
Assets		
Cash	$ 4,407	$ 4,876
Other assets	36,057	33,278
Total assets	$40,464	$38,154
Liabilities		
Total liabilities	$36,301	$33,924
Stockholders' Equity		
Common stock	$ 1,369	$ 1,517
Retained earnings	2,794	2,713
Total liabilities and stockholders' equity	$40,464	$38,154

2. Calculate Charles Schwab's net income for 2001. (**Hint:** Reconstruct the statement of retained earnings.)

 Group Activity: After groups discuss **1,** have them compete to see which one can come up with the answer to **2** first.

International Company

FRA 4.
LO1 The Goal of Profitability

In 1998, the celebrated Danish toy company Lego Group <www.lego.com> reported its first loss since the 1930s. In subsequent years, Lego's performance continued to be erratic with profits in 1999, but with a loss in 2000. While its bright plastic bricks were still famous around the globe, Lego was rapidly losing market share to computer and video games. The company's president said, "The Lego Group is not in critical condition, but action is needed. . . . We have to acknowledge that growth and innovation are not enough. We also have to be a profitable business."[16] Discuss the meaning of *profitability*. What other goal must a business achieve? Why is the goal of profitability important to Lego's president? What is the accounting measure of profitability, and on which statement is it determined?

Toys "R" Us Annual Report

FRA 5.
LO6 The Four Basic Financial Statements

Refer to the Toys "R" Us <www.tru.com> annual report in the Supplement to Chapter 1 to answer the questions below. Keep in mind that every company, while following basic principles, adapts financial statements and terminology to its own needs. Thus, the complexity of the financial statements and the terminology in the Toys "R" Us statements will sometimes differ from those in the text. (Note that 2002 refers to the year ended February 1, 2003, and 2001 refers to the year ended February 2, 2002.)

1. What names does Toys "R" Us give its four basic financial statements? (Note that the word *consolidated* in the names of the financial statements means that these statements combine those of several companies owned by Toys "R" Us.)
2. Prove that the accounting equation works for Toys "R" Us on February 1, 2003, by finding the appropriate amounts for it: Assets = Liabilities + Stockholders' Equity.

3. What were the total revenues of Toys "R" Us for the year ended February 1, 2003?
4. Was Toys "R" Us profitable in the year ended February 1, 2003? How much was net income (loss) in that year, and did it increase or decrease from the year ended February 2, 2002?
5. Did the company's cash and cash equivalents increase from February 2, 2002, to February 1, 2003? By how much? In what two places in the statements can this number be found or computed?
6. Did cash flows from operating activities, cash flows from investing activities, and cash flows from financing activities increase or decrease from 2001 to 2002?

Group Activity: Assign the above questions to in-class groups of three or four students. Set a time limit. The first group to answer all questions correctly wins.

Comparison cases ask you to read the financial statements of Toys "R" Us and Walgreens in the supplement to Chapter 1 and to compare these companies on key financial performance measures and financial disclosures.

Comparison Case: Toys "R" Us and Walgreen Co.

FRA 6. Refer to the Toys "R" Us <www.tru.com> annual report and the financial statements of Walgreens <www.walgreens.com> at the end of this chapter to answer these questions:

LO1 **Performance Measures**
LO5 **and Financial Statements**
LO7

1. Which company is larger in terms of assets and in terms of revenues? What do you think is the best way to measure the size of a company?
2. Which company is more profitable in terms of net income? What is the trend of profitability over the past three years for both companies?
3. Which company has more cash? Which increased cash most in the last year? Which has more liquidity as measured by cash flows from operating activities?
4. Who is the auditor for each company? Why is the auditor's report that accompanies the financial statements important?

Use the professional software Fingraph® to analyze financial data.

Fingraph® Financial Analyst™

FRA 7. Choose a company from the list of Fingraph companies on the Needles Accounting Resource Center Web Site at http://accounting.college.hmco.com/students. Click on the company you selected to access the Microsoft Excel spreadsheet for that company. You will find the company's URL (Internet address) in the heading of the spreadsheet. Click on the URL for a link to the company's web site and annual report.

LO1 **Financial Statements,**
LO6 **Business Activities, and Goals**

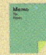

1. In the company's annual report, find a description of the business. What business is the company in? How would you describe its operating activities?
2. Find the company's four basic financial statements. Which statement shows the resources of the business and the claims to those resources? From the balance sheet, prove the accounting equation by showing that the company's assets equal its liabilities plus stockholders' equity. What is the company's largest category of assets? Which statement shows changes in all or part of the stockholders' equity during the year? Did the company pay any dividends in the last year?
3. Which statement is most closely associated with the company's profitability goal? How much net income did the company earn in the last year? Which statement is most closely associated with the company's liquidity goal? Did cash (and cash equivalents) increase in the last year? Which provided the most positive cash flows in the last year: operating, investing, or financing activities?
4. Prepare a one-page "executive summary" from steps **1, 2,** and **3.** An executive summary is a short, easy-to-read report that emphasizes important data and conclusions by putting them in numbered paragraphs or bulleted lists.

Use the Internet to research concepts and applications presented in the chapter.

Internet Case

FRA 8. Microsoft <www.microsoft.com> and Intel <www.intel.com> are two very successful high-tech corporations. Access their web sites using the URLs listed here or go to the Needles Accounting Resource Center Web Site at http://accounting.college.hmco.com/students for a link to their web sites. Access each company's annual report and locate the consolidated balance sheet and consolidated statement of income. Find the amount of total assets, revenues, and net income for the most recent year shown. Then compute net income to revenues (divide net income by revenues) and net income to total assets (divide net income by total assets) for both companies. Which company is larger? Which is more profitable?

LO1 **Financial Performance**
LO5 **Comparison of Two High-Tech Companies**

Supplement to Chapter 1
How to Read an Annual Report

More than 4 million corporations are chartered in the United States. Most of these are small, family-owned businesses. They are called *private* or *closely held corporations* because their common stock is held by only a few people and is not available for sale to the public. Larger companies usually find it desirable to raise investment funds from many investors by issuing common stock to the public. These companies are called *public companies*. Although they are fewer in number than private companies, their total economic impact is much greater.

Public companies must register their common stock with the Securities and Exchange Commission (SEC), which regulates the issuance and subsequent trading of the stock of public companies. One important responsibility of the management of public companies under SEC rules is to report each year to the company's stockholders on the financial performance of the company. This report, called an *annual report*, contains the annual financial statements and other information about the company. Annual reports, which are a primary source of financial information about public companies, are distributed to all the company's stockholders and filed with the SEC. When filed with the SEC, the annual report is called the 10-K because a Form 10-K is used to file the report. The general public may obtain an annual report by calling or writing the company or accessing it online at the company's web site. If a company has filed its 10-K electronically with the SEC, it may be accessed at http://www.sec.gov/edgar.shtml. Many libraries also maintain files of annual reports or have them available on electronic media, such as *Compact Disclosure*.

This supplement describes the major sections of the typical annual report and contains the annual report of one of the most successful retailers of this generation, Toys "R" Us, Inc. In addition to operating stores that sell toys and other items for children, the company has a chain of stores that sell children's clothes, called Kids "R" Us and a chain of stores devoted exclusively to babies, called Babies "R" Us. The Toys "R" Us annual report should be referred to in completing the case assignments related to the company in each chapter. For purposes of comparison, the supplement also includes the financial statements and notes to the financial statements of Walgreens, one of the largest drugstore chains in the United States.

THE COMPONENTS OF AN ANNUAL REPORT

In addition to listing the corporation's directors and officers, an annual report contains a letter to the stockholders, a multiyear summary of financial highlights, a description of the company, management's discussion of operating results and financial conditions, the financial statements, notes to the financial statements, a report of management's responsibilities, the auditors' report, and supplementary information notes.

LETTER TO THE STOCKHOLDERS

Traditionally, an annual report begins with a letter in which the top officers of the corporation tell stockholders about the performance and prospects of the company. In its 2001 annual report, the president and chief executive officer of Toys "R" Us wrote to the stockholders about the highlights of the past year, the key priorities for the new year, store format and redeployment plans, corporate citizenship, and other aspects of the business. He reported on future prospects as follows:

2002 was a year of encouraging progress, but a time of disappointments as well. Three divisions in our portfolio of businesses — Babies "R" Us, Toys "R" Us International and Toysrus.com — enjoyed the best performances in their history. Those results, coupled with improved expense discipline, resulted in a 19% gain in net earnings, before restructuring and other charges in 2001, for Toys "R" Us, Inc. However, weaker results in Toys "R" Us U.S. and Kids "R" Us were very disappointing, despite progress in strategic execution in both divisions. . . .

Nonetheless, we were encouraged by the progress we made in the execution of our strategy, which we believe further strengthened our ability to improve our performance in 2003 and beyond.

FINANCIAL HIGHLIGHTS

The financial highlights section of an annual report presents key statistics for a ten-year period and is often accompanied by graphs. The Toys "R" Us annual report, for example, gives key figures for operations, financial position, and number of stores at year end. Note that the financial highlights section often includes nonfinancial data, such as the number of stores.

DESCRIPTION OF THE COMPANY

An annual report contains a detailed description of the products and divisions of the company. Some analysts tend to scoff at this section of the annual report because it often contains glossy photographs and other image-building material, but it should not be overlooked because it may provide useful information about past results and future plans.

MANAGEMENT'S DISCUSSION AND ANALYSIS

Management also presents a discussion and analysis of financial condition and results of operations. In this section, management explains the difference from one year to the next. For example, the management of Toys "R" Us describes the company's net sales in the following way:

Comparison of Fiscal Year 2002 to 2001

We reported consolidated net sales of $11.3 billion for the 52-week fiscal year ended February 1, 2003 versus $11.0 billion for the 52-week fiscal year ended February 2, 2002, or a 3% increase in consolidated net sales. Our consolidated net sales were $11.2 billion for 2002, after excluding the impact of foreign currency translation, representing a 1% increase over 2001 net sales.

 Its management of cash flows is described as follows:

The seasonal nature of our business typically causes cash balances to decline from the beginning of the year through October as inventory increases for the holiday selling season and funds are used for construction of new stores, remodeling and other initiates that normally occur in this period. The fourth quarter, including the holiday season, accounts for more than 40% of our net sales and substantially all of our operating earnings.

FINANCIAL STATEMENTS

All companies present four basic financial statements in their annual reports. As you can see in the annual report included with this supplement, Toys "R" Us presents statements of earnings (income statements), balance sheets, statements of cash flows, and statements of stockholders' equity (retained earnings).

The headings of all Toys "R" Us financial statements are preceded by the word *consolidated*. A corporation issues *consolidated* financial statements when it consists of more than one company and has combined their data for reporting purposes. For example, Toys "R" Us has combined the financial data of Kids "R" Us and Babies "R" Us with those of the Toys "R" Us stores.

Toys "R" Us provides several years of data for each financial statement: two years for the balance sheet and three years for the others. Financial statements presented in this fashion are called *comparative financial statements*. Such statements are in accordance with generally accepted accounting principles and help readers assess the company's performance over several years.

You may notice that the fiscal year for Toys "R" Us ends on the Saturday nearest the end of January, rather than on the same date each year. The reason is that Toys "R" Us is a retail company. It is common for retailers to end their fiscal years at a slow period after the busiest time of year.

In a note at the bottom of each page of the financial statements, Toys "R" Us reminds the reader that the accompanying notes are an integral part of the statements and must be consulted in interpreting the data.

■ **STATEMENTS OF EARNINGS** Toys "R" Us uses a multistep form of the income statement that shows gross margin as the difference between net sales and cost of sales (goods sold). Total operating expenses are deducted from gross margin to arrive at operating earnings (income). Interest expense is shown separately, and income taxes are deducted in another step. *Net earnings* is an alternative name for *net income*. The company also discloses the earnings per share, which is the net earnings divided by the weighted average number of shares of common stock held by stockholders during the year.

■ **BALANCE SHEETS** Toys "R" Us has a typical balance sheet for a merchandising company. In the assets and liabilities sections, the company separates out the current assets and the current liabilities. Current assets will become available as cash or be used up in the next year; current liabilities will have to be paid or satisfied in the next year. These groupings help in understanding the company's liquidity.

Several items in the stockholders' equity section need additional explanation. Common stock represents the number of shares outstanding at par value. Additional paid-in capital represents amounts invested by stockholders in excess of the par value of the common stock. Treasury shares is a deduction from stockholders' equity that represents the cost of previously issued shares that have been bought back and held by the company.

■ **STATEMENTS OF CASH FLOWS** Whereas the income statement reflects a company's profitability, the statement of cash flows reflects its liquidity. This statement provides information about a company's cash receipts, cash payments, and investing and financing activities during an accounting period.

Refer to the consolidated statements of cash flows in the Toys "R" Us annual report. The first major section shows cash flows from operating activities. It begins with the net earnings (income) from the consolidated statements of earnings and adjusts that figure to a figure that represents the net cash from operating activities. Among the adjustments are increases for depreciation and amortization, which are expenses that do not require the use of cash, and increases and decreases for the changes in the working capital accounts. In the year ended February 1, 2003, Toys "R" Us had net earnings of $229,000,000, and its net cash from operating activities was $574,000,000. Added to net income are such expenses as depreciation and amortization. Two small negative items were more than offset by a positive amount associated with deferred income taxes. Accounts and other receivables showed little change. Increases in merchandise inventories, prepaid expenses, and other operating assets contributed to declines in cash, as did a decrease in income taxes payable. An increase of $112,000,000 in accounts payable, accrued expenses, and other liabilities was a significant source of cash.

The second major section of the consolidated statements of cash flows is cash flows from investing activities. The main item in this category is capital expenditures, net, of $388,000,000. This figure demonstrates that Toys "R" Us is a growing company.

The third major section of the consolidated statements of cash flows is cash flows from financing activities. You can see here that the sources of cash from financing are long-term borrowings of $548,000,000, and issuance of stock options of $266,000,000, which were helpful in making debt repayments of $141,000,000. In total, the company generated $613,000,000 in cash from financing activities during the year.

At the bottom of the consolidated statements of cash flows, the net effect of the operating, investing, and financing activities on the cash balance may be seen. Toys "R" Us had an increase in cash and cash equivalents during the year of $740,000,000 and ended the year with $1,023,000,000 of cash and cash equivalents on hand.

The supplemental disclosures of cash flow information show income tax and interest payments for the last three years.

■ **STATEMENTS OF STOCKHOLDERS' EQUITY** Instead of a simple statement of retained earnings, Toys "R" Us presents a *statement of stockholders' equity*. This statement explains the changes in five components of stockholders' equity.

NOTES TO FINANCIAL STATEMENTS

To meet the requirements of full disclosure, a company must add *notes to the financial statements* to help users interpret some of the more complex items. The notes are considered an integral part of the financial statements. In recent years, the need for explanation and further details has become so great that the notes often take more space than the statements themselves. The notes to the financial statements include a summary of significant accounting policies and explanatory notes.

■ **SUMMARY OF SIGNIFICANT ACCOUNTING POLICIES** Generally accepted accounting principles require that the financial statements include a *Summary of Significant Accounting Policies*. In most cases, this summary is presented in the first note to the financial statements or as a separate section just before the notes. In this summary, the company tells which generally accepted accounting principles it has followed in preparing the statements. For example, in the Toys "R" Us report, the company states the principles followed for property and equipment:

> Property and equipment are recorded at cost. Leasehold improvements represent capital inprovements made to leased locations. Depreciation and amortization are provided using the straight-line method over the estimated useful lives of the assets or, where applicable, the terms of the respective leases, whichever is shorter.

Other important accounting policies listed by Toys "R" Us deal with fiscal year; reclassification; principles of consolidation; uses of estimates; revenue recognition; advertising costs; cash and cash equivalents; merchandise inventories; credits and allowances received from vendors; cost of sales and selling, general, and administrative expenses; costs of computer software; financial instruments; and stock options.

■ **EXPLANATORY NOTES** Other notes explain some of the items in the financial statements. For example, Toys "R" Us showed the details of its Property and Equipment account, which is reproduced at the top of the next page.

Other notes had to do with restricted cash, merchandise inventories, goodwill, investment in Toys–Japan, seasonal financing and long-term debt, derivative instruments and hedging activities, issuance of common stock and equity security units,

	Property and Equipment		
	Useful Life (in years)	February 1, 2003	February 2, 2002
Land		$ 825	$ 811
Buildings	45–50	2,009	1,980
Furniture and equipment	5–20	1,786	1,800
Leasehold improvements	12½–35	1,726	1,542
Cost of computer software	5	192	127
Construction in progress		33	41
Leased property and equipment under capital lease		53	53
		6,624	6,354
Less accumulated depreciation and amortization		1,861	1,810
		$4,763	$4,544

stockholders' equity, earnings per share, stock purchases warrants, leases, taxes on income, stock options, replacement of certain stock options grants with restricted stock, profit-sharing plan, Toysrus.com, segments, restructuring and other charges, gain from initial public offering of Toys–Japan, subsequent events, and other matters.

REPORT OF MANAGEMENT'S RESPONSIBILITIES

A statement of management's responsibility for the financial statements and the internal control structure may accompany the financial statements. The management report of Toys "R" Us acknowledges management's responsibility for the integrity and objectivity of the financial information and for the system of internal controls. It mentions the company's internal audit program and its distribution of company policies to employees. It also mentions the Audit Committee of the Board of Directors and states that the company's financial statements have been audited.

REPORT OF CERTIFIED PUBLIC ACCOUNTANTS

The *independent auditors' report* deals with the credibility of the financial statements. This report prepared by independent certified public accountants gives the accountants' opinion about how fairly these statements have been presented. Using financial statements prepared by managers without an independent audit would be like having a judge hear a case in which he or she was personally involved. Management, through its internal accounting system, is logically responsible for recordkeeping because it needs similar information for its own use in operating the business. The certified public accountants, acting independently, add the necessary credibility to management's figures for interested third parties. They report to the board of directors and the stockholders rather than to management.

In form and language, most auditors' reports are like the one shown in Figure 8. Usually such a report is short, but its language is very important. The report is usually divided into three parts, but it can have a fourth part if there is a need for further explanation.

1. The first paragraph identifies the financial statements subject to the auditors' report. This paragraph also identifies responsibilities. Company management is responsible for the financial statements, and the auditor is responsible for expressing an opinion on the financial statements based on the audit.

FIGURE 8
Auditors' Report for Toys "R" Us, Inc.

REPORT OF INDEPENDENT AUDITORS

To the Board of Directors and Stockholders
Toys"R"Us, Inc.

① We have audited the accompanying consolidated balance sheets of Toys"R"Us, Inc. and subsidiaries as of February 1, 2003 and February 2, 2002, and the related consolidated statements of earnings, stockholders' equity and cash flows for each of the three years in the period ended February 1, 2003. These financial statements are the responsibility of the company's management. Our responsibility is to express an opinion on these financial statements based on our audits.

② We conducted our audits in accordance with auditing standards generally accepted in the United States. Those standards require that we plan and perform the audit to obtain reasonable assurance about whether the financial statements are free of material misstatement. An audit includes examining, on a test basis, evidence supporting the amounts and disclosures in the financial statements. An audit also includes assessing the accounting principles used and significant estimates made by management, as well as evaluating the overall financial statement presentation. We believe that our audits provide a reasonable basis for our opinion.

③ In our opinion, the financial statements referred to above present fairly, in all material respects, the consolidated financial position of Toys"R"Us, Inc. and subsidiaries at February 1, 2003 and February 2, 2002, and the consolidated results of their operations and their cash flows for each of the three years in the period ended February 1, 2003, in conformity with accounting principles generally accepted in the United States.

④ As discussed in the note entitled "Goodwill," the company adopted SFAS No. 142, Goodwill and Other Intangible Assets, effective February 3, 2002.

Ernst & Young LLP

Ernst & Young LLP
New York, New York
March 5, 2003

Source: Reprinted by permission of Toys "R" Us. The notes to the financial statement, which are an integral part of the report, are not included.

2. The second paragraph, or *scope section*, states that the examination was made in accordance with generally accepted auditing standards. These standards call for an acceptable level of quality in ten areas established by the American Institute of Certified Public Accountants. This paragraph also contains a brief description of the objectives and nature of the audit.

3. The third paragraph, or *opinion section*, states the results of the auditors' examination. The use of the word *opinion* is very important because the auditor does not certify or guarantee that the statements are absolutely correct. To do so would go beyond the truth, since many items, such as depreciation, are based on estimates. Instead, the auditors simply give an opinion about whether, overall, the financial statements "present fairly," in all material respects, the financial position, results of operations, and cash flows. This means that the statements are prepared in accordance with generally accepted accounting principles. If, in the auditors' opinion, the statements do not meet accepted standards, the auditors must explain why and to what extent.

4. The optional fourth paragraph mentions the adoption of a new accounting standard.

SUPPLEMENTARY INFORMATION NOTES

In recent years, the FASB and the SEC have ruled that certain supplemental information must be presented with financial statements. Examples are the quarterly reports that most companies present to their stockholders and to the SEC. These quarterly reports, called *interim financial statements*, are in most cases reviewed but not audited by the company's independent CPA firm. In its annual report, Toys "R"

Company Profile

We are one of the world's leading retailers of toys, children's apparel and baby products based on our consolidated net sales in 2002. As of February 1, 2003, we operated 1,595 "R"Us retail stores worldwide. These consist of 1,051 United States locations comprised of 681 toy stores under the name "Toys"R"Us," 183 infant-toddler stores under the name "Babies"R"Us," 146 children's clothing stores under the name "Kids"R"Us," 37 educational specialty stores under the name "Imaginarium" and 4 "Geoffrey" stores that include products from Toys"R"Us, Kids"R"Us and Babies"R"Us as well as many interactive events. Internationally, as of February 1, 2003, we operated 544 stores, including licensed and franchised stores, under the "R"Us name. We also sell merchandise through Internet sites at www.toysrus.com, www.babiesrus.com, www.imaginarium.com and www.giftsrus.com. Toys"R"Us, Inc. is incorporated in the state of Delaware.

Our History

Toys"R"Us got its start in 1948 when founder Charles Lazarus opened a baby furniture store, Children's Bargain Town, in Washington D.C. Lazarus quickly realized the potential of fulfilling customer's requests for baby toys and toys for older children.

In 1957, Lazarus introduced a "supermarket environment." That same year, the Toys"R"Us name made its debut, complete with a backwards "R". By 1966, Lazarus had four stores with approximately $12 million in annual sales. Around this time, Lazarus sold his stores to retail conglomerate Interstate Stores. He maintained responsibility for running Toys"R"Us, which continued to grow profitably. Interstate, however, faced major difficulties and was forced to declare bankruptcy. During this critical period, Lazarus led and restructured the company. In 1978, when Interstate emerged from bankruptcy it was renamed Toys"R"Us, Inc.

The 1980s were a time of major expansion for Toys"R"Us, Inc. In 1983, the company had 169 toy stores in 26 states and had added four stores under its new Kids"R"Us brand. The company opened its first international stores in Singapore and Canada in 1984. Just 10 years later, the company completed its 1993 fiscal year with 581 U.S. toy stores, 217 Kids"R"Us stores and 234 stores in international locations. In 2001, Toys"R"Us opened its flagship store in Times Square.

In 1996, the company opened its first Babies"R"Us store. The acquisition of Baby Superstore in 1997 added 76 locations and helped Babies"R"Us become the undisputed leader in the juvenile market. Imaginarium was acquired in 1998 to bring the learning and educational toy categories to the "R"Us family of retail stores. Between 2000 and 2002, Imaginarium boutiques were added to U.S. toy stores as part of the division's Mission Possible renovation. In addition, Imaginarium also operates 37 freestanding locations.

Geoffrey the Giraffe was first introduced in 1960. However, he didn't receive his name until 1970 when a contest was held among company associates to name him. In 2000, Geoffrey was reintroduced, in his current animatronic form, as the company's lovable wisecracking "spokesanimal." Today he's one of the world's most recognized icons by kids and grown-ups alike, representative of a worldwide chain of stores that has forever changed the way the world shops for toys.

financial highlights

Toys"R"Us, Inc. and Subsidiaries

(Dollars in millions, except per share data) — Fiscal Year Ended

	Feb. 1, 2003	Feb. 2, 2002	Feb. 3, 2001	Jan. 29, 2000	Jan. 30, 1999	Jan. 31, 1998	Feb. 1, 1997	Feb. 3, 1996	Jan. 28, 1995	Jan. 29, 1994
Operations										
Total Enterprise Sales*	$13,067	$12,630	$12,774	$12,118	$11,459	$11,315	$10,113	$9,498	$8,819	$8,018
Net Sales	11,305	11,019	11,332	11,862	11,170	11,038	9,932	9,427	8,746	7,946
Net Earnings/(Loss)	229	67	404	279	(132)	490	427	148	532	483
Basic Earnings/(Loss) Per Share	1.10	0.34	1.92	1.14	(0.50)	1.72	1.56	0.54	1.88	1.66
Diluted Earnings/(Loss) Per Share	1.09	0.33	1.88	1.14	(0.50)	1.70	1.54	0.53	1.85	1.63
Financial Position at Year End										
Working Capital	$ 1,182	$ 657	$ 575	$ 35	$ 106	$ 579	$ 619	$ 326	$ 484	$ 633
Real Estate - Net	2,398	2,313	2,348	2,342	2,354	2,435	2,411	2,336	2,271	2,036
Total Assets	9,397	8,076	8,003	8,353	7,899	7,963	8,023	6,738	6,571	6,150
Long-Term Debt	2,139	1,816	1,567	1,230	1,222	851	909	827	785	724
Stockholders' Equity	4,030	3,414	3,418	3,680	3,624	4,428	4,191	3,432	3,429	3,148
Common Shares Outstanding	212.5	196.7	197.5	239.3	250.6	282.4	287.8	273.1	279.8	289.5
Number of Stores at Year End										
Toys"R"Us – U.S.	681	701	710	710	704	700	682	653	618	581
Toys"R"Us – International**	544	507	491	462	452	441	396	337	293	234
Babies"R"Us – U.S.	183	165	145	131	113	98	82	–	–	–
Kids"R"Us – U.S.	146	184	198	205	212	215	212	213	204	217
Imaginarium – U.S.	37	42	37	40	–	–	–	–	–	–
Geoffrey – U.S.	4	–	–	–	–	–	–	–	–	–
Total Stores	1,595	1,599	1,581	1,548	1,481	1,454	1,372	1,203	1,115	1,032

*Total enterprise sales consist of all Toys"R"Us branded net sales, which include net sales from all the company's stores and from the company's internet businesses, in addition to net sales from licensed and franchised stores.

**Includes licensed and franchised stores.

contents

Financial Highlights . . . . page 1

Letter to Our Shareholders . . . . page 3

Divisional Highlights . . . . page 7

Corporate Philanthropy and Corporate Responsibility . . . . page 19

Management's Discussion and Analysis
of Results of Operations and Financial Condition . . . . . . page 22

Financial Statements . . . . page 31

Report of Management and
Report of Independent Auditors . . . . page 45

Directors and Officers . . . . page 46

Quarterly Financial Data and Market Information . . . . . . page 48

Store Locations, Corporate Data
and Stockholder Information . . . . page 49

Building our portfolio of brands

letter to our shareholders

Performance *and Progress*

A year in review

2002 was a year of encouraging progress, but a time of disappointments as well. Three divisions in our portfolio of businesses – Babies"R"Us, Toys"R"Us International and Toysrus.com – enjoyed the best performances in their history. Those results, coupled with improved expense discipline resulted in a 19% gain in net earnings, before restructuring and other charges in 2001, for Toys"R"Us, Inc. However, weaker results in Toys"R"Us U.S. and Kids"R"Us were very disappointing, despite progress in strategic execution in both divisions.

The performance of our U.S. toy stores did not meet our expectations. Our comparable store sales declined 1% for the year and, in a difficult retail environment, our operating earnings declined as well.

Nonetheless, we were encouraged by the progress we made in the execution of our strategy; which we believe further strengthened our ability to improve our performance in 2003 and beyond. For example, by working closely with our vendors last year, we gained market share in core toy, defined as the Boys and Girls, Learning (i.e. Imaginarium) and Preschool categories. Our core toy sales outpaced toy industry performance, as reported by the Toy Industry Association, by 4% for the year.

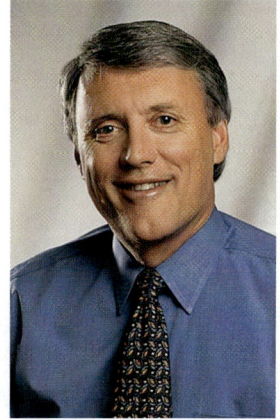

John Eyler
Chairman and Chief Executive Officer

We continued to improve our in-stock position, content, presentation and service levels. In addition, we experienced significant improvements in customer satisfaction scores related to pricing and value perception. Both messages were effectively reinforced through our award-winning television commercials featuring our charismatic "spokesanimal," Geoffrey the Giraffe.

We enjoyed historically high levels of success in several of our divisions in 2002. Babies"R"Us and Toys"R"Us International both turned in record-setting operating earnings for the fourth quarter and full year of 2002. In addition, Toysrus.com achieved operating profitability in the fourth quarter – a full year ahead of schedule. Our Kids"R"Us division has been struggling in its stand-alone stores for some time now, but we have seen positive results from sourcing apparel through Kids"R"Us for our Babies"R"Us stores as well as our Toys"R"Us/Kids"R"Us combo stores. Currently, our total apparel business represents approximately $900 million in sales per year, at above company average profit margins, and we expect continued growth. Approximately 65% of these sales come from exclusive products that generate higher margins than nationally branded items. We'll talk about these divisions in greater detail in this report.

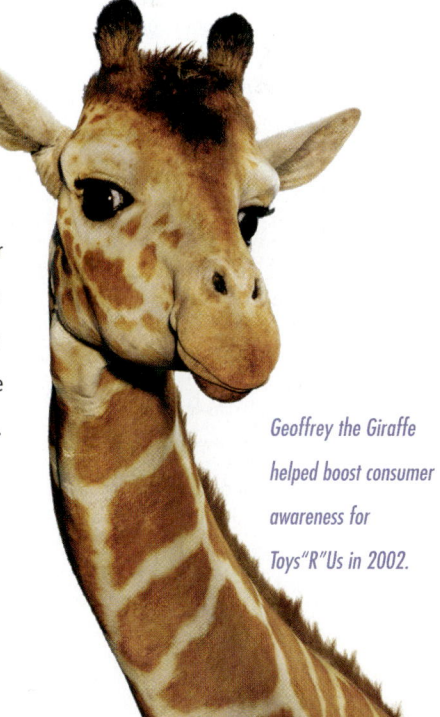

Geoffrey the Giraffe helped boost consumer awareness for Toys"R"Us in 2002.

letter to our shareholders

We worked diligently in 2002 to improve our productivity, reduce expenses and enhance our financial strength.

We took steps to strengthen our balance sheet and improve our liquidity. As a result, we had substantial excess liquidity in early November during our seasonal borrowing peak, and ended the fiscal year with more than $1 billion in cash.

We reduced capital spending significantly in 2002. Net capital expenditures were $398 million in 2002 as compared to $705 million in 2001.

We made solid progress on our commitment to reduce selling, general and administrative (SG&A) expenses by 200 basis points by 2005. We were able to achieve a reduction of 70 basis points in 2002, so we're approximately a third of the way to achieving our four-year objectives in the first year.

We will also continue to find ways to strengthen and expand our portfolio, and, in fact, made progress in the development of new businesses for the future in 2002. Our test of Toys"R"Us ToyBox, our store concept within grocery stores which first opened in the summer of 2001, is generating positive results. By the end of the year, we expanded our initial test to more than 30 stores, and we are currently evaluating further expansion opportunities for 2003.

The customer response to our recently launched Geoffrey stores has been positive.

We also launched Geoffrey, which is a combination Toys"R"Us, Kids"R"Us and Babies"R"Us store, in four smaller markets in 2002. The customer response has been positive, and we've already derived some key learnings from Geoffrey that may be applicable to our other divisions. We plan to move forward carefully with this concept, but we are encouraged by the results we've seen.

Challenges for 2003

We are committed to doing all it takes to turn the U.S. toy stores around and to expand further on the successes that we've seen. This progress clearly indicates that we are on the right track with our strategies. Our challenge and our commitment is to build on what we've accomplished. We will accelerate execution of our merchandising, presentation, customer service, pricing and advertising efforts designed to drive traffic and increase profitable sales. Knowing that we also need the support of our vendor community to succeed, we continue to work in partnership with them to build excitement for their brands and to re-energize underperforming product categories.

We will accelerate execution of our strategies in 2003.

letter to our shareholders

We will also continue to improve our cost effectiveness to reduce our SG&A even further in 2003. In March, we reduced our national headquarters staff by approximately 200 positions, or 10%. We also announced that we would combine our Kids"R"Us and Babies"R"Us management teams into one group. This will help Kids"R"Us reduce its operating costs. In addition, we will ensure that our balance sheet remains strong and that we have ample liquidity now and into the future.

I think it truly says something about the strength of our portfolio that even in a year where we did not see the kind of success we expected in the largest division of our company, we were still able to announce a meaningful earnings increase. As we look to the future, I'm very proud of the steps that we've taken to manage the business in an undeniably difficult operating environment.

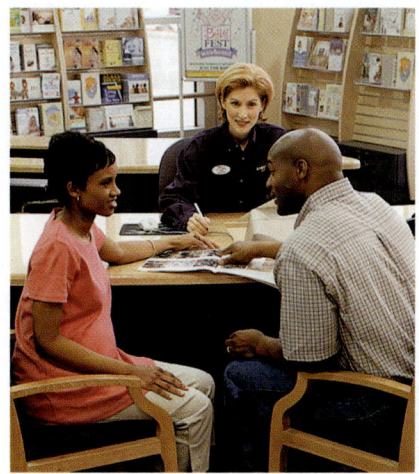

Babies"R"Us registers more expectant parents than any other retailer in the U.S.

Conclusion

As I write this letter, our associates from all divisions and all disciplines are working with tremendous commitment to make ours a more profitable organization. They share my absolute conviction that in 2003 we will seize upon every opportunity to drive sales and profits across every division. Given the solid improvement in our earnings in 2002, despite very difficult and uncertain economic and world environments, we believe we have ample evidence that we're on the right track. We will build on that progress, and we will not stop until we can deliver a better value for your investment and repay your faith in our company.

[signature]

John H. Eyler, Jr.
Chairman, President and Chief Executive Officer
March 29, 2003

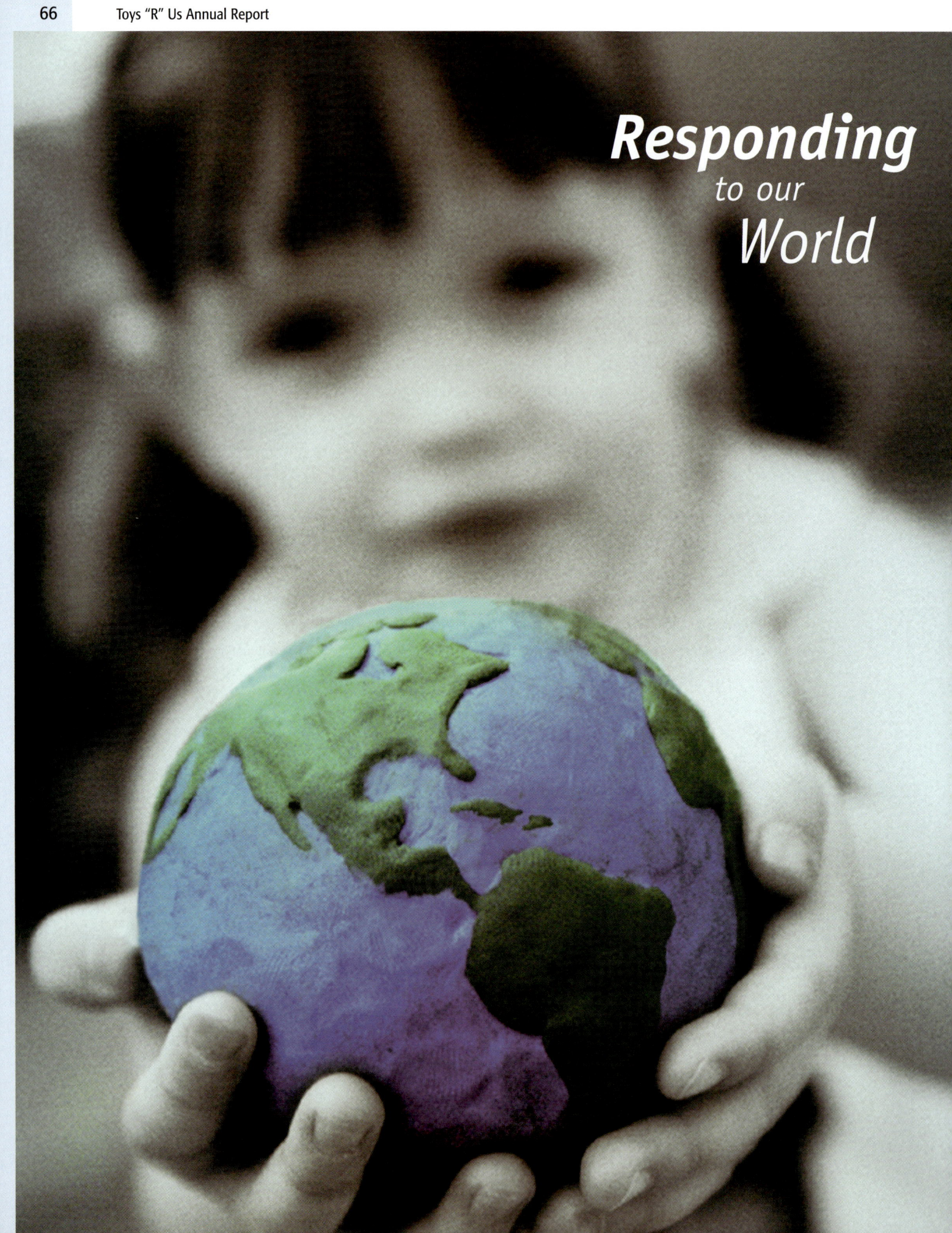

corporate responsibility

The Demand for Corporate **Responsibility**

Corporate Governance

Corporate governance is a joint responsibility requiring the involvement of and interaction between the Board of Directors and the senior management of the company.

Toys"R"Us, Inc. is fortunate to have a talented Board of Directors committed to the success of the company. For example, during fiscal year 2002, 11 Board meetings and 34 additional Board committee meetings were held. At several of the Board meetings, the Board met in executive session, outside the presence of senior management, to further discuss and examine issues of importance to the company.

After many months of careful research, investigation and thought, the Board adopted Corporate Governance Guidelines of the company in March 2002 to reflect the Board's commitment to monitor the effectiveness of policy and decision-making, both at the Board and management level, and to enhance stockholder value over the long term. Those Guidelines covered such issues as conflicts of interest, the compensation of the company's Chief Executive Officer and other Board members, the process and criteria for selecting Board members and the requirements that the Audit, Compensation and former Corporate Governance Committees be comprised solely of independent Board members and that independent Board members constitute a substantial majority of the Board.

In the past year, the Board has adopted Amended and Restated Corporate Governance Guidelines of the company that further address those issues and cover such issues as director orientation and continuing education and the Board's retention of independent advisors, as well as the requirement that the new Corporate Governance and Nominating Committee be comprised solely of independent Board members. The current Guidelines and committee charters are published in the company's proxy materials filed with the SEC in 2003.

The Toys"R"Us Board of Directors is fully engaged in and focused on the strategic issues facing our business. Each year, the Board devotes one meeting to develop, discuss and refine the company's long-range operating plan and overall corporate strategy. Following the Board's annual strategic meeting, the Board reviews the progress of one or more strategic initiatives at each scheduled meeting. Through the established procedures, the Board, consistent with good corporate governance, encourages the long-term success of the company by exercising sound and independent business judgment on the strategic issues that are important to the company's business.

Code of Conduct for Suppliers

There is growing concern in the global community about working conditions in many nations, including the United States, which may fall below the basic standards of fair and humane treatment. In an effort to source products in a manner that is both socially responsible and profitable, Toys"R"Us, Inc. developed its Code of Conduct for Suppliers program in 1997.

Implementation of the Code and the use of SA8000®, an independent monitoring and factory certification program, enable the company and its business partners to continually improve their performance in relation to workers' rights, labor standards and other human rights issues integral to the manufacturing process.

Developed by Social Accountability International (SAI) in 1998 and currently in use by businesses and governments around the world, SA8000® assessments are widely recognized by trade unions and non-governmental organizations as a powerful tool for creating environments where both workers and management benefit. Facilities in more than 20 nations and 15 industries have been SA8000® certified.

Participation in the Toys"R"Us Code of Conduct program and compliance with all of its provisions is mandatory for all suppliers who sell products, for the purpose of resale, to any Toys"R"Us, Inc. division. The company will terminate its business relationship with any supplier that elects not to participate in the Code of Conduct program or fails to abide by any of its stated provisions.

The Toys"R"Us Code of Conduct includes provisions covering the following issues: Child Labor, Forced Labor, Worker Environment, Working Conditions, Discrimination, Wages & Hours, and Freedom of Association.

Suppliers must post copies of the Toys"R"Us Code of Conduct for all workers to view. The company also encourages suppliers to implement their own Code of Conduct that meets or exceeds the provisions of the Toys"R"Us, Inc. program.

Inquiries about the Toys"R"Us Code of Conduct can be directed to: Vice President of Product Development, Safety Assurance & Imports, Toys"R"Us, Inc., 461 From Road, Paramus, NJ 07652.

Management's Discussion and Analysis
of Results of Operations and Financial Condition

RESULTS OF OPERATIONS

Comparison of Fiscal Year 2002 to 2001

We reported consolidated net sales of $11.3 billion for the 52-week fiscal year ended February 1, 2003 versus $11.0 billion for the 52-week fiscal year ended February 2, 2002, or a 3% increase in consolidated net sales. Our consolidated net sales were $11.2 billion for 2002, after excluding the impact of foreign currency translation, representing a 1% increase over 2001 net sales.

Total enterprise sales consist of all Toys"R"Us branded net sales from all of our stores and from our internet businesses, and the net sales from international licensed and franchised stores. We believe that enterprise sales are useful in analyzing the worldwide strength of our family of brands:

(In billions)	2002	2001	2000
Consolidated net sales	**$ 11.3**	$ 11.0	$ 11.3
Licensed and franchised net sales	**1.8**	1.6	1.5
Total enterprise sales	**$ 13.1**	$ 12.6	$ 12.8

Our consolidated comparable store sales, in local currencies, were flat for the fourth quarter and the fiscal year. Comparable store sales for our U.S. toy store division declined 1% for both the fourth quarter and the full year. Video game sales, which include sales of video hardware, software and accessories, were the primary factor contributing to these decreases. The video game category posted an 18% decline for the fourth quarter and a 13% decline for the year. The introduction of three video platforms (X-Box, Gamecube and Gameboy Advance) drove strong video sales in 2001. The performance of the video game category was also negatively impacted by significant reductions in the retail prices of video game platforms this year, such as the reduction in retail price from $299 to $199 for X-Box and PlayStation 2, and a reduction in retail price from $199 to $149 for Gamecube. Video game sales accounted for approximately 19% of our total U.S. toy store sales, excluding apparel sales, in the fourth quarter of 2002, down from 22% in 2001. Juvenile product sales in our U.S. toy stores declined 8% for the full year, mainly due to a shift of some sales to Babies"R"Us stores in the same markets. However, our core toy sales, which include boys and girls, learning and preschool toy categories, increased 3% in 2002.

Our International division reported comparable toy store sales increases, in local currencies, of 5% for the fourth quarter and 6% for the full year. These increases were primarily driven by the strong performance of our toy stores in the United Kingdom and Spain. We continued to expand the presence of in-store shops, such as Universe of Imagination (learning and educational products), Animal Alley (plush), Teentronics (electronic entertainment products) and Babies"R"Us (newborn and infant products). In addition, the penetration of exclusive products in the International division continues to grow, and, as a result, contributed to the improvement of our gross margin in this division.

Our Babies"R"Us division reported 12% net sales growth for the full year, primarily driven by the opening of 19 new Babies"R"Us stores in the United States this year. This division reported a 2% increase in comparable store sales for the fourth quarter and a 3% increase for the full year. A variety of initiatives helped to drive sales and guest traffic, including the rollout of extended apparel sizing to all stores and the addition of in-store photo studios in 21 Babies"R"Us stores.

Toysrus.com reported a net sales increase of 11% for the fourth quarter and 23% for the full year. Growth in the on-line toy business and the Babiesrus.com (baby products), Imaginarium.com (learning products) and the new Giftsrus.com (personalized gifts) on-line stores were factors in the sales performance of Toysrus.com.

We record the costs associated with operating our distribution network as a part of selling, general and administrative expenses (SG&A), including those costs that primarily relate to moving merchandise from distribution centers to stores. Therefore, our consolidated gross margin may not be comparable to some other retailers which include similar costs in their cost of sales. Our consolidated gross margin, as a percentage of sales, increased by 0.4% for the fourth quarter and was flat at 31.0% for the full year. Our consolidated gross margin for the fourth quarter of 2001 included $27 million of store closing markdowns, which were recorded as part of the restructuring and other charges announced in January 2002. Credits and allowances from vendors, which are netted against our cost of sales, have a positive impact on our consolidated gross margin. These credits and allowances increased our consolidated gross margin by 0.4% for the year, primarily in support of our increased promotional activities. Our U.S. toy store division reported a 0.7% decline in gross margin for the fourth quarter and a 0.8% decline for the full year. These declines were primarily attributed to the impact of increased promotional activity, such as our "Low Price Super Stars" pricing campaign, as well as the impact of higher markdowns recorded to keep our inventories fresh. Our International toy store division reported a 0.3% increase in gross margin to 32.2% for the year, primarily due to our continued emphasis on exclusive products which carry higher margins. Our Babies"R"Us division reported a 1.0% improvement in gross margin to 36.0%, primarily due to a shift in sales mix to higher margin import product. Gross margin for Toysrus.com improved 2.7% to 24.8%, reflecting an ongoing mix shift toward higher margin juvenile and learning products, as well as lower markdowns due to decreased inventory levels this year.

Our consolidated SG&A, as a percentage of net sales, increased 0.3% to 18.3% for the fourth quarter of 2002. This increase was primarily due to an increase in net advertising expense as a result of our decision to defer certain of our advertising activities to this year's fourth quarter. Our consolidated SG&A, as a percentage of sales, decreased 0.7% to 24.0% for the full year, primarily as a result of our continued focus on expense control. During 2002, we implemented shared services in a variety of functional groups, which, along with other efforts, helped us to achieve the overall reduction in SG&A as a percentage of sales. Advertising allowances, which are netted against *management's discussion and analysis*

SG&A and have a positive impact on our SG&A, did not significantly vary year over year. SG&A for our U.S. toy store division decreased in absolute dollars, however it remained flat as a percentage of sales at 22.6% for the year. SG&A for the Babies"R"Us division decreased 0.2% to 23.6% for the year, primarily as a function of expense control coupled with higher sales productivity. SG&A for our International toy store business was reduced by 0.2% to 22.6% for the year. SG&A for Toysrus.com decreased for the year, due to lower fulfillment costs associated with product bundling, and a reduction in net advertising costs. The SG&A decrease, as well as an increase in Toysrus.com's net sales for the year, contributed to the overall reduction in consolidated SG&A, as a percentage of sales.

Depreciation and amortization increased by $9 million to $317 million for the year. Depreciation and amortization for 2001 included $13 million related to the amortization of goodwill. We ceased amortizing this goodwill on February 3, 2002 when we adopted the provisions of Statement of Financial Accounting Standard No. 142, "Goodwill and Other Intangible Assets,"(SFAS No. 142) (see the section "Recent Accounting Pronouncements"). Therefore, excluding the 2001 goodwill amortization, depreciation and amortization increased by $22 million for the year. This increase was primarily due to our Mission Possible store remodeling program, new store openings, and strategic investments to improve our management information systems. These increases were partially offset by the impact of closed stores. As part of the restructuring initiatives announced in January 2002, we closed 37 Kids"R"Us stores and 27 Toys"R"Us stores in the United States.

Interest expense, net of interest income, increased by $4 million to $23 million for the fourth quarter of 2002 and increased by $1 million to $110 million for the full year. These increases in net interest expense are mainly attributable to increased long-term borrowings, partly offset by increased cash investments, lower short-term borrowings and a decrease in interest rates.

Our effective tax rate was 36.5% versus 26.9% in the prior year. Our 2001 effective tax rate was impacted by the reversal of prior years' charges included in restructuring and other charges recorded in 2001.

Foreign currency translation had a 3% favorable impact on our consolidated net earnings for the fourth quarter of 2002 and a 4% favorable impact on our consolidated net earnings for the full year of 2002. Inflation did not have a significant impact on our full year consolidated net earnings for 2002.

Fourth Quarter Results

Our business is highly seasonal, with net sales and net earnings typically highest in the fourth quarter due to the inclusion of the holiday selling season. Fourth quarter 2002 net earnings were $278 million compared with $158 million in 2001. Diluted earnings per share were $1.30 for the fourth quarter of 2002 compared with $0.78 in 2001. Total consolidated comparable store sales, in local currencies, were flat in the fourth quarter of 2002 compared with an increase of 2% in 2001. Our results for 2001 included restructuring and other charges of $213 million ($126 million, net of taxes). Excluding the impact of these charges, net earnings were $284 million and diluted earnings per share were $1.39 for the fourth quarter of 2001.

Fourth Quarter Net Sales by Segment

(In millions)	2002	2001	2000
Toys"R"Us – U.S.	$3,114	$3,202	$3,270
Toys"R"Us – International	1,069	915	907
Babies"R"Us	381	342	335
Toysrus.com[1]	193	174	140
Other[2]	112	126	147
Total	$4,869	$4,759	$4,799

Fourth Quarter Operating Earnings by Segment

(In millions)	2002	2001	2000
Toys"R"Us – U.S.[3]	$ 271	$ 331	$ 335
Toys"R"Us – International	157	131	128
Babies"R"Us	40	29	29
Toysrus.com, net of minority interest[4]	3	(17)	(54)
Other[3], [5]	(9)	(35)	(13)
Restructuring and other charges	–	(186)	–
Total	$ 462	$ 253	$ 425

(1) Includes the sales of Toysrus.com – Japan.
(2) Includes the sales of the Kids"R"Us and Geoffrey divisions.
(3) Includes markdowns related to the store closings announced as part of the restructuring in 2001.
(4) Includes the operations of Toysrus.com – Japan, net of minority interest.
(5) Includes corporate expenses, the operating results of the Kids"R"Us and Geoffrey divisions and the equity in net earnings of Toys"R"Us – Japan, Ltd. (Toys – Japan).

management's discussion and analysis

Comparison of Fiscal Year 2001 to 2000

We reported consolidated net sales of $11.0 billion for the 52-week fiscal year ended February 2, 2002 versus $11.3 billion for the 53-week fiscal year ended February 3, 2001. Net sales of Toys – Japan, which has been accounted for on the "equity method" since its initial public offering, are included in our consolidated net sales in the first quarter of 2000 and excluded from our net sales thereafter. Our consolidated net sales were $11.0 billion for both years, after excluding sales of Toys – Japan. Currency translation did not have a significant impact on our consolidated net sales in 2001.

Total enterprise sales, which consist of all Toys"R"Us branded net sales from all of our stores and from our internet businesses, and the net sales from international licensed and franchised stores, were $12.6 billion in 2001 versus $12.8 billion in 2000.

Our consolidated comparable store sales, in local currencies, declined 1%. Comparable store sales for our U.S. toy store division increased 2% for the fourth quarter and declined 1% for the fiscal year. Video game sales were the primary drivers of the fourth quarter increase due to the introduction of X-Box, Gamecube and Gameboy Advance in the latter half of the year. Video game sales accounted for approximately 22% of our total U.S. toy store sales, excluding apparel sales, in the fourth quarter of 2001 as compared to 18% in the fourth quarter of the prior year. We had 433 stores in the Mission Possible format by the start of the 2001 holiday season, which also contributed to the comparable store sales increase in the fourth quarter. This gain partially offset the negative impact of 268 stores under construction during the first nine months of 2001 that were retrofitted to the Mission Possible format, as well as the negative impact resulting from the events of the September 11th terrorist attacks. Our International division reported comparable toy store sales increases of 5%, in local currencies, primarily driven by the performance of our toy stores in the United Kingdom, which reported double-digit comparable store sales growth. Our Babies"R"Us division reported 8% net sales growth, primarily driven by the opening of 20 new Babies"R"Us stores in the United States this year, as well as a 2% comparable store sales increase. Toysrus.com reported a net sales increase of 24% for the fourth quarter and 54% for the full year, which continued to reflect increases in its market share and the impact of the Toysrus.com alliance with Amazon.com that began in 2000.

Our consolidated gross margin, as a percentage of net sales, remained flat at 31.0%. Our consolidated margin for 2001 included $27 million of store closing markdowns, which were recorded as part of the restructuring and other charges announced in January 2002, and our consolidated margin for 2000 included $10 million of markdowns resulting from the alliance between Toysrus.com and Amazon.com. Excluding the impact of these items, our consolidated gross margin would have increased from 31.0% to 31.2%. Credits and allowances from our vendors, which are netted against our gross margin and have a positive impact on our cost of sales, did not vary significantly. Gross margin for the U.S. toy store division decreased 0.2% to 30.1% due to the impact of $15 million in store closing markdowns, that we recorded with the 2001 restructuring and other charges. The Babies"R"Us division reported a 1.2% improvement in gross margin to 35.0%, primarily due to a favorable sales shift to higher margin juvenile import and proprietary product. Our International toy store business reported a 0.2% increase in gross margin to 31.9%, primarily due to our continued emphasis on exclusive products.

Our consolidated SG&A, as a percentage of net sales, remained flat at 24.7% for the full year. Our consolidated SG&A for 2000 included $85 million of non-recurring charges related to the alliance between Toysrus.com and Amazon.com. Excluding these charges, our 2000 consolidated SG&A would have been 24.0% of sales. A reduction in advertising allowances, which are netted against SG&A and have a positive impact on SG&A, accounted for 0.3% of the increase in consolidated SG&A. SG&A for our U.S. toy store division increased 1.1% to 22.6%, reflecting the strategic investments we made in our business, including the renovation of our U.S. toy stores to the Mission Possible format and certain guest focused initiatives, both of which accounted for approximately 1.0% of this increase. Additional SG&A expenses resulting from the September 11th events accounted for approximately 0.1% of this increase. SG&A for our International toy store business increased 0.1% to 22.8%. SG&A for the Babies"R"Us division increased 0.4% to 23.8%, primarily attributable to increased payroll costs to support our emphasis on guest focused initiatives.

Depreciation and amortization increased by $18 million, primarily due to the Mission Possible store remodeling program, continued new store expansion and strategic investments to improve our management information systems.

Interest expense decreased by $10 million, primarily due to lower interest rates, partially offset by the impact of higher average total debt outstanding during the year. Interest and other income decreased by $15 million, primarily due to lower average investments outstanding, as well as lower interest rates.

Our effective tax rate declined to 26.9% from 36.5%. The reduction in our effective tax rate was due to the impact of the restructuring and other charges recorded in 2001.

Neither foreign currency exchange nor inflation had a significant impact on our consolidated net earnings in 2001.

Restructuring and Other Charges

In January 2002, we announced plans to reposition our business and, as part of this plan, we closed 27 non-Mission Possible format Toys"R"Us stores and 37 Kids"R"Us stores. In conjunction with the Kids"R"Us store closings in most all of these locations, we converted the nearest Toys"R"Us store into a Toys"R"Us/Kids"R"Us combo store.

As part of this plan, we eliminated approximately 1,700 staff positions in our stores and our headquarters. In addition, these plans included the costs of consolidating five of our store support center facilities into our new headquarters in Wayne, New Jersey, in 2003.

The costs associated with the facilities' consolidation, elimination of positions, and other actions designed to improve efficiency in support functions were $79 million, of which $15 million related to severance. The costs associated with store closings were $73 million for Kids"R"Us and $85 million for Toys"R"Us, of which $27 million was recorded in

management's discussion and analysis

cost of sales. The fair value of the facilities to be consolidated and stores identified for closure were obtained from third party appraisals. We also reversed $24 million of previously accrued charges ($11 million from the 1998 charge and $13 million from the 1995 charge) that we determined to be no longer needed. Accordingly, based on these actions, we recorded $213 million of pre-tax ($126 million after-tax) restructuring and other charges in the fourth quarter of the fiscal year ending February 2, 2002. Details on the components of the charges are as follows:

Description (in millions)	Initial charge	Utilized in 2001	Reserve balance at 2/02/02	Utilized in 2002	Adjustments to charge in 2002	Reserve balance at 2/01/03
Store closing:						
Lease commitments	$ 52	$ –	$ 52	$ (11)	$ –	$ 41
Severance	4	–	4	(4)	–	–
Write-down of property and equipment	75	(75)	–	–	–	–
Markdowns	27	–	27	(27)	–	–
Store support center consolidation:						
Lease commitments	28	–	28	–	11*	39
Write-down of property and equipment	29	(29)	–	–	–	–
Severance	15	–	15	(9)	(1)	5
Other	7	(7)	–	–	–	–
Total restructuring and other charges	$237	$(111)	$126	$ (51)	$ 10	$ 85

*In the fourth quarter of 2002, we determined that the reserve for lease costs for the disposition of one of our store support center facilities needed to be increased and, accordingly, recorded an additional charge of $11 million.

In 2000, Toysrus.com, our internet subsidiary, recorded $118 million in non-recurring charges as a result of the transition to its co-branded on-line store with Amazon.com, of which $10 million was included in cost of sales and $108 million was included in SG&A. These costs and charges related primarily to the closure of three distribution centers, as well as web-site asset write-offs and other costs. We had remaining lease commitment reserves of $3 million at February 1, 2003, that will be utilized in 2003 and thereafter.

We previously announced strategic initiatives to reposition our worldwide business and recorded related restructuring and other charges of $698 million in 1998 and $396 million in 1995 to complete these initiatives. As of February 1, 2003, we substantially completed all announced initiatives. We reversed reserves of $10 million in the fourth quarter of 2002 that were determined to no longer be needed. We also reversed reserves of $29 million in 2001, $24 million of which were reversed in the fourth quarter of 2001 and is discussed above, and $11 million in 2000 that were determined to no longer be needed. We had $42 million of reserves remaining at February 1, 2003, primarily for long-term lease commitments that will be utilized in 2003 and thereafter.

We believe that the remaining reserves at February 1, 2003 are reasonable estimates of what is required to complete all remaining initiatives.

Liquidity and Capital Resources

Our contractual obligations mainly consist of operating leases related to real estate used in the operation of our business and long-term debt. The table below shows the amounts we are obligated to pay for operating leases and principal amounts due under long-term debt issuances by fiscal period:

Contractual Obligations at February 1, 2003 (in millions)

	Amounts due in Fiscal 2003	Amounts due in Fiscal 2004 and Fiscal 2005	Amounts due in Fiscal 2006 and Fiscal 2007	Amounts due subsequent to 2007	Total
Operating leases*	$ 317	$ 615	$ 552	$ 1,786	$ 3,270
Sub-leases to third parties	17	26	20	40	103
Net operating lease obligations	300	589	532	1,746	3,167
Capital lease obligations	6	9	2	1	18
Long-term debt	367	541	697**	723	2,328
Minimum royalty obligations	14	7	–	–	21
Other obligations	2	4	–	–	6
Total contractual obligations	$ 689	$ 1,150	$ 1,231	$ 2,470	$ 5,540

*Includes synthetic lease obligation for our new headquarters facility in Wayne, New Jersey as described in the section "Critical Accounting Policies" and the note to our consolidated financial statements entitled "LEASES."
**Includes $390 million of equity security units, due 2007, which we are obligated to remarket in 2005. See the section "Financing Activities" and the note to our consolidated financial statements entitled "ISSUANCE OF COMMON STOCK AND EQUITY UNITS."

We are in compliance with all covenants associated with the above contractual obligations. The covenants include, among other things, requirements to provide financial information and public filings, and to comply with specified financial ratios. Non-compliance with associated covenants could give rise to accelerated payments, requirements to provide collateral, or changes in terms contained in the respective agreements.

At February 1, 2003, we had available over $1 billion of cash and cash equivalents. Our current portion of long-term debt of $379 million at February 1, 2003 includes a 475 million Swiss Franc note, due on January 28, 2004. In addition, our long-term debt at February 1, 2003 includes a 500 million Euro bond, due on February 13, 2004. See the section "Other Matters" and the note to our consolidated financial statements entitled "SUBSEQUENT EVENTS" for a discussion regarding the registration of $800 million of debt securities in March 2003 and the sale and issuance of $400 million of notes in April 2003.

We have $985 million in unsecured committed revolving credit facilities from a syndicate of financial institutions. These credit facilities are available for seasonal borrowings. There were no outstanding balances under these credit facilities at the end of fiscal 2002, 2001 or 2000. Additionally, we have lines of credit with various banks to meet certain of the short-term financing needs of our foreign subsidiaries. The following table shows our commercial commitments with their related expirations and availability:

Commercial Commitments at February 1, 2003 (in millions)

			Amount of commitment expiration per fiscal period			
	Total amounts committed	Fiscal 2003	Fiscal 2004 and Fiscal 2005	Fiscal 2006 and Fiscal 2007	Fiscal 2008 and subsequent	Amounts available at February 1, 2003
Unsecured revolving credit facilities:						
Facility expiring in September 2006	$ 685	$ –	$ –	$ 685	$ –	$ 685
364-day facility expiring August 25, 2003	300	300	–	–	–	300
Total unsecured revolving credit facilities	$ 985	$ 300	$ –	$ 685	$ –	$ 985

Cash requirements for operating and investing activities will be met primarily through use of our exisiting cash and cash equivalents, cash flows from operating activities, and utilization of our unsecured committed revolving credit facilities. At February 1, 2003, we had in place stand-by letters of credit of $360 million, primarily as a guarantee for a debt obligation and $75 million of outstanding letters of credit related to import merchandise.

Credit Ratings

	Moody's	Standard & Poor's
Long-term debt	Baa3	BBB-
Commercial paper	P-3	A-3
Outlook	Negative	Stable
Date of last rating update	March 19, 2003	March 5, 2003

Our debt instruments do not contain provisions requiring acceleration of payment upon a debt rating downgrade. We continue to be confident in our ability to refinance maturing debt. Other credit ratings for our debt are available; however we disclosed above only ratings of the two largest nationally recognized statistical rating organizations because we believe these are the most relevant to our business.

The seasonal nature of our business typically causes cash balances to decline from the beginning of the year through October as inventory increases for the holiday selling season and funds are used for construction of new stores, remodeling and other initiatives that normally occur in this period. The fourth quarter, including the holiday season, accounts for more than 40% of our net sales and substantially all of our operating earnings.

Operating Activities

Our net cash inflows from operating activities increased to $574 million in 2002 from net cash inflows of $504 million in 2001 and net cash outflows of $151 in 2000. Net earnings, as adjusted for non-cash items, of $600 million in 2002 and $425 million in 2001 were the primary drivers of the net cash inflows from operations in those years. The net cash outflows from operations in 2000 were primarily driven by an increase in merchandise inventories of $486 million, and a net decrease in accounts payable, accrued expenses and other liabilities of $178 million, and was partially offset by net earnings, as adjusted for non-cash items, of $444 million for that year.

Investing Activities

Capital expenditures, net of dispositions, were $398 million in 2002, $705 million in 2001 and $402 million in 2000. Capital expenditures during these periods include investments to: open 55 new Babies"R"Us stores in the United States; open 18 new Toys"R"Us stores internationally; reformat our existing Toys"R"Us store base in the United States to our Mission Possible format and remodel 41 existing Kids"R"Us stores to our R-Generation store format; convert 286 existing Toys"R"Us stores into Toys"R"Us/Kids"R"Us combo stores; improve and enhance our management information systems.

During 2003, we plan to reduce our capital expenditures for our business to less than $350 million. We plan to open approximately 20 new Babies"R"Us stores in the United States and approximately five new international Toys"R"Us stores, and we also plan to continue to improve and enhance our management information systems in 2003.

Financing Activities

Net cash inflows from financing activities were $613 million in 2002, primarily driven by net long-term borrowings of $407 million, as well as proceeds received from the issuance of our common stock and contracts to purchase common stock totaling $266 million. In May 2002, we issued 14,950,000 shares of our common stock at a price of $17.65 per share and received net proceeds of $253 million. On the same date, we issued 8,050,000 equity security units with a stated amount of $50 per unit and received net proceeds of $390 million. Each security unit consists of a contract to purchase, for $50, a specified number of shares of Toys"R"Us common stock in August 2005, and a senior note due in 2007 with a principal amount of $50. The fair value of the contract to purchase shares of Toys"R"Us common stock was estimated at $1.77 per equity security unit. The fair value of the senior note was estimated at $48.23 per equity security unit. Interest on the senior notes is payable quarterly at an initial rate of 6.25%. We are obligated to remarket the notes in May 2005 at the then prevailing interest rate for similar notes. If the remarketing were not to be successful, we would be entitled to take possession of the senior notes, and the holder's obligation under the contracts to purchase shares of our common stock would be deemed to have been satisfied. The net proceeds from these public offerings were used to refinance short-term borrowings and for other general corporate purposes.

management's discussion and analysis

Net cash inflows from financing activities were $191 million in 2001, primarily as a result of net borrowings of $216 million during the year. In July 2001, we issued and sold $750 million of notes, comprised of $500 million of notes bearing interest at 7.625% per annum, maturing in 2011, and $250 million of notes bearing interest at 6.875% per annum, maturing in 2006. The proceeds from these notes were used to reduce outstanding commercial paper obligations. Simultaneously with the sale of the notes, we entered into interest rate swap agreements. As a result of the interest rate swap agreements, interest on the $500 million notes accrues at an effective rate of LIBOR plus 1.5120% and interest on the $250 million notes accrues at an effective rate of LIBOR plus 1.1515%. In October 2002, we terminated a portion of the interest rate swap agreeements and received a payment of $27 million, which is being amortized over the remaining lives of the related notes. Concurrently, we entered into new interest rate swap agreements. Of the $500 million notes, $200 million accrues interest at an effective rate of LIBOR plus 3.06%, and $125 million of the $250 million notes accrues interest at an effective rate of LIBOR plus 3.54%. Interest is payable on both notes semi-annually on February 1 and August 1 of each year. In February 2001, we borrowed 500 million EURO through the public issuance of a EURO bond bearing interest at 6.375% per annum. The obligation was swapped into a $466 million fixed rate obligation with an effective rate of 7.43% per annum with interest payments due annually and principal due February 13, 2004.

Net cash outflows from financing activities were $2 million for 2000. Net borrowings for 2000 were $521 million and were used primarily to repurchase 42 million shares of our common stock, to fund increased inventory levels, and to fund our Toysrus.com internet subsidiary. In 2000, we received a total of $97 million from SOFTBANK Venture Capital and affiliates representing their 20% minority interest investment in Toysrus.com.

Other Matters

On March 24, 2003, we filed a "shelf" registration statement with the Securities and Exchange Commission giving us the capability to sell up to $800 million of debt securities that would be used to repay outstanding debt and for general corporate purposes. In April 2003, we sold and issued $400 million in notes bearing interest at a coupon rate of 7.875%, maturing on April 15, 2013. The notes were sold at a price of 98.305%, resulting in an effective yield of 8.125%. Simultaneously with the sale of the notes, we entered into interest rate swap agreements. As a result of these swap agreements, interest will accrue at the effective rate of LIBOR plus 3.622%. Interest is payable semi-annually commencing on October 15, 2003. We plan to use the proceeds from these notes for the repayment of indebtedness maturing in the 2004 calendar year, and pending such repayment, for working capital needs and other general corporate purposes.

In August 2000, eleven purported class action lawsuits were filed (six in the United States District Court for the District of New Jersey, three in the United States District Court for the Northern District of California, one in the United States District Court for the Western District of Texas and one in the Superior Court of the State of California, County of San Bernardino), against us and our affiliates Toysrus.com, Inc. and Toysrus.com, LLC. In September 2000, three additional purported class action lawsuits were filed (two in the United States District Court for the District of New Jersey and one in the United States District Court for the Western District of Texas). These actions generally purport to bring claims under federal privacy and computer fraud statutes, as well as under state statutory and common law, on behalf of all persons who have visited one or more of our websites and either made an online purchase or allegedly had information about them unlawfully "intercepted," "monitored," "transmitted," or "used." All the suits (except one filed in the United States District Court for the District of New Jersey) also named Coremetrics, Inc. (Coremetrics) as a defendant. Coremetrics is an internet marketing company with whom we have an agreement. These suits seek damages in unspecified amounts and other relief under state and federal law.

With Coremetrics, we filed a joint application with the Multidistrict litigation panel which resulted in all of the federal actions being consolidated and transferred to the United States District Court for the Northern District of California. Plaintiffs voluntarily dismissed the action in the Superior Court of the State of California, County of San Bernardino without prejudice. On October 16, 2001, plaintiffs filed an amended complaint in the United States District Court for the Northern District of California. We believe that we have substantial defenses to all of these claims. On November 13, 2002, we entered into a settlement agreement with plaintiffs in connection with all causes of action. This settlement agreement is subject to the court's review and approval and will not have a material impact on our consolidated financial statements.

We are party to certain other litigation, which, in our judgment, based in part on the opinion of legal counsel, will not have a material adverse effect on our consolidated financial statements.

In August 2000, Toysrus.com entered into a 10-year strategic alliance with Amazon.com to operate a co-branded toy and video game on-line store, which was launched in the third quarter of 2000. In addition, a co-branded baby products on-line store was launched in May 2001 and a co-branded creative and learning products on-line store was launched in July 2001. Under this alliance, Toysrus.com and Amazon.com are responsible for specific aspects of the on-line stores. Toysrus.com is responsible for merchandising, marketing and content for the co-branded store. Toysrus.com also identifies, buys, owns and manages the inventory. Amazon.com handles web-site development, order fulfillment, guest service, and the housing of Toysrus.com's inventory in Amazon.com's U.S. distribution centers. Also in August 2000, Amazon.com was granted a warrant entitling it to acquire up to 5% (subject to dilution under certain circumstances) of the capital of Toysrus.com at the then market value. This warrant has not been exercised.

We recorded a non-operating gain of $315 million ($200 million net of taxes) resulting from the initial public offering of shares of Toys – Japan, which was completed in April 2000. Of this gain, $91 million resulted from an adjustment to the basis of our investment in Toys – Japan, and $224 million was related to the sale of a portion of company-owned common stock of Toys – Japan, for which we received net cash proceeds of $267 million. In connection with this transaction, we recorded a provision for current income taxes of $82 million and a provision for deferred income taxes of $33 million. As a result of this transaction, our ownership percentage in the common stock of Toys – Japan was reduced from 80% to 48%. Toys – Japan is a licensee of our company.

Quantitative and Qualitative Disclosures About Market Risks

We are exposed to market risk from potential changes in interest rates and foreign exchange rates. The countries in which we own assets and operate stores are politically stable, and we regularly evaluate these risks and have taken the following measures to mitigate these risks: our foreign exchange risk management objectives are to stabilize cash flow from the effects of foreign currency fluctuations; we do not participate in speculative hedges; and we will, whenever practical, offset local investments in foreign currencies with liabilities denominated in the same currencies. We also enter into derivative financial instruments to hedge a variety of risk exposures, including interest rate and currency risks.

Our foreign currency exposure is primarily concentrated in the United Kingdom, Europe, Canada, Australia and Japan. We face currency exposures that arise from translating the results of our worldwide operations into U.S. dollars from exchange rates that have fluctuated from the beginning of the period. We also face transactional currency exposures relating to merchandise that we purchase in foreign currencies. We enter into forward exchange contracts to minimize and manage the currency risks associated with these transactions. The counter-parties to these contracts are highly rated financial institutions and we do not have significant exposure to any one counter-party. Gains or losses on these derivative instruments are largely offset by the gains or losses on the underlying hedged transactions. For foreign currency derivative instruments, market risk is determined by calculating the impact on fair value of an assumed one-time change in foreign rates relative to the U.S. dollar. Fair values were estimated based on market prices, where available, or dealer quotes. With respect to derivative instruments outstanding at February 1, 2003, a 10% appreciation of the U.S. dollar would have increased pre-tax earnings in 2002 by $39 million, while a 10% depreciation of the U.S. dollar would have decreased pre-tax earnings in 2002 by $42 million. Comparatively, considering our derivative instruments outstanding at February 2, 2002, a 10% appreciation of the U.S. dollar would have increased pre-tax earnings in 2001 by $13 million, while a 10% depreciation of the U.S. dollar would have decreased pre-tax earnings in 2001 by $13 million.

We are faced with interest rate risks resulting from interest rate fluctuations. We have a variety of fixed and variable rate debt instruments. In an effort to manage interest rate exposures, we strive to achieve an acceptable balance between fixed and variable rate debt and have entered into interest rate swaps to maintain that balance. For interest rate derivative instruments, market risk is determined by calculating the impact to fair value of an assumed one-time change in interest rates across all maturities. Fair values were estimated based on market prices, where available, or dealer quotes. A change in interest rates on variable rate debt is assumed to impact earnings and cash flow, but not the fair value of debt. A change in interest rates on fixed rate debt is assumed to impact the fair value of debt, but not earnings and cash flow. Based on our overall interest rate exposure at February 1, 2003 and February 2, 2002, a 1% increase in interest rates would have decreased pre-tax earnings by $15 million in 2002 and $11 million in 2001, respectively. A 1% decrease in interest rates would have increased pre-tax earnings by $15 million in 2002 and $11 million in 2001. A 1% increase in interest rates would decrease the fair value of our long-term debt at February 1, 2003 and February 2, 2002 by approximately $90 million and $79 million, respectively. A 1% decrease in interest rates would increase the fair value of our long-term debt at February 1, 2003 and February 2, 2002 by approximately $98 million and $87 million, respectively.

See notes to our consolidated financial statements for additional discussion of our outstanding derivative financial instruments at February 1, 2003.

Critical Accounting Policies

Our consolidated financial statements have been prepared in accordance with accounting principles generally accepted in the United States. The preparation of these financial statements requires us to make certain estimates and assumptions that affect the reported amounts of assets, liabilities, revenues and expenses, and the related disclosure of contingent assets and liabilities as of the date of the financial statements and during the applicable periods. We base these estimates on historical experience and on other various assumptions that we believe to be reasonable under the circumstances. Actual results may differ materially from these estimates under different assumptions or conditions and could have a material impact on our consolidated financial statements.

We believe the following are some of the critical accounting policies that include significant judgments and estimates used in the preparation of our consolidated financial statements.

Inventories and Vendor Allowances:

Merchandise inventories for the U.S. toy store division, which represent approximately 60% of total merchandise inventories, are stated at the lower of LIFO (last-in, first-out) cost or market value, as determined by the retail inventory method. All other merchandise inventories are stated at the lower of FIFO (first-in, first-out) cost or market value, as determined by the retail inventory method.

We receive various types of merchandise and other types of allowances from our vendors, which are based on negotiated terms. We use estimates at interim periods to record our provisions for inventory shortage and to record vendor funded merchandise allowances. These estimates are based on available data and other factors and are adjusted to actual amounts at the completion of our physical inventories and finalization of all vendor allowances.

management's discussion and analysis

Deferred Tax Assets:
As part of the process of preparing our consolidated financial statements, we are required to estimate our income taxes in each of the jurisdictions in which we operate. This process involves estimating our actual current tax exposure, together with assessing temporary differences resulting from differing treatment of items for tax and accounting purposes. These differences result in deferred tax assets and liabilities, which are included within our consolidated balance sheet. The measurement of deferred tax assets is adjusted by a valuation allowance to recognize the extent to which, more likely than not, the future tax benefits will be recognized.

At February 1, 2003, we recorded deferred tax assets, net of valuation allowances, of $317 million. We believe it is more likely than not that we will be able to realize these assets through the reduction of future taxable income. We base this belief upon the levels of taxable income historically generated by our businesses, as well as projections of future taxable income. If future levels of taxable income are not consistent with our expectations, we may be required to record an additional valuation allowance, which could reduce our net earnings by a material amount.

Derivatives and Hedging Activities:
We enter into derivative financial arrangements to hedge a variety of risk exposures, including interest rate and currency risks associated with our long-term debt, as well as foreign currency risk relating to import merchandise purchases. We account for these hedges in accordance with SFAS No. 133, "Accounting for Derivative Instruments and Hedging Activities," and we record the fair value of these instruments within our consolidated balance sheet. Gains and losses from derivative financial instruments are largely offset by gains and losses on the underlying transactions. At February 1, 2003, we increased the carrying amount of our long-term debt by $172 million, representing the fair value of debt in excess of the carrying amount on that date. Also at February 1, 2003, we recorded derivative assets of $158 million and derivative liabilities of $10 million. While we intend to continue to meet the conditions for hedge accounting, if hedges were not to be highly effective in offsetting cash flows attributable to the hedged risk, the changes in the fair value of the derivatives used as hedges could have a material effect on our consolidated financial statements.

Insurance Risks:
We insure a substantial portion of our general liability and workers' compensation risks through a wholly-owned insurance subsidiary, in addition to third party insurance coverage. Provisions for losses related to self-insured risks are based upon independent actuarially determined estimates. While we believe these provisions for losses to be adequate, the ultimate liabilities may be in excess of, or less than, the amounts recorded.

Stock Options:
We account for stock options under Accounting Principles Board Opinion No. 25, "Accounting for Stock Issued to Employees", which does not require compensation costs related to stock options to be recorded in net income, as all options granted under the various stock option plans had an exercise price equal to the market value of the underlying common stock at grant date. SFAS No. 148 "Accounting for Stock-Based Compensation – Transition and Disclosure – an amendment of SFAS No. 123," provides guidance on acceptable approaches to the implementation of SFAS No. 123, and requires more prominent disclosures of pro forma net earnings and earnings per share determined as if the fair value method of accounting for stock options had been applied in measuring compensation cost. Stock options are further detailed in the note to our consolidated financial statements entitled "STOCK OPTIONS."

Synthetic Lease:
Our new corporate headquarters facility, located in Wayne, New Jersey, is financed under a lease arrangement commonly referred to as a "synthetic lease." Under this lease, unrelated third parties, arranged by Wachovia Development Corporation, a multi-purpose real estate investment company, will fund up to $125 million for the acquisition and construction of the facility. Upon completion of the construction, which is expected to be in 2003, we will begin to pay rent on the facility until the lease expires in 2011. The rent will be based on a mix of fixed and variable interest rates, which will be applied against the final amount funded. Upon expiration of the lease, we would expect to either: renew the lease arrangement; purchase the facility from the lessor; or remarket the property on behalf of the owner. The lease agreement provides the lessor with a residual value guarantee equal to the funding for the acquisition and construction of the facility. Under accounting principles generally accepted in the United States, this arrangement is required to be treated as an operating lease for accounting purposes and as a financing for tax purposes.

Recent Accounting Pronouncements

In 2002, the FASB Emerging Issues Task Force issued EITF issue No. 02-16, "Accounting by a Reseller for Cash Consideration Received from a Vendor" (EITF 02-16). EITF 02-16 considers vendor allowances as a reduction in the price of a vendor's product that should be recognized as a reduction of cost of sales. Advertising allowances that are received for specific, identifiable and incremental costs are considered a reduction of advertising expenses and should be recognized as a reduction of SG&A. The provisions of EITF 02-16 are effective for all new arrangements, or modifications to existing arrangements, beginning after December 31, 2002. We are currently evaluating the potential impact of the provisions of EITF 02-16 on our consolidated financial statements for 2003.

In January 2003, the Financial Accounting Standards Board (FASB) issued Interpretation No. 46, "Consolidation of Variable Interest Entities" (FIN 46), which will require the consolidation of entities that are controlled by a company through interests other than voting interests. Under the requirements of this interpretation, an entity that maintains a majority of the risks or rewards associated with Variable Interest Entities (VIEs), commonly known as special purpose entities, is effectively in the same position as the parent in a parent-subsidiary relationship. Disclosure requirements of VIEs are effective in all financial statements issued after January 31, 2003. The consolidation requirements apply to all VIEs created after January 31, 2003. FIN 46 requires public companies to apply the consolidation requirements to VIEs that existed prior to February 1, 2003 and remained in existence as of the beginning of annual or interim periods beginning after June 15, 2003. Our new corporate headquarters facility, located in Wayne, New Jersey, is leased from unrelated third parties, arranged by a multi-purpose real estate investment company that we do not control. In addition, we do not have the majority of the associated risks or rewards. Accordingly, we believe that FIN 46 will have no impact on the accounting for this synthetic lease. The synthetic lease is discussed above and in the note to our consolidated financial statements entitled "LEASES." We believe that FIN 46 will not have a material impact on our consolidated financial statements.

In November 2002, the FASB issued Interpretation No. 45, "Guarantor's Accounting and Disclosure Requirements for Guarantees, Including Indirect Guarantees of Indebtedness of Others" (FIN 45), which imposes new disclosure and liability-recognition requirements for financial guarantees, performance guarantees, indemnifications and indirect guarantees of the indebtedness of others. FIN 45 requires certain guarantees to be recorded at fair value. This is different from previous practice, where a liability would typically be recorded only when a loss is probable and reasonably estimable. The initial recognition and initial measurement provisions are applicable on a prospective basis to guarantees issued or modified after December 31, 2002. FIN 45 also requires new disclosures, even when the likelihood of making any payments under the guarantee is remote. The disclosure requirements are effective for interim and annual periods ending after December 15, 2002. We have procedures to identify guarantees contained in the various legal documents and agreements that have been executed, and those to be executed in the future, that fall within the scope of FIN 45. We expect that FIN 45 will not have a material impact on our consolidated financial statements.

In July 2002, the FASB issued SFAS No. 146, "Accounting for Costs Associated with Exit or Disposal Activities" (SFAS No. 146), which addresses the recognition, measurement, and reporting of costs associated with exit or disposal activities and supercedes Emerging Issues Task Force issue No. 94-3, "Liability Recognition for Certain Employee Termination Benefits and Other Costs to Exit an Activity (including Certain Costs Incurred in a Restructuring)," (EITF No. 94-3). The fundamental difference between SFAS No. 146 and EITF No. 94-3 is the requirement that a liability for a cost associated with an exit or disposal activity be recognized when the liability is incurred rather than at the date an entity commits to an exit plan. A fundamental conclusion of SFAS No. 146 is that an entity's commitment to a plan, by itself, does not create an obligation that meets the definition of a liability. SFAS No. 146 also establishes that the initial measurement of a liability recognized be recorded at fair value. The provisions of this statement are effective for exit or disposal activities that are initiated after December 31, 2002, with early application encouraged. We believe that the adoption of this pronouncement will not have a significant effect on our consolidated financial statements.

In August 2001, the FASB issued SFAS No. 144, "Accounting for the Impairment or Disposal of Long-Lived Assets" (SFAS No. 144), which addresses financial accounting and reporting for the impairment or disposal of long-lived assets and supersedes SFAS No. 121, "Accounting for the Impairment of Long-Lived Assets and for Long-Lived Assets to be Disposed Of." We adopted SFAS No. 144 as of February 3, 2002 and the adoption did not have a significant effect on our consolidated financial statements.

In July 2001, the FASB issued SFAS No. 142, "Goodwill and Other Intangible Assets" (SFAS No. 142), which is effective for fiscal years beginning after December 15, 2001. SFAS No. 142 changes the accounting for goodwill from an amortization method to an impairment only approach. We adopted this pronouncement on February 3, 2002. As a result of this adoption, amortization of $348 million of goodwill, which was to be amortized ratably through 2037, ceased. Based on the historical and projected operating results of the reporting units to which the goodwill relates, we determined that no impairment of this goodwill exists. Application of the non-amortization provisions of SFAS No. 142 resulted in an increase in net earnings of $2 million for the fourth quarter of 2002 and $8 million for the 2002 fiscal year.

Forward Looking Statements

This annual report contains "forward looking" statements within the meaning of Section 27A of the Securities Act of 1933, as amended, and Section 21E of the Securities Exchange Act of 1934, which are intended to be covered by the safe harbors created thereby. All statements that are not historical facts, including statements about our beliefs or expectations, are forward-looking statements. We generally identify these statements by words or phrases such as "anticipate," "estimate," "plan," "expect," "believe," "intend," "foresee," "will," "may," and similar words or phrases. These statements discuss, among other things, our strategy, store openings and renovations, future performance and anticipated cost savings, results of our restructuring, anticipated international development and other goals and targets. Such statements involve risks and uncertainties that exist in our operations and business environment that could render actual outcomes and results materially different than predicted. Our forward-looking statements are based on assumptions about many factors, including, but not limited to, ongoing competitive pressures in the retail industry, changes in consumer spending and consumer preferences, general economic conditions in the United States and other jurisdictions in which we conduct our business (such as interest rates, currency exchange rates and consumer confidence) and normal business uncertainty. While we believe that our assumptions are reasonable at the time forward-looking statements were made, we caution that it is impossible to predict the actual outcome of numerous factors and, therefore, readers should not place undue reliance on such statements. Forward-looking statements speak only as of the date they are made, and we undertake no obligation to update such statements in light of new information or future events that involve inherent risks and uncertainties. Actual results may differ materially from those contained in any forward-looking statement.

consolidated financial statements

Consolidated Statements of Earnings
Toys"R"Us, Inc. and Subsidiaries

		Year Ended	
(in millions, except per share data)	**February 1, 2003**	February 2, 2002	February 3, 2001
Net sales	$ **11,305**	$ 11,019	$ 11,332
Cost of sales	**7,799**	7,604	7,815
Gross margin	**3,506**	3,415	3,517
Selling, general and administrative expenses	**2,718**	2,721	2,801
Depreciation and amortization	**317**	308	290
Restructuring and other charges	**–**	186	–
Total operating expenses	**3,035**	3,215	3,091
Operating earnings	**471**	200	426
Other (expense) income:			
Interest expense	**(119)**	(117)	(127)
Interest and other income	**9**	8	23
Gain from IPO of Toys – Japan	**–**	–	315
Earnings before income taxes	**361**	91	637
Income taxes	**132**	24	233
Net earnings	$ **229**	$ 67	$ 404
Basic earnings per share	$ **1.10**	$ 0.34	$ 1.92
Diluted earnings per share	$ **1.09**	$ 0.33	$ 1.88

See notes to consolidated financial statements.

Consolidated Balance Sheets
Toys"R"Us, Inc. and Subsidiaries

(In millions)	February 1, 2003	February 2, 2002
Assets		
Current Assets:		
Cash and cash equivalents	$ 1,023	$ 283
Restricted cash	60	–
Accounts and other receivables	202	210
Merchandise inventories	2,190	2,041
Prepaid expenses and other current assets	85	97
Total current assets	3,560	2,631
Property and Equipment:		
Real estate, net	2,398	2,313
Other, net	2,365	2,231
Total property and equipment	4,763	4,544
Goodwill, net	348	348
Derivative assets	158	42
Other assets	568	511
	$ 9,397	$ 8,076
Liabilities and Stockholders' Equity		
Current Liabilities:		
Short-term borrowings	$ –	$ –
Accounts payable	896	878
Accrued expenses and other current liabilities	824	738
Income taxes payable	279	319
Current portion of long-term debt	379	39
Total current liabilities	2,378	1,974
Long-term debt	2,139	1,816
Deferred income taxes	545	447
Derivative liabilities	10	122
Other liabilities	282	276
Minority interest in Toysrus.com	13	27
Stockholders' Equity:		
Common stock	30	30
Additional paid-in capital	414	444
Retained earnings	5,457	5,228
Accumulated other comprehensive loss	(149)	(267)
Treasury shares, at cost	(1,722)	(2,021)
Total stockholders' equity	4,030	3,414
	$ 9,397	$ 8,076

See notes to consolidated financial statements.

consolidated financial statements

Consolidated Statements of Cash Flows
Toys"R"Us, Inc. and Subsidiaries

		Year Ended	
(In millions)	**February 1, 2003**	February 2, 2002	February 3, 2001
Cash Flows from Operating Activities			
Net earnings	$ 229	$ 67	$ 404
Adjustments to reconcile net earnings to net cash from operating activities:			
Depreciation and amortization	317	308	290
Deferred income taxes	99	(6)	67
Minority interest in Toysrus.com	(14)	(24)	(52)
Other non-cash items	(31)	(29)	50
Restructuring and other charges	–	109	–
Gain from initial public offering of Toys – Japan	–	–	(315)
Changes in operating assets and liabilities:			
Accounts and other receivables	8	15	(69)
Merchandise inventories	(100)	217	(486)
Prepaid expenses and other operating assets	(18)	36	(54)
Accounts payable, accrued expenses and other liabilities	112	(241)	(178)
Income taxes payable	(28)	52	192
Net cash from operating activities	574	504	(151)
Cash Flows from Investing Activities			
Capital expenditures, net	(398)	(705)	(402)
Net proceeds from sale of Toys – Japan common stock	–	–	267
Reduction in cash due to deconsolidation of Toys – Japan	–	–	(15)
Net cash from investing activities	(398)	(705)	(150)
Cash Flows from Financing Activities			
Short-term borrowings, net	–	(588)	419
Long-term borrowings	548	1,214	147
Long-term debt repayment	(141)	(410)	(45)
Proceeds from issuance of stock and contracts to purchase stock	266	–	–
Increase in restricted cash	(60)	–	–
Exercise of stock options	–	19	2
Proceeds received from investors in Toysrus.com	–	–	97
Share repurchase program	–	(44)	(632)
Issuance of stock warrants	–	–	10
Net cash from financing activities	613	191	(2)
Effect of exchange rate changes on cash and cash equivalents	(49)	18	(6)
Cash and Cash Equivalents			
Increase/(decrease) during year	740	8	(309)
Beginning of year	283	275	584
End of year	$ 1,023	$ 283	$ 275
Supplemental Disclosures of Cash Flow Information			
Income tax payments (refunds), net	$ 32	$ (22)	$ (2)
Interest payments	$ 93	$ 85	$ 128

See notes to consolidated financial statements.

Consolidated Statements of Stockholders' Equity
Toys"R"Us, Inc. and Subsidiaries

(In millions)	Common Stock Issued Shares	Common Stock Issued Amount	Common Stock In Treasury Shares	Common Stock In Treasury Amount	Additional paid-in capital	Accumulated other comprehensive loss	Retained earnings	Total stockholders' equity
Balance, January 29, 2000	300.4	$ 30	(61.1)	$ (1,423)	$ 453	$ (137)	$ 4,757	$ 3,680
Net earnings for the year	–	–	–	–	–	–	404	404
Foreign currency translation adjustments	–	–	–	–	–	(74)	–	(74)
Comprehensive income								330
Share repurchase program	–	–	(42.1)	(632)	–	–	–	(632)
Issuance of restricted stock, net	–	–	–	50	(21)	–	–	29
Exercise of stock options, net	–	–	0.3	4	(3)	–	–	1
Issuance of stock warrants	–	–	–	–	10	–	–	10
Balance, February 3, 2001	300.4	$ 30	(102.9)	$ (2,001)	$ 439	$ (211)	$ 5,161	$ 3,418
Net earnings for the year	–	–	–	–	–	–	67	67
Foreign currency translation adjustments	–	–	–	–	–	(55)	–	(55)
Unrealized loss on hedged transactions	–	–	–	–	–	(1)	–	(1)
Comprehensive income								11
Share repurchase program	–	–	(2.1)	(44)	–	–	–	(44)
Issuance of restricted stock, net	–	–	0.5	5	4	–	–	9
Exercise of stock options, net	–	–	0.8	19	1	–	–	20
Balance, February 2, 2002	300.4	$ 30	(103.7)	$ (2,021)	$ 444	$ (267)	$ 5,228	$ 3,414
Net earnings for the year	–	–	–	–	–	–	229	229
Foreign currency translation adjustments	–	–	–	–	–	127	–	127
Unrealized loss on hedged transactions	–	–	–	–	–	(9)	–	(9)
Comprehensive income								347
Common stock equity offering	–	–	14.9	301	(35)	–	–	266
Issuance of restricted stock, net	–	–	0.9	(2)	5	–	–	3
Balance, February 1, 2003	300.4	$ 30	(87.9)	$(1,722)	$ 414	$ (149)	$ 5,457	$ 4,030

See notes to consolidated financial statements.

Notes to Consolidated Financial Statements
Toys"R"Us, Inc. and Subsidiaries

(Amounts in millions, except per share data)
SUMMARY OF SIGNIFICANT ACCOUNTING POLICIES

Fiscal Year
The company's fiscal year ends on the Saturday nearest to January 31. References to 2002, 2001, and 2000 are for the 52 weeks ended February 1, 2003 and February 2, 2002 and the 53 weeks ended February 3, 2001.

Reclassification
Certain reclassifications have been made to prior periods to conform to current presentations.

Principles of Consolidation
The consolidated financial statements include the accounts for the company and its subsidiaries. All material intercompany balances and transactions have been eliminated. Assets and liabilities of foreign operations are translated at current rates of exchange at the balance sheet date while results of operations are translated at average rates in effect for the period. Unrealized translation gains or losses are shown as a component of accumulated other comprehensive loss within stockholders' equity.

Use of Estimates
The preparation of financial statements in conformity with accounting principles generally accepted in the United States requires management to make estimates and assumptions that affect the amounts reported in the consolidated financial statements and accompanying notes. Actual results could differ from those estimates.

Revenue Recognition
The company recognizes sales revenue at the time the guest takes possession of merchandise or at the point of sale in our stores, or at the time of delivery for products purchased from our web-sites. Layaway transactions are recognized as revenue when the guest satisfies all payment obligations and takes possession of the merchandise. Revenues from the sale of gift cards and issuance of store credits are recognized as they are redeemed.

Advertising Costs
Net advertising costs are included in selling, general and administrative expenses and are expensed at the point of first broadcast or distribution. Net advertising costs were $147, $160, and $135 for 2002, 2001 and 2000, respectively.

Cash and Cash Equivalents
The company considers its highly liquid investments with original maturities of less than three months to be cash equivalents.

Merchandise Inventories
Merchandise inventories for the U.S. toy store division, which represent approximately 60% of total inventories, are stated at the lower of LIFO (last-in, first-out) cost or market, as determined by the retail inventory method. All other merchandise inventories are stated at the lower of FIFO (first-in, first-out) cost or market, as determined by the retail inventory method.

Credits and Allowances Received from Vendors
Credits and allowances are received from vendors and are related to formal agreements negotiated with such vendors. These credits and allowances are predominantly for cooperative advertising, promotions, and volume related purchases. These credits and allowances, excluding advertising allowances, are netted against cost of sales. The company's policy is to recognize credits, that are related directly to inventory purchases, as the related inventory is sold. Cooperative advertising allowances offset the cost of cooperative advertising that is agreed to by the company and its vendors, and are netted against advertising expenses included in selling, general and administrative expenses. The company's policy is to recognize cooperative advertising allowances in the period that the related advertising media is run.

Cost of Sales and Selling, General and Administrative Expenses
The significant components of the line item "Cost of sales" include the cost to acquire merchandise from vendors; freight in; markdowns; provision for inventory shortages; and discounts and allowances related to merchandise inventories.

The significant components of the line item "Selling, general and administrative expenses" include store payroll and related payroll benefits; rent and other store operating expenses; net advertising expenses; costs associated with operating the company's distribution network that primarily relate to moving merchandise from distribution centers to stores; and other corporate-related expenses.

Property and Equipment
Property and equipment are recorded at cost. Leasehold improvements represent capital improvements made to leased locations. Depreciation and amortization are provided using the straight-line method over the estimated useful lives of the assets or, where applicable, the terms of the respective leases, whichever is shorter. Accelerated depreciation methods are used for income tax reporting purposes with recognition of deferred income taxes for the resulting temporary differences. The company periodically evaluates the need to recognize impairment losses relating to long-lived assets. If indications of impairment exist and if the value of the assets are impaired, an impairment loss would be recognized.

Costs of Computer Software
The company capitalizes certain costs associated with computer software developed or obtained for internal use in accordance with the provisions of Statement Of Position No. 98-1, "Accounting for the Costs of Computer Software Developed or Obtained for Internal Use," issued by the American Institute of Certified Public Accountants. The company's policy provides for the capitalization of costs from the acquisition of external materials and services associated with developing or obtaining internal use computer software. Certain payroll costs for employees that are directly associated with internal use computer software projects are capitalized once specific criteria are met. The amount of payroll costs capitalized is limited to the time directly

spent on computer software projects. Costs associated with preliminary stage activities, training, maintenance and all other post-implementation stage activities are expensed as incurred. All costs capitalized in connection with internal use computer software projects are amortized on a straight-line basis over a useful life of five years.

Financial Instruments

The company adopted the provisions of Statement of Financial Accounting Standards No. 133, "Accounting for Derivative Instruments and Hedging Activities" (SFAS No. 133), as amended, effective February 4, 2001, as discussed in the footnote entitled "DERIVATIVE INSTRUMENTS AND HEDGING ACTIVITIES." This statement requires that all derivatives be recorded on the balance sheet at fair value and that changes in fair value be recognized currently in earnings unless specific hedge accounting criteria is met.

The company enters into forward foreign exchange contracts to minimize the risk associated with currency movement relating to its short-term intercompany loan program with foreign subsidiaries. Gains and losses, which offset the movement in the underlying transactions, are recognized as part of such transactions. Gross deferred unrealized losses on the forward contracts were not material at either February 1, 2003 or at February 2, 2002. The related receivable, payable and deferred gain or loss are included on a net basis in the balance sheet. The company had $205 and $108 of short-term outstanding forward contracts at February 1, 2003 and February 2, 2002, maturing in 2003 and 2002, respectively. These contracts are entered into with counter-parties that have high credit ratings and with which the company has the contractual right to net forward currency settlements.

Stock Options

The company accounts for stock options in accordance with the provisions of Accounting Principles Board Opinion No. 25, "Accounting for Stock Options Issued to Employees" (APB 25). The company has adopted the disclosure only provisions of SFAS No. 123 "Accounting for Stock Based Compensation" (FAS 123), issued in 1995.

In accordance with the provisions of SFAS No. 123, the company applies APB Opinion No. 25 and related interpretations in accounting for its stock option plans and, accordingly, does not recognize compensation cost. If the company had elected to recognize compensation cost based on the fair value of the options granted at grant date as prescribed by SFAS No. 123, net earnings and earnings per share would have been reduced to the pro forma amounts indicated in the following table:

	2002	2001	2000
Net earnings – as reported	$ 229	$ 67	$ 404
Net earnings – pro forma	190	28	385
Basic earnings per share – as reported	1.10	0.34	1.92
Basic earnings per share – pro forma	0.92	0.14	1.83
Diluted earnings per share – as reported	1.09	0.33	1.88
Diluted earnings per share – pro forma	0.91	0.14	1.79

The weighted-average fair value at the date of grant for options granted in 2002, 2001, 2000 was $6.42, $9.16 and $5.88, respectively. The fair value of each option grant is estimated on the date of grant using the Black-Scholes option pricing model. As there were a number of options granted during the years of 2000 through 2002, a range of assumptions are provided below:

	2002	2001	2000
Expected stock price volatility	.407 –.507	.407 –.567	.434 –.585
Risk-free interest rate	2.6% – 5.0%	3.6% – 5.1%	5.0% – 6.8%
Weighted average expected life of options	5 years	5 years	5 years

The effects of applying SFAS No. 123 and the results obtained through the use of the Black-Scholes option pricing model are not necessarily indicative of future values.

RESTRICTED CASH

The company had restricted cash of $60 at February 1, 2003. Included in this amount is $45 being used as support for a letter of credit in exchange for reduced letter of credit fees. This letter of credit partially supports the company's 475 Swiss Franc note, due January 28, 2004. The remaining $15 relates to a pending real estate transaction that is expected to close in 2003.

MERCHANDISE INVENTORIES

Merchandise inventories for the U.S. toy store division are stated at the lower of LIFO (last-in, first-out) cost or market. If inventories had been valued at the lower of FIFO (first-in, first-out) cost or market, inventories would show no change at February 1, 2003 or February 2, 2002.

	February 1, 2003	February 2, 2002
Toys"R"Us – U.S.	$ 1,387	$ 1,328
Toys"R"Us – International	362	278
Babies"R"Us	287	282
Toysrus.com	34	52
Other	120	101
	$ 2,190	$ 2,041

PROPERTY AND EQUIPMENT

	Useful life (in years)	February 1, 2003	February 2, 2002
Land		$ 825	$ 811
Buildings	45-50	2,009	1,980
Furniture and equipment	5-20	1,786	1,800
Leasehold improvements	12½-35	1,726	1,542
Costs of computer software	5	192	127
Construction in progress		33	41
Leased property and equipment under capital lease		53	53
		6,624	6,354
Less accumulated depreciation and amortization		1,861	1,810
		$ 4,763	$ 4,544

GOODWILL

In July 2001, the Financial Accounting Standards Board ("FASB") issued SFAS No. 142, "Goodwill and Other Intangible Assets" (SFAS No. 142), which is effective for fiscal years beginning after December 15, 2001. SFAS No. 142 changes the accounting for goodwill from an amortization method to an impairment only approach. The company adopted this pronouncement on February 3, 2002. As a result of this adoption, amortization of $348 of goodwill, which was to be amortized ratably through 2037, ceased. The carrying amount of goodwill at February 1, 2003 relates to the acquisition of Baby Super Stores, Inc. in 1997 ($319), which is now part of the Babies"R"Us division, and the acquisition of Imaginarium Toy Centers, Inc. in 1999 ($29), which is part of the Toys"R"Us – U.S. division. Based on the estimated fair market values (calculated using historical operating results of the reporting units to which the goodwill relates and relative industry multiples) of these divisions compared with the related book values, the company has determined that no impairment of this goodwill exists. Application of the non-amortization provisions of SFAS No. 142 resulted in an increase in net earnings of $8 for 2002. Had the non-amortization provisions of SFAS No. 142 been applied for 2001 and 2000, the company would have reported net earnings of $75 and $412, respectively, and diluted earnings per share of $0.36 and $1.92, respectively.

INVESTMENT IN TOYS – JAPAN

The company is accounting for its 48% ownership investment in the common stock of Toys – Japan on the "equity method" of accounting since the initial public offering in April 2000. Toys – Japan operates as a licensee of the company. As part of the initial public offering, Toys – Japan issued 1.3 shares of common stock to the public at a price of 12,000 yen or $113.95 per share. In November 2001, the common stock of Toys - Japan split 3 for 1. The company's accounting policy for the sales of subsidiaries' stock is to recognize gains or losses for value received in excess of or less than its basis in such subsidiary. No similar issuances of subsidiaries' stock are contemplated at this time. The carrying value of the investment is reflected on the consolidated balance sheets as part of "Other Assets" and was $140 and $123 at February 1, 2003 and February 2, 2002, respectively. At February 1, 2003, the quoted market value of the company's investment was $188, which exceeds the carrying value of the investment. The valuation represents a mathematical calculation based on the closing quotation published by the Tokyo over-the-counter market and is not necessarily indicative of the amount that could be realized upon sale. The company is a guarantor of 80% of a 10 billion yen ($84) loan from third parties in Japan with an annual rate of 6.47%, due in 2012, for which Toys – Japan is the borrower.

SEASONAL FINANCING AND LONG-TERM DEBT

	February 1, 2003	February 2, 2002
7.625% notes, due fiscal 2011	$ 554	$ 505
6.875% notes, due fiscal 2006	267	254
500 Euro bond, due February 13, 2004	538	431
475 Swiss Franc note, due January 28, 2004[a]	348	277
Equity Security Units	408	–
8¾% debentures, due fiscal 2021, net of expenses[b]	198	198
Note at an effective cost of 2.32% due in semi-annual installments through fiscal 2005[c]	158	126
Industrial revenue bonds, net of expenses	21	34
Obligation under capital leases	18	21
Mortgage notes at annual interest rates from 10.16% to 11.00%	8	9
	2,518	1,855
Less current portion	379	39
	$ 2,139	$ 1,816

Long-term debt balances as of February 1, 2003 and February 2, 2002 have been impacted by certain interest rate and currency swaps that have been designated as fair value and cash flow hedges, as discussed in the note entitled, "DERIVATIVE INSTRUMENTS AND HEDGING ACTIVITIES."

(a) Supported by a 475 Swiss Franc bank letter of credit. This note has been converted by an interest rate and currency swap to a floating rate, U.S. dollar obligation at 3 month LIBOR.

(b) Fair value was $192 and $204 at February 1, 2003 and February 2, 2002, respectively. The fair value was estimated using quoted market rates for publicly traded debt and estimated interest rates for non-public debt.

(c) Amortizing note secured by the expected future yen cash flows from license fees due from Toys – Japan.

On May 28, 2002, the company completed public offerings of Toys"R"Us common stock and equity security units, as described in the note entitled "ISSUANCE OF COMMON STOCK AND EQUITY SECURITY UNITS."

In February 2001, the company issued and sold 500 EURO through the public issuance of a EURO bond bearing interest at 6.375% per annum. Through the use of derivative instruments, this obligation was swapped into a $466 fixed rate obligation at an effective rate of 7.43% per annum with interest payments due annually and principal due on February 13, 2004.

In July 2001, the company issued and sold $750 of notes comprised of $500 of notes bearing interest at 7.625% per annum, maturing in August 2011, and $250 of notes bearing interest at 6.875% per annum, maturing in August 2006. Simultaneously with the issuance of these notes, the company entered into interest rate swap agreements. As a result of the interest rate swap agreements, interest on the $500 notes will accrue at the rate of LIBOR plus 1.5120% per annum and interest on the $250 notes accrues at the rate of LIBOR plus 1.1515% per annum. Interest is payable on both notes semi-annually on February 1 and August 1, commencing on February 1, 2002. In October 2002, the company terminated a portion of the interest rate swap agreements and received a payment of $27, which is being amortized over the lives of the related notes. Concurrently, the company entered into new interest rate swap agreements. Of the $500 notes, $200 accrues interest at the rate of LIBOR plus 3.06%, and $125 of the $250 notes accrues interest at the rate of LIBOR plus 3.54%.

As of February 1, 2003, the company had $985 in unsecured committed revolving credit facilities from a syndicate of financial institutions. These credit facilities consist of a $685 facility expiring September 2006 and a $300 facility expiring on August 25, 2003. The facilities are used for seasonal borrowings and to support the company's domestic commercial paper borrowings. As of February 1, 2003, all of the $685 facility expiring September 2006 and all of the $300 facility expiring on August 25, 2003 were available.

The annual maturities of long-term debt at February 1, 2003 are as follows:

	Annual maturities	Fair value hedging adjustment	Annual maturities, including fair value hedging adjustment
2003	$ 373	$ 6	$ 379
2004	499	75	574
2005	51	–	51
2006	279	17	296
2007	420*	19	439
2008 and subsequent	724	55	779
	$ 2,346	$ 172	$ 2,518

Long-term debt balances as of February 1, 2003 have been impacted by certain interest rate and currency swaps that have been designated as fair value and cash flow hedges, as discussed in the note entitled, "DERIVATIVE INSTRUMENTS AND HEDGING ACTIVITIES."

*Includes $390 of equity security units, due 2007, which the company is obligated to remarket in 2005. See the note entitled "ISSUANCE OF COMMON STOCK AND EQUITY SECURITY UNITS."

DERIVATIVE INSTRUMENTS AND HEDGING ACTIVITIES

The company is exposed to market risk from potential changes in interest rates and foreign exchange rates. The company continues to regularly evaluate these risks and continues to take measures to mitigate these risks, including, among other measures, entering into derivative financial instruments to hedge a variety of risk exposures including interest rate and currency risks. The company enters into forward exchange contracts to minimize and manage the currency risks related to its import merchandise purchase program. The company enters into interest rate swaps to manage interest rate risk and strives to achieve what it believes is an acceptable balance between fixed and variable rate debt.

The company purchases forward exchange contracts to minimize and manage the foreign currency risks related to its import merchandise purchase program. The counter-parties to these contracts are highly rated financial institutions and the company does not have significant exposure to any one counter-party. These forward exchange contracts are designated as cash flow hedges, as defined by SFAS No. 133, and are effective as hedges. Accordingly, changes in the effective portion of the fair value of these forward exchange contracts are included in other comprehensive income. Once the hedged transactions are completed, or when merchandise is sold, the unrealized gains and losses on the forward contracts are reclassified from accumulated other comprehensive income and recognized in earnings. The unrealized losses related to the import merchandise purchase program contracts, that were recorded in other comprehensive income, were not material at February 1, 2003 or February 2, 2002.

The company is faced with interest rate risks resulting from interest rate fluctuations. The company has a variety of fixed and variable rate debt instruments. In an effort to manage interest rate exposures, the company strives to achieve an acceptable balance between fixed and variable rate debt and has entered into interest rate swaps to maintain that balance.

On May 28, 2002, the company entered into an interest rate swap agreement on its Equity-Linked Securities. Under the agreement, the company will pay interest at a variable rate in exchange for fixed rate payments, effectively transforming these debentures to floating rate obligations. This swap is designated as a highly effective fair value hedge, as defined by SFAS No. 133. Changes in the fair value of the interest rate swap offset changes in the fair value of the fixed rate debt due to changes in market interest rates with some ineffectiveness present. The amount of ineffectiveness did not have a material effect on earnings.

On March 19, 2002, the company refinanced a note payable originally due in 2005 and increased the amount outstanding to $160 from $100. This borrowing is repayable in semi-annual installments of principal and interest, with the final installment due on February 20, 2008. The effective cost of this borrowing is 2.23% and is secured by expected future cash flows from license fees due from Toys – Japan. The company also entered into a contract to swap yen to U.S. dollars, within exact terms of the loan. This cross currency swap has been designated as a foreign currency cash flow hedge, as defined by SFAS No. 133, and is effective as a hedge.

In July 2001, the company entered into interest rate swap agreements on its 7.625% $500 notes, due August 1, 2011, and its 6.875% $250 notes, due August 1, 2006. Under these agreements, the company will pay interest at a variable rate in exchange for fixed rate payments, effectively transforming the debentures to floating rate obligations. These swaps are designated as highly effective fair value hedges, as defined by SFAS No. 133. Changes in the fair value of the interest rate swaps perfectly offset changes in the fair value of the fixed rate debt due to changes in market interest rates. As such, there were no ineffective hedge portions recognized in earnings during 2001.

notes to consolidated financial statements

In February 2001, the company issued and sold 500 EURO through the public issuance of a EURO bond bearing interest at 6.375% per annum. The obligation was swapped into a $466 fixed rate obligation with an effective rate of 7.43% per annum with interest payments due annually and principal due February 13, 2004. This cross currency swap is designated as a cash flow hedge, as defined by SFAS No. 133, and is effective as a hedge. The portion of the fair value of the swap attributable to changes in the spot rate is matched in earnings against changes in the fair value of debt.

The company entered into a Swiss Franc floating rate loan with a financial institution in January 1999, due January, 28 2004. The company also entered into a contract to swap U.S. dollars to Swiss Francs, within exact terms of the loan. This cross currency swap has been designated as a foreign currency fair value hedge, as defined by SFAS No. 133, and is effective as a hedge.

The company increased the carrying amount of its long-term debt by $172 at February 1, 2003, representing the fair value of debt in excess of the carrying amount on that date. Also at February 1, 2003, the company recorded derivative assets of $158 and derivative liabilities of $10, representing the fair value of these derivatives at that date.

ISSUANCE OF COMMON STOCK AND EQUITY SECURITY UNITS

On May 28, 2002, the company completed public offerings of Toys"R"Us common stock and equity security units. On that date, the company issued 15.0 shares of its common stock at a price of $17.65 per share and received net proceeds of $253. Also on that date, the company issued 8.0 equity security units with a stated amount of $50 per unit and received net proceeds of $390. Each security unit consists of a contract to purchase, for $50, a specified number of shares of Toys"R"Us common stock in August 2005, and a senior note due in 2007 with a principal amount of $50. The fair value of the contract to purchase shares of Toys"R"Us common stock was estimated at $1.77 per equity security unit. The fair value of the senior note was estimated at $48.23 per equity security unit. Interest on the senior notes is payable quarterly at an initial rate of 6.25%, which commenced in August 2002. The company is obligated to remarket the notes in May 2005 at the then prevailing market interest rate for similar notes. If the remarketing were not to be successful, the company would be entitled to take possession of the senior notes, and the holder's obligation under the contracts to purchase shares of Toys"R"Us common stock would be deemed to have been satisfied. The proceeds allocated to the purchase contracts were recorded in stockholders' equity on the consolidated balance sheet. The fair value of the senior notes is reflected as long-term debt on the consolidated balance sheet. The net proceeds from the public offerings were used to refinance short-term borrowings and for other general corporate purposes. As a result of the interest rate swap agreements, interest on the senior notes will accrue at the rate of LIBOR plus 3.43% per annum. Interest is payable quarterly each year, beginning in August 2002.

STOCKHOLDERS' EQUITY

The common shares of the company, par value $0.10 per share, were as follows:

	February 1, 2003	February 2, 2002
Authorized shares	650.0	650.0
Issued shares	300.4	300.4
Treasury shares	87.9	103.7
Issued and outstanding shares	212.5	196.7

EARNINGS PER SHARE

The following table sets forth the computation of basic and diluted earnings per share:

	2002	2001	2000
Numerator:			
Net earnings available to common stockholders	$ 229	$ 67	$ 404
Denominator for basic earnings per share – weighted average shares	207.6	197.6	210.9
Impact of dilutive securities	2.0	8.4	4.1
Denominator for diluted earnings per share – weighted average shares	209.6	206.0	215.0
Basic earnings per share	$ 1.10	$ 0.34	$ 1.92
Diluted earnings per share	$ 1.09	$ 0.33	$ 1.88

Options to purchase approximately 32.5, 10.3 and 3.0 shares of common stock were outstanding during 2002, 2001 and 2000, respectively, but were not included in the computation of diluted earnings per share because the option exercise prices were greater than the average market price of the common shares.

STOCK PURCHASE WARRANTS

The company issued 1.2 stock purchase warrants to SOFTBANK Venture Capital and affiliates ("SOFTBANK") for $8.33 per warrant. Each warrant gives the holder thereof the right to purchase one share of Toys"R"Us common stock at an exercise price of $13 per share, until the expiration date of February 24, 2010. In addition, the company granted a warrant on August 9, 2000 entitling Amazon.com to acquire up to 5% (subject to dilution under certain circumstances) of the capital of Toysrus.com at the then market value. As of February 1, 2003, none of these warrants have been exercised.

LEASES

The company leases a portion of the real estate used in its operations. Most leases require the company to pay real estate taxes and other expenses; some require additional amounts based on percentages of sales.

Minimum rental commitments under noncancelable operating leases having a term of more than one year as of February 1, 2003 are as follows:

	Gross minimum rentals	Sublease income	Net minimum rentals
2003	$ 317	$ 17	$ 300
2004	314	14	300
2005	301	12	289
2006	285	11	274
2007	267	9	258
2008 and subsequent	1,786	40	1,746
	$ 3,270	$ 103	$ 3,167

Total rent expense, net of sublease income, was $267, $261 and $291 in 2002, 2001 and 2000, respectively. The company remains contingently liable for lease payments related to the sub-lease of locations to third parties. To the extent that sub-lessees fail to perform, the company's total net rent expense would be increased.

The company's new corporate headquarters facility, located in Wayne, New Jersey, is financed under a lease arrangement commonly referred to as a "synthetic lease." Under this lease, unrelated third parties, arranged by Wachovia Development Corporation, a multi-purpose real estate investment company, will fund up to $125 for the acquisition and construction of the facility. Upon completion of the construction, which is expected to be in 2003, the company will begin to pay rent on the facility until the lease expires in 2011. The rent will be based on a mix of fixed and variable interest rates that will be applied against the final amount funded. Upon expiration of the lease, the company would expect to either: renew the lease arrangement; purchase the facility from the lessor; or remarket the property on behalf of the owner. The lease agreement provides the lessor with a residual value guarantee equal to the funding for the acquisition and construction of the facility. Under accounting principles generally accepted in the United States, this arrangement is required to be treated as an operating lease for accounting purposes and as a financing for tax purposes.

TAXES ON INCOME

The provisions for income taxes consist of the following:

	2002	2001	2000
Current:			
Federal	$ 4	$ 63	$ 120
Foreign	31	10	36
State	(2)	9	10
	$ 33	$ 82	$ 166
Deferred:			
Federal	62	(61)	50
Foreign	23	16	13
State	14	(13)	4
	99	(58)	67
Total tax provision	$ 132	$ 24	$ 233

At February 1, 2003 and February 2, 2002, the company had gross deferred tax assets, before valuation allowances, of $612 and $576, respectively, and gross deferred tax liabilities of $600 and $484, respectively. Deferred tax assets of $32 and $45 were included in "Prepaid Expenses and Other Current Assets" at February 1, 2003 and February 2, 2002, respectively. Deferred tax assets, net of valuation allowances, of $285 and $245 were included in "Other Assets" at February 1, 2003 and February 2, 2002, respectively. Deferred tax liabilities of $55 and $36 were included in "Accrued Expenses and Other Current Liabilities" at February 1, 2003 and February 2, 2002, respectively. The tax effects of temporary differences and carryforwards that give rise to significant portions of deferred tax assets and liabilities consist of the following:

	February 1, 2003	February 2, 2002
Deferred tax assets:		
Foreign loss carryforwards	$ 305	$ 296
Restructuring	116	131
Other	143	115
Depreciation and amortization	30	22
Derivative instruments and hedging activities	11	–
LIFO reserves	7	12
Valuation allowances, related to foreign loss carryforwards	(295)	(287)
	$ 317	$ 289
Deferred tax liabilities:		
Depreciation and amortization	$ (404)	$ (344)
Other	(169)	(131)
LIFO reserves	(27)	(9)
	$ (600)	$ (484)
Net deferred liabilities	$ (283)	$ (195)

On February 1, 2003, the company had foreign loss carryforwards available to reduce future taxable income of certain foreign subsidiaries. The foreign loss carryforwards, as well as the related tax benefits associated with the foreign loss carryforwards, will expire as follows:

Expiration	Net operating loss carryforwards	Tax benefit
1 – 5 years	$ 208	$ 71
6 – 7 years	9	4
Indefinitely	572	230
	$ 789	$ 305

At February 1, 2003, the company had valuation allowances of $295 against the tax benefit of foreign loss carryforwards of $305.

A reconciliation of the federal statutory tax rate with the effective tax rate follows:

	2002	2001	2000
Statutory tax rate	35.0%	35.0%	35.0%
State income taxes, net of federal income tax benefit	1.4	1.8	1.4
Foreign taxes, net of valuation allowance	(2.4)	(9.4)	1.1
Reversal of deferred tax asset	–	(6.5)	–
Subpart F income	1.5	5.4	0.6
Amortization of goodwill	–	3.5	0.5
Other, net	1.0	(2.9)	(2.1)
Effective tax rate	36.5%	26.9%	36.5%

reports

Report of Management

Responsibility for the integrity and objectivity of the financial information presented in this Annual Report resides with the management of Toys"R"Us. The accompanying financial statements have been prepared from accounting records which management believes fairly and accurately reflect the operations and financial position of the company.

Management has established a system of internal controls to provide reasonable assurance that assets are maintained and accounted for in accordance with its policies and that transactions are recorded accurately on the company's books and records. The company's disclosure controls provide reasonable assurance that appropriate information is accumulated and communicated to senior management to allow decisions regarding accurate, complete and timely financial disclosures.

The company's comprehensive internal audit program provides for constant evaluation of the adequacy of the adherence to management's established policies and procedures. The company has distributed to key employees its policies for conducting business affairs in a lawful and ethical manner.

The Audit Committee of the Board of Directors, which is comprised solely of outside directors, provides oversight of the financial reporting process through periodic meetings with our independent auditors, internal auditors, and management.

The financial statements of the company have been audited by Ernst & Young LLP, the company's independent auditors, in accordance with auditing standards generally accepted in the United States, including a review of financial reporting matters and internal controls to the extent necessary to express an opinion on the consolidated financial statements.

John H. Eyler, Jr.
Chairman, President and
Chief Executive Officer
March 5, 2003

Louis Lipschitz
Executive Vice President
and Chief Financial Officer

Report of Independent Auditors

The Board of Directors and Stockholders
Toys"R"Us, Inc.

We have audited the accompanying consolidated balance sheets of Toys"R"Us, Inc. and subsidiaries as of February 1, 2003 and February 2, 2002, and the related consolidated statements of earnings, stockholders' equity and cash flows for each of the three years in the period ended February 1, 2003. These financial statements are the responsibility of the company's management. Our responsibility is to express an opinion on these financial statements based on our audits.

We conducted our audits in accordance with auditing standards generally accepted in the United States. Those standards require that we plan and perform the audit to obtain reasonable assurance about whether the financial statements are free of material misstatement. An audit includes examining, on a test basis, evidence supporting the amounts and disclosures in the financial statements. An audit also includes assessing the accounting principles used and significant estimates made by management, as well as evaluating the overall financial statement presentation. We believe that our audits provide a reasonable basis for our opinion.

In our opinion, the financial statements referred to above present fairly, in all material respects, the consolidated financial position of Toys"R"Us, Inc. and subsidiaries at February 1, 2003 and February 2, 2002, and the consolidated results of their operations and their cash flows for each of the three years in the period ended February 1, 2003, in conformity with accounting principles generally accepted in the United States.

As discussed in the note entitled "Goodwill", the company adopted SFAS No. 142, Goodwill and Other Intangible Assets, effective February 3, 2002.

Ernst & Young LLP
New York, New York
March 5, 2003

board of directors

The Board of Directors

Charles Lazarus
Chairman Emeritus and founder
Toys"R"Us, Inc.
Board member since 1969

Charles Lazarus, founder of Toys"R"Us, Inc., is a pioneer of off-price specialty retailing. He opened his first retail establishment totally dedicated to children's needs in 1948 in Washington D.C. Mr. Lazarus continued to lead Toys"R"Us, Inc. as Chairman of the Board and Chief Executive Officer until 1994. Under his leadership, the company expanded internationally and launched its Kids"R"Us and Babies"R"Us brands. Mr. Lazarus remained Chairman of the Board from 1994 until 1998 when he became Chairman Emeritus.

Mr. Lazarus is a Director of Loral Space Systems and has served on the boards of Wal-Mart and Automatic Data Processing. He also served on the Advisory Board for Trade Policy under both President George Bush and President Bill Clinton. He is a member of the Toy Industry Hall of Fame.

John H. Eyler, Jr. [1]
Chairman, President and
Chief Executive Officer
Toys"R"Us, Inc.
Board member since 2000

John H. Eyler Jr. joined Toys"R"Us, Inc. as President and Chief Executive Officer in January 2000. He was named Chairman of the Board in 2001. Prior to joining the company, Mr. Eyler was Chairman and Chief Executive Officer of FAO Schwarz in New York, where he had been employed since 1992.

Mr. Eyler's previous positions include Chief Executive Officer of Chicago's Hartmarx retail subsidiary, and Chairman and Chief Executive Officer of MainStreet, a division of Federated Department Stores, Inc.

He serves on the Board of Directors for the National Retail Federation and The Andre Agassi Charitable Foundation. Mr. Eyler is also on the Board of NYC 2012, an effort to bring the 2012 Olympic Games to New York City. He holds a degree in Finance from the University of Washington and an M.B.A. from Harvard Business School.

RoAnn Costin [2]
President
Reservoir Capital Management, Inc.
Board member since 1996

RoAnn Costin is the President of Reservoir Capital Management, Inc., an investment advisory firm. She has worked in investment management since 1981, holding the position of Senior Vice President, Investment Manager for The Putnam Companies and Portfolio Manager for State Street Research and Management, Inc.

Ms. Costin holds an M.B.A. from the Stanford University Graduate School of Business and a B.A. in Government from Harvard University. In addition to Toys"R"Us, Inc., she serves on the Board of Directors for the Paul Taylor Dance Company in New York and on the Board of Trustees for The Boston Conservatory.

Roger N. Farah [1,4]
President and Chief Operating Officer
Polo Ralph Lauren
Board member since 2001

Roger N. Farah, has been President and Chief Operating Officer of Polo Ralph Lauren and a member of its Board of Directors since 2000.

From 1994 to 2000, Mr. Farah was Chairman of the Board and Chief Executive Officer of Venator Group, Inc. Prior to that, he held positions as President and Chief Operating Officer of Macy's Inc., Chairman and Chief Executive Officer of Federated Merchandising Services, and Chairman and Chief Executive Officer of Rich's Department Stores. From 1998 until 2000, he served on the Board of Directors at Liz Claiborne, Inc.

Mr. Farah received his B.S. in Economics from the University of Pennsylvania, Wharton School. He currently serves on the Wharton School's Board of Directors.

Peter A. Georgescu [2,4]
Chairman Emeritus
Young & Rubicam, Inc.
Board member since 2001

Peter A. Georgescu is Chairman Emeritus of Young & Rubicam, Inc. where he served as the company's Chairman and CEO from 1994 until 2000. He also served as President of Young and Rubicam Advertising and President of the company's former International division. Under Mr. Georgescu's tenure, Young & Rubicam transformed from a private to a publicly-held company and built an extensive database for global branding.

Mr. Georgescu also serves on the Board of Directors for EMI Group PLC, International Flavors & Fragrances Inc. and Levi Strauss & Co. He is Vice Chairman/Director of New York Presbyterian Hospital and a Director of A Better Chance. He received his B.A. from Princeton and an M.B.A. from the Stanford Business School. He was elected to the Advertising Hall of Fame in 2001.

Michael Goldstein [1]
Chairman, The Toys"R"Us
Children's Fund, Inc.
Board member since 1989

Michael Goldstein is Chairman of The Toys"R"Us Children's Fund, Inc. and Toys"R"Us.com, Inc. He has spent 19 years with Toys"R"Us, Inc. serving as both Chairman of the Board and Chief Executive Officer. Prior to 1983, Mr. Goldstein held positions as Sr. Executive Vice President-Operations & Finance with Lerner Stores Corporation and as a Partner with Ernst & Young.

Mr. Goldstein is a Director of Finlay Enterprises, Inc., United Retail Group, 4 Kids Entertainment, Inc. and Columbia House. He is President-elect of the 92nd Street Y, a Director of The Special Contributions Fund of the NAACP, and serves on the Advisory Boards of the For All Kids Foundation, USA Tennis Foundation and the New York Restoration Project. Mr. Goldstein is President and Director of the Northside Center for Child Development. He serves on the Board and Executive Committee of Reading is Fundamental and on the Board and Executive Committee of the Queens College Foundation. He is an inductee into the Toy Industry Hall of Fame and was appointed by President George W. Bush to serve on the Advisory Committee for Trade Policy and Negotiation. He is a graduate of Queens College with a B.S. in Economics.

Calvin Hill [3]
Consultant
Board member since 1997

Calvin Hill is a consultant to The Dallas Cowboys Football Club, Mental Health Management, Inc., Fleet Financial Services and Alexander & Associates, Inc. Mr. Hill was Vice President with the Baltimore Orioles from 1987 to 1994, also serving on its Board of Directors. From 1993 to 2000, he served on President Bill Clinton's Council on Physical Fitness.

Mr. Hill currently serves on the Boards of the Rand Corporation Drug Policy and Research Center, the NCAA Foundation, Duke Divinity School, and International Special Olympics. He launched his professional athletic career with the Dallas Cowboys in 1969 and has played professional football in both the World Football League and the NFL. He is a graduate of Yale University.

Nancy Karch [2,4]
Senior Partner (retired)
McKinsey & Company
Board member since 2000

Nancy Karch is a retired Director of the international consulting firm McKinsey & Company and a member of the McKinsey Advisory Council, comprised of former partners who provide advice to the firm. During 26 years with McKinsey, she held several leadership positions, including Managing Partner of the Retail and Consumer Industries Sector, and Managing Partner of McKinsey Southeast United States.

Ms. Karch is a recognized expert in the field of general merchandise retailing and an active speaker in the retailing and consumer goods fields. She also serves on the Board of Directors of Liz Claiborne, Inc., Gillette, and the Corporate Executive Board, a business research firm. Ms. Karch holds a B.A. in mathematics from Cornell University, an M.S. in mathematics from Northeastern University, and an M.B.A. from Harvard Business School.

company officers

Norman S. Matthews [1,3,4]
Consultant
Board member since 1996

Norman S. Matthews has worked in consulting and venture capital since 1989. Prior to that he held various executive positions with Federated Department stores, including President, Vice Chairman and Executive Vice President. He was also Chairman of Federated's Gold Circle Stores Division.

In addition to Toys"R"Us, Inc., Mr. Matthews serves on the Board of Directors for The Progressive Corporation, Sunoco, Eye Care Centers of America, Finlay Enterprises, Inc., Galyan's Trading Company, and Henry Schein, Inc. He holds a B.A. degree from Princeton University and an M.B.A. from Harvard Business School.

Arthur B. Newman [1,2,3]
Senior Managing Director,
The Blackstone Group, L.P.
Board member since 1997

Arthur B. Newman has been a Senior Managing Director and head of The Restructuring Group of The Blackstone Group, L.P., a private investment bank, since 1991. Previously, Mr. Newman was a Managing Director and head of the Restructuring and Reorganization Group of Chemical Bank and a senior partner at Ernst & Young. Mr. Newman has been an advisor in many of this country's largest reorganizations, including AMF Bowling, Arch Wireless, The Charter Company, Chiquita Banana, Dow Corning Corporation, Eastern Airlines, Exide Technologies, Global Crossing, Iridium, LTV Corporation, Levitz Furniture, Macy's, Manville Corporation, Mobile Media Corporation, Montgomery Ward, Texaco, Inc., White Motor Corporation and the Wickes Corporation.

Mr. Newman is a member of the America College of Bankruptcy and was the recipient of the 1990 award by the Bankruptcy & Reorganization Group, Lawyers Division of UJA-Federation. Mr. Newman holds a B.S. degree in economics and an M.B.A. from Rutgers University. He is a certified public accountant in New York.

1 *Executive Committee*
2 *Audit Committee*
3 *Compensation & Organizational Development Committee*
4 *Corporate Governance and Nominating Committee*

Corporate and Administrative Officers

John H. Eyler, Jr.
Chairman, President and Chief Executive Officer

Francesca L. Brockett
Executive Vice President – Strategic Planning & Business Development

Michael D'Ambrose
Executive Vice President – Human Resources

Karen Duvall
Executive Vice President – Supply Chain

John Holohan
Executive Vice President – Chief Information Officer

Christopher K. Kay
Executive Vice President – Operations & General Counsel, Corporate Secretary

Warren F. Kornblum
Executive Vice President – Chief Marketing Officer

Louis Lipschitz
Executive Vice President – Chief Financial Officer

Jon W. Kimmins
Sr. Vice President – Treasurer

Dorvin D. Lively
Sr. Vice President – Corporate Controller

Peter W. Weiss
Sr. Vice President – Taxes

Rebecca A. Caruso
Vice President – Corporate Communications

Ursula H. Moran
Vice President – Investor Relations

Divisional Officers

Richard L. Markee
Executive Vice President and President – Specialty Businesses and International Operations

Raymond L. Arthur
President – Toysrus.com

John Barbour
Executive Vice President and President – Toys"R"Us International

James E. Feldt
Executive Vice President and President – Merchandising and Marketing, Toys"R"Us U.S.

Elliott Wahle
President – Babies"R"Us & Kids"R"Us

Joan W. Donovan
Sr. Vice President – General Merchandise Manager, Toys"R"Us International

Jonathan M. Friedman
Sr. Vice President – Chief Financial Officer, Toys"R"Us U.S.

Andrew R. Gatto
Sr. Vice President – Product Development, Toys"R"Us U.S.

Steven J. Krajewski
Sr. Vice President – Operations, Toys"R"Us U.S.

James G. Parros
Sr. Vice President – Stores & Distributions Center Operations, Kids"R"Us

David Schoenbeck
Sr. Vice President – Operations, Babies"R"Us

Pamela B. Wallack
Sr. Vice President – General Merchandise Manager, Babies"R"Us & Kids"R"Us

International Country Presidents and Managing Directors

David Rurka
Managing Director – Toys"R"Us U.K.

Jacques LeFoll
President – Toys"R"Us France

Monika Merz
President – Toys"R"Us Canada

John Schryver
Managing Director – Toys"R"Us Australia

Michael C. Taylor
Managing Director – Toys"R"Us Central Europe

Antonio Urcelay
Managing Director – Toys"R"Us Iberia

A Heartfelt Tribute

After decades of much appreciated leadership and service, Charles Lazarus and Michael Goldstein will be leaving the Board at the end of this year's (2002-2003) term. Charles and Mike have both served many years as Chief Executive Officer and as Chairman of the Board of Directors of Toys"R"Us, Inc., where they both played significant roles in the growth of the company. Thereafter, they served the company with distinction as members of the Board of Directors. We are extremely grateful for their leadership, their inspiration, their compassion and their commitment to the Toys"R"Us family of stockholders, colleagues and guests.

financial data

Quarterly Financial Data and Market Information
Toys"R"Us, Inc. and Subsidiaries

Quarterly Financial Data
(In millions except per share data)

The following table sets forth certain unaudited quarterly financial information:

	First Quarter	Second Quarter	Third Quarter	Fourth Quarter
Year Ended February 1, 2003				
Net Sales	$ 2,095	$ 2,070	$ 2,271	$ 4,869
Gross Margin	682	670	722	1,432
Net (Loss)/Earnings	(4)	(17)	(28)	278
Basic (Loss)/ Earnings per Share	$ (0.02)	$ (0.08)	$ (0.13)	$ 1.31
Diluted (Loss)/ Earnings per Share	$ (0.02)	$ (0.08)	$ (0.13)	$ 1.30

	First Quarter	Second Quarter	Third Quarter	Fourth Quarter[a]
Year Ended February 2, 2002				
Net Sales	$ 2,061	$ 2,021	$ 2,178	$ 4,759
Gross Margin	665	661	710	1,379
Net (Loss)/Earnings	(18)	(29)	(44)	158
Basic (Loss)/ Earnings per Share	$ (0.09)	$ (0.15)	$ (0.22)	$ 0.80
Diluted (Loss)/ Earnings per Share	$ (0.09)	$ (0.15)	$ (0.22)	$ 0.78

(a) Includes restructuring and other charges of $213 ($126 net of tax, or $0.61 per share).

Market Information

The company's common stock is listed on the New York Stock Exchange. The following table reflects the high and low prices (rounded to the nearest hundredth) based on New York Stock Exchange trading since February 3, 2001.

The company has not paid any cash dividends, however, the Board of Directors of the company periodically reviews this policy.

The company had approximately 30,736 Stockholders of Record on March 12, 2003.

			High	Low
2001	1st	Quarter	$ 26.52	$ 23.00
	2nd	Quarter	31.00	22.30
	3rd	Quarter	25.10	16.81
	4th	Quarter	24.00	18.25
2002	1st	Quarter	$ 20.31	$ 16.18
	2nd	Quarter	18.28	12.58
	3rd	Quarter	14.09	8.70
	4th	Quarter	13.81	9.04

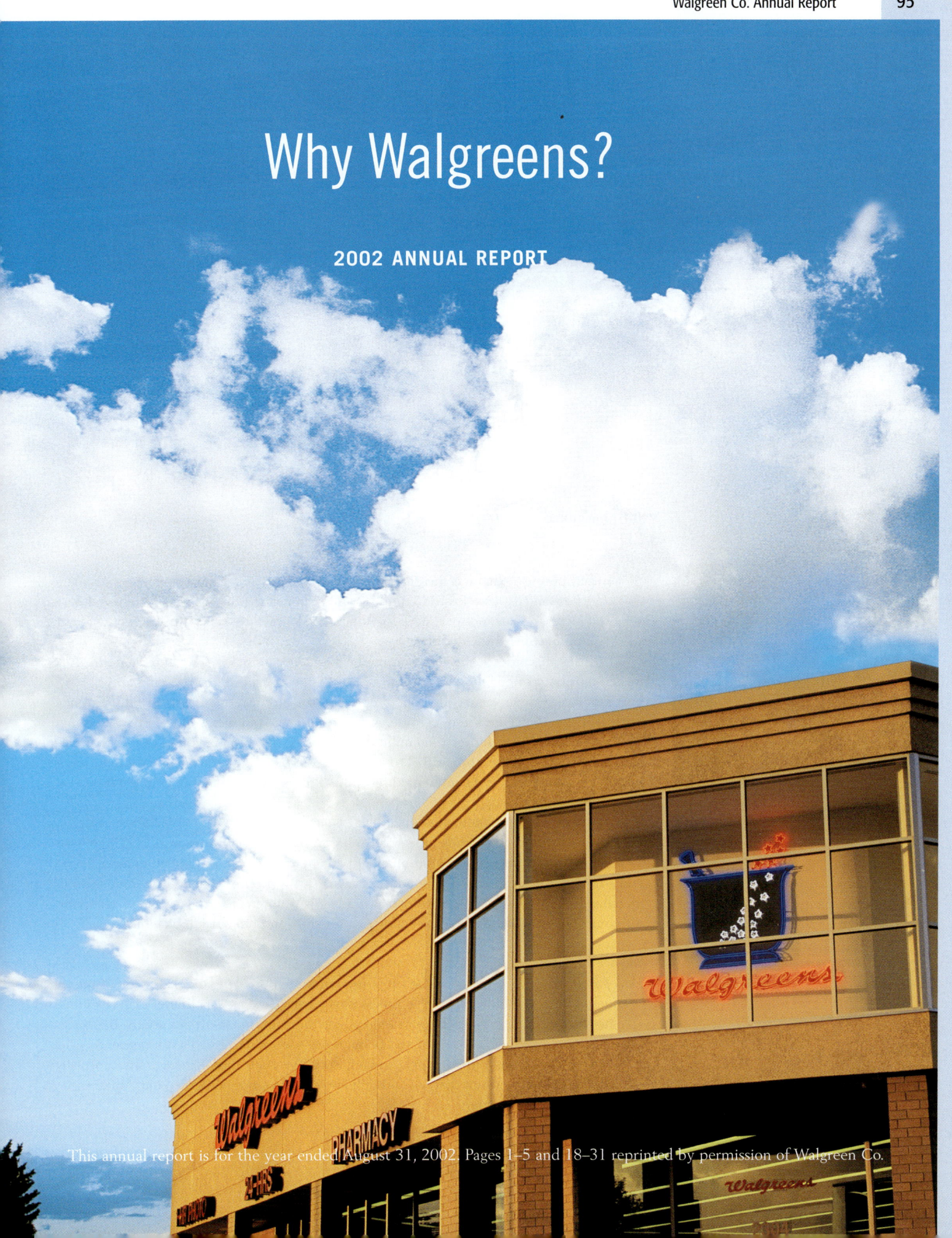

Why Walgreens?

2002 ANNUAL REPORT

This annual report is for the year ended August 31, 2002. Pages 1–5 and 18–31 reprinted by permission of Walgreen Co.

Financial Highlights
For the Years Ended August 31, 2002 and 2001

(In Millions, except per share data)	2002	2001	Increase
Net Sales	$28,681.1	$24,623.0	16.5%
Net Earnings	$ 1,019.2	$ 885.6	15.1%
Net Earnings per Common Share (diluted)	$ .99	$ .86	15.1%
Shareholders' Equity	$ 6,230.2	$ 5,207.2	19.6%
Return on Average Shareholders' Equity	17.8%	18.8%	
Closing Stock Price per Common Share	$ 34.75	$ 34.35	
Total Market Value of Common Stock	$ 35,616	$ 35,017	1.7%
Dividends Declared per Common Share	$ .145	$ .140	3.6%
Average Shares Outstanding (diluted)	1,032.3	1,028.9	0.3%

Questions and Answers for Our Shareholders
November 18, 2002

Chairman L. Daniel Jorndt (left) with president and chief executive officer David W. Bernauer.

"Beautifully boring" – that was the description of Walgreens and other companies who made *Bloomberg Personal Finance's* "Profit Champ" list this fall. Each of the 51 firms recognized has achieved increased earnings per share for at least 10 consecutive years. In Walgreens case, the streak is approaching three decades.

During this past rocky year, when the bears ruled the stock market and economic news turned morning coffee bitter, we completed our 28th consecutive record year – and first billion-dollar earnings year – while opening 471 stores and investing nearly $1 billion in new stores, distribution centers and technology improvements. And in a world where cash is now king, we ended 2002 with over $400 million in the bank, nearly $3 billion in owned real estate, virtually no debt and the wherewithal to self-finance accelerating growth and customer service innovations. As one analyst commented recently: "Profits are opinion, but cash is a fact."

It was a record year, but fourth quarter earnings came in a penny light of expectations. Why?
Dave Bernauer: Pure and simple, this was a sales problem. Prescriptions were excellent – up 20 percent for the quarter and more than 21 percent for the year. But fourth quarter front-end – non-pharmacy – sales were anemic, particularly for promotional and summer seasonal merchandise. Those weak sales held our profit below Wall Street's expectations. A company with our stock market valuation isn't allowed a toe-stub, and our stock took a hit.

Why the weak sales?
Dan Jorndt: The easiest culprit is the economy, but we're not taking that bait. One of the beauties of our admittedly "boring" business is its staying power – we sell everyday, consumable items that people *need* more than *want*. Some times are tougher than others, but since the mid-1970s – through recessions and boom times – we've never had a down year. So when sales are tight, we look in the mirror…and adjust. We've made lots of corrections, especially in our advertising, to ensure that fall and holiday sales are more "Walgreen-like," that is, good, strong front-end sales.

Quite frankly, we got out of balance this summer. We were less promotion-oriented, which helped increase our gross profits, but hurt the top sales line. Advertising is always a delicate balance and we're moving the pendulum a little more in favor of traffic building. But we're seeking middle ground. Walgreens is not a retailer that sacrifices all to drive sales. We will get the top line moving…sensibly.

Walgreens keeps adding stores despite the economic slowdown. Is this smart?

Bernauer: There's never been a better time for us to expand. We have the sites, the cash, the people…and America has the need. The only retail segment where sales are outpacing store growth is drugstores. In 2001, the number of retail prescriptions climbed 5 percent, while drugstore outlets grew only 1 percent. Although we're the largest prescription provider in the nation, we still fill only 12 percent of the total, which gives us outstanding growth opportunity.

What about Wal*Mart?

Bernauer: What about *any* competitor? Any store that sells what we sell is on our radar screen. Our strategy has always been to define our segment – convenient healthcare and basic need retailing – and do it better than anyone else. We've seriously – and successfully – competed head-on with Wal*Mart for a quarter century now. They're not new competition. They *are* excellent, respected competition…and they're also one of the few retailers expanding at the same pace we are. Top competitors like Wal*Mart make us better. We watch them… they watch us.

Inventory was high going into fiscal 2002. How did you end up?

Bernauer: A chunk of our positive cash position is due to a big improvement in inventory levels. We had a bad case of indigestion last year, but ended 2002 with inventories up just 5 percent, despite a 16.5 percent sales increase and opening a record 363 net new stores plus new distribution centers in Jupiter, Florida, and Waxahachie, Texas. More importantly, we didn't just blow out product with severe price cuts. We used our systems to attack overages on an orderly basis without hurting gross profit margins and in-stock conditions.

Short-term borrowings of $441 million were completely repaid during the year. For my money, the beauty of our 2002 balance sheet rivals Monet, showing a positive cash swing from borrowing to investing of nearly $900 million.

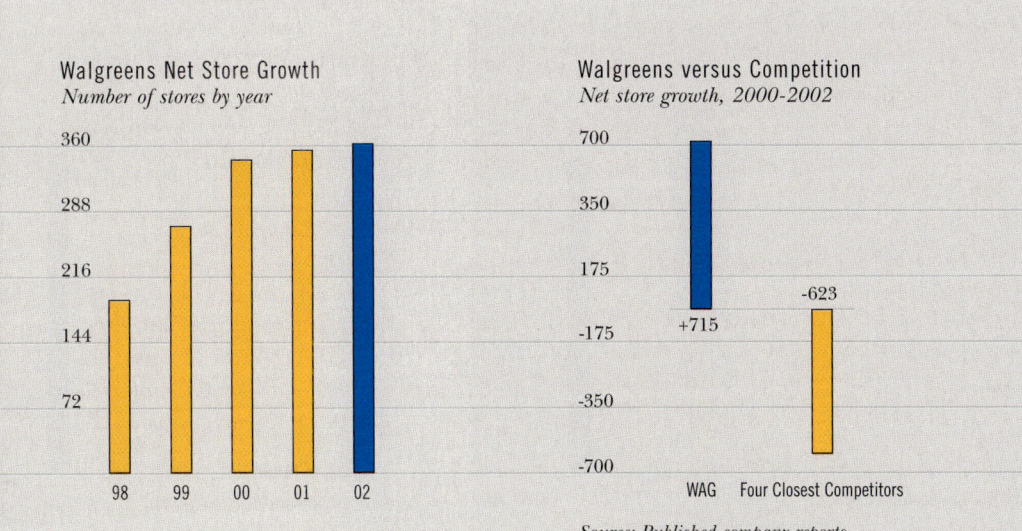

3,883 AND GROWING

Walgreens is the most "national" – and fastest growing – drugstore chain in America. In 2002, we filled 361 million prescriptions – 12 percent of the U.S. retail market and more per store than all major competitors. Our stores average $7.1 million or $654 per square foot in annual sales. Looking ahead, in 2003 we plan to open 450 new stores (approximately 360 net), add 12,000 new jobs and open our third new distribution center in just two years.

Dan Jorndt retires in January after 40 years with Walgreens. Since 1990 he's served as president, CEO and then chairman, leading this company through its period of greatest expansion and innovation. Dan Jorndt's two favorite words are "thank you." On behalf of all shareholders, we thank him for his leadership, honesty, retail savvy, tough decisions, long days and nights, sense of humor and the example he's set. Quite simply, he's made all of those whose lives he's touched a little richer. We wish him and his wife, Pat, the best — and most active — of retirements.

What was the impact of generic drug introductions last year?
Jorndt: Very positive. Generics save money for patients and their providers, both private insurance companies and state Medicaid plans. For Walgreens, while the higher mix of generics to brands slowed our top-line sales growth trend slightly last year, it had a healthy impact on the bottom line. The most important metric in pharmacy is the number of prescriptions. We filled 361 million in 2002, up almost 12 percent from the previous year, and more than double the national increase.

Is there still a pharmacist shortage?
Bernauer: There is a shortage…a big one. But aside from a few markets, we're in good shape. At the end of fiscal 2002, we had 1,600 more pharmacists working for us than a year ago. We're meeting ongoing needs and staffing over 360 net new drugstores a year. We also have the pharmacists to cover 900 24-hour stores. That's more than half of *all* 24-hour pharmacies in America.

If you could stress just one thing to shareholders this year, what would it be?
Jorndt: The quality of our earnings. Warren Buffet has a good quote: "It's only when the tide goes out that you learn who's been swimming naked." A lot of skinny-dippers have surfaced in the past year, bringing down high-flying companies and millions of shareholders. Believe me, we at Walgreens have our swimsuits on, and they're those scratchy knee-to-neck getups beach lovers wore in the 1920s. More boring than bikinis and thongs? You'd better believe it. But accounting works best when it's boring.

Our earnings are all about quality. Our financial statements are straightforward…what you see is what you get. We pay as we go and, other than store leases, everything is on our balance sheet. With no one-time charges and virtually no debt, WAG made the "Top 10" on a recent Merrill Lynch list of firms with quality earnings.

What worries you?
Bernauer: Mostly, stuff that's difficult to control. That includes the current economy as well as government actions. As our population ages, healthcare costs are going up, up, up. This will require government at all levels to make some very tough decisions about resource allocation. We believe it's our job to invest, create jobs, serve customer needs and get a return for these efforts, a return on which we pay significant taxes. It's the government's job to provide social

WHAT ARE WE WORTH?

As of August 31, 2002, Walgreens market capitalization was $35.6 billion. That ranks us third among U.S. retailers and third in the world. In terms of sales volume, we rank No. 78 in the *Fortune 100*. Walgreens has paid dividends in every quarter since 1933 and has raised them for 27 consecutive years. Since 1980, we've had seven two-for-one stock splits.

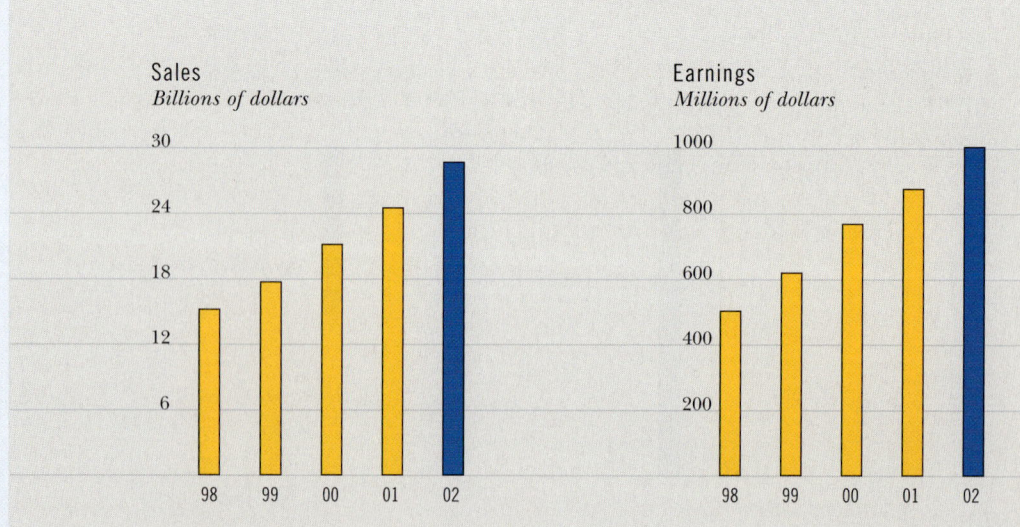

Sales — Billions of dollars (98–02)

Earnings — Millions of dollars (98–02)

2002 WALGREENS ANNUAL REPORT

WALGREENS STOCK PERFORMANCE

10 YEARS
On August 31, 1992, 100 shares of Walgreen stock sold for $3,838. Ten years later, on August 31, 2002, those 100 shares, having split three times, were 800 shares worth $27,800, for a gain of 624 percent.

20 YEARS
On August 31, 1982, 100 shares of Walgreen stock sold for $3,600. Twenty years later, those 100 shares, having split six times, were 6,400 shares worth $222,400, for a gain of 6,078 percent.

services. Although pharmacy consumes only 10 percent of the nation's healthcare bill and is the most cost-effective form of treatment, there have been moves recently to slash state Medicaid reimbursement to levels below the filling cost. We and other community pharmacies cannot accept plans – public or private – on which we lose money.

January marks a new era, as Dan Jorndt retires and Dave Bernauer adds "chairman" to his CEO position. What will change?
Jorndt: I've had a great 40-year run with this company, but it's time for new blood. Same core strategy, same execution…someone else calling the shots. These moves are part of our long-term succession plan. We're blessed in not having to go outside for CEOs. Dave Bernauer and our new president, Jeff Rein, are both pharmacists who started in the stores and have spent long careers here. They, and what I call the "new generation" of Walgreen leaders behind them, are among the top retailers in the country. These men and women know drugstores inside out and bring amazing energy and relentless character to their work. It will be a pleasure to watch their progress.

Jeffrey A. Rein will become president and chief operating officer in January 2003.

IN A TOUGH BUSINESS ENVIRONMENT, where confidence in corporate America has plummeted, we feel compelled to say, "No, Chicken Little, the sky isn't falling." We read volumes about the failures…while the thousands of successful companies receive little press. We can't solve the world's ills, but we can promise you, our shareholders and employees, that we'll do our level best to restore faith in what's good about American business. At Walgreens, we know who we are and what we're about. We have a competitive format and clearly defined strategy…a growing demand for our products and services…healthy cash and inventory positions…superior real estate and technology…and motivated, seasoned people at every level. Thanks for your faith in our long-term future…it's a solid one.

L. Daniel Jorndt
Chairman

David W. Bernauer
President and Chief Executive Officer

Eleven-Year Summary of Selected Consolidated Financial Data

Walgreen Co. and Subsidiaries (Dollars in Millions, except per share data)

Fiscal Year		2002	2001	2000
Net Sales		**$28,681.1**	$24,623.0	$21,206.9
Costs and Deductions	Cost of sales	21,076.1	18,048.9	15,465.9
	Selling, occupancy and administration	5,980.8	5,175.8	4,516.9
	Other (income) expense (1)	(13.1)	(24.4)	(39.2)
	Total Costs and Deductions	27,043.8	23,200.3	19,943.6
Earnings	Earnings before income tax provision and cumulative effect of accounting changes	1,637.3	1,422.7	1,263.3
	Income tax provision	618.1	537.1	486.4
	Earnings before cumulative effect of accounting changes	1,019.2	885.6	776.9
	Cumulative effect of accounting changes (2)	—	—	—
	Net Earnings	$ 1,019.2	$ 885.6	$ 776.9
Per Common Share (3)	Net earnings (2)			
	Basic	$ 1.00	$ .87	$ .77
	Diluted	.99	.86	.76
	Dividends declared	.15	.14	.14
	Book value	6.08	5.11	4.19
Non-Current Liabilities	Long-term debt	$ 11.2	$ 20.8	$ 18.2
	Deferred income taxes	176.5	137.0	101.6
	Other non-current liabilities	505.7	457.2	446.2
Assets and Equity	Total assets	$ 9,878.8	$ 8,833.8	$ 7,103.7
	Shareholders' equity	6,230.2	5,207.2	4,234.0
	Return on average shareholders' equity	17.8%	18.8%	20.1%
Drugstore Units	Year-end: Units (4)	3,883	3,520	3,165

(1) Fiscal 2002, 2001 and 2000 include pre-tax income of $6.2 million ($.004 per share), $22.1 million ($.01 per share) and $33.5 million ($.02 per share), respectively, from the partial payments of the brand name prescription drugs litigation settlement. Fiscal 1998 includes a pre-tax gain of $37.4 million ($.02 per share) from the sale of the company's long-term care pharmacy business.

(2) Fiscal 1998 includes the after-tax $26.4 million ($.03 per share) charge from the cumulative effect of accounting change for system development costs. Fiscal 1993 includes the after-tax $23.6 million ($.02 per share) costs from the cumulative effect of accounting changes for postretirement benefits and income taxes.

(3) Per share data have been adjusted for two-for-one stock splits in 1999, 1997 and 1995.

(4) Units include mail service facilities.

	1999	1998	1997	1996	1995	1994	1993	1992
	$17,838.8	$15,306.6	$13,363.0	$11,778.4	$10,395.1	$9,235.0	$8,294.8	$7,475.0
	12,978.6	11,139.4	9,681.8	8,514.9	7,482.3	6,614.4	5,959.0	5,377.7
	3,844.8	3,332.0	2,972.5	2,659.5	2,392.7	2,164.9	1,929.6	1,738.8
	(11.9)	(41.9)	(3.9)	(2.9)	(3.6)	(2.7)	6.5	5.5
	16,811.5	14,429.5	12,650.4	11,171.5	9,871.4	8,776.6	7,895.1	7,122.0
	1,027.3	877.1	712.6	606.9	523.7	458.4	399.7	353.0
	403.2	339.9	276.1	235.2	202.9	176.5	154.4	132.4
	624.1	537.2	436.5	371.7	320.8	281.9	245.3	220.6
	—	(26.4)	—	—	—	—	(23.6)	—
	$ 624.1	$ 510.8	$ 436.5	$ 371.7	$ 320.8	$ 281.9	$ 221.7	$ 220.6
	$ .62	$ .51	$ .44	$ .38	$ .33	$ .29	$ .23	$ .22
	.62	.51	.44	.37	.32	.29	.23	.22
	.13	.13	.12	.11	.11	.09	.08	.07
	3.47	2.86	2.40	2.08	1.82	1.60	1.40	1.25
	$ 18.0	$ 13.6	$ 3.3	$ 3.4	$ 2.4	$ 1.8	$ 6.2	$ 18.7
	74.8	89.1	112.8	145.2	142.3	137.7	144.2	171.8
	405.8	369.9	279.2	259.9	237.6	213.8	176.2	103.8
	$ 5,906.7	$ 4,901.6	$ 4,207.1	$ 3,633.6	$ 3,252.6	$2,872.8	$2,506.0	$2,346.9
	3,484.3	2,848.9	2,373.3	2,043.1	1,792.6	1,573.6	1,378.8	1,233.3
	19.7%	19.6%	19.8%	19.4%	19.1%	19.1%	18.8%	19.1%
	2,821	2,549	2,358	2,193	2,085	1,968	1,836	1,736

Management's Discussion and Analysis of Results of Operations and Financial Condition

Results of Operations

Fiscal 2002 was the 28th consecutive year of record sales and earnings. Net earnings were $1.019 billion or $.99 per share (diluted), an increase of 15.1% from last year's earnings of $885.6 million or $.86 per share. Included in this year's results was a $6.2 million pre-tax gain ($.004 per share) for a partial payment of the company's share of the brand name prescription drugs antitrust litigation settlement. Last year's results included a $22.1 million ($.01 per share) comparable payment. Excluding these gains, fiscal year earnings rose 16.5%.

Total net sales increased by 16.5% to $28.7 billion in fiscal 2002 compared to increases of 16.1% in 2001 and 18.9% in 2000. Drugstore sales increases resulted from sales gains in existing stores and added sales from new stores, each of which include an indeterminate amount of market-driven price changes. Comparable drugstore (those open at least one year) sales were up 10.5% in 2002, 10.5% in 2001 and 11.7% in 2000. New store openings accounted for 9.6% of the sales gains in 2002, 11.3% in 2001 and 10.6% in 2000. The company operated 3,883 drugstores as of August 31, 2002, compared to 3,520 a year earlier.

Prescription sales increased 21.2% in 2002, 20.9% in 2001 and 25.3% in 2000. Comparable drugstore prescription sales were up 16.3% in 2002, 17.6% in 2001 and 19.0% in 2000. Prescription sales were 59.8% of total sales for fiscal 2002 compared to 57.5% in 2001 and 55.2% in 2000. Third party sales, where reimbursement is received from managed care organizations and government and private insurance, were 89.8% of pharmacy sales in 2002, 88.4% in 2001 and 86.1% in 2000. Pharmacy sales trends are expected to continue primarily because of increased penetration in existing markets, availability of new drugs and demographic changes such as the aging population.

Gross margins as a percent of total sales were 26.5% in 2002, 26.7% in 2001 and 27.1% in 2000. The decrease in gross margin was caused by a number of factors. Non-pharmacy margins declined as a result of more aggressive advertising and in-store promotions. Although prescription margins increased, due in part to the shift to more generic medications, the trend in sales mix continued toward pharmacy, which carries lower margins than the rest of the store. Within the pharmacy, third party sales, which typically have lower profit margins than cash prescriptions, continue to become a larger portion of prescription sales.

The company uses the last-in, first-out (LIFO) method of inventory valuation. The effective LIFO inflation rates were 1.42% in 2002, 1.93% in 2001 and 1.36% in 2000, which resulted in charges to cost of sales of $55.9 million in 2002, $62.8 million in 2001 and $38.8 million in 2000. Inflation on prescription inventory was 4.3% in 2002, 4.9% in 2001 and 3.5% in 2000.

Selling, occupancy and administration expenses were 20.9% of sales in fiscal 2002, 21.0% of sales in fiscal 2001 and 21.3% of sales in fiscal 2000. The decrease in fiscal 2002, as a percent to sales, was caused by lower store direct expenses, which were partially offset by higher occupancy costs. The decline in fiscal 2001 resulted from lower advertising and headquarters expense. Fixed costs continue to be spread over a larger base of stores.

SG&A Expense (as a percent to sales)

Interest income net of interest expense increased in 2002 principally due to higher investment levels. Average net investment levels were approximately $162 million in 2002, $31 million in 2001 and $64 million in 2000.

The fiscal 2002 and 2001 effective income tax rates were 37.75% compared to 38.50% in 2000. The decrease in rates compared to 2000 was principally the result of lower state income taxes and the settlement of various IRS matters.

Critical Accounting Policies

The consolidated financial statements are prepared in accordance with accounting principles generally accepted in the United States of America and include amounts based on management's prudent judgments and estimates. Actual results may differ from these estimates. Management believes that any reasonable deviation from those judgments and estimates would not have a material impact on the company's consolidated financial position or results of operations. However, to the extent that the estimates used differ from actual results, adjustments to the statement of earnings and corresponding balance sheet accounts would be necessary. Some of the more significant estimates include liability for closed locations, liability for insurance reserves, vendor allowances, allowance for doubtful accounts, and cost of sales. The company uses the following techniques to determine estimates:

Liability for closed locations – The present value of future rent obligations and other related costs to the first lease option date or estimated sublease date.

Liability for insurance reserves – Incurred losses by policy year extended by historical growth factors to derive ultimate losses.

Vendor allowances – Vendor allowances are principally received as a result of meeting defined purchase levels or promoting vendors' products. Those received as a result of purchase levels are accrued as a reduction of merchandise purchase prices over the incentive period based on estimates. Those received for promoting vendors' products are offset against advertising expense and result in a reduction of selling, occupancy and administration expense.

Allowance for doubtful accounts – Based on both specific receivables and historic write-off percents.

Cost of sales – Based primarily on point-of-sale scanning information with an estimate for shrinkage and adjusted based on periodic inventories.

Financial Condition

Cash and cash equivalents were $449.9 million at August 31, 2002, compared to $16.9 million at August 31, 2001. Short-term investment objectives are to minimize risk, maintain liquidity and maximize after-tax yields. To attain these objectives, investment limits are placed on the amount, type and issuer of securities. Investments are principally in top-tier money market funds, tax exempt bonds and commercial paper.

Net cash provided by operating activities for fiscal 2002 was $1.5 billion compared to $719.2 million a year ago. The change between periods was principally due to tighter control over inventory levels. The company's profitability is the principal source for providing funds for expansion and remodeling programs, dividends to shareholders and funding for various technological improvements.

Net cash used for investing activities was $551.9 million in fiscal 2002 and $1.1 billion in 2001. Additions to property and equipment were $934.4 million compared to $1.2 billion last year. During the year, 471 new or relocated drugstores were opened. This compares to 474 new or relocated drugstores opened in the same period last year. New stores are owned or leased. There were 150 owned locations opened during the year or under construction at August 31, 2002, versus 245 for the same period last year. During the year, two new distribution centers opened, one in West Palm Beach (Jupiter), Florida, and the other in the Dallas metropolitan area.

During fiscal 2002, the company entered into two sale-leaseback transactions. These transactions involved 86 drugstore locations and resulted in proceeds of $302 million.

Capital expenditures for fiscal 2003 are expected to exceed $1 billion. The company expects to open more than 450 new stores in fiscal 2003 and have a total of 7,000 drugstores by the year 2010. The company is continuing to relocate stores to more convenient and profitable freestanding locations. In addition to new stores, a significant portion of the expenditures will be made for technology and distribution centers. A new distribution center is under construction in Ohio. Another is planned in Southern California.

Net cash used for financing activities was $488.9 million compared to $419.4 million provided a year ago. The change was principally due to payments of short-term borrowings this year versus proceeds from borrowings last year. There were no short-term borrowings at August 31, 2002, compared to $440.7 million at August 31, 2001. Borrowings were needed during each year to support working capital needs and store and distribution center growth, which included purchases of new store property, equipment and inventory. At August 31, 2002, the company had a syndicated bank line of credit facility of $600 million to support the company's short-term commercial paper program. On July 2, 2002, the company deregistered the remaining $100 million of unissued authorized debt securities, previously filed with the Securities and Exchange Commission.

Recent Accounting Pronouncements

During the first quarter of 2002, the company adopted Statement of Financial Accounting Standards (SFAS) No. 142, "Goodwill and Other Intangible Assets." Under this pronouncement, goodwill is no longer amortized but periodically tested for impairment. No significant impact to the consolidated financial position or results of operations occurred as a result of adopting this standard.

The adoption of SFAS No. 144, "Accounting for the Impairment or Disposal of Long-Lived Assets," resulted in additional disclosures which can be found under "Impaired Assets and Liabilities for Store Closings" in the Summary of Major Accounting Policies.

During the fourth quarter of 2002, the company early adopted SFAS No. 146, "Accounting for Costs Associated with Exit or Disposal Activity." As a result, beginning in June 2002, the remaining lease obligations for closed locations were no longer recognized at the time management made the decision to close the location but were recognized at the time of closing. The adoption of this pronouncement did not have a material impact in the fourth quarter and is not expected to have a material impact on the company's consolidated financial position or results of operations in the future.

Cautionary Note Regarding Forward-Looking Statements

Certain statements and projections of future results made in this report constitute forward-looking information that is based on current market, competitive and regulatory expectations that involve risks and uncertainties. Those risks and uncertainties include changes in economic conditions generally or in the markets served by the company; consumer preferences and spending patterns; changes in state or federal legislation or regulations; the availability and cost of real estate and construction; competition; and risks of new business areas. Please see Walgreen Co.'s Form 10-K for the period ended August 31, 2002, for a discussion of certain other important factors as they relate to forward-looking statements. Actual results could differ materially.

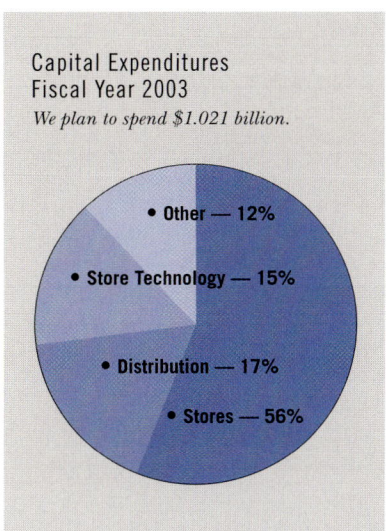

Capital Expenditures Fiscal Year 2003
We plan to spend $1.021 billion.

- Other — 12%
- Store Technology — 15%
- Distribution — 17%
- Stores — 56%

Consolidated Statements of Earnings and Shareholders' Equity

Walgreen Co. and Subsidiaries for the Years Ended August 31, 2002, 2001 and 2000 (Dollars in Millions, except per share data)

	Earnings	2002	2001	2000
Net Sales		**$28,681.1**	$24,623.0	$21,206.9
Costs and Deductions	Cost of sales	21,076.1	18,048.9	15,465.9
	Selling, occupancy and administration	5,980.8	5,175.8	4,516.9
		27,056.9	23,224.7	19,982.8
Other (Income) Expense	Interest income	(6.9)	(5.4)	(6.1)
	Interest expense	—	3.1	.4
	Other income	(6.2)	(22.1)	(33.5)
		(13.1)	(24.4)	(39.2)
Earnings	Earnings before income tax provision	1,637.3	1,422.7	1,263.3
	Income tax provision	618.1	537.1	486.4
	Net Earnings	$ 1,019.2	$ 885.6	$ 776.9
Net Earnings per Common Share	Basic	$ 1.00	$ .87	$ .77
	Diluted	.99	.86	.76
	Average shares outstanding	1,022,554,460	1,016,197,785	1,007,393,572
	Dilutive effect of stock options	9,716,486	12,748,828	12,495,236
	Average shares outstanding assuming dilution	1,032,270,946	1,028,946,613	1,019,888,808

	Common Stock Shares	Common Stock Amount	Paid-in Capital	Retained Earnings
Shareholders' Equity				
Balance, August 31, 1999	1,004,022,258	$78.4	$258.9	$3,147.0
Net earnings	—	—	—	776.9
Cash dividends declared ($.135 per share)	—	—	—	(136.1)
Employee stock purchase and option plans	6,796,632	.6	108.3	—
Balance, August 31, 2000	1,010,818,890	79.0	367.2	3,787.8
Net earnings	—	—	—	885.6
Cash dividends declared ($.14 per share)	—	—	—	(142.5)
Employee stock purchase and option plans	8,606,162	.6	229.5	—
Balance, August 31, 2001	1,019,425,052	79.6	596.7	4,530.9
Net earnings	—	—	—	1,019.2
Cash dividends declared ($.145 per share)	—	—	—	(148.4)
Employee stock purchase and option plans	5,483,224	.5	151.7	—
Balance, August 31, 2002	1,024,908,276	$80.1	$748.4	$5,401.7

The accompanying Summary of Major Accounting Policies and the Notes to Consolidated Financial Statements are integral parts of these statements.

Consolidated Balance Sheets

Walgreen Co. and Subsidiaries at August 31, 2002 and 2001 (Dollars in Millions)

	Assets	2002	2001
Current Assets	Cash and cash equivalents	$ 449.9	$ 16.9
	Accounts receivable, net	954.8	798.3
	Inventories	3,645.2	3,482.4
	Other current assets	116.6	96.3
	Total Current Assets	5,166.5	4,393.9
Non-Current Assets	Property and equipment, at cost, less accumulated depreciation and amortization	4,591.4	4,345.3
	Other non-current assets	120.9	94.6
	Total Assets	$9,878.8	$8,833.8
	Liabilities and Shareholders' Equity		
Current Liabilities	Short-term borrowings	$ —	$ 440.7
	Trade accounts payable	1,836.4	1,546.8
	Accrued expenses and other liabilities	1,017.9	937.5
	Income taxes	100.9	86.6
	Total Current Liabilities	2,955.2	3,011.6
Non-Current Liabilities	Deferred income taxes	176.5	137.0
	Other non-current liabilities	516.9	478.0
	Total Non-Current Liabilities	693.4	615.0
Shareholders' Equity	Preferred stock, $.0625 par value; authorized 32 million shares; none issued	—	—
	Common stock, $.078125 par value; authorized 3.2 billion shares; issued and outstanding 1,024,908,276 in 2002 and 1,019,425,052 in 2001	80.1	79.6
	Paid-in capital	748.4	596.7
	Retained earnings	5,401.7	4,530.9
	Total Shareholders' Equity	6,230.2	5,207.2
	Total Liabilities and Shareholders' Equity	$9,878.8	$8,833.8

The accompanying Summary of Major Accounting Policies and the Notes to Consolidated Financial Statements are integral parts of these statements.

Consolidated Statements of Cash Flows

Walgreen Co. and Subsidiaries for the Years Ended August 31, 2002, 2001 and 2000 (In Millions)

Fiscal Year		2002	2001	2000
Cash Flows from Operating Activities	Net earnings	$1,019.2	$ 885.6	$ 776.9
	Adjustments to reconcile net earnings to net cash provided by operating activities –			
	Depreciation and amortization	307.3	269.2	230.1
	Deferred income taxes	22.9	46.9	21.0
	Income tax savings from employee stock plans	56.8	67.3	38.5
	Other	(8.6)	2.1	13.6
	Changes in operating assets and liabilities –			
	Inventories	(162.8)	(651.6)	(368.2)
	Trade accounts payable	289.6	182.8	233.7
	Accounts receivable, net	(170.6)	(177.3)	(135.4)
	Accrued expenses and other liabilities	75.0	82.2	101.2
	Income taxes	14.3	(5.4)	28.6
	Other	30.7	17.4	31.7
	Net cash provided by operating activities	1,473.8	719.2	971.7
Cash Flows from Investing Activities	Additions to property and equipment	(934.4)	(1,237.0)	(1,119.1)
	Disposition of property and equipment	368.1	43.5	22.9
	Net proceeds from corporate-owned life insurance	14.4	59.0	58.8
	Net cash used for investing activities	(551.9)	(1,134.5)	(1,037.4)
Cash Flows from Financing Activities	(Payments of) proceeds from short-term borrowings	(440.7)	440.7	—
	Cash dividends paid	(147.0)	(140.9)	(134.6)
	Proceeds from employee stock plans	111.1	126.1	79.2
	Other	(12.3)	(6.5)	(7.9)
	Net cash (used for) provided by financing activities	(488.9)	419.4	(63.3)
Changes in Cash and Cash Equivalents	Net increase (decrease) in cash and cash equivalents	433.0	4.1	(129.0)
	Cash and cash equivalents at beginning of year	16.9	12.8	141.8
	Cash and cash equivalents at end of year	$ 449.9	$ 16.9	$ 12.8

The accompanying Summary of Major Accounting Policies and the Notes to Consolidated Financial Statements are integral parts of these statements.

Summary of Major Accounting Policies

Description of Business
The company is principally in the retail drugstore business and its operations are within one reportable segment. Stores are located in 43 states and Puerto Rico. At August 31, 2002, there were 3,880 retail drugstores and 3 mail service facilities. Prescription sales were 59.8% of total sales for fiscal 2002 compared to 57.5% in 2001 and 55.2% in 2000.

Basis of Presentation
The consolidated statements include the accounts of the company and its subsidiaries. All significant intercompany transactions have been eliminated. The consolidated financial statements are prepared in accordance with accounting principles generally accepted in the United States of America and include amounts based on management's prudent judgments and estimates. While actual results may differ from these estimates, management does not expect the differences, if any, to have a material effect on the consolidated financial statements.

Cash and Cash Equivalents
Cash and cash equivalents include cash on hand and all highly liquid investments with an original maturity of three months or less. The company's cash management policy provides for the bank disbursement accounts to be reimbursed on a daily basis. Checks issued but not presented to the banks for payment of $317 million and $233 million at August 31, 2002 and 2001, respectively, are included in cash and cash equivalents as reductions of other cash balances.

Financial Instruments
The company had approximately $37 million and $53 million of outstanding letters of credit at August 31, 2002 and 2001, respectively, which guaranteed foreign trade purchases. Additional outstanding letters of credit of $84 million and $71 million at August 31, 2002 and 2001, respectively, guaranteed payments of casualty claims. The casualty claim letters of credit are annually renewable and will remain in place until the casualty claims are paid in full. The company pays a nominal facility fee to the financing bank to keep this line of credit facility active. The company also had purchase commitments of approximately $70 million and $162 million at August 31, 2002 and 2001, respectively, related to the purchase of store locations. There were no investments in derivative financial instruments during fiscal 2002 and 2001.

Inventories
Inventories are valued on a lower of last-in, first-out (LIFO) cost or market basis. At August 31, 2002 and 2001, inventories would have been greater by $693.5 million and $637.6 million, respectively, if they had been valued on a lower of first-in, first-out (FIFO) cost or market basis. Included in inventory are product cost and in-bound freight. Cost of sales is primarily derived based upon point-of-sale scanning information with an estimate for shrinkage and adjusted based on periodic inventories. At August 31, 2001 and 2000, the company experienced lower inventory levels in certain LIFO pools compared with the previous year-end inventory levels which caused a liquidation of LIFO inventories which were carried at lower costs prevailing in prior years. The effect of this liquidation was a reduction in cost of sales of $4.2 million in fiscal 2001 and $3.1 million in fiscal 2000.

Vendor Allowances
The company receives vendor allowances principally as a result of meeting defined purchase levels or promoting vendors' products. Those received as a result of purchase levels are accrued as a reduction of merchandise purchase price over the incentive period and result in a reduction of cost of sales. Those received for promoting vendors' products are offset against advertising expense and result in a reduction of selling, occupancy and administration expense.

Property and Equipment
Depreciation is provided on a straight-line basis over the estimated useful lives of owned assets. Leasehold improvements and leased properties under capital leases are amortized over the estimated physical life of the property or over the term of the lease, whichever is shorter. Estimated useful lives range from 12½ to 39 years for land improvements, buildings and building improvements and 5 to 12½ years for equipment. Major repairs, which extend the useful life of an asset, are capitalized in the property and equipment accounts. Routine maintenance and repairs are charged against earnings. The composite method of depreciation is used for equipment; therefore, gains and losses on retirement or other disposition of such assets are included in earnings only when an operating location is closed, completely remodeled or impaired. Fully depreciated property and equipment are removed from the cost and related accumulated depreciation and amortization accounts.

Property and equipment consists of *(In Millions)*:

	2002	2001
Land and land improvements		
Owned stores	**$1,080.4**	$1,109.2
Distribution centers	**57.8**	38.7
Other locations	**9.3**	18.6
Buildings and building improvements		
Owned stores	**1,185.9**	1,156.6
Leased stores (leasehold improvements only)	**425.6**	411.1
Distribution centers	**364.9**	309.1
Other locations	**58.2**	70.6
Equipment		
Stores	**1,609.6**	1,440.3
Distribution centers	**499.4**	350.2
Other locations	**464.9**	462.7
Capitalized system development costs	**144.1**	117.4
Capital lease properties	**17.8**	18.8
	5,917.9	5,503.3
Less: accumulated depreciation and amortization	**1,326.5**	1,158.0
	$4,591.4	$4,345.3

The company capitalizes application stage development costs for significant internally developed software projects, including "SIMS Plus," an inventory management system, and "Basic Department Management," a marketing system. These costs are amortized over a five-year period. Amortization of these costs was $19.5 million in 2002, $17.3 million in 2001 and $13.1 million in 2000. Unamortized costs as of August 31, 2002 and 2001, were $73.2 million and $66.1 million, respectively.

Revenue Recognition
For all sales other than third party pharmacy sales, the company recognizes revenue at the time of the sale. For third party sales, revenue is recognized at the time the prescription is filled, adjusted by an estimate for those that will be unclaimed by customers. Customer returns are immaterial.

Impaired Assets and Liabilities for Store Closings
The company tests long-lived assets for impairment whenever events or circumstances indicate. Store locations that have been open at least five years are periodically reviewed for impairment indicators. Once identified, the amount of the impairment is computed by comparing the carrying value of the assets to the fair value, which is based on the discounted estimated future cash flows. Included in selling, occupancy and administration expense were impairment charges of $8.4 million in 2002, $9.7 million in 2001, and $15.1 million in 2000.

Summary of Major Accounting Policies
(continued)

During the fourth quarter of fiscal 2002, the company implemented SFAS No. 146, "Accounting for Costs Associated with Exit or Disposal Activities." Since implementation, the present value of expected future lease costs are charged against earnings when the location is closed. Prior to this, the liability was recognized at the time management made the decision to relocate or close the store.

Insurance
The company obtains insurance coverage for catastrophic exposures as well as those risks required to be insured by law. It is the company's policy to retain a significant portion of certain losses related to worker's compensation, property losses, business interruptions relating from such losses and comprehensive general, pharmacist and vehicle liability. Provisions for these losses are recorded based upon the company's estimates for claims incurred. The provisions are estimated in part by considering historical claims experience, demographic factors and other actuarial assumptions.

Pre-Opening Expenses
Non-capital expenditures incurred prior to the opening of a new or remodeled store are charged against earnings as incurred.

Advertising Costs
Advertising costs, which are reduced by the portion funded by vendors, are expensed as incurred. Net advertising expenses which are included in selling, occupancy and administration expense were $64.5 million in 2002, $54.1 million in 2001 and $76.7 million in 2000.

Stock-Based Compensation Plans
As permitted by SFAS No. 123, the company applies Accounting Principles Board (APB) Opinion No. 25 and related interpretations in accounting for its plans. Under APB 25, compensation expense is recognized for stock option grants if the exercise price is below the fair value of the underlying stock at the date of grant. The company complies with the disclosure provisions of SFAS No. 123, which requires presentation of pro forma information applying the fair-value based method of accounting.

Income Taxes
The company provides for federal and state income taxes on items included in the Consolidated Statements of Earnings regardless of the period when such taxes are payable. Deferred taxes are recognized for temporary differences between financial and income tax reporting based on enacted tax laws and rates.

Earnings Per Share
In fiscal year 2002 and 2001, the diluted earnings per share calculation excluded certain stock options, because the options' exercise price was greater than the average market price of the common shares for the year. If they were included, anti-dilution would have resulted. At August 31, 2002 and August 31, 2001, options to purchase 3,186,227 and 3,316,906 common shares granted at a price ranging from $35.90 to $45.625 and $36.875 to $45.625 per share were excluded from the fiscal year 2002 and 2001 calculations, respectively.

Notes to Consolidated Financial Statements

Interest Expense
The company capitalized $8.5 million, $15.6 million and $4.0 million of interest expense as part of significant construction projects during fiscal 2002, 2001 and 2000, respectively. Interest paid, net of amounts capitalized, was $.3 million in 2002, $3.4 million in 2001 and $.2 million in 2000.

Other Income
In fiscal 2002, 2001 and 2000, the company received partial payments of the brand name prescription drug antitrust litigation settlement for pre-tax income of $6.2 million ($.004 per share), $22.1 million ($.01 per share) and $33.5 million ($.02 per share), respectively. These payments, which are now concluded, were a result of a pharmacy class action against drug manufacturers, which resulted in a $700 million settlement for all recipients.

Leases
Although some locations are owned, the company generally operates in leased premises. Original non-cancelable lease terms typically are 20-25 years and may contain escalation clauses, along with options that permit renewals for additional periods. The total amount of the minimum rent is expensed on a straight-line basis over the term of the lease. In addition to minimum fixed rentals, most leases provide for contingent rentals based upon sales.

Minimum rental commitments at August 31, 2002, under all leases having an initial or remaining non-cancelable term of more than one year are shown below (In Millions):

2003	$ 897.9
2004	943.3
2005	933.4
2006	914.0
2007	895.0
Later	10,659.2
Total minimum lease payments	$15,242.8

The above minimum lease payments include minimum rental commitments related to capital leases amounting to $10.7 million at August 31, 2002. Total minimum lease payments have not been reduced by minimum sublease rentals of approximately $49.1 million on leases due in the future under non-cancelable subleases.

During fiscal 2002, the company entered into two sale-leaseback transactions. The properties were sold at net book value and resulted in proceeds of $302 million. The related leases are accounted for as operating leases.

Rental expense was as follows (In Millions):

	2002	2001	2000
Minimum rentals	**$873.0**	$730.1	$605.7
Contingent rentals	**23.6**	26.2	31.4
Less: Sublease rental income	**(11.1)**	(10.4)	(7.6)
	$885.5	$745.9	$629.5

Notes to Consolidated Financial Statements
(continued)

Income Taxes

The provision for income taxes consists of the following *(In Millions)*:

	2002	2001	2000
Current provision –			
Federal	**$510.2**	$417.1	$400.9
State	**85.0**	73.1	64.5
	595.2	490.2	465.4
Deferred provision –			
Federal	**24.0**	47.1	17.7
State	**(1.1)**	(.2)	3.3
	22.9	46.9	21.0
	$618.1	$537.1	$486.4

The deferred tax assets and liabilities included in the Consolidated Balance Sheets consist of the following *(In Millions)*:

	2002	2001
Deferred tax assets –		
Employee benefit plans	**$106.2**	$146.3
Accrued rent	**56.5**	52.7
Insurance	**82.7**	68.3
Inventory	**35.6**	28.1
Other	**95.3**	39.0
	376.3	334.4
Deferred tax liabilities –		
Accelerated depreciation	**401.9**	341.7
Inventory	**98.9**	92.9
Other	**14.7**	16.1
	515.5	450.7
Net deferred tax liabilities	**$139.2**	$116.3

Income taxes paid were $528.0 million, $432.1 million and $398.4 million during the fiscal years ended August 31, 2002, 2001 and 2000, respectively. The difference between the statutory income tax rate and the effective tax rate is principally due to state income tax provisions.

Short-Term Borrowings

The company obtained funds through the placement of commercial paper, as follows *(Dollars in Millions)*:

	2002	2001	2000
Average outstanding during the year	**$250.2**	$304.9	$14.0
Largest month-end balance	**689.0**	461.2	98.0
	(Nov)	(Nov)	(Nov)
Weighted-average interest rate	**2.3%**	5.2%	5.9%

At August 31, 2002, the company had a syndicated bank line of credit facility of $600 million to support the company's short-term commercial paper program. On July 2, 2002, the company deregistered the remaining $100 million of unissued authorized debt securities, previously filed with the Securities and Exchange Commission.

Contingencies

The company is involved in various legal proceedings incidental to the normal course of business. Company management is of the opinion, based upon the advice of General Counsel, that although the outcome of such litigation cannot be forecast with certainty, the final disposition should not have a material adverse effect on the company's consolidated financial position or results of operations.

Capital Stock

The company's common stock is subject to a Rights Agreement under which each share has attached to it a Right to purchase one one-hundredth of a share of a new series of Preferred Stock, at a price of $37.50 per Right. In the event an entity acquires or attempts to acquire 15% of the then outstanding shares, each Right, except those of an acquiring entity, would entitle the holder to purchase a number of shares of common stock pursuant to a formula contained in the Agreement. These non-voting Rights will expire on August 21, 2006, but may be redeemed at a price of $.0025 per Right at any time prior to a public announcement that the above event has occurred.

As of August 31, 2002, 102,738,392 shares of common stock were reserved for future stock issuances under the company's various employee benefit plans. Preferred stock of 10,249,083 shares has been reserved for issuance upon the exercise of Preferred Share Purchase Rights.

Stock Compensation Plans

The Walgreen Co. Executive Stock Option Plan provides to key employees the granting of options to purchase company common stock over a 10-year period, at a price not less than the fair market value on the date of the grant. Under this Plan, options may be granted until October 9, 2006, for an aggregate of 38,400,000 shares of common stock of the company. Compensation expense related to the plan was less than $1 million in fiscal 2002, $1.4 million in fiscal 2001 and less than $1 million in fiscal 2000. The options granted during fiscal 2002, 2001 and 2000 have a minimum three-year holding period.

The Walgreen Co. Stock Purchase/Option Plan (Share Walgreens) provides for the granting of options to purchase company common stock over a period of 10 years to eligible employees upon the purchase of company shares subject to certain restrictions. Under the terms of the Plan, the option price cannot be less than 85% of the fair market value at the date of grant. Compensation expense related to the Plan was $10.9 million in fiscal 2002, $9.6 million in fiscal 2001 and less than $1 million in fiscal 2000. Options may be granted under this Plan until September 30, 2012, for an aggregate of 42,000,000 shares of common stock of the company. The options granted during fiscal 2002, 2001 and 2000 have a two-year holding period.

The Walgreen Co. Restricted Performance Share Plan provides for the granting of up to 32,000,000 shares of common stock to certain key employees, subject to restrictions as to continuous employment except in the case of death, normal retirement or total and permanent disability. Restrictions generally lapse over a four-year period from the date of grant. Compensation expense is recognized in the year of grant. Compensation expense related to the Plan was $5.4 million in fiscal 2002, $3.6 million in fiscal 2001 and $5.1 million in fiscal 2000. The number of shares granted was 81,416 in 2002, 61,136 in 2001 and 84,746 in 2000.

Under the Walgreen Co. 1982 Employees Stock Purchase Plan, eligible employees may purchase company stock at 90% of the fair market value at the date of purchase. Employees may purchase shares through cash purchases, loans or payroll deductions up to certain limits. The aggregate number of shares for which all participants have the right to purchase under this Plan is 64,000,000.

On May 11, 2000, substantially all employees, in conjunction with opening the company's 3,000th store, were granted a stock option award to purchase from 75 to 500 shares, based on years of service. The stock option award, issued at fair market value on the date of the grant, represents a total of 14,859,275 shares of Walgreen Co. common stock. The options vest after three years and are exercisable up to 10 years after the grant date.

The Walgreen Co. Broad Based Employee Stock Option Plan provides for the granting of options to eligible employees to purchase common stock over a 10-year period, at a price not less than the fair market value on the date of the grant, in connection with the achievement of store opening milestones. Options may be granted for an aggregate of 15,000,000 shares of company common stock until all options have either been exercised or have expired. There is a holding period of three years for options granted under this plan.

Notes to Consolidated Financial Statements
(continued)

A summary of information relative to the company's stock option plans follows:

	Options Outstanding		Options Exercisable	
	Shares	Weighted-Average Exercise Price	Shares	Weighted-Average Exercise Price
August 31, 1999	28,479,238	$ 7.89		
Granted	17,040,383	28.43		
Exercised	(5,055,842)	5.59		
Canceled/Forfeited	(1,086,118)	27.39		
August 31, 2000	39,377,661	$16.55	19,267,211	$6.45
Granted	5,354,388	36.68		
Exercised	(5,532,895)	5.75		
Canceled/Forfeited	(2,943,030)	28.02		
August 31, 2001	36,256,124	$20.24	14,824,227	$7.40
Granted	2,886,365	34.05		
Exercised	(3,525,955)	7.28		
Canceled/Forfeited	(1,315,499)	30.32		
August 31, 2002	34,301,035	$22.35	13,786,657	$9.71

Net options granted as a percentage of outstanding shares at fiscal year-end were 0.2% in fiscal 2002, 0.2% in fiscal 2001 and 1.6% in fiscal 2000.

The following table summarizes information concerning currently outstanding and exercisable options:

	Options Outstanding			Options Exercisable	
Range of Exercise Prices	Number Outstanding at 8/31/02	Weighted-Average Remaining Contractual Life	Weighted-Average Exercise Price	Number Exercisable at 8/31/02	Weighted-Average Exercise Price
$ 4 to 14	11,511,707	3.13 yrs.	$ 7.64	11,511,707	$ 7.64
15 to 30	14,869,487	7.31	26.65	2,212,570	19.81
31 to 46	7,919,841	8.48	35.67	62,380	34.17
$ 4 to 46	34,301,035	6.18 yrs.	$22.35	13,786,657	$ 9.71

The company applies Accounting Principles Board (APB) Opinion No. 25 and related interpretations in accounting for its plans. Accordingly, no compensation expense has been recognized based on the fair value of its grants under these plans. Had compensation costs been determined consistent with the method of SFAS No. 123 for options granted in fiscal 2002, 2001 and 2000, pro forma net earnings and net earnings per common share would have been as follows (In Millions, except per share data):

	2002	2001	2000
Net earnings			
As reported	$1,019.2	$885.6	$776.9
Pro forma	958.7	833.3	754.3
Net earnings per common share – Basic			
As reported	1.00	.87	.77
Pro forma	.94	.82	.75
Net earnings per common share – Diluted			
As reported	.99	.86	.76
Pro forma	.93	.81	.74

The weighted-average fair value and exercise price of options granted for fiscal 2002, 2001 and 2000 were as follows:

	2002	2001	2000
Granted at market price –			
Weighted-average fair value	$13.60	$14.28	$12.17
Weighted-average exercise price	34.40	32.88	28.44
Granted below market price –			
Weighted-average fair value	11.86	20.78	10.56
Weighted-average exercise price	33.21	38.78	24.12

The fair value of each option grant used in the pro forma net earnings and net earnings per share was determined using the Black-Scholes option pricing model with weighted-average assumptions used for grants in fiscal 2002, 2001 and 2000:

	2002	2001	2000
Risk-free interest rate	4.56%	6.16%	6.64%
Average life of option (years)	7	7	7
Volatility	27.58%	25.95%	25.86%
Dividend yield	.22%	.16%	.27%

Retirement Benefits

The principal retirement plan for employees is the Walgreen Profit-Sharing Retirement Trust to which both the company and the employees contribute. The company's contribution, which is determined annually at the discretion of the Board of Directors, has historically related to pre-tax income. The profit-sharing provision was $145.7 million in 2002, $126.6 million in 2001 and $112.4 million in 2000.

The company provides certain health and life insurance benefits for retired employees who meet eligibility requirements, including age and years of service. The costs of these benefits are accrued over the period earned. The company's postretirement health and life benefit plans currently are not funded.

Components of net periodic benefit costs (In Millions):

	2002	2001	2000
Service cost	$ 6.0	$ 4.8	$ 4.7
Interest cost	10.5	8.7	7.7
Amortization of actuarial loss	1.4	.3	—
Amortization of prior service cost	(0.4)	—	—
Total postretirement benefit cost	$17.5	$13.8	$12.4

Change in benefit obligation (In Millions):

	2002	2001
Benefit obligation at September 1	$142.7	$118.6
Service cost	6.0	4.8
Interest cost	10.5	8.7
Amendments	—	(7.1)
Actuarial loss	72.6	23.1
Benefit payments	(6.6)	(6.3)
Participants contributions	1.2	.9
Benefit obligation at August 31	$226.4	$142.7

Notes to Consolidated Financial Statements
(continued)

Change in plan assets *(In Millions)*:

	2002	2001
Plan assets at fair value at September 1	$ —	$ —
Plan participants contributions	1.2	.9
Employer contributions	5.4	5.4
Benefits paid	(6.6)	(6.3)
Plan assets at fair value at August 31	$ —	$ —

Funded status *(In Millions)*:

	2002	2001
Funded status	$(226.4)	$(142.7)
Unrecognized actuarial loss	99.1	27.9
Unrecognized prior service cost	(6.7)	(7.1)
Accrued benefit cost at August 31	$(134.0)	$(121.9)

The discount rate assumptions used to compute the postretirement benefit obligation at year-end were 7.0% for 2002 and 7.5% for 2001.

Future benefit costs were estimated assuming medical costs would increase at a 9% annual rate decreasing to 5.25% over the next seven years and then remaining at a 5.25% annual growth rate thereafter. A one percentage point change in the assumed medical cost trend rate would have the following effects *(In Millions)*:

	1% Increase	1% Decrease
Effect on service and interest cost	$ 4.0	$ (3.0)
Effect on postretirement obligation	49.0	(37.8)

Supplementary Financial Information

Included in the Consolidated Balance Sheets captions are the following assets and liabilities *(In Millions)*:

	2002	2001
Accounts receivable –		
Accounts receivable	$ 974.9	$819.2
Allowances for doubtful accounts	(20.1)	(20.9)
	$ 954.8	$798.3
Accrued expenses and other liabilities –		
Accrued salaries	$ 323.8	$272.7
Taxes other than income taxes	179.9	155.5
Profit sharing	143.3	122.1
Other	370.9	387.2
	$1,017.9	$937.5

Summary of Quarterly Results *(Unaudited)*
(Dollars in Millions, except per share data)

		Quarter Ended				
		November	February	May	August	Fiscal Year
Fiscal 2002	Net sales	$6,559.4	$7,488.5	$7,397.9	$7,235.3	$28,681.1
	Gross profit	1,697.9	2,033.9	1,937.2	1,936.0	7,605.0
	Net earnings	185.9	326.6	259.0	247.7	1,019.2
	Per Common Share – Basic	$ .18	$ .32	$ .25	$ .25	$ 1.00
	Diluted	.18	.32	.25	.24	.99
Fiscal 2001	Net sales	$5,614.2	$6,429.0	$6,296.2	$6,283.6	$24,623.0
	Gross profit	1,488.1	1,770.8	1,651.6	1,663.6	6,574.1
	Net earnings	158.4	296.9	213.4	216.9	885.6
	Per Common Share – Basic	$ .16	$ .29	$ .21	$ .21	$ .87
	Diluted	.15	.29	.21	.21	.86

Comments on Quarterly Results: In further explanation of and supplemental to the quarterly results, the 2002 fourth quarter LIFO adjustment was a credit of $9.9 million compared to a 2001 charge of $2.8 million. If the 2002 interim results were adjusted to reflect the actual inventory inflation rates and inventory levels as computed at August 31, 2002, earnings per share would have increased in the first quarter by $.01 and decreased in the fourth quarter by $.01. Similar adjustments in 2001 would have increased earnings per share in the second quarter by $.01 and decreased earnings per share in the fourth quarter by $.01.

The quarter ended November 30, 2001, includes the pre-tax income of $5.5 million (less than $.01 per share) from the partial payment of the brand name prescription drugs antitrust litigation settlement. The quarter ended August 31, 2002, includes the pre-tax income of $.7 million (less than $.01 per share). The quarter ended February 28, 2001, includes the pre-tax income of $22.1 million ($.01 per share) from the second partial payment.

Common Stock Prices
Below is the New York Stock Exchange high and low sales price for each quarter of fiscal 2002 and 2001.

		Quarter Ended				
		November	February	May	August	Fiscal Year
Fiscal 2002	High	$36.00	$40.70	$40.29	$39.49	$40.70
	Low	28.70	30.72	36.10	30.20	28.70
Fiscal 2001	High	$45.75	$45.00	$45.29	$42.40	$45.75
	Low	32.75	35.38	37.13	31.00	31.00

Reports of Independent Public Accountants

To the Board of Directors and Shareholders of Walgreen Co.:

We have audited the accompanying consolidated balance sheet of Walgreen Co. and subsidiaries (the "Company") as of August 31, 2002, and the related consolidated statements of earnings, shareholders' equity, and cash flows for the year then ended. These consolidated financial statements are the responsibility of the Company's management. Our responsibility is to express an opinion on these consolidated financial statements based on our audit. The consolidated financial statements of the Company for the years ended August 31, 2001 and 2000 were audited by other auditors who have ceased operations. Those auditors expressed in their report dated September 28, 2001 an unqualified opinion on those statements.

We conducted our audit in accordance with auditing standards generally accepted in the United States of America. Those standards require that we plan and perform the audit to obtain reasonable assurance about whether the consolidated financial statements are free of material misstatement. An audit includes examining, on a test basis, evidence supporting the amounts and disclosures in the financial statements. An audit also includes assessing the accounting principles used and significant estimates made by management, as well as evaluating the overall financial statement presentation. We believe that our audit provides a reasonable basis for our opinion.

In our opinion, such consolidated financial statements present fairly, in all material respects, the financial position of Walgreen Co. and subsidiaries as of August 31, 2002, and the results of their operations and their cash flows for the year then ended, in conformity with accounting principles generally accepted in the United States of America.

Deloitte & Touche LLP
Chicago, Illinois
September 27, 2002

To the Board of Directors and Shareholders of Walgreen Co.:

We have audited the accompanying consolidated balance sheets of Walgreen Co. (an Illinois corporation) and Subsidiaries as of August 31, 2001 and 2000, and the related consolidated statements of earnings, shareholders' equity and cash flows for each of the three years in the period ended August 31, 2001. These financial statements are the responsibility of the company's management. Our responsibility is to express an opinion on these financial statements based on our audits.

We conducted our audits in accordance with auditing standards generally accepted in the United States. Those standards require that we plan and perform the audit to obtain reasonable assurance about whether the financial statements are free of material misstatement. An audit includes examining, on a test basis, evidence supporting the amounts and disclosures in the financial statements. An audit also includes assessing the accounting principles used and significant estimates made by management, as well as evaluating the overall financial statement presentation. We believe that our audits provide a reasonable basis for our opinion.

In our opinion, the financial statements referred to above present fairly, in all material respects, the financial position of Walgreen Co. and Subsidiaries as of August 31, 2001 and 2000 and the results of their operations and their cash flows for each of the three years in the period ended August 31, 2001 in conformity with accounting principles generally accepted in the United States.

Arthur Andersen LLP (1)
Chicago, Illinois
September 28, 2001

(1) This report is a copy of the previously issued report covering fiscal years 2001 and 2000. The predecessor auditor has not reissued their report.

Management's Report

The primary responsibility for the integrity and objectivity of the consolidated financial statements and related financial data rests with the management of Walgreen Co. The financial statements were prepared in conformity with accounting principles generally accepted in the United States of America appropriate in the circumstances and included amounts that were based on management's most prudent judgments and estimates relating to matters not concluded by fiscal year-end. Management believes that all material uncertainties have been either appropriately accounted for or disclosed. All other financial information included in this annual report is consistent with the financial statements.

The firm of Deloitte & Touche LLP, independent public accountants, was engaged to render a professional opinion on Walgreen Co.'s consolidated financial statements as of August 31, 2002. Their report contains an opinion based on their audit, which was made in accordance with auditing standards generally accepted in the United States of America and procedures, which they believed were sufficient to provide reasonable assurance that the consolidated financial statements, considered in their entirety, are not misleading and do not contain material errors. The financial statements for the years ended August 31, 2001 and 2000 were audited by other auditors whose report expressed an unqualified opinion on those statements.

Four outside members of the Board of Directors constitute the company's Audit Committee, which meets at least quarterly and is responsible for reviewing and monitoring the company's financial and accounting practices. Deloitte & Touche LLP and the company's General Auditor meet alone with the Audit Committee, which also meets with the company's management to discuss financial matters, auditing and internal accounting controls.

The company's systems are designed to provide an effective system of internal accounting controls to obtain reasonable assurance at reasonable cost that assets are safeguarded from material loss or unauthorized use and transactions are executed in accordance with management's authorization and properly recorded. To this end, management maintains an internal control environment which is shaped by established operating policies and procedures, an appropriate division of responsibility at all organizational levels, and a corporate ethics policy which is monitored annually. The company also has an Internal Control Evaluation Committee, composed primarily of senior management from the Accounting and Auditing Departments, which oversees the evaluation of internal controls on a company-wide basis. Management believes it has appropriately responded to the internal auditors' and independent public accountants' recommendations concerning the company's internal control system.

David W. Bernauer
President
and Chief Executive Officer

William M. Rudolphsen
Controller
and Chief Accounting Officer

Roger L. Polark
Senior Vice President
and Chief Financial Officer

Board of Directors
As of November 18, 2002

Directors

L. Daniel Jorndt*
Chairman
Elected 1990

David W. Bernauer*
President and
Chief Executive Officer
Elected 1999

William C. Foote
Chairman of the Board,
Chief Executive Officer
and President
USG Corporation
Elected 1997

James J. Howard
Chairman Emeritus
Xcel Energy, Inc.
Elected 1986

Alan G. McNally
Chairman
Harris Bankcorp Inc.
Elected 1999

Cordell Reed
Former Senior Vice President
Commonwealth Edison Co.
Elected 1994

David Y. Schwartz
Former Partner
Arthur Andersen LLP
Elected 2000

John B. Schwemm
Former Chairman and
Chief Executive Officer
R.R. Donnelley & Sons Co.
Elected 1985

Marilou M. von Ferstel
Former Executive Vice President
and General Manager
Ogilvy Adams & Rinehart
Elected 1987

Charles R. Walgreen III
Chairman Emeritus
Elected 1963

* L. Daniel Jorndt will retire in January 2003. David W. Bernauer will become chairman and chief executive officer. Jeffrey A. Rein will become president and chief operating officer. George J. Riedl will become senior vice president–Marketing.

Committees

Audit Committee
John B. Schwemm,
 Chairman
William C. Foote
David Y. Schwartz
Marilou M. von Ferstel

Compensation Committee
Cordell Reed,
 Chairman
James J. Howard
John B. Schwemm

Finance Committee
David Y. Schwartz,
 Chairman
David W. Bernauer
L. Daniel Jorndt
Alan G. McNally
Cordell Reed
Charles R. Walgreen III

Nominating and Governance Committee
William C. Foote,
 Chairman
James J. Howard
Alan G. McNally
John B. Schwemm
Marilou M. von Ferstel

Officers
As of November 18, 2002

Corporate

Chairman
L. Daniel Jorndt*

President
David W. Bernauer*
 Chief Executive Officer

Executive Vice Presidents
Jerome B. Karlin
 Store Operations
Jeffrey A. Rein*
 Marketing

Senior Vice Presidents
R. Bruce Bryant
 Western Store Operations
George C. Eilers
 Eastern Store Operations
J. Randolph Lewis
 Distribution & Logistics
Julian A. Oettinger
 General Counsel and
 Corporate Secretary
Roger L. Polark
 Chief Financial Officer
William A. Shiel
 Facilities Development
Trent E. Taylor
 Chief Information Officer
Mark A. Wagner
 Central Store Operations

Vice Presidents
John W. Gleeson
 Corporate Strategy and Treasurer
Dana I. Green
 Human Resources
Dennis R. O'Dell
 Health Services
Gregory D. Wasson
 President
 Walgreens Health Initiatives

Operational and Divisional

Store Operations Vice Presidents
James F. Cnota
Kermit R. Crawford
George C. Eilers Jr.
Debra M. Ferguson
John J. Foley
David L. Gloudemans
John W. Grant
Frank C. Grilli
William M. Handal
Patrick E. Hanifen
Barry L. Markl
Richard Robinson
Michael D. Tovian
Kevin P. Walgreen
Christine D. Whelan
Bruce C. Zarkowsky
Barry W. Zins

Divisional Vice Presidents
Thomas L. Bergseth
 Facilities Planning and Design
Donald A. Churchill
 Construction and Facilities
Thomas J. Connolly
 Real Estate
Robert M. Kral
 Operations/Merchandising Development
Laurie L. Meyer
 Corporate Communications
Allan M. Resnick
 Law
George J. Riedl*
 Purchasing
Robert E. Rogan
 Distribution Centers
Jerry A. Rubin
 Real Estate
William M. Rudolphsen
 Controller
James M. Schultz
 Performance Development
Craig M. Sinclair
 Advertising
Patrick W. Tupa
 Real Estate
Terry R. Watkins
 Distribution Centers
Kenneth R. Weigand
 Employee Relations
Denise K. Wong
 Supply Chain Systems
Chester G. Young
 General Auditor
Robert G. Zimmerman
 Vice President – Administration
 Walgreens Health Initiatives

2

Chapter 2 continues the exploration of accounting measurement by focusing on the problems of recognition, valuation, and classification and how they are solved in the measuring and recording of business transactions.

Measuring Business Transactions

LEARNING OBJECTIVES

LO1 Explain, in simple terms, the generally accepted ways of solving the measurement issues of recognition, valuation, and classification.

LO2 Describe the chart of accounts and recognize commonly used accounts.

LO3 Define *double-entry system* and state the rules for double entry.

LO4 Apply the steps for transaction analysis and processing to simple transactions.

LO5 Prepare a trial balance and describe its value and limitations.

SUPPLEMENTAL OBJECTIVE

SO6 Record transactions in the general journal and post transactions from the general journal to the ledger.

DECISION POINT A USER'S FOCUS

Continental Airlines, Inc. <www.continental.com> **& The Boeing Co.** <www.boeing.com>   In October 2000, Continental Airlines, Inc., announced that it had ordered 15 Boeing 757-300 jetliners.[1] The $1.2 billion order was part of an exclusive agreement Boeing negotiated with Continental. This exclusive 20-year agreement to purchase only Boeing aircraft was Boeing's fourth such agreement with a major airline and positioned the company favorably against Airbus, its European competitor. How should this important order have been recorded, if at all, in the records of Continental and Boeing? When should the purchase and sale that result from this order be recorded in the companies' records?

The order obviously was an important event, one with long-term consequences for both companies. But, as you will see in this chapter, it was not recorded in the accounting records of either company. At the time the order was placed, the aircraft were yet to be manufactured, and the first of them would not be delivered for several years. Even for "firm" orders, Boeing has cautioned that "an economic downturn could result in airline equipment requirements less than currently anticipated resulting in requests to negotiate the rescheduling or possible cancellation of firm orders."[2] The aircraft were not assets of Continental, and the company had not incurred a liability. No aircraft had been delivered or even built, so Continental was not obligated to pay at that point. And Boeing could not record any revenue until it manufactured and delivered the aircraft to Continental, and title to them shifted from Boeing to Continental.

When does Continental record the purchase of a new aircraft it orders from Boeing? When does Boeing record the revenue from the sale?

In fact, Boeing later experienced cancellation or extension of large, previously firm orders because of the economic slowdown in Asia, and also because of the 9-11 attacks and the war in Iraq.[3]

To understand and effectively use financial statements, it is important to know how to analyze events in order to determine the extent of their impact on those statements.

MEASUREMENT ISSUES

LO1 Explain, in simple terms, the generally accepted ways of solving the measurement issues of recognition, valuation, and classification.

RELATED TEXT ASSIGNMENTS
Q: 1, 2, 3, 4, 5
SE: 1, 2
E: 1, 2
P: 3, 4, 7
SD: 1, 2, 3
FRA: 4, 5

Business transactions are economic events that affect the financial position of a business entity. To measure a business transaction, the accountant must decide when the transaction occurred (the recognition issue), what value to place on the transaction (the valuation issue), and how the components of the transaction should be categorized (the classification issue).

These three issues—recognition, valuation, and classification—underlie almost every major decision in financial accounting today. They lie at the heart of accounting for pension plans, for mergers of giant companies, and for international transactions. In discussing the three basic issues, we follow generally accepted accounting principles and use an approach that promotes an understanding of the basic ideas of accounting. Keep in mind, however, that controversy does exist, and that solutions to some problems are not as cut-and-dried as they appear.

THE RECOGNITION ISSUE

TERMINOLOGY NOTE: In accounting, *recognize* means to record a transaction or event.

The **recognition** issue refers to the difficulty of deciding when a business transaction should be recorded. Often the facts of a situation are known, but there is disagreement about *when* the event should be recorded. Suppose, for instance, that a company orders, receives, and pays for an office desk. Which of the following actions constitutes a recordable event?

No 1. An employee sends a purchase requisition to the purchasing department.
No 2. The purchasing department sends a purchase order to the supplier.
Yes 3. The supplier ships the desk.
4. The company receives the desk.
5. The company receives the bill from the supplier.
6. The company pays the bill.

KEY POINT: A purchase should not be recognized (recorded) before title is transferred because until that point, the vendor has not fulfilled its contractual obligation and the buyer has no liability.

The answer to this question is important because the date on which a purchase is recorded affects amounts in the financial statements. According to accounting tradition, the transaction is recorded when title to the desk passes from the supplier to the purchaser, creating an obligation to pay. Thus, depending on the details of the shipping agreement, the transaction is recognized (recorded) at the time of either action 3 or action 4. This is the guideline that we generally use in this book. However, in many small businesses that have simple accounting systems, the transaction is not recorded until the bill is received (action 5) or paid (action 6) because these are the implied points of title transfer. The predetermined time at which a transaction should be recorded is the **recognition point**.

The recognition issue is not always easy to resolve. Consider an advertising agency that prepares a major advertising campaign for a client. Employees may work on the campaign several hours a day for a number of weeks. They add value to the plan as they develop it. Should this added value be recognized as the campaign is being produced or at the time it is completed? Normally, the increase in value is recorded at the time the plan is finished and the client is billed for it. However, if a plan is going to take a long period to develop, the agency and the client may agree

FOCUS ON BUSINESS PRACTICE

Accounting Policies: Where Do You Find Them?
As noted in the Decision Point at the beginning of this chapter, Continental Airlines' <www.continental.com> order of jetliners from Boeing <www.boeing.com> was not an event that either company should have recorded as a transaction. But when do companies record such events as sales or purchase transactions? The answer to this question and others about a company's accounting policies may be found in the Summary of Significant Accounting Policies in the company's annual report. For example, under the heading "Sales and Other Operating Expenses," Boeing's Summary of Significant Accounting Policies states that "commercial aircraft sales are recorded as deliveries are made."[4]

that the client will be billed at key points during its development. A transaction is recorded at each billing.

Here are some more examples of the distinction between business events and transactions:

Business Events That Are *Not* Transactions	Business Events That *Are* Transactions
A customer inquires about the availability of a service.	A customer buys a service.
A company orders a product from a supplier.	A company receives a product previously ordered.
A company hires a new employee.	A company pays an employee for work performed.

THE VALUATION ISSUE

ENRICHMENT NOTE: The value of a transaction usually is based on a business document—a canceled check or an invoice. In general, appraisals or other subjective amounts are not recorded.

Valuation is perhaps the most controversial issue in accounting. The **valuation** issue focuses on assigning a monetary value to a business transaction. Generally accepted accounting principles state that the original cost (often called *historical cost*) is the appropriate value to assign to all business transactions—and therefore to all assets, liabilities, and components of stockholders' equity, including revenues and expenses, recorded by a business.

Cost is defined here as the exchange price associated with a business transaction at the point of recognition. According to this guideline, the purpose of accounting is not to account for value in terms of worth, which can change after a transaction occurs, but to account for value in terms of cost at the time of the transaction. For example, the cost of an asset is recorded when the asset is acquired, and the value is held at that level until the asset is sold, expires, or is consumed. In this context, *value* means the cost at the time of the transaction. The practice of recording transactions at cost is referred to as the **cost principle**.

●**STOP AND THINK!**
Which is the most important issue in recording a transaction: recognition, valuation, or classification?

No issue is more important than another. Each must be resolved satisfactorily for a transaction to be recorded correctly.■

Suppose that a person offers a building for sale at $120,000. It may be valued for real estate taxes at $75,000, and it may be insured for $90,000. One prospective buyer may offer $100,000 for the building, and another may offer $105,000. At this point, several different, unverifiable opinions of value have been expressed. Finally, suppose the seller and a buyer settle on a price and complete the sale for $110,000. All these figures are values of one kind or another, but only the last is sufficiently reliable to be used in the records. The market value of the building may vary over the years, but the building will remain on the new buyer's records at $110,000 until it is sold again. At that point, the accountant will record the new transaction at the new exchange price, and a profit or loss will be recognized.

FOCUS ON INTERNATIONAL BUSINESS

No Dollar Amount: How Can That Be?

Determining the valuation of a sale or purchase transaction is often not difficult because it equals the amount of cash, or dollar amount, that changes hands. However, in some areas of the world, valuation is not so easy to determine. In a country where the currency is declining in value and inflation is high, companies often are forced to resort to barter transactions, in which one good or service is traded for another. In Russia, for example, perhaps as many as two-thirds of all transactions are barters. It is not uncommon for Russian companies to end up with piles of goods stacked around their offices and warehouses. In one case, an electric utility company provided a textile-machinery plant with electricity in exchange for wool blankets, which the plant had received in exchange for equipment sold to another company. Determining the value can be difficult in such cases because it becomes a matter of determining the fair value of the goods being traded.[5]

Focus on Business Practice

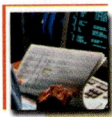

Is It Always Cost?

There are sometimes exceptions to the general rules of accounting. For instance, the cost principle is not followed in all parts of the financial statements. Investments, for example, are often accounted for at fair or market value because these investments are available for sale. The fair or market value is the best measure of the potential benefit to the company. Intel Corp. <www.intel.com>, the large microprocessor company, states in its annual report:

> Investments designated as available-for-sale on the balance sheet date are reported at fair value.[6]

KEY POINT: Assets, liabilities, and the components of stockholders' equity are not accounts, but account *classifications*. For example, Cash is a type of asset account, and Accounts Payable is a type of liability account.

The cost principle is used because the cost is verifiable. It results from the actions of independent buyers and sellers who come to an agreement on price. An exchange price is an objective price that can be verified by evidence created at the time of the transaction. It is this final price, verified by agreement of the two parties, at which the transaction is recorded.

The Classification Issue

The **classification** issue has to do with assigning all the transactions in which a business engages to appropriate categories, or accounts. Classification of debts can affect a company's ability to borrow money. And classification of purchases can affect its income; for example, purchases of tools may be considered repair expenses (a component of stockholders' equity) or equipment (assets).

Proper classification depends not only on correctly analyzing the effect of each transaction on the business, but also on maintaining a system of accounts that reflects that effect. The rest of this chapter explains the classification of accounts and the analysis and recording of transactions.

 Check out ACE for a Review Quiz at http://accounting.college.hmco.com/students.

Accounts and the Chart of Accounts

LO2 Describe the chart of accounts and recognize commonly used accounts.

RELATED TEXT ASSIGNMENTS
Q: 6, 7, 8, 23
SE: 3
E: 3
FRA: 1, 6

Measuring business transactions often involves gathering large amounts of data. These data require a method of storage that allows businesspeople to retrieve transaction data quickly and in usable form—in other words, a filing system that classifies all transactions according to accounts. Recall that accounts are the basic storage units for accounting data and are used to accumulate amounts from similar transactions. An accounting system has a separate account for each asset, each liability, and each component of stockholders' equity, including revenues and expenses. Whether a company keeps records by hand or by computer, management must be able to refer to accounts so that it can study the company's financial history and plan for the future. A very small company may need only a few dozen accounts; a multinational corporation may need thousands.

In a manual accounting system, each account is kept on a separate page or card. These pages or cards are placed together in a book or file called the **general ledger**. In the computerized systems that most companies have today, accounts are maintained on magnetic tapes or disks. However, as a matter of convenience, accountants still refer to the group of company accounts as the *general ledger*, or simply the *ledger*.

KEY POINT: A chart of accounts is a table of contents for the ledger. Typically, it lists accounts in the order they appear in the ledger, which is usually the order in which they appear on the financial statements, and the numbering scheme allows for some flexibility.

To help identify accounts in the ledger and to make them easy to find, the accountant often numbers them. A list of these numbers with the corresponding account names is called a **chart of accounts**. A very simple chart of accounts appears in Exhibit 1. Notice that the first digit refers to the major financial statement classification. An account number that begins with the digit 1 represents an asset, an account number that begins with a 2 represents a liability, and so forth. The second and third digits refer to individual accounts. Also notice the gaps in the sequence of numbers. These gaps allow the accountant to expand the number of accounts.

In this chapter and in the next two, we refer to the accounts listed in Exhibit 1 as we discuss the sample case of the Joan Miller Advertising Agency, Inc.

EXHIBIT 1
Chart of Accounts for a Small Business

Account Number	Account Name	Description
		Assets
111	Cash	Money and any medium of exchange, including coins, currency, checks, postal and express money orders, and money on deposit in a bank
112	Notes Receivable	Amounts due from others in the form of promissory notes (written promises to pay definite sums of money at fixed future dates)
113	Accounts Receivable	Amounts due from others for revenues or sales on credit (sales on account)
115	Art Supplies	Prepaid expense; art supplies purchased and not used
116	Office Supplies	Prepaid expense; office supplies purchased and not used
117	Prepaid Rent	Prepaid expense; rent paid in advance and not used
118	Prepaid Insurance	Prepaid expense; insurance purchased and not expired; unexpired insurance
141	Land	Property owned for use in the business
142	Buildings	Structures owned for use in the business
143	Accumulated Depreciation, Buildings	Sum of the periodic allocation of the cost of buildings to expense
144	Art Equipment	Art equipment owned for use in the business
145	Accumulated Depreciation, Art Equipment	Sum of the periodic allocation of the cost of art equipment to expense
146	Office Equipment	Office equipment owned for use in the business
147	Accumulated Depreciation, Office Equipment	Sum of the periodic allocation of the cost of office equipment to expense
		Liabilities
211	Notes Payable	Amounts due to others in the form of promissory notes
212	Accounts Payable	Amounts due to others for purchases on credit
213	Unearned Art Fees	Unearned revenue; advance deposits for artwork to be provided in the future
214	Wages Payable	Amounts due to employees for wages earned and not paid
215	Income Taxes Payable	Amounts due to government for income taxes owed and not paid
221	Mortgage Payable	Amounts due on loans that are backed by the company's property and buildings
		Stockholders' Equity
311	Common Stock	Stockholders' investments in a corporation for which they receive shares of capital stock
312	Retained Earnings	Stockholders' claims against company assets derived from profitable operations
313	Dividends	Distributions of assets (usually cash) that reduce retained earnings
314	Income Summary	Temporary account used to summarize the revenues and expenses at the end of the accounting period
		Revenues
411	Advertising Fees Earned	Revenues derived from performing advertising services
412	Art Fees Earned	Revenues derived from performing art services

(continued)

Exhibit 1
Chart of Accounts for a Small Business *(continued)*

Account Number	Account Name	Description
		Expenses
511	Wages Expense	Amounts earned by employees
512	Utilities Expense	Amounts of utilities, such as water, electricity, and gas, used
513	Telephone Expense	Amounts of telephone services used
514	Rent Expense	Amounts of rent on property and buildings used
515	Insurance Expense	Amounts for insurance expired
516	Art Supplies Expense	Amounts for art supplies used
517	Office Supplies Expense	Amounts for office supplies used
518	Depreciation Expense, Buildings	Amount of buildings' cost allocated to expense
519	Depreciation Expense, Art Equipment	Amount of art equipment cost allocated to expense
520	Depreciation Expense, Office Equipment	Amount of office equipment cost allocated to expense
521	Income Taxes Expense	Amount of tax on income

● **Stop and Think!**
How would the asset accounts in the chart of accounts for Joan Miller Advertising Agency, Inc., differ if it were a retail company that sold advertising products instead of a service company?

If it were a retail company, it would have an account for inventory. ■

KEY POINT: Although dividends are a component of stockholders' equity, they normally appear only in the statement of retained earnings, not in the stockholders' equity section of the balance sheet. In addition, they do not appear as an expense on the income statement.

STOCKHOLDERS' EQUITY ACCOUNTS

In the chart of accounts shown in Exhibit 1, the revenue and expense accounts are separated from the stockholders' equity accounts. Figure 1 illustrates the relationships of these accounts to each other and to the financial statements. The distinctions among them are important for legal and financial reporting purposes.

First, the stockholders' equity accounts represent legal claims by the stockholders against the assets of the company. Common Stock is a capital stock account (corporations may have more than one type of capital stock) that represents stockholders' claims arising from their investments in the company, and Retained Earnings represents stockholders' claims arising from profitable operations. Both are claims against the general assets of the company, not against specific assets. They do not represent pools of funds that have been set aside. Dividends are included among the stockholders' equity accounts because they are distributions of assets that reduce stockholders' claims on retained earnings and are shown on the statement of retained earnings.

Second, by law, capital investments and dividends must be separated from revenues and expenses for income tax and financial reporting and other purposes.

Third, management needs a detailed breakdown of revenues and expenses for budgeting and operating purposes. From these accounts, which are included on the income statement, management can identify the sources of all revenues and the nature of all expenses. In this way, accounting gives management information about whether it has achieved its primary goal of earning a net income.

ACCOUNT TITLES

Account titles often confuse beginning students because the words are new to them or have technical meanings. Also, different terms may be used for the same type of account. For example, Fixed Assets, Plant and Equipment, Capital Assets, and Long-Lived Assets are all titles for long-term assets. Moreover, even the most acceptable titles change over time, but out of habit, some companies continue to use them.

FIGURE 1
Relationships of Stockholders' Equity Accounts

KEY POINT: Although revenues and expenses are components of stockholders' equity, they appear on the income statement, *not* on the stockholders' equity section of the balance sheet. Figure 1 illustrates this point.

KEY POINT: Account names must be both concise and descriptive. Although some account names, such as Cash and Land, generally are fixed, others are not.

In general, an account title should describe what is recorded in the account. When you come across an account title that you do not recognize, examine the context of the name—whether it is classified as an asset, liability, or stockholders' equity component, including revenue or expense, on the financial statements—and look for the kind of transaction that gave rise to the account.

 Check out ACE for a Review Quiz at http://accounting.college.hmco.com/students.

THE DOUBLE-ENTRY SYSTEM: THE BASIC METHOD OF ACCOUNTING

LO3 Define *double-entry system* and state the rules for double entry.
RELATED TEXT ASSIGNMENTS
Q: 9, 10, 11, 12, 13
SE: 2
FRA: 5

KEY POINT: Each transaction must include at least one debit and one credit, and the debit totals must equal the credit totals.

The double-entry system, the backbone of accounting, evolved during the Renaissance. The first systematic description of double-entry bookkeeping appeared in 1494, two years after Columbus discovered America, in a mathematics book by Fra Luca Pacioli. Goethe, the famous German poet and dramatist, referred to double-entry bookkeeping as "one of the finest discoveries of the human intellect." Werner Sombart, an eminent economist-sociologist, believed that "double-entry bookkeeping is born of the same spirit as the system of Galileo and Newton."

What is the significance of the double-entry system? The system is based on the *principle of duality*, which means that every economic event has two aspects—effort and reward, sacrifice and benefit, source and use—that offset or balance each other. In the **double-entry system**, each transaction must be recorded with at least one debit and one credit, so that the total dollar amount of debits and the total dollar amount of credits equal each other. Because of the way it is designed, the whole system is always in balance. All accounting systems, no matter how sophisticated, are based on the principle of duality.

THE T ACCOUNT

The T account is a good place to begin the study of the double-entry system. In its simplest form, an account has three parts: (1) a **title**, which describes the asset, the

> **KEY POINT:** A T account is simply an abbreviated version of a ledger account. T accounts are used by accountants, instructors, students, and textbooks to quickly analyze a set of transactions; ledger accounts are used in the accounting records.

> **KEY POINT:** Many students have preconceived ideas about what *debit* and *credit* mean. They think that *debit* means "decrease" (or implies something bad) and that *credit* means "increase" (or implies something good). It is important to realize that *debit* simply means "left side" and *credit* simply means "right side."

liability, or the stockholders' equity account; (3) a left side, which is called the **debit** side; and (3) a right side, which is called the **credit** side. This form of an account, called a **T account** because it resembles the letter *T*, is used to analyze transactions. It looks like this:

```
           Title of Account
       ─────────────┬─────────────
           Debit    │    Credit
        (left) side │  (right) side
```

Any entry made on the left side of the account is a debit, or debit entry, and any entry made on the right side of the account is a credit, or credit entry. The terms *debit* (abbreviated Dr., from the Latin *debere*) and *credit* (abbreviated Cr., from the Latin *credere*) are simply the accountant's words for "left" and "right" (not for "increase" or "decrease"). We present a more formal version of the T account, the ledger account form, later in this chapter.

THE T ACCOUNT ILLUSTRATED

As discussed in the chapter on uses of accounting information and the financial statements, Shannon Realty, Inc., had several transactions that involved the receipt or payment of cash. These transactions can be summarized in the Cash account by recording receipts on the left (debit) side of the account and payments on the right (credit) side:

```
                        Cash
        ─────────────────────┬─────────────────────
        (1)    50,000        │ (2)    35,000
        (5)     1,500        │ (4)       200
        (7)     1,000        │ (8)     1,000
                             │ (9)       400
                             │ (11)      600
        ─────────────────────┼─────────────────────
               52,500        │        37,200
        Bal.   15,300        │
```

> **KEY POINT:** Notice that the debits and credits do not act independently. That is, one is netted out against the other to produce the account balance.

The cash receipts on the left total $52,500. (The total is written in small figures so that it cannot be confused with an actual debit entry.) The cash payments on the right side total $37,200. These totals are simply working totals, or **footings**. Footings, which are calculated at the end of each month, are an easy way to determine cash on hand. The difference in dollars between the total debit footing and the total credit footing is called the **balance**, or *account balance*. If the balance is a debit, it is written on the left side. If it is a credit, it is written on the right side. Notice that Shannon Realty's Cash account has a debit balance of $15,300 ($52,500 − $37,200). This is the amount of cash the business has on hand at the end of the month.

ANALYZING AND PROCESSING TRANSACTIONS

The two rules of double-entry bookkeeping are that every transaction affects at least two accounts and that total debits must equal total credits. In other words, for every transaction, one or more accounts must be debited and one or more accounts must be credited, and the total dollar amount of the debits must equal the total dollar amount of the credits.

Look again at the accounting equation:

$$\text{Assets} = \text{Liabilities} + \text{Stockholders' Equity}$$

You can see that if a debit increases assets, then a credit must be used to increase liabilities or stockholders' equity because they are on opposite sides of the equal sign. Likewise, if a credit decreases assets, then a debit must be used to decrease liabilities or stockholders' equity. These rules can be shown as follows:

	Assets		=	Liabilities		+	Stockholders' Equity	
	Debit for increases (+)	Credit for decreases (−)		Debit for decreases (−)	Credit for increases (+)		Debit for decreases (−)	Credit for increases (+)

● **STOP AND THINK!**
How are assets and expenses related, and why are the debit and credit effects for assets and expenses the same?

Assets and expenses are closely related because many assets are expenses that have not yet been used. Examples are prepaid assets and plant and equipment. As a result, debits increase assets and expenses, and credits decrease assets and expenses. They appear on opposite sides of the accounting equation. ■

1. Debit increases in assets to asset accounts. Credit decreases in assets to asset accounts.
2. Credit increases in liabilities and stockholders' equity to liability and stockholders' equity accounts. Debit decreases in liabilities and stockholders' equity to liability and stockholders' equity accounts.

One of the more difficult points to understand is the application of double-entry rules to the stockholders' equity components. The key is to remember that dividends and expenses are deductions from stockholders' equity. Thus, transactions that *increase* dividends or expenses *decrease* stockholders' equity. Consider this expanded version of the accounting equation:

$$\text{Assets} = \text{Liabilities} + \overbrace{\text{Common Stock} + \text{Retained Earnings} - \text{Dividends} + \text{Revenues} - \text{Expenses}}^{\text{Stockholders' Equity}}$$

This equation may be rearranged by shifting dividends and expenses to the left side, as follows:

Assets	+	Dividends	+	Expenses	=	Liabilities	+	Common Stock	+	Retained Earnings	+	Revenues
+ (debits)	− (credits)	+ (debits)	− (credits)	+ (debits)	− (credits)	− (debits)	+ (credits)	− (debits)	+ (credits)	− (debits)	+ (credits)	− (debits)	+ (credits)

Note that the rules for double entry for all the accounts on the left of the equal sign are just the opposite of the rules for all the accounts on the right of the equal sign. Assets, dividends, and expenses are increased by debits and decreased by credits. Liabilities, common stock, retained earnings, and revenues are increased by credits and decreased by debits.

With this basic information about double entry, it is possible to analyze and process transactions by following the five steps illustrated in Figure 2. To show how the steps are applied, assume that on June 1, Koenig Art Supplies borrows $100,000 from its bank on a promissory note. The list that follows describes how this transaction is analyzed and processed.

FIGURE 2
Analyzing and Processing Transactions

1. *Analyze the transaction to determine its effect on assets, liabilities, and stockholders' equity.* In this case, both an asset (Cash) and a liability (Notes Payable) increase. A transaction is usually supported by some kind of **source document**—an invoice, receipt, check, or contract; here, it would be a copy of the signed note.

2. *Apply the rules of double entry.* Increases in assets are recorded by debits. Increases in liabilities are recorded by credits.

3. *Record the entry.* Transactions are recorded in chronological order in a journal. In one form of journal, which is explained in more detail later in this chapter, the date, debit account, and debit amount are recorded on one line and the credit account and credit amount, indented, on the next line, as follows:

A = L + OE
+   +

		Dr.	Cr.
June 1	Cash	100,000	
	Notes Payable		100,000
	Issued note payable for cash		

This form is called **journal form.** An explanation appears right after the entry. If more than one account is debited or credited, more lines are used.

4. *Post the entry.* The entry is posted to the general ledger by transferring the date and amounts to the proper accounts. The T account is one form of ledger account.

Cash	Notes Payable
June 1 100,000	June 1 100,000

In formal records, step **3** is never omitted. However, for purposes of analysis, accountants often bypass step **3** and record entries directly in T accounts because doing so clearly and quickly shows the effects of transactions on the accounts. Some of the assignments in this chapter use the same approach to emphasize the analytical aspects of double entry.

5. *Prepare the trial balance to confirm the balance of the accounts.* Periodically, accountants prepare a trial balance to confirm that the accounts are still in balance after the recording and posting of transactions. Preparation of the trial balance is explained later in this chapter.

 Check out ACE for a Review Quiz at http://accounting.college.hmco.com/students.

TRANSACTION ANALYSIS ILLUSTRATED

LO4 Apply the steps for transaction analysis and processing to simple transactions.

RELATED TEXT ASSIGNMENTS
Q: 14, 15, 16, 20, 24
SE: 5, 6
E: 4, 5, 7, 12
P: 1, 2, 3, 4, 5, 6, 7, 8
SD: 2, 4, 5
FRA: 1, 2, 3, 5, 6

KEY POINT: For this transaction, many students incorrectly credit Stockholders' Equity rather than Common Stock. Stockholders' equity is an account *classification*, not an account title.

In the next few pages, we examine the transactions for Joan Miller Advertising Agency, Inc., during the month of July. In the discussion, we illustrate the principle of duality and show how transactions are recorded in the accounts.

July 1: Joan Miller obtains a charter from the state and invests $20,000 in her own advertising agency in exchange for 20,000 shares of $1 par value common stock.

A = L + OE
+   +

		Dr.	Cr.
July 1	Cash	20,000	
	Common Stock		20,000

Cash
July 1 20,000

Common Stock
July 1 20,000

Transaction: Investment in business.
Analysis: Assets increase. Stockholders' equity increases.
Rules: Increases in assets are recorded by debits. Increases in stockholders' equity are recorded by credits.
Entry: The increase in assets is recorded by a debit to Cash. The increase in stockholders' equity is recorded by a credit to Common Stock.

Analysis: If Joan Miller had invested assets other than cash in the business, the appropriate asset accounts would be debited.

July 2: Rents an office, paying two months' rent, $1,600, in advance.

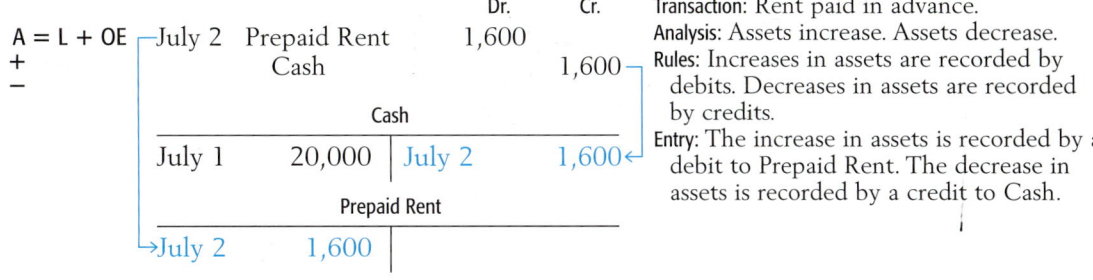

Transaction: Rent paid in advance.
Analysis: Assets increase. Assets decrease.
Rules: Increases in assets are recorded by debits. Decreases in assets are recorded by credits.
Entry: The increase in assets is recorded by a debit to Prepaid Rent. The decrease in assets is recorded by a credit to Cash.

July 3: Purchases art equipment, $4,200, with cash.

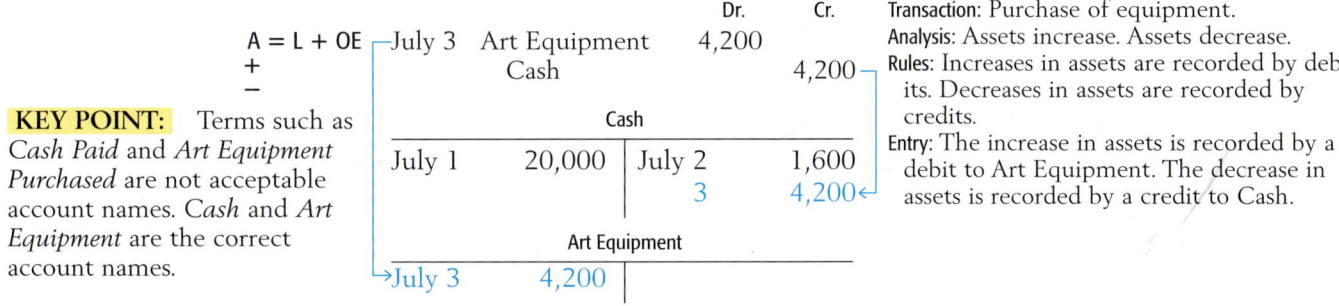

Transaction: Purchase of equipment.
Analysis: Assets increase. Assets decrease.
Rules: Increases in assets are recorded by debits. Decreases in assets are recorded by credits.
Entry: The increase in assets is recorded by a debit to Art Equipment. The decrease in assets is recorded by a credit to Cash.

KEY POINT: Terms such as *Cash Paid* and *Art Equipment Purchased* are not acceptable account names. *Cash* and *Art Equipment* are the correct account names.

July 4: Orders art supplies, $1,800, and office supplies, $800.

Analysis: No entry is made because no transaction has occurred. According to the recognition issue, there is no liability until the supplies are shipped or received and there is an obligation to pay for them.

July 5: Purchases office equipment, $3,000, from Morgan Equipment; pays $1,500 in cash and agrees to pay the rest next month.

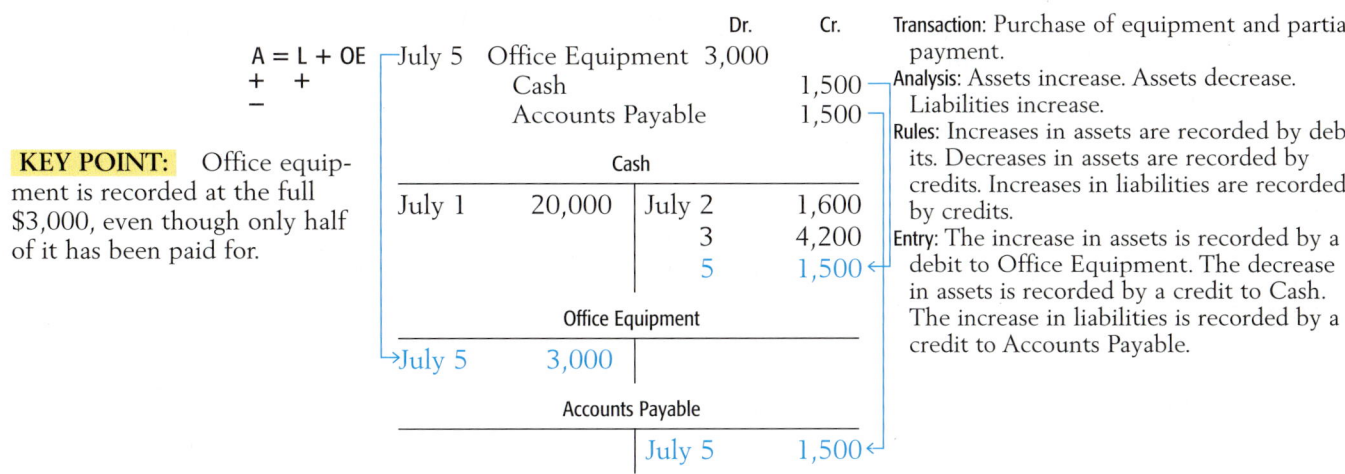

Transaction: Purchase of equipment and partial payment.
Analysis: Assets increase. Assets decrease. Liabilities increase.
Rules: Increases in assets are recorded by debits. Decreases in assets are recorded by credits. Increases in liabilities are recorded by credits.
Entry: The increase in assets is recorded by a debit to Office Equipment. The decrease in assets is recorded by a credit to Cash. The increase in liabilities is recorded by a credit to Accounts Payable.

KEY POINT: Office equipment is recorded at the full $3,000, even though only half of it has been paid for.

FOCUS ON BUSINESS ETHICS

Are Financial Statements Always Truthful?

The accounting concepts related to recognition (when a transaction should be recorded), valuation (what value to place on the transaction), and classification (how the components of the transaction should be categorized) are not only important for good financial reporting; they are also designed to help a company's management fulfill its responsibilities to the owners and the public.

A prime example of this responsibility was recently demonstrated at Lucent Technologies <www.lucent.com>, a major telecommunications equipment manufacturer. After years of excellent results, Lucent surprised its investors by admitting that because of returns of equipment that distributors had been unable to sell, it was going to have to erase $452 million in equipment sales from the $679 million it had reported for the year.

The problem related to how and when Lucent recognizes proceeds from sales. The company's chief executive officer explained that to meet short-term growth targets, "We mortgaged future sales and revenue in a way we are paying for now."[7] In the aftermath, the company's stock dropped from $80 per share to less than $5 per share, and more than 10,000 employees were laid off.

July 6: Purchases art supplies, $1,800, and office supplies, $800, from Taylor Supply Company, on credit.

	Dr.	Cr.
July 6 Art Supplies	1,800	
Office Supplies	800	
Accounts Payable		2,600

A = L + OE
+   +
+

Art Supplies

| July 6 | 1,800 | |

Office Supplies

| July 6 | 800 | |

Accounts Payable

| | | July 5 | 1,500 |
| | | 6 | 2,600 |

KEY POINT: Accounts Payable is used when there is a delay between purchase and payment.

Transaction: Purchase of supplies on credit.
Analysis: Assets increase. Liabilities increase.
Rules: Increases in assets are recorded by debits. Increases in liabilities are recorded by credits.
Entry: The increase in assets is recorded by debits to Art Supplies and Office Supplies. The increase in liabilities is recorded by a credit to Accounts Payable.

July 8: Pays for a one-year life insurance policy, $960, with coverage effective July 1.

Transaction: Insurance purchased in advance.
Analysis: Assets increase. Assets decrease.
Rules: Increases in assets are recorded by debits. Decreases in assets are recorded by credits.
Entry: The increase in assets is recorded by a debit to Prepaid Insurance. The decrease in assets is recorded by a credit to Cash.

July 9: Pays Taylor Supply Company $1,000 of the amount owed.

A = L + OE
−   −

KEY POINT: Accounts Payable, not Art Supplies or Office Supplies, is debited. Also, a liability usually is credited before it can be debited.

	Dr.	Cr.
July 9 Accounts Payable	1,000	
Cash		1,000

Cash

July 1	20,000	July 2	1,600
		3	4,200
		5	1,500
		8	960
		9	1,000

Accounts Payable

July 9	1,000	July 5	1,500
		6	2,600

Transaction: Partial payment on a liability.
Analysis: Assets decrease. Liabilities decrease.
Rules: Decreases in liabilities are recorded by debits. Decreases in assets are recorded by credits.
Entry: The decrease in liabilities is recorded by a debit to Accounts Payable. The decrease in assets is recorded by a credit to Cash.

July 10: Performs a service for an automobile dealer by placing advertisements in a newspaper and collects a fee, $1,400.

A = L + OE
+   +

	Dr.	Cr.
July 10 Cash	1,400	
Advertising Fees Earned		1,400

Cash

July 1	20,000	July 2	1,600
10	1,400	3	4,200
		5	1,500
		8	960
		9	1,000

Advertising Fees Earned

		July 10	1,400

Transaction: Revenue earned and cash collected.
Analysis: Assets increase. Stockholders' equity increases.
Rules: Increases in assets are recorded by debits. Increases in stockholders' equity are recorded by credits.
Entry: The increase in assets is recorded by a debit to Cash. The increase in stockholders' equity is recorded by a credit to Advertising Fees Earned.

July 12: Pays the secretary two weeks' wages, $1,200.

A = L + OE
−   −

	Dr.	Cr.
July 12 Wages Expense	1,200	
Cash		1,200

Cash

July 1	20,000	July 2	1,600
10	1,400	3	4,200
		5	1,500
		8	960
		9	1,000
		12	1,200

Wages Expense

July 12	1,200		

Transaction: Payment of wages expense.
Analysis: Assets decrease. Stockholders' equity decreases.
Rules: Decreases in stockholders' equity are recorded by debits. Decreases in assets are recorded by credits.
Entry: The decrease in stockholders' equity is recorded by a debit to Wages Expense. The decrease in assets is recorded by a credit to Cash.

July 15: Accepts an advance fee, $1,000, for artwork to be done for another agency.

A = L + OE
+   +

	Dr.	Cr.
July 15 Cash	1,000	
Unearned Art Fees		1,000

Cash

July 1	20,000	July 2	1,600
10	1,400	3	4,200
15	1,000	5	1,500
		8	960
		9	1,000
		12	1,200

Unearned Art Fees

		July 15	1,000

Transaction: Payment received for future services.
Analysis: Assets increase. Liabilities increase.
Rules: Increases in assets are recorded by debits. Increases in liabilities are recorded by credits.
Entry: The increase in assets is recorded by a debit to Cash. The increase in liabilities is recorded by a credit to Unearned Art Fees.

●Stop and Think!
In what way are **unearned revenues** the opposite of prepaid expenses?

With unearned revenues (a liability), cash is received *in advance* for a service to be performed later. With prepaid expenses (an asset), cash is *paid* in advance of receiving a service. ■

July 19: Performs a service by placing several major advertisements for Ward Department Stores. The fee, $4,800, is billed now but will be collected next month.

A = L + OE
+   +

	Dr.	Cr.
July 19 Accounts Receivable	4,800	
Advertising Fees Earned		4,800

Accounts Receivable

July 19	4,800		

Advertising Fees Earned

		July 10	1,400
		19	4,800

Transaction: Revenue earned, to be received later.
Analysis: Assets increase. Stockholders' equity increases.
Rules: Increases in assets are recorded by debits. Increases in stockholders' equity are recorded by credits.
Entry: The increase in assets is recorded by a debit to Accounts Receivable. The increase in stockholders' equity is recorded by a credit to Advertising Fees Earned.

KEY POINT: Revenue is recognized even though payment has not been received yet. Accounts Receivable is used when there is a delay between the sale of services or merchandise and payment.

July 26: Pays the secretary two more weeks' wages, $1,200.

A = L + OE
−   −

	Dr.	Cr.
July 26 Wages Expense	1,200	
Cash		1,200

Cash

July 1	20,000	July 2	1,600
10	1,400	3	4,200
15	1,000	5	1,500
		8	960
		9	1,000
		12	1,200
		26	1,200

Wages Expense

July 12	1,200		
26	1,200		

Transaction: Payment of wages expense.
Analysis: Assets decrease. Stockholders' equity decreases.
Rules: Decreases in stockholders' equity are recorded by debits. Decreases in assets are recorded by credits.
Entry: The decrease in stockholders' equity is recorded by a debit to Wages Expense. The decrease in assets is recorded by a credit to Cash.

July 29: Receives and pays the utility bill, $200.

A = L + OE
− −

	Dr.	Cr.
July 29 Utilities Expense	200	
Cash		200

Cash

July 1	20,000	July 2	1,600
10	1,400	3	4,200
15	1,000	5	1,500
		8	960
		9	1,000
		12	1,200
		26	1,200
		29	200

Utilities Expense

| July 29 | 200 | | |

Transaction: Payment of utilities expense.
Analysis: Assets decrease. Stockholders' equity decreases.
Rules: Decreases in stockholders' equity are recorded by debits. Decreases in assets are recorded by credits.
Entry: The decrease in stockholders' equity is recorded by a debit to Utilities Expense. The decrease in assets is recorded by a credit to Cash.

July 30: Receives (but does not pay) the telephone bill, $140.

A = L + OE
    + −

	Dr.	Cr.
July 30 Telephone Expense	140	
Accounts Payable		140

Accounts Payable

July 9	1,000	July 5	1,500
		6	2,600
		30	140

Telephone Expense

| July 30 | 140 | | |

KEY POINT: The expense and liability are recognized at this point, even though payment has not yet been made, because an expense has been incurred. Telephone services have been used, and the obligation to pay exists.

Transaction: Expense incurred, to be paid later.
Analysis: Liabilities increase. Stockholders' equity decreases.
Rules: Decreases in stockholders' equity are recorded by debits. Increases in liabilities are recorded by credits.
Entry: The decrease in stockholders' equity is recorded by a debit to Telephone Expense. The increase in liabilities is recorded by a credit to Accounts Payable.

July 31: Declared and paid a dividend of $1,400.

A = L + OE
− −

	Dr.	Cr.
July 31 Dividends	1,400	
Cash		1,400

Cash

July 1	20,000	July 2	1,600
10	1,400	3	4,200
15	1,000	5	1,500
		8	960
		9	1,000
		12	1,200
		26	1,200
		29	200
		31	1,400

Dividends

| July 31 | 1,400 | | |

KEY POINT: Dividends are not considered expenses. Expenses are costs of operating a business, but dividends are assets distributed to the stockholders of the business.

Transaction: Declaration and payment of dividends.
Analysis: Assets decrease. Stockholders' equity decreases.
Rules: Decreases in stockholders' equity are recorded by debits. Decreases in assets are recorded by credits.
Entry: The decrease in stockholders' equity is recorded by a debit to Dividends. The decrease in assets is recorded by a credit to Cash.

EXHIBIT 2
Summary of Transactions for Joan Miller Advertising Agency, Inc.

Assets	=	Liabilities	+	Stockholders' Equity

Cash

July 1	20,000	July 2	1,600
10	1,400	3	4,200
15	1,000	5	1,500
		8	960
		9	1,000
		12	1,200
		26	1,200
		29	200
		31	1,400
	22,400		13,260
Bal.	9,140		

Accounts Receivable

July 19	4,800

Art Supplies

July 6	1,800

Office Supplies

July 6	800

Prepaid Rent

July 2	1,600

Prepaid Insurance

July 8	960

Art Equipment

July 3	4,200

Office Equipment

July 5	3,000

Accounts Payable

July 9	1,000	July 5	1,500
		6	2,600
		30	140
	1,000		4,240
		Bal.	3,240

Unearned Art Fees

	July 15	1,000

This account links to the statement of cash flows.

Common Stock

	July 1	20,000

Dividends

July 31	1,400

Advertising Fees Earned

	July 10	1,400
	19	4,800
	Bal.	6,200

Wages Expense

July 12	1,200
26	1,200
Bal.	2,400

Utilities Expense

July 29	200

Telephone Expense

July 30	140

These accounts link to the income statement.

Exhibit 2 shows the transactions for July in their accounts and in relation to the accounting equation. Note that all transactions have been recorded on the date they are recognized. Most of these transactions involve either the receipt or payment of cash, as reflected in the Cash account. There are important exceptions, however. For instance, on July 19 Advertising Fees were earned, but receipt of cash for these fees will come later. Also, on July 5, 6, and 30 there were transactions recognized that totaled $4,240 in Accounts Payable. This means the company can wait to pay. At the end of the month, only the $1,000 recorded on July 9 had been paid. These lags between recognition of transactions and the subsequent cash inflows or outflows have an impact on achieving the goal of liquidity.

 Check out ACE for a Review Quiz at http://accounting.college.hmco.com/students.

THE TRIAL BALANCE

LO5 Prepare a trial balance and describe its value and limitations.

RELATED TEXT ASSIGNMENTS
Q: 17, 18, 19, 24
SE: 4, 7, 8
E: 3, 6, 8, 9, 10, 11
P: 2, 3, 4, 5, 7, 8
SD: 5

KEY POINT: The trial balance is prepared at the end of the accounting period. It is an initial check that the ledger is in balance.

For every amount debited, an equal amount must be credited. This means that the total of debits and credits in the T accounts must be equal. To test this, the accountant periodically prepares a **trial balance**. Exhibit 3 shows a trial balance for Joan Miller Advertising Agency, Inc. It was prepared from the accounts in Exhibit 2.

A trial balance may be prepared at any time but is usually prepared on the last day of the month. Here are the steps in preparing a trial balance:

1. List each T account that has a balance, with debit balances in the left column and credit balances in the right column. Accounts are listed in the order in which they appear in the ledger.
2. Add each column.
3. Compare the totals of the columns.

In accounts in which increases are recorded by debits, the **normal balance** (the usual balance) is a debit balance; in accounts in which increases are recorded by credits, the normal balance is a credit balance. Table 1 summarizes the normal account balances of the major account categories. According to the table, the T account Accounts Payable (a liability) typically has a credit balance and is copied into the trial balance as a credit balance.

EXHIBIT 3
Trial Balance

Joan Miller Advertising Agency, Inc.
Trial Balance
July 31, 20xx

Cash	$ 9,140	
Accounts Receivable	4,800	
Art Supplies	1,800	
Office Supplies	800	
Prepaid Rent	1,600	
Prepaid Insurance	960	
Art Equipment	4,200	
Office Equipment	3,000	
Accounts Payable		$ 3,240
Unearned Art Fees		1,000
Common Stock		20,000
Dividends	1,400	
Advertising Fees Earned		6,200
Wages Expense	2,400	
Utilities Expense	200	
Telephone Expense	140	
	$30,440	$30,440

● **STOP AND THINK!**
Which account category would be most likely to have an account balance that is not normal?

Retained Earnings is the most likely account to have an abnormal balance (debit) because of situations in which expenses exceed revenues (net loss). It is unusual for any of the other accounts to have abnormal balances. ■

TABLE 1. Normal Account Balances of Major Account Categories

Account Category	Increases Recorded by		Normal Balance	
	Debit	Credit	Debit	Credit
Assets	x		x	
Liabilities		x		x
Stockholders' equity:				
Common stock		x		x
Retained earnings		x		x
Dividends	x		x	
Revenues		x		x
Expenses	x		x	

Once in a while, a transaction leaves an account with a balance that is not "normal." For example, when a company overdraws its account at the bank, its Cash account (an asset) will show a credit balance instead of a debit balance. The "abnormal" balance should be copied into the trial balance columns as it stands, as a debit or a credit.

The trial balance proves whether or not the ledger is in balance. *In balance* means that the total of all debits recorded equals the total of all credits recorded. But the trial balance does not prove that the transactions were analyzed correctly or recorded in the proper accounts. For example, there is no way of determining from the trial balance that a debit should have been made in the Art Equipment account rather than the Office Equipment account. And the trial balance does not detect whether transactions have been omitted, because equal debits and credits will have been omitted. Also, if an error of the same amount is made in both a debit and a credit, it will not be discovered by the trial balance. The trial balance proves only that the debits and credits in the accounts are in balance.

If the debit and credit columns of the trial balance are not equal, look for one or more of the following errors: (1) a debit was entered in an account as a credit, or vice versa; (2) the balance of an account was computed incorrectly; (3) an error was made in carrying the account balance to the trial balance; or (4) the trial balance was summed incorrectly.

Other than simply adding the columns incorrectly, the two most common mistakes in preparing a trial balance are (1) recording an account with a debit balance as a credit, or vice versa, and (2) transposing two digits when transferring an amount to the trial balance (for example, entering $23,459 as $23,549). The first of these mistakes causes the trial balance to be out of balance by an amount evenly divisible by 2. The second error causes the trial balance to be out of balance by a number divisible by 9. Thus, if a trial balance is out of balance and the addition has been verified, determine the amount by which the trial balance is out of balance and divide it first by 2 and then by 9. If the amount is divisible by 2, look in the trial balance for an amount that is equal to the quotient. If you find such an amount, chances are it is probably in the wrong column. If the amount is divisible by 9, trace each amount back to the ledger account balance, checking carefully for a transposition error. If neither of these techniques is successful in identifying the error, first recompute the balance of each account in the ledger.

FOCUS ON BUSINESS TECHNOLOGY

Are All Trial Balances Created Equal?
In computerized accounting systems, posting is done automatically, and the trial balance can be easily prepared as often as needed. Any accounts with abnormal balances are highlighted for investigation. Some general ledger software packages for small businesses list the trial balance amounts in a single column, with credit balances shown as minuses. In such cases, the trial balance is in balance if the total is zero.

Then, if you still have not found the error, retrace each posting from the journal to the ledger.

 Check out ACE for a Review Quiz at http://accounting.college.hmco.com/students.

RECORDING AND POSTING TRANSACTIONS

SO6 Record transactions in the general journal and post transactions from the general journal to the ledger.

RELATED TEXT ASSIGNMENTS
Q: 20, 21, 22, 23, 24
SE: 9, 10
E: 12, 13
P: 5, 8

KEY POINT: The journal is a chronological record of events. Only the general journal is discussed in this chapter.

Let us now take a look at the formal process of recording transactions in the general journal and posting them to the ledger.

THE GENERAL JOURNAL

As you have seen, transactions can be entered directly into the accounts. But this method makes identifying individual transactions or finding errors very difficult because the debit is recorded in one account and the credit in another. The solution is to record all transactions chronologically in a *journal*. The journal is sometimes called the *book of original entry* because it is where transactions first enter the accounting records. Later, the debit and credit portions of each transaction can be transferred to the appropriate accounts in the ledger. A separate *journal entry* is used to record each transaction, and the process of recording transactions is called *journalizing*.

Most businesses have more than one kind of journal. Several types of journals are discussed in the appendix on special-purpose journals. The simplest and most flexible type is the *general journal*, the one we focus on in this chapter. Entries in the general journal include the following information about each transaction:

1. The date
2. The names of the accounts debited and the dollar amounts on the same lines in the debit column
3. The names of the accounts credited and the dollar amounts on the same lines in the credit column
4. An explanation of the transaction
5. The account identification numbers, if appropriate

Exhibit 4 displays two of the transactions for Joan Miller Advertising Agency, Inc., that we discussed earlier. The procedure for recording transactions in the general journal is as follows:

1. Record the date by writing the year in small figures on the first line at the top of the first column, the month on the next line of the first column, and the day in the second column opposite the month. For subsequent entries on the same page for the same month and year, the month and year can be omitted.
2. Write the exact names of the accounts debited and credited in the Description column. Starting on the same line as the date, write the name(s) of the account(s) that are debited next to the left margin and indent the name(s) of the account(s) credited. The explanation is placed on the next line and is further indented. The explanation should be brief but sufficient to explain and identify the transaction. A transaction can have more than one debit or credit entry; this is called a *compound entry*. In a compound entry, all debit accounts are listed before any credit accounts. (The July 6 transaction of Joan Miller Advertising Agency, Inc., in Exhibit 4 is an example of a compound entry.)
3. Write the debit amounts in the Debit column opposite the accounts to be debited, and write the credit amounts in the Credit column opposite the accounts to be credited.

EXHIBIT 4
The General Journal

		General Journal			Page 1
Date		Description	Post. Ref.	Debit	Credit
20xx July	6	Art Supplies		1,800	
		Office Supplies		800	
		Accounts Payable			2,600
		Purchase of art and office supplies on credit			
	8	Prepaid Insurance		960	
		Cash			960
		Paid one-year life insurance premium			

A = L + OE
+   +
+

A = L + OE
+
−

4. At the time the transactions are recorded, nothing is placed in the Post. Ref. (posting reference) column. (This column is sometimes called *LP* or *Folio*.) Later, if the company uses account numbers to identify accounts in the ledger, fill in the account numbers to provide a convenient cross-reference from the general journal to the ledger and to indicate that the entry has been posted to the ledger. If the accounts are not numbered, use a checkmark (✔).

5. It is customary to skip a line after each journal entry.

THE GENERAL LEDGER

The general journal is used to record the details of each transaction. The general ledger is used to update each account.

■ **THE LEDGER ACCOUNT FORM** The T account is a simple, direct means of recording transactions. In practice, a somewhat more complicated form of the account is needed in order to record more information. The **ledger account form**, which contains four columns for dollar amounts, is illustrated in Exhibit 5.

The account title and number appear at the top of the account form. As in the journal, the transaction date appears in the first two columns. The Item column is

EXHIBIT 5
Accounts Payable in the General Ledger

General Ledger

Accounts Payable   Account No. 212

Date		Item	Post. Ref.	Debit	Credit	Balance Debit	Balance Credit
20xx July	5		J1		1,500		1,500
	6		J1		2,600		4,100
	9		J1	1,000			3,100
	30		J2		140		3,240

EXHIBIT 6
Posting from the General Journal to the Ledger

$A = L + OE$
$\quad +\quad -$

General Journal — Page 2

Date	Description	Post. Ref.	Debit	Credit
20xx July 30	Telephone Expense	513	140	
	Accounts Payable	212		140
	Received bill for telephone expense			

General Ledger

Accounts Payable — Account No. 212

Date	Item	Post. Ref.	Debit	Credit	Balance Debit	Balance Credit
20xx July 5		J1		1,500		1,500
6		J1		2,600		4,100
9		J1	1,000			3,100
30		J2		140		3,240

General Ledger

Telephone Expense — Account No. 513

Date	Item	Post. Ref.	Debit	Credit	Balance Debit	Balance Credit
20xx July 30		J2	140		140	

rarely used to identify transactions, because explanations already appear in the journal. The Post. Ref. column is used to note the journal page where the original entry for the transaction can be found. The dollar amount is entered in the appropriate Debit or Credit column, and a new account balance is computed in the final two columns after each entry. The advantage of this account form over the T account is that the current balance of the account is readily available.

■ **POSTING TO THE LEDGER** After transactions have been entered in the journal, they must be transferred to the ledger. The process of transferring journal entry information from the journal to the ledger is called **posting**. Posting is usually done after several entries have been made—for example, at the end of each day or less frequently, depending on the number of transactions. As shown in Exhibit 6, through posting, each amount in the Debit column of the journal is transferred into the Debit column of the appropriate account in the ledger, and each amount in the

Credit column of the journal is transferred into the Credit column of the appropriate account in the ledger. The steps in the posting process are as follows:

1. In the ledger, locate the debit account named in the journal entry.
2. Enter the date of the transaction and, in the Post. Ref. column of the ledger, the journal page number from which the entry comes.
3. Enter in the Debit column of the ledger account the amount of the debit as it appears in the journal.
4. Calculate the account balance and enter it in the appropriate Balance column.
5. Enter in the Post. Ref. column of the journal the account number to which the amount has been posted.
6. Repeat the same five steps for the credit side of the journal entry.

Notice that step **5** is the last step in the posting process for each debit and credit. In addition to serving as an easy reference between the journal entry and the ledger account, this entry in the Post. Ref. column of the journal indicates that all steps for the transaction have been completed. This allows accountants who have been called away from their work to easily find where they were before they were interrupted.

SOME NOTES ON PRESENTATION

A ruled line appears in financial reports before each subtotal or total to indicate that the amounts above are added or subtracted. It is common practice to use a double line under a final total to show that it has been checked, or verified.

Dollar signs ($) are required in all financial statements, including the balance sheet and income statement, and in the trial balance and other schedules. On these statements, a dollar sign should be placed before the first amount in each column and before the first amount in a column following a ruled line. Dollar signs in the same column are aligned. Dollar signs are not used in journals and ledgers.

On unruled paper, commas and decimal points are used in dollar amounts. On paper with ruled columns—like the paper in journals and ledgers—commas and decimal points are not needed. In this book, because most problems and illustrations are in whole dollar amounts, the cents column usually is omitted. When accountants deal with whole dollars, they often use a dash in the cents column to indicate whole dollars rather than taking the time to write zeros.

 Check out ACE for a Review Quiz at http://accounting.college.hmco.com/students.

Chapter Review

REVIEW OF LEARNING OBJECTIVES

LO1 Explain, in simple terms, the generally accepted ways of solving the measurement issues of recognition, valuation, and classification.

To measure a business transaction, the accountant determines when the transaction should be recorded (the recognition issue), what value should be placed on the transaction (the valuation issue), and how the components of the transaction should be categorized (the classification issue). In general, recognition occurs when title passes, and a transaction is valued at the exchange price, the cost at the time the transaction is recognized. Classification refers to the categorizing of transactions according to a system of accounts.

LO2 Describe the chart of accounts and recognize commonly used accounts.

An account is a device for storing data from transactions. There is one account for each asset, liability, and component of stockholders' equity, including revenues and expenses. The ledger is a book or file containing all of a company's accounts, arranged according to a chart of accounts. Commonly used asset accounts are Cash, Notes Receivable,

Accounts Receivable, Prepaid Expenses, Land, Buildings, and Equipment. Common liability accounts are Notes Payable, Accounts Payable, Wages Payable, and Mortgage Payable. Common stockholders' equity accounts are Common Stock, Retained Earnings, Dividends, and revenue and expense accounts.

LO3 Define *double-entry system* and state the rules for double entry.

In the double-entry system, each transaction must be recorded with at least one debit and one credit, so that the total dollar amount of the debits equals the total dollar amount of the credits. The rules for double entry are (1) increases in assets are debited to asset accounts; decreases in assets are credited to asset accounts; and (2) increases in liabilities and stockholders' equity are credited to those accounts; decreases in liabilities and stockholders' equity are debited to those accounts.

LO4 Apply the steps for transaction analysis and processing to simple transactions.

The procedure for analyzing transactions is (1) analyze the effect of the transaction on assets, liabilities, and stockholders' equity; (2) apply the appropriate double-entry rule; (3) record the entry; (4) post the entry; and (5) prepare a trial balance.

LO5 Prepare a trial balance and describe its value and limitations.

A trial balance is used to check that the debit and credit balances are equal. It is prepared by listing each account with its balance in the Debit or Credit column. Then the two columns are added and the totals compared to test the balances. The major limitation of the trial balance is that even if debit and credit balances are equal, this does not guarantee that the transactions were analyzed correctly or recorded in the proper accounts.

Supplemental Objective

SO6 Record transactions in the general journal and post transactions from the general journal to the ledger.

The general journal is a chronological record of all transactions. That record contains the date of each transaction, the names of the accounts and the dollar amounts debited and credited, an explanation of each entry, and the account numbers to which postings have been made. After transactions have been entered in the general journal, they are posted to the ledger. Posting is done by transferring each amount in the Debit column of the general journal to the Debit column of the appropriate account in the ledger, and transferring each amount in the Credit column of the general journal to the Credit column of the appropriate account in the ledger. After each entry is posted, a new balance is entered in the appropriate Balance column.

Review of Concepts and Terminology

The following concepts and terms were introduced in this chapter:

LO3 **Balance:** The difference in dollars between the total debit footing and the total credit footing of an account. Also called *account balance*.

LO2 **Chart of accounts:** A scheme that assigns a unique number to each account to facilitate finding the account in the ledger; also, the list of account numbers and titles.

LO1 **Classification:** The process of assigning transactions to the appropriate accounts.

SO6 **Compound entry:** An entry that has more than one debit or credit entry.

LO1 **Cost:** The exchange price associated with a business transaction at the point of recognition.

LO1 **Cost principle:** The practice of recording transactions at cost.

LO3 **Credit:** The right side of an account.

LO3 **Debit:** The left side of an account.

LO3 **Double-entry system:** The accounting system in which each transaction is recorded with at least one debit and one credit, so that the total dollar amount of debits and the total dollar amount of credits equal each other.

LO3 **Footings:** Working totals of columns of numbers. *To foot* means to total a column of numbers.

SO6 **General journal:** The simplest and most flexible type of journal.

LO2 **General ledger:** The book or file that contains all of the company's accounts, arranged in the order of the chart of accounts. Also called *ledger*.

SO6 **Journal:** A chronological record of all transactions; the place where transactions first enter the accounting records. Also called *book of original entry*.

SO6 **Journal entry:** Journal notations that record a single transaction.

LO3 **Journal form:** A form of journal in which the date, the debit account, and the debit amount of a transaction are recorded on one line and the credit account and credit amount on the next line.

SO6 **Journalizing:** The process of recording transactions in a journal.

SO6 **Ledger account form:** The form of account that has four dollar amount columns: one column for debit entries, one column for credit entries, and two columns (debit and credit) for showing the balance of the account.

LO5 **Normal balance:** The usual balance of an account; also the side (debit or credit) that increases the account.

SO6 **Posting:** The process of transferring journal entry information from the journal to the ledger.

LO1 **Recognition:** The determination of when a business transaction should be recorded.

LO1 **Recognition point:** The predetermined time at which a transaction should be recorded; usually, the point at which title passes to the buyer.

LO3 **Source document:** An invoice, check, receipt, or other document that supports a transaction.

LO3 **T account:** The simplest form of an account, used to analyze transactions.

LO5 **Trial balance:** A comparison of the total of debit and credit balances in the accounts to check that they are equal.

LO1 **Valuation:** The process of assigning a monetary value to a business transaction.

REVIEW PROBLEM

Transaction Analysis, Journalizing, T Accounts, and Trial Balance

LO4
LO5 After graduation from veterinary school, Laura Cox entered private practice. The transactions of the business through May 27 are as follows:

20xx
May 1   Laura Cox invested $2,000 in 2,000 shares of $1 par value common stock of her newly chartered company, Pet Clinic, Inc.
     3   Paid $300 for two months' rent in advance for an office.
     9   Purchased medical supplies for $200 in cash.
    12   Purchased $400 of equipment on credit, making a 25 percent down payment.
    15   Delivered a calf for a fee of $35 on credit.
    18   Made a partial payment of $50 on the equipment purchased May 12.
    27   Paid a utility bill of $40.

REQUIRED ▶
1. Record these transactions in journal form.
2. Post the transactions to the following T accounts: Cash; Accounts Receivable; Medical Supplies; Prepaid Rent; Equipment; Accounts Payable; Common Stock; Veterinary Fees Earned; and Utilities Expense.
3. Prepare a trial balance as of May 31.

4. How does the transaction of May 15 relate to recognition and cash flows? Also compare the transactions of May 9 and May 27 with regard to classification.

ANSWER TO REVIEW PROBLEM

1. Transactions recorded in journal form

Date	Account	Debit	Credit
May 1	Cash	2,000	
	Common Stock		2,000
	Invested $2,000 in 2,000 shares of $1 par value common stock		
3	Prepaid Rent	300	
	Cash		300
	Paid two months' rent in advance for an office		
9	Medical Supplies	200	
	Cash		200
	Purchased medical supplies for cash		
12	Equipment	400	
	Accounts Payable		300
	Cash		100
	Purchased equipment on credit, paying 25 percent down		
15	Accounts Receivable	35	
	Veterinary Fees Earned		35
	Fee on credit for delivery of a calf		
18	Accounts Payable	50	
	Cash		50
	Partial payment for equipment purchased May 12		
27	Utilities Expense	40	
	Cash		40
	Paid utility bill		

2. Transactions posted to T accounts

Cash			
May 1	2,000	May 3	300
		9	200
		12	100
		18	50
		27	40
	2,000		690
Bal.	1,310		

Accounts Receivable	
May 15	35

Medical Supplies	
May 9	200

Prepaid Rent	
May 3	300

Equipment	
May 12	400

Accounts Payable			
May 18	50	May 12	300
		Bal.	250

Common Stock			
		May 1	2,000

Veterinary Fees Earned			
		May 15	35

Utilities Expense			
May 27	40		

3. Trial balance prepared

Pet Clinic, Inc.
Trial Balance
May 31, 20xx

Cash	$1,310	
Accounts Receivable	35	
Medical Supplies	200	
Prepaid Rent	300	
Equipment	400	
Accounts Payable		$ 250
Common Stock		2,000
Veterinary Fees Earned		35
Utilities Expense	40	
	$2,285	$2,285

4. The transaction is recorded, or recognized, on May 15, even though no cash is received. The revenue is earned because the service was provided to and accepted by the buyer. The customer now has an obligation to pay the provider of the service. It is recorded as an accounts receivable because the customer has been allowed to pay later. The transaction on May 9 is classified as an asset, Medical Supplies, because these supplies will benefit the company in the future. The transaction on May 27 is classified as an expense, Utilities Expense, because the utilities have already been used and will not benefit the company in the future.

Chapter Assignments

Building Your Knowledge Foundation

Questions

1. What three issues underlie most accounting measurement decisions?
2. Why is recognition an issue for accountants?
3. A customer asks the owner of a store to save an item for him and says that he will pick it up and pay for it next week. The owner agrees to hold it. Should this transaction be recorded as a sale? Explain your answer.
4. Why is it practical for accountants to rely on original cost for valuation purposes?
5. Under the cost principle, changes in value after a transaction is recorded are not usually recognized in the accounts. Comment on this possible limitation of using original cost in accounting measurements.
6. What is an account, and how is it related to the ledger?
7. Tell whether each of the following accounts is an asset account, a liability account, or a stockholders' equity account:
   a. Notes Receivable
   b. Land
   c. Dividends
   d. Mortgage Payable
   e. Prepaid Rent
   f. Insurance Expense
   g. Service Revenue

8. In the stockholders' equity accounts, why do accountants maintain separate accounts for revenues and expenses rather than using the Retained Earnings account?
9. Why is the system of recording entries called the double-entry system? What is significant about this system?
10. "Double-entry accounting refers to entering a transaction in both the journal and the ledger." Comment on this statement.
11. "Debits are bad; credits are good." Comment on this statement.
12. What are the rules of double entry for (a) assets, (b) liabilities, and (c) stockholders' equity?
13. Why are the rules of double entry the same for liabilities and stockholders' equity?
14. What is the meaning of the statement, "The Cash account has a debit balance of $500"?
15. Explain why debits, which decrease stockholders' equity, also increase expenses, which are a component of stockholders' equity.
16. What are the five steps in analyzing and processing a transaction?
17. What does a trial balance prove?
18. What is the normal balance of Accounts Payable? Under what conditions could Accounts Payable have a debit balance?
19. Is it possible for errors to be present even though a trial balance balances? Explain your answer.
20. Is it a good idea to forgo the journal and enter a transaction directly into the ledger? Explain your answer.
21. In recording entries in a journal, which is written first, the debit or the credit? How is indentation used in the journal?
22. What is the relationship between the journal and the ledger?
23. Describe each of the following:
    a. Account
    b. Journal
    c. Ledger
    d. Book of original entry
    e. Post. Ref. column
    f. Journalizing
    g. Posting
    h. Footings
    i. Compound entry
24. List the following six items in sequence to illustrate the flow of events through the accounting system:
    a. Analysis of the transaction
    b. Debits and credits posted from the journal to the ledger
    c. Occurrence of the business transaction
    d. Preparation of the financial statements
    e. Entry made in the journal
    f. Preparation of the trial balance

Short Exercises

LO1 Recognition

SE 1. Which of the following events would be recognized and entered in the accounting records of Thorpe Corporation? Why?

Jan. 10 Thorpe Corporation places an order for office supplies.
Feb. 15 Thorpe Corporation receives the office supplies and a bill for them.
Mar. 1   Thorpe Corporation pays for the office supplies.

Chapter 2 Measuring Business Transactions

LO1 **Recognition, Valuation,**
LO3 **and Classification**

SE 2. Tell how the concepts of recognition, valuation, and classification apply to this transaction:

Cash			Supplies	
June 1	250	June 1	250	

LO2 **Classification of Accounts**

SE 3. Tell whether each of the following accounts is an asset, a liability, a revenue, an expense, or none of these:

a. Accounts Payable
b. Supplies
c. Dividends
d. Fees Earned
e. Supplies Expense
f. Accounts Receivable
g. Unearned Revenue
h. Equipment

LO5 **Normal Balances**

SE 4. Tell whether the normal balance of each account in **SE 3** is a debit or a credit.

LO4 **Transaction Analysis**

SE 5. For each transaction below, tell which account is debited and which account is credited.

May 2 Han Kim started a computer programming business, Kim's Programming Service, Inc., by investing $5,000 in exchange for common stock.
   5 Purchased a computer for $2,500 in cash.
   7 Purchased supplies on credit for $300.
  19 Received cash for programming services performed, $500.
  22 Received cash for programming services to be performed, $600.
  25 Paid the rent for May, $650.
  31 Billed a customer for programming services performed, $250.

LO4 **Recording Transactions in T Accounts**

SE 6. Set up T accounts and record each transaction in **SE 5**. Determine the balance of each account.

LO5 **Preparing a Trial Balance**

SE 7. From the T accounts created in **SE 6**, prepare a trial balance dated May 31, 20x4.

LO5 **Correcting Errors in a Trial Balance**

SE 8. The trial balance that follows is out of balance. Assuming all balances are normal, place the accounts in proper order and correct the trial balance so that debits equal credits.

Serowik Boating Service, Inc.
Trial Balance
January 31, 20x4

Cash	$2,000	
Accounts Payable	400	
Fuel Expense	800	
Unearned Service Revenue	250	
Accounts Receivable		$1,300
Prepaid Rent		150
Common Stock		1,500
Service Revenue	1,750	
Wages Expense		300
Retained Earnings	650	
	$5,850	$3,250

SO6 **Recording Transactions in the General Journal**

SE 9. Prepare a general journal form like the one in Exhibit 4 and label it Page 4. Record the following transactions in the journal:

Sept. 6 Billed a customer for services performed, $1,900.
  16 Received partial payment from the customer billed on Sept. 6, $900.

SO6 **Posting to the Ledger Accounts**

SE 10. Prepare ledger account forms like the ones in Exhibit 5 for the following accounts: Cash (111), Accounts Receivable (113), and Service Revenue (411). Post the transactions that are recorded in **SE 9** to the ledger accounts, at the same time making the proper posting references.

EXERCISES

LO1 **Recognition**

E 1. Which of the following events would be recognized and recorded in the accounting records of Friese Corporation on the date indicated?

Jan. 15 Friese Corporation offers to purchase a tract of land for $140,000. There is a high likelihood that the offer will be accepted.
Feb. 2 Friese Corporation receives notice that its rent will be increased from $500 per month to $600 per month effective March 1.
Mar. 29 Friese Corporation receives its utility bill for the month of March. The bill is not due until April 9.
June 10 Friese Corporation places a firm order for new office equipment costing $21,000.
July 6 The office equipment ordered on June 10 arrives. Payment is not due until August 1.

LO1 **Application of Recognition Point**

E 2. Dempsey's Parts Shop, Inc., uses a large amount of supplies in its business. The following table summarizes selected transaction data for supplies that Dempsey's Parts Shop purchased:

Order	Date Shipped	Date Received	Amount
a	June 26	July 5	$ 600
b	July 10	15	1,500
c	16	22	800
d	23	30	1,200
e	27	Aug. 1	1,500
f	Aug. 3	7	1,000

Determine the total purchases of supplies for July alone under each of the following assumptions:

1. Dempsey's Parts Shop, Inc., recognizes purchases when orders are shipped.
2. Dempsey's Parts Shop, Inc., recognizes purchases when orders are received.

LO2 **LO5** **Classification of Accounts**

E 3. The following ledger accounts are for Arif Service Corporation:

a. Cash
b. Wages Expense
c. Accounts Receivable
d. Common Stock
e. Service Revenue
f. Prepaid Rent
g. Accounts Payable
h. Investments in Securities
i. Income Taxes Payable
j. Income Taxes Expense
k. Land
l. Supplies Expense
m. Prepaid Insurance

n. Utilities Expense
o. Fees Earned
p. Dividends
q. Wages Payable
r. Unearned Revenue
s. Office Equipment
t. Rent Payable
u. Notes Receivable
v. Interest Expense
w. Notes Payable
x. Supplies
y. Interest Receivable
z. Rent Expense

Complete the table that appears at the top of the next page, using Xs to indicate each account's classification and normal balance (whether a debit or a credit increases the account).

	Type of Account						Normal Balance (increases balance)	
			Stockholders' Equity					
			Common Stock	Retained Earnings				
Item	Asset	Liability		Dividends	Revenue	Expense	Debit	Credit
a.	X						X	

LO4 Transaction Analysis

E 4. Analyze transactions **a–g**, following the example below.
a. Harry Boka established Whiskers Barber Shop, Inc., by incorporating and investing $1,200 in exchange for 120 shares of $10 par value common stock.
b. Paid two months' rent in advance, $840.
c. Purchased supplies on credit, $60.
d. Received cash for barbering services, $300.
e. Paid for supplies purchased in c.
f. Paid utility bill, $36.
g. Declared and paid a dividend of $50.

Example:
a. The asset Cash was increased. Increases in assets are recorded by debits. Debit Cash $1,200. A component of stockholders' equity, Common Stock, was increased. Increases in stockholders' equity are recorded by credits. Credit Common Stock $1,200.

LO4 Recording Transactions in T Accounts

E 5. Open the following T accounts: Cash; Repair Supplies; Repair Equipment; Accounts Payable; Common Stock; Dividends; Repair Fees Earned; Salaries Expense; and Rent Expense. Record the following transactions for the month of June directly in the T accounts; use the letters to identify the transactions in your T accounts. Determine the balance in each account.

a. Ella Clunie opened Ceramics Repair Service, Inc., by investing $4,300 in cash and $1,600 in repair equipment in return for 5,900 shares of the company's $1 par value common stock.
b. Paid $400 for the current month's rent.
c. Purchased repair supplies on credit, $500.
d. Purchased additional repair equipment for cash, $300.
e. Paid salary to a helper, $450.
f. Paid $200 of amount purchased on credit in c.
g. Accepted cash for repairs completed, $1,860.
h. Declared and paid a dividend of $600.

LO5 Trial Balance

E 6. After recording the transactions in E 5, prepare a trial balance in proper sequence for Ceramics Repair Service, Inc., as of June 30, 20xx.

LO4 Analysis of Transactions

E 7. Explain each transaction **(a–h)** entered in the following T accounts:

Cash				Accounts Receivable				Equipment			
a.	60,000	b.	15,000	c.	6,000	g.	1,500	b.	15,000	h.	900
g.	1,500	e.	3,000					d.	9,000		
h.	900	f.	4,500								

Accounts Payable				Common Stock				Service Revenue			
f.	4,500	d.	9,000			a.	60,000			c.	6,000

Wages Expense	
e. 3,000	

LO5 Preparing a Trial Balance

E 8. The list that follows presents the accounts of the Gobi Metal Corporation as of March 31, 20xx, in alphabetical order. The list does not include the amount of Accounts Payable.

Accounts Payable	?
Accounts Receivable	$ 3,000
Building	34,000
Cash	9,000
Common Stock	20,000
Equipment	12,000
Land	5,200
Notes Payable	20,000
Prepaid Insurance	1,100
Retained Earnings	11,450

Prepare a trial balance with the proper heading (see Exhibit 3) and with the accounts listed in the chart of accounts sequence (see Exhibit 1). Compute the balance of Accounts Payable.

LO5 Effects of Errors on a Trial Balance

E 9. Which of the following errors would cause a trial balance to have unequal totals? Explain your answers.

a. A payment to a creditor was recorded as a debit to Accounts Payable for $86 and as a credit to Cash for $68.
b. A payment of $100 to a creditor for an account payable was debited to Accounts Receivable and credited to Cash.
c. A purchase of office supplies of $280 was recorded as a debit to Office Supplies for $28 and as a credit to Cash for $28.
d. A purchase of equipment for $300 was recorded as a debit to Supplies for $300 and as a credit to Cash for $300.

LO5 Correcting Errors in a Trial Balance

E 10. This was the trial balance for Maxx Services, Inc., at the end of July:

Maxx Services, Inc.
Trial Balance
July 31, 20xx

Cash	$ 1,920	
Accounts Receivable	2,830	
Supplies	60	
Prepaid Insurance	90	
Equipment	4,200	
Accounts Payable		$ 2,270
Common Stock		2,000
Retained Earnings		3,780
Dividends		350
Revenues		2,960
Salaries Expense	1,300	
Rent Expense	300	
Advertising Expense	170	
Utilities Expense	13	
	$10,883	$11,360

The trial balance does not balance because of a number of errors. Maxx's accountant compared the amounts in the trial balance with the ledger, recomputed the account balances, and compared the postings. He found the following errors:

a. The balance of Cash was understated by $200.
b. A cash payment of $210 was credited to Cash for $120.
c. A debit of $60 to Accounts Receivable was not posted.

d. Supplies purchased for $30 were posted as a credit to Supplies.
e. A debit of $90 to Prepaid Insurance was not posted.
f. The Accounts Payable account had debits of $2,660 and credits of $4,590.
g. The Notes Payable account, with a credit balance of $1,200, was not included on the trial balance.
h. The debit balance of Dividends was listed in the trial balance as a credit.
i. A $100 debit to Dividends was posted as a credit.
j. The actual balance of Utilities Expense, $130, was listed as $13 in the trial balance.

Prepare a corrected trial balance.

LO5 Preparing a Trial Balance

E 11. The Loreau Construction Corporation builds foundations for buildings and parking lots. The following alphabetical list shows Loreau Construction's account balances as of April 30, 20xx:

Accounts Payable	$ 3,900	Office Trailer	$ 2,200
Accounts Receivable	10,120	Prepaid Insurance	4,600
Cash	?	Retained Earnings	10,000
Common Stock	30,000	Supplies Expense	7,200
Construction Supplies	1,900	Revenue Earned	17,400
Dividends	7,800	Utilities Expense	420
Equipment	24,500	Wages Expense	8,800
Notes Payable	20,000		

Prepare a trial balance for the company with the proper heading and with the accounts in balance sheet sequence. Determine the correct balance for the Cash account on April 30, 20xx.

LO4 Analysis of Unfamiliar
SO6 Transactions

E 12. Managers and accountants often encounter transactions with which they are unfamiliar. Use your analytical skills to analyze and record in journal form the transactions that follow, which have not yet been discussed in the text.

May 1 Purchased merchandise inventory on account, $2,400.
2 Purchased marketable securities for cash, $5,600.
3 Returned part of merchandise inventory purchased in a for full credit, $500.
4 Sold merchandise inventory on account, $1,600 (record sale only).
5 Purchased land and a building for $600,000. Payment is $120,000 cash, and there is a thirty-year mortgage for the remainder. The purchase price is allocated as follows: $200,000 to the land and $400,000 to the building.
6 Received an order for $24,000 in services to be provided. With the order was a deposit of $8,000.

SO6 Recording Transactions in the General Journal and Posting to the Ledger Accounts

E 13. Open a general journal form like the one in Exhibit 4, and label it Page 10. After opening the form, record the following transactions in the journal:

Dec. 14 Purchased an item of equipment for $6,000, paying $2,000 as a cash down payment.
28 Paid $3,000 of the amount owed on the equipment.

Prepare three ledger account forms like the one shown in Exhibit 5. Use the following account numbers: Cash, 111; Equipment, 144; and Accounts Payable, 212. Then post the two transactions from the general journal to the ledger accounts, being sure to make proper posting references.

Assume that the Cash account has a debit balance of $8,000 on the day prior to the first transaction.

Problems

LO4 Transaction Analysis

P 1. The following accounts are applicable to Walter's Chimney Sweeps, Inc.:
1. Cash
2. Accounts Receivable
3. Supplies
4. Prepaid Insurance
5. Equipment

6. Notes Payable
7. Accounts Payable
8. Common Stock
9. Retained Earnings
10. Dividends
11. Service Revenue
12. Rent Expense
13. Repair Expense

Walter's Chimney Sweeps, Inc., completed the following transactions:

	Debit	Credit
a. Paid for supplies purchased on credit last month.	7	1
b. Billed customers for services performed.		
c. Paid the current month's rent.		
d. Purchased supplies on credit.		
e. Received cash from customers for services performed but not yet billed.		
f. Purchased equipment on account.		
g. Received a bill for repairs.		
h. Returned part of the equipment purchased in f for a credit.		
i. Received payments from customers previously billed.		
j. Paid the bill received in g.		
k. Received an order for services to be performed.		
l. Paid for repairs with cash.		
m. Made a payment to reduce the principal of the note payable.		
n. Declared and paid a dividend.		

REQUIRED ▶ Analyze each transaction and show the accounts affected by entering the corresponding numbers in the appropriate debit or credit column as shown in transaction **a**. Indicate no entry, if appropriate.

P 2. Bob Lutz opened a secretarial school called Best Secretarial Training, Inc.

LO4 **Transaction Analysis,**
LO5 **T Accounts, and Trial Balance**

a. He contributed the following assets to the business in exchange for 13,600 shares of $1 par value common stock:

Cash	$5,700
Computers	4,300
Office Equipment	3,600

b. Found a location for his business and paid the first month's rent, $260.
c. Paid for an advertisement announcing the opening of the school, $190.
d. Received applications from three students for a four-week secretarial program and two students for a ten-day keyboarding course. The students will be billed a total of $1,300.
e. Purchased supplies on credit, $330.
f. Billed the enrolled students, $1,300.
g. Paid an assistant one week's salary, $220.
h. Purchased a second-hand computer, $480, and office equipment, $380, on credit.
i. Paid for the supplies purchased on credit in e, $330.
j. Paid cash to repair a broken computer, $40.
k. Billed new students who enrolled late in the course, $440.
l. Received partial payment from students previously billed, $1,080.
m. Paid the utility bill for the current month, $90.
n. Paid an assistant one week's salary, $220.
o. Received cash revenue from another new student, $250.
p. Declared and paid a dividend of $300.

REQUIRED ▶
1. Set up the following T accounts: Cash; Accounts Receivable; Supplies; Computers; Office Equipment; Accounts Payable; Common Stock; Dividends; Tuition Revenue; Salaries Expense; Utilities Expense; Rent Expense; Repair Expense; and Advertising Expense.
2. Record the transactions directly in the T accounts, using the transaction letter to identify each debit and credit.
3. Prepare a trial balance using today's date.

LO1 Transaction Analysis, T
LO4 Accounts, and Trial
LO5 Balance

P 3. Hiroshi Tanaka began an upholstery-cleaning business on October 1 and engaged in the following transactions during the month:

Oct. 1 Began business by depositing $6,000 in a bank account in the name of the corporation in exchange for 6,000 shares of $1 par value common stock.
2 Ordered cleaning supplies, $500.
3 Purchased cleaning equipment for cash, $1,400.
4 Leased a van by making two months' lease payment in advance, $600.
7 Received the cleaning supplies ordered on October 2 and agreed to pay half the amount in ten days and the rest in thirty days.
9 Paid for repairs on the van with cash, $40.
12 Received cash for cleaning upholstery, $480.
17 Paid half the amount owed on supplies purchased on October 7, $250.
21 Billed customers for cleaning upholstery, $670.
24 Paid cash for additional repairs on the van, $40.
27 Received $300 from the customers billed on October 21.
31 Declared and paid a dividend of $350.

REQUIRED
1. Set up the following T accounts: Cash; Accounts Receivable; Cleaning Supplies; Prepaid Lease; Cleaning Equipment; Accounts Payable; Common Stock; Dividends; Cleaning Revenue; and Repair Expense.
2. Record transactions directly in the T accounts. Identify each entry by date.
3. Prepare a trial balance for Tanaka Upholstery-Cleaning, Inc., as of October 31, 20xx.
4. Compare and contrast how the issue of recognition, valuation, and classification are settled in the transactions of October 7 and 9.

LO1 Transaction Analysis,
LO4 Journal Form, T Accounts,
LO5 and Trial Balance

P 4. Sonny Hales is a house painter. During the month of April, he completed the following transactions:

Apr. 2 Began his business by contributing equipment valued at $1,230 and depositing $7,100 in a checking account in the name of the corporation in exchange for 833 shares of $10 par value common stock of the corporation.
3 Purchased a used truck costing $1,900. Paid $500 cash and signed a note for the balance. 1400 A/P
4 Purchased supplies on account for $320.
5 Completed a painting job and billed the customer $480.
7 Received $150 in cash for painting two rooms.
8 Hired an assistant at $6 per hour. NO TRANSACTION
10 Purchased supplies for $160 in cash.
11 Received a $480 check from the customer billed on April 5.
12 Paid $400 for an insurance policy for eighteen months' coverage.
13 Billed a customer $620 for a painting job.
14 Paid the assistant $150 for twenty-five hours' work.
15 Paid $40 for a tune-up for the truck.
18 Paid for the supplies purchased on April 4.
20 Purchased a new ladder (equipment) for $60 and supplies for $290, on account.
22 Received a telephone bill for $60, due next month.
23 Received $330 in cash from the customer billed on April 13.
25 Received $360 in cash for painting a five-room apartment.
27 Paid $200 on the note signed for the truck.
29 Paid the assistant $180 for thirty hours' work.
30 Declared and paid a dividend of $300.

REQUIRED
1. Prepare entries to record these transactions in journal form.
2. Set up the following T accounts and post all the entries: Cash; Accounts Receivable; Supplies; Prepaid Insurance; Equipment; Truck; Notes Payable; Accounts Payable; Common Stock; Dividends; Painting Fees Earned; Wages Expense; Telephone Expense; and Repair Expense.
3. Prepare a trial balance for Hales Painting Service, Inc., as of April 30, 20xx.
4. Compare how recognition applies to the transactions of April 5 and 7 and their effects on cash flow and how classification applies to the transactions of April 12 and 14.

LO4 Transaction Analysis,
LO5 General Journal, Ledger
SO6 Accounts, and Trial Balance

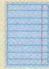

P 5. The Acorn Nursery School Corporation provides baby-sitting and child-care programs. On January 31, 20xx, the company had the following trial balance:

Acorn Nursery School Corporation
Trial Balance
January 31, 20xx

Cash (111)	$ 1,870	
Accounts Receivable (113)	1,700	
Equipment (141)	1,040	
Buses (143)	17,400	
Notes Payable (211)		$15,000
Accounts Payable (212)		1,640
Common Stock (311)		4,000
Retained Earnings (312)		1,370
	$22,010	$22,010

During the month of February, the company completed the following transactions:

Feb. 2 Paid this month's rent, $270.
3 Received fees for this month's services, $650.
4 Purchased supplies on account, $85.
5 Reimbursed the bus driver for gas expenses, $40.
6 Ordered playground equipment, $1,000.
8 Made a payment on account, $170.
9 Received payments from customers on account, $1,200.
10 Billed customers who had not yet paid for this month's services, $700.
11 Paid for the supplies purchased on February 4.
12 Paid part-time assistants for two weeks' services, $230.
13 Purchased playground equipment for cash, $1,000.
17 Purchased equipment on account, $290.
19 Paid this month's utility bill, $145.
22 Received payment for one month's services from customers previously billed, $500.
26 Paid part-time assistants for two weeks' services, $230.
27 Purchased gas and oil for the bus on account, $35.
28 Paid for a one-year insurance policy, $290.
28 Declared and paid a dividend of $110.

REQUIRED ▶
1. Open accounts in the ledger for the accounts in the trial balance plus the following ones: Supplies (115); Prepaid Insurance (116); Dividends (313); Service Revenue (411); Rent Expense (511); Gas and Oil Expense (512); Wages Expense (513); and Utilities Expense (514).
2. Enter the January 31, 20xx, account balances from the trial balance.
3. Enter the above transactions in the general journal (Pages 17 and 18).
4. Post the entries to the ledger accounts. Be sure to make the appropriate posting references in the journal and ledger as you post.
5. Prepare a trial balance as of February 28, 20xx.

Alternate Problems

LO4 Transaction Analysis

P 6. The following accounts are applicable to Dale's Lawn Service, Inc., a company that maintains condominium grounds:

1. Cash
2. Accounts Receivable

3. Supplies
4. Prepaid Insurance
5. Equipment
6. Accounts Payable
7. Common Stock
8. Retained Earnings
9. Dividends
10. Lawn Services Revenue
11. Wages Expense
12. Rent Expense
13. Utilities Expense

Dale's Lawn Service, Inc., completed the following transactions:

		Debit	Credit
a.	Received cash from customers billed last month.	1	2
b.	Made a payment on accounts payable.		
c.	Purchased a new one-year insurance policy in advance.		
d.	Purchased supplies on credit.		
e.	Billed a client for lawn services.		
f.	Made a rent payment for the current month.		
g.	Received cash from customers for lawn services.		
h.	Paid wages for the staff.		
i.	Ordered equipment.		
j.	Paid the current month's utility bill.		
k.	Received and paid for the equipment ordered in **i**.		
l.	Returned for full credit some of the supplies purchased in **d** because they were defective.		
m.	Paid for supplies purchased in **d**, less the return in **l**.		
n.	Declared and paid a dividend.		

REQUIRED ▶ Analyze each transaction and show the accounts affected by entering the corresponding numbers in the appropriate debit or credit columns as shown in transaction **a**. Indicate no entry, if appropriate.

LO1 **Transaction Analysis,**
LO4 **Journal Form, T Accounts,**
LO5 **and Trial Balance**

P 7. Nomar Parra won a concession to rent bicycles in the local park during the summer. During the month of June, Parra completed the following transactions for his bicycle rental business:

June 2 Began business by placing $7,200 in a business checking account in the name of the corporation in exchange for 7,200 shares of $1 par value common stock.
3 Purchased supplies on account for $150.
4 Purchased ten bicycles for $2,500, paying $1,200 down and agreeing to pay the rest in thirty days.
5 Paid $2,900 in cash for a small shed to store the bicycles and to use for other operations.
6 Received $470 in cash for rentals during the first week of operation.
8 Paid $400 in cash for shipping and installation costs (considered an addition to the cost of the shed) to place the shed at the park entrance.
9 Hired a part-time assistant to help out on weekends at $8 per hour.
10 Paid a maintenance person $75 to clean the grounds.
13 Received $500 in cash for rentals during the second week of operation.
15 Paid the assistant $80 for a weekend's work.
17 Paid $150 for the supplies purchased on June 3.
18 Paid a $55 repair bill on bicycles.
20 Received $550 in cash for rentals during the third week of operation.
22 Paid the assistant $80 for a weekend's work.
23 Billed a company $110 for bicycle rentals for an employee outing.
25 Paid the $100 fee for June to the Park District for the right to the bicycle concession.
27 Received $410 in cash for rentals during the week.
29 Paid the assistant $80 for a weekend's work.
30 Declared and paid a dividend of $500.

REQUIRED
1. Prepare entries to record these transactions in journal form.
2. Set up the following T accounts and post all the entries: Cash; Accounts Receivable; Supplies; Shed; Bicycles; Accounts Payable; Common Stock; Dividends; Rental Revenue; Wages Expense; Maintenance Expense; Repair Expense; and Concession Fee Expense.
3. Prepare a trial balance for Parra Rentals, Inc., as of June 30, 20xx.
4. Compare and contrast how the issues of recognition, valuation, and classification are settled in the transactions of June 3 and 10.

LO4 Transaction Analysis,
LO5 General Journal, Ledger
SO6 Accounts, and Trial Balance

P 8. Yury Wagoner Corporation is a marketing firm. On July 31, 20xx, the company's trial balance was as follows:

Yury Wagoner Corporation
Trial Balance
July 31, 20xx

Cash (111)	$10,200	
Accounts Receivable (113)	5,500	
Supplies (115)	610	
Office Equipment (141)	4,200	
Accounts Payable (212)		$ 2,600
Common Stock (311)		12,000
Retained Earnings (312)		5,910
	$20,510	$20,510

During the month of August, the company completed the following transactions:

Aug. 2 Paid rent for August, $650.
   3 Received cash from customers on account, $2,300.
   7 Ordered supplies, $380.
  10 Billed customers for services provided, $2,800.
  12 Made a payment on accounts payable, $1,100.
  14 Received the supplies ordered on August 7 and agreed to pay for them in 30 days, $380.
  15 Paid salaries for the first half of August, $1,900.
  17 Discovered some of the supplies were not as ordered and returned them for full credit, $80.
  19 Received cash from a customer for services provided, $4,800.
  24 Paid the utility bill for August, $160.
  25 Paid the telephone bill for August, $120.
  26 Received a bill, to be paid in September, for advertisements placed in the local newspaper during the month of August to promote Yury Wagoner Corporation, $700.
  29 Billed a customer for services provided, $2,700.
  30 Paid salaries for the last half of August, $1,900.
  31 Declared and paid a dividend of $1,200.

REQUIRED
1. Open accounts in the ledger for the accounts in the trial balance plus the following accounts: Dividends (313); Public Relations Fees (411); Salaries Expense (511); Rent Expense (512); Utilities Expense (513); Telephone Expense (514); and Advertising Expense (515).
2. Enter the July 31, 20xx, account balances from the trial balance.
3. Enter the above transactions in the general journal (Pages 22 and 23).
4. Post the entries to the ledger accounts. Be sure to make the appropriate posting references in the journal and ledger as you post.
5. Prepare a trial balance as of August 31, 20xx.

Skills Development Cases

Conceptual Analysis

LO1 Valuation Issue

SD 1. Nike, Inc., <www.nike.com> manufactures athletic shoes and related products. In one of its annual reports, Nike made this statement: "Property, plant, and equipment are recorded at cost."[8] Given that the property, plant, and equipment undoubtedly were purchased over several years and that the current value of those assets was likely to be very different from their original cost, tell what authoritative basis there is for carrying the assets at cost. Does accounting generally recognize changes in value after the purchase of property, plant, and equipment? Assume you are a Nike accountant. Write a memo to management explaining the rationale underlying Nike's approach.

LO1 Valuation and Classification
LO4 Issues for Dot-Coms

SD 2. The dot-com business has raised many issues about accounting practices, some of which are of great concern to both the SEC and the FASB. Important ones relate to the valuation and classification of revenue transactions. Many dot-com companies seek to report as much revenue as possible because revenue growth is seen as a key performance measure for these companies. Amazon.com is a good example. Consider the following situations:

a. An Amazon.com <www.amazon.com> customer orders and pays $28 for a Gameboy® electronic game on the Internet. Amazon sends an email to the company that makes the product, which sends the Gameboy to the customer. Amazon collects $28 from the customer and pays $24 to the other company. Amazon never owns the Gameboy.

b. Amazon agrees to place a banner advertisement on its web site for another dot-com company. Instead of paying cash for the advertisement, the other company agrees to let Amazon advertise on its web site.

c. Assume the same facts as in situation **b** except that Amazon agrees to accept the other company's common stock in this barter transaction. Over the next six months, the price of the stock received goes down.

Discuss the valuation and classification issues that arise in each of these situations, including how Amazon should account for each transaction.

 Group Activity: Divide the class into groups. Assign each group one of the above cases so that one-third of the groups have each case. Debrief and discuss.

Ethical Dilemma

LO1 Recognition Point and Ethical Considerations

SD 3. Jerry Hasbrow, a sales representative for Penn Office Supplies Corporation, is compensated on a commission basis and receives a substantial bonus for meeting his annual sales goal. The company's recognition point for sales is the day of shipment. On December 31, Hasbrow realizes he needs sales of $2,000 to reach his sales goal and receive the bonus. He calls a purchaser for a local insurance company, whom he knows well, and asks him to buy $2,000 worth of copier paper today. The purchaser says, "But Jerry, that's more than a year's supply for us." Hasbrow says, "Buy it today. If you decide it's too much, you can return however much you want for full credit next month." The purchaser says, "Okay, ship it." The paper is shipped on December 31 and recorded as a sale. On January 15, the purchaser returns $1,750 worth of paper for full credit (approved by Hasbrow) against the bill. Should the shipment on December 31 be recorded as a sale? Discuss the ethics of Hasbrow's action.

 Group Activity: Divide the class into informal groups to discuss and report on the ethical issues of this case.

Research Activity

LO4 Transactions in a Business Article

SD 4. Locate an article on a company you recognize or on a company in a business that interests you in one of the following sources: a recent issue of a business publication (such as *Barron's*, *Fortune*, *The Wall Street Journal*, *BusinessWeek*, or *Forbes*) or the Needles Accounting Resource Center Web Site at http://accounting.college.hmco.com/students.

Read the article carefully, noting any references to transactions in which the company engages. These may be normal transactions (such as sales or purchases) or unusual transactions (such as a merger or the purchase of another company). Bring a copy of the article to class and be prepared to describe how you would analyze and record the transactions you have noted.

Decision-Making Practice

SD 5.

LO4 **Transaction Analysis**
LO5 **and Evaluation of a Trial Balance**

Luis Ruiz hired an attorney to help him start Ruiz Repair Service Corporation. On March 1, Ruiz deposited $11,500 cash in a bank account in the name of the corporation in exchange for 1,150 shares of $10 par value common stock. When he paid the attorney's bill of $700, the attorney advised him to hire an accountant to keep his records. Ruiz was so busy that it was March 31 before he asked you to straighten out his records. Your first task is to develop a trial balance based on the March transactions, which are described in the next two paragraphs.

After investing in his business and paying his attorney, Ruiz borrowed $5,000 from the bank. He later paid $260, including interest of $60, on this loan. He also purchased a used pickup truck in the company's name, paying $2,500 down and financing $7,400. The first payment on the truck is due April 15. Ruiz then rented an office and paid three months' rent, $900, in advance. Credit purchases of office equipment of $800 and repair tools of $500 must be paid by April 10.

In March, Ruiz Repair Service completed repairs of $1,300, of which $400 were cash transactions. Of the credit transactions, $300 were collected during March, and $600 remained to be collected at the end of March. Wages of $450 were paid to employees. On March 31, the company received a $75 bill for the March utilities expense and a $50 check from a customer for work to be completed in April.

1. Record all of the transactions for March in journal form. Label each of the entries alphabetically.
2. Set up T accounts. Then post the entries to the T accounts. Identify each posting with the letter corresponding to the transaction.
3. Determine the balance of each account.
4. Prepare a trial balance for Ruiz Repair Service Corporation as of March 31.
5. Luis Ruiz is unsure how to evaluate the trial balance. His Cash account balance is $12,440, which exceeds his original investment of $11,500 by $940. Did he make a profit of $940? Explain why the Cash account is not an indicator of business earnings. Cite specific examples to show why it is difficult to determine net income by looking solely at figures in the trial balance.

FINANCIAL REPORTING AND ANALYSIS CASES

Interpreting Financial Reports

FRA 1.

LO2 **Interpreting a Bank's**
LO4 **Financial Statements**

Mellon Bank <www.mellon.com> is a large bank holding company. Selected accounts from a recent annual report are as follows (in millions):[9]

Cash and Due from Banks	$ 3,506	Securities Available for Sale	$ 7,910
Loans to Customers	26,369	Deposits by Customers	36,890

1. Indicate whether each of the accounts just listed is an asset, a liability, or a component of stockholders' equity on Mellon Bank's balance sheet.
2. Assume that you are in a position to do business with this large company. Prepare the entry on Mellon Bank's books in journal form to record each of the following transactions:
   a. You sell securities in the amount of $2,000 to the bank.
   b. You deposit the $2,000 received in step **a** in the bank.
   c. You borrow $5,000 from the bank.

International Company

LO4 Transaction Analysis

FRA 2. Ajinomoto Company <www.ajinomoto.com>, a Japanese company with operations in 22 countries, is primarily engaged in the manufacture and sale of food products. The following selected aggregate cash transactions were reported in the statement of cash flows in Ajinomoto's annual report (amounts in millions of yen):[10]

Dividends paid	¥ 7,793
Purchase of property, plant, and equipment	46,381
Proceeds from issuance of long-term debt	10,357
Repayment of long-term debt	11,485

Prepare entries in journal form to record the above transactions.

Toys "R" Us Annual Report

LO4 Transaction Analysis

FRA 3. Refer to the balance sheet in the Toys "R" Us <www.tru.com> annual report in the Supplement to Chapter 1. Prepare T accounts for the accounts Cash and Cash Equivalents, Accounts and Other Receivables, Prepaid Expenses and Other Current Assets, Accounts Payable, and Income Taxes Payable. Properly place the balance of the account at February 1, 2003, in the T accounts. Below are some typical transactions in which Toys "R" Us would engage. Analyze each transaction, enter it in the T accounts, and determine the balance of each account. Assume all entries are in thousands.

a. Paid cash in advance for certain expenses, $20,000.
b. Received cash from customers billed previously, $35,000.
c. Paid cash for income taxes previously owed, $70,000.
d. Paid cash to suppliers for amounts owed, $120,000.

Comparison Case: Toys "R" Us and Walgreen Co.

LO1 Recognition, Valuation, and Classification

FRA 4. Refer to the Summary of Significant Accounting Policies in the notes to the financial statements in the Toys "R" Us <www.tru.com> annual report and to the financial statements of Walgreen Co. <www.walgreens.com> to answer these questions:

1. How does the concept of recognition apply to advertising costs for both Toys "R" Us and Walgreens?
2. How does the concept of valuation apply to property and equipment for both companies?
3. How does the concept of classification apply to cash and cash equivalents for both companies?

Discuss any differences that you may observe.

Fingraph® Financial Analyst™

LO1
LO3
LO4 Transaction Identification

FRA 5. Choose a company from the list of Fingraph companies on the Needles Accounting Resource Center Web Site at http://accounting.college.hmco.com/students. Click on the company you selected to access the Microsoft Excel spreadsheet for that company. You will find the company's URL (Internet address) in the heading of the spreadsheet. Click on the URL for a link to the company's web site and annual report.

1. From the company's annual report, determine the industry(ies) in which the company operates.
2. Find the summary of significant accounting policies that follows the financial statements. In these policies, find examples of the application of recognition, valuation, and classification.
3. Identify six types of transactions the company would commonly engage in. Are any of these transactions more common in the industry in which the company operates than in other industries? For each transaction, tell what account would typically be debited and what account would be credited.
4. Prepare a one-page executive summary that highlights what you have learned from steps **1**, **2**, and **3**.

Internet Case

LO2 Comparison of
LO4 Contrasting Companies

FRA 6. Sun Microsystems <www.sun.com> and Oracle Corporation <www.oracle.com> are leading computer and software companies. Go to their web sites directly using the URLs shown here, or go to the Needles Accounting Resource Center Web Site at http://accounting.college.hmco.com/students for a link to their web sites. Access each company's annual report and find its balance sheet.

1. What differences and similarities do you find in the account titles used by Sun Microsystems and those used by Oracle? What differences and similarities do you find in the account titles used by the two companies and those used in this text?
2. Although the companies are in the same general industry, their businesses differ. How are these differences reflected on the balance sheets? What types of transactions resulted in the differences?

3

Chapter 3 defines the accounting concept of business income, discusses the role of adjusting entries in the measurement of income, and demonstrates the preparation of financial statements.

Measuring Business Income

LEARNING OBJECTIVES

LO1 Define *net income* and its two major components, *revenues* and *expenses.*

LO2 Explain how the income measurement issues of accounting period, continuity, and matching are resolved.

LO3 Define *accrual accounting* and explain three broad ways of accomplishing it.

LO4 State four principal situations that require adjusting entries and prepare typical adjusting entries.

LO5 Prepare financial statements from an adjusted trial balance.

SUPPLEMENTAL OBJECTIVE

SO6 Analyze cash flows from accrual-based information.

DECISION POINT
A USER'S FOCUS

Kelly Services <www.kellyservices.com> Kelly Services is one of the most successful temporary employment agencies. During any given year, Kelly incurs various operating expenses that are recorded as expenses when they are paid. However, at the end of the year, some expenses—including, for example, the wages of employees during the last days before the end of the year—will have been incurred but will not be paid until the next year. If these expenses are not accounted for correctly, they will appear in the wrong year—the year in which they are paid instead of the year in which Kelly benefited from them. The result is a misstatement of the company's income, a key profitability performance measure. How is this problem avoided?

According to the concepts of accrual accounting and the matching rule, which you will learn in this chapter, the amount of expenses that have been incurred but not paid must be determined and then recorded as expenses of the current year with corresponding liabilities to be paid the next year. The accompanying figure shows the liabilities, called *accrued liabilities,* that resulted from this process at Kelly Services.[1] Total accrued liabilities for payroll and related expenses, accrued insurance, and income and other taxes were $227,033,000 in 2001 and $257,215,000 in 2002. If these items had not been recorded in their respective years, income would have been misstated by a significant amount.

How does Kelly Services record wages that have been incurred in December but won't be paid until January?

Financial Highlights: Notes to the Financial Statements
3. ACCRUED LIABILITIES
(In thousands)

	2002	2001
Payroll and related expenses	$181,686	$154,813
Accrued insurance	27,912	24,071
Income and other taxes	47,617	48,149
Total accrued liabilities	$257,215	$227,033

PROFITABILITY MEASUREMENT: THE ROLE OF BUSINESS INCOME

LO1 Define *net income* and its two major components, *revenues* and *expenses*.

RELATED TEXT ASSIGNMENTS
Q: 1
SD: 5
FRA: 5

KEY POINT: Accounting measures and reports a business's profitability. The extent of the reported profit or loss communicates the company's success or failure in meeting this business goal.

 STOP AND THINK!
When a company has net income, what happens to assets and/or liabilities?
Stockholders' equity increases, but there is also an increase in assets and/or a decrease in liabilities. ■

Profitability is one of the two major goals of a business (the other being liquidity). For a business to succeed, or even to survive, it must earn a profit. The word **profit**, though, has many meanings. One is the increase in stockholders' equity that results from business operations. However, even this definition can be interpreted differently by economists, lawyers, businesspeople, and the public. Because the word *profit* has more than one meaning, accountants prefer to use the term *net income*, which can be precisely defined from an accounting point of view. Net income is reported on the income statement and is a performance measure used by management, stockholders, and others to monitor a business's progress in meeting the goal of profitability. Readers of income statements need to understand how the accountant defines net income and to be aware of its strengths and weaknesses as a measure of company performance.

NET INCOME

Net income is the net increase in stockholders' equity that results from the operations of a company and is accumulated in the Retained Earnings account. Net income, in its simplest form, is measured by the difference between revenues and expenses when revenues exceed expenses:

$$\text{Net Income} = \text{Revenues} - \text{Expenses}$$

When expenses exceed revenues, a **net loss** occurs.

REVENUES

KEY POINT: The essence of revenue is that something has been *earned* through the sale of goods or services. That is why cash received through a loan does not constitute revenue.

Revenues are increases in stockholders' equity resulting from selling goods, rendering services, or performing other business activities. In the simplest case, revenues equal the price of goods sold or services rendered over a specific period of time. When a business delivers a product or provides a service to a customer, it usually receives either cash or a promise to pay cash in the near future. The promise to pay is recorded in either Accounts Receivable or Notes Receivable. The revenue for a given period equals the total of cash and receivables from goods and services provided to customers during that period.

Liabilities generally are not affected by revenues, and some transactions that increase cash and other assets are not revenues. For example, a bank loan increases liabilities and cash but does not produce revenue. The collection of accounts receivable, which increases cash and decreases accounts receivable, does not produce revenue either. Remember that when a sale on credit takes place, the asset account Accounts Receivable increases; at the same time, a stockholders' equity revenue account increases. So counting the collection of the receivable as revenue later would be counting the same sale twice.

Not all increases in stockholders' equity arise from revenues. Stockholders' investments increase stockholders' equity but are not revenue.

EXPENSES

KEY POINT: The primary purpose of an expense is to generate revenue.

Expenses are decreases in stockholders' equity resulting from the costs of selling goods, rendering services, or performing other business activities. In other words, expenses are the costs of the goods and services used up in the course of earning revenues. Often called the *cost of doing business*, expenses include the costs of goods sold, the costs of activities necessary to carry on a business, and the costs of attracting and serving customers. Examples of expenses are salaries, rent, advertising, telephone service, and depreciation (allocation of cost) of a building or office equipment.

BUSINESS-WORLD EXAMPLE: Income measurement is difficult in many industries because of the uncertainties associated with their revenues and expenses. For example, construction companies must estimate their revenues based on a project's percentage of completion.

Just as not all cash receipts are revenues, not all cash payments are expenses. A cash payment to reduce a liability does not result in an expense. The liability, however, may have come from incurring a previous expense, such as advertising, that is to be paid later. There may also be two steps before an expenditure of cash becomes an expense. For example, prepaid expenses and plant assets (such as machinery and equipment) are recorded as assets when they are acquired. Later, as their usefulness expires in the operation of the business, their cost is allocated to expenses. In fact, expenses sometimes are called *expired costs*.

Not all decreases in stockholders' equity arise from expenses. Dividends decrease stockholders' equity, but they are not expenses.

 Check out ACE for a Review Quiz at http://accounting.college.hmco.com/students.

INCOME MEASUREMENT ISSUES

LO2 Explain how the income measurement issues of accounting period, continuity, and matching are resolved.

RELATED TEXT ASSIGNMENTS
Q: 2, 3, 4
SE: 1
E: 1
SD: 1, 3
FRA: 1, 3, 5, 6

KEY POINT: Accounting periods must be of equal length so that one period can be compared with the next.

Several issues must be addressed in the measurement of income. These include the accounting period issue, the continuity issue, and the matching issue.

THE ACCOUNTING PERIOD ISSUE

The **accounting period issue** addresses the difficulty of assigning revenues and expenses to a short period of time, such as a month or a year. Not all transactions can be easily assigned to specific time periods. Purchases of buildings and equipment, for example, have effects that extend over many years. Accountants solve this problem by estimating the number of years the buildings or equipment will be in use and the cost that should be assigned to each year. In the process, they make an assumption about **periodicity**: that the net income for any period of time less than the life of the business, although tentative, is still a useful estimate of the entity's profitability for the period.

Generally, to make comparisons easier, the time periods are of equal length. Financial statements may be prepared for any time period. Accounting periods of less than one year—for example, a month or a quarter—are called *interim periods*. The 12-month accounting period used by an organization is called its **fiscal year**. Many organizations use the calendar year, January 1 to December 31, for their fiscal year. Others find it convenient to choose a fiscal year that ends during a slack season rather than a peak season. In this case, the fiscal year corresponds to the yearly cycle of business activity. The time period should always be noted in the financial statements.

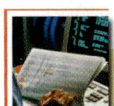

FOCUS ON BUSINESS PRACTICE

Fiscal Year-Ends Vary.
The table below shows the diverse fiscal years used by some well-known companies. Many governmental and educational units use fiscal years that end June 30 or September 30.

Company	Last Month of Fiscal Year
Caesars World Inc. <www.caesarsworld.com>	July
The Walt Disney Company <www.disney.go.com>	September
Fleetwood Enterprises, Inc. <www.fleetwood.com>	April
H.J. Heinz, Inc. <www.heinz.com>	March
Kelly Services <www.kellyservices.com>	December
MGM-UA Communications Co. <www.mgm.com>	August
Toys "R" Us <www.tru.com>	January

THE CONTINUITY ISSUE

The process of measuring business income requires that certain expense and revenue transactions be allocated over several accounting periods. The number of accounting periods raises the **continuity issue**. How long will the business entity last? Many businesses last less than five years; in any given year, thousands of businesses go bankrupt. To prepare financial statements for an accounting period, the accountant must make an assumption about the ability of the business to survive. Specifically, unless there is evidence to the contrary, the accountant assumes that the business will continue to operate indefinitely—that it is a **going concern**. Justification for all the techniques

BUSINESS-WORLD EXAMPLE: The continuity assumption is set aside when an organization is formed for a limited venture, such as a World's Fair or the Olympics.

of income measurement rests on the assumption of continuity. For example, this assumption allows the cost of certain assets to be held on the balance sheet until a future year, when it will become an expense on the income statement.

Another example has to do with the value of assets on the balance sheet. The accountant records assets at cost and does not record subsequent changes in their value. But the value of assets to a going concern is much higher than the value of assets to a firm facing bankruptcy. In the latter case, the accountant may be asked to set aside the assumption of continuity and to prepare financial statements based on the assumption that the firm will go out of business and sell all of its assets at liquidation value—that is, for what they will bring in cash.

THE MATCHING ISSUE

KEY POINT: Although the cash basis often is used for tax purposes, it seldom produces an accurate measurement of a business's performance for financial reporting purposes.

Revenues and expenses can be accounted for on a cash received and cash paid basis. This practice is known as the **cash basis of accounting**. Individuals and some businesses may use the cash basis of accounting for income tax purposes. Under this method, revenues are reported in the period in which cash is received, and expenses are reported in the period in which cash is paid. Taxable income, therefore, is calculated as the difference between cash receipts from revenues and cash payments for expenses.

Although the cash basis of accounting works well for some small businesses and many individuals, it does not meet the needs of most businesses. As explained above, revenues can be earned in a period other than the one in which cash is received, and expenses can be incurred in a period other than the one in which cash is paid. To measure net income adequately, revenues and expenses must be assigned to the appropriate accounting period. The accountant solves this problem by applying the **matching rule**:

Revenues must be assigned to the accounting period in which the goods are sold or the services performed, and expenses must be assigned to the accounting period in which they are used to produce revenue.

🛑 **STOP AND THINK!**
Why must a company that gives a guaranty or warranty with its product or service show an expense in the year of sale rather than in a later year when a repair or replacement is made?

To measure a company's performance (net income) accurately, each expense (in this case, guaranty or warranty expense) must be matched with the related revenue in the year in which the product or service was sold. Otherwise, net income will be overstated, and the related liability will be understated. ■

Direct cause-and-effect relationships seldom can be demonstrated for certain, but many costs appear to be related to particular revenues. The accountant recognizes these expenses and the related revenues in the same accounting period. Examples are the costs of goods sold and sales commissions. When there is no direct means of connecting expenses and revenues, the accountant tries to allocate costs in a systematic way among the accounting periods that benefit from the costs. For example, a building is converted from an asset to an expense by allocating its cost over the years that the company benefits from its use.

 Check out ACE for a Review Quiz at http://accounting.college.hmco.com/students.

ACCRUAL ACCOUNTING

LO3 Define *accrual accounting* and explain three broad ways of accomplishing it.

RELATED TEXT ASSIGNMENTS
Q: 5, 6, 7, 8
SE: 1
E: 1, 2
P: 2, 7
SD: 1, 2, 3
FRA: 3

To apply the matching rule, accountants have developed accrual accounting. **Accrual accounting** "attempts to record the financial effects on an enterprise of transactions and other events and circumstances . . . in the periods in which those transactions, events, and circumstances occur rather than only in the periods in which cash is received or paid by the enterprise."[2] That is, accrual accounting consists of all the techniques developed by accountants to apply the matching rule. It is done in the following general ways: (1) by recording revenues when earned, (2) by recording expenses when incurred, and (3) by adjusting the accounts.

RECOGNIZING REVENUES WHEN EARNED

The process of determining when revenue is earned, and consequently when it should be recorded, is called **revenue recognition**. The Securities and Exchange

Commission has said that all the following conditions must exist before revenue is recognized:

- Persuasive evidence of an arrangement exists.
- Delivery has occurred or services have been rendered.
- The seller's price to the buyer is fixed or determinable.
- Collectibility is reasonably assured.[3]

For example, when Joan Miller Advertising Agency, Inc., bills a customer for placing an advertisement, it is recorded as revenue because the transaction meets these four criteria. It is agreed that the customer owes for the service, the service has been rendered, the parties understand the price, and there is a reasonable expectation that the customer will pay the bill. Revenue is recorded by debiting Accounts Receivable and crediting Advertising Fees Earned. Note that it is not necessary for cash to be collected for revenue to be recorded. There only needs to be a reasonable expectation that it will be collected.

RECOGNIZING EXPENSES WHEN INCURRED

Expenses are recorded when there is an agreement to purchase goods or services, the goods have been delivered or the services rendered, a price is established or can be determined, and the goods or services have been used to produce revenue. For example, when Joan Miller Advertising Agency receives its telephone bill, the expense is recognized both as having been incurred and as helping to produce revenue. The transaction is recorded by debiting Telephone Expense and crediting Accounts Payable. Until the bill is paid, Accounts Payable serves as a holding account. Notice that recognition of the expense does not depend on the payment of cash.

ADJUSTING THE ACCOUNTS

A third application of accrual accounting is adjusting the accounts. Adjustments are necessary because the accounting period, by definition, ends on a particular day. The balance sheet must list all assets and liabilities as of the end of that day, and the income statement must contain all revenues and expenses applicable to the period ending on that day. Although operating a business is a continuous process, there must be a cutoff point for the periodic reports. Some transactions invariably span the cutoff point; thus, some accounts need adjustment.

For example, some of the accounts in the end-of-the-period trial balance for Joan Miller Advertising Agency (Exhibit 1) do not show the correct balances for

ENRICHMENT NOTE: The accountant waits until the end of an accounting period to update certain revenues and expenses even though the revenues and expenses theoretically have changed during the period. There usually is no need to adjust them until the end of the period, when the financial statements are prepared. In fact, it would be impractical, even impossible, to adjust the accounts each time they are affected.

FOCUS ON BUSINESS ETHICS

Aggressive Accounting or Deception? You Judge.

Accounting principles, such as revenue recognition and the matching rule, should not be applied in a way that will distort or obscure financial information. Accounting practices are meant to inform readers of financial statements, not to deceive them. In recent years, the Securities and Exchange Commission <www.sec.gov> has been waging a public campaign against corporate accounting practices that manage or manipulate earnings to meet the expectations of Wall Street analysts.[4] Corporations engage in such practices in the hope of avoiding shortfalls that might cause serious declines in their stock price. The following describes a few of the corporate accounting practices that the SEC has challenged:

- Lucent Technologies <www.lucent.com> sold telecommunications equipment to companies from which there was no reasonable expectation of collection because of the companies' poor financial condition.
- America Online (AOL) <www.aol.com> recorded advertising as an asset rather than as an expense.
- Eclipsys <www.eclipsys.com> recorded software contracts as revenue even though it had not yet rendered the services.
- KnowledgeWare <knowledgeware.itil.com> recorded revenue from sales of software even though it told customers they did not have to pay until they had the software.

EXHIBIT 1
Trial Balance for Joan Miller Advertising Agency, Inc.

Joan Miller Advertising Agency, Inc.
Trial Balance
July 31, 20xx

Cash	$ 9,140	
Accounts Receivable	4,800	
Art Supplies	1,800	
Office Supplies	800	
Prepaid Rent	1,600	
Prepaid Insurance	960	
Art Equipment	4,200	
Office Equipment	3,000	
Accounts Payable		$ 3,240
Unearned Art Fees		1,000
Common Stock		20,000
Dividends	1,400	
Advertising Fees Earned		6,200
Wages Expense	2,400	
Utilities Expense	200	
Telephone Expense	140	
	$30,440	$30,440

preparing the financial statements. The July 31 trial balance lists prepaid rent of $1,600. At $800 per month, this represents rent for the months of July and August. So on July 31, one-half of the $1,600, or $800, represents rent expense for July; the remaining $800 represents an asset that will be used in August. An adjustment is needed to reflect the $800 balance in the Prepaid Rent account on the balance sheet and the $800 rent expense on the income statement. As you will see on the following pages, several other accounts in the Joan Miller Advertising Agency trial balance do not reflect their correct balances. Like the Prepaid Rent account, they need to be adjusted.

ACCRUAL ACCOUNTING AND PERFORMANCE MEASURES

Accrual accounting can be difficult to understand. The related adjustments take time to calculate and enter in the records. Also, adjusting entries do not affect cash flows in the current period because they never involve the Cash account. You might ask, "Why go to all the trouble of making them? Why worry about them?" The Securities and Exchange Commission, in fact, has identified issues related to accrual accounting and adjustments as an area of utmost importance because of the potential for abuse and misrepresentation.[5]

All adjustments are important because they are necessary to measure key profitability performance measures. Adjusting entries affect net income on the income statement, and they affect profitability comparisons from one accounting period to the next. They also affect assets and liabilities on the balance sheet and thus provide information about a company's *future* cash inflows and outflows. This information is needed to assess management's short-term goal of achieving sufficient liquidity to meet its need for cash to pay ongoing obligations. The potential for abuse arises because considerable judgment underlies the application of adjusting entries. Misuse of this judgment can result in misleading measures of performance.

● **STOP AND THINK!**
Is accrual accounting more closely related to a company's goal of profitability or liquidity?
It is more closely related to profitability because the purpose of accrual accounting is to measure net income. Cash accounting is more closely related to the goal of liquidity. ■

 Check out ACE for a Review Quiz at http://accounting.college.hmco.com/students.

The Adjustment Process

LO4 State four principal situations that require adjusting entries and prepare typical adjusting entries.

RELATED TEXT ASSIGNMENTS
Q: 9, 10, 11, 12, 13, 14, 15, 16, 17, 18, 19, 20
SE: 2, 3, 4, 5, 6
E: 1, 3, 4, 5, 6, 7, 8, 9
P: 1, 2, 3, 4, 5, 6, 7, 8
SD: 1, 2, 3, 4, 5
FRA: 1, 2, 4, 5, 6, 7

KEY POINT: Each adjusting entry must include at least one balance sheet account and one income statement account. By definition, it cannot include a debit or a credit to Cash. Because adjusting entries never involve the Cash account, they never affect cash flows.

Accountants use **adjusting entries** to apply accrual accounting to transactions that span more than one accounting period. There are four situations in which adjusting entries are required, as illustrated in Figure 1. As shown, each situation affects one balance sheet account and one income statement account. Adjusting entries never involve the Cash account. The four types of adjusting entries may be stated as follows:

1. Costs have been recorded that must be allocated between two or more accounting periods. Examples are prepaid rent, prepaid insurance, supplies, and costs of a building. The adjusting entry in this case involves an asset account and an expense account.
2. Expenses have been incurred but are not yet recorded. Examples are the wages earned by employees in the current accounting period but after the last pay period. The adjusting entry involves an expense account and a liability account.
3. Revenues have been recorded that must be allocated between two or more accounting periods. An example is payments collected for services yet to be rendered. The adjusting entry involves a liability account and a revenue account.
4. Revenues have been earned but are not yet recorded. An example is fees earned but not yet collected or billed to customers. The adjusting entry involves an asset account and a revenue account.

Accountants often refer to adjusting entries as deferrals or accruals. A **deferral** is the postponement of the recognition of an expense already paid (Type 1 adjustment) or of a revenue received in advance (Type 3 adjustment). Recording of the receipt or payment of cash precedes the adjusting entry. An **accrual** is the recognition of a revenue (Type 4 adjustment) or expense (Type 2 adjustment) that has arisen but has not yet been recorded. No cash was received or paid prior to the adjusting entry; this will occur in a future accounting period. Once again, we use Joan Miller Advertising Agency, Inc., to illustrate the kinds of adjusting entries that most businesses make.

TYPE 1: ALLOCATING RECORDED COSTS BETWEEN TWO OR MORE ACCOUNTING PERIODS (DEFERRED EXPENSES)

Companies often make expenditures that benefit more than one period. These expenditures are usually debited to an asset account. At the end of the accounting period, the amount that has been used is transferred from the asset account to an

FIGURE 1
The Four Types of Adjustments

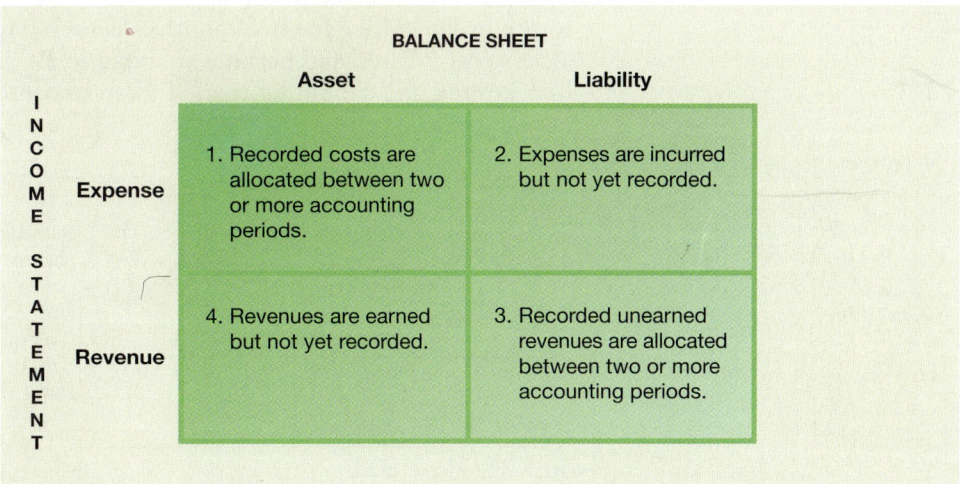

FIGURE 2
Adjustment for Prepaid (Deferred) Expenses

expense account. Two of the more important kinds of adjustments are those for prepaid expenses and the depreciation of plant and equipment.

KEY POINT: The expired portion of a prepayment is converted to an expense; the unexpired portion remains an asset.

■ **PREPAID EXPENSES** Some expenses customarily are paid in advance. These expenditures are called **prepaid expenses**. Among them are rent, insurance, and supplies. At the end of an accounting period, a portion (or all) of these goods or services will have been used up or will have expired. An adjusting entry reducing the asset and increasing the expense, as shown in Figure 2, is always required. The amount of the adjustment equals the cost of the goods or services used up or expired. If adjusting entries for prepaid expenses are not made at the end of the period, both the balance sheet and the income statement will present incorrect information; the assets of the company will be overstated, and the expenses of the company will be understated. This means that stockholders' equity on the balance sheet and net income on the income statement will be overstated.

At the beginning of the month, Joan Miller Advertising Agency paid two months' rent in advance. This expenditure resulted in an asset consisting of the right to occupy the office for two months. As each day in the month passed, part of the asset's cost expired and became an expense. By July 31, one-half of the asset's cost had expired and should be treated as an expense. Here is the analysis of this economic event:

Prepaid Rent (Adjustment a)

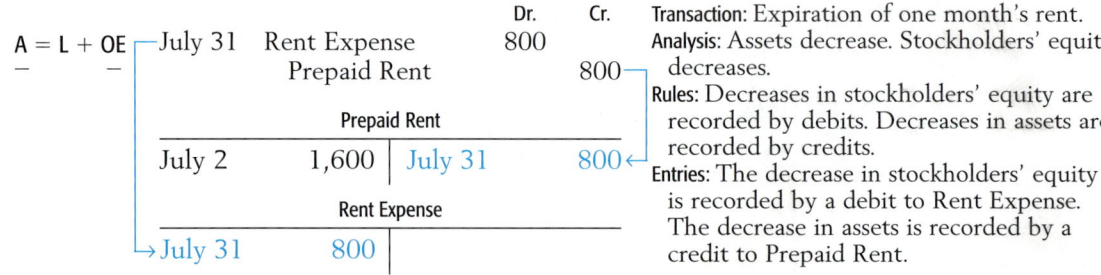

The Prepaid Rent account now has a balance of $800, which represents one month's rent paid in advance. The Rent Expense account reflects the $800 expense for the month of July.

Besides rent, Joan Miller Advertising Agency prepaid expenses for insurance, art supplies, and office supplies, all of which call for adjusting entries.

On July 8, the agency purchased a one-year life insurance policy, paying for it in advance. Like prepaid rent, prepaid insurance offers benefits (in this case, protection) that expire day by day. By the end of the month, one-twelfth of the insurance protection had expired. The adjustment is analyzed and recorded like this:

Prepaid Insurance (Adjustment b)

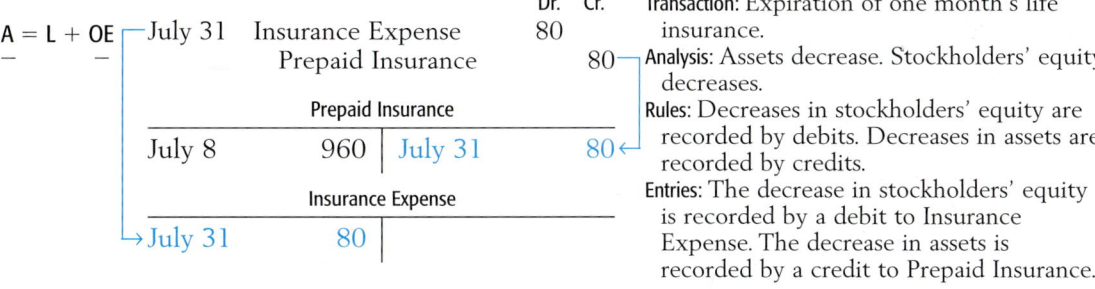

The Prepaid Insurance account now shows the correct balance, $880, and Insurance Expense reflects the expired cost, $80 for the month of July.

Early in the month, Joan Miller Advertising Agency purchased art supplies and office supplies. As Joan Miller prepared advertising designs for various clients, art supplies were consumed, and her secretary used office supplies. There is no need to account for these supplies every day because the financial statements are not prepared until the end of the month and the recordkeeping would involve too much work. Instead, Joan Miller makes a careful inventory of the art and office supplies at the end of the month. This inventory records the number and cost of those supplies that are still assets of the company—that are yet to be consumed.

KEY POINT: Notice that the cost of supplies consumed is inferred, not observed.

Suppose the inventory shows that art supplies costing $1,300 and office supplies costing $600 are still on hand. This means that of the $1,800 of art supplies originally purchased, $500 worth were used up (became an expense) in July. Of the original $800 of office supplies, $200 worth were consumed. These transactions are analyzed and recorded as follows:

Art Supplies and Office Supplies (Adjustments c and d)

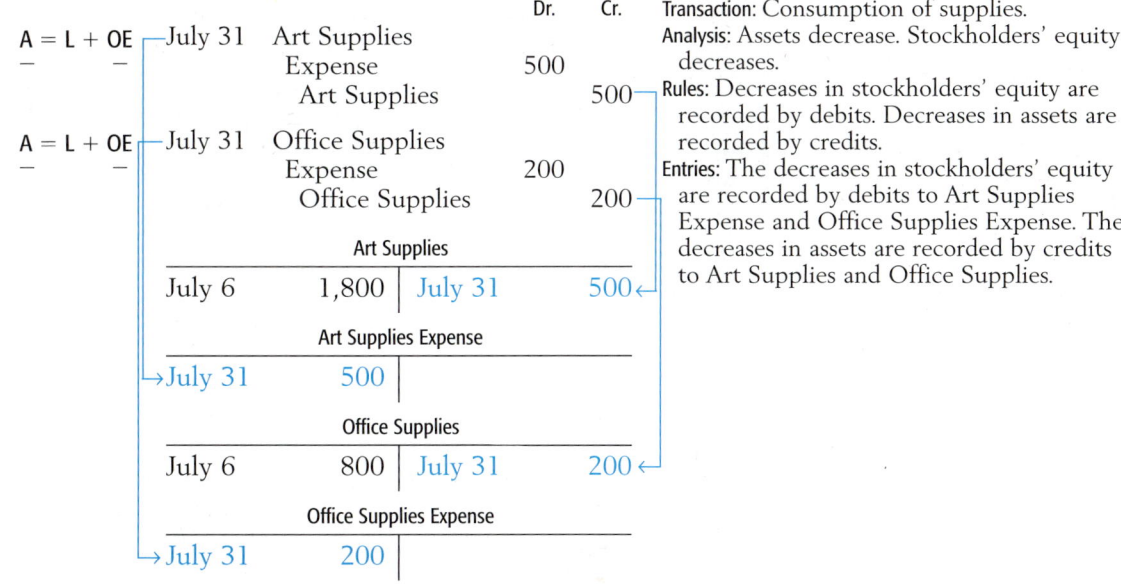

The asset accounts Art Supplies and Office Supplies now reflect the correct balances, $1,300 and $600, respectively, of supplies that are yet to be consumed. In addition, the amount of art supplies used up during the month of July is shown as $500, and the amount of office supplies used up is shown as $200.

■ **DEPRECIATION OF PLANT AND EQUIPMENT** When a company buys a long-term asset—a building, trucks, computers, store fixtures, or furniture—it is, in effect, prepaying for the usefulness of that asset for as long as it benefits the company. Because a long-term asset is a deferral of an expense, the accountant must allocate the cost of the asset over its estimated useful life. The amount allocated to any one accounting period is called **depreciation** or *depreciation expense*. Depreciation, like other expenses, is incurred during an accounting period to produce revenue.

> **KEY POINT:** In accounting, depreciation refers only to the *allocation* of an asset's cost, not to the decline in its value.

> **KEY POINT:** The difficulty in estimating an asset's useful life is further evidence that the bottom-line figure is, at best, an estimate.

It is often impossible to tell how long an asset will last or how much of the asset is used in any one period. For this reason, depreciation must be estimated. Accountants have developed a number of methods for estimating depreciation and for dealing with the related complex problems. Here we look at the simplest case, depreciation on the art and office equipment for Joan Miller Advertising Agency.

Art Equipment and Office Equipment (Adjustments e and f)

Suppose, for example, that Joan Miller estimates that the art equipment and office equipment for which she paid $4,200 and $3,000, respectively, will last five years (60 months) and will have zero value at the end of that time. The monthly

FIGURE 3
Adjustment for Depreciation

depreciation of art equipment and office equipment is $70 ($4,200 ÷ 60 months) and $50 ($3,000 ÷ 60 months), respectively. These amounts represent the costs allocated to July, and they are the amounts by which the asset accounts must be reduced and the expense accounts increased (reducing stockholders' equity).

■ **ACCUMULATED DEPRECIATION—A CONTRA ACCOUNT** Notice that in the previous analysis, the asset accounts are not credited directly. Instead, as shown in Figure 3, new accounts—Accumulated Depreciation, Art Equipment; and Accumulated Depreciation, Office Equipment—are credited. These accumulated depreciation accounts are contra-asset accounts used to total the past depreciation expense on specific long-term assets. A contra account is a separate account that is paired with a related account—in this case an asset account. The balance of the contra account is shown on the financial statement as a deduction from the related account.

There are several types of contra accounts. In this case, the balance of Accumulated Depreciation, Art Equipment is shown on the balance sheet as a deduction from the associated account Art Equipment. Likewise, Accumulated

FOCUS ON INTERNATIONAL BUSINESS

Who Needs Accounting Knowledge?

The privatization of businesses in Eastern Europe and the republics of the former Soviet Union has created a great need for Western accounting knowledge. Many managers from these countries are anxious to study accounting. Under the old governmental systems, the concept of net income as Westerners know it did not exist because the state owned everything and there was no such thing as income.

The new businesses, because they are private, require accounting systems that recognize the importance of net income. In these new systems, it is necessary to make adjusting entries to record such things as depreciation and accrued expenses. Many Eastern European businesses have been suffering losses for years without knowing it and, as a result, are now in poor financial condition.

EXHIBIT 2
Plant and Equipment Section of the Balance Sheet

Joan Miller Advertising Agency, Inc.
Partial Balance Sheet
July 31, 20xx

Plant and equipment		
Art equipment	$4,200	
Less accumulated depreciation	70	$4,130
Office equipment	$3,000	
Less accumulated depreciation	50	2,950
Total plant and equipment		$7,080

● **STOP AND THINK!**
Will the carrying value of a long-term asset normally equal its market value?

The carrying value will equal the market value of the asset only by coincidence because the goal of recording depreciation is to allocate the cost of the asset over its life, not to determine its market value. ■

Depreciation, Office Equipment is a deduction from Office Equipment. Exhibit 2 shows the plant and equipment section of the balance sheet for Joan Miller Advertising Agency, Inc., after these adjusting entries have been made.

A **contra account is used for two very good reasons**. First, it **recognizes that depreciation is an estimate**. Second, a contra account **preserves the original cost of an asset**. In combination with the asset account, it shows both how much of the asset has been allocated as an expense and the balance left to be depreciated. As the months pass, the amount of the accumulated depreciation grows, and the net amount shown as an asset declines. In six months, Accumulated Depreciation, Art Equipment will show a balance of $420; when this amount is subtracted from the balance of Art Equipment, a net amount of $3,780 will remain. The net amount is called the **carrying value**, or *book value*, of the asset.

TYPE 2: RECOGNIZING UNRECORDED EXPENSES (ACCRUED EXPENSES)

At the end of an accounting period, there usually are expenses that have been incurred but not recorded in the accounts. These expenses require adjusting entries. One such case is interest on borrowed money. Each day, interest accumulates on the debt. As shown in Figure 4, at the end of the accounting period, an adjusting entry is made to record this accumulated interest, which is an expense of the period, and the corresponding liability to pay the interest. Other common unrecorded expenses are taxes, wages, and utilities. As the expense and the corresponding liability accumulate, they are said to *accrue*—hence the term **accrued expenses**.

■ **ACCRUED WAGES** Suppose the calendar for the month of July looks like the calendar that follows.

July

Su	M	T	W	Th	F	Sa
	1	2	3	4	5	6
7	8	9	10	11	12	13
14	15	16	17	18	19	20
21	22	23	24	25	26	27
28	29	30	31			

By the end of business on July 31, the secretary at Joan Miller Advertising Agency will have worked three days (Monday, Tuesday, and Wednesday) beyond the last

FIGURE 4
Adjustment for Unrecorded (Accrued) Expenses

biweekly pay period, which ended on July 26. The employee has earned the wages for these days, but she will not be paid until the regular payday in August. The wages for these three days are rightfully an expense for July, and the liabilities should reflect that the company owes the secretary for those days. Because the secretary's wage rate is $1,200 every two weeks, or $120 per day ($1,200 ÷ 10 working days), the expense is $360 ($120 × 3 days).

Accrued Wages (Adjustment g)

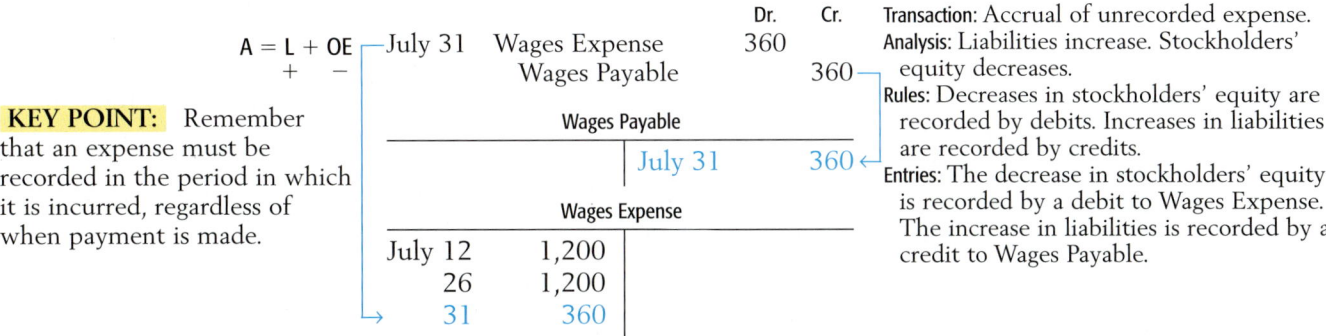

KEY POINT: Remember that an expense must be recorded in the period in which it is incurred, regardless of when payment is made.

Transaction: Accrual of unrecorded expense.
Analysis: Liabilities increase. Stockholders' equity decreases.
Rules: Decreases in stockholders' equity are recorded by debits. Increases in liabilities are recorded by credits.
Entries: The decrease in stockholders' equity is recorded by a debit to Wages Expense. The increase in liabilities is recorded by a credit to Wages Payable.

The liability of $360 is now reflected correctly in the Wages Payable account. The actual expense incurred for wages during July, $2,760, is also correct.

■ **ESTIMATED INCOME TAXES** As a corporation, Joan Miller Advertising Agency is subject to federal income taxes. Although the actual amount owed cannot be determined until after net income is computed at the end of the fiscal year, each month should bear its part of the total year's expense, in accordance with the matching rule. Therefore, the amount of income taxes expense for the current month must be estimated. Assume that after analyzing the first month's operations and conferring with her CPA, Joan Miller estimates July's share of federal income taxes for the year to be $400. This estimated expense can be analyzed and recorded as shown next.

Estimated Income Taxes (Adjustment h)

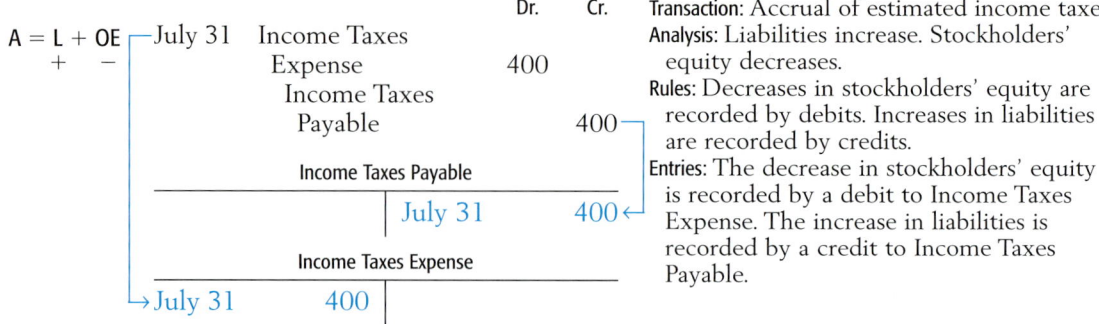

Transaction: Accrual of estimated income taxes.
Analysis: Liabilities increase. Stockholders' equity decreases.
Rules: Decreases in stockholders' equity are recorded by debits. Increases in liabilities are recorded by credits.
Entries: The decrease in stockholders' equity is recorded by a debit to Income Taxes Expense. The increase in liabilities is recorded by a credit to Income Taxes Payable.

Expenses for July will now reflect the estimated income taxes attributable to that month, and the liability for these taxes will appear on the balance sheet.

As noted in this chapter's Decision Point, Kelly Services, like Joan Miller Advertising Agency, has accrued liabilities for payroll and for income taxes. However, unlike Joan Miller Advertising Agency, which has *prepaid* insurance, Kelly has *accrued* insurance. This means Kelly does not pay for insurance in advance but recognizes that it has an expense for insurance that it will have to pay later.

www.kellyservices.com

TYPE 3: ALLOCATING RECORDED UNEARNED REVENUES BETWEEN TWO OR MORE ACCOUNTING PERIODS (DEFERRED REVENUES)

KEY POINT: Unearned Revenue is a liability because there is an obligation to deliver goods or perform a service, or to return the payment. Once the goods have been delivered or the service performed, the liability is converted into revenue.

Just as expenses can be paid before they are used, revenues can be received before they are earned. When revenues are received in advance, the company has an obligation to deliver goods or perform services. Therefore, **unearned revenues** are shown in a liability account. For example, publishing companies usually receive payment in advance for magazine subscriptions. These receipts are recorded in a liability account. If the company fails to deliver the magazines, subscribers are entitled to their money back. As the company delivers each issue of the magazine, it earns a part of the advance payments. This earned portion must be transferred from the

FIGURE 5
Adjustment for Unearned (Deferred) Revenues

Unearned Subscriptions (liability) account to the Subscription Revenue account, as shown in Figure 5.

During the month of July, Joan Miller Advertising Agency received $1,000 as an advance payment for advertising designs to be prepared for another agency. Assume that by the end of the month, $400 of the design was completed and accepted by the other agency. Here is the transaction analysis:

Unearned Art Fees (Adjustment i)

The liability account Unearned Art Fees now reflects the amount of work still to be performed, $600. The revenue account Art Fees Earned reflects the services performed and the revenue earned for them during July, $400.

TYPE 4: RECOGNIZING UNRECORDED REVENUES (ACCRUED REVENUES)

Accrued revenues are revenues for which a service has been performed or goods delivered but for which no entry has been recorded. Any revenues earned but not recorded during the accounting period call for an adjusting entry that debits an asset account and credits a revenue account, as shown in Figure 6. For example, the interest on a note receivable is earned day by day but may not be received until another accounting period. Interest Receivable should be debited and Interest Income should be credited for the interest accrued at the end of the current period.

FIGURE 6
Adjustment for Unrecorded (Accrued) Revenues

FOCUS ON BUSINESS TECHNOLOGY

Ecommerce: What's Its Impact?

Electronic commerce has received much attention in recent years. Sales and purchases involving Internet-based companies like Amazon.com <www.amazon.com> and Travelocity.com <www.travelocity.com> have grown steadily. The total value of goods and services traded over the Internet was $433 billion in 2002, of which $94 billion were retail sales.[6] It is important to realize that when transactions are made electronically, they are analyzed and recorded just as if they had taken place in a physical store. Internet companies require insurance, employee payrolls, buildings, and other assets and liabilities, and they must make the adjusting entries in the same way as any other business.

Suppose that Joan Miller Advertising Agency has agreed to place a series of advertisements for Marsh Tire Company and that the first ad appears on July 31, the last day of the month. The fee of $200 for this advertisement, which has been earned but not recorded, should be recorded this way:

Accrued Advertising Fees (Adjustment j)

Now both the asset and the revenue accounts show the correct balance: The $5,000 in Accounts Receivable is owed to the company, and the $6,400 in Advertising Fees Earned has been earned by the company during July. Marsh Tire Company will be billed for the series of advertisements when they are completed.

A NOTE ABOUT JOURNAL ENTRIES

Thus far, we have presented a full analysis of each journal entry. The analyses showed you the thought process behind each entry. By now, you should be fully aware of the effects of transactions on the accounting equation and the rules of debit and credit. For this reason, in the rest of the book, we present journal entries without full analysis.

 Check out ACE for a Review Quiz at http://accounting.college.hmco.com/students.

USING THE ADJUSTED TRIAL BALANCE TO PREPARE FINANCIAL STATEMENTS

LO5 Prepare financial statements from an adjusted trial balance.

RELATED TEXT ASSIGNMENTS
Q: 21
SE: 7, 8
E: 10
P: 4, 5

After adjusting entries have been recorded and posted, an **adjusted trial balance** is prepared by listing all accounts and their balances. If the adjusting entries have been posted to the accounts correctly, the adjusted trial balance should have equal debit and credit totals.

The adjusted trial balance for Joan Miller Advertising Agency, Inc., is shown on the left side of Exhibit 3. Notice that some accounts, such as Cash and Accounts Payable, have the same balances as they have in the trial balance (see Exhibit 1) because no adjusting entries affected them. Some new accounts, such as depreciation accounts and Wages Payable, appear in the adjusted trial balance, and other

Exhibit 3
Relationship of Adjusted Trial Balance to Income Statement

Joan Miller Advertising Agency, Inc.
Adjusted Trial Balance
July 31, 20xx

Cash	$ 9,140	
Accounts Receivable	5,000	
Art Supplies	1,300	
Office Supplies	600	
Prepaid Rent	800	
Prepaid Insurance	880	
Art Equipment	4,200	
Accumulated Depreciation, Art Equipment		$ 70
Office Equipment	3,000	
Accumulated Depreciation, Office Equipment		50
Accounts Payable		3,240
Unearned Art Fees		600
Wages Payable		360
Income Taxes Payable		400
Common Stock		20,000
Dividends	1,400	
Advertising Fees Earned		6,400
Art Fees Earned		400
Wages Expense	2,760	
Utilities Expense	200	
Telephone Expense	140	
Rent Expense	800	
Insurance Expense	80	
Art Supplies Expense	500	
Office Supplies Expense	200	
Depreciation Expense, Art Equipment	70	
Depreciation Expense, Office Equipment	50	
Income Taxes Expense	400	
	$31,520	$31,520

Joan Miller Advertising Agency, Inc.
Income Statement
For the Month Ended July 31, 20xx

Revenues

Advertising fees earned	$6,400	
Art fees earned	400	
Total revenues		$6,800

Expenses

Wages expense	$2,760	
Utilities expense	200	
Telephone expense	140	
Rent expense	800	
Insurance expense	80	
Art supplies expense	500	
Office supplies expense	200	
Depreciation expense, Art equipment	70	
Depreciation expense, Office equipment	50	
Income taxes expense	400	
Total expenses		5,200
Net income		**$1,600**

KEY POINT: The net income figure from the income statement is needed to prepare the statement of retained earnings, and the bottom-line figure of that statement is needed to prepare the balance sheet. Thus, the income statement is prepared before the statement of retained earnings, and that statement is prepared before the balance sheet.

🛑 **STOP AND THINK!**
Why is Retained Earnings not listed on the trial balance for Joan Miller Advertising Agency, Inc., in Exhibits 3 and 4?

It is not listed because it begins with a zero balance in Joan Miller's first month of operation. It does not yet reflect the amounts of revenues, expenses, and dividends for the year, which are listed in the adjusted trial balance. ■

accounts, such as Art Supplies, Office Supplies, Prepaid Rent, and Prepaid Insurance, have balances that differ from those in the trial balance because adjusting entries did affect them.

Using the adjusted trial balance, the financial statements can be easily prepared. The income statement is prepared from the revenue and expense accounts, as shown in Exhibit 3. Then, as shown in Exhibit 4, the statement of retained earnings and the balance sheet are prepared. Notice that the net income from the income statement is combined with dividends on the statement of retained earnings to give the net change in Joan Miller Advertising Agency's Retained Earnings account. The resulting balance of Retained Earnings at July 31 is used on the balance sheet, as are the asset and liability accounts.

EXHIBIT 4
Relationship of Adjusted Trial Balance to Balance Sheet and Statement of Retained Earnings

Joan Miller Advertising Agency, Inc.
Adjusted Trial Balance
July 31, 20xx

Cash	$ 9,140	
Accounts Receivable	5,000	
Art Supplies	1,300	
Office Supplies	600	
Prepaid Rent	800	
Prepaid Insurance	880	
Art Equipment	4,200	
Accumulated Depreciation, Art Equipment		$ 70
Office Equipment	3,000	
Accumulated Depreciation, Office Equipment		50
Accounts Payable		3,240
Unearned Art Fees		600
Wages Payable		360
Income Taxes Payable		400
Common Stock		20,000
Dividends	1,400	
Advertising Fees Earned		6,400
Art Fees Earned		400
Wages Expense	2,760	
Utilities Expense	200	
Telephone Expense	140	
Rent Expense	800	
Insurance Expense	80	
Art Supplies Expense	500	
Office Supplies Expense	200	
Depreciation Expense, Art Equipment	70	
Depreciation Expense, Office Equipment	50	
Income Taxes Expense	400	
	$31,520	$31,520

KEY POINT: Notice that the figure for Retained Earnings does not appear on the adjusted trial balance. The balance is updated when the closing entries are prepared.

KEY POINT: The adjusted trial balance is a second check that the ledger is still in balance. Because it reflects updated information from the adjusting entries, it may be used to prepare the formal statements.

Joan Miller Advertising Agency, Inc.
Balance Sheet
July 31, 20xx

Assets

Cash			$ 9,140
Accounts receivable			5,000
Art supplies			1,300
Office supplies			600
Prepaid rent			800
Prepaid insurance			880
Art equipment		$ 4,200	
Less accumulated depreciation		70	4,130
Office equipment		$ 3,000	
Less accumulated depreciation		50	2,950
Total assets			$24,800

Liabilities

Accounts payable		$ 3,240
Unearned art fees		600
Wages payable		360
Income taxes payable		400
Total liabilities		$ 4,600

Stockholders' Equity

Common stock	$20,000	
Retained earnings	200	
Total stockholders' equity		20,200
Total liabilities and stockholders' equity		$24,800

Joan Miller Advertising Agency, Inc.
Statement of Retained Earnings
For the Month Ended July 31, 20xx

Retained earnings, July 1, 20xx	—
Net income	$1,600
Subtotal	$1,600
Less dividends	1,400
Retained earnings, July 31, 20xx	$ 200

From Income Statement in Exhibit 3

FOCUS ON BUSINESS TECHNOLOGY

Entering Adjustments With the Touch of a Button

In a computerized accounting system, adjusting entries can be entered just like any other transactions. However, when the adjusting entries are similar for each accounting period, such as those for insurance expense and depreciation expense, or when they always involve the same accounts, such as those for accrued wages, the computer can be programmed to display them automatically. All the accountant has to do is verify the amounts or enter the correct amounts. The adjusting entries are then entered and posted, and the adjusted trial balance is prepared with the touch of a button.

 Check out ACE for a Review Quiz at http://accounting.college.hmco.com/students.

CASH FLOWS FROM ACCRUAL-BASED INFORMATION

SO6 Analyze cash flows from accrual-based information.

RELATED TEXT ASSIGNMENTS
Q: 22
SE: 9, 10
E: 11, 12
FRA: 6

Management has the short-range goal of achieving sufficient liquidity to meet its needs for cash to pay its ongoing obligations. It is important for managers to be able to use accrual-based financial information to analyze cash flows in order to plan payments to creditors and assess the need for short-term borrowing.

Every revenue or expense account on the income statement has one or more related accounts on the balance sheet. For instance, Supplies Expense is related to Supplies, Wages Expense is related to Wages Payable, and Art Fees Earned is related to Unearned Art Fees. As we have shown, these accounts are related through adjusting entries whose purpose is to apply the matching rule in the measurement of net income. The cash flows generated or paid by company operations may also be determined by analyzing these relationships. For example, suppose that after receiving the financial statements in Exhibits 3 and 4, management wants to know how much cash was expended for art supplies. On the income statement, Art Supplies Expense is $500, and on the balance sheet, Art Supplies is $1,300. Because July was the company's first month of operation, there was no prior balance of art supplies, so the amount of cash expended for art supplies during the month was $1,800. The cash flow used to purchase art supplies ($1,800) was much greater than the amount expensed in determining income ($500). In planning for August, management can anticipate that the cash needed may be less than the amount expensed because, given the large inventory of art supplies, it will probably not be necessary to buy art supplies for more than a month. Understanding these cash flow effects enables management to better predict the business's need for cash in August.

The general rule for determining the cash flow received from any revenue or paid for any expense (except depreciation, which is a special case not covered here) is to determine the potential cash payments or cash receipts and deduct the amount not paid or received. The application of the general rule varies with the type of asset or liability account, which is shown as follows:

Type of Account	Potential Payment or Receipt		Not Paid or Received	Result
Prepaid Expense	Ending Balance	+ Expense for the Period	− Beginning Balance	= Cash Payments for Expenses
Unearned Revenue	Ending Balance	+ Revenue for the Period	− Beginning Balance	= Cash Receipts from Revenues
Accrued Payable	Beginning Balance	+ Expense for the Period	− Ending Balance	= Cash Payments for Expenses
Accrued Receivable	Beginning Balance	+ Revenue for the Period	− Ending Balance	= Cash Receipts from Revenues

For instance, assume that on May 31 a company had a balance of $480 in Prepaid Insurance and that on June 30 the balance was $670. If the insurance expense during June was $120, the amount of cash expended on insurance during June can be computed as follows:

Prepaid Insurance at June 30	$670
Insurance Expense during June	120
Potential cash payments for insurance	$790
Less Prepaid Insurance at May 31	480
Cash payments for insurance during June	$310

The beginning balance is deducted because it was paid in a prior accounting period. Note that the cash payments equal the expense plus the increase in the balance of the Prepaid Insurance account [$120 + ($670 − $480) = $310]. In this case, the cash paid was almost three times the amount of insurance expense. In future months, cash payments are likely to be less than the expense.

✓ Check out ACE for a Review Quiz at http://accounting.college.hmco.com/students.

Chapter Review

REVIEW OF LEARNING OBJECTIVES

LO1 Define *net income* and its two major components, *revenues* and *expenses*.

Net income is the net increase in stockholders' equity that results from the operations of a company. Net income equals revenues minus expenses, unless expenses exceed revenues, in which case a net loss results. Revenues equal the price of goods sold and services rendered during a specific period. Expenses are the costs of goods and services used up in the process of producing revenues.

LO2 Explain how the income measurement issues of accounting period, continuity, and matching are resolved.

The accounting period issue recognizes that net income measurements for short periods of time are necessarily tentative. The continuity issue recognizes that even though businesses face an uncertain future, without evidence to the contrary, accountants must assume that a business will continue indefinitely. The matching issue has to do with the difficulty of assigning revenues and expenses to a period of time. It is addressed by applying the matching rule: Revenues must be assigned to the accounting period in which the goods are sold or the services performed, and expenses must be assigned to the accounting period in which they are used to produce revenue.

LO3 Define *accrual accounting* and explain three broad ways of accomplishing it.

Accrual accounting consists of all the techniques developed by accountants to apply the matching rule. Three broad ways of accomplishing it are by recognizing revenues when earned, recognizing expenses when incurred, and adjusting the accounts.

LO4 State four principal situations that require adjusting entries and prepare typical adjusting entries.

Adjusting entries are required when (1) recorded costs have to be allocated between two or more accounting periods, (2) unrecorded expenses exist, (3) recorded unearned revenues must be allocated between two or more accounting periods, and (4) unrecorded revenues exist. The preparation of adjusting entries is summarized as follows:

Type of Adjusting Entry	Type of Account Debited	Type of Account Credited	Balance Sheet Account Examples
1. Allocating recorded costs (previously paid, expired)	Expense	Asset (or contra-asset)	Prepaid Rent Prepaid Insurance Supplies Accumulated Depreciation, Buildings Accumulated Depreciation, Equipment
2. Accrued expenses (incurred, not paid)	Expense	Liability	Wages Payable Income Taxes Payable
3. Allocating recorded unearned revenues (previously received, earned)	Liability	Revenue	Unearned Art Fees
4. Accrued revenues (earned, not received)	Asset	Revenue	Accounts Receivable Interest Receivable

LO5 Prepare financial statements from an adjusted trial balance.

An adjusted trial balance is prepared after adjusting entries have been posted to the accounts. Its purpose is to test whether the adjusting entries are posted correctly before the financial statements are prepared. The income statement is prepared from the revenue and expense accounts in the adjusted trial balance. The balance sheet is prepared from the asset and liability accounts in the adjusted trial balance and from the statement of retained earnings.

SUPPLEMENTAL OBJECTIVE

SO6 Analyze cash flows from accrual-based information.

Cash flow information relates to management's liquidity goal. The general rule for determining the cash flow effect of any revenue or expense (except depreciation, which is a special case not covered here) is to determine the potential cash payments or cash receipts and deduct the amount not paid or received.

REVIEW OF CONCEPTS AND TERMINOLOGY

The following concepts and terms were introduced in this chapter:

LO2 **Accounting period issue:** The difficulty of assigning revenues and expenses to a short period of time.

LO4 **Accrual:** The recognition of an expense or revenue that has arisen but has not yet been recorded.

LO3 **Accrual accounting:** The attempt to record the financial effects of transactions and other events in the periods in which those transactions or events occur, rather than only in the periods in which cash is received or paid by the business; all the techniques developed by accountants to apply the matching rule.

LO4 **Accrued expenses:** Expenses incurred but not recognized in the accounts; unrecorded expenses.

LO4 **Accrued revenues:** Revenues for which a service has been performed or goods delivered but for which no entry has been made; unrecorded revenues.

LO4 **Accumulated depreciation accounts:** Contra-asset accounts used to accumulate the depreciation expense of specific long-lived assets.

LO5 **Adjusted trial balance:** A trial balance prepared after all adjusting entries have been recorded and posted to the accounts.

LO4 **Adjusting entries:** Entries made to apply accrual accounting to transactions that span more than one accounting period.

LO4 **Carrying value:** The unexpired portion of the cost of an asset. Also called *book value*.

LO2 **Cash basis of accounting:** Accounting for revenues and expenses on a cash received and cash paid basis.

LO2 **Continuity issue:** The difficulty associated with not knowing how long a business entity will survive.

LO4 **Contra account:** An account whose balance is subtracted from an associated account in the financial statements.

LO4 **Deferral:** The postponement of the recognition of an expense that already has been paid or of a revenue that already has been received.

LO4 **Depreciation:** The portion of the cost of a tangible long-term asset allocated to any one accounting period. Also called *depreciation expense*.

LO1 **Expenses:** Decreases in stockholders' equity resulting from the costs of goods and services used up in the course of earning revenues. Also called *cost of doing business* or *expired costs*.

LO2 **Fiscal year:** Any 12-month accounting period used by an economic entity.

LO2 **Going concern:** The assumption, unless there is evidence to the contrary, that a business entity will continue to operate indefinitely.

LO2 **Matching rule:** Revenues must be assigned to the accounting period in which the goods are sold or the services performed, and expenses must be assigned to the accounting period in which they are used to produce revenue.

LO1 **Net income:** The net increase in stockholders' equity that results from business operations and is accumulated in the Retained Earnings account; revenues less expenses when revenues exceed expenses.

LO1 **Net loss:** The net decrease in stockholders' equity that results from business operations when expenses exceed revenues. It is accumulated in the Retained Earnings account.

LO2 **Periodicity:** The recognition that net income for any period less than the life of the business, although tentative, is still a useful measure.

LO4 **Prepaid expenses:** Expenses paid in advance that have not yet expired; an asset account.

LO1 **Profit:** The increase in stockholders' equity that results from business operations.

LO3 **Revenue recognition:** In accrual accounting, the process of determining when revenue is earned.

LO1 **Revenues:** Increases in stockholders' equity resulting from selling goods, rendering services, or performing other business activities.

LO4 **Unearned revenues:** Revenues received in advance for which the goods have not yet been delivered or the services performed; a liability account.

REVIEW PROBLEM

Determining Adjusting Entries, Posting to T Accounts, Preparing Adjusted Trial Balance, and Preparing Financial Statements

LO4
LO5 The following is the unadjusted trial balance for Certified Answering Service, Inc., on December 31, 20x2:

Certified Answering Service, Inc.
Trial Balance
December 31, 20x2

Cash	$2,160	
Accounts Receivable	1,250	
Office Supplies	180	
Prepaid Insurance	240	
Office Equipment	3,400	
Accumulated Depreciation, Office Equipment		$ 600
Accounts Payable		700
Unearned Revenue		460
Common Stock		2,000
Retained Earnings		2,870
Dividends	400	
Answering Service Revenue		2,900
Wages Expense	1,500	
Rent Expense	400	
	$9,530	$9,530

The following information is also available:
a. Insurance that expired during December amounted to $40.
b. Office supplies on hand at the end of December totaled $75.

		SE 3.	The Supplies account began the year with a balance of $190. During the year, supplies in the amount of $490 were purchased. At the end of the year (December 31), the inventory of supplies on hand was $220. Make the year-end entry in journal form to record the adjustment for supplies expense for the year.
LO4	**Adjustment for Supplies**		
		SE 4.	The depreciation expense on office equipment for the month of March is $50. This is the third month that the office equipment, which cost $950, has been owned. Prepare the adjusting entry in journal form to record depreciation for March and show the balance sheet presentation for office equipment and related accounts after the adjustment.
LO4	**Adjustment for Depreciation**		
		SE 5.	Wages are paid each Saturday for a six-day work week. Wages are currently running $690 per week. Make the adjusting entry required on June 30, assuming July 1 falls on a Tuesday.
LO4	**Adjustment for Accrued Wages**		
		SE 6.	During the month of August, deposits in the amount of $550 were received for services to be performed. By the end of the month, services in the amount of $380 had been performed. Prepare the necessary adjustment for Service Revenue at the end of the month.
LO4	**Adjustment for Unearned Revenue**		
		SE 7.	The adjusted trial balance for Reingold Company on December 31, 20x3, contains the following accounts and balances: Retained Earnings, $4,300; Dividends, $350; Service Revenue, $2,600; Rent Expense, $400; Wages Expense, $900; Utilities Expense, $200; Telephone Expense, $50; and Income Taxes Expense, $350. Prepare an income statement in proper form for the month of December.
LO5	**Preparation of an Income Statement from an Adjusted Trial Balance**		
		SE 8.	Using the data in **SE 7**, prepare a statement of retained earnings for Reingold Company.
LO5	**Preparation of a Statement of Retained Earnings**		
		SE 9.	Wages Payable was $590 at the end of May and $920 at the end of June. Wages Expense for June was $2,300. How much cash was paid for wages during June?
SO6	**Determination of Cash Flows**		
		SE 10.	Unearned Revenue was $1,300 at the end of November and $900 at the end of December. Service Revenue was $5,100 for the month of December. How much cash was received for services provided during December?
SO6	**Determination of Cash Flows**		

EXERCISES

		E 1.	The accountant for Ampere Company makes the assumptions or performs the activities listed below. Tell which of the following concepts of accrual accounting most directly relates to each assumption or action: (a) periodicity, (b) going concern, (c) matching rule, (d) revenue recognition, (e) deferral, and (f) accrual.
LO2	**Applications of Accounting**		
LO3	**Concepts Related to Accrual**		
LO4	**Accounting**		

1. In estimating the life of a building, assumes that the business will last indefinitely
2. Records a sale when the customer is billed
3. Postpones the recognition of a one-year insurance policy as an expense by initially recording the expenditure as an asset
4. Recognizes the usefulness of financial statements prepared on a monthly basis even though they are based on estimates
5. Recognizes, by making an adjusting entry, wages expense that has been incurred but not yet recorded
6. Prepares an income statement that shows the revenues earned and the expenses incurred during the accounting period

		E 2.	Four conditions must be met before revenue should be recognized. In each of the following cases, tell which condition has *not* been met:
LO3	**Application of Conditions for Revenue Recognition**		

a. Company A accepts a contract to perform services in the future for $1,000.
b. Company B ships products to another company worth $1,500 without an order from the other company but tells the company that it can return the products if it does not sell them.
c. Company C performs services totaling $5,000 for a company that is in financial difficulty.
d. Company D agrees to work out a price later for services that it performs for another company.

		E 3.	City Fun Company of Canton, Ohio, publishes a monthly magazine featuring local restaurant reviews and upcoming social, cultural, and sporting events. Subscribers pay for subscriptions either one year or two years in advance. Cash received from subscribers is credited to an account called Magazine Subscriptions Received in Advance. On
LO4	**Adjusting Entry for Unearned Revenue**		

December 31, 20x3, the end of the company's fiscal year, the balance of this account was $1,000,000. Expiration of subscriptions revenue is as follows:

During 20x3 $200,000
During 20x4   500,000
During 20x5   300,000

Prepare the adjusting entry in journal form for December 31, 20x3.

E 4.
LO4 Adjusting Entries for Prepaid Insurance

An examination of the Prepaid Insurance account shows a balance of $4,112 at the end of an accounting period, before adjustment. Prepare entries in journal form to record the insurance expense for the period under the following independent assumptions:

1. An examination of the insurance policies shows unexpired insurance that cost $1,974 at the end of the period.
2. An examination of the insurance policies shows that insurance that cost $694 has expired during the period.

E 5.
LO4 Supplies Account: Missing Data

Each of the following columns represents a Supplies account:

	a	b	c	d
Supplies on hand at July 1	$132	$217	$98	$?
Supplies purchased during the month	26	?	87	964
Supplies consumed during the month	97	486	?	816
Supplies on hand at July 31	?	218	28	594

1. Determine the amounts indicated by the question marks.
2. Make the adjusting entry for column a, assuming supplies purchased are debited to an asset account.

E 6.
LO4 Adjusting Entry for Accrued Salaries

Oland has a five-day work week and pays salaries of $35,000 each Friday.

1. Make the adjusting entry required on May 31, assuming that June 1 falls on a Wednesday.
2. Make the entry to pay the salaries on June 3.

E 7.
LO4 Revenue and Expense Recognition

Remini Company produces computer software that is sold by Elton Comp, Inc. Remini receives a royalty of 15 percent of sales. Royalties are paid by Elton Comp and received by Remini semiannually on May 1 for sales made in July through December of the previous year and on November 1 for sales made in January through June of the current year. Royalty expense for Elton Comp and royalty income for Remini in the amount of $12,000 were accrued on December 31, 20x2. Cash in the amounts of $12,000 and $20,000 was paid and received on May 1 and November 1, 20x3, respectively. Software sales during the July to December 20x3 period totaled $300,000.

1. Calculate the amount of royalty expense for Elton Comp and royalty income for Remini during 20x3.
2. Record the adjusting entry made by each company on December 31, 20x3.

E 8.
LO4 Adjusting Entries

Prepare year-end adjusting entries for each of the following:

1. Office Supplies had a balance of $84 on January 1. Purchases debited to Office Supplies during the year amount to $415. A year-end inventory reveals supplies of $285 on hand.
2. Depreciation of office equipment is estimated to be $2,130 for the year.
3. Property taxes for six months, estimated at $875, have accrued but have not been recorded.
4. Unrecorded interest receivable on U.S. government bonds is $850.
5. Unearned Revenue has a balance of $900. Services for $300 received in advance have now been performed.
6. Services totaling $200 have been performed; the customer has not yet been billed.

E 9.
LO4 Accounting for Revenue Received in Advance

Olaf Bjorn, a lawyer, was paid $24,000 on October 1 to represent a client in real estate negotiations over the next 12 months.

1. Record the entries required in Bjorn's records on October 1 and at the end of the fiscal year, December 31.
2. How would this transaction be reflected on the income statement and balance sheet on December 31?

E 10.
LO5 Preparation of Financial Statements

Prepare the monthly income statement, statement of retained earnings, and balance sheet for Totally Clean, Inc., from the data provided in the following adjusted trial balance:

Totally Clean, Inc.
Adjusted Trial Balance
August 31, 20xx

Cash	$ 2,295	
Accounts Receivable	1,296	
Prepaid Insurance	190	
Prepaid Rent	100	
Cleaning Supplies	76	
Cleaning Equipment	1,600	
Accumulated Depreciation, Cleaning Equipment		$ 160
Truck	3,600	
Accumulated Depreciation, Truck		360
Accounts Payable		210
Wages Payable		40
Unearned Janitorial Revenue		460
Income Taxes Payable		400
Common Stock		2,000
Retained Earnings		5,517
Dividends	1,000	
Janitorial Revenue		7,310
Wages Expense	2,840	
Rent Expense	600	
Gas, Oil, and Other Truck Expenses	290	
Insurance Expense	190	
Supplies Expense	1,460	
Depreciation Expense, Cleaning Equipment	160	
Depreciation Expense, Truck	360	
Income Taxes Expense	400	
	$16,457	$16,457

E 11.
SO6 Determination of Cash Flows

After adjusting entries had been made, the balance sheets of Yun Company showed the following asset and liability amounts at the end of 20x3 and 20x4:

	20x4	20x3
Prepaid insurance	$2,400	$2,900
Wages payable	1,200	2,200
Unearned fees	4,200	1,900

The following amounts were taken from the 20x4 income statement:

Insurance expense	$ 3,800
Wages expense	19,500
Fees earned	8,900

Calculate the amount of cash paid for insurance and wages and the amount of cash received for fees during 20x4.

E 12.
SO6 Relationship of Expenses to Cash Paid

The income statement for Libra Company included the following expenses for 20xx:

Rent expense	$ 2,600
Interest expense	3,900
Salaries expense	41,500

Listed below are the related balance sheet account balances at year end for last year and this year.

	Last Year	This Year
Prepaid rent	—	$ 450
Interest payable	$ 600	—
Salaries payable	2,500	4,800

1. Compute the cash paid for rent during the year.
2. Compute the cash paid for interest during the year.
3. Compute the cash paid for salaries during the year.

PROBLEMS

P 1. At the end of its fiscal year, the trial balance for Roosevelt Cleaners, Inc., appears as follows:

LO4 Determining Adjustments

Roosevelt Cleaners, Inc.
Trial Balance
September 30, 20x4

Cash	$ 11,788	
Accounts Receivable	26,494	
Prepaid Insurance	3,400	
Cleaning Supplies	7,374	
Land	18,000	
Building	185,000	
Accumulated Depreciation, Building		$ 45,600
Accounts Payable		20,400
Unearned Dry Cleaning Revenue		1,600
Mortgage Payable		110,000
Common Stock		40,000
Retained Earnings		16,560
Dividends	10,000	
Dry Cleaning Revenue		120,334
Laundry Revenue		37,300
Wages Expense	101,330	
Cleaning Equipment Rental Expense	6,000	
Delivery Truck Expense	4,374	
Interest Expense	11,000	
Other Expenses	7,034	
	$391,794	$391,794

The following information is also available:

a. A study of the company's insurance policies shows that $680 is unexpired at the end of the year.
b. An inventory of cleaning supplies shows $1,244 on hand.
c. Estimated depreciation on the building for the year is $12,800.
d. Accrued interest on the mortgage payable amounts to $1,000.
e. On September 1, the company signed a contract, effective immediately, with Kings County Hospital to dry clean, for a fixed monthly charge of $400, the uniforms used by doctors in surgery. The hospital paid for four months' service in advance.
f. Sales and delivery wages are paid on Saturday. The weekly payroll is $2,520. September 30 falls on a Thursday and the company has a six-day pay week.
g. Federal income taxes for the period are estimated to be $2,000.

REQUIRED ▶ All adjustments affect one balance sheet account and one income statement account. For each of the above situations, show the accounts affected, the amount of the adjustment (using a + or − to indicate an increase or decrease), and the balance of the account after the adjustment in the following format:

Balance Sheet Account	Amount of Adjustment (+ or −)	Balance after Adjustment	Income Statement Account	Amount of Adjustment (+ or −)	Balance after Adjustment

P 2.
LO3 Preparing Adjusting Entries
LO4

On June 30, the end of the current fiscal year, the following information was available to aid the Sterling Company's accountants in making adjusting entries:

a. Among the liabilities of the company is a mortgage payable in the amount of $240,000. On June 30, the accrued interest on this mortgage amounted to $12,000.
b. On Friday, July 2, the company, which is on a five-day workweek and pays employees weekly, will pay its regular salaried employees $19,200.
c. On June 29, the company completed negotiations and signed a contract to provide services to a new client at an annual rate of $3,600.
d. The Supplies account showed a beginning balance of $1,615 and purchases during the year of $3,766. The end-of-year inventory revealed supplies on hand of $1,186.
e. The Prepaid Insurance account showed the following entries on June 30:

Beginning Balance $1,530
January 1   2,900
May 1   3,366

The beginning balance represents the unexpired portion of a one-year policy purchased the previous year. The January 1 entry represents a new one-year policy, and the May 1 entry represents the additional coverage of a three-year policy.

f. The following table contains the cost and annual depreciation for buildings and equipment, all of which were purchased before the current year:

Account	Cost	Annual Depreciation
Buildings	$185,000	$ 7,300
Equipment	218,000	21,800

g. On June 1, the company completed negotiations with another client and accepted a payment of $21,000, representing one year's services paid in advance. The $21,000 was credited to Services Collected in Advance.
h. The company calculated that as of June 30 it had earned $3,500 on a $7,500 contract that will be completed and billed in August.
i. Federal income taxes for the year are estimated to be $7,500.

REQUIRED
1. Prepare adjusting entries in journal form for each item listed above.
2. Explain how the conditions for revenue recognition are applied to transactions **c** and **h**.

P 3.
LO4 Determining Adjusting Entries, Posting to T Accounts, and Preparing an Adjusted Trial Balance

The trial balance for Financial Strategies Service, Inc., on December 31 is presented below.

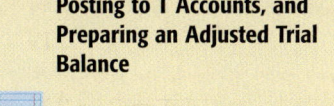

Financial Strategies Service, Inc.
Trial Balance
December 31, 20xx

Cash	$ 16,500	
Accounts Receivable	8,250	
Office Supplies	2,662	
Prepaid Rent	1,320	
Office Equipment	9,240	
Accumulated Depreciation, Office Equipment		$ 1,540
Accounts Payable		5,940
Notes Payable		11,000
Unearned Service Revenue		2,970
Common Stock		10,000
Retained Earnings		14,002
Dividends	22,000	
Service Revenue		72,600
Salaries Expense	49,400	
Rent Expense	4,400	
Utilities Expense	4,280	
	$118,052	$118,052

The following information is also available:

a. Ending inventory of office supplies, $264.
b. Prepaid rent expired, $440.
c. Depreciation of office equipment for the period, $660.
d. Accrued interest expense at the end of the period, $550.
e. Accrued salaries at the end of the period, $330.
f. Service revenue still unearned at the end of the period, $1,166.
g. Service revenue earned but unrecorded, $2,200.
h. Management estimates income taxes for the period to be $4,000.

REQUIRED

1. Open T accounts for the accounts in the trial balance plus the following: Interest Payable; Salaries Payable; Income Taxes Payable; Office Supplies Expense; Depreciation Expense, Office Equipment; Interest Expense; and Income Taxes Expense. Enter the balances shown on the trial balance.
2. Determine the adjusting entries and post them directly to the T accounts.
3. Prepare an adjusted trial balance.

P 4.
LO4 Determining Adjusting Entries
LO5 and Tracing Their Effects to Financial Statements

Having graduated from college with a degree in accounting, Joyce Ozaki opened a small tax-preparation service. At the end of its second year of operation, Ozaki Tax Service, Inc., had the trial balance shown below.

Ozaki Tax Service, Inc.
Trial Balance
December 31, 20x4

Cash	$ 2,268	
Accounts Receivable	1,031	
Prepaid Insurance	240	
Office Supplies	782	
Office Equipment	4,100	
Accumulated Depreciation, Office Equipment		$ 410
Copier	3,000	
Accumulated Depreciation, Copier		360
Accounts Payable		635
Unearned Tax Fees		219
Common Stock		2,000
Retained Earnings		3,439
Dividends	6,000	
Tax Fees Revenue		21,926
Office Salaries Expense	8,300	
Advertising Expense	650	
Rent Expense	2,400	
Telephone Expense	218	
	$28,989	$28,989

The following information was also available:

a. Office supplies on hand, December 31, 20x4, were $227.
b. Insurance still unexpired amounted to $120.
c. Estimated depreciation of office equipment was $410.
d. Estimated depreciation of the copier was $360.
e. The telephone expense for December was $19. Bill was received but not recorded.
f. The services for all unearned tax fees had been performed by the end of the year.
g. Federal income taxes for the year were estimated to be $1,800.

REQUIRED

1. Open T accounts for the accounts in the trial balance plus the following: Income Taxes Payable; Insurance Expense; Office Supplies Expense; Depreciation Expense, Office Equipment; Depreciation Expense, Copier; and Income Taxes Expense. Record the balances shown in the trial balance.

2. Determine the adjusting entries and post them directly to the T accounts.
3. Prepare an adjusted trial balance, an income statement, a statement of retained earnings, and a balance sheet.

P 5.
LO4 Determining Adjusting Entries
LO5 and Tracing Their Effects to Financial Statements

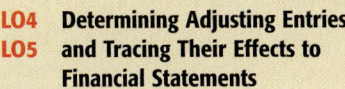

The Elite Livery Service, Inc., was organized to provide limousine service between the airport and various suburban locations. It has just completed its second year of business. Its trial balance appears below.

Elite Livery Service, Inc.
Trial Balance
June 30, 20x4

Cash (111)	$ 9,812	
Accounts Receivable (112)	14,227	
Prepaid Rent (117)	12,000	
Prepaid Insurance (118)	4,900	
Prepaid Maintenance (119)	12,000	
Spare Parts (141)	11,310	
Limousines (142)	200,000	
Accumulated Depreciation, Limousines (143)		$ 25,000
Notes Payable (211)		45,000
Unearned Passenger Service Revenue (212)		30,000
Common Stock (311)		30,000
Retained Earnings (312)		48,211
Dividends (313)	20,000	
Passenger Service Revenue (411)		428,498
Gas and Oil Expense (511)	89,300	
Salaries Expense (512)	206,360	
Advertising Expense (513)	26,800	
	$606,709	$606,709

The following information is also available:

a. To obtain space at the airport, Elite paid two years' rent in advance when it began the business.
b. An examination of insurance policies reveals that $2,800 expired during the year.
c. To provide regular maintenance for the vehicles, a deposit of $12,000 was made with a local garage. Examination of maintenance invoices reveals that there are $10,944 in charges against the deposit.
d. An inventory of spare parts shows $1,902 on hand.
e. All of the Elite Livery Service's limousines are to be depreciated at the rate of 12.5 percent per year. There were no limousines purchased during the year.
f. A payment of $10,500 for one full year's interest on notes payable is now due.
g. Unearned Passenger Service Revenue on June 30 includes $17,815 in tickets that were purchased by employers for use by their executives and have not been redeemed.
h. Federal income taxes for the year are estimated to be $12,000.

REQUIRED

1. Determine adjusting entries and enter them in the general journal (Page 14).
2. Open ledger accounts for the accounts in the trial balance plus the following: Interest Payable (213); Income Taxes Payable (214); Rent Expense (514); Insurance Expense (515); Spare Parts Expense (516); Depreciation Expense, Limousines (517); Maintenance Expense (518); Interest Expense (519); and Income Taxes Expense (520). Record the balances shown in the trial balance.
3. Post the adjusting entries from the general journal to the ledger accounts, showing proper references.
4. Prepare an adjusted trial balance, an income statement, a statement of retained earnings, and a balance sheet.

ALTERNATE PROBLEMS

LO4 Determining Adjustments

P 6. At the end of the first three months of operation, the trial balance of Metropolitan Answering Service, Inc., appears as shown below. Oscar Rienzo, the owner of Metropolitan, has hired an accountant to prepare financial statements to determine how well the company is doing after three months. Upon examining the accounting records, the accountant finds the following items of interest:

a. An inventory of office supplies reveals supplies on hand of $133.
b. The Prepaid Rent account includes the rent for the first three months plus a deposit for April's rent.
c. Depreciation on the equipment for the first three months is $208.
d. The balance of the Unearned Answering Service Revenue account represents a 12-month service contract paid in advance on February 1.
e. On March 31, accrued wages total $80.
f. Federal income taxes for the three months are estimated to be $1,500.

Metropolitan Answering Service, Inc.
Trial Balance
March 31, 20xx

Cash	$ 3,482	
Accounts Receivable	4,236	
Office Supplies	903	
Prepaid Rent	800	
Equipment	4,700	
Accounts Payable		$ 2,673
Unearned Answering Service Revenue		888
Common Stock		5,933
Dividends	2,130	
Answering Service Revenue		9,002
Wages Expense	1,900	
Office Cleaning Expense	345	
	$18,496	$18,496

REQUIRED ▶ All adjustments affect one balance sheet account and one income statement account. For each of the above situations, show the accounts affected, the amount of the adjustment (using a + or − to indicate an increase or decrease), and the balance of the account after the adjustment in the following format.

Balance Sheet Account	Amount of Adjustment (+ or −)	Balance after Adjustment	Income Statement Account	Amount of Adjustment (+ or −)	Balance after Adjustment

LO3 LO4 Preparing Adjusting Entries

P 7. On November 30, the end of the current fiscal year, the following information was available to assist Pinder Corporation's accountants in making adjusting entries:

a. Pinder Corporation's Supplies account showed a beginning balance of $2,174. Purchases during the year were $4,526. The end-of-year inventory revealed supplies on hand of $1,397.
b. The Prepaid Insurance account showed the following on November 30:

Beginning Balance	$3,580
July 1	4,200
October 1	7,272

The beginning balance represents the unexpired portion of a one-year policy purchased the previous year. The July 1 entry represents a new one-year policy, and the October 1 entry represents additional coverage in the form of a three-year policy.

c. The following table contains the cost and annual depreciation for buildings and equipment, all of which were purchased before the current year:

Account	Cost	Annual Depreciation
Buildings	$286,000	$14,500
Equipment	374,000	35,400

d. On September 1, the company completed negotiations with a client and accepted a payment of $16,800, which represented one year's services paid in advance. The $16,800 was credited to Unearned Services Revenue.

e. The company calculated that as of November 30, it had earned $4,000 on an $11,000 contract that will be completed and billed in January.

f. Among the liabilities of the company is a note payable in the amount of $300,000. On November 30, the accrued interest on this note amounted to $15,000.

g. On Saturday, December 2, the company, which is on a six-day workweek, will pay its regular salaried employees $12,300.

h. On November 29, the company completed negotiations and signed a contract to provide services to a new client at an annual rate of $17,500.

i. Management estimates income taxes for the year to be $25,000.

REQUIRED

1. Prepare adjusting entries for each item listed above.
2. Explain how the conditions for revenue recognition are applied to transactions **e** and **h**.

P 8.
LO4 Determining Adjusting Entries, Posting to T Accounts, and Preparing an Adjusted Trial Balance

The schedule below presents the trial balance for the Sigma Consultants Corporation on December 31, 20x4.

Sigma Consultants Corporation
Trial Balance
December 31, 20x4

Cash	$ 12,786	
Accounts Receivable	24,840	
Office Supplies	991	
Prepaid Rent	1,400	
Office Equipment	6,700	
Accumulated Depreciation, Office Equipment		$ 1,600
Accounts Payable		1,820
Notes Payable		10,000
Unearned Service Revenue		2,860
Common Stock		10,000
Retained Earnings		19,387
Dividends	15,000	
Service Revenue		58,500
Salaries Expense	33,000	
Utilities Expense	1,750	
Rent Expense	7,700	
	$104,167	$104,167

The following information is also available:

a. Ending inventory of office supplies, $86.
b. Prepaid rent expired, $700.
c. Depreciation of office equipment for the period, $600.
d. Interest accrued on the note payable, $600.
e. Salaries accrued at the end of the period, $200.
f. Service revenue still unearned at the end of the period, $1,410.
g. Service revenue earned but not billed, $600.
h. Estimated federal income taxes for the period, $3,000.

REQUIRED
1. Open T accounts for the accounts in the trial balance plus the following: Interest Payable; Salaries Payable; Income Taxes Payable; Office Supplies Expense; Depreciation Expense, Office Equipment; Interest Expense; and Income Taxes Expense. Enter the account balances.
2. Determine the adjusting entries and post them directly to the T accounts.
3. Prepare an adjusted trial balance.

SKILLS DEVELOPMENT CASES

Conceptual Analysis

LO2 **Importance of Adjustments**
LO3
LO4

SD 1. Never Flake Company, which operated in the northeastern part of the United States, provided a rust-prevention coating for the underside of new automobiles. The company advertised widely and offered its services through new car dealers. When a dealer sold a new car, the salesperson attempted to sell the rust-prevention coating as an option. The protective coating was supposed to make cars last longer in the severe northeastern winters. A key selling point was Never Flake's warranty, which stated that it would repair any damage due to rust at no charge for as long as the buyer owned the car.

During the 1990s, Never Flake was very successful in generating enough cash to continue operations. But in 2001 the company suddenly declared bankruptcy. Company officials said that the firm had only $5.5 million in assets against liabilities of $32.9 million. Most of the liabilities represented potential claims under the company's lifetime warranty. It seemed that owners were keeping their cars longer now than previously. Therefore, more damage was being attributed to rust. Discuss what accounting decisions could have helped Never Flake to survive under these circumstances.

 Group Activity: Divide the class into groups to discuss this case. Then debrief as a class by asking a person from each group to comment.

LO3 **Application of Accrual**
LO4 **Accounting**

SD 2. The Lyric Opera of Chicago <www.lyricopera.com> is one of the largest and best-managed opera companies in the United States. Managing opera productions requires advance planning, including the development of scenery, costumes, and stage properties and the sale of tickets. To measure how well the company is operating in any given year, accrual accounting must be applied to these and other transactions. At year end, April 30, 2001, Lyric Opera's balance sheet showed Deferred Production Costs of $1,639,949 and Deferred Ticket Revenue of $19,100,781.[7] Be prepared to discuss what accounting policies and adjusting entries are applicable to these accounts. Why are they important to Lyric Opera's management?

Ethical Dilemma

LO2 **Importance of Adjustments**
LO3
LO4

SD 3. Central Appliance Service Co., Inc., has achieved fast growth in the St. Louis area by selling service contracts on large appliances, such as washers, dryers, and refrigerators. For a fee, Central Appliance agrees to provide all parts and labor on an appliance after the regular warranty runs out. For example, by paying a fee of $200, a person who buys a dishwasher can add two years (years 2 and 3) to the regular one-year (year 1) warranty on the appliance. In 2004, the company sold service contracts in the amount of $1.8 million, all of which applied to future years. Management wanted all the sales recorded as revenues in 2004, contending that the amount of the contracts could be determined and the cash had been received. Discuss whether you agree with this logic. How would you record the cash receipts? What assumptions do you think should be made? Would you consider it unethical to follow management's recommendation? Who might be hurt or helped by this action?

Research Activity

LO4 **Real-World Observation of**
Business Activities

SD 4. Choose a company with which you are familiar. Visit the company and observe its operations. For example, it can be where you work, where you eat, or where you buy things. Identify at least two sources of revenue for the company and six types of expenses. For

each type of revenue and each type of expense, determine whether it is probable that an adjusting entry is required at the end of the accounting period and specify the adjusting entry as a deferred revenue, deferred expense, accrued revenue, or accrued expense.

Decision-Making Practice

SD 5.
LO1 Adjusting Entries, Dividend
LO4 Performance Evaluation, and Dividend Policy

Karen Jamison, the owner of a newsletter for managers of hotels and restaurants, has prepared the following condensed amounts from her company's financial statements for 20x3:

Revenues	$346,000
Expenses	282,000
Net income	$ 64,000
Total assets	$172,000
Liabilities	$ 48,000
Stockholders' equity	124,000
Total liabilities and stockholders' equity	$172,000

Given these figures, Jamison is planning a cash dividend of $50,000. However, Jamison's accountant has found that the following items were overlooked:

a. Although the balance of the Printing Supplies account is $32,000, only $14,000 in supplies is on hand at the end of the year.
b. Depreciation of $20,000 on equipment has not been recorded.
c. Wages of $9,400 have been earned by Jamison's employees but not recognized in the accounts.
d. No provision has been made for estimated income taxes payable of $10,800.
e. A liability account called Unearned Subscriptions has a balance of $16,200, although it has been determined that one-third of these subscriptions have been mailed to subscribers.

1. Prepare the necessary adjusting entries.
2. Recast the condensed financial statement figures after you have made the necessary adjustments.
3. Discuss the performance of Jamison's business after the adjustments have been made. (**Hint:** Compare net income to revenues (divide net income by revenues) and total assets (divide net income by total assets) before and after the adjustments.) Do you think that paying the dividend is advisable?

FINANCIAL REPORTING AND ANALYSIS CASES

Interpreting Financial Reports

FRA 1.
LO2 Analysis of an Asset Account
LO4

The Walt Disney Company <www.disney.go.com> is engaged in the financing, production, and distribution of motion pictures and television programming. In Disney's annual report, the balance sheet contains an asset called Film and Television Costs. Film and Television Costs, which consist of the cost associated with producing films and television programs less the amount expensed, were $3,606,000,000. The statement of cash flows reveals that the amount of film and television costs expensed (amortized) during the year was $2,469,000,000. The amount spent for new film productions was $2,679,000,000.[8]

1. What are Film and Television Costs, and why would they be classified as an asset?
2. Prepare an entry in T account form to record the amount the company spent on new film and television production during the year (assume all expenditures are paid for in cash).
3. Prepare an adjusting entry in T account form to record the expense for film and television productions.
4. Can you suggest a method by which The Walt Disney Company might have determined the amount of the expense in **3** in accordance with the matching rule?

FRA 2.
LO4 Identification of Accruals

H.J. Heinz Company, <www.heinz.com>, a major food company, had a net income in 2001 of $478,012,000 and the following current liabilities at the end of 2001:[9]

Current Liabilities (in thousands):	2001
Short-term debt	$1,555,869
Portion of long-term debt due within one year	314,965
Accounts payable	962,497
Salaries and wages	54,036
Accrued marketing	146,138
Accrued restructuring costs	134,550
Other accrued liabilities	388,582
Income taxes	98,460
Total current liabilities	$3,655,097

1. Which of the current liabilities definitely arose as the result of an adjusting entry at the end of the year? Which ones may partially have arisen from an adjusting entry? Which ones probably did not arise from an adjusting entry?
2. What effect do adjustments that create new liabilities have on net income or loss? Based on your answer in 1, what percentage of current liabilities was definitely the result of an adjusting entry? Assuming the adjusting entries for these items had not been performed, what would Heinz's net income or loss have been?

International Company

FRA 3.
LO2 Account Identification and
LO3 Accrual Accounting

Takashimaya Company, Ltd. <www.takashimaya.co.jp> is Japan's largest department store chain. An account on Takashimaya's balance sheet called Gift Certificates contains ¥41,657 million ($404 million).[10] Is this account an asset or a liability? What transaction gives rise to the account? How is this account an example of the application of accrual accounting? Explain the conceptual issues that must be resolved for an adjusting entry to be valid.

Toys "R" Us Annual Report

FRA 4.
LO4 Analysis of Balance Sheet and Adjusting Entries

Refer to the balance sheet in the Toys "R" Us <www.tru.com> annual report. Examine the accounts listed in the current assets, property and equipment, and current liabilities sections. Which accounts are most likely to have had year-end adjusting entries? Describe the nature of the adjusting entries. For more information about the property and equipment section, refer to the notes to the consolidated financial statements.

Comparison Case: Toys "R" Us and Walgreen Co.

FRA 5.
LO1 Depreciation Expense and
LO2 Estimates
LO4

Depreciation expense is recorded by an adjusting entry and is one of the most important expenses for many companies. In the supplement to Chapter 1, refer to the Summary of Significant Accounting Policies in the notes to the financial statements in the Toys "R" Us <www.tru.com> annual report and to Walgreens' <www.walgreens.com> financial statements to answer these questions:

1. Where is depreciation (and amortization) expense disclosed on the financial statements for each company? Note that depreciation expense is not listed on Walgreens' income statement. Does this mean it is not a factor in computing net income for the company? (Also, note that amortization expense is similar to depreciation expense and is often included with it.)
2. Determine the importance of depreciation and amortization expense to each company by dividing depreciation and amortization expense by net sales. Why do you think the percentages are small?
3. Each company has a statement on the "Use of Estimates" in its Summary of Significant Accounting Policies. Read these statements and tell how important estimates are to the determination of depreciation expense. What assumptions do accountants make that allow these estimates to be made?

Fingraph® Financial Analyst™

FRA 6.
LO2 Income Measurement and
LO4 Adjustments
SO6

Choose a company from the list of Fingraph companies on the Needles Accounting Resource Center Web Site at http://accounting.college.hmco.com/students. Click on the company you selected to access the Microsoft Excel spreadsheet for that company. You will find the company's URL (Internet address) in the heading of the spreadsheet. Click on the URL for a link to the company's web site and annual report.

1. Identify the type of fiscal year that the company uses. Do you think the year end corresponds to the company's natural business year?
2. Find the company's balance sheet. From the asset accounts and liability accounts, find four examples of accounts that might have been related to an adjusting entry at the end of the year. For each example, tell whether it is a deferral or an accrual and suggest an income statement account that might be associated with it.
3. Find the summary of significant accounting policies that appears following the financial statements. In these policies, find examples of the application of going concern and accrual accounting. Explain your choices of examples.
4. Prepare a one-page executive summary that highlights what you have learned from parts **1**, **2**, and **3**.

Internet Case

FRA 7.
LO4 Comparison of Accrued Expenses

How important are accrued expenses? Randomly choose four different companies from the Needles Accounting Resource Center Web Site at http://accounting.college.hmco.com/students. Use the links to get to each company's web site and annual report. For each company, find the section of the balance sheet labeled "Current Liabilities" and identify the current liabilities that are accrued expenses (sometimes called *accrued liabilities*). More than one account may be involved. On a pad, write the information you find in four columns: name of company, total current liabilities, total accrued liabilities, and total accrued liabilities as a percentage of total current liabilities. Write a memorandum to your instructor listing the companies you chose, telling how you obtained their reports, reporting the data you have gathered in the form of a table, and stating a conclusion, with reasons, as to the importance of accrued expenses to the companies you studied. (**Hint:** Compute the average percentage of total accrued expenses for the four companies.)

4

Chapter 4 focuses on the principles of designing accounting information systems and on the preparation of closing entries and the completion of the accounting cycle.

Accounting Information Systems

LEARNING OBJECTIVES

LO1 Identify the principles of designing accounting information systems.

LO2 State all the steps in the accounting cycle.

LO3 Describe the use and structure of spreadsheet software and general ledger systems in computerized accounting systems.

LO4 Explain how accountants and businesses use the Internet.

LO5 Explain the purposes of closing entries and prepare required closing entries.

LO6 Prepare the post-closing trial balance.

SUPPLEMENTAL OBJECTIVES

SO7 Prepare reversing entries as appropriate.

SO8 Prepare and use a work sheet.

DECISION POINT

A USER'S FOCUS

Hershey Foods Corp. <www.hersheys.com> is a large multinational company well known for its chocolate products. As a company whose shares are traded on the New York Stock Exchange, Hershey must prepare both annual and quarterly financial statements for its stockholders and file them with the Securities and Exchange Commission. Note the interim income statement from Hershey's quarterly report that appears on the opposite page.[1] This statement shows that Hershey's net sales for the third quarter ended September 28, 2003, were greater than those for the same period of the preceding year, and that net income increased by approximately 16.7 percent, from $123,065,000 to $143,604,000, for the same period.

Whether required by law or not, the preparation of *interim financial statements* every quarter, or even every month, is a good idea for all businesses because such reports give management an ongoing view of a company's financial performance. What are the costs and time involved in preparing interim financial statements?

The preparation of interim financial statements throughout the year requires more effort than the preparation of a single set of financial statements for the entire year. Each time the financial statements are prepared, adjusting entries must be determined, prepared, and recorded. Also, the ledger accounts must be prepared to begin the next accounting period. These procedures are time-consuming and costly. However, the advantages of preparing interim finan-

Why is it important for Hershey Foods to prepare interim financial statements throughout the year?

cial statements, even when they are not required, usually outweigh the costs, because such statements give management timely information for making decisions that will improve operations. This chapter explains the accounting information systems used to process data and prepare financial statements at the end of an accounting period, whether that period is a month, a quarter, or a year.

Financial Highlights: Interim Income Statement
(Unaudited—in thousands)

	Third Quarter	
	2003	2002
Net Sales	$1,191,019	$1,152,321
Costs and Expenses:		
Cost of sales	724,185	717,197
Selling, marketing and administrative	212,107	218,052
Business realignment charge, net	8,564	8,536
Gain on sale of business	(8,330)	—
Total costs and expenses	936,526	943,785
Income before Interest and Income Taxes	254,493	208,536
Interest expense, net	17,258	14,120
Income before Income Taxes	237,235	194,416
Provision for income taxes	86,263	71,351
Income before Cumulative Effect of Accounting Change	150,972	123,065
Cumulative effect of accounting change, net of $4,933 tax benefit	7,368	—
Net Income	$ 143,604	$ 123,065

Accounting Information Systems: Principles of Design

LO1 Identify the principles of designing accounting information systems.

RELATED TEXT ASSIGNMENTS
Q: 1, 2
SE: 1
FRA: 6

www.sap.com
www.peoplesoft.com
www.oracle.com

Accounting information systems summarize financial data about a business and organize the data into useful forms. Accountants communicate the results to management. The means by which an accounting system accomplishes these objectives is called **data processing**. Management uses the resulting information to make a variety of business decisions.

As businesses have grown larger and more complex, the role of accounting information systems has grown. Today, many organizations use comprehensive, computerized information systems that integrate financial and nonfinancial information about customers, operations, and suppliers in a single database. Though integrated with a wide variety of other information, accounting information serves as the base for these integrated information systems, which are known as **enterprise resource planning (ERP) systems**. Three companies that specialize in ERP software are the German-based company SAP and the U.S.-based companies PeopleSoft and Oracle.

ERP systems are most often set up, monitored, and operated by accountants. The primary purpose of these systems is to integrate all functions of a company to provide timely information to decision makers throughout the organization. For this reason, accountants must understand all phases of their company's operations as well as the latest developments in systems design and technology. Additionally, while a computerized accounting system may automate many or all bookkeeping functions, it does not eliminate the need to understand the accounting process. In fact, it is impossible to use any accounting information system, manual or computerized, without a basic knowledge of accounting.

The design of an accounting information system involves four general principles: (1) the cost-benefit principle, (2) the control principle, (3) the compatibility principle, and (4) the flexibility principle.

● Stop and Think!
Certainly, it is important to make right decisions and avoid wrong decisions, but what is the cost of making no decisions?

The cost can be high. For example, assume a product suddenly becomes so popular that it will soon be sold out. If the retailer's accounting information system is not set up to provide this information to the sales manager quickly, the sales manager's failure to make the decision to reorder could cause the company to lose valuable sales. ■

Cost-Benefit Principle

The most important systems principle, the **cost-benefit principle**, holds that the benefits derived from an accounting information system must be equal to or greater than the system's cost. In addition to performing certain routine tasks—preparing payroll and tax reports and financial statements, and maintaining internal control—the accounting system may be called upon to provide other information that management wants or needs. The benefits from that information must be weighed against both the tangible and the intangible costs of gathering it.

Among the tangible costs are those for personnel, forms, and equipment. One of the intangible costs is the cost of wrong decisions stemming from the lack of good information. For instance, wrong decisions can lead to loss of sales, production stoppages, or inventory losses. Some companies have spent thousands of dollars on computerized systems that do not offer enough benefits. On the other hand, some have failed to realize the important benefits that could be gained from investing in more advanced systems. It is the job of the accountant and the systems designer or analyst to weigh the costs and benefits.

KEY POINT: The cost of making a wrong decision is an intangible cost that can easily be overlooked in designing an accounting system. It is the systems analyst's job to strike the optimal balance between expected benefits and costs.

Control Principle

KEY POINT: An accounting information system should help protect the company's assets and provide reliable data.

The **control principle** requires that an accounting information system provide all the features of internal control needed to protect a firm's assets and to ensure that data are reliable. For example, before expenditures are made, a responsible member of management should approve them.

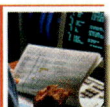

FOCUS ON BUSINESS PRACTICE

How Much Is a Used Computerized Accounting System Worth?

Apparently, a second-hand computerized accounting system has value in the marketplace, if it's a good one. When it declared bankruptcy, the old-line retailer Montgomery Ward had many problems, but accounting, inventory, and sales software wasn't one of them. When the company auctioned off its custom-designed software system, bids started at $100 million.[2]

KEY POINT: A systems analyst must carefully consider a business's activities, objectives, and performance measures, as well as the behavioral characteristics of its employees.

KEY POINT: To work effectively with a computerized accounting system, you must understand how a manual accounting system works. A computerized system functions exactly like a manual system, except that it processes information at lightning speed.

COMPATIBILITY PRINCIPLE

The **compatibility principle** holds that the design of an accounting information system must be in harmony with the organizational and human factors of the business. The organizational factors have to do with the nature of a company's business and the formal roles its units play in meeting business objectives. For example, a company can organize its marketing efforts by region or by product. If a company is organized by region, its accounting information system should report revenues and expenses by region. If a company is organized by product, its system should report revenues and expenses first by product and then by region.

The human factors of business have to do with the people within the organization and their abilities, behaviors, and personalities. The interest, support, and competence of a company's employees are very important to the success or failure of systems design. In changing systems or installing new ones, the accountant must deal with the people who are carrying out or supervising existing procedures. Such people must understand, accept, and, in many cases, be trained in the new procedures. The new system cannot succeed unless the system and the people in the organization are compatible.

FLEXIBILITY PRINCIPLE

The **flexibility principle** holds that an accounting information system must be flexible enough to allow for growth in the volume of transactions and for organizational changes. Businesses do not stay the same. They grow, they offer new products, they add new branch offices, they sell existing divisions, or they make other changes that require adjustments in the accounting system. A carefully designed accounting system allows a business to grow and change without having to make major alterations in the system. For example, the chart of accounts should be designed to accommodate the addition of new asset, liability, stockholders' equity, revenue, and expense accounts.

 Check out ACE for a Review Quiz at http://accounting.college.hmco.com/students.

OVERVIEW OF THE ACCOUNTING CYCLE

LO2 State all the steps in the accounting cycle.

RELATED TEXT ASSIGNMENTS
Q: 3
SE: 2
P: 3
SD: 1, 3, 4, 5
FRA: 3, 4

🛑 **STOP AND THINK!**
Why is the accounting cycle called a "cycle"?

It is so called because its steps are repeated each accounting period. Step 1 of one period follows step 6 of the prior period. ■

The **accounting cycle** is a series of steps in the accounting information system whose purpose is to measure business activities in the form of transactions and to transform these transactions into financial statements that will communicate useful information to decision makers. The steps in the accounting cycle, illustrated in Figure 1, are as follows:

1. *Analyze* business transactions from source documents.
2. *Record* the entries in the journal.
3. *Post* the entries to the ledger and prepare a trial balance.
4. *Adjust* the accounts and prepare an adjusted trial balance.
5. *Close* the accounts and prepare a post-closing trial balance.
6. *Prepare* financial statements.

You are already familiar with steps 1 through 4 and 6. Step 5 is covered in this chapter. The order of these steps can vary to some extent depending on the system

Figure 1
Overview of the Accounting Cycle

Computerized Accounting Systems

KEY POINT: Steps 1 through 3 are carried out throughout the period, whereas steps 4 through 6 are carried out at the end of the period only.

in place. For instance, the financial statements (step 6) may be completed before the closing entries are prepared (step 5). In fact, in a computerized system, step 6 usually must be performed before step 5. The point is that all these steps must be accomplished to complete the accounting cycle. At key points in the accounting cycle, trial balances are prepared to ensure that the ledger remains in balance.

 Check out ACE for a Review Quiz at http://accounting.college.hmco.com/students.

COMPUTERIZED ACCOUNTING SYSTEMS

LO3 Describe the use and structure of spreadsheet software and general ledger systems in computerized accounting systems.

RELATED TEXT ASSIGNMENTS
Q: 4, 5, 6
SE: 3
FRA: 6

Businesses use computerized systems for accounting and many other purposes. Large, multinational companies have vast computer resources and use very powerful computers that are linked together to provide communication and data transfer around the world. However, even in these large companies and in most small companies, the microcomputer, or PC, is a critical element in the processing of information. It has become even more critical as companies have expanded their use of the Internet to communicate and transact business directly with vendors, suppliers, and clients. Two kinds of microcomputer programs on which accountants rely heavily are spreadsheet software and general ledger systems.

SPREADSHEET SOFTWARE

Spreadsheet software is used to analyze data. A **spreadsheet** is a computerized grid of columns and rows into which the user places data or formulas related to financial planning, cost estimating, and other accounting tasks. Windows® Excel and Lotus are popular commercial spreadsheet programs used for financial analysis and other purposes.

GENERAL LEDGER SYSTEMS

KEY POINT: Five kinds of transactions—credit sales, credit purchases, cash receipts, cash payments, and miscellaneous—are common in the typical business. In a manual system, a separate journal is used for each of the first four types of transactions and a general journal is used for miscellaneous transactions. In a computerized system, a separate function is chosen for each type.

General ledger systems is the terminology commonly used to identify the group of integrated software programs that accountants use to perform major functions, such as accounting for sales and accounts receivable, purchases and accounts payable, cash receipts and disbursements, and payroll.

Today, most general ledger systems are written using the Windows® operating system, which has a **graphical user interface (GUI)**. A graphical user interface employs symbols, called **icons**, to represent operations. Examples of icons include a file folder, eraser, hourglass, and magnifying glass. The keyboard can be used in the traditional way, or a *mouse* or *trackball* may be used. When a program uses Windows as its graphical user interface, the program is termed *Windows-compatible*. The visual format and the ability to use a mouse or trackball make Windows-compatible software easy to use.

FOCUS ON BUSINESS TECHNOLOGY

Networking: How to Get It Done

Many businesses achieve the computing power of mainframes (large computers) by linking many microcomputers in a network. In a daisy chain network, the microcomputers are linked in a type of circle, or daisy chain. With this network, a person may have to go through several other microcomputers to reach a file or communicate with a person at another computer. In a home base, or star, network, all microcomputers are linked to a central switching point, or home base. A separate microcomputer called a *server* contains all the common data files, such as the accounting records. The server is also connected to the home base. All users can access accounting records and other data files by going through the home base. This type of network is faster and more efficient than the daisy chain network.

FIGURE 2
Graphical User Interface

1. **Title Bar:** The title bar at the top of the screen identifies the program and the company under consideration.

2. **Menu Bar:** When you click on one of the menu bar headings, a submenu of options opens. You select an option with a mouse or by holding down the <Alt> key and pressing the letter underlined in the desired option.

3. **Active Window:** This bar shows what window is open, or "active." Here, the "General Journal Entry" window is active.

4. **Icon Bar:** The icon bar shows visual images that pertain to the window. Some icons are common to all windows, whereas others are specific to a particular window. You click on an icon to perform the associated function.

5. **Entry Area:** This part of the screen is where you enter information for the journal entry.

6. **Navigation Aid:** The navigation aid offers a graphical supplement to the menu bar. The major functions of the program are represented as icons or pictures that show you how tasks flow through the system.

7. **Status Bar:** The gray bar (screen colors may vary) at the bottom of the window shows the current date and the current accounting period.

Source: "Graphical User Interface" from *Peachtree Complete Accounting*™ *for Windows*®. Reprinted by permission of Peachtree Software.

● **Stop and Think!**
Why is knowledge of accounting necessary when a computerized general ledger system will do the steps in the accounting cycle automatically?
Knowledge of accounting is necessary for two reasons. First, transactions must be entered in the proper way and in the proper accounts. Second, an understanding of the financial statements that the system produces is a necessary component in making business decisions. ■

KEY POINT: At least one source document should support each business transaction entered in the records. The accounting system should provide easy reference to the source documents to facilitate subsequent examination (e.g., by an auditor). For instance, canceled checks should be filed by check number.

Figure 2 shows how Peachtree Complete Accounting™ for Windows (PCW) uses a combination of text and icons. It is an example of what a graphical user interface looks like on your computer.

One of the benefits of Windows-compatible programs is that they use standardized terms and operations. Once you have mastered one Windows-compatible program, such as Peachtree Complete, you will be able to use other Windows-compatible applications.

Three software programs available for this book are (1) General Ledger Software, (2) Peachtree Complete Accounting for Windows, and (3) Quickbooks®. General Ledger Software is used to work end-of-chapter problems. It is designed for educational use and cannot be purchased commercially. Peachtree Complete and Quickbooks can be purchased through retail stores. They, too, can be used with selected end-of-chapter problems.

STRUCTURE OF GENERAL LEDGER SYSTEMS

Most general ledger systems are organized so that each module performs a major task of the accounting information system. Figure 3 shows a typical configuration of general ledger systems. Note that there is a software module for each major accounting function: sales/accounts receivable, purchases/accounts payable, cash receipts, cash disbursements, payroll, and general journal. When these features interact with one another, the software is called an *integrated program*.

Source documents, or written evidence, should support each transaction entered into the accounting system. Source documents verify that a transaction occurred and provide the details of the transaction. For example, a customer's invoice should support each sale on account, and a vendor's invoice should support each purchase. Even though the transactions are recorded in a computer file

FIGURE 3
Microcomputer Accounting Information System Using a General Ledger System

(on floppy disks or hard disks), the original documents should be stored so that they can be examined at a later date if a question arises about the accuracy of the accounting records.

After transactions are processed in a general ledger system, there is a procedure for posting them, updating the ledgers, and preparing the trial balance. Finally, the financial statements and other accounting reports are printed.

Peachtree Complete Accounting for Windows allows either *batch* posting or *real-time* posting. In a batch posting system, source documents are recorded in the appropriate journal and saved; posting is done at the end of the day, week, or month. In a real-time posting system, documents are posted as they are recorded in the journal. The basic goal of a general ledger system is to make accounting tasks less time-consuming and more accurate and dependable. However, it is important to understand just what the computer is accomplishing. Knowledge of the underlying accounting process helps ensure that the accounting records are accurate and that the assets of the business are protected.

 Check out ACE for a Review Quiz at http://accounting.college.hmco.com/students.

ACCOUNTANTS, BUSINESSES, AND THE INTERNET

LO4 Explain how accountants and businesses use the Internet.

RELATED TEXT ASSIGNMENTS
Q: 7
SE: 4
FRA: 2

www.sec.gov/edgar.shtml

STOP AND THINK!
Why do you think small businesses may be reluctant to establish their own web sites?
There are several possible reasons. A web site is costly to set up and maintain; management may lack knowledge or expertise about web sites and may fail to see their benefits; or the business may be of a type that would not benefit from the principal features of a web site. ■

The **Internet** is the world's largest computer network. The Internet allows any computer on the network to communicate with any other computer on the network. Computer access to the Internet is generally gained via a modem connected to a phone line or cable.

Most people are well aware of the Internet's ability to provide access to the World Wide Web (WWW), electronic mail (email), and electronic bulletin boards. Recent research shows that even businesses with fewer than ten employees are users of the Internet. More than 50 percent of these small businesses have Internet access, and more than 20 percent have their own web sites.[3] Among the ways in which accountants and businesses of all sizes use the Internet are the following:

- **Financial reporting.** Companies today commonly make their financial statements available on the Internet. Large companies are required to file their financial information electronically with the SEC, and it is available on Edgar, the SEC's online warehouse of financial information. Additionally, most companies publish electronic versions of their annual reports on their web sites.

- **XBRL. Extensible Business Reporting Language (XBRL)** is a new computer language developed by accountants and others for the express purpose of identifying and communicating financial information. It allows businesses to post information on the Web in a uniform way so that users can access the information, summarize it, perform computations, and format the output in any manner they wish.

- **Ecommerce. Electronic commerce (ecommerce)** is the conduct of business transactions on computer networks, including the Internet. Most people are familiar with the buying and selling of products from business to consumers (B to C) on the Internet, but the Internet is used far more widely in business-to-business (B to B) and business to government (B to G) transactions. These transactions include buying and selling products and services, collecting receivables, and paying bills.

- **EDI.** Ecommerce is often facilitated through private links, referred to as **Electronic Data Interchange (EDI).** For example, companies in many industries, such as retail chemicals, oil, and automobile parts, have formed private networks to use EDI for buying and selling goods and services.

- **Supply-chain management. Supply-chain management** is a system that uses the Internet to track the supplies and materials a manufacturer will need on a day-to-day—sometimes hour-to-hour—basis. Such a system may also link the manufacturer to its customers.

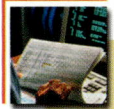

FOCUS ON BUSINESS PRACTICE

B to B and EDI: How Much Can They Save?

An officer of Target Corporation <www.target.com>, the large discount retailer, is quoted as saying, B to B is "real, and it's big, and it's growing. In five years all of our purchasing activity will be done over the Internet." Most executives agree with this statement. Sales and purchases that in the past would have been made by telephone or fax are now transacted by electronic data interchange (EDI). For example, Target participates in the worldwide Retail Exchange, an electronic marketplace formed by over 50 large retailers, including J.C. Penney <www.jcpenney.com> and Safeway Inc. <www.safeway.com>. The purpose of the Retail Exchange is to provide a market for online sales and purchases. When Target wants to purchase something—for instance, fax paper, cleaning products, or jeans—it posts its needs, and other companies bid on the business. Retailers participating in the exchange have seen a 12 to 15 percent reduction in purchasing costs. Even greater reductions are likely because at present only about 50 percent of purchases are made this way.[4]

- **E2K.** **Event-to-knowledge (E2K) management** means that the Internet is used to get information to users within and outside a company in the quickest possible way after an event like a sale or a purchase has occurred.
- **Document-less transactions.** One of the limitations on the growth of electronic commerce is that although the transactions are conducted electronically, source documents, such as those used in general ledger systems, are still often needed to back up the transactions. For example, a purchase is made on the Internet, but a confirmation is emailed, faxed, or mailed to provide documentation of the transaction. Gradually, methods that eliminate the need for source documents are being developed.

 Check out ACE for a Review Quiz at http://accounting.college.hmco.com/students.

CLOSING ENTRIES

LO5 Explain the purposes of closing entries and prepare required closing entries.

RELATED TEXT ASSIGNMENTS
Q: 8, 9, 10, 11
SE: 5, 6, 7, 8, 10
E: 1, 8
P: 1, 2, 3, 4, 5, 6, 7, 8
SD: 4
FRA: 1, 3, 5

Balance sheet accounts are considered **permanent accounts**, or *real accounts*, because they carry their end-of-period balances into the next accounting period. On the other hand, revenue and expense accounts are considered **temporary accounts**, or *nominal accounts*, because they begin each accounting period with a zero balance, accumulate a balance during the period, and are then cleared by means of closing entries.

Closing entries are journal entries made at the end of an accounting period. They have two purposes. First, closing entries set the stage for the next accounting period by clearing revenue, expense, and Dividends accounts of their balances. Remember that the income statement reports net income (or loss) for a single accounting period and shows revenues and expenses for that period only. For the income statement to present the activity of a single accounting period, the revenue

FOCUS ON BUSINESS TECHNOLOGY

E2K: How Much Time Can It Save?

E2K, or event-to-knowledge, is the concept of the time it takes to turn the results of a transaction, such as a sale or a purchase, into useful information for managers. It involves the application of the just-in-time management philosophy to accounting. The goal of just-in-time accounting (JITA) is to reduce the time it takes to produce and distribute financial reports from days or weeks to a single business day so that managers receive them when they need them, or "just in time." Cisco Systems <www.cisco.com>, the large software company, believes it has achieved a breakthrough with a "virtual close" program that gives managers the financial results of one day by 2 P.M. the next day. A reduction in E2K time means that managers have more time to consider the information and can thus make better decisions.[5]

FIGURE 4
Overview of the Closing Process

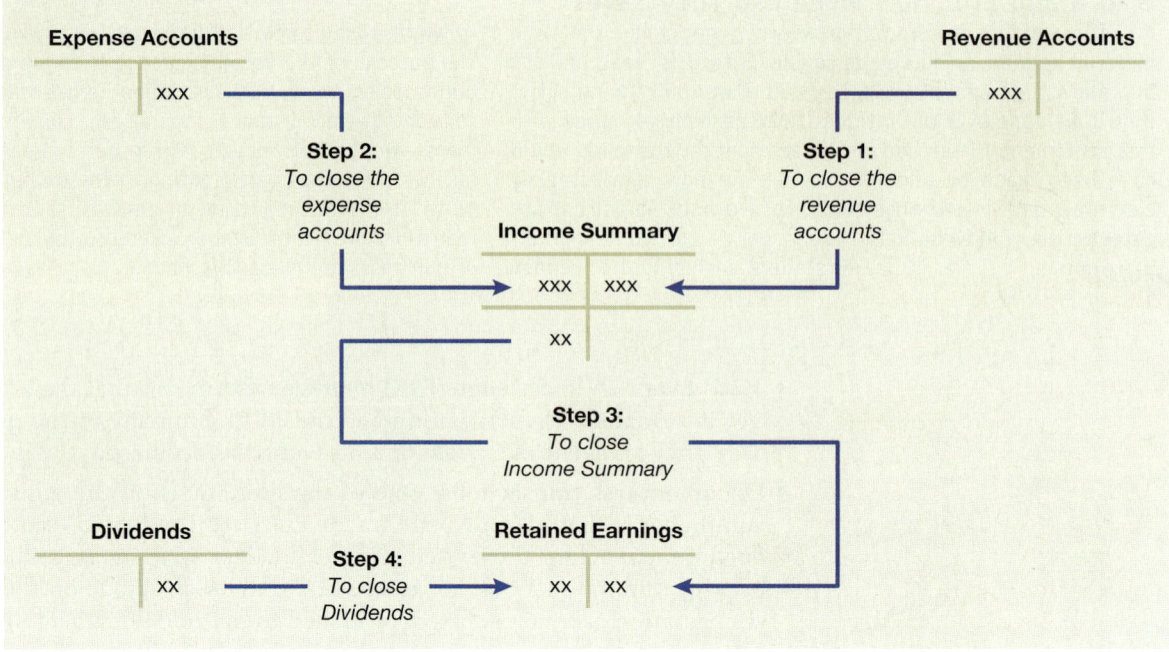

> **STOP AND THINK!**
> Could closing entries be done without using the Income Summary account?
>
> *Since the Income Summary account is used to accumulate a balance (steps 1 and 2) that is subsequently transferred to Retained Earnings (step 3), it would be possible to eliminate the use of the Income Summary account by closing the accounts in steps 1 and 2 directly to the Retained Earnings account and eliminating step 3.* ■
>
> www.hersheys.com

and expense accounts must begin each new period with zero balances. The zero balances are obtained by using closing entries to clear the balances in the revenue and expense accounts at the end of each accounting period. The Dividends account is closed in a similar manner.

Second, closing entries summarize a period's revenues and expenses. This is done by transferring the balances of revenue and expense accounts to the Income Summary account. This temporary account, which appears in the chart of accounts between the Dividends account and the first revenue account, provides a place to summarize all revenues and expenses. It is used only in the closing process and never appears in the financial statements.

The balance of the Income Summary account equals the net income or loss reported on the income statement. The net income or loss is then transferred to the Retained Earnings account. This is done because even though revenues and expenses are recorded in revenue and expense accounts, they actually represent increases and decreases in stockholders' equity. Closing entries transfer the net effect of increases (revenues) and decreases (expenses) to stockholders' equity. An overview of the closing process is illustrated in Figure 4.

Closing entries are required at the end of any period for which financial statements are prepared. As noted in the Decision Point at the beginning of the chapter, Hershey Foods prepares financial statements each quarter; when it does so, it must close its books. Such interim information is helpful to investors and creditors in assessing the ongoing financial performance of a company. Many companies, including Hershey, also close their books monthly to give management a more timely view of ongoing operations.

REQUIRED CLOSING ENTRIES

There are four important steps in closing the accounts:
1. Closing the credit balances from income statement accounts to the Income Summary account

Exhibit 1
Preparing Closing Entries from the Adjusted Trial Balance

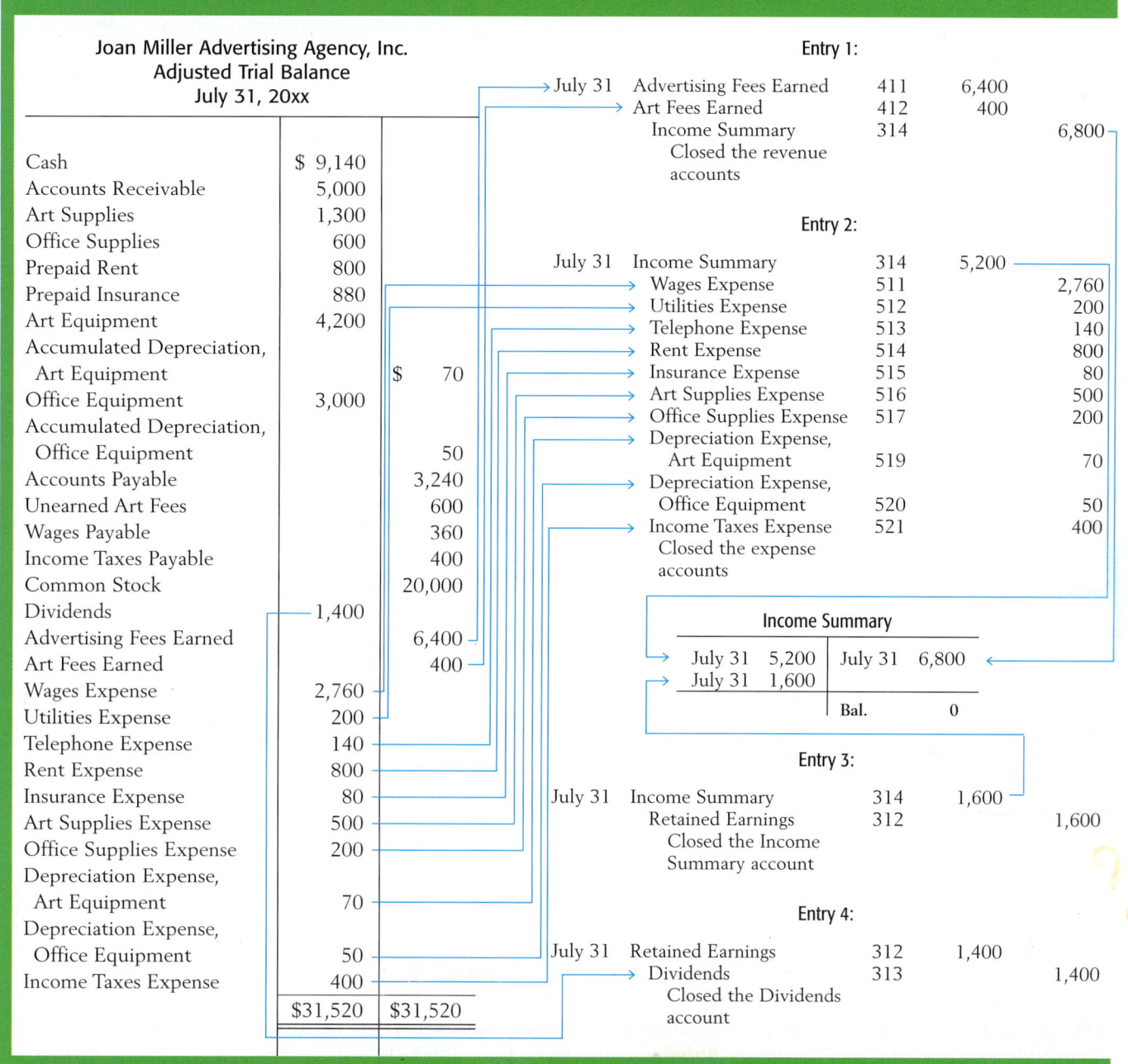

ENRICHMENT NOTE: It is not absolutely necessary to use the Income Summary account when preparing closing entries. However, it does simplify the procedure. The Income Summary account is opened and closed with the preparation of closing entries.

2. Closing the debit balances from income statement accounts to the Income Summary account
3. Closing the Income Summary account balance to the Retained Earnings account
4. Closing the Dividends account balance to the Retained Earnings account

Each step is accomplished by a closing entry. All the data needed to record the closing entries are found in the adjusted trial balance. The relationships of the four kinds of entries to the adjusted trial balance are shown in Exhibit 1.

EXHIBIT 2
Posting the Closing Entry of the Credit Balances from the Income Statement Accounts to the Income Summary Account

Advertising Fees Earned — Account No. 411

Date	Item	Post. Ref.	Debit	Credit	Balance Debit	Balance Credit
July 10		J2		1,400		1,400
19		J2		4,800		6,200
31	Adj. (j)	J3		200		6,400
31	Closing	J4	6,400			—

Art Fees Earned — Account No. 412

Date	Item	Post. Ref.	Debit	Credit	Balance Debit	Balance Credit
July 31	Adj. (i)	J3		400		400
31	Closing	J4	400			—

→ 6,400
  400 ←
  6,800

Income Summary — Account No. 314

Date	Item	Post. Ref.	Debit	Credit	Balance Debit	Balance Credit
July 31	Closing	J4		6,800		6,800

KEY POINT: The Income Summary account now reflects the account balances that the revenue accounts contained before they were closed.

STUDY NOTE: In steps 1 and 2, the words "credit balances" and "debit balances" are used in place of "revenue accounts" and "expense accounts," respectively, because as you will learn in future chapters, not all credit balances are revenue accounts and not all debit balances are expense accounts.

■ **STEP 1: CLOSING THE CREDIT BALANCES FROM INCOME STATEMENT ACCOUNTS TO THE INCOME SUMMARY ACCOUNT** On the credit side of the adjusted trial balance in Exhibit 1, two revenue accounts show balances: Advertising Fees Earned and Art Fees Earned. To close these two accounts, an entry must be made debiting each account in the amount of its balance and crediting the total to the Income Summary account. The effect of posting the entry is illustrated in Exhibit 2. Notice that the entry (1) sets the balances of the revenue accounts to zero and (2) transfers the total revenues to the credit side of the Income Summary account.

■ **STEP 2: CLOSING THE DEBIT BALANCES FROM INCOME STATEMENT ACCOUNTS TO THE INCOME SUMMARY ACCOUNT** Several expense accounts show balances on the debit side of the adjusted trial balance in Exhibit 1. A compound entry is needed to credit each of these expense accounts for its balance and to debit the Income Summary account for the total. The effect of posting the closing entry is shown in Exhibit 3.

EXHIBIT 3
Posting the Closing Entry of the Debit Balances from the Income Statement Accounts to the Income Summary Account

Wages Expense					Account No. 511			Income Summary					Account No. 314	
		Post.			Balance					Post.			Balance	
Date	Item	Ref.	Debit	Credit	Debit	Credit		Date	Item	Ref.	Debit	Credit	Debit	Credit
July 12		J2	1,200		1,200			July 31	Closing	J4		6,800		6,800
26		J2	1,200		2,400			31	Closing	J4	5,200			1,600
31	Adj. (g)	J3	360		2,760									
31	Closing	J4		2,760	—									

Utilities Expense					Account No. 512		
		Post.			Balance		
Date	Item	Ref.	Debit	Credit	Debit	Credit	
July 29		J2	200		200		→ 2,760
31	Closing	J4		200	—		→ 200

→ 140
→ 800
→ 80

Telephone Expense					Account No. 513		
		Post.			Balance		
Date	Item	Ref.	Debit	Credit	Debit	Credit	
July 30		J2	140		140		→ 500
31	Closing	J4		140	—		→ 200

→ 400
→ 50
→ 70
5,200

Rent Expense					Account No. 514	
		Post.			Balance	
Date	Item	Ref.	Debit	Credit	Debit	Credit
July 31	Adj. (a)	J3	800		800	
31	Closing	J4		800	—	

Insurance Expense					Account No. 515			Depreciation Expense, Art Equipment					Account No. 519	
		Post.			Balance					Post.			Balance	
Date	Item	Ref.	Debit	Credit	Debit	Credit		Date	Item	Ref.	Debit	Credit	Debit	Credit
July 31	Adj. (b)	J3	80		80			July 31	Adj. (e)	J3	70		70	
31	Closing	J4		80	—			31	Closing	J4		70	—	

Art Supplies Expense					Account No. 516			Depreciation Expense, Office Equipment					Account No. 520	
		Post.			Balance					Post.			Balance	
Date	Item	Ref.	Debit	Credit	Debit	Credit		Date	Item	Ref.	Debit	Credit	Debit	Credit
July 31	Adj. (c)	J3	500		500			July 31	Adj. (f)	J3	50		50	
31	Closing	J4		500	—			31	Closing	J4		50	—	

Office Supplies Expense					Account No. 517			Income Taxes Expense					Account No. 521	
		Post.			Balance					Post.			Balance	
Date	Item	Ref.	Debit	Credit	Debit	Credit		Date	Item	Ref.	Debit	Credit	Debit	Credit
July 31	Adj. (d)	J3	200		200			July 31	Adj. (h)	J3	400		400	
31	Closing	J4		200	—			31	Closing	J4		400	—	

KEY POINT: The credit balance of the Income Summary account at this point ($1,600) represents the key performance measure of net income.

Notice how the entry (1) reduces the expense account balances to zero and (2) transfers the total of the account balances to the debit side of the Income Summary account.

■ **STEP 3: CLOSING THE INCOME SUMMARY ACCOUNT BALANCE TO THE RETAINED EARNINGS ACCOUNT** After the entries closing the revenue and expense accounts have been posted, the balance of the Income Summary account equals the net

EXHIBIT 4
Posting the Closing Entry of the Income Summary Account Balance to the Retained Earnings Account

Income Summary					Account No. 314		Retained Earnings					Account No. 312	
		Post.			Balance				Post.			Balance	
Date	Item	Ref.	Debit	Credit	Debit	Credit	Date	Item	Ref.	Debit	Credit	Debit	Credit
July 31	Closing	J4		6,800		6,800	July 31	Closing	J4		1,600		1,600
31	Closing	J4	5,200			1,600							
31	Closing	J4	1,600			—							

income or loss for the period. Since revenues are represented by the credit to Income Summary and expenses are represented by the debit to Income Summary, a net income is indicated by a credit balance (where revenues exceed expenses) and a net loss by a debit balance (where expenses exceed revenues). At this point, the Income Summary account balance, whatever its nature, must be closed to the Retained Earnings account, as shown in Exhibit 1. The effect of posting the closing entry when the company has a net income is shown in Exhibit 4. Notice the dual effect of (1) closing the Income Summary account and (2) transferring the balance, net income in this case, to Retained Earnings.

> **KEY POINT:** In a net loss situation, debit the Retained Earnings account (to reduce it) and credit Income Summary (to close it).

> **KEY POINT:** Notice that the Dividends account is closed to the Retained Earnings account, not to the Income Summary account.

■ **STEP 4: CLOSING THE DIVIDENDS ACCOUNT BALANCE TO THE RETAINED EARNINGS ACCOUNT** The Dividends account shows the amount by which retained earnings are reduced during the accounting period by cash dividends. The debit balance of the Dividends account is closed to the Retained Earnings account, as illustrated in Exhibit 1. The effect of this closing entry, as shown in Exhibit 5, is to (1) close the Dividends account and (2) transfer the balance to the Retained Earnings account.

THE ACCOUNTS AFTER CLOSING

After all the steps in the closing process have been completed and all closing entries have been posted to the accounts, everything is ready for the next accounting period. The ledger accounts of Joan Miller Advertising Agency, Inc., as they appear at this point, are shown in Exhibit 6. The revenue, expense, and Dividends accounts

EXHIBIT 5
Posting the Closing Entry of the Dividends Account Balance to the Retained Earnings Account

Dividends					Account No. 313		Retained Earnings					Account No. 312	
		Post.			Balance				Post.			Balance	
Date	Item	Ref.	Debit	Credit	Debit	Credit	Date	Item	Ref.	Debit	Credit	Debit	Credit
July 31		J2	1,400		1,400		July 31	Closing	J4		1,600		1,600
31	Closing	J4		1,400	—		31	Closing	J4	1,400			200

EXHIBIT 6
The Accounts After Closing Entries Are Posted

Cash — Account No. 111

Date	Item	Post. Ref.	Debit	Credit	Balance Debit	Balance Credit
July 1		J1	20,000		20,000	
2		J1		1,600	18,400	
3		J1		4,200	14,200	
5		J1		1,500	12,700	
8		J1		960	11,740	
9		J1		1,000	10,740	
10		J2	1,400		12,140	
12		J2		1,200	10,940	
15		J2	1,000		11,940	
26		J2		1,200	10,740	
29		J2		200	10,540	
31		J2		1,400	9,140	

Accounts Receivable — Account No. 113

Date	Item	Post. Ref.	Debit	Credit	Balance Debit	Balance Credit
July 19		J2	4,800		4,800	
31	Adj. (j)	J3	200		5,000	

Art Supplies — Account No. 115

Date	Item	Post. Ref.	Debit	Credit	Balance Debit	Balance Credit
July 6		J1	1,800		1,800	
31	Adj. (c)	J3		500	1,300	

Office Supplies — Account No. 116

Date	Item	Post. Ref.	Debit	Credit	Balance Debit	Balance Credit
July 6		J1	800		800	
31	Adj. (d)	J3		200	600	

Prepaid Rent — Account No. 117

Date	Item	Post. Ref.	Debit	Credit	Balance Debit	Balance Credit
July 2		J1	1,600		1,600	
31	Adj. (a)	J3		800	800	

Prepaid Insurance — Account No. 118

Date	Item	Post. Ref.	Debit	Credit	Balance Debit	Balance Credit
July 8		J1	960		960	
31	Adj. (b)	J3		80	880	

Art Equipment — Account No. 144

Date	Item	Post. Ref.	Debit	Credit	Balance Debit	Balance Credit
July 3		J1	4,200		4,200	

Accumulated Depreciation, Art Equipment — Account No. 145

Date	Item	Post. Ref.	Debit	Credit	Balance Debit	Balance Credit
July 31	Adj. (e)	J3		70		70

Office Equipment — Account No. 146

Date	Item	Post. Ref.	Debit	Credit	Balance Debit	Balance Credit
July 5		J1	3,000		3,000	

Accumulated Depreciation, Office Equipment — Account No. 147

Date	Item	Post. Ref.	Debit	Credit	Balance Debit	Balance Credit
July 31	Adj. (f)	J3		50		50

Accounts Payable — Account No. 212

Date	Item	Post. Ref.	Debit	Credit	Balance Debit	Balance Credit
July 5		J1		1,500		1,500
6		J1		2,600		4,100
9		J1	1,000			3,100
30		J2		140		3,240

Unearned Art Fees — Account No. 213

Date	Item	Post. Ref.	Debit	Credit	Balance Debit	Balance Credit
July 15		J2		1,000		1,000
31	Adj. (i)	J3	400			600

Wages Payable — Account No. 214

Date	Item	Post. Ref.	Debit	Credit	Balance Debit	Balance Credit
July 31	Adj. (g)	J3		360		360

Income Taxes Payable — Account No. 215

Date	Item	Post. Ref.	Debit	Credit	Balance Debit	Balance Credit
July 31	Adj. (h)	J3		400		400

Common Stock — Account No. 311

Date	Item	Post. Ref.	Debit	Credit	Balance Debit	Balance Credit
July 1		J1		20,000		20,000

(continued)

Exhibit 6
The Accounts After Closing Entries Are Posted (continued)

Retained Earnings — Account No. 312

Date	Item	Post. Ref.	Debit	Credit	Balance Debit	Balance Credit
July 31	Closing	J4		1,600		1,600
31	Closing	J4	1,400			200

Dividends — Account No. 313

Date	Item	Post. Ref.	Debit	Credit	Balance Debit	Balance Credit
July 31		J2	1,400		1,400	
31	Closing	J4		1,400	—	

Income Summary — Account No. 314

Date	Item	Post. Ref.	Debit	Credit	Balance Debit	Balance Credit
July 31	Closing	J4		6,800		6,800
31	Closing	J4	5,200			1,600
31	Closing	J4	1,600			—

Advertising Fees Earned — Account No. 411

Date	Item	Post. Ref.	Debit	Credit	Balance Debit	Balance Credit
July 10		J2		1,400		1,400
19		J2		4,800		6,200
31	Adj. (j)	J3		200		6,400
31	Closing	J4	6,400			—

Art Fees Earned — Account No. 412

Date	Item	Post. Ref.	Debit	Credit	Balance Debit	Balance Credit
July 31	Adj. (i)	J3		400		400
31	Closing	J4	400			—

Wages Expense — Account No. 511

Date	Item	Post. Ref.	Debit	Credit	Balance Debit	Balance Credit
July 12		J2	1,200		1,200	
26		J2	1,200		2,400	
31	Adj. (g)	J3	360		2,760	
31	Closing	J4		2,760	—	

Utilities Expense — Account No. 512

Date	Item	Post. Ref.	Debit	Credit	Balance Debit	Balance Credit
July 29		J2	200		200	
31	Closing	J4		200	—	

Telephone Expense — Account No. 513

Date	Item	Post. Ref.	Debit	Credit	Balance Debit	Balance Credit
July 30		J2	140		140	
31	Closing	J4		140	—	

Rent Expense — Account No. 514

Date	Item	Post. Ref.	Debit	Credit	Balance Debit	Balance Credit
July 31	Adj. (a)	J3	800		800	
31	Closing	J4		800	—	

Insurance Expense — Account No. 515

Date	Item	Post. Ref.	Debit	Credit	Balance Debit	Balance Credit
July 31	Adj. (b)	J3	80		80	
31	Closing	J4		80	—	

Art Supplies Expense — Account No. 516

Date	Item	Post. Ref.	Debit	Credit	Balance Debit	Balance Credit
July 31	Adj. (c)	J3	500		500	
31	Closing	J4		500	—	

Office Supplies Expense — Account No. 517

Date	Item	Post. Ref.	Debit	Credit	Balance Debit	Balance Credit
July 31	Adj. (d)	J3	200		200	
31	Closing	J4		200	—	

Depreciation Expense, Art Equipment — Account No. 519

Date	Item	Post. Ref.	Debit	Credit	Balance Debit	Balance Credit
July 31	Adj. (e)	J3	70		70	
31	Closing	J4		70	—	

Depreciation Expense, Office Equipment — Account No. 520

Date	Item	Post. Ref.	Debit	Credit	Balance Debit	Balance Credit
July 31	Adj. (f)	J3	50		50	
31	Closing	J4		50	—	

Income Taxes Expense — Account No. 521

Date	Item	Post. Ref.	Debit	Credit	Balance Debit	Balance Credit
July 31	Adj. (h)	J3	400		400	
31	Closing	J4		400	—	

(temporary accounts) have zero balances. Retained Earnings has been increased to reflect the agency's net income and decreased for dividends. The balance sheet accounts (permanent accounts) show the correct balances, which are carried forward to the next period.

 Check out ACE for a Review Quiz at http://accounting.college.hmco.com/students.

FOCUS ON INTERNATIONAL BUSINESS

Closing Doesn't Have to Be Such a Headache.
For companies with extensive international operations, like Caterpillar Inc. <www.caterpillar.com>, Dow Chemical <www.dow.com>, Phillips Petroleum <www.phillips66.com>, Gillette <www.gillette.com>, and Bristol-Myers Squibb <www.bms.com>, closing the records and preparing financial statements on a timely basis used to be a problem. It was common practice for foreign divisions of companies like these to end their fiscal year one month before the end of the fiscal year of their counterparts in the United States. This gave them the extra time they needed to perform closing procedures and mail the results back to U.S. headquarters to be used in preparation of the company's overall financial statements. This setup is usually unnecessary today because high-speed computers and electronic communications enable companies to close records and prepare financial statements for both foreign and domestic operations in less than a week.

THE POST-CLOSING TRIAL BALANCE

LO6 Prepare the post-closing trial balance.

RELATED TEXT ASSIGNMENTS
Q: 12, 13
P: 3
SD: 4

Because it is possible to make errors in posting the closing entries to the ledger accounts, it is necessary to determine that all temporary accounts have zero balances and to double-check that total debits equal total credits by preparing a new trial balance. This final trial balance, called the **post-closing trial balance**, is shown in Exhibit 7 for Joan Miller Advertising Agency, Inc. Notice that only the balance sheet accounts show balances because the income statement accounts and the Dividends account have all been closed. Also, notice that Retained Earnings is shown on the post-closing trial balance but was not shown on the adjusted trial balance in Exhibit 1. This is because it is the company's first month of operation and the account had a zero beginning balance. At the end of the month, after income and dividends are posted, Retained Earnings has a balance of $200.

EXHIBIT 7
Post-Closing Trial Balance

STOP AND THINK!
Why does the post-closing trial balance contain only balance sheet accounts?

All the income statement, or temporary, accounts have been closed, thus leaving only the balance sheet, or permanent, accounts to carry over to the next accounting period. ∎

KEY POINT: Notice that Retained Earnings now reflects the correct month-end balance, $200.

Joan Miller Advertising Agency, Inc.
Post-Closing Trial Balance
July 31, 20xx

Cash	$ 9,140	
Accounts Receivable	5,000	
Art Supplies	1,300	
Office Supplies	600	
Prepaid Rent	800	
Prepaid Insurance	880	
Art Equipment	4,200	
Accumulated Depreciation, Art Equipment		$ 70
Office Equipment	3,000	
Accumulated Depreciation, Office Equipment		50
Accounts Payable		3,240
Unearned Art Fees		600
Wages Payable		360
Income Taxes Payable		400
Common Stock		20,000
Retained Earnings		200
	$24,920	$24,920

 Check out ACE for a Review Quiz at http://accounting.college.hmco.com/students.

Reversing Entries: The Optional First Step in the Next Accounting Period

SO7 Prepare reversing entries as appropriate.

RELATED TEXT ASSIGNMENTS
Q: 14, 15
SE: 9
E: 3, 7
P: 4, 5, 8
SD: 2, 4

At the end of each accounting period, adjusting entries are made to bring revenues and expenses into conformity with the matching rule. A **reversing entry** is a general journal entry made on the first day of a new accounting period; it is the exact reverse of an adjusting entry made at the end of the previous accounting period. Reversing entries are optional. They simplify the bookkeeping process for transactions involving certain types of adjustments. Not all adjusting entries can be reversed. Under the recording system used in this book, only adjustments for accruals (accrued revenues and accrued expenses) can be reversed. Deferrals cannot be reversed because such reversals would not simplify the bookkeeping process in future accounting periods.

To see how reversing entries can be helpful, consider the adjusting entry made in the records of Joan Miller Advertising Agency, Inc., to accrue wages expense:

A = L + OE
+ −

July 31	Wages Expense	360	
	Wages Payable		360
	Accrued unrecorded wages		

When the secretary is paid on the next regular payday, the accountant would make this entry:

A = L + OE
− − −

Aug. 9	Wages Payable	360	
	Wages Expense	840	
	Cash		1,200
	Paid two weeks' wages to secretary, $360 of which accrued in the previous period		

KEY POINT: Reversing entries are the opposite of adjusting entries and are dated the first day of the new period. They apply only to certain adjusting entries and are never required.

Notice that when the payment is made, if there is no reversing entry, the accountant must look in the records to find out how much of the $1,200 applies to the current accounting period and how much is applicable to the previous period. This may seem easy in our example, but think how difficult and time-consuming it would be if a company had hundreds of employees working on different schedules. A reversing entry helps solve the problem of applying revenues and expenses to the correct accounting period. It is exactly what its name implies: a reversal made by debiting the credits and crediting the debits of a previously made adjusting entry.

For example, notice the following sequence of entries and their effects on the ledger account Wages Expense:

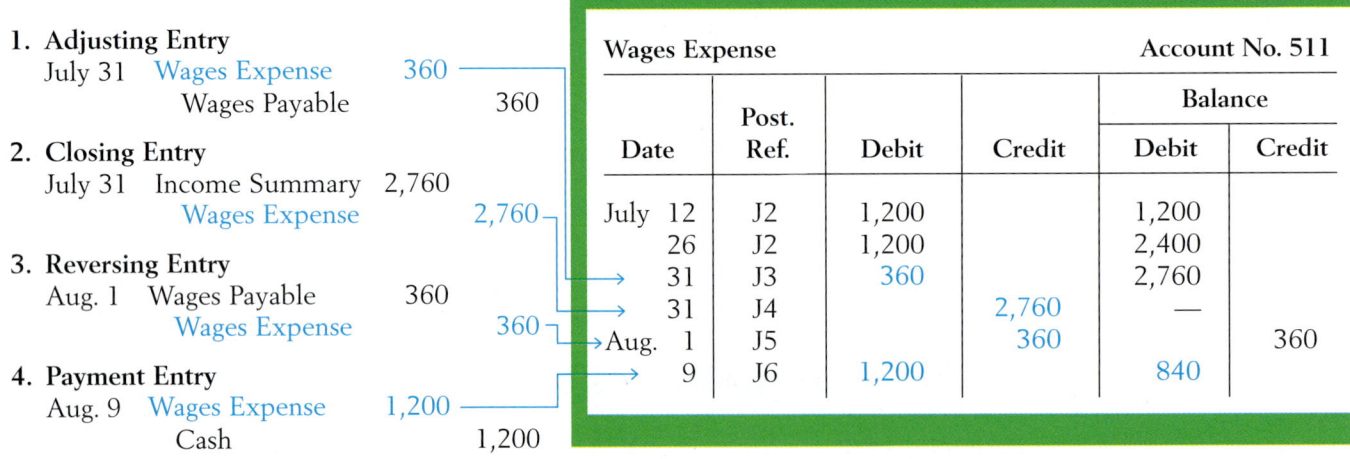

1. **Adjusting Entry**
   July 31 Wages Expense   360
                  Wages Payable   360

2. **Closing Entry**
   July 31 Income Summary 2,760
                  Wages Expense   2,760

3. **Reversing Entry**
   Aug. 1 Wages Payable   360
                  Wages Expense   360

4. **Payment Entry**
   Aug. 9 Wages Expense   1,200
                  Cash   1,200

Wages Expense — Account No. 511

Date	Post. Ref.	Debit	Credit	Balance Debit	Balance Credit
July 12	J2	1,200		1,200	
26	J2	1,200		2,400	
31	J3	360		2,760	
31	J4		2,760	—	
Aug. 1	J5		360		360
9	J6	1,200		840	

Entry **1** adjusted Wages Expense to accrue $360 in the July accounting period.

Entry **2** closed the $2,760 in Wages Expense for July to Income Summary, leaving a zero balance.

KEY POINT: Notice the abnormal credit balance as of August 1. This situation is "corrected" with the August 9 entry, an entry the bookkeeper can easily make.

Entry **3**, the reversing entry, set up a credit balance of $360 on August 1 in Wages Expense, which is the expense recognized through the adjusting entry in July (and also reduced the liability account Wages Payable to a zero balance). The reversing entry always sets up an abnormal balance in the income statement account and produces a zero balance in the balance sheet account.

Entry **4** recorded the $1,200 payment of two weeks' wages as a debit to Wages Expense, automatically leaving a balance of $840, which represents the correct wages expense to date in August.

The reversing entry simplified the process of making the payment entry on August 9.

Reversing entries apply to any accrued expenses or revenues. In the case of Joan Miller Advertising Agency, Inc., Income Taxes Expense is also an accrued expense that can be reversed. The adjusting entry for accrued revenue (advertising fees earned) can be reversed as well. The two additional reversing entries are as follows:

A = L + OE				
− +	Aug. 1	Income Taxes Payable	400	
		Income Taxes Expense		400
		Reversed adjusting entry for estimated income taxes		

A = L + OE				
− −	1	Advertising Fees Earned	200	
		Accounts Receivable		200
		Reversed adjusting entry for accrued fees earned		

When the series of advertisements is finished, the company can credit all the proceeds to Advertising Fees Earned without regard to the amount accrued in the previous period. The credit will automatically be reduced to the amount earned during August by the $200 debit in the account.

As noted earlier, under our system of recording, reversing entries apply only to accruals. They do not apply to deferrals, such as the entries that involve supplies, prepaid rent, prepaid insurance, depreciation, and unearned art fees.

 Check out ACE for a Review Quiz at http://accounting.college.hmco.com/students.

THE WORK SHEET: AN ACCOUNTANT'S TOOL

SO8 Prepare and use a work sheet.

RELATED TEXT ASSIGNMENTS
Q: 16, 17, 18, 19, 20, 21, 22, 23, 24, 25
SE: 10
E: 2, 4, 5, 6, 7, 8
P: 4, 5, 8
SD: 4

KEY POINT: The work sheet is extremely useful when an accountant must prepare numerous adjustments. It is not a financial statement, it is not required, and it is not made public.

Accountants must collect relevant data to determine what should be included in financial reports. For example, they must examine insurance policies to see how much prepaid insurance has expired, examine plant and equipment records to determine depreciation, take an inventory of supplies on hand, and calculate the amount of accrued wages. These calculations, along with other computations, analyses, and preliminary drafts of statements, make up the accountants' **working papers**. Working papers are important for two reasons. First, they help accountants organize their work and thus avoid omitting important data or steps that affect the financial statements. Second, they provide evidence of past work so that accountants or auditors can retrace their steps and support the information in the financial statements.

The **work sheet** is a special kind of working paper. It is often used as a preliminary step in the preparation of financial statements. Using a work sheet lessens the possibility of leaving out an adjustment, helps the accountant check the arithmetical accuracy of the accounts, and facilitates the preparation of financial statements. The work sheet is never published and is rarely seen by management. It is a tool for the accountant. Because preparing a work sheet is a very mechanical process, many accountants use a microcomputer for this purpose. In some cases, accountants use

EXHIBIT 8
Entering the Account Balances in the Trial Balance Columns

Joan Miller Advertising Agency, Inc.
Work Sheet
For the Month Ended July 31, 20xx

Account Name	Trial Balance		Adjustments		Adjusted Trial Balance		Income Statement		Balance Sheet	
	Debit	Credit	Debit	Credit	Debit	Credit	Debit	Credit	Debit	Credit
Cash	9,140									
Accounts Receivable	4,800									
Art Supplies	1,800									
Office Supplies	800									
Prepaid Rent	1,600									
Prepaid Insurance	960									
Art Equipment	4,200									
Accumulated Depreciation, Art Equipment										
Office Equipment	3,000									
Accumulated Depreciation, Office Equipment										
Accounts Payable		3,240								
Unearned Art Fees		1,000								
Common Stock		20,000								
Dividends	1,400									
Advertising Fees Earned		6,200								
Wages Expense	2,400									
Utilities Expense	200									
Telephone Expense	140									
	30,440	30,440								

a spreadsheet program to prepare the work sheet. In other cases, they use a general ledger system to prepare financial statements from the adjusted trial balance.

PREPARING THE WORK SHEET

So far, adjusting entries for Joan Miller Advertising Agency, Inc., have been entered directly in the journal and posted to the ledger, and the financial statements have been prepared from the adjusted trial balance. The process has been relatively simple because of the small size of the company. For larger companies, which may require many adjusting entries, a work sheet is essential. To illustrate the preparation of the work sheet, we continue with the Joan Miller Advertising Agency example.

A common form of work sheet has one column for account names and/or numbers and ten more columns with the headings shown in Exhibit 8. Notice that the work sheet is identified by a heading that consists of the name of the company, the title "Work Sheet," and the period of time covered (as on the income statement).

Preparation of a work sheet involves the following five steps:

KEY POINT: The work sheet Trial Balance columns take the place of the "traditional" trial balance.

1. **Enter and total the account balances in the Trial Balance columns.** The titles and balances of the accounts as of July 31 are copied directly from the ledger into the Trial Balance columns, as shown in Exhibit 8. When accountants use a work sheet, they do not have to prepare a separate trial balance.

the text? When the interview is finished, organize and write up your findings and be prepared to present them in class.

 Group Activity: Divide the class into groups and have each group investigate a different type of business, such as a shoe store, grocery store, hardware store, and fast-food restaurant. Have the groups give presentations in class.

Decision-Making Practice

SD 5.

LO2 Conversion from Accrual to Cash Statement

Adele's Secretarial Service, Inc., provides word processing services for students at the local university. Adele's accountant prepared the income statement that appears below for the year ended June 30, 20x4.

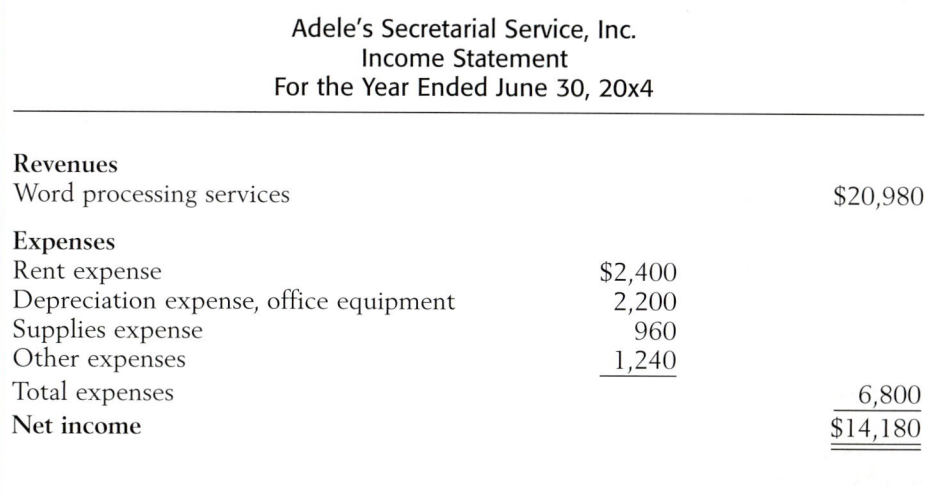

Adele's Secretarial Service, Inc.
Income Statement
For the Year Ended June 30, 20x4

Revenues		
Word processing services		$20,980
Expenses		
Rent expense	$2,400	
Depreciation expense, office equipment	2,200	
Supplies expense	960	
Other expenses	1,240	
Total expenses		6,800
Net income		$14,180

In reviewing this statement, Adele is puzzled. She knows the company paid cash dividends of $15,600 to her, the sole stockholder, yet the cash balance in the company's bank account increased from $460 to $3,100 from last June 30 to this June 30. She wants to know how her net income could be less than the cash dividends she took out of the business if there is an increase in the cash balance.

Her accountant has completed the closing entries and shows her the balance sheets for June 30, 20x4, and June 30, 20x3. The accountant explains that besides the change in the cash balance, Accounts Receivable decreased by $1,480 and Accounts Payable increased by $380 (supplies are the only items Adele buys on credit). The only other asset or liability account that changed during the year was Accumulated Depreciation, Office Equipment, which increased by $2,200.

1. Verify the cash balance increase by preparing a statement that lists the receipts of cash and the expenditures of cash during the year.
2. Write a memorandum to Adele explaining why the accountant is pointing out year-to-year changes in the balance sheet. Include an explanation of your treatment of depreciation expense, giving your reasons for the treatment.

FINANCIAL REPORTING AND ANALYSIS CASES

Interpreting Financial Reports

FRA 1.

LO5 Closing Entries

H&R Block, Inc., <www.hrblock.com> is the world's largest tax preparation service firm. Adapted information from the statement of earnings (in thousands, without earnings per share information) in its annual report for the year ended April 30, 2002, is shown on the next page.[6]

Revenues	
Service revenues	$2,333,064
Other revenues	986,084
Total revenues	$3,319,148
Expenses	
Employee compensation and benefits	$1,308,705
Occupancy and equipment expense	305,387
Depreciation expense	155,386
Marketing and advertising expense	155,729
Supplies, freight, and postage expense	75,710
Bad debt	76,804
Interest expense	116,141
Other operating expenses	408,446
Total expenses	$2,602,308
Earnings before income taxes	$ 716,840
Income taxes	282,435
Net earnings	$ 434,405

The company reported distributing cash in the amount of $115,725 to the owners in 2002.

1. Prepare, in journal form, the closing entries that H&R Block would have made on April 30, 2002.
2. Based on the way you handled expenses and cash distributions in step 1 and their ultimate effect on stockholders' equity, what theoretical reason can you give for not including expenses and cash distributions in the same closing entry?

FRA 2.

LO4 Uses of the Internet

Baxter International <www.baxter.com> is one of the largest and most successful pharmaceutical companies in the world. Its annual sales are more than $8 billion. One of the company's goals is to use the Internet as much as possible to improve the efficiency of its operations. In what ways do you think Baxter International may be using the Internet in its operations?

International Company

FRA 3.

LO2 Accounting Cycle and Closing
LO5 Entries

Nestlé S.A. <www.nestle.com>, maker of such well-known products as Nescafé, Lean Cuisine, and Perrier, is one of the largest and most internationally diverse companies in the world. Only 2 percent of its $81.4 billion in revenues comes from its home country of Switzerland; the rest comes from sales in almost every other country of the world. Nestlé has over 224,000 employees in 70 countries and is highly decentralized; that is, many of its divisions operate as separate companies.⁷ Managing the accounting operations of such a vast empire is a tremendous challenge. In what ways do you think the accounting cycle, including the closing process, would be the same for Nestlé as it is for Joan Miller Advertising Agency, Inc., and in what ways would it be different?

Toys "R" Us Annual Report

FRA 4.

LO2 Fiscal Year, Closing Process, and Interim Reports

Refer to the notes to the financial statements in the Toys "R" Us <www.tru.com> annual report. When does Toys "R" Us end its fiscal year? What reasons can you give for the company's having chosen this date? From the standpoint of completing the accounting cycle, what advantages does this date have? Does Toys "R" Us prepare interim financial statements? What are the implications of interim financial statements for the accounting cycle?

Financial Reporting and Analysis Cases

Comparison Case: Toys "R" Us and Walgreen Co.

FRA 5.

LO5 **Interim Financial Reporting and Seasonality**

Like Hershey Foods <www.hersheys.com> and many other companies, both Walgreens <www.walgreens.com> and Toys "R" Us <www.tru.com> provide quarterly financial information in their financial statements. Quarterly financial reports provide important information about the "seasonality" of a company's operations. *Seasonality* refers to how dependent a company is on sales during one season of the year, such as the Christmas season, and it affects a company's need to plan for cash flows and inventory. From the quarterly financial information for Walgreens and for Toys "R" Us in the Supplement to Chapter 1, determine which company has more seasonal sales and income by calculating for the most recent year the percentage of quarterly net sales and net earnings to annual net sales and net earnings. Discuss the results.

Fingraph® Financial Analyst™

This activity is not applicable to this chapter.

Internet Case

FRA 6.

LO1
LO3 **Enterprise Resource Planning (ERP) Systems**

We defined enterprise resource planning (ERP) systems as "comprehensive, computerized information systems that integrate financial and nonfinancial information about customers, operations, and suppliers in a single database." Explore further what this concept means by visiting the web site of a company that produces ERP software, such as SAP <www.sap.com>, PeopleSoft <www.peoplesoft.com>, or Oracle <www.oracle.com>. After accessing one of these web sites, find out what products the company offers and explain how these products relate to the definition of ERP. In addition to financial systems, what other business functions are included in ERP? Take notes and be prepared to discuss your findings in class.

5

Chapter 5 introduces the objectives and qualitative aspects of financial information and demonstrates how much more useful classified financial statements are than simple financial statements in presenting information to statement users.

Financial Reporting and Analysis

LEARNING OBJECTIVES

LO1 State the objectives of financial reporting.

LO2 State the qualitative characteristics of accounting information and describe their interrelationships.

LO3 Define and describe the conventions of *comparability* and *consistency, materiality, conservatism, full disclosure,* and *cost-benefit.*

LO4 Explain management's responsibility for ethical financial reporting and define *fraudulent financial reporting.*

LO5 Identify and describe the basic components of a classified balance sheet.

LO6 Prepare multistep and single-step classified income statements.

LO7 Evaluate liquidity and profitability using classified financial statements.

DECISION POINT
A USER'S FOCUS

General Mills, Inc. <www.generalmills.com> The management of a corporation is judged by the company's financial performance. Financial performance is reported to stockholders and others outside the business in the company's annual report, which includes the financial statements and other relevant information. Performance measures are usually based on the relationships of key data in the financial statements. For large companies, this often means condensing a tremendous amount of information to a few numbers that management considers important. For example, what key measures does the management of General Mills, Inc., a successful food products company that recently acquired its long-time rival Pillsbury and offers such well-known brands as Cheerios, Wheaties, Hamburger Helper, and Progresso Soups, choose to focus on as its goals?

In its letter to shareholders, General Mills states its financial goals as follows:

> Our target is 7 percent compound annual sales growth between now and 2010. With this faster topline growth, ... our Earnings Per Share (EPS) growth should accelerate, too. Our target is to deliver 11 to 15 percent annual earnings per share growth over the balance of this decade. We believe achieving these goals will represent superior performance when benchmarked against major consumer products companies.[1]

General Mills' management has thus set forth measurable performance goals by which it can be evaluated. The graph on the opposite page shows that the company reached its growth in sales target in only

What key performance measures does the management of General Mills choose to focus on as its goals?

one of the past three years. However, it reached its growth in EPS in all three years.

Of course, investors and creditors will want to do their own analysis of General Mills. This will require reading and interpreting the financial statements and calculating other ratios. However, the analysis will be meaningless unless the reader understands financial statements and generally accepted accounting principles, on which the statements are based. Also important to learning how to read and interpret financial statements is a comprehension of the categories and classifications used in balance sheets and income statements. Key financial ratios used in financial statement analysis are based on those categories. This chapter begins by describing the objectives, characteristics, and conventions that underlie the preparation of financial statements.

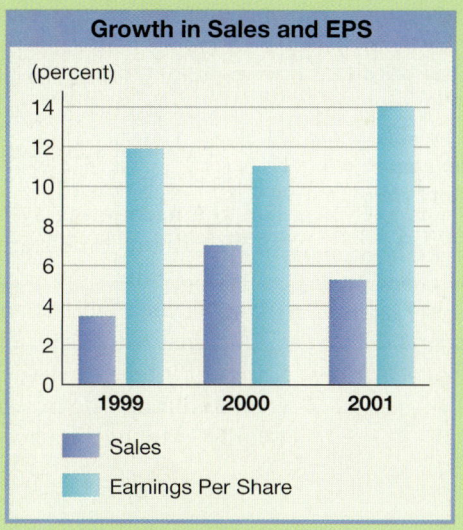

OBJECTIVES OF FINANCIAL INFORMATION

LO1 State the objectives of financial reporting.

RELATED TEXT ASSIGNMENTS
Q: 1
SE: 1
E: 1

The United States has a highly developed exchange economy. In this kind of economy, most goods and services are exchanged for money or claims to money instead of being used or bartered by their producers. Most business is carried on through corporations, including many extremely large firms that buy, sell, and obtain financing in U.S. and world markets.

By issuing stocks and bonds that are traded in financial markets, businesses can raise capital for production and marketing activities. Investors are interested mainly in returns from dividends and increases in the market price of their investments. Creditors want to know if the business can repay a loan plus interest in accordance with required terms. Thus, both investors and creditors need to know if a company can generate adequate cash flows. Financial statements are important to both groups in making that judgment. They offer valuable information about a company's ability to pay dividends and repay debts with interest. In this way, the market puts scarce resources to work in the companies that can use them most efficiently.

The information needs of users and the general business environment are the basis for the three objectives of financial reporting established by the Financial Accounting Standards Board (FASB):[2]

KEY POINT: Although reading financial reports requires some understanding of business, it does not require the skills of a CPA.

1. *To furnish information that is useful in making investment and credit decisions.* Financial reporting should offer information that can help current and potential investors and creditors make rational investment and credit decisions. The reports should be in a form that makes sense to those who have some understanding of business and are willing to study the information carefully.

2. *To provide information useful in assessing cash flow prospects.* Financial reporting should supply information to help current and potential investors and creditors judge the amounts, timing, and risk of expected cash receipts from dividends or interest and the proceeds from the sale, redemption, or maturity of stocks or loans.

● **STOP AND THINK!**
How do the four basic financial statements meet the third objective of financial reporting?
The balance sheet provides information about a company's resources (assets) and claims to those resources (liabilities and stockholders' equity). The income statement, statement of cash flows, and statement of retained earnings provide information about changes in resources and claims to them. ■

3. *To provide information about business resources, claims to those resources, and changes in them.* Financial reporting should give information about the company's assets, liabilities, and stockholders' equity, and the effects of transactions on the company's assets, liabilities, and stockholders' equity.

Financial statements are the most important way of periodically presenting to parties outside the business the information that has been gathered and processed in the accounting system. For this reason, the financial statements—the balance sheet, the income statement, the statement of retained earnings, and the statement of cash flows—are the most important output of the accounting system. These financial statements are "general purpose" because of their wide audience. They are "external" because their users are outside the business. Because of a potential conflict of interest between managers, who must prepare the statements, and investors or creditors, who invest in or lend money to the business, these statements often are audited by outside accountants to increase confidence in their reliability.

 Check out ACE for a Review Quiz at http://accounting.college.hmco.com/students.

QUALITATIVE CHARACTERISTICS OF ACCOUNTING INFORMATION

LO2 State the qualitative characteristics of accounting information and describe their interrelationships.

RELATED TEXT ASSIGNMENTS
Q: 2
SE: 1
E: 1

It is easy for students in their first accounting course to get the idea that accounting is 100 percent accurate. This idea is reinforced by the fact that all the problems in this and other introductory books can be solved. The numbers all add up; what is supposed to equal something else does. Accounting seems very much like mathematics in its precision. In this book, the basics of accounting are presented in a simple form to help you understand them. In practice, however, accounting information

FIGURE 1
Qualitative Characteristics and the Conventions of Accounting Information

> **Stop and Think!**
> What are some areas that require estimates to record transactions under the matching rule?
>
> To record depreciation expense, it is necessary to estimate the useful life of the asset. To record the amount of unearned revenue that is now earned or the amount of accrued revenue on a project in process, it is necessary to estimate the amount of revenue earned. ■
>
> **KEY POINT:** Financial statements should be free of material misstatements.

is neither simple nor precise, and it rarely satisfies all criteria. The FASB emphasizes this fact in the following statement:

> The information provided by financial reporting often results from approximate, rather than exact, measures. The measures commonly involve numerous estimates, classifications, summarizations, judgments and allocations. The outcome of economic activity in a dynamic economy is uncertain and results from combinations of many factors. Thus, despite the aura of precision that may seem to surround financial reporting in general and financial statements in particular, with few exceptions the measures are approximations, which may be based on rules and conventions, rather than exact amounts.[3]

The goal of accounting information—to provide the basic data that different users need to make informed decisions—is an ideal. The gap between the ideal and the actual provides much of the interest and controversy in accounting. To facilitate interpretation, the FASB has described the **qualitative characteristics** of accounting information, which are standards for judging that information. In addition, there are generally accepted conventions for recording and reporting that simplify interpretation. The relationships among these concepts are shown in Figure 1.

The most important qualitative characteristics are understandability and usefulness. **Understandability** depends on both the accountant and the decision maker. The accountant prepares the financial statements in accordance with accepted practices, generating important information that is believed to be understandable. But the decision maker must interpret the information; in making decisions, he or she must judge what information to use, how to use it, and what it means.

For accounting information to meet the standard of **usefulness**, it must have two major qualitative characteristics: relevance and reliability. **Relevance** means that the information can affect the outcome of a decision. In other words, a different decision would be made if the relevant information were not available. To be relevant, information must provide feedback, help predict future conditions, and be timely. For example, the income statement provides information about how a company performed over the past year (feedback), and it helps in planning for the next year (prediction). To be useful, however, it also must be communicated soon enough after the end of the accounting period to enable the reader to make decisions (timeliness).

In addition to being relevant, accounting information must have **reliability**. In other words, the user must be able to depend on the information. It must represent what it is meant to represent. It must be credible and verifiable by independent parties using the same methods of measuring. It also must be neutral. Accounting should convey information about business activity as faithfully as possible without influencing anyone in a specific direction. For example, the balance sheet should represent the economic resources, obligations, and stockholders' equity of a business as faithfully as possible in accordance with generally accepted accounting principles, and it should be verifiable by an auditor.

✓ Check out ACE for a Review Quiz at http://accounting.college.hmco.com/students.

CONVENTIONS THAT HELP IN THE INTERPRETATION OF FINANCIAL INFORMATION

LO3 Define and describe the conventions of *comparability* and *consistency, materiality, conservatism, full disclosure,* and *cost-benefit*.

RELATED TEXT ASSIGNMENTS
Q: 3
SE: 2
E: 1, 2
P: 1, 6
SD: 1, 2

To a large extent, financial statements are based on estimates and the application of accounting rules for recognition and allocation. In this book, we point out a number of difficulties with financial statements. One is failing to recognize the changing value of the dollar caused by inflation. Another is treating intangibles, such as research and development costs, as assets if they are purchased outside the company and as expenses if they are developed within the company. Such problems do not mean that financial statements are useless; they are essential. However, users must know how to interpret them. To help in this interpretation, accountants depend on five **conventions**, or rules of thumb, in recording transactions and preparing financial statements: (1) comparability and consistency, (2) materiality, (3) conservatism, (4) full disclosure, and (5) cost-benefit.

COMPARABILITY AND CONSISTENCY

A characteristic that increases the usefulness of accounting information is comparability. Information about a company is more useful if it can be compared with similar facts about the same company over several time periods or about another company for the same time period. **Comparability** means that the information is presented in such a way that a decision maker can recognize similarities, differences, and trends over different time periods or between different companies.

Consistent use of accounting measures and procedures is important in achieving comparability. The **consistency** convention requires that once an accounting procedure is adopted by a company, it remain in use from one period to the next unless users of the financial statements are informed of the change. Thus, without a note to the contrary, the users can assume that there has been no change in the treatment of a particular transaction, account, or item that would affect the interpretation of the statements.

● **STOP AND THINK!**
How can financial information be consistent but not comparable?

Consistency in accounting applies only to the use of the accounting principles for presenting the financial information. It does not apply to the conditions that are represented in the financial statements. For example, changes in business operations or the economy may make financial information incomparable from year to year, even though the same accounting policies have been followed. ■

If management decides that a certain procedure is no longer appropriate and should be changed, generally accepted accounting principles require that the change and its dollar effect be described in the notes to the financial statements:

> The nature of and justification for a change in accounting principle and its effect on income should be disclosed in the financial statements of the period in which the change is made. The justification for the change should explain clearly why the newly adopted accounting principle is preferable.[4]

www.goodyeartires.com

For example, Goodyear Tire & Rubber Co. recently reported that it changed its method of accounting for inventories because management felt the new method improved the matching of revenues and costs.

Focus on Business Practice

How Much Is Material? It's Not Only a Matter of Numbers.

The materiality issue has been a pet peeve of the SEC <www.sec.gov>, which contends that companies have increasingly abused the convention to protect their stocks from taking a pounding when earnings do not reach their targets. Over the years, companies have excluded from earnings any losses that they deem so small as to have virtually no effect on net income. Accountants and companies have typically used a rule of thumb of 5 percent of net income. The SEC has issued a new rule that puts stricter requirements on the use of materiality in that it calls for qualitative considerations in addition to quantitative guides. The percentage assessment is acceptable as an initial screening, but now companies cannot decline to book items in order to meet earnings estimates, preserve a growing earnings trend, convert a loss to a profit, increase management compensation, or hide an illegal transaction, such as a bribe.[5]

MATERIALITY

BUSINESS-WORLD EXAMPLE: By definition, a $10 stapler is a long-term asset that, theoretically, should be capitalized and depreciated over its useful life. However, the convention of materiality allows the stapler to be expensed entirely in the year of purchase because its cost is small and writing it off in one year has no effect on anyone's decision making.

KEY POINT: Illegal acts involving even small dollar amounts should be investigated.

Materiality refers to the relative importance of an item or event. If an item or event is material, it is probably relevant to users of the financial statements. In other words, an item is material if users would have done something differently if they had not known about the item. The accountant is often faced with decisions about small items or events that make little difference to users no matter how they are handled. For example, a large company may decide that expenditures for durable items of less than $500 should be charged as expenses rather than recorded as long-term assets and depreciated.

In general, an item is material if there is a reasonable expectation that knowing about it would influence the decisions of users of financial statements. The materiality of an item normally is determined by relating its dollar value to an element of the financial statements, such as net income or total assets. Some accountants feel that when an item is 5 percent or more of net income, it is material. However, materiality also depends on the nature of the item, not just its value. For example, in a multimillion-dollar company, a mistake of $5,000 in recording an item may not be important, but the discovery of a $5,000 bribe or theft can be very important. Also, many small errors can combine into a material amount. Accountants judge the materiality of many things, and the users of financial statements depend on their judgments being fair and accurate. The SEC has recently questioned whether a desire to avoid showing certain items in the financial statements has influenced some companies' judgment about materiality.

CONSERVATISM

KEY POINT: The purpose of conservatism is not to produce the lowest net income and lowest asset value. It is a guideline for choosing among GAAP alternatives, and it should be used with care.

KEY POINT: Expensing a long-term asset in the period of purchase is not a GAAP alternative.

Accountants try to base their decisions on logic and evidence that lead to the fairest report of what happened. In judging and estimating, however, accountants often are faced with uncertainties. In these cases, they look to the convention of **conservatism**. This convention means that when accountants face major uncertainties about which accounting procedure to use, they generally choose the one that is least likely to overstate assets and income.

One of the most common applications of the conservatism convention is the use of the lower-of-cost-or-market method in accounting for inventories. Under this method, if an item's market value is greater than its cost, the more conservative cost figure is used. If the market value falls below the cost, the more conservative market value is used. The latter situation often occurs in the computer industry.

Conservatism can be a useful tool in doubtful cases, but its abuse leads to incorrect and misleading financial statements. Suppose that someone incorrectly applies the conservatism convention by expensing a long-term asset of material cost in the period of purchase. In this case, there is no uncertainty. Income and assets for the current period would be understated, and income in future periods would be overstated. For this reason, accountants depend on the conservatism convention only when there is uncertainty about which accounting procedure to use.

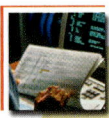

FOCUS ON BUSINESS PRACTICE

When Is "Full Disclosure" Too Much? It's a Matter of Cost and Benefits.

The large accounting firm of Ernst & Young <www.ey.com> reports that over a 20-year period, the total number of pages in the annual reports of 25 large, well-known companies has increased an average of 84 percent and the number of pages of notes has increased 325 percent—from 4 to 17 pages. Management's discussion and analysis increased 300 percent, from 3 pages to 12.[6] Because some people feel that "these documents are so daunting that people don't read them at all," the SEC allows companies to issue to the public "summary reports" in which the bulk of the notes can be reduced. Although more accessible and less costly, summary reports are controversial because many analysts feel that it is in the notes that one gets the detailed information necessary to understand complex business operations. One analyst remarked, "To banish the notes for fear they will turn off readers would be like eliminating fractions from math books on the theory that the average student prefers to work with whole numbers."[7] Where this controversy will end, nobody knows. Detailed reports still must be filed with the SEC, but more and more companies are providing summary reports to the public.

> **ENRICHMENT NOTE:** Significant events arising after the balance sheet date must be disclosed in the statements. Suppose a firm has purchased a piece of land for a future subdivision. Shortly after the end of its fiscal year, the firm is served papers to halt construction because the Environmental Protection Agency asserts that the land was once a toxic waste dump. This information, which obviously affects the users of the financial statements, must be disclosed in the statements for the just-ended fiscal year.

FULL DISCLOSURE

The convention of **full disclosure** requires that financial statements and their notes present all information that is relevant to the users' understanding of the statements. That is, the statements should offer any explanation needed to keep them from being misleading. Explanatory notes are considered an integral part of the financial statements. For instance, a change from one accounting procedure to another should be reported. In general, the form of the financial statements can affect their usefulness in making certain decisions—for example, the categories used to group accounts in the statements convey information about the accounts. Also, certain items, such as the amount of depreciation expense on the income statement and the accumulated depreciation on the balance sheet, are essential to the readers of financial statements.

Other examples of disclosures required by the FASB and other official bodies are the accounting procedures used in preparing the statements, important terms of the company's debt, commitments and contingencies, and important events taking place after the date of the statements. However, the statements can become so cluttered with notes that they impede rather than help understanding. Beyond required disclosures, the application of the full-disclosure convention is based on the judgment of management and of the accountants who prepare the financial statements.

In recent years, the principle of full disclosure also has been influenced by investors and creditors. To protect them, independent auditors, the stock exchanges, and the SEC have made more demands for disclosure by publicly owned companies. The SEC has been pushing especially hard for the enforcement of full disclosure. As a result, more and better information about corporations is available to the public today than ever before.

> **BUSINESS-WORLD EXAMPLE:** Firms use the convention of cost-benefit for both accounting and nonaccounting decisions. Department stores could almost completely stop shoplifting if they were to hire five times as many clerks to watch customers. The benefit would be reduced shoplifting. The cost would be reduced sales (customers do not like being watched closely) and increased wages expense. Although shoplifting is a serious problem for department stores, the benefit of reducing shoplifting in this way does not outweigh the cost.

COST-BENEFIT

The **cost-benefit** convention underlies all the qualitative characteristics and conventions. It holds that the benefits to be gained from providing accounting information should be greater than the costs of providing it. Of course, minimum levels of relevance and reliability must be reached if accounting information is to be useful. Beyond the minimum levels, however, it is up to the FASB and the SEC, which require the information, and the accountant, who provides the information, to judge the costs and benefits in each case. Most of the costs of providing information fall at first on the preparers; the benefits are reaped by both preparers and users. Finally, both the costs and the benefits are passed on to society in the form of prices and social benefits from more efficient allocation of resources.

The costs and benefits of a particular requirement for accounting disclosure are both direct and indirect, immediate and deferred. For example, it is hard to judge the final costs and benefits of a far-reaching and costly regulation. The FASB, for instance, allows certain large companies to make a supplemental disclosure in their financial statements of the effects of changes in current costs. Most companies choose not to present this information because they believe the costs of producing and providing it exceed its benefits to the readers of their financial statements. Cost-benefit is a question faced by all regulators, including the FASB and the SEC. Even though there are no definitive ways of measuring costs and benefits, much of an accountant's work deals with these concepts.

✓ Check out ACE for a Review Quiz at http://accounting.college.hmco.com/students.

Management's Responsibility for Ethical Reporting

LO4 Explain management's responsibility for ethical financial reporting and define *fraudulent financial reporting*.

RELATED TEXT ASSIGNMENTS
Q: 4
SD: 3, 4, 5

www.generalmills.com

● **Stop and Think!**
What is the difference between aggressive accounting and fraudulent financial reporting?
There is often a fine line between aggressive accounting, which is the use of legitimate accounting methods to achieve business purposes, and fraudulent financial reporting, which is the intentional misrepresentation of financial information. The former is acceptable, whereas the latter is unethical and sometimes illegal. ■

The users of financial statements depend on the good faith of those who prepare these statements. This dependence places a duty on a company's management and its accountants to act ethically in the reporting process. That duty is often expressed in the report of management that accompanies financial statements. For example, the report of the management of General Mills, Inc., a company known for strong financial reporting and controls, states:

> The management . . . is responsible for the fairness and accuracy of the consolidated financial statements. The consolidated financial statements have been prepared in accordance with accounting principles that are generally accepted in the United States, using management's best estimates and judgments where appropriate.[8]

General Mills' management also tells how it meets this responsibility:

> Management has established a system of internal controls that provides reasonable assurance that assets are adequately safeguarded and transactions are recorded accurately in all material respects, in accordance with management's authorization. We maintain a strong audit program that independently evaluates the adequacy and effectiveness of internal controls.[9]

The intentional preparation of misleading financial statements is called **fraudulent financial reporting**.[10] It can result from the distortion of records (e.g., the manipulation of inventory records), falsified transactions (e.g., fictitious sales), or the misapplication of accounting principles (e.g., treating as an asset an item that should be expensed). There are a number of possible motives for fraudulent reporting—for instance, to obtain a higher price when a company is sold, to meet the expectations of stockholders, or to obtain a loan. Sometimes, the incentive is personal gain, such as additional compensation, promotion, or avoidance of penalties for poor performance. The personal costs of such actions can be high. Individuals who authorize or prepare fraudulent financial statements may face prison sentences

Focus on Business Ethics

Questionable Accounting Practices Are Under Scrutiny.

There is a difference between management's choosing to follow accounting principles that are favorable to its actions and fraudulent financial reporting. Because of recent, highly visible accounting misstatements by such companies as WorldCom <www.worldcom.com>, Enron <www.enron.com>, Sunbeam Corporation <www.sunbeam.com>, and many others attempting to meet the earnings expectations of stock analysts, the SEC is cracking down on what it sees as the main abuses, which the chairman of the SEC has called "accounting hocus-pocus." These are cases in which real transactions are accounted for in such a way as to distort reality. Examples include one-time "big bath" restructuring charges that overstate current expenses to benefit future periods, creative acquisition accounting in mergers, writing off purchased research and development inappropriately, miscellaneous "cookie jar reserves" involving unrealistic assumptions about such items as sales returns and warranty costs, and the abuse of the materiality convention.[11] The SEC brings about 100 accounting actions each year. In recent times, executives at WorldCom and Sunbeam have been indicted. Executives at Enron are under investigation.[12]

and fines. A company's investors and lenders, employees, and customers suffer from fraudulent financial reporting as well.

Due to recent abuses in financial reporting that have come to light in companies like WorldCom and Enron, Congress passed the Sarbanes-Oxley Act in 2002. This legislation orders the SEC to draw up rules requiring chief executives and chief financial officers of all 15,000 publicly traded companies to file statements each quarter swearing that, based on their knowledge, their company's quarterly and annual statements are accurate and complete. Violation can result in criminal penalties. To comply with this law and meet ethical reporting requirements, a company's accountants and auditors must apply financial accounting concepts in such a way as to present a fair view of the company's operations and financial position and to avoid misleading readers of the financial statements.

www.worldcom.com
www.enron.com

Check out ACE for a Review Quiz at http://accounting.college.hmco.com/students.

CLASSIFIED BALANCE SHEET

LO5 Identify and describe the basic components of a classified balance sheet.

RELATED TEXT ASSIGNMENTS
Q: 5, 6, 7, 8, 9, 10, 11, 12
SE: 3, 4
E: 3, 4
P: 3, 5
FRA: 4, 5

The balance sheets you have seen in the chapters thus far categorize accounts as assets, liabilities, and stockholders' equity. Because even a fairly small company can have hundreds of accounts, simply listing accounts in these broad categories is not particularly helpful to a statement user. Setting up subcategories within the major categories often makes financial statements much more useful. Investors and creditors study and evaluate the relationships among the subcategories. General-purpose external financial statements that are divided into subcategories are called **classified financial statements**.

The balance sheet presents the financial position of a company at a particular time. The subdivisions of the classified balance sheet shown in Exhibit 1 are typical of those used by most companies in the United States. The subdivisions under owners' or stockholders' equity depend, of course, on the form of business.

ASSETS

A company's assets are often divided into four categories: (1) current assets; (2) investments; (3) property, plant, and equipment; and (4) intangible assets. These categories are listed in the order of their presumed ease of conversion into cash. For example, current assets are usually more easily converted to cash than are property, plant, and equipment. For simplicity, some companies group investments, intangible assets, and other miscellaneous assets into a category called "**other assets**."

■ **CURRENT ASSETS** **Current assets** are cash and other assets that are reasonably expected to be converted to cash, sold, or consumed within one year or within the normal operating cycle of the business, whichever is longer. The normal operating cycle of a company is the average time needed to go from cash to cash. For example, cash is used to buy merchandise inventory, which is sold for cash or for a promise of cash if the sale is made on account. If a sale is made on account, the resulting receivable must be collected before the cycle is completed.

KEY POINT: Use one year as the current period unless the normal operating cycle happens to be longer.

The normal operating cycle for most companies is less than one year, but there are exceptions. Tobacco companies, for example, must age their tobacco for two or three years before it can be sold. The tobacco inventory is nonetheless considered a current asset because it will be sold within the normal operating cycle. Another example is a company that sells on the installment basis. The payments for a television set or a refrigerator can be extended over 24 or 36 months, but these receivables are still considered current assets.

Cash is obviously a current asset. Short-term investments, notes and accounts receivable, and inventory are also current assets because they are expected to be converted to cash within the next year or during the normal operating cycle. On the balance sheet, they are listed in the order of their ease of conversion into cash.

Exhibit 1
Classified Balance Sheet for Shafer Auto Parts Corporation

Study

Shafer Auto Parts Corporation
Balance Sheet
December 31, 20xx

Assets

Current assets
Cash		$10,360
Short-term investments		2,000
Notes receivable		8,000
Accounts receivable		35,300
Merchandise inventory		60,400
Prepaid insurance		6,600
Store supplies		1,060
Office supplies		636
Total current assets			$124,356

Investments
Land held for future use		5,000

Property, plant, and equipment
Land			$ 4,500
Building	$20,650		
Less accumulated depreciation	8,640	12,010	
Delivery equipment	$18,400		
Less accumulated depreciation	9,450	8,950	
Office equipment	$ 8,600		
Less accumulated depreciation	5,000	3,600	
Total property, plant, and equipment			29,060

Intangible assets
Trademark		500
Total assets		$158,916

Liabilities

Current liabilities
Notes payable		$15,000
Accounts payable		25,683
Salaries payable		2,000
Total current liabilities			$ 42,683

Long-term liabilities
Mortgage payable		17,800
Total liabilities		$ 60,483

Stockholders' Equity

Contributed capital
Common stock, $10 par value, 5,000 shares authorized, issued, and outstanding		$50,000
Additional paid-in capital		10,000
Total contributed capital		$60,000

Retained earnings 38,433

Total stockholders' equity		98,433
Total liabilities and stockholders' equity		$158,916

Prepaid expenses, such as rent and insurance paid in advance, and inventories of supplies bought for use rather than for sale also should be classified as current assets. Such assets are current in the sense that if they had not been bought earlier, a current outlay of cash would be needed to obtain them.[13]

In deciding whether an asset is current or noncurrent, the idea of "reasonable expectation" is important. For example, Short-Term Investments, also called "Marketable Securities," is an account used for temporary investments of "idle" cash—that is, cash not immediately required for operating purposes. Management can reasonably expect to sell these securities as cash needs arise over the next year or operating cycle. Investments in securities that management does not expect to sell within the next year and that do not involve the temporary use of idle cash should be shown in the investments category of a classified balance sheet.

KEY POINT: For an investment to be classified as current, management must intend to sell it within the next year or the current operating cycle, and it must be readily marketable.

◆ **STOP AND THINK!**
Why is it that land held for future use and equipment not currently used in the business are classified as investments rather than as property, plant, and equipment?

They are classified as investments because doing so helps users of financial statements assess the performance of the company using such measures as return on assets. Also, the investment category gives users some idea of resources the company may be able to draw on without disturbing the current business operations. ■

■ **INVESTMENTS** The **investments** category includes assets, usually long term, that are not used in the normal operation of the business and that management does not plan to convert to cash within the next year. Items in this category are securities held for long-term investment, long-term notes receivable, land held for future use, plant or equipment not used in the business, and special funds established to pay off a debt or buy a building. Also included are large permanent investments in another company for the purpose of controlling that company.

■ **PROPERTY, PLANT, AND EQUIPMENT** **Property, plant, and equipment** are tangible long-term assets used in the continuing operation of the business. They represent a place to operate (land and buildings) and the equipment to produce, sell, deliver, and service the company's goods. They are therefore also called *operating assets* or, sometimes, *fixed assets, tangible assets, long-lived assets,* or *plant assets.* Through depreciation, the costs of these assets (except land) are spread over the periods they benefit. Past depreciation is recorded in the Accumulated Depreciation accounts. The order in which property, plant, and equipment are listed on the balance sheet is not the same everywhere. In practice, accounts are often combined to make the financial statements less cluttered. For example:

Property, Plant, and Equipment

Land		$ 4,500
Buildings and equipment	$47,650	
Less accumulated depreciation	23,090	24,560
Total property, plant, and equipment		$29,060

Many companies simply show a single line with a total for property, plant, and equipment and provide the details in a note to the financial statements.

The property, plant, and equipment category also includes natural resources owned by the company, such as forest lands, oil and gas properties, and coal mines, if they are used in the regular course of business. If they are not, they are listed in the investments category, as noted above.

■ **INTANGIBLE ASSETS** **Intangible assets** are long-term assets with no physical substance whose value stems from the rights or privileges they extend to their owners. Examples are patents, copyrights, goodwill, franchises, and trademarks. They are recorded at cost, which is spread over the expected life of the right or privilege.

LIABILITIES

Liabilities are divided into two categories, based on when the liabilities fall due: current liabilities and long-term liabilities.

■ **CURRENT LIABILITIES** The category of **current liabilities** consists of obligations due to be paid or performed within one year or within the normal operating cycle of the business, whichever is longer. Current liabilities are typically paid from

BUSINESS-WORLD EXAMPLE: The portion of a mortgage paid monthly for 120 months that is due during the next year or the current operating cycle would be classified as a current liability; the portion due after the next year or the current operating cycle would be classified as a long-term liability.

current assets or by incurring new short-term liabilities. They include notes payable, accounts payable, the current portion of long-term debt, salaries and wages payable, taxes payable, and customer advances (unearned revenues).

■ **LONG-TERM LIABILITIES** The debts of a business that fall due more than one year in the future or beyond the normal operating cycle, which will be paid out of noncurrent assets, are **long-term liabilities**. Mortgages payable, long-term notes, bonds payable, employee pension obligations, and long-term lease liabilities generally fall into the category of long-term liabilities. Deferred income taxes are often disclosed as a separate category in the long-term liability section of the balance sheet of publicly held corporations. This liability arises because the rules for measuring income for tax purposes differ from those for financial reporting. The cumulative annual difference between the income taxes payable to governments and the income taxes expense reported on the income statement is included in the account Deferred Income Taxes.

STOCKHOLDERS' EQUITY

The stockholders' equity section for a corporation would appear as shown in the balance sheet for Shafer Auto Parts Corporation (see Exhibit 1). As you learned earlier, corporations are separate legal entities owned by their stockholders. The stockholders' equity section of a balance sheet has two parts: contributed capital and retained earnings. Generally, contributed capital is shown on corporate balance sheets as two amounts: the par value of the issued stock, and the paid-in capital in excess of the par value per share.

OTHER FORMS OF BUSINESS ORGANIZATION

Although the form of business organization does not usually affect the accounting treatment of assets and liabilities, the equity section of the balance sheet of a sole proprietorship or partnership is very different from that of a corporation.

■ **SOLE PROPRIETORSHIP** The equity section for a sole proprietorship simply shows the capital in the owner's name at an amount equal to the net assets of the company. It might appear as follows:

Owner's Equity

Hershell Serton, Capital $57,390

Because there is no legal separation between an owner and his or her sole proprietorship, there is no need for contributed capital to be separated from earnings retained for use in a business. This capital account is increased by both the owner's investments and net income. It is decreased by net losses and withdrawals of assets from the business for personal use by the owner. In this kind of business, the formality of declaring and paying dividends is not required.

In fact, the terms *owner's equity, proprietorship, capital,* and *net worth* are used interchangeably. They all stand for the owner's interest in the company. The first three terms are preferred to *net worth* because most assets are recorded at original cost rather than at current value. For this reason, the ownership section will not represent "worth." It is really a claim against the assets of the company.

KEY POINT: The only difference in equity between a sole proprietorship and a partnership is in the number of capital accounts.

■ **PARTNERSHIP** The equity section of the balance sheet for a partnership is called *partners' equity* and is much like that for the sole proprietorship. It might appear as follows:

Partners' Equity

A. J. Martin, Capital	$21,666
R. C. Moore, Capital	35,724
Total partners' equity	$57,390

EXHIBIT 2
Balance Sheet for Dell Computer Corporation

Dell Computer Corporation
Consolidated Statement of Financial Position
(in millions)

	January 31, 2003	February 1, 2002
ASSETS		
Current assets:		
Cash and cash equivalents	$ 4,232	$ 3,641
Short-term investments	406	273
Accounts receivable, net	2,586	2,269
Inventories	306	278
Other	1,394	1,416
Total current assets	8,924	7,877
Property, plant and equipment, net	913	826
Investments	5,267	4,373
Other non-current assets	366	459
Total assets	$15,470	$13,535
LIABILITIES AND STOCKHOLDERS' EQUITY		
Current liabilities:		
Accounts payable	$ 5,989	$ 5,075
Accrued and other	2,944	2,444
Total current liabilities	8,933	7,519
Long-term debt	506	520
Other liabilities	1,158	802
Total liabilities	10,597	8,841
Stockholders' equity:		
Common stock and capital in excess of $.01 par value; shares authorized: 7,000; shares issued: 2,681 and 2,654, respectively	6,018	5,605
Treasury stock, at cost; 102 and 52 shares, respectively	(4,539)	(2,249)
Retained earnings	3,486	1,364
Other comprehensive income (loss)	(33)	38
Other	(59)	(64)
Total stockholders' equity	4,873	4,694
Total liabilities and stockholders' equity	$15,470	$13,535

Source: Dell Computer Corporation, *Annual Report,* 2002.

READING AND GRAPHING REAL COMPANY BALANCE SHEETS

Although financial statements usually follow the same general form as illustrated for Shafer Auto Parts Corporation, no two companies have statements that are exactly alike. The balance sheet of Dell Computer Corporation, the world's leading direct seller of computer systems, is a good example of some of the variations. As shown in Exhibit 2, it provides data for two years so that the change from one year to the next can be evaluated. Note that its major classifications are similar but not identical to Shafer's. For instance, Shafer's assets include investments and intangible assets categories, whereas Dell has an asset category called "other non-current

www.dell.com

FIGURE 2
Graphic Presentation of Dell Computer Corporation's Balance Sheet

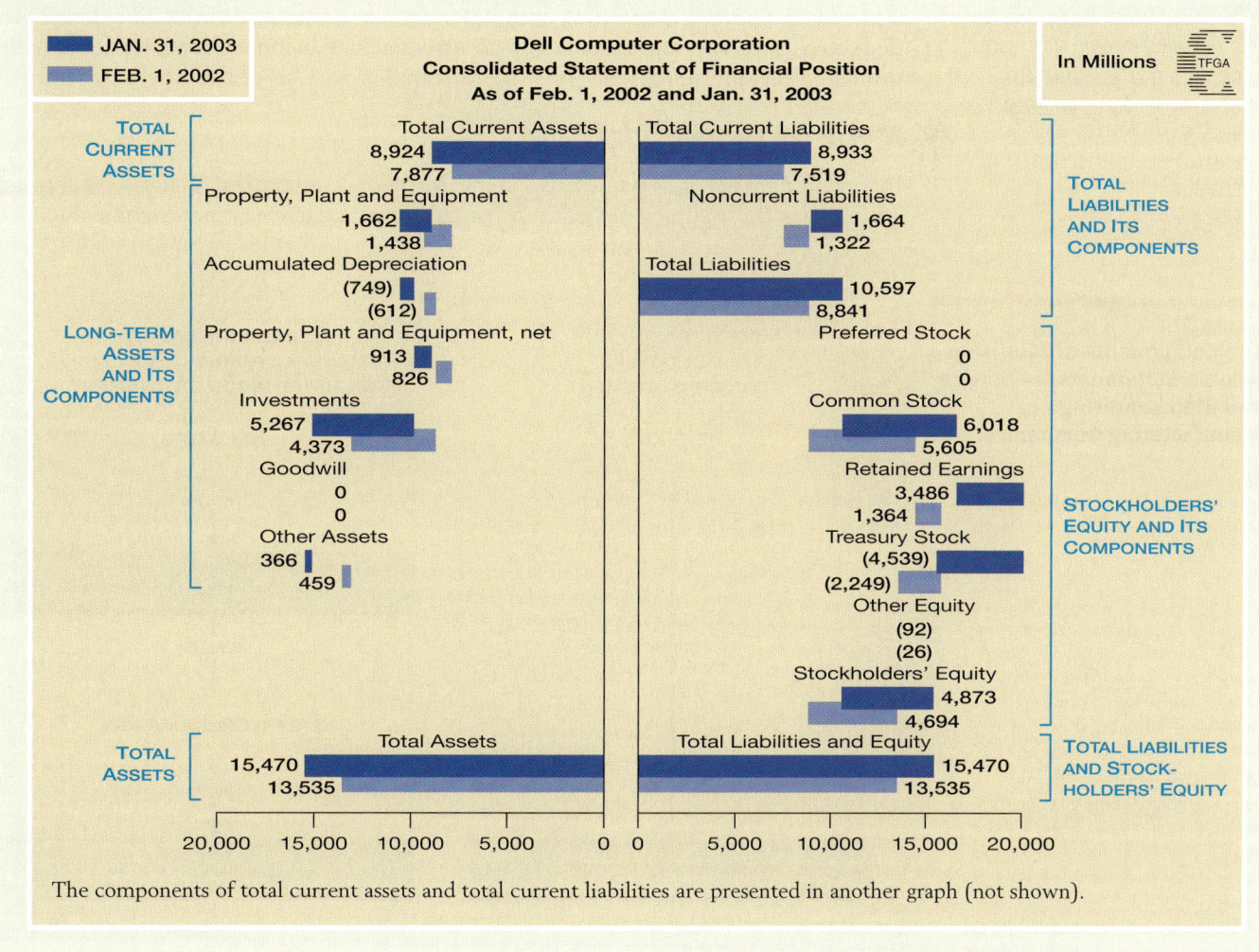

The components of total current assets and total current liabilities are presented in another graph (not shown).

assets," which is a small amount of its total assets. Also note that Dell has a category called "other liabilities." Because this category appears after long-term debt, it represents longer-term liabilities, due more than one year from the balance sheet dates.

Dell's stockholders' equity section also differs from that of Shafer Auto Parts in that it subtracts a category called "other" from common stock, retained earnings, and other comprehensive income. However, it is possible to look at the total stockholders' equity and know that this amount relates to the stockholders' claims on the company.

When looking at columns of numbers, it may be hard to see the patterns of change in a company's financial position; graphic presentation of the numbers can help clarify them. Figure 2, prepared with the Fingraph® Financial Analyst™ CD-ROM software that accompanies this text, is a graphic presentation of a portion of the balance sheet in Exhibit 2. Total assets and its components are graphed on the left side; total liabilities and its components, together with total stockholders' equity, are on the right. The composition of the assets and liabilities, their relation to stockholders' equity, and the changes in them from 2001 to 2002 are easily seen. These graphs show that overall Dell was relatively stable in both totals and components from 2001 to 2002, but overall the assets increased. Also note that the graphic presentation of the balance sheet reduces the detailed clutter of the statement. For instance, all current assets are combined and represented by a single component line.

Check out ACE for a Review Quiz at http://accounting.college.hmco.com/students.

FORMS OF THE INCOME STATEMENT

LO6 Prepare multistep and single-step classified income statements.

RELATED TEXT ASSIGNMENTS
Q: 13, 14, 15, 16, 17, 18, 19, 20
SE: 5, 6, 7
E: 5, 6, 7
P: 2, 5, 7
FRA: 5

Thus far, we have presented income statements in single-step form: all expenses are deducted from revenue in one step to arrive at net income. Here, we look at the multistep income statement and a more complex version of the single-step form.

Multistep Income Statement

In practice, many companies use some form of a **multistep income statement**, which goes through a series of steps, or subtotals, to arrive at net income. Figure 3

FIGURE 3
The Components of Multistep Income Statements for Service and Merchandising or Manufacturing Companies

SERVICE COMPANY MULTISTEP INCOME STATEMENT	MERCHANDISING OR MANUFACTURING COMPANY MULTISTEP INCOME STATEMENT
REVENUES	NET SALES
minus	minus
	COST OF GOODS SOLD
	equals
	STEP 1: GROSS MARGIN
	minus
OPERATING EXPENSES	OPERATING EXPENSES
equals	equals
STEP 1: INCOME FROM OPERATIONS	STEP 2: INCOME FROM OPERATIONS
plus or minus	plus or minus
OTHER REVENUES AND EXPENSES	OTHER REVENUES AND EXPENSES
equals	equals
STEP 2: INCOME BEFORE INCOME TAXES	STEP 3: INCOME BEFORE INCOME TAXES
minus	minus
INCOME TAXES	INCOME TAXES
equals	equals
STEP 3: NET INCOME	STEP 4: NET INCOME

EXHIBIT 3
Multistep Income Statement for Shafer Auto Parts Corporation

Shafer Auto Parts Corporation
Income Statement
For the Year Ended December 31, 20xx

Net sales		$289,656
Cost of goods sold		181,260
Step 1: Gross margin		$108,396
Operating expenses		
Selling expenses	$54,780	
General and administrative expenses	34,504	
Total operating expenses		89,284
Step 2: Income from operations		$ 19,112
Other revenues and expenses		
Interest income	$ 1,400	
Less interest expense	2,631	
Excess of other expenses over other revenues		1,231
Step 3: Income before income taxes		$ 17,881
Income taxes		3,381
Step 4: Net income		$ 14,500
Earnings per share		$ 2.90

BUSINESS-WORLD EXAMPLE: The multistep income statement is a valuable analytical tool that is often overlooked. Analysts frequently convert a single-step statement into a multistep one because the latter separates operating sources of income from nonoperating ones. Investors want income to result primarily from operations, not from one-time gains or losses.

compares the multistep income statement for service companies with that for **merchandising companies**, which buy and sell products, and **manufacturing companies**, which make and sell products. Note that in the multistep income statement for service companies, the operating expenses are deducted from revenues in a single step to arrive at income from operations. In contrast, because manufacturing and merchandising companies make or buy goods for sale, they must include an additional step in the multistep income statement for the cost of these goods that are sold. In the following discussion of these components, the income statement presented in Exhibit 3 for Shafer Auto Parts Corporation, a merchandising company, will serve as an example of a multistep income statement.

■ **NET SALES** The first major part of the multistep income statement for a merchandising or manufacturing company is **net sales** [REAL SALES], often simply called *sales*. Net sales consist of the gross proceeds from sales of merchandise, or **gross sales, less sales returns and allowances** and any discounts allowed. **Gross sales** consist of total cash sales and total credit sales during an accounting period. Even though the cash may not be collected until the following accounting period, under the revenue recognition rule, revenue is recorded as earned when title for merchandise passes from seller to buyer at the time of sale. Sales returns and allowances are cash refunds, credits on account, and allowances off selling prices made to customers who have received defective products or products that are otherwise unsatisfactory. If other discounts or allowances are given to customers, they also should be deducted from gross sales.

Management, investors, and others often use the amount of sales and trends suggested by sales as indicators of a firm's progress. Increasing sales suggest growth; decreasing sales indicate the possibility of decreased future earnings and other financial problems. To detect trends, comparisons are frequently made between the net sales of different accounting periods.

KEY POINT: The matching rule precludes the cost of inventory from being expensed until the inventory has been sold.

KEY POINT: For a merchandiser or manufacturer, net income equals gross margin less operating expenses plus or minus other revenue or expenses and income taxes.

KEY POINT: Gross margin is an important measure of profitability. When it is less than operating expenses, the company has suffered a net loss from operations.

www.samsclub.com
www.costco.com

www.neimanmarcus.com
www.tiffany.com

BUSINESS-WORLD EXAMPLE: Companies that are restructuring their operations often focus on reducing operating expenses.

KEY POINT: The most common types of operating expenses are selling expenses and general and administrative expenses. They are deducted from gross margin on the income statement.

KEY POINT: Financial analysts often focus on income from operations as a key profitability measure.

■ **COST OF GOODS SOLD** The second part of the multistep income statement for a merchandiser or manufacturer is **cost of goods sold**, or simply *cost of sales*. Cost of goods sold (an expense) is the amount a merchandiser paid for the merchandise it sold during an accounting period or the cost to a manufacturer of making the products it sold during an accounting period.

■ **GROSS MARGIN** The third major part of the multistep income statement for a merchandiser or manufacturer is **gross margin**, or *gross profit*, which is the difference between net sales and cost of goods sold (Step 1 in Exhibit 3). To be successful, companies must achieve a gross margin that is sufficient to cover operating expenses and provide an adequate after-tax income.

Management is interested in both the amount and the percentage of gross margin. The percentage of gross margin is computed by dividing the amount of gross margin by net sales. In the case of Shafer Auto Parts Corporation, the amount of gross margin is $108,396 and the percentage of gross margin is 37.4 percent ($108,396 ÷ $289,656). This information is useful in planning business operations. For instance, management may try to increase total sales dollars by reducing the selling price. This strategy reduces the percentage of gross margin, but it will work if the total of items sold increases enough to raise the absolute amount of gross margin. This is the strategy followed by discount warehouse stores like Sam's Clubs and Costco Wholesale Corporation. On the other hand, management may decide to keep a high gross margin from sales and attempt to increase sales and the amount of gross margin by increasing operating expenses, such as advertising. This is the strategy followed by upscale specialty stores like Neiman Marcus and Tiffany & Co. Other strategies to increase gross margin from sales include reducing cost of goods sold by using better purchasing methods.

■ **OPERATING EXPENSES** The next major area of the multistep income statement consists of **operating expenses**, which are the expenses other than cost of goods sold that are incurred in running a business. It is customary to group operating expenses into categories, such as selling expenses and general and administrative expenses. Selling expenses include the costs of storing goods and preparing them for sale; preparing displays, advertising, and otherwise promoting sales; making sales; and delivering goods to the buyer, if the seller pays the cost of delivery. The latter cost is often called **freight out expense**, or *delivery expense*. Among general and administrative expenses are general office expenses, which include expenses for accounting, personnel, and credit and collections, and any other expenses that apply to overall operations. Although general occupancy expenses, such as rent expense, insurance expense, and utilities expense, are often classified as general and administrative expenses, they may also be allocated between the selling and the general and administrative categories. Careful planning and control of operating expenses can improve a company's profitability.

■ **INCOME FROM OPERATIONS** **Income from operations**, or simply *operating income*, is the difference between gross margin and operating expenses (Step 2 in Exhibit 3). It represents the income from a company's normal, or main, business. Because companies may have significant other revenues and expenses and different income tax rates, income from operations is often used to compare the profitability of two or more companies or divisions within a company.

■ **OTHER REVENUES AND EXPENSES** **Other revenues and expenses**, or *nonoperating revenues and expenses*, are not part of a company's operating activities. This section of the multistep income statement includes revenues from investments (such as dividends and interest on stocks, bonds, and savings accounts) and interest earned on credit or notes extended to customers. It also includes interest expense and other expenses that result from borrowing money or from credit extended to the company. If the company has yet other kinds of revenues and expenses not related to the company's normal business operations, they, too, are included in this part of the income statement. An analyst who wants to compare two companies independent of their financing methods—that is, before considering other revenues and expenses—would focus on income from operations.

■ **INCOME BEFORE INCOME TAXES** **Income before income taxes** is the amount a company has earned from all activities—operating and nonoperating—before taking into account the amount of income taxes it incurred (Step 3 in Exhibit 3). Because companies may be subject to different income tax rates, income before income taxes is often used to compare the profitability of two or more companies or divisions within a company.

■ **INCOME TAXES** **Income taxes**, also called *provision for income taxes*, represent the expense for federal, state, and local taxes on corporate income. Income taxes are shown as a separate item on the income statement. Usually the word *expense* is not used. Income taxes do not appear on the income statements of sole proprietorships and partnerships because they are not tax-paying units. The individuals who own these businesses are the tax-paying units, and they pay income taxes on their share of the business income. Corporations, however, must report and pay income taxes on earnings. Because federal, state, and local income taxes for corporations are substantial, they have a significant effect on business decisions. Current federal income tax rates for corporations vary from 15 percent to 38 percent, depending on the amount of income before income taxes and other factors. Most other taxes, such as property and employment taxes, are included in the operating expenses.

● **STOP AND THINK!**
Which is the better measure of a company's performance: income from operations or net income?
Neither measure is better than the other. Both measure different aspects of profitability. Income from operations measures the income from a company's ongoing operations before considering issues of financing (interest expense), nonoperating revenues, and income taxes. Net income measures whether a business has been operating successfully. ■

■ **NET INCOME** **Net income**, the final figure, or "bottom line," of the income statement, is what remains of the gross margin after operating expenses are deducted, other revenues and expenses are added or deducted, and income taxes are deducted (Step 4 in Exhibit 3). It is an important performance measure because it represents the amount of business earnings that accrue to stockholders. It is the amount that is transferred to retained earnings from all the income-generating activities during the year. Both management and investors often use net income to measure whether a business has operated successfully during the past accounting period.

ENRICHMENT NOTE:
Earnings per share is the most commonly cited performance measure in the business press because it is a shorthand measure of profitability.

■ **EARNINGS PER SHARE** **Earnings per share**, often called *net income per share*, is the net income earned on each share of common stock. It is unique to corporate reporting. Ownership in corporations is represented by shares of stock, and the net income per share is reported immediately below net income on the income statement. In the simplest case, it is computed by dividing the net income by the average number of shares of common stock outstanding during the year. For example, Shafer's earnings per share of $2.90 was computed by dividing the net income of $14,500 by the 5,000 shares of common stock outstanding (see the stockholders' equity section of the balance sheet in Exhibit 1). Investors find the figure useful as a quick way of assessing both a company's profit-earning success and its earnings in relation to the market price of its stock.

READING AND GRAPHING REAL COMPANY INCOME STATEMENTS

www.dell.com

Income statements, like balance sheets, vary among companies. You will rarely, if ever, find an income statement exactly like the one for Shafer Auto Parts Corporation. You will encounter terms and structure that differ, such as those on the multistep income statement for Dell Computer Corporation in Exhibit 4, in which management provides three years of data for comparison purposes. You may also encounter components that are not covered in this chapter. If this occurs, refer to the index at the end of the book to find the topic and read about it.

EXHIBIT 4
Income Statement for Dell Computer Corporation

Dell Computer Corporation
Consolidated Statement of Income
(in millions, except per share amounts)

	Fiscal Year Ended		
	January 31, 2003	February 1, 2002	February 2, 2001
Net revenue	$35,404	$31,168	$31,888
Cost of revenue	29,055	25,661	25,445
Gross margin	6,349	5,507	6,443
Operating expenses:			
Selling, general and administrative	3,050	2,784	3,193
Research, development and engineering	455	452	482
Special charges	—	482	105
Total operating expenses	3,505	3,718	3,780
Operating income	2,844	1,789	2,663
Investment and other income (loss), net	183	(58)	531
Income before income taxes and cumulative effect of change in accounting principle	3,027	1,731	3,194
Provision for income taxes	905	485	958
Income before cumulative effect of change in accounting principle	2,122	1,246	2,236
Cumulative effect of change in accounting principle, net	—	—	(59)
Net income	$ 2,122	$ 1,246	$ 2,177

Source: Dell Computer Corporation, *Annual Report,* 2002.

Figure 4, which was prepared with the Fingraph® Financial Analyst™ CD-ROM software that is available with this text, is a graphic presentation of a portion of Dell's income statement. It helps show the company's progress in meeting its profitability objectives. On the left side of the graph are the components of income from operations, beginning with net revenues at the top and ending with income from operations at the bottom. The right side graphs the percentage changes in the components. Increases are shown on the right of the vertical column, and decreases are shown on the left. Except for special charges, there was little change in the components from 2001 to 2002, but overall the company grew during the year.

SINGLE-STEP INCOME STATEMENT

The **single-step income statement**, illustrated for Shafer Auto Parts Corporation in Exhibit 5, derives income before income taxes in a single step by putting the major categories of revenues in the first part of the statement and the major categories of costs and expenses in the second part. Income taxes are shown as a separate item, as on the multistep income statement. Both the multistep form and the single-step form have advantages: the multistep form shows the components used in deriving net income, and the single-step form has the advantage of simplicity.

www.nike.com

Exhibit 6 shows the single-step income statement used by Nike, Inc., the footwear company. When a company uses the single-step form, most analysts will

Figure 4
Graphic Presentation of a Portion of Dell Computer Corporation's Income Statement

Dell Computer Corporation — Consolidated Income from Operations (In Millions)

Legend: JAN. 31, 2003 / FEB. 1, 2001

Gross Margin and Its Components:
- Net Revenues: 35,404 / 31,168 — change: 4,236
- Cost of Goods Sold: 29,055 / 25,661 — change: 3,394
- Gross Margin: 6,349 / 5,507 — change: 842

Operating Expenses, Other Charges, and Income from Operations:
- Operating Expenses: 3,505 / 3,236 — change: 269
- Other Charges: 482 / — change: 482
- Income from Operations: 2,844 / 1,789 — change: 1,055

Decreases / Increases axis: −10,000 to 10,000

Other components and net income are presented in another graph (not shown).

Exhibit 5
Single-Step Income Statement for Shafer Auto Parts Corporation

Shafer Auto Parts Corporation
Income Statement
For the Year Ended December 31, 20xx

Revenues		
Net sales		$289,656
Interest income		1,400
Total revenues		$291,056
Costs and expenses		
Cost of goods sold	$181,260	
Selling expenses	54,780	
General and administrative expenses	34,504	
Interest expense	2,631	
Total costs and expenses		273,175
Income before income taxes		$ 17,881
Income taxes		3,381
Net income		$ 14,500
Earnings per share		$ 2.90

EXHIBIT 6
Single-Step Income Statement for Nike, Inc.

Nike, Inc.
Consolidated Statements of Income
(In millions, except per share data)

	Year Ended May 31,		
	2002	2001	2000
Revenues	$9,893.0	$9,488.8	$8,995.1
Costs and expenses:			
Costs of sales	6,004.7	5,784.9	5,403.8
Selling and administrative	2,820.4	2,689.7	2,606.4
Interest expense	47.6	58.7	45.0
Other income/expense, net	3.0	34.1	20.7
Total costs and expenses	8,875.7	8,567.4	8,075.9
Income before income taxes	1,017.3	921.4	919.2
Income taxes	349.0	331.7	340.1
Net income	$ 668.3	$ 589.7	$ 579.1
Basic income per common share	$ 2.50	$ 2.18	$ 2.10

Source: Nike, Inc., *Annual Report,* 2002.
The accompanying notes to consolidated financial statements are an integral part of this statement.

still calculate gross margin, income from operations, and each component's percentage of revenues. Such calculations for Nike would be as follows (in millions):

	2002	Percent	2001	Percent
Revenues	$9,893.0	100.0	$9,488.8	100.0
Cost of sales	6,004.7	60.7	5,784.9	61.0
Gross margin	$3,888.3	39.3	$3,703.9	39.0
Selling and administrative expenses	2,820.4	28.5	2,689.7	28.3
Income from operations	$1,067.9	10.8	$1,014.2	10.7

This analysis shows that Nike's income from operations increased slightly, from 10.7 to 10.8 percent. The difference of 0.1 percent may not seem like a lot, but on revenues of $9,893.0 million, it amounts to almost $10.0 million. The company's efficiency declined by 0.2 percent (28.5 − 28.3) as measured by selling and administrative expenses, but this was more than offset by the increase in gross margin of 0.3 percent (39.3 − 39.0).

 Check out ACE for a Review Quiz at http://accounting.college.hmco.com/students.

USING CLASSIFIED FINANCIAL STATEMENTS

LO7 Evaluate liquidity and profitability using classified financial statements.

RELATED TEXT ASSIGNMENTS
Q: 21, 22, 23, 24, 25
SE: 8, 9, 10
E: 8, 9, 10
P: 4, 5, 8
SD: 6
FRA: 1, 2, 3, 4, 5, 6, 7, 8

As noted earlier, the objectives of financial reporting established by the Financial Accounting Standards Board are to provide information useful in making investment and credit decisions, judging cash flow prospects, and understanding business resources, claims to those resources, and changes in them. These objectives are related to two important goals of management: maintaining adequate liquidity and achieving satisfactory profitability. Investors and creditors base their decisions largely on their assessment of a firm's potential liquidity and profitability. The following analysis shows how ratios use the components in classified financial statements to reflect a firm's performance with respect to these important goals.

KEY POINT: It is imperative that accounts be classified correctly before the ratios are computed. If accounts are not classified correctly, the ratios will not be correct.

EVALUATION OF LIQUIDITY

Liquidity means having enough money on hand to pay bills when they are due and to take care of unexpected needs for cash. Two measures of liquidity are working capital and the current ratio.

■ **WORKING CAPITAL** **Working capital** is the amount by which total current assets exceed total current liabilities. This is an important measure of liquidity because current liabilities are debts that must be paid or obligations that must be performed within one year, and current assets are assets that will be realized in cash or used up within one year or one operating cycle, whichever is longer. By definition, current liabilities are paid out of current assets. So the excess of current assets over current liabilities is the net current assets, or working capital, on hand to continue business operations. Working capital can be used to buy inventory, obtain credit, and finance expanded sales. Lack of working capital can lead to a company's failure. For Shafer Auto Parts, working capital is computed as follows:

Current assets	$124,356
Less current liabilities	42,683
Working capital	$ 81,673

BUSINESS-WORLD EXAMPLE: Some successful firms, such as McDonald's, manage to have very low current ratios by carefully planning their cash flows.

■ **CURRENT RATIO** The second measure of liquidity, the current ratio, is closely related to working capital and is believed by many bankers and other creditors to be a good indicator of a company's ability to pay its bills and to repay outstanding loans. The **current ratio** is the ratio of current assets to current liabilities. For Shafer Auto Parts Corporation, it would be computed like this:

$$\text{Current Ratio} = \frac{\text{Current Assets}}{\text{Current Liabilities}} = \frac{\$124{,}356}{\$42{,}683} = 2.9$$

ENRICHMENT NOTE: It is inadvisable to have too high a current ratio because the firm could probably use the excess funds more effectively to increase its overall profit.

Thus, Shafer has $2.90 of current assets for each $1.00 of current liabilities. Is that good or bad? The answer requires the comparison of this year's ratio with ratios for earlier years and with similar measures for successful companies in the same industry. The average current ratio varies widely from industry to industry, as shown in Figure 5. For the advertising industry, which has no merchandise inventory, the current ratio is 1.4. In contrast, auto and home supply, which carries large merchandise inventories, has an average current ratio of 2.3. The current ratio for Shafer Auto Parts Corporation, 2.9, exceeds the average for its industry. A very low current ratio, of course, can be unfavorable, but so can a very high one. The latter may indicate that the company is not using its assets effectively.

FIGURE 5
Average Current Ratio for Selected Industries

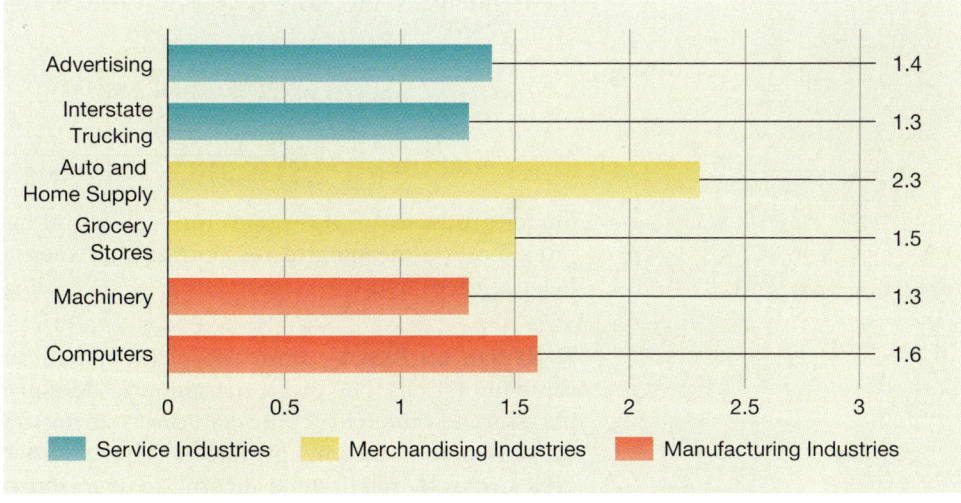

Source: Data from Dun & Bradstreet, *Industry Norms and Key Business Ratios,* 2001–2002.

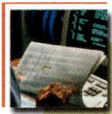

FOCUS ON BUSINESS PRACTICE

Who Is Right: The Credit-Worthiness Analyst or the Profitability Analyst?

The answer depends on your point of view. For example, the future of Amazon.com, the online retailer, has sparked controversy in the big investment company of Lehman Brothers Inc. <www.lehman.com>. One Lehman analyst, who focuses on debt and credit worthiness, has provided a very bearish prediction of the future of Amazon.com because of the company's high level of debt and lack of cash flows to make debt payments. Another Lehman analyst, who focuses on growth and future profitability, is bullish on Amazon.com because the company is growing fast and reducing costs, which should lead to future profitability. Credit analysts tend to look at the downside of future prospects, whereas profitability analysts look at the upside. Which view of Amazon.com's future will prevail? Only time will tell.[14]

EVALUATION OF PROFITABILITY

Just as important as paying bills on time is **profitability**—the ability to earn a satisfactory income. As a goal, profitability competes with liquidity for managerial attention because liquid assets, although important, are not the best profit-producing resources. Cash, for example, means purchasing power, but a satisfactory profit can be made only if purchasing power is used to buy profit-producing (and less liquid) assets, such as inventory and long-term assets.

Among the common measures of a company's ability to earn income are (1) profit margin, (2) asset turnover, (3) return on assets, (4) debt to equity ratio, and (5) return on equity. To evaluate a company meaningfully, one must relate its profit performance to its past performance and prospects for the future as well as to the averages for other companies in the same industry.

■ **PROFIT MARGIN** The **profit margin** shows the percentage of each sales dollar that results in net income. It is figured by dividing net income by net sales. It should not be confused with gross margin, which is not a ratio but rather the amount by which revenues exceed the cost of goods sold.

Shafer Auto Parts Corporation has a profit margin of 5.0 percent:

$$\text{Profit Margin} = \frac{\text{Net Income}}{\text{Net Sales}} = \frac{\$14,500}{\$289,656} = .050 \ (5.0\%)$$

On each dollar of net sales, Shafer made 5.0 cents. A difference of 1 or 2 percent in a company's profit margin can mean the difference between a fair year and a very profitable one.

■ **ASSET TURNOVER** **Asset turnover** measures how efficiently assets are used to produce sales. Computed by dividing net sales by average total assets, it shows how many dollars of sales were generated by each dollar of assets. A company with a higher asset turnover uses its assets more productively than one with a lower asset turnover. Average total assets is computed by adding total assets at the beginning of the year to total assets at the end of the year and dividing by 2.

Assuming that total assets for Shafer Auto Parts Corporation were $148,620 at the beginning of the year, its asset turnover is computed as follows:

$$\text{Asset Turnover} = \frac{\text{Net Sales}}{\text{Average Total Assets}}$$

$$= \frac{\$289,656}{(\$158,916 + \$148,620) \div 2} = \frac{\$289,656}{\$153,768} = 1.9 \text{ times}$$

KEY POINT: Average total assets equals assets at the beginning of the year plus assets at the end of the year, divided by 2.

Shafer produces $1.90 in sales for each $1.00 invested in average total assets. This ratio shows a meaningful relationship between an income statement figure and a balance sheet figure.

■ **RETURN ON ASSETS** Both the profit margin and the asset turnover ratios have some limitations. The profit margin ratio does not take into consideration the assets necessary to produce income, and the asset turnover ratio does not take into account the amount of income produced. The **return on assets** ratio overcomes these deficiencies by relating net income to average total assets. For Shafer Auto Parts, it is computed like this:

FIGURE 6
Average Profit Margin for Selected Industries

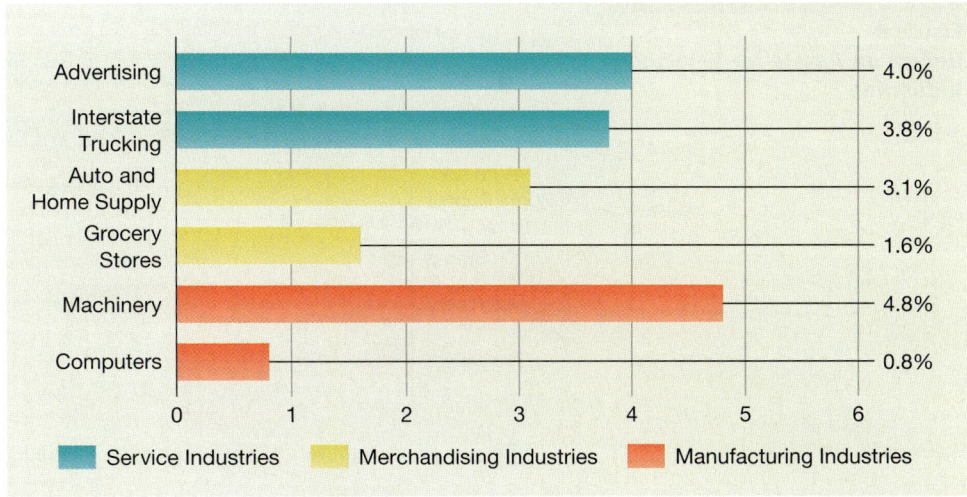

Source: Data from Dun & Bradstreet, *Industry Norms and Key Business Ratios,* 2001–2002.

$$\text{Return on Assets} = \frac{\text{Net Income}}{\text{Average Total Assets}}$$

$$= \frac{\$14{,}500}{(\$158{,}916 + \$148{,}620) \div 2} = \frac{\$14{,}500}{\$153{,}768} = .094 \; (9.4\%)$$

KEY POINT: Return on assets is one of the most widely used measures of profitability because it reflects both the profit margin and asset turnover.

For each dollar invested, Shafer's assets generated 9.4 cents of net income. This ratio indicates the income-generating strength (profit margin) of the company's resources and how efficiently the company is using all its assets (asset turnover).

Return on assets, then, combines profit margin and asset turnover:

$$\frac{\text{Net Income}}{\text{Net Sales}} \times \frac{\text{Net Sales}}{\text{Average Total Assets}} = \frac{\text{Net Income}}{\text{Average Total Assets}}$$

| Profit Margin | × | Asset Turnover | = | Return on Assets |
| 5.0% | × | 1.9 times | = | 9.5%* |

*The slight difference between 9.4 and 9.5 is due to rounding.

Thus, a company's management can improve overall profitability by increasing the profit margin, the asset turnover, or both. Similarly, in evaluating a company's overall profitability, the financial statement user must consider the interaction of both ratios to produce return on assets.

Careful study of Figures 6, 7, and 8 shows the different ways in which the selected industries combine profit margin and asset turnover to produce return on

FIGURE 7
Asset Turnover for Selected Industries

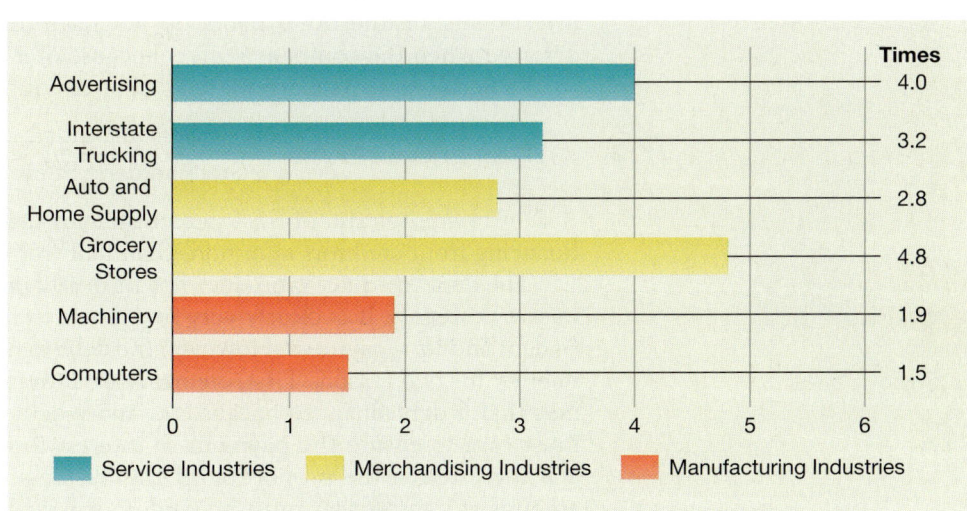

Source: Data from Dun & Bradstreet, *Industry Norms and Key Business Ratios,* 2001–2002.

FIGURE 8
Return on Assets for Selected Industries

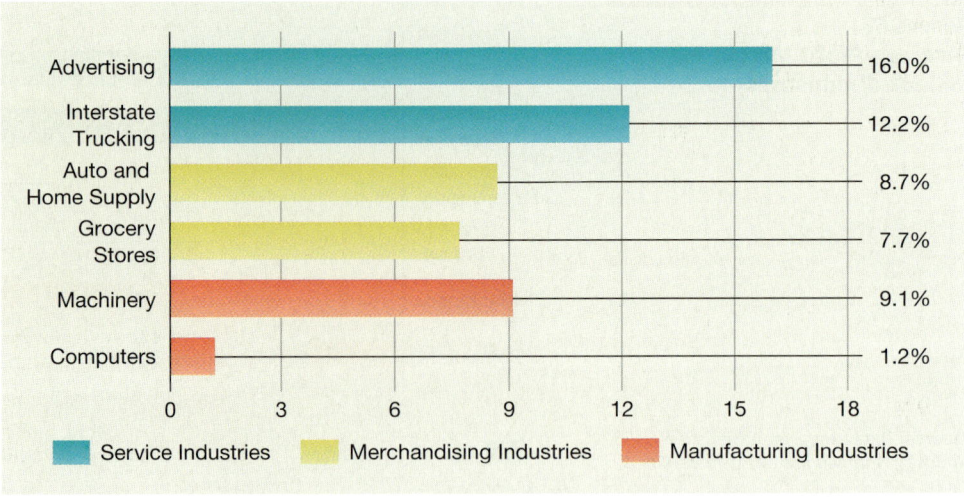

Source: Data from Dun & Bradstreet, *Industry Norms and Key Business Ratios*, 2001–2002.

● **STOP AND THINK!**
Why is it important to compare a company's financial performance with industry averages?

When calculating ratios to measure performance, analysts need benchmarks to measure whether the performance was good or bad. Past performance of the company is one measure, but a better measure is the financial performance of similar companies. This is done by examining industry averages. ■

KEY POINT: A company with a low debt to equity ratio has a better chance of surviving in rough times. Debt requires additional expenses (interest) that must be paid.

assets. For instance, by comparing the return on assets for grocery stores and machinery manufacturers, you can see how they achieve it in very different ways. The grocery store industry has a profit margin of 1.6 percent, which when multiplied by an asset turnover of 4.8 times, gives a return on assets of 7.7 percent. The machinery industry, on the other hand, has a higher profit margin, 4.8 percent, and a lower asset turnover, 1.9 times, and produces a return on assets of 9.1 percent.

Shafer's profit margin of 5.0 percent is well above the auto and home supply industry average of 3.1 percent, but its asset turnover of 1.9 times lags behind the industry average of 2.8 times. Shafer is sacrificing asset turnover to achieve a higher profit margin. It is clear that this strategy is working, because Shafer's return on assets of 9.4 percent exceeds the industry average of 8.7 percent.

■ **DEBT TO EQUITY RATIO** Another useful measure of profitability is the **debt to equity ratio**, which shows the proportion of the company financed by creditors in comparison with that financed by stockholders. This ratio is computed by dividing total liabilities by stockholders' equity. Since the balance sheets of most public companies do not show total liabilities, a short way of determining total liabilities is to deduct the total stockholders' equity from total assets. A debt to equity ratio of 1.0 means that total liabilities equal stockholders' equity—that half of the company's assets are financed by creditors. A ratio of .5 means that one-third of the assets are financed by creditors. A company with a high debt to equity ratio is at risk in poor economic times because it must continue to repay creditors. Stockholders' investments, on the other hand, do not have to be repaid, and dividends can be deferred when the company suffers because of a poor economy.

Shafer Auto Parts Corporation's debt to equity ratio is computed as follows:

$$\text{Debt to Equity Ratio} = \frac{\text{Total Liabilities}}{\text{Stockholders' Equity}} = \frac{\$60,483}{\$98,433} = .614 \ (61.4\%)$$

A debt to equity ratio of 61.4 percent means that Shafer receives less than half its financing from creditors and more than half from its investors.

The debt to equity ratio does not fit neatly into either the liquidity or the profitability category. It is clearly very important to liquidity analysis because it relates to debt and its repayment. However, the debt to equity ratio is also relevant to profitability for two reasons. First, creditors are interested in the proportion of the business that is debt-financed because the more debt a company has, the more profit it must earn to ensure the payment of interest to its creditors. Second, stockholders are interested in the proportion of the business that is debt-financed because the amount of interest that must be paid on the debt affects the amount of profit that

FIGURE 9
Average Debt to Equity Ratio for Selected Industries

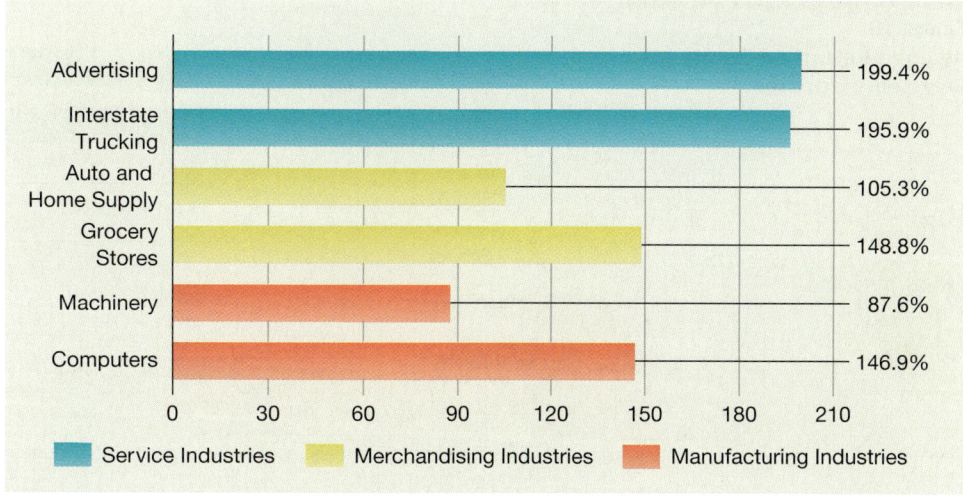

Source: Data from Dun & Bradstreet, *Industry Norms and Key Business Ratios,* 2001–2002.

is left to provide a return on stockholders' investments. The debt to equity ratio also shows how much expansion is possible by borrowing additional long-term funds. Figure 9 shows that the debt to equity ratio in our selected industries varies from a low of 87.6 percent in the machinery industry to a high of 199.4 percent in the advertising industry.

■ **RETURN ON EQUITY** Of course, stockholders are interested in how much they have earned on their investment in the business. Their **return on equity** is measured by the ratio of net income to average stockholders' equity. Taking the ending stockholders' equity from the balance sheet and assuming that beginning stockholders' equity is $100,553, Shafer's return on equity is computed as follows:

$$\text{Return on Equity} = \frac{\text{Net Income}}{\text{Average Stockholders' Equity}}$$

$$= \frac{\$14,500}{(\$98,433 + \$100,553) \div 2} = \frac{\$14,500}{\$99,493} = .146 \ (14.6\%)$$

In 20xx, Shafer earned 14.6 cents for every dollar invested by stockholders.

Whether this is an acceptable return depends on several factors, such as how much the company earned in previous years and how much other companies in the same industry earned. As measured by return on equity (Figure 10), the advertising industry is the most profitable of our sample industries, with a return on equity of

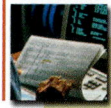

FOCUS ON BUSINESS PRACTICE

To What Level of Profitability Should a Company Aspire?

At one time, a company earning a 20 percent return on equity ranked among the elite. Only Disney <www.disney.go.com>, Wal-Mart <www.walmart.com>, Coca-Cola <www.coca-cola.com>, and a few other companies were able to achieve this level of profitability. However, in the first quarter of 1995, for the first time, the average company of the Standard & Poor's 500 companies made a return on equity of 20.12 percent. *The Wall Street Journal* described this performance as "akin to the average ball player hitting .350."[15] This meant that stockholders' equity would double every four years.

Why did this happen? First, a good business environment and cost cutting led to more profitable operations. Second, special charges and other accounting transactions reduced stockholders' equity for many companies. In this way, the denominator of the ratio is reduced, thus increasing the ratio.

Until 2000, the number of companies with a return on equity of more than 20 percent continued to increase, but during 2001, 2002, and 2003, this number declined. When earnings are declining, companies tend to emphasize measures of performance other than profitability.

FIGURE 10
Average Return on Equity for Selected Industries

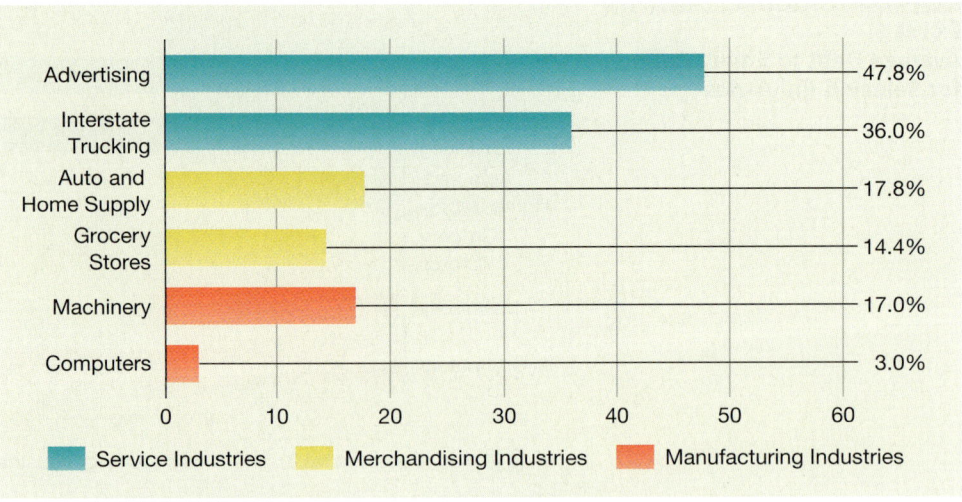

Source: Data from Dun & Bradstreet, *Industry Norms and Key Business Ratios,* 2001–2002.

47.8 percent. Shafer Auto Parts Corporation's average return on equity of 14.6 percent is less than the average of 17.8 percent for the auto and home supply industry.

■ **GRAPHING RATIO ANALYSIS** Figure 11, prepared with the Fingraph® Financial Analyst™ software that is available with this text, graphically presents Dell Computer Corporation's profitability ratios involving net income. It helps us

www.dell.com

FIGURE 11
Graphic Presentation of Dell Computer Corporation's Profitability Ratios

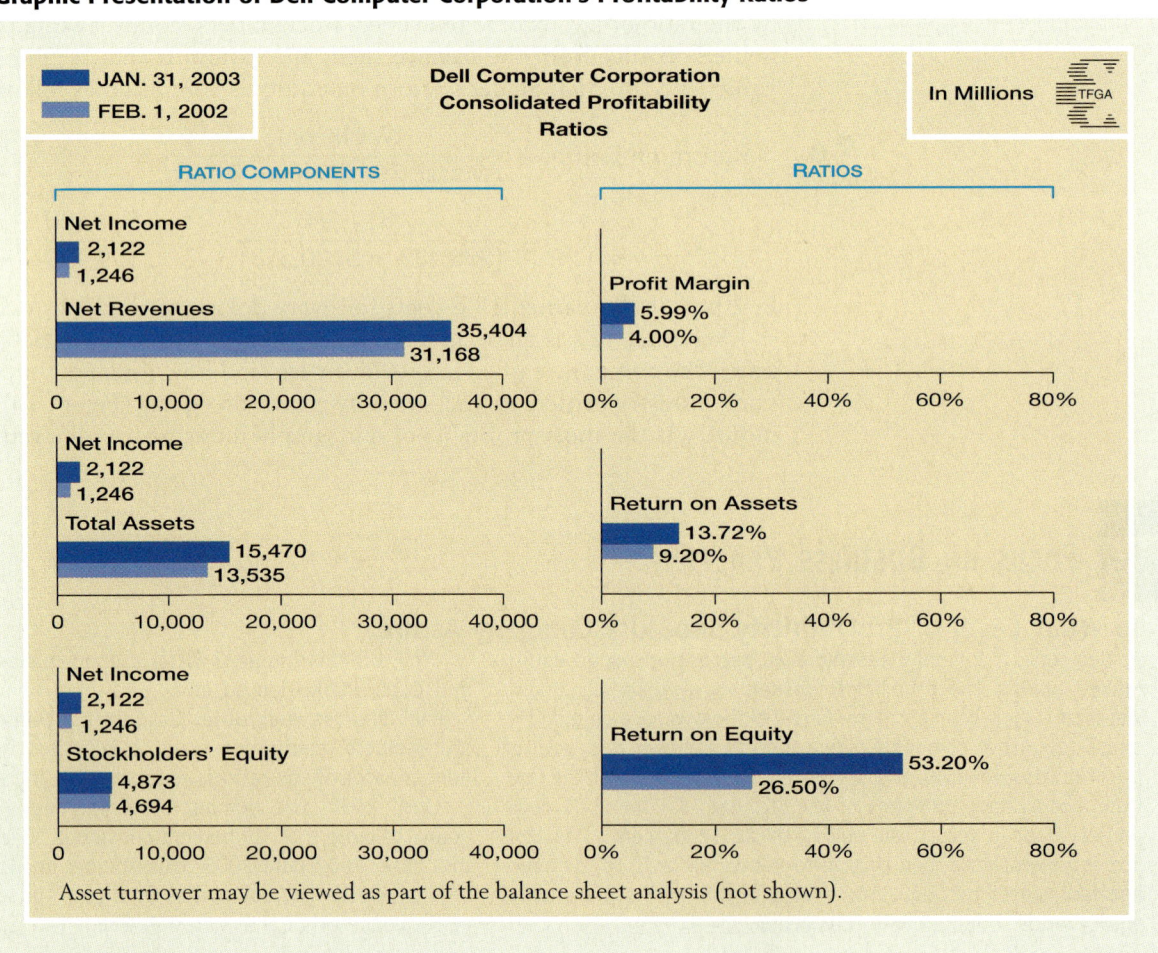

visualize the progress of the company in meeting its profitability objectives. On the left of the figure are the components of the ratios. On the right are the ratios for the past two years. Notice that the changes in return on equity and return on assets are linked to changes in profit margin or asset turnover. The Fingraph Financial Analyst CD-ROM software graphs all the ratios used in this book and provides narrative analysis. The asset turnover ratio is shown graphically with the Fingraph balance sheet analysis.

 Check out ACE for a Review Quiz at http://accounting.college.hmco.com/students.

Chapter Review

REVIEW OF LEARNING OBJECTIVES

LO1 State the objectives of financial reporting.

The objectives of financial reporting are (1) to furnish information that is useful in making investment and credit decisions, (2) to provide information that can be used to assess cash flow prospects, and (3) to provide information about business resources, claims to those resources, and changes in them.

LO2 State the qualitative characteristics of accounting information and describe their interrelationships.

Understandability depends on the knowledge of the user and the ability of the accountant to provide useful information. Usefulness is a function of two primary characteristics, relevance and reliability. Information is relevant when it affects the outcome of a decision. Information that is relevant has feedback value and predictive value, and is timely. To be reliable, information must represent what it is supposed to represent and be verifiable and neutral.

LO3 Define and describe the conventions of *comparability* and *consistency, materiality, conservatism, full disclosure,* and *cost-benefit.*

Because accountants' measurements are not exact, certain conventions are applied in current practice to help users interpret financial statements. The first of these conventions is comparability and consistency. Consistency requires the use of the same accounting procedures from period to period and enhances the comparability of financial statements. The second is materiality, which has to do with the relative importance of an item. The third is conservatism, which entails using the procedure that is least likely to overstate assets and income. The fourth is full disclosure, which means including all relevant information in the financial statements. The fifth is cost-benefit, which suggests that above a minimum level of information, additional information should be provided only if the benefits derived from the information exceed the costs of providing it.

LO4 Explain management's responsibility for ethical financial reporting and define *fraudulent financial reporting.*

Management is responsible for the preparation of financial statements in accordance with generally accepted accounting principles and for the internal controls that provide assurance that this objective is achieved. Fraudulent financial reporting is the intentional preparation of misleading financial statements.

LO5 Identify and describe the basic components of a classified balance sheet.

The classified balance sheet is subdivided as follows:

Assets	Liabilities
Current assets	Current liabilities
Investments	Long-term liabilities
Property, plant, and equipment	**Stockholders' Equity**
Intangible assets	Contributed capital
(Other assets)	Retained earnings

A current asset is an asset that can reasonably be expected to be realized in cash or consumed during the next year or the normal operating cycle, whichever is longer. Investments are assets, usually long term, that are not used in the normal operation of a business. Property, plant, and equipment are tangible long-term assets used in day-to-day operations. Intangible assets are long-term assets with no physical substance whose value stems from the rights or privileges they extend to stockholders. A current liability is an obligation that can reasonably be expected to be paid or performed during the next year or the normal operating cycle, whichever is longer. Long-term liabilities are debts that fall due more than one year in the future or beyond the normal operating cycle. The equity section of the balance sheet for a corporation differs from that for a proprietorship or partnership in that it has subdivisions of contributed capital (the value of assets invested by stockholders) and retained earnings (stockholders' claim to assets earned from operations and reinvested in operations).

LO6 Prepare multistep and single-step classified income statements.

Classified income statements for external reporting can be in multistep or single-step form. The multistep form arrives at income before income taxes through a series of steps; the single-step form arrives at income before income taxes in a single step. There is usually a separate section in the multistep form for other revenues and expenses.

LO7 Evaluate liquidity and profitability using classified financial statements.

One important use of classified financial statements is to evaluate a company's liquidity and profitability. Two measures of liquidity are working capital and the current ratio. Five measures of profitability are profit margin, asset turnover, return on assets, debt to equity ratio, and return on equity. Referring to industry averages aids interpretation of these ratios.

REVIEW OF CONCEPTS AND TERMINOLOGY

The following concepts and terms were introduced in this chapter:

LO7 Asset turnover: A measure of profitability that shows how efficiently assets are used to produce sales; net sales divided by average total assets.

LO5 Classified financial statements: General-purpose external financial statements that are divided into subcategories.

LO3 Comparability: The convention of presenting information in a way that enables decision makers to recognize similarities, differences, and trends over different time periods or between different companies.

LO3 Conservatism: The convention that when faced with two equally acceptable alternatives, the accountant must choose the one least likely to overstate assets and income.

LO3 Consistency: The convention requiring that once an accounting procedure is adopted, it not be changed from one period to the next unless users of the financial statements are informed of the change.

LO3 Conventions: Rules of thumb, or general principles, for recording transactions and preparing financial statements.

LO3 Cost-benefit: The convention that the benefits gained from providing accounting information should be greater than the costs of providing that information.

LO6 Cost of goods sold: The amount a merchandiser paid for the merchandise it sold during an accounting period or the cost to a manufacturer of making the products it sold during an accounting period. Also called *cost of sales*.

LO5 Current assets: Cash and other assets that are reasonably expected to be converted to cash, sold, or consumed within one year or within a normal operating cycle, whichever is longer.

LO5 Current liabilities: Obligations due to be paid or performed within one year or within the normal operating cycle, whichever is longer.

LO7 Current ratio: A measure of liquidity; current assets divided by current liabilities.

LO7 Debt to equity ratio: A measure of profitability that shows the relationship of assets financed by creditors to those financed by stockholders; total liabilities divided by stockholders' equity.

LO6 Earnings per share: Net income earned on each share of common stock; net income divided by the average number of common shares outstanding during the year. Also called *net income per share*.

LO4 Fraudulent financial reporting: The intentional preparation of misleading financial statements.

LO6 Freight out expense: The cost to the seller of shipping goods to the buyer. Also called *delivery expense*.

LO3 **Full disclosure:** The convention requiring that a company's financial statements and their notes present all information relevant to the users' understanding of the statements.

LO6 **Gross margin:** The difference between net sales and cost of goods sold. Also called *gross profit*.

LO6 **Gross sales:** Total sales for cash and on credit during an accounting period.

LO6 **Income before income taxes:** The amount a company has earned from all activities—operating and nonoperating—before taking into account the amount of income taxes incurred.

LO6 **Income from operations:** Gross margin less operating expenses. Also called *operating income*.

LO6 **Income taxes:** A category for the expense of federal, state, and local taxes that appears only on income statements of corporations. Also called *provision for income taxes*.

LO5 **Intangible assets:** Long-term assets with no physical substance whose value stems from the rights or privileges they extend to their owners.

LO5 **Investments:** Assets, usually long term, that are not used in the normal operation of a business and that management does not intend to convert to cash within the next year.

LO7 **Liquidity:** Having enough money on hand to pay bills when they are due and to take care of unexpected needs for cash.

LO5 **Long-term liabilities:** Debts that fall due more than one year in the future or beyond the normal operating cycle.

LO6 **Manufacturing companies:** Companies that make and sell products.

LO3 **Materiality:** The convention that refers to the relative importance of an item or event in a financial statement and its influence on the decisions of the users of financial statements.

LO6 **Merchandising companies:** Companies, including both wholesalers and retailers, that buy and sell products.

LO6 **Multistep income statement:** An income statement that goes through a series of steps to arrive at income before income taxes.

LO6 **Net income:** What remains of gross margin after operating expenses are deducted, other revenues and expenses are added or deducted, and income taxes are deducted. Also referred to as the "bottom line."

LO6 **Net sales:** The gross proceeds from sales of merchandise, or gross sales, less sales returns and allowances and any discounts allowed. Often simply called *sales*.

LO6 **Operating expenses:** Expenses other than cost of goods sold that are incurred in running a business.

LO5 **Other assets:** A balance sheet category that some companies use to group all assets other than current assets and property, plant, and equipment.

LO6 **Other revenues and expenses:** The section of a multistep income statement that includes revenues and expenses not related to business operations. Also called *nonoperating revenues and expenses*.

LO7 **Profitability:** The ability of a business to earn a satisfactory income.

LO7 **Profit margin:** A measure of profitability that shows the percentage of each sales dollar that results in net income; net income divided by net sales.

LO5 **Property, plant, and equipment:** Tangible long-term assets used in the continuing operation of a business. Also called *operating assets, fixed assets, tangible assets, long-lived assets,* or *plant assets*.

LO2 **Qualitative characteristics:** Standards for judging the information that accountants give to decision makers.

LO2 **Relevance:** The qualitative characteristic of information that bears directly on the outcome of a decision.

LO2 **Reliability:** The qualitative characteristic of information that represents what it is supposed to represent and is verifiable and neutral.

LO7 **Return on assets:** A measure of profitability that shows how efficiently a company uses its assets to produce income; net income divided by average total assets.

LO7 **Return on equity:** A measure of profitability that relates the amount earned by a business to the stockholders' investment in the business; net income divided by average stockholders' equity.

LO6 **Single-step income statement:** An income statement that arrives at income before income taxes in a single step.

LO2 **Understandability:** The qualitative characteristic of information that communicates an intended meaning.

LO2 **Usefulness:** The qualitative characteristic of information that is relevant and reliable.

LO7 **Working capital:** A measure of liquidity that shows the net current assets on hand to continue business operations; total current assets minus total current liabilities.

REVIEW PROBLEM

Analyzing Liquidity and Profitability Using Ratios

LO7 Flavin Shirt Company has faced increased competition from overseas shirtmakers in recent years. Presented below is summary information for the last two years:

	20x2	20x1
Current Assets	$ 200,000	$ 170,000
Total Assets	880,000	710,000
Current Liabilities	90,000	50,000
Long-Term Liabilities	150,000	50,000
Stockholders' Equity	640,000	610,000
Sales	1,200,000	1,050,000
Net Income	60,000	80,000

Total assets and stockholders' equity at the beginning of 20x1 were $690,000 and $590,000, respectively.

REQUIRED ▶ Use (1) liquidity analysis and (2) profitability analysis to document the declining financial position of Flavin Shirt Company.

ANSWER TO REVIEW PROBLEM

1. Liquidity analysis

	Current Assets	Current Liabilities	Working Capital	Current Ratio
20x1	$170,000	$50,000	$120,000	3.40
20x2	200,000	90,000	110,000	2.22
Decrease in working capital			$ 10,000	
Decrease in current ratio				1.18

Both working capital and the current ratio declined from 20x1 to 20x2 because the $40,000 increase in current liabilities ($90,000 − $50,000) was greater than the $30,000 increase in current assets.

2. Profitability analysis

	Net Income	Sales	Profit Margin	Average Total Assets	Asset Turnover	Return on Assets	Average Stockholders' Equity	Return on Equity
20x1	$80,000	$1,050,000	7.6%	$700,000[1]	1.50	11.4%	$600,000[3]	13.3%
20x2	60,000	1,200,000	5.0	795,000[2]	1.51	7.5	625,000[4]	9.6
Increase (decrease)	($20,000)	$ 150,000	(2.6)%	$ 95,000	0.01	(3.9)%	$ 25,000	(3.7)%

[1] ($710,000 + $690,000) ÷ 2
[2] ($880,000 + $710,000) ÷ 2
[3] ($610,000 + $590,000) ÷ 2
[4] ($640,000 + $610,000) ÷ 2

Net income decreased by $20,000 despite an increase in sales of $150,000 and an increase in average total assets of $95,000. The results were decreases in profit margin from 7.6 percent to 5.0 percent and in return on assets from 11.4 percent to 7.5 percent. Asset turnover showed almost no change and so did not contribute to the decline in profitability. The decrease in return on equity, from 13.3 percent to 9.6 percent, was not as great as the decrease in return on assets because the growth in total assets was financed mainly by debt instead of by stockholders' equity, as shown by the capital structure analysis below.

	Total Liabilities	Stockholders' Equity	Debt to Equity Ratio
20x1	$100,000	$610,000	16.4%
20x2	240,000	640,000	37.5
Increase	$140,000	$ 30,000	21.1%

Total liabilities increased by $140,000, while stockholders' equity increased by $30,000. As a result, the amount of the business financed by debt in relation to the amount of the business financed by stockholders' equity increased from 20x1 to 20x2.

Chapter Assignments

BUILDING YOUR KNOWLEDGE FOUNDATION

QUESTIONS

1. What are the three objectives of financial reporting?
2. What are the qualitative characteristics of accounting information, and what is their significance?
3. What are the accounting conventions? How does each help in the interpretation of financial information?

4. Who is responsible for the preparation of reliable financial statements, and what is a principal way of achieving this objective?
5. What is the purpose of classified financial statements?
6. What are four common categories of assets?
7. What criteria must an asset meet to be classified as current? Under what condition is an asset considered current even though it will not be realized as cash within a year? What are two examples of assets that fall into this category?
8. In what order should current assets be listed?
9. What is the difference between a short-term investment in the current assets section of the balance sheet and a security in the investments section?
10. What is an intangible asset? Give at least three examples.
11. Name the two major categories of liabilities.
12. What are the primary differences between the equity section of the balance sheet for a sole proprietorship or partnership and the corresponding section for a corporation?
13. What is the primary difference between the operations of a merchandising business and those of a service business? How is this difference reflected on the income statement?
14. Define *gross margin*. Why is it important?
15. During its first year in operation, Kumler Nursery had a cost of goods sold of $64,000 and a gross margin equal to 40 percent of sales. What was the dollar amount of the company's sales?
16. Could Kumler Nursery (in Question 15) have a net loss for the year? Explain your answer.
17. Explain how the multistep form of income statement differs from the single-step form. What are the relative merits of each?
18. Why are other revenues and expenses separated from operating revenues and expenses on the multistep income statement?
19. What are some of the differences between the income statement for a sole proprietorship and that for a corporation?
20. Explain earnings per share and indicate how this figure appears on the income statement.
21. Define *liquidity* and name two measures of liquidity.
22. How is the current ratio computed, and why is it important?
23. Which is the more important goal, liquidity or profitability? Explain your answer.
24. Name five measures of profitability.
25. "Return on assets is a better measure of profitability than profit margin." Evaluate this statement.

Short Exercises

LO1 **Objectives and Qualitative**
LO2 **Characteristics**

SE 1. Identify each of the following statements as either an objective (O) of financial information or a qualitative (Q) characteristic of accounting information:
1. Information about business resources, claims to those resources, and changes in them should be provided.
2. Decision makers must be able to interpret accounting information.
3. Information that is useful in making investment and credit decisions should be furnished.
4. Accounting information must be relevant and reliable.
5. Information useful in assessing cash flow prospects should be provided.

LO3 **Accounting Conventions**

SE 2. State which of the accounting conventions—comparability and consistency, materiality, conservatism, full disclosure, or cost-benefit—is being followed in each of the cases listed below.
1. Management provides detailed information about the company's long-term debt in the notes to the financial statements.

2. A company does not account separately for discounts received for prompt payment of accounts payable because few of these transactions occur and the total amount of the discounts is small.
3. Management eliminates a weekly report on property, plant, and equipment acquisitions and disposals because no one finds it useful.
4. A company follows the policy of recognizing a loss on inventory when the market value of an item falls below its cost but does nothing if the market value rises.
5. When several accounting methods are acceptable, management chooses a single method and follows that method from year to year.

SE 3.
LO5 Classification of Accounts: Balance Sheet

Tell whether each of the following accounts is a current asset; an investment; property, plant, and equipment; an intangible asset; a current liability; a long-term liability; stockholders' equity; or not on the balance sheet:

1. Delivery Trucks
2. Accounts Payable
3. Note Payable (due in 90 days)
4. Delivery Expense
5. Common Stock
6. Prepaid Insurance
7. Trademark
8. Investment to Be Held Six Months
9. Income Taxes Payable
10. Factory Not Used in Business

SE 4.
LO5 Classified Balance Sheet

Using the following accounts, prepare a classified balance sheet at year end, May 31, 20xx: Accounts Payable, $400; Accounts Receivable, $550; Accumulated Depreciation, Equipment, $350; Cash, $100; Common Stock, $500; Equipment, $2,000; Franchise, $100; Investments (long-term), $250; Merchandise Inventory, $300; Notes Payable (long-term), $200; Retained Earnings, ?; Wages Payable, $50.

SE 5.
LO6 Classification of Accounts: Income Statement

Tell whether each of the following accounts is part of net sales, cost of goods sold, operating expenses, other revenues and expenses, or is not on the income statement:

1. Delivery Expense
2. Interest Expense
3. Unearned Revenue
4. Sales Returns and Allowances
5. Cost of Goods Sold
6. Depreciation Expense
7. Investment Income
8. Retained Earnings

SE 6.
LO6 Single-Step Income Statement

Using the following accounts, prepare a single-step income statement at year end, May 31, 20xx: Cost of Goods Sold, $280; General Expenses, $150; Income Taxes, $35; Interest Expense, $70; Interest Income, $30; Net Sales, $800; Selling Expenses, $185. Ignore earnings per share.

SE 7.
LO6 Multistep Income Statement

Using the accounts presented in **SE 6,** prepare a multistep income statement.

SE 8.
LO7 Liquidity Ratios

Using the following accounts and balances taken from a year-end balance sheet, compute working capital and the current ratio:

Accounts Payable	$ 7,000
Accounts Receivable	10,000
Cash	4,000
Common Stock	20,000
Marketable Securities (CURRENT ASSET)	2,000
Merchandise Inventory	12,000
Notes Payable in Three Years	13,000
Property, Plant, and Equipment	40,000
Retained Earnings	28,000

SE 9.
LO7 Profitability Ratios

Using the following information from a balance sheet and an income statement, compute the (1) profit margin, (2) asset turnover, (3) return on assets, (4) debt to equity ratio, and (5) return on equity. (The previous year's total assets were $100,000 and stockholders' equity was $70,000.)

Total assets	$120,000
Total liabilities	30,000
Total stockholders' equity	90,000
Net sales	130,000
Cost of goods sold	70,000
Operating expenses	40,000
Income taxes	5,000

SE 10.
LO7 Relationship of Profitability Ratios

Assume that a company has a profit margin of 6.0 percent, an asset turnover of 3.2 times, and a debt to equity ratio of 50 percent. What are the company's return on assets and return on equity?

Exercises

LO1 **Financial Accounting Concepts**
LO2
LO3

E 1. The lettered items below represent a classification scheme for the concepts of financial accounting. Match each numbered term with the letter of the category in which it belongs.

a. Decision makers (users of accounting information)
b. Business activities or entities relevant to accounting measurement
c. Objectives of accounting information
d. Accounting measurement considerations
e. Accounting processing considerations
f. Qualitative characteristics
g. Accounting conventions
h. Financial statements

1. Conservatism
2. Verifiability
3. Statement of cash flows
4. Materiality
5. Reliability
6. Recognition
7. Cost-benefit
8. Understandability
9. Business transactions
10. Consistency
11. Full disclosure
12. Furnishing information that is useful to investors and creditors
13. Specific business entities
14. Classification
15. Management
16. Neutrality
17. Internal accounting control
18. Valuation
19. Investors
20. Timeliness
21. Relevance
22. Furnishing information that is useful in assessing cash flow prospects

LO3 **Accounting Concepts and Conventions**

E 2. Each of the statements below violates a convention in accounting. State which of the following accounting conventions is violated: comparability and consistency, materiality, conservatism, full disclosure, or cost-benefit.

1. A series of reports that are time-consuming and expensive to prepare is presented to the board of directors each month even though the reports are never used.
2. A company changes its method of accounting for depreciation.
3. The company in **2** does not indicate in the financial statements that the method of depreciation was changed, nor does it specify the effect of the change on net income.
4. A new office building next to the factory is debited to the Factory account because it represents a fairly small dollar amount in relation to the factory.
5. The asset account for a pickup truck still used in the business is written down to what the truck could be sold for even though the carrying value under conventional depreciation methods is higher.

LO5 **Classification of Accounts: Balance Sheet**

E 3. The lettered items below represent a classification scheme for a balance sheet, and the numbered items are account titles. Match each account with the letter of the category in which it belongs.

a. Current assets
b. Investments
c. Property, plant, and equipment
d. Intangible assets
e. Current liabilities
f. Long-term liabilities
g. Stockholders' equity
h. Not on balance sheet

1. Patent
2. Building Held for Sale
3. Prepaid Rent
4. Wages Payable
5. Note Payable in Five Years
6. Building Used in Operations
7. Fund Held to Pay Off Long-Term Debt
8. Inventory
9. Prepaid Insurance
10. Depreciation Expense
11. Accounts Receivable
12. Interest Expense
13. Unearned Revenue
14. Short-Term Investments
15. Accumulated Depreciation
16. Retained Earnings

LO5 **Classified Balance Sheet Preparation**

E 4. The following data pertain to Mia, Inc.: Accounts Payable, $51,000; Accounts Receivable, $38,000; Accumulated Depreciation, Building, $14,000; Accumulated Depreciation, Equipment, $17,000; Bonds Payable, $60,000; Building, $70,000; Cash, $31,200; Common Stock, $10 par, 10,000 shares authorized, issued, and outstanding, $100,000;

Copyright, $6,200; Equipment, $152,000; Inventory, $40,000; Investment in Corporate Securities (long-term), $20,000; Investment in Six-Month Government Securities, $16,400; Land, $8,000; Paid-in Capital in Excess of Par Value, $50,000; Prepaid Rent, $1,200; Retained Earnings, $88,200; and Revenue Received in Advance, $2,800.

Prepare a classified balance sheet at December 31, 20xx.

LO6 Classification of Accounts: Income Statement

E 5. Using the classification scheme below for a multistep income statement, match each account with the letter of the category in which it belongs.

a. Net sales
b. Cost of goods sold
c. Selling expenses
d. General and administrative expenses
e. Other revenues and expenses
f. Not on income statement

1. Sales Discounts
2. Cost of Goods Sold
3. Dividend Income
4. Advertising Expense
5. Office Salaries Expense
6. Freight Out Expense
7. Prepaid Insurance
8. Utilities Expense
9. Sales Salaries Expense
10. Rent Expense
11. Depreciation Expense, Delivery Equipment
12. Taxes Payable
13. Interest Expense

LO6 Preparation of Income Statements

E 6. The following data pertain to a corporation: net sales, $810,000; cost of goods sold, $440,000; selling expenses, $180,000; general and administrative expenses, $120,000; income taxes, $15,000; interest expense, $8,000; interest income, $6,000; and common stock outstanding, 100,000 shares.

1. Prepare a single-step income statement.
2. Prepare a multistep income statement.

LO6 Multistep Income Statement

E 7. A single-step income statement appears below. Present the information in a multistep income statement, and tell what insights can be obtained from the multistep form as opposed to the single-step form.

Skye Linens Corporation
Income Statement
For the Year Ended December 31, 20xx

Revenues		
Net sales		$598,566
Interest income		2,860
Total revenues		$601,426
Costs and expenses		
Cost of goods sold	$388,540	
Selling expenses	101,870	
General and administrative expenses	50,344	
Interest expense	6,780	
Total costs and expenses		547,534
Income before income taxes		$ 53,892
Income taxes		12,000
Net income		$ 41,892
Earnings per share		$ 4.19

LO7 Liquidity Ratios

E 8. The accounts and balances that follow are from the general ledger of Lake Corporation. Compute the (1) working capital and (2) current ratio.

Accounts Payable	$16,600
Accounts Receivable	10,200
Cash	1,500
Current Portion of Long-Term Debt	10,000
Long-Term Investments	10,400
Marketable Securities	12,600
Merchandise Inventory	25,400
Notes Payable, 90 days	15,000
Notes Payable, 2 years	20,000
Notes Receivable, 90 days	26,000
Notes Receivable, 2 years	10,000
Prepaid Insurance	400
Property, Plant, and Equipment	60,000
Property Taxes Payable	1,250
Retained Earnings	28,300
Salaries Payable	850
Supplies	350
Unearned Revenue	750

LO7 Profitability Ratios

E 9. The following end-of-year amounts are from the financial statements of Parto Corporation: total assets, $426,000; total liabilities, $172,000; stockholders' equity, $254,000; net sales, $782,000; cost of goods sold, $486,000; operating expenses, $178,000; income taxes, $24,000; and dividends, $40,000. During the past year, total assets increased by $75,000. Total stockholders' equity was affected only by net income and dividends. Compute the (1) profit margin, (2) asset turnover, (3) return on assets, (4) debt to equity ratio, and (5) return on equity.

LO7 Computation of Ratios

E 10. The simplified balance sheet and income statement for a corporation appear below.

Balance Sheet
December 31, 20xx

Assets		Liabilities	
Current assets	$100,000	Current liabilities	$ 40,000
Investments	20,000	Long-term liabilities	60,000
Property, plant, and equipment	293,000	Total liabilities	$100,000
Intangible assets	27,000	**Stockholders' Equity**	
		Common stock	$200,000
		Retained earnings	140,000
		Total stockholders' equity	$340,000
Total assets	$440,000	Total liabilities and stockholders' equity	$440,000

Income Statement
For the Year Ended December 31, 20xx

Net sales	$820,000
Cost of goods sold	500,000
Gross margin	$320,000
Operating expenses	260,000
Income before income taxes	$ 60,000
Income taxes	10,000
Net income	$ 50,000

Total assets and stockholders' equity at the beginning of 20xx were $360,000 and $280,000, respectively.

1. Compute the following liquidity measures: (a) working capital and (b) current ratio.
2. Compute the following profitability measures: (a) profit margin, (b) asset turnover, (c) return on assets, (d) debt to equity ratio, and (e) return on equity.

PROBLEMS

P 1.
LO3 Accounting Conventions

In each case below, accounting conventions *may* have been violated.

1. Arinno Manufacturing Company uses the cost method for computing the balance sheet amount of inventory unless the market value of the inventory is less than the cost, in which case the market value is used. At the end of the current year, the market value is $77,000, and the cost is $80,000. Arinno uses the $77,000 figure to compute current assets because management feels it is the more cautious approach.
2. Shuess Company has annual sales of $5,000,000. It follows the practice of charging any items costing less than $100 to expenses in the year purchased. During the current year, it purchased several chairs for the executive conference rooms at $97 each, including freight. Although the chairs were expected to last for at least ten years, they were charged as an expense in accordance with company policy.
3. Wong Company closed its books on December 31, 20x3, before preparing its annual report. A day later, a fire destroyed one of its two factories. Although Wong had fire insurance and would not suffer a loss on the building, it expected a significant decrease in sales in 20x4 because of the fire. It did not report the fire damage in its 20x3 financial statements because the fire did not affect that years's operations.
4. Duffy Drug Company spends a substantial portion of its profits on research and development. The company has been reporting its $2,500,000 expenditure for research and development as a lump sum, but management recently decided to begin classifying the expenditures by project even though the recordkeeping costs will increase.
5. During the current year, Himall Company changed from one generally accepted method of accounting for inventories to another method.

REQUIRED ▶ In each case, identify the convention that applies, state whether or not the treatment is in accord with the convention and GAAP, and briefly explain why.

P 2.
LO6 Forms of the Income Statement

Ivy Nursery Corporation's single-step income statements for 20x4 and 20x3 follow.

Ivy Nursery Corporation
Income Statements
For the Years Ended April 30, 20x4 and 20x3

	20x4	20x3
Revenues		
Net sales	$525,932	$475,264
Interest income	800	700
Total revenues	$526,732	$475,964
Costs and expenses		
Cost of goods sold	$234,948	$171,850
Selling expenses	161,692	150,700
General and administrative expenses	62,866	42,086
Interest expense	3,600	850
Total costs and expenses	$463,106	$365,486
Income before income taxes	$ 63,626	$110,478
Income taxes	15,000	27,600
Net income	$ 48,626	$ 82,878
Earnings per share	$ 2.43	$ 4.14

Ivy Nursery Corporation had 20,000 shares of common stock outstanding during both 20x4 and 20x3.

REQUIRED
1. From the information provided, prepare multistep income statements for 20x3 and 20x4 showing percentages of net sales for each component.
2. Did income from operations increase or decrease from 20x3 to 20x4? Write a short explanation of why this change occurred.
3. What effect did other revenues and expenses have on the change in income before income taxes? What action by management probably caused this change?

LO5 Classified Balance Sheet

P 3. The following information is from the June 30, 20x4, post-closing trial balance of Olcott Hardware Corporation.

Account Name	Debit	Credit
Cash	$ 24,000	
Short-Term Investments	13,150	
Notes Receivable	45,000	
Accounts Receivable	76,570	
Merchandise Inventory	156,750	
Prepaid Rent	2,000	
Prepaid Insurance	1,200	
Sales Supplies	426	
Office Supplies	97	
Land Held for Future Expansion	11,500	
Selling Fixtures	72,400	
Accumulated Depreciation, Selling Fixtures		$ 22,000
Office Equipment	24,100	
Accumulated Depreciation, Office Equipment		12,050
Trademark	4,000	
Accounts Payable		109,745
Salaries Payable		787
Interest Payable		600
Notes Payable (due in three years)		36,000
Common Stock, $1 par value, 20,000 shares authorized, issued, and outstanding		20,000
Paid-in Capital in Excess of Par Value		130,000
Retained Earnings		100,011

REQUIRED From the information provided, prepare a classified balance sheet.

LO7 Ratio Analysis: Liquidity and Profitability

P 4. Below is a summary of data from the income statements and balance sheets for Gamber Construction Supply, Inc., for 20x4 and 20x3.

	20x4	20x3
Current assets	$ 183,000	$ 155,000
Total assets	1,160,000	870,000
Current liabilities	90,000	60,000
Long-term liabilities	300,000	200,000
Stockholders' equity	670,000	520,000
Net sales	2,300,000	1,740,000
Net income	150,000	102,000

Total assets and stockholders' equity at the beginning of 20x3 were $680,000 and $420,000, respectively.

REQUIRED
1. Compute the following liquidity measures for 20x3 and 20x4: (a) working capital and (b) current ratio. Comment on the differences between the years.

2. Compute the following measures of profitability for 20x3 and 20x4: (a) profit margin, (b) asset turnover, (c) return on assets, (d) debt to equity ratio, and (e) return on equity. Comment on the change in performance from 20x3 to 20x4.

LO5 **Classified Financial**
LO6 **Statement Preparation**
LO7 **and Evaluation**

P 5. Sol Corporation is in the auto supply business. At the December 31, 20x6, year end, the following financial information was available from the income statement: administrative expenses, $161,600; cost of goods sold, $700,840; income taxes, $14,000; interest expense, $45,280; interest income, $5,600; net sales, $1,428,780; and selling expenses, $440,400.

The following information was available from the balance sheet (after closing entries were made): accounts payable, $65,200; accounts receivable, $209,600; accumulated depreciation, delivery equipment, $34,200; accumulated depreciation, store fixtures, $84,440; cash, $56,800; common stock, $1 par value, 20,000 shares authorized, issued, and outstanding, $20,000; delivery equipment, $177,000; inventory, $273,080; investment in securities (long-term), $112,000; investment in U.S. government securities (short-term), $79,200; long-term notes payable, $200,000; paid-in capital in excess of par value, $180,000; retained earnings, $518,600 (ending balance); notes payable (short-term), $100,000; prepaid expenses (short-term), $11,520; and store fixtures, $283,240.

Total assets and total stockholders' equity at December 31, 20x5, were $1,048,800 and $766,340, respectively, and dividends for the year were $120,000.

REQUIRED
1. From the information above, prepare (a) an income statement in single-step form, (b) a statement of retained earnings, and (c) a classified balance sheet.
2. From the statements you have prepared, compute the following measures: (a) working capital and current ratio (for liquidity); and (b) profit margin, asset turnover, return on assets, debt to equity ratio, and return on equity (for profitability).
3. Using the industry averages for the auto and home supply business in Figures 5-10 in this chapter, determine whether Sol Corporation needs to improve its liquidity or its profitability. Explain your answer, making recommendations as to specific areas on which Sol Corporation should concentrate.

Alternate Problems

LO3 **Accounting Conventions**

P 6. In each case below, accounting conventions *may* have been violated.
1. After careful study, Murphy Company, which has offices in forty states, has determined that in the future its method of depreciating office furniture should be changed. The new method is adopted for the current year, and the change is noted in the financial statements.
2. In the past, Bofti Corporation has recorded operating expenses in general accounts for each classification (e.g., Salaries Expense, Depreciation Expense, and Utilities Expense). Management has determined that despite the additional recordkeeping costs, the company's income statement should break down each operating expense into its components of selling expense and administrative expense.
3. Lilly Soo, the auditor of Norto Corporation, discovered that an official of the company had authorized the payment of a $1,000 bribe to a local government official. The management of Norto Corporation argued that because the item was so small in relation to the size of the company ($1,000,000 in sales), the illegal payment should not be disclosed.
4. Hayley's Bookstore built a small addition to its main building to house a new computer games section. Because no one could be sure that the computer games section would succeed, the accountant took a conservative approach and recorded the addition as an expense.
5. Since its origin ten years ago, Tor Company has used the same generally accepted inventory method. Because there has been no change in the inventory method, the company does not declare in its financial statements what inventory method it uses.

REQUIRED In each case, identify the convention that applies, state whether or not the treatment is in accord with the convention and generally accepted accounting principles, and briefly explain why.

LO6 Forms of the Income Statement

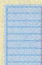

P 7. The income statements that follow are for Fitz Hardware Corporation.

Fitz Hardware Corporation
Income Statements
For the Years Ended July 31, 20x5 and 20x4

	20x5	20x4
Revenues		
Net sales	$464,200	$388,466
Interest income	420	500
Total revenues	$464,620	$388,966
Costs and expenses		
Cost of goods sold	$243,880	$198,788
Selling expenses	95,160	55,644
General and administrative expenses	90,840	49,286
Interest expense	5,600	1,100
Total costs and expenses	$435,480	$304,818
Income before income taxes	$ 29,140	$ 84,148
Income taxes	7,000	21,000
Net income	$ 22,140	$ 63,148
Earnings per share	$ 2.21	$ 6.31

REQUIRED
1. From the information provided, prepare a multistep income statement for 20x4 and 20x5 showing percentages of net sales for each component.
2. Did income from operations increase or decrease from 20x4 to 20x5? Write a short explanation of why this change occurred.
3. What effect did other revenues and expenses have on the change in income before income taxes? What action by Fitz Hardware's management probably accounted for this change?

LO7 Ratio Analysis: Liquidity and Profitability

P 8. Murillo Products Corporation has had poor operating results for the past two years. As the accountant for Murillo Products Corporation, you have the following information available to you:

	20x4	20x3
Current assets	$ 90,000	$ 70,000
Total assets	290,000	220,000
Current liabilities	40,000	20,000
Long-term liabilities	40,000	—
Stockholders' equity	210,000	200,000
Net sales	524,000	400,000
Net income	32,000	22,000

Total assets and stockholders' equity at the beginning of 20x3 were $180,000 and $160,000, respectively.

REQUIRED
1. Compute the following measures of liquidity for 20x3 and 20x4: (a) working capital and (b) current ratio. Comment on the differences between the years.

2. Compute the following measures of profitability for 20x3 and 20x4: (a) profit margin, (b) asset turnover, (c) return on assets, (d) debt to equity ratio, and (e) return on equity. Comment on the change in performance from 20x3 to 20x4.

Skills Development Cases

Conceptual Analysis

LO3 Accounting Conventions

SD 1. Central Parking, which operates a seven-story parking building in downtown Chicago, has a calendar year end. It serves daily and hourly parkers, as well as monthly parkers who pay a fixed monthly rate in advance. The company traditionally has recorded all cash receipts as revenues when received. Most monthly parkers pay in full during the month prior to that in which they have the right to park. The company's auditors have said that beginning in 20x3, the company should consider recording the cash receipts from monthly parking on an accrual basis, crediting Unearned Revenues. Total cash receipts for 20x3 were $2,500,000, and the cash receipts received in 20x3 and applicable to January 20x4 were $125,000. Discuss the relevance of the accounting conventions of consistency, materiality, and full disclosure to the decision to record the monthly parking revenues on an accrual basis.

LO3 Materiality

SD 2. Sophia Electronics, Inc., operates a chain of consumer electronics stores in the Atlanta area. This year the company achieved annual sales of $50 million, on which it earned a net income of $2 million. At the beginning of the year, management implemented a new inventory system that enabled it to track all purchases and sales. At the end of the year, a physical inventory revealed that the actual inventory was $80,000 below what the new system indicated it should be. The inventory loss, which probably resulted from shoplifting, is reflected in a higher cost of goods sold. The problem concerns management but seems to be less important to the company's auditors. What is materiality? Why might the inventory loss concern management more than it does the auditors? Do you think the amount is material?

Ethical Dilemma

LO4 Ethics and Financial Reporting

SD 3. Sensor Software, located outside Boston, develops computer software and licenses it to financial institutions. The firm uses an aggressive accounting method that records revenues from the software it has developed on a percentage of completion basis. Consequently, revenue for partially completed projects is recognized based on the proportion of the project that is completed. If a project is 50 percent completed, then 50 percent of the contracted revenue is recognized. In 20x4, preliminary estimates for a $5 million project are that the project is 75 percent complete. Because the estimate of completion is a matter of judgment, management asks for a new report showing the project to be 90 percent complete. The change will enable senior managers to meet their financial goals for the year and thus receive substantial year-end bonuses. Do you think management's action is ethical? If you were the company controller and were asked to prepare the new report, would you do it? What action would you take?

Group Activity: Use in-class groups to debate the ethics of the action.

LO4 Ethics and Financial Reporting

SD 4. The SEC is conducting an investigation into possible fraudulent accounting practices at Lucent Technologies, Inc. <www.lucent.com>. The probe focuses on whether Lucent improperly booked $679 million in revenue. The SEC is looking at how Lucent recognized revenue on sales to its distribution partners, who may not have sold the products or even may not have been able to sell the products. This practice is known as "stuffing the channels." In an adjustment, the company took back $452 million in revenue it had sent to its distribution partners but never actually sold to end customers. Normal accounting practice does not allow recording as revenue shipments to distributors on consignment—that is, with the right of return if not sold. It is not clear what rights of return exist in this case, but analysts have been critical of Lucent's aggressive practice. Lucent maintains the practice is legal.¹⁶ What is the difference between aggressive accounting and fraudulent financial reporting? Can Lucent's revenue recognition practice follow accounting rules but also be fraudulent?

Research Activity

LO4 Accounting and Fraud

SD 5. Most university and public libraries have access to indexes of leading newspapers, such as *The Wall Street Journal* and *The New York Times*, on CD-ROM. Go to a library and do a search for a recent year using the key words "accounting and fraud," "accounting and restatement," or "accounting and irregularities." Choose one of the articles you find and read it. What company is involved, and how is accounting connected with the fraud, restatement, or irregularity? Describe the situation. Does it involve an apparently legal or illegal activity? Does it involve fraudulent financial reporting? Explain your answer and be prepared to discuss it in class.

Decision-Making Practice

LO7 Financial Analysis for Loan Decision

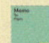

SD 6. Steve Sulong was recently promoted to loan officer at First National Bank. He has authority to issue loans up to $50,000 without approval from a higher bank official. This week two small companies, Handy Harvey, Inc., and Sheila's Fashions, Inc., have each submitted a proposal for a six-month, $50,000 loan. To prepare financial analyses of the two companies, Sulong has obtained the information summarized below.

Handy Harvey, Inc., is a local lumber and home improvement company. Because sales have increased so much during the past two years, Handy Harvey has had to raise additional working capital, especially as represented by receivables and inventory. The $50,000 loan is needed to assure the company of enough working capital for the next year. Handy Harvey began the year with total assets of $740,000 and stockholders' equity of $260,000. During the past year, the company had a net income of $40,000 on net sales of $760,000. Handy Harvey's unclassified balance sheet as of the current date appears as follows:

Assets		Liabilities and Stockholders' Equity	
Cash	$ 30,000	Accounts payable	$200,000
Accounts receivable (net)	150,000	Notes payable	
Inventory	250,000	(short term)	100,000
Land	50,000	Notes payable	
Buildings (net)	250,000	(long term)	200,000
Equipment (net)	70,000	Common stock	250,000
		Retained earnings	50,000
		Total liabilities and	
Total assets	$800,000	stockholders' equity	$800,000

Sheila's Fashions, Inc., has for three years been a successful clothing store for young professional women. The leased store is located in the downtown financial district. Sheila's loan proposal asks for $50,000 to pay for stocking a new line of women's suits during the coming season. At the beginning of the year, the company had total assets of $200,000 and total stockholders' equity of $114,000. Over the past year, the company earned a net income of $36,000 on net sales of $480,000. The firm's unclassified balance sheet at the current date is as follows:

Assets		Liabilities and Stockholders' Equity	
Cash	$ 10,000	Accounts payable	$ 80,000
Accounts receivable (net)	50,000	Accrued liabilities	10,000
Inventory	135,000	Common stock	50,000
Prepaid expenses	5,000	Retained earnings	100,000
Equipment (net)	40,000	Total liabilities and	
Total assets	$240,000	stockholders' equity	$240,000

1. Prepare a financial analysis of each company's liquidity before and after receiving the proposed loan. Also compute profitability ratios before and after, as appropriate. Write a brief summary of the effect of the proposed loan on each company's financial position.
2. Assume you are Sulong and can make a loan to only one of these companies. Write a memorandum to the bank's vice president outlining your decision and naming the company to which you would lend $50,000. Be sure to state what positive and negative factors could affect each company's ability to pay back the loan in the next year. Also indicate what other information of a financial or nonfinancial nature would be helpful in making a final decision.

FINANCIAL REPORTING AND ANALYSIS CASES

Interpreting Financial Reports

FRA 1.
LO7 Comparison of Profitability

Two of the largest chains of grocery stores in the United States are Albertson's Inc. <www.albertsons.com> and the Great Atlantic & Pacific Tea Company (A&P) <www.aptea.com>. In a recent fiscal year, Albertson's had a net income of $765 million, and A&P had a net income of $14 million. It is difficult to judge which company is more profitable from those figures alone because they do not take into account the relative sales, sizes, and investments of the companies. Data (in millions) to complete a financial analysis of the two companies follow:[17]

	Albertson's	A&P
Net sales	$36,762	$10,151
Beginning total assets	15,719	3,335
Ending total assets	16,078	3,309
Beginning total liabilities	10,017	2,489
Ending total liabilities	10,394	2,512
Beginning stockholders' equity	5,702	846
Ending stockholders' equity	5,684	797

1. Determine which company was more profitable by computing profit margin, asset turnover, return on assets, debt to equity ratio, and return on equity for the two companies. Comment on the relative profitability of the two companies.
2. What do the ratios tell you about the factors that go into achieving an adequate return on assets in the grocery industry? For industry data, refer to Figures 6 through 10 in this chapter.
3. How would you characterize the use of debt financing in the grocery industry and the use of debt by the two companies?

 Group Activity: Assign each ratio or company to a group and hold a class discussion.

FRA 2.
LO7 Evaluation of Profitability

Carla Cruz is the principal stockholder and president of Cruz Tapestries, Inc., which wholesales fine tapestries to retail stores. Because Cruz was not satisfied with the company earnings in 20x3, she raised prices in 20x4, increasing gross margin from sales from

30 percent in 20x3 to 35 percent in 20x4. Cruz is pleased that net income went up from 20x3 to 20x4, as shown in the following comparative income statements:

	20x4	20x3
Revenues		
Net sales	$611,300	$693,200
Costs and expenses		
Cost of goods sold	$397,345	$485,240
Selling and administrative expenses	154,199	152,504
Total costs and expenses	$551,544	$637,744
Income before income taxes	$ 59,756	$ 55,456
Income taxes	15,000	14,000
Net income	$ 44,756	$ 41,456

Total assets for Cruz Tapestries, Inc., at year end for 20x2, 20x3, and 20x4 were $623,390, $693,405, and $768,455, respectively.

Has Cruz Tapestries' profitability really improved? (**Hint:** Compute profit margin and return on assets, and comment.) What factors has Cruz overlooked in evaluating the profitability of the company? (**Hint:** Compute asset turnover and comment on the role it plays in profitability.)

FRA 3.
LO7 Financial Analysis with Industry Comparison

Exhibits 2 and 4 in this chapter contain the comparative balance sheet and income statement for Dell Computer Corporation <www.dell.com>. Assume you are the chief financial officer.

1. Compute liquidity ratios (working capital and current ratio) and profitability ratios (profit margin, asset turnover, return on assets, debt to equity ratio, and return on equity) for 2001 and 2002 and show the industry ratios (except working capital) from Figures 5 to 10 in this chapter. Use income from continuing operations and end-of-year assets and stockholders' equity to compute the ratios.
2. Write a memorandum to the board of directors in executive summary form describing changes in Dell's liquidity and profitability performance from 2001 to 2002 compared with the industry averages.

International Company

FRA 4.
LO5 Interpretation and Analysis
LO7 of British Financial Statements

Presented on the opposite page are the classified balance sheets for the British company GlaxoSmithKline PLC <www.gsk.com>, a pharmaceutical firm with marketing and manufacturing operations in 57 countries.[18]

In the United Kingdom, the format of classified financial statements usually differs from that used in the United States. To compare the financial statements of companies in different countries, it is important to know how to interpret a variety of formats.

1. For each line on GlaxoSmithKline's balance sheet, indicate the corresponding term that would be found on a U.S. balance sheet. (For this exercise, consider Provisions for liabilities and Charges to be long-term liabilities.) What is the focus or rationale behind the format of the U.K. balance sheet?
2. Assuming that GlaxoSmithKline earned a net income of £4,147 million and £2,543 million in 2000 and 1999, respectively, compute the current ratio, debt to equity

GlaxoSmithKline PLC and Subsidiaries
Consolidated Balance Sheets

	2000 £m	1999 £m
Goodwill	170	160
Intangible assets	966	926
Tangible assets	6,642	6,402
Investments	2,544	1,804
Fixed assets	**10,322**	**9,292**
Equity investments	171	52
Stocks	2,277	2,243
Debtors	5,399	4,828
Liquid investments	2,138	1,780
Cash at bank	1,283	579
Current assets	**11,268**	**9,482**
Loans and overdrafts	(2,281)	(2,819)
Other creditors	(6,803)	(5,629)
Creditors: amounts due within one year	**(9,084)**	**(8,448)**
Net current assets	**2,184**	**1,034**
Total assets less current liabilities	**12,506**	**10,326**
Loans	(1,751)	(1,897)
Other creditors	(143)	(147)
Creditors: amounts due after one year	**(1,894)**	**(2,044)**
Provisions for liabilities and charges	**(1,657)**	**(1,675)**
Net assets	**8,955**	**6,607**
Called up share capital	1,556	1,549
Share premium account	30	—
Other reserves	6,125	3,915
Equity shareholders' funds	**7,711**	**5,464**
Non-equity minority interest	1,039	961
Equity minority interests	205	182
Capital employed	**8,955**	**6,607**

ratio, return on assets, and return on equity for 2000 and 1999. (Use year-end amounts to compute ratios.)

Toys "R" Us Annual Report

FRA 5.

LO5 Reading and Analyzing an
LO6 Annual Report
LO7

Refer to the Toys "R" Us <www.tru.com> annual report in the Supplement to Chapter 1 to answer the following questions. (Note that 2001 refers to the year ended February 2, 2002, and 2002 refers to the year ended February 1, 2003.)

1. Consolidated balance sheets: (a) Did the amount of working capital increase or decrease from 2001 to 2002? By how much? (b) Did the current ratio improve from 2001 to 2002? (c) Does the company have long-term investments or intangible assets? (d) Did the debt to equity ratio of Toys "R" Us change from 2001 to 2002? (e) What is the contributed capital for 2002? How does contributed capital compare with retained earnings?
2. Consolidated statements of earnings: (a) Does Toys "R" Us use a multistep or single-step income statement? (b) Is it a comparative statement? (c) What is the trend of net earnings? (d) How significant are income taxes for Toys "R" Us? (e) Did the profit margin increase from 2001 to 2002? (f) Did asset turnover improve from 2001 to 2002? (g) Did the return on assets increase from 2001 to 2002? (h) Did the return on equity increase from 2001 to 2002? Total assets and total stockholders' equity for 2000 may be obtained from the financial highlights.
3. Multistep income statement: In the 1987 Toys "R" Us annual report, management stated that the company's "[operating] expense levels were among the best controlled in retailing [at] 18.8 percent. . . . We were able to operate with lower merchandise margins and still increase our earnings and return on sales."[19] Prepare a multistep income statement for Toys "R" Us down to income from operations for 2001 and 2002, and compute the ratios of gross margin, operating expenses, and income from operations to net sales. Comment on whether the company continued, as of 2002, to maintain the level of performance indicated by management in 1987. In 1987, gross margin was 31.2 percent and income from operations was 12.4 percent of net sales.

Comparison Case: Toys "R" Us and Walgreen Co.

FRA 6.

LO7 Financial Analysis
Comparison: Toys "R" Us vs.
Walgreens

Compare the financial performance of Toys "R" Us <www.tru.com> and Walgreens <www.walgreens.com> on the basis of liquidity and profitability for 2002 and 2001. Use the following ratios: working capital, current ratio, debt to equity ratio, profit margin, asset turnover, return on assets, and return on equity. In 2000, Walgreens' total assets were $7,103,700,000, and total stockholders' equity was $4,234,000,000. Comment on the relative performance of the two companies. (If you have done **FRA 5,** use the computations you made in that solution for Toys "R" Us.) In general, how does Walgreens' performance compare to Toys "R" Us with respect to liquidity and profitability? What distinguishes Walgreens' profitability performance from that of Toys "R" Us?

Fingraph® Financial Analyst™

FRA 7.

LO7 Analysis of Dell Computer
Corporation or Toys "R" Us

Choose one or both of the following analyses:

1. *Alternative to FRA 3:* Analyze the balance sheet and income statement of Dell Computer Corporation <www.dell.com> using Fingraph Financial Analyst CD-ROM software. To do this assignment, you will need to enter the data from Dell's financial statements shown in this chapter. Complete part 1 of **FRA 3.** Prepare the memorandum required in part 2 of **FRA 3** separately.
2. *Alternative to FRA 5:* Refer to the Toys "R" Us <www.tru.com> annual report in the Supplement to Chapter 1. Analyze the Toys "R" Us balance sheet and income statement using Fingraph Financial Analyst CD-ROM software. Your instructor will specify which year to analyze. Complete requirements 1, 2, and 3 of **FRA 5.**

Internet Case

LO7 Annual Reports and Financial Analysis

FRA 8. Select a large, well-known company and access its annual report online. Or, choose a company on the Needles Accounting Resource Center Web Site at http://accounting.college.hmco.com/students and use the links provided there to access the company's web site and its annual report. In the annual report of the company you have chosen, identify the four basic financial statements and the notes to the financial statements. Perform a liquidity analysis, including the calculation of working capital and the current ratio. Perform a profitability analysis, calculating profit margin, asset turnover, return on assets, debt to equity ratio, and return on equity. Be prepared to present your findings in class.

6

Chapter 6 introduces the operating cycle, the perpetual and periodic inventory systems, and internal control for merchandising businesses.

Merchandising Operations and Internal Control

Learning Objectives

LO1 Identify the management issues related to merchandising businesses.

LO2 Define and distinguish the terms of sale for merchandising transactions.

LO3 Prepare an income statement and record merchandising transactions under the perpetual inventory system.

LO4 Prepare an income statement and record merchandising transactions under the periodic inventory system.

LO5 Define *internal control* and its basic components, give examples of control activities, and describe the limitations of internal control.

LO6 Apply internal control activities to common merchandising transactions.

Supplemental Objective

SO7 Apply sales and purchases discounts to merchandising transactions.

DECISION POINT
A USER'S FOCUS

Target Stores <www.target.com> Merchandising businesses have two key decisions to make: the price at which they sell merchandise and the level of service they provide. A department store may set the price of its merchandise at a relatively high level and provide a great deal of service. A discount store, on the other hand, may price its merchandise at a relatively low level and provide limited service. Target Stores, a division of Target Corp., is a successful discount retailer, as the figures in the Financial Highlights show.[1] What decisions did Target Stores' management make about pricing and service to achieve this success?

Target distinguishes itself from other discounters by providing its customers with high-quality, name-brand merchandise, superior service, a convenient shopping experience, and competitive prices. Target's merchandise might be sold at full price in specialty stores; Target sells it at prices that are competitive with those of other discount stores that sell less well-known merchandise. Target's chief executive officer says, "We continue to open stores across the country. . . . Even in our most populated states, our market presence has expanded by 40 percent [since 1997] indicating ample opportunity for profitable growth well into the future."[2]

What decisions did Target's management make about pricing and service that resulted in Target's becoming a leading discount retailer?

Financial Highlights
(In millions, except stores and square feet)

	2002	2001
Revenues	**$43,917**	$39,826
Net earnings	**1,654**	$1,386
Stores	**1,475**	1,381
Retail square feet*	**176,525**	161,624

*In thousands, reflects total square feet, less office, warehouse, and vacant space.

MANAGEMENT ISSUES IN MERCHANDISING BUSINESSES

LO1 Identify the management issues related to merchandising businesses.

RELATED TEXT ASSIGNMENTS
Q: 1, 2, 3, 4
SE: 1
E: 1, 2
P: 1, 3, 7, 9
SD: 1, 2, 4, 5
FRA: 1, 2, 5, 6, 7, 8

A **merchandising business** earns income by buying and selling goods. Such a company, whether wholesale or retail, uses the same basic accounting methods as service companies, but the buying and selling of goods adds to the complexity of the process. As a foundation for discussing the accounting issues of merchandising businesses, we must first identify the management issues involved in running such a business. It is also important to note that analyses, systems, and controls for merchandising businesses are equally relevant to manufacturing companies.

CASH FLOW MANAGEMENT

Cash flow management involves planning a company's receipts and payments of cash. If a company is not able to pay its bills when they are due, it may be forced out of business. This is particularly true for merchandising businesses, which differ from service businesses in that they must have goods on hand so that they are available for sale to customers. These goods are called **merchandise inventory**.

KEY POINT: The operating cycle is average day's inventory on hand plus the average number of days to collect credit sales.

Merchandising businesses engage in a series of transactions called the **operating cycle**, which is illustrated in Figure 1. The transactions in the operating cycle consist of (1) purchases of merchandise inventory for cash or on credit, (2) payment for purchases made on credit, (3) sales of merchandise inventory for cash or on credit, and (4) collection of cash from credit sales. Purchases of merchandise are usually made on credit, so the merchandiser has a period of time before payment is due, but this period is generally less than the time it takes to sell the merchandise. To finance the inventory until it is sold and the resulting cash is collected, management must plan for cash flows from within the company or from borrowing.

The need for cash flow management is demonstrated in Figure 2, which shows the financing period. Sometimes referred to as the *cash gap*, the **financing period** is the amount of time from the purchase of inventory until it is sold and payment is collected, less the amount of time creditors give the company to pay for the inventory. Thus, if it takes 60 days to sell inventory, 60 days to collect for the sale, and creditors' payment terms are 30 days, the financing period is 90 days. During the financing period, the company will be without cash from this series of transactions and will need either to have funds available internally or to borrow from a bank.

FIGURE 1
The Operating Cycle of Merchandising Businesses

Video Case

Claire's Stores, Inc. <www.clairestores.com>

Objectives

- To become familiar with the nature of merchandising operations.
- To identify the management issues associated with a merchandising business.
- To show how gross margin and operating expenses affect the business goal of profitability.

Background for the Case

Claire's Stores, Inc. is a leading international retailer offering value-priced costume jewelry, accessories, and cosmetics to fashion-aware teens and young adults. Claire's Accessories is the company's core business. In the 1980s, the company sold its capital-intensive manufacturing businesses to concentrate on the specialty retailing of women's fashion accessories. The company has grown steadily and now has about 2,200 stores throughout North America, Europe, and Japan. Claire's Accessories stores are approximately 1,000 square feet in size in North America and 600 square feet in Europe and Japan. Claire's expansion into Europe has been particularly successful, with high store traffic and sales per square foot at 250 percent of that in North America. Keys to the company's success are the merchandising and marketing practices that reinforce its position as the place for customers to find new accessories. Constant product testing, test placement of successful items in all departments, and an efficient distribution system all enable Claire's to make quick responses to "what's new." The company's North American distribution center receives and ships merchandise on the same day, and the retail outlets receive shipments three to five times per week.

For more information about Claire's Stores, Inc., visit the company's web site through the Needles Accounting Resource Center Web Site at **http://accounting.college.hmco.com/students**.

Required

View the video on Claire's Stores, Inc., that accompanies this book. As you are watching the video, take notes related to the following questions:

1. All merchandising companies have inventories. What is inventory, and why is it important to implement controls over it? Identify the types of products that Claire's Accessories stores typically have in inventory and some ways in which the company might control its inventory.
2. All merchandising companies have an operating cycle. Describe the operating cycle and explain how Claire's successfully manages its operating cycle.
3. All merchandising companies try to achieve the goal of profitability by producing a satisfactory gross margin and maintaining acceptable levels of operating expenses. Describe how Claire's operations affect gross margin and operating expenses in a way that enables the company to achieve superior profitability.

---

www.dillards.com

www.target.com

The financing period for a merchandising company can be less than 120 days. For example, Dillard Dept. Stores, Inc., a successful chain of U.S. department stores, has a financing period of 101 days. It consists of inventory on hand for an average of 102 days, plus an average of 42 days to collect its receivables, minus an average of 43 days to pay for its merchandise. Target, on the other hand, has a much shorter

Figure 2
The Financing Period

> **STOP AND THINK!**
> Can a company have a "negative" financing period?
> *Yes, if its merchandise is held for a very short time, if its sales are made mostly for cash, or if it has long terms to pay its suppliers. For example, Dell makes its computers to order (resulting in small inventories), sells on credit cards (which reduces accounts receivable), and takes 30 days or more to pay its suppliers.* ■

KEY POINT: A sale takes place when title to the goods transfers to the buyer.

financing period, only 29 days. Its period consists of inventory on hand for an average of 61 days, plus an average of 20 days to collect its receivables, minus an average of 52 days to pay for its merchandise. Target derives its advantage from selling most of its merchandise for cash, which results in very low receivables.

As Target demonstrates, a company can help its cash flow by reducing its financing period. Many retailers, including Target, do this by selling as much as possible for cash. Cash sales include sales on bank credit cards, such as Visa or MasterCard, and on debit cards, which draw directly on the purchaser's bank account. They are considered cash sales because funds from them are available to the merchandiser immediately. In the case of credit sales, the company must wait a period of time before receiving the cash. Small retail stores may have mostly cash sales and very few credit sales, whereas large wholesale concerns may have almost all credit sales. Most merchandising concerns, however, have a combination of cash and credit sales.

PROFITABILITY MANAGEMENT

In addition to managing cash flow, management must achieve a satisfactory level of profitability. It must sell merchandise at a price that exceeds its cost by a sufficient margin to pay operating expenses and have enough left to provide sufficient income, or profitability. **Profitability management** is a complex activity that includes, first, achieving a satisfactory gross margin and, second, maintaining acceptable levels of operating expenses. Achieving a satisfactory gross margin depends on setting appropriate prices for merchandise and purchasing merchandise at favorable prices and terms. Maintaining acceptable levels of operating expenses depends on controlling expenses and operating efficiently.

KEY POINT: An operating budget is a financial plan for achieving the goal of profitability.

One of the more effective ways of controlling expenses is to use operating budgets. An **operating budget** reflects management's operating plans and consists of detailed listings of projected selling expenses and general and administrative expenses. At key times during the year and at the end of the year, management should compare the budget with actual expenses and make adjustments to operations as appropriate. Exhibit 1 shows an operating budget for Fenwick Fashions Corporation, a merchandising company that we use as an example throughout this chapter. Fenwick's total selling expenses exceeded the budget by only $80, but four of its selling expense categories exceeded the budget by a total of $2,080. Management should investigate the possibility that underspending in advertising of $2,000 hid inefficiencies and waste in other areas. Also, sales may have been penalized by not spending the budgeted amount on advertising. Total general and administrative expenses exceeded the budget by $6,904. Management should determine why large differences occurred for office salaries expense, insurance expense, and office supplies expense. The amount of insurance expense is usually set by the insurance company; thus, an error in the initial budgeting of insurance expense may have caused the unfavorable result. The operating budget helps management focus on specific areas that need attention.

CHOICE OF INVENTORY SYSTEM

Another issue the management of a merchandising business must address is the choice of inventory system. Management must choose the system or combination of systems that is best for achieving the company's goals. There are two basic systems of accounting for the many items in the merchandise inventory: the perpetual inventory system and the periodic inventory system.

KEY POINT: Under the perpetual inventory system, the Merchandise Inventory account and the Cost of Goods Sold account are updated with every sale.

Under the **perpetual inventory system**, continuous records are kept of the quantity and, usually, the cost of individual items as they are bought and sold. The detailed data available from the perpetual inventory system enable management to respond to customers' inquiries about product availability, to order inventory more effectively and thus avoid running out of stock, and to control the financial costs associated with investments in inventory. Under this system, the cost of each item is recorded in the Merchandise Inventory account when it is purchased. As mer-

EXHIBIT 1
An Example of an Operating Budget

Fenwick Fashions Corporation
Operating Budget
For the Year Ended December 31, 20x3

Operating Expenses	Budget	Actual	Difference Under (Over) Budget
Selling Expenses			
Sales Salaries Expense	$22,000	$22,500	($ 500)
Freight Out Expense	5,500	5,740	(240)
Advertising Expense	12,000	10,000	2,000
Insurance Expense, Selling	800	1,600	(800)
Store Supplies Expense	1,000	1,540	(540)
Total Selling Expenses	$41,300	$41,380	($ 80)
General and Administrative Expenses			
Office Salaries Expense	$23,000	$26,900	($3,900)
Insurance Expense, General	2,100	4,200	(2,100)
Office Supplies Expense	500	1,204	(704)
Depreciation Expense, Building	2,600	2,600	—
Depreciation Expense, Office Equipment	2,000	2,200	(200)
Total General and Administrative Expenses	$30,200	$37,104	($6,904)
Total Operating Expenses	$71,500	$78,484	($6,984)

KEY POINT: The valuation of ending inventory on the balance sheet is determined by multiplying the quantity of each inventory item by its unit cost.

chandise is sold, its cost is transferred from the Merchandise Inventory account to the Cost of Goods Sold account. Thus, at all times the balance of the Merchandise Inventory account equals the cost of goods on hand, and the balance in Cost of Goods Sold equals the cost of merchandise sold to customers.

Under the **periodic inventory system**, the inventory not yet sold, or on hand, is counted periodically, usually at the end of the accounting period. No detailed records of the inventory on hand are maintained during the accounting period. The figure for inventory on hand is accurate only on the balance sheet date. As soon as any purchases or sales are made, the inventory figure becomes a historical amount, and it remains so until the new ending inventory amount is entered at the end of the next accounting period.

Some retail and wholesale businesses use the periodic inventory system because it reduces the amount of clerical work. If a business is fairly small, management can maintain control over its inventory simply through observation or by using an offline system of cards or computer records. But for larger businesses, the lack of detailed records may lead to lost sales or high operating costs.

FOCUS ON BUSINESS TECHNOLOGY

Bar Codes—How Have They Influenced Choice of Inventory Systems?

Many grocery stores, which traditionally used the periodic inventory system, now employ bar coding to update the physical inventory as items are sold. At the checkout counter, the cashier scans the electronic marking on each product, called a *bar code* or *universal product code* (UPC), into the cash register, which is linked to a computer that records the sale. Bar coding has become common in all types of retail companies, and in manufacturing firms and hospitals as well. It has also become a major factor in the increased use of the perpetual inventory system. Interestingly, some retail businesses now use the perpetual inventory system for keeping track of the physical flow of inventory and the periodic inventory system for preparing their financial statements.

KEY POINT: Although computerization has made the perpetual inventory system more popular in recent years, a physical count still should be made periodically to ensure that the actual number of goods on hand matches the quantity indicated by the computer records.

Because of the difficulty and expense of accounting for the purchase and sale of each item, companies that sell items of low value in high volume have traditionally used the periodic inventory system. Examples of such companies are drugstores, automobile parts stores, department stores, and discount stores. In contrast, companies that sell items of high unit value, such as appliances or automobiles, have tended to use the perpetual inventory system. The distinction between high and low unit value for inventory systems has blurred considerably in recent years because of the widespread use of computers. Although the periodic inventory system is still widely used, use of the perpetual inventory system has increased greatly.

CONTROL OF MERCHANDISING OPERATIONS

Buying and selling, the principal transactions of merchandising businesses, involve assets—cash, accounts receivable, and merchandise inventory—that are vulnerable to theft and embezzlement. One reason for this vulnerability is that cash and inventory may be fairly easy to steal. Another is the difficulty of monitoring the large number of transactions (including cash receipts, receipts on account, payments for purchases, and receipts and shipments of inventory) in which these assets are usually involved. If a merchandising company does not take steps to protect its assets, it may suffer high losses of cash and inventory. Management's responsibility is to establish an environment, accounting systems, and control procedures that will protect the company's assets. These systems and procedures are called *internal controls*.

Maintaining control over merchandise inventory is facilitated by taking a **physical inventory.** This process involves an actual count of all merchandise on hand. It can be a difficult task because it is easy to accidentally omit items or to count them twice. A physical inventory must be taken under both the periodic and the perpetual inventory systems. Under the perpetual inventory system, the records need to be compared with the physical inventory to determine whether any inventory shortages exist.

Merchandise inventory includes all goods intended for sale that are owned by a business, regardless of where they are located—on shelves, in storerooms, in warehouses, or in trucks between warehouses and stores. It also includes goods in transit from suppliers if title to the goods has passed to the merchant. Ending inventory does not include merchandise that has been sold but not yet delivered to customers or goods that cannot be sold because they are damaged or obsolete. If the damaged or obsolete goods can be sold at a reduced price, however, they should be included in ending inventory at their reduced value.

The actual count is usually taken after the close of business on the last day of the fiscal year. To facilitate taking the physical inventory, many companies end their fiscal year in a slow season, when inventories are at relatively low levels. Retail department stores often end their fiscal year in January or February, for example. After hours, at night, or on the weekend, employees count all items and record the results on numbered inventory tickets or sheets, following procedures to ensure no items will be missed. Sometimes a store closes for all or part of a day for inventory taking. The use of bar coding to take inventory electronically has greatly facilitated the process in many companies.

ENRICHMENT NOTE: Inventory shortages can result from honest mistakes, such as accidentally tagging inventory with the wrong number.

Most companies experience losses of merchandise inventory from spoilage, shoplifting, and theft by employees. When such losses occur, the periodic inventory system provides no means of identifying them because the costs are automatically included in the cost of goods sold. For example, assume that a company has lost $1,250 in stolen merchandise during an accounting period. When the physical inventory is taken, the missing items are not in stock, so they cannot be counted. Because the ending inventory does not contain these items, the amount subtracted from goods available for sale is less than it would be if the goods were in stock. The cost of goods sold, then, is overstated by $1,250. In a sense, the cost of goods sold is inflated by the amount of merchandise that has been lost.

KEY POINT: An adjustment to the Merchandise Inventory account will be needed if the physical inventory reveals a difference between the actual inventory and the amount in the records.

The perpetual inventory system makes it easier to identify such losses. Because the Merchandise Inventory account is continuously updated for sales, purchases, and returns, the loss will show up as the difference between the inventory records and the physical inventory taken at the end of the accounting period. Once the amount of the loss has been identified, the ending inventory is updated by crediting the Merchandise Inventory account. The offsetting debit is usually an increase in Cost of Goods Sold because the loss is considered a cost that reduces the company's gross margin.

 Check out ACE for a Review Quiz at http://accounting.college.hmco.com/students.

TERMS OF SALE

LO2 Define and distinguish the terms of sale for merchandising transactions.

RELATED TEXT ASSIGNMENTS
Q: 5, 6, 16
SE: 2, 7
E: 3

KEY POINT: A trade discount applies to the list or catalogue price. A sales discount applies to the sales price.

ENRICHMENT NOTE: Early collection also has the advantage of reducing the probability of a customer's defaulting.

When goods are sold on credit, both parties should understand the amount and timing of payment as well as other terms of the purchase, such as who pays delivery charges and what warranties or rights of return apply. Sellers quote prices in different ways. Many merchants quote the price at which they expect to sell their goods. Others, particularly manufacturers and wholesalers, quote prices as a percentage (usually 30 percent or more) off their list or catalogue prices. Such a reduction is called a **trade discount**. For example, if an article is listed at $1,000 with a trade discount of 40 percent, or $400, the seller records the sale at $600 and the buyer records the purchase at $600. The seller may raise or lower the trade discount depending on the quantity purchased. The list or catalogue price and related trade discount are used only to arrive at the agreed-upon price; they do not appear in the accounting records.

The terms of sale are usually printed on the sales invoice and thus constitute part of the sales agreement. Customary terms differ from industry to industry. In some industries, payment is expected in a short period of time, such as 10 or 30 days. In these cases, the invoice is marked "n/10" ("net 10") or "n/30" ("net 30"), meaning that the amount of the invoice is due either 10 days or 30 days after the invoice date. If the invoice is due 10 days after the end of the month, it is marked "n/10 eom."

FOCUS ON BUSINESS TECHNOLOGY

How Are Web Sales Doing?
In spite of the well-publicized dot-com meltdown and the demise of "pure-play" Internet retailers like eToys.com and Pets.com, merchandise sales over the Internet are thriving. Internet sales amounted to $44.5 billion in 2001 and were expected to double in the next few years. As it has turned out, the most successful Internet retailing companies are established retailers that use the Internet to enhance their current operations. For example, mail-order catalogue companies like Lands' End <www.landsend.com> and L.L. Bean <www.llbean.com> have profitable Internet operations. Circuit City <www.circuitcity.com> allows customers to purchase online and pick up the products at stores near their homes. Office Depot <www.officedepot.com>, which focuses primarily on business-to-business Internet sales, has set up customized web pages for 37,000 corporate clients. These web sites allow customers to make online purchases or to check store inventories.³ Although Internet transactions are recorded in the same way as on-site transactions, the technology adds a level of complexity to the transaction.

In some industries, it is customary to give a discount for early payment. This discount, called a **sales discount**, is intended to increase the seller's liquidity by reducing the amount of money tied up in accounts receivable. An invoice that offers a sales discount might be labeled "2/10, n/30," which means that the buyer either can pay the invoice within 10 days of the invoice date and take a 2 percent discount or can wait 30 days and pay the full amount of the invoice. It is almost always advantageous for a buyer to take the discount because the saving of 2 percent over a period of 20 days (from the eleventh day to the thirtieth day) represents an effective annual rate of 36.5 percent (365 days ÷ 20 days × 2% = 36.5%). Most companies would be better off borrowing money to take the discount. The practice of giving sales discounts has been declining because it is costly to the seller and because, from the buyer's viewpoint, the amount of the discount is usually very small in relation to the price of the purchase. Accounting for sales discounts is covered in supplemental objective 7.

In some industries, the seller usually pays transportation costs and charges a price that includes those

> **STOP AND THINK!**
> Assume a large shipment of uninsured merchandise to your company was destroyed when the delivery truck had an accident and burned. Would you want the terms to be FOB shipping point or FOB destination?
>
> *You would want the terms to be FOB destination because the loss of merchandise would be the responsibility of the seller. If the terms were FOB shipping point, the merchandise would belong to you when it left the seller and would be your loss.* ■

costs. In other industries, it is customary for the purchaser to pay transportation charges. Special terms designate whether the seller or the purchaser pays the freight charges. **FOB shipping point** means that the seller places the merchandise "free on board" at the point of origin and the buyer bears the shipping costs. The title to the merchandise passes to the buyer at that point. For example, when the sales agreement for the purchase of a car says "FOB factory," the buyer must pay the freight from where the car was made to wherever he or she is located, and the buyer owns the car from the time it leaves the factory.

On the other hand, **FOB destination** means that the seller bears the transportation costs to the place where the merchandise is delivered. The seller retains title until the merchandise reaches its destination and usually prepays the shipping costs, in which case the buyer makes no accounting entry for freight. The effects of these special shipping terms are summarized as follows:

Shipping Term	Where Title Passes	Who Pays the Cost of Transportation
FOB shipping point	At origin	Buyer
FOB destination	At destination	Seller

Many retailers allow customers to charge their purchases to a third-party company that the customer will pay later. These transactions are normally handled with credit cards. Five of the most widely used credit cards are American Express, Discover Card, Diners Club, MasterCard, and Visa. The customer establishes credit with the lender (the credit card issuer) and receives a plastic card to use in making charge purchases. If the seller accepts the card, an invoice is prepared and signed by the customer at the time of the sale. The sale is communicated to the seller's bank, resulting in a cash deposit in the seller's bank account. Thus, the seller does not have to establish the customer's credit, collect from the customer, or tie up money in accounts receivable. As payment, the lender, rather than paying the total amount of the credit card sales, takes a discount of 2 to 6 percent. The discount is a selling expense for the merchandiser. For example, assume that a restaurant made sales of $1,000 on Visa credit cards and that Visa takes a 4 percent discount on the sales. Assume also that the sales invoices are deposited in a special Visa bank account in the name of the company, in much the same way that checks from cash sales are deposited. The sales are recorded as follows:

```
A = L + OE    Cash                                960
+        −    Credit Card Discount Expense         40
         +        Sales                                      1,000
                    Made sales on Visa cards
```

✓ Check out ACE for a Review Quiz at http://accounting.college.hmco.com/students.

APPLYING THE PERPETUAL INVENTORY SYSTEM

LO3 Prepare an income statement and record merchandising transactions under the perpetual inventory system.

RELATED TEXT ASSIGNMENTS
Q: 7, 8, 9, 10, 14, 15
SE: 3
E: 4, 5, 6
P: 1, 2, 7, 8
SD: 4, 5
FRA: 1, 2, 7, 8

Exhibit 2 shows the income statement for Fenwick Fashions Corporation as it would appear if the company used the perpetual inventory system. The focal point of this income statement is cost of goods sold, which is deducted from net sales to arrive at gross margin. Under the perpetual inventory system, this account is continually updated during the accounting period as purchases, sales, and other inventory transactions take place. The Merchandise Inventory account on the balance sheet is updated at the same time.

TRANSACTIONS RELATED TO PURCHASES OF MERCHANDISE

The following sections illustrate the recording of typical transactions related to purchases of merchandise under the perpetual inventory system. Transactions related to sales made by Fenwick Fashions Corporation follow.

EXHIBIT 2
Income Statement Under the Perpetual Inventory System

Fenwick Fashions Corporation
Income Statement
For the Year Ended December 31, 20x3

Net sales		$239,325
Cost of goods sold*		131,360
Gross margin		$107,965
Operating Expenses		
Selling expenses	$41,380	
General and administrative expenses	37,104	
Total operating expenses		78,484
Income before income taxes		$ 29,481
Income taxes		5,000
Net income		$ 24,481

*Freight in has been included in cost of goods sold.

KEY POINT: The Merchandise Inventory account is increased when a purchase is made.

A = L + OE
+   +

● **STOP AND THINK!**
Under the perpetual inventory system, the Merchandise Inventory account is constantly updated. What would cause it to have the wrong balance?
The balance would be wrong if an error were made in updating the account or if merchandise had been lost or stolen. ■

A = L + OE
+   −

KEY POINT: Freight in is included in cost of goods sold on the income statement, and freight out expense appears as a selling expense.

Purchases of Merchandise on Credit

Oct. 3 Received merchandise purchased on credit from Neebok Company, invoice dated October 1, terms n/10, FOB shipping point, $4,890.

Oct. 3 Merchandise Inventory   4,890
          Accounts Payable   4,890
          Purchased merchandise from
          Neebok Company, terms n/10, FOB
          shipping point, invoice dated Oct. 1

Under the perpetual inventory system, the cost of merchandise purchased is placed in the Merchandise Inventory account at the time of purchase.

Transportation Costs on Purchases

Oct. 4 Received bill from Transfer Freight Company for transportation costs on October 3 shipment, invoice dated October 1, terms n/10, $160.

Oct. 4 Freight In   160
          Accounts Payable   160
          Received transportation charges on
          Oct. 3 purchase, Transfer Freight
          Company, terms n/10,
          invoice dated Oct. 1

Freight in, also called *transportation in*, is the transportation cost of receiving merchandise. Transportation costs are accumulated in a Freight In account because most shipments contain multiple items. It is usually not practical to identify the specific cost of shipping each item of inventory. In Exhibit 2, freight in is included in cost of goods sold. Theoretically, freight in should be allocated between ending inventory and cost of goods sold, but most companies choose to include the cost of freight in with the cost of goods sold on the income statement because it is a relatively small amount.

In some cases, the seller pays the freight charges and bills them to the buyer as a separate item on the invoice. When this occurs, the entry is the same as in the October 3 example, except that an additional debit is made to Freight In for the amount of the freight charges and Accounts Payable is increased by a like amount.

Purchases Returns and Allowances

Oct. 6 Returned merchandise received from Neebok Company on October 3 for credit, $480.

A = L + OE
−   −

Oct. 6	Accounts Payable	480	
	Merchandise Inventory		480
	Returned merchandise from purchase of Oct. 3 to Neebok Company for full credit		

If a seller sends the wrong product or one that is otherwise unsatisfactory, the buyer may be allowed to return the item for a cash refund or credit on account, or the buyer may be given an allowance off the sales price. Under the perpetual inventory system, the returned merchandise is removed from the Merchandise Inventory account.

Payments on Account

Oct. 10 Paid in full the amount due to Neebok Company for the purchase of October 3, part of which was returned on October 6.

A = L + OE
−   −

Oct. 10	Accounts Payable	4,410	
	Cash		4,410
	Made payment on account to Neebok Company $4,890 − $480 = $4,410		

TRANSACTIONS RELATED TO SALES OF MERCHANDISE

KEY POINT: The Cost of Goods Sold account is increased and the Merchandise Inventory account is decreased when a sale is made.

Under the perpetual inventory system, at the time of a sale, the cost of the merchandise is transferred from the Merchandise Inventory account to the Cost of Goods Sold account. In the case of a return of sold merchandise, the cost of the merchandise is transferred from Cost of Goods Sold back to Merchandise Inventory. Transactions related to sales made by Fenwick Fashions follow.

Sales of Merchandise on Credit

Oct. 7 Sold merchandise on credit to Gonzales Distributors, terms n/30, FOB destination, $1,200; the cost of the merchandise was $720.

A = L + OE
+   +

Oct. 7	Accounts Receivable	1,200	
	Sales		1,200
	Sold merchandise to Gonzales Distributors, terms n/30, FOB destination		

A = L + OE
−   −

	Cost of Goods Sold (EXPENSE)	720	
	Merchandise Inventory (DECREASED INVENTORY)		720
	Transferred cost of merchandise inventory sold to Cost of Goods Sold account		

RELIEVE INVENTORY

Under the perpetual inventory system, two entries are necessary. First, the sale is recorded. Second, Cost of Goods Sold is updated by a transfer from Merchandise Inventory. In the case of cash sales, Cash rather than Accounts Receivable is debited for the amount of the sale.

Payment of Delivery Costs

Oct. 8 Paid transportation costs for the sale on October 7, $78.

A = L + OE
−   −

Oct. 8	Freight Out Expense	78	
	Cash		78
	Paid delivery costs on Oct. 7 sale		

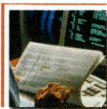

Focus on Business Practice

Are Sales Returns Worth Accounting For?

Some industries routinely have a high percentage of sales returns. More than 6 percent of all nonfood items sold in stores are eventually returned to vendors. This amounts to more than $100 billion a year, or more than the gross national product of two-thirds of the world's nations.[4] Book publishers like Simon & Schuster <www.simonsays.com> often have returns as high as 30 to 50 percent of books shipped because to gain the attention of potential buyers, large numbers of copies must be distributed to various outlets. Magazine publishers like AOL Time Warner <www.aoltw.com> expect to sell no more than 35 to 38 percent of the magazines they send to newsstands and other outlets.[5] In all these businesses, it pays for management to scrutinize the Sales Returns and Allowances account for ways to reduce returns and increase profitability.

A seller will often absorb delivery or freight out costs in the belief that doing so will facilitate the sale of its products. These costs are accumulated in an account called **Freight Out Expense**, or *Delivery Expense*, which is shown as a selling expense on the income statement.

Returns of Merchandise Sold

Oct. 9   Return of merchandise sold on October 7 accepted from Gonzales Distributors for full credit and returned to merchandise inventory, $300; the cost of the merchandise was $180.

A = L + OE
−   −

Oct. 9	Sales Returns and Allowances	300	
	Accounts Receivable		300
	Accepted returns of merchandise from Gonzales Distributors		

A = L + OE
+   +

Oct. 9	Merchandise Inventory	180	
	Cost of Goods Sold		180
	Transferred cost of merchandise returned to the Merchandise Inventory account		

KEY POINT: Because the Sales account is established with a credit, its contra account, Sales Returns and Allowances, is established with a debit.

Returns and allowances to customers for wrong or unsatisfactory merchandise are often an indicator of customer dissatisfaction. Such amounts are accumulated in a **Sales Returns and Allowances** account, which gives management a readily available measure of unsatisfactory products and dissatisfied customers. This contra-revenue account has a normal debit balance and is deducted from sales on the income statement. Under the perpetual inventory system, the cost of the merchandise must also be transferred from the Cost of Goods Sold account back into the Merchandise Inventory account. If an allowance is made instead of accepting a return, or if the merchandise cannot be returned to inventory and resold, this transfer is not made.

Receipts on Account

Nov. 5   Received payment in full from Gonzales Distributors for sale of merchandise on October 7, less the return on October 9.

A = L + OE
+
−

Nov. 5	Cash	900	
	Accounts Receivable		900
	Received on account from Gonzales Distributors		
	$1,200 − $300 = $900		

 Check out ACE for a Review Quiz at http://accounting.college.hmco.com/students.

Applying the Periodic Inventory System

WILL NOT BE TESTED ON PERIODIC SYSTEM — OMIT

LO4 Prepare an income statement and record merchandising transactions under the periodic inventory system.

RELATED TEXT ASSIGNMENTS
Q: 11, 12, 13, 14, 15
SE: 4, 5, 6
E: 7, 8, 9, 10
P: 3, 4, 6, 9, 10
SD: 4, 5
FRA: 1, 4

Exhibit 3 shows the income statement for Fenwick Fashions Corporation as it would appear if the company used the periodic inventory system. A major feature of this income statement is the computation of cost of goods sold. Cost of goods sold must be computed because it is not updated for purchases, sales, and other transactions during the accounting period, as it is under the perpetual inventory system. Figure 3 illustrates the components of cost of goods sold.

To calculate cost of goods sold, the **goods available for sale** must first be determined. The goods available for sale during the year is the sum of two factors, beginning inventory and the net cost of purchases during the year. In this case, the goods available for sale is $179,660 ($52,800 + $126,860).

If a company sold all the goods available for sale during an accounting period, the cost of goods sold would equal the goods available for sale. In most businesses, however, some merchandise remains unsold and on hand at the end of the period. This merchandise, or ending inventory, must be deducted from the goods available for sale to determine the cost of goods sold. In the case of Fenwick Fashions Corporation, the ending inventory on December 31, 20x3, is $48,300. Thus, the cost of goods sold is $131,360 ($179,660 − $48,300).

An important component of the cost of goods sold section is **net cost of purchases**, which consists of net purchases plus any freight charges on the purchases. **Net purchases** equal total purchases less any deductions, such as purchases returns

---

EXHIBIT 3
Income Statement Under the Periodic Inventory System

ENRICHMENT NOTE:
Most published financial statements are condensed, eliminating much of the detail shown here.

Study COGS

Fenwick Fashions Corporation
Income Statement
For the Year Ended December 31, 20x3

Net sales		$239,325
Cost of goods sold		
Merchandise inventory, December 31, 20x2		$ 52,800 *BEGINNING*
Purchases	$126,400	
Less purchases returns and allowances	7,776	
Net purchases	$118,624	
Freight in	8,236	
Net cost of purchases		126,860 + 52,800
Goods available for sale		$179,660
Less merchandise inventory, December 31, 20x3		48,300
Cost of goods sold		131,360
Gross margin		$107,965
Operating expenses		
Selling expenses	$ 41,380	
General and administrative expenses	37,104	
Total operating expenses		78,484
Income before income taxes		$ 29,481
Income taxes		5,000
Net income		$ 24,481

FIGURE 3
The Components of Cost of Goods Sold

Beginning inventory 12/31/20x2: $52,800

Net cost of purchases for 20x3: $126,860

Cost of goods available for sale: $179,660

Cost of goods sold in 20x3: $131,360 — Merchandise sold to customers

Ending inventory 12/31/20x3: $48,300 — Merchandise carried over to next year

● **STOP AND THINK!**
Why is a physical inventory needed under both the periodic and perpetual inventory systems?

Under the periodic inventory system, a physical inventory is needed to determine the cost of goods sold. Under the perpetual inventory system, a physical inventory is required to verify the inventory as shown in the accounting records. ■

and allowances and any discounts allowed by suppliers for early payment (see supplemental objective 7). Because transportation charges, or freight in, are a necessary cost of receiving merchandise for sale, they are added to net purchases to arrive at the net cost of purchases, as shown in Exhibit 3.

TRANSACTIONS RELATED TO PURCHASES OF MERCHANDISE

The primary difference between the perpetual and periodic inventory systems is that in the perpetual inventory system, the Merchandise Inventory account is adjusted each time a purchase, sale, or other inventory transaction occurs, whereas in the periodic inventory system, the Merchandise Inventory account stays at its beginning balance until the physical inventory is recorded at the end of the period. In the periodic system, a Purchases account is used to accumulate the purchases of merchandise during the accounting period, and a Purchases Returns and Allowances account is used to accumulate returns of and allowances on purchases.

The following sections illustrate how purchase transactions made by Fenwick Fashions Corporation would be recorded under the periodic inventory system.

KEY POINT: The Purchases account is increased when a purchase is made under the periodic inventory system.

A = L + OE
     +   −

Purchases of Merchandise on Credit

Oct. 3   Received merchandise purchased on credit from Neebok Company, invoice dated October 1, terms n/10, FOB shipping point, $4,890.

Oct. 3   Purchases   4,890
            Accounts Payable   4,890
                Purchased merchandise from Neebok
                Company, terms n/10, FOB shipping
                point, invoice dated Oct. 1

Purchases is a temporary account used under the periodic inventory system. Its sole purpose is to accumulate the total cost of merchandise purchased for resale during an accounting period. (Purchases of other assets, such as equipment, are recorded in the appropriate asset account, not in the Purchases account.) The Purchases account does not indicate whether merchandise has been sold or is still on hand.

Transportation Costs on Purchases

Oct. 4   Received bill from Transfer Freight Company for transportation costs on October 3 shipment, invoice dated October 1, terms n/10, $160.

A = L + OE
     +   −

Oct. 4   Freight In   160
            Accounts Payable   160
                Received transportation charges on Oct. 3
                purchase, Transfer Freight Company,
                terms n/10, invoice dated Oct. 1

Transportation costs on purchases are usually accumulated in a Freight In account. In some cases, the seller pays the freight charges and bills them to the buyer as a separate item on the invoice. When this occurs, the entry is the same as in the October 3 example, except that an additional debit is made to Freight In for the amount of the freight charges and Accounts Payable is increased by a like amount.

Purchases Returns and Allowances

ENRICHMENT NOTE: Accounts such as Purchases and Purchases Returns and Allowances are used only in conjunction with a periodic inventory system.

Oct. 6 Returned merchandise received from Neebok Company on October 3 for credit, $480.

A = L + OE
−   +

Oct. 6 Accounts Payable   480
        Purchases Returns and Allowances   480
           Returned merchandise from purchase
           of Oct. 3 to Neebok Company for
           full credit

KEY POINT: Because the Purchases account is established with a debit, its contra account, Purchases Returns and Allowances, is established with a credit.

If a seller sends the wrong product or one that is otherwise unsatisfactory, the buyer may be allowed to return the item for a cash refund or credit on account, or the buyer may be given an allowance off the sales price. Under the periodic inventory system, the amount of the return or allowance is recorded in the **Purchases Returns and Allowances** account. This account is a contra-purchases account with a normal credit balance, and it is deducted from purchases on the income statement.

Payments on Account

Oct. 10 Paid in full the amount due to Neebok Company for the purchase of October 3, part of which was returned on October 6.

A = L + OE
−   −

Oct. 10 Accounts Payable   4,410
        Cash   4,410
           Made payment on account to
           Neebok Company
           $4,890 − $480 = $4,410

TRANSACTIONS RELATED TO SALES OF MERCHANDISE

The Cost of Goods Sold account, which is updated for sales and returns under the perpetual inventory system, is not used under the periodic inventory system because the Merchandise Inventory account is not updated until the end of the accounting period. Transactions related to sales made by Fenwick Fashions Corporation follow.

Sales of Merchandise on Credit

Oct. 7 Sold merchandise on credit to Gonzales Distributors, terms n/30, FOB destination, $1,200.

A = L + OE
+   +

Oct. 7 Accounts Receivable   1,200
        Sales   1,200
           Sold merchandise to Gonzales
           Distributors, terms n/30,
           FOB destination

In the case of cash sales, Cash rather than Accounts Receivable is debited for the amount of the sale.

Payment of Delivery Costs

Oct. 8 Paid transportation costs for the sale on October 7, $78.

A = L + OE
−   −

Oct. 8 Freight Out Expense   78
        Cash   78
           Paid delivery costs on Oct. 7 sale

Delivery costs are accumulated in the Freight Out Expense account. This account is shown as a selling expense on the income statement.

Returns of Merchandise Sold

Oct. 9 Return of Merchandise sold on October 7 accepted from Gonzales Distributors for full credit and returned to merchandise inventory, $300.

A = L + OE
−   −

Oct. 9   Sales Returns and Allowances   300
             Accounts Receivable   300
             Accepted return of merchandise from
             Gonzales Distributors

Returns and allowances to customers for wrong or unsatisfactory merchandise are accumulated in the Sales Returns and Allowances account. This account is a contra-revenue account with a normal debit balance and is deducted from sales on the income statement.

Receipts on Account

Nov. 5 Received payment in full from Gonzales Distributors for sale of merchandise on October 7, less the return on October 9.

A = L + OE
+
−

Nov. 5   Cash   900
             Accounts Receivable   900
             Received on account from
             Gonzales Distributors
             $1,200 − $300 = $900

✓ Check out ACE for a Review Quiz at http://accounting.college.hmco.com/students.

INTERNAL CONTROL: BASIC COMPONENTS AND CONTROL ACTIVITIES

LO5 Define *internal control* and its basic components, give examples of control activities, and describe the limitations of internal control.

RELATED TEXT ASSIGNMENTS
Q: 17, 18, 19, 20
SE: 8, 9
E: 11, 12, 13
P: 5
SD: 4, 5
FRA: 3

A merchandising company can have inaccurate accounting records as well as high losses of cash and inventory if it does not take steps to protect its assets. The best way to do this is to set up and maintain a good system of internal control.

MANAGEMENT'S RESPONSIBILITY FOR INTERNAL CONTROL

Management is responsible for establishing a satisfactory system of internal control. **Internal control** is defined as all the policies and procedures management uses to ensure the reliability of financial reporting, compliance with laws and regulations, and the effectiveness and efficiency of operations. In other words, management must safeguard the firm's assets and have reliable accounting records. It must ensure that employees comply with legal requirements and operate the company in the best way possible.

Management comments on its responsibility and effectiveness in achieving the goals of internal control in the "Report of Management" in the company's annual report to stockholders. A portion of this statement from the annual report of Circuit City Stores, Inc., follows:

www.circuitcity.com

> Management is responsible for maintaining an internal control structure designed to provide reasonable assurance that the books and records reflect the transactions of the Company and that the Company's established policies and procedures are carefully followed. Because of inherent limitations in any system, there can be no absolute assurance that errors or irregularities will not occur. Nevertheless, management believes that the internal control structure provides reasonable assurance that assets are safeguarded and that financial information is objective and reliable.[6]

COMPONENTS OF INTERNAL CONTROL

To accomplish the objectives of internal control, management must establish five interrelated components of internal control:[7]

1. *Control environment*   The **control environment** is created by the overall attitude, awareness, and actions of management. It includes management's integrity and ethics, philosophy and operating style, organizational structure, method of assigning authority and responsibility, and personnel policies and practices. Personnel should be qualified to handle responsibilities, which means that employees must be trained and informed. For example, the manager of a retail store should train employees to follow prescribed procedures for handling cash sales, credit card sales, and returns and refunds.

2. *Risk assessment*   **Risk assessment** is the identification of areas in which risks of loss of assets or inaccuracies in the accounting records are high so that adequate controls can be implemented. Among the greater risks in a retail store are that employees will take cash or that customers will shoplift merchandise.

3. *Information and communication*   **Information and communication** relates to the accounting system established by management to identify, assemble, analyze, classify, record, and report a company's tramsactions, and to the need for clear communication of individual responsibilities in performing the accounting functions.

4. *Control activities*   **Control activities** are the policies and procedures management puts in place to see that its directives are carried out. Control activities are discussed in more detail below.

5. *Monitoring*   **Monitoring** involves management's regular assessment of the quality of internal control, including periodic review of compliance with all policies and procedures. For example, large companies often have a staff of internal auditors who review the company's system of internal control to determine if it is working properly and if procedures are being followed. In smaller businesses, owners and managers conduct these reviews.

● **STOP AND THINK!**
Which of the following accounts would be assigned a higher level of risk: Buildings or Merchandise Inventory?
Merchandise Inventory would because there is a greater risk of human error in recording the large number of transactions involved and because there is a greater risk of theft. ■

CONTROL ACTIVITIES

Control activities are a principal way in which internal control is implemented in an accounting information system. They safeguard a company's assets and ensure the reliability of accounting records. These control activities include the following:

1. *Authorization*   All transactions and activities should be properly authorized by management. In a retail store, for example, some transactions, such as normal cash sales, are authorized routinely; others, such as issuing a refund, may require a manager's approval.

2. *Recording transactions*   To facilitate preparation of financial statements and to establish accountability for assets, all transactions should be recorded. For example, in a retail store, the cash register records sales, refunds, and other transactions internally on a paper tape or computer disk so that the cashier can be held responsible for the cash received and the merchandise removed during his or her shift.

3. *Documents and records*   Using well-designed documents helps ensure the proper recording of transactions. For example, to ensure that all transactions are recorded, invoices and other documents should be prenumbered, and all numbers should be accounted for.

4. *Physical controls*   Physical controls permit access to assets only with management's authorization. For example, retail stores should use cash registers, and only the cashier responsible for the cash in a register should have access to it. Other employees should not be able to open the cash drawer if the cashier is not present. Likewise, warehouses and storerooms should be accessible only to

FOCUS ON BUSINESS ETHICS

Which Frauds Are Most Common?

A survey of 5,000 large U.S. businesses disclosed that 21 percent suffered frauds in excess of $1 million. The most common were credit card frauds, check frauds, inventory theft, false invoices and phantom vendors, and expense account abuse. Major factors in allowing these frauds to take place were poor internal controls, management override of internal controls, and collusion. The most common methods of detection were notification by an employee, internal controls, internal auditor review, notification by a customer, and accidental discovery. Companies successful in preventing fraud have a good system of internal control and a formal code of ethics with a program to monitor compliance that includes a system for reporting incidents of fraud. These companies routinely communicate the existence of the program to their employees.[8]

authorized personnel. Access to accounting records, including those stored in company computers, should also be controlled.

5. *Periodic independent verification* The records should be periodically checked against the assets by someone other than the persons responsible for those records and assets. For example, at the end of each shift or day, the owner or store manager should count the cash in the cash drawer and compare the amount with the amount recorded on the tape or computer disk in the cash register. Other examples of independent verification are the monthly bank reconciliation and periodic counts of physical inventory.

6. *Separation of duties* The organizational plan should separate functional responsibilities. Within a department, no one person should be in charge of authorizing transactions, operating the department, handling assets, and keeping records of assets. For example, in a stereo store, each employee should oversee only a single part of a transaction. A sales employee takes the order and creates an invoice. Another employee receives the customer's cash or credit card payment and issues a receipt. Once the customer has a paid receipt, and only then, a third employee obtains the item from the warehouse and gives it to the customer. A person in the accounting department subsequently records the sales from the tape or disk in the cash register, comparing them with the sales invoices and updating the inventory in the records. The separation of duties means that a mistake, careless or not, cannot be made without being seen by at least one other person.

KEY POINT: No control procedure can guarantee the prevention of theft. However, the more procedures there are in place, the less likely it is that a theft will occur.

7. *Sound personnel procedures* Sound practices should be followed in managing the people who carry out the functions of each department. Among those practices are supervision, rotation of key people among different jobs, insistence that employees take vacations, and bonding of personnel who handle cash or inventories. **Bonding** is the process of carefully checking an employee's background and insuring the company against theft by that person. Bonding does not guarantee against theft, but it does prevent or reduce economic loss if theft occurs. Prudent personnel procedures help ensure that employees know their jobs, are honest, and will find it difficult to carry out and conceal embezzlement over time.

LIMITATIONS OF INTERNAL CONTROL

No system of internal control is without weaknesses. As long as control procedures are performed by people, the internal control system will be vulnerable to human error. Errors may arise from misunderstandings, mistakes in judgment, carelessness, distraction, or fatigue. Separation of duties can be defeated through collusion by employees who secretly agree to deceive the company. In addition, established procedures may be ineffective against employees' errors or dishonesty, and controls that were initially effective may become ineffective when conditions change.[9] In some cases, the costs of establishing and maintaining elaborate systems may exceed the benefits. In a small business, for example, active involvement by the owner can be a practical substitute for the separation of some duties.

 Check out ACE for a Review Quiz at http://accounting.college.hmco.com/students.

INTERNAL CONTROL OVER MERCHANDISING TRANSACTIONS

LO6 Apply internal control activities to common merchandising transactions.

RELATED TEXT ASSIGNMENTS
Q: 21, 22, 23
SE: 8
E: 12
P: 5
SD: 4, 5

Sound internal control activities are needed in all aspects of a business, but particularly when assets are involved. Assets are especially vulnerable when they enter or leave a business. When sales are made, for example, cash or other assets enter the business, and goods or services leave the business. Activities must be set up to prevent theft during those transactions.

Likewise, purchases of assets and payments of liabilities must be controlled. The majority of those transactions can be safeguarded by adequate purchasing and payment systems. In addition, assets on hand, such as cash, investments, inventory, plant, and equipment, must be protected.

In this section, you will see how internal control activities are applied to such merchandising transactions as cash sales, receipts, purchases, and cash payments. Similar activities are applicable to service and manufacturing businesses.

INTERNAL CONTROL AND MANAGEMENT GOALS

When a system of internal control is applied effectively to merchandising transactions, it can achieve important management goals. For example, two key goals for the success of a merchandising business are:

1. To prevent losses of cash or inventory owing to theft or fraud
2. To provide accurate records of merchandising transactions and account balances

Three broader goals for management are:

1. To keep enough inventory on hand to sell to customers without overstocking
2. To keep enough cash on hand to pay for purchases in time to receive discounts
3. To keep credit losses as low as possible by making credit sales only to customers who are likely to pay on time

KEY POINT: Maintaining internal control is especially complex and difficult for a merchandiser. Management must not only establish controls for cash sales receipts, purchases, and cash payments, but also go to great lengths to manage and protect its inventory.

One control used in meeting broad management goals is the cash budget, which projects future cash receipts and disbursements. By maintaining adequate cash balances, a company is able to take advantage of discounts on purchases, prepare to borrow money when necessary, and avoid the damaging effects of being unable to pay bills when they are due. By investing excess cash, the company can earn interest until the cash is needed.

A more specific accounting control is the separation of duties that involve the handling of cash. Such separation makes theft without detection extremely unlikely, unless two or more employees conspire. The separation of duties is easier in large businesses than in small ones, where one person may have to carry out several duties. The effectiveness of internal control over cash varies, based on the size and nature of the company. Most firms, however, should use the following procedures:

1. Separate the functions of authorization, recordkeeping, and custodianship of cash.
2. Limit the number of people who have access to cash.
3. Designate specific people who are responsible for handling cash.
4. Use banking facilities as much as possible, and keep the amount of cash on hand to a minimum.
5. Bond all employees who have access to cash.

Internal Control over Merchandising Transactions

6. Physically protect cash on hand by using cash registers, cashiers' cages, and safes.
7. Have a person who does not handle or record cash make periodic independent verifications of the cash on hand.
8. Record all cash receipts promptly.
9. Deposit all cash receipts promptly.
10. Make payments by check rather than by currency.
11. Have a person who does not authorize, handle, or record cash transactions reconcile the Cash account.

Notice that each of the foregoing procedures helps safeguard cash by making it more difficult for any one individual who has access to cash to steal or misuse it without being detected.

Control of Cash Sales Receipts

Cash payments for sales of goods and services can be received by mail or over the counter in the form of checks, credit or debit cards, or currency. Whatever the source of the payments, cash should be recorded immediately upon receipt. This is usually done by making an entry in a cash receipts journal. Such a journal establishes a written record of cash receipts that should prevent errors and make theft more difficult.

> **● Stop and Think!**
> Why is it important to write down the amount of cash received through the mail or over the counter?
> *It is important because until there is a written record of the cash, there is no accountability. This is why some stores offer a reward to customers who report making a purchase without receiving a receipt.* ■

■ **Control of Cash Received Through the Mail** Payment by mail is increasing because of the expansion of mail-order sales. Cash receipts that arrive by mail are vulnerable to theft by the employees who handle them. To control mailed receipts, customers should be urged to pay by check or credit card instead of with currency.

Cash received through the mail should be handled by two or more employees. The employee who opens the mail should make a list in triplicate of the money received. The list should contain each payer's name, the purpose for which the money was sent, and the amount. One copy goes with the cash to the cashier, who deposits the money. The second copy goes to the accounting department for recording. The third copy is kept by the person who opens the mail. Errors can be easily caught because the amount deposited by the cashier must agree with the amount received and the amount recorded in the cash receipts journal.

> **KEY POINT:** The cashier should not be allowed to remove the cash register tape or to record the day's cash receipts.

■ **Control of Cash Received over the Counter** Two common tools for controlling cash sales receipts are cash registers and prenumbered sales tickets. The amount of a cash sale should be rung up on a cash register at the time of the sale. The cash register should be placed so that the customer can see the amount recorded. Each cash register should have a locked-in tape on which it prints the day's transactions. At the end of the day, the cashier counts the cash in the cash register and turns it in to the cashier's office. Another employee takes the tape out of the cash register and records the cash receipts for the day in the cash receipts journal. The amount of cash turned in and the amount recorded on the tape should agree; if not, any differences must be explained. Large retail chains commonly monitor cash receipts by having each cash register tied directly into a computer that records each transaction as it occurs. Whether the elements are performed manually or by computer, separating responsibility for cash receipts, cash deposits, and recordkeeping is necessary to ensure good internal control.

In some stores, internal control is further strengthened by the use of prenumbered sales tickets and a central cash register or cashier's office, where all sales are rung up and collected by a person who does not participate in the sale. The salesperson completes a prenumbered sales ticket at the time of the sale, giving one copy to the customer and keeping a copy. At the end of the day, all sales tickets must be accounted for, and the sales total computed from the sales tickets should equal the total sales recorded on the cash register.

FIGURE 4
Internal Control for Purchasing and Paying for Goods and Services

CONTROL OF PURCHASES AND CASH DISBURSEMENTS

 Cash disbursements are particularly vulnerable to fraud and embezzlement. In one case, the treasurer of one of the nation's largest jewelry retailers was charged with having stolen over $500,000 by systematically overpaying federal income taxes and keeping the refund checks as they came back to the company.

To avoid such theft, cash should be paid only after the receipt of specific authorization supported by documents that establish the validity and amount of the claim. In addition, maximum possible use should be made of the principle of separation of duties in the purchase of goods and services and the payment for them. The degree of separation of duties varies, depending on the size of the business. Figure 4 shows how separation of duties can be maximized in large companies. Five

FOCUS ON BUSINESS TECHNOLOGY

How Do Computers Influence Internal Controls?

One of the more difficult challenges facing computer programmers is to build good internal controls into computerized accounting programs. Such computer programs must include controls that prevent unintentional errors as well as unauthorized access and tampering. The programs prevent errors through reasonableness checks (such as not allowing any transactions over a specified amount), mathematical checks that verify the arithmetic of transactions, and sequence checks that require documents and transactions to be in proper order. They typically use passwords and questions about randomly selected personal data to prevent unauthorized access to computer records. They may also use firewalls, which are strong electronic barriers to unauthorized access, as well as data encryption. Data encryption is a way of coding data so that if they are stolen, they are useless to the thief.

internal units (the requesting department, the purchasing department, the accounting department, the receiving department, and the treasurer) and two external contacts (the supplier and the banking system) all play a role in the internal control plan. Notice that business documents are also crucial components of the plan.

As shown in Figure 5 (on the following pages), every action is documented and verified by at least one other person. Thus, the requesting department cannot work out a kickback scheme to make illegal payments to the vendor because the receiving department independently records receipts and the accounting department verifies prices. The receiving department cannot steal goods because the receiving report must equal the invoice. For the same reason, the vendor cannot bill for more goods than it ships. The accounting department's work is verified by the treasurer, and the treasurer ultimately is checked by the accounting department.

Figure 5 illustrates the typical sequence of documents used in an internal control plan for purchases and cash disbursements. To begin, the credit office (requesting department) of Fenwick Fashions Corporation fills out a formal request for a purchase, or **purchase requisition**, for 20 boxes of fax paper rolls (item 1). The department head approves it and forwards it to the purchasing department. The people in the purchasing department prepare a **purchase order**, as shown in item 2. The purchase order is addressed to the vendor (seller) and contains a description of the items ordered; the expected price, terms, and shipping date; and other shipping instructions. Fenwick Fashions Corporation does not pay any bill that is not accompanied by a purchase order number.

KEY POINT: A purchase requisition is not the same as a purchase order. A purchase requisition is sent to the purchasing department; a purchase order is sent to the vendor.

After receiving the purchase order, the vendor, Henderson Supply Company, ships the goods and sends an **invoice** or bill (item 3) to Fenwick Fashions Corporation. The invoice gives the quantity and description of the goods delivered, the price, and the terms of payment. If goods cannot all be shipped immediately, the estimated date for shipment of the remainder is indicated.

KEY POINT: *Invoice* is the business term for "bill." Every business document must have a number for purposes of reference.

When the goods reach the receiving department of Fenwick Fashions Corporation, an employee writes the description, quantity, and condition of the goods on a form called a **receiving report** (item 4). The receiving department does not receive a copy of the purchase order or the invoice, so its employees do not know what should be received or its value. Thus, they are not tempted to steal any excess that may be delivered.

The receiving report is sent to the accounting department, where it is compared with the purchase order and the invoice. If everything is correct, the accounting department completes a **check authorization** and attaches it to the three supporting documents. The check authorization form shown in item 5 has a space for each item to be checked off as it is examined. Notice that the accounting department has all the documentary evidence for the transaction but does not have access to the assets purchased. Nor does it write the check for payment. This means that the people performing the accounting function cannot gain by falsifying documents in an effort to conceal fraud.

Finally, the treasurer examines all the documents and issues an order to the bank for payment, called a **check** (item 6), for the amount of the invoice less any appropriate discount. In some systems, the accounting department fills out the check so that all the treasurer has to do is inspect and sign it. The check is then sent to the vendor, with a remittance advice that shows what the check is for. A vendor who is not paid the proper amount will complain, of course, thus providing a form of outside control over the payment. Using a deposit ticket, the vendor deposits the check in the bank, which returns the canceled check with Fenwick Fashions Corporation's next bank statement (item 7). If the treasurer has made the check out for the wrong amount (or altered a pre-filled-in check), the problem will show up in the bank reconciliation.

There are many variations of the system just described. This example is offered as a simple system that provides adequate internal control.

 Check out ACE for a Review Quiz at http://accounting.college.hmco.com/students.

FIGURE 5
Internal Control Plan for Purchases and Cash Disbursements

Business Document	Prepared by	Sent to	Verification and Related Procedures
① Purchase requisition	Requesting department	Purchasing department	Purchasing verifies authorization.
② Purchase order	Purchasing department	Vendor	Vendor sends goods or services in accordance with purchase order.
③ Invoice	Vendor	Accounting department	Accounting receives invoice from vendor.
④ Receiving report	Receiving department	Accounting department	Accounting compares invoice, purchase order, and receiving report. Accounting verifies prices.
⑤ Check authorization	Accounting department	Treasurer	Accounting attaches check authorization to invoice, purchase order, and receiving report.
⑥ Check	Treasurer	Vendor	Treasurer verifies all documents before preparing check.
⑦ Bank statement	Buyer's bank	Accounting department	Accounting compares amount and payee's name on returned check with check authorization.

⑦ Statement of Account with
THE LAKE PARK NATIONAL BANK
Chicago, Illinois

Fenwick Fashions Corporation
8428 Rocky Island Avenue
Chicago, Illinois 60643

Checking Acct No
8030-647-4
Period covered
Sept. 30–Oct. 31, 20xx

Previous Balance	Checks/Debits—No.	Deposits/Credits—No.	S.C.	Current Balance
$2,645.78	$4,319.33 —16	$5,157.12 —7	$12.50	$3,471.07

CHECKS/DEBITS | DEPOSITS/CREDITS | DAILY BALANCES

Posting Date	Check No.	Amount	Posting Date	Amount	Date	Amount
					09/30	2,645.78
10/01	2564	100.00	10/01	586.00	10/01	2,881.78
10/01	2565	250.00	10/05	1,500.00	10/04	2,825.60
10/04	2567	56.18	10/06	300.00	10/05	3,900.46
10/05	2566	425.14	10/16	1,845.50	10/06	4,183.34
10/06	2568	17.12	10/21	600.00	10/12	2,242.34
10/12	2569	1,705.80	10/24	300.00CM	10/16	3,687.84
10/12	2570	235.20	10/31	25.62IN	10/17	3,589.09
10/16	2571	400.00			10/21	4,189.09
10/17	2572	29.75			10/24	3,745.59
10/17	2573	69.00			10/25	3,586.09
10/24	2574	738.50			10/28	3,457.95
10/24		5.00DM			10/31	3,471.07
10/25	2575	7.50				
10/25	2577	152.00				
10/28		118.14NSF				
10/28		10.00DM				
10/31		12.50SC				

Explanation of Symbols:

CM – Credit Memo
DM – Debit Memo
NSF – Non-Sufficient Funds
SC – Service Charge
EC – Error Correction
OD – Overdraft
IN – Interest on Average Balance

The last amount in this column is your balance.

Please examine; if no errors are reported within ten (10) days, the account will be considered to be correct.

ACCOUNTING FOR DISCOUNTS

SO7 Apply sales and purchases discounts to merchandising transactions.

RELATED TEXT ASSIGNMENTS
Q: 24
SE: 10
E: 14, 15, 16
P: 6
SD: 3

SALES DISCOUNTS

As mentioned earlier, sales discounts for early payment are customary in some industries. Because it usually is not possible to know at the time of the sale whether the customer will pay in time to take advantage of sales discounts, the discounts are recorded only at the time the customer pays. For example, assume that Fenwick Fashions Corporation sells merchandise to a customer on September 20 for $300, on terms of 2/10, n/60. This is the entry at the time of the sale:

A = L + OE
+   +

Sept. 20	Accounts Receivable	300	
	Sales		300
	Sold merchandise on credit, terms 2/10, n/60		

The customer can take advantage of the sales discount any time on or before September 30, ten days after the date of the invoice. If the customer pays on September 29, the entry in Fenwick's records would look like this:

A = L + OE
+   −

Sept. 29	Cash	294	
	Sales Discounts	6	
	Accounts Receivable		300
	Received payment for Sept. 20 sale; discount taken		

KEY POINT: Accounts Receivable must be credited for the full $300 even though only $294 has been received.

If the customer does not take advantage of the sales discount but waits until November 19 to pay for the merchandise, the entry would be as follows:

A = L + OE
+   −

Nov. 19	Cash	300	
	Accounts Receivable		300
	Received payment for Sept. 20 sale; no discount taken		

At the end of the accounting period, the Sales Discounts account has accumulated all the sales discounts taken during the period. Because sales discounts reduce revenues from sales, Sales Discounts is a contra-revenue account with a normal debit balance that is deducted from sales on the income statement.

PURCHASES DISCOUNTS

Merchandise purchases are usually made on credit and sometimes involve **purchases discounts** for early payment. Purchases discounts are discounts taken for early payment for merchandise purchased for resale. They are to the buyer what sales discounts are to the seller. The amount of discounts taken is recorded in a separate account. Assume that Fenwick made a credit purchase of merchandise on November 12 for $1,500 with terms of 2/10, n/30 and returned $200 in merchandise on November 14. When payment is made within the discount period, Fenwick's journal entry looks like this:

A = L + OE
−   −   +

Nov. 22	Accounts Payable	1,300	
	Purchases Discounts		26
	Cash		1,274
	Paid the invoice of Nov. 12		
	Purchase Nov. 12	$1,500	
	Less return Nov. 14	200	
	Net purchase	$1,300	
	Discount: 2%	26	
	Cash paid	$1,274	

KEY POINT: Accounts Payable must be debited for the full $1,300 even though only $1,274 has been paid.

If Fenwick does not pay for the purchase within the discount period, the entry would be as follows:

A = L + OE	Dec. 12	Accounts Payable	1,300
– –		Cash	1,300
		Paid the invoice of Nov. 12, less the return, on due date; no discount taken	

Like Purchases Returns and Allowances, Purchases Discounts is a contra-purchases account with a normal credit balance that is deducted from purchases on the income statement. If a company makes only a partial payment on an invoice, most creditors allow the company to take the discount applicable to the partial payment. The discount usually does not apply to freight, postage, taxes, or other charges that might appear on the invoice.

✓ Check out ACE for a Review Quiz at http://accounting.college.hmco.com/students.

Chapter Review

REVIEW OF LEARNING OBJECTIVES

LO1 Identify the management issues related to merchandising businesses.

Merchandising companies differ from service companies in that they earn income by buying and selling goods. The buying and selling of goods adds to the complexity of the business and raises four issues that management must address. First, the series of transactions in which merchandising companies engage (the operating cycle) requires careful cash flow management. Second, to achieve the goal of profitability, management must price goods and control operating costs by using budgets to ensure an adequate income after operating expenses and income taxes have been paid. Third, management must choose whether to use the perpetual or the periodic inventory system. Fourth, management must establish an internal control structure that protects the company's assets—its cash, merchandise inventory, and accounts receivable.

LO2 Define and distinguish the terms of sale for merchandising transactions.

A trade discount is a reduction from the list or catalogue price of a product. A sales discount is a discount given for early payment of a sale on credit. FOB shipping point means that the buyer bears the cost of transportation and that title to the goods passes to the buyer at the shipping origin. FOB destination means that the seller bears the cost of transportation and that title does not pass to the buyer until the goods reach their destination.

LO3 Prepare an income statement and record merchandising transactions under the perpetual inventory system.

The Merchandise Inventory account is continuously adjusted by entering purchases, sales, and other inventory transactions as they occur. Purchases increase the Merchandise Inventory account, and purchases returns decrease it. As goods are sold, their cost is transferred from the Merchandise Inventory account to the Cost of Goods Sold account.

LO4 Prepare an income statement and record merchandising transactions under the periodic inventory system.

When the periodic inventory system is used, the cost of goods sold section of the income statement must include the following elements:

$$\text{Purchases} - \text{Purchases returns and allowances} + \text{Freight in} = \text{Net cost of purchases}$$

$$\text{Beginning merchandise inventory} + \text{Net cost of purchases} = \text{Goods available for sale}$$

$$\text{Goods available for sale} - \text{Ending merchandise inventory} = \text{Cost of goods sold}$$

Under the periodic inventory system, the Merchandise Inventory account stays at the beginning level until the physical inventory is recorded at the end of the accounting period. A Purchases account is used to accumulate purchases of merchandise during the accounting period, and a Purchases Returns and Allowances account is used to accumulate returns of and allowances on purchases.

LO5 Define *internal control* and its basic components, give examples of control activities, and describe the limitations of internal control.	Internal control consists of all the policies and procedures a company uses to ensure the reliability of financial reporting, compliance with laws and regulations, and the effectiveness and efficiency of operations. Internal control has five components: the control environment, risk assessment, information and communication, control activities, and monitoring. Examples of control activities are proper authorization of transactions; recording all transactions to facilitate preparation of financial statements and to establish accountability for assets; use of well-designed documents to ensure proper recording of transactions; physical controls; periodic checks of records and assets; separation of duties into the functions of authorization, operations, custody of assets, and recordkeeping; and use of sound personnel policies. A system of internal control relies on the people who implement it. Thus, the effectiveness of internal control is limited by the people involved. Human error, collusion, and failure to recognize changed conditions all can contribute to a system's failure.
LO6 Apply internal control activities to common merchandising transactions.	Certain procedures strengthen internal control over sales, cash receipts, purchases, and cash disbursements. First, the functions of authorization, recordkeeping, and custody should be kept separate. Second, the accounting system should provide for physical protection of assets (especially cash and merchandise inventory), use of banking services, prompt recording and deposit of cash receipts, and payment by check. Third, the people who have access to cash and merchandise inventory should be specifically designated and their number limited. Fourth, employees who have access to cash or merchandise inventory should be bonded. Fifth, the Cash account should be reconciled each month, and unannounced audits of cash on hand should be made by an individual who does not authorize, handle, or record cash transactions.

Supplemental Objective

SO7 Apply sales and purchases discounts to merchandising transactions.	Sales discounts are discounts for early payment. Terms of 2/10, n/30 mean that the buyer can take a 2 percent discount if the invoice is paid within ten days of the invoice date. Otherwise, the buyer is obligated to pay the full amount in 30 days. Discounts on sales are recorded in the Sales Discounts account, and discounts on purchases are recorded in the Purchases Discounts account.

Review of Concepts and Terminology

The following concepts and terms were introduced in this chapter:

LO5 **Bonding:** The process of carefully checking an employee's background and insuring the company against theft by that person.

LO1 **Cash flow management:** The planning of a company's receipts and payments of cash.

LO6 **Check:** A written order to a bank to pay the amount specified from funds on deposit.

LO6 **Check authorization:** A form prepared by the accounting department after it has compared the receiving report with the purchase order and the invoice. It permits the issuance of a check to pay the invoice.

LO5 **Control activities:** Policies and procedures established by management to ensure that the objectives of internal control are met.

LO5 **Control environment:** The overall attitude, awareness, and actions of management, as reflected in the company's philosophy and operating style, organizational structure, method of assigning authority and responsibility, and personnel policies and practices.

LO1 **Financing period:** The amount of time from the purchase of inventory until it is sold and payment is collected, less the amount of time creditors allow for payment of the inventory. Also called the *cash gap*.

LO2 **FOB destination:** A shipping term that means that the seller bears transportation costs to the place of delivery.

LO2 **FOB shipping point:** A shipping term that means that the buyer bears transportation costs from the point of origin.

- **LO3** **Freight in:** The transportation cost of receiving merchandise. Also called *transportation in*.
- **LO3** **Freight Out Expense:** The account that accumulates transportation charges on merchandise sold, which are shown as a selling expense. Also called *Delivery Expense*.
- **LO4** **Goods available for sale:** The sum of beginning inventory and the net cost of purchases during the period; the total goods available for sale to customers during an accounting period.
- **LO5** **Information and communication:** The accounting system established by management and the communication of responsibilities with regard to the accounting system.
- **LO5** **Internal control:** All the policies and procedures a company uses to ensure the reliability of financial reporting, compliance with laws and regulations, and the effectiveness and efficiency of operations.
- **LO6** **Invoice:** A form sent to the purchaser by the vendor describing the goods delivered, the quantity, price, and terms of payment.
- **LO1** **Merchandise inventory:** The goods on hand at any one time that are available for sale to customers.
- **LO1** **Merchandising business:** A business that earns income by buying and selling goods.
- **LO5** **Monitoring:** Management's regular assessment of the quality of internal control.
- **LO4** **Net cost of purchases:** Net purchases plus any freight charges on the purchases.
- **LO4** **Net purchases:** Total purchases less any deductions, such as purchases returns and allowances and purchases discounts.
- **LO1** **Operating budget:** Management's operating plans as reflected by detailed listings of projected selling expenses and general and administrative expenses.
- **LO1** **Operating cycle:** A series of transactions that includes purchases of merchandise inventory for cash or on credit, payment for purchases made on credit, sales of merchandise inventory for cash or on credit, and collection of cash from the sales.
- **LO1** **Periodic inventory system:** A system for determining inventory on hand by taking a physical count at the end of an accounting period.
- **LO1** **Perpetual inventory system:** A system for determining inventory on hand by keeping continuous records of the quantity and, usually, the cost of individual items as they are bought and sold.
- **LO1** **Physical inventory:** An actual count of all merchandise on hand.
- **LO1** **Profitability management:** The process of achieving a satisfactory gross margin and maintaining acceptable levels of operating expenses.
- **LO6** **Purchase order:** A form prepared by a company's purchasing department and sent to a vendor describing the items ordered; the expected price, terms, and shipping date; and other shipping instructions.
- **LO6** **Purchase requisition:** A formal written request for a purchase, prepared by the requesting department in an organization and sent to the purchasing department.
- **LO4** **Purchases:** A temporary account used under the periodic inventory system to accumulate the total cost of merchandise purchased for resale during an accounting period.
- **SO7** **Purchases discounts:** Discounts taken for prompt payment for merchandise purchased for resale; the Purchases Discounts account is a contra-purchases account.
- **LO4** **Purchases Returns and Allowances:** A contra-purchases account used under the periodic inventory system to accumulate cash refunds, credits on account, and other allowances made by suppliers.
- **LO6** **Receiving report:** A form prepared by the receiving department of a company describing the quantity and condition of goods received.
- **LO5** **Risk assessment:** The identification of areas in which risks of loss of assets or inaccuracies in the accounting records are high.

LO2 **Sales discount:** A discount given to a buyer for early payment of a sale made on
SO7 credit; the Sales Discounts account is a contra-revenue account.

LO3 **Sales Returns and Allowances:** A contra-revenue account used to accumulate cash refunds, credits on account, and other allowances made to customers who have received defective or otherwise unsatisfactory products.

LO2 **Trade discount:** A deduction (usually 30 percent or more) off a list or catalogue price that is not recorded in the accounting records.

REVIEW PROBLEM

Merchandising Transactions: Perpetual and Periodic Inventory Systems

LO3
LO4
Dawkins Company engaged in the following transactions during October.

Oct. 1 Sold merchandise to Ernie Devlin on credit, terms n/30, FOB shipping point, $1,050 (cost, $630).
2 Purchased merchandise on credit from Ruland Company, terms n/30, FOB shipping point, $1,900.
2 Paid Custom Freight $145 for freight charges on merchandise received.
6 Purchased store supplies on credit from Arizin Supply House, terms n/30, $318.
9 Purchased merchandise on credit from LNP Company, terms n/30, FOB shipping point, $1,800, including $100 freight costs paid by LNP Company.
11 Accepted from Ernie Devlin a return of merchandise, which was returned to inventory, $150 (cost, $90).
14 Returned for credit $300 of merchandise received on October 2.
15 Returned for credit $100 of store supplies purchased on October 6.
16 Sold merchandise for cash, $500 (cost, $300).
22 Paid Ruland Company for purchase of October 2 less return of October 14.
23 Received full payment from Ernie Devlin for his October 1 purchase, less return on October 11.

REQUIRED
1. Prepare entries in journal form to record the transactions, assuming the perpetual inventory system is used.
2. Prepare entries in journal form to record the transactions, assuming the periodic inventory system is used.

ANSWER TO REVIEW PROBLEM

Accounts that differ under the two systems are highlighted.

	1. Perpetual Inventory System			2. Periodic Inventory System		

Oct. 1	Accounts Receivable
	    Sales
	Sold merchandise on account to Ernie Devlin, terms n/30, FOB shipping point
		1,050	1,050	Accounts Receivable
				    Sales
				Sold merchandise on account to Ernie Devlin, terms n/30, FOB shipping point
					1,050	1,050

	Cost of Goods Sold Merchandise Inventory Transferred cost of merchandise sold to Cost of Goods Sold account	630	630			

2	Merchandise Inventory
	    Accounts Payable
	Purchased merchandise on account from Ruland Company, terms n/30, FOB shipping point
		1,900	1,900	Purchases
				    Accounts Payable
				Purchased merchandise on account from Ruland Company, terms n/30, FOB shipping point
					1,900	1,900

	Freight In
	    Cash
	Paid freight on previous purchase
		145	145	Freight In
				    Cash
				Paid freight on previous purchase
					145	145

	1. Perpetual Inventory System			2. Periodic Inventory System		

Oct. 6	Store Supplies
	   Accounts Payable
	      Purchased store supplies
	      on account from Arizin
	      Supply House, terms n/30
		318	318	Store Supplies
				   Accounts Payable
				      Purchased store supplies
				      on account from Arizin
				      Supply House, terms n/30
					318	318

9	Merchandise Inventory
	Freight In
	   Accounts Payable
	      Purchased merchandise on
	      account from LNP Company,
	      terms n/30, FOB shipping
	      point, freight paid by supplier
		1,700
		100
			1,800	Purchases
				Freight In
				   Accounts Payable
				      Purchased merchandise on
				      account from LNP Company,
				      terms n/30, FOB shipping
				      point, freight paid by supplier
					1,700
					100
						1,800

11	Sales Returns and Allowances
	   Accounts Receivable
	      Accepted return of merchandise
	      from Ernie Devlin
		150	150	Sales Returns and Allowances
				   Accounts Receivable
				      Accepted return of merchandise
				      from Ernie Devlin
					150	150

	Merchandise Inventory
	   Cost of Goods Sold
	      Transferred cost of merchandise
	      returned to Merchandise
	      Inventory account
		90	90			

14	Accounts Payable
	   Merchandise Inventory
	      Returned portion of
	      merchandise purchased
	      from Ruland Company
		300	300	Accounts Payable
				   Purchases Returns and
				     Allowances
				      Returned portion of
				      merchandise purchased
				      from Ruland Company
					300	300

15	Accounts Payable
	   Store Supplies
	      Returned store supplies (not
	      merchandise) purchased on
	      October 6 for credit
		100	100	Accounts Payable
				   Store Supplies
				      Returned store supplies (not
				      merchandise) purchased
				      on October 6 for credit
					100	100

16	Cash
	   Sales
	      Sold merchandise for cash
		500	500	Cash
				   Sales
				      Sold merchandise for cash
					500	500

	Cost of Goods Sold
	   Merchandise Inventory
	      Transferred cost of merchandise
	      sold to Cost of Goods Sold
	      account
		300	300			

22	Accounts Payable
	   Cash
	      Made payment on account
	      to Ruland Company
	      $1,900 − $300 = $1,600
		1,600	1,600	Accounts Payable
				   Cash
				      Made payment on account
				      to Ruland Company
				      $1,900 − $300 = $1,600
					1,600	1,600

23	Cash
	   Accounts Receivable
	      Received payment on
	      account from Ernie Devlin
	      $1,050 − $150 = $900
		900	900	Cash
				   Accounts Receivable
				      Received payment on
				      account from Ernie Devlin
				      $1,050 − $150 = $900
					900	900

Chapter Assignments

BUILDING YOUR KNOWLEDGE FOUNDATION

QUESTIONS

1. What four issues must managers of merchandising businesses address?
2. What is the operating cycle of a merchandising business, and why is it important?
3. What are two important elements in achieving a satisfactory profit in a merchandising business?
4. What is an operating budget, and how does it help management improve a company's profitability?
5. What is the difference between a trade discount and a sales discount?
6. Two companies quoted the following prices and terms on 50 units of product:

	Price	Terms
Supplier A	$20 per unit	FOB shipping point
Supplier B	$21 per unit	FOB destination

   Which supplier is quoting the better deal? Explain your answer.
7. Under which inventory system is a Cost of Goods Sold account maintained? Explain why.
8. Discuss this statement: "The perpetual inventory system is the best system because management always needs to know how much inventory it has."
9. Why is it advisable to maintain a Sales Returns and Allowances account when the same result could be obtained by debiting each return or allowance to the Sales account?
10. Is freight in an operating expense? Explain your answer.
11. Under the periodic inventory system, an important figure in computing cost of goods sold is goods available for sale. What are the two main components of goods available for sale, and what is the relationship of ending inventory to goods available for sale?
12. Under the periodic inventory system, how must the amount of inventory at the end of the year be determined?
13. Hornberger Hardware purchased the following items: (a) a delivery truck, (b) two dozen hammers, (c) supplies for its office workers, and (d) a broom for the janitor. Which items should be debited to the Purchases account under the periodic inventory system?
14. What is the difference between the perpetual inventory system and the periodic inventory system?
15. What are the principal differences in the handling of merchandise inventory in the accounting records under the perpetual inventory system and the periodic inventory system?
16. Merchants who accept credit cards from customers must allow the credit card companies a 2 to 6 percent discount on the sales. Why are they willing to do this?
17. Most people think of internal control as a means of making fraud harder to commit and easier to detect. What are some other important purposes of internal control?
18. What are the five components of internal control?
19. What are some examples of control activities?
20. Why is the separation of duties necessary to ensure sound internal control? What does this principle assume about the relationships of employees in a company and the possibility of two or more of them stealing from the company?
21. In a small business, it is sometimes impossible to separate duties completely. What are three other practices that a small business can follow to achieve the objectives of internal control over cash?

22. At Thrifty Variety Store, each sales clerk counts the cash in his or her cash drawer at the end of the day, then removes the cash register tape and prepares a daily cash form, noting any discrepancies. This information is checked by an employee in the cashier's office, who counts the cash, compares the total with the form, and then gives the cash to the cashier. What is the weakness in this system of internal control?

23. How does a movie theater control cash receipts?

24. Is the normal balance of the Sales Discounts account a debit or a credit balance? Is it an asset, liability, expense, or contra-revenue account?

SHORT EXERCISES

SE 1.
LO1 Identification of Management Issues

Identify each of the following decisions as most directly related to (a) cash flow management, (b) profitability management, (c) choice of inventory system, or (d) control of merchandising operations:

1. Determination of how to protect cash from theft or embezzlement
2. Determination of the selling price of goods for sale
3. Determination of policies governing sales of merchandise on credit
4. Determination of whether to use the periodic or the perpetual inventory system

SE 2.
LO2 Terms of Sale

A dealer buys tooling machines from a manufacturer and resells them to its customers.

a. The manufacturer sets a list or catalogue price of $6,000 for a machine. The manufacturer offers its dealers a 40 percent trade discount.
b. The manufacturer sells the machine under terms of FOB shipping point. The cost of shipping is $350.
c. The manufacturer offers a sales discount of 2/10, n/30. The sales discount does not apply to shipping costs.

What is the net cost of the tooling machine to the dealer, assuming it is paid for within ten days of purchase?

SE 3.
LO3 Purchases of Merchandise: Perpetual Inventory System

Record in journal form each of the following transactions, assuming the perpetual inventory system is used:

Aug. 2 Purchased merchandise on credit from Foxx Company, invoice dated August 1, terms n/10, FOB shipping point, $2,300.
     3 Received bill from Main Shipping Company for transportation costs on August 2 shipment, invoice dated August 1, terms n/30, $210.
     7 Returned damaged merchandise received from Foxx Company on August 2 for credit, $360.
    10 Paid in full the amount due to Foxx Company for the purchase of August 2, part of which was returned on August 7.

SE 4.
LO4 Purchases of Merchandise: Periodic Inventory System

Record in journal form the transactions in **SE 3,** assuming the periodic inventory system is used.

SE 5.
LO4 Cost of Goods Sold: Periodic Inventory System

Using the following data and assuming cost of goods sold is $230,000, prepare the cost of goods sold section of a merchandising income statement (periodic inventory system), including computation of the amount of purchases for the month of October:

Freight in	$12,000
Merchandise inventory, Sept. 30, 20xx	33,000
Merchandise inventory, Oct. 31, 20xx	44,000
Purchases	?
Purchases returns and allowances	9,000

SE 6.
LO4 Sales of Merchandise: Periodic Inventory System

Record in journal form the following four transactions, assuming the periodic inventory system is used:

Aug. 4 Sold merchandise on credit to Bonds Corporation, terms n/30, FOB destination, $1,200.
     5 Paid transportation costs for sale of August 4, $110.
     9 Part of the merchandise sold on August 4 was accepted back from Bonds Corporation for full credit and returned to the merchandise inventory, $350.

Sept. 3 Received payment in full from Bonds Corporation for merchandise sold on August 4, less the return on August 9.

SE 7. Record in journal form the following transaction for Jenny's Cards Store:

LO2 Credit Card Sales Transaction

Apr. 19 A tabulation of invoices at the end of the day showed $400 in Visa invoices, which are deposited in a special bank account at full value less 5 percent discount.

SE 8. Match the check-writing policies for a small business described below to these control activities:

LO5 Internal Control Activities
LO6

a. Authorization
b. Recording transactions
c. Documents and records
d. Physical controls

e. Periodic independent check
f. Separation of duties
g. Sound personnel policies

1. The person who writes the checks to pay bills is different from the persons who authorize the payments and who keep the records of the payments.
2. The checks are kept in a locked drawer. The only person who has the key is the person who writes the checks.
3. The person who writes the checks is bonded.
4. Once each month the owner compares and reconciles the amount of money shown in the accounting records with the amount in the bank account.
5. Each check is approved by the owner of the business before it is mailed.
6. A check stub recording pertinent information is completed for each check.
7. Every day, all checks are recorded in the accounting records, using the information on the check stubs.

SE 9. Internal control is subject to several inherent limitations. Indicate whether each of the following situations is an example of (a) human error, (b) collusion, (c) changed conditions, or (d) cost-benefit considerations:

LO5 Limitations of Internal Control

1. Effective separation of duties in a restaurant is impractical because the business is too small.
2. The cashier and the manager of a retail shoe store work together to circumvent the internal controls for the purpose of embezzling funds.
3. The cashier in a pizza shop does not understand the procedures for operating the cash register and thus fails to ring up all sales and to count the cash at the end of the day.
4. At a law firm, computer supplies were mistakenly delivered to the reception area instead of the receiving area because the supplier began using a different means of shipment. As a result, the receipt of supplies was not recorded.

SE 10. On April 15, Eiji Company sold merchandise to Pinto Company for $1,500 on terms of 2/10, n/30. Record the entries in both Eiji's and Pinto's records for (1) the sale, (2) a return of merchandise on April 20 of $300, and (3) payment in full on April 25. Assume both companies use the periodic inventory system.

SO7 Sales and Purchases Discounts

Exercises

E 1. The decisions that follow were made by the management of Cotton Gold Company. Indicate whether each decision pertains primarily to (a) cash flow management, (b) profitability management, (c) choice of inventory system, or (d) control of merchandise operations.

LO1 Management Issues and Decisions

1. Decided to mark each item of inventory with a magnetic tag that sets off an alarm if the tag is removed from the store before being deactivated
2. Decided to reduce the credit terms offered to customers from 30 days to 20 days to speed up collection of accounts
3. Decided that the benefits of keeping track of each item of inventory as it is bought and sold would exceed the costs of such a system
4. Decided to raise the price of each item of inventory to achieve a higher gross margin to offset an increase in rent expense
5. Decided to purchase a new type of cash register that can be operated only by a person who knows a predetermined code
6. Decided to switch to a new cleaning service that will provide the same service at a lower cost

Chapter Assignments

LO1 Operating Budget

E 2. The operating budget and actual performance for the six months ended June 30, 20x3, for Kobe Hardware Corporation appear below.

	Budget	Actual
Selling Expenses		
Sales Salaries Expense	$ 90,000	$102,030
Sales Supplies Expense	2,000	1,642
Rent Expense, Selling Space	18,000	18,000
Utilities Expense, Selling Space	12,000	11,256
Advertising Expense	15,000	21,986
Depreciation Expense, Selling Fixtures	6,500	6,778
Total Selling Expenses	$143,500	$161,692
General and Administrative Expenses		
Office Salaries Expense	$ 50,000	$ 47,912
Office Supplies Expense	1,000	782
Rent Expense, Office Space	4,000	4,000
Depreciation Expense, Office Equipment	3,000	3,251
Utilities Expense, Office Space	3,000	3,114
Postage Expense	500	626
Insurance Expense	2,000	2,700
Miscellaneous Expense	500	481
Total General and Administrative Expenses	$ 64,000	$ 62,866
Total Operating Expenses	$207,500	$224,558

1. Prepare an operating report that shows budget, actual, and difference.
2. Discuss the results. Which differences should management investigate?

LO2 Terms of Sale

E 3. A household appliance dealer buys refrigerators from a manufacturer and resells them to its customers.

a. The manufacturer sets a list or catalogue price of $1,000 for a refrigerator. The manufacturer offers its dealers a 30 percent trade discount.
b. The manufacturer sells the machine under terms of FOB destination. The cost of shipping is $100.
c. The manufacturer offers a sales discount of 2/10, n/30. Sales discounts do not apply to shipping costs.

What is the net cost of the refrigerator to the dealer, assuming it is paid for within ten days of purchase?

LO3 Preparation of the Income Statement: Perpetual Inventory System

E 4. Using the selected account balances at December 31, 20xx, for Tents, Etc. that follow, prepare an income statement for the year ended December 31, 20xx. Show detail of net sales. The company uses the perpetual inventory system, and Freight In has not been included in Cost of Goods Sold.

Account Name	Debit	Credit
Sales		$237,500
Sales Returns and Allowances	$ 11,750	
Cost of Goods Sold	140,000	
Freight In	6,750	
Selling Expenses	21,500	
General and Administrative Expenses	43,500	
Income Taxes	5,000	

LO3 Recording Purchases: Perpetual Inventory System

E 5. Give the entries to record each of the following transactions under the perpetual inventory system:
a. Purchased merchandise on credit, terms n/30, FOB shipping point, $2,500.
b. Paid freight on the shipment in transaction **a**, $135.
c. Purchased merchandise on credit, terms n/30, FOB destination, $1,400.
d. Purchased merchandise on credit, terms n/30, FOB shipping point, $2,600, which includes freight paid by the supplier of $200.
e. Returned part of the merchandise purchased in transaction **c**, $500.
f. Paid the amount owed on the purchase in transaction **a**.
g. Paid the amount owed on the purchase in transaction **d**.
h. Paid the amount owed on the purchase in transaction **c** less the return in **e**.

LO3 Recording Sales: Perpetual Inventory System

E 6. On June 15, Ohio Company sold merchandise for $1,300 on terms of n/30 to Whist Company. On June 20, Whist Company returned some of the merchandise for a credit of $300, and on June 25, Whist paid the balance owed. Give Ohio's entries to record the sale, return, and receipt of payment under the perpetual inventory system. The cost of the merchandise sold on June 15 was $750, and the cost of the merchandise returned to inventory on June 20 was $175.

LO4 Preparation of the Income Statement: Periodic Inventory System

E 7. Using the selected year-end account balances at December 31, 20x4, for the Happ General Store shown below, prepare a 20x4 income statement. Show detail of net sales. The company uses the periodic inventory system. Beginning merchandise inventory was $52,000; ending merchandise inventory is $44,000.

Account Name	Debit	Credit
Sales		$594,000
Sales Returns and Allowances	$ 30,400	
Purchases	229,600	
Purchases Returns and Allowances		8,000
Freight In	11,200	
Selling Expenses	97,000	
General and Administrative Expenses	74,400	
Income Taxes	30,000	

LO4 Merchandising Income Statement: Missing Data, Multiple Years

E 8. Determine the missing data for each letter in the following three income statements for Iron Wholesale Paper Company (in thousands):

	20x4	20x3	20x2
Sales	$ p	$ h	$286
Sales returns and allowances	24	19	a
Net sales	q	317	b
Merchandise inventory, beginning	r	i	38
Purchases	192	169	c
Purchases returns and allowances	31	j	17
Freight in	s	29	22
Net cost of purchases	189	k	d
Goods available for sale	222	212	182
Merchandise inventory, ending	39	l	42
Cost of goods sold	t	179	e
Gross margin	142	m	126
Selling expenses	u	78	f
General and administrative expenses	39	n	33
Total operating expenses	130	128	g
Income before income taxes	v	o	27
Income taxes	3	2	5
Net income	w	8	22

LO4 **Recording Purchases: Periodic Inventory System**

E 9. Using the data in **E 5,** give the entries to record each of the transactions under the periodic inventory system.

LO4 **Recording Sales: Periodic Inventory System**

E 10. Using the relevant data in **E 6,** give the entries to record each of the transactions under the periodic inventory system.

LO5 **Use of Accounting Records in Internal Control**

E 11. Careful scrutiny of accounting records and financial statements can lead to the discovery of fraud or embezzlement. Each of the following situations may indicate a breakdown in internal control. Indicate the nature of the possible fraud or embezzlement in each of these situations.

1. Wages expense for a branch office was 30 percent higher in 20x5 than in 20x4, even though the office was authorized to employ only the same four employees and raises were only 5 percent in 20x5.
2. Sales returns and allowances increased from 5 percent to 20 percent of sales in the first two months of 20x5, after record sales in 20x4 resulted in large bonuses for the sales staff.
3. Gross margin decreased from 40 percent of net sales in 20x4 to 20 percent in 20x5, even though there was no change in pricing. Ending inventory was 50 percent less at the end of 20x5 than it was at the beginning of the year. There is no immediate explanation for the decrease in inventory.
4. A review of daily records of cash register receipts shows that one cashier consistently accepts more discount coupons for purchases than do the other cashiers.

LO5 **LO6** **Control Procedures**

E 12. Ned Remy, who operates a small grocery store, has established the following policies with regard to the checkout cashiers:

1. Each cashier has his or her own cash drawer, to which no one else has access.
2. Each cashier may accept checks for purchases under $50 with proper identification. Checks over $50 must be approved by Remy before they are accepted.
3. Every sale must be rung up on the cash register and a receipt given to the customer. Each sale is recorded on a tape inside the cash register.
4. At the end of each day, Remy counts the cash in the drawer and compares it with the amount on the tape inside the cash register.

Match the following conditions for internal control to each of the policies listed above:

a. Transactions are executed in accordance with management's general or specific authorization.
b. Transactions are recorded as necessary to permit preparation of financial statements and maintain accountability for assets.
c. Access to assets is permitted only as allowed by management.
d. At reasonable intervals, the records of assets are compared with the existing assets.

LO5 **Internal Control Procedures**

E 13. Lessing Video Store maintains the following policies with regard to purchases of new videotapes at each of its branch stores:

1. Employees are required to take vacations, and the duties of employees are rotated periodically.
2. Once each month a person from the home office visits each branch store to examine the receiving records and to compare the inventory of videos with the accounting records.
3. Purchases of new videos must be authorized by purchase order in the home office and paid for by the treasurer in the home office. Receiving reports are prepared in each branch and sent to the home office.
4. All new personnel receive one hour of training in how to receive and catalogue new videos.
5. The company maintains a perpetual inventory system that keeps track of all videos purchased, sold, and on hand.

Match the following control procedures to each of the above policies. (Some may have several answers.)

a. Authorization
b. Recording transactions
c. Documents and records
d. Limited access
e. Periodic independent verification
f. Separation of duties
g. Sound personnel policies

SO7 Sales Involving Discounts

E 14. Give the entries to record the following transactions engaged in by Rios Company, which uses the periodic inventory system:

Mar. 1 Sold merchandise on credit to Bee Company, terms 2/10, n/30, FOB shipping point, $1,000.
3 Accepted a return from Bee Company for full credit, $400.
10 Received payment from Bee Company for the sale, less the return and discount.
11 Sold merchandise on credit to Bee Company, terms 2/10, n/30, FOB shipping point, $1,600.
31 Received payment for amount due from Bee Company for the sale of March 11.

SO7 Purchases Involving Discounts

E 15. Give the entries to record the following transactions engaged in by Pecan Company, which uses the periodic inventory system:

July 2 Purchased merchandise on credit from Ensur Company, terms 2/10, n/30, FOB destination, invoice dated July 1, $1,600.
6 Returned some merchandise to Ensur Company for full credit, $200.
11 Paid Ensur Company for purchase of July 2 less return and discount.
14 Purchased merchandise on credit from Ensur Company, terms 2/10, n/30, FOB destination, invoice dated July 12, $1,800.
31 Paid amount owed Ensur Company for purchase of July 14.

SO7 Purchases and Sales Involving Discounts

E 16. Tanweiczk Company purchased $4,600 of merchandise, terms 2/10, n/30, from A&G Company and paid for the merchandise within the discount period. Give the entries (1) by Tanweiczk Company to record the purchase and payment and (2) by A&G Company to record the sale and receipt of payment. Both companies use the periodic inventory system.

PROBLEMS

LO1 Merchandising Income
LO3 Statement: Perpetual Inventory System

P 1. At the end of the fiscal year, June 30, 20x4, selected accounts from the adjusted trial balance for Bear Camera Store, Inc., appeared as shown below.

Bear Camera Store, Inc.
Partial Adjusted Trial Balance
June 30, 20x4

Sales		$433,912
Sales Returns and Allowances	$ 11,250	
Cost of Goods Sold	221,185	
Freight In	10,078	
Store Salaries Expense	107,550	
Office Salaries Expense	26,500	
Advertising Expense	18,200	
Rent Expense	14,400	
Insurance Expense	2,800	
Utilities Expense	8,760	
Store Supplies Expense	2,464	
Office Supplies Expense	1,814	
Depreciation Expense, Store Equipment	1,800	
Depreciation Expense, Office Equipment	1,850	
Income Taxes	2,500	

REQUIRED

1. Prepare a multistep income statement for Bear Camera Store, Inc. Freight In should be combined with Cost of Goods Sold. Store Salaries Expense; Advertising Expense;

Store Supplies Expense; and Depreciation Expense, Store Equipment are selling expenses. The other expenses are general and administrative expenses. The company uses the perpetual inventory system. Show details of net sales and operating expenses.

2. Based on your knowledge at this point in the course, how would you use the income statement for Bear Camera Store to evaluate the company's profitability? What other financial statement should be considered and why?

P 2.

LO3 Merchandising Transactions: Perpetual Inventory System

Sweet Company engaged in the following transactions in July 20xx:

July 1 Sold merchandise to Rick Lee on credit, terms n/30, FOB shipping point, $4,200 (cost, $2,520).
3 Purchased merchandise on credit from Cobalt Company, terms n/30, FOB shipping point, $7,600.
5 Paid Mix Freight for freight charges on merchandise received, $580.
6 Purchased store supplies on credit from DGE Supply Company, terms n/20, $1,272.
8 Purchased merchandise on credit from Holt Company, terms n/30, FOB shipping point, $7,200, which includes $400 freight costs paid by Holt Company.
12 Returned some of the merchandise purchased on July 3 for credit, $1,200.
15 Sold merchandise on credit to Bob Wagner, terms n/30, FOB shipping point, $2,400 (cost, $1,440).
16 Returned some of the store supplies purchased on July 6 for credit, $400.
17 Sold merchandise for cash, $2,000 (cost, $1,200).
18 Accepted for full credit a return from Rick Lee and returned merchandise to inventory, $400 (cost, $240).
24 Paid Cobalt Company for purchase of July 3 less return of July 12.
25 Received full payment from Rick Lee for his July 1 purchase less the return on July 18.

REQUIRED ▶ Prepare entries in journal form to record the transactions, assuming use of the perpetual inventory system.

P 3.

LO1 Merchandising Income
LO4 Statement: Periodic Inventory System

The data below are from the adjusted trial balance of Pat's Sports Equipment, Inc., on September 30, 20x5, the fiscal year end. The company's beginning merchandise inventory was $243,666 and ending merchandise inventory is $229,992 for the period.

Pat's Sports Equipment, Inc.
Partial Adjusted Trial Balance
September 30, 20x5

Sales		$1,301,736
Sales Returns and Allowances	$ 33,750	
Purchases	663,555	
Purchases Returns and Allowances		90,714
Freight In	30,234	
Store Salaries Expense	322,650	
Office Salaries Expense	79,500	
Advertising Expense	54,600	
Rent Expense	43,200	
Insurance Expense	8,400	
Utilities Expense	56,280	
Store Supplies Expense	1,392	
Office Supplies Expense	2,442	
Depreciation Expense, Store Equipment	5,400	
Depreciation Expense, Office Equipment	5,550	
Income Taxes	15,000	

REQUIRED ▶ 1. Prepare a multistep income statement for Pat's Sports Equipment, Inc. Store Salaries Expense; Advertising Expense; Store Supplies Expense; and Depreciation Expense,

Store Equipment are selling expenses. The other expenses are general and administrative expenses. The company uses the periodic inventory system. Show details of net sales and operating expenses.

2. Based on your knowledge at this point in the course, how would you use the income statement for Pat's Sports Equipment to evaluate the company's profitability? What other financial statements should be considered and why?

P 4. Use the relevant data in **P 2** for this problem.

LO4 Merchandising Transactions: Periodic Inventory System

REQUIRED ▶ Prepare entries in journal form to record the transactions, assuming use of the periodic inventory system.

P 5.

LO5 Internal Control Evaluation
LO6

Equipment Services Company provides maintenance services to factories in the Newark, New Jersey, area. The company, which buys a large amount of cleaning supplies, consistently has been over budget in its expenditures for these items. In the past, supplies were left open in the warehouse to be taken each evening as needed by the onsite supervisors. A clerk in the accounting department periodically ordered additional supplies from a long-time supplier. No records were maintained other than to record purchases. Once a year, an inventory of supplies was made for the preparation of the financial statements.

To solve the budgetary problem, management implemented a new system for controlling and purchasing supplies. A supplies clerk was put in charge of a secured storeroom for cleaning supplies. Supervisors use a purchase requisition to request supplies for the jobs they oversee. Each job receives a predetermined amount of supplies based on a study of its needs. In the storeroom, the supplies clerk notes the levels of supplies and completes the purchase requisition when supplies are needed. The purchase requisition goes to the purchasing clerk, a new position, who is solely responsible for authorizing purchases and who prepares the purchase orders. Supplier prices are monitored constantly to ensure that the lowest price is obtained. When supplies are received, the supplies clerk checks them in and prepares a receiving report, which is sent to accounting, where each payment to a supplier is documented by the purchase requisition, the purchase order, and the receiving report. The accounting department also maintains a record of supplies inventory, supplies requisitioned by supervisors, and supplies received. Once each month, a physical inventory of cleaning supplies in the storeroom is made by the warehouse manager and compared against the supplies inventory records maintained by the accounting department.

REQUIRED ▶ Show how the new system applies or does not apply to the seven control activities described in this chapter. Is each new control activity better than the old system?

P 6.

LO4 Merchandising Transactions,
SO7 Including Discounts: Periodic Inventory System

The following is a list of transactions for Image Products, Inc., for the month of March 20xx:

Mar. 1 Sold merchandise on credit to D. Brody, terms 2/10, n/60, FOB shipping point, $2,200.
3 Purchased merchandise on credit from Isle Company, terms 2/10, n/30, FOB shipping point, $12,800.
4 Received freight bill for shipment received on March 3, $900.
6 Sold merchandise for cash, $1,100.
7 Sold merchandise on credit to R. Guido, terms 2/10, n/60, $2,400.
9 Purchased merchandise from Maskel Company, terms 1/10, n/30, FOB shipping point, $6,180, which includes freight charges of $400.
10 Sold merchandise on credit to B. Viola, terms 2/10, n/20, $4,400.
10 Received check from D. Brody for payment in full for sale of March 1.
11 Purchased merchandise from Isle Company, terms 2/10, n/30, FOB shipping point, $16,400.
12 Received freight bill for shipment of March 11, $1,460.
13 Paid Isle Company for purchase of March 3.
14 Returned merchandise from the March 9 shipment that was the wrong size and color, for credit, $580.
16 B. Viola returned some of the merchandise sold to him on March 10 for credit, $400.

Mar. 17 Received payment from R. Guido for half of her purchase on March 7. A discount is allowed on partial payment.
18 Paid Maskel Company balance due on account from transactions on March 9 and 14.
20 In checking the purchase of March 11 from Isle Company, Image Products' accounting department found an overcharge of $800. Isle Company agreed to issue a credit.
21 Paid freight company for freight charges of March 4 and 12.
23 Purchased cleaning supplies on credit from Liu Company, terms n/5, $500.
24 Discovered that some of the cleaning supplies purchased on March 23 had not been ordered. Returned them to Liu Company for credit, $100.
25 Sold merchandise for cash, $1,600.
27 Paid Liu Company for the March 23 purchase less the March 24 return.
28 Received payment in full from B. Viola for transactions on March 10 and 16.
29 Paid Isle Company for purchase of March 11 less allowance of March 20.
31 Received payment for balance of amount owed from R. Guido from transactions of March 7 and 17.

REQUIRED Prepare entries in journal form to record the transactions, assuming that the periodic inventory system is used.

ALTERNATE PROBLEMS

P 7. At the end of the fiscal year, August 31, 20x4, selected accounts from the adjusted trial balance for Holiday Merchandise, Inc., appeared as follows:

LO1 Merchandising Income
LO3 Statement: Perpetual Inventory System

Holiday Merchandise, Inc.
Partial Adjusted Trial Balance
August 31, 20x4

Sales		$324,000
Sales Returns and Allowances	$ 4,000	
Cost of Goods Sold	122,800	
Freight In	4,600	
Store Salaries Expense	65,250	
Office Salaries Expense	25,750	
Advertising Expense	48,600	
Rent Expense	4,800	
Insurance Expense	2,400	
Utilities Expense	3,120	
Store Supplies Expense	5,760	
Office Supplies Expense	2,350	
Depreciation Expense, Store Equipment	2,100	
Depreciation Expense, Office Equipment	1,600	
Income Taxes	4,000	

REQUIRED
1. Using the information given, prepare an income statement for Holiday Merchandise, Inc. Combine Freight In with Cost of Goods Sold. Store Salaries Expense; Advertising Expense; Store Supplies Expense; and Depreciation Expense, Store Equipment are selling expenses. The other expenses are general and administrative expenses. The company uses the perpetual inventory system. Show details of net sales and operating expenses.
2. Based on your knowledge at this point in the course, how would you use the income statement for Holiday Merchandise to evaluate the company's profitability? What other financial statement should be considered and why?

P 8. Garden Company engaged in the following transactions in October 20xx:

LO3 **Merchandising Transactions: Perpetual Inventory System**

Oct. 7 Sold merchandise on credit to Sonia Mendes, terms n/30, FOB shipping point, $6,000 (cost, $3,600).
8 Purchased merchandise on credit from DaCosta Company, terms n/30, FOB shipping point, $12,000.
9 Paid Jay Company for shipping charges on merchandise purchased on October 8, $508.
10 Purchased merchandise on credit from Paige Company, terms n/30, FOB shipping point, $19,200, including $1,200 freight costs paid by Paige.
13 Purchased office supplies on credit from Hayami Company, terms n/30, $4,800.
14 Sold merchandise on credit to Eliza Samms, terms n/30, FOB shipping point, $4,800 (cost, $2,880).
14 Returned damaged merchandise received from DaCosta Company on October 8 for credit, $1,200.
17 Received check from Sonia Mendes for her purchase of October 7.
18 Returned a portion of the office supplies purchased on October 13 for credit because the wrong items were sent, $800.
19 Sold merchandise for cash, $3,600 (cost, $2,160).
20 Paid Paige Company for purchase of October 10.
21 Paid DaCosta Company the balance from the transactions of October 8 and October 14.
24 Accepted from Eliza Samms a return of merchandise, which was put back in inventory, $400 (cost, $240).

REQUIRED ▶ Prepare entries in journal form to record the transactions, assuming the perpetual inventory system is used.

P 9. Selected accounts from the adjusted trial balance for Gourmet Gadgets Shop, Inc., as of March 31, 20x4, the end of the fiscal year, are shown below. The merchandise inventory for Gourmet Gadgets Shop was $38,200 at the beginning of the year and $29,400 at the end of the year.

LO1 **Merchandising Income Statement: Periodic Inventory System**
LO4

Gourmet Gadgets Shop, Inc.
Partial Adjusted Trial Balance
March 31, 20x4

Sales		$165,000
Sales Returns and Allowances	$ 2,000	
Purchases	70,200	
Purchases Returns and Allowances		2,600
Freight In	2,300	
Store Salaries Expense	32,625	
Office Salaries Expense	12,875	
Advertising Expense	24,300	
Rent Expense	2,400	
Insurance Expense	1,200	
Utilities Expense	1,560	
Store Supplies Expense	2,880	
Office Supplies Expense	1,175	
Depreciation Expense, Store Equipment	1,050	
Depreciation Expense, Office Equipment	800	
Income Taxes	1,000	

REQUIRED ▶ 1. Using the information given, prepare an income statement for Gourmet Gadgets Shop, Inc. Store Salaries Expense; Advertising Expense; Store Supplies Expense; and

Depreciation Expense, Store Equipment are selling expenses. The other expenses are general and administrative expenses. The company uses the periodic inventory system. Show details of net sales and operating expenses.

2. Based on your knowledge at this point in the course, how would you use the income statement for Gourmet Gadgets Shop to evaluate the company's profitability? What other financial statements should be considered and why?

P 10. Use the relevant data in **P 8** for this problem.

LO4 Merchandising Transactions: Periodic Inventory System

REQUIRED ▶ Prepare entries in journal form to record the transactions, assuming the periodic inventory system is used.

SKILLS DEVELOPMENT CASES

Conceptual Analysis

SD 1. Matson Audio and Video Source, Inc., has operated in a middle-size Midwest city for 30 years. The company has always prided itself on individual attention to its customers. It carries a large inventory so it can offer a good selection and deliver purchases quickly. It accepts credit cards and checks in payment but also provides 90 days credit to reliable customers who have purchased from the company in the past. The company maintains good relations with suppliers by paying invoices soon after they are received. In the past year, the company has been strapped for cash and has had to borrow from the bank to pay its bills. An analysis of its financial statements reveals that, on average, inventory is on hand for 70 days before being sold and receivables are held for 90 days before being paid. Accounts payable are paid, on average, in 20 days. What are the operating cycle and the financing period, and how long are Matson's? In what three ways can Matson improve its cash flow management? Make a suggestion for implementing each.

LO1 Cash Flow Management

SD 2. Books Unlimited is a well-established chain of 20 bookstores in eastern Michigan. In recent years the company has grown rapidly, adding five new stores in regional malls. Management has relied on the manager of each store to place orders keyed to the market in his or her region; the managers select from a master list of available titles provided by the central office. Every six months, a physical inventory is taken, and financial statements are prepared using the periodic inventory system. At that time, books that have not sold well are placed on sale or, whenever possible, returned to the publisher. As a result of the company's fast growth, there are many new store managers, and management has found that they are not as able to judge the market as are managers of the older, established stores. Thus, management is considering a recommendation to implement a perpetual inventory system and carefully monitor sales from the central office. Do you think Books Unlimited should switch to the perpetual inventory system or stay with the periodic inventory system? Discuss the advantages and disadvantages of each system.

LO1 Periodic Versus Perpetual Inventory Systems

Ethical Dilemma

SD 3. The purchasing power of some customers is such that they can exert pressure on suppliers to go beyond the suppliers' customary allowances. For example, Wal-Mart <www.walmart.com> represents more than 10 percent of annual sales for many suppliers, including Fruit of the Loom <www.fruit.com>, Sunbeam <www.sunbeam.com>, Rubbermaid <www.rubbermaid.com>, and Coleman <www.coleman.com>. *Forbes* magazine reports that while many of these suppliers allow a 2 percent discount if bills are paid within 15 days, "Wal-Mart routinely pays its bills closer to 30 days and takes the 2 percent discount anyway on the gross amount of the invoice, not the net amount, which deducts for [trade] discounts and things like freight costs."[10]

SO7 Ethics and Purchases Discounts

Identify two ways in which Wal-Mart's practice benefits Wal-Mart. Do you think this practice is unethical, or is it just good cash management on the part of Wal-Mart? Are the suppliers harmed by it?

Research Activity

SD 4.

LO1 **Inventory Systems and**
LO3 **Internal Controls**
LO4
LO5
LO6

Go to a retail business, such as a bookstore, a clothing shop, a gift shop, a grocery, a hardware store, or a car dealership, in your local shopping area or a local shopping mall. Ask to speak to someone who is knowledgeable about the store's inventory methods. Find out the answers to the following questions and be prepared to discuss your findings in class:

1. *Inventory systems* How is each item of inventory identified? Does the business have a computerized or a manual inventory system? Which inventory system, periodic or perpetual, is used? How often do employees take a physical inventory? What procedures are followed in taking a physical inventory? What kinds of inventory reports are prepared or received?
2. *Internal control structure* How does the company protect against inventory theft and loss? What control activities, including authorization, recording transactions, documents and records, physical controls, periodic checks, separation of duties, and sound personnel policies, does the company use? Can you see these control procedures in use?

Group Activity: Assign teams to carry out the above assignments.

Decision-Making Practice

SD 5.

LO1 **Analysis of Merchandising**
LO3 **Income Statement**
LO4
LO5
LO6

In 20x5, Mark Fischer opened a small retail store in a suburban mall. Called Fischer Garb Company, the shop sold designer jeans. Mark Fischer worked 14 hours a day and controlled all aspects of the operation. All sales were for cash or bank credit card. Fischer Garb Company was such a success that in 20x6, Fischer decided to open a second store in another mall. Because the new shop needed his attention, he hired a manager to work in the original store with two sales clerks. During 20x6, the new store was successful, but the operations of the original store did not match the first year's performance.

Concerned about this turn of events, Fischer compared the two years' results for the original store. The figures were as follows:

	20x6	20x5
Net sales	$325,000	$350,000
Cost of goods sold	225,000	225,000
Gross margin	$100,000	$125,000
Operating expenses	75,000	50,000
Income before income taxes	$ 25,000	$ 75,000

In addition, Fischer's analysis revealed that the cost and selling price of jeans were about the same in both years and that the level of operating expenses was roughly the same in both years, except for the new manager's $25,000 salary. Sales returns and allowances were insignificant amounts in both years.

Studying the situation further, Fischer discovered the following facts about the cost of goods sold:

	20x6	20x5
Purchases	$200,000	$271,000
Total purchases allowances	15,000	20,000
Freight in	19,000	27,000
Physical inventory, end of year	32,000	53,000

Still not satisfied, Fischer went through all the individual sales and purchase records for the year. Both sales and purchases were verified. However, the 20x6 ending inventory should have been $57,000, given the unit purchases and sales during the year. After puzzling over all this information, Fischer comes to you for accounting help.

1. Using Fischer's new information, recompute the cost of goods sold for 20x5 and 20x6, and account for the difference in income before income taxes between 20x5 and 20x6.
2. Suggest at least two reasons for the discrepancy in the 20x6 ending inventory. How might Fischer improve the management of the original store?

FINANCIAL REPORTING AND ANALYSIS CASES

Interpreting Financial Reports

FRA 1.
LO1 Comparison of Operating
LO3 Performance
LO4

Wal-Mart <www.walmart.com> and Kmart <www.kmartcorp.com>, two of the largest retailers in the United States, have different approaches to retailing. Their success has been different also. At one time, Kmart was larger than Wal-Mart. Today, Wal-Mart is almost three times as large and Kmart has declared bankruptcy. You can see the difference by analyzing their respective income statements and merchandise inventories. Selected information from their annual reports for the year ended January 31, 2001, is presented below.[11] (All amounts are in millions.)

Wal-Mart: Net sales, $191,329; Cost of goods sold, $150,255; Operating expenses, $31,550; Ending inventory, $21,442

Kmart: Net sales, $37,028; Cost of goods sold, $29,658; Operating expenses, $7,415; Ending inventory, $6,412

1. Prepare a schedule computing the gross margin and income from operations for both companies as dollar amounts and as percentages of net sales. Also compute inventory as a percentage of the cost of goods sold.
2. From what you know about the different retailing approaches of these two companies, do the gross margins and incomes from operations you computed in 1 seem compatible with these approaches? What is it about the nature of Wal-Mart's operations that produces higher gross margin and lower operating expenses in percentages in comparison to Kmart? Which company's approach was more successful in the fiscal year ending January 31, 2001? Explain your answer.
3. Both companies have chosen a fiscal year that ends on January 31. Why do you suppose they made this choice? How realistic do you think the inventory figures are as indicators of inventory levels during the rest of the year? Which company appears to make the most efficient use of its inventory?

FRA 2.
LO1 Business Objectives and
LO3 Income Statements

Superior Products, Inc., is one of the nation's largest discount retailers, operating 216 stores in 30 states. In a letter to stockholders in the 2003 annual report (fiscal year ended January 31, 2004), the chairman and chief executive officer of the company stated, "Our operating plan for fiscal 2004 (year ended January 30, 2005) calls for moderate sales increases, continued improvement in gross margins, and a continuation of aggressive expense reduction programs." The following data are from the income statements presented in the 2004 annual report (dated January 30, 2005) (in millions):

	Year Ended		
	January 30, 2005	January 31, 2004	February 1, 2003
Net sales	$2,067	$2,142	$2,235
Cost of goods sold	1,500	1,593	1,685
Operating expenses	466	486	502

Did Superior Products achieve the objectives stated by its chairman? (**Hint:** Prepare an income statement for each year and compute gross margin and operating expenses as percentages of net sales.)

FRA 3.
LO5 Internal Control Lapse

Starbucks Corporation <www.starbucks.com> has accused an employee and her husband of embezzling $3.7 million by billing the company for services from a fictitious consulting firm. The employee and her husband created a phony company called RAD Services Inc. and charged Starbucks for work they never provided. The employee worked in the information technology department. RAD Services Inc. charged

Starbucks for as much as $492,800 in consulting services in a single week.[12] For such a fraud to have taken place, certain control activities were likely not implemented. Identify and describe these activities.

International Company

FRA 4.
LO4 British Terminology for Merchandising Transactions

Harrods <www.harrods.com> is a large British retailer with department stores throughout the United Kingdom and Europe. British and American merchandising terms differ. For instance, in the United Kingdom, the income statement is called the *profit and loss account*, sales is called *turnover*, merchandise inventory is called *stocks*, accounts receivable is called *debtors*, and accounts payable is called *creditors*. Of course, the amounts are stated in terms of the pound (£). In today's business world, it is important to understand terminology employed by professionals from other countries. Explain in your own words why the British may use the terms *profit and loss account, turnover, stocks, debtors,* and *creditors* rather than the American equivalents.

Toys "R" Us Annual Report

FRA 5.
LO1 Operating Cycle and Financing Period

Refer to the Toys "R" Us <www.tru.com> annual report in the Supplement to Chapter 1 and to Figures 1 and 2 in this chapter. Write a memorandum to your instructor briefly describing the Toys "R" Us operating cycle and financing period. This memorandum should identify the most common transactions in the operating cycle as it applies to Toys "R" Us. It should refer to the importance of accounts receivable, accounts payable, and merchandise inventory in the Toys "R" Us financial statements. Complete the memorandum by explaining why the operating cycle and financing period are favorable to the company.

Comparison Case: Toys "R" Us and Walgreen Co.

FRA 6.
LO1 Income Statement Analysis

Refer to the Toys "R" Us <www.tru.com> annual report and the financial statements of Walgreen Co. <www.walgreens.com> in the Supplement to Chapter 1. Determine which company—Toys "R" Us or Walgreens—has more profitable merchandising operations by preparing a schedule that compares the companies based on net sales, cost of sales, gross margin, total operating expenses, and income from operations as a percentage of sales. (*Hint:* You should put the income statements in comparable formats.) In addition, for each company, compute inventory as a percentage of the cost of sales. Which company has the highest prices in relation to costs of sales? Which company is more efficient in its operating expenses? Which company manages its inventory better? Overall, on the basis of the income statement, which company is more profitable? Explain your answers.

Fingraph® Financial Analyst™

FRA 7.
LO1 Income Statement Analysis
LO3

Choose any retail company from the list of Fingraph companies on the Needles Accounting Resource Center Web Site at http://accounting.college.hmco.com/students. Access the Microsoft Excel spreadsheets for the company you selected. Using the Fingraph CD-ROM software, display the Income Statements Analysis: Income from Operations in tabular and graphic form for the company.

Write an executive summary that analyzes the change in the company's income from operations from the first to the second year. In preparing the summary, focus on the reasons the change occurred by answering the following questions: Did the company's income from operations improve or decline from the first to the second year? What was the relationship of the change to the change in net sales? Was the change in income from operations primarily due to a change in gross margin or to a change in operating expenses? Suggest some possible reasons for the change in gross margin or operating expenses. Use percentages to support your answer.

Internet Case

LO1 Comparison of Traditional
LO3 Merchandising with Ecommerce

FRA 8. *Ecommerce* is a word coined to describe business conducted over the Internet. Ecommerce is similar in some ways to traditional retailing, but it presents new challenges. Choose a company with traditional retail outlets that is also selling over the Internet and go to its web site. Some examples are Wal-Mart <www.walmart.com>, Kmart <www.kmartcorp.com>, Toys "R" Us <www.tru.com>, Barnes & Noble <www.bn.com>, and Lands' End <www.landsend.com>. Investigate and list the steps a customer makes to purchase an item on the site. How do these steps differ from those in a traditional retail store? What are some of the accounting challenges in recording Internet transactions? Be prepared to discuss your results in class.

7

Chapter 7 focuses on management of, and accounting for, several types of short-term assets: cash and cash equivalents, short-term investments, accounts receivable, and notes receivable.

Short-Term Financial Assets

LEARNING OBJECTIVES

LO1 Identify and explain the management issues related to short-term financial assets.

LO2 Explain *cash, cash equivalents,* and the importance of electronic funds transfer.

LO3 Identify types of short-term investments and explain the financial reporting implications.

LO4 Define *accounts receivable* and apply the allowance method of accounting for uncollectible accounts.

LO5 Define *promissory note,* and compute and record promissory notes receivable.

SUPPLEMENTAL OBJECTIVE

SO6 Prepare a bank reconciliation.

DECISION POINT A USER'S FOCUS

Pioneer Corporation <www.pioneer.co.jp> A company must use its assets to maximize income earned while maintaining liquidity. Pioneer Corporation, a leading Japanese manufacturer of electronics for home, commerce, and industry, manages about $2.4 billion in short-term financial assets. **Short-term financial assets** are assets that arise from cash transactions, the investment of cash, and the extension of credit. What is the composition of these assets? Why are they important to Pioneer's management?

Pioneer's short-term financial assets, as reported on the balance sheet in the company's annual report, are shown in the table on the opposite page.[1] These assets make up almost 41 percent of Pioneer's total assets, and they are very important to the company's strategy for meeting its goals. Effective asset management techniques ensure that these assets remain liquid and usable for the company's operations.

A commonly used ratio for measuring the adequacy of short-term financial assets is the quick ratio. The **quick ratio** is the ratio of short-term financial assets to current liabilities. Because Pioneer's current liabilities are (in millions) ¥177,825 ($1,434.1), its quick ratio is 1.39, which is computed as follows:

$$\text{Quick Ratio} = \frac{\text{Short-Term Financial Assets}}{\text{Current Liabilities}}$$

$$= \frac{\$1,995,200,000}{\$1,434,100,000} = 1.39$$

A quick ratio of about 1.0 has historically been the minimum common benchmark. However, it is more

How does Pioneer Electric, a leading manufacturer of electronics for the home, manage its short-term financial assets?

important to look at industry characteristics and at the trends for a particular company to see if the ratio is improving or not. A lower ratio may mean that a company is a very good manager of its short-term financial assets. Pioneer has maintained a quick ratio of over 1.0 for several years. Through good cash management, the company has not tied up excess funds in quick assets relative to current liabilities. This chapter emphasizes management of, and accounting for, short-term financial assets to achieve liquidity.

Financial Highlights
(In millions)

	Yen	Dollars
Cash and cash equivalents	¥121,127	$ 976.8
Short-term investments	1,598	12.9
Accounts receivable, net of allowances of ¥5,895 ($47.5)	116,594	940.3
Notes receivable	8,079	65.2
Total short-term financial assets	¥247,398	$1,995.2

MANAGEMENT ISSUES RELATED TO SHORT-TERM FINANCIAL ASSETS

LO1 Identify and explain the management issues related to short-term financial assets.

RELATED TEXT ASSIGNMENTS
Q: 1, 2
SE: 1, 2
E: 1, 2
P: 2, 7
SD: 1, 2, 3, 4, 5
FRA: 1, 3, 4, 5, 6

The management of short-term financial assets is critical to the goal of maintaining adequate liquidity. In dealing with short-term financial assets, management must address three key issues: managing cash needs during seasonal cycles, setting credit policies, and financing receivables.

Managing Cash Needs During Seasonal Cycles

Most companies experience seasonal cycles of business activity during the year. During some periods, sales are weak; during others, they are strong. There are also periods when expenditures are high and periods when expenditures are low. For toy companies, college textbook publishers, amusement parks, construction companies, and sports equipment companies, the cycles are dramatic, but all companies experience them to some degree.

Seasonal cycles require careful planning of cash inflows, cash outflows, borrowing, and investing. Figure 1 shows the seasonal cycles typical of a home improvement company, such as The Home Depot, Inc. As you can see, cash receipts from sales are highest in the late spring, summer, and fall because that is when most people make home improvements. Sales are relatively low in the winter months. On the other hand, cash expenditures are highest in late winter and spring as the company builds up inventory for spring and summer selling. During the late summer, fall, and winter, the company has excess cash on hand that it needs to invest in a way that will earn a return but still permit access to cash as needed. During the late spring

www.homedepot.com

FIGURE 1
Seasonal Cycles and Cash Requirements for a Home Improvement Company

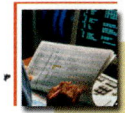

FOCUS ON BUSINESS PRACTICE

What a Difference a Year Makes!

It's hard to know how much cash reserve a company should have. Analysts are often critical of companies that build cash reserves because the cash is not earning as much as other assets might. But having a cash reserve may be a good thing, especially in a cyclical industry like the auto industry. For example, just about two years ago, the Big Three automakers—General Motors <www.gm.com>, Ford <www.ford.com>, and DaimlerChrysler <www.daimlerchrysler.com>—were awash in cash. However, in little over two years, the three companies went through $28 billion in cash through various purchases, losses, dividends, and share buybacks. Then, with increasing losses from rising costs, big rebates, and 0 percent financing, the companies were suddenly faced with a shortage of cash. As a result, Standard & Poor's lowered their credit ratings, which raises the interest cost of borrowing money. Perhaps the Big Three should have held on to some of that cash.[2]

ENRICHMENT NOTE:
Here is a chance to apply the economic concept of profit maximization. Profit is maximized when marginal revenue equals marginal cost. Thus, credit policy should equate the additional gross profit from credit sales with the cost of credit sales (i.e., bad debts).

● **STOP AND THINK!**
To increase sales, a company decides to increase its credit terms from 15 days to 30 days. What effect will this change in policy have on receivable turnover, average days' sales uncollected, and cash flows?

Receivable turnover will become smaller because average net accounts receivable will increase relative to sales. Consequently, the average days' sales uncollected will increase. This will have an adverse effect on cash flows because, on average, the company will have to wait longer to receive cash from sales. ■

and early summer, the company needs to plan for short-term borrowing to tide it over until cash receipts pick up later in the year. The discussion in this chapter of accounting for cash and cash equivalents and for short-term investments is directly related to managing the seasonal cycles of a business.

SETTING CREDIT POLICIES

Companies that sell on credit do so to be competitive and to increase sales. In setting credit terms, management must keep in mind both the terms the company's competitors are offering and the needs of customers. Obviously, companies that sell on credit want to have customers who will pay the debts they incur. To increase the likelihood of selling only to customers who will pay on time, most companies develop control procedures and maintain a credit department. The credit department's responsibilities include the examination of each person or company that applies for credit and the approval or rejection of a credit sale to that customer. Typically, the credit department asks for information about the customer's financial resources and debts. It may also check personal references and credit bureaus for further information. Then, based on the information it has gathered, the credit department decides whether to extend credit to the customer.

Two common measures of the effect of a company's credit policies are **receivable turnover** and **average days' sales uncollected**. The receivable turnover reflects the relative size of a company's accounts receivable and the success of its credit and collection policies. It may also be affected by external factors, such as seasonal conditions and interest rates. It shows how many times, on average, the receivables were turned into cash during the accounting period. The average days' sales uncollected is a related measure that shows, on average, how long it takes to collect accounts receivable.

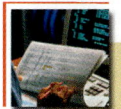

FOCUS ON BUSINESS PRACTICE

Why Powerful Buyers Can Cause Headaches for Small Businesses

Big buyers often have significant power over small suppliers, and their cash management decisions can cause severe cash flow problems for the little companies that depend on them. For instance, in an effort to control costs and optimize cash flow, Ameritech Corp. <www.ameritech.com> told 70,000 suppliers that it would begin paying its bills in 45 days instead of 30. Other large companies routinely take 90 days or more to pay. Some small suppliers are so anxious to get the big companies' business that they fail to realize the implications of the deals they make until it is too late. When Earthly Elements, Inc., accepted a $10,000 order for dried floral gifts from a national home shopping network, its management was ecstatic because the deal increased sales by 25 percent. But in four months, the resulting cash crunch forced the company to close down. When the shopping network finally paid for the big order six months later, it was too late to revive Earthly Elements.[3]

www.pioneer.co.jp

Turnover ratios usually consist of one balance sheet account and one income statement account. The receivable turnover is computed by dividing net sales by average net accounts receivable. Theoretically, the numerator should be net credit sales, but the amount of net credit sales is rarely made available in public reports, so total net sales is used. Pioneer Corporation, discussed in the Decision Point at the start of the chapter, had net sales in 2001 of $5,052,700,000. Its net trade accounts receivable in 2001 and 2000 were $940,300,000 and $805,564,000, respectively. Its receivable turnover is computed as follows:[4]

$$\text{Receivable Turnover} = \frac{\text{Net Sales}}{\text{Average Net Accounts Receivable}}$$

$$= \frac{\$5,052,700,000}{(\$940,300,000 + \$805,564,000) \div 2}$$

$$= \frac{\$5,052,700,000}{\$872,932,000} = 5.8 \text{ times}$$

BUSINESS-WORLD EXAMPLE: For many businesses with seasonal sales activity, such as Nordstrom, Dillard, Marshall Field's, and Macy's, the fourth quarter produces more than 25 percent of annual sales. For such businesses, receivables are highest at the balance sheet date, resulting in an artificially low receivable turnover and high average days' sales uncollected.

To find the average days' sales uncollected, the number of days in a year is divided by the receivable turnover, as follows:

$$\text{Average Days' Sales Uncollected} = \frac{365 \text{ days}}{\text{Receivable Turnover}} = \frac{365 \text{ days}}{5.8} = 62.9 \text{ days}$$

Pioneer turns its receivables 5.8 times a year, for an average of every 62.9 days. While this turnover period is longer than that of many companies, it is not unusual for electronics companies because their credit terms allow retail outlets to receive and sell products before paying for them. This example demonstrates the need to interpret ratios in light of the specific industry's practice.

As Figure 2 shows, the receivable turnover ratio varies substantially from industry to industry. Grocery stores, for example, have a high turnover because that type of business has few receivables; the turnover in interstate trucking is 11.4 times because the typical credit terms in that industry are 30 days. The turnover in the machinery and computer industries is lower because those industries tend to have longer credit terms.

Figure 3 shows the average days' sales uncollected for the industries listed in Figure 2. Grocery stores, which have the lowest ratio (3.8 days) require the least amount of receivables financing; the computer industry, with average days' sales uncollected of 52.9 days, requires the most.

FIGURE 2
Receivable Turnover for Selected Industries

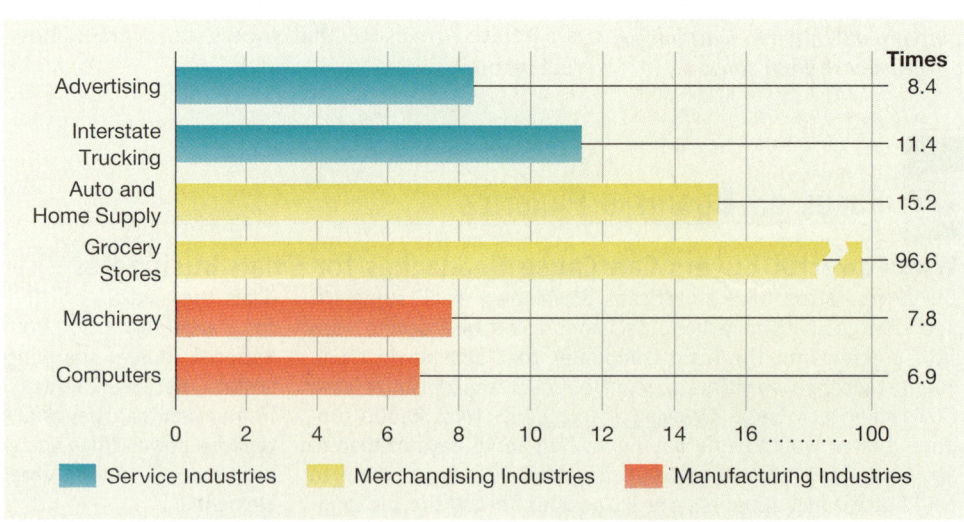

Source: Data from Dun and Bradstreet, *Industry Norms and Key Business Ratios,* 2001–2002.

FIGURE 3
Average Days' Sales Uncollected for Selected Industries

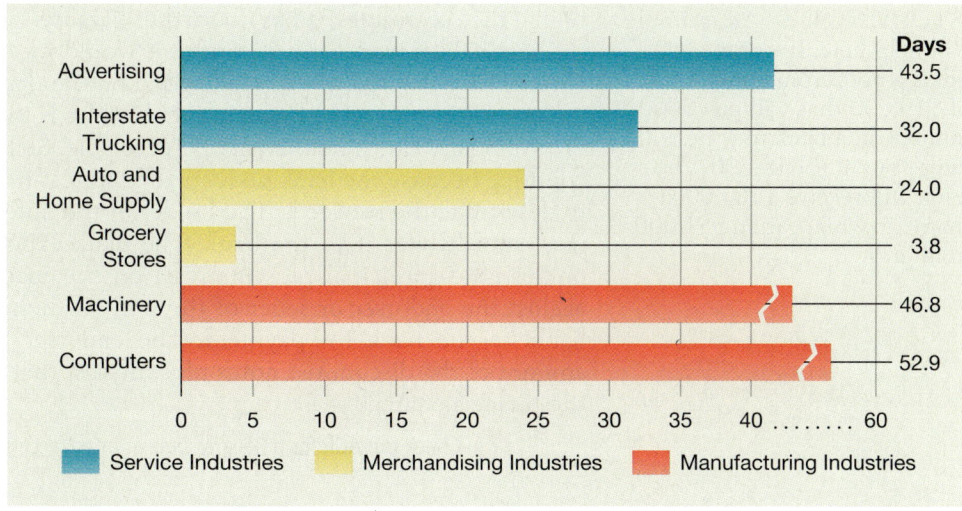

Source: Data from Dun and Bradstreet, *Industry Norms and Key Business Ratios,* 2001–2002.

FINANCING RECEIVABLES

Financial flexibility is important to most companies. Companies that have significant amounts of assets tied up in accounts receivable may be unwilling or unable to wait until cash from the receivables is collected. Many companies have set up finance companies to help their customers pay for the purchase of their products; for example, Ford has set up Ford Motor Credit Co. (FMCC), General Motors has set up General Motors Acceptance Corp. (GMAC), and Sears has set up Sears Roebuck Acceptance Corp. (SRAC). Some companies borrow funds by pledging their accounts receivable as collateral. If a company does not pay back its loan, the creditor can take the collateral (in this case, the accounts receivable) and convert it to cash to satisfy the loan.

www.ford.com
www.gm.com
www.sears.com

Companies can also raise funds by selling or transferring accounts receivable to another entity, called a **factor**. The sale or transfer of accounts receivable, called **factoring**, can be done with or without recourse. *With recourse* means that the seller of the receivables is liable to the purchaser if a receivable is not collected. *Without recourse* means that the factor that buys the accounts receivable bears any losses from uncollectible accounts. A company's acceptance of credit cards like Visa, MasterCard, or American Express is an example of factoring without recourse because the credit card issuers accept the risk of nonpayment.

KEY POINT: The receivable turnover and average days' sales uncollected will appear better for a company that factors receivables than for a company that does not factor.

The factor, of course, charges a fee for its service. The fee for sales with recourse is usually about 1 percent of the accounts receivable. The fee is higher for sales without recourse because the factor's risk is greater. In accounting terminology, the seller of the receivables with recourse is said to be contingently liable. A **contingent liability** is a potential liability that can develop into a real liability if a particular subsequent event occurs. In this case, the subsequent event would be nonpayment of the receivable by the customer. A contingent liability generally requires disclosure in the notes to the financial statements.

www.circuitcity.com

Circuit City Stores, Inc., is one of the nation's largest electronics and appliance retailers. To sell its products, the company offers generous terms through its installment programs, under which customers pay over a number of months. The company is growing rapidly and needs the cash from these installment receivables sooner than the customers have agreed to pay. To generate cash immediately from these receivables, the company sells them through a process called securitization. Under **securitization**, the company groups its receivables in batches and sells them at a discount to companies and investors. When the receivables are paid, the buyers of the receivables receive the full amount; their revenue is the amount of the discount. Circuit City sells all its receivables without recourse, which means that after

STUDY NOTE: An example will help here. If Company A holds a note from company B of $10,000 that will pay $600 in interest, a bank may be willing to buy it for $9,600. The bank will receive $10,600 at maturity while earning $1,000 in interest.

selling the receivables, it has no further liability, even if the customers do not pay. If the receivables were with recourse, it would mean that if a customer did not pay, Circuit City would have to make good on the debt.[5]

Another method of financing receivables is through the **discounting**, or selling, of promissory notes held as notes receivable. Selling notes receivable is called discounting because the bank deducts the interest from the maturity value of the note to determine the proceeds. The holder of the note (usually the payee) endorses the note and delivers it to the bank. The bank expects to collect the maturity value of the note (principal plus interest) on the maturity date but also has recourse against the endorser or seller of the note. If the maker fails to pay, the endorser is liable to the bank for payment. The endorser has a contingent liability in the amount of the discounted notes plus interest that must be disclosed in the notes to the financial statements.

✓ Check out ACE for a Review Quiz at http://accounting.college.hmco.com/students.

CASH AND CASH EQUIVALENTS

LO2 Explain *cash, cash equivalents,* and the importance of electronic funds transfer.

RELATED TEXT ASSIGNMENTS
Q: 3, 4
SE: 3
E: 3
SD: 1
FRA: 4

ENRICHMENT NOTE:
Most reporting practices are set by the FASB. This is an example of an SEC requirement for disclosure of information.

www.pioneer.co.jp

🔴 **STOP AND THINK!**
A cash register can be considered a type of imprest system. If a cashier in a supermarket started the day with $100 in change, what should the amount of cash in the drawer equal at the end of the day?
The amount of cash in the drawer should equal the total cash sales less any refunds plus $100. ∎

The annual report of Pioneer Corporation refers to *cash and cash equivalents.* Of the two terms, *cash* is the easier to understand. It is the most liquid of all assets and the most readily available to pay debts. On the balance sheet, **cash** normally consists of currency and coins on hand, checks and money orders from customers, and deposits in bank checking and savings accounts. Cash may also include a **compensating balance**, an amount that is not entirely free to be spent. A compensating balance is a minimum amount that a bank requires a company to keep in its bank account as part of a credit-granting arrangement. Such an arrangement restricts cash; in effect, increases the interest of the loan; and reduces a company's liquidity. Therefore, the SEC requires companies to disclose the amount of any compensating balances in a note to the financial statements.

The term *cash equivalents* is a little harder to understand. At times a company may find that it has more cash on hand than it needs to pay current obligations. Excess cash should not remain idle, especially during periods of high interest rates. Thus, management may periodically invest idle funds in time deposits or certificates of deposit at banks and other financial institutions, in government securities (such as U.S. Treasury notes), or in other securities. Such actions are rightfully called investments. However, if the investments have a term of 90 days or less when they are purchased, they are called **cash equivalents** because the funds revert to cash so quickly that they are regarded as cash on the balance sheet. Pioneer Corporation follows this practice. Its policy is stated as follows: "The Company considers all highly liquid investments with a maturity of 90 days or less when purchased to be cash equivalents. Cash equivalents are stated at cost, which approximates market value."[6] A survey of 600 large U.S. corporations found that 53 of them, or 9 percent, used the term *cash* as the balance sheet caption and 510, or 85 percent, used the phrase *cash and cash equivalents* or *cash and equivalents.* Twenty-seven companies, or 5 percent, combined cash with marketable securities.[7] The average amount of cash held can also vary by industry.

Most companies need to keep some currency and coins on hand. Currency and coins are needed for cash registers, for paying expenses that are impractical to pay by check, and for situations that require cash advances—for example, when sales representatives need cash for travel expenses. One way to control a cash fund or cash advances is through the use of an imprest system. A common form of imprest system is a petty cash fund, which is established at a fixed amount. Each cash payment from the fund is documented by a receipt. The fund is periodically reimbursed, based on the documented expenditures, by the exact amount necessary to restore its original cash balance. The person responsible for the petty cash fund must

Focus on Business Ethics

What About the Unlawful Use of EFT?

Electronic Funds Transfer (EFT) has made it easy to transfer funds around the world. It has facilitated the huge growth in international business, but what about the unlawful use of EFT? To combat the laundering of money by drug dealers, U.S. law requires banks to report cash transactions in excess of $10,000. However, terrorist groups have circumvented this law by electronically transferring amounts of less than $10,000. In response, the Treasury Department has set up rules that require banks to keep records about the sources and recipients of electronic transfers. But it is questionable how much effect this action will have. Since most of the millions of EFT transactions that occur every day look pretty much alike, looking for transactions that support illegal activities is like looking for a needle in a haystack.

---

always be able to account for its contents by having cash and receipts whose total equals the originally fixed amount.

All businesses rely on banks to control cash receipts and cash disbursements. Banks serve as safe depositories for cash, negotiable instruments, and other valuable business documents, such as stocks and bonds. The checking accounts that banks provide improve control by minimizing the amount of currency a company needs to keep on hand and by supplying permanent records of all cash payments. Banks also serve as agents in a variety of transactions, such as the collection and payment of certain kinds of debts and the exchange of foreign currencies.

Many companies commonly conduct transactions through a type of electronic communication called **electronic funds transfer (EFT)**. Instead of writing checks to pay for purchases or to repay loans, the company arranges to have cash transferred electronically from its bank to another company's bank. Wal-Mart Stores, Inc., for example, makes 75 percent of its payments to suppliers through EFT. The actual cash, of course, is not transferred. For the banks, an electronic transfer is simply a bookkeeping entry.

www.walmart.com

In serving customers, banks also offer automated teller machines (ATMs) for making deposits, withdrawing cash, transferring funds among accounts, and paying bills. Large consumer banks like Citibank, BankOne, and Bank of America process hundreds of thousands of ATM transactions each week. Many banks also give customers the option of paying bills over the telephone and with *debit cards*. When a customer makes a retail purchase using a debit card, the amount of the purchase is deducted directly from the buyer's bank account. The bank usually documents debit card transactions for the retailer, but the retailer must develop new internal controls to ensure that the transactions are recorded properly and that unauthorized transfers are not permitted. It is expected that within a few years, 25 percent of all retail activity will be handled electronically.

www.citigroup.com
www.bankone.com
www.bankofamerica.com

✓ Check out ACE for a Review Quiz at http://accounting.college.hmco.com/students.

SHORT-TERM INVESTMENTS

LO3 Identify types of short-term investments and explain the financial reporting implications.

RELATED TEXT ASSIGNMENTS
Q: 5, 6
SE: 4, 5
E: 4, 5
P: 1, 6
SD: 1, 5, 6

When investments have a maturity of more than 90 days but are intended to be held only until cash is needed for current operations, they are called **short-term investments** or **marketable securities**. Investments intended to be held for more than one year are called *long-term investments*. Long-term investments are reported in an investments section of the balance sheet, not in the current assets section. Although long-term investments may be just as marketable as short-term assets, management intends to hold them for an indefinite period of time.

Securities that may be held as short-term or long-term investments fall into three categories, as specified by the Financial Accounting Standards Board: held-to-maturity securities, trading securities, and available-for-sale securities.[8] Trading securities are classified as short-term investments. Held-to-maturity securities and available-for-sale securities may be classified as either short-term or long-term investments, depending on their length to maturity or management's intent to hold them. The three categories of securities when held as short-term investments are discussed here.

HELD-TO-MATURITY SECURITIES

KEY POINT: Any broker costs or taxes paid to acquire securities are part of the cost of the securities.

Held-to-maturity securities are debt securities that management intends to hold to their maturity date and whose cash value is not needed until that date. Such securities are recorded at cost and valued on the balance sheet at cost adjusted for the effects of interest. For example, suppose that on December 1, 20x4, Webber Company pays $97,000 for U.S. Treasury bills, which are short-term debt of the federal government. The bills will mature in 120 days at $100,000. Webber would make the following entry:

A = L + OE
+
−

```
20x4
Dec. 1   Short-Term Investments              97,000
              Cash                                    97,000
          Purchase of U.S. Treasury bills
          that mature in 120 days
```

At Webber's year end on December 31, the entry to accrue the interest income earned to date would be as follows:

A = L + OE
+   +

```
20x4
Dec. 31  Short-Term Investments                 750
              Interest Income                          750
          Accrual of interest on U.S. Treasury bills
          $3,000 × 30/120 = $750
```

On December 31, the U.S. Treasury bills would be shown on the balance sheet as a short-term investment at their amortized cost of $97,750 ($97,000 + $750). When Webber receives the maturity value on March 31, 20x5, the entry is as follows:

A = L + OE
+   +
−

```
20x5
Mar. 31  Cash                                 100,000
              Short-Term Investments                97,750
              Interest Income                         2,250
          Receipt of cash at maturity of
          U.S. Treasury bills and recognition
          of related income
```

TRADING SECURITIES

Trading securities are debt and equity securities bought and held principally for the purpose of being sold in the near term. Debt securities are to be redeemed at a specified time and pay a return in the form of interest. Equity securities are an ownership interest in an entity and are subject to market fluctuations. Return takes the form of dividends and increases in the price of the securities.

Trading securities are frequently bought and sold to generate profits on short-term changes in their prices. Trading securities are classified as current assets on the balance sheet and are valued at fair value, which is usually the same as market value—for example, when securities are traded on a stock exchange or in the over-the-counter market.

An increase or decrease in the fair value of the total trading portfolio (the group of securities held for trading purposes) is included in net income in the accounting period in which the increase or decrease occurs. For example, assume that Franklin Company purchases 10,000 shares of Exxon Mobil Corporation for $900,000 ($90 per share) and 5,000 shares of Texaco Inc. for $300,000 ($60 per share) on October 25, 20x4. The purchase is made for trading purposes; that is, management intends

www.exxonmobil.com
www.texaco.com

to realize a gain by holding the shares for only a short period. The entry to record the investment at cost follows:

A = L + OE
+
−

20x4
Oct. 25   Short-Term Investments   1,200,000
                Cash   1,200,000
                    Investment in stocks for trading
                    ($900,000 + $300,000 = $1,200,000)

Assume that at year end Exxon Mobil's stock price has decreased to $80 per share and Texaco's has risen to $64 per share. The trading portfolio is now valued at $1,120,000:

Security	Market Value	Cost	Gain (Loss)
Exxon Mobil (10,000 shares)	$ 800,000	$ 900,000	
Texaco (5,000 shares)	320,000	300,000	
Totals	$1,120,000	$1,200,000	($80,000)

Because the current fair value of the portfolio is $80,000 less than the original cost of $1,200,000, an adjusting entry is needed, as follows:

A = L + OE
−   −

20x4
Dec. 31   Unrealized Loss on Investments   80,000
                Allowance to Adjust Short-Term
                    Investments to Market   80,000
                    Recognition of unrealized loss
                    on trading portfolio

KEY POINT: The Allowance to Adjust Short-Term Investments to Market account is never changed when securities are sold. It changes only with an adjusting entry at year end.

The unrealized loss will appear on the income statement as a reduction in income. The loss is unrealized because the securities have not been sold; unrealized gains are treated the same way if they occur. The Allowance to Adjust Short-Term Investments to Market account appears on the balance sheet as a contra-asset, as follows:

Short-term investments (at cost) $1,200,000
Less allowance to adjust short-term investments to market   80,000
Short-term investments (at market) $1,120,000

or, more simply,

Short-term investments (at market value, cost is $1,200,000) $1,120,000

If Franklin sells its 5,000 shares of Texaco for $70 per share on March 2, 20x5, a realized gain on trading securities is recorded as follows:

A = L + OE
+   +
−

20x5
Mar. 2   Cash   350,000
                Short-Term Investments   300,000
                Realized Gain on Investments   50,000
                    Sale of 5,000 shares of Texaco
                    for $70 per share; cost was $60 per share

The realized gain will appear on the income statement. Note that the realized gain is unaffected by the adjustment for the unrealized loss at the end of 20x4. The two transactions are treated independently. If the stock had been sold for less than cost, a realized loss on investments would have been recorded. Realized losses also appear on the income statement.

www.bp.com

Let's assume that during 20x5 Franklin buys 2,000 shares of BP Corporation at $64 per share and has no transactions involving Exxon Mobil. Also assume that by December 31, 20x5, the price of Exxon Mobil's stock has risen to $95 per share, or $5 per share more than the original cost, and that BP's stock price has fallen to $58, or $6 less than the original cost. The trading portfolio now can be analyzed as follows:

Security	Market Value	Cost	Gain (Loss)
Exxon Mobil (10,000 shares)	$ 950,000	$ 900,000	
BP (2,000 shares)	116,000	128,000	
Totals	$1,066,000	$1,028,000	$38,000

KEY POINT: The entry to the Allowance to Adjust Short-Term Investments to Market account is equal to the change in the market value. Compute the new allowance, and then compute the amount needed to change the account. The unrealized loss or gain is the other half of the entry.

$A = L + OE$
  $+$ $+$

The market value of the portfolio now exceeds the cost by $38,000 ($1,066,000 − $1,028,000). This amount represents the targeted ending balance for the Allowance to Adjust Short-Term Investments to Market account. Recall that at the end of 20x4, that account had a credit balance of $80,000, meaning that the market value of the trading portfolio was less than the cost. The account has no entries during 20x5 and thus retains its balance until adjusting entries are made at the end of the year. The adjustment for 20x5 must be $118,000—enough to result in a debit balance of $38,000 in the allowance account.

20x5				
Dec. 31	Allowance to Adjust Short-Term Investments to Market		118,000	
	Unrealized Gain on Investments			118,000
	Recognition of unrealized gain on trading portfolio			
	($80,000 + $38,000 = $118,000)			

● **STOP AND THINK!**
What would cause an Allowance to Adjust Short-Term Investments to Market account that has a negative (credit) balance at the beginning of the year to have a positive (debit) balance at the end of the year?

The total market value of the portfolio of trading securities would have increased enough during the year to exceed the negative (credit) balance at the beginning of the year. ■

The 20x5 ending balance of the allowance account may be determined as follows:

Allowance to Adjust Short-Term Investments to Market

Dec. 31, 20x5 adj.	118,000	Dec. 31, 20x4 bal.	80,000
Dec. 31, 20x5 bal.	**38,000**		

The balance sheet presentation of short-term investments is as follows:

Short-term investments (at cost)	$1,028,000
Plus allowance to adjust short-term investments to market	38,000
Short-term investments (at market)	$1,066,000

or, more simply,

Short-term investments (at market value, cost is $1,028,000)	$1,066,000

If the company also holds held-to-maturity securities, they are included in short-term investments at cost adjusted for the effects of interest if they will mature within one year.

AVAILABLE-FOR-SALE SECURITIES

Available-for-sale securities are debt and equity securities that do not meet the criteria for either held-to-maturity or trading securities. They are accounted for in exactly the same way as trading securities, except that the unrealized gain or loss is not reported on the income statement, but as a special item in the stockholders' equity section of the balance sheet. For example, Pioneer Corporation states in its annual report that "all debt securities and marketable equity securities held by the Company are classified as available-for-sale securities, and are carried at their fair values with unrealized gains and losses reported as a component of shareholders' equity."[9] This component is called accumulated other comprehensive income.

www.pioneer.co.jp

DIVIDEND AND INTEREST INCOME

Dividend and interest income for all three categories of investments appears in the other income and expenses section of the income statement.

 Check out ACE for a Review Quiz at http://accounting.college.hmco.com/students.

Accounts Receivable

LO4 Define *accounts receivable* and apply the allowance method of accounting for uncollectible accounts.

RELATED TEXT ASSIGNMENTS
Q: 7, 8, 9, 10, 11, 12, 13, 14, 15, 16, 17
SE: 6, 7, 8
E: 6, 7, 8, 9, 10, 11
P: 2, 3, 7, 8
SD: 2, 4
FRA: 1, 2, 4, 7

www.jcpenney.com
www.sears.com

The other major types of short-term financial assets are accounts receivable and notes receivable. Both result from credit sales to customers. Retailers like Sears, Roebuck and Co. have made credit available to nearly every responsible person in the United States. Every field of retail trade has expanded by allowing customers to make payments a month or more after the date of sale. What is not so apparent is that credit has expanded even more in the wholesale and manufacturing industries than at the retail level. The levels of accounts receivable in selected industries are shown in Figure 4.

Accounts receivable are short-term financial assets that arise from sales on credit to customers by wholesalers or retailers. This type of credit is often called **trade credit**. Terms on trade credit usually range from 5 to 60 days, depending on industry practice. For some companies that sell to consumers, **installment accounts receivable** constitute a significant portion of accounts receivable. Installment accounts receivable arise from the sale of goods on terms that allow the buyer to make a series of time payments. Department stores, appliance stores, furniture stores, used car companies, and other retail businesses often offer installment credit. Retailers like J.C. Penney Company, Inc., and Sears, Roebuck and Co. have millions of dollars in installment accounts receivable. Although the payment period may be 24 months or more, installment accounts receivable are classified as current assets if such credit policies are customary in the industry.

On the balance sheet, the title "accounts receivable" is used for amounts arising from credit sales made to customers in the ordinary course of business. If loans or credit sales are made to employees, officers of the corporation, or owners, they should be shown separately, with an asset title like "receivables from employees," because of the increased risk of uncollectibility and conflict of interest.

Normally, individual customer accounts receivable have debit balances, but sometimes customers overpay their accounts either by mistake or in anticipation of future purchases. When these accounts show credit balances, the total of the credits should be shown on the balance sheet as a current liability because the amounts must be refunded if future sales are not made to those customers.

UNCOLLECTIBLE ACCOUNTS AND THE DIRECT CHARGE-OFF METHOD

A company will always have some customers who cannot or will not pay their debts. The accounts owed by such customers are called **uncollectible accounts**, or *bad debts*, and are a loss or an expense of selling on credit. Why does a company sell

FIGURE 4
Accounts Receivable as a Percentage of Total Assets for Selected Industries

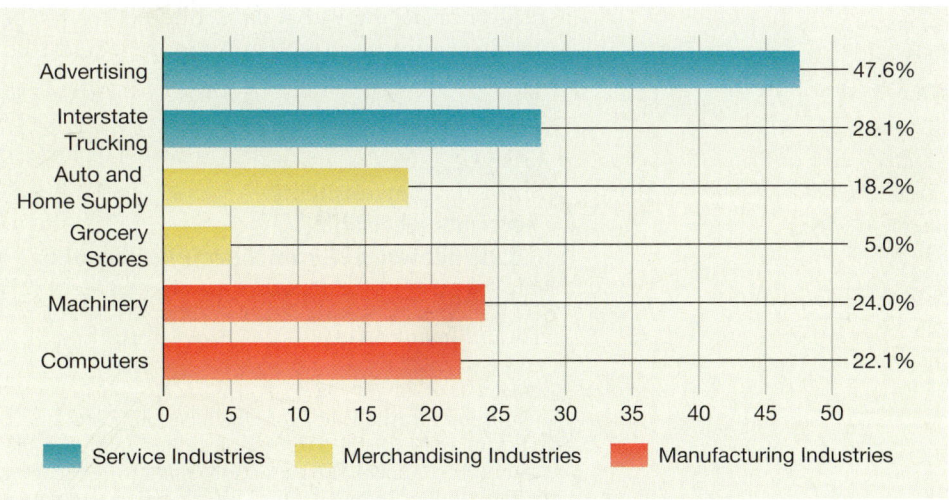

Source: Data from Dun and Bradstreet, *Industry Norms and Key Business Ratios*, 2001–2002.

on credit if it expects that some of its accounts will not be paid? The answer is that the company expects to sell much more than it would if it did not sell on credit, thereby increasing its earnings.

Some companies recognize the loss from an uncollectible account receivable at the time it is determined to be uncollectible by reducing Accounts Receivable directly and increasing Uncollectible Accounts Expense. Many small companies use this method, called the **direct charge-off method**, because it is required in computing taxable income under federal tax regulations. However, companies that follow generally accepted accounting principles do not use it in their financial statements because it does not conform to the matching rule. The direct charge-off is often recorded in a different accounting period from the one in which the sale takes place. Companies that follow GAAP prefer the allowance method, which is explained in the next section.

KEY POINT: The direct charge-off method does not conform to the matching rule.

UNCOLLECTIBLE ACCOUNTS AND THE ALLOWANCE METHOD

KEY POINT: The allowance method relies on an estimate of uncollectible accounts but is in accord with the matching rule.

Under the **allowance method** of accounting for uncollectible accounts, bad debt losses are matched against the sales they help to produce. As mentioned earlier, when management extends credit to increase sales, it knows that it will incur some losses from uncollectible accounts. Those losses are expenses that occur at the time sales on credit are made and should be matched to the revenues they help to generate. Of course, at the time the sales are made, management cannot identify which customers will not pay their debts, nor can it predict the exact amount of money that will be lost. Therefore, to observe the matching rule under generally accepted accounting principles, losses from uncollectible accounts must be estimated, and the estimate becomes an expense in the fiscal year in which the sales are made.

For example, let us assume that Cottage Sales Company made most of its sales on credit during its first year of operation, 20x4. At the end of the year, accounts receivable amounted to $100,000. On December 31, 20x4, management reviewed the collectible status of the accounts receivable. Approximately $6,000 of the $100,000 of accounts receivable were estimated to be uncollectible. Therefore, the uncollectible accounts expense for the first year of operation was estimated to be $6,000. The following adjusting entry would be made on December 31 of that year:

A = L + OE
− −

	20x4			
	Dec. 31	Uncollectible Accounts Expense	6,000	
		Allowance for Uncollectible Accounts		6,000
		To record the estimated uncollectible accounts expense for the year		

Uncollectible Accounts Expense appears on the income statement as an operating expense. **Allowance for Uncollectible Accounts** appears on the balance sheet as a contra account that is deducted from accounts receivable.* It reduces the accounts receivable to the amount expected to be realized, or collected, in cash, as follows:

Current assets		
Cash		$ 10,000
Short-term investments		15,000
Accounts receivable	$100,000	
Less allowance for uncollectible accounts	6,000	94,000
Inventory		56,000
Total current assets		$175,000

---

*The purpose of Allowance for Uncollectible Accounts is to reduce the gross accounts receivable to the amount estimated to be collectible (net realizable value). The purpose of another contra account, Accumulated Depreciation, is *not* to reduce the gross plant and equipment accounts to realizable value. Rather, its purpose is to show how much of the cost of the plant and equipment has been allocated as an expense to previous accounting periods.

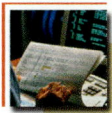

FOCUS ON BUSINESS PRACTICE

Selling Goods and Services Is Only Half the Problem.

To be profitable, a company must not only sell goods and services; it must also generate cash flows by collecting on those sales. The latter has been a problem for the five leading North American manufacturers of telecommunications equipment. In the late 1990s, to make sales to start-up telecom companies, these manufacturers made loans of $17 billion to their customers. Nortel Networks <www.nortelnetworks.com> had $4.1 billion in customer financing; Cisco Systems <www.cisco.com>, $2.4 billion; Lucent Technologies <www.lucent.com>, $5.4 billion; Motorola <www.motorola.com>, $3.8 billion; and Qualcomm <www.qualcomm.com>, $1.18 billion. While not all of these loans were bad debts, many became so when the telecom industry experienced a major recession in 2001. All five companies had to increase their allowances for uncollectible accounts, actions that eliminated previously reported earnings and caused the companies' stock prices to fall.[10]

Accounts receivable may also be shown on the balance sheet as follows:

Accounts receivable (net of allowance for uncollectible accounts of $6,000) $94,000

Or they may be shown at "net," with the amount of the allowance for uncollectible accounts identified in a note to the financial statements. The estimated uncollectible amount cannot be identified with any particular customer; therefore, it is credited to a separate contra-asset account—Allowance for Uncollectible Accounts.

The allowance account often has other titles, such as *Allowance for Doubtful Accounts* and *Allowance for Bad Debts*. Once in a while, the older phrase *Reserve for Bad Debts* will be seen, but in modern practice it should not be used. *Bad Debts Expense* is a title often used for Uncollectible Accounts Expense.

ESTIMATING UNCOLLECTIBLE ACCOUNTS EXPENSE

KEY POINT: The accountant looks at the local economic conditions as well as national conditions in setting the estimated-uncollectible accounts expense.

● **STOP AND THINK!**
How might the receivable turnover and the average days' sales uncollectible ratios reveal that management is consistently underestimating the amount of losses from uncollectible accounts?

A decrease in receivables turnover and an increase in average days' sales uncollectible from period to period, especially in the absence of changes in credit policies, might mean that management is underestimating the amount of losses from uncollectible accounts. ■

As noted, it is necessary to estimate the expense to cover the expected losses for the year. Of course, estimates can vary widely. If management takes an optimistic view and projects a small loss from uncollectible accounts, the resulting net accounts receivable will be larger than if management takes a pessimistic view. The net income will also be larger under the optimistic view because the estimated expense will be smaller. The company's accountant makes an estimate based on past experience and current economic conditions. For example, losses from uncollectible accounts are normally expected to be greater in a recession than during a period of economic growth. The final decision, made by management, on the amount of the expense will depend on objective information, such as the accountant's analyses, and on certain qualitative factors, such as how investors, bankers, creditors, and others may view the performance of the debtor company. Regardless of the qualitative considerations, the estimated losses from uncollectible accounts should be realistic.

Two common methods of estimating uncollectible accounts expense are the percentage of net sales method and the accounts receivable aging method.

KEY POINT: The percentage of net sales method can be described as the income statement method to emphasize that the percentage of the net sales calculated is the amount expensed. That is, any previous balance in the allowance account is irrelevant in preparing the adjustment.

■ **PERCENTAGE OF NET SALES METHOD**   The **percentage of net sales method** asks the question, How much of this year's net sales will not be collected? The answer determines the amount of uncollectible accounts expense for the year. For example, the following balances represent the ending figures for Hassel Company for 20x9:

Sales		Sales Returns and Allowances	
	Dec. 31 645,000	Dec. 31 40,000	

Sales Discounts		Allowance for Uncollectible Accounts	
Dec. 31 5,000			Dec. 31 3,600

PARENTHETICAL NOTE:
The percentage of net sales method, unlike the direct charge-off method, matches revenues with expenses.

Below are Hassel's actual losses from uncollectible accounts for the past three years:

Year	Net Sales	Losses from Uncollectible Accounts	Percentage
20x6	$ 520,000	$10,200	1.96
20x7	595,000	13,900	2.34
20x8	585,000	9,900	1.69
Total	$1,700,000	$34,000	2.00

In many businesses, net sales is understood to approximate net credit sales. If there are substantial cash sales, then net credit sales should be used because they generate accounts receivable. Hassel's management believes that uncollectible accounts will continue to average about 2 percent of net sales. The uncollectible accounts expense for the year 20x9 is therefore estimated to be

$$.02 \times (\$645,000 - \$40,000 - \$5,000) = .02 \times \$600,000 = \$12,000$$

The entry to record this estimate is as follows:

A = L + OE
− −

20x9			
Dec. 31	Uncollectible Accounts Expense	12,000	
	Allowance for Uncollectible Accounts		12,000
	To record uncollectible accounts expense at 2 percent of $600,000 net sales		

After the above entry is posted, Allowance for Uncollectible Accounts will have a balance of $15,600:

Allowance for Uncollectible Accounts		
	Dec. 31	3,600
	Dec. 31 adj.	12,000
	Dec. 31 bal.	15,600

The balance consists of the $12,000 estimated uncollectible accounts receivable from 20x9 sales and the $3,600 estimated uncollectible accounts receivable from previous years.

■ **ACCOUNTS RECEIVABLE AGING METHOD** The **accounts receivable aging method** asks the question, How much of the year-end balance of accounts receivable will not be collected? Under this method, the year-end balance of Allowance for Uncollectible Accounts is determined directly by an analysis of accounts receivable. The difference between the amount determined to be uncollectible and the actual balance of Allowance for Uncollectible Accounts is the expense for the year. In theory, this method should produce the same result as the percentage of net sales method, but in practice it rarely does.

The **aging of accounts receivable** is the process of listing each customer's receivable account according to the due date of the account. If the customer's account is past due, there is a possibility that the account will not be paid. And that possibility increases as the account extends further beyond the due date. The aging of accounts receivable helps management evaluate its credit and collection policies and alerts it to possible problems.

FOCUS ON INTERNATIONAL BUSINESS

Why Companies in Emerging Economies Must Adapt Accounting Practices

Companies in emerging economies do not always follow the accounting practices accepted in the United States. The Shanghai Stock Exchange is one of the fastest-growing stock markets in the world. Few Chinese companies acknowledge that uncollected receivables are not worth full value even when the receivables have been outstanding for a year or more. It is common practice in the United States to write off receivables more than six months old. Now that Chinese companies like Shanghai Steel Tube and Shanghai Industrial Sewing Machine are making their shares of stock available to outsiders, they must estimate uncollectible accounts in accordance with international accounting standards. Recognition of this expense could easily wipe out annual earnings.[11]

EXHIBIT 1
Analysis of Accounts Receivable by Age

Myer Company
Analysis of Accounts Receivable by Age
December 31, 20x5

Customer	Total	(Current) Not Yet Due	1–30 Days Past Due	31–60 Days Past Due	61–90 Days Past Due	Over 90 Days Past Due
A. Arnold	$ 150		$ 150			
M. Benoit	400			$ 400		
J. Connolly	1,000	$ 900	100			
R. Deering	250				$ 250	
Others	42,600	21,000	14,000	3,800	2,200	$1,600
Totals	$44,400	$21,900	$14,250	$4,200	$2,450	$1,600
Estimated percentage uncollectible		1.0	2.0	10.0	30.0	50.0
Allowance for Uncollectible Accounts	$ 2,459	$ 219	$ 285	$ 420	$ 735	$ 800

ENRICHMENT NOTE: The aging method is often superior to the percentage of net sales method during changing economic times. For example, during a recession, more bad debts occur. The aging method automatically reflects the economic change as accounts receivable age because customers are unable to pay. A company using the percentage of net sales method must anticipate the change and modify the percentage it uses.

KEY POINT: When the write-offs in an accounting period exceed the amount of the allowance, a debit balance in the Allowance for Uncollectible Accounts account results.

A = L + OE
−   −

The aging of accounts receivable for Myer Company is illustrated in Exhibit 1. Each account receivable is classified as being not yet due or as being 1–30 days, 31–60 days, 61–90 days, or over 90 days past due. The estimated percentage uncollectible in each of these catagories is multiplied by the amount in each category in order to determine the estimated, or target, balance of Allowance for Uncollectible Accounts. In total, it is estimated that $2,459 of the $44,400 accounts receivable will not be collected.

Once the target balance for Allowance for Uncollectible Accounts has been found, it is necessary to determine how much the adjustment is. The amount of the adjustment depends on the current balance of the allowance account. Let us assume two cases for the December 31 balance of Myer Company's Allowance for Uncollectible Accounts: (1) a credit balance of $800 and (2) a debit balance of $800.

In the first case, an adjustment of $1,659 is needed to bring the balance of the allowance account to a $2,459 credit balance, calculated as follows:

Targeted balance for allowance for uncollectible accounts	$2,459
Less current credit balance of allowance for uncollectible accounts	800
Uncollectible accounts expense	$1,659

The uncollectible accounts expense is recorded as follows:

20x5
Dec. 31   Uncollectible Accounts Expense   1,659
              Allowance for Uncollectible Accounts   1,659
              To bring the allowance for
              uncollectible accounts to the
              level of estimated losses

The resulting balance of Allowance for Uncollectible Accounts is $2,459, as follows:

Allowance for Uncollectible Accounts		
	Dec. 31	800
	Dec. 31 adj.	1,659
	Dec. 31 bal.	**2,459**

In the second case, because Allowance for Uncollectible Accounts has a debit balance of $800, the estimated uncollectible accounts expense for the year will have to be $3,259 to reach the targeted balance of $2,459. This calculation is as follows:

Targeted balance for allowance for uncollectible accounts	$2,459
Plus current debit balance of allowance for uncollectible accounts	800
Uncollectible accounts expense	$3,259

The uncollectible accounts expense is recorded as follows:

A = L + OE
– –

20x5				
Dec. 31	Uncollectible Accounts Expense		3,259	
	Allowance for Uncollectible Accounts			3,259
	To bring the allowance for uncollectible accounts to the level of estimated losses			

After this entry, Allowance for Uncollectible Accounts has a credit balance of $2,459:

Allowance for Uncollectible Accounts			
Dec. 31	800	Dec. 31 adj.	3,259
		Dec. 31 bal.	**2,459**

■ **COMPARISON OF THE TWO METHODS** Both the percentage of net sales method and the accounts receivable aging method estimate the uncollectible accounts expense in accordance with the matching rule, but as shown in Figure 5, they do so in different ways. The percentage of net sales method is an income statement

FIGURE 5
Two Methods of Estimating Uncollectible Accounts

*Add current debit balance or subtract current credit balance to determine uncollectible accounts expense.

KEY POINT: Describing the aging method as the balance sheet method emphasizes that the computation is based on ending accounts receivable, rather than on net sales for the period.

approach. It assumes that a certain proportion of sales will not be collected, and this proportion is the *amount of Uncollectible Accounts Expense* for the accounting period. The accounts receivable aging method is a balance sheet approach. It assumes that a certain proportion of accounts receivable outstanding will not be collected. This proportion is the *targeted balance of the Allowance for Uncollectible Accounts account*. The expense for the accounting period is the difference between the targeted balance and the current balance of the allowance account.

■ **WHY ACCOUNTS WRITTEN OFF WILL DIFFER FROM ESTIMATES** Regardless of the method used to estimate uncollectible accounts, the total of accounts receivable written off in any given year will rarely equal the estimated uncollectible amount. The allowance account will show a credit balance when the total of accounts written off is less than the estimated uncollectible amount. The allowance account will show a debit balance when the total of accounts written off is greater than the estimated uncollectible amount.

WRITING OFF AN UNCOLLECTIBLE ACCOUNT

When it becomes clear that a specific account receivable will not be collected, the amount should be written off to Allowance for Uncollectible Accounts. Remember that the uncollectible amount was already accounted for as an expense when the allowance was established. For example, assume that on January 15, 20x6, R. Deering, who owes Myer Company $250, is declared bankrupt by a federal court. The entry to *write off* this account is as follows:

A = L + OE
+
−

20x6			
Jan. 15	Allowance for Uncollectible Accounts	250	
	Accounts Receivable		250
	To write off receivable from R. Deering as uncollectible; Deering declared bankrupt on January 15		

KEY POINT: When writing off an individual account, debit Allowance for Uncollectible Accounts, not Uncollectible Accounts Expense.

Although the write-off removes the uncollectible amount from Accounts Receivable, it does not affect the estimated net realizable value of accounts receivable. The write-off simply reduces R. Deering's account to zero and reduces Allowance for Uncollectible Accounts by a similar amount, as shown below:

	Balances Before Write-off	Balances After Write-off
Accounts receivable	$44,400	$44,150
Less allowance for uncollectible accounts	2,459	2,209
Estimated net realizable value of accounts receivable	$41,941	$41,941

RECOVERY OF ACCOUNTS RECEIVABLE WRITTEN OFF

Occasionally, a customer whose account has been written off as uncollectible will later be able to pay some or all of the amount owed. When this happens, two entries must be made: one to reverse the earlier write-off (which is now incorrect) and another to show the collection of the account. For example, assume that on September 1, 20x6, R. Deering, after his bankruptcy on January 15, notified Myer Company that he could pay $100 of his account and sent a check for $50. The entries to record this transaction are as follows:

		20x6		

A = L + OE
+
−
	Sept. 1	Accounts Receivable
		    Allowance for Uncollectible Accounts
		      To reinstate the portion of
		      the account of R. Deering
		      now considered collectible;
		      originally written off January 15
			100	100

A = L + OE
+
−
	Sept. 1	Cash
		    Accounts Receivable
		      Collection from R. Deering
			50	50

The collectible portion of R. Deering's account must be restored to his account and credited to Allowance for Uncollectible Accounts for two reasons. First, it turned out to be wrong to write off the full $250 on January 15 because only $150 was actually uncollectible. Second, the accounts receivable subsidiary account for R. Deering should reflect his ability to pay a portion of the money he owed despite his declaration of bankruptcy. Documentation of this action will give a clear picture of R. Deering's credit record for future credit action.

 Check out ACE for a Review Quiz at http://accounting.college.hmco.com/students.

NOTES RECEIVABLE

LO5 Define *promissory note,* and compute and record promissory notes receivable.

RELATED TEXT ASSIGNMENTS
Q: 18, 19
SE: 9
E: 12, 13, 14, 15
P: 4, 9

A **promissory note** is an unconditional promise to pay a definite sum of money on demand or at a future date. The entity who signs the note and thereby promises to pay is called the *maker* of the note. The entity to whom payment is to be made is called the *payee*.

The promissory note illustrated in Figure 6 is dated May 20, 20x5, and is an unconditional promise by the maker, Samuel Mason, to pay a definite sum, or principal ($1,000), to the payee, Cook County Bank & Trust Company, on the future date of August 18, 20x5. The promissory note bears an interest rate of 8 percent. The payee regards all promissory notes it holds that are due in less than one year as **notes receivable** in the current assets section of the balance sheet. The maker regards them as **notes payable** in the current liabilities section of the balance sheet.

This portion of the chapter is concerned primarily with notes received from customers. The nature of a company's business generally determines how frequently it receives promissory notes from customers. Firms selling durable goods of high value, such as farm machinery and automobiles, will often accept promissory notes. Among the advantages of promissory notes are that they produce interest income and represent a stronger legal claim against a debtor than do accounts receivable. In addition, selling, or discounting, promissory notes to banks is a common financing method. Almost all companies occasionally receive a note, and many companies obtain notes receivable in settlement of past-due accounts.

COMPUTATIONS FOR PROMISSORY NOTES

In accounting for promissory notes, the following terms are important to remember: (1) *maturity date,* (2) *duration of note,* (3) *interest and interest rate,* and (4) *maturity value.*

■ **MATURITY DATE** The **maturity date** is the date on which a promissory note must be paid. This date must either be stated on the note or be determinable from the facts stated on the note. Among the most common statements of maturity date are the following:

1. A specific date, such as "November 14, 20xx"
2. A specific number of months after the date of the note, for example, "three months after date"

FIGURE 6
A Promissory Note

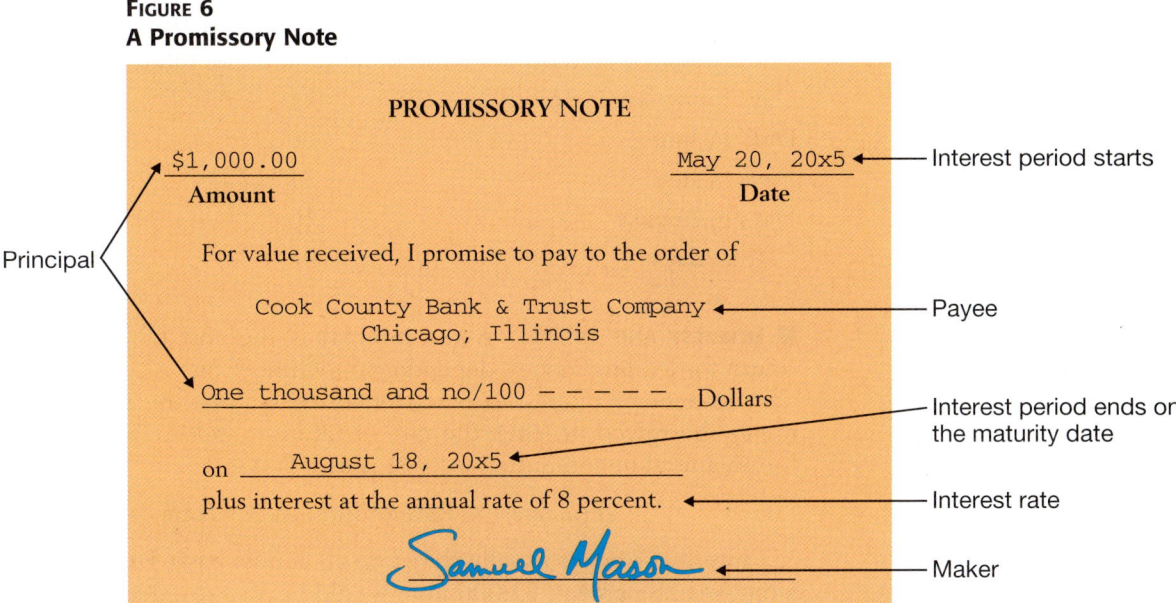

3. A specific number of days after the date of the note, for example, "60 days after date"

The maturity date is obvious when a specific date is stated. And when the maturity date is a number of months from the date of the note, one simply uses the same day in the appropriate future month. For example, a note that is dated January 20 and that is due in two months would be due on March 20.

When the maturity date is a specific number of days from the date of the note, however, the exact maturity date must be determined. In computing the maturity date, it is important to exclude the date of the note. For example, a note dated May 20 and due in 90 days would be due on August 18, computed as follows:

Days remaining in May (31 − 20)	11
Days in June	30
Days in July	31
Days in August	18
Total days	90

■ **DURATION OF NOTE** The **duration of note** is the length of time in days between a promissory note's issue date and its maturity date. Knowing the duration of the note is important because interest is calculated for the exact number of days. Identifying the duration is easy when the maturity date is stated as a specific number of days from the date of the note because the two numbers are the same.

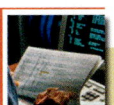

FOCUS ON BUSINESS PRACTICE

How Long Is a Year? It Depends.

Most banks use a 365-day year to compute interest for all loans, but some use a 360-day year for commercial loans. For example, the brokerage firm of May SWS Securities <www.maysws.com> of Dallas, Texas, states in its customer loan agreement, "Interest is calculated on a 360-day basis." In Europe, use of a 360-day year is common. Financial institutions that use the 360-day basis earn slightly more interest than those that use the 365-day basis. In this book, we use a 360-day year to keep the computations simple.

STUDY NOTE: Another way to compute the duration of notes is to begin with the interest period, as follows:

90	Interest period
−11	days remaining in May (31 − 20)
79	
−30	days in June
49	
−31	days in July
18	due date in August

However, if the maturity date is stated as a specific date, the exact number of days must be determined. Assume that a note issued on May 10 matures on August 10. The duration of the note is 92 days, determined as follows:

Days remaining in May (31 − 10)	21
Days in June	30
Days in July	31
Days in August	10
Total days	92

■ **INTEREST AND INTEREST RATE** *Interest* is the cost of borrowing money or the return for lending money, depending on whether one is the borrower or the lender. The amount of interest is based on three factors: the principal (the amount of money borrowed or lent), the rate of interest, and the loan's length of time. The formula used in computing interest is as follows:

$$\text{Principal} \times \text{Rate of Interest} \times \text{Time} = \text{Interest}$$

Interest rates are usually stated on an annual basis. For example, the interest on a one-year, 8 percent, $1,000 note would be $80 ($1,000 × 8/100 × 1 = $80). If the term, or time period, of the note is three months instead of a year, the interest charge would be $20 ($1,000 × 8/100 × 3/12 = $20).

When the term of a note is expressed in days, the exact number of days must be used in computing the interest. To keep the computation simple, let us compute interest on the basis of 360 days per year. Therefore, if the term of the above note were 45 days, the interest would be $10, computed as follows: $1,000 × 8/100 × 45/360 = $10.

■ **MATURITY VALUE** The **maturity value** is the total proceeds of a promissory note—face value plus interest—at the maturity date. The maturity value of a 90-day, 8 percent, $1,000 note is computed as follows:

$$\begin{aligned}\text{Maturity Value} &= \text{Principal} + \text{Interest} \\ &= \$1{,}000 + (\$1{,}000 \times 8/100 \times 90/360) \\ &= \$1{,}000 + \$20 \\ &= \$1{,}020\end{aligned}$$

There are also so-called non-interest-bearing notes. The maturity value is the face value, or principal amount. In this case, the principal includes an implied interest cost.

ACCOUNTING ENTRIES FOR PROMISSORY NOTES

The accounting entries for promissory notes receivable fall into four groups: (1) recording receipt of a note, (2) recording collection on a note, (3) recording a dishonored note, and (4) recording adjusting entries.

■ **RECORDING RECEIPT OF A NOTE** Assume that on June 1, a 30-day, 12 percent note is received from a customer, J. Halsted, in settlement of an existing account receivable of $4,000. The entry for this transaction is as follows:

KEY POINT: The entry to record receipt of a note does not include interest because no interest has yet been earned.

A = L + OE
\+
−

June 1	Notes Receivable	4,000	
	Accounts Receivable		4,000
	Received 30-day, 12 percent note in payment of account of J. Halsted		

■ **RECORDING COLLECTION ON A NOTE** When the note plus interest is collected 30 days later, the entry is as follows:

A = L + OE
\+   +
\-

July 1 Cash   4,040
            Notes Receivable   4,000
            Interest Income   40
                Collected 30-day, 12 percent
                note from J. Halsted

STUDY NOTE: Dishonored notes are, in effect, not written off. The amounts are merely transferred to accounts receivable, which can be written off later.

■ **RECORDING A DISHONORED NOTE** When the maker of a note does not pay the note at maturity, the note is said to be dishonored. The holder, or payee, of a **dishonored note** should make an entry to transfer the total amount due from Notes Receivable to an account receivable from the debtor. If J. Halsted dishonors her note on July 1, the following entry would be made:

A = L + OE
\+   +
\-

July 1 Accounts Receivable   4,040
            Notes Receivable   4,000
            Interest Income   40
                30-day, 12 percent note
                dishonored by J. Halsted

The interest earned is recorded because although J. Halsted did not pay the note, she is still obligated to pay both the principal and the interest.

Two things are accomplished by transferring a dishonored note receivable into an Accounts Receivable account. First, it leaves only notes that have not matured and are presumably negotiable and collectible in the Notes Receivable account. Second, it establishes a record in the borrower's accounts receivable account that he or she has dishonored a note receivable. Such information may be helpful in deciding whether to extend future credit to the customer.

ENRICHMENT NOTE: The interest rate on the account receivable is usually higher than the rate on the note.

● **STOP AND THINK!**
Under what circumstances would an accrual of interest income on an interest-bearing note receivable not be required at the end of an accounting period?
It would not be required if the interest to date were paid on the last day of the accounting period. ■

■ **RECORDING ADJUSTING ENTRIES** A promissory note received in one period may not be due until a following accounting period. Because the interest on a note accrues by a small amount each day of the note's duration, it is necessary, according to the matching rule, to apportion the interest earned to the periods in which it belongs. For example, assume that on August 31 a 60-day, 8 percent, $2,000 note was received and that the company prepares financial statements monthly. The following adjusting entry is necessary on September 30 to show how the interest earned for September has accrued:

A = L + OE
\+   +

Sept. 30 Interest Receivable   13.33
              Interest Income   13.33
                  To accrue 30 days' interest
                  earned on a note receivable
                  $2,000 × 8/100 × 30/360 = $13.33

The Interest Receivable account is a current asset on the balance sheet. When payment of the note plus interest is received on October 30, the following entry is made:*

A = L + OE
\+   +
\-
\-

Oct. 30 Cash   2,026.67
             Notes Receivable   2,000.00
             Interest Receivable   13.33
             Interest Income   13.34
                 Receipt of note receivable
                 plus interest

As can be seen from these transactions, both September and October receive the benefit of one-half the interest earned.

✓ Check out ACE for a Review Quiz at http://accounting.college.hmco.com/students.

---

*Some firms may follow the practice of reversing the September 30 adjusting entry. Here we assume that a reversing entry is not made.

Preparing a Bank Reconciliation

SO6 Prepare a bank reconciliation.
RELATED TEXT ASSIGNMENTS
SE: 10
E: 16
P: 5, 10

Rarely will the balance of a company's Cash account exactly equal the cash balance shown on the bank statement. Certain transactions shown in the company's records may not have been recorded by the bank, and certain bank transactions may not appear in the company's records. Therefore, a necessary step in internal control is to prove both the balance shown on the bank statement and the balance of Cash in the accounting records. A **bank reconciliation** is the process of accounting for the difference between the balance appearing on the bank statement and the balance of the Cash account in the company's records. This process involves making additions to and subtractions from both balances to arrive at the adjusted cash balance.

The most common transactions shown in the company's records but not entered in the bank's records are the following:

1. *Outstanding checks* These are checks that the company has issued and recorded but that do not yet appear on the bank statement.
2. *Deposits in transit* These are deposits mailed or taken to the bank but not received in time to be recorded on the bank statement.

Transactions that may appear on the bank statement but not in the company's records include the following:

1. *Service charges (SC)* Banks often charge a fee, or service charge, for the use of a checking account. Many banks base the service charge on a number of factors, such as the average balance of the account during the month or the number of checks drawn.
2. *NSF (nonsufficient funds) checks* An NSF check is a check that the company has deposited but that is not paid when the bank presents it to the issuer's bank. The bank charges the company's account and returns the check so that the company can try to collect the amount due. If the bank has deducted the NSF check from the bank statement but the company has not deducted it from its book balance, an adjustment must be made in the bank reconciliation. The company usually reclassifies the NSF check from Cash to Accounts Receivable because it must now collect from the person or company that wrote the check.
3. *Miscellaneous debits and credits* Banks also charge for other services, such as stopping payment on checks and printing checks. The bank notifies the depositor of each deduction by including a debit memorandum with the monthly statement. A bank will also sometimes serve as an agent in collecting on promissory notes for the depositor. In such a case, a credit memorandum will be included in the statement, along with a debit memorandum of the service charge.
4. *Interest income* Banks commonly pay interest on a company's average balance. Accounts that pay interest are sometimes called NOW or money market accounts. Such interest is reported on the bank statement.

An error by either the bank or the depositor will, of course, require immediate correction.

KEY POINT: The ending bank statement balance does not represent the amount that should appear on the balance sheet for cash. There are events and items, such as deposits in transit and outstanding checks, that the bank is unaware of at the cutoff date. This is why a bank reconciliation must be prepared.

■ **Illustration of a Bank Reconciliation** Assume that the October bank statement for Martin Maintenance Company indicates a balance on October 31 of $3,471.07, and that in its records, Martin Maintenance Company has a cash balance on October 31 of $2,415.91. The purpose of a bank reconciliation is to identify the items that make up the difference between these amounts and to determine the correct cash balance. The bank reconciliation for Martin Maintenance is shown in Exhibit 2. The numbered items in the exhibit refer to the following:

1. A deposit in the amount of $276.00 was mailed to the bank on October 31 and has not been recorded by the bank.

EXHIBIT 2
Bank Reconciliation

Martin Maintenance Company
Bank Reconciliation
October 31, 20xx

Balance per bank, October 31		$3,471.07
① Add deposit of October 31 in transit		276.00
		$3,747.07
② Less outstanding checks:		
No. 551	$150.00	
No. 576	40.68	
No. 578	500.00	
No. 579	370.00	
No. 580	130.50	1,191.08
Adjusted bank balance, October 31		**$2,555.89**
Balance per books, October 31		$2,415.91
Add:		
④ Note receivable collected by bank	$280.00	
④ Interest income on note	20.00	
⑦ Interest income	15.62	315.62
		$2,731.53
Less:		
③ Overstatement of deposit of October 6	$ 30.00	
④ Collection fee	5.00	
⑤ NSF check of Arthur Clubb	128.14	
⑥ Service charge	12.50	175.64
Adjusted book balance, October 31		**$2,555.89**

Note: The circled numbers refer to the items listed in the text.

STUDY NOTE: It is possible to place an item in the wrong section of a bank reconciliation and still have it balance. The *correct* adjusted balance must be obtained.

KEY POINT: Even though the September 14 check was deducted on the September 30 reconciliation, it must be deducted again in each subsequent month in which it remains outstanding.

STUDY NOTE: A credit memorandum means that an amount was *added* to the bank balance; a debit memorandum means that an amount was *deducted*.

2. Five checks issued in October or prior months have not yet been paid by the bank, as follows:

Check No.	Date	Amount
551	Sept. 14	$150.00
576	Oct. 30	40.68
578	Oct. 31	500.00
579	Oct. 31	370.00
580	Oct. 31	130.50

3. The deposit for cash sales of October 6 was incorrectly recorded in Martin Maintenance Company's records as $330.00. The bank correctly recorded the deposit as $300.00.

4. Among the returned checks was a credit memorandum showing that the bank had collected a promissory note from A. Jacobs in the amount of $280.00, plus $20.00 in interest on the note. A debit memorandum was also enclosed for the $5.00 collection fee. No entry had been made on Martin Maintenance Company's records.

5. Also returned with the bank statement was an NSF check for $128.14. This check had been received from a customer named Arthur Clubb. The NSF check from Clubb was not reflected in the company's accounting records.

6. A debit memorandum was enclosed for the regular monthly service charge of $12.50. The company had not yet recorded this charge.
7. Interest earned by the company on the average balance was reported as $15.62.

Note in Exhibit 2 that starting from their separate balances, both the bank and book amounts are adjusted to the amount of $2,555.89. This adjusted balance is the amount of cash owned by the company on October 31 and thus is the amount that should appear on its October 31 balance sheet.

■ **RECORDING TRANSACTIONS AFTER RECONCILIATION** The adjusted balance of cash differs from both the bank statement and Martin Maintenance Company's records. The bank balance will automatically become correct when outstanding checks are presented for payment and the deposit in transit is received and recorded by the bank. Entries must be made, however, for the transactions necessary to update the book balance. All the items reported by the bank but not yet recorded by the company must be recorded in the general journal by means of the following entries:

KEY POINT: Notice that only those transactions the company has not recorded before receiving the bank statement are recorded.

Oct. 31	Cash		300.00	
	Notes Receivable			280.00
	Interest Income			20.00
	Note receivable of $280.00 and interest of $20.00 collected by bank from A. Jacobs			
31	Cash		15.62	
	Interest Income			15.62
	Interest on average bank account balance			
31	Sales		30.00	
	Cash			30.00
	Correction of error in recording a $300.00 deposit as $330.00			
31	Accounts Receivable		128.14	
	Cash			128.14
	NSF check of Arthur Clubb returned by bank			
31	Bank Service Charges Expense		17.50	
	Cash			17.50
	Bank service charge ($12.50) and collection fee ($5.00) for October			

It is acceptable to record these entries in one or two compound entries to save time and space.

✓ Check out ACE for a Review Quiz at http://accounting.college.hmco.com/students.

Chapter Review

REVIEW OF LEARNING OBJECTIVES

LO1 Identify and explain the management issues related to short-term financial assets.

In managing short-term financial assets, management must (1) consider the need for short-term investing and borrowing as the business's balance of cash fluctuates during seasonal cycles, (2) establish credit policies that balance the need for sales with the ability to collect, and (3) assess the need to increase cash flows through the financing of receivables.

2. Toys "R" Us does not disclose an allowance for uncollectible accounts. How do you explain the lack of disclosure?
3. Compute the quick ratios for 2002 and 2001 and comment on them.
4. Compute receivable turnover and average days' sales uncollected for 2002 and 2001 and comment on Toys "R" Us credit policies. Accounts Receivable in 2000 were $225,000,000.

Comparison Case: Toys "R" Us and Walgreen Co.

FRA 5.
LO1 Quick Ratio and Seasonality of Cash Flows

Refer to the Toys "R" Us <www.tru.com> annual report and the financial statements of Walgreens <www.walgreens.com> in the Supplement to Chapter 1 to answer the following questions:

1. What is the quick ratio for both companies for the last two years? Comment on the results of your calculation. (If you were assigned **FRA 4**, use the calculation from that case for Toys "R" Us.)
2. Do you think the seasonal need for cash is different or the same for Toys "R" Us and Walgreens? Explain. Identify the place in the financial statements where the seasonality of sales is discussed.

Fingraph® Financial Analyst™

FRA 6.
LO1 Comparison and Analysis of Short-Term Financial Assets

Choose any two companies in the same industry from the list of Fingraph companies on the Needles Accounting Resource Center Web Site at http://accounting.college.hmco.com/students. The industry should be one in which accounts receivable is likely to be an important current asset—for example, manufacturing, consumer products, consumer food and beverage, or computers. Retail companies should be avoided because they usually have low accounts receivables. Access the Microsoft Excel spreadsheets for the companies you selected. Click on the URL at the top of each company's spreadsheet for a link to the company's web site and annual report.

1. In the summary of significant accounting policies or notes to the financial statements in the annual reports of the companies you have selected, find any reference to cash and cash equivalents, short-term (marketable) securities, and accounts receivable.
2. Using the Fingraph Financial Analyst CD-ROM software, display and print for the companies you have selected (a) the Current Assets and Current Liabilities Analysis page and (b) the Liquidity and Asset Utilization Analysis page in tabular and graphic form. Prepare a table that compares the quick ratio, receivable turnover, and average days' sales uncollected for both companies for two years.
3. Find and read the liquidity analysis section of management's discussion and analysis in each annual report.
4. Write a one-page executive summary that highlights the accounting policies for short-term financial assets and compares the short-term liquidity position of the two companies. Include your assessment of the companies' relative liquidity, and make reference to management's assessment. Include the Fingraph pages and your table with your report.

Internet Case

FRA 7.
LO4 Comparison of J.C. Penney and Sears

Access the annual reports of J.C. Penney, Inc. <www.jcpenney.com> and Sears, Roebuck and Co. <www.sears.com> directly, or go to the Needles Accounting Resource Center Web Site at http://accounting.college.hmco.com/students for a link to their web sites. Find the accounts receivable and marketable securities (if any) on each company's balance sheet and the notes related to these accounts in the notes to the financial statements. If either company has marketable securities, what is their cost and market value? Does the company currently have a gain or loss on the securities? Which company has the most accounts receivable as a percentage of total assets? What is the percentage of the allowance account to gross accounts receivable for each company? Which company experienced the highest loss rate on its receivables? Why do you think there is a difference? Do the companies finance their receivables? Be prepared to discuss your findings in class.

8

Chapter 8 presents the management issues associated with inventories, including the costing of inventories for financial reporting.

Inventories

LEARNING OBJECTIVES

LO1 Identify and explain the management issues associated with accounting for inventories.

LO2 Define *inventory cost* and relate it to goods flow and cost flow.

LO3 Calculate the pricing of inventory, using the cost basis under the periodic inventory system.

LO4 Apply the perpetual inventory system to the pricing of inventories at cost.

LO5 State the effects of inventory methods and misstatements of inventory on income determination, income taxes, and cash flows.

LO6 Apply the lower-of-cost-or-market (LCM) rule to inventory valuation.

SUPPLEMENTAL OBJECTIVE

SO7 Estimate the cost of ending inventory using the retail method and gross profit method.

DECISION POINT
A USER'S FOCUS

J.C. Penney Company, Inc. <www.jcpenney.com> Managing inventory for profit is one of management's most complex and challenging tasks. In terms of dollars, the inventory of goods held for sale is one of the largest assets of a merchandising business. As may be seen in the financial highlights on the opposite page, J.C. Penney Company, Inc., a major retailer with department stores in all 50 states and Puerto Rico, devotes more than 27 percent, or $4.9 billion, of its $17.9 billion in assets to inventories. What challenges does J.C. Penney's management face in managing its inventory?

Not only must J.C. Penney's management purchase merchandise that customers will want to buy; it must also have the merchandise available in the right locations at the times when customers want to buy it. Management also must try to minimize the cost of inventory while maintaining quality. To these ends, J.C. Penney maintains purchasing offices in cities throughout the world, including Hong Kong, Taipei, Osaka, Seoul, Bangkok, Singapore, Bombay, and Florence. Further, because of the high cost of borrowing funds and storing inventory, management must control the amount of money tied up in inventory. Important accounting decisions include what assumptions to make about the flow of inventory costs, what prices to put on inventory, what inventory systems to use, and how to protect inventory against loss.

Proper management of inventory has helped J.C. Penney reduce its inventory (and total assets) and increase its level of retail sales. The company has

What challenges does J.C. Penney's management face in managing its inventory?

improved its income from operations from a negative $886 million in 2000 to a positive $584 million in 2002. The company plans to improve the profitability of its core department stores by further improving inventory management, controlling costs, and closing underperforming stores.[1]

Financial Highlights
(In millions)

	2002	2001	2000
Retail sales, net	$32,347	$32,004	$31,846
Cost of goods sold	22,573	22,789	23,031
(Loss)/income from operations	584	203	(886)
Merchandise inventories	4,945	4,930	5,269
Total assets	$17,867	$18,048	$19,742

MANAGEMENT ISSUES ASSOCIATED WITH ACCOUNTING FOR INVENTORIES

LO1 Identify and explain the management issues associated with accounting for inventories.

RELATED TEXT ASSIGNMENTS
Q: 1, 2, 3
SE: 1, 2
E: 1, 2
P: 1, 2, 6, 7
SD: 1, 4
FRA: 1, 4, 5, 6, 7

www.jcpenney.com
www.tru.com
www.itwinc.com

Inventory is considered a current asset because it is normally sold within a year or within a company's operating cycle. For a merchandising business like J.C. Penney or Toys "R" Us, **merchandise inventory** consists of all goods owned and held for sale in the regular course of business.

Inventories are important for manufacturing companies as well. Because manufacturers are engaged in the actual making of products, they have three kinds of inventory: raw materials to be used in the production of goods, partially completed products (often called *work in process*), and finished goods ready for sale. For example, in its annual report for the year 2002, Illinois Tool Works, Inc., disclosed the following inventories:[2]

Financial Highlights
(In thousands)

	2002	2001
Inventories		
Raw materials	$275,902	$287,067
Work in process	98,678	101,418
Finished goods	588,166	605,671
Total inventories	$962,746	$994,156

In manufacturing operations, the costs of the work in process and the finished goods inventories include not only the cost of the raw materials that go into the product, but also the cost of the labor used to convert the raw materials to finished goods and the overhead costs that support the production process. Included in this last category are such costs as indirect materials (e.g., paint, glue, and nails), indirect labor (such as the salaries of supervisors), factory rent, depreciation of plant assets, utilities costs, and insurance costs. The methods for maintaining and pricing inventory explained in this chapter are applicable to manufactured goods, but because the details of accounting for manufacturing companies are usually covered as a management accounting topic, this chapter focuses on accounting for merchandising firms.

APPLYING THE MATCHING RULE TO INVENTORIES

The American Institute of Certified Public Accountants states, "A major objective of accounting for inventories is the proper determination of income through the process of matching appropriate costs against revenues."[3] Note that the objective is the proper determination of income through the matching of costs and revenues, not the determination of the most realistic inventory value. These two objectives are sometimes incompatible, in which case the objective of income determination takes precedence.

KEY POINT: Merchandise inventory affects both the income statement and the balance sheet.

The reason inventory accounting is so important to income measurement is linked to the way income is measured on the merchandising income statement. Recall that gross margin is computed as the difference between net sales and cost of goods sold and that cost of goods sold is dependent on the cost assigned to inventory or goods not sold. Because of those relationships, the higher the cost of ending inventory, the lower the cost of goods sold and the higher the resulting gross margin. Conversely, the lower the value assigned to ending inventory, the higher the cost of goods sold and the lower the gross margin. Because the amount of gross mar-

Video Case

J.C. Penney Company, Inc.
<www.jcpenney.com>

Objectives

- To explain why merchandise inventories represent one of the most important assets of a retail company
- To understand the difference between goods flow and cost flow
- To identify and explain four methods of determining inventory cost
- To define and explain the lower-of-cost-or-market (LCM) rule

Background for the Case

J.C. Penney Company, Inc., as profiled in the Decision Point in this chapter, is a major department store retailer. Merchandise inventories represent a substantial portion of the company's assets. J.C. Penney stores sell fashion at value prices. The company's target customers fall in the middle of the American population. They have a household income ranging from $30,000 to $80,000. The company's goal is "to be the customer's first choice for its products and services." The company faces intense competition not only from other department stores like Sears <www.sears.com> or Macy's <www.macys.com>, but also from discount stores like Target <www.target.com> and specialty stores like The Limited <www.limitedbrands.com>. To a great extent, J.C. Penney's future success depends on its ability to manage its inventory. Proper management of inventory has helped the company reduce its inventory (and total assets) and increase its level of retail sales, but the company still faces challenges. The company has announced plans to improve the profitability of its core department stores by further improving inventory management, controlling costs, and closing underperforming stores.

For more information about J.C. Penney Company, Inc., visit the company's web site through the Needles Accounting Resource Center Web Site at **http://accounting.college.hmco.com/students**.

Required

View the video on J.C. Penney Company, Inc., that accompanies this book. As you are watching the video, take notes related to the following questions:

1. Merchandise inventories make up more than 25 percent of J.C. Penney's assets. Explain how inventories affect the profitability of a retailer like J.C. Penney, and give both positive and negative reasons why the level of inventory is important to the company's operations.

2. Explain the difference between goods flow and cost flow as they relate to inventories, and tell which is more important in determining the cost of inventory.

3. Identify and explain the four methods of determining the cost of inventory available to J.C. Penney. Which method does J.C. Penney use?

4. What is the lower-of-cost-or-market (LCM) rule and why is it appropriate for J.C. Penney to use it? Why is LCM considered a conservative approach to inventory valuation?

---

gin has a direct effect on the amount of net income, the amount assigned to ending inventory directly affects the amount of net income. In effect, the value assigned to the ending inventory determines what portion of the cost of goods available for sale is assigned to cost of goods sold and what portion is assigned to the balance sheet as inventory to be carried over into the next accounting period.

Assessing the Impact of Inventory Decisions

Figure 1 summarizes the choices management has with regard to inventory systems and methods. The decisions usually result in different amounts of reported net income. Thus, the choices affect both the external evaluation of the company by investors and creditors and such internal evaluations as performance reviews, which determine bonuses and executive compensation. Because income is affected, the valuation of inventory may also have a considerable effect on the amount of income taxes paid. Federal income tax authorities have specific regulations about the acceptability of different methods. As a result, management is sometimes faced with balancing the goal of proper income determination with that of minimizing income taxes. Another consideration is that since the choice of inventory valuation method affects the amount of income taxes paid, it also affects a company's cash flows.

FIGURE 1
Management Choices in Accounting for Inventories

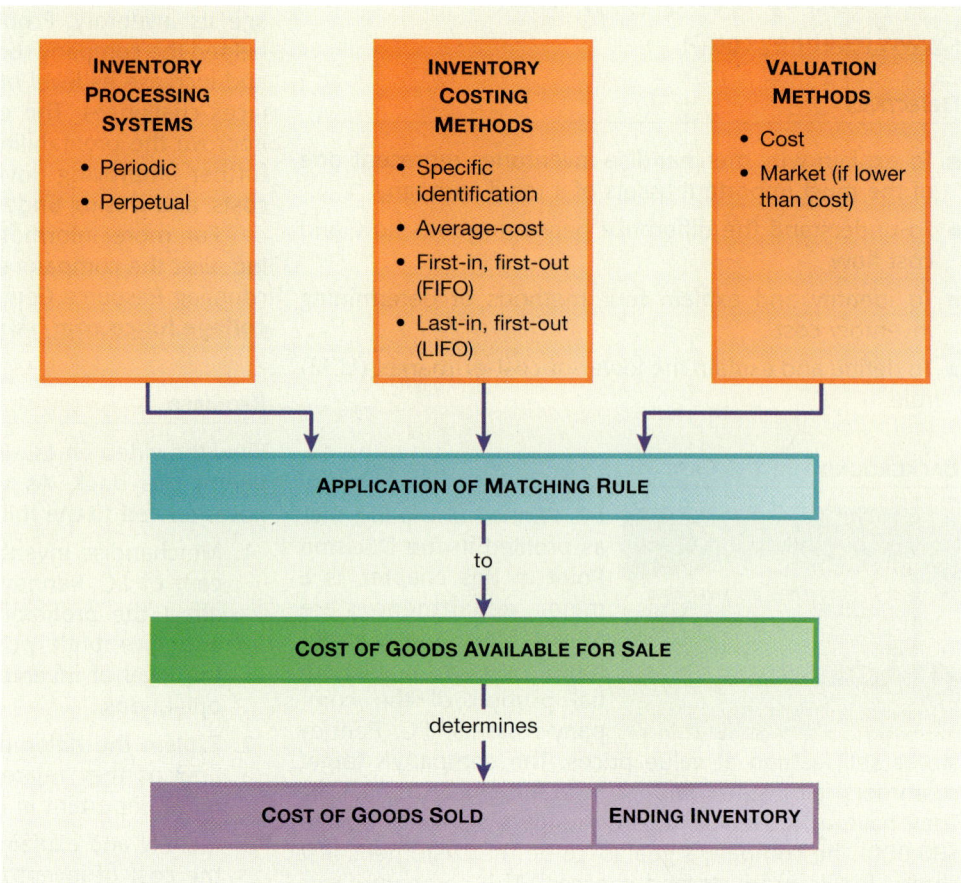

ENRICHMENT NOTE: Management considers the behavior of inventory prices over time when selecting inventory costing methods.

Evaluating the Level of Inventory

The level of inventory has important economic consequences for a company. Ideally, a company should have a great variety and quantity on hand so that customers have a large choice and do not have to wait for an item to be restocked. Such an inventory policy is not costless, however. Handling and storage costs and the interest on the funds needed to maintain high inventory levels can be substantial. But low inventory levels may result in disgruntled customers and lost sales. Common measures for evaluating inventory levels are inventory turnover and its related measure, average days' inventory on hand. **Inventory turnover** is similar to receivable turnover. It indicates the number of times a company's average inventory is sold during an accounting period. It is computed by dividing cost of goods sold by average inventory. For example, J.C. Penny's cost of goods sold was

ENRICHMENT NOTE: Some of the costs associated with carrying inventory are insurance, property taxes, and storage costs. There is also the possibility of additional spoilage and employee theft.

Focus on Business Technology

Dell's Inventory Turnover Can Make Your Head Spin.

Dell Computer <www.dell.com> turns its inventory every six days. How can it do this when other companies have inventory on hand for 60, 100, or even more days? Technology and good inventory management are a big part of the answer.

Dell's speed from order to delivery sets the industry standard. Consider that a computer ordered by 9 A.M. can be delivered the next day by 9 P.M. How can Dell do this when it does not start ordering components and assembling computers until an order is placed? First, Dell's suppliers keep components warehoused just minutes from Dell's factories, making efficient, just-in-time operations possible. Another time and money saver is the handling of computer monitors. Monitors are no longer shipped first to Dell and then on to buyers. Dell sends an email message to a shipper, such as United Parcel Service <www.ups.com>, and the shipper picks up a monitor from a supplier and schedules it to arrive with the PC. In addition to contributing to a high inventory turnover, this practice saves Dell about $30 per monitor in freight costs. Dell is showing the world how to run a business in the cyber age by selling more than $1 million worth of computers a day on its web site.[4]

FIGURE 2
Inventory Turnover for Selected Industries

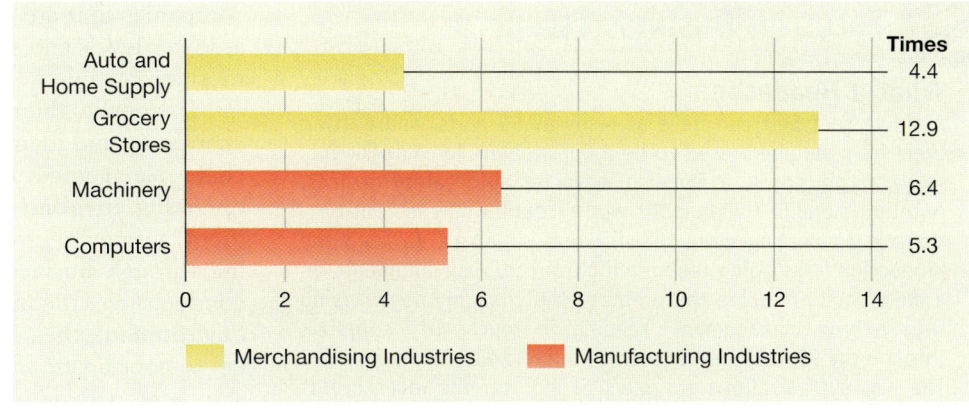

Source: Data from Dun & Bradstreet, *Industry Norms and Key Business Ratios,* 2001–2002.

ENRICHMENT NOTE:
Inventory turnover will be systematically higher if year-end inventory levels are low. For example, Toys "R" Us inventory levels on January 30 are at their lowest point of the year.

● **STOP AND THINK!**
Is it good or bad for a retail store to have a large inventory? *It depends. Obviously, a large inventory means customers have choices, and they are less likely to be disappointed because the items they want are out of stock. On the other hand, maintaining a large inventory is expensive, and if the items do not sell, they may have to be sold at a discount. The challenge to management is finding the right balance in the size of inventory.* ■

$22,573 million in 2002; its ending inventory was $4,945 million in 2002 and $4,930 million in 2001. Its inventory turnover is computed as follows:

$$\text{Inventory Turnover} = \frac{\text{Cost of Goods Sold}}{\text{Average Inventory}}$$

$$= \frac{\$22,573,000,000}{(\$4,945,000,000 + \$4,930,000,000) \div 2}$$

$$= \frac{\$22,573,000,000}{\$4,937,500,000} = 4.6 \text{ times}$$

The **average days' inventory on hand** indicates the average number of days required to sell the inventory on hand. It is found by dividing the number of days in a year by the inventory turnover, as follows:

$$\text{Average Days' Inventory on Hand} = \frac{\text{Number of Days in a Year}}{\text{Inventory Turnover}}$$

$$= \frac{365 \text{ days}}{4.6 \text{ times}} = 79.3 \text{ days}$$

J.C. Penney turned its inventory over 4.6 times in 2002, or, on average, every 79.3 days. These figures represent an improvement over the previous two years, and they are also reasonable because J.C. Penney is in a business in which fashions change every season, or about every 90 days. Management wants to sell all of each season's inventory within 80 to 90 days, even while purchasing inventory for the next season.

There are natural levels of inventory in every industry, as shown for selected merchandising and manufacturing industries in Figures 2 and 3. Nonetheless,

FIGURE 3
Average Days' Inventory on Hand for Selected Industries

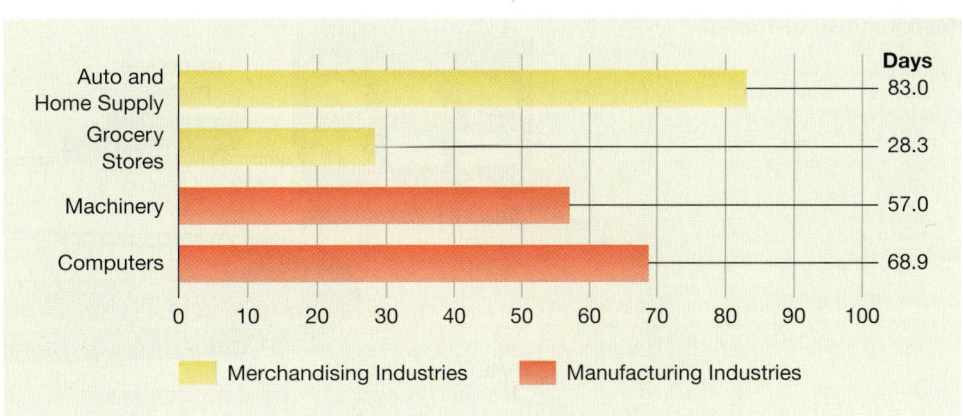

Source: Data from Dun & Bradstreet, *Industry Norms and Key Business Ratios,* 2001–2002.

FOCUS ON BUSINESS TECHNOLOGY

What a Headache!

A single seat belt can have as many as 50 parts, and getting them from suppliers used to be a big problem for Autoliv, Inc. <www.autoliv.com>, a Swedish maker of auto safety devices. Autoliv's plant in Indianapolis was encountering constant bottlenecks in dealing with 125 different suppliers. To keep the production lines going required high-priced, rush shipments on a daily basis. To solve the problem, the company began using supply-chain management, keeping in touch with suppliers through the Internet rather than through faxes and phone calls. The new system allows suppliers to monitor the inventory at Autoliv and thus to anticipate problems. It also provides information on quantity and time of recent shipments, as well as continuously updated forecasts of parts that will be needed in the next 12 weeks. With the new system, Autoliv has reduced inventory by 75 percent and rush freight costs by 95 percent.[5]

companies that are able to maintain their inventories at lower levels and still satisfy customer needs are the most successful.

To reduce their levels of inventory, many merchandising and manufacturing companies use supply-chain management in conjunction with a just-in-time operating environment. With **supply-chain management**, a company manages its inventory and purchasing through business-to-business transactions that it conducts over the Internet. In a **just-in-time operating environment**, the company works closely with suppliers to coordinate and schedule shipments so that the shipments arrive just at the time they are needed. The benefits of using supply-chain management in a just-in-time operating environment are that the company has less money tied up in inventory, and the cost associated with carrying the inventory is reduced.

 Check out ACE for a Review Quiz at http://accounting.college.hmco.com/students.

INVENTORY COST AND GOODS FLOW

LO2 Define *inventory cost* and relate it to goods flow and cost flow.

RELATED TEXT ASSIGNMENTS
Q: 4, 5, 6
SD: 5
FRA: 1

BUSINESS-WORLD EXAMPLE: When customers order merchandise from a catalogue company, they pay not only the price listed in the catalogue, but also such charges as shipping and insurance. Consequently, the cost is greater than the catalogue price.

According to the AICPA, "The primary basis of accounting for inventories is cost, which has been defined generally as the price paid or consideration given to acquire an asset."[6] This definition of **inventory cost** has generally been interpreted as including the following costs: invoice price less purchases discounts; freight in, including insurance in transit; and applicable taxes and tariffs. Other costs—for ordering, receiving, and storing—should in principle also be included in inventory cost, but in practice it is so difficult to allocate such costs to specific inventory items that they are instead usually considered expenses of the accounting period.

MERCHANDISE IN TRANSIT

Because merchandise inventory includes all items owned by a company and held for sale, the status of any merchandise in transit, whether the company is selling it or buying it, must be examined to determine if the merchandise should be included in the inventory count. As Figure 4 illustrates, neither the seller nor the buyer has *phys-*

FIGURE 4
Merchandise in Transit

ical possession of merchandise in transit. Ownership of goods in transit is determined by the terms of the shipping agreement, which indicate when title passes. Outgoing goods shipped FOB (free on board) destination would be included in the seller's merchandise inventory, whereas those shipped FOB shipping point would not. Conversely, incoming goods shipped FOB shipping point would be included in the buyer's merchandise inventory, but those shipped FOB destination would not.

MERCHANDISE ON HAND NOT INCLUDED IN INVENTORY

At the time a company takes a physical inventory, it may have merchandise on hand to which it does not hold title. One category of such goods is merchandise that has been sold and is awaiting delivery to the buyer. Since the sale has been completed, title to the goods has passed to the buyer, and the merchandise should be included in the inventory of the buyer, not of the seller. A second category is goods held on consignment. A **consignment** is merchandise that its owner (known as the *consignor*) places on the premises of another company (the *consignee*) with the understanding that payment is expected only when the merchandise is sold and that unsold items may be returned to the consignor. Title to consigned goods remains with the consignor until the consignee sells the goods. Consigned goods should not be included in the physical inventory of the consignee because they still belong to the consignor.

KEY POINT: The consignor will count as inventory all merchandise placed (consigned) at other locations.

GOODS FLOW VERSUS COST FLOW

KEY POINT: The assumed flow of costs for inventory pricing does not have to correspond to the natural flow of goods.

The prices of most kinds of merchandise vary during the year. Identical lots of merchandise may have been purchased at different prices. Also, when identical items are bought and sold, it is often impossible to tell which have been sold and which are still in inventory. It is therefore necessary to make an assumption about the order in which items have been sold. Because the assumed order of sale may or may not be the same as the actual order of sale, the assumption is really about the *flow of costs* rather than the *flow of physical inventory.*

The term **goods flow** refers to the actual physical movement of goods in the operations of a company, and the term **cost flow** refers to the association of costs with their *assumed* flow in the operations of a company. The assumed cost flow may or may not be the same as the actual goods flow. The possibility of a difference between cost flow and goods flow may seem strange at first, but it arises because several choices of assumed cost flow are available under generally accepted accounting principles. In fact, it is sometimes preferable to use an assumed cost flow that bears no relationship to goods flow because it gives a better estimate of income, which is the main goal of inventory valuation.

● **STOP AND THINK!**
Which is more important from the standpoint of inventory costing: the flow of goods or the flow of costs?
Flow of costs is more important because inventory costing ignores the actual flow of goods and assumes a flow of costs. ■

✓ Check out ACE for a Review Quiz at http://accounting.college.hmco.com/students.

METHODS OF PRICING INVENTORY AT COST UNDER THE PERIODIC INVENTORY SYSTEM

LO3 Calculate the pricing of inventory, using the cost basis under the periodic inventory system.

RELATED TEXT ASSIGNMENTS
Q: 7, 8, 9
SE: 3, 4, 5, 6
E: 3, 4, 5, 7, 9
P: 1, 2, 6, 7
SD: 7

The value assigned to ending inventory is the result of two measurements: quantity and price. Quantity is determined by taking a physical inventory. The pricing of inventory is usually based on the assumed cost flow of the goods as they are bought and sold. Accountants usually price inventory by using one of the following generally accepted methods, each based on a different assumption of cost flow: (1) specific identification method; (2) average-cost method; (3) first-in, first-out (FIFO) method; and (4) last-in, first-out (LIFO) method. The choice of method depends on the nature of the business, the financial effects of the method, and the cost of implementing the method. To illustrate the four methods under the periodic inventory system, we use the following data for the month of June:

Inventory Data—June 30

June			
1	Inventory	50 units @ $1.00	$ 50
6	Purchase	50 units @ $1.10	55
13	Purchase	150 units @ $1.20	180
20	Purchase	100 units @ $1.30	130
25	Purchase	150 units @ $1.40	210
Goods available for sale		500 units	$625
Sales		280 units	
On hand June 30		220 units	

Notice that a total of 500 units is available for sale at a total cost of $625. Stated simply, the problem of inventory pricing is to divide the $625 between the 280 units sold and the 220 units on hand. Recall that under the periodic inventory system, the inventory is not updated after each purchase and sale. Thus, it is not necessary to know when the individual sales take place.

SPECIFIC IDENTIFICATION METHOD

If the units in the ending inventory can be identified as coming from specific purchases, the **specific identification method** may be used. This method prices the inventory by identifying the cost of each item in ending inventory. For instance, if the June 30 inventory consisted of 50 units from the June 1 inventory, 100 units from the June 13 purchase, and 70 units from the June 25 purchase, the specific identification method would assign a cost of $268 to the inventory, as follows:

Periodic Inventory System—Specific Identification Method

50 units @ $1.00	$ 50	Cost of goods available for sale	$625
100 units @ $1.20	120		
70 units @ $1.40	98	Less June 30 inventory	268
220 units at a cost of	$268	Cost of goods sold	$357

BUSINESS-WORLD EXAMPLE: Even if it were possible to track each individual inventory item, a company would not do so because it would be excessively expensive to track which items were left in inventory. The cost would clearly exceed the benefit.

The specific identification method may appear logical, and it might be used in the purchase and sale of high-priced articles, such as automobiles and works of art, but it is not used by many companies because of two definite disadvantages. First, it is often difficult and impractical to keep track of the purchase and sale of individual items. Second, when a company deals in items that are identical but that it bought at different costs, deciding which items were sold becomes arbitrary; thus, the company can raise or lower income by choosing the lower- or higher-cost items.

AVERAGE-COST METHOD

BUSINESS-WORLD EXAMPLE: The physical flow of goods may sometimes seem to dictate a particular method, such as in a milk producer's operations in which the perishable nature of the product apparently requires a *physical flow* of FIFO. However, the milk producer's management can choose an inventory method based on an assumed *cost flow* that differs from FIFO, such as average-cost or LIFO.

Under the **average-cost method,** inventory is priced at the average cost of the goods available for sale during the period. Average cost is computed by dividing the total cost of goods available for sale by the total units available for sale. This gives an average unit cost that is applied to the units in ending inventory. In our illustration, the ending inventory would be $275, or $1.25 per unit, determined as follows:

Periodic Inventory System—Average-Cost Method

Cost of Goods Available for Sale ÷ Units Available for Sale = Average Unit Cost

$625 ÷ 500 units = $1.25

Ending inventory: 220 units @ $1.25 =	$275
Cost of goods available for sale	$625
Less June 30 inventory	275
Cost of goods sold	$350

The average-cost method tends to level out the effects of cost increases and decreases because the cost for the ending inventory calculated under this method is influenced by all the prices paid during the year and by the beginning inventory price. Some, however, criticize the average-cost method because they believe recent costs are more relevant for income measurement and decision making.

FIRST-IN, FIRST-OUT (FIFO) METHOD

The **first-in, first-out (FIFO) method** is based on the assumption that the costs of the first items acquired should be assigned to the first items sold. The costs of the goods on hand at the end of a period are assumed to be from the most recent purchases, and the costs assigned to goods that have been sold are assumed to be from beginning inventory and the earliest purchases. The FIFO method of determining inventory cost may be adopted by any business, regardless of the actual physical flow of goods, because the assumption is made regarding the flow of costs and not the flow of goods. In our illustration, the June 30 inventory would be $301 when the FIFO method is used. It is computed as follows:

Periodic Inventory System—First-In, First-Out Method

150 units @ $1.40 from purchase of June 25	$210
70 units @ $1.30 from purchase of June 20	91
220 units at a cost of	$301
Cost of goods available for sale	$625
Less June 30 inventory	301
Cost of goods sold	$324

ENRICHMENT NOTE: When you make a FIFO cost flow assumption, you use it even if you can prove that one of the first-purchased items is still in inventory. Let's say that for the first week of January, perfume was packaged in blue boxes, and then the company changed to red packaging. When you price inventory using the FIFO method, you assume the blue boxes (the older merchandise) were sold, even if you have some of them left in inventory.

The effect of the FIFO method is to value the ending inventory at the most recent costs and include earlier costs in cost of goods sold. During periods of consistently rising prices, the FIFO method yields the highest possible amount of net income because cost of goods sold will show the earliest costs incurred, which are lower during periods of inflation. Another reason for this result is that businesses tend to increase selling prices as costs rise, even when inventories were purchased before the price rise. The reverse effect occurs in periods of price decreases. Consequently, a major criticism of FIFO is that it magnifies the effects of the business cycle on income.

LAST-IN, FIRST-OUT (LIFO) METHOD

The **last-in, first-out (LIFO) method** of costing inventories is based on the assumption that the costs of the last items purchased should be assigned to the first items sold and that the cost of ending inventory reflects the cost of the goods purchased earliest. Under LIFO, the June 30 inventory would be $249, computed as follows:

Periodic Inventory System—Last-In, First-Out Method

50 units @ $1.00 from June 1 inventory	$ 50
50 units @ $1.10 from purchase of June 6	55
120 units @ $1.20 from purchase of June 13	144
220 units at a cost of	$249
Cost of goods available for sale	$625
Less June 30 inventory	249
Cost of goods sold	$376

BUSINESS-WORLD EXAMPLE: Physical flow under LIFO can be likened to the changes in a gravel pile. As gravel on top is sold, more is purchased and added on top. The gravel on the bottom may never be sold. Despite the physical flow of LIFO, any acceptable cost flow assumption may be made.

The effect of LIFO is to value inventory at the earliest prices and to include in cost of goods sold the cost of the most recently purchased goods. This assumption, of course, does not agree with the actual physical movement of goods in most businesses.

FIGURE 5
Impact of Cost Flow Assumptions on the Income Statement and Balance Sheet Using the Periodic Inventory System

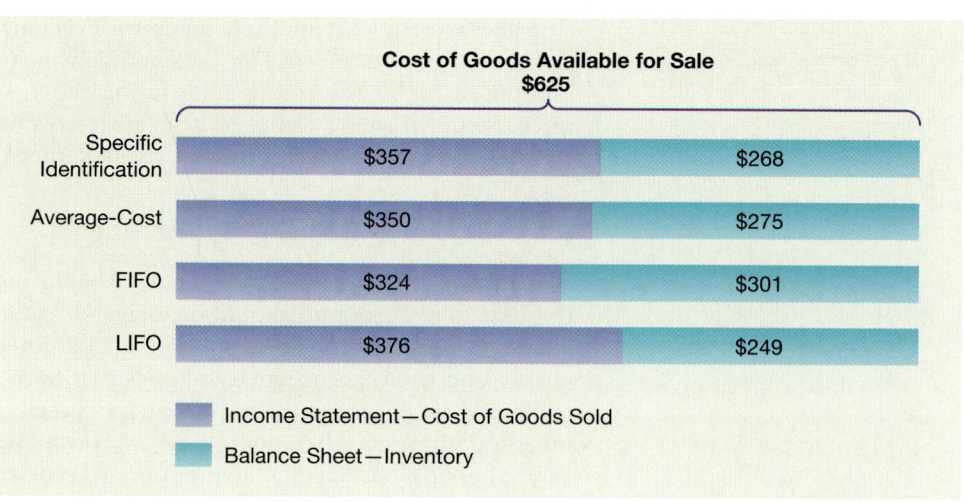

There is, however, a strong logical argument to support LIFO, based on the fact that a certain size of inventory is necessary in a going concern. When inventory is sold, it must be replaced with more goods. The supporters of LIFO reason that the fairest determination of income occurs if the current costs of merchandise are matched against current sales prices, regardless of which physical units of merchandise are sold. When prices are moving either upward or downward, the cost of goods sold will, under LIFO, show costs closer to the price level at the time the goods were sold. As a result, the LIFO method tends to show a smaller net income during inflationary times and a larger net income during deflationary times than other methods of inventory valuation. The peaks and valleys of the business cycle tend to be smoothed out. In inventory valuation, the flow of costs—and hence income determination—is more important than the physical movement of goods and balance sheet valuation.

An argument may also be made against LIFO. Because the inventory valuation on the balance sheet reflects earlier prices, it often gives an unrealistic picture of the current value of the inventory. Such balance sheet measures as working capital and current ratio may be distorted and must be interpreted carefully.

Figure 5 summarizes the impact of the four inventory cost allocation methods on the cost of goods sold as reported on the income statement and on inventory as reported on the balance sheet when a company uses the periodic inventory system. In periods of rising prices, the FIFO method yields the highest inventory valuation, the lowest cost of goods sold, and hence a higher net income; the LIFO method yields the lowest inventory valuation, the highest cost of goods sold, and thus a lower net income.

● **STOP AND THINK!**
Under what condition would all four methods of inventory pricing produce exactly the same results?
They would produce the same results if there were no price changes after the purchase of beginning inventory. ■

Check out ACE for a Review Quiz at http://accounting.college.hmco.com/students.

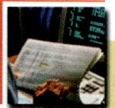

FOCUS ON BUSINESS PRACTICE

What's a "Category Killer?"

A new type of retail company called the "category killer" seems to ignore the tenets of good inventory management. The category killers include Home Depot <www.homedepot.com>, Barnes & Noble <www.bn.com>, Wal-Mart <www.walmart.com>, Toys "R" Us <www.tru.com>, and Blockbuster Entertainment Corporation <www.blockbuster.com>. These retailers maintain huge inventories of the goods in which they specialize and sell them at such low prices that smaller competitors find it hard to compete. Although the category killers have large amounts of money tied up in inventories, they maintain very sophisticated just-in-time operating environments that require suppliers to meet demanding standards for delivery of products and reduction of inventory costs. Some suppliers are required to stock the shelves and keep track of inventory levels. By minimizing handling and overhead costs and buying at favorably low prices, the category killers achieve great success.

PRICING INVENTORY UNDER THE PERPETUAL INVENTORY SYSTEM

LO4 Apply the perpetual inventory system to the pricing of inventories at cost.

RELATED TEXT ASSIGNMENTS
Q: 10
SE: 7, 8, 9
E: 6, 7
P: 3, 8
SD: 5

The pricing of inventories under the perpetual inventory system differs from pricing under the periodic inventory system. The difference occurs because under the perpetual inventory system, a continuous record of quantities and costs of merchandise is maintained as purchases and sales are made. Under the periodic inventory system, only the ending inventory is counted and priced, and cost of goods sold is determined by deducting the cost of the ending inventory from the cost of goods available for sale. Under the perpetual inventory system, cost of goods sold is accumulated as sales are made and costs are transferred from the Inventory account to the Cost of Goods Sold account. The cost of the ending inventory is the balance of the Inventory account. To illustrate pricing methods under the perpetual inventory system, we use the same data as in the last section, but we add specific sales dates and amounts, as follows:

Inventory Data—June 30

June			
	1	Inventory	50 units @ $1.00
	6	Purchase	50 units @ $1.10
	10	Sale	70 units
	13	Purchase	150 units @ $1.20
	20	Purchase	100 units @ $1.30
	25	Purchase	150 units @ $1.40
	30	Sale	210 units
	30	Inventory	220 units

Pricing the inventory and cost of goods sold using the specific identification method is the same under the perpetual system as under the periodic system because cost of goods sold and ending inventory are based on the cost of the identified items sold and on hand. The perpetual system facilitates the use of the specific identification method because detailed records of purchases and sales are maintained.

ENRICHMENT NOTE: An automated perpetual system has considerable costs. They include the costs of automating the system, maintaining the system, and taking a physical inventory to check against the perpetual records.

Pricing the inventory and cost of goods sold using the average-cost method differs when the perpetual system is used. Under the periodic system, the average cost is computed for all goods available for sale during the month. Under the perpetual system, an average is computed after each purchase or series of purchases, as follows:

Perpetual Inventory System—Average-Cost Method

June	1	Inventory	50 units @ $1.00	$ 50.00
	6	Purchase	50 units @ $1.10	55.00
	6	Balance	100 units @ $1.05	$105.00
	10	Sale	70 units @ $1.05	(73.50)
	10	Balance	30 units @ $1.05	$ 31.50
	13	Purchase	150 units @ $1.20	180.00
	20	Purchase	100 units @ $1.30	130.00
	25	Purchase	150 units @ $1.40	210.00
	25	Balance	430 units @ $1.28*	$551.50
	30	Sale	210 units @ $1.28	(268.80)
	30	Inventory	220 units @ $1.29*	$282.70
Cost of goods sold			($73.50 + $268.80)	$342.30

*Rounded.

● **STOP AND THINK!**
Under the perpetual inventory system, why is the cost of goods sold not determined by deducting the ending inventory from goods available for sale, as it is under the periodic method?

Under the perpetual inventory system, the cost of goods sold and the inventory balance are determined after every transaction. ■

The sum of the costs applied to sales becomes the cost of goods sold, $342.30. The ending inventory is the balance, or $282.70.

When pricing the inventory using the FIFO and LIFO methods, it is necessary to keep track of the components of inventory at each step of the way because as sales are made, the costs must be assigned in the proper order. To apply the FIFO method, the approach is as follows:

Perpetual Inventory System—FIFO Method

June 1	Inventory	50 units @ $1.00		$ 50.00	
6	Purchase	50 units @ $1.10		55.00	
10	Sale	50 units @ $1.00	($ 50.00)		
		20 units @ $1.10	(22.00)		(72.00)
10	Balance	30 units @ $1.10		$ 33.00	
13	Purchase	150 units @ $1.20		180.00	
20	Purchase	100 units @ $1.30		130.00	
25	Purchase	150 units @ $1.40		210.00	
30	Sale	30 units @ $1.10	($ 33.00)		
		150 units @ $1.20	(180.00)		
		30 units @ $1.30	(39.00)		(252.00)
30	Inventory	70 units @ $1.30		$ 91.00	
		150 units @ $1.40		210.00	$301.00
Cost of goods sold		($72.00 + $252.00)			$324.00

Note that the ending inventory of $301 and the cost of goods sold of $324 are the same as the figures computed earlier under the periodic inventory system. This will always occur because the ending inventory under both systems consists of the last items purchased—in this case, the entire purchase of June 25 and 70 units from the purchase of June 20.

To apply the LIFO method, the approach is as follows:

Perpetual Inventory System—LIFO Method

June 1	Inventory	50 units @ $1.00		$ 50.00	
6	Purchase	50 units @ $1.10		55.00	
10	Sale	50 units @ $1.10	($ 55.00)		
		20 units @ $1.00	(20.00)		(75.00)
10	Balance	30 units @ $1.00		$ 30.00	
13	Purchase	150 units @ $1.20		180.00	
20	Purchase	100 units @ $1.30		130.00	
25	Purchase	150 units @ $1.40		210.00	
30	Sale	150 units @ $1.40	($210.00)		
		60 units @ $1.30	(78.00)		(288.00)
30	Inventory	30 units @ $1.00		$ 30.00	
		150 units @ $1.20		180.00	
		40 units @ $1.30		52.00	$262.00
Cost of goods sold		($75.00 + $288.00)			$363.00

Note that the ending inventory of $262 includes 30 units from the beginning inventory, all units from the June 13 purchase, and 40 units from the June 20 purchase.

A comparison of the average-cost, FIFO, and LIFO methods using the perpetual inventory system is shown in Figure 6. The results are the same as under the periodic inventory system, but some amounts have changed. For example, LIFO has

FOCUS ON BUSINESS TECHNOLOGY

More Companies Enjoy LIFO!

Using the LIFO method under the perpetual inventory system is a tedious process, especially if done manually. The development of faster and less expensive computer systems has made it easier for many companies to switch to LIFO and still use the perpetual inventory system. The availability of better technology may partially account for the increasing use of LIFO in the United States and may enable more companies to enjoy LIFO's economic benefits.

FIGURE 6
Impact of Cost Flow Assumptions on the Income Statement and Balance Sheet Using the Perpetual Inventory System

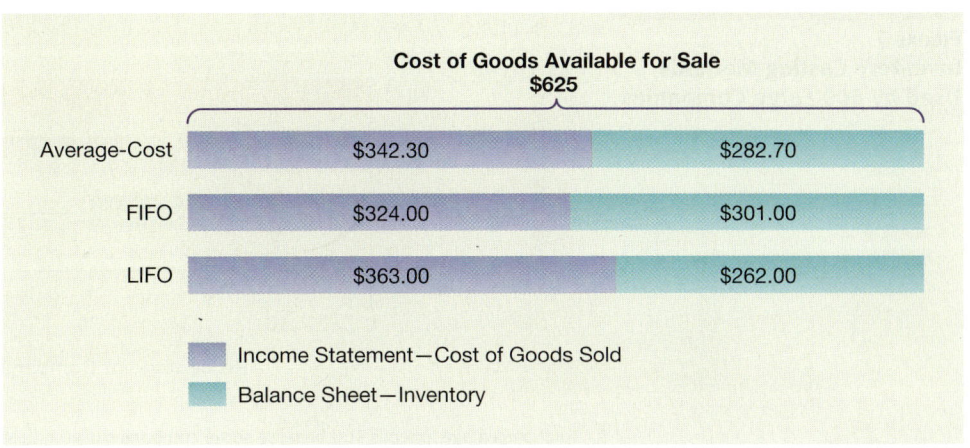

the lowest inventory valuation regardless of the inventory system used, but the amount is $262 using the perpetual system versus $249 using the periodic system.

✓ Check out ACE for a Review Quiz at http://accounting.college.hmco.com/students.

COMPARISON AND IMPACT OF INVENTORY DECISIONS AND MISSTATEMENTS

LO5 State the effects of inventory methods and misstatements of inventory on income determination, income taxes, and cash flows.

RELATED TEXT ASSIGNMENTS
Q: 11, 12, 13, 14
SE: 10
E: 8, 9, 10
SD: 2, 4, 6, 7
FRA: 1, 2, 3, 4, 5, 8

Exhibit 1 shows how the specific identification, average-cost, FIFO, and LIFO methods of pricing inventory under both the periodic and the perpetual inventory systems affect gross margin. The exhibit uses the same data as before and assumes June sales of $500. Because the specific identification method is based on actual cost, it is the same under both systems.

Keeping in mind that June was a period of rising prices, we can see that LIFO, which charges the most recent, and, in this case, the highest, prices to cost of goods sold, resulted in the lowest gross margin under both systems. Conversely, FIFO, which charges the earliest, and, in this case, the lowest, prices to cost of goods sold,

EXHIBIT 1
Effects of Inventory Systems and Costing Methods on Gross Margin

		Periodic Inventory System				Perpetual Inventory System*		
	Specific Identification Method	Average-Cost Method	First-In, First-Out Method	Last-In, First-Out Method		Average-Cost Method	First-In, First-Out Method	Last-In, First-Out Method
Sales	$500	$500	$500	$500		$500	$500	$500
Cost of goods sold								
Beginning inventory	$ 50	$ 50	$ 50	$ 50				
Purchases	575	575	575	575				
Cost of goods available for sale	$625	$625	$625	$625				
Less ending inventory	268	275	301	249		$283†	$301	$262
Cost of goods sold	$357	$350	$324	$376		$342†	$324	$363
Gross margin	$143	$150	$176	$124		$158	$176	$137

*Ending inventory under the perpetual inventory system is provided for comparison only. It is not used in the computation of cost of goods sold.
†Rounded.

FIGURE 7
Inventory Costing Methods Used by 600 Large Companies

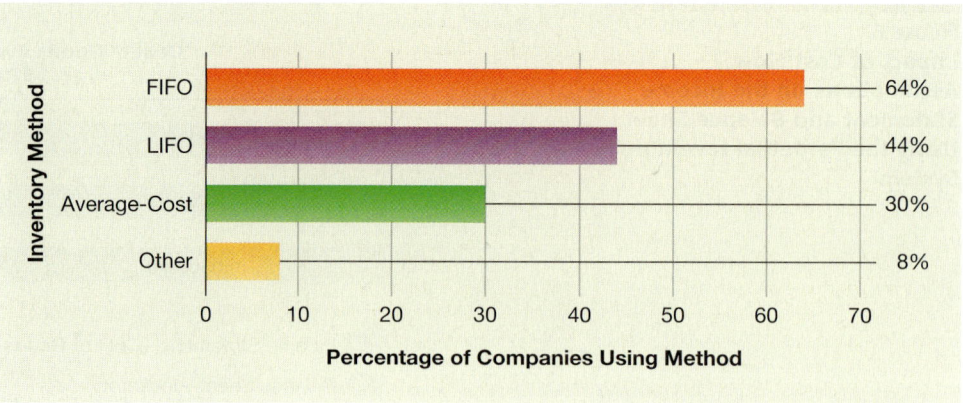

Total percentage exceeds 100 because some companies used different methods for different types of inventory.
Source: "Inventory Costing Methods Used by 600 Large Companies." Reprinted with permission from *Accounting Trends and Techniques*. Copyright © 2002 by the American Institute of Certified Public Accountants, Inc.

produced the highest gross margin. The gross margin under the average-cost method is in between the gross margins under LIFO and FIFO; thus, this method clearly has a less pronounced effect. Note that ending inventory and gross margin under FIFO are the same under both the periodic and the perpetual inventory systems.

During a period of declining prices, the reverse would occur. The LIFO method would produce a higher gross margin than the FIFO method. It is apparent that the method of inventory valuation has the greatest importance during prolonged periods of price changes in one direction, either up or down.

Because the specific identification method depends on the particular items sold, no generalization can be made about the effect of changing prices.

EFFECTS ON THE FINANCIAL STATEMENTS

KEY POINT: The assumption of inventory cost flows is necessary because of changes in merchandise prices.

Each of the four methods of inventory pricing is acceptable for use in published financial statements. The FIFO, LIFO, and average-cost methods are widely used, as can be seen in Figure 7, which shows the inventory costing methods used by 600 large companies. Each method has its advantages and disadvantages, and none can be considered best or perfect. The factors that should be considered in choosing an inventory method are the trend of prices and the effects of each method on financial statements, income taxes, and cash flows.

A basic problem in determining the best inventory measure for a particular company is that inventory affects both the balance sheet and the income statement. As we have seen, the LIFO method is best suited for the income statement because it matches revenues and cost of goods sold. But it is not the best measure of the current balance sheet value of inventory, particularly during a prolonged period of price increases or decreases. FIFO, on the other hand, is best suited to the balance sheet because the ending inventory is closest to current values and thus gives a more realistic view of the current financial assets of a business. Readers of financial statements must be alert to inventory methods and be able to assess their effects.

EFFECTS ON INCOME TAXES

The Internal Revenue Service has developed several rules for valuing inventories for federal income tax purposes. A company has a wide choice of methods, including specific identification, average-cost, FIFO, and LIFO, as well as lower-of-cost-or-market, discussed later in the chapter. But once a method has been chosen, it must be used consistently from one year to the next. The IRS must approve any change in the inventory valuation method for income tax purposes.* This requirement

---
*A single exception to this rule is that although taxpayers must notify the IRS of a change to LIFO from another method, they do not need to have advance IRS approval.

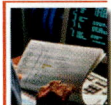

Focus on Business Practice

Does a Company's Accounting Method Affect Management's Operating Decisions?

It certainly does when taxes are involved! Research has shown that among firms that use the LIFO inventory method, those with high tax rates are more likely to buy extra inventory at year end than are those with low tax rates.[7] This behavior is predictable because LIFO deducts the most recent purchases, which are likely to have higher costs than earlier purchases, in determining taxable income. This action will result in lower income taxes.

KEY POINT: In periods of rising prices, LIFO results in lower net income and thus lower taxes.

agrees with the consistency convention, since changes in inventory method may cause income to fluctuate too much and would make income statements hard to interpret from year to year. A company may change its inventory method if there is a good reason for doing so. The nature and effect of the change must be shown on the company's financial statements.

Many accountants believe that using the FIFO and average-cost methods in periods of rising prices causes businesses to report more than their true profit, resulting in the payment of excess income taxes. The profit is overstated because cost of goods sold is understated relative to current prices. The company must buy replacement inventory at higher prices, but additional funds are also needed to pay income taxes. During the rapid inflation of 1979 to 1982, billions of dollars reported as profits and paid in income taxes were believed to be the result of poor matching of current costs and revenues under the FIFO and average-cost methods. Consequently, many companies, believing that prices would continue to rise, switched to the LIFO inventory method.

If a company uses the LIFO method in reporting income for tax purposes, the IRS requires that the same method be used in the accounting records. Also, the IRS will not allow the use of the lower-of-cost-or-market rule if LIFO is used to determine inventory cost. In such a case, only the LIFO cost can be used. This rule, however, does not preclude a company from using lower-of-LIFO-cost-or-market for financial reporting purposes (discussed later in this chapter).

Over a period of rising prices, a business that uses the LIFO method may find that for balance sheet purposes, its inventory is valued at a cost figure far below what it currently pays for the same items. Management must monitor this situation carefully, because if it should let the inventory quantity at year end fall below the beginning-of-the-year level, the company will find itself paying higher income taxes. Higher income before taxes results because the company expenses historical costs of inventory, which are below current costs. When this occurs, it is called a **LIFO liquidation** because sales have reduced inventories below the levels set in prior years; that is, units sold exceed units purchased for the period.

A LIFO liquidation may be prevented by making enough purchases prior to year end to restore the desired inventory level. Sometimes a LIFO liquidation cannot be avoided because products are discontinued or supplies are interrupted, as in the case of a strike. In a recent year, 27 out of 600 large companies reported a LIFO liquidation in which net income was increased because of the matching of older historical cost with present sales dollars.[8]

Effects of Misstatements in Inventory Measurement

The basic problem of separating goods available for sale into two components—goods sold and goods not sold—is that of assigning a cost to the goods not sold, the ending inventory. The portion of the goods available for sale not assigned to the ending inventory is used to determine the cost of goods sold.

Because the figures for ending inventory and cost of goods sold are related, a misstatement in the inventory figure at the end of the period will cause an equal misstatement in gross margin and income before income taxes on the income statement. The amount of assets and owner's equity on the balance sheet will also be misstated by the same amount. The consequences of overstatement and understatement of inventory are illustrated in the three simplified examples that follow. In each case, beginning inventory, net cost of purchases, and cost of goods available for sale have been stated correctly. In the first example, ending inventory has been stated correctly. In the second example, ending inventory is overstated by $6,000; in the third example, ending inventory is understated by $6,000.

Example 1. Ending Inventory Correctly Stated at $10,000

Cost of Goods Sold for the Year		Income Statement for the Year	
Beginning inventory	$12,000	Net sales	$100,000
Net cost of purchases	58,000	Cost of goods sold	60,000
Cost of goods available for sale	$70,000	Gross margin	$ 40,000
Ending inventory	10,000	Operating expenses	32,000
Cost of goods sold	$60,000	Income before income taxes	$ 8,000

Example 2. Ending Inventory Overstated by $6,000

Cost of Goods Sold for the Year		Income Statement for the Year	
Beginning inventory	$12,000	Net sales	$100,000
Net cost of purchases	58,000	Cost of goods sold	54,000
Cost of goods available for sale	$70,000	Gross margin	$ 46,000
Ending inventory	16,000	Operating expenses	32,000
Cost of goods sold	$54,000	Income before income taxes	$ 14,000

Example 3. Ending Inventory Understated by $6,000

Cost of Goods Sold for the Year		Income Statement for the Year	
Beginning inventory	$12,000	Net sales	$100,000
Net cost of purchases	58,000	Cost of goods sold	66,000
Cost of goods available for sale	$70,000	Gross margin	$ 34,000
Ending inventory	4,000	Operating expenses	32,000
Cost of goods sold	$66,000	Income before income taxes	$ 2,000

KEY POINT: A misstatement in inventory affects not only the current year, but also has the opposite effect on the next year.

KEY POINT: Inventory errors will correct (counterbalance) themselves over a two-year period.

In all three examples, the total cost of goods available for sale was $70,000. The difference in income before income taxes resulted from how this $70,000 was divided between ending inventory and cost of goods sold.

Because the ending inventory in one period becomes the beginning inventory in the following period, it is important to recognize that a misstatement in inventory valuation affects not only the current period but also the following period. Over a two-year period, the errors in income before income taxes will offset, or counterbalance, each other. If we assume that Example 2 represents year 1, for instance, the overstatement of ending inventory in year 1 will cause a $6,000 overstatement of beginning inventory in year 2, resulting in an understatement of income by $6,000 in the second year.

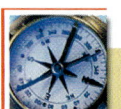

Focus on Business Ethics

The Temptation to Overstate Inventories

Net income can be easily manipulated when accounting for inventory. For example, it is easy to overstate or understate inventory by including end-of-the-year purchase and sales transactions in the wrong fiscal year or by simply misstating inventory. In one spectacular case, Rite Aid Corp. <www.riteaid.com>, the large drugstore chain, falsified income by manipulating its computerized inventory system to cover losses from shrinkage, which includes shoplifting, employee theft, and spoilage. In another case, bookkeepers at RentWay, Inc. <www.rentway.com>, a company that rents furniture to apartment dwellers, boosted income artificially over several years by overstating inventory in small increments that were not noticed by top management.[9]

Stop and Think!

Why is misstatement of inventory one of the most common means of financial statement fraud?

For one thing, the value put on inventory has a direct dollar-for-dollar effect on net income. For another, it is relatively easy to falsify the value placed on the ending inventory and to cover up the falsification. ■

Because the total income before income taxes for the two years is the same, it may appear that one need not worry about inventory misstatements. However, the misstatements violate the matching rule. In addition, management, creditors, and investors make many decisions on an annual basis and depend on the accountant's determination of net income. The accountant has an obligation to make the net income figure for each year as useful as possible.

The effects of misstatements in inventory on income before income taxes are as follows:

Year 1	Year 2
Ending inventory overstated	**Beginning inventory overstated**
Cost of goods sold understated	Cost of goods sold overstated
Income before income taxes overstated	Income before income taxes understated
Ending inventory understated	**Beginning inventory understated**
Cost of goods sold overstated	Cost of goods sold understated
Income before income taxes understated	Income before income taxes overstated

A misstatement in inventory results in a misstatement in income before income taxes of the same amount. Thus, the measurement of inventory is important.

INVENTORY MEASUREMENT AND CASH FLOWS

www.internationalpaper.com

A company's inventory methods affect not only its reported profitability but also its reported liquidity and cash flows. In the case of a large company like International Paper Co., these effects can be complex and material. In a note on inventories, International Paper provides more detail about these effects:

> The last-in, first-out inventory method is used to value most of International Paper's U.S. inventories. Approximately 68% of total raw materials and finished products inventories were valued using this method. If the first-in, first-out method had been used, it would have increased total inventory balances by approximately $264 million and $250 million at December 31, 2000 and 1999, respectively.[10]

By using LIFO, the company usually reports a lower income before taxes. This will have a favorable effect on cash flows because of the lower amount of income taxes to be paid. The reader of the financial statements may determine what International Paper's inventory value would have been if it were valued at current prices under FIFO rather than older prices under LIFO. Thus, a more realistic comparison of the company's liquidity ratios can be made. For example, the more realistic FIFO figure would show a better short-term liquidity position as measured by the current ratio than the LIFO figures reported on the balance sheet would seem to indicate. However, the company's inventory turnover and average days' inventory on hand will be adversely affected if the more realistic FIFO figures are used.

✓ Check out ACE for a Review Quiz at http://accounting.college.hmco.com/students.

VALUING INVENTORY AT THE LOWER OF COST OR MARKET (LCM)

LO6 Apply the lower-of-cost-or-market (LCM) rule to inventory valuation.

RELATED TEXT ASSIGNMENTS
Q: 15, 16
SE: 11
E: 11
SD: 3
FRA: 5

Although cost is usually the most appropriate basis for valuation of inventory, there are times when inventory may properly be shown in the financial statements at less than its cost. If the market value of inventory falls below its cost because of physical deterioration, obsolescence, or decline in price level, a loss has occurred. This loss may be recognized by writing the inventory down to **market**, or current replacement cost, of inventory. For a merchandising company, market is the amount that the company would pay at the present time for the same goods, purchased from the usual suppliers and in the usual quantities. The **lower-of-cost-or-market (LCM) rule**

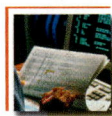

Focus on Business Practice

How Bad Can It Get?

Pretty bad! When the lower-of-cost-or-market rule comes into play, it can be an indicator of how bad. For example, when the market for Internet and telecommunications equipment soured in 2001, Cisco Systems, Inc. <www.cisco.com>, found itself faced with probably the largest inventory loss in history. It had to write down to zero almost two-thirds of its $2.5 billion inventory, 80 percent of which consisted of raw materials that would never be made into final product. In another case, through poor management, a downturn in the economy, and underperforming stores, Kmart <www.kmartcorp.com> found itself with a huge amount of excess merchandise, including more than 5,000 truckloads of goods stored in parking lots, which it could not sell except at drastically reduced prices. The company had to mark down its inventory by $1 billion in order to sell it, resulting in a loss for the year.[12]

● **Stop and Think!**
Given that the LCM rule is an application of the conservatism convention in the current accounting period, is the effect of this application also conservative in the next period?

It probably is not because a reduction in inventory in the current period resulting in lower net income will cause the beginning inventory in the next period to be smaller and will thus increase net income in that period. ■

STUDY NOTE: Cost must first be determined by the specific identification, FIFO, LIFO, or average-cost method before it can be compared with replacement cost.

requires that when the replacement cost of inventory falls below historical cost, based on one of the conventional inventory costing methods, the inventory is written down to the lower value and a loss is recorded. This rule is an example of the application of the convention of conservatism because the loss is recognized before an actual transaction takes place. Under historical cost accounting, the inventory remains at cost until it is sold. It may help in applying the LCM rule to think of it as the "lower-of-cost-or-replacement-cost" rule.* Approximately 90 percent of 600 large companies report applying the LCM rule to their inventories.[11]

There are two basic methods of valuing inventories at the lower of cost or market accepted both by GAAP and the IRS for federal income tax purposes: (1) the item-by-item method and (2) the major category method. For example, a stereo shop could determine lower of cost or market for each kind of speaker, receiver, and turntable (item by item) or for all speakers, all receivers, and all turntables (major categories).

Item-by-Item Method

When the **item-by-item method** is used, cost and market values are compared for each item in inventory. Each individual item is then valued at its lower price, as shown in Table 1:

TABLE 1. Lower of Cost or Market with Item-by-Item Method

		Per Unit		Lower of
	Quantity	Cost	Market	Cost or Market
Category I				
Item a	200	$1.50	$1.70	$ 300
Item b	100	2.00	1.80	180
Item c	100	2.50	2.60	250
Category II				
Item d	300	5.00	4.50	1,350
Item e	200	4.00	4.10	800
Inventory at the lower of cost or market				$2,880

Major Category Method

Under the **major category method**, the total cost and total market values for each category of items are compared. Each category is then valued at its lower amount, as shown in Table 2:

---

*In some cases, the *realizable value* of the inventory determines the *market value*—the amount for which the goods can be sold—rather than by the amount for which the goods can be replaced. The circumstances in which realizable value determines market value are encountered in practice only occasionally, and the valuation procedures are technical enough to be addressed in a more advanced accounting course.

TABLE 2. Lower of Cost or Market with Major Category Method

	Quantity	Per Unit Cost	Per Unit Market	Total Cost	Total Market	Lower of Cost or Market
Category I						
Item a	200	$1.50	$1.70	$ 300	$ 340	
Item b	100	2.00	1.80	200	180	
Item c	100	2.50	2.60	250	260	
Totals				$ 750	$ 780	$ 750
Category II						
Item d	300	5.00	4.50	$1,500	$1,350	
Item e	200	4.00	4.10	800	820	
Totals				$2,300	$2,170	2,170
Inventory at the lower of cost or market						$2,920

 Check out ACE for a Review Quiz at http://accounting.college.hmco.com/students.

VALUING INVENTORY BY ESTIMATION

SO7 Estimate the cost of ending inventory using the retail method and gross profit method.

RELATED TEXT ASSIGNMENTS
Q: 17, 18, 19
E: 12, 13
P: 4, 5
FRA: 5

It is sometimes necessary or desirable to estimate the value of ending inventory. The retail method and gross profit method are most commonly used for this purpose.

RETAIL METHOD OF INVENTORY ESTIMATION

The **retail method**, as its name implies, is used in retail merchandising businesses to estimate the cost of ending inventory by using the ratio of cost to retail price. There are two principal reasons for its use. First, since preparing financial statements each month requires a knowledge of the cost of inventory, the retail method can be used to estimate the cost without the time or expense of determining the cost of items in the inventory. Second, because items in a retail store normally have a price tag or a universal product code, it is common practice to take the physical inventory at retail from these price tags or codes and to reduce the total value to cost through use of the retail method. The term *at retail* means the amount of the inventory at the marked selling prices of the inventory items.

KEY POINT: When estimating inventory by the retail method, the inventory need not be counted.

When the retail method is used to estimate ending inventory, the records must show the beginning inventory at cost and at retail. The records must also show the amount of goods purchased during the period both at cost and at retail. The net sales at retail is, of course, the balance of the Sales account less returns and allowances. A simple example of the retail method is shown in Table 3.

Goods available for sale is determined both at cost and at retail by listing beginning inventory and net purchases for the period at cost and at their expected selling price, adding freight to the cost column, and totaling. The ratio of these two amounts (cost to retail price) provides an estimate of the cost of each dollar of retail sales value. The estimated ending inventory at retail is then determined by deducting sales for the period from the retail price of the goods that were available for sale during the period. The inventory at retail is then converted to cost on the basis of the ratio of cost to retail.

The cost of ending inventory may also be estimated by applying the ratio of cost to retail price to the total retail value of the physical count of the ending inventory.

TABLE 3. Retail Method of Inventory Estimation

	Cost	Retail
Beginning inventory	$ 40,000	$ 55,000
Net purchases for the period (excluding freight in)	107,000	145,000
Freight in	3,000	
Merchandise available for sale	$150,000	$200,000
Ratio of cost to retail price: $\frac{\$150,000}{\$200,000} = 75\%$		
Net sales during the period		160,000
Estimated ending inventory at retail		$ 40,000
Ratio of cost to retail		75%
Estimated cost of ending inventory		$ 30,000

STUDY NOTE: Freight in is not placed under the Retail column when using the retail method of inventory estimation because businesses automatically price their goods high enough to cover freight charges.

Applying the retail method in practice is often more difficult than this simple example because of such complications as changes in retail price during the year, different markups on different types of merchandise, and varying volumes of sales for different types of merchandise.

GROSS PROFIT METHOD OF INVENTORY ESTIMATION

The **gross profit method** (also known as the *gross margin method*) assumes that the ratio of gross margin for a business remains relatively stable from year to year. The gross profit method is used in place of the retail method when records of the retail prices of beginning inventory and purchases are not kept. It is considered acceptable for estimating the cost of inventory for interim reports, but it is not acceptable for valuing inventory in the annual financial statements. It is also useful in estimating the amount of inventory lost or destroyed by theft, fire, or other hazards. Insurance companies often use this method to verify loss claims.

As Table 4 shows, the gross profit method is simple to use. First, figure the cost of goods available for sale in the usual way (add purchases to beginning inventory). Second, estimate the cost of goods sold by deducting the estimated gross margin of 30 percent from sales. Finally, deduct the estimated cost of goods sold from the goods available for sale to arrive at the estimated cost of ending inventory.

BUSINESS-WORLD EXAMPLE: It is highly desirable to maintain financial records off site. If records were destroyed, it would be difficult, if not impossible, to reconstruct the data necessary for an insurance claim.

TABLE 4. Gross Profit Method of Inventory Estimation

1. Beginning inventory at cost		$ 50,000
Purchases at cost (including freight in)		290,000
Cost of goods available for sale		$340,000
2. Less estimated cost of goods sold		
Sales at selling price	$400,000	
Less estimated gross margin (30% × 400,000)	120,000	
Estimated cost of goods sold		280,000
3. Estimated cost of ending inventory		$ 60,000

✓ Check out ACE for a Review Quiz at http://accounting.college.hmco.com/students.

Chapter Review

REVIEW OF LEARNING OBJECTIVES

LO1 Identify and explain the management issues associated with accounting for inventories.

Included in inventory are goods owned, whether produced or purchased, that are held for sale in the normal course of business. Manufacturing companies also include raw materials and work in process. Among the issues management must face in accounting for inventories are allocating the cost of inventories in accordance with the matching rule, assessing the impact of inventory decisions, and evaluating the level of inventory. The objective of accounting for inventories is the proper determination of income through the matching of costs and revenues, not the determination of the most realistic inventory value. Because the valuation of inventory has a direct effect on a company's net income, the choice of inventory systems and methods affects not only the amount of income taxes and cash flows, but also the external and internal evaluation of the company. The level of inventory as measured by the inventory turnover and its related measure, average days' inventory on hand, is important to managing the amount of investment a company needs.

LO2 Define *inventory cost* and relate it to goods flow and cost flow.

The cost of inventory includes (1) invoice price less purchases discounts; (2) freight in, including insurance in transit; and (3) applicable taxes and tariffs. Goods flow refers to the actual physical flow of merchandise, whereas cost flow refers to the assumed flow of costs in the operations of the business.

LO3 Calculate the pricing of inventory, using the cost basis under the periodic inventory system.

The value assigned to ending inventory is the result of two measurements: quantity and price. Quantity is determined by taking a physical inventory. The pricing of inventory is usually based on the assumed cost flow of the goods as they are bought and sold. One of four assumptions is usually made regarding cost flow. These assumptions are represented by four inventory methods. Inventory pricing can be determined by the specific identification method, which associates the actual cost with each item of inventory, but this method is rarely used. The average-cost method assumes that the cost of inventory is the average cost of goods available for sale during the period. The first-in, first-out (FIFO) method assumes that the costs of the first items acquired should be assigned to the first items sold. The last-in, first-out (LIFO) method assumes that the costs of the last items acquired should be assigned to the first items sold. The inventory method chosen may or may not be equivalent to the actual physical flow of goods.

LO4 Apply the perpetual inventory system to the pricing of inventories at cost.

The pricing of inventories under the perpetual and periodic inventory systems differs because under the perpetual system a continuous record of quantities and costs of merchandise is maintained as purchases and sales are made. Cost of goods sold is accumulated as sales are made and costs are transferred from the Inventory account to the Cost of Goods Sold account. The cost of the ending inventory is the balance of the Inventory account. The specific identification method and the FIFO method produce the same results under the perpetual and periodic inventory systems. The results differ for the average-cost method because an average is calculated after each purchase rather than at the end of the accounting period, and for the LIFO method because the cost components of inventory change constantly as goods are bought and sold.

LO5 State the effects of inventory methods and misstatements of inventory on income determination, income taxes, and cash flows.

During periods of rising prices, the LIFO method will show the lowest net income; FIFO, the highest; and average-cost, in between. The opposite effects occur in periods of falling prices. No generalization can be made regarding the specific identification method. The Internal Revenue Service requires that if LIFO is used for tax purposes, it must also be used for financial statements; it also does not allow the lower-of-cost-or-market rule to be applied to the LIFO method. If the value of ending inventory is understated or overstated, a corresponding error—dollar for dollar—will be made in income before income taxes. Furthermore, because the ending inventory of one period is the beginning inventory of the next, the misstatement affects two accounting periods, although the effects are opposite.

LO6 Apply the lower-of-cost-or-market (LCM) rule to inventory valuation.

The lower-of-cost-or-market rule can be applied to the above methods of determining inventory at cost. This rule states that if the replacement cost (market) of the inventory is lower than the inventory cost, the lower figure should be used. Valuation can be determined on an item-by-item or major category basis.

SUPPLEMENTAL OBJECTIVE

SO7 Estimate the cost of ending inventory using the retail method and gross profit method.

Two methods of estimating the value of inventory are the retail method and the gross profit method. Under the retail method, inventory is determined at retail prices and is then reduced to estimated cost by applying a ratio of cost to retail price. Under the gross profit method, cost of goods sold is estimated by reducing sales by estimated gross margin. The estimated cost of goods sold is then deducted from the cost of goods available for sale to estimate the inventory.

REVIEW OF CONCEPTS AND TERMINOLOGY

The following concepts and terms were introduced in this chapter:

LO3 **Average-cost method:** An inventory costing method in which inventory is priced at the average cost of the goods available for sale during the period.

LO1 **Average days' inventory on hand:** The average number of days required to sell the inventory on hand; number of days in a year divided by inventory turnover.

LO2 **Consignment:** Merchandise that its owner (the *consignor*) places on the premises of another company (the *consignee*) with the understanding that payment is expected only when the merchandise is sold and that unsold items may be returned to the consignor.

LO2 **Cost flow:** The association of costs with their assumed flow in the operations of a company.

LO3 **First-in, first-out (FIFO) method:** An inventory costing method based on the assumption that the costs of the first items acquired should be assigned to the first items sold.

LO2 **Goods flow:** The actual physical movement of goods in the operations of a company.

SO7 **Gross profit method:** A method of inventory estimation based on the assumption that the ratio of gross margin for a business remains relatively stable from year to year. Also called *gross margin method*.

LO2 **Inventory cost:** The price paid or consideration given to acquire an asset; includes invoice price less purchases discounts, plus freight in, plus applicable taxes and tariffs.

LO1 **Inventory turnover:** A ratio indicating the number of times a company's average inventory is sold during an accounting period; cost of goods sold divided by average inventory.

LO6 **Item-by-item method:** A lower-of-cost-or-market method of valuing inventory in which cost and market values are compared for each item in inventory and each item is then valued at its lower price.

LO1 **Just-in-time operating environment:** A system of reducing levels of inventory by working closely with suppliers to coordinate and schedule deliveries so that goods arrive just at the time they are needed.

LO3 **Last-in, first-out (LIFO) method:** An inventory costing method based on the assumption that the costs of the last items purchased should be assigned to the first items sold.

LO5 **LIFO liquidation:** The reduction of inventory below previous levels so that income is increased by the amount by which current prices exceed the historical cost of the inventory under LIFO.

LO6 **Lower-of-cost-or-market (LCM) rule:** A method of valuing inventory at an amount less than cost when the replacement cost falls below historical cost.

LO6 Major category method: A lower-of-cost-or-market method of valuing inventory in which the total cost and total market values for each category of items are compared and each category is then valued at its lower amount.

LO6 Market: Current replacement cost of inventory.

LO1 Merchandise inventory: All goods owned and held for sale in the regular course of business.

SO7 Retail method: A method of inventory estimation, used in retail merchandising businesses, in which inventory at retail value is reduced by the ratio of cost to retail price.

LO3 Specific identification method: An inventory costing method in which the price of inventory is computed by identifying the cost of each item in ending inventory as coming from a specific purchase.

LO1 Supply-chain management: A system of managing inventory and purchasing through business-to-business transactions conducted over the Internet.

REVIEW PROBLEM

Periodic and Perpetual Inventory Systems

LO1 LO3 LO4 The table below summarizes the beginning inventory, purchases, and sales of Psi Company's single product during January.

Date		Beginning Inventory and Purchases			Sales Units
		Units	Cost	Total	
Jan. 1	Inventory	1,400	$19	$26,600	
4	Sale				300
8	Purchase	600	20	12,000	
10	Sale				1,300
12	Purchase	900	21	18,900	
15	Sale				150
18	Purchase	500	22	11,000	
24	Purchase	800	23	18,400	
31	Sale				1,350
Totals		4,200		$86,900	3,100

REQUIRED
1. Assuming that the company uses the periodic inventory system, compute the cost that should be assigned to ending inventory and to cost of goods sold using (a) the average-cost method, (b) the FIFO method, and (c) the LIFO method.
2. Assuming that the company uses the perpetual inventory system, compute the cost that should be assigned to ending inventory and to cost of goods sold using (a) the average-cost method, (b) the FIFO method, and (c) the LIFO method.
3. Compute inventory turnover and average days' inventory on hand under each of the inventory cost flow assumptions in 1. What conclusion can be made from this comparison?

ANSWER TO REVIEW PROBLEM

	Units	Amount
Beginning inventory	1,400	$26,600
Purchases	2,800	60,300
Available for sale	4,200	$86,900
Sales	3,100	
Ending inventory	1,100	

1. Periodic inventory system:
   a. Average-cost method

Cost of goods available for sale	$86,900
Less ending inventory consisting of 1,100 units at $20.69*	22,759
Cost of goods sold	$64,141

   *$86,900 ÷ 4,200 = $20.69 (rounded).

   b. FIFO method

Cost of goods available for sale		$86,900
Less ending inventory consisting of		
Jan. 24 purchase (800 × $23)	$18,400	
Jan. 18 purchase (300 × $22)	6,600	25,000
Cost of goods sold		$61,900

   c. LIFO method

Cost of goods available for sale	$86,900
Less ending inventory consisting of beginning inventory (1,100 × $19)	20,900
Cost of goods sold	$66,000

2. Perpetual inventory system:
   a. Average-cost method

Date		Units	Cost*	Amount*
Jan. 1	Inventory	1,400	$19.00	$26,600
4	Sale	(300)	19.00	(5,700)
4	Balance	1,100	19.00	$20,900
8	Purchase	600	20.00	12,000
8	Balance	1,700	19.35	$32,900
10	Sale	(1,300)	19.35	(25,155)
10	Balance	400	19.36	$ 7,745
12	Purchase	900	21.00	18,900
12	Balance	1,300	20.50	$26,645
15	Sale	(150)	20.50	(3,075)
15	Balance	1,150	20.50	$23,570
18	Purchase	500	22.00	11,000
24	Purchase	800	23.00	18,400
24	Balance	2,450	21.62	$52,970
31	Sale	(1,350)	21.62	(29,187)
31	Inventory	1,100	21.62	$23,783

   Cost of goods sold ($5,700 + $25,155 + $3,075 + $29,187) $63,117

   *Rounded.

   b. FIFO method

Date		Units	Cost	Amount
Jan. 1	Inventory	1,400	$19	$26,600
4	Sale	(300)	19	(5,700)
4	Balance	1,100	19	$20,900
8	Purchase	600	20	12,000

			Units	Cost	Amount
Jan. 8	Balance		1,100	19	
			600	20	$32,900
10	Sale		(1,100)	19	
			(200)	20	(24,900)
10	Balance		400	20	$ 8,000
12	Purchase		900	21	18,900
12	Balance		400	20	
			900	21	$26,900
15	Sale		(150)	20	(3,000)
15	Balance		250	20	
			900	21	$23,900
18	Purchase		500	22	11,000
24	Purchase		800	23	18,400
24	Balance		250	20	
			900	21	
			500	22	
			800	23	$53,300
31	Sale		(250)	20	
			(900)	21	
			(200)	22	(28,300)
31	Inventory		300	22	
			800	23	$25,000

Cost of goods sold ($5,700 + $24,900 + $3,000 + $28,300) $61,900

c. LIFO method

Date		Units	Cost	Amount
Jan. 1	Inventory	1,400	$19	$26,600
4	Sale	(300)	19	(5,700)
4	Balance	1,100	19	$20,900
8	Purchase	600	20	12,000
8	Balance	1,100	19	
		600	20	$32,900
10	Sale	(600)	20	
		(700)	19	(25,300)
10	Balance	400	19	$ 7,600
12	Purchase	900	21	18,900
12	Balance	400	19	
		900	21	$26,500
15	Sale	(150)	21	(3,150)
15	Balance	400	19	
		750	21	$23,350
18	Purchase	500	22	11,000
24	Purchase	800	23	18,400
24	Balance	400	19	
		750	21	
		500	22	
		800	23	$52,750
31	Sale	(800)	23	
		(500)	22	
		(50)	21	(30,450)
31	Inventory	400	19	
		700	21	$22,300

Cost of goods sold ($5,700 + $25,300 + $3,150 + $30,450) $64,600

3. Ratios computed:

	Average-Cost	FIFO	LIFO
Cost of goods sold	$64,141	$61,900	$66,000
Average inventory	$24,680*	$25,800	$23,750
	($22,759 + $26,600) ÷ 2	($25,000 + $26,600) ÷ 2	($20,900 + $26,600) ÷ 2
Inventory turnover	2.6 times	2.4 times	2.8 times
	($64,141 ÷ $24,680)	($61,900 ÷ $25,800)	($66,000 ÷ $23,750)
Average days' inventory on hand	140.4 days	152.1 days	130.4 days
	(365 days ÷ 2.6 times)	(365 days ÷ 2.4 times)	(365 days ÷ 2.8 times)

*Rounded.

In periods of rising prices, the LIFO method will always result in a higher inventory turnover and lower average days' inventory on hand. When comparing inventory ratios for two or more companies, the inventory methods used by the companies should be considered.

Chapter Assignments

BUILDING YOUR KNOWLEDGE FOUNDATION

QUESTIONS

1. What is merchandise inventory, and what is the primary objective of inventory measurement?
2. How does inventory for a manufacturing company differ from that for a merchandising company?
3. Why is the level of inventory important, and what are two common measures of inventory level?
4. What items should be included in the cost of inventory?
5. Fargo Sales Company is very busy at the end of its fiscal year on June 30. It has an order for 130 units of product in its warehouse. Although the shipping department tries, it cannot ship the product by June 30, and title has not yet passed. Should the 130 units be included in the year-end count of inventory? Why or why not?
6. What is the difference between goods flow and cost flow?
7. Do the FIFO and LIFO inventory methods result in different quantities of ending inventory?
8. Under which method of cost flow are (a) the earliest costs assigned to inventory, (b) the latest costs assigned to inventory, and (c) the average costs assigned to inventory?
9. What are the relative advantages and disadvantages of FIFO and LIFO from management's point of view?
10. Why do you think it is more expensive to maintain a perpetual inventory system?
11. In periods of steadily rising prices, which inventory method—average-cost, FIFO, or LIFO—will give the (a) highest ending inventory cost, (b) lowest ending inventory cost, (c) highest net income, and (d) lowest net income?
12. May a company change its inventory cost method from year to year? Explain.
13. What is the relationship between income tax rules and the inventory valuation methods?
14. If the merchandise inventory is mistakenly overstated at the end of 20x0, what is the effect on the (a) 20x0 net income, (b) 20x0 year-end balance sheet value, (c) 20x1 net income, and (d) 20x1 year-end balance sheet value?
15. In the phrase *lower of cost or market*, what is meant by the word *market*?

How would inventory method affect your evaluation if you were to compare Pioneer and Yamaha to a U.S. company? What could you do to make the results comparable?

Toys "R" Us Annual Report

FRA 5.

LO1 **Retail Method and Inventory**
LO5 **Ratios**
LO6
SO7

Refer to the note related to inventories in the Toys "R" Us <www.tru.com> annual report in the Supplement to Chapter 1 to answer the following questions: What inventory method(s) does Toys "R" Us use? If LIFO inventories had been valued at FIFO, why would there be no difference? Do you think many of the company's inventories are valued at market? Few companies use the retail method; why do you think Toys "R" Us uses it? Compute and compare the inventory turnover and average days' inventory on hand for Toys "R" Us for 2001 and 2002. Beginning 2001 inventory was $1,902 million.

Comparison Case: Toys "R" Us and Walgreen Co.

FRA 6.

LO1 **Inventory Efficiency**

Refer to the financial statements for Toys "R" Us <www.tru.com> and Walgreens <www.walgreens.com> in the Supplement to Chapter 1. Beginning inventory for 2001 for Toys "R" Us was $2,307 million and for Walgreens, $2,830.8 million. Calculate inventory turnover and average days' inventory on hand for the past two years. If you did **FRA 5**, refer to your answer there for Toys "R" Us. Has either company improved its performance over the past two years? If so, what advantage does it have? Which company seems to make the most efficient use of inventory? Explain.

Fingraph® Financial Analyst™

FRA 7.

LO1 **Comparative Analysis of Inventories and Operating Cycle**

Select any two companies from the same industry from the list of Fingraph companies on the Needles Accounting Resource Center Web Site at http://accounting.college.hmco.com/students. Choose an industry, such as manufacturing, consumer products, consumer food and beverage, or computers, in which inventory is likely to be an important current asset. Access the Microsoft Excel spreadsheets for the companies you selected. Click on the URL at the top of each company's spreadsheet for a link to the company's web site and annual report.

1. In the annual reports of the companies you have selected, read any reference to inventories in the summary of significant accounting policies or notes to the financial statements. What inventory method does the company use? What are the changes in and the relative importance of raw materials, work in process, and finished goods inventories?
2. Using the Fingraph Financial Analyst CD-ROM software, display and print in tabular and graphic form the Liquidity and Asset Utilization Analysis page. Prepare a table that compares the inventory turnover and average days' inventory on hand for both companies for two years. Also include in your table the operating cycle by combining average days' inventory on hand with average days' sales uncollected.
3. Find and read references to inventories in the liquidity analysis section of management's discussion and analysis in each annual report.
4. Write a one-page executive summary that highlights the accounting policies for inventories, the relative importance and changes in raw materials, work in process, and finished goods, and compares the inventory utilization of the two companies, including reference to management's assessment. Comment specifically on the financing implications of the companies' relative operating cycles. Include the Fingraph page and your table with your report.

Internet Case

FRA 8.

LO5 **Effect of LIFO on Income and Cash Flows**

Maytag Corporation <www.maytag.com>, an appliance manufacturer, uses the LIFO inventory method. Go to its web site and select "About Maytag." Then select "Financial Center." After finding the income statement and inventory note, calculate what net income would have been had the company used FIFO. Calculate how much cash the company saved for the year and cumulatively by using LIFO. What is the difference between the LIFO and FIFO gross margin and profit margin results? Which reporting alternative is better for the company?

9

Chapter 9 presents the management issues associated with current liabilities and payroll accounting.

Current Liabilities

Learning Objectives

LO1 Identify the management issues related to recognition, valuation, classification, and disclosure of current liabilities.

LO2 Identify, compute, and record definitely determinable and estimated current liabilities.

LO3 Distinguish *contingent liabilities* from *commitments*.

Supplemental Objective

SO4 Compute and record the liabilities associated with payroll accounting.

DECISION POINT
A USER'S FOCUS

US Airways, Inc. <www.usairways.com> Liabilities are one of the three major parts of the balance sheet. They are legal obligations for the future payment of assets or the future performance of services that result from past transactions. The current and long-term liabilities of US Airways, Inc., which has total assets of almost $8 billion, are shown in the Financial Highlights.[1] Current maturities of long-term debt; accounts payable; accrued aircraft rent; accrued salaries, wages, and vacation; and other accrued expenses will for the most part require an outlay of cash in the next year. Traffic balances payable will require payments to other airlines, but those may be partially offset by amounts owed by other airlines. Unused tickets are tickets already paid for by passengers and represent services that must be performed. Long-term debt will require cash outlays in future years. Altogether these liabilities represent over 75 percent of total assets. How does the decision of US Airways' management to incur so much debt relate to the goals of the business?

Liabilities are important because they are closely related to the goals of profitability and liquidity. Liabilities are sources of cash for operating and financing activities when they are incurred, but they are also obligations that use cash when they are paid. Achieving the appropriate level of liabilities is critical to business success. A company that has too few liabilities may not be earning up to its potential. A company that has too many liabilities, however, may be incurring excessive risks. In the case of US Airways, the company became vulnerable when there was a down-received is slightly less ($4,900 in Case 2 versus $5,000 in Case 1). Discount on Notes Payable is a contra account to Notes Payable and is deducted from Notes Payable on the balance sheet.

On October 30, when the note is paid, each alternative is recorded as follows:

	Case 1—Interest Stated Separately				Case 2—Interest in Face Amount		
Case 1 A = L + OE − − −	Oct. 30	Notes Payable Interest Expense Cash Payment of note with interest stated separately $5,000 × .12 × $\frac{60}{360}$ = $100	5,000 100	5,100	Oct. 30	Notes Payable Cash Payment of note with interest included in face amount	5,000 5,000
Case 2 A = L + OE − − A = L + OE + −					30	Interest Expense Discount on Notes Payable Interest expense on note payable	100 100

■ **ACCRUED LIABILITIES** A key reason for making adjusting entries at the end of an accounting period is to recognize and record any liabilities that are not already in the accounting records. This practice applies to any type of liability. As you will see, accrued liabilities can include estimated liabilities.

Here the focus is on interest payable, a definitely determinable liability. Interest accrues daily on interest-bearing notes. At the end of the accounting period, an adjusting entry should be made in accordance with the matching rule to record the interest obligation up to that point. Let us again use the example of the two notes presented in Figure 3. If we assume that the accounting period ends on September 30, or 30 days after the issuance of the 60-day notes, the adjusting entries for each case would be as follows:

	Case 1—Interest Stated Separately			Case 2—Interest in Face Amount		
Case 1 A = L + OE + −	Sept. 30	Interest Expense Interest Payable To record interest expense for 30 days on note with interest stated separately $5,000 × .12 × $\frac{30}{360}$ = $50	50 50	Sept. 30	Interest Expense Discount on Notes Payable To record interest expense for 30 days on note with interest included in face amount $100 × $\frac{30}{60}$ = $50	50 50
Case 2 A = L + OE + −						

KEY POINT: Both of these entries have exactly the same impact on the financial statements.

In Case 2, Discount on Notes Payable will now have a debit balance of $50, which will become interest expense during the next 30 days.

■ **DIVIDENDS PAYABLE** Cash dividends are a distribution of earnings by a corporation. The payment of dividends is solely the decision of the corporation's board of directors. A liability does not exist until the board declares the dividends. There is usually a short time between the date of declaration and the date of payment of dividends. During that short time, the dividends declared are considered current liabilities of the corporation.

■ **SALES AND EXCISE TAXES PAYABLE** Most states and many cities levy a sales tax on retail transactions. There is a federal excise tax on some products, such as automobile tires. A merchant who sells goods subject to these taxes must collect the taxes and forward them periodically to the appropriate government agency. The amount of tax collected represents a current liability until it is remitted to the government. For example, assume that a merchant makes a $100 sale that is subject to a 5 percent sales tax and a 10 percent excise tax. Assuming that the sale takes place on June 1, the entry to record the sale is as follows:

A = L + OE	June 1	Cash	115	
+ + +		Sales		100
+		Sales Tax Payable		5
		Excise Tax Payable		10
		Sales of merchandise and collection of sales and excise tax		

The sale is properly recorded at $100, and the taxes collected are recorded as liabilities to be remitted at the proper times to the appropriate government agencies.

■ **CURRENT PORTIONS OF LONG-TERM DEBT** If a portion of long-term debt is due within the next year and is to be paid from current assets, then that current portion is properly classified as a current liability. For example, suppose that a $500,000 debt is to be paid in installments of $100,000 per year for the next five years. The $100,000 installment due in the current year should be classified as a current liability. The remaining $400,000 should be classified as a long-term liability. Note that no journal entry is necessary. The total debt of $500,000 is simply reclassified when the financial statements are prepared, as follows:

Current liabilities
    Current portion of long-term debt $100,000
Long-term liabilities
    Long-term debt   400,000

■ **PAYROLL LIABILITIES** For most organizations, the cost of labor and related payroll taxes is a major expense. In some industries, such as banking and airlines, payroll costs represent more than half of all operating costs. Payroll accounting is important because complex laws and significant liabilities are involved. The employer is liable to employees for wages and salaries and to various agencies for amounts withheld from wages and salaries and for related taxes. The term **wages** refers to payment for the services of employees at an hourly rate. The term **salaries** refers to the compensation of employees who are paid at a monthly or yearly rate.

Because payroll accounting applies only to the employees of an organization, it is important to distinguish between employees and independent contractors. Employees are paid a wage or salary by the organization and are under its direct supervision and control. Independent contractors are not employees of the organization, so they are not accounted for under the payroll system. They offer services to the organization for a fee, but they are not under its direct control or supervision. Certified public accountants, advertising agencies, and lawyers, for example, may act as independent contractors.

Figure 4 provides an illustration of payroll liabilities and their relationship to employee earnings and employer taxes and other costs. Two important observations may be made. First, the amount payable to employees is less than the amount of earnings. This occurs because employers are required by law or are requested by employees to withhold certain amounts from wages and send them directly to government agencies or other organizations. Second, the total employer liabilities exceed employee earnings because the employer must pay additional taxes and make other contributions, such as for pensions and medical care, that increase the cost and liabilities. The most common withholdings, taxes, and other payroll costs are described next.

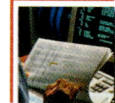

FOCUS ON BUSINESS PRACTICE

Small Businesses Offer Benefits, Too.
A survey of small businesses in the Midwest shows the percentages of respondents that offer the following benefits:[6]

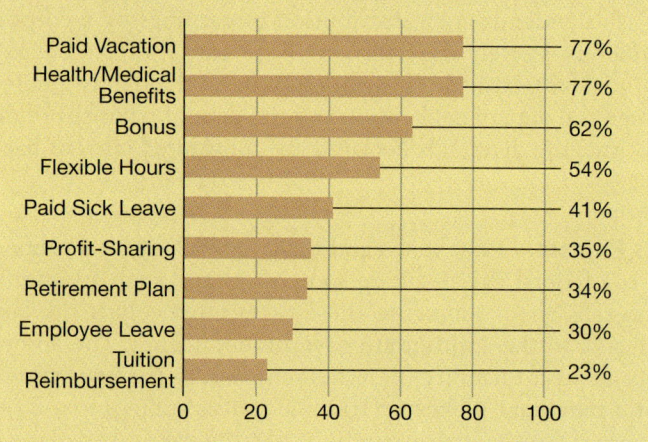

FIGURE 4 Illustration of Payroll Liabilities

KEY POINT: The employee bears all the tax for federal, state, and local income taxes. The employer and employee share FICA and Medicare taxes. The employer bears FUTA and state unemployment taxes.

ENRICHMENT NOTE: For many organizations, a large portion of the cost of labor is not reflected in employees' regular paychecks. Vacation pay, sick pay, personal days, health insurance, life insurance, and pensions are some of the additional costs that may be negotiated between employers and employees.

Federal Income Taxes Federal income taxes are collected on a "pay as you go" basis. Employers are required to withhold appropriate taxes from employees' paychecks and pay them to the United States Treasury.

State and Local Income Taxes Most states and some local governments have income taxes. In most cases, the procedures for withholding are similar to those for federal income taxes.

Social Security (FICA) Tax The social security program (the Federal Insurance Contribution Act) offers retirement and disability benefits and survivor's benefits. About 90 percent of the people working in the United States fall under the provisions of this program. The 2003 social security tax rate of 6.2 percent was paid by *both* employee and employer on the first $87,000 earned by an employee during the calendar year. Both the rate and the base to which it applies are subject to change in future years.

Medicare Tax A major extension of the social security program is Medicare, which provides hospitalization and medical insurance for persons over age 65. In 2003, the Medicare tax rate was 1.45 percent of gross income, with no limit, paid by *both* employee and employer.

Medical Insurance Many organizations provide medical benefits to employees. Often, the employee contributes a portion of the cost through withholdings from income and the employer pays the rest, usually a greater amount, to the insurance company.

Pension Contributions Many organizations also provide pension benefits to employees. In a manner similar to that for medical insurance, a portion of the pension contribution is withheld from the employee's income and the rest is paid by the organization to the pension fund.

Federal Unemployment Insurance (FUTA) Tax This tax is intended to pay for programs to help unemployed workers. It is paid *only* by employers and recently was 6.2 percent of the first $7,000 earned by each employee (this amount may vary from state to state). Against this federal tax, the employer is allowed a credit for unemployment taxes paid to the state. The maximum credit is 5.4 percent of the first $7,000 earned by each employee. Most states set their rate at this maximum. Thus, the FUTA tax most often paid is .8 percent (6.2 percent − 5.4 percent) of the taxable wages.

State Unemployment Insurance Tax All state unemployment programs provide for unemployment compensation to be paid to eligible unemployed workers. This compensation is paid out of the fund provided by the 5.4 percent of the first $7,000 (or whatever amount the state sets) earned by each employee. In some states, employers with favorable employment records may be entitled to pay less than 5.4 percent.

To illustrate the recording of the payroll, assume that on February 15 total employee wages are $32,500, with withholdings of $5,400 for federal income taxes, $1,200 for state income taxes, $2,015 for social security tax, $471 for Medicare tax, $900 for medical insurance, and $1,300 for pension contributions. The entry to record this payroll follows:

A = L + OE
+ −
+
+
+
+
+

Feb. 15	Wages Expense	32,500	
	Employees' Federal Income Taxes Payable		5,400
	Employees' State Income Taxes Payable		1,200
	Social Security Tax Payable		2,015
	Medicare Tax Payable		471
	Medical Insurance Premiums Payable		900
	Pension Contributions Payable		1,300
	Wages Payable		21,214
	To record payroll		

Note that the employees' take-home pay is $21,214, although $32,500 was earned.

May 16	Cash		39,000	
	Discount on Notes Payable		1,000	
	Notes Payable			40,000
	Obtained loan from bank by signing			
	90-day, 10% note; discount equals			
	$40,000 × .10 × 90/360 = $1,000			
June 30	Interest Expense		900	
	Interest Payable			900
	Accrued interest expense			
	$54,000 × .12 × 50/360 = $900			
30	Interest Expense		500	
	Discount on Notes Payable			500
	Recognized interest on note			
	$1,000 × 45/90 = $500			
30	Income Summary		1,400	
	Interest Expense			1,400
	Closed interest expense			
July 10	Notes Payable		54,000	
	Interest Payable		900	
	Interest Expense		180	
	Cash			55,080
	Paid note on equipment			
	$54,000 × .12 × 10/360 = $180			
Aug. 14	Notes Payable		40,000	
	Cash			40,000
	Paid bank loan			
14	Interest Expense		500	
	Discount on Notes Payable			500
	Interest expense on matured note			
	$1,000 − $500 = $500			

Chapter Assignments

BUILDING YOUR KNOWLEDGE FOUNDATION

QUESTIONS

1. What are liabilities?
2. Why is the timing of liability recognition important in accounting?
3. At the end of the accounting period, Janson Company had a legal obligation to accept delivery of and pay for a truckload of hospital supplies the following week. Is this legal obligation a liability?
4. Ned Johnson, a star college basketball player, received a contract from the Midwest Blazers to play professional basketball. The contract calls for a salary of $300,000 a year for four years, dependent on his making the team in each of those years. Should this contract be considered a liability and recorded on the books of the basketball team?
5. What is the rule for classifying a liability as current?
6. What are a line of credit and commercial paper? Where do they appear on the balance sheet?
7. A bank is offering Diane Wedge two alternatives for borrowing $2,000. The first alternative is a $2,000, 12 percent, 30-day note. The second alternative is a $2,000, 30-day note discounted at 12 percent. (a) What entries are required by

Diane Wedge to record the two loans? (b) What entries are needed by Wedge to record the payment of the two loans? (c) Which alternative favors Wedge, and why?

8. Where should the Discount on Notes Payable account appear on the balance sheet?
9. When can a portion of long-term debt be classified as a current liability?
10. What are three types of employer-related payroll liabilities?
11. How does an employee differ from an independent contractor?
12. Who pays social security and Medicare taxes?
13. Why are unearned revenues classified as liabilities?
14. What is definite about an estimated liability?
15. Why are income taxes payable considered to be estimated liabilities?
16. When does a company incur a liability for a product warranty?
17. What is a contingent liability, and how does it differ from a commitment?
18. What are some examples of contingent liabilities? For what reason is each a contingent liability?
19. What role does the W-4 form play in determining the withholding for estimated federal income taxes?
20. How can the payroll register be used as a special-purpose journal?
21. Why is an employee earnings record necessary, and how does it relate to the W-2 form?

SHORT EXERCISES

LO1 Issues in Accounting for Liabilities

SE 1. Indicate whether each of the following actions relates to (a) managing liquidity and cash flow, (b) recognition of liabilities, (c) valuation of liabilities, (d) classification of liabilities, or (e) disclosure of liabilities:
1. Determining that a liability will be paid in less than one year
2. Estimating the amount of a liability
3. Providing information about when liabilities are due and their interest rates
4. Determining when a liability arises
5. Assessing working capital and payables turnover

LO1 Measuring Short-Term Liquidity

SE 2. Stratton Company has current assets of $130,000 and current liabilities of $80,000, of which accounts payable are $70,000. Stratton's cost of goods sold is $460,000, its merchandise inventory increased by $20,000, and accounts payable were $50,000 the prior year. Calculate Stratton's working capital, payables turnover, and average days' payable.

LO2 Types of Liabilities
LO3

SE 3. Indicate whether each of the following is (a) a definitely determinable liability, (b) an estimated liability, (c) a commitment, or (d) a contingent liability:
1. Dividends Payable
2. Pending litigation
3. Income Taxes Payable
4. Current portion of long-term debt
5. Vacation Pay Liability
6. Guaranteed loans of another company
7. Purchase agreement

LO2 Interest Expense: Interest Not Included in Face Value of Note

SE 4. On the last day of August, Swift Company borrowed $60,000 on a bank note for 60 days at 10 percent interest. Assume that interest is stated separately. Prepare the following entries in journal form: (1) August 31, recording of note; and (2) October 30, payment of note plus interest.

LO2 Interest Expense: Interest Included in Face Value of Note

SE 5. Assume the same facts as in **SE 4,** except that interest of $1,000 is included in the face amount of the note and the note is discounted at the bank on August 31. Prepare the following entries in journal form: (1) August 31, recording of note; and (2) October 30, payment of note and recording of interest expense.

LO2 Payroll Entries

SE 6. The following payroll totals for the month of April are from the payroll register of Corelli Corporation: salaries, $223,000.00; federal income taxes withheld, $31,440.00; social security tax withheld, $13,826.00; Medicare tax withheld, $3,233.50; medical insurance deductions, $6,580.00; and salaries subject to unemployment taxes, $156,600.00. Prepare entries in journal form to record (1) the monthly payroll and (2) employer's payroll expense, assuming social security and Medicare taxes equal to the amounts for employees, a federal unemployment insurance tax of .8 percent, a state unemployment tax of 5.4 percent, and medical insurance premiums for which the employer pays 80 percent of the cost.

LO2 Product Warranty Liability

SE 7. Diamante Corp. manufactures and sells travel clocks. Each clock costs $25 to produce and sells for $50. In addition, each clock carries a warranty that provides for free replacement if it fails during the two years following the sale. In the past, 5 percent of the clocks sold have had to be replaced under the warranty. During October, Diamante sold 52,000 clocks, and 2,800 clocks were replaced under the warranty. Prepare entries in journal form to record the estimated liability for product warranties during the month and the clocks replaced under warranty during the month.

LO2 Vacation Pay Liability

SE 8. The employees of Larue Services receive two weeks of paid vacation each year. Seventy percent of the employees qualify for vacation. Assuming the September payroll is $150,000, including $12,000 paid to employees on vacation, how much is the vacation pay expense for September? What is the ending balance of the Estimated Liability for Vacation Pay account, assuming a beginning balance of $16,000?

SO4 Payroll Taxes

SE 9. Karma Company and its employees are subject to a 6.2 percent social security tax on wages up to $87,000 and a 1.45 percent Medicare tax with no limit. The company is subject to a 5.4 percent state unemployment tax and a .8 percent federal unemployment tax up to $7,000 per employee. The company has two employees: A. Ballo, who has cumulative earnings of $88,000 and earned $7,000 in the month of December, and C. Dureo, who has cumulative earnings of $5,000 and earned $1,000 during December. Compute the total payroll taxes for the employees and the employer for December.

SO4 Payroll Earnings, Withholdings, and Taxes

SE 10. Last week, Manuel Karmelo worked 44 hours. He is paid $10 per hour and receives one and one-half times his regular rate for hours worked over 40. Karmelo has withholdings of $45 for federal income taxes, $10 for state income taxes, $23 for health insurance, 6.2 percent for social security tax, and 1.45 percent for Medicare tax. Compute Karmelo's take-home pay. Also compute the total cost of Karmelo to his employer, assuming that Karmelo's cumulative wages are over the limit for unemployment taxes and that the company makes a health-care contribution of $75.

Exercises

LO1 Issues in Accounting for Liabilities

E 1. Indicate whether each of the following actions relates to (a) managing liquidity and cash flows, (b) recognition of liabilities, (c) valuation of liabilities, (d) classification of liabilities, or (e) disclosure of liabilities:

1. Setting a liability at the fair market value of goods to be delivered
2. Relating the payment date of a liability to the length of the operating cycle
3. Recording a liability in accordance with the matching rule
4. Providing information about financial instruments on the balance sheet
5. Estimating the amount of "cents-off" coupons that will be redeemed
6. Categorizing a liability as long-term debt
7. Measuring working capital
8. Comparing average days' payable with last year

LO1 Measuring Short-Term Liquidity

E 2. In 20x1, Telos Company had current assets of $310,000 and current liabilities of $200,000, of which accounts payable were $130,000. Cost of goods sold was $850,000, merchandise inventory increased by $40,000, and accounts payable were $110,000 in the prior year. In 20x2, Telos had current assets of $420,000 and current liabilities of $320,000, of which accounts payable were $150,000. Cost of goods sold was $950,000, and merchandise inventory decreased by $30,000. Calculate Telos's working capital, payables turnover, and average days' payable for 20x1 and 20x2. Assess Telos's liquidity and cash flows in relation to the change in payables turnover from 20x1 to 20x2.

E 3.
LO2 Interest Expense: Interest Not Included in Face Value of Note

On the last day of October, Shealy Company borrows $30,000 on a bank note for 60 days at 12 percent interest. Interest is not included in the face amount. Prepare the following entries in journal form: (1) October 31, recording of note; (2) November 30, accrual of interest expense; and (3) December 30, payment of note plus interest.

E 4.
LO2 Interest Expense: Interest Included in Face Value of Note

Assume the same facts as in **E 3**, except that interest is included in the face amount of the note and the note is discounted at the bank on October 31. Prepare the following entries in journal form: (1) October 31, recording of note; (2) November 30, recognition of interest accrued on note; and (3) December 30, payment of note and recording of interest expense.

E 5.
LO2 Sales and Excise Taxes

Web Design Service billed its customers a total of $980,400 for the month of August, including 9 percent federal excise tax and 5 percent sales tax.

1. Determine the proper amount of service revenue to report for the month.
2. Prepare an entry in journal form to record the revenue and related liabilities for the month.

E 6.
LO2 Payroll Entries

At the end of October, the payroll register for Lakeside Tool and Die Corporation contained the following totals: wages, $185,500; federal income taxes withheld, $47,442; state income taxes withheld, $7,818; social security tax withheld, $11,501; Medicare tax withheld, $2,689.75; medical insurance deductions, $6,435; and wages subject to unemployment taxes, $28,620.

Prepare entries in journal form to record the (1) monthly payroll and (2) employer payroll expenses, assuming social security and Medicare taxes equal to the amount for employees, a federal unemployment insurance tax of .8 percent, a state unemployment tax of 5.4 percent, and medical insurance premiums for which the employer pays 80 percent of the cost.

E 7.
LO2 Product Warranty Liability

Hoopes Company manufactures and sells electronic games. Each game costs $25 to produce and sells for $45. In addition, each game carries a warranty that provides for free replacement if it fails during the two years following the sale. In the past, 7 percent of the games sold had to be replaced under the warranty. During July, Hoopes sold 26,000 games, and 2,800 games were replaced under the warranty.

1. Prepare an entry in journal form to record the estimated liability for product warranties during the month.
2. Prepare an entry in journal form to record the games replaced under warranty during the month.

E 8.
LO2 Vacation Pay Liability

Syracuse Corporation gives three weeks' paid vacation to each employee who has worked at the company for one year. Based on studies of employee turnover and previous experience, management estimates that 65 percent of the employees will qualify for vacation pay this year.

1. Assume that Syracuse's July payroll is $600,000, of which $40,000 is paid to employees on vacation. Figure the estimated employee vacation benefit for the month.
2. Prepare an entry in journal form to record the employee benefit for July.
3. Prepare an entry in journal form to record the pay to employees on vacation.

E 9.
SO4 Social Security, Medicare, and Unemployment Taxes

Munro Company is subject to a 5.4 percent state unemployment insurance tax and a .8 percent federal unemployment insurance tax after credits. Assume both federal and state unemployment taxes apply to the first $7,000 earned by each employee. Social security and Medicare taxes in effect at this time are 6.2 and 1.45 percent, respectively. The social security tax is levied for both employee and employer on the first $87,000 earned by each employee during the year.

During the current year, the cumulative earnings for each employee of the company are as follows:

Employee	Cumulative Earnings	Employee	Cumulative Earnings
Basmani, J.	$28,620	Van Trapp, M.	$16,760
Cohen, A.	5,260	Harwit, P.	6,420
Derbye, G.	32,820	Lemaire, C.	51,650
Carbone, R.	30,130	Papyani, D.	32,100
Sourdiffe, B.	89,000	Menzek, V.	36,645
Conniger, N.	5,120	Woo, S.	5,176

1. Prepare and complete a schedule with the following columns: Employee Name, Cumulative Earnings, Earnings Subject to Social Security Tax, Earnings Subject to Medicare Tax, and Earnings Subject to Unemployment Taxes. Total the columns.
2. Compute the social security and Medicare taxes and the federal and state unemployment taxes for Munro Company for the year.

SO4 Net Pay Calculation and Payroll Entries

E 10. Lynne Featherstone is an employee whose overtime pay is regulated by the Fair Labor Standards Act. Her hourly rate is $8, and during the week ended July 11, she worked 42 hours. She claims two exemptions on her W-4 form. So far this year she has earned $8,650. Each week $12 is deducted from her paycheck for medical insurance.

1. Compute the following items related to the pay for Lynne Featherstone for the week of July 11: (a) total pay, (b) federal income taxes withholding (use Figure 4), (c) social security and Medicare taxes (assume rates of 6.2 percent and 1.45 percent, respectively), and (d) net pay.
2. Prepare an entry in journal form to record the wages expense and related liabilities for Lynne Featherstone for the week ended July 11.

SO4 Payroll Transactions

E 11. Jian-Jin Loo earns a salary of $90,000 per year. Social security and Medicare taxes are, respectively, 6.2 percent on salary up to $87,000 and 1.45 percent on total salary. Federal unemployment insurance taxes are 6.2 percent of the first $7,000; however, a credit is allowed equal to the state unemployment insurance taxes of 5.4 percent on the $7,000. During the year, $15,000 was withheld for federal income taxes, $3,000 for state income taxes, and $1,500 for medical insurance.

1. Prepare an entry in journal form summarizing the payment of $90,000 to Loo during the year.
2. Prepare an entry in journal form summarizing the employer payroll taxes and other costs on Loo's salary for the year. Assume the company pays 80 percent of the total premiums for medical insurance.
3. Determine the total amount paid by Jian-Jin Loo's employer to employ Loo for the year.

PROBLEMS

LO1 Identification of Current
LO2 Liabilities

P 1. Neil Fusco opened a small television repair shop, Fusco Television Repair, on January 2, 20x0. The shop also sells a limited number of television sets. In January 20x1, Fusco realized he had never filed any tax reports for his business and therefore probably owes a considerable amount of taxes. Since he has limited experience in running a business, he has brought you all his business records, including a checkbook, canceled checks, deposit slips, suppliers' invoices, a notice of annual property taxes of $4,620 due to the city, and a promissory note to his father-in-law for $5,000. He wants you to determine what his business owes the government and other parties.

You analyze all his records and determine the following as of December 31, 20x0:

Unpaid invoices for televisions	$ 18,000
Television sales (excluding sales tax)	88,540
Cost of Televisions Sold	62,250
Workers' salaries	20,400
Repair revenues	120,600
Current assets	32,600
Television inventory	23,500

You learn that the company has deducted $952 from the two employees' salaries for federal income taxes owed to the government. The current social security tax is 6.2 percent on maximum earnings of $87,000 for each employee, and the current Medicare tax is 1.45 percent (no maximum earnings). The FUTA tax is 5.4 percent to the state and .8 percent to the federal government on the first $7,000 earned by each employee, and each employee earned more than $7,000. Fusco has not filed a sales tax report to the state (5 percent of sales).

REQUIRED
1. Given these limited facts, determine Fusco Television Repair's current liabilities as of December 31, 20x0.
2. What additional information would you want from Fusco to satisfy yourself that all current liabilities have been identified?

3. Evaluate Fusco's liquidity by calculating working capital, payables turnover, and average days' payable. Comment on the results. (Assume average accounts payable were the same as year-end accounts payable.)

LO2 Notes Payable Transactions and End-of-Period Entries

P 2. Iron's Paper Company, whose fiscal year ends December 31, completed the following transactions involving notes payable:

20x3
Nov. 25 Purchased a new loading cart by issuing a 60-day, 10 percent note for $43,200.
Dec. 16 Borrowed $50,000 from the bank to finance inventory by signing a 90-day note. The face value of the note includes interest of $1,500. Proceeds received were $48,500.
     31 Made the end-of-year adjusting entry to accrue interest expense.
     31 Made the end-of-year adjusting entry to recognize the discount expired on the note.

20x4
Jan. 24 Paid off the loading cart note.
Mar. 16 Paid off the inventory note to the bank.

REQUIRED
1. Prepare entries in journal form for the notes payable transactions.
2. In the transaction of December 16, would the bank be better off making the loan with the interest stated separately instead of included in the $50,000? Why or why not?

LO2 Product Warranty Liability

P 3. The Galway Company manufactures and sells food processors, which it guarantees for five years. If a processor fails, it is replaced free, but the customer is charged a service fee for handling. In the past, management has found that only 3 percent of the processors sold required replacement under the warranty. The average food processor costs the company $240. At the beginning of September, the account for estimated liability for product warranties had a credit balance of $208,000. During September, 250 processors were returned under the warranty. Service fees of $9,860 were collected for handling. During the month, the company sold 2,800 food processors.

REQUIRED
1. Prepare entries in journal form to record (a) the cost of food processors replaced under warranty and (b) the estimated liability for product warranties for processors sold during the month.
2. Compute the balance of the Estimated Product Warranty Liability account at the end of the month.
3. If the company's product warranty liability is underestimated, what are the effects on current and future years' income?

LO2 Payroll Entries

P 4. At the end of October, the payroll register for Golinski Corporation contained the following totals: sales salaries, $176,220; office salaries, $80,880; administrative salaries, $113,900; federal income taxes withheld, $94,884; state income taxes withheld, $15,636; social security tax withheld, $23,002; Medicare tax withheld, $5,379.50; medical insurance premiums, $12,870; life insurance premiums, $11,712; union dues deductions, $1,368; and salaries subject to unemployment taxes, $57,240. Fifty percent of medical and life insurance premiums are paid by the employer.

REQUIRED
Prepare entries in journal form to record the (1) accrual of the monthly payroll, (2) payment of the net payroll, (3) accrual of employer's payroll taxes and expenses (assuming social security and Medicare taxes equal to the amount for employees, a federal unemployment insurance tax of .8 percent, and a state unemployment tax of 5.4 percent), and (4) payment of all liabilities related to the payroll (assuming that all are paid at the same time).

SO4 Payroll Register and Related Entries

P 5. Hendrik Dairy Company has seven employees. Employees paid hourly receive a set rate for regular hours plus one and one-half times their hourly rate for overtime hours. They are paid every two weeks. The salaried employees are paid monthly on the last biweekly payday of each month. The employees and company are subject to social security tax of 6.2 percent up to a maximum of $87,000 for each employee and to Medicare tax of 1.45 percent. The unemployment insurance tax rates are 5.4 percent for the state and .8 percent for the federal government. The unemployment insurance tax applies to the first $7,000 earned by each employee and is levied only on the employer.

The company maintains a supplemental benefits plan that includes medical insurance, life insurance, and additional retirement funds for employees. Under the plan, each employee contributes 4 percent of her or his gross income as a payroll withholding, and the company matches the amount. Data for the November 30 payroll, the last payday of November, follow.

Employee	Hours Regular	Hours Overtime	Pay Rate	Cumulative Gross Pay Excluding Current Pay Period	Federal Income Taxes to Be Withheld
Eggers, D.	80	5	$ 8.00	$ 4,867.00	$ 71.00
Gosligan, W.	80	4	6.50	3,954.00	76.00
Valmont, P.*	Salary	—	5,000.00	55,000.00	985.00
Norelli, V.	80	—	5.00	8,250.00	32.00
Appia, L.*	Salary	—	2,000.00	20,000.00	294.00
Tou, M.	80	20	10.00	12,000.00	103.00
Voss, B.*	Salary	—	1,500.00	15,000.00	210.00

*Denotes administrative personnel; the rest are sales. P. Valmont's cumulative gross pay includes a $5,000 bonus paid early in the year.

REQUIRED
1. Prepare a payroll register for the pay period ended November 30. The payroll register should have the following columns:

   Employee
   Total Hours
   Earnings
     Regular
     Overtime
     Gross
     Cumulative

   Deductions
     Federal Income Taxes
     Social Security Tax
     Medicare Tax
     Supplemental Benefits Plan

   Net Pay
   Distribution
     Sales Wages Expense
     Administrative Salaries Expense

2. Prepare an entry in journal form to record the payroll and related liabilities for deductions for the period ended November 30.
3. Prepare entries in journal form to record the employer's payroll taxes and contribution to the supplemental benefits plan.
4. Prepare the November 30 entries (a) to transfer sufficient cash from the company's regular checking account to a special payroll disbursement account and (b) to pay the employees.

ALTERNATE PROBLEMS

LO2 **Notes Payable Transactions and End-of-Period Entries**

P 6. Aragian Corporation, whose fiscal year ends June 30, completed the following transactions involving notes payable:

20xx
May 11 Signed a 90-day, $132,000 note payable to Eastern Shore Bank for a working capital loan. The face value included interest of $3,960. Proceeds received were $128,040.
     21 Obtained a 60-day extension on a $36,000 trade account payable owed to a supplier by signing a 60-day, $36,000 note. Interest is in addition to the face value, at the rate of 14 percent.
June 30 Made the end-of-year adjusting entry to accrue interest expense.
     30 Made the end-of-year adjusting entry to recognize discount expired on the note.
July 20 Paid off the note plus interest due the supplier.
Aug. 9 Paid the amount due to the bank on the 90-day note.

REQUIRED
1. Prepare entries in journal form for the notes payable transactions.
2. In the transaction of May 11, would the bank be better off making the loan with the interest stated separately or with it included in the loan amount? Why or why not?

LO2 Product Warranty Liability

P 7. Sparkle Bright Company is engaged in the retail sale of washing machines. Each machine has a 24-month warranty on parts. If a repair under warranty is required, a charge for the labor is made. Management has found that 20 percent of the machines sold require some work before the warranty expires. Furthermore, the average cost of replacement parts has been $120 per repair. At the beginning of June, the account for the estimated liability for product warranties had a credit balance of $28,600. During June, 112 machines were returned under the warranty. The cost of the parts used in repairing the machines was $17,530, and $18,884 was collected as service revenue for the labor involved. During the month, Sparkle Bright Company sold 450 new machines.

REQUIRED
1. Prepare entries in journal form to record each of the following: (a) the warranty work completed during the month, including related revenue; (b) the estimated liability for product warranties for machines sold during the month.
2. Compute the balance of the Estimated Product Warranty Liability account at the end of the month.
3. If the company's product warranty liability is overestimated, what are the effects on current and future years' income?

LO2 Payroll Entries

P 8. The following payroll amounts for the month of April were taken from the payroll register of Weiskauf Corporation: sales salaries, $116,400; office salaries, $57,000; general salaries, $49,600; social security tax withheld, $13,826; Medicare tax withheld, $3,233.50; income taxes withheld, $31,440; medical insurance premiums, $3,290; life insurance premiums, $1,880; salaries subject to unemployment taxes, $156,600. Fifty percent of medical and life insurance premiums are paid by the employee. The rest are paid by the employer.

REQUIRED Prepare entries in journal form to record the following: (1) accrual of the monthly payroll, (2) payment of the net payroll, (3) accrual of employer's payroll taxes and expenses (assuming social security and Medicare taxes equal to the amounts for employees, a federal unemployment insurance tax of .8 percent, and a state unemployment tax of 5.4 percent), and (4) payment of all liabilities related to the payroll (assuming that all are paid at the same time).

SKILLS DEVELOPMENT CASES

Conceptual Analysis

LO2 Frequent-Flier Plan

SD 1. America South Airways instituted a frequent-flier program under which passengers accumulate points toward a free flight based on the number of miles they fly on the airline. One point was awarded for each mile flown, with a minimum of 750 miles being given for any flight. Because of competition in 2001, the company began a bonus plan under which passengers receive triple the normal mileage points. In the past, about 1.5 percent of passenger miles were flown by passengers who had converted points to free flights. With the triple mileage program, it is expected that a 2.5 percent rate will be more appropriate for future years. During 2001, the company had passenger revenues of $966.3 million and passenger transportation operating expenses of $802.8 million before depreciation and amortization. Operating income was $86.1 million. What is the appropriate rate to use to estimate free miles? What would be the effect of the estimated liability for free travel by frequent fliers on 2001 net income? Describe several ways to estimate the amount of this liability. Be prepared to discuss the arguments for and against recognizing this liability.

LO2
LO3 Nature and Recognition of an Estimated Liability

SD 2. The decision to recognize and record a liability is sometimes a matter of judgment. People who use General Motors <www.gm.com> credit cards earn rebates toward the purchase or lease of GM vehicles in relation to the amount of purchases they make with their cards. General Motors chooses to treat these outstanding rebates as a commitment in the notes to its financial statements:

> GM sponsors a credit card program . . . that offers rebates that can be applied primarily against the purchase or lease of GM vehicles. The amount of rebates available to qualified cardholders (net of deferred program income) was $4.0 billion, $3.9 billion, and $3.8 billion at December 31, 2002, 2001, and 2000, respectively.[14]

Using the two criteria established by the FASB for recording a contingency, explain GM's reasoning in treating this liability as a commitment in the notes, where it will likely receive less attention by analysts, rather than including it on the income statement as an expense and on the balance sheet as an estimated liability. Do you agree with this position? (**Hint:** Apply the matching rule.)

Ethical Dilemma

LO2 Known Legal Violations

SD 3. Chop Shop Restaurant is a large steak restaurant in the suburbs of Chicago. Joe Murray, an accounting student at a nearby college, recently secured a full-time accounting job at the restaurant. He felt fortunate to have a good job that accommodated his class schedule because the local economy was very bad. After a few weeks on the job, Murray realized that his boss, the owner of the business, was paying the kitchen workers in cash and was not withholding federal and state income taxes or social security and Medicare taxes. Murray understands that federal and state laws require these taxes to be withheld and paid to the appropriate agency in a timely manner. He also realizes that if he raises this issue, he could lose his job. What alternatives are available to Murray? What action would you take if you were in his position? Why did you make this choice?

 Group Activity: Use in class groups. Debrief by asking each group for an alternative. Then debate the ethics of each alternative.

Research Activity

LO2 Basic Research Skills
LO3

SD 4. Indexes for business periodicals, in which you can look up topics of interest, are available in your school library. Three of the most important of these indexes are the *Business Periodicals Index*, *The Wall Street Journal Index*, and the *Accountants' Index*. Using one or more of these indexes, locate and photocopy two articles related to bank financing, commercial paper, product warranties, airline frequent-flier plans, or contingent liabilities. Keep in mind that you may have to look under related topics to find an article. For example, to find articles about contingent liabilities, you might look under litigation, debt guarantees, or environmental losses. For each of the two articles, write a short summary of the situation and tell how it relates to accounting for the topic as described in the text. Be prepared to discuss your results in class.

Decision-Making Practice

LO1 Identification of Current
LO2 Liabilities
SO4

SD 5. Sandra Miller opened a bicycle repair shop, Miller Bicycles, in 20x3. She also sold bicycles. The new business was such a success that she hired two assistants on June 1, 20x3. In December, Miller realized that she had failed to file any tax reports for her business since its inception and therefore probably owed a considerable amount of taxes. Since Miller has limited experience in running a business, she has brought all her business records to you and is asking for help. The records include a checkbook, canceled checks, deposit slips, invoices from her suppliers, a notice of annual property taxes of $9,240 due to the city on January 1, 20x4, and a one-year promissory note to the bank for $10,000. She wants you to determine what her business owes the government and other parties. You analyze all her records and determine the following:

Unpaid supplies invoices	$ 6,320
Sales (excluding sales tax)	177,080
Workers' salaries	40,800
Repair revenues	241,200

You learn that the company has deducted $1,904 from the two employees' salaries for federal income taxes owed to the government. The current social security tax is 6.2 percent on maximum earnings of $87,000 for each employee, and the current Medicare tax is 1.45 percent (no maximum earnings). The FUTA tax is 5.4 percent to the state and .8 percent to the federal government on the first $7,000 earned by each employee, and each employee earned more than $7,000. Miller has not filed a sales tax report to the state (5 percent of sales).

1. Given these limited facts, determine Miller Bicycle's current liabilities as of December 31, 20x4.
2. What additional information would you want from Miller to satisfy yourself that all current liabilities have been identified?

Financial Reporting and Analysis Cases

Interpreting Financial Reports

FRA 1. Both Sun Microsystems Inc. <www.sun.com> and Cisco Systems <www.cisco.com> are in the computer industry. These data (in thousands) are for their fiscal year ends:[15]

LO1 Comparison of Two Companies' Ratios with Industry Ratios

	Sun	Cisco
Accounts payable	$ 1,050,000	$ 644,000
Cost of goods sold	10,049,000	11,221,000
Increase (decrease) in inventory	492,000	452,000

Compare the payables turnover ratio and average days' payable for both companies. Comment on the results. How are cash flows affected by average days' payable? How do Sun Microsystems' and Cisco Systems' ratios compare with the computer industry ratios shown in Figures 1 and 2 in this chapter? (Use year-end amounts for ratios.)

FRA 2. In its 1986 annual report, Texaco, Inc. <www.texaco.com>, one of the world's largest oil companies, reported its loss in the biggest damage judgment rendered to that date:

LO3 Classic Case: Contingent Liabilities

> **Note 17.** Contingent Liabilities
> Pennzoil Litigation
>
> *State Court Action.* On December 10, 1985, the 151st District Court of Harris County, Texas, entered judgment for Pennzoil Company of $7.5 billion actual damages, $3 billion punitive damages, and approximately $600 million prejudgment interest in *Pennzoil Company v. Texaco, Inc.*, an action in which Pennzoil claims that Texaco, Inc., tortiously interfered with Pennzoil's alleged contract to acquire a 3/7ths interest in Getty. Interest began accruing on the judgment at the simple rate of 10% per annum from the date of judgment. Texaco, Inc., believes that there is no legal basis for the judgment, which it believes is contrary to the evidence and applicable law. Texaco, Inc., is pursuing all available remedies to set aside or to reverse the judgment. . . .
>
> The outcome of the appeal on the preliminary injunction and the ultimate outcome of the Pennzoil litigation are not presently determinable, but could have a material adverse effect on the consolidated financial position and the results of the consolidated operations of Texaco, Inc.[16]

At December 31, 1986, Texaco's retained earnings were $12.882 billion, and its cash and marketable securities totaled $3.0 billion. Its net income for 1986 was $.725 billion.

After a series of court reversals and filing for bankruptcy in 1987, Texaco announced in December 1987 an out-of-court settlement with Pennzoil for $3.0 billion. Although less than the original amount, it is still the largest damage payment in history.

1. What two conditions established by the FASB must a contingent liability meet before it is recorded in the accounting records? Does the situation described in "Note 17. Contingent Liabilities" meet those conditions? Explain your answer.
2. Do the events of 1987 change your answer to **1**? Explain your response.
3. How would the settlement have affected Texaco's retained earnings, cash and marketable securities, and net income?

International Company

FRA 3. Man Nutzfahrzeuge Aktiengesellschaft <www.mannutzfahrzeuge.de>, a German firm, is one of the world's largest truck companies. Accounting in Germany differs in some respects from that in the United States. A good example is the placement and classification of liabilities. On the balance sheet, Man places liabilities below a detailed stockholders' equity section. Man does not distinguish between current and long-term liabilities; however, a note to the financial statements does disclose the amount of the liabilities due within one year. Those liabilities are primarily what we call *definitely determinable liabilities,* such as loans, accounts payable, and notes payable. Estimated liabilities do not seem to appear in this category. There is an asset category called *current assets,* similar to that used in the United States. In another note to the financial statements, Man lists what it calls *contingent liabilities,* which have not been recorded and do not appear on the balance sheet. These include liabilities for hire and leasing contracts, guarantees of loans of other companies, and warranties on trucks.[17] What do you think of

LO1 Classification and Disclosure
LO2 of Current Liabilities and
LO3 Contingent Liabilities

combining all liabilities, short- and long-term, in a single item on the balance sheet? Should any contingent liabilities be recorded and shown on the balance sheet?

Toys "R" Us Annual Report

FRA 4.
LO1 Short-Term Liabilities and Seasonality

Refer to the balance sheet and the liquidity and capital resources section of management's discussion in the Toys "R" Us annual report <www.tru.com>. Compute the payables turnover for 2002 for Toys "R" Us. How does it compare with the payables turnover ratios for the industries shown in Figure 1? Toys "R" Us is a seasonal business. Would you expect short-term borrowings and accounts payable to be unusually high or unusually low at the balance sheet date of February 1, 2003? How does management use short-term financing to meet its needs for cash during the year?

Comparison Case: Toys "R" Us and Walgreen Co.

FRA 5.
LO1 Payables Analysis and
LO3 Commitments and Contingencies

Refer to the financial statements and notes for Toys "R" Us <www.tru.com> and Walgreens <www.walgreens.com> in the Supplement to Chapter 1.

1. Compute the payables turnover and average days' payable for Toys "R" Us and Walgreens for the past two years. Accounts payable in 2000 were $1,152 million for Toys "R" Us and $1,364.0 million for Walgreens. The merchandise inventory for Toys "R" Us in 2000 was $2,307 million, and for Walgreens, $2,830.8 million. Which company makes most use of creditors to finance the operating cycle's needs?
2. Read each company's note on commitments and contingencies. What commitments and contingencies do the companies have in common? For which company does this information seem to be most important? Why is it important to consider this information in connection with payables analysis?

Fingraph® Financial Analyst™

FRA 6.
LO1 Comparison of Current
LO2 Liabilities and Working
LO3 Capital

Choose any two companies from the list of Fingraph companies on the Needles Accounting Resource Center Web Site at http://accounting.college.hmco.com/students. The industry should be one in which current liabilities are likely to be important, such as the airline, manufacturing, consumer products, or computer industry. Access the Microsoft Excel spreadsheets for the companies you selected. Click the URL at the top of each company's spreadsheet to link to the company's web site and annual report.

1. In the annual reports of the companies you have selected, read the current liability section of the balance sheet and any reference to current liabilities in the summary of significant accounting policies or notes to the financial statements. What are the most important current liabilities for each company? Do any current liabilities appear to be characteristic of the industry? Which current liabilities are definitely determinable, and which appear to be accrued liabilities?
2. Using the Fingraph CD-ROM software, display and print in tabular and graphic form the Current Assets and Current Liabilities Analysis page. Prepare a table that compares the current ratio and working capital for both companies for two years.
3. Find and read references to current liabilities in the liquidity analysis section of management's discussion and analysis in each annual report.
4. Write a one-page executive summary that highlights the most important types of current liabilities for this industry and that compares the current ratio and working capital trends of the two companies, including reference to management's assessment. Include the Fingraph page and your table with your report.

Internet Case

FRA 7.
LO3 Investigation of Status of Famous Contingencies

In addition to the Texaco <www.texaco.com> case in **FRA 2**, other famous contingency liability cases include suits against RJR Nabisco <www.nabisco.com>, Philip Morris <www.philipmorris.com>, and Waste Management, Inc. <www.wm.com>. Investigate the current status of any one of these cases by going to the company's web site and finding its latest annual report. Look in the notes to the financial statements under "Contingencies." Report what you find about the case, including whether it has been settled or is no longer being reported.

10

Chapter 10 explores the management issues associated with the acquisition, operation, and disposal of property, plant, and equipment, natural resources, and intangible assets, as well as the concepts and techniques of depreciation, depletion, and amortization.

Long-Term Assets

LEARNING OBJECTIVES

LO1 Identify the types of long-term assets and explain the management issues related to accounting for them.

LO2 Distinguish between capital and revenue expenditures, and account for the cost of property, plant, and equipment.

LO3 Define *depreciation* and compute depreciation under the straight-line, production, and declining-balance methods.

LO4 Account for the disposal of depreciable assets.

LO5 Identify the issues related to accounting for natural resources and compute depletion.

LO6 Identify the issues related to accounting for intangible assets, including research and development costs and goodwill.

SUPPLEMENTAL OBJECTIVE

SO7 Apply depreciation methods to problems of partial years, revised rates, groups of similar items, special types of capital expenditures, and cost recovery.

DECISION POINT
A USER'S FOCUS

H. J. Heinz Company <www.heinz.com> The effects of management's decisions regarding long-term assets are most apparent in the areas of reported total assets, net income, and cash flows related to investing activities. How does one learn about the significance of those items to a company? An idea of the extent of a company's long-term assets and their importance can be gained from the financial statements. For example, the list of assets in the Financial Highlights is from the annual report of H. J. Heinz Company, one of the world's largest food companies. Of the company's $10 billion in total assets, property, plant, and equipment represent about 23 percent, and other non-current assets represent about 47 percent.

With 69 percent of Heinz's total assets classified as long-term, management's decisions regarding choice of expected useful life and residual value of the assets can have a material impact on the amount expensed on the income statement. The income statement shows that depreciation and amortization expenses associated with those assets are more than $207 million, or about 25 percent of net income. While depreciation and amortization expenses have no cash effect, the statement of cash flows indicates the amount paid for newly purchased property, plant, and equipment and to what extent a company is reinvesting in its operations. Heinz spent more than $213 million on new long-term assets. In addition to annual expense recognition, long-term assets are reviewed annually to determine if the assets have lost some of their service potential, resulting in asset impairment. Finally, disposals of long-term assets may result in

What do Heinz's financial statements reveal about the company's long-term assets?

gains or losses on the income statement. Each of these financial-statement issues falls within the scope of accounting for the acquisition, use, and disposal of long-term assets and the related management judgments.[1]

Financial Highlights (In thousands)

	2002	2001
Total Current Assets	$ 3,373,566	$3,116,814
Property, Plant, and Equipment:		
Land	$ 63,075	$ 54,774
Buildings and leasehold improvements	880,490	878,028
Equipment, furniture, and other	2,929,082	2,947,978
	3,872,647	3,880,780
Less accumulated depreciation	1,622,573	1,712,400
Total property, plant, and equipment, net	$ 2,250,074	$2,168,380
Other Noncurrent Assets:		
Goodwill (net of amortization: 2002—$393,972 and 2001—$334,907)	$ 2,528,942	$2,077,451
Trademarks (net of amortization: 2002—$144,884 and 2001—$118,254)	808,884	567,692
Other intangibles (net of amortization: 2002—$160,230 and 2001—$157,678)	152,249	120,749
Other noncurrent assets	1,164,639	984,064
Total other noncurrent assets	$ 4,654,714	$3,749,956
Total Assets	$10,278,354	$9,035,150

Management Issues Related to Accounting for Long-Term Assets

LO1 Identify the types of long-term assets and explain the management issues related to accounting for them.

RELATED TEXT ASSIGNMENTS
Q: 1, 2, 3, 4, 5, 6, 7
SE: 1
E: 1, 2
SD: 1, 6, 7
FRA: 3, 4, 5

STUDY NOTE: For an asset to be classified as property, plant, and equipment, it must be "put in use." This means that it is available for its intended purpose. An emergency generator is "put in use" when it is available for emergencies, even if it is never used.

KEY POINT: A computer used in the office would be considered plant and equipment, whereas an identical computer held for sale to customers would be considered inventory.

◆ **Stop and Think!**
Is carrying value ever the same as market value?
On the date of acquisition, the carrying value equals the current market value. After that, it would be a coincidence if it equaled the market value. ■

Long-term assets are assets that (1) have a useful life of more than one year, (2) are acquired for use in the operation of a business, and (3) are not intended for resale to customers. For many years, it was common to refer to long-term assets as *fixed assets*, but use of this term is declining because the word *fixed* implies that they last forever. The relative importance of long-term assets to various industries is shown in Figure 1. Long-term assets range from 17.7 percent of total assets in the advertising industry to 51.2 percent in interstate trucking.

Although there is no strict rule for defining the useful life of a long-term asset, the most common criterion is that the asset be capable of repeated use for at least a year. Included in this category is equipment used only in peak or emergency periods, such as generators.

Assets not used in the normal course of business should not be included in this category. Thus, land held for speculative reasons or buildings no longer used in ordinary business operations should not be included in the property, plant, and equipment category. Instead, they should be classified as long-term investments.

Finally, if an item is held for resale to customers, it should be classified as inventory—not plant and equipment—no matter how durable it is. For example, a printing press held for sale by a printing press manufacturer would be considered inventory, whereas the same printing press would be considered plant and equipment if a printing company buys it for use in operations.

Long-term assets differ from current assets in that they support the operating cycle instead of being a part of it. They are also expected to benefit the business for a longer period than do current assets. Current assets are expected to be used up or converted to cash within one year or during the operating cycle, whichever is longer. Long-term assets are expected to last beyond that period. Long-term assets and their related expenses are summarized in Figure 2 on page 456.

Generally, long-lived assets are reported at carrying value, as presented in Figure 3 on page 456. **Carrying value** is the unexpired part of the cost of an asset, not its market value; it is also called *book value*. If a long-lived asset loses some or all of its revenue-generating potential before the end of its useful life, the asset may be deemed impaired, and its carrying value reduced. **Asset impairment** occurs when the sum of the expected cash flows from the asset is less than the carrying value of the asset.[2] Reducing carrying value to fair value, as measured by the present value

FIGURE 1
Long-Term Assets as a Percentage of Total Assets for Selected Industries

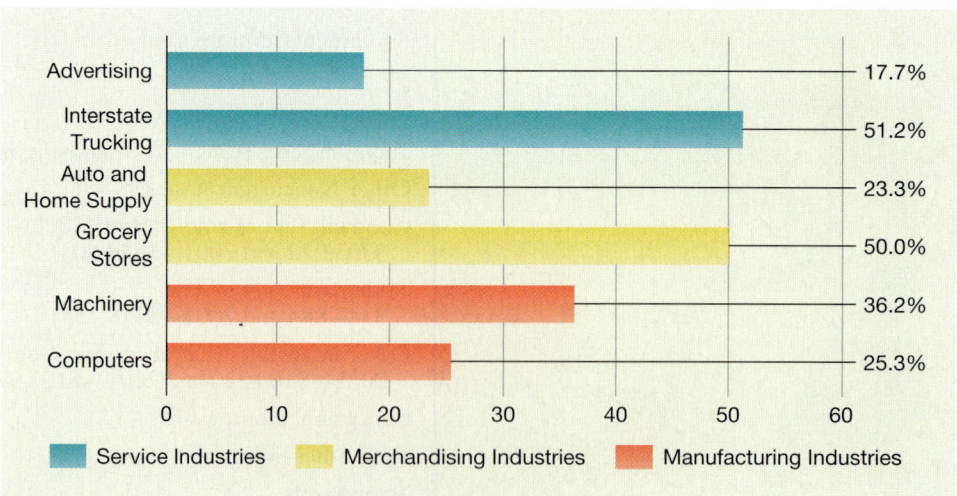

Source: Data from Dun & Bradstreet, *Industry Norms and Key Business Ratios,* 2001–02.

Video Case

Fermi National Accelerator Laboratory <www.fnal.gov>

Objectives

- To describe the characteristics of long-term assets
- To identify the four issues that must be addressed in applying the matching rule to long-term assets
- To define depreciation and state the principal causes of depreciation
- To identify the issues related to intangible assets, including research and development

Background for the Case

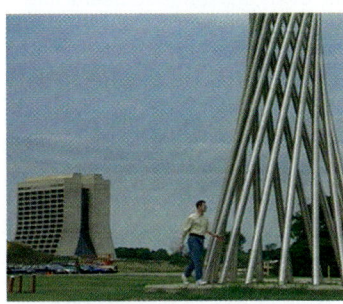

Fermi National Accelerator Laboratory (Fermilab), located 30 miles west of Chicago, is run by the U.S. Department of Energy. Its primary mission is to advance the understanding of the fundamental nature of matter and energy.

Fermilab operates the world's highest-energy particle accelerator, the Trevatron, or "atom-smasher." Circling through rings of magnets four miles in circumference, particle beams generate experimental conditions equivalent to those that existed in the first quadrillionth of a second after the birth of the universe. This capability to re-create such high energy levels places Fermilab at the frontier of global physics research. The facility provides leadership and resources for qualified experimenters to conduct basic research at the leading edge of high-energy physics and related disciplines. In the year 2000, with Collider Run II, scientists at Fermilab began probing the smallest dimensions that humans have ever examined. These scientists have the opportunity to make discoveries that could answer some important questions in particle physics.

Although a unit of the U.S. government, Fermilab is a financially independent nonprofit corporation with a governing body consisting of the presidents of 87 affiliated research universities. With annual revenues of about $300 million, consisting mostly of government contracts, and annual expenses of about $260 million, Fermilab faces the same management challenges as a for-profit corporation. It must make huge investments in long-term assets. Other than salaries, depreciation is the lab's largest expense. In addition, Fermilab creates intellectual capital through basic research that it shares with U.S. industry to encourage economic development.

For more information about Fermi National Accelerator Laboratory, visit its web site through the Needles Accounting Resource Center Web Site at **http://accounting.college.hmco.com/students** or directly through Fermilab's web site.

Required

View the video on Fermi National Accelerator Laboratory that accompanies this book. As you are watching the video, take notes related to the following questions:

1. What characteristics distinguish long-term assets? What are some examples of long-term assets at Fermilab?
2. What four issues must be addressed in applying the matching rule to long-term assets?
3. What is depreciation, and what are its two major causes?
4. What are research and development costs, and how does Fermilab account for them? How might this method understate the assets of Fermilab?

---

of future cash flows, is an application of conservatism. All long-term assets are subject to an asset impairment evaluation. A reduction in carrying value as a result of impairment is recorded as a loss.

Because of a slowdown in the growth of Internet, telecommunications, and technology companies, companies like Amazon.com, Cisco Systems, and Lucent Technologies took write-downs totaling billions of dollars. The carrying value of certain long-term tangible and intangible assets no longer exceeded the cash flows that they would help generate, due to declining revenues or slowing revenue growth. The write-downs caused the companies to report operating losses.[3]

www.amazon.com
www.cisco.com
www.lucent.com

Deciding to Acquire Long-Term Assets

The decision to acquire a long-term asset involves a complex process. Methods of evaluating data to make rational decisions in this area are grouped under a topic called capital budgeting, which is usually covered as a managerial accounting topic. However, an awareness of the general nature of the problem can be helpful in

Figure 2
Classification of Long-Term Assets and Corresponding Expenses

BALANCE SHEET
Long-Term Assets

INCOME STATEMENT
Expenses

Tangible Assets: long-term assets that have physical substance
- Land
- Plant, Buildings, Equipment (plant assets)

} Land is not expensed because it has an unlimited life.

} **Depreciation:** periodic allocation of the cost of a tangible long-lived asset (other than land and natural resources) over its estimated useful life

Natural Resources: long-term assets purchased for the economic value that can be taken from the land and used up, as with ore, lumber, oil, and gas or other resources contained in the land
- Mines
- Timberland
- Oil and Gas Fields

} **Depletion:** exhaustion of a natural resource through mining, cutting, pumping, or other extraction, and the way in which the cost is allocated

Intangible Assets: long-term assets that have no physical substance but have a value based on rights or advantages accruing to the owner
- Patents, Copyrights, Trademarks, Franchises, Leaseholds, Leasehold Improvements, Goodwill

} **Amortization:** periodic allocation of the cost of an intangible asset to the periods it benefits

} Goodwill is not expensed, but its value is reviewed annually.

KEY POINT: For an asset to be classified as intangible, it must lack physical substance, be long term, and (normally) represent a legal right or advantage.

understanding the accounting issues related to long-term assets. To illustrate the acquisition decision, let us assume that Irena Markova, M.D., is considering the purchase of a $5,000 computer system for her office. She estimates that if she purchases the computer, she can reduce the hours of a part-time employee sufficiently to save net cash flows of $2,000 per year for four years and that the computer will be worth $1,000 at the end of that period. These data are summarized as follows:

Figure 3
Carrying Value of Long-Term Assets on the Balance Sheet

Plant Assets	Natural Resources	Intangible Assets
Less Accumulated Depreciation	Less Accumulated Depletion	Less Accumulated Amortization
Carrying Value	Carrying Value	Carrying Value

	20x4	20x5	20x6	20x7
Acquisition cost	($5,000)			
Net annual savings in cash flows	2,000	$2,000	$2,000	$2,000
Disposal price				1,000
Net cash flows	($3,000)	$2,000	$2,000	$3,000

To place the cash flows on a comparable basis, it is helpful to use present value tables, such as Tables 3 and 4 in the appendix on future value and present value tables. Assuming that the appropriate interest rate is 10 percent compounded annually, the purchase may be evaluated as follows:

		Present Value
Acquisition cost	Present value factor = 1.000 1.000 × $5,000	($5,000)
Net annual savings in cash flows	Present value factor = 3.170 (Table 4: 4 periods, 10%) 3.170 × $2,000	6,340
Disposal price	Present value factor = .683 (Table 3: 4 periods, 10%) .683 × $1,000	683
Net present value		$2,023

As long as the net present value is positive, Dr. Markova will earn at least 10 percent on the investment. In this case, the return is greater than 10 percent because the net present value is a positive $2,023. Based on this analysis, Dr. Markova makes the decision to purchase. However, there are other important considerations that have to be taken into account, such as the costs of training and maintenance, and the possibility that because of unforeseen circumstances, the savings may not be as great as expected. In Dr. Markova's case, the decision to purchase is likely to be a good one because the net present value is both positive and large relative to the investment.

Information about a company's acquisitions of long-term assets may be found under investing activities in the statement of cash flows. For example, in referring to this section of its 2002 annual report, the management of H. J. Heinz Company makes the following statement:

www.heinz.com

> Capital expenditures totaled $213.4 million compared to $411.3 million last year. . . . In fiscal 2003, the company expects capital expenditures to be consistent with fiscal 2002.[4]

FINANCING LONG-TERM ASSETS

In addition to deciding whether to acquire a long-term asset, management must decide how to finance the asset if it is acquired. Some companies are profitable enough to pay for long-term assets out of cash flows from operations, but when financing is needed, some form of long-term arrangement related to the life of the asset is usually most appropriate. For example, an automobile loan generally spans 4 or 5 years, whereas a mortgage on a house may span as many as 30 years.

For a major long-term acquisition, a company may issue capital stock, long-term notes, or bonds. A good place to study a company's long-term financing is in the financing activities section of the statement of cash flows. For instance, in discussing this section, Ford Motor Company's management states, "At December 31, 2002, the Automotive sector had total debt of $14.2 billion, up $400 million from a year ago. The weighted average maturity of our long-term debt . . . is approximately 27 years."[5]

www.ford.com

FIGURE 4
Issues of Accounting for Long-Term Assets

APPLYING THE MATCHING RULE TO LONG-TERM ASSETS

Accounting for long-term assets requires the proper application of the matching rule through the resolution of two important issues. The first is how much of the total cost to allocate to expense in the current accounting period. The second is how much to retain on the balance sheet as an asset to benefit future periods. To resolve these issues, four important questions about the acquisition, use, and disposal of each long-term asset must be answered (see Figure 4):

1. How is the cost of the long-term asset determined?
2. How should the expired portion of the cost of the long-term asset be allocated against revenues over time?
3. How should subsequent expenditures, such as repairs and additions, be treated?
4. How should disposal of the long-term asset be recorded?

STUDY NOTE: Useful life is measured by the service units a business expects to receive from an asset. It should not be confused with physical life, which is often much longer. If the management of a new business is having difficulty determining an asset's estimated useful life, it may obtain help from trade magazines. Nearly every industry has at least one.

Because of the long life of long-term assets and the complexity of the transactions relating to them, management has many choices and estimates to make. For example, acquisition cost may be complicated by group purchases, trade-ins, or construction costs. In addition, to allocate the cost of the asset to future periods effectively, management must estimate how long the asset will last and what it will be worth at the end of its use. In making such estimates, it is helpful to think of a long-term asset as a bundle of services to be used in the operation of the business over a period of years. A delivery truck may provide 100,000 miles of service over its life. A piece of equipment may have the potential to produce 500,000 parts. A building may provide shelter for 50 years. As each of those assets is purchased, the company is paying in advance for 100,000 miles, the capacity to produce 500,000 parts, or 50 years of service. In essence, each asset is a type of long-term prepaid expense. The accounting problem is to spread the cost of the services over the useful life of the asset. As the services benefit the company over the years, the cost becomes an expense rather than an asset.

 Check out ACE for a Review Quiz at http://accounting.college.hmco.com/students.

ACQUISITION COST OF PROPERTY, PLANT, AND EQUIPMENT

LO2 Distinguish between capital and revenue expenditures, and account for the cost of property, plant, and equipment.

RELATED TEXT ASSIGNMENTS
Q: 8, 9, 10
SE: 2, 3
E: 3, 4, 5, 14
P: 1, 6
SD: 4, 5, 6
FRA: 3

STUDY NOTE: Although dyeing a carpet may make it look almost new, it is not considered a capital expenditure because even though the carpet looks better, its fibers are not stronger, and it probably will not last significantly longer than it would have before the color was changed.

STUDY NOTE: The cost of mailing lists may be recorded as an asset because the mailing lists will be used over and over and will benefit future accounting periods.

KEY POINT: Expenditures necessary to prepare an asset for its intended use are a cost of the asset.

Expenditure refers to a payment or an obligation to make future payment for an asset, such as a truck, or a service, such as a repair. Expenditures may be classified as capital expenditures or revenue expenditures. A **capital expenditure** is an expenditure for the purchase or expansion of a long-term asset. Capital expenditures are recorded in the asset accounts because they benefit several future accounting periods. A **revenue expenditure** is an expenditure related to the repair, maintenance, and operation of a long-term asset. These expenditures do not extend the asset's original useful life but are necessary to enable the asset to fulfill its original useful life. Revenue expenditures are recorded in the expense accounts because their benefits are realized in the current period.

THE IMPORTANCE OF CLASSIFYING EXPENDITURES CORRECTLY

Careful distinction between capital and revenue expenditures is important to the proper application of the matching rule. For example, if the purchase of an automobile is mistakenly recorded as a revenue expenditure, the total cost of the automobile is recorded as an expense on the income statement. As a result, current net income is reported at a lower amount (understated) and assets are understated. In future periods net income will be overstated because depreciation expense is understated. Assets are also understated because the asset was completely expensed in the period that it was purchased. If, on the other hand, a revenue expenditure, such as the painting of a building, were charged to an asset account, the expense of the current period would be understated. Current net income and assets would be overstated by the same amount, and the net income of future periods would be understated because of the erroneous future depreciation expense that was recorded.

Determining when a payment is an expense and when it is an asset is a matter of judgment, in the exercise of which management takes a leading role. For example, inconsistencies have existed in accounting for the costs of computer programs that run the systems for businesses. Some companies immediately write off the expenditure as an expense, whereas others treat it as a long-term intangible asset and amortize it year after year. Companies spend billions of dollars a year on this type of software, and it is an important variable in the profitability of many companies. Although the AICPA has issued new rules to try to bring more standardization to these accounting issues, considerable latitude does still exist, such as in determining how long the economic life of the software will be.[6]

GENERAL APPROACH TO ACQUISITION COSTS

The acquisition cost of property, plant, and equipment includes all expenditures reasonable and necessary to get the asset in place and ready for use. For example, the cost of installing and testing a machine is a legitimate cost of the machine. However, if the machine is damaged during installation, the cost of repairs is an operating expense and not an acquisition cost.

Cost is easiest to determine when a purchase is made for cash. In that case, the cost of the asset is equal to the cash paid for the asset plus expenditures for freight, insurance while in transit, installation, and other necessary related costs. If a debt is incurred in the purchase of the asset, the interest charges are not a cost of the asset, but a cost of borrowing the money to buy the asset. They are therefore an operating expense. An exception to this principle is that interest costs incurred during the construction of an asset are properly included as a cost of the asset.[7]

Expenditures like freight, insurance while in transit, and installation are included in the cost of the asset because they are necessary if the asset is to function. Following the matching rule, they are allocated to the useful life of the asset rather than charged as expenses in the current period.

For practical purposes, many companies establish policies defining when an expenditure should be recorded as an expense or an asset. For example, small expenditures for items that would normally be treated as assets may be treated as expenses because the amounts involved are not material in relation to net income. Thus, a wastebasket, which might last for years, would be recorded as a supplies expense rather than as a depreciable asset.

Some of the problems of determining the cost of long-lived plant assets are discussed in the next sections.

KEY POINT: Many costs may be incurred to prepare land for its intended use and condition. All such costs are a cost of land.

■ **LAND** There are often expenditures in addition to the purchase price of land that should be debited to the Land account. Some examples are commissions to real estate agents; lawyers' fees; accrued taxes paid by the purchaser; costs of preparing the land to build on, such as the costs of tearing down old buildings and draining, clearing, and grading the land; and assessments for local improvements, such as putting in streets and sewage systems. The cost of landscaping is usually debited to the Land account because such improvements are relatively permanent. Land is not subject to depreciation because it does not have a limited useful life.

ENRICHMENT NOTE: The costs of tearing down existing buildings can be major. For example, companies may spend millions of dollars imploding buildings so they can remove them and build new ones.

Let us assume that a company buys land for a new retail operation. It pays a net purchase price of $170,000, pays brokerage fees of $6,000 and legal fees of $2,000, pays $10,000 to have an old building on the site torn down, receives $4,000 salvage from the old building, and pays $1,000 to have the site graded. The cost of the land is $185,000:

Net purchase price		$170,000
Brokerage fees		6,000
Legal fees		2,000
Tearing down old building	$10,000	
Less salvage	4,000	6,000
Grading		1,000
Total cost		$185,000

■ **LAND IMPROVEMENTS** Some improvements to real estate, such as driveways, parking lots, and fences, have a limited life and are thus subject to depreciation. They should be recorded in an account called Land Improvements rather than in the Land account.

■ **BUILDINGS** When an existing building is purchased, its cost includes the purchase price plus all repairs and other expenditures required to put it in usable condition. Buildings are subject to depreciation because they have a limited useful life. When a business constructs its own building, the cost includes all reasonable and necessary expenditures, such as those for materials, labor, part of the overhead and other indirect costs, architects' fees, insurance during construction, interest on construction loans during the period of construction, lawyers' fees, and building permits. If outside contractors are used in the construction, the net contract price plus other expenditures necessary to put the building in usable condition are included in the cost.

ENRICHMENT NOTE: The electrical wiring and plumbing of a dental chair are included in the cost of the asset because they are a necessary cost of preparing the asset for use.

■ **EQUIPMENT** The cost of equipment includes all expenditures connected with purchasing the equipment and preparing it for use. Those expenditures include the invoice price less cash discounts; freight, including insurance; excise taxes and tariffs; buying expenses; installation costs; and test runs to ready the equipment for operation. Equipment is subject to depreciation.

Focus on Business Ethics

Is It an Asset or Expense? The Answer Matters.

Determining whether an expenditure is a long-term asset or an expense is not always as clear-cut as some might imagine. Management has considerable leeway in how to record transactions, but the financial statements must be prepared in accordance with generally accepted accounting principles and the result cannot be deceptive. If management's choices are questioned, the results can sometimes have drastic consequences.

For example, *The Wall Street Journal* reported that the chief financial officer of WorldCom <www.worldcom.com> used an unorthodox and unusually aggressive technique to account for one of the long-distance company's biggest expenses. The company recorded charges paid to local telephone networks to complete calls as long-term assets instead of operating expenses. This increased income in the year in question by deferring the costs to a future year, effectively turning a net loss for the year into a net income. In total, the company says that at least $3.8 billion was accounted for in this way. As a result of the report, the company's stock price dropped from a high of $64.50 to less than one dollar. The SEC filed civil fraud charges against WorldCom, saying the company "falsely portrayed itself as a profitable business."[8] Criminal charges may follow and the company will likely face bankruptcy.

This and other notable cases show that accounting is not a passive part of business that can be manipulated at will, but must be taken seriously. The financial statements must reveal the substance of the business's activities.

● **Stop and Think!**
What incentive does a company have to allocate more of a group purchase price to the land rather than to the building?

A higher land valuation has the effect of increasing income because a smaller building valuation results in a lower amount to depreciate over its useful life. ■

■ **Group Purchases** Land and other assets are sometimes purchased for a lump sum. Because land is a nondepreciable asset that has an unlimited life, it must have a separate ledger account, and the lump-sum purchase price must be apportioned between the land and the other assets. For example, assume that a building and the land on which it is situated are purchased for a lump-sum payment of $85,000. The apportionment can be made by determining the price of each if purchased separately and applying the appropriate percentages to the lump-sum price. Assume that appraisals yield estimates of $10,000 for the land and $90,000 for the building if purchased separately. In that case, 10 percent of the lump-sum price, or $8,500, would be allocated to the land, and 90 percent, or $76,500, would be allocated to the building, as follows:

	Appraisal	Percentage	Apportionment
Land	$ 10,000	10% ($10,000 ÷ $100,000)	$ 8,500 ($85,000 × 10%)
Building	90,000	90% ($90,000 ÷ $100,000)	76,500 ($85,000 × 90%)
Totals	$100,000	100%	$85,000

 Check out ACE for a Review Quiz at http://accounting.college.hmco.com/students.

Accounting for Depreciation

LO3 Define *depreciation* and compute depreciation under the straight-line, production, and declining-balance methods.

RELATED TEXT ASSIGNMENTS
Q: 11, 12, 13, 14, 15, 16
SE: 4, 5, 6
E: 5, 6, 7, 10
P: 2, 3, 7, 8
SD: 1, 2, 6
FRA: 1, 3, 5, 6

The AICPA describes depreciation accounting as follows:

> The cost of a productive facility is one of the costs of the services it renders during its useful economic life. Generally accepted accounting principles require that this cost be spread over the expected useful life of the facility in such a way as to allocate it as equitably as possible to the periods during which services are obtained from the use of the facility. This procedure is known as depreciation accounting, a system of accounting which aims to distribute the cost or other basic value of tangible capital assets, less salvage (if any), over the estimated useful life of the unit . . . in a systematic and rational manner. It is a process of allocation, not of valuation.[9]

This description contains several important points. First, all tangible assets except land have a limited useful life. Because of this, their costs must be distributed as expenses over the years they benefit. Physical deterioration and obsolescence are the major causes of the limited useful life of a depreciable asset. The

PARENTHETICAL NOTE: An older computer may be functioning as well as it did on the day of purchase, but it has become obsolete because much faster, more efficient computers are now available.

physical deterioration of tangible assets results from use and from exposure to the elements, such as wind and sun. Periodic repairs and a sound maintenance policy may keep buildings and equipment in good operating order and extract the maximum useful life from them, but every machine or building at some point must be discarded. Repairs do not eliminate the need for depreciation. **Obsolescence** is the process of becoming out of date. Because of fast-changing technology and fast-changing demands, machinery and even buildings often become obsolete before they wear out. Accountants do not distinguish between physical deterioration and obsolescence because they are interested in the length of an asset's useful life, not in what limits that useful life.

Second, the term *depreciation*, as used in accounting, does not refer to an asset's physical deterioration or decrease in market value over time. Depreciation means the allocation of the cost of a plant asset to the periods that benefit from the services of that asset. The term is used to describe the gradual conversion of the cost of the asset into an expense.

KEY POINT: Depreciation is the allocation of the acquisition cost of an asset, and any similarity between undepreciated cost and current market value is pure coincidence.

Third, depreciation is not a process of valuation. Accounting records are kept in accordance with the cost principle; they are not indicators of changing price levels. It is possible that because of an advantageous purchase and specific market conditions, the market value of a building may rise. Nevertheless, depreciation must continue to be recorded because it is the result of an allocation, not a valuation, process. Eventually, the building will wear out or become obsolete regardless of interim fluctuations in market value.

FACTORS THAT AFFECT THE COMPUTATION OF DEPRECIATION

Four factors affect the computation of depreciation: (1) cost, (2) residual value, (3) depreciable cost, and (4) estimated useful life.

- **COST** As explained earlier in the chapter, cost is the net purchase price plus all reasonable and necessary expenditures to get the asset in place and ready for use.

KEY POINT: Residual value is the portion of an asset's acquisition cost expected to be recovered at the asset's disposal date.

- **RESIDUAL VALUE** The **residual value** of an asset is its estimated net scrap, salvage, or trade-in value as of the estimated date of disposal. Other terms often used to describe residual value are *salvage value* and *disposal value*. IN REAL WORLD USUALLY $0

KEY POINT: It is depreciable cost, not acquisition cost, that is allocated over the useful life of a plant asset.

- **DEPRECIABLE COST** The **depreciable cost** of an asset is its cost less its residual value. For example, a truck that costs $12,000 and has a residual value of $3,000 would have a depreciable cost of $9,000. Depreciable cost must be allocated over the useful life of the asset.

- **ESTIMATED USEFUL LIFE** **Estimated useful life** is the total number of service units expected from a long-term asset. Service units may be measured in terms of years

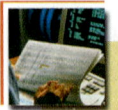

FOCUS ON BUSINESS PRACTICE

The Useful Life of an Aircraft Is How Long?

Most airlines depreciate airplanes over an estimated useful life of 10 to 20 years. But how long will a properly maintained airplane really last? Western Airlines <www.westernairlines.com> paid $3.3 million for a new Boeing 737 in July 1968. More than 78,000 flights and 30 years later, this aircraft was still flying for Vanguard Airlines <www.flyvanguard.com>, a no-frills airline. Among the other airlines that have owned this aircraft during the course of its life are Piedmont, Delta <www.delta.com>, and US Airways <www.usairways.com>. Virtually every part of the plane has been replaced over the years. Boeing believes the plane could theoretically make double the number of flights before it is retired.

The useful lives of many types of assets can be extended indefinitely if the assets are correctly maintained, but proper accounting in accordance with the matching rule requires depreciation over a "reasonable" useful life. Each airline that owned the plane would have accounted for the plane in this way.

the asset is expected to be used, units expected to be produced, miles expected to be driven, or similar measures. In computing the estimated useful life of an asset, an accountant should consider all relevant information, including (1) past experience with similar assets, (2) the asset's present condition, (3) the company's repair and maintenance policy, (4) current technological and industry trends, and (5) local conditions, such as weather.

Depreciation is recorded at the end of the accounting period by an adjusting entry that takes the following form:

A = L + OE
− −

Depreciation Expense, Asset Name	xxx	
Accumulated Depreciation, Asset Name		xxx
To record depreciation for the period		

METHODS OF COMPUTING DEPRECIATION

Many methods are used to allocate the cost of plant assets to accounting periods through depreciation. Each is proper for certain circumstances. The most common methods are (1) the straight-line method, (2) the production method, and (3) an accelerated method known as the declining-balance method.

CLARIFICATION NOTE: The straight-line depreciation method should be used when approximately equal asset benefit is obtained each year.

■ **STRAIGHT-LINE METHOD** When the **straight-line method** is used to calculate depreciation, the depreciable cost of the asset is spread evenly over the estimated useful life of the asset. The straight-line method is based on the assumption that depreciation depends only on the passage of time. The depreciation expense for each period is computed by dividing the depreciable cost (cost of the depreciating asset less its estimated residual value) by the number of accounting periods in the asset's estimated useful life. The rate of depreciation is the same in each year. Suppose, for example, that a delivery truck costs $10,000 and has an estimated residual value of $1,000 at the end of its estimated useful life of five years. The annual depreciation would be $1,800 under the straight-line method, calculated as follows:

KEY POINT: Residual value and useful life are, at best, educated guesses.

$$\frac{\text{Cost} - \text{Residual Value}}{\text{Estimated Useful Life}} = \frac{\$10,000 - \$1,000}{5 \text{ years}} = \$1,800 \text{ per year}$$

The depreciation for the five years would be as follows:

Depreciation Schedule, Straight-Line Method

	Cost	Yearly Depreciation	Accumulated Depreciation	Carrying Value
Date of purchase	$10,000	—	—	$10,000
End of first year	10,000	$1,800	$1,800	8,200
End of second year	10,000	1,800	3,600	6,400
End of third year	10,000	1,800	5,400	4,600
End of fourth year	10,000	1,800	7,200	2,800
End of fifth year	10,000	1,800	9,000	1,000

There are three important points to note from the depreciation schedule for the straight-line depreciation method. First, the depreciation is the same each year. Second, the accumulated depreciation increases uniformly. Third, the carrying value decreases uniformly until it reaches the estimated residual value.

■ **PRODUCTION METHOD** The **production method** of depreciation is based on the assumption that depreciation is solely the result of use and that the passage of time plays no role in the depreciation process. If we assume that the delivery truck in the previous example has an estimated useful life of 90,000 miles, the depreciation cost per mile would be determined as follows:

$$\frac{\text{Cost} - \text{Residual Value}}{\text{Estimated Units of Useful Life}} = \frac{\$10,000 - \$1,000}{90,000 \text{ miles}} = \$.10 \text{ per mile}$$

PARENTHETICAL NOTE: The production method is appropriate when a company has widely fluctuating rates of production. For example, carpet mills often close during the first two weeks in July. Charging a full month's depreciation would not achieve the goal of matching cost with revenue. Conversely, the same mills may run double shifts in September. At that time, twice the usual amount of depreciation should be charged.

If we assume that the use of the truck was 20,000 miles for the first year, 30,000 miles for the second, 10,000 miles for the third, 20,000 miles for the fourth, and 10,000 miles for the fifth, the depreciation schedule for the delivery truck would be as follows:

Depreciation Schedule, Production Method

	Cost	Miles	Yearly Depreciation	Accumulated Depreciation	Carrying Value
Date of purchase	$10,000	—	—	—	$10,000
End of first year	10,000	20,000	$2,000	$2,000	8,000
End of second year	10,000	30,000	3,000	5,000	5,000
End of third year	10,000	10,000	1,000	6,000	4,000
End of fourth year	10,000	20,000	2,000	8,000	2,000
End of fifth year	10,000	10,000	1,000	9,000	1,000

There is a direct relation between the amount of depreciation each year and the units of output or use. Also, the accumulated depreciation increases each year in direct relation to units of output or use. Finally, the carrying value decreases each year in direct relation to units of output or use until it reaches the estimated residual value.

Under the production method, the unit of output or use employed to measure the estimated useful life of each asset should be appropriate for that asset. For example, the number of items produced may be an appropriate measure for one machine, but the number of hours of use may be a better measure for another. The production method should be used only when the output of an asset over its useful life can be estimated with reasonable accuracy.

PARENTHETICAL NOTE: Accelerated depreciation is appropriate for assets that provide the greatest benefits in their early years. Under such a method, depreciation charges will be high in years when revenue generation from the asset is high.

■ **DECLINING-BALANCE METHOD** An **accelerated method** of depreciation results in relatively large amounts of depreciation in the early years of an asset's life and smaller amounts in later years. Such a method, which is based on the passage of time, assumes that many kinds of plant assets are most efficient when new, and so provide more and better service in the early years of their useful life. It is consistent with the matching rule to allocate more depreciation to earlier years than to later years if the benefits or services received in the earlier years are greater than those received later.

An accelerated method also recognizes that fast-changing technologies cause some equipment to become obsolescent and lose service value rapidly. Thus, it is realistic to allocate more to depreciation in earlier years than in later ones. Another argument in favor of an accelerated method is that repair expense is likely to be greater in later years than in earlier years. Thus, the total of repair and depreciation expense remains fairly constant over a period of years. This result naturally assumes that the services received from the asset are roughly equal from year to year.

The **declining-balance method** is the most common accelerated method of depreciation. Under this method, depreciation is computed by applying a fixed rate to the carrying value (the declining balance) of a tangible long-lived asset, resulting in higher depreciation charges during the early years of the asset's life. Though any fixed rate can be used, the most common rate is a percentage equal to twice the straight-line depreciation percentage. When twice the straight-line rate is used, the method is usually called the **double-declining-balance method**.

KEY POINT: The double-declining-balance method is the only method presented in which the residual value is not deducted before beginning the depreciation calculation.

In our earlier example, the delivery truck had an estimated useful life of five years. Consequently, under the straight-line method, the depreciation rate for each year was 20 percent (100 percent ÷ 5 years).

Under the double-declining-balance method, the fixed rate is 40 percent (2 × 20 percent). This fixed rate is applied to the *remaining carrying value* at the end of each year. Estimated residual value is not taken into account in figuring depreciation except in a year when calculated depreciation exceeds the amount necessary to is required because the asset was used until that date and, under the matching rule, the accounting period should receive the proper allocation of depreciation expense.

In this illustration, MGC Company disposes of the machinery on September 30. The entry to record the depreciation for the first nine months of 20x7 (nine-twelfths of a year) is as follows:

A = L + OE
−   −

Sept. 30	Depreciation Expense, Machinery	450	
	Accumulated Depreciation, Machinery		450
	To record depreciation up to date of disposal		

$$\frac{\$6{,}500 - \$500}{10} \times \frac{9}{12} = \$450$$

The relevant accounts appear as follows after the entry is posted:

Machinery		Accumulated Depreciation, Machinery	
6,500			4,650

After updating the depreciation, it is then necessary to remove the carrying value of the asset as shown in the following sections.

KEY POINT: When it disposes of an asset, a company must do two things. First, it must bring the depreciation up to date. Second, it must remove all evidence of ownership of the asset, including the contra account Accumulated Depreciation.

KEY POINT: A fully depreciated asset is kept on the books as long as it is still being used in the business. When a physical count of plant assets is made and reconciled with the general ledger control account and the subsidiary ledger, all assets must be accounted for.

■ **DISCARDED PLANT ASSETS**   A plant asset rarely lasts exactly as long as its estimated life. If it lasts longer than its estimated life, it is not depreciated past the point at which its carrying value equals its residual value. The purpose of depreciation is to spread the depreciable cost of an asset over the estimated life of the asset. Thus, the total accumulated depreciation should never exceed the total depreciable cost. If an asset remains in use beyond the end of its estimated life, its cost and accumulated depreciation remain in the ledger accounts. Proper records will thus be available for maintaining control over plant assets. If the residual value is zero, the carrying value of a fully depreciated asset is zero until the asset is disposed of. If such an asset is discarded, no gain or loss results.

In the illustration, however, the discarded equipment has a carrying value of $1,850 at the time of its disposal. The carrying value is computed from the T accounts above as machinery of $6,500 less accumulated depreciation of $4,650. A loss equal to the carrying value should be recorded when the machine is discarded, as follows:

A = L + OE
+   −
−

Sept. 30	Accumulated Depreciation, Machinery	4,650	
	Loss on Disposal of Machinery	1,850	
	Machinery		6,500
	Discarded machine no longer used in the business		

Gains and losses on disposals of plant assets are classified as other revenues and expenses on the income statement.

● **STOP AND THINK!**
When would the disposal of long-term assets result in no gain or loss?
If cash received for the assets equals their residual value, then no gain or loss occurs. ■

■ **PLANT ASSETS SOLD FOR CASH**   The entry to record a plant asset sold for cash is similar to the one just illustrated, except that the receipt of cash should also be recorded. The following entries show how to record the sale of a machine under three assumptions about the selling price. In the first case, the $1,850 cash received is exactly equal to the $1,850 carrying value of the machine; therefore, no gain or loss occurs.

A = L + OE
+
+
−

Sept. 30	Cash	1,850	
	Accumulated Depreciation, Machinery	4,650	
	Machinery		6,500
	Sale of machine for carrying value; no gain or loss		

In the second case, the $1,000 cash received is less than the carrying value of $1,850, so a loss of $850 is recorded.

A = L + OE
+   −
+
−

Sept. 30	Cash	1,000	
	Accumulated Depreciation, Machinery	4,650	
	Loss on Sale of Machinery	850	
	Machinery		6,500
	Sale of machine at less than carrying value; loss of $850 ($1,850 − $1,000) recorded		

KEY POINT: For an asset discarded or sold for cash, the gain (loss) on disposal of the asset equals cash received minus carrying value.

In the third case, the $2,000 cash received exceeds the carrying value of $1,850, so a gain of $150 is recorded.

A = L + OE
+   +
+
−

Sept. 30	Cash	2,000	
	Accumulated Depreciation, Machinery	4,650	
	Gain on Sale of Machinery		150
	Machinery		6,500
	Sale of machine at more than the carrying value; gain of $150 ($2,000 − $1,850) recorded		

EXCHANGES OF PLANT ASSETS

Businesses also dispose of plant assets by trading them in on the purchase of other plant assets. Exchanges may involve similar assets, such as an old machine traded in on a newer model, or dissimilar assets, such as a cement mixer traded in on a truck. In either case, the purchase price is reduced by the amount of the trade-in allowance.

Basically, accounting for exchanges of plant assets is similar to accounting for sales of plant assets for cash. If the trade-in allowance received is greater than the carrying value of the asset surrendered, there has been a gain. If the allowance is less, there has been a loss. There are special rules for recognizing these gains and losses, depending on the nature of the assets exchanged:

Exchange	Losses Recognized	Gains Recognized
For financial accounting purposes		
Of dissimilar assets	Yes	Yes
Of similar assets	Yes	No
For income tax purposes		
Of dissimilar assets	Yes	Yes
Of similar assets	No	No

CLARIFICATION NOTE: For assets to be similar, they must be used for similar purposes. A desktop computer, for example, is similar to a laptop computer. Dissimilar assets, such as a truck and a cement mixer, are not used for similar purposes.

PARENTHETICAL NOTE: Recognizing losses but not gains on similar assets follows the convention of conservatism.

KEY POINT: For exchanges of dissimilar assets, the gain or loss on exchange equals the trade-in allowance minus carrying value of the old asset.

For both financial accounting and income tax purposes, both gains and losses are recognized when a company exchanges dissimilar assets. Assets are dissimilar when they perform different functions or do not meet specific monetary and business criteria for being considered similar assets. For financial accounting purposes, most exchanges are considered exchanges of dissimilar assets. In rare cases, when exchanges meet the specific criteria for exchanges of similar assets, the gains are not recognized. In these cases, you could think of the trade-in as an extension of the life and usefulness of the original machine. Instead of recognizing a gain at the time of the exchange, the company records the new machine at the sum of the carrying value of the older machine plus any cash paid.[10]

For income tax purposes, similar assets are defined as those performing the same function. Neither gains nor losses on exchanges of these assets are recognized in computing a company's income tax liability. Thus, in practice, accountants face cases in which both gains and losses are recognized (exchanges of dissimilar assets), cases in which losses are recognized and gains are not (exchanges of similar assets for financial reporting purposes), and cases in which neither gains nor losses are recognized (exchanges of similar assets for income tax purposes). Since all these options are used in practice, they are all illustrated in the following sections.

LOSS ON THE EXCHANGE RECOGNIZED A loss is recognized for financial accounting purposes on all exchanges in which a material loss occurs. A loss occurs when the trade-in allowance is less than the carrying value of the old asset. To illustrate the recognition of a loss, let us assume that the firm in our earlier example exchanges the machine for a newer, more modern machine on the following terms:

List price of new machine	$12,000
Trade-in allowance for old machine	(1,000)
Cash payment required	$11,000

> **CLARIFICATION NOTE:** There is no relationship between carrying value and trade-in value. Carrying value is original cost minus accumulated depreciation to date, whereas trade-in value is fair market value on the date of the exchange.

In this case, the trade-in allowance ($1,000) is less than the carrying value ($1,850) of the old machine. The loss on the exchange is $850 ($1,850 − $1,000). This entry records the transaction under the assumption that the loss is to be recognized:

A = L + OE
+
+
−
−

Sept. 30	Machinery (new)	12,000	
	Accumulated Depreciation, Machinery	4,650	
	Loss on Exchange of Machinery	850	
	Machinery (old)		6,500
	Cash		11,000
	Exchange of machines		

LOSS ON THE EXCHANGE NOT RECOGNIZED In the previous example, in which a loss was recognized, the new asset was recorded at the purchase price of $12,000 and a loss of $850 was recorded. If the transaction involves similar assets and is to be recorded for income tax purposes, the loss should not be recognized. In this case, the cost basis of the new asset will reflect the effect of the unrecorded loss. The cost basis is computed by adding the cash payment to the carrying value of the old asset:

> **KEY POINT:** For income tax purposes, gains and losses on the exchange of similar assets are not recognized.

Carrying value of old machine	$ 1,850
Cash paid	11,000
Cost basis of new machine	$12,850

Note that no loss is recognized in the entry to record this transaction:

A = L + OE
+
+
−
−

Sept. 30	Machinery (new)	12,850	
	Accumulated Depreciation, Machinery	4,650	
	Machinery (old)		6,500
	Cash		11,000
	Exchange of machines		

Note that the new machinery is reported at the purchase price of $12,000 plus the unrecognized loss of $850. The nonrecognition of the loss on the exchange is, in effect, a postponement of the loss. Since depreciation of the new machine will be computed based on a cost of $12,850 instead of $12,000, the "unrecognized" loss results in more depreciation each year on the new machine than if the loss had been recognized.

> **KEY POINT:** For exchanges of assets, the cash payment on the exchange equals list price of the new asset minus trade-in allowance of the old asset.

GAIN ON THE EXCHANGE RECOGNIZED Gains on exchanges are recognized for accounting purposes when dissimilar assets are involved. To illustrate the recognition of a gain, we continue with our example, assuming the following terms and assuming the machines being exchanged serve different functions:

List price of new machine	$12,000
Trade-in allowance for old machine	(3,000)
Cash payment required	$ 9,000

Here, the trade-in allowance ($3,000) exceeds the carrying value ($1,850) of the old machine by $1,150. Thus, there is a gain on the exchange, assuming the price of the new machine has not been inflated to allow for an excessive trade-in value. In other words, a gain exists if the trade-in allowance represents the fair market value of the old machine. In that case, the transaction is recorded as follows:

A = L + OE
+
+
−

Sept. 30	Machinery (new)	12,000	
	Accumulated Depreciation, Machinery	4,650	
	Gain on Exchange of Machinery		1,150
	Machinery (old)		6,500
	Cash		9,000
	Exchange of machines		

■ **GAIN ON THE EXCHANGE NOT RECOGNIZED** When similar assets are exchanged, gains are not recognized for either accounting or income tax purposes. The cost basis of the new machine must reflect the effect of the unrecorded gain. This cost basis is computed by adding the cash payment to the carrying value of the old asset:

Carrying value of old machine	$ 1,850
Cash paid	9,000
Cost basis of new machine	$10,850

The entry to record the transaction is as follows:

A = L + OE
+
+
−

Sept. 30	Machinery (new)	10,850	
	Accumulated Depreciation, Machinery	4,650	
	Machinery (old)		6,500
	Cash		9,000
	Exchange of machines		

As with the nonrecognition of losses, the nonrecognition of the gain on an exchange is, in effect, a postponement of the gain. In this illustration, when the new machine is eventually discarded or sold, its cost basis will be $10,850 instead of its original price of $12,000. Since depreciation will be computed on the cost basis of $10,850, the "unrecognized" gain is reflected in lower depreciation each year on the new machine than if the gain had been recognized.

✓ Check out ACE for a Review Quiz at http://accounting.college.hmco.com/students.

ACCOUNTING FOR NATURAL RESOURCES

LO5 Identify the issues related to accounting for natural resources and compute depletion.

RELATED TEXT ASSIGNMENTS
Q: 19, 20
SE: 9
E: 10
FRA: 5

CLARIFICATION NOTE:
Natural resources are not intangible assets. Natural resources are correctly classified as components of property, plant, and equipment.

Natural resources are shown on the balance sheet as long-term assets with such descriptive titles as Timberlands, Oil and Gas Reserves, and Mineral Deposits. The distinguishing characteristic of these assets is that they are converted to inventory by cutting, pumping, mining, or other extraction methods. Natural resources are recorded at acquisition cost, which may include some costs of development. As the resource is extracted and converted to inventory, the asset account must be proportionally reduced. The carrying value of oil reserves on the balance sheet, for example, is reduced by a small amount for each barrel of oil pumped. As a result, the original cost of the oil reserves is gradually reduced, and depletion is recognized in the amount of the decrease.

DEPLETION

The term *depletion* is used to describe not only the exhaustion of a natural resource but also the proportional allocation of the cost of a natural resource to the units extracted. The costs are allocated in a way that closely resembles the production method used to calculate depreciation. When a natural resource is purchased or developed, there must be an estimate of the total units that will be available, such as barrels of oil, tons of coal, or board-feet of lumber. The depletion cost per unit is determined by dividing the cost of the natural resource (less residual value, if any) by the estimated number of units available. The amount of the depletion cost for each accounting period is then computed by multiplying the depletion cost per unit by the number of units extracted and sold. For example, for a mine having an estimated 1,500,000 tons of coal, a cost of $1,800,000, and an estimated residual value of $300,000, the depletion charge per ton of coal is $1:

$$\frac{\$1,800,000 - \$300,000}{1,500,000 \text{ tons}} = \$1 \text{ per ton}$$

Thus, if 115,000 tons of coal are mined and sold during the first year, the depletion charge for the year is $115,000. This charge is recorded as follows:

> **ENRICHMENT NOTE:**
> When determining the total units available for depletion, management uses only the total units that are economically feasible to extract. This follows the cost-benefit principle—that is, when the cost of extracting a mineral is greater than the expected profit from the sale of the mineral, the company stops extracting it.

A = L + OE
− −

Dec. 31	Depletion Expense, Coal Deposits	115,000	
	Accumulated Depletion, Coal Deposits		115,000
	To record depletion of coal mine: $1 per ton for 115,000 tons mined and sold		

On the balance sheet, data for the mine would be presented as follows:

Coal deposits	$1,800,000	
Less accumulated depletion	115,000	$1,685,000

Sometimes a natural resource is not sold in the year it is extracted. It is important to note that it would then be recorded as a depletion *expense* in the year it is *sold*. The part not sold is considered inventory.

> **KEY POINT:** The matching rule dictates that the extracted resource be treated as an asset until it is sold. At that point, the asset cost is converted into an expense.

DEPRECIATION OF CLOSELY RELATED PLANT ASSETS

The extraction of natural resources generally requires special on-site buildings and equipment (e.g., conveyors, drills, and pumps). If the useful life of those assets is longer than the estimated time it will take to deplete the resource, a special problem arises. Because such long-term assets are often abandoned and have no useful purpose once all the resources have been extracted, they should be depreciated on the same basis as the depletion. For example, if machinery with a useful life of ten years is installed on an oil field that is expected to be depleted in eight years, the machinery should be depreciated over the eight-year period, using the production method. That way, each year's depreciation will be proportional to the year's depletion. If one-sixth of the oil field's total reserves is pumped in one year, then the depreciation should be one-sixth of the machinery's cost minus the residual value. If the useful life of a long-term plant asset is less than the expected life of the resource, the shorter life should be used to compute depreciation. In such cases, or when an asset will not be abandoned once all reserves have been depleted, other depreciation methods, such as straight-line or declining-balance, are appropriate.

> **PARENTHETICAL NOTE:**
> A company may abandon equipment that is still in good working condition. It may cost the company more to dismantle the equipment and move it to another site than to abandon it.

DEVELOPMENT AND EXPLORATION COSTS IN THE OIL AND GAS INDUSTRY

The costs of exploring and developing oil and gas resources can be accounted for under one of two methods. Under the **successful efforts method**, the cost of successful exploration—for example, producing an oil well—is a cost of the resource. It should be recorded as an asset and depleted over the estimated life of the resource. The cost of an unsuccessful exploration—such as the cost of a dry well—is written off immediately as a loss. Because of these immediate write-offs, successful efforts accounting is considered the more conservative method and is used by most large oil companies. Exploration-minded independent oil companies, on the other hand, argue that the cost of dry wells is part of the overall cost of the systematic development of an oil field and is thus a part of the cost of producing wells. Under this **full-costing method**, all costs, including the cost of dry wells, are

> **STOP AND THINK!**
> When would annual depletion not equal depletion expense?
> *Annual depletion refers to units extracted, but depletion expense includes only units sold. So annual depletion does not equal depletion expense when units extracted do not equal units sold.* ∎

recorded as assets and depleted over the estimated life of the producing resources. This method tends to improve a company's earnings performance in its early years. Either method is permitted by the Financial Accounting Standards Board.[11]

 Check out ACE for a Review Quiz at http://accounting.college.hmco.com/students.

ACCOUNTING FOR INTANGIBLE ASSETS

LO6 Identify the issues related to accounting for intangible assets, including research and development costs and goodwill.

RELATED TEXT ASSIGNMENTS
Q: 21, 22, 23, 24, 25, 26
SE: 10
E: 11
P: 5
SD: 3, 5, 6
FRA: 2, 3, 5, 6

www.heinz.com

KEY POINT: Generally, intangible assets, including goodwill, are recorded only when purchased. An exception is the cost of internally developed computer software after a working prototype has been developed.

The purchase of an intangible asset is a special kind of capital expenditure. An intangible asset is both long term and nonphysical. Its value comes from the long-term rights or advantages it offers its owner. The most common examples—goodwill, trademarks, brand names, copyrights, patents, licenses or franchises, leaseholds, leasehold improvements, technology, noncompete covenants, and customer lists—are described in Table 1. Some current assets, such as accounts receivable and certain prepaid expenses, also have no physical substance, but they are not classified as intangible assets because they are short term.

Figure 7 shows the percentage of companies that report the various types of intangible assets. For some companies, intangible assets make up a substantial portion of total assets. As noted in the Decision Point at the beginning of the chapter, goodwill, trademarks, and other intangible assets of H. J. Heinz Company amount to almost $3.5 billion, or 35 percent of total assets. How these assets are accounted for will have a substantial effect on Heinz's performance.

Intangible assets are accounted for at acquisition cost—that is, the amount that was paid for them. Some intangible assets, such as goodwill and trademarks, may be acquired at little or no cost. Even though they may have great value and be needed for profitable operations, they should not appear on the balance sheet unless they have been purchased from another party at a price established in the marketplace.

The accounting issues connected with intangible assets, other than goodwill, are the same as those connected with other long-lived assets. The Accounting Principles Board, in its *Opinion No. 17*, lists them as (1) determining an initial carrying amount, (2) accounting for that amount after acquisition under normal business conditions—that is through periodic write-off or amortization—in a manner similar to depreciation, and (3) accounting for that amount if the value declines substantially and permanently.[12] In addition to these three problems, an intangible

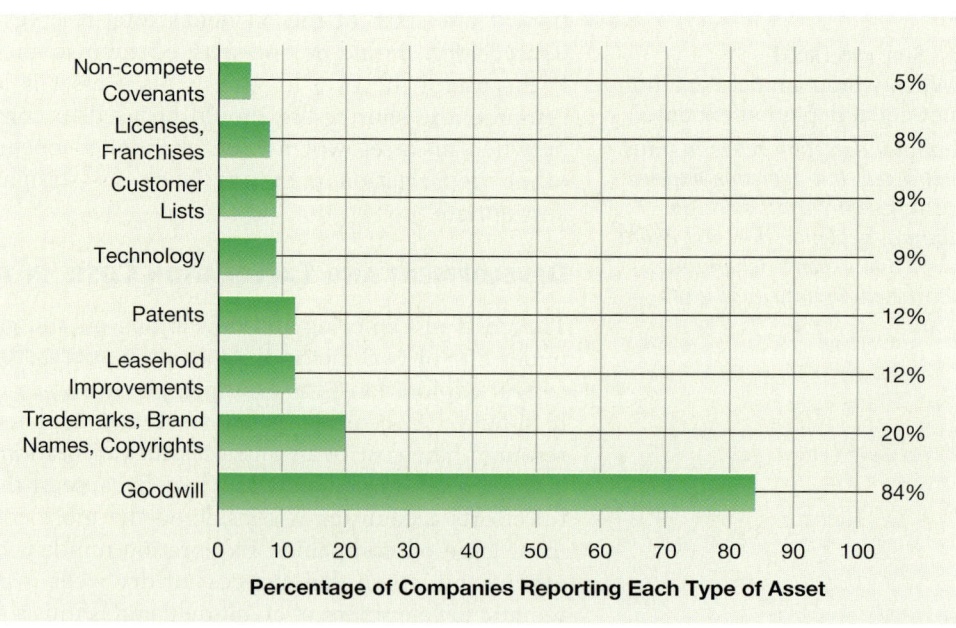

FIGURE 7
Intangible Assets Separately Reported by 600 Large Companies

Source: Data from *Accounting Trends and Techniques*, 2002

TABLE 1. Accounting for Intangible Assets

Type	Description	Accounting Treatment
Goodwill	The excess of the amount paid for the purchase of a business over the fair market value of the net assets.	Debit Goodwill for the acquisition cost, and perform impairment review annually.
Trademark, brand name	A registered symbol or name that can be used only by its owner to identify a product or service.	Debit Trademark or Brand Name for the acquisition cost, and amortize it over a reasonable life.
Copyright	An exclusive right granted by the federal government to reproduce and sell literary, musical, and other artistic materials and computer programs for a period of the author's life plus 70 years.	Record at acquisition cost, and amortize over the useful life, which is often much shorter than the legal life. For example, the cost of paperback rights to a popular novel would typically be amortized over a useful life of two to four years.
Patent	An exclusive right granted by the federal government for a period of 20 years to make a particular product or use a specific process. A design may be granted a patent for 14 years.	The cost of successfully defending a patent in a patent infringement suit is added to the acquisition cost of the patent. Amortize over the useful life, which may be less than the legal life.
License, franchise	A right to an exclusive territory or market, or the right to use a formula, technique, process, or design.	Debit License or Franchise for the acquisition cost, and amortize it over a reasonable life.
Leasehold	A right to occupy land or buildings under a long-term rental contract. For example, Company A, which owns the right to use but does not want to use a retail location, sells or subleases to Company B the right to use it for ten years in return for one or more rental payments. Company B has purchased a leasehold.	Debit Leasehold for the amount of the rental payment, and amortize it over the remaining life of the lease. Payments to the lessor during the life of the lease should be debited to Lease Expense.
Leasehold improvements	Improvements to leased property that become the property of the lessor (the owner of the property) at the end of the lease.	Debit Leasehold Improvements for the cost of improvements, and amortize the cost of the improvements over the remaining life of the lease.
Technology	Capitalized costs associated with software developed for sale, lease, or internal use.	Record the amount of capitalizable software production costs, and amortize over the estimated economic life of the product.
Noncompete covenant	A contract limiting the rights of others to compete in a specific industry or line of business for a specified period.	Record at the acquisition cost, and amortize over the contract period.
Customer list	A list of customers or subscribers.	Debit Customer Lists for amount paid, and amortize over the expected life.

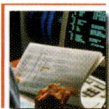

FOCUS ON BUSINESS PRACTICE

Take a Closer Look at Subscriber Lists!
One of the most valuable intangible assets some companies have is a list of subscribers. For example, the Newark Morning Ledger Co., a newspaper chain, purchased a chain of Michigan newspapers whose list of 460,000 subscribers was valued at $68 million. The U.S. Supreme Court upheld the company's right to amortize the value of the subscriber list because the company showed that the list had a limited useful life. The Internal Revenue Service had argued that the list had an indefinite life and therefore could not provide tax deductions through amortization. This ruling will benefit other types of businesses that purchase everything from bank deposits to pharmacy prescription files.[13]

CLARIFICATION NOTE:
Useful life refers to how long an intangible asset will be contributing income to a firm.

asset, because it has no physical substance, may sometimes be impossible to identify. For these reasons, its value and its useful life may be quite hard to estimate.

The Accounting Principles Board has decided that a company should record the costs of intangible assets acquired from others as assets. However, the company should record as expenses the costs of developing intangible assets. Also, intangible assets that have a determinable useful life, such as patents, copyrights, and leaseholds, should be written off through periodic amortization over that useful life in much the same way that plant assets are depreciated. Even though some intangible assets, such as brand names and trademarks, have no measurable limit on their lives, they should still be amortized over a reasonable length of time.

To illustrate these procedures, assume that Soda Bottling Company purchases a patent on a unique bottle cap for $18,000. The entry to record the patent would include $18,000 in the asset account Patents. Note that if Soda Bottling Company had developed the bottle cap internally instead of purchasing it from others, the costs of developing the cap, such as salaries of researchers, supplies used in testing, and costs of equipment, would have been expensed as incurred.

Assume now that Soda's management determines that although the patent for the bottle cap will last for 20 years, the product using the cap will be sold only for the next six years. The entry to record the annual amortization expense would be for $3,000 ($18,000 ÷ 6 years). Note that the Patents account is reduced directly by the amount of the amortization expense. This is in contrast to the treatment of other long-term asset accounts, for which depreciation or depletion is accumulated in separate contra accounts.

If the patent becomes worthless before it is fully amortized, the remaining carrying value is written off as a loss by removing it from the Patents account.

RESEARCH AND DEVELOPMENT COSTS

Most successful companies carry out research and development (R&D) activities, often in a separate department. R&D activities include development of new products, testing of existing and proposed products, and pure research. The costs of these activities are substantial for many companies. In a recent year, General Motors spent $6.6 billion on R&D, or about 4 percent of its revenues.[14] R&D costs can be even greater in high-tech fields like pharmaceuticals. For example, Abbott Laboratories recently spent $1.4 billion, or almost 10 percent of revenues, on R&D, and Roche Group spent almost $4 billion, or 14 percent of revenues.[15]

www.gm.com

www.abbott.com

www.roche.com

In the past, some companies recorded as assets R&D costs that could be directly traced to the development of specific patents, formulas, or other rights. Other costs,

FOCUS ON INTERNATIONAL BUSINESS

Lack of Comparability Is a Real Problem!
Worldwide variability in accounting practice causes problems for those who want to compare the financial statements of companies from different countries. For example, the method of accounting for R&D costs differs, depending on the country in which a company files its financial report. In Germany, Mexico, and the United States, a company must expense its R&D costs, whereas in France, Australia, and Japan, a company may expense R&D or capitalize it (record it as an asset) if it meets certain criteria. Companies complying with the European Directives (European laws affecting financial reporting) have a choice of expensing or capitalizing R&D costs, but companies complying with International Accounting Standards (IAS) must expense research costs and capitalize development costs that meet certain conditions.[16]

such as those for testing and pure research, were treated as expenses of the accounting period and deducted from income. Since then, the Financial Accounting Standards Board has stated that all R&D costs should be treated as revenue expenditures and charged to expense in the period in which they are incurred.[17] The board argues that it is too hard to trace specific costs to specific profitable developments. Also, the costs of research and development are continuous and necessary for the success of a business and so should be treated as current expenses. To support this conclusion, the board cites studies showing that 30 to 90 percent of all new products fail and that 75 percent of new-product expenses go to unsuccessful products. Thus, their costs do not represent future benefits.

COMPUTER SOFTWARE COSTS

The costs that companies incur in developing computer software for sale or lease or for their own internal use are considered research and development costs until the product has proved technologically feasible. Thus, costs incurred before that point should be charged to expense when incurred. A product is deemed technologically feasible when a detailed working program has been designed. Once that occurs, all software production costs are recorded as assets, such as Technology, and are amortized over the estimated economic life of the product using the straight-line method. If at any time the company cannot expect to realize from a software product the amount of its unamortized costs on the balance sheet, the asset should be written down to the amount expected to be realized.[18]

LEASEHOLD IMPROVEMENTS

As noted in Table 1, improvements to leased property that become the property of the lessor (the owner of the property) at the end of the lease are called leasehold improvements. Such improvements are common for both small and large businesses. A study of large companies showed that 19 percent list leasehold improvements separately; the percentage is likely to be much higher for small businesses, since they generally operate in leased premises.[19] The improvement costs are amortized over the remaining term of the lease or the useful life of the improvement, whichever is shorter. Leasehold improvements are often classified as tangible assets in the property, plant, and equipment section of the balance sheet but are included in the intangible asset section because the improvements revert to the lessor at the end of the lease and are therefore more of a right than a tangible asset.

GOODWILL

● **STOP AND THINK!**
Why would a company spend millions of dollars on goodwill?
The company must be paying for anticipated superior earnings and believes it will more than recoup the goodwill it purchased. ■

The term *goodwill* means different things to different people. In most cases, the term is taken to mean the good reputation of a company. From an accounting standpoint, goodwill exists when a purchaser pays more for a business than the fair market value of the net assets if purchased individually. Because the purchaser has paid more than the fair market value of the physical assets, there must be intangible assets. If the company being purchased does not have patents, copyrights, trademarks, or other identifiable intangible assets of value, the excess payment is assumed to be for goodwill. Goodwill exists because most businesses are worth more as going concerns than as collections of assets. Goodwill reflects all the factors that allow a company to earn a higher-than-market rate of return on its assets, including customer satisfaction, good management, manufacturing efficiency, the advantages of holding a monopoly, good locations, and good employee relations. The payment above and beyond the fair market value of the tangible assets and other specific intangible assets is properly recorded in the Goodwill account.

The FASB has stated that purchased goodwill is an asset to be reported as a separate line item on the balance sheet and is subject to an annual impairment review. The impairment review requires a company to determine the reporting-unit level

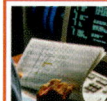

FOCUS ON BUSINESS PRACTICE

Wake up, Goodwill Is Growing!

As Figure 7 shows, 84 percent of 600 large companies separately report goodwill as an asset. Because much of the growth of these companies has come through purchasing other companies, goodwill as a percentage of total assets has also grown. For some, the amount of goodwill is material:[20]

	Goodwill (in billions)	Percentage of Total Assets
General Mills <www.generalmills.com>	$8,473	51.2
Sara Lee Corporation <www.saralee.com>	$3,314	24.1
Tribune Company <www.tribune.com>	$5,419	38.5

KEY POINT: Goodwill equals purchase price minus adjusted net asset value.

on which goodwill is to be tested and the specific methodology to calculate the fair value of the reporting unit. If the fair value of goodwill is less than its carrying value on the balance sheet, then goodwill is considered impaired. Impairment results in reducing goodwill to its fair value and reporting the impairment charge on the income statement. A company can perform the fair value measurement for each reporting unit at any time as long as the measurement date is consistent from year to year.[21]

Goodwill should not be recorded unless it is paid for in connection with the purchase of a whole business. The amount to be recorded as goodwill can be determined by writing the identifiable net assets up to their fair market values at the time of purchase and subtracting the total from the purchase price. For example, assume that the owners of Company A agree to sell the company for $11,400,000. If the net assets (total assets − total liabilities) are fairly valued at $10,000,000, then the amount of the goodwill is $1,400,000 ($11,400,000 − $10,000,000). If the fair market value of the net assets is later determined to be more or less than $10,000,000, an entry is made in the accounting records to adjust the assets to the fair market value. The goodwill would then represent the difference between the adjusted net assets and the purchase price of $11,400,000.

 Check out ACE for a Review Quiz at http://accounting.college.hmco.com/students.

SPECIAL PROBLEMS OF DEPRECIATING PLANT ASSETS

SO7 Apply depreciation methods to problems of partial years, revised rates, groups of similar items, special types of capital expenditures, and cost recovery.

RELATED TEXT ASSIGNMENTS
Q: 27, 28, 29, 30, 31, 32
E: 12, 13, 14, 15
P: 3, 8
FRA: 1

The illustrations used so far in this chapter have been simplified to explain the concepts and methods of depreciation. In actual business practice, there is often a need to (1) calculate depreciation for partial years, (2) revise depreciation rates based on new estimates of useful life or residual value, (3) group like items when calculating depreciation, (4) account for special types of capital expenditures, and (5) use the accelerated cost recovery method for tax purposes. The next sections discuss these five cases.

DEPRECIATION FOR PARTIAL YEARS

So far, most illustrations of depreciation methods have assumed that plant assets were purchased at the beginning or end of an accounting period. Usually, however, businesses buy assets when they are needed and sell or discard them when they are no longer useful or needed. The time of year is normally not a factor in the decision. Consequently, it is often necessary to calculate depreciation for partial years.

For example, assume that a piece of equipment is purchased for $3,600 and that it has an estimated useful life of six years and an estimated residual value of $600. Assume also that it is purchased on September 5 and that the yearly accounting period ends on December 31. Depreciation must be recorded for four months, September through December, or four-twelfths of the year. This factor is applied to the calculated depreciation for the entire year. The four months' depreciation under the straight-line method is calculated as follows:

$$\frac{\$3,600 - \$600}{6 \text{ years}} \times 4/12 = \$167$$

For the other depreciation methods, most companies compute the first year's depreciation and then multiply by the partial year factor. For example, if the company

LO1   **Amortization:** The periodic allocation of the cost of an intangible asset to the periods it benefits.

LO1   **Asset impairment:** Loss of revenue-generating potential of a long-lived asset before the end of its useful life; the difference between an asset's carrying value and its fair value, as measured by the present value of the expected cash flows.

SO7   **Betterment:** An improvement that does not add to the physical layout of a plant asset.

LO6   **Brand name:** A registered name that can be used only by its owner to identify a product or service.

LO2   **Capital expenditure:** An expenditure for the purchase or expansion of a long-term asset, recorded in an asset account.

LO1   **Carrying value:** The unexpired part of the cost of an asset, not its market value. Also called *book value*.

LO6   **Copyright:** An exclusive right granted by the federal government to reproduce and sell literary, musical, and other artistic materials and computer programs for a period of the author's life plus 70 years.

LO6   **Customer list:** A list of customers or subscribers.

LO3   **Declining-balance method:** An accelerated method of depreciation in which depreciation is computed by applying a fixed rate to the carrying value (the declining balance) of a tangible long-lived asset.

LO1   **Depletion:** The exhaustion of a natural resource through mining, cutting, pumping, or other extraction, and the way in which the cost is allocated.

LO3   **Depreciable cost:** The cost of an asset less its residual value.

LO1   **Depreciation:** The periodic allocation of the cost of a tangible long-lived asset (other than land and natural resources) over its estimated useful life.

LO3   **Double-declining-balance method:** An accelerated method of depreciation in which a fixed rate equal to twice the straight-line percentage is applied to the carrying value (the declining balance) of a tangible long-lived asset.

LO3   **Estimated useful life:** The total number of service units expected from a long-term asset.

LO2   **Expenditure:** A payment or an obligation to make future payment for an asset or a service.

SO7   **Extraordinary repairs:** Repairs that affect the estimated residual value or estimated useful life of an asset thereby increasing its carrying value.

LO6   **Franchise:** The right or license to an exclusive territory or market.

LO5   **Full-costing method:** A method of accounting for the costs of exploring and developing oil and gas resources in which all costs are recorded as assets and depleted over the estimated life of the producing resources.

LO6   **Goodwill:** The excess of the cost of a group of assets (usually a business) over the fair market value of the net assets if purchased individually.

SO7   **Group depreciation:** The grouping of similar items to calculate depreciation.

LO1   **Intangible assets:** Long-term assets with no physical substance whose value is based on rights or advantages accruing to the owner.

LO6   **Leasehold:** A right to occupy land or buildings under a long-term rental contract.

LO6   **Leasehold improvements:** Improvements to leased property that become the property of the lessor at the end of the lease.

LO6   **License:** The right to use a formula, technique, process, or design.

LO1   **Long-term assets:** Assets that have a useful life of more than one year, are acquired for use in the operation of a business, and are not intended for resale. Less commonly called *fixed assets*.

SO7 **Modified Accelerated Cost Recovery System (MACRS):** A mandatory system of depreciation for income tax purposes, enacted by Congress in 1986, that requires a cost recovery allowance to be computed (1) on the unadjusted cost of property being recovered, and (2) over a period of years prescribed by the law for all property of similar types.

LO1 **Natural resources:** Long-term assets purchased for the economic value that can be taken from the land and used up.

LO6 **Noncompete covenant:** A contract limiting the rights of others to compete in a specific industry or line of business for a specified period.

LO3 **Obsolescence:** The process of becoming out of date, which is a factor in the limited useful life of tangible assets.

SO7 **Ordinary repairs:** Repairs necessary to maintain an asset in good operating condition, which are recorded as current period expenses.

LO6 **Patent:** An exclusive right granted by the federal government for a period of 20 years to make a particular product or use a specific process or design.

LO3 **Physical deterioration:** Limitations on the useful life of a depreciable asset resulting from use and from exposure to the elements.

LO3 **Production method:** A method of depreciation that assumes depreciation is solely the result of use and that allocates depreciation based on the units of output or use during each period of an asset's useful life.

LO3 **Residual value:** The estimated net scrap, salvage, or trade-in value of a tangible asset at the estimated date of disposal. Also called *salvage value* or *disposal value*.

LO2 **Revenue expenditure:** An expenditure related to repair, maintenance, and operation of a long-term asset, recorded by a debit to an expense account.

LO3 **Straight-line method:** A method of depreciation that assumes depreciation depends only on the passage of time and that allocates an equal amount of depreciation to each accounting period in an asset's useful life.

LO5 **Successful efforts method:** A method of accounting for the costs of exploring and developing oil and gas resources in which successful exploration is recorded as an asset and depleted over the estimated life of the resource and all unsuccessful efforts are immediately written off as losses.

LO1 **Tangible assets:** Long-term assets that have physical substance.

LO6 **Technology:** Capitalized costs associated with software developed for sale, lease, or internal use and amortized over the estimated economic life of the software.

LO6 **Trademark:** A registered symbol or brand name that can be used only by its owner to identify a product or service.

REVIEW PROBLEM

Comparison of Depreciation Methods

LO3 Norton Construction Company purchased a cement mixer on January 2, 20x4, for $14,500. The mixer was expected to have a useful life of five years and a residual value of $1,000. The company engineers estimated that the mixer would have a useful life of 7,500 hours. It was used 1,500 hours in 20x4, 2,625 hours in 20x5, 2,250 hours in 20x6, 750 hours in 20x7, and 375 hours in 20x8. Norton Construction Company's year end is December 31.

REQUIRED ▶
1. Compute the depreciation expense and carrying value for 20x4 to 20x8, using the following methods: (a) straight-line, (b) production, and (c) double-declining-balance.
2. Prepare the adjusting entry to record the depreciation for 20x4 that you calculated in 1(a).

3. Show the balance sheet presentation for the cement mixer after the entry in **2** on December 31, 20x4.
4. What conclusions can you draw from the patterns of yearly depreciation?

Answer to Review Problem

1. Depreciation computed:

Depreciation Method	Year	Computation	Depreciation	Carrying Value
a. Straight-line	20x4	$13,500 × 1/5	$2,700	$11,800
	20x5	13,500 × 1/5	2,700	9,100
	20x6	13,500 × 1/5	2,700	6,400
	20x7	13,500 × 1/5	2,700	3,700
	20x8	13,500 × 1/5	2,700	1,000
b. Production	20x4	$13,500 × $\frac{1,500}{7,500}$	$2,700	$11,800
	20x5	13,500 × $\frac{2,625}{7,500}$	4,725	7,075
	20x6	13,500 × $\frac{2,250}{7,500}$	4,050	3,025
	20x7	13,500 × $\frac{750}{7,500}$	1,350	1,675
	20x8	13,500 × $\frac{375}{7,500}$	675	1,000
c. Double-declining-balance	20x4	$14,500 × .4	$5,800	$ 8,700
	20x5	8,700 × .4	3,480	5,220
	20x6	5,220 × .4	2,088	3,132
	20x7	3,132 × .4	1,253*	1,879
	20x8		879*†	1,000

*Rounded.
†Remaining depreciation to reduce carrying value to residual value ($1,879 − $1,000 = $879).

2. Adjusting entry prepared—straight-line method:

20x4
Dec. 31 Depreciation Expense, Cement Mixer   2,700
             Accumulated Depreciation, Cement Mixer   2,700
         To record depreciation expense,
         straight-line method

3. Balance sheet presentation for 20x4 shown:

Property, plant, and equipment
   Cement mixer $14,500
   Less accumulated depreciation   2,700
                                         $11,800

4. Conclusions drawn from depreciation patterns: The pattern of depreciation for the straight-line method differs significantly from that for the double-declining-balance method. In the earlier years, the amount of depreciation under the double-declining-balance method is significantly greater than the amount under the straight-line method. In the later years, the opposite is true. The carrying value under the straight-line method is greater than that under the double-declining-balance method at the end of all years except the fifth year. Depreciation under the production method differs from that under the other methods in that it follows no regular pattern. It varies with the amount of use. Consequently, depreciation is greatest in 20x5 and 20x6, which are the years of greatest use. Use declined significantly in the last two years.

Chapter Assignments

BUILDING YOUR KNOWLEDGE FOUNDATION

QUESTIONS

1. What are the characteristics of long-term assets?
2. Which of the following items would be classified as plant assets on the balance sheet? (a) A truck held for sale by a truck dealer, (b) an office building that was once the company headquarters but is now to be sold, (c) a typewriter used by a secretary of the company, (d) a machine that is used in manufacturing operations but is now fully depreciated, (e) pollution-control equipment that does not reduce the cost or improve the efficiency of a factory, (f) a parking lot for company employees.
3. Why is land different from other long-term assets?
4. What do accountants mean by the term *depreciation*, and what is its relationship to depletion and amortization?
5. What is asset impairment, and how does it affect the valuation of long-term assets?
6. How do cash flows relate to the decision to acquire a long-term asset, and how does the useful life of an asset relate to the means of financing it?
7. Why is it useful to think of a plant asset as a bundle of services?
8. What is the distinction between revenue expenditures and capital expenditures, why is it important, and what in general is included in the cost of a long-term asset?
9. Which of the following expenditures stemming from the purchase of a computer system would be charged to the asset account? (a) The purchase price of the equipment, (b) interest on the debt incurred to purchase the equipment, (c) freight charges, (d) installation charges, (e) the cost of special communications outlets at the computer site, (f) the cost of repairing a door that was damaged during installation, (g) the cost of adjustments to the system during the first month of operation.
10. Bert's Grocery obtained bids on the construction of a receiving dock at the back of its store. The lowest bid was $22,000. The company decided to build the dock itself, however, and was able to do so for $20,000, which it borrowed. The activity was recorded as a debit to Buildings for $22,000 and credits to Notes Payable for $20,000 and Gain on Construction for $2,000. Do you agree with the entry?
11. A firm buys technical equipment that is expected to last twelve years. Why might the equipment have to be depreciated over a shorter period of time?
12. A company purchased a building five years ago. The market value of the building is now greater than it was when the building was purchased. Explain why the company should continue depreciating the building.
13. Evaluate the following statement: "A parking lot should not be depreciated because adequate repairs will make it last forever."
14. Is the purpose of depreciation to determine the value of equipment? Explain your answer.
15. Contrast the assumption underlying the straight-line depreciation method with the assumption underlying the production depreciation method.
16. What is the principal argument supporting an accelerated depreciation method?
17. If a plant asset is sold during the year, why should depreciation be computed for the partial year prior to the date of the sale?
18. If a plant asset is discarded before the end of its useful life, how is the amount of loss measured?
19. Blackfeet Mining Company computes the depletion rate of ore to be $2 per ton. During 20xx the company mined 400,000 tons of ore and sold 370,000 tons. What is the total depletion expense for the year?
20. Under what circumstances can a mining company depreciate its plant assets over a period of time that is less than their useful lives?

21. Because accounts receivable have no physical substance, can they be classified as intangible assets?
22. Under what circumstances can a company have intangible assets that do not appear on the balance sheet?
23. How does the Financial Accounting Standards Board recommend that research and development costs be treated?
24. After spending three years developing a new software program for designing office buildings, Drew Mason Architects recently completed the detailed working program. How does accounting for the costs of software development differ before and after the completion of a successful working program?
25. How is accounting for software development costs similar to and different from accounting for research and development costs?
26. Under what conditions should goodwill be recorded? Should it remain in the records permanently once it is recorded?
27. What basic procedure should be followed in revising a depreciation rate?
28. On what basis can depreciation be taken on a group of assets rather than on individual items?
29. What will be the effect on future years' income of charging an addition to a building to repair expense?
30. In what ways do an addition, a betterment, and an extraordinary repair differ?
31. How does an extraordinary repair differ from an ordinary repair? What is the accounting treatment for each?
32. What is the difference between depreciation for accounting purposes and the Modified Accelerated Cost Recovery System for income tax purposes?

SHORT EXERCISES

LO1 Management Issues

SE 1. Indicate whether each of the following actions is primarily related to (a) acquisition of long-term assets, (b) financing of long-term assets, or (c) choosing methods and estimates related to long-term assets:

1. Deciding between common stock and long-term notes for the raising of funds
2. Relating the acquisition cost of a long-term asset to the cash flows generated by the asset
3. Determining how long an asset will benefit the company
4. Deciding to use cash flows from operations to purchase long-term assets
5. Determining how much an asset will sell for when it is no longer useful to the company

LO2 Determining Cost of Long-Term Assets

SE 2. Standard Auto purchased a neighboring lot for a new building and parking lot. Indicate whether each of the following expenditures is properly charged to (a) Land, (b) Land Improvements, or (c) Buildings.

1. Paving costs
2. Architects' fee for building design
3. Cost of clearing the property
4. Cost of the property
5. Building construction costs
6. Lights around the property
7. Building permit
8. Interest on the construction loan

LO2 Group Purchase

SE 3. Arney Company purchased property with a warehouse and parking lot for $750,000. An appraiser valued the components of the property if purchased separately as follows:

Land	$200,000
Land improvements	100,000
Building	500,000
Total	$800,000

Determine the cost to be assigned to each component.

LO3 Straight-Line Method

SE 4. Waybury Fitness Center purchased a new step machine for $5,500. The apparatus is expected to last four years and have a residual value of $500. What will be the depreciation expense for each year under the straight-line method?

SE 5.
LO3 Production Method

Assuming that the step machine in **SE 4** has an estimated useful life of 8,000 hours and was used for 2,400 hours in year 1, for 2,000 hours in year 2, for 2,200 hours in year 3, and for 1,400 hours in year 4, how much would depreciation expense be in each year?

SE 6.
LO3 Double-Declining-Balance Method

Assuming that the step machine in **SE 4** is depreciated using the double-declining-balance method, how much would depreciation expense be in each year?

SE 7.
LO4 Disposal of Plant Assets: No Trade-In

West Coast Printing had a piece of equipment that cost $8,100 and on which $4,500 of accumulated depreciation had been recorded. The equipment was disposed of on January 4, the first day of business of the current year.

1. Calculate the carrying value of the equipment.
2. Calculate the gain or loss on the disposal under each of the following assumptions:
   a. It was discarded as having no value.
   b. It was sold for $1,500 cash.
   c. It was sold for $4,000 cash.

SE 8.
LO4 Disposal of Plant Assets: Trade-In

For each of the following assumptions and referring to the equipment mentioned in **SE 7**, compute the gain (loss) on the exchange, the cash payment required, and the amount at which the new equipment would be recorded:

1. The equipment was traded in on dissimilar equipment that had a list price of $12,000. A $3,800 trade-in was allowed, and the balance was paid in cash. Gains and losses are to be recognized.
2. The equipment was traded in on dissimilar equipment that had a list price of $12,000. A $1,750 trade-in was allowed, and the balance was paid in cash. Gains and losses are to be recognized.
3. Same as **2**, except the items are similar and gains and losses are not to be recognized.

SE 9.
LO5 Natural Resources

Ledgemore Company purchased land containing an estimated 4,000,000 tons of ore for $8,000,000. The land will be worth $1,200,000 without the ore after eight years of active mining. Although the equipment needed for the mining will have a useful life of 20 years, it is not expected to be usable and will have no value after the mining on this site is complete. Compute the depletion charge per ton and the amount of depletion expense for the first year of operation, assuming that 600,000 tons of ore were mined and sold. Also, compute the first-year depreciation on the mining equipment using the production method, assuming a cost of $9,600,000 with no residual value.

SE 10.
LO6 Intangible Assets: Computer Software

Osaka created a new software application for PCs. Its costs during research and development were $500,000, and its costs after the working program was developed were $350,000. Although its copyright may be amortized over 40 years, management believes that the product will be viable for only five years. How should the costs be accounted for? At what value will the software appear on the balance sheet after one year?

EXERCISES

E 1.
LO1 Management Issues

Indicate whether each of the following actions is primarily related to (a) acquisition of long-term assets, (b) financing of long-term assets, or (c) choosing methods and estimates related to long-term assets:

1. Deciding to use the production method of depreciation
2. Allocating costs on a group purchase
3. Determining the total units a machine will produce
4. Deciding to borrow funds to purchase equipment
5. Estimating the savings a new machine will yield and comparing the amount to cost
6. Deciding whether to rent or buy a piece of equipment

E 2.
LO1 Purchase Decision—Present Value Analysis

Management is considering the purchase of a new machine for a cost of $12,000. It is estimated that the machine will generate positive net cash flows of $3,000 per year for five years and will have a disposal price at the end of that time of $1,000. Assuming an interest rate of 9 percent, determine if management should purchase the machine. Use Tables 3 and 4 in the appendix on future value and present value tables to determine the net present value of the new machine.

E 3.
LO2 Determining Cost of Long-Term Assets

Denver Manufacturing purchased land next to its factory to be used as a parking lot. Expenditures were as follows: purchase price, $150,000; broker's fees, $12,000; title search and other fees, $1,100; demolition of a shack on the property, $4,000; general grading of property, $2,100; paving parking lots, $20,000; lighting for parking lots,

$16,000; and signs for parking lots, $3,200. Determine the amounts that should be debited to the Land account and the Land Improvements account.

LO2 Group Purchase

E 4. Jodie Williams purchased a car wash for $480,000. If purchased separately, the land would have cost $120,000, the building $270,000, and the equipment $210,000. Determine the amount that should be recorded in the new business's records for land, building, and equipment.

LO2 Cost of Long-Term Asset
LO3 and Depreciation

E 5. Dewees Brown purchased a used tractor for $35,000. Before the tractor could be used, it required new tires, which cost $2,200, and an overhaul, which cost $2,800. Its first tank of fuel cost $150. The tractor is expected to last six years and have a residual value of $4,000. Determine the cost and depreciable cost of the tractor and calculate the first year's depreciation under the straight-line method.

LO3 Depreciation Methods

E 6. North End Oil Company purchased a drilling truck for $90,000. North End expected the truck to last five years or 200,000 miles, with an estimated residual value of $15,000 at the end of that time. During 20x5, the truck was driven 48,000 miles. North End's year end is December 31. Compute the depreciation for 20x5 under each of the following methods, assuming that the truck was purchased on January 13, 20x4: (1) straight-line, (2) production, and (3) double-declining-balance. Using the amount computed in **3**, prepare the entry in journal form to record depreciation expense for the second year and show how the Drilling Truck account would appear on the 20x5 balance sheet.

LO3 Double-Declining-Balance Method

E 7. Aburri Burglar Alarm Systems Company purchased a word processor for $2,240. It has an estimated useful life of four years and an estimated residual value of $240. Compute the depreciation charge for each of the four years using the double-declining-balance method.

LO4 Disposal of Plant Assets

E 8. A piece of equipment that cost $32,400 and on which $18,000 of accumulated depreciation had been recorded was disposed of on January 2, the first day of business of the current year. For each of the following assumptions, compute the gain (loss) on the disposal or exchange. In addition, for assumptions **4, 5** and **6**, compute the cash payment required and the amount at which the new equipment would be recorded.

1. It was discarded as having no value.
2. It was sold for $6,000 cash.
3. It was sold for $18,000 cash.
4. It was traded in on dissimilar equipment having a list price of $48,000. A $16,200 trade-in was allowed, and the balance was paid in cash. Gains and losses are to be recognized.
5. It was traded in on dissimilar equipment having a list price of $48,000. A $7,500 trade-in was allowed, and the balance was paid in cash. Gains and losses are to be recognized.
6. Same as **5,** except the items are similar and gains and losses are not to be recognized.

LO4 Disposal of Plant Assets

E 9. Sunshire Company purchased a computer on January 2, 20x4, at a cost of $5,000. It is expected to have a useful life of five years and a residual value of $500. Assuming that the computer is disposed of on July 1, 20x7, record the partial year's depreciation for 20x7 using the straight-line method, and record the disposal under each of the following assumptions:

1. The computer is discarded.
2. The computer is sold for $800.
3. The computer is sold for $2,200.
4. The computer is exchanged for a new computer with a list price of $9,000. A $1,200 trade-in is allowed on the cash purchase. The accounting approach to gains and losses is followed.
5. Same as **4,** except a $2,400 trade-in is allowed.
6. Same as **4,** except the income tax approach is followed.
7. Same as **5,** except the income tax approach is followed.
8. Same as **4,** except the computer is exchanged for dissimilar office equipment.
9. Same as **5,** except the computer is exchanged for dissimilar office equipment.

LO3 Natural Resource Depletion
LO5 and Depreciation of Related Plant Assets

E 10. Seropoulos Mining Company purchased land containing an estimated 10 million tons of ore for a cost of $8,800,000. The land without the ore is estimated to be worth $1,600,000. The company expects that all the usable ore can be mined in 10 years. Buildings costing $1,000,000 with an estimated useful life of 30 years were erected on the site. Equipment costing $960,000 with an estimated useful life of 10 years was installed. Because of the remote location, neither the buildings nor the equipment has an estimated residual value. During its first year of operation, the company mined and sold 800,000 tons of ore.

1. Compute the depletion charge per ton.
2. Compute the depletion expense that Seropoulos Mining should record for the year.
3. Determine the depreciation expense for the year for the buildings, making it proportional to the depletion.
4. Determine the depreciation expense for the year for the equipment under two alternatives: (a) making the expense proportional to the depletion and (b) using the straight-line method.

E 11.
LO6 Amortization of Copyrights and Trademarks

1. Maddox Publishing Company purchased the copyright to a basic computer textbook for $20,000. The usual life of a textbook is about four years. However, the copyright will remain in effect for another 50 years. Calculate the annual amortization of the copyright.
2. Weyland Company purchased a trademark from a well-known supermarket for $160,000. The management of the company argued that because the trademark's value would last forever and might even increase, no amortization should be charged. Calculate the minimum amount of annual amortization that should be charged, according to guidelines of the appropriate Accounting Principles Board opinion.

E 12.
SO7 Depreciation Methods and Partial Years

Using the data given for North End Oil Company in **E 6,** compute the depreciation for calendar year 20x4 under each of the following methods, assuming that the truck was purchased on July 1, 20x4, and was driven 20,000 miles during 20x4: (1) straight-line, (2) production, and (3) double-declining-balance.

E 13.
SO7 Revision of Depreciation Rates

Mt. Sinai Hospital purchased a special x-ray machine. The machine, which cost $311,560, was expected to last ten years, with an estimated residual value of $31,560. After two years of operation (and depreciation charges using the straight-line method), it became evident that the x-ray machine would last a total of only seven years. The estimated residual value, however, would remain the same. Given this information, determine the new depreciation charge for the third year on the basis of the revised estimated useful life.

E 14.
LO2 Special Types of Capital
SO7 Expenditures

Tell whether each of the following transactions related to an office building is a revenue expenditure (RE) or a capital expenditure (CE). In addition, indicate whether each transaction is an ordinary repair (OR), an extraordinary repair (ER), an addition (A), a betterment (B), or none of these (N).

1. The hallways and ceilings in the building are repainted at a cost of $8,300.
2. The hallways, which have tile floors, are carpeted at a cost of $28,000.
3. A new wing is added to the building at a cost of $175,000.
4. Furniture is purchased for the entrance to the building at a cost of $16,500.
5. The air-conditioning system is overhauled at a cost of $28,500. The overhaul extends the useful life of the air-conditioning system by ten years.
6. A cleaning firm is paid $200 per week to clean the newly installed carpets.

E 15.
SO7 Extraordinary Repairs

Marino Manufacturing has an incinerator that originally cost $187,200 and now has accumulated depreciation of $132,800. The incinerator has completed its 15th year of service in an estimated useful life of 20 years. At the beginning of the 16th year, the company spent $42,800 repairing and modernizing the incinerator to comply with pollution-control standards. Therefore, the incinerator is now expected to last 10 more years instead of 5. It will not, however, have more capacity than it did in the past or a residual value at the end of its useful life.

1. Prepare the entry in journal form to record the cost of the repair.
2. Compute the carrying value of the incinerator after the entry.
3. Prepare the entry to record straight-line depreciation for the current year.

PROBLEMS

P 1.
LO2 Determining Cost of Assets

Constanza Computers constructed a new training center in 20x4. You have been hired to manage the training center. A review of the accounting records shows the following expenditures debited to an asset account called Training Center:

Attorney's fee, land acquisition		$ 17,450
Cost of land		299,000
Architect's fee, building design		51,000
Building		510,000
Parking lot and sidewalk		67,800
Electrical wiring, building		82,000
Landscaping		27,500
Cost of surveying land		4,600
Training equipment, tables, and chairs		68,200
Installation of training equipment		34,000
Cost of grading the land		7,000
Cost of changes in building to soundproof rooms		29,600
Total account balance		$1,198,150

During the center's construction, an employee of Constanza Computers worked full time overseeing the project. He spent two months on the purchase and preparation of the site, six months on the construction, one month on land improvements, and one month on equipment installation and training room furniture purchase and setup. His salary of $32,000 during this ten-month period was charged to Administrative Expense. The training center was placed in operation on November 1.

REQUIRED ▶ Prepare a schedule with the following four column (Account) headings: Land, Land Improvements, Building, and Equipment. Place each of the above expenditures in the appropriate column. Total the columns.

P 2.
LO3 Comparison of Depreciation Methods

Harrington Manufacturing Company purchased a robot for $720,000 at the beginning of year 1. The robot has an estimated useful life of four years and an estimated residual value of $60,000. The robot, which should last 20,000 hours, was operated 6,000 hours in year 1; 8,000 hours in year 2; 4,000 hours in year 3; and 2,000 hours in year 4.

REQUIRED ▶
1. Compute the annual depreciation and carrying value for the robot for each year assuming the following depreciation methods: (a) straight-line, (b) production, and (c) double-declining-balance.
2. Prepare the adjusting entry in journal form that would be made each year to record the depreciation calculated under the straight-line method.
3. Show the balance sheet presentation for the robot after the adjusting entry in year 2 using the straight-line method.
4. What conclusions can you draw from the patterns of yearly depreciation and carrying value in **1**?

P 3.
LO3 Depreciation Methods and
SO7 Partial Years

Ellen Leblanc purchased a laundry company. In addition to the washing machines, Leblanc installed a tanning machine and a refreshment center. Because each type of asset performs a different function, Leblanc has decided to use different depreciation methods. Data on each type of asset are summarized in the table below. The tanning machine was operated for 2,100 hours in 20x5, 3,000 hours in 20x6, and 2,400 hours in 20x7.

Asset	Date Purchased	Cost	Installation Cost	Residual Value	Estimated Life	Depreciation Method
Washing machines	3/5/x5	$15,000	$2,000	$2,600	4 years	Straight-line
Tanning machine	4/1/x5	34,000	3,000	1,000	7,500 hours	Production
Refreshment center	10/1/x5	3,400	600	600	10 years	Double-declining-balance

REQUIRED ▶ Assume the fiscal year ends December 31. Compute the depreciation expense for each item and the total depreciation expense for 20x5, 20x6, and 20x7. Round your answers to the nearest dollar and present them in a table with the headings shown below.

			Depreciation		
Asset	Year	Computations	20x5	20x6	20x7

P 4.
LO4 Recording Disposals

Masterson Construction Company purchased a road grader for $29,000. The machine is expected to have a useful life of five years and a residual value of $2,000.

REQUIRED ▶ Prepare entries in journal form to record the disposal of the road grader at the end of the second year, after the depreciation is recorded, assuming that the straight-line method is used and making the following separate assumptions:

a. The road grader is sold for $20,000 cash.
b. The road grader is sold for $16,000 cash.
c. The road grader is traded in on a dissimilar piece of machinery costing $33,000, a trade-in allowance of $20,000 is given, the balance is paid in cash, and gains or losses are recognized.
d. The road grader is traded in on a dissimilar piece of machinery costing $33,000, a trade-in allowance of $16,000 is given, the balance is paid in cash, and gains or losses are recognized.
e. Same as **c,** except it is traded for a similar road grader and Masterson Construction Company follows accounting rules for the recognition of gains or losses.
f. Same as **d,** except it is traded for a similar road grader and Masterson Construction Company follows accounting rules for the recognition of gains or losses.
g. Same as **c,** except it is traded for a similar road grader and gains or losses are not recognized for income tax purposes.
h. Same as **d,** except it is traded for a similar road grader and gains or losses are not recognized for income tax purposes.

P 5.

LO6 Amortization of License, Leasehold, and Leasehold Improvements

Part A: On January 2, Baby Doll, Inc., purchased the exclusive license to make dolls based on the characters in a popular new television series called "Sky Pirates." The license cost $2,100,000, and there was no termination date on the rights. Immediately after signing the contract, the company sued a rival firm that claimed it had already received the exclusive license to the series characters. Baby Doll successfully defended its rights at a cost of $360,000.

During the first year and the next, Baby Doll marketed toys based on the series. Because a successful television series lasts about five years, the company felt it could market the toys for three more years. However, before the third year of the series could get under way, a controversy arose between its two stars and its producer. As a result, the stars refused to work the third year, and the show was canceled, rendering the exclusive rights worthless.

REQUIRED ▶ Prepare entries in journal form to record the following: (a) purchase of the exclusive license; (b) successful defense of the license; (c) amortization expense, if any, for the first year; and (d) write-off of the license as worthless.

Part B: Valerie Spare purchased a six-year sublease on a building from the estate of the former tenant. It was a good location for her business, and the annual rent of $3,600, which had been established ten years before, was low. The cost of the sublease was $9,450.

To use the building, Spare had to make certain alterations. She moved some panels at a cost of $1,700 and installed others for $6,100. She also added carpet, lighting fixtures, and a sign at costs of $2,900, $3,100, and $1,200, respectively. All items except the carpet would last for at least twelve years. The expected life of the carpet was six years. None of the improvements would have a residual value.

REQUIRED ▶ Prepare entries in journal form to record the following: (a) the payment for the sublease; (b) the payments for the alterations, panels, carpet, lighting fixtures, and sign; (c) the lease payment for the first year; (d) the amortization expense, if any, associated with the sublease; and (e) the amortization expense, if any, associated with the alterations, panels, carpet, lighting fixtures, and sign.

Alternate Problems

P 6.

LO2 Determining Cost of Assets

Patroni Company began operation on January 2 of 20x5. At the end of the year, the company's auditor discovered that all expenditures involving long-term assets had been debited to an account called Fixed Assets. An analysis of the Fixed Assets account, which had a year-end balance of $5,289,944, disclosed that it contained the following items:

Cost of land	$ 633,200
Surveying costs	8,200
Transfer of title and other fees required by the county	1,840
Broker's fees for land	42,288
Attorney's fees associated with land acquisition	14,096
Cost of removing timber from land	100,800
Cost of grading land	8,400
Cost of digging building foundation	69,200
Architect's fee for building and land improvements (80 percent building)	129,600
Cost of building construction	1,420,000
Cost of sidewalks	22,800
Cost of parking lots	108,800
Cost of lighting for grounds	160,600
Cost of landscaping	23,600
Cost of machinery	1,978,000
Shipping cost on machinery	110,600
Cost of installing machinery	352,400
Cost of testing machinery	44,200
Cost of changes in building to comply with safety regulations pertaining to machinery	25,080
Cost of repairing building that was damaged in the installation of machinery	17,800
Cost of medical bill for injury received by employee while installing machinery	4,800
Cost of water damage to building during heavy rains prior to opening the plant for operation	13,640
Account balance	$5,289,944

Patroni Company sold the timber it cleared from the land to a firewood dealer for $10,000. This amount was credited to Miscellaneous Income.

During the construction period, two of Patroni's supervisors devoted full time to the construction project. They earn annual salaries of $96,000 and $84,000, respectively. They spent two months on the purchase and preparation of the land, six months on the construction of the building (approximately one-sixth of which was devoted to improvements on the grounds), and one month on machinery installation. The plant began operation on October 1, and the supervisors returned to their regular duties. Their salaries were debited to Factory Salaries Expense.

REQUIRED ▶ Prepare a schedule with the following column headings: Land, Land Improvements, Buildings, Machinery, and Expense. Place each of the above expenditures in the appropriate column. Negative amounts should be shown in parentheses. Total the columns.

P 7.

LO3 Comparison of Depreciation Methods

Mount Royal Construction Company purchased a new crane for $360,500 at the beginning of year 1. The crane has an estimated residual value of $35,000 and an estimated useful life of six years. The crane is expected to last 10,000 hours. It was used 1,800 hours in year 1; 2,000 in year 2; 2,500 in year 3; 1,500 in year 4; 1,200 in year 5; and 1,000 in year 6.

REQUIRED ▶
1. Compute the annual depreciation and carrying value for the new crane for each of the six years (round to nearest dollar where necessary) under each of the following methods: (a) straight-line, (b) production, and (c) double-declining-balance.
2. Prepare the adjusting entry that would be made each year to record the depreciation calculated under the straight-line method.
3. Show the balance sheet presentation for the crane after the adjusting entry in year 2 using the straight-line method.
4. What conclusions can you draw from the patterns of yearly depreciation and carrying value in 1?

P 8.

LO3 Depreciation Methods and SO7 Partial Years

Sao Company operates three types of equipment. Because of the equipment's varied functions, company accounting policy requires the application of three different depreciation methods. Data on this equipment are summarized in the table that follows.

Equipment	Date Purchased	Cost	Installation Cost	Estimated Residual Value	Estimated Life	Depreciation Method
1	1/12/x4	$171,000	$ 9,000	$18,000	10 years	Double-declining-balance
2	7/9/x4	191,100	15,900	21,000	10 years	Straight-line
3	10/2/x4	290,700	8,100	33,600	20,000 hours	Production

Equipment 3 was used for 2,000 hours in 20x4; for 4,200 hours in 20x5; and for 3,200 hours in 20x6.

REQUIRED ▶ Assuming that the fiscal year ends December 31, compute the depreciation expense on each type of equipment and the total depreciation expense for 20x4, 20x5, and 20x6 by filling in a table with the headings shown below.

		Depreciation		
Equipment No.	Computations	20x4	20x5	20x6

SKILLS DEVELOPMENT CASES

Conceptual Analysis

SD 1.

LO1 **Nature of Depreciation and**
LO3 **Amortization and Estimated Useful Lives**

A change in the estimated useful lives of long-term assets can have a significant effect. For instance, General Motors Corp. <www.gm.com> states,

> ... the Corporation revised the estimated service lives of its plants and equipment and special tools retroactive to January 1, 1987. These revisions, which were based on 1987 studies of actual useful lives and periods of use, recognized current estimates of service lives of the assets and had the effect of reducing 1987 depreciation and amortization charges by $1,236.6 million or $2.53 per share of $1⅔ par value common stock.[23]

General Motors' income before income taxes for the year was $2,005.4 million. Discuss the purpose of depreciation and amortization. What is estimated service life, and on what basis did General Motors change the estimates of the service lives of plants and equipment and special tools? What was the effect of this change on the corporation's income before income taxes? Is it likely that the company is in better condition economically as a result of the change? Does the company have more cash at the end of the year as a result? (Ignore income tax effects.)

SD 2.

LO3 **Change of Depreciation Method**

Several years ago, Polaroid Corporation <www.polaroid.com>, a manufacturer of instant cameras and film, changed from an accelerated depreciation method for financial reporting purposes to the straight-line method for newly acquired assets. As noted in its annual report:

> The company changed its method of depreciation for financial reporting for the cost of buildings, machinery, and equipment ... from a primarily accelerated method to the straight-line method.[24]

What reasons can you give for Polaroid's choosing to switch to a straight-line method of depreciation? Discuss which of the two depreciation methods is more conservative. Polaroid's deteriorating financial position led it to declare bankruptcy in 2001. Could this accounting change have been a signal that the company was in trouble?

SD 3.

LO6 **Brands**

Hilton Hotels Corporation <www.hilton.com> and Marriott International <www.marriott.com> provide hospitality services. Hilton Hotels' well-known brands include Hilton, Doubletree, Hampton Inn, Embassy Suites, Red Lion Hotels and Inns, and Homewood Suites. Marriott also owns or manages properties with recognizable brand names, such as Marriott Hotels, Resorts and Suites; Ritz-Carlton; Renaissance Hotels; Residence Inn; Courtyard; and Fairfield Inn.

On its balance sheet, Hilton Hotels Corporation includes brands (net of amortization) of $1,048 million, or 11.3 percent of total assets. Marriott International, however, does not list brands among its intangible assets.[25] What principles of accounting for intangibles would cause Hilton to record brands as an asset while Marriott does not? How will these differences in accounting for brands generally affect the net income and return on assets of these two competitors?

Ethical Dilemma

LO2 Ethics and Allocation of Acquisition Costs

SD 4. Signal Company has purchased land and a warehouse for $18,000,000. The warehouse is expected to last 20 years and to have a salvage value equal to 10 percent of its cost. The chief financial officer (CFO) and the controller are discussing the allocation of the purchase price. The CFO believes that the largest amount possible should be assigned to the land because this action will improve reported net income in the future. Depreciation expense will be lower because land is not depreciated. He suggests allocating one-third, or $6,000,000, of the cost to the land. This results in depreciation expense each year of $540,000 [($12,000,000 − $1,200,000) ÷ 20 years]. The controller disagrees, arguing that the smallest amount possible, say one-fifth of the purchase price, should be allocated to the land, thereby saving income taxes, since the depreciation, which is tax deductible, will be greater. Under this plan, annual depreciation would be $648,000 [($14,400,000 − $1,440,000) ÷ 20 years]. The annual tax savings at a 30 percent tax rate is $32,400 [($648,000 − $540,000) × .30]. How will this decision affect the company's cash flows? Ethically, how should the purchase cost be allocated? Who will be affected by the decision?

 Group Activity: Divide the class into groups and have each develop the position of the CFO or controller for presentation and debate.

LO2 Ethics of Aggressive
LO6 Accounting Policies

SD 5. Is it ethical to choose aggressive accounting practices to advance a company's business? During the 1990s, America Online (AOL) <www.aol.com>, the largest Internet service provider in the United States, was one of the hottest stocks on Wall Street. After its initial stock offering in 1992, its stock price shot up several thousand percent. Accounting is very important to a company like AOL because earnings enable it to sell shares of stock and raise more cash to fund its growth. In its early years, AOL was one of the most aggressive companies in its choice of accounting principles. AOL's strategy called for building the largest customer base in the industry. Consequently, it spent many millions of dollars each year marketing its services to new customers. Such costs are usually recognized as operating expenses in the year in which they are incurred. However, AOL treated these costs as long-term assets, called "deferred subscriber acquisition costs," and expensed them over several years, because it said the average customer was going to stay with the company for three years or more. The company also recorded research and development costs as "product development costs" and amortized them over five years. Both of these practices are justifiable theoretically, but they are not common practice. If the standard, more conservative practice had been followed, the company would have had a net loss in every year it has been in business.[26] This result would have greatly limited AOL's ability to raise money and grow.

Explain in your own words AOL management's rationale for adopting the accounting policies that it did. What could go wrong with such a plan? How would you evaluate the ethics of AOL's actions? Who benefits from the actions? Who is harmed by these actions?

Research Activity

LO1
LO2 Individual Field Trip
LO3
LO6

SD 6. Visit a fast-food restaurant. Make a list of all the intangible and property, plant, and equipment assets you can identify. For each one, identify one management issue that relates to that asset. In addition, give examples of at least one capital expenditure and one revenue expenditure that is applicable to property, plant, and equipment assets. Bring your list to class for discussion.

Decision-Making Practice

SD 7.
LO1 Purchase Decision and Time Value of Money

Morningside Machine Works has obtained a subcontract to manufacture parts for a new military aircraft. The parts are to be delivered over the next five years, and the company will be paid as the parts are delivered.

To make the parts, Morningside Machine Works will have to purchase new equipment. Two types are available. Type A is conventional equipment that can be put into service immediately; Type B requires one year to be put into service but is more efficient than Type A. Type A requires an immediate cash investment of $1,000,000 and will produce enough parts to provide net cash receipts of $340,000 each year for the five years. Type B may be purchased by signing a two-year non-interest-bearing note for $1,346,000. It is projected that Type B will produce net cash receipts of zero in year 1, $500,000 in year 2, $600,000 in year 3, $600,000 in year 4, and $200,000 in year 5. Neither type of equipment can be used on other contracts or will have any useful life remaining at the end of the contract. Morningside currently pays an interest rate of 16 percent to borrow money.

1. What is the present value of the investment required for each type of equipment? (Use Table 3 in the appendix on future value and present value tables.)
2. Compute the net present value of each type of equipment based on your answer in 1 and the present value of the net cash receipts projected to be received. (Use Tables 3 and 4 in the appendix on future value and present value tables.)
3. Write a memorandum to the board of directors that recommends the option that appears to be best for Morningside. Explain your reasoning and include 1 and 2 as attachments.

FINANCIAL REPORTING AND ANALYSIS CASES

Interpreting Financial Reports

FRA 1.
LO3 Effects of Change in
SO7 Accounting Method

Depreciation expense is a significant cost for companies in which plant assets are a high proportion of assets. The amount of depreciation expense in a given year is affected by estimates of useful life and choice of depreciation method. In 2004, Century Steelworks Company, a major integrated steel producer, changed the estimated useful lives for its major production assets. It also changed the method of depreciation for other steel-making assets from straight-line to the production method.

The company's 2004 annual report states, "A recent study conducted by management shows that actual years-in-service figures for our major production equipment and machinery are, in most cases, higher than the estimated useful lives assigned to these assets. We have recast the depreciable lives of such assets so that equipment previously assigned a useful life of 8 to 26 years now has an extended depreciable life of 10 to 32 years."

The report goes on to explain that the new production method of depreciation "recognizes that depreciation of production equipment and machinery correlates directly to both physical wear and tear and the passage of time. The production method of depreciation, which we have now initiated, more closely allocates the cost of these assets to the periods in which products are manufactured."

The report summarizes the effects of both actions on the year 2004 as shown in the following table:

Incremental Increase in Net Income	In Millions	Per Share
Lengthened lives	$11.0	$ .80
Production method		
Current year	7.3	.53
Prior years	2.8	.20
Total increase	$21.1	$1.53

During 2004, Century Steelworks reported a net loss of $83,156,500 ($6.03 per share). Depreciation expense for 2004 was $87,707,200.

In explaining the changes the company has made, the controller of Century Steelworks was quoted in an article in *Business Journal* as follows: "There is no reason for Century Steelworks to continue to depreciate our assets more conservatively than our competitors do." But the article also quotes an industry analyst who argues that by slowing its method of depreciation, Century Steelworks could be viewed as reporting lower-quality earnings.

1. Explain the accounting treatment when there is a change in the estimated lives of depreciable assets. What circumstances must exist for the production method to produce the effect it did in relation to the straight-line method? What would Century Steelworks' net income or loss have been if the changes had not been made? What might have motivated management to make the changes?
2. What does the controller of Century Steelworks mean when he says that Century had been depreciating "more conservatively than our competitors do"? Why might the changes at Century Steelworks indicate, as the analyst asserts, "lower-quality earnings"? What risks might Century face as a result of its decision to use the production method of depreciation?

International Company

FRA 2.

LO6 Accounting for Goodwill: U.S. and IAS rules

For most pharmaceutical companies, intangible assets, such as goodwill, patents, licenses, and trademarks, make up a significant percentage of total assets. For example, for Roche Group <www.roche.com>, intangible assets constitute 22.8 percent of total assets, and for Baxter International <www.baxter.com>, 14.2 percent.[27] For both companies, goodwill represents the largest portion of intangible assets.

Before 2000, Roche Group, a Swiss company, charged any goodwill resulting from acquisitions against equity immediately. However, in 2000, in accordance with a change in International Accounting Standards (IAS), Roche began recording goodwill as an asset and amortizing it over a period of up to 20 years. This IAS change brought U.S. and IAS companies into closer agreement on accounting for goodwill. At that time, companies like Baxter International, which comply with U.S. GAAP, recorded goodwill resulting from acquisitions as an asset and amortized it over periods not to exceed 40 years. However, as of 2002, U.S. companies, while continuing to record purchased goodwill as an asset, were no longer required to amortize any existing or new goodwill. Both IAS and U.S. GAAP require companies to apply the impairment test annually to ensure that goodwill is not overvalued.

What impact did accounting for goodwill under IAS and U.S. GAAP have on cash flows and net income in the year 2002? In your opinion, which accounting treatment for goodwill (U.S. or IAS) is better? State your reasons.

Toys "R" Us Annual Report

FRA 3.

LO1 Long-Term Assets
LO2
LO3
LO6

1. Refer to the balance sheets and to the note on property and equipment in the notes to the financial statements in the Toys "R" Us <www.tru.com> annual report to answer the following questions: What percentage of total assets in the most recent year was property and equipment? What is the most significant type of property and equipment? Does Toys "R" Us have a significant investment in land? What other kinds of things are included in the property and equipment category? (Ignore leased property under capital leases for now.)
2. Refer to the summary of significant accounting policies and to the note on property and equipment in the Toys "R" Us annual report. What method of depreciation does Toys "R" Us use? How long does management estimate its buildings to last as compared with furniture and equipment? What does this say about the company's need to remodel its stores?
3. Refer again to the note on property and equipment. What are leasehold improvements? How significant are leasehold improvements, and what are their effects on the earnings of the company?

Comparison Case: Toys "R" Us and Walgreen Co.

FRA 4. Refer to the annual report of Toys "R" Us <www.tru.com> and to the financial statements of Walgreens <www.walgreens.com> in the Supplement to Chapter 1 to answer the following:

LO1 **Long-Term Assets and Cash Flows**

1. Prepare a table that shows the net amount each company spent on property and equipment (from the statement of cash flows), the total property and equipment (from the balance sheet), and the percentage of the first figure to the second for each of the past two years. Which company grew its property and equipment at a faster rate?
2. Which other note to the financial statements is helpful in evaluating the cash flows related to property and equipment? (**Hint:** In what way do Toys "R" Us and Walgreens gain use of property and equipment other than by purchase?) How important is this method of obtaining use of assets to these companies? Which company makes greater use of the method?

Fingraph® Financial Analyst™

FRA 5. Choose any two companies from the list of Fingraph companies on the Needles Accounting Resource Center Web Site at http://accounting.college.hmco.com/students. The industry should be one in which long-term assets are likely to be important, such as the airline, manufacturing, consumer products, consumer food and beverage, or computer industry. Access the Microsoft Excel spreadsheets for the companies you selected. For parts 1, 3, and 4, click on the URL at the top of each company's spreadsheet for a link to the company's web site and annual report.

LO1 **Comparison of Long-Term Assets**
LO3
LO5
LO6

1. In the annual reports of the companies you have selected, read the long-term asset section of the balance sheet and any reference to long-term assets in the summary of significant accounting policies or notes to the financial statements. What are the most important long-term assets for each company? What depreciation methods do the companies use? Do any long-term assets appear to be characteristic of the industry? What intangible assets do the companies have, and how important are they?
2. Using the Fingraph CD-ROM software, display and print in tabular and graphic form the Balance Sheet Analysis page. Prepare a table that compares the gross and net amounts for property, plant, and equipment.
3. Locate the statements of cash flows in the two companies' annual reports. Prepare another table that compares depreciation (and amortization) expense from the operating activities section with the net purchases of property, plant, and equipment (net capital expenditures) from the investing activities section for two years. Does depreciation (and amortization) expense exceed replacement of long-term assets? Are the companies expanding or reducing their property, plant, and equipment?
4. Find and read references to long-term assets and capital expenditures in management's discussion and analysis in each annual report.
5. Write a one-page executive summary that highlights the most important long-term assets and the accounting policies for long-term assets, and that compares the investing activities of the two companies, including reference to management's assessment. Include the Fingraph page and your tables with your report.

Internet Case

FRA 6. Public corporations are required not only to communicate with their stockholders by means of an annual report but also to submit an annual report to the Securities and Exchange Commission (SEC). The annual report to the SEC is called a Form 10-K and is a source of the latest information about a company. Through the Needles Accounting Resource Center Web Site at http://accounting.college.hmco.com/students, access the SEC's EDGAR files to locate either H. J. Heinz Company's <www.heinz.com> or Ford Motor Company's <www.ford.com> Form 10-K. Find the financial statements and the notes to the financial statements. Scan through the notes to the financial statements and prepare a list of information related to long-term assets, including intangibles. For

LO3 **SEC and Forms 10-K**
LO4
LO6

instance, what depreciation methods does the company use? What are the useful lives of its property, plant, and equipment? What intangible assets does the company have? Does the company have goodwill? How much does the company spend on research and development? In the statement of cash flows, how much did the company spend on new property, plant, and equipment (capital expenditures)? Summarize your results and be prepared to discuss them as well as your experience in using the SEC's EDGAR database.

Group Activity: Divide students into groups according to the company researched and have each group compile a comprehensive list of information about its company.

11

Chapter 11 covers the management issues related to sources of long-term financing, with an emphasis on bond liabilities.

Long-Term Liabilities

LEARNING OBJECTIVES

LO1 Identify the management issues related to issuing long-term debt.
LO2 Identify and contrast the major characteristics of bonds.
LO3 Record the issuance of bonds at face value and at a discount or premium.
LO4 Use present values to determine the value of bonds.
LO5 Amortize bond discounts and bond premiums using the straight-line and effective interest methods.
LO6 Record bonds issued between interest dates and year-end adjustments.

SUPPLEMENTAL OBJECTIVES

SO7 Account for the retirement of bonds and the conversion of bonds into stock.
SO8 Explain the basic features of mortgages payable, long-term leases, and pensions and other postretirement benefits as long-term liabilities.

DECISION POINT
A USER'S FOCUS

AT&T Corporation <www.att.com> During 2002, AT&T Corporation reduced its debt financing. How much to borrow and how much debt should be financed long term are two questions management must consider. What is the impact of AT&T's lower debt level on its capital structure and its interest-paying ability?

Decisions related to the issuance of long-term debt are among the most important that management has to make because, next to the success or failure of a company's operations, how the company finances its operations is the most important factor in the company's long-term viability. Long-term liabilities, or long-term debt, are obligations of a business that are due to be paid after one year or beyond the operating cycle, whichever is longer. Even after reducing its debt, AT&T's capital structure includes a large amount of long-term debt, as shown by the figures for 2002 in the Financial Highlights.[1] Total liabilities are greater than stockholders' equity, and the debt to equity ratio is 3.5 ($42,960 ÷ $12,312). What factors might have influenced AT&T's management to incur a large amount of debt?

In the past, AT&T was the nation's largest long-distance telephone company. The investments in power lines, transformers, computers, and other types of property, plant, and equipment required for this business are enormous. These are mostly long-term assets, and the most sensible way to finance them is through long-term financing. When the business was protected from competition, management could reasonably predict sufficient earnings and cash flow to

Now that AT&T is facing competition for its markets, why must management reassess the company's long-term liabilities?

meet the debt and interest obligations. Now that AT&T is facing open competition for its markets, the company must reassess not only the kind of business it is but also the amount and kinds of debt it carries. The amount and type of debt a company incurs depends on many factors, including the nature of the business, its competitive environment, the state of the financial markets, and the predictability of its earnings.

Financial Highlights: Capital Structure
(In millions)

Liabilities	
Total current liabilities	$12,024
Long-term debt	$18,812
Long-term benefit-related liabilities	4,001
Deferred income taxes	4,739
Other long-term liabilities and deferred credits	3,384
Total long-term liabilities	$30,936
Total liabilities	$42,960
Stockholders' equity	12,312
Total liabilities and stockholders' equity	$55,272

Management Issues Related to Issuing Long-Term Debt

LO1 Identify the management issues related to issuing long-term debt.

RELATED TEXT ASSIGNMENTS
Q: 1
SE: 1
E: 1
SD: 6
FRA: 1, 3, 4, 5, 6

Profitable operations and short-term credit seldom provide sufficient cash for a growing business. Growth often requires investment in long-term assets and in research and development and other activities that will produce income in future years. To finance such assets and activities, the company requires funds that will be available for longer periods. Two key sources of long-term funds are the issuance of capital stock and the issuance of long-term debt in the form of bonds, notes, mortgages, and leases. The management issues related to issuing long-term debt are (1) whether to take on long-term debt, (2) how much long-term debt to carry, (3) what types of long-term debt to incur, and (4) how to handle debt repayment.

The Decision to Issue Long-Term Debt

A key decision for management is whether to rely solely on stockholders' equity—capital stock issued and retained earnings—for long-term funds for the business or to rely partially on long-term debt for those funds. Since long-term debts represent financial commitments that must be paid at maturity and interest or other payments that must be paid periodically, common stock would seem to have two advantages over long-term debt: it does not have to be paid back, and dividends on common stock are usually paid only if the company earns sufficient income. Long-term debt does, however, have the following advantages over common stock:

KEY POINT: Although carrying a lot of debt is risky, there are some advantages to issuing bonds instead of stock. First, bond interest expense is tax-deductible for the issuing corporation, whereas dividends paid on stock are not. Second, issuing bonds is a way to raise capital without diluting ownership of the corporation. The challenge is to determine the optimal balance between stocks and bonds so that the advantages of each can be enjoyed.

1. **Stockholder control.** Since bondholders and other creditors do not have voting rights, common stockholders do not relinquish any control of the company.

2. **Tax effects.** The interest on debt is tax-deductible, whereas dividends on common stock are not. For example, if a corporation pays $100,000 in interest and the income tax rate is 30 percent, the net cost to the corporation is $70,000 because it will save $30,000 on its income taxes. To pay $100,000 in dividends, the company would have to earn $142,857 before taxes ($100,000 ÷ .70).

3. **Financial leverage.** If a corporation is able to earn more on its assets than it pays in interest on debt, the excess will increase its earnings for stockholders. This concept is called **financial leverage** or *trading on the equity*. For example, if a company is able to earn 12 percent, or $120,000, on a $1,000,000 investment financed by long-term 10 percent notes, it will earn $20,000 before taxes ($120,000 − $100,000). Financial leverage makes heavily debt-financed investments in office buildings and shopping centers attractive to investors, who hope to earn a return that exceeds the cost of the interest on the underlying debt. The debt to equity ratio is considered an overall measure of the financial leverage of a company.

www.continental.com

Despite these advantages, using debt financing is not always in a company's best interest. First, since cash is required to make periodic interest payments and to pay back the principal amount of the debt at the maturity date, a company whose plans for earnings do not pan out, whose operations are subject to ups and downs, or whose cash flow is weak can be in danger. If the company fails to meet its obligations, it can be forced into bankruptcy by creditors. In other words, a company may become overcommitted. Consider, for example, the heavily debt-financed airline industry. Both TWA and Continental Airlines filed for bankruptcy protection because they could not make payments on their long-term debt and other liabilities. (While in bankruptcy both firms restructured their debt and interest payments, but only Continental survived.) And Swiss Air and Midway Airlines shut down all operations because of insufficient cash to pay creditors and employees. Second, financial leverage can work against a company if the earnings from its investments do not exceed its interest payments. This happened during the savings and loan crisis when long-term debt was used to finance the construction of office buildings that subsequently could not be leased for enough money to cover interest payments.

FOCUS ON INTERNATIONAL BUSINESS

Pushed to the Brink of Failure

Due to recent declines in passenger revenue, a record number of airlines are shutting down operations, operating under bankruptcy protection, seeking purchase by another airline, or relying on government loan guarantees for their short-term survival. Air Afrique, Canada 3000, Swiss Air, and Midway Airlines have been among those hardest hit.[2] Subsequently, TWA and US Airways joined the group as the largest airline bankruptcies. In a weak economy, the large amount of debt financing that airlines use to fund operations and purchases of aircraft adds to their troubles. With lower cash flows, the airlines find it harder to make payments of interest and principal on debt, thereby increasing the risk of default.

HOW MUCH DEBT TO CARRY

The amount of total debt that companies carry varies widely. Many companies carry less than 100 percent of their stockholders' equity. However, as can be seen from Figure 1, the average debt to equity for these selected industries exceeds 100 percent of stockholders' equity. The range is from about 105 percent to 200 percent of equity. Clearly the use of debt financing varies widely across industries. Firms that own a high percentage of long-term assets would be looking to long-term financing as an option. We saw previously that AT&T has a debt to equity ratio of 3.5 times. Financial leverage makes it advantageous to have long-term debt so long as the company earns a satisfactory income and is able to make interest payments and repay the debt at maturity. Since failure to make timely interest payments could force a company into bankruptcy, it is important for companies to assess the risk of default or nonpayment of interest or principal.

www.att.com

A common measure of how much risk a company is undertaking with its debt is the **interest coverage ratio**. It measures the degree of protection a company has from default on interest payments. For AT&T, which in 2002 had income before taxes and special items of $2,836 million and interest expense of $1,448 million, this ratio is computed as follows:

$$\text{Interest Coverage Ratio} = \frac{\text{Income Before Taxes} + \text{Interest Expense}}{\text{Interest Expense}}$$

$$= \frac{\$2,836,000,000 + \$1,448,000,000}{\$1,448,000,000}$$

$$= 3.0 \text{ times}$$

This ratio shows that the interest expense for AT&T was covered 3.0 times in 2002. AT&T's interest coverage ratio was much higher in 2001 (6.1 times). Its income

FIGURE 1
Average Debt to Equity for Selected Industries

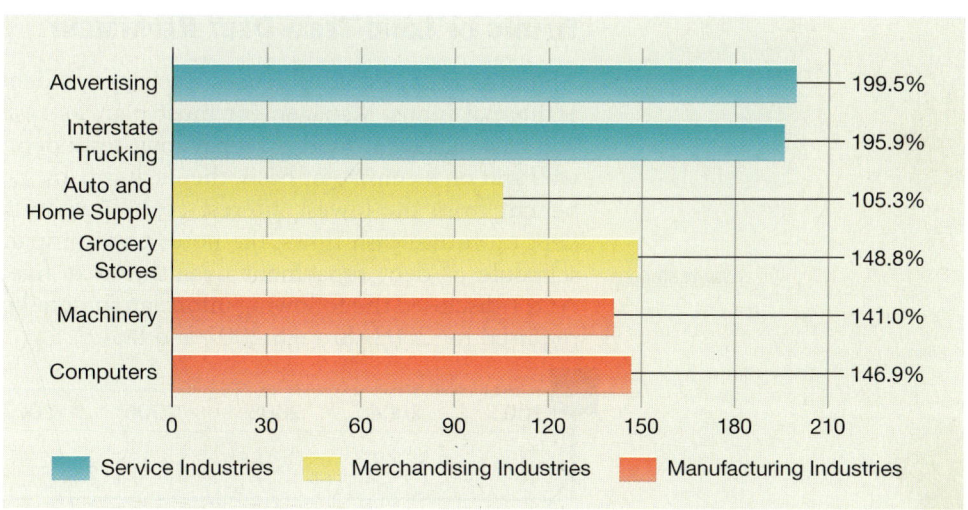

Source: Data from Dun & Bradstreet, *Industry Norms and Key Business Ratios,* 2000–2001.

> **STOP AND THINK!**
> How does a lender assess the risk that a borrower may default—that is, not pay interest and principal when due?
>
> *The lender reviews the enterprise's current earnings and cash flows as well as its debt to equity and interest coverage ratios. The analysis may also include a historical comparison that reflects both good and poor economic times. The lender can then judge how well the company has met its past debt obligations.* ∎

before taxes in 2002 was 63 percent lower, and its interest expense was about the same, resulting in the dramatic decline in interest coverage. The risk for lenders increased substantially, and a lower debt rating is likely if earnings before taxes do not return to levels of previous years.

TYPES OF LONG-TERM DEBT

Long-term bonds (most of which are also called debentures) are the most common type of long-term debt. They can have many different characteristics, including the time until repayment, amount of interest, whether the company can elect to repay early, and whether they can be converted into common stock or other securities. But there are many other types of long-term debt, such as long-term notes, mortgages, and long-term leases. AT&T, for example, has a mixture of long-term obligations, as shown by the following excerpt from its 2002 annual report:[3]

www.att.com

Financial Highlights: Long-Term Obligations
(This table shows the outstanding long-term debt obligations, in millions, at December 31.)

Interest Rates (b)	Maturities	2002
Debentures and Notes		
4.59%–6.00%	2004–2009	$ 1,455
6.06%–6.50%	2004–2029	6,678
6.75%–7.50%	2004–2006	2,449
7.75%–8.85%	2003–2031	6,796
9.90%–19.95%	2004–2004	13
Variable rate	2003–2054	3,012
Total debentures and notes		20,403
Other		105
Less: Unamortized discount—net		(115)
Total long-term obligations		20,393
Less: Currently maturing long-term debt		1,581
Net long-term obligations		$18,812

To structure long-term financing to the best advantage of their companies, managers must know the characteristics of the various types of long-term debt.

TIMING OF LONG-TERM DEBT REPAYMENT

Ability to repay debt influences a company's debt rating and the cost of borrowing additional funds. Management must plan its cash flows carefully to ensure that it will have sufficient funds to repay long-term debt when it comes due. If this is done well and on a consistent basis, then a company can achieve the best debt rating and benefit from the lowest interest cost. To show the potential effects of long-term debt on future cash flows, the notes to a company's financial statements provide a schedule of debt repayment over the next five years. For example, in its notes, AT&T disclosed the following information detailing cash payments totaling $20,393 required for 2003 through 2007 and later:[4]

www.att.com

2003	2004	2005	2006	2007	Later years
$1,581	$2,437	$1,185	$4,328	$296	$10,566

 Check out ACE for a Review Quiz at http://accounting.college.hmco.com/students.

THE NATURE OF BONDS

LO2 Identify and contrast the major characteristics of bonds.
RELATED TEXT ASSIGNMENTS
Q: 2, 3
SD: 4, 6
FRA: 6, 7

● **STOP AND THINK!**
If a company with a high debt to equity ratio wants to increase its debt when the economy is weak, what kind of bond might it issue?
It would most likely issue a secured bond because, rather than being issued on the company's general credit, certain assets are pledged as a guarantee of repayment. ■

TERMINOLOGY NOTE:
Do not confuse the terms *indenture* and *debenture*. They sound alike, but an indenture is a bond contract, whereas a debenture is an unsecured bond.

STUDY NOTE: A debenture of a solid company actually might be a less risky investment than a secured bond of an unstable company.

STUDY NOTE: An advantage of issuing serial bonds is that the organization retires the bonds over a period of years, rather than all at once.

 A **bond** is a security, usually long term, representing money that a corporation or other entity borrows from the investing public. (Bonds are also issued by the U.S. government, state and local governments, and foreign countries to raise money.) A bond must be repaid at a specified time and requires periodic payments of interest.* Interest is usually paid semiannually (twice a year). Bonds must not be confused with stocks. Because stocks are shares of ownership, stockholders are owners. Bondholders are creditors. Bonds are promises to repay the amount borrowed, called the *principal*, and interest at a specified rate on specified future dates.

Often, a bondholder receives a **bond certificate** as evidence of the organization's debt. In most cases, the face value (denomination) of the bond is $1,000 or some multiple of $1,000. A **bond issue** is the total value of bonds issued at one time. For example, a $1,000,000 bond issue could consist of a thousand $1,000 bonds. Because a bond issue can be bought and held by many investors, the organization usually enters into a supplementary agreement called a **bond indenture**. The bond indenture defines the rights, privileges, and limitations of the bondholders. It generally describes such things as the maturity date of the bonds, interest payment dates, and interest rate. It may also cover repayment plans and restrictions.

The prices of bonds are stated in terms of a percentage of face value. A bond issue quoted at 103½ means that a $1,000 bond costs $1,035 ($1,000 × 1.035). When a bond sells at exactly 100, it is said to sell at face or par value. When it sells above 100, it is said to sell at a premium; below 100, at a discount. A $1,000 bond quoted at 87.62 would be selling at a discount and would cost the buyer $876.20.

A bond indenture can be written to fit the financing needs of an individual organization. As a result, the bonds being issued in today's financial markets have many different features. Several of the more important ones are described in the following paragraphs.

SECURED OR UNSECURED BONDS

Bonds can be either secured or unsecured. If issued on the general credit of the organization, they are **unsecured bonds** (also called *debenture bonds*). **Secured bonds** give the bondholders a pledge of certain assets as a guarantee of repayment. The security identified by a secured bond can be any specific asset of the organization or a general category of asset, such as property, plant, or equipment.

TERM OR SERIAL BONDS

When all the bonds of an issue mature at the same time, they are called **term bonds**. For instance, an organization may decide to issue $1,000,000 worth of bonds, all due 20 years from the date of issue. When the bonds in an issue mature on different dates, the bonds are called **serial bonds**. An example of serial bonds would be a $1,000,000 issue that calls for retiring $200,000 of the principal every five years. This arrangement means that after the first $200,000 payment is made, $800,000 of the bonds would remain outstanding for the next five years. In other words, $1,000,000 is outstanding for the first five years, $800,000 for the second five years, and so on. An organization may issue serial bonds to ease the task of retiring its debt.

REGISTERED OR COUPON BONDS

Most bonds issued today are **registered bonds**. The names and addresses of the owners of such bonds must be recorded with the issuing organization. The organization keeps a register of the owners and pays interest by check to the bondholders

---

*At the time this chapter was written, the market interest rates on corporate bonds were volatile. We therefore use a variety of interest rates to demonstrate the concepts.

Focus on International Business

Choice of Bank Debt Cripples Japanese Firms.
When U.S. companies need cash, one ready source is a bond issue, but this source of funds is not available in many other countries. For instance, surprising as it may seem, Japan, with one of the world's largest economies and financial systems, has only a fledgling corporate bond market. Whereas corporate bonds account for 31 percent of U.S. corporate debt, only 57 of the 2,500 publicly listed companies in Japan have any domestic bonds outstanding. Japanese companies have traditionally relied on loans from big Japanese banks when they need cash. Reliance on bank debt has caused problems for Japanese companies because, as a result of the collapse of the real estate industry in Japan, Japanese banks do not have the funds to lend them.[5] Similar problems have occurred recently in other Asian countries.

of record on the interest payment date. **Coupon bonds** generally are not registered with the organization; instead, they bear interest coupons stating the amount of interest due and the payment date. The bondholder removes the coupons from the bonds on the interest payment dates and presents them at a bank for collection.

 Check out ACE for a Review Quiz at http://accounting.college.hmco.com/students.

Accounting for Bonds Payable

LO3 Record the issuance of bonds at face value and at a discount or premium.

RELATED TEXT ASSIGNMENTS
Q: 4, 5
SE: 2, 3, 5, 7
E: 2, 3, 4, 5, 10, 12
P: 1, 2, 3, 4, 5, 6, 7, 8
SD: 1, 5

When the board of directors of a public corporation decides to issue bonds, the company must submit the appropriate legal documents to the Securities and Exchange Commission for permission to borrow the funds. The SEC reviews the corporation's financial health and the specific terms of the bond agreement. Once approved, the company has a limited time in which to issue the authorized bonds. It is not necessary to make an entry for the bond authorization, but most companies prepare a memorandum in the Bonds Payable account describing the issue. This note lists the number and value of bonds authorized, the interest rate, the interest payment dates, and the life of the bonds.

Once the bonds are issued, the corporation must pay interest to the bondholders over the life of the bonds (in most cases, semiannually) and the principal of the bonds at maturity.

Balance Sheet Disclosure of Bonds

KEY POINT: Bonds payable are presented on the balance sheet as either a current or a long-term liability, depending on the maturity date and method of retiring the bonds.

Bonds payable and unamortized discounts or premiums (which we explain later) are typically shown on a company's balance sheet as long-term liabilities. However, if the maturity date of the bond issue is one year or less and the bonds will be retired using current assets, bonds payable should be listed as a current liability. If the issue is to be paid with segregated assets or replaced by another bond issue, the bonds should still be shown as a long-term liability.

www.att.com

Important provisions of the bond indenture are reported in the notes to the financial statements, as illustrated by the Financial Highlights excerpted from the AT&T annual report. Often reported with them is a list of all bond issues, the kinds of bonds, any securities connected with the bonds, interest payment dates, maturity dates, and interest rates.

Bonds Issued at Face Value

Suppose that the Vason Corporation has authorized the issuance of $100,000 of 9 percent, five-year bonds on January 1, 20x4. According to the bond indenture, interest is to be paid on January 1 and July 1 of each year. Assume that the bonds are sold on January 1, 20x4, for their face value. The entry to record the issuance is as follows:

A = L + OE
+   +
	20x4
	Jan. 1
		Cash
		   Bonds Payable
		      Sold $100,000 of 9%, 5-year bonds
		      at face value
			100,000
			               100,000

STUDY NOTE: When calculating semiannual interest, do not use the annual rate (9 percent in this case) by mistake. Rather, use half the annual rate.

As stated above, interest is paid on January 1 and July 1 of each year. Therefore, the corporation would owe the bondholders $4,500 interest on July 1, 20x4:

$$\text{Interest} = \text{Principal} \times \text{Rate} \times \text{Time}$$
$$= \$100{,}000 \times .09 \times \frac{6}{12} \text{ year}$$
$$= \$4{,}500$$

The interest paid to the bondholders on each semiannual interest payment date (January 1 or July 1) would be recorded as follows:

A* = L + OE
−   −
*assumes cash paid

Bond Interest Expense	4,500	
Cash (or Interest Payable)		4,500
Paid (or accrued) semiannual interest to bondholders of 9%, 5-year bonds		

FACE INTEREST RATE AND MARKET INTEREST RATE

KEY POINT: A bond sells at face value when the face interest rate of the bond is identical to the market interest rate for similar bonds on the date of issue.

KEY POINT: When bonds with an interest rate different from the market rate are issued, they sell at a discount or premium. The discount or premium acts as an equalizing factor.

When issuing bonds, most organizations try to set the face interest rate as close as possible to the market interest rate. The **face interest rate** is the rate of interest paid to bondholders based on the face value, or principal, of the bonds. The rate and amount are fixed over the life of the bond. An organization must decide in advance what the face interest rate will be to allow time to file with regulatory bodies, publicize the issue, and print the certificates.

The **market interest rate** is the rate of interest paid in the market on bonds of similar risk. It is also referred to as the *effective interest rate*. The market interest rate fluctuates daily. Because an organization has no control over the market interest rate, it often differs from the face interest rate on the issue date. As a result, the issue price of the bonds does not always equal their face value. If the market interest rate is higher than the face interest rate, the issue price will be less than the face value and the bonds are said to be issued at a **discount**. The discount equals the excess of the face value over the issue price. On the other hand, if the market interest rate is

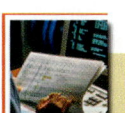

FOCUS ON BUSINESS PRACTICE

Check Out Those Bond Prices!

The price of many bonds can be found daily in business publications like *The Wall Street Journal*. For instance, shown to the right are the quotations for a number of AT&T <www.att.com> bonds. The first is a bond with a face interest rate of 6¾ percent that is due in 2004. The current yield is 6.5 percent based on the closing price of 103. The volume of $1,000 bonds traded was 70, and the last sale was up by .22 point from the previous day's last sales.

Corporation bond price/change (5/30/03), from *Wall Street Journal*. Copyright 2003 by Dow Jones & Co. Inc. Reproduced with permission of Dow Jones & Co. Inc. in the format textbook via Copyright Clearance Center.

Bonds	Cur Yld	Vol	Close	Net Chg
ATT 6¾04	6.5	70	103	0.22
ATT 5⅝04	5.5	15	102.06	...
ATT 7½04	7.2	37	103.59	0.06
ATT 7½06	6.8	362	111.13	1.13
ATT 7¾07	6.9	25	111.75	...
ATT 6s09	5.8	1136	103.63	0.13
ATT 6½13	6.2	86	105.25	0.38
ATT 8⅛22	7.9	200	102.75	0.25
ATT 8⅛24	7.9	190	103.25	...
ATT 8.35s25	7.9	101	105.13	0.63
ATT 6½29	6.7	263	97.50	0.75
ATT 8⅝31	8.3	41	104.25	0.63

lower than the face interest rate, the issue price will be more than the face value and the bonds are said to be issued at a **premium**. The premium equals the excess of the issue price over the face value.

BONDS ISSUED AT A DISCOUNT

Suppose that the Vason Corporation issues $100,000 of 9 percent, five-year bonds at 96.149 on January 1, 20x4, when the market interest rate is 10 percent. In this case, the bonds are being issued at a discount because the market interest rate exceeds the face interest rate. The following entry records the issuance of the bonds at a discount:

A = L + OE
+ +
    −

KEY POINT: The carrying amount is always the face value of the bonds plus the unamortized premium or less the unamortized discount. The carrying amount always approaches the face value over the life of the bond.

```
20x4
Jan. 1  Cash                                      96,149
        Unamortized Bond Discount                  3,851
            Bonds Payable                                   100,000
        Sold $100,000 of 9%, 5-year
          bonds at 96.149
        Face amount of bonds            $100,000
        Less purchase price of bonds
          ($100,000 × .96149)             96,149
        Unamortized bond discount       $  3,851
```

In the entry, Cash is debited for the amount received ($96,149), Bonds Payable is credited for the face amount ($100,000) of the bond liability, and the difference ($3,851) is debited to Unamortized Bond Discount. If a balance sheet is prepared right after the bonds are issued at a discount, the liability for bonds payable is reported as follows:

KEY POINT: The unamortized bond discount is subtracted from bonds payable on the balance sheet. The carrying value will be below the face value until the maturity date.

```
Long-term liabilities
  9% bonds payable, due 1/1/x9          $100,000
  Less unamortized bond discount           3,851     $96,149
```

Unamortized bond discount is a contra-liability account: its balance is deducted from the face amount of the bonds to arrive at the carrying value, or present value, of the bonds. The bond discount is described as unamortized because it will be amortized (written off) over the life of the bonds.

● **STOP AND THINK!**
What determines whether bonds are issued at a discount, premium, or face value?
The relationship between the prevailing market interest rate and the face interest rate on the issue date is the determinant. ■

BONDS ISSUED AT A PREMIUM

When bonds have a face interest rate above the market interest rate for similar investments, they are issued at a price above the face value, or at a premium. For example, assume that the Vason Corporation issues $100,000 of 9 percent, five-year bonds for $104,100 on January 1, 20x4, when the market interest rate is 8 percent. This means that investors will purchase the bonds at 104.1 percent of their face value. The issuance would be recorded as follows:

A = L + OE
+ +
    +

```
20x4
Jan. 1  Cash                                      104,100
            Unamortized Bond Premium                          4,100
            Bonds Payable                                   100,000
        Sold $100,000 of 9%, 5-year bonds
          at 104.1 ($100,000 × 1.041)
```

Right after this entry is made, bonds payable would be presented on the balance sheet as follows:

KEY POINT: The unamortized bond premium is *added* to bonds payable on the balance sheet. The carrying value will be above the face value until the maturity date.

```
Long-term liabilities
  9% bonds payable, due 1/1/x9          $100,000
  Unamortized bond premium                 4,100     $104,100
```

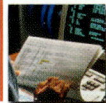

FOCUS ON BUSINESS PRACTICE

100-Year Bonds Are Not for Everyone.
In 1993, interest rates on long-term debt were at historically low levels, which induced some companies to attempt to lock in those low costs for long periods. One of the most aggressive companies in that regard was The Walt Disney Company <www.disney.go.com>, which issued $150 million of 100-year bonds at a yield of only 7.5 percent. It was the first time since 1954 that 100-year bonds had been issued. Among the others that followed Walt Disney's lead by issuing 100-year bonds were the Coca-Cola Company <www.coca-cola.com>, Columbia HCA Healthcare <www.hcahealthcare.com>, Bell South <www.bellsouth.com>, IBM <www.ibm.com>, and even the People's Republic of China. Some analysts wondered if even Mickey Mouse could survive 100 years. Investors who purchase such bonds take a financial risk because if interest rates rise, which would seem likely, then the market value of the bonds will decrease.[6]

The carrying value of the bonds payable is $104,100, which equals the face value of the bonds plus the unamortized bond premium. The cash received from the bond issue is also $104,100. This means that the purchasers were willing to pay a premium of $4,100 to buy these bonds because their face interest rate was higher than the market interest rate.

BOND ISSUE COSTS

KEY POINT: A separate Bond Issue Costs account is usually established and amortized over the life of the issue.

Most bonds are sold through underwriters, who receive a fee for taking care of the details of marketing the issue or for taking a chance on receiving the selling price. Such costs are connected with the issuance of bonds. Because bond issue costs benefit the whole life of a bond issue, it makes sense to spread the costs over that period. It is generally accepted practice to establish a separate account for bond issue costs and to amortize them over the life of the bonds. However, issue costs decrease the amount of money a company receives from a bond issue. They have the effect, then, of raising the discount or lowering the premium on the issue. As a result, bond issue costs can be spread over the life of the bonds through the amortization of a discount or premium. Because this method simplifies recordkeeping, we assume in the text and problems of this book that all bond issue costs increase the discounts or decrease the premiums of bond issues.

 Check out ACE for a Review Quiz at http://accounting.college.hmco.com/students.

USING PRESENT VALUE TO VALUE A BOND

LO4 Use present values to determine the value of bonds.
RELATED TEXT ASSIGNMENTS
SE: 4
E: 6, 7, 8, 13

Present value is relevant to the study of bonds because the value of a bond is based on the present value of two components of cash flow: (1) a series of fixed interest payments and (2) a single payment at maturity. The amount of interest a bond pays is fixed over its life. However, the market interest rate varies from day to day. Thus, the amount investors are willing to pay for a bond changes as well.

Assume, for example, that a bond has a face value of $10,000 and pays fixed interest of $450 every six months (a 9 percent annual rate). The bond is due in five years. If the market interest rate today is 14 percent, what is the present value of the bond?

To determine the present value of the bond, we use Table 4 in the appendix on future value and present value tables to calculate the present value of the periodic interest payments of $450, and we use Table 3 in the same appendix to calculate the present value of the single payment of $10,000 at maturity. Since interest payments are made every six months, the compounding period is half a year. Because of this, it is necessary to convert the annual rate to a semiannual rate of 7 percent (14 percent divided by two six-month periods per year) and to use ten periods (five

STUDY NOTE: The amount buyers are willing to pay for an investment is normally based on what they expect to receive in return, taken at present value. In the case of a bond, the theoretical value equals the present value of the periodic interest payments plus the present value of the maturity value. The discount rate is set at the market rate (what investors are looking for), not at the face rate.

years multiplied by two six-month periods per year). Using this information, we compute the present value of the bond as follows:

Present value of 10 periodic payments at 7% (from Table 4 in the appendix on future value and present value tables): $450 × 7.024	$3,160.80
Present value of a single payment at the end of 10 periods at 7% (from Table 3 in the appendix on future value and present value tables): $10,000 × .508	5,080.00
Present value of $10,000 bond	$8,240.80

The market interest rate has increased so much since the bond was issued (from 9 percent to 14 percent) that the value of the bond is only $8,240.80 today. That amount is all investors would be willing to pay at this time for a bond that provides income of $450 every six months and a return of the $10,000 principal in five years.

If the market interest rate falls below the face interest rate, say to 8 percent (4 percent semiannually), the present value of the bond will be greater than the face value of $10,000:

Present value of 10 periodic payments at 4% (from Table 4 in the appendix on future value and present value tables): $450 × 8.111	$ 3,649.95
Present value of a single payment at the end of 10 periods at 4% (from Table 3 in the appendix on future value and present value tables): $10,000 × .676	6,760.00
Present value of $10,000 bond	$10,409.95

● **STOP AND THINK!**
Why do bond prices vary over time?
Bond price is the present value of the principal and interest cash flows at the market interest rate; therefore, as the market interest rate changes over time, bond prices will change. ■

 Check out ACE for a Review Quiz at http://accounting.college.hmco.com/students.

AMORTIZATION OF BOND DISCOUNTS AND PREMIUMS

LO5 Amortize bond discounts and bond premiums using the straight-line and effective interest methods.
RELATED TEXT ASSIGNMENTS
Q: 6, 7
SE: 2, 3, 7
E: 2, 3, 4, 5, 9, 12
P: 1, 2, 3, 4, 5, 6, 7, 8
SD: 2

A bond discount or premium represents the amount by which the total interest cost is higher or lower than the total interest payments. To record interest expense properly and ensure that at maturity the carrying value of bonds payable equals its face value, systematic reduction of the bond discount or premium over the bond term is required. That is, the discount or premium has to be amortized over the life of the bonds. This is accomplished by using either the straight-line method or the effective interest method.

AMORTIZING A BOND DISCOUNT

In one of the examples on page 506, Vason Corporation issued $100,000 of five-year bonds at a discount because the market interest rate of 10 percent exceeded the face interest rate of 9 percent. The bonds were sold for $96,149, resulting in an unamortized bond discount of $3,851. Because this discount affects interest expense in each year of the bond issue, the bond discount should be amortized (reduced gradually) over the life of the issue. This means that the unamortized bond discount will decrease gradually over time, and that the carrying value of the bond issue (face value less unamortized discount) will increase gradually. By the maturity date of the bond, the carrying value of the issue will equal its face value, and the unamortized bond discount will be zero. In the following sections, the total interest cost is calculated, and the bond discount is amortized using the straight-line and the effective interest methods.

KEY POINT: A bond discount is considered a component of total interest cost because a bond discount represents the amount in excess of the issue price that the corporation must pay on the maturity date.

■ **CALCULATION OF TOTAL INTEREST COST** When bonds are issued at a discount, the effective (or market) interest rate paid by the company is greater than the face interest rate on the bonds. The reason is that the interest cost to the company is the stated interest payments *plus* the amount of the bond discount. That is, although the company does not receive the full face value of the bonds on issue, it still must pay back the full face value at maturity. The difference between the issue price and the face value must be added to the total interest payments to arrive at the actual interest expense. The full cost to the corporation of issuing the bonds at a discount is as follows:

Cash to be paid to bondholders
  Face value at maturity $100,000
  Interest payments ($100,000 × .09 × 5 years)   45,000
Total cash paid to bondholders $145,000
Less cash received from bondholders   96,149
Total interest cost $ 48,851

Or, alternatively:

Interest payments ($100,000 × .09 × 5 years) $ 45,000
Bond discount   3,851
Total interest cost $ 48,851

The total interest cost of $48,851 is made up of $45,000 in interest payments and the $3,851 bond discount, so the bond discount increases the interest paid on the bonds from the face interest rate to the market interest rate. The *market (effective) interest rate* is the real interest cost of the bond over its life.

For each year's interest expense to reflect the market interest rate, the discount must be allocated over the remaining life of the bonds as an increase in the interest expense each period. The process of allocation is called *amortization of the bond discount*. Thus, interest expense for each period will exceed the actual payment of interest by the amount of the bond discount amortized over the period.

Some companies and governmental units issue bonds that do not require periodic interest payments. These bonds, called **zero coupon bonds**, are simply a promise to pay a fixed amount at the maturity date. They are issued at a large discount because the only interest earned by the buyer or paid by the issuer is the discount. For example, a five-year, $100,000 zero coupon bond issued at a time when the market rate is 14 percent, compounded semiannually, would sell for only $50,800. That amount is the present value of a single payment of $100,000 at the end of five years. The discount of $49,200 ($100,000 − $50,800) is the total interest cost; it is amortized over the life of the bond.

KEY POINT: The discount on a zero coupon bond represents the interest that will be paid (in its entirety) on the maturity date.

■ **STRAIGHT-LINE METHOD** The **straight-line method** assumes equal amortization of the bond discount for each interest period. Suppose that the interest payment dates for the Vason Corporation bond issue are January 1 and July 1. The amount of the bond discount amortized and the interest expense for each semiannual period are calculated in four steps:

1. Total Interest Payments = Interest Payments per Year × Life of Bonds
   = 2 × 5 = 10

2. Amortization of Bond Discount per Interest Period = $\dfrac{\text{Bond Discount}}{\text{Total Interest Payments}}$

   = $\dfrac{\$3,851}{10}$ = $385*

*Rounded.

3. Cash Interest Payment = Face Value × Face Interest Rate × Time
   = $100,000 × .09 × 6/12 = $4,500

4. Interest Expense per Interest Period = Interest Payment + Amortization of Bond Discount
   = $4,500 + $385 = $4,885

On July 1, 20x4, the first semiannual interest date, the entry would be as follows:

A* = L + OE
− + −
*assumes cash paid

20x4			
July 1	Bond Interest Expense	4,885	
	Unamortized Bond Discount		385
	Cash (or Interest Payable)		4,500
	Paid (or accrued) semiannual interest to bondholders and amortized the discount on 9%, 5-year bonds		

Notice that the bond interest expense is $4,885, but the amount paid to the bondholders is the $4,500 face interest payment. The difference of $385 is the credit to Unamortized Bond Discount. This lowers the debit balance of Unamortized Bond Discount and raises the carrying value of the bonds payable by $385 each interest period. Assuming that no changes occur in the bond issue, this entry will be made every six months for the life of the bonds. When the bond issue matures, there will be no balance in the Unamortized Bond Discount account, and the carrying value of the bonds will be $100,000—exactly equal to the amount due the bondholders.

The straight-line method has long been used, but it has a certain weakness. Because the carrying value goes up each period and the bond interest expense stays the same, the rate of interest falls over time. Conversely, when the straight-line method is used to amortize a premium, the rate of interest rises over time. Therefore, the Accounting Principles Board has ruled that the straight-line method can be used only when it does not lead to a material difference from the effective interest method.[7] An amount is material if it affects a decision on the evaluation of the company.

🔴 **STOP AND THINK!**
When is it acceptable to use the straight-line method to amortize a bond discount or premium?
It is acceptable only when it does not produce a result materially different from that produced by the effective interest method. ∎

■ **EFFECTIVE INTEREST METHOD** To compute the interest and amortization of a bond discount for each interest period under the **effective interest method**, a constant interest rate is applied to the carrying value of the bonds at the beginning of the interest period. This constant rate equals the market rate, or effective rate, at the time the bonds were issued. The amount to be amortized each period is the difference between the interest computed by using the market rate and the actual interest paid to bondholders. As an example, we use the same facts presented earlier—a $100,000 bond issue at 9 percent, with a five-year maturity and interest to be paid twice a year. The market, or effective, interest rate at the time the bonds were issued was 10 percent. The bonds were sold for $96,149, a discount of $3,851. The interest and amortization of the bond discount are shown in Table 1.

The amounts in the table (using period 1) were computed as follows:

Column A: The carrying value of the bonds is their face value less the unamortized bond discount ($100,000 − $3,851 = $96,149).

Column B: The interest expense to be recorded is the effective interest. It is found by multiplying the carrying value of the bonds by the effective (market) interest rate for one-half year ($96,149 × .10 × 6/12 = $4,807).

Column C: The interest paid in the period is a constant amount computed by multiplying the face value of the bonds by their face interest rate by the interest time period ($100,000 × .09 × 6/12 = $4,500).

Column D: The discount amortized is the difference between the effective interest expense to be recorded and the interest to be paid on the interest payment date ($4,807 − $4,500 = $307).

TABLE 1. Interest and Amortization of a Bond Discount: Effective Interest Method

	A	B	C	D	E	F
Semiannual Interest Period	Carrying Value at Beginning of Period	Semiannual Interest Expense at 10% to Be Recorded* (5% × A)	Semiannual Interest Payment to Bondholders (4½% × $100,000)	Amortization of Bond Discount (B − C)	Unamortized Bond Discount at End of Period (E − D)	Carrying Value at End of Period (A + D)
0					$3,851	$ 96,149
1	$96,149	$4,807	$4,500	$307	3,544	96,456
2	96,456	4,823	4,500	323	3,221	96,779
3	96,779	4,839	4,500	339	2,882	97,118
4	97,118	4,856	4,500	356	2,526	97,474
5	97,474	4,874	4,500	374	2,152	97,848
6	97,848	4,892	4,500	392	1,760	98,240
7	98,240	4,912	4,500	412	1,348	98,652
8	98,652	4,933	4,500	433	915	99,085
9	99,085	4,954	4,500	454	461	99,539
10	99,539	4,961†	4,500	461	—	100,000

*Rounded to the nearest dollar.
†Last period's interest expense equals $4,961 ($4,500 + $461); it does not equal $4,977 ($99,539 × .05) because of the cumulative effect of rounding.

Column E: The unamortized bond discount is the balance of the bond discount at the beginning of the period less the current period amortization of the discount ($3,851 − $307 = $3,544). The unamortized discount decreases each interest payment period because it is amortized as a portion of interest expense.

Column F: The carrying value of the bonds at the end of the period is the carrying value at the beginning of the period plus the amortization during the period ($96,149 + $307 = $96,456). Notice that the sum of the carrying value and the unamortized discount (Column F + Column E) always equals the face value of the bonds ($96,456 + $3,544 = $100,000).

The entry to record the interest expense is like the one used with the straight-line method, but the amounts debited and credited to the various accounts differ. With the effective interest method, the entry for July 1, 20x4, would be as follows:

A* = L + OE
− + −
*assumes cash paid

```
20x4
July 1   Bond Interest Expense                    4,807
             Unamortized Bond Discount                    307
             Cash (or Interest Payable)                 4,500
         Paid (or accrued) semiannual
         interest to bondholders and
         amortized the discount on 9%,
         5-year bonds
```

KEY POINT: The bond interest expense recorded exceeds the amount of interest paid because of the amortization of the bond discount. The matching rule dictates that the discount be amortized over the life of the bond.

Notice that it is not necessary to prepare an interest and amortization table to determine the amortization of a discount for any one interest payment period. It is necessary only to multiply the carrying value by the effective interest rate and subtract the interest payment from the result. For example, the amount of discount to be amortized in the seventh interest payment period is $412, calculated as follows: ($98,240 × .05) − $4,500.

■ **VISUAL SUMMARY OF THE EFFECTIVE INTEREST METHOD** The effect on carrying value and interest expense of the amortization of a bond discount using the effective

FIGURE 2
Carrying Value and Interest Expense—Bonds Issued at a Discount

KEY POINT: The bond interest expense *increases* each period because the carrying value of the bonds (the principal on which the interest is calculated) increases each period.

interest method can be seen in Figure 2 (which is based on the data from Table 1). Notice that initially the carrying value (the issue price) is less than the face value, but that it gradually increases toward the face value over the life of the bond issue. Notice also that interest expense exceeds interest payments by the amount of the bond discount amortized. Interest expense increases gradually over the life of the bond because it is based on the gradually increasing carrying value (multiplied by the market interest rate).

AMORTIZING A BOND PREMIUM

In our example of bonds issued at a premium, Vason Corporation issued $100,000 of five-year bonds at a premium because the market interest rate of 8 percent was less than the face interest rate of 9 percent. The bonds were sold for $104,100, which resulted in an unamortized bond premium of $4,100. Like a discount, a premium must be amortized over the life of the bonds so that it can be matched to its effects on interest expense during that period. In the following sections, the total interest cost is calculated, and the bond premium is amortized using the straight-line and the effective interest methods.

■ **CALCULATION OF TOTAL INTEREST COST** Because the bondholders paid more than face value for the bonds, the premium of $4,100 ($104,100 − $100,000) represents an amount that the bondholders will not receive at maturity. The premium is in effect a reduction, in advance, of the total interest paid on the bonds over the life of the bond issue. The total interest cost over the issue's life can be computed as follows:

KEY POINT: The bond interest expense recorded is less than the amount of the interest paid because of the amortization of the bond premium. The matching rule dictates that the premium be amortized over the life of the bond.

KEY POINT: A bond premium is deducted from interest payments in calculating total interest cost because a bond premium represents an amount over the face value of a bond that the corporation never has to return to the bondholders. In effect, it reduces the higher-than-market interest the corporation is paying on the bond.

Cash to be paid to bondholders
Face value at maturity	$100,000
Interest payments ($100,000 × .09 × 5 years)	45,000
Total cash paid to bondholders	$145,000
Less cash received from bondholders	104,100
Total interest cost	$ 40,900

Or, alternatively:

Interest payments ($100,000 × .09 × 5 years)	$ 45,000
Less bond premium	4,100
Total interest cost	$ 40,900

Notice that the total interest payments of $45,000 exceed the total interest cost of $40,900 by $4,100, the amount of the bond premium.

■ **STRAIGHT-LINE METHOD** Under the straight-line method, the bond premium is spread evenly over the life of the bond issue. As with bond discounts, the amount of the bond premium amortized and the interest expense for each semiannual period are computed in four steps:

1. Total Interest Payments = Interest Payments per Year × Life of Bonds
   = 2 × 5 = 10

2. Amortization of Bond Premium per Interest Period = $\dfrac{\text{Bond Premium}}{\text{Total Interest Payments}}$

   $= \dfrac{\$4,100}{10} = \$410$

3. Cash Interest Payment = Face Value × Face Interest Rate × Time
   = $100,000 × .09 × 6/12 = $4,500

4. Interest Expense per Interest Period = Interest Payment − Amortization of Bond Premium
   = $4,500 − $410 = $4,090

On July 1, 20x4, the first semiannual interest date, the entry would be as follows:

$A^* = L + OE$
$- \quad -$
*assumes cash paid

20x4			
July 1	Bond Interest Expense	4,090	
	Unamortized Bond Premium	410	
	Cash (or Interest Payable)		4,500
	Paid (or accrued) semiannual interest		
	to bondholders and amortized the		
	premium on 9%, 5-year bonds		

Notice that the bond interest expense is $4,090, but the amount received by the bondholders is the $4,500 face interest payment. The difference of $410 is the debit to Unamortized Bond Premium. This lowers the credit balance of the Unamortized Bond Premium account and the carrying value of the bonds payable by $410 each interest period. Assuming that the bond issue remains unchanged, the same entry will be made on every semiannual interest date over the life of the bond issue. When the bond issue matures, there will be no balance in the Unamortized Bond Premium account, and the carrying value of the bonds payable will be $100,000, exactly equal to the amount due the bondholders.

STUDY NOTE: Whether a bond is sold at a discount or a premium, its carrying value will equal its face value on the maturity date.

As noted earlier, the straight-line method should be used only when it does not lead to a material difference from the effective interest method.

■ **EFFECTIVE INTEREST METHOD** Under the straight-line method, the effective interest rate changes constantly, even though the interest expense is fixed, because

TABLE 2. Interest and Amortization of a Bond Premium: Effective Interest Method

	A	B	C	D	E	F
Semiannual Interest Period	Carrying Value at Beginning of Period	Semiannual Interest Expense at 8% to Be Recorded* (4% × A)	Semiannual Interest Payment to Bondholders (4½% × $100,000)	Amortization of Bond Premium (C − B)	Unamortized Bond Premium at End of Period (E − D)	Carrying Value at End of Period (A − D)
0					$4,100	$104,100
1	$104,100	$4,164	$4,500	$336	3,764	103,764
2	103,764	4,151	4,500	349	3,415	103,415
3	103,415	4,137	4,500	363	3,052	103,052
4	103,052	4,122	4,500	378	2,674	102,674
5	102,674	4,107	4,500	393	2,281	102,281
6	102,281	4,091	4,500	409	1,872	101,872
7	101,872	4,075	4,500	425	1,447	101,447
8	101,447	4,058	4,500	442	1,005	101,005
9	101,005	4,040	4,500	460	545	100,545
10	100,545	3,955†	4,500	545	—	100,000

*Rounded to the nearest dollar.
†Last period's interest expense equals $3,955 ($4,500 − $545); it does not equal $4,022 ($100,545 × .04) because of the cumulative effect of rounding.

the effective interest rate is determined by comparing the fixed interest expense with a carrying value that changes as a result of amortizing the discount or premium. To apply a fixed interest rate over the life of the bonds based on the actual market rate at the time of the bond issue requires the use of the effective interest method. Under this method, the interest expense decreases slightly each period (see Table 2, Column B) because the amount of the bond premium amortized increases slightly (Column D). This occurs because a fixed rate is applied each period to the gradually decreasing carrying value (Column A).

The first interest payment is recorded as follows:

```
                          20x4
A* = L + OE     July 1    Bond Interest Expense              4,164
 −    −   −               Unamortized Bond Premium             336
*assumes cash paid          Cash (or Interest Payable)                4,500
                          Paid (or accrued) semiannual interest
                          to bondholders and amortized the
                          premium on 9%, 5-year bonds
```

FOCUS ON BUSINESS TECHNOLOGY

Speed Up the Calculations!
Interest and amortization tables like those in Tables 1 and 2 are ideal applications for computer spreadsheet software, such as Lotus and Microsoft Excel. Once the tables have been set up with the proper formula in each cell, only five variables must be entered to produce the entire table. These variables are the face value of the bonds, selling price, life of the bonds, face interest rate, and market interest rate.

Notice that the unamortized bond premium (Column E) decreases gradually to zero as the carrying value decreases to the face value (Column F). To find the amount of premium amortized in any one interest payment period, subtract the effective interest expense (the carrying value times the effective interest rate, Column B) from the interest payment (Column C). In semiannual interest period 5, for example, the amortization of premium is $393, which is calculated in the following manner: $4,500 − ($102,674 × .04).

FIGURE 3
Carrying Value and Interest Expense—Bonds Issued at a Premium

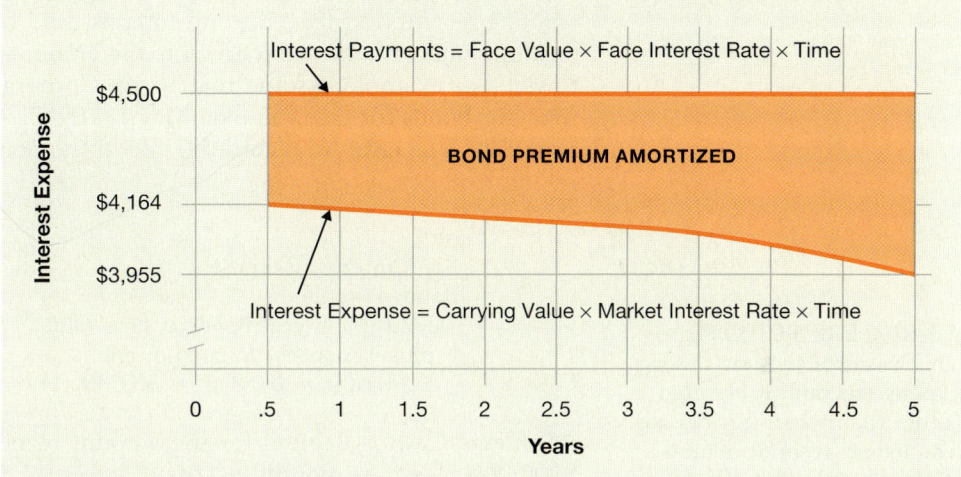

KEY POINT: Over the life of a bond, the premium or discount amortized increases each period.

■ **VISUAL SUMMARY OF THE EFFECTIVE INTEREST METHOD** The effect on carrying value and interest expense of the amortization of a bond premium using the effective interest method can be seen in Figure 3 (which is based on data from Table 2). Notice that initially the carrying value (issue price) is greater than the face value, but that it gradually decreases toward the face value over the life of the bond issue. Notice also that interest payments exceed interest expense by the amount of the premium amortized and that interest expense decreases gradually over the life of the bond because it is based on the gradually decreasing carrying value (multiplied by the market interest rate).

 Check out ACE for a Review Quiz at http://accounting.college.hmco.com/students.

OTHER BONDS PAYABLE ISSUES

LO6 Record bonds issued between interest dates and year-end adjustments.

RELATED TEXT ASSIGNMENTS
Q: 8
SE: 3, 5, 6, 7
E: 4, 5, 9, 10, 11, 12
P: 1, 2, 3, 5, 6, 7, 8

Several other issues arise in accounting for bonds payable. Among them are the sale of bonds between interest payment dates and the year-end accrual of bond interest expense.

SALE OF BONDS BETWEEN INTEREST DATES

Bonds may be issued on an interest payment date, as in the previous examples, but they are often issued between interest payment dates. The generally accepted method of handling bonds issued in this manner is to collect from investors the interest that would have accrued for the partial period preceding the issue date.

Then, when the first interest period is completed, the corporation pays investors the interest for the entire period. Thus, the interest collected when bonds are sold is returned to investors on the next interest payment date.

There are two reasons for following this procedure. The first is a practical one. If a company issued bonds on several different days and did not collect the accrued interest, records would have to be maintained for each bondholder and date of purchase. In such a case, the interest due each bondholder would have to be computed on the basis of a different time period. Clearly, large bookkeeping costs would be incurred under this kind of system. On the other hand, if accrued interest is collected when the bonds are sold, the corporation can pay the interest due for the entire period on the interest payment date, eliminating the extra computations and costs.

The second reason for collecting accrued interest in advance is that when that amount is netted against the full interest paid on the interest payment date, the resulting interest expense represents the amount for the time the money was borrowed. For example, assume that Vason Corporation sold $100,000 of 9 percent, five-year bonds for face value on May 1, 20x4, rather than on January 1, 20x4, the issue date. The entry to record the sale of the bonds is as follows:

A = L + OE
+   +   +

20x4
May 1   Cash   103,000
            Bond Interest Expense   3,000
            Bonds Payable   100,000
            Sold 9%, 5-year bonds at face value
            plus 4 months' accrued interest
            $100,000 × .09 × 4/12 = $3,000

ENRICHMENT NOTE:
This is one of the few times an expense account is credited (other than when it is closed). The ledger account demonstrates that the net effect is the recording of two months' interest (May and June).

As shown, Cash is debited for the amount received, $103,000 (the face value of $100,000 plus four months' accrued interest of $3,000). Bond Interest Expense is credited for the $3,000 of accrued interest, and Bonds Payable is credited for the face value of $100,000.

When the first semiannual interest payment date arrives, this entry is made:

A* = L + OE
 −   −

*assumes cash paid

20x4
July 1   Bond Interest Expense   4,500
            Cash (or Interest Payable)   4,500
            Paid (or accrued) semiannual interest
            $100,000 × .09 × 6/12 = $4,500

Notice that the entire half-year interest is both debited to Bond Interest Expense and credited to Cash because the corporation pays bond interest only once every six months, in full six-month amounts. This process is illustrated in Figure 4. The actual interest expense for the two months that the bonds were outstanding is $1,500. This amount is the net balance of the $4,500 debit to Bond Interest Expense on July 1 less the $3,000 credit to Bond Interest Expense on May 1. You can see these steps clearly in the following T account:

Bond Interest Expense			
Bal.	0	May 1	3,000
July 1	4,500		
Bal.	1,500		

YEAR-END ACCRUAL OF BOND INTEREST EXPENSE

Bond interest payment dates rarely correspond with a company's fiscal year. Therefore, an adjustment must be made at the end of the accounting period to

FIGURE 4
Effect on Bond Interest Expense When Bonds Are Issued Between Interest Dates

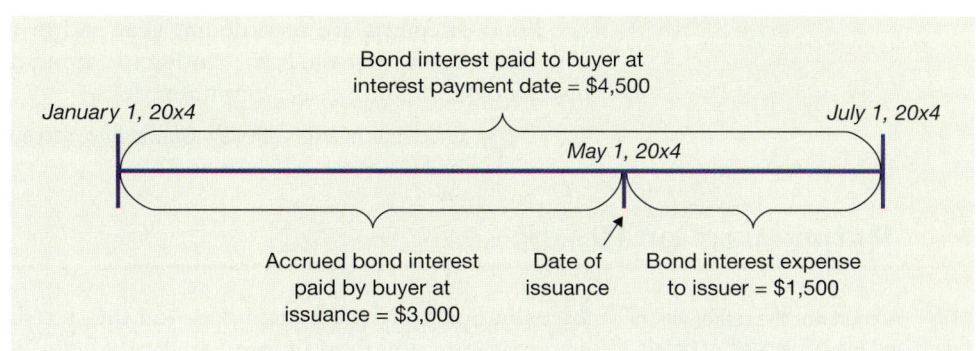

accrue the interest expense on the bonds from the last payment date to the end of the fiscal year. Further, if there is any discount or premium on the bonds, it must also be amortized for the fractional period.

KEY POINT: Remember that adjusting entries never affect cash.

Remember that in the example of bonds issued at a premium, Vason Corporation issued $100,000 in bonds on January 1, 20x4, at 104.1 percent of face value. Suppose the company's fiscal year ends on September 30, 20x4. In the period since the interest payment and amortization of the premium on July 1, three months' worth of interest has accrued, and the following adjusting entry under the effective interest method must be made:

```
20x0
A = L + OE   Sept. 30   Bond Interest Expense              2,075.50
 -   -                  Unamortized Bond Premium             174.50
     +                     Interest Payable                             2,250.00
                              To record accrual of interest on
                              9% bonds payable for 3 months and
                              amortization of one-half of the
                              premium for the second interest
                              payment period
```

CLARIFICATION NOTE: The matching rule dictates that both the accrued interest and the amortization of a premium or discount be recorded at year end.

This entry covers one-half of the second interest period. Unamortized Bond Premium is debited for $174.50, which is one-half of $349, the amortization of the premium for the second period from Table 2. Interest Payable is credited for $2,250, three months' interest on the face value of the bonds ($100,000 × .09 × 3/12). The net debit figure of $2,075.50 ($2,250.00 − $174.50) is the bond interest expense for the three-month period.

When the January 1, 20x5, payment date arrives, the entry to pay the bondholders and amortize the premium is as follows:

```
20x1
A = L + OE   Jan. 1    Bond Interest Expense              2,075.50
 -   -  -              Interest Payable                   2,250.00
                       Unamortized Bond Premium             174.50
                          Cash                                        4,500.00
                          Paid semiannual interest, including
                          interest previously accrued, and
                          amortized the premium for the
                          period since the end of the fiscal
                          year
```

STOP AND THINK!
Why must the accrual of bond interest expense be recorded?
Bond interest expense must be accrued at the close of each accounting period to ensure proper matching of all the borrowing costs associated with bonds payable. Interest payment dates rarely coincide with the end of the accounting period. ∎

As shown here, one-half ($2,250) of the amount paid ($4,500) was accrued on September 30. Unamortized Bond Premium is debited for $174.50, the remaining amount to be amortized for the period ($349.00 − $174.50). The resulting bond interest expense is the amount that applies to the three-month period from October 1 to December 31.

Bond discounts are recorded at year end in the same way as bond premiums. The difference is that the amortization of a bond discount increases interest expense instead of decreasing it as a premium does.

 Check out ACE for a Review Quiz at http://accounting.college.hmco.com/students.

RETIREMENT OF BONDS

SO7 Account for the retirement of bonds and the conversion of bonds into stock.

RELATED TEXT ASSIGNMENTS
Q: 9, 10
SE: 8, 9
E: 13, 14, 15
P: 4, 5
FRA: 2

ENRICHMENT NOTE: When interest rates drop, corporations frequently refinance their bonds at the lower rate, much like homeowners who refinance their mortgage loans when interest rates go down. Even though a call premium is usually paid to extinguish the bonds, the interest saved makes the refinancing cost-effective in the long run.

Usually, bonds are paid when due—on the stated maturity date. However, it can be advantageous not to wait until maturity, as is sometimes the case with callable bonds and convertible bonds.

CALLABLE BONDS

Callable bonds give the issuer the right to buy back and retire the bonds at a specified **call price**, usually above face value, before maturity. Such bonds give the company flexibility in financing its operations. For example, if bond interest rates drop, the company can call its bonds and reissue debt at a lower interest rate. A company might also call its bonds if it has earned enough to pay off the debt, if the reason for having the debt no longer exists, or if it wants to restructure its debt to equity ratio. The bond indenture states the time period and the prices at which the bonds can be redeemed. The retirement of a bond issue before its maturity date is called **early extinguishment of debt**.

Let's assume that Vason Corporation can call or retire at 105 the $100,000 of bonds it issued at a premium (104.1) and that it decides to do so on July 1, 20x7. (To simplify the example, the retirement is made on an interest payment date.) Because the bonds were issued on January 1, 20x4, the retirement takes place on the seventh interest payment date. Assume that the entry for the required interest payment and the amortization of the premium has been made. The entry to retire the bonds is as follows:

A = L + OE
− − −

	20x7			
	July 1	Bonds Payable	100,000	
		Unamortized Bond Premium	1,447	
		Loss on Retirement of Bonds	3,553	
		Cash		105,000
		Retired 9% bonds at 105		

In this entry, the cash paid is the face value times the call price ($100,000 × 1.05 = $105,000). The unamortized bond premium can be found in Column E of Table 2. The loss on retirement of bonds occurs because the call price of the bonds is greater than the carrying value ($105,000 − $101,447 = $3,553).

Sometimes, a rise in the market interest rate can cause the market value of bonds to fall considerably below their face value. If it has the cash to do so, the company may find it advantageous to purchase the bonds on the open market and retire them, rather than wait and pay them off at face value. A gain is recognized for the difference between the purchase price of the bonds and the carrying value of the retired bonds. For example, assume that because of a rise in interest rates, Vason Corporation is able to purchase the $100,000 bond issue on the open market at 85. The entry would be as follows:

STUDY NOTE: The goal is to eliminate from the books any reference to the bonds being retired.

A = L + OE
− − +

	20x7			
	July 1	Bonds Payable	100,000	
		Unamortized Bond Premium	1,447	
		Cash		85,000
		Gain on Retirement of Bonds		16,447
		Purchased and retired		
		9% bonds at 85		

CONVERTIBLE BONDS

Bonds that can be exchanged for common stock or other securities of the corporation are called **convertible bonds**. Convertibility enables an investor to make more money if the market price of the common stock rises, because the value of the bonds then rises. However, if the common stock price does not rise, the investor still holds the bonds and receives both the periodic interest payments and the principal at the maturity date.

Several factors related to the issuance of convertible bonds are favorable to the company. First, the interest rate is usually less than the company would have to offer if the bonds were not convertible. An investor is willing to give up some current interest for the prospect that the value of the stock will increase and therefore the value of the bonds will also increase. Another advantage is that management will not have to give up any current control of the company. Unlike stockholders, bondholders do not have voting rights. A third benefit is tax savings. Interest paid on bonds is fully deductible for income tax purposes, whereas cash dividends on common stock are not. Fourth, the company's income will be affected favorably if the company earns a return that exceeds the interest cost of the bonds. Finally, the convertible feature offers financial flexibility. If the market value of the stock rises to a level at which the bond is worth more than face value, management can avoid repaying the bonds by calling them for redemption, thereby forcing the bondholders to convert their bonds into common stock. The bondholders will agree to convert because no gain or loss results from the transaction.

One major disadvantage of bonds is that interest must be paid semiannually. Inability to make an interest payment could force the company into bankruptcy. Common stock dividends are declared and paid only when the board of directors decides to do so. Another disadvantage of bonds is that when the bonds are converted, they become new outstanding common stock. These new shares give the bondholders stockholders' rights and reduce the proportional ownership of the existing stockholders.

When a bondholder wishes to convert bonds into common stock, the common stock is recorded at the carrying value of the bonds. The bond liability and the associated unamortized discount or premium are written off the books. For this reason, no gain or loss on the transaction is recorded. For example, suppose that Vason Corporation's bonds are not called on July 1, 20x7. Instead, the corporation's bondholders decide to convert all the bonds to $8 par value common stock under a convertible provision of 40 shares of common stock for each $1,000 bond. The entry would be as follows:

A = L + OE
    − +
    − +

20x7			
July 1	Bonds Payable	100,000	
	Unamortized Bond Premium	1,447	
	Common Stock		32,000
	Paid-in Capital in Excess of Par		
	Value, Common		69,447
	Converted 9% bonds payable into		
	$8 par value common stock at a rate		
	of 40 shares for each $1,000 bond		

STUDY POINT: The credits to the contributed capital accounts are based on the carrying value of the bonds converted. As a result, no gain or loss is recognized. If only a portion of the bonds had been converted, proportionate shares of the balances in Bonds Payable and Unamortized Bond Premium would be eliminated.

The unamortized bond premium is found in Column E of Table 2. At a rate of 40 shares for each $1,000 bond, 4,000 shares will be issued, with a total par value of $32,000 (4,000 × $8). The Common Stock account is credited for the amount of the par value of the stock issued. In addition, Paid-in Capital in Excess of Par Value, Common is credited for the difference between the carrying value of the bonds and the par value of the stock issued ($101,447 − $32,000 = $69,447). No gain or loss is recorded.

 Check out ACE for a Review Quiz at http://accounting.college.hmco.com/students.

OTHER LONG-TERM LIABILITIES

SO8 Explain the basic features of mortgages payable, long-term leases, and pensions and other post-retirement benefits as long-term liabilities.

RELATED TEXT ASSIGNMENTS
Q: 11, 12, 13, 14, 15
SE: 10
E: 16, 17
SD: 3, 6
FRA: 4, 6

A company may have other long-term liabilities besides bonds. The most common are mortgages payable, long-term leases, and pensions and other postretirement benefits.

MORTGAGES PAYABLE

A **mortgage** is a long-term debt secured by real property. It is usually paid in equal monthly installments. Each monthly payment includes interest on the debt and a reduction in the debt. Table 3 shows the first three monthly payments on a $50,000, 12 percent mortgage. The mortgage was obtained on June 1, and the monthly payments are $800. According to the table, the entry to record the July 1 payment would be as follows:

A = L + OE
− − −

July 1	Mortgage Payable	300	
	Mortgage Interest Expense	500	
	Cash		800
	Made monthly mortgage payment		

Notice from the entry and from Table 3 that the July 1 payment represents interest expense of $500 ($50,000 × .12 × 1/12) and a reduction in the debt of $300 ($800 − $500). Therefore, the unpaid balance is reduced to $49,700 by the July payment. August's interest expense is slightly less than July's because of the decrease in the debt.

LONG-TERM LEASES

A company can obtain new operating assets in several ways. One way is to borrow money and buy the asset. Another is to rent the equipment on a short-term lease. A third way is to obtain the equipment on a long-term lease. The first two methods do not create accounting problems. In the first case, the asset and liability are recorded at the amount paid, and the asset is subject to periodic depreciation. In the second case, the lease is short term in relation to the useful life of the asset, and the risks of ownership remain with the lessor. This type of agreement is called an **operating lease**. It is proper accounting procedure to treat operating lease payments as an expense and to debit the amount of each monthly payment to Rent Expense.

The third alternative, a long-term lease, is one of the fastest-growing ways of financing operating equipment in the United States today. It has several advantages.

TABLE 3. Monthly Payment Schedule on a $50,000, 12 Percent Mortgage

	A	B	C	D	E
Payment Date	Unpaid Balance at Beginning of Period	Monthly Payment	Interest for 1 Month at 1% on Unpaid Balance* (1% × A)	Reduction in Debt (B − C)	Unpaid Balance at End of Period (A − D)
June 1					$50,000
July 1	$50,000	$800	$500	$300	49,700
Aug. 1	49,700	800	497	303	49,397
Sept. 1	49,397	800	494	306	49,091

*Rounded to the nearest dollar.

LO6 Record bonds issued between interest dates and year-end adjustments.

When bonds are sold on dates between the interest payment dates, the issuing corporation collects from investors the interest that has accrued since the last interest payment date. When the next interest payment date arrives, the corporation pays the bondholders interest for the entire interest period.

When the end of a corporation's fiscal year does not fall on an interest payment date, the corporation must accrue bond interest expense from the last interest payment date to the end of the company's fiscal year. This accrual results in the inclusion of the interest expense in the year incurred.

SUPPLEMENTAL OBJECTIVES

SO7 Account for the retirement of bonds and the conversion of bonds into stock.

Callable bonds can be retired before maturity at the option of the issuing corporation. The call price is usually an amount greater than the face value of the bonds, in which case the corporation recognizes a loss on the retirement of the bonds. A gain can be recognized on the early extinguishment of debt when a company purchases its bonds on the open market at a price below carrying value. This happens when a rise in the market interest rate causes the market value of the bonds to fall below face value.

Convertible bonds allow the bondholder to convert bonds to common stock in the issuing corporation. In this case, the common stock issued is recorded at the carrying value of the bonds being converted. No gain or loss is recognized.

SO8 Explain the basic features of mortgages payable, long-term leases, and pensions and other postretirement benefits as long-term liabilities.

A mortgage is a long-term debt secured by real property. It usually is paid in equal monthly installments. Each payment is partly interest expense and partly debt repayment. If a long-term lease is a capital lease, the risks of ownership lie with the lessee. Like a mortgage payment, each lease payment is partly interest and partly a reduction of debt. For a capital lease, both an asset and a long-term liability should be recorded. The liability should be equal to the present value at the beginning of the lease of the total lease payments over the lease term. The recorded asset is subject to depreciation. Pension expense must be recorded in the current period. Other postretirement benefits should be estimated and accrued while the employee is still working.

REVIEW OF CONCEPTS AND TERMINOLOGY

The following concepts and terms were introduced in this chapter:

LO2 **Bond:** A security, usually long term, representing money that a corporation or other entity borrows from the investing public.

LO2 **Bond certificate:** Evidence of an organization's debt to a bondholder.

LO2 **Bond indenture:** A supplementary agreement to a bond issue that defines the rights, privileges, and limitations of bondholders.

LO2 **Bond issue:** The total value of bonds issued at one time.

SO7 **Callable bonds:** Bonds that an organization can buy back and retire at a call price before maturity.

SO7 **Call price:** A specified price, usually above face value, at which a corporation may buy back and retire bonds before maturity.

SO8 **Capital lease:** A long-term lease in which the risk of ownership lies with the lessee and whose terms resemble those of a purchase or sale on installment.

SO7 **Convertible bonds:** Bonds that can be exchanged for common stock or other securities of the corporation.

LO2 **Coupon bonds:** Bonds that are usually not registered with the issuing organization but instead bear interest coupons stating the amount of interest due and the payment date.

LO3 **Discount:** The amount by which the face value of a bond exceeds the issue price, which occurs when the market interest rate is higher than the face interest rate.

SO7 **Early extinguishment of debt:** The retirement of a bond issue before its maturity date.

LO5 **Effective interest method:** A method of amortizing bond discounts or premiums that applies a constant interest rate (the market rate at the time the bonds were issued) to the carrying value of the bonds at the beginning of each interest period.

LO3 **Face interest rate:** The rate of interest paid to bondholders based on the face value of the bonds.

LO1 **Financial leverage:** The ability to increase earnings for stockholders by earning more on assets than is paid in interest on debt incurred to finance the assets. Also called *trading on the equity*.

LO1 **Interest coverage ratio:** A measure of the degree of protection a company has from default on interest payments; income before taxes plus interest expense divided by interest expense.

LO3 **Market interest rate:** The rate of interest paid in the market on bonds of similar risk. Also called *effective interest rate*.

SO8 **Mortgage:** A long-term debt secured by real property.

SO8 **Operating lease:** A short-term lease in which the risks of ownership remain with the lessor and whose payments are recorded as rent expense.

SO8 **Other postretirement benefits:** Health care and other nonpension benefits paid to a worker after retirement but earned while the employee is still working.

SO8 **Pension fund:** A fund established through contributions by an employer, and often by employees, from which payments are made to employees after retirement or on disability or death.

SO8 **Pension plan:** A contract between a company and its employees under which the company agrees to pay benefits to the employees after they retire.

LO3 **Premium:** The amount by which the issue price of a bond exceeds its face value, which occurs when the market interest rate is lower than the face interest rate.

LO2 **Registered bonds:** Bonds for which the names and addresses of bondholders are recorded with the issuing organization.

LO2 **Secured bonds:** Bonds that give the bondholders a pledge of certain assets as a guarantee of repayment.

LO2 **Serial bonds:** Bonds in an issue that mature on different dates.

LO5 **Straight-line method:** A method of amortizing bond discounts or premiums that allocates the discount or premium equally over each interest period of the life of a bond.

LO2 **Term bonds:** Bonds in an issue that mature at the same time.

LO2 **Unsecured bonds:** Bonds issued on the general credit of an organization. Also called *debenture bonds*.

LO5 **Zero coupon bonds:** Bonds that do not pay periodic interest but that promise to pay a fixed amount on the maturity date.

REVIEW PROBLEM

Interest and Amortization of a Bond Discount, Bond Retirement, and Bond Conversion

LO3
LO5
SO7
When Merrill Manufacturing Company was expanding its metal window division, it did not have enough capital to finance the expansion. So, management sought and received approval from the board of directors to issue bonds. The company planned to issue $5,000,000 of 8 percent, five-year bonds in 20x4. Interest would be paid on June 30 and December 31 of each year. The bonds would be callable at 104, and each $1,000 bond would be convertible into 30 shares of $10 par value common stock.

On January 1, 20x4, the bonds were sold at 96 because the market rate of interest for similar investments was 9 percent. The company decided to amortize the bond discount by using the effective interest method. On July 1, 20x6, management called and retired half the bonds, and investors converted the other half into common stock.

REQUIRED
1. Prepare an interest and amortization schedule for the first five interest periods.
2. Prepare entries in journal form to record the sale of the bonds, the first two interest payments, the bond retirement, and the bond conversion.

ANSWER TO REVIEW PROBLEM

1. Schedule prepared for the first five interest periods:

Interest and Amortization of Bond Discount

Semiannual Interest Payment Date	Carrying Value at Beginning of Period	Semiannual Interest Expense* (9% × ½)	Semiannual Interest Payment (8% × ½)	Amortization of Discount	Unamortized Bond Discount at End of Period	Carrying Value at End of Period
Jan. 1, 20x4					$200,000	$4,800,000
June 30, 20x4	$4,800,000	$216,000	$200,000	$16,000	184,000	4,816,000
Dec. 31, 20x4	4,816,000	216,720	200,000	16,720	167,280	4,832,720
June 30, 20x5	4,832,720	217,472	200,000	17,472	149,808	4,850,192
Dec. 31, 20x5	4,850,192	218,259	200,000	18,259	131,549	4,868,451
June 30, 20x6	4,868,451	219,080	200,000	19,080	112,469	4,887,531

*Rounded to the nearest dollar.

2. Entries made in journal form:

```
20x4
Jan.  1   Cash                                      4,800,000
          Unamortized Bond Discount                   200,000
              Bonds Payable                                       5,000,000
          Sold $5,000,000 of 8%,
          5-year bonds at 96

June 30   Bond Interest Expense                      216,000
              Unamortized Bond Discount                              16,000
              Cash                                                  200,000
          Paid semiannual interest and
          amortized the discount on 8%,
          5-year bonds

Dec. 31   Bond Interest Expense                      216,720
              Unamortized Bond Discount                              16,720
              Cash                                                  200,000
          Paid semiannual interest and
          amortized the discount on 8%,
          5-year bonds

20x6
July  1   Bonds Payable                            2,500,000
          Loss on Retirement of Bonds                156,235
              Unamortized Bond Discount                              56,235
              Cash                                                2,600,000
          Called $2,500,000 of 8% bonds and
          retired them at 104
          $112,469 × ½ = $56,235*

      1   Bonds Payable                            2,500,000
              Unamortized Bond Discount                              56,234
              Common Stock                                          750,000
              Paid-in Capital in Excess of Par
                Value, Common                                     1,693,766
          Converted $2,500,000 of 8% bonds into
          common stock:
          2,500 × 30 shares = 75,000 shares
          75,000 shares × $10 = $750,000
          $112,469 − $56,235 = $56,234
          $2,500,000 − ($56,234 + $750,000) =
          $1,693,766
```

*Rounded.

Chapter Assignments

BUILDING YOUR KNOWLEDGE FOUNDATION

QUESTIONS

1. What are the advantages and disadvantages of issuing long-term debt?
2. What are a bond certificate, a bond issue, and a bond indenture? What information is in a bond indenture?
3. What are the essential differences between (a) secured and debenture bonds, (b) term and serial bonds, and (c) registered and coupon bonds?
4. Napier Corporation sold $500,000 of 5 percent $1,000 bonds on the interest payment date. What would the proceeds from the sale be if the bonds were issued at 95, at 100, and at 102?
5. If you were about to buy bonds on which the face interest rate was less than the market interest rate, would you expect to pay more or less than par value for the bonds?
6. Why does the amortization of a bond discount increase interest expense to an amount greater than interest paid? Why does the amortization of a premium have the opposite effect?
7. When the effective interest method of amortizing a bond discount or premium is used, why does the amount of interest expense change from period to period?
8. When bonds are issued between interest dates, why is it necessary for the issuer to collect an amount equal to accrued interest from the buyer?
9. Why would a company want to exercise the call provision of a bond when it can wait to pay off the debt?
10. What are the advantages of convertible bonds to the company issuing them and to the investor?
11. What are the two components of a uniform monthly mortgage payment?
12. What is a capital lease? Why should an accountant record both an asset and a liability in connection with this type of lease? What items should appear on the income statement as the result of a capital lease?
13. What is a pension plan? What is a pension fund?
14. What is the difference between a defined contribution plan and a defined benefit plan? In general, how is expense determined under each plan? What assumptions must be made to account for the expenses of a defined benefit plan?
15. What are other postretirement benefits, and how is the matching rule applied?

SHORT EXERCISES

SE 1.
LO1 Bond Versus Common Stock Financing

Indicate whether each of the following is an advantage or a disadvantage of using long-term bond financing rather than issuing common stock:

1. Interest paid on bonds is tax deductible.
2. Investments are sometimes not as successful as planned.
3. Financial leverage can have a negative effect when investments do not earn as much as the interest payments on the related debt.
4. Bondholders do not have voting rights in a corporation.
5. Positive financial leverage may be achieved.

SE 2.
LO3 Entries for Interest Using
LO5 the Straight-Line Method

On April 1, 20x4, Agaki Corporation issued $4,000,000 in 8.5 percent, five-year bonds at 98. The semiannual interest payment dates are April 1 and October 1. Prepare entries in journal form for the issue of the bonds by Agaki on April 1, 20x4, and the first two interest payments on October 1, 20x4, and April 1, 20x5. Use the straight-line method and ignore year-end accruals.

Chapter Assignments

SE 3.
LO3 LO5 LO6 Entries for Interest Using the Effective Interest Method

On March 1, 20xx, Westward Freight Company sold $100,000 of its 9.5 percent, 20-year bonds at 106. The semiannual interest payment dates are March 1 and September 1. The market interest rate is about 8.9 percent. The company's fiscal year ends August 31. Prepare entries in journal form to record the sale of the bonds on March 1, the accrual of interest and amortization of premium on August 31, and the first interest payment on September 1. Use the effective interest method to amortize the premium.

[Handwritten annotations: "INDICATES Premium" → 106, "INTEREST EXPENSE" → 8.9%, "STATED RATE / FACE RATE" → 9.5]

SE 4.
LO4 Valuing Bonds Using Present Value

Cap Art, Inc., is considering the sale of two bond issues. Choice A is a $400,000 bond issue that pays semiannual interest of $32,000 and is due in 20 years. Choice B is a $400,000 bond issue that pays semiannual interest of $30,000 and is due in 15 years. Assume that the market interest rate for each bond is 12 percent. Calculate the amount that Cap Art will receive if both bond issues occur. (Calculate the present value of each bond issue and sum.)

SE 5.
LO3 LO6 Entries for Bond Issues

League Company is authorized to issue $900,000 in bonds on June 1. The bonds carry a face interest rate of 8 percent, with interest to be paid on June 1 and December 1. Prepare entries in journal form for the issue of the bonds under the independent assumptions that (a) the bonds are issued on September 1 at 100 and (b) the bonds are issued on June 1 at 103.

SE 6.
LO6 Sale of Bonds Between Interest Dates

Eisley Corporation sold $200,000 of 9 percent, ten-year bonds for face value on September 1, 20xx. The issue date of the bonds was May 1, 20xx. The company's fiscal year ends on December 31, and this is its only bond issue. Record the sale of the bonds on September 1 and the first semiannual interest payment on November 1, 20xx. What is the bond interest expense for the year ended December 31, 20xx?

SE 7.
LO3 LO5 LO6 Year-End Accrual of Bond Interest

On October 1, 20x4, Knight Corporation issued $500,000 of 9 percent bonds at 96. The bonds are dated October 1 and pay interest semiannually. The market rate of interest is 10 percent, and the company's year end is December 31. Prepare the entries to record the issuance of the bonds, the accrual of the interest on December 31, 20x4, and the payment of the first semiannual interest on April 1, 20x5. Assume that the company does not use reversing entries and uses the effective interest method to amortize the bond discount.

SE 8.
SO7 Entry for Bond Retirement

Ross Corporation has outstanding $800,000 of 8 percent bonds callable at 104. On December 1, immediately after the payment of the semiannual interest and the amortization of the bond discount were recorded, the unamortized bond discount equaled $21,000. On that date, $480,000 of the bonds were called and retired. Prepare the entry to record the retirement of the bonds on December 1.

SE 9.
SO7 Entry for Bond Conversion

Hui Corporation has $1,000,000 of 6 percent bonds outstanding. There is $20,000 of unamortized discount remaining on the bonds after the March 1, 20x5, semiannual interest payment. The bonds are convertible at the rate of 20 shares of $10 par value common stock for each $1,000 bond. On March 1, 20x5, bondholders presented $600,000 of the bonds for conversion. Prepare the entry to record the conversion of the bonds.

SE 10.
SO8 Mortgage Payable

Sedaka Corporation purchased a building by signing a $300,000 long-term mortgage with monthly payments of $2,400. The mortgage carries an interest rate of 8 percent. Prepare a monthly payment schedule showing the monthly payment, the interest for the month, the reduction in debt, and the unpaid balance for the first three months. (Round to the nearest dollar.)

Exercises

E 1.
LO1 Interest Coverage Ratio

Compute the interest coverage ratios for 20x4 and 20x5 from the partial income statements of Ivy Wall Company that appear below. State whether the ratio improved or worsened over time.

	20x5	20x4
Income from operations	$23,890	$18,460
Interest expense	5,800	3,300
Income before income taxes	$18,090	$15,160
Income taxes	5,400	4,500
Net income	$12,690	$10,660

E 2.
LO3 Entries for Interest Using the
LO5 Straight-Line Method

Agga Corporation issued $4,000,000 in 10.5 percent, ten-year bonds on February 1, 20x4, at 104. The semiannual interest payment dates are February 1 and August 1. Prepare entries in journal form for the issue of bonds by Agga on February 1, 20x4, and the first two interest payments on August 1, 20x4, and February 1, 20x5. Use the straight-line method and ignore year-end accruals.

E 3.
LO3 Entries for Interest Using
LO5 the Straight-Line Method

Famina Corporation issued $8,000,000 in 8.5 percent, five-year bonds on March 1, 20x5, at 96. The semiannual interest payment dates are March 1 and September 1. Prepare entries in journal form for the issue of the bonds by Famina on March 1, 20x5, and the first two interest payments on September 1, 20x5, and March 1, 20x6. Use the straight-line method and ignore year-end accruals.

E 4.
LO3 Entries for Interest Using the
LO5 Effective Interest Method
LO6

Whistle Toy Company sold $500,000 of 9.5 percent, 20-year bonds on April 1, 20xx, at 106. The semiannual interest payment dates are April 1 and October 1. The market interest rate is 8.9 percent. The company's fiscal year ends September 30. Prepare entries in journal form to record the sale of the bonds on April 1, the accrual of interest and amortization of premium on September 30, and the first interest payment on October 1. Use the effective interest method to amortize the premium.

E 5.
LO3 Entries for Interest Using
LO5 the Effective Interest Method
LO6

On March 1, 20x4, Eddy Corporation issued $1,200,000 of 10 percent, five-year bonds. The semiannual interest payment dates are March 1 and September 1. Because the market rate for similar investments was 11 percent, the bonds had to be issued at a discount. The discount on the issuance of the bonds was $48,670. The company's fiscal year ends February 28. Prepare entries in journal form to record the bond issue on March 1, 20x4; the payment of interest and the amortization of the discount on September 1, 20x4; the accrual of interest and the amortization of the discount on February 28, 20x5; and the payment of interest on March 1, 20x5. Use the effective interest method. (Round answers to the nearest dollar.)

E 6.
LO4 Valuing Bonds Using Present Value

Octogon, Inc., is considering the sale of two bond issues. Choice A is an $800,000 bond issue that pays semiannual interest of $64,000 and is due in 20 years. Choice B is an $800,000 bond issue that pays semiannual interest of $60,000 and is due in 15 years. Assume that the market interest rate for each bond is 12 percent. Calculate the amount that Octogon, Inc., will receive if both bond issues are made. (**Hint:** Calculate the present value of each bond issue and sum.)

E 7.
LO4 Valuing Bonds Using Present Value

Use the present value tables in the appendix on future value and present value tables to calculate the issue price of a $1,200,000 bond issue in each of the following independent cases, assuming that interest is paid semiannually:

a. A ten-year, 8 percent bond issue; the market interest rate is 10 percent.
b. A ten-year, 8 percent bond issue; the market interest rate is 6 percent.
c. A ten-year, 10 percent bond issue; the market interest rate is 8 percent.
d. A 20-year, 10 percent bond issue; the market interest rate is 12 percent.
e. A 20-year, 10 percent bond issue; the market interest rate is 6 percent.

E 8.
LO4 Zero Coupon Bonds

The state of Idaho needs to raise $100,000,000 for highway repairs. Officials are considering issuing zero coupon bonds, which do not require periodic interest payments. The current market interest rate for the bonds is 10 percent. What face value of bonds must be issued to raise the needed funds, assuming the bonds will be due in 30 years and compounded annually? How would your answer change if the bonds were due in 50 years? How would both answers change if the market interest rate were 8 percent instead of 10 percent?

E 9.
LO5 Entries for Interest Payments
LO6 Using the Effective Interest Method

The long-term debt section of the Sanchos Corporation's balance sheet at the end of its fiscal year, December 31, 2005, was as follows:

Long-term liabilities
   Bonds payable—8%, interest payable
     1/1 and 7/1, due 12/31/13 $1,000,000
   Less unamortized bond discount   80,000 $920,000

Prepare entries in journal form relevant to the interest payments on July 1, 2006, December 31, 2006, and January 1, 2007. Use the effective interest rate method and assume a market interest rate of 10 percent.

E 10.
LO3 Entries for Bond Issue
LO6

Water Symphonics, Inc., is authorized to issue $1,800,000 in bonds on June 1. The bonds carry a face interest rate of 9 percent, which is to be paid on June 1 and December 1. Prepare entries in journal form for the issue of the bonds by Water Symphonics, Inc., under the assumptions that (a) the bonds are issued on September 1 at 100 and (b) the bonds are issued on June 1 at 105.

E 11.
LO6 Sale of Bonds Between Interest Dates

Margi Corporation sold $400,000 of 12 percent, ten-year bonds at face value on September 1, 20xx. The issue date of the bonds was May 1, 20xx.

1. Record the sale of the bonds on September 1 and the first semiannual interest payment on November 1, 20xx.
2. The company's fiscal year ends on December 31, and this is its only bond issue. What is the bond interest expense for the year ended December 31, 20xx?

E 12.
LO3 Year-End Accrual of Bond
LO5 Interest
LO6

Lon Corporation issued $1,000,000 of 9 percent bonds on October 1, 20x3, at 96. The bonds are dated October 1 and pay interest semiannually. The market interest rate is 10 percent, and Lon's fiscal year ends on December 31. Prepare the entries to record the issuance of the bonds, the accrual of the interest on December 31, 20x3, and the first semiannual interest payment on April 1, 20x4. Assume the company does not use reversing entries and uses the effective interest method to amortize the bond discount.

E 13.
LO4 Time Value of Money and
SO7 Early Extinguishment of Debt

Brown, Inc., has a $1,400,000, 8 percent bond issue that was issued a number of years ago at face value. There are now ten years left on the bond issue, and the market interest rate is 16 percent. Interest is paid semiannually.

1. Using present value tables, figure the current market value of the bond issue.
2. Record the retirement of the bonds, assuming the company purchases the bonds on the open market at the calculated value.

E 14.
SO7 Entry for Bond Retirement

The Pucinski Corporation has outstanding $1,600,000 of 8 percent bonds callable at 104. On September 1, immediately after recording the payment of the semiannual interest and the amortization of the discount, the unamortized bond discount equaled $42,000. On that date, $960,000 of the bonds were called and retired. Prepare the entry to record the retirement of the bonds on September 1.

E 15.
SO7 Entry for Bond Conversion

The Daglar Corporation has $400,000 of 6 percent bonds outstanding. There is $20,000 of unamortized discount remaining on these bonds after the July 1, 20x8, semiannual interest payment. The bonds are convertible at the rate of 40 shares of $5 par value common stock for each $1,000 bond. On July 1, 20x8, bondholders presented $300,000 of the bonds for conversion. Prepare the entry to record the conversion of the bonds.

E 16.
SO8 Mortgage Payable

Fiery Corporation purchased a building by signing a $150,000 long-term mortgage with monthly payments of $2,000. The mortgage carries an interest rate of 12 percent.

1. Prepare a monthly payment schedule showing the monthly payment, the interest for the month, the reduction in debt, and the unpaid balance for the first three months. (Round to the nearest dollar.)
2. Prepare entries in journal form to record the purchase and the first two monthly payments.

E 17.
SO8 Recording Lease Obligations

Foxx Corporation has leased a piece of equipment that has a useful life of 12 years. The terms of the lease are $43,000 per year for 12 years. Foxx currently is able to borrow money at a long-term interest rate of 15 percent. Round answers to the nearest dollar.)

1. Calculate the present value of the lease.
2. Prepare the entry to record the lease agreement.
3. Prepare the entry to record depreciation of the equipment for the first year using the straight-line method.
4. Prepare the entries to record the lease payments for the first two years.

PROBLEMS

P 1.
LO3 Bond Transactions—Straight-
LO5 Line Method
LO6

Gala Corporation has $30,000,000 of 10.5 percent, 20-year bonds dated June 1, with interest payment dates of May 31 and November 30. The company's fiscal year ends on December 31. It uses the straight-line method to amortize bond premiums or discounts.

REQUIRED ▶

1. Assume the bonds are issued at 103 on June 1. Prepare entries in journal form for June 1, November 30, and December 31.
2. Assume the bonds are issued at 97 on June 1. Prepare entries in journal form for June 1, November 30, and December 31.
3. Assume the bonds are issued at face value plus accrued interest on August 1. Prepare entries in journal form for August 1, November 30, and December 31.

Chapter 11 Long-Term Liabilities

P 2.
LO3 Bond Transactions—Effective
LO5 Interest Method
LO6

Paco Corporation has $16,000,000 of 9.5 percent, 25-year bonds dated March 1, with interest payable on March 1 and September 1. The company's fiscal year ends on November 30. It uses the effective interest method to amortize bond premiums or discounts. (Round amounts to the nearest dollar.)

REQUIRED
1. Assume the bonds are issued at 102.5 on March 1 to yield an effective interest rate of 9.2 percent. Prepare entries in journal form for March 1, September 1, and November 30.
2. Assume the bonds are issued at 97.5 on March 1 to yield an effective interest rate of 9.8 percent. Prepare entries in journal form for March 1, September 1, and November 30.
3. Assume the bonds are issued on June 1 at face value plus accrued interest. Prepare entries in journal form for June 1, September 1, and November 30.

P 3.
LO3 Bonds Issued at a Discount
LO5 and a Premium
LO6

Reiser Corporation issued bonds twice during 20x4. A summary of the transactions involving the bonds follows.

20x4
Jan. 1 Issued $3,000,000 of 9.9 percent, 10-year bonds dated January 1, 20x4, with interest payable on June 30 and December 31. The bonds were sold at 102.6, resulting in an effective interest rate of 9.4 percent.
Mar. 1 Issued $2,000,000 of 9.2 percent, 10-year bonds dated March 1, 20x4, with interest payable March 1 and September 1. The bonds were sold at 98.2, resulting in an effective interest rate of 9.5 percent.
June 30 Paid semiannual interest on the January 1 issue and amortized the premium, using the effective interest method.
Sept. 1 Paid semiannual interest on the March 1 issue and amortized the discount, using the effective interest method.
Dec. 31 Paid semiannual interest on the January 1 issue and amortized the premium, using the effective interest method.
31 Made an end-of-year adjusting entry to accrue interest on the March 1 issue and to amortize two-thirds of the discount applicable to the second interest period.

20x5
Mar. 1 Paid semiannual interest on the March 1 issue and amortized the remainder of the discount applicable to the second interest period.

REQUIRED Prepare entries in journal form to record the bond transactions. (Round amounts to the nearest dollar.)

P 4.
LO3 Bond Interest and
LO5 Amortization Table, and
SO7 Bond Retirements

In 20x3, the Boston Corporation was authorized to issue $60,000,000 of six-year unsecured bonds. The bonds carried a face interest rate of 9 percent, payable semiannually on June 30 and December 31. The bonds were callable at 105 any time after June 30, 20x6. All of the bonds were issued on July 1, 20x3 at 95.568, a price yielding an effective interest rate of 10 percent. On July 1, 20x6, the company called and retired half the outstanding bonds.

REQUIRED
1. Prepare a table similar to Table 1 to show the interest and amortization of the bond discount for 12 interest payment periods, using the effective interest method. (Round results to the nearest dollar.)
2. Calculate the amount of loss on early retirement of one-half of the bonds on July 1, 20x6.

P 5.
LO3 Comprehensive Bond
LO5 Transactions
LO6
SO7

The Ingolls Corporation, a company whose fiscal year ends on June 30, engaged in the following long-term bond transactions over a three-year period:

20x3
Nov. 1 Issued $40,000,000 of 12 percent debenture bonds at face value plus accrued interest. Interest is payable on January 31 and July 31, and the bonds are callable at 104.

20x4
Jan. 31 Made the semiannual interest payment on the 12 percent bonds.
June 30 Made the year-end accrual of interest payment on the 12 percent bonds.
July 1 Issued $20,000,000 of 10 percent, 15-year convertible bonds at 105. Interest is payable on June 30 and December 31, and each $1,000 bond is convertible into 30 shares of $10 par value common stock. The market rate of interest is 9 percent.

July 31 Made the semiannual interest payment on the 12 percent bonds.
Dec. 31 Made the semiannual interest payment on the 10 percent bonds and amortized the bond premium.

20x5
Jan. 31 Made the semiannual interest payment on the 12 percent bonds.
Feb. 28 Called and retired all of the 12 percent bonds, including accrued interest.
June 30 Made the semiannual interest payment on the 10 percent bonds and amortized the bond premium.
July 1 Accepted for conversion into common stock all of the 10 percent bonds.

REQUIRED ▶ Prepare entries in journal form to record the bond transactions, making all necessary accruals and using the effective interest method. (Round all calculations to the nearest dollar.)

ALTERNATE PROBLEMS

P 6. Raol Corporation has $4,000,000 of 9.5 percent, 25-year bonds dated March 1, with interest payable on March 1 and September 1. The company's fiscal year ends on November 30, and it uses the straight-line method to amortize bond premiums or discounts.

LO3 **Bond Transactions—Straight-**
LO5 **Line Method**
LO6

REQUIRED ▶
1. Assume the bonds are issued at 103.5 on March 1. Prepare entries in journal form for March 1, September 1, and November 30.
2. Assume the bonds are issued at 96.5 on March 1. Prepare entries in journal form for March 1, September 1, and November 30.
3. Assume the bonds are issued on June 1 at face value plus accrued interest. Prepare entries in journal form for June 1, September 1, and November 30.

P 7. Dubchec Corporation has $10,000,000 of 10.5 percent, 20-year bonds dated June 1, with interest payment dates of May 31 and November 30. The company's fiscal year ends December 31. It uses the effective interest method to amortize bond premiums or discounts.

LO3 **Bond Transactions—Effective**
LO5 **Interest Method**
LO6

REQUIRED ▶
1. Assume the bonds are issued at 103 on June 1 to yield an effective interest rate of 10.1 percent. Prepare entries in journal form for June 1, November 30, and December 31. (Round amounts to the nearest dollar.)
2. Assume the bonds are issued at 97 on June 1 to yield an effective interest rate of 10.9 percent. Prepare entries in journal form for June 1, November 30, and December 31. (Round amounts to the nearest dollar.)
3. Assume the bonds are issued at face value plus accrued interest on August 1. Prepare entries in journal form for August 1, November 30, and December 31. (Round amounts to the nearest dollar.)

P 8. Fils Corporation issued bonds twice during 20x3. The transactions were as follows:

LO3 **Bonds Issued at a Discount**
LO5 **and a Premium**
LO6

20x3
Jan. 1 Issued $1,000,000 of 9.2 percent, 10-year bonds dated January 1, 20x3, with interest payable on June 30 and December 31. The bonds were sold at 98.1, resulting in an effective interest rate of 9.5 percent.
Apr. 1 Issued $2,000,000 of 9.8 percent, 10-year bonds dated April 1, 20x3, with interest payable on March 31 and September 30. The bonds were sold at 102, resulting in an effective interest rate of 9.5 percent.
June 30 Paid semiannual interest on the January 1 issue and amortized the discount, using the effective interest method.
Sept. 30 Paid semiannual interest on the April 1 issue and amortized the premium, using the effective interest method.
Dec. 31 Paid semiannual interest on the January 1 issue and amortized the discount, using the effective interest method.
     31 Made an end-of-year adjusting entry to accrue interest on the April 1 issue and to amortize half the premium applicable to the second interest period.

20x4
Mar. 31 Paid semiannual interest on the April 1 issue and amortized the premium applicable to the second half of the second interest period.

REQUIRED ▶ Prepare entries in journal form to record the bond transactions. (Round amounts to the nearest dollar.)

Skills Development Cases

Conceptual Analysis

LO3 Bond Interest Rates and Market Prices

SD 1. Safeway Inc. <www.safeway.com> is one of the largest food and drug retailers in North America. Among its long-term liabilities is a bond due in 2004 that carries a face interest rate of 9.65 percent. Recently this bond sold on the New York Stock Exchange at 108%. Does this bond sell at a discount or a premium? Assuming the bond was originally issued at face value, have interest rates risen or declined since the date of issue? Do you expect the market interest rate on this bond to be more or less than 9.65 percent? Does the current market price affect either the amount that the company pays in semi-annual interest or the amount of interest expense for the same period? Explain your answers.

LO5 Nature of Zero Coupon Notes

SD 2. *The Wall Street Journal* reported, "Financially ailing Trans World Airlines has renegotiated its agreement to sell its 40 landing and takeoff slots and three gates at O'Hare International Airport to American Airlines." Instead of receiving a lump-sum cash payment in the amount of $162.5 million, TWA elected to receive a zero coupon note from American <www.aa.com> that would be paid off in monthly installments over a 20-year period. Since the 240 monthly payments totaled $500 million, TWA placed a value of $500 million on the note and indicated that the bankruptcy court would not have accepted the lower lump-sum cash payment.

How does this zero coupon note differ from the zero coupon bonds that we described earlier in this chapter? Explain the difference between the $162.5 million cash payment and the $500 million note. Do you think TWA was right in placing a $500 million price on the sale?[12]

SO8 Lease Financing

SD 3. FedEx Corporation <www.fedex.com>, known for overnight delivery and distribution of high-priority goods and documents throughout the world, has an extensive fleet of aircraft and vehicles. In its 2001 annual report, the company stated that it "utilizes certain aircraft, land, facilities, and equipment under capital and operating leases which expire at various dates through 2038. In addition, supplemental aircraft are leased under agreements which generally provide for cancellation upon 30 days' notice." The annual report further stated that the minimum commitments for capital leases and noncancelable operating leases for 2002 were $15,416,000 and $1,246,936,000, respectively.[13] What is the difference between a capital lease and an operating lease? How do the accounting procedures for the two types of leases differ? How do you interpret management's reasoning in acquiring some aircraft under capital leases and others under operating leases? Why do you think the management of FedEx leases most of its aircraft instead of buying them?

Ethical Dilemma

LO2 Bond Indenture and Ethical Reporting

SD 4. CellWorks Technology, Inc., a biotech company, has a $24,000,000 bond issue outstanding. The bond indenture has several restrictive provisions, including requirements that current assets exceed current liabilities by a ratio of 2 to 1 and that income before income taxes exceed the annual interest on the bonds by a ratio of 3 to 1. If those requirements are not met, the bondholders can force the company into bankruptcy. The company is still awaiting Food and Drug Administration (FDA) approval of its new product CMZ-12, a cancer treatment drug. Management had been counting on sales of CMZ-12 this year to meet the provisions of the bond indenture. As the end of the fiscal year approaches, the company does not have sufficient current assets or income before taxes to meet the requirements. Roger Landon, the chief financial officer, proposes, "Since we can assume that FDA approval will occur early next year, I suggest we book sales and receivables from our major customers now in anticipation of next year's sales. This action will increase our current assets and our income before taxes. It is essential that we do this to save the company. Look at all the people who will be hurt if we don't do it."

Is Landon's proposal acceptable accounting? Is it ethical? Who could be harmed by it? What steps might management take?

Research Activity

LO3 Reading the Bond Markets

SD 5. Obtain a recent issue of *The Wall Street Journal* and turn to the page on which the New York Exchange Bonds are listed. Notice, first, the Dow Jones Bond Averages of 20 bonds, ten utilities, and ten industrials. Are the averages above or below 100? Is this a premium or a discount? Is the market interest rate above or below the face rate of the average bond? Now, choose three bonds from those listed—one that sells at a discount, one that sells at a premium, and one that sells for approximately 100. For each bond, write the name of the company, the face interest rate, the year the bond is due, the current yield (market interest rate), and the current closing market price. (Some bonds have the letters *cv* in the Yield column, which means the bonds are convertible into common stock and the yield may not be meaningful.) For each bond, explain the relationships between the face interest rate, the current yield, and the closing price. What other factors affect the current yield of a bond? Be prepared to discuss your findings in class.

Decision-Making Practice

LO1 Issuance of Long-Term Bonds
LO2 Versus Leasing
SO8

SD 6. The Weiss Chemical Corporation plans to build or lease a new plant that will produce liquid fertilizer for the agricultural market. The plant is expected to cost $800,000,000 and will be located in the southwestern United States. The company's chief financial officer, Sharon Weiss, has spent the last several weeks studying different means of financing the plant. From her talks with bankers and other financiers, she has decided that there are two basic choices: the plant can be financed through the issuance of a long-term bond or through a long-term lease. Details for the two options are as follows:

1. Issue $800,000,000 of 25-year, 16 percent bonds secured by the new plant. Interest on the bonds would be payable semiannually.
2. Sign a 25-year lease for an existing plant calling for lease payments of $65,400,000 on a semiannual basis.

Weiss wants to know what the effect of each choice will be on the company's financial statements. She estimates that the useful life of the plant is 25 years, at which time it is expected to have an estimated residual value of $80,000,000.

Weiss plans a meeting to discuss the alternatives. Write a short memorandum to her identifying the issues that should be considered at this meeting. (**Note:** You are not asked to make any calculations, discuss the factors, or recommend an action.)

FINANCIAL REPORTING AND ANALYSIS CASES

Interpreting Financial Reports

LO1 Debt Repayment

FRA 1. During economic recessions, occupancy rates of hotels generally decline, and the hotels are forced to reduce their room prices. The impact on a hotel's cash flows may be such that it is unable to pay its debts when they come due. A study of the financial statements of 3,300 hotels by the Hospitality Research Group found that 16 percent of hotels were unable to generate enough cash from operations to make debt repayments in 2000. The group estimated that this figure would increase to 20.9 percent in 2001 and 36.5 percent in 2002.[14] What alternative sources of cash might be available to hotels whose cash flows from operations are inadequate to cover debt repayments?

SO7 Characteristics of Convertible Debt

FRA 2. Amazon.com, Inc. <www.amazon.com>, gained renown as an online marketplace for books, records, and other products. Although the increase in its stock price was initially meteoric, the company has yet to earn a profit. To support its enormous growth, the company issued $1,250,000,000 in 4¾ percent convertible notes due in 2009 at face value. Interest is payable on February 1 and August 1. The notes are convertible into common stock at a price of $156 per share, which is 27 percent above the market price of $123 for the common stock on the date of issue. The market value of Amazon.com's common stock has been quite volatile; earlier it was $200 per share.[15]

What reasons can you suggest for Amazon.com's management choosing notes that are convertible into common stock rather than simply issuing nonconvertible notes or issuing common stock directly? Are there any disadvantages to this approach? If the price of the company's common stock returns to $200 per share, what would be the total theoretical value of the notes? If the holders of the notes were to elect to convert the notes into common stock, what would be the effect on the company's debt to equity ratio, and what would be the effect on the percentage ownership of the company by other stockholders?

International Company

FRA 3.

LO1 **Comparison of Interest Coverage**

Japanese companies have historically relied more on debt financing and are more highly leveraged than U.S. companies. For instance, NEC Corporation <www.nec.com> and Sanyo Electric Co. <www.sanyo.com>, two large Japanese electronics companies, had debt to equity ratios of about 4.3 and 3.5, respectively, in 2001. From the selected data from the companies' annual reports shown below (in millions of yen), compute the interest coverage ratios for the two companies for the two years. Comment on the riskiness of the companies and on the trends they show.[16]

	NEC		Sanyo	
	2001	2000	2001	2000
Interest expense	63,873	70,211	26,427	27,914
Income before income taxes	92,323	30,183	73,484	36,953

Group Activity: Assign the two companies to different groups to calculate the ratios and discuss the results. Debrief by discussing the advantages and disadvantages of a debt-laden capital structure.

Toys "R" Us Annual Report

FRA 4.

LO1 **Business Practice, Long-Term**
SO8 **Debt, and Leases**

Refer to the financial statements and the notes to the financial statements in the Toys "R" Us <www.tru.com> annual report to answer the following questions:

1. Is it the practice of Toys "R" Us to own or lease most of its property and equipment?
2. Does Toys "R" Us lease property predominantly under capital leases or under operating leases? How much was rental expense for operating leases in 2002?

Comparison Case: Toys "R" Us and Walgreen Co.

FRA 5.

LO1 **Use of Debt Financing**

Refer to the annual report of Toys "R" Us <www.tru.com> and the financial statements of Walgreens <www.walgreens.com> in the Supplement to Chapter 1. Calculate the debt to equity ratio and the interest coverage ratio for both companies' most recent two years. Evaluate and comment on the relative performance of the two companies with regard to debt financing. Which company has more risk of not being able to meet its interest obligations? Explain.

FRA 6.

LO1 **Long-Term Liabilities**
LO2
SO8

Fingraph® Financial Analyst™

Select any two companies from the same industry from the list of Fingraph companies on the Needles Accounting Resource Center Web Site at http://accounting.college.hmco.com/students. Access the Microsoft Excel spreadsheets for the companies you selected. For parts 1, 3, and 4, click on the URL at the top of each company's spreadsheet for a link to the company's web site and annual report.

1. In the annual reports of the companies you have selected, identify the long-term liabilities on the balance sheet and read any reference to long-term liabilities in the summary of significant accounting policies or notes to the financial statements. There is likely to be a separate note for each type of long-term liability. What are the most important long-term liabilities for each company?
2. Using the Fingraph CD-ROM software, display and print in tabular and graphic form the Balance Sheet Analysis page. Prepare a table that compares the debt to equity and interest coverage ratios for both companies for two years.
3. Read the statements of cash flows in both annual reports. Have the companies been increasing or decreasing their long-term debt? If increasing, what were each com-

pany's most important sources of long-term financing over the past two years? If decreasing, which liabilities are being decreased?
4. Find and read references to long-term liabilities in management's discussion and analysis in each annual report.
5. Write a one-page executive summary that highlights the most important types of long-term liabilities for these companies, identifies their accounting policies for specific long-term liabilities, and compares their debt to equity and interest coverage trends. The summary should refer to management's assessment. Include the Fingraph page and your table with your report.

Internet Case

LO2 Bond Rating Changes

FRA 7. Go to the Needles Accounting Resource Center Web Site at http://accounting.college.hmco.com/students. Under Web Links, select Standard & Poor's or access their web site directly at <www.standardandpoors.com>. In times of economic or industry recessions, it is common to see downward revisions of bond ratings. From the Standard & Poor's list of companies with lowered bond ratings, identify three whose names you recognize. For each company, give reasons that you believe contributed to the ratings downgrade.

12

Chapter 12 focuses on long-term equity financing, including the types of equity securities and transactions that affect the stockholders' equity section of the balance sheet, such as stock issues, dividends, and treasury stock purchases.

Contributed Capital

Learning Objectives

LO1 Identify and explain the management issues related to contributed capital.

LO2 Identify the components of stockholders' equity.

LO3 Account for cash dividends.

LO4 Identify the characteristics of preferred stock, including the effect on distribution of dividends.

LO5 Account for the issuance of stock for cash and other assets.

LO6 Account for treasury stock.

DECISION POINT
A USER'S FOCUS

Cisco Systems, Inc. <www.cisco.com> One way corporations raise new capital is by issuing stock. Cisco Systems, Inc., a major manufacturer of telecommunications equipment, issued almost $3.5 billion of common stock in a recent three-year period, as shown in the Financial Highlights on the opposite page.[1] Why does Cisco Systems' management choose to issue common stock to satisfy some of its needs for new capital? What are some of the advantages and disadvantages of this approach?

Financing with common stock has several advantages. First, it is less risky than financing with bonds because dividends on common stock are not paid unless the board of directors decides to pay them. Cisco Systems does not currently pay any dividends. In contrast, if the interest on bonds is not paid, a company can be forced into bankruptcy. Second, when a company does not pay a cash dividend, the cash generated by profitable operations can be invested in the company's operations. Third, a company may need the proceeds of a common stock issue to maintain or improve the balance between liabilities and stockholders' equity. By issuing common stock in 2001, Cisco Systems offset the impact on stockholders' equity of a $1 billion net loss in 2001. The balance between total liabilities and total equity remains a relatively low 30 percent.

On the other hand, issuing common stock comes with certain disadvantages. Unlike the interest on bonds, dividends paid on stock are not tax-deductible. Furthermore, when it issues more stock, the corpora-

Why does Cisco Systems, Inc. choose to issue common stock to satisfy some of its needs for new capital?

tion dilutes its ownership. This means that the current stockholders must yield some control to the new stockholders. It is important for accountants to understand the nature and characteristics of corporations as well as the process of accounting for a stock issue and other types of stock transactions.

Financial Highlights
(In millions)

	2002	2001	2000
Issuance of common stock	$655	$1,262	$1,564

MANAGEMENT ISSUES RELATED TO CONTRIBUTED CAPITAL

LO1 Identify and explain the management issues related to contributed capital.

RELATED TEXT ASSIGNMENTS
Q: 1, 2, 3, 4, 5, 6, 7, 8, 9
SE: 1, 2, 3, 4
E: 1
P: 1, 2, 3, 4, 5, 6, 7, 8
SD: 1, 4, 5, 6
FRA: 1, 4, 5, 6, 7

A **corporation** is defined as a body of persons granted a charter recognizing them as a separate legal entity having its own rights, privileges, and liabilities distinct from those of its members.[2] In other words, a corporation is a legal entity separate and distinct from its owners.

Contributed capital is a critical component in financing a corporation. Important management issues related to this area are managing under the corporate form of business, using equity financing, determining dividend policies, evaluating performance using return on equity, and using stock options as compensation.

FORMING A CORPORATION

To form a corporation, most states require individuals, called incorporators, to sign an application and file it with the proper state official. This application contains the **articles of incorporation**. If approved by the state, these articles become, in effect, a contract, called the company charter, between the state and the incorporators. The company is then authorized to do business. The authority to manage the corporation is delegated by the stockholders to the board of directors and by the board of directors to the corporate officers (see Figure 1). That is, the stockholders elect the board of directors, which sets company policies and chooses the corporate officers, who in turn carry out the corporate policies by managing the business.

■ **STOCKHOLDERS** A unit of ownership in a corporation is called a **share of stock**. The articles of incorporation state the maximum number of shares of stock that the corporation will be allowed, or authorized, to issue. The number of shares held by stockholders is the outstanding capital stock; this is generally less than the number authorized in the articles of incorporation. To invest in a corporation, a stockholder transfers cash or other resources to the corporation. In return, the stockholder receives shares of stock representing a proportionate share of ownership in the corporation. The stockholder may then transfer the shares at will. Corporations may have more than one kind of capital stock, but we will refer only to common stock.

■ **BOARD OF DIRECTORS** As noted, the stockholders elect the board of directors, which in turn decides on the major business policies of the corporation. Among the specific duties of the board are authorizing contracts, setting executive salaries, and arranging major loans with banks. The declaration of dividends is also an important function. Only the board has the authority to declare dividends. **Dividends** are distributions of resources, generally in the form of cash, to the stockholders. Paying dividends is one way of rewarding stockholders for their investment when the corporation has been successful in earning a profit. (The other way is through a rise in the market value of the stock.) There is usually a delay of two or three weeks between the time the board declares a dividend and the date of the actual payment.

The board of directors usually includes several corporate officers and several outsiders. Today, the formation of an **audit committee** with several outside directors is encouraged to ensure that the board will be objective in evaluating management's performance. One function of the audit committee is to engage independent auditors and review their work. Another is to ensure that proper systems safeguard the company's resources and that accounting records are reliable.

■ **MANAGEMENT** The board of directors appoints managers to carry out the corporation's policies and run day-to-day operations. The management consists of the operating officers, generally the president, vice presidents, controller, treasurer, and secretary. Besides being responsible for running the business, management must report the financial results of its administration to the board and stockholders. Though management must make at least one comprehensive annual report, it

FIGURE 1
The Corporate Form of Business

generally reports more often. The annual reports of large public corporations are available to the public. Excerpts from many of them appear throughout this book.

MANAGING UNDER THE CORPORATE FORM OF BUSINESS

Although sole proprietorships and partnerships outnumber corporations in the United States, corporations dominate the economy in total dollars of assets and output of goods and services. Corporations are well suited to today's trends toward large organizations, international trade, and professional management. Figure 2 shows the amount and sources of new funds raised by corporations in recent years.

FIGURE 2
Sources of Capital Raised by Corporations in the United States

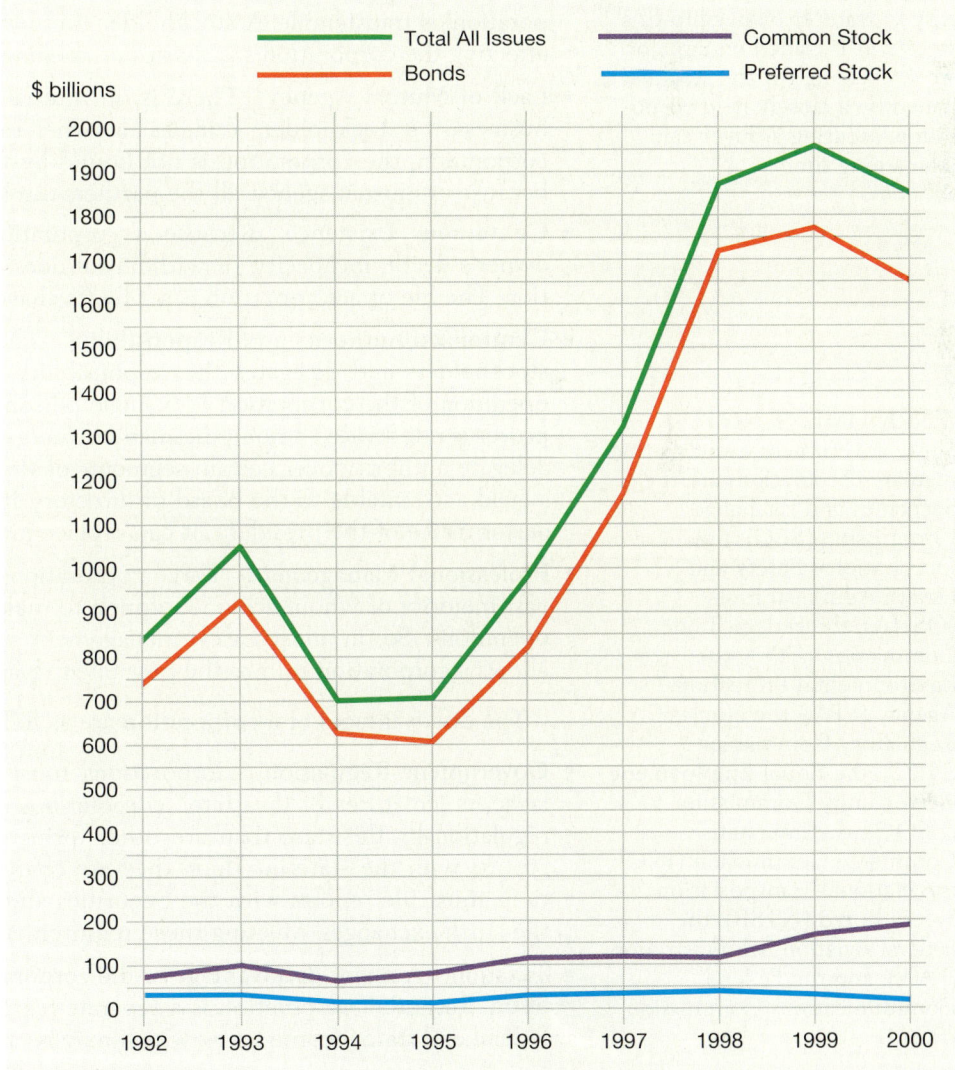

Source: Securities Industry Yearbook 1999–2000 (New York: Securities Industry Association, 1999), p. 895.

The amount raised increased dramatically after 1995. In 2000, the amount of new corporate capital was $1,851.0 billion, of which $1,646.6 billion, or 89 percent, came from new bond issues; $189.1 billion, or 10 percent, came from new common stock issues; and $15.4 billion, or 1 percent, came from preferred stock issues.

In managing a corporation, the advantages and disadvantages of this form of business must be considered. Some of the advantages are as follows:

- **Separate Legal Entity**   A corporation is a separate legal entity. As such, it can buy, sell, or own property; sue and be sued; enter into contracts; hire and fire employees; and be taxed.

- **Limited Liability**   Because a corporation is a separate legal entity, it is responsible for its own actions and liabilities. This means that a corporation's creditors can satisfy their claims only against the assets of the corporation, not against the personal property of the corporation's owners. Because the owners are not responsible for the corporation's debts, their liability is limited to the amount of their investment. The personal property of sole proprietors and partners, however, generally is available to creditors.

> **STUDY NOTE:** Lenders qualify a corporation for a loan as they would a person. If a corporation does not have a credit history or a good credit rating, a loan will not be granted in its name only. Others, such as the corporation's officers, will be required to co-sign the note and will therefore be personally liable.

- **Ease of Capital Generation**   It is fairly easy for a corporation to raise capital because shares of ownership in the business are available to a great number of potential investors for a small amount of money. As a result, a single corporation can be owned by many people.

- **Ease of Transfer of Ownership**   A share of stock, a unit of ownership in a corporation, is transferable. A stockholder can normally buy and sell shares without affecting the corporation's activities or needing the approval of other owners.

> **ENRICHMENT NOTE:** It is easy to transfer ownership of a stock if it is traded on a major stock exchange. If the stock is issued by a closely held corporation, securing a buyer can take a long time.

- **Lack of Mutual Agency**   There is no mutual agency in the corporate form of business. If a stockholder, acting as an owner, tries to enter into a contract for the corporation, the corporation is not bound by the contract. But in a partnership, because of mutual agency, all the partners can be bound by one partner's actions.

- **Continuous Existence**   Because a corporation is a separate legal entity, an owner's death, incapacity, or withdrawal does not affect the life of the corporation. The life of a corporation is set by its charter and regulated by state laws.

- **Centralized Authority and Responsibility**   The board of directors represents the stockholders and delegates the responsibility and authority for the day-to-day operation of the corporation to a single person, usually the president. Operating power is not divided among the many owners of the business. The president may delegate authority over certain segments of the business to others, but he or she is held accountable to the board of directors. If the board is dissatisfied with the performance of the president, it can replace him or her.

> **ENRICHMENT NOTE:** Some government agencies that regulate corporations are the Securities and Exchange Commission (SEC), the Occupational Safety and Health Administration (OSHA), the Federal Trade Commission (FTC), the Environmental Protection Agency (EPA), the Nuclear Regulatory Commission (NRC), the Equal Employment Opportunity Commission (EEOC), the Interstate Commerce Commission (ICC), the National Transportation Safety Board (NTSB), the Federal Aviation Administration (FAA), and the Federal Communications Commission (FCC).

- **Professional Management**   Large corporations are owned by many people, the vast majority of whom are unequipped to make timely decisions about business operations. So, in most cases, management and ownership are separate. This allows a corporation to hire the best talent available to manage the business.

The disadvantages of a corporation are as follows:

- **Government Regulation**   Corporations must meet the requirements of state laws. As "creatures of the state," corporations are subject to greater control and regulation by the state than are other forms of business. They must file many reports with the state in which they are chartered. Also, publicly held corporations must file reports with the Securities and Exchange Commission and with the stock exchanges. Meeting those requirements is very costly.

- **Taxation**   A major disadvantage of the corporate form of business is **double taxation**. Because a corporation is a separate legal entity, its earnings are subject to federal and state income taxes, which may be as much as 35 percent of corporate

Management Issues Related to Contributed Capital

earnings. If any of the corporation's after-tax earnings are then paid out as dividends, the earnings are taxed again as income to the stockholders. In contrast, the earnings of sole proprietorships and partnerships are taxed only once, as personal income to the owners.

- **Limited Liability** Although limited liability is an advantage of incorporation, it also can be a disadvantage. Limited liability restricts the ability of a small corporation to borrow money. Because creditors can lay claim only to the assets of the corporation, they limit their loans to the level secured by those assets or ask stockholders to guarantee the loans personally.

- **Separation of Ownership and Control** Just as limited liability can be a drawback, so can the separation of ownership and control. Management sometimes makes decisions that are not good for the corporation as a whole. Poor communication can also make it hard for stockholders to exercise control over the corporation or even to recognize that management's decisions are harmful.

USING EQUITY FINANCING

A share of stock is a unit of ownership in a corporation. A **stock certificate** is issued to the owner. It shows the number of shares of the corporation's stock that the stockholder owns. Stockholders can transfer their ownership at will. When they do, they must sign their stock certificate and send it to the corporation's secretary. In large corporations that are listed on the organized stock exchanges, stockholders' records are hard to maintain. Such companies can have millions of shares of stock, thousands of which change ownership every day. Therefore, they often appoint independent registrars and transfer agents (usually banks and trust companies) to help perform the secretary's duties. The outside agents are responsible for transferring the corporation's stock, maintaining stockholders' records, preparing a list of stockholders for stockholders' meetings, and paying dividends.

www.cisco.com

When a corporation applies for a charter, the articles of incorporation specify the maximum number of shares of stock the corporation is allowed to issue. This number represents **authorized stock**. Most corporations are authorized to issue more shares of stock than are necessary at the time of organization, which allows for future stock issues to raise additional capital. For example, Cisco Systems has 20 billion shares of stock authorized and only 7.3 billion shares issued. If Cisco Systems needs cash to expand in the future, it can sell its unissued shares. If a corporation issues all of its authorized stock, it cannot issue more stock without a change in its state charter.

KEY POINT: Par value is usually a small amount, $.01 up to $10. The amount is arbitrary and has primarily legal significance.

The charter also shows the par value of the stock that has been authorized. **Par value** is an arbitrary amount assigned to each share of stock. It must be recorded in the capital stock accounts and constitutes the legal capital of a corporation. **Legal capital** equals the number of shares issued times the par value; it is the minimum amount that can be reported as contributed capital. Par value usually bears little if any relationship to the market value or book value of the shares. The par value of Cisco Systems' common stock is only $.001 per share, and its legal capital is $7.3 million (7.3 billion shares × $.001). When a corporation is formed, a memorandum entry may be made in the general journal giving the number and description of authorized shares.

ENRICHMENT NOTE: In effect, the underwriter buys the stock from the corporation at a set price. The stock price in the secondary markets can be above or below the commitment to the corporation. Thus, the underwriter can gain or lose on the transaction and is exposed to a certain amount of risk.

■ **INITIAL PUBLIC OFFERING** To help with the initial issue of capital stock, called an **initial public offering (IPO)**, a corporation often uses an **underwriter**—an intermediary between the corporation and the investing public. For a fee—usually less than 1 percent of the selling price—the underwriter guarantees the sale of the stock. The corporation records the amount of the net proceeds of the offering—what the public paid less the underwriter's fees, legal and printing expenses, and any other direct costs of the offering—in its capital stock and additional paid-in capital accounts. When Goldman, Sachs, & Co., the renowned 130-year-old investment bank, went public, it had one of the largest IPOs ever recorded, amounting to about $3.6 billion.

■ **START-UP AND ORGANIZATION COSTS** The costs of forming a corporation are called **start-up and organization costs**. Such costs, which are incurred before the corporation begins operations, include state incorporation fees and attorneys' fees for drawing up the articles of incorporation. They also include the cost of printing stock certificates, accountants' fees for services rendered in registering the firm's initial stock, and other expenditures that are necessary for the formation of the corporation.

Theoretically, start-up and organization costs benefit the entire life of the corporation. For that reason, a case can be made for recording them as intangible assets and amortizing them over the years of the life of the corporation. However, the life of a corporation normally is not known, so accountants expense start-up and organization costs as they are incurred.[3]

KEY POINT: Start-up and organization costs are expensed when incurred.

DETERMINING DIVIDEND POLICIES

The board of directors has sole authority to declare dividends, but the dividend policies are influenced by senior managers, who usually serve as members of the board. Receiving dividends from a corporation is one of two ways in which stockholders can earn a return on their investment in the company. The other way is to sell their shares of stock for more than they paid for them.

Investors evaluate the amount of dividends received with the ratio **dividends yield**. Dividends yield measures the current return to an investor in the form of dividends and is computed by dividing the dividends per share by the market price per share. For instance, the dividends yield (shown in Figure 3) for Abbott Laboratories, a large, successful pharmaceutical company, is computed as follows:

$$\text{Dividends Yield} = \frac{\text{Dividends per Share}}{\text{Market Price per Share}} = \frac{\$.98}{\$43.22} = 2.3\%$$

Since the yield on corporate bonds exceeds 7 percent, the shareholders of Abbott Labs must expect some of their return to come from increases in the price of the shares.

A measure of investors' confidence in a company's future is the **price/earnings (P/E) ratio**, which is calculated by dividing the market price per share by the earnings per share. The price/earnings ratio will vary as market price per share fluctuates daily and the amount of earnings per share changes. Figure 3 shows a P/E ratio of 25 for Abbott Labs. It was computed using the most recent earnings per share amount available at the time, as follows:

ENRICHMENT NOTE: Due to the rise in prices of stocks during the 1990s, the average dividends yield has declined and the average P/E ratio has increased.

$$\text{Price/Earnings (P/E) Ratio} = \frac{\text{Market Price per Share}}{\text{Earnings per Share}} = \frac{\$43.22}{\$1.73} = 25 \text{ times}$$

Since the market price is 25 times earnings, investors are paying a relatively high price in relation to earnings. They do so in the expectation that this drug company will continue to be successful. Caution must be taken in interpreting high P/E ratios because unusually low earnings can produce a high result.

Companies usually pay dividends to stockholders only when they have had profitable operations. For example, Apple Computer, Inc., paid a dividend beginning in 1987 but suspended its dividend payments in 1996 to conserve cash after large operating losses in 1995. Factors other than earnings affect the decision to pay dividends. First, a company may change its dividend policy to bring it into line with the prevailing industry policy. For example, despite positive earnings, AT&T Corporation slashed its dividends 83 percent. This action put AT&T's policy more in line with

FIGURE 3
Stock Quotations on the New York Stock Exchange

NYSE COMPOSITE TRANSACTIONS

YTD % CHG	52 WEEKS HI	52 WEEKS LO	STOCK (SYM)	DIV	YLD %	PE	VOL 100S	LAST	NET CHG
5.9	21.50	1.25	AMR **AMR**		...	dd	120058	6.99	0.39
1.7	20.13	8.70	AOL Time **AOL**		...	dd	192018	13.32	0.30
1.7	3.10	1.10	APT Satelt **ATS**	.05e	2.9	...	1614	1.75	0.24
21.2	8.44	3.15	AT&T Wrls **AWE**		...	dd	66961	6.85	0.12
−36.9	29.52	13.45	AT&T T s	.75	4.6	dd	62766	16.47	−0.04
6.0	23.60	7.31	AVX Cp **AVX**	.15	1.4	dd	1196	10.39	0.01
13.2	21.97	9.05	♦ AXA ADS **AXA**	.37e	2.4	...	3010	15.22	0.04
−13.5	19.60	8.30	AZZ **AZZ**		...	7	37	10.74	−0.01
14.2	28.49	17.05	AaronRent **RNT**	.04	.2	18	1027	24.98	1.93
− 3.9	27.10	18.80	AaronRent A **RNTA**	.04	.2	16	39	22	0.60
19.5	9.84	1.10	ABB ADS **ABB**		...	dd	666	3.43	−0.02
8.1	52.50	29.80	AbbottLab **ABT**	.98f	2.3	25	33759	43.22	−0.16
51.0	33.65	14.97	Abercrombie A **ANF**		...	16	26051	30.90	0.81
− 9.2	9.63	5.92	Abitibi **ABY**	.40g	...	...	2452	7	−0.02
23.6	9.22	6.77	♦ AcadiaRlty **AKR**	.58f	6.3	12	58	9.17	−0.02
− 7.2	23.08	11.30	Accenture **ACN**		...	19	18982	16.70	−0.15

Source: Stock quotations on the New York Stock Exchange (5/13/03). *Wall Street Journal*, *Eastern Edition* by Wall Street Journal. Copyright © 2003 by Dow Jones & Co., Inc. Reproduced with permission of Dow Jones & Co., Inc. via Copyright Clearance Center.

the policies of its peers in the telecommunications industry, most of which do not pay dividends.[4] Second, the expected volatility of earnings is a factor. If a company has years of good earnings followed by years of poor earnings, the board may want to keep dividends low to avoid giving a false impression of sustained high earnings. For years, General Motors Corporation followed the practice of having a fairly stable dividend yield and paying a bonus dividend in especially good years. Third, the level of dividends affects cash flows. Some companies may not have the cash to pay higher dividends because operations are not generating cash at the level of earnings or because the companies are investing the cash in future operations. For instance, Abbott Labs pays a dividend of $.98 per share on earnings of $1.79 per share. Management believes a portion of the cash generated by the earnings is better spent for other purposes, such as researching and developing new drugs that will generate revenue in the future. It is partly due to Abbott's investment in new products that stockholders are willing to pay a high price for its stock. In recent years, because the tax rates are more favorable to capital gains made by selling shares than to dividend income, many investors have shown a preference for companies like Cisco Systems that have strong earnings growth but that pay no dividends.

www.gm.com

www.cisco.com

EVALUATING PERFORMANCE USING RETURN ON EQUITY

Return on equity is the most important ratio associated with stockholders' equity because it is a common measure of management's performance. For instance, when *BusinessWeek* and *Forbes* rate companies on their success, return on equity is the major basis of their evaluations. Also, the compensation of top executives is often tied to return on equity benchmarks. This ratio is computed for Abbott Labs from information in the company's 2002 annual report, as follows:[5]

www.abbott.com

$$\text{Return on Equity} = \frac{\text{Net Income}}{\text{Average Stockholders' Equity}}$$

$$= \frac{\$2{,}793{,}703{,}000}{(\$10{,}664{,}553{,}000 + \$9{,}059{,}432{,}000) \div 2}$$

$$= 28.3\%$$

KEY POINT: A company can improve its return on equity by increasing net income or by reducing average stockholders' equity.

Abbott Labs' healthy return on equity of 28.3 percent depends, of course, on the amount of net income the company earns. But it also depends on the level of stockholders' equity, which depends, in turn, on management decisions about the amount of stock the company sells to the public. Management can keep the stockholders' equity at a minimum by financing the business with cash flows from operations and with debt instead of with stock. However, the use of debt to finance the business increases a company's risk because the interest and principal of the debt must be paid in a timely manner. In the case of common stock, dividends may be suspended if there is a cash shortage. Abbott Labs has a debt to equity ratio of 127.5% and thus is taking advantage of the leverage provided by debt.

In addition, management can reduce the number of shares in the hands of the public by buying back the company's shares on the open market. The cost of these shares, which are called *treasury stock*, has the effect of reducing the amount of stockholders' equity and thereby increasing the return on equity. Many companies follow this practice instead of paying or increasing dividends. Their reason for doing so is that it puts money into the hands of stockholders in the form of market price appreciation without creating a commitment to higher dividends in the future. For example, during the three years ended 2002, Abbott Labs purchased its common stock at a cost of $.5 billion.[6] Abbott Labs' stock repurchases improved the company's return on equity, increased its earnings per share, and lowered its price/earnings ratio.

USING STOCK OPTIONS AS COMPENSATION

● **STOP AND THINK!**
Why do companies like to give options as compensation?
Companies do not have to record compensation expense on stock options, which can improve profitability. (There is a proposal to change this rule.) Also, salaries require a cash outflow, but stock options do not. Finally, companies get a tax deduction for the difference between the option price and the market price on the exercise date. Tax deductions decrease taxes owed and increase cash flows. ■

More than 97 percent of public companies encourage the ownership of their common stock through a **stock option plan**, which is an agreement to issue stock to employees according to specified terms.[7] In most cases, the stock option plan gives employees the right to purchase stock in the future at a fixed price. This type of plan, which is usually offered only to management personnel, both compensates and motivates management because the market value of a company's stock is tied to the company's performance. As the market value of the stock goes up, the difference between the option price and the market price grows, which increases management's compensation. Another key benefit of stock options for corporations is a tax deduction for the amount of compensation expense, which lowers income taxes owed.

On the date stock options are granted, the fair value of the options must be estimated, and the amount in excess of the exercise price must be either recorded as compensation expense over the grant period or reported in the notes to the financial statements.[8] If a company chooses to record compensation expense, additional paid-in capital will increase as a result. Almost all companies report the excess of fair value over exercise price in the notes to the financial statements. The notes must include the impact on net income and earnings per share of not recording compensation expense in the income statement.

If note disclosure is the preferred method of reporting compensation costs, then when an option eventually is exercised and the stock is issued, the entry is the same as for issuance of common stock to any outsider. For example, assume that on July 1, 20x4, a company grants its key management personnel the option to purchase 50,000 shares of $10 par value common stock at its then-current market value of $15 per share. Suppose that one of the firm's vice presidents exercises the option to purchase 2,000 shares on March 30, 20x7, when the market price is $25 per share. Although the vice president has a gain of $20,000 (the $50,000 market value less the $30,000 option price), no compensation expense is recorded. Estimation of the fair value of options at the grant date is the subject of more advanced courses.*

---

*Stock options are discussed here in the context of employee compensation. They can also be important features of complex corporate capitalization arrangements.

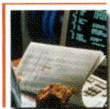

FOCUS ON BUSINESS PRACTICE

When Are Stock Options Worthless? Apparently Never!

Stock options are supposed to reward employees for good performance. They also act as an incentive for continued good performance, thus aligning the interests of owners and employees. When stock prices rise, the rewards can be handsome; some executives have made staggering sums on stock options. For example, the CEO of Cisco Systems <www.cisco.com> made $156 million in option-related profits in fiscal 2000, dwarfing his salary of about $1.3 million. To keep employees happy when stock prices decline, companies often change the stock-option rules to accommodate them. When their stock prices fell, Amazon <www.amazon.com>, Sprint Corp. <www.sprint.com>, and Real Networks Inc. <www.realnetworks.com> repriced options at a lower value or allowed employees to turn in worthless options to be issued later at a lower price. Yet other companies let employees cancel already exercised options. Actions like these anger owners who believe employees should be held accountable for the company's poor performance and not rewarded for unsatisfactory results.[9]

 Check out ACE for a Review Quiz at http://accounting.college.hmco.com/students.

COMPONENTS OF STOCKHOLDERS' EQUITY

LO2 Identify the components of stockholders' equity.

RELATED TEXT ASSIGNMENTS
Q: 16
SE: 5
E: 2, 3, 4
P: 1, 4, 5, 6, 8
SD: 1, 5, 6
FRA: 1, 3, 4, 6

In a corporation's balance sheet, the owners' claims to the business are called *stockholders' equity*. Look at the sample stockholders' equity section of a balance sheet that follows.

Stockholders' Equity

Contributed capital		
Preferred stock, $50 par value, 1,000 shares authorized, issued, and outstanding		$ 50,000
Common stock, $5 par value, 30,000 shares authorized, 20,000 shares issued and outstanding	$100,000	
Paid-in capital in excess of par value, common	50,000	150,000
Total contributed capital		$200,000
Retained earnings		60,000
Total stockholders' equity		$260,000

FOCUS ON INTERNATIONAL BUSINESS

Hot New European Stock Markets Have Cooled!

In 1996, to bring capital to cash-starved growth-stock companies, Europe's stock exchanges began setting up a series of four new exchanges, including France's Nouveau Marche and Germany's Neuer Markt. More than 160 companies went public via this "Euro new market" network. Most owners of these stocks are individual investors, rather than institutional fund managers, as is the case in the United States. The new markets rose quickly, causing a good deal of excitement.[10] However, when they failed to meet expectations, they seemed to fall even faster than they had risen. Case in point, Germany has announced the closing of the Neuer Markt.

Notice that the equity section of the corporate balance sheet is divided into two parts: (1) contributed capital and (2) retained earnings. Contributed capital represents the stockholders' investments in the corporation. Retained earnings are the earnings of the corporation since its inception, less any losses, dividends, or transfers to contributed capital. Retained earnings are not a pool of funds to be distributed to the stockholders; instead, they represent the stockholders' claim to the assets from earnings reinvested in the corporation.

In keeping with the convention of full disclosure, the contributed-capital portion of the stockholders' equity section of the balance sheet gives a great deal

FIGURE 4
Relationship of Authorized, Unissued, Issued, Outstanding, and Treasury Shares

of information about the corporation's stock: the kinds of stock; their par value; and the number of shares authorized, issued, and outstanding.

A corporation can issue two basic types of stock: common stock and preferred stock. If only one kind of stock is issued by the corporation, it is called **common stock**. Common stock is the company's **residual equity**. This means that all creditors' and usually preferred stockholders' claims to the company's assets rank ahead of those of the common stockholders in case of liquidation. Because common stock is generally the only stock that carries voting rights, it represents the means of controlling the corporation.

The second kind of stock a company can issue is called **preferred stock**. Preferred stock has preference over common stock in one or more areas. These "preferences" will be described later in the chapter. Both common stock and preferred stock are sold to raise money. But investors in preferred stock and investors in common stock have different investment goals; preferred stock investors place more value on one or more of the preferences attached to the preferred stock.

The **issued stock** of a corporation is the shares sold or otherwise transferred to stockholders. For example, a corporation can be authorized to issue 500,000 shares of stock but may choose to issue only 300,000 shares when the company is organized. The holders of those 300,000 shares own 100 percent of the corporation. The remaining 200,000 shares of stock are unissued shares. No rights or privileges are associated with them until they are issued.

Outstanding stock is stock that has been issued and is still in circulation. A share of stock is not outstanding if the issuing corporation has repurchased it or if a stockholder has given it back to the company that issued it, so a company can have more shares issued than are currently outstanding. Issued shares that are bought back and held by the corporation are called *treasury stock*, which we discuss in detail later in this chapter. The relationship of authorized, issued, unissued, outstanding, and treasury shares is illustrated in Figure 4.

 Check out ACE for a Review Quiz at http://accounting.college.hmco.com/students.

KEY POINT: A corporation may have more shares issued than it has outstanding because it has repurchased some shares, which are called *treasury stock*.

● **STOP AND THINK!**
Why are issued shares not the same amount as authorized shares?
Authorized shares usually far exceed a corporation's need for immediate capital. Issuing fewer shares than authorized provides a corporation with greater flexibility in raising additional contributed capital in the future. ■

DIVIDENDS

LO3 Account for cash dividends.
RELATED TEXT ASSIGNMENTS
Q: 10, 11
SE: 6
E: 5, 6
P: 1, 4, 5, 6, 8
SD: 5
FRA: 3, 7

Dividends can be paid quarterly, semiannually, annually, or at other times decided on by the board. Most states do not allow the board to declare a dividend that exceeds retained earnings. When a dividend that exceeds retained earnings is declared, the corporation is, in essence, returning to the stockholders part of their contributed capital. It is called a **liquidating dividend** and is usually paid when a company is going out of business or reducing its operations. Having sufficient retained earnings in itself does not justify the distribution of a dividend. If cash or other readily distributable assets are not available for distribution, the company might have to borrow money to pay a dividend—an action most boards of directors want to avoid.

Three important dates are associated with dividends. In order of occurrence, they are (1) the date of declaration, (2) the date of record, and (3) the date of pay-

ENRICHMENT NOTE:
Some reasons that the board of directors of a corporation with sufficient cash and retained earnings might not declare a dividend include the following: the cash is needed for expansion; the board wants to liquidate debt and improve the overall financial position of the company; major uncertainties threaten the corporation (such as a pending lawsuit or strike); the economy is poor, and the board wants to preserve resources.

● **Stop and Think!**
If an investor sells shares after the declaration date but before the date of record, does the seller still receive the dividend?
Yes, but it comes in the form of a higher price for the stock, not in a dividend distribution. After the declaration date, the stock price adjusts upward to include the dividend declared. As a result, the seller receives the dividend even though on the distribution date, the check for the dividend will go to the buyer. ■

ment. The **date of declaration** is the date on which the board of directors formally declares that a dividend is going to be paid. The **date of record** is the date on which ownership of the stock of a company, and therefore of the right to receive a dividend, is determined. Individuals who own the stock on the date of record will receive the dividend. Between that date and the date of payment, the stock is said to be **ex-dividend**. If the owner on the date of record later sells the shares of stock, the right to the cash dividend remains with that person; it does not transfer with the shares to the second owner. The **date of payment** is the date on which the dividend is paid to the stockholders of record.

To illustrate accounting for cash dividends, we assume that the board of directors has decided that sufficient cash is available to pay a $56,000 cash dividend to the common stockholders. The process has two steps. First, the board declares the dividend as of a certain date. Second, the dividend is paid. Assume that the dividend is declared on February 21, 20xx, for stockholders of record on March 1, 20xx, to be paid on March 11, 20xx. Here are the entries to record the declaration and payment of the cash dividend:

Date of Declaration

A = L + OE
+ −

Feb. 21	Cash Dividends Declared		56,000	
	Cash Dividends Payable			56,000
	Declared cash dividend			
	to common stockholders			

Date of Record

Mar. 1 No entry is required. This date is used simply to determine the owners of the stock who will receive the dividends. After this date (starting March 2), the shares are ex-dividend.

Date of Payment

A = L + OE
− −

Mar. 11	Cash Dividends Payable		56,000	
	Cash			56,000
	Paid cash dividends			
	declared on February 21			

Notice that the liability for the dividend is recorded on the date of declaration because the legal obligation to pay the dividend is established on that date. No entry is required on the date of record. The liability is liquidated, or settled, on the date of payment. The Cash Dividends Declared account is a temporary stockholders' equity account that is closed at the end of the accounting period by debiting Retained Earnings and crediting Cash Dividends Declared. Retained Earnings are thereby reduced by the total dividends declared during the period.

 Check out ACE for a Review Quiz at http://accounting.college.hmco.com/students.

The Characteristics of Preferred Stock

LO4 Identify the characteristics of preferred stock, including the effect on distribution of dividends.

RELATED TEXT ASSIGNMENTS
Q: 12, 13
SE: 7
E: 3, 7, 8
P: 2, 4, 5, 7, 8
SD: 2, 5
FRA: 2, 7

Most preferred stock has one or more of the following characteristics: preference as to dividends, preference as to assets of the business in liquidation, convertibility, and a callable option. In fact, a corporation may offer several different classes of preferred stock, each with distinctive characteristics to attract different investors.

Preference as to Dividends

Preferred stocks ordinarily have a preference over common stock in the receipt of dividends; that is, the holders of preferred shares must receive a certain amount of

KEY POINT: Preferred stock has many different characteristics. They are rarely exactly the same from company to company.

dividends before the holders of common shares can receive dividends. The amount that preferred stockholders must be paid before common stockholders can be paid is usually stated in dollars per share or as a percentage of the par value of the preferred shares. For example, a corporation can issue a preferred stock and pay an annual dividend of $4 per share, or it might issue a preferred stock at $50 par value and pay a yearly dividend of 8 percent of par value, also $4 per share.

Preferred stockholders have no guarantee of ever receiving dividends. The company must have earnings and the board of directors must declare dividends on preferred shares before any liability arises. The consequences of not declaring a dividend to preferred stockholders in the current year vary according to the exact terms under which the shares were issued. In the case of **noncumulative preferred stock**, if the board of directors fails to declare a dividend to preferred stockholders in a given year, the company is under no obligation to make up the missed dividend in future years. In the case of **cumulative preferred stock**, however, the fixed dividend amount per share accumulates from year to year, and the whole amount must be paid before any dividends on common stock can be paid. Dividends not paid in the year they are due are called **dividends in arrears**.

Assume that a corporation has been authorized to issue 10,000 shares of $100 par value, 5 percent cumulative preferred stock and that the shares have been issued and are outstanding. If no dividends were paid in 20x4, at the end of the year there would be preferred dividends of $50,000 (10,000 shares × $100 × .05 = $50,000) in arrears. If dividends are paid in 20x5, the preferred stockholders' dividends in arrears plus the 20x5 preferred dividends must be paid before any dividends on common stock can be paid.

Dividends in arrears are not recognized as liabilities because no liability exists until the board declares a dividend. A corporation cannot be sure it is going to make a profit, so, of course, it cannot promise dividends to stockholders. However, if a company has dividends in arrears, the amount should be reported either in the body of the financial statements or in a note. The following note appeared in a steel company's annual report:

> On January 1, 20xx, the company was in arrears by $37,851,000 ($1.25 per share) on dividends to its preferred stockholders. The company must pay all dividends in arrears to preferred stockholders before paying any dividends to common stockholders.

Suppose that on January 1, 20x4, a corporation issued 10,000 shares of $10 par, 6 percent cumulative preferred stock and 50,000 shares of common stock. The first year's operations resulted in income of only $4,000. The corporation's board of directors declared a $3,000 cash dividend to the preferred stockholders. The dividend picture at the end of 20x4 was as follows:

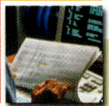

Focus on Business Practice

Why Did Microsoft Issue Preferred Stock?

Preferred stock represents a flexible means of achieving goals that cannot be achieved with common stock. For example, Microsoft Corporation <www.microsoft.com> issued almost $1 billion in preferred stock even though the company probably did not need the cash.[11] Since Microsoft does not pay and has no plans to pay a dividend on its common stock, this preferred stock satisfies the desire of investors who want to own Microsoft stock but who want to buy stocks that pay a dividend. The preferred stock pays a fixed dividend and is convertible into common stock or convertible notes. If it is not converted, the company guarantees it can be redeemed at face value for cash in three years. In return for this flexibility and low risk, the company puts a limit of 25 to 30 percent on the gain that can be realized from converting the preferred stock into common stock. As a Microsoft vice president put it, "If you own the preferred, you get a dividend yield and downside protection, but the upside is capped."[12]

20x4 dividends due preferred stockholders ($100,000 × .06)	$6,000
Less 20x4 dividends declared to preferred stockholders	3,000
20x4 preferred stock dividends in arrears	$3,000

Now suppose that in 20x5 the corporation earned income of $30,000 and wanted to pay dividends to both the preferred and the common stockholders. Because the preferred stock is cumulative, the corporation must pay the $3,000 in arrears on the preferred stock, plus the current year's dividends on its preferred stock, before it can distribute a dividend to the common stockholders. For example, assume that the corporation's board of directors declared a $12,000 dividend to be distributed to preferred and common stockholders. It would be distributed as follows:

20x5 declaration of dividends	$12,000
Less 20x4 preferred stock dividends in arrears	3,000
Available for 20x5 dividends	$ 9,000
Less 20x5 dividends due preferred stockholders ($100,000 × .06)	6,000
Remainder available to common stockholders	$ 3,000

This is the entry when the dividend is declared:

A = L + OE
     + −

Dec. 31	Cash Dividends Declared	12,000	
	Cash Dividends Payable		12,000
	Declared a $9,000 cash dividend to preferred stockholders and a $3,000 cash dividend to common stockholders		

PREFERENCE AS TO ASSETS

ENRICHMENT NOTE: Many companies that liquidate do not have enough assets to pay creditors. Consequently, there is nothing left for shareholders, common or preferred.

Many preferred stocks have preference in terms of the assets of the corporation in the case of liquidation. If the corporation's existence is terminated, the preferred stockholders have a right to receive the par value of their stock or a larger stated liquidation value per share before the common stockholders receive any share of the corporation's assets. This preference can also extend to any dividends in arrears owed to the preferred stockholders.

CONVERTIBLE PREFERRED STOCK

A corporation can make its preferred stock more attractive to investors by adding convertibility. People who hold **convertible preferred stock** can exchange their shares of preferred stock for shares of the company's common stock at a ratio stated in the preferred stock contract. Convertibility appeals to investors for two reasons. First, like all preferred stockholders, owners of convertible preferred stock are more likely to receive regular dividends than are common stockholders. Second, if the market value of a company's common stock rises, the conversion feature allows the preferred stockholders to share in the increase. The rise in value would come either through increases in the value of the preferred stock or through conversion to common stock.

    For example, suppose that a company issues 1,000 shares of 8 percent, $100 par value convertible preferred stock for $100 per share. Each share of stock can be converted into five shares of the company's common stock at any time. The market value of the common stock is now $15 per share. In the past, an owner of the common stock could expect dividends of about $1 per share per year. The owner of one share of preferred stock, on the other hand, now holds an investment that is

ENRICHMENT NOTE:
When a preferred shareholder converts to common stock, he or she gains voting rights but loses the dividend and liquidation preference. Conversion back to preferred stock is not an option.

approaching a value of $100 on the market and is more likely to receive dividends than is the owner of common stock.

Assume that in the next several years, the corporation's earnings increase, and the dividends paid to common stockholders rise to $3 per share. Assume also that the market value of a share of common stock rises from $15 to $30. Preferred stockholders can convert each of their preferred shares into five common shares and increase their dividends from $8 on each preferred share to the equivalent of $15 ($3 on each of five common shares). Further, the market value of each share of preferred stock will be close to the $150 value of the five shares of common stock because each share can be converted into five shares of common stock.

Callable Preferred Stock

Most preferred stock is **callable preferred stock**. That is, it can be redeemed or retired at the option of the issuing corporation at a price stated in the preferred stock contract. A stockholder must surrender nonconvertible preferred stock to the corporation when asked to do so. If the preferred stock is convertible, the stockholder can either surrender the stock to the corporation or convert it into common stock when the corporation calls the stock. The *call price*, or redemption price, is usually higher than the par value of the stock. For example, a $100 par value preferred stock might be callable at $103 per share. When preferred stock is called and surrendered, the stockholder is entitled to (1) the par value of the stock, (2) the call premium, (3) any dividends in arrears, and (4) a portion of the current period's dividend, prorated by the proportion of the year to the call date.

● **Stop and Think!**
Why would a company want to issue callable preferred stock?
Callable preferred stock gives the company greater flexibility. The company can eliminate the related dividends at some future date by redeeming the shares at a specified call price. ■

A corporation may call its preferred stock for several reasons. First, it may want to force conversion of the preferred stock to common stock because the cash dividend paid on the equivalent common stock is lower than the dividend paid on the preferred shares. Second, it may be able to replace the outstanding preferred stock on the current market with a preferred stock at a lower dividend rate or with long-term debt, which can have a lower after-tax cost. Third, the corporation may simply be profitable enough to retire the preferred stock.

 Check out ACE for a Review Quiz at http://accounting.college.hmco.com/students.

Accounting for Stock Issuance

LO5 Account for the issuance of stock for cash and other assets.
RELATED TEXT ASSIGNMENTS
Q: 14
SE: 8, 9
E: 4, 9, 10
P: 1, 4, 5, 6, 8
SD: 5
FRA: 1, 7

KEY POINT: Legal capital is the minimum amount that can be reported as contributed capital. For the protection of creditors, dividends that would reduce capital below the amount of legal capital cannot be declared.

A share of capital stock may be either par or no-par. The value of par stock is stated in the corporate charter and must be printed on each share of stock. Par value can be $.01, $1, $5, $100, or any other amount established by the organizers of the corporation. The par values of common stocks tend to be lower than those of preferred stocks.

As noted earlier, par value is the amount per share that is entered into a corporation's capital stock accounts and that makes up the legal capital of the corporation. A corporation cannot declare a dividend that would cause stockholders' equity to fall below the firm's legal capital. Par value is thus a minimum cushion of capital that protects the corporation's creditors. Any amount in excess of par value received from the issuance of stock is recorded in the Paid-in Capital in Excess of Par Value account and represents a portion of the company's contributed capital.

No-par stock is capital stock that does not have a par value. There are several reasons for issuing stock without a par value. One is that some investors confuse par value with the market value of stock instead of recognizing it as an arbitrary figure. Another reason is that most states do not allow an original stock issue below par value and thereby limit a corporation's flexibility in obtaining capital.

KEY POINT: When stock is issued with no par and no stated value, all proceeds represent legal capital and are recorded as capital stock. Because stock may be issued at different prices, the legal capital per share varies.

● **STOP AND THINK!**
What relevance does par value or stated value have to a financial ratio, such as return on equity or debt to equity?
Return on equity and debt to equity are computed using total stockholders' equity, which includes par or stated value. Financial analysis does not generally find par or stated value of any relevance. ∎

No-par stock can be issued with or without a stated value. The board of directors of a corporation issuing no-par stock may be required by state law to place a **stated value** on each share of stock or may choose to do so as a matter of convenience. The stated value can be any value set by the board unless the state specifies a minimum amount, which is sometimes the case. The stated value can be set before or after the shares are issued if the state law is not specific.

If a company issues no-par stock without a stated value, all proceeds are recorded in the Capital Stock account. That amount becomes the corporation's legal capital unless a different amount is specified by state law. Because additional shares of the stock can be issued at different prices, the per-share credit to the Capital Stock account will not be uniform. This is a key way in which no-par stock without a stated value differs from par value stock or no-par stock with a stated value.

When no-par stock with a stated value is issued, the shares are recorded in the Capital Stock account at the stated value. Any amount received in excess of the stated value is recorded in the Paid-in Capital in Excess of Stated Value account. The amount in excess of the stated value is part of the corporation's contributed capital. However, the stated value is normally considered to be the legal capital of the corporation.

PAR VALUE STOCK

When par value stock is issued, the appropriate capital stock account (usually Common Stock or Preferred Stock) is credited for the par value regardless of whether the proceeds are more or less than the par value. For example, assume that Bradley Corporation is authorized to issue 20,000 shares of $10 par value common stock and issues 10,000 shares at $10 per share on January 1, 20xx. The entry to record the stock issue at par value would be as follows:

A = L + OE
\+   +

Jan. 1	Cash	100,000
	Common Stock	100,000
	Issued 10,000 shares of $10 par value common stock for $10 per share	

Cash is debited for $100,000 (10,000 shares × $10), and Common Stock is credited for an equal amount because the stock was sold for par value.

When stock is issued for a price greater than par, the proceeds in excess of par are credited to a capital account called Paid-in Capital in Excess of Par Value, Common. For example, assume that the 10,000 shares of Bradley common stock sold for $12 per share on January 1, 20xx. The entry to record the issuance of the stock at the price in excess of par value would be as follows:

TERMINOLOGY NOTE:
Many companies refer to paid-in capital in excess of par value as additional paid-in capital.

A = L + OE
\+   +
             +

Jan. 1	Cash	120,000
	Common Stock	100,000
	Paid-in Capital in Excess of Par Value, Common	20,000
	Issued 10,000 shares of $10 par value common stock for $12 per share	

KEY POINT: Common stock and paid-in capital in excess of par value are separated for legal purposes. Their effect on the company's balance sheet is the same.

Cash is debited for the proceeds of $120,000 (10,000 shares × $12), and Common Stock is credited for the total par value of $100,000 (10,000 shares × $10). Paid-in Capital in Excess of Par Value, Common is credited for the difference of $20,000 (10,000 shares × $2). The amount in excess of par value is part of the corporation's contributed capital and will be included in the stockholders' equity section of the balance sheet. The stockholders' equity section for Bradley Corporation immediately following the stock issue would appear as follows:

Contributed capital
 Common stock, $10 par value, 20,000 shares
  authorized, 10,000 shares issued and outstanding $100,000
 Paid-in capital in excess of par value, common   20,000
 Total contributed capital $120,000
Retained earnings   —
Total stockholders' equity $120,000

If a corporation issues stock for less than par, an account called Discount on Capital Stock is debited for the difference. The issuance of stock at a discount rarely occurs; it is illegal in many states.

NO-PAR STOCK

As mentioned earlier, stock can be issued without a par value. However, most states require that all or part of the proceeds from the issuance of no-par stock be designated as legal capital, which cannot be withdrawn except in liquidation. The purpose of this requirement is to protect the corporation's assets for creditors. Assume that Bradley Corporation's capital stock is no-par common and that 10,000 shares are issued on January 1, 20xx, at $15 per share. The $150,000 (10,000 shares × $15) in proceeds would be recorded as shown in the following entry:

A = L + OE
+ +

Jan. 1	Cash	150,000	
	Common Stock		150,000
	Issued 10,000 shares of no-par		
	common stock for $15 per share		

Because the stock does not have a stated or par value, all proceeds of the issue are credited to Common Stock and are part of the company's legal capital.

  Most states allow the board of directors to put a stated value on no-par stock, and that value represents the corporation's legal capital. Assume that Bradley's board puts a $10 stated value on its no-par stock. The entry to record the issue of 10,000 shares of no-par common stock with a $10 stated value for $15 per share would appear as follows:

KEY POINT: When no-par stock has a stated value, the stated value serves the same purpose as par value.

A = L + OE
+ +
  +

Jan. 1	Cash	150,000	
	Common Stock		100,000
	Paid-in Capital in Excess of		
	Stated Value, Common		50,000
	Issued 10,000 shares of no-par		
	common stock with $10 stated value		
	for $15 per share		

Notice that the legal capital credited to Common Stock is the stated value decided by the board of directors. Notice also that the account Paid-in Capital in Excess of Stated Value, Common is credited for $50,000. The $50,000 is the difference between the proceeds ($150,000) and the total stated value ($100,000). Paid-in Capital in Excess of Stated Value is presented on the balance sheet in the same way as Paid-in Capital in Excess of Par Value.

ISSUANCE OF STOCK FOR NONCASH ASSETS

Stock can be issued for assets or services other than cash. The problem is to determine the dollar amount that should be recorded for the exchange. The generally preferred rule is to record the transaction at the fair market value of what the corporation is giving up—in this case, the stock. If the fair market value of the stock cannot be determined, the fair market value of the assets or services received can be used. Transactions of this kind usually involve the use of stock to pay for land or buildings or for the services of attorneys and others who helped organize the company.

KEY POINT: The board of directors may not arbitrarily establish the fair market value of property that is exchanged for stock; it must do so prudently, using all the information at its disposal.

When there is an exchange of stock for noncash assets, the board of directors has the right to determine the fair market value of the property. Suppose that when Bradley Corporation was formed on January 1, 20xx, its attorney agreed to accept 100 shares of its $10 par value common stock for services rendered. At the time the stock was issued, its market value could not be determined. However, for similar services the attorney would have billed the company $1,500. The entry to record the noncash transaction is as follows:

A = L + OE
      +
  −   +

Jan. 1	Start-up and Organization Expense	1,500	
	Common Stock		1,000
	Paid-in Capital in Excess of		
	Par Value, Common		500
	Issued 100 shares of $10 par		
	value common stock for attorney's		
	services		

Now suppose that two years later Bradley Corporation exchanged 1,000 shares of its $10 par value common stock for a piece of land. At the time of the exchange, the stock was selling on the market for $16 per share. The following entry records the exchange:

A = L + OE
+   +
      +

Jan. 1	Land	16,000	
	Common Stock		10,000
	Paid-in Capital in Excess of		
	Par Value, Common		6,000
	Issued 1,000 shares of $10 par value		
	common stock with a market value		
	of $16 per share for a piece of land		

 Check out ACE for a Review Quiz at http://accounting.college.hmco.com/students.

ACCOUNTING FOR TREASURY STOCK

LO6 Account for treasury stock.
RELATED TEXT ASSIGNMENTS
Q: 15, 16
SE: 10, 11
E: 2, 6, 11, 12
P: 3, 4, 5, 8
SD: 3, 4
FRA: 4, 6, 7

Treasury stock is capital stock, either common or preferred, that the issuing company has reacquired. The company normally gets the stock back by purchasing the shares on the market. It is common for companies to buy and hold their own stock. In a recent year, 410, or 68 percent, of 600 large companies held treasury stock.[13] Although the purchase of treasury stock can be a severe drain on cash, a company may purchase its own stock for several reasons:

1. It may want stock to distribute to employees through stock option plans.
2. It may be trying to maintain a favorable market for its stock.
3. It may want to increase its earnings per share or stock price per share.
4. It may want to have additional shares of stock available for such activities as purchasing other companies.
5. It may want to prevent a hostile takeover.

KEY POINT: Treasury stock is not the same as unissued stock. Treasury stock represents shares that have been issued but are no longer outstanding. Unissued shares, on the other hand, have never been in circulation.

A treasury stock purchase reduces the assets and stockholders' equity of the company. It is not considered a purchase of assets, as the purchase of shares in another company would be. Treasury stock is capital stock that has been issued but is no longer outstanding. Treasury shares can be held for an indefinite period, reissued, or retired. Like unissued stock, treasury stock has no rights until it is reissued. It does not have voting rights, rights to cash dividends and stock dividends, or rights to share in assets during liquidation of the company, and it is not considered to be outstanding in the calculation of book value. However, there is one major difference between unissued shares and treasury shares: A share of stock that originally was issued at par value or greater and fully paid for, and that then was reacquired as treasury stock, can be reissued at less than par value without negative consequences.

Purchase of Treasury Stock

When treasury stock is purchased, it is normally recorded at cost. The transaction reduces the firm's assets as well as stockholders' equity. For example, assume that on September 15 Caprock Corporation purchases 1,000 shares of its common stock on the market at a price of $50 per share. The purchase would be recorded as follows:

A = L + OE
−   −

Sept. 15	Treasury Stock, Common	50,000	
	Cash		50,000
	Acquired 1,000 shares of the company's common stock for $50 per share		

ENRICHMENT NOTE: Since treasury stock reduces stockholders' equity—the denominator of the return on equity ratio—the return on equity will increase when treasury shares are purchased even though there is no increase in earnings.

The treasury shares are recorded at cost. The par value, stated value, or original issue price of the stock is ignored.

The stockholders' equity section of Caprock's balance sheet shows the cost of the treasury stock as a deduction from the total of contributed capital and retained earnings:

Contributed capital	
Common stock, $5 par value, 100,000 shares authorized, 30,000 shares issued, 29,000 shares outstanding	$ 150,000
Paid-in capital in excess of par value, common	30,000
Total contributed capital	$ 180,000
Retained earnings	900,000
Total contributed capital and retained earnings	$1,080,000
Less treasury stock, common (1,000 shares at cost)	50,000
Total stockholders' equity	$1,030,000

Notice that the number of shares issued, and therefore the legal capital, has not changed, although the number of outstanding shares has decreased as a result of the transaction.

Sale of Treasury Stock

Treasury shares can be sold at cost, above cost, or below cost. For example, assume that on November 15, Caprock Corporation sells its 1,000 treasury shares for $50 per share. The following entry records the transaction:

A = L + OE
+   +

Nov. 15	Cash	50,000	
	Treasury Stock, Common		50,000
	Reissued 1,000 shares of treasury stock for $50 per share		

When treasury shares are sold for an amount greater than their cost, the excess of the sales price over cost should be credited to Paid-in Capital, Treasury Stock. No gain should be recorded. For example, suppose that on November 15, Caprock sells its 1,000 treasury shares for $60 per share. The entry for the reissue would be as follows:

A = L + OE
+   +

Nov. 15	Cash	60,000	
	Treasury Stock, Common		50,000
	Paid-in Capital, Treasury Stock		10,000
	Sold 1,000 shares of treasury stock for $60 per share; cost was $50 per share		

If treasury shares are sold below their cost, the difference is deducted from Paid-in Capital, Treasury Stock. When this account does not exist or its balance is

FOCUS ON BUSINESS PRACTICE

When Are Share Buybacks a Bad Idea?

Corporate America set share repurchase records in 2000 of $123 billion. As recently as 1991, share repurchases totaled only $10 billion. Among the companies that spent billions to boost their stock prices were Hewlett-Packard <www.hp.com>, AT&T <www.att.com>, Intel <www.intel.com>, and Microsoft <www.microsoft.com>—all to no avail.

According to renowned investor Warren Buffet, share buybacks are ill-advised when companies buy high and sell low. Such action is the exact opposite of good investment theory (to buy when stocks are cheap and to sell when prices rise).

But in 2000, to avoid increased shares outstanding and the resulting lower earnings per share, companies were buying stock at record high prices and then selling it to employees at much lower prices.

Another bad idea is to borrow money to buy back stock. In 2000, many companies were borrowing money to repurchase stock, thereby increasing their debt to equity ratio. These companies are now suffering credit rating reductions and severe stock price declines.[14]

KEY POINT: Gains and losses on the reissue of treasury stock are never recognized as such. Instead, the accounts Retained Earnings and Paid-in Capital, Treasury Stock are used.

insufficient to cover the excess of cost over the reissue price, Retained Earnings absorbs the excess. No loss is recorded. For example, suppose that on September 15, Caprock bought 1,000 shares of its common stock on the market at a price of $50 per share. The company sold 400 shares on October 15 for $60 per share and the remaining 600 shares on December 15 for $42 per share. The entries for these transactions are as follows:

```
A = L + OE    Sept. 15   Treasury Stock, Common              50,000
 −       −                  Cash                                         50,000
                            Purchased 1,000 shares of
                            treasury stock at $50 per share

A = L + OE    Oct. 15    Cash                                 24,000
 +       +                  Treasury Stock, Common                       20,000
                            Paid-in Capital, Treasury Stock               4,000
                            Sold 400 shares of treasury
                            stock for $60 per share; cost
                            was $50 per share

A = L + OE    Dec. 15    Cash                                 25,200
 +       −                  Paid-in Capital, Treasury Stock    4,000
         +                  Retained Earnings                    800
                            Treasury Stock, Common                       30,000
                            Sold 600 shares of treasury
                            stock for $42 per share; cost
                            was $50 per share
```

STUDY NOTE: Retained Earnings is debited only when the Paid-in Capital, Treasury Stock account has been depleted. In this case, the credit balance of $4,000 is exhausted completely before Retained Earnings absorbs the excess.

In the entry for the December 15 transaction, Retained Earnings is debited for $800 because the 600 shares were sold for $4,800 less than cost. That amount is $800 greater than the $4,000 of paid-in capital generated by the sale of the 400 shares of treasury stock on October 15.

RETIREMENT OF TREASURY STOCK

◆ **STOP AND THINK!**
Why might a company choose to retire its treasury stock?

A company that does not plan to reissue the shares might decide to retire them. ■

If a company determines that it will not reissue treasury stock, it can, with the approval of its stockholders, retire the stock. When shares of stock are retired, all items related to those shares are removed from the related capital accounts. When treasury stock whose acquisition price is less than the original contributed capital is retired, the difference is recognized in Paid-in Capital, Retirement of Stock. If the acquisition price is more than was received when the stock was first issued, the difference is a reduction in stockholders' equity and is debited to Retained Earnings. For instance, suppose that instead of selling the 1,000 shares of treasury stock it purchased for $50,000, Caprock Corporation decides to retire the shares on November

15. Assuming that the $5 par value common stock was originally issued at $6 per share, this entry records the retirement:

A = L + OE	Nov. 15	Common Stock	5,000	
−		Paid-in Capital in Excess of		
−		Par Value, Common	1,000	
+		Retained Earnings	44,000	
		Treasury Stock, Common		50,000
		Retired 1,000 shares that cost $50 per share and were issued originally at $6 per share		

✓ Check out ACE for a Review Quiz at http://accounting.college.hmco.com/students.

Chapter Review

REVIEW OF LEARNING OBJECTIVES

LO1 Identify and explain the management issues related to contributed capital.

The management of contributed capital is a critical component in corporate financing. The issues faced by management in the area of contributed capital are forming a corporation, managing under the corporate form of business, using equity financing, determining dividend policies, evaluating performance using return on equity, and using stock options as compensation.

LO2 Identify the components of stockholders' equity.

Stockholders' equity consists of contributed capital and retained earnings. Contributed capital includes two basic types of stock: common stock and preferred stock. When only one type of security is issued, it is common stock. Common stockholders have voting rights; they also share in the earnings of the corporation. Preferred stock, like common stock, is sold to raise capital. But the investors in preferred stock have different objectives. To attract such investors, corporations usually give them a preference—in terms of receiving dividends and assets—over common stockholders.

Retained earnings, the other component of stockholders' equity, represents the claim of stockholders to the assets of the company resulting from profitable operations. These are earnings that have been invested in the corporation.

LO3 Account for cash dividends.

The liability for payment of cash dividends arises on the date of declaration by the board of directors. The declaration is recorded with a debit to Cash Dividends Declared and a credit to Cash Dividends Payable. The date of record requires no entry; it is the date on which ownership of the stock, and thus of the right to receive a dividend, is determined. Date of payment is recorded with a debit to Cash Dividends Payable and a credit to Cash.

LO4 Identify the characteristics of preferred stock, including the effect on distribution of dividends.

The dividend on preferred stock is generally figured first; the remainder goes to common stock. If the preferred stock is cumulative and in arrears, the amount in arrears must be allocated to preferred stockholders before any allocation is made to common stockholders. In addition, certain preferred stock is convertible. Preferred stock is often callable at the option of the corporation.

LO5 Account for the issuance of stock for cash and other assets.

A corporation's stock is normally issued for cash and other assets. Most states require that stock be issued at a minimum value called *legal capital*. Legal capital is represented by the par or stated value of the stock.

When stock is issued for cash at par or stated value, Cash is debited and Common Stock or Preferred Stock is credited. When stock is sold at an amount greater than par or stated value, the excess is recorded in Paid-in Capital in Excess of Par or Stated Value.

Stock is sometimes issued for noncash assets. In these cases, the board of directors must decide how to value the stock. The general rule is to record the stock at its market value. If this value cannot be determined, the fair market value of the asset received is used to record the transaction.

LO6 Account for treasury stock.

Treasury stock is stock that the issuing company has reacquired. A company may buy its own stock for several reasons, including a desire to create stock option plans, maintain a favorable market for the stock, increase earnings per share, or purchase other companies. Treasury stock is similar to unissued stock in that it does not have rights until it is reissued. However, treasury stock can be resold at less than par value without penalty. The accounting treatment for treasury stock is as follows:

Treasury Stock Transaction	Accounting Treatment
Purchase of treasury stock	Debit Treasury Stock and credit Cash for the cost of the shares.
Sale of treasury stock at the same price as the cost of the shares	Debit Cash and credit Treasury Stock for the cost of the shares.
Sale of treasury stock at an amount greater than the cost of the shares	Debit Cash for the reissue price of the shares, and credit Treasury Stock for the cost of the shares and Paid-in Capital, Treasury Stock for the excess.
Sale of treasury stock at an amount less than the cost of the shares	Debit Cash for the reissue price; debit Paid-in Capital, Treasury Stock for the difference between the reissue price and the cost of the shares; and credit Treasury Stock for the cost of the shares. If Paid-in Capital, Treasury Stock does not exist or its balance is not large enough to cover the difference, Retained Earnings should absorb the difference.
Retirement of treasury stock	Debit Common Stock and Paid-in Capital in Excess of Par Value, Common for the original issue price and Retained Earnings for the remainder to bring the total to the cost of the treasury stock. Credit Treasury Stock for its total cost.

REVIEW OF CONCEPTS AND TERMINOLOGY

The following concepts and terms were introduced in this chapter:

LO1 **Articles of incorporation:** An official document filed with and approved by a state that authorizes the incorporators to do business as a corporation.

LO1 **Audit committee:** A subgroup of the board of directors of a corporation charged with ensuring that the board will be objective in reviewing management's performance; it engages the company's independent auditors and reviews their work.

LO1 **Authorized stock:** The maximum number of shares a corporation can issue without a change in its state charter.

LO4 **Callable preferred stock:** Preferred stock that can be redeemed or retired at a stated price at the option of the issuing corporation.

LO2 **Common stock:** Shares of stock that carry voting rights but that rank below preferred stock in terms of dividends and the distribution of assets.

LO4 **Convertible preferred stock:** Preferred stock that can be exchanged for common stock at the option of the holder.

LO1 **Corporation:** A separate legal entity having its own rights, privileges, and liabilities distinct from those of its owners.

LO4 **Cumulative preferred stock:** Preferred stock on which unpaid dividends accumulate over time and must be satisfied before a dividend can be paid to common stockh

- **LO3** **Date of declaration:** The date on which the board of directors declares a dividend.
- **LO3** **Date of payment:** The date on which payment of a dividend is made.
- **LO3** **Date of record:** The date on which ownership of stock for the purpose of receiving a dividend is determined.
- **LO1** **Dividends:** The distribution of a corporation's assets (usually cash generated by past earnings) to its stockholders.
- **LO4** **Dividends in arrears:** Past dividends on cumulative preferred stock that remain unpaid.
- **LO1** **Dividends yield:** Current return to stockholders in the form of dividends; dividends per share divided by market price per share.
- **LO1** **Double taxation:** Taxation of corporate earnings twice—once as income of the corporation and once again as income to stockholders based on the dividends they receive.
- **LO3** **Ex-dividend:** A description of capital stock between the date of record and the date of payment, when the right to a dividend already declared on the stock remains with the person who sells the stock and does not transfer to the person who buys it.
- **LO1** **Initial public offering (IPO):** A company's first issue of capital stock to the public.
- **LO2** **Issued stock:** The shares of stock sold or otherwise transferred to stockholders.
- **LO1** **Legal capital:** The number of shares of stock issued times the par value; the minimum amount that can be reported as contributed capital.
- **LO3** **Liquidating dividend:** A dividend that exceeds retained earnings; usually paid when a corporation goes out of business or reduces its operations.
- **LO4** **Noncumulative preferred stock:** Preferred stock that does not oblige the issuer to make up a missed dividend in a subsequent year.
- **LO5** **No-par stock:** Capital stock that does not have a par value.
- **LO2** **Outstanding stock:** Stock that has been issued and is still in circulation.
- **LO1** **Par value:** An arbitrary amount assigned to each share of stock; constitutes the legal capital of a corporation.
- **LO2** **Preferred stock:** Stock that has preference over common stock, usually in terms of dividends and the distribution of assets.
- **LO1** **Price/earnings (P/E) ratio:** A measure of confidence in a company's future; market price per share divided by earnings per share.
- **LO2** **Residual equity:** The common stock of a corporation.
- **LO1** **Return on equity:** A measure of management performance; net income divided by average stockholders' equity.
- **LO1** **Share of stock:** A unit of ownership in a corporation.
- **LO1** **Start-up and organization costs:** The costs of forming a corporation.
- **LO5** **Stated value:** A value assigned by the board of directors of a corporation to no-par stock.
- **LO1** **Stock certificate:** A document issued to a stockholder indicating the number of shares of stock the stockholder owns.
- **LO1** **Stock option plan:** An agreement to issue stock to employees according to specified terms.
- **LO6** **Treasury stock:** Capital stock, either common or preferred, that the issuing company has reacquired but has not subsequently resold or retired.
- **LO1** **Underwriter:** An intermediary between the corporation and the investing public who facilitates an issue of stock or other securities for a fee.

Review Problem

Stock Entries and Stockholders' Equity

LO1 LO2 LO3 LO4 LO5 LO6 The Beta Corporation was organized in 20x4 in the state of Arizona. Its charter authorized the corporation to issue 1,000,000 shares of $1 par value common stock and an additional 25,000 shares of 4 percent, $20 par value cumulative convertible preferred stock. Here are the transactions related to the company's stock during 20x4:

Feb. 1 Issued 100,000 shares of common stock for $125,000.
     15 Issued 3,000 shares of common stock for accounting and legal services. The services were billed to the company at $3,600.
Mar. 15 Issued 120,000 shares of common stock to Edward Jackson in exchange for a building and land appraised at $100,000 and $25,000, respectively.
Apr. 2 Purchased 20,000 shares of common stock for the treasury at $1.25 per share from a person who changed his mind about investing in the company.
July 1 Issued 25,000 shares of preferred stock for $500,000.
Sept. 30 Sold 10,000 of the shares in the treasury for $1.50 per share.
Dec. 31 The board declared dividends of $24,910 payable on January 15 to stockholders of record on January 8. Dividends included preferred stock cash dividends for one-half year.

For the period ended December 31, 20x4, the company reported net income of $40,000 and earnings per common share of $.14. At December 31, the market price per common share was $1.60.

REQUIRED
1. Record these transactions in journal form. In the explanation for the December 31 entry to record dividends, show dividends payable to each class of stock.
2. Prepare the stockholders' equity section of the Beta Corporation balance sheet as of December 31, 20x4. (**Hint:** Use net income and dividends to calculate retained earnings.)
3. Calculate dividends yield on common stock, price/earnings ratio of common stock, and return on equity.

Answer to Review Problem

1. Entries prepared in journal form:

Feb.	1	Cash	125,000	
		Common Stock		100,000
		Paid-in Capital in Excess of		
		Par Value, Common		25,000
		Issued 100,000 shares of		
		$1 par value common		
		stock for $1.25 per share		
	15	Start-up and Organization Expense	3,600	
		Common Stock		3,000
		Paid-in Capital in Excess of		
		Par Value, Common		600
		Issued 3,000 shares of		
		$1 par value common stock		
		for billed accounting and		
		legal services of $3,600		
Mar.	15	Building	100,000	
		Land	25,000	
		Common Stock		120,000
		Paid-in Capital in Excess of		
		Par Value, Common		5,000
		Issued 120,000 shares of		
		$1 par value common stock		
		for a building and land		
		appraised at $100,000 and		
		$25,000, respectively		

Apr. 2	Treasury Stock, Common		25,000	
	Cash			25,000
	Purchased 20,000 shares of common stock for the treasury at $1.25 per share			
July 1	Cash		500,000	
	Preferred Stock			500,000
	Issued 25,000 shares of $20 par value preferred stock for $20 per share			
Sept. 30	Cash		15,000	
	Treasury Stock, Common			12,500
	Paid-in Capital, Treasury Stock			2,500
	Sold 10,000 shares of treasury stock at $1.50 per share; original cost was $1.25 per share			
Dec. 31	Cash Dividends Declared		24,910	
	Cash Dividends Payable			24,910
	Declared a $24,910 cash dividend to preferred and common stockholders			

Total dividend	$24,910
Less preferred stock cash dividend	
$500,000 × .04 × 6/12	10,000
Common stock cash dividend	$14,910

2. Stockholders' equity section of the balance sheet prepared:

Beta Corporation
Balance Sheet
December 31, 20x4

Stockholders' Equity

Contributed capital
  Preferred stock, 4 percent cumulative convertible, $20 par value, 25,000 shares authorized, issued, and outstanding $500,000
  Common stock, $1 par value, 1,000,000 shares authorized, 223,000 shares issued, and 213,000 shares outstanding $223,000
  Paid-in capital in excess of par value, common   30,600
  Paid-in capital, treasury stock   2,500   256,100

Total contributed capital $756,100
Retained earnings   15,090*

Total contributed capital and retained earnings $771,190
Less treasury stock, common (10,000 shares, at cost)   12,500
Total stockholders' equity $758,690

*Retained Earnings = $40,000 − $24,910 = $15,090.

3. Dividends yield on common stock, price/earnings ratio of common stock, and return on equity calculated:

$$\text{Dividends per Share} = \$14{,}910 \text{ Common Stock Dividend} \div 213{,}000 \text{ Common Shares Outstanding} = \$.07$$

$$\text{Dividends Yield} = \frac{\text{Dividends per Share}}{\text{Market Price per Share}} = \frac{\$.07}{\$1.60} = 4.4\%$$

$$\text{Price/Earnings (P/E) Ratio} = \frac{\text{Market Price per Share}}{\text{Earnings per Share}} = \frac{\$1.60}{\$.14} = 11.4 \text{ times}$$

The opening balance of stockholders' equity on February 1, 20x1, was $125,000.

$$\text{Return on Equity} = \frac{\text{Net Income}}{\text{Average Stockholders' Equity}}$$

$$= \frac{\$40{,}000}{(\$758{,}690 + \$125{,}000) \div 2}$$

$$= 9.1\%$$

Chapter Assignments

BUILDING YOUR KNOWLEDGE FOUNDATION

QUESTIONS

1. What management issues are related to contributed capital?
2. Identify and explain several advantages of the corporate form of business.
3. Identify and explain several disadvantages of the corporate form of business.
4. What is dividends yield, and what do investors learn from it?
5. What is the price/earnings (P/E) ratio, and what does it measure?
6. What are the start-up and organization costs of a corporation?
7. What is the proper accounting treatment of start-up and organization costs?
8. What is a stock option plan, and why would a company have one?
9. What is the legal capital of a corporation, and what is its significance?
10. Describe the significance of the following dates as they relate to dividends: (a) date of declaration, (b) date of record, and (c) date of payment.
11. Explain the accounting treatment of cash dividends.
12. What are dividends in arrears, and how should they be disclosed in the financial statements?
13. Define *cumulative, convertible,* and *callable* as they apply to preferred stock.
14. How is the value of stock determined when stock is issued for noncash assets?
15. Define *treasury stock* and explain why a company would purchase its own stock.
16. What is the proper classification of the accounts listed below on the balance sheet? Indicate whether stockholders' equity accounts are contributed capital, retained earnings, or contra stockholders' equity.
    a. Common Stock
    b. Treasury Stock
    c. Paid-in Capital, Treasury Stock
    d. Paid-in Capital in Excess of Par Value, Common
    e. Paid-in Capital in Excess of Stated Value, Common
    f. Retained Earnings

SHORT EXERCISES

SE 1.
LO1 Management Issues

Indicate whether each of the following actions is related to (a) managing under the corporate form of business, (b) using equity financing, (c) determining dividend policies, or (d) evaluating performance using return on equity:

1. Considering whether to make a distribution to stockholders
2. Controlling day-to-day operations
3. Determining whether to issue preferred or common stock
4. Compensating management based on the company's meeting or exceeding the targeted return on equity
5. Issuing shares
6. Transferring shares without the approval of other owners

SE 2.
LO1 Advantages and Disadvantages of a Corporation

Identify whether each of the following characteristics is an advantage or a disadvantage of the corporate form of business:

1. Ease of transfer of ownership
2. Taxation
3. Separate legal entity
4. Lack of mutual agency
5. Government regulation
6. Continuous existence

SE 3.
LO1 Effect of Start-up and Organization Costs

At the beginning of 20x3, Shiran Company incurred the following start-up and organization costs: (1) attorneys' fees with a market value of $5,000, paid with 3,000 shares of $1 par value common stock, and (2) incorporation fees paid of $3,000. Calculate total start-up and organization costs. What will be the effect of these costs on the balance sheet and income statement?

SE 4.
LO1 Exercise of Stock Options

On June 6, Heda Corday exercised her option to purchase 10,000 shares of Antonia Corporation $1 par value common stock at an option price of $4. The market price per share was $4 on the grant date and $18 on the exercise date. Record the transaction on Antonia's books.

SE 5.
LO2 Stockholders' Equity

Prepare the stockholders' equity section of Keech Corporation's balance sheet from the following accounts and balances on December 31, 20xx:

Account	Balance Debit	Balance Credit
Common Stock, $10 par value, 60,000 shares authorized, 40,000 shares issued, and 39,000 shares outstanding		$400,000
Paid-in Capital in Excess of Par Value, Common		200,000
Retained Earnings		30,000
Treasury Stock, Common (1,000 shares, at cost)	$15,000	

SE 6.
LO3 Cash Dividends

Powers Corporation has authorized 100,000 shares of $1 par value common stock, of which 80,000 are issued and 70,000 are outstanding. On May 15, the board of directors declared a cash dividend of $.10 per share payable on June 15 to stockholders of record on June 1. Prepare the entries, as necessary, for each of the three dates.

SE 7.
LO4 Preferred Stock Dividends with Dividends in Arrears

Maddox Corporation has 1,000 shares of $100, 8 percent cumulative preferred stock outstanding and 20,000 shares of $1 par value common stock outstanding. In the company's first three years of operation, its board of directors paid cash dividends as follows: 20x3, none; 20x4, $20,000; and 20x5, $40,000. Determine the total cash dividends and dividends per share paid to the preferred and common stockholders during each of the three years.

SE 8.
LO5 Issuance of Stock

Brianna Corporation is authorized to issue 100,000 shares of common stock. The company sold 5,000 shares at $12 per share. Prepare entries in journal form to record the sale of stock for cash under each of the following independent alternatives: (1) The stock has a par value of $5, and (2) the stock has no par value but a stated value of $1 per share.

LO5 Issuance of Stock for Noncash Assets

SE 9. Rheimes Corporation issued 8,000 shares of its $1 par value common stock in exchange for land that had a fair market value of $50,000. Prepare in journal form the entries necessary to record the issuance of the stock for the land under each of the following conditions: (1) The stock was selling for $7 per share on the day of the transaction, and (2) management attempted to place a value on the common stock but could not do so.

LO6 Treasury Stock Transactions

SE 10. Prepare in journal form the entries necessary to record the following stock transactions of Oahanii Company during 20xx:

Oct. 1 Purchased 1,000 shares of its own $2 par value common stock for $20 per share, the current market price.
  17 Sold 250 shares of treasury stock purchased on October 1 for $25 per share.
  21 Sold 400 shares of treasury stock purchased on October 1 for $18 per share.

LO6 Retirement of Treasury Stock

SE 11. On October 28, 20xx, Oahanii Company (**SE 10**) retired the remaining 350 shares of treasury stock. The shares were originally issued at $5 per share. Prepare the necessary entry in journal form.

EXERCISES

LO1 Dividends Yield and Price/Earnings Ratio

E 1. In 20x5, Palladin Corporation earned $2.20 per share and paid a dividend of $1.00 per share. At year end, the price of its stock was $33 per share. Calculate the dividends yield and the price/earnings ratio.

LO2 Stockholders' Equity
LO6

E 2. The following accounts and balances are from the records of Halloran Corporation on December 31, 20xx:

Account	Balance Debit	Balance Credit
Preferred Stock, $100 par value, 9 percent cumulative, 20,000 shares authorized, 12,000 shares issued and outstanding		$1,200,000
Common Stock, $12 par value, 90,000 shares authorized, 60,000 shares issued, and 57,000 shares outstanding		720,000
Paid-in Capital in Excess of Par Value, Common		388,000
Retained Earnings		46,000
Treasury Stock, Common (3,000 shares, at cost)	$60,000	

Prepare the stockholders' equity section for Halloran Corporation's balance sheet.

LO2 Characteristics of Common
LO4 and Preferred Stock

E 3. Indicate whether each of the following characteristics is more closely associated with common stock (C) or preferred stock (P):

1. Often receives dividends at a set rate
2. Is considered the residual equity of a company
3. Can be callable
4. Can be convertible
5. More likely to have dividends that vary in amount from year to year
6. Can be entitled to receive dividends not paid in past years
7. Likely to have full voting rights
8. Receives assets first in liquidation
9. Generally receives dividends before other classes of stock

LO2 Stock Entries Using
LO5 T Accounts; Stockholders' Equity

E 4. The Wallace Hospital Supply Corporation was organized in 20xx. It was authorized to issue 100,000 shares of no-par common stock with a stated value of $5 per share, and 20,000 shares of $100 par value, 6 percent noncumulative preferred stock. On March 1, the company issued 60,000 shares of its common stock for $15 per share and 8,000 shares of its preferred stock for $100 per share.

1. Record the issuance of the stock in T accounts.
2. Prepare the stockholders' equity section of Wallace Hospital Supply Corporation's balance sheet as it would appear immediately after the company issued the common and preferred stock.

LO3 Cash Dividends

E 5. Estey Corporation secured authorization from the state for 200,000 shares of $10 par value common stock. It has 160,000 shares issued and 140,000 shares outstanding. On June 5, the board of directors declared a $.50 per share cash dividend to be paid on June 25 to stockholders of record on June 15. Prepare entries in journal form to record these events.

LO3 Cash Dividends
LO6

E 6. Santori Corporation has 500,000 authorized shares of $1 par value common stock, of which 400,000 are issued, including 40,000 shares of treasury stock. On October 15, the board of directors declared a cash dividend of $.25 per share payable on November 15 to stockholders of record on November 1. Prepare entries in journal form for each of the three dates.

LO4 Cash Dividends with Dividends in Arrears

E 7. Amsco Corporation has 10,000 shares of its $100 par value, 7 percent cumulative preferred stock outstanding, and 50,000 shares of its $1 par value common stock outstanding. In Amsco's first four years of operation, its board of directors paid cash dividends as follows: 20x3, none; 20x4, $120,000; 20x5, $140,000; 20x6, $140,000. Determine the dividends per share and total cash dividends paid to the preferred and common stockholders during each of the four years.

LO4 Cash Dividends on Preferred and Common Stock

E 8. Caron Corporation pays dividends at the end of each year. The dividends that it paid for 20x3, 20x4, and 20x5 were $80,000, $60,000, and $180,000, respectively. Calculate the total amount of dividends the Caron Corporation paid in each of these years to its common and preferred stockholders under both of the following capital structures: (1) 20,000 shares of $100 par, 6 percent noncumulative preferred stock and 60,000 shares of $10 par common stock; (2) 10,000 shares of $100 par, 7 percent cumulative preferred stock and 60,000 shares of $10 par common stock. No dividends were in arrears at the beginning of 20x3.

LO5 Issuance of Stock

E 9. Montana Company is authorized to issue 200,000 shares of common stock. On August 1, the company issued 10,000 shares at $25 per share. Prepare entries in journal form to record the issuance of stock for cash under each of the following alternatives:

1. The stock has a par value of $25.
2. The stock has a par value of $10.
3. The stock has no par value.
4. The stock has a stated value of $1 per share.

LO5 Issuance of Stock for Noncash Assets

E 10. On July 1, 20xx, Florine, a new corporation, issued 20,000 shares of its common stock to finance a corporate headquarters building. The building has a fair market value of $600,000 and a book value of $400,000. Because Florine is a new corporation, it is not possible to establish a market value for its common stock. Record the issuance of stock for the building, assuming the following conditions: (1) the par value of the stock is $10 per share; (2) the stock is no-par stock; and (3) the stock has a stated value of $4 per share.

LO6 Treasury Stock Transactions

E 11. Record in T accounts the following stock transactions of Mahtani Company, which represent all the company's treasury stock transactions during 20xx:

May 5 Purchased 400 shares of its own $2 par value common stock for $20 per share, the current market price.
17 Sold 150 shares of treasury stock purchased on May 5 for $22 per share.
21 Sold 100 shares of treasury stock purchased on May 5 for $20 per share.
28 Sold the remaining 150 shares of treasury stock purchased on May 5 for $19 per share.

LO6 Treasury Stock Transactions Including Retirement

E 12. Record in T accounts the following stock transactions of Theoharis Corporation, which represent all its treasury stock transactions for the year:

June 1 Purchased 2,000 shares of its own $30 par value common stock for $70 per share, the current market price.
10 Sold 500 shares of treasury stock purchased on June 1 for $80 per share.
20 Sold 700 shares of treasury stock purchased on June 1 for $58 per share.
30 Retired the remaining shares purchased on June 1. The original issue price was $42 per share.

PROBLEMS

P 1.
LO1 LO2 LO3 LO5 **Start-up and Organization Costs, Stock and Dividend Entries Using T Accounts, and Stockholders' Equity**

On March 1, 20xx, Jung Corporation began operations with a charter from the state that authorized 100,000 shares of $2 par value common stock. Over the next quarter, the firm engaged in the following transactions:

Mar. 1 Issued 30,000 shares of common stock, $100,000.
     2 Paid fees associated with obtaining the charter and starting up and organizing the corporation, $12,000.
Apr. 10 Issued 13,000 shares of common stock, $65,000.
May 31 The board of directors declared a $.10 per share cash dividend to be paid on June 15 to shareholders of record on June 10.

REQUIRED
1. Record the above transactions in T accounts.
2. Prepare the stockholders' equity section of Jung Corporation's balance sheet on May 31, 20xx. Net income earned during the first quarter was $15,000.

P 2.
LO1 LO4 **Preferred and Common Stock Dividends and Dividends Yield**

Taswell Corporation had the following stock outstanding from 20x3 through 20x6:

Preferred stock: $50 par value, 8 percent cumulative, 10,000 shares authorized, issued, and outstanding

Common stock: $5 par value, 200,000 shares authorized, issued, and outstanding

The company paid $30,000, $30,000, $94,000, and $130,000 in dividends during 20x3, 20x4, 20x5, and 20x6, respectively. The market price per common share was $7.25 and $8.00 per share at year end 20x5 and 20x6, respectively.

REQUIRED
1. Determine the dividends per share and the total dividends paid to common stockholders and preferred stockholders in 20x3, 20x4, 20x5, and 20x6.
2. Perform the same computations, with the assumption that the preferred stock was noncumulative.
3. Calculate the 20x5 and 20x6 dividends yield for common stock, using the dividends per share computed in **2**.
4. How are cumulative preferred stock and noncumulative preferred stock similar to long-term bonds? How do they differ from long-term bonds?

P 3.
LO1 LO6 **Treasury Stock Transactions**

Bendix Company was involved in the following treasury stock transactions during 20xx:

Jan. 10 Purchased 52,000 shares of its $2 par value common stock on the market for $40 per share.
    20 Sold 16,000 shares of the treasury stock for $42 per share.
Feb. 8 Sold 12,000 shares of the treasury stock for $38 per share.
    16 Sold 20,000 shares of the treasury stock for $34 per share.
Mar. 14 Purchased an additional 8,000 shares for $36 per share.
    25 Retired all the remaining shares of treasury stock. All shares originally were issued at $16 per share.

REQUIRED
1. Record these transactions in journal form.
2. What effect does the purchase of treasury stock have on return on equity? Why might management prefer to buy treasury stock rather than pay dividends?

P 4.
LO1 LO2 LO3 LO4 LO5 LO6 **Comprehensive Stockholders' Equity Transactions and Financial Ratios**

Arkazian, Inc., was organized and authorized to issue 10,000 shares of $100 par value, 9 percent preferred stock and 100,000 shares of no-par, $10 stated value common stock on July 1, 20xx. Stock-related transactions for Arkazian were as follows:

July 1 Issued 20,000 shares of common stock at $22 per share.
    1 Issued 1,000 shares of common stock at $22 per share for services rendered in connection with the organization of the company.
    2 Issued 4,000 shares of preferred stock at par value for cash.
    10 Issued 5,000 shares of common stock for land on which the asking price was $120,000. Market value of the stock was $24. Management wishes to record the land at full market value of the stock.
Aug. 2 Purchased 3,000 shares of its common stock at $26 per share.
    10 Declared a cash dividend for one month on the outstanding preferred stock and $.04 per share on common stock outstanding, payable on August 22 to stockholders of record on August 12.
    12 Date of record for cash dividends.
    22 Paid cash dividends.

REQUIRED
1. Record the transactions in T accounts.
2. Prepare the stockholders' equity section of the balance sheet as it would appear on August 31, 20xx. Net income for July and August was $50,000.
3. Calculate dividends yield, price/earnings ratio, and return on equity. Assume earnings per common share are $1.97 and market price per common share is $25. For beginning stockholders' equity, use the balance at the close of business on July 1, 20xx.

P 5.
LO1 **Comprehensive Stockholders'**
LO2 **Equity Transactions and**
LO3 **T Accounts**
LO4
LO5
LO6

In January 20xx, Hammond Corporation was organized and authorized to issue 2,000,000 shares of no-par common stock and 50,000 shares of 5 percent, $50 par value, noncumulative preferred stock. The stock-related transactions for the first year's operations were as follows:

Jan. 19 Sold 15,000 shares of the common stock for $31,500. State law requires a minimum of $1 stated value per share.
    21   Issued 5,000 shares of common stock to attorneys and accountants for services valued at $11,000 and provided during the organization of the corporation.
Feb. 7   Issued 30,000 shares of common stock for a building that had an appraised value of $78,000.
Mar. 22 Purchased 10,000 shares of its common stock at $3 per share.
July 15 Issued 5,000 shares of common stock to employees under a stock option plan that allows any employee to buy shares at the current market price, which is now $3 per share.
Aug. 1   Sold 2,500 shares of treasury stock for $4 per share.
Sept. 1 Declared a cash dividend of $.15 per common share to be paid on September 25 to stockholders of record on September 15.
    15   Cash dividends date of record.
    25   Paid cash dividends to stockholders of record on September 15.
Oct. 30 Issued 4,000 shares of common stock for a piece of land. The stock was selling for $3 per share, and the land had a fair market value of $12,000.
Dec. 15 Issued 2,200 shares of preferred stock for $50 per share.

REQUIRED
1. Record the above transactions in T accounts. Prepare T accounts for Cash; Land; Building; Cash Dividends Payable; Preferred Stock; Common Stock; Paid-in Capital in Excess of Stated Value, Common; Paid-in Capital, Treasury Stock; Retained Earnings; Treasury Stock, Common; Cash Dividends Declared; and Start-up and Organization Expense.
2. Prepare the stockholders' equity section of Hammond Corporation's balance sheet as of December 31, 20xx. Net income earned during the year was $100,000.

Alternate Problems

P 6.
LO1 **Start-up and Organization**
LO2 **Costs, Stock and Dividend**
LO3 **Entries, and Stockholders'**
LO5 **Equity**

Quesnel Corporation began operations on September 1, 20xx. The corporation's charter authorized 300,000 shares of $8 par value common stock. Quesnel Corporation engaged in the following transactions during its first quarter:

Sept. 1 Issued 50,000 shares of common stock, $500,000.
     1   Paid an attorney $32,000 to help start up and organize the corporation and obtain a corporate charter from the state.
Oct. 2   Issued 80,000 shares of common stock, $960,000.
Nov. 30 Declared a cash dividend of $.40 per share to be paid on December 15 to stockholders of record on December 10.

REQUIRED
1. Prepare entries in journal form to record the above transactions.
2. Prepare the stockholders' equity section of Quesnel Corporation's balance sheet on November 30, 20xx. Net income for the quarter was $80,000.

P 7.
LO1 **Preferred and Common Stock**
LO4 **Dividends and Dividends Yield**

DeMarcello Corporation had both common stock and preferred stock outstanding from 20x2 through 20x4. Information about each stock for the three years is as follows:

Type	Par Value	Shares Outstanding	Other
Preferred	$100	40,000	7% cumulative
Common	20	600,000	

The company paid $140,000, $800,000, and $1,100,000 in dividends for 20x2 through 20x4, respectively. The market price per common share was $15 and $17 per share at the end of years 20x3 and 20x4, respectively.

REQUIRED
1. Determine the dividends per share and total dividends paid to the common and preferred stockholders each year.
2. Assuming that the preferred stock was noncumulative, repeat the computations performed in **1**.
3. Calculate the 20x3 and 20x4 dividends yield for common stock using dividends per share computed in **2**.
4. How are cumulative preferred stock and noncumulative preferred stock similar to long-term bonds? How do they differ from long-term bonds?

P 8.
LO1 **Comprehensive Stockholders'**
LO2 **Equity Transactions**
LO3
LO4
LO5
LO6

Czerepak, Inc., was organized and authorized to issue 10,000 shares of $100 par value, 9 percent preferred stock and 100,000 shares of no-par, $5 stated value common stock on July 1, 20xx. Stock-related transactions for Czerepak are as follows:

July 1   Issued 20,000 shares of common stock at $11 per share.
      1   Issued 1,000 shares of common stock at $11 per share for services rendered in connection with the organization of the company.
      2   Issued 2,000 shares of preferred stock at par value for cash.
    10   Issued 5,000 shares of common stock for land on which the asking price was $70,000. Market value of the stock was $12. Management wishes to record the land at full market value of the stock.
Aug. 2   Purchased 3,000 shares of its common stock at $13 per share.
    10   Declared a cash dividend for one month on the outstanding preferred stock and $.02 per share on common stock outstanding, payable on August 22 to stockholders of record on August 12.
    12   Date of record for cash dividends.
    22   Paid cash dividends.

REQUIRED
1. Record the transactions in journal form.
2. Prepare the stockholders' equity section of the balance sheet as it would appear on August 31, 20xx. Net income for July and August was $25,000.

SKILLS DEVELOPMENT CASES

Conceptual Analysis

SD 1.
LO1 **Reasons for Issuing Common**
LO2 **Stock**

In a recent year, Avaya, Inc. <www.avaya.com>, an East Coast telecommunications company, issued 34,300,000 shares of common stock for a total of $212,000,000.[15] As a growing company, Avaya could have raised this significant amount of money by issuing long-term bonds, but the company's bond rating had recently been lowered. What are some advantages of issuing common stock as opposed to bonds? What are some disadvantages?

SD 2.
LO4 **Reasons for Issuing Preferred**
Stock

Preferred stock is a hybrid security; it has some of the characteristics of stock and some of the characteristics of bonds. Historically, preferred stock has not been a popular means of financing. In the past few years, however, it has become more attractive to companies and individual investors alike, and investors are buying large amounts because of high yields. Large preferred stock issues have been made by such banking firms as Chase <www.chase.com>, Citibank <www.citigroup.com>, HSBC Bank USA <www.us.hsbc.com>, and Wells Fargo <www.wellsfargo.com>, as well as by other companies. The dividends yields on these stocks are over 9 percent, higher than the interest rates on bonds of comparable risk.[16] Especially popular are preferred equity redemption convertible stocks, or PERCs, which are automatically convertible into common stock after three years if the company does not call them first and retire them. What reasons can you give for the popularity of preferred stock, and of PERCs in particular, when the tax-deductible interest on bonds is lower? Discuss from both the company's and the investor's standpoint.

SD 3.
LO6 **Purposes of Treasury Stock**

Many companies in recent years have bought back their common stock. For example, IBM <www.ibm.com>, with large cash holdings, spent almost $27 billion over five years repurchasing its stock. What are the reasons companies buy back their own shares? What is the effect of common stock buybacks on earnings per share, return on equity, return on assets, debt to equity, and the current ratio?

Ethical Dilemma

SD 4.

LO1 Ethics, Management
LO6 Compensation, and Treasury Stock

Compensation of senior management is often tied to earnings per share or return on equity. Treasury stock purchases have a favorable impact on both these measures. In the recent buyback boom, many companies borrowed money to purchase treasury shares, resulting in a higher debt to equity ratio. In some cases, the motivation for the borrowing and repurchase of shares was the desire of executives to secure their year-end cash bonuses. Did these executives act ethically? Were their actions in the best interests of stockholders? Why or why not? How might such behavior be avoided in the future?

Research Activity

SD 5.

LO1 Comparison of Stockholders'
LO2 Equity Characteristics
LO3
LO4
LO5

Select the annual reports of three corporations from sources in your library or from the Fingraph® Financial Analyst™ CD-ROM software that accompanies this text. You can choose them from the same industry or at random, at the direction of your instructor. (**Note:** You may be asked to use these companies again in the Research Activity cases in later chapters.) Prepare a table with a column for each corporation. Then answer the following questions for each corporation: Does it have preferred stock? If so, what are the preferred stock's par value and dividend, and is the stock cumulative or convertible? Is the common stock par value or no-par? What is its par value or stated value? What cash dividends, if any, did the corporation pay in the past year? What is the dividends yield? From the notes to the financial statements, determine whether the corporation has an employee stock option plan. If so, what are some of its provisions? What is the return on equity? Be prepared to discuss the characteristics of the stocks and dividends of the three corporations in class.

Decision-Making Practice

SD 6.

LO1 Analysis of Alternative
LO2 Financing Methods

Northeast Servotech Corporation, which offers services to the computer industry, has expanded rapidly in recent years. Because of its profitability, the company has been able to grow without obtaining external financing. This fact is reflected in its current balance sheet, which contains no long-term debt. The liabilities and stockholders' equity sections of the balance sheet on March 31, 20xx, appear below.

Northeast Servotech Corporation
Balance Sheet
March 31, 20xx

Liabilities

Current liabilities		$ 500,000

Stockholders' Equity

Common stock, $10 par value, 500,000 shares authorized, 100,000 shares issued and outstanding	$1,000,000	
Paid-in capital in excess of par value, common	1,800,000	
Retained earnings	1,700,000	
Total stockholders' equity		4,500,000
Total liabilities and stockholders' equity		$5,000,000

The company now has the opportunity to double its size by purchasing the operations of a rival company for $4,000,000. If the purchase goes through, Northeast Servotech will become one of the top companies in its specialized industry. The problem for management is how to finance the purchase. After much study and discussion with bankers and underwriters, management has prepared the following three financing alternatives to present to the board of directors, which must authorize the purchase and the financing:

Alternative A   The company could issue $4,000,000 of long-term debt. Given the company's financial rating and the current market rates, management believes the company will have to pay an interest rate of 12 percent on the debt.

Alternative B   The company could issue 40,000 shares of 8 percent, $100 par value preferred stock.

Alternative C   The company could issue 100,000 additional shares of $10 par value common stock at $40 per share.

Management explains to the board that the interest on the long-term debt is tax-deductible and that the applicable income tax rate is 40 percent. The board members know that a dividend of $.80 per share of common stock was paid last year, up from $.60 and $.40 per share in the two years before that. The board has had a policy of regular increases in dividends of $.20 per share. It believes each of the three financing alternatives is feasible and now wants to study the financial effects of each one.

1. Prepare a schedule to show how the liabilities and stockholders' equity sections of Northeast Servotech's balance sheet would look under each alternative, and compute the debt to equity ratio (total liabilities ÷ total stockholders' equity) for each.
2. Compute and compare the cash needed to pay the interest or dividends for each kind of new financing, net of income taxes, in the first year.
3. How might the cash needed to pay for the financing change in future years under each alternative?
4. Prepare a memorandum to the board of directors that evaluates the alternatives in order of preference based on cash flow effects, giving arguments for and against each.

 Group Activity: Assign the alternatives to different groups to analyze and present to members of the class who act as the board of directors.

FINANCIAL REPORTING AND ANALYSIS CASES

Interpreting Financial Reports

LO1 Effect of Stock Issue
LO2
LO5

FRA 1.   Netscape Communications Corporation <www.netscape.com>, now part of AOL–Time Warner, is a leading provider of software that links people and information over the Internet and intranets. It is one of the great success stories of the Internet age. When Netscape went public with an IPO, it issued stock at $14 per share. In its second year as a public company, it advertised a common stock issue in *The Wall Street Journal*:

6,440,000 Shares
NETSCAPE
Common Stock
Price $53¾ a share

If Netscape sold all these shares at the offering price of $53.75, the net proceeds before issue costs would have been $346.15 million. Below is a portion of the stockholders' equity section of the balance sheet adapted from Netscape's annual report, which was issued prior to this stock offering.

Stockholders' Equity
(In thousands)

Common stock, $.0001 par value, 200,000,000 shares authorized, 81,063,158 shares issued and outstanding	$ 8
Additional paid-in capital	196,749
Accumulated deficit	(16,314)

1. Assume the net proceeds from the sale of 6,440,000 shares at $53.75 were $342.6 million after issue costs. Record the stock issuance on Netscape's accounting records in journal form.
2. Prepare the portion of the stockholders' equity section of the balance sheet shown at the bottom of the previous page after the issue of the common stock, based on the information given. Round all answers to the nearest thousand.
3. Based on your answer in **2**, did Netscape have to increase its authorized shares to undertake this stock issue?
4. What amount per share did Netscape receive and how much did Netscape's underwriters receive to help in issuing the stock if investors paid $53.75 per share? What do underwriters do to earn their fee?

FRA 2.
LO4 Effect of Deferring Preferred Dividends

US Airways <www.usairways.com> had indefinitely deferred the quarterly dividend on its $358 million of cumulative convertible 9¼ percent preferred stock.[17] According to a US Airways spokesperson, the company did not want to "continue to pay a dividend while the company is losing money." Others interpreted the action as "an indication of a cash crisis situation."

At the time, Berkshire Hathaway <www.berkshirehathaway.com>, the large company run by Warren Buffett and the owner of the preferred stock, was not happy, but US Airways was able to turn around, become profitable, and return to paying its cumulative dividends on preferred stock. Berkshire Hathaway was able to convert the preferred stock into 9.24 million common shares of US Airways' common stock at $38.74 per share at a time when the market value had risen to $62.[18]

What is cumulative convertible preferred stock? Why is deferring dividends on those shares a drastic action? What is the impact on profitability and liquidity? Why did using preferred stock instead of long-term bonds as a financing method probably save the company from bankruptcy? What was Berkshire Hathaway's gain on its investment at the time of the conversion?

International Company

FRA 3.
LO2 Stockholders' Equity and
LO3 Dividends

Roche Group <www.roche.com> is a giant Swiss pharmaceutical company. Its stockholders' equity shows how little importance common stock, which the Swiss call *share capital*, typically has in the financing of Swiss companies:[19]

	2001	2000
Shareholders' equity (in millions of Swiss francs)		
Share capital	160	160
Retained earnings	32,273	31,614
Total shareholders' equity	32,433	31,774

When Swiss companies need financing, they often rely on debt financing from large Swiss banks and other debt markets. With only 160 million Swiss francs (835 million shares) in share capital, Roche has had few stock issues in its history. In contrast, the company has over 42 billion Swiss francs in liabilities. Roche has been profitable, having built up retained earnings of more than 32 billion Swiss francs over the years. The company also pays a substantial dividend that totaled 981 million Swiss francs in 2001. Calculate the dividends per share and dividends yield assuming a share price of 118.5 Swiss francs. Assuming that dividends and net income were the only factors that affected retained earnings during 2001, how much did Roche earn in 2001 in U.S. dollars (use an exchange rate of 1.7 Swiss francs to the dollar)? What was Roche's return on equity? Comment on Roche's dividend policy and its level of earnings.

Financial Reporting and Analysis Cases

Toys "R" Us Annual Report

FRA 4. Refer to the Toys "R" Us <www.tru.com> annual report to answer the following questions:

LO1 **Stockholders' Equity**
LO2
LO6

1. What type of capital stock does Toys "R" Us have? What is the par value? How many shares were authorized, issued, and outstanding at the end of fiscal 2002?
2. What is the dividends yield for Toys "R" Us and its relationship to the investors' total return? Does the company rely mostly on stock or on earnings for its stockholders' equity?
3. Does the company have a stock option plan? To whom do the stock options apply? Do employees have significant stock options? Given the market price of the stock shown in the report, do these options represent significant value to the employees?
4. Calculate and discuss the price/earnings ratio and return on equity for 2001 and 2002. The average share price for the fourth quarter was $21.13 and $11.43 for 2001 and 2002, respectively.

Comparison Case: Toys "R" Us and Walgreen Co.

FRA 5. Refer to the annual report of Toys "R" Us <www.tru.com> and the financial statements and notes of Walgreens <www.walgreens.com> in the Supplement to Chapter 1.

LO1 **Return on Equity, Treasury Stock, and Dividends Policy**

1. Compute the return on equity for both companies for the most recent two years.
2. Did either company purchase treasury stock during these years? How will the purchase of treasury stock affect return on equity and earnings per share?
3. Did either company issue stock during these years? What are the details?
4. Compare the dividend policy of the two companies.

Fingraph® Financial Analyst™

FRA 6. Select any two companies from the list of Fingraph companies on the Needles Accounting Resource Center Web Site at http://accounting.college.hmco.com/students. Access the Microsoft Excel spreadsheets for the companies you selected.

LO1 **Comparative Analysis of**
LO2 **Stockholders' Equity**
LO6

1. In the Fingraph spreadsheet for each company, identify the equity section of the balance sheet information. Do the companies have more than one kind of capital stock? Do the companies have treasury stock?
2. Using the Fingraph CD-ROM software, prepare a page of text that summarizes the price/earnings ratio and dividends yield for each company.
3. Using the Fingraph CD-ROM software, prepare a page of text that summarizes the financing section of each company's statement of cash flows.
4. Write a one-page summary highlighting the types of capital stock and the significance of treasury stock for these companies. Mention the extent to which they raised cash from recent stock issues or used cash to repurchase capital stock. Describe the impact on total equity. Also compare the price/earnings ratio and dividends yield trends of the two companies. Include your Fingraph pages with your report.

Internet Case

FRA 7. Many Internet start-up companies have gone public in recent years. These companies are generally unprofitable and require a great deal of cash to finance expansion. They also reward their employees with stock options. Choose any two of the following Internet companies: Amazon.com <www.amazon.com>, Yahoo! <www.yahoo.com>, eBay Inc. <www.ebay.com>, or AOL-Time Warner <www.aoltw.com>. Go to the web sites of the two companies you have selected. In their latest annual reports, look at the financing section of the statement of cash flows for the last three years. How have these two companies financed their businesses? Have they issued stock or long-term debt? Have they purchased treasury stock, paid dividends, or issued stock under stock option plans? Are the companies profitable (see net income or earnings at the top of the statement)? Are your findings in line with your expectations about these Internet companies? Find each company's stock price, either on its web site or in a newspaper, and compare it with the average issue price of that company's past stock issues. Summarize your findings.

LO1 **Comparison of Financing of**
LO3 **Internet Companies**
LO4
LO5
LO6

13

Chapter 13 focuses on the components of the corporate income statement and the statement of stockholders' equity within the context of evaluating quality of earnings. The chapter also covers earnings per share, stock dividends, stock splits, and book value per share.

The Corporate Income Statement and the Statement of Stockholders' Equity

LEARNING OBJECTIVES

LO1 Prepare a corporate income statement and identify the issues related to evaluating the quality of earnings.

LO2 Show the relationships among income taxes expense, deferred income taxes, and net of taxes.

LO3 Describe the disclosure on the income statement of discontinued operations, extraordinary items, and accounting changes.

LO4 Compute earnings per share.

LO5 Prepare a statement of stockholders' equity.

LO6 Account for stock dividends and stock splits.

LO7 Calculate book value per share.

DECISION POINT

A USER'S FOCUS

AMR Corporation <www.amrcorp.com> AMR Corporation, American Airlines' parent company, is one of the two largest airline companies in the United States. Its operating results are of interest to many people, but interpreting these results is not always easy. Net earnings per share is the "bottom line" by which many investors judge a company's success or failure. For instance, we know that during 2001 and 2002, the airline industry was adversely affected by the 9/11 attacks and the impending war in Iraq. This is reflected in AMR's basic earnings per share over the past three years, as shown in the Financial Highlights. Net earnings (loss) per share have declined from a positive in 2000 to substantial losses in 2001 and 2002. Note, however, that other factors affect earnings per share. The results in 2002 were also adversely affected by the cumulative effect of an accounting change of $6.35 per share, which made the results appear worse than the company's loss from continuing operations of $16.22. Also, in 2000, the company had discontinued operations and an extraordinary loss.[1] To truly understand a company's "bottom line," it is important to know the various components. In fact, many analysts consider income (loss) from continuing operations to be a better indicator than the "bottom-line" numbers of a company's future operations. In this chapter, we examine the components of the corporate income statement and the statement of stockholders' equity with a view to understanding their impact on a company's future operations.

Is American Airlines' income from operations a better measure than its "bottom-line" numbers?

Financial Highlights			
Earnings (Loss) per Share: Basic	2002	2001	2000
Income (loss) from continuing operations	$(16.22)	$(11.43)	$ 5.20
Discontinued operations	—	—	0.30
Extraordinary loss	—	—	(0.07)
Cumulative effect of accounting change	(6.35)	—	—
Net earnings (loss)	$(22.57)	$(11.43)	$ 5.43

PERFORMANCE MEASUREMENT: QUALITY OF EARNINGS ISSUES

LO1 Prepare a corporate income statement and identify the issues related to evaluating the quality of earnings.

RELATED TEXT ASSIGNMENTS
Q: 1, 2, 3, 4, 5
SE: 1, 2
E: 1, 2, 3
P: 1, 2, 3, 6
SD: 1, 2, 4
FRA: 1, 4, 6, 7

The Financial Accounting Standards Board (FASB) has taken the position that income for a period should be all-inclusive, comprehensive income, which is different from net income.[2] **Comprehensive income** is the change in a company's equity from sources other than owners during a period; it includes net income, changes in unrealized investment gains and losses, and other items affecting equity. Companies are reporting comprehensive income and its components as a separate financial statement or as a part of another financial statement.

In a recent survey of 600 large companies, 519 reported comprehensive income. Of these, 81 percent reported comprehensive income on the statement of stockholders' equity, 13 percent reported it on a separate statement, and only 6 percent reported it on the income statement.[3] In the illustration of comprehensive income later in this chapter, we follow the most common practice and show it as a part of the statement of stockholders' equity.

THE CORPORATE INCOME STATEMENT

www.aimr.org

Net income is the most commonly used measure of earnings because current and expected earnings are important factors in evaluating a company's performance and analyzing its prospects. In fact, a survey of 2,000 members of the Association for Investment Management and Research indicated that the two most important economic measures in evaluating common stocks were expected changes in earnings per share and expected return on equity;[4] net income is a key component of both measures. The corporate income statement is the statement that shows how a company's net income is derived.

KEY POINT: It is important to know which items included in earnings are recurring and which are one-time items. Income from continuing operations before nonoperating items gives a clear signal about future results. In assessing the company's future earnings potential, nonoperating items are excluded because they are not expected to continue.

Net income or loss for a period includes all revenues, expenses, gains, and losses over the period, with the exception of prior period adjustments. Thus, the corporate income statement may consist of several components, as illustrated in Exhibit 1. When a company has both continuing and discontinued operations, the operating income section is called **income from continuing operations**. Income from continuing operations before income taxes is affected by choices of accounting methods and estimates and may contain such items as gains and losses, write-downs, and restructurings. The income taxes expense section of the statement is also subject to special accounting rules. The lower part of the statement may contain such nonoperating items as discontinued operations, extraordinary gains and losses, and effects of accounting changes. Another item that may appear in this section is the write-off of goodwill when its value has been impaired. Finally, earnings per share information appears at the bottom of the statement. We discuss these components of the corporate income statement in more detail later in the chapter.

Because of the importance of net income, or the "bottom line," in measuring a company's prospects, there is significant interest in evaluating the quality of the net income figure, or the **quality of earnings**. The quality of a company's earnings refers to the substance of earnings and their sustainability into future accounting periods. For example, if earnings increase because of a gain on the sale of an asset, analysts may not view this portion of earnings as sustainable. The quality of earnings may be affected by the accounting methods and estimates the company's management chooses and by the gains and losses, the write-downs and restructurings, and the nature of the nonoperating items reported on the income statement. Since management has choices in the content and positioning of these income-

FOCUS ON BUSINESS PRACTICE

Why Do Investors Study Quality of Earnings?
Analysts for Twentieth Century Mutual Funds, a major investment company, now merged with American Century Services Corp. <www.americancentury.com>, make adjustments to a company's reported financial performance to create a more accurate picture of the company's ongoing operations. Assume a paper company reports earnings of $1.30 per share, which makes year-to-year comparisons unusually strong. Upon further investigation, however, it is found that the per share number includes a one-time gain on the sale of assets of $.25 per share. Twentieth Century would list the company in its data base as earning only $1.05 per share. "These kinds of adjustments help assure long-term decisions aren't based on one-time events."[5]

Exhibit 1
Corporate Income Statement

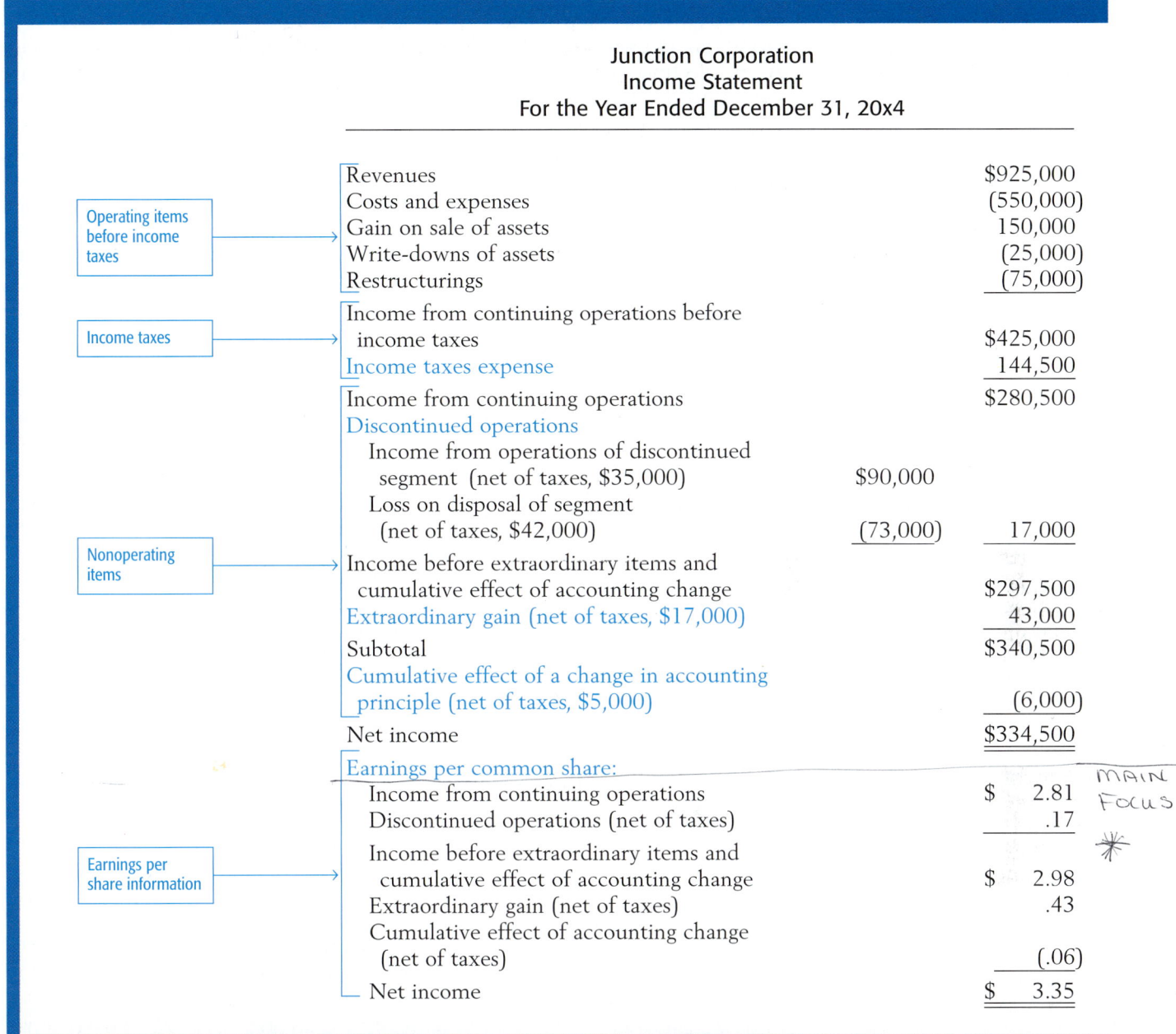

ENRICHMENT NOTE:
Management is responsible for the content of financial statements. Financial statements report on the performance of management. When a group is responsible for reporting on its own activity, usually the best or most favorable position will be reported.

statement categories, there is the potential for managing earnings to achieve specific income targets. Thus, users of income statements must understand these factors and take them into consideration when evaluating a company's performance.

CHOICE OF ACCOUNTING METHODS AND ESTIMATES

Choices of accounting methods and estimates affect a firm's operating income. To assure proper matching of revenues and expenses, accounting requires cost allocations and estimates of data that will not be known with certainty until some future date. For example, accountants estimate the useful life of assets when they are acquired. However, technological obsolescence could shorten the expected useful life, and excellent maintenance and repairs could lengthen it. The actual useful life will not be known with certainty until some future date. The estimate affects both current and future operating income.

Because there is considerable latitude in assumptions underlying estimates, management and other financial statement users must be aware of the impact of accounting estimates on reported operating income. Estimates include percentage of uncollectible accounts receivable, sales returns, useful life, residual or salvage value, total units of production, total recoverable units of natural resources, amortization period, expected warranty claims, and expected environmental cleanup costs.

These estimates are not equally important to all firms. Their relative importance depends on the industry in which a firm operates. For example, the estimate of uncollectible receivables for a credit card firm, such as American Express, or a financial services firm, such as Bank of America, can have a material impact on earnings, but the estimate of useful life may be less important because depreciable assets represent only a small percentage of total assets. Toys "R" Us has very few receivables, but it has substantial investment in depreciable assets; thus, estimates of useful life and residual value are much more important than the estimate of uncollectible accounts receivable.

www.americanexpress.com
www.bankofamerica.com

www.tru.com

The choice of methods also affects a firm's operating income. Generally accepted accounting methods include uncollectible receivable methods (percentage of net sales and aging of accounts receivable), inventory methods (last-in, first-out [LIFO]; first-in, first-out [FIFO]; and average-cost), depreciation methods (accelerated, production, and straight-line), and revenue recognition methods. These methods are designed to match revenues and expenses. Costs are allocated based on a determination of the benefits to the current period (expenses) versus the benefits to future periods (assets). The expenses are estimates, and the period or periods benefited cannot be demonstrated conclusively. The estimates are also subjective, because in practice it is hard to justify one method of estimation over another.

KEY POINT: Two companies in the same industry may have comparable earnings quantity but not comparable earnings quality. To assess the quality of reported earnings, one must know the methods and estimates used to compute income. GAAP allow several methods and estimates, all yielding different results.

For these reasons, management, the accountant, and the financial statement user need to understand the possible effects of different accounting procedures on net income and financial position. Some methods and estimates are more conservative than others because they tend to produce a lower net income in the current period. For example, suppose that two companies have similar operations, but one uses FIFO for inventory costing and straight-line (SL) for computing depreciation, whereas the other uses LIFO for inventory costing and double-declining-balance (DDB) for computing depreciation. The income statements of the two companies might appear as follows:

	FIFO and SL	LIFO and DDB
Net sales	$875,000	$875,000
Goods available for sale	$400,000	$400,000
Less ending inventory	60,000	50,000
Cost of goods sold	$340,000	$350,000
Gross margin	$535,000	$525,000
Less depreciation expense	$ 40,000	$ 80,000
Less other expenses	170,000	170,000
Total operating expenses	$210,000	$250,000
Income from continuing operations before income taxes	$325,000	$275,000

The income from continuing operations before income taxes (operating income) for the firm using LIFO and DDB is lower because in periods of rising prices, the LIFO inventory costing method produces a higher cost of goods sold, and, in the early years of an asset's useful life, accelerated depreciation yields a higher depreciation expense. The result is lower operating income. However, future operating income is expected to be higher. It is also important that the choice of accounting method does not affect cash flows except for possible differences in income taxes caused by the use of one method instead of another.

The $50,000 difference in operating income stems only from the differences in accounting methods. Differences in the estimated lives and residual values of the plant assets could lead to an even greater variation. In practice, of course, differences in net income occur for many reasons, but the user must be aware of the discrepancies that can occur as a result of the accounting methods chosen by management. In general, an accounting method or estimate that results in lower current earnings is considered to produce a better quality of operating income.

The existence of such alternatives could cause problems in the interpretation of financial statements were it not for the conventions of full disclosure and consistency. As noted in an earlier chapter, full disclosure requires that management explain the significant accounting policies used in preparing the financial statements in a note to the statements. Consistency requires that the same accounting procedures be followed from year to year. If a change in procedure is made, the nature of the change and its monetary effect must be explained in a note.

GAINS AND LOSSES

When a company sells or otherwise disposes of operating assets or marketable securities, a gain or loss generally results. These gains or losses appear in the operating portion of the income statement, but they usually represent one-time events. They are not sustainable, ongoing operations, and management often has some choice as to their timing. Thus, from an analyst's point of view, they should be ignored when considering operating income.

WRITE-DOWNS AND RESTRUCTURINGS

Management has considerable latitude in deciding when an asset is no longer of value to the company. If the value of an asset is impaired, management may decide to record a write-down. A **write-down**, also referred to as a *write-off*, is the recording of a decrease in the value of an asset below the carrying value on the balance sheet and the reduction of income in the current period by the amount of the decrease. If operations have changed, management may decide to record a restructuring. A **restructuring** is the estimated cost associated with a change in a company's operations, usually involving the closing of facilities and the laying off of personnel. Both write-downs and restructurings reduce current operating income and boost future income by shifting future costs to the current accounting period.

Write-downs and restructurings are important to consider because they often are an indication of bad management decisions in the past, such as paying too much for the assets of another company or making operational changes that do not work out. Companies sometimes take all possible losses in the current year so that future years will be "clean" of these costs. Such "big baths," as they are called, commonly occur when a company is having a bad year. They also often occur in years when there is a change in management. The new management takes a "big bath" in the current year so it can show improved results in future years.

Write-downs and restructurings are common. In a recent year, 27 percent of 600 large companies had write-downs, and 26 percent had restructurings. Another 24 percent had write-downs or charges involving intangible assets.[6] As discussed in the chapter on long-term assets, goodwill is subject to an annual impairment test to determine if its current fair value is below cost.

NATURE OF NONOPERATING ITEMS

The nonoperating items that appear on the income statement, such as discontinued operations, extraordinary gains and losses, and effects of accounting changes, can also significantly affect the bottom line, or net income. In fact, in Exhibit 1, earnings

● **STOP AND THINK!**
Is it unethical for new management to take a "big bath" in order to enhance future performance?

It is not unethical as long as new management stays within the accounting rules and properly discloses its actions. An investor or analyst must be aware of these actions and take them into consideration when evaluating the company's performance. ■

Focus on Business Ethics

Whistle-Blowing

External users of financial statements depend on management's honesty and openness in disclosing factual information about a company. In the vast majority of cases, management's reports are reliable, but there are exceptions. Whistle-blowers—employees who step forward to disclose such exceptions and other types of wrongdoing they observe in their companies—run various risks, including losing their jobs, with no assurance that their actions will have any effect. In the recent Enron case, the largest bankruptcy in U.S. history, the whistle-blower was a company accountant who, well before the firm's collapse, informed her CEO and the firm's external auditors of Enron's questionable accounting practices. Although her warnings were ignored then, they made headlines during the SEC and congressional investigations, as well as the criminal prosecutions that followed the collapse.[7]

ENRICHMENT NOTE:
Discontinued operations, extraordinary items, and cumulative effects of a change in accounting principle are more likely to occur in large, public corporations. A knowledge of these items is important when analyzing the financial results of such companies. These items do not occur as frequently in small, private corporations.

www.sears.com

per common share for income from continuing operations are $2.81, but net income per share is $3.35 when all the nonoperating items are taken into consideration.

For practical reasons, the calculations of trends and ratios are based on the assumption that net income and other components are comparable from year to year and from company to company. However, in making interpretations, the astute analyst will always look beyond the ratios to the quality of the components. For example, write-downs, restructurings, and nonoperating items, if the charges are large enough, can have a significant effect on a company's return on equity.

A company may boost income by including one-time gains. For example, Sears, Roebuck and Co. used a gain from the change of an accounting principle to bolster its net income by $136 million or by $.35 per share. Without the gain, earnings per share (EPS) would have decreased from $3.12 to $2.92, not increased as Sears reported.[8] The quality of Sears's earnings is, in fact, lower than it might appear on the surface. Unless analysts are prepared to go beyond the "bottom line" in analyzing and interpreting financial reports, they can come to the wrong conclusions.

Effect of Quality of Earnings on Cash Flows and Performance Measures

The reason for considering quality of earnings issues is to assess their effects on cash flows and performance measures. Generally speaking, except for possible income tax effects, none of the gains and losses, asset write-downs, restructurings, and nonoperating items has any effect on cash flows. The cash expenditures for these items were made previously. For this reason, the focus of analysis is on sustainable earnings, which generally have a relationship to future cash flows.

Since management's performance and compensation are often linked to return on assets or return on equity, it is important to understand the nature of both the numerator and denominator of these performance measures. Most commonly, the numerator in these ratios is net income. However, when a company has a complex income statement with items that affect quality of earnings, such as those discussed above, it is important not to take net income at face value. Consider the example of Junction Corporation in Exhibit 1. The reported net income is $334,500, whereas income from continuing operations is $280,500. Even the latter amount is a questionable measure of sustainable earnings because of the gain, write-down, and restructuring, which collectively added $50,000 to income from continuing operations before income taxes. With a tax rate of 34 percent, the sustainable earnings after income taxes are probably close to $247,500 [$280,500 − ($50,000 × .66)].

It also pays to examine how quality of earnings issues affect the denominator of the return on assets and return on equity ratios. If a company has a write-down or restructuring of assets, in addition to a reduction in net income, there is also a reduction in assets and in stockholders' equity, which tends to improve these ratios in both current and future years. This contributes to the motivation to take "big-bath" write-

> **STOP AND THINK!**
> What is one action a company can take to improve its earnings per share without improving its earnings or net income?
>
> Many companies attempt to improve their earnings per share by reducing the number of shares outstanding through buybacks of their own stock. ■

Assume that the company had 100,000 shares of common stock outstanding for the entire year. The earnings per share of common stock is computed as follows:

$$\text{Earnings per Share} = \frac{\$334,500}{100,000} = \$3.35 \text{ per share}$$

If the number of shares outstanding changes during the year, it is necessary to figure the weighted-average number of shares outstanding for the year. Suppose that during various periods of the year, Junction Corporation had the following amounts of common shares outstanding: January–March, 100,000 shares; April–September, 120,000 shares; and October–December, 130,000 shares. The weighted-average number of common shares outstanding and basic earnings per share would be calculated this way:

100,000 shares × 3/12 year	25,000
120,000 shares × 6/12 year	60,000
130,000 shares × 3/12 year	32,500
Weighted-average common shares outstanding	117,500

$$\text{Basic Earnings per Share} = \frac{\text{Net Income}}{\text{Weighted-Average Common Shares Outstanding}}$$

$$= \frac{\$334,500}{117,500 \text{ shares}} = \$2.85 \text{ per share}$$

If a company has nonconvertible preferred stock outstanding, the dividend for that stock must be subtracted from net income before earnings per share for common stock are computed. Suppose that Junction Corporation has preferred stock on which the annual dividend is $23,500. Earnings per share on common stock would be $2.65 [($334,500 − $23,500) ÷ 117,500 shares].

Companies with a capital structure in which there are no bonds, stocks, or stock options that can be converted into common stock are said to have a **simple capital structure**. The earnings per share for these companies is computed as shown above. Some companies, however, have a **complex capital structure**, which includes exercisable stock options or convertible preferred stocks and bonds. Those convertible securities have the potential of diluting the earnings per share of common stock. *Potential dilution* means that a stockholder's proportionate share of ownership in a company could be reduced through the conversion of stocks or bonds or the exercise of stock options, which would increase the total number of shares the company has outstanding.

For example, suppose that a person owns 10,000 shares of a company, which equals 2 percent of the outstanding shares of 500,000. Now suppose that holders of convertible bonds convert the bonds into 100,000 shares of stock. The person's 10,000 shares would then equal only 1.67 percent (10,000 ÷ 600,000) of the outstanding shares. In addition, the added shares outstanding would lower earnings per share and would most likely lower market price per share.

Because stock options and convertible preferred stocks or bonds have the potential to dilute earnings per share, they are referred to as **potentially dilutive securities**. When a company has a complex capital structure, it must report two earnings per share figures: basic earnings per share and diluted earnings per share.[19] **Diluted earnings per share** are calculated by adding all potentially dilutive securities to the denominator of the basic earnings per share calculation. This figure shows stockholders the maximum potential effect of dilution on their ownership position in the company.

The difference between basic and diluted earnings per share can be significant. For example, consider the results reported by Tribune Company:

> **KEY POINT:** A company with potentially dilutive securities (such as convertible preferred stock or bonds) has a complex capital structure and must present two earnings per share figures—basic and diluted. The latter figure is the more conservative of the two.
>
> www.amrcorp.com

Financial Highlights

	2002	2001	2000
Basic earnings per share	$1.38	$.28	$.74
Diluted earnings per share	1.30	.28	.70

Note that in 2000 and 2002, diluted earnings per share are about 5-6 percent less than basic earnings per share.[20] The basic earnings per share is used in various ratios, including the price/earnings ratio.

The computation of diluted earnings per share is a complex process and is reserved for more advanced courses.

 Check out ACE for a Review Quiz at http://accounting.college.hmco.com/students.

THE STATEMENT OF STOCKHOLDERS' EQUITY

LO5 Prepare a statement of stockholders' equity.

RELATED TEXT ASSIGNMENTS
Q: 14, 15, 16
SE: 5, 6, 7
E: 7, 8
P: 4, 5, 7, 8
SD: 4, 5
FRA: 1, 3, 4, 6, 7

The **statement of stockholders' equity**, also called the *statement of changes in stockholders' equity*, summarizes the changes in the components of the stockholders' equity section of the balance sheet. More and more companies are using this statement in place of the statement of retained earnings because it reveals much more about the year's stockholders' equity transactions. In the statement of stockholders' equity in Exhibit 2, for example, the first line shows the beginning balance of each account in the stockholders' equity section. Each subsequent line discloses the effects of transactions on those accounts. Tri-State earned net income of $270,000 and had a foreign currency translation loss of $10,000, reported as accumulated other comprehensive income. These two items together resulted in comprehensive income of $260,000. The statement also shows that during 20x4 Tri-State Corporation issued 5,000 shares of common stock for $250,000, had a conversion of $100,000 of preferred stock into common stock, declared and issued a 10 percent stock dividend on common stock, had a net purchase of treasury shares of $24,000, and paid cash dividends on both preferred and common stock. The ending balances of the accounts are presented at the bottom of the statement. Those accounts and balances make up the stockholders' equity section of Tri-State's balance sheet on December 31, 20x4, as shown in Exhibit 3.

RETAINED EARNINGS

Notice that in Exhibit 2 the Retained Earnings column has the same components as the statement of retained earnings. The **retained earnings** of a company are the part of stockholders' equity that represents stockholders' claims to assets arising from the earnings of the business. Retained earnings equal a company's profits since the date of its inception, less any losses, dividends to stockholders, or transfers to contributed capital.

It is important to remember that retained earnings are not the assets themselves. The existence of retained earnings means that assets generated by profitable operations have been kept in the company to help it grow or meet other business needs. A credit balance in Retained Earnings is *not* directly associated with a specific amount of cash or designated assets. Rather, such a balance means that assets as a whole have been increased.

Retained Earnings can carry a debit balance. Generally, this happens when a company's dividends and subsequent losses are greater than its accumulated profits from operations. In such a case, the firm is said to have a **deficit** (debit balance) in Retained Earnings. A deficit is shown in the stockholders' equity section of the balance sheet as a deduction from contributed capital.

● **STOP AND THINK!**
In Exhibit 2, what is the total amount of comprehensive income?
The total amount of comprehensive income includes all changes in stockholders' equity not involving the owners. In Exhibit 2, it is the net income of $270,000 and accumulated other comprehensive income (foreign currency translation adjustment) of ($10,000), or $260,000. ■

KEY POINT: In accounting, a deficit is a negative (debit) balance in Retained Earnings. It is not the same thing as a net loss, which reflects the performance in just one accounting period.

light of legislated changes in income tax laws and regulations. If changes have occurred, an adjusting entry to bring the account balance into line with current laws is required. For example, a decrease in corporate income tax rates, like the one that occurred in 1987, means that a company with a deferred income taxes liability will pay less in taxes in future years than the amount indicated by the credit balance of its Deferred Income Taxes account. As a result, the company would debit Deferred Income Taxes to reduce the liability and credit Gain from Reduction in Income Tax Rates. This credit increases the reported income on the income statement. If the tax rate increases in future years, a loss would be recorded and the deferred income taxes liability would be increased.

In any given year, the amount a company pays in income taxes is determined by subtracting (or adding, as the case may be) the deferred income taxes for that year, as reported in the notes to the financial statements, from (or to) income taxes expense, which is reported in the financial statements. In subsequent years, the amount of deferred income taxes can vary based on changes in tax laws and rates.

Some understanding of the importance of deferred income taxes to financial reporting can be gained from studying a survey of the financial statements of 600 large companies. About 65 percent reported deferred income taxes with a credit balance in the long-term liability section of the balance sheet.[10]

NET OF TAXES

The phrase **net of taxes**, as used in Exhibit 1, means that the effect of applicable taxes (usually income taxes) has been considered in determining the overall effect of an item on the financial statements. The phrase is used on the corporate income statement when a company has items that must be disclosed in a separate section. Each such item should be reported net of the applicable income taxes to avoid distorting the income taxes expense associated with ongoing operations and the resulting net operating income. For example, assume that a corporation with operating income before income taxes of $120,000 has a total tax expense of $66,000 and that the total income includes a gain of $100,000 on which a tax of $30,000 is due. Also assume that the gain is not part of normal operations and must be disclosed separately on the income statement as an extraordinary item (explained later). This is how the income taxes expense would be reported on the income statement:

Operating income before income taxes	$120,000
Income taxes expense	36,000
Income before extraordinary item	$ 84,000
Extraordinary gain (net of taxes, $30,000)	70,000
Net income	$154,000

If all the income taxes expense were deducted from operating income before income taxes, both the income before extraordinary item and the extraordinary gain would be distorted.

A company follows the same procedure in the case of an extraordinary loss. For example, assume the same facts as before except that the total income taxes expense is only $6,000 because of a $100,000 extraordinary loss. The result is a $30,000 tax savings, shown as follows:

Operating income before income taxes	$120,000
Income taxes expense	36,000
Income before extraordinary item	$ 84,000
Extraordinary loss (net of taxes, $30,000)	(70,000)
Net income	$ 14,000

In Exhibit 1, the total of the income tax items for Junction Corporation is $149,500. That amount is allocated among five statement components, as follows:

Income taxes expense on income from continuing operations	$144,500
Income taxes on income from a discontinued segment	35,000
Income tax savings on the loss on the disposal of the segment	(42,000)
Income taxes on the extraordinary gain	17,000
Income tax savings on the cumulative effect of a change in accounting principle	(5,000)
Total income taxes expense	$149,500

 Check out ACE for a Review Quiz at http://accounting.college.hmco.com/students.

NONOPERATING ITEMS

LO3 Describe the disclosure on the income statement of discontinued operations, extraordinary items, and accounting changes.

RELATED TEXT ASSIGNMENTS
Q: 8, 9, 10
E: 3
P: 2, 3, 6
SD: 2, 4
FRA: 4, 6

Nonoperating items are items not related to the company's normal operations. They appear in a separate section of the income statement because they are considered one-time items that will not affect future results. There are three principal kinds of nonoperating items: discontinued operations, extraordinary items, and accounting changes.

DISCONTINUED OPERATIONS

Large companies in the United States usually have many **segments**. A segment may be a separate major line of business or serve a separate class of customer. For example, a company that makes heavy drilling equipment may also have another line of business, such as the manufacture of mobile homes. A large company may discontinue or otherwise dispose of certain segments of its business that do not fit its future plans or are not profitable. **Discontinued operations** are segments of a business that are no longer part of its ongoing operations. Generally accepted accounting principles require that gains and losses from discontinued operations be reported separately on the income statement. Such separation makes it easier to evaluate the ongoing activities of the business. For example, the Financial Highlights in the Decision Point in this chapter show that AMR's discontinued operations are a significant factor in its "bottom-line" earnings per share. The discontinued operations are AMR's Sabre reservation services, one of the steadiest and most profitable parts of the company's business, which it is divesting to the shareholders of the company. For the analyst, this important piece of information means that in the future, the company is going to be more dependent on the volatile airline business.

www.amrcorp.com

🔴 **STOP AND THINK!**
Why is it useful to disclose discontinued operations separately on the income statement?
Users of financial statements want to assess the effects of past performance on the future performance of a company. Separating discontinued operations on the income statement helps accomplish that objective. ∎

In Exhibit 1, the disclosure of discontinued operations has two parts. One part shows that after the decision to discontinue, the income from operations of the disposed segment was $90,000 (net of $35,000 taxes). The other part shows that the loss from the disposal of the segment was $73,000 (net of $42,000 tax savings). Computation of the gains or losses is covered in more advanced accounting courses. We have described the disclosure to give a complete view of the corporate income statement.

EXTRAORDINARY ITEMS

In its *Opinion No. 30*, the Accounting Principles Board defines **extraordinary items** as "events or transactions that are distinguished by their unusual nature *and* by the infrequency of their occurrence."[11] Unusual and infrequent occurrences are explained in the opinion as follows:

> Unusual Nature—the underlying event or transaction should possess a high degree of abnormality and be of a type clearly unrelated to, or only incidentally related to, the ordinary and typical activities of the entity, taking into account the environment in which the entity operates.

KEY POINT: To qualify as extraordinary, an event must be unusual (not in the ordinary course of business) and must not be expected to occur again in the foreseeable future. Occasionally, it is not clear whether an event meets these two criteria, and the decision then becomes a matter of judgment.

Infrequency of Occurrence—the underlying event or transaction should be of a type that would not reasonably be expected to recur in the foreseeable future, taking into account the environment in which the entity operates.[12]

If an item is both unusual and infrequent (and material in amount), it should be reported separately from continuing operations on the income statement. The disclosure allows readers to identify gains or losses in income that would not be expected to happen again soon. Items usually treated as extraordinary include (1) an uninsured loss from flood, earthquake, fire, or theft; (2) a gain or loss resulting from the passage of a new law; and (3) the expropriation (taking) of property by a foreign government.

Gains or losses from extraordinary items should be reported on the income statement after discontinued operations. And they should be shown net of applicable taxes. In a recent year, 78 (13 percent) of 600 large companies reported extraordinary items on their income statements.[13] In Exhibit 1, the extraordinary gain was $43,000 after applicable taxes of $17,000.

ACCOUNTING CHANGES

ENRICHMENT NOTE: A change in accounting method (principle) violates the convention of consistency. Such a change is allowed, however, when it can be demonstrated that the new method will produce more useful financial statements. The effect of the change is disclosed just above net income on the income statement.

ETHICAL CONSIDERATION: Some accounting changes can produce a significant increase in net income without an accompanying improvement in performance. The user of financial statements should be aware that some businesses implement an accounting change solely for the increase in net income that results.

In a departure from the consistency convention, a company is allowed to make accounting changes if current procedures are incorrect or inappropriate. For example, a change from the FIFO to the LIFO inventory method can be made if there is adequate justification for the change. Adequate justification usually means that if the change occurs, the financial statements will better show the financial activities of the company. A company's desire to lower the amount of income taxes it pays is not considered adequate justification for an accounting change. If justification does exist and an accounting change is made, generally accepted accounting principles require the disclosure of the change in the financial statements.

The **cumulative effect of an accounting change** is the effect that the new accounting principle would have had on net income in prior periods if it had been applied instead of the old principle. This effect is shown on the income statement immediately after extraordinary items.[14] For example, assume that in the five years prior to 20x4, Junction Corporation had used the straight-line method to depreciate its machinery. This year, the company retroactively changed to the double-declining-balance method of depreciation. The controller computed the cumulative effect of the change in depreciation charges (net of taxes) as $6,000, as follows:

Cumulative, five-year double-declining-balance depreciation	$29,000
Less cumulative, five-year straight-line depreciation	18,000
Before tax effect	$11,000
Income tax savings	5,000
Cumulative effect of accounting change	$ 6,000

FOCUS ON INTERNATIONAL BUSINESS

Were Preussag's Year-End Results Really "Remarkable"?

The big German travel company Preussag <www.preussag.com> reported that the year 2000 was "a remarkable year" in which the company achieved "all-time high" results and "profit rose by 16.5 percent." The financial reports reveal that profits would not have been so remarkable if the effects of four voluntary accounting changes had not been taken into account. Profits would have increased by only 6.7 percent if Preussag had not made these changes. The company began recognizing revenue from holiday packages at the beginning of the holiday instead of at the stage of completion, but it began deferring the cost of brochures over future tourist seasons. In addition, the cost of "empty-leg flights" at the beginning and the end of each tourist season are now amortized over the season. Finally the inventory method was changed from LIFO to the average-cost method. None of these cosmetic changes affect future cash flows or change the company's operations for the better.[15]

Relevant information about the accounting change is shown in the notes to the financial statements. The change results in $11,000 of depreciation expense for prior years being deducted in the current year, in addition to the current year's depreciation costs included in the $550,000 costs and expenses section of the income statement. This expense must be shown in the current year's income statement as a reduction in income (see Exhibit 1). In a recent year, over 90 percent of 600 large companies reported changes in accounting procedures, mostly in order to conform to new FASB pronouncements.[16] Further study of accounting changes is left to more advanced accounting courses.

✓ Check out ACE for a Review Quiz at http://accounting.college.hmco.com/students.

EARNINGS PER SHARE

LO4 Compute earnings per share.
RELATED TEXT ASSIGNMENTS
Q: 11, 12, 13
SE: 4
E: 3, 6
P: 2, 3, 6
FRA: 6, 7

Readers of financial statements use earnings per share information to judge a company's performance and to compare it with the performance of other companies. Because such information is so important, the Accounting Principles Board concluded that earnings per share of common stock should be presented on the face of the income statement.[17] As shown in Exhibit 1, the information is usually disclosed just below the net income.

An earnings per share amount is always shown for (1) income from continuing operations, (2) income before extraordinary items and cumulative effect of accounting change, (3) cumulative effect of accounting change, and (4) net income. If the statement shows a gain or loss from discontinued operations or a gain or loss on extraordinary items, earnings per share amounts can also be presented for them.

The following per share data from the income statement of Minnesota Mining and Manufacturing Company (3M) show why it is a good idea to study the components of earnings per share:[18]

www.3m.com

ENRICHMENT NOTE:
Earnings per share is a measure of a corporation's profitability. It is one of the most closely watched financial statement ratios in the business world. Its disclosure on the income statement is required.

Financial Highlights

	2000	1999	1998
Earnings per share—basic			
Income before extraordinary loss and cumulative effect of accounting change	$ 4.69	$ 4.39	$ 3.01
Extraordinary loss	—	—	(.10)
Cumulative effect of accounting change	(.19)	—	—
Net income	$ 4.50	$ 4.39	$ 2.91

Note that net income was influenced by special items in 1998 and 2000: An extraordinary loss decreased income from continuing operations by $.10 per share in 1998, and the cumulative effect of an accounting change decreased earnings by $.19 in 2000. In 1999, the company had no special items; thus, 100 percent of 3M's basic earnings per share were attributable to continuing operations.

Basic earnings per share is net income applicable to common stock divided by the weighted-average number of common shares outstanding. To compute this figure, one must determine if the number of common shares outstanding changed during the year, and if the company paid preferred stock dividends.

When a company has only common stock and has the same number of shares outstanding throughout the year, the earnings per share computation is simple. From Exhibit 1, we know that Junction Corporation reported net income of $334,500.

EXHIBIT 2
Statement of Stockholders' Equity

Tri-State Corporation
Statement of Stockholders' Equity
For the Year Ended December 31, 20x4

	Preferred Stock $100 Par Value 8% Convertible	Common Stock $10 Par Value	Paid-in Capital in Excess of Par Value, Common	Retained Earnings	Treasury Stock	Accumulated Other Comprehensive Income	Total
Balance, December 31, 20x3	$400,000	$300,000	$300,000	$600,000	—		$1,600,000
Net income				270,000			270,000
Foreign currency translation adjustment						($10,000)	(10,000)
Issuance of 5,000 shares of common stock		50,000	200,000				250,000
Conversion of 1,000 shares of preferred stock to 3,000 shares of common stock	(100,000)	30,000	70,000				—
10 percent stock dividend on common stock, 3,800 shares		38,000	152,000	(190,000)			—
Purchase of 500 shares of treasury stock					($24,000)		(24,000)
Cash dividends							
Preferred stock				(24,000)			(24,000)
Common stock				(47,600)			(47,600)
Balance, December 31, 20x4	$300,000	$418,000	$722,000	$608,400	($24,000)	($10,000)	$2,014,400

EXHIBIT 3
Stockholders' Equity Section of a Balance Sheet

KEY POINT: The ending balances on the statement of stockholders' equity are transferred to the stockholders' equity section of the balance sheet.

Tri-State Corporation
Stockholders' Equity
December 31, 20x4

Contributed capital			
Preferred stock, $100 par value, 8 percent convertible, 10,000 shares authorized, 3,000 shares issued and outstanding			$ 300,000
Common stock, $10 par value, 100,000 shares authorized, 41,800 shares issued, 41,300 shares outstanding		$418,000	
Paid-in capital in excess of par value, common		722,000	1,140,000
Total contributed capital			$1,440,000
Retained earnings			608,400
Total contributed capital and retained earnings			$2,048,400
Less: Treasury stock, common (500 shares, at cost)		$ 24,000	
Foreign currency translation adjustment		10,000	34,000
Total stockholders' equity			$2,014,400

FOCUS ON INTERNATIONAL BUSINESS

Why Are Reserves Common in Other Countries?

Restrictions on retained earnings, called *reserves,* are much more common in some foreign countries than in the United States. In Sweden, for instance, reserves are used to respond to fluctuations in the economy. The Swedish tax code allows companies to set up contingency reserves for the purpose of maintaining financial stability. Appropriations to those reserves reduce taxable income and income taxes. The reserves become taxable when they are reversed, but they are available to absorb losses should they occur. For example, Skandia Group <www.skandia.com>, a large Swedish insurance company, reported a net income of only SK2,826 million in 2000, considerably less than the SK3,456 million in 1999. An examination of its statement of stockholders' equity shows restricted reserves in 2000 of SK10.2 billion. Skandia also increased its dividends in 2000 to SK512 million and still had SK9.5 billion in unrestricted reserves.[21]

RESTRICTION ON RETAINED EARNINGS

A corporation may be required or may want to restrict all or a portion of its retained earnings. A **restriction on retained earnings** means that dividends can be declared only to the extent of the *unrestricted* retained earnings. The following are reasons a company might restrict retained earnings:

1. *A contractual agreement.* For example, bond indentures may place a limitation on the dividends the company can pay.

2. *State law.* Many states do not allow a corporation to distribute dividends or purchase treasury stock if doing so reduces equity to a level that would impair the legal capital of the company.

3. *Voluntary action by the board of directors.* Often, a board decides to retain assets in the business for future needs. For example, the company may want to limit dividends to save enough money for a new building or to offset a possible future loss of assets resulting from a lawsuit.

A restriction on retained earnings does not change the total retained earnings or stockholders' equity of the company. It simply divides retained earnings into two parts: restricted and unrestricted. The unrestricted amount represents earnings kept in the business that the company can use for dividends and other purposes. Also, the restriction of retained earnings does not restrict cash or other assets in any way. It simply explains to the readers of the financial statements that a certain amount of assets generated by earnings will remain in the business for the purpose stated. It is still management's job to make sure enough cash or assets are on hand to fulfill the purpose. The removal of a restriction does not necessarily mean that the board of directors can then declare a dividend.

The most common way to disclose restricted retained earnings is by reference to a note to the financial statements. For example:

Retained earnings (Note 15) $900,000

> Note 15:
> Because of plans to expand the capacity of the company's clothing division, the board of directors has restricted retained earnings available for dividends by $300,000.

 Check out ACE for a Review Quiz at http://accounting.college.hmco.com/students.

ACCOUNTING FOR STOCK DIVIDENDS AND STOCK SPLITS

LO6 Account for stock dividends and stock splits.

RELATED TEXT ASSIGNMENTS
Q: 17, 18
SE: 6, 8, 9
E: 9, 10, 11
P: 4, 5, 7, 8
SD: 3, 4, 5
FRA: 6

Two common transactions that can modify the content of stockholders' equity are stock dividends and stock splits.

Stock Dividends

A **stock dividend** is a proportional distribution of shares among a corporation's stockholders. Unlike a cash dividend, it involves no distribution of assets, so it has no effect on a firm's assets and liabilities. A board of directors may declare a stock dividend for several reasons:

1. It may want to give stockholders some evidence of the company's success without paying a cash dividend, which would affect working capital.

2. It may want to reduce the stock's market price by increasing the number of shares outstanding. (This goal is, however, more often met by a stock split.)
3. It may want to make a nontaxable distribution to stockholders. Stock dividends that meet certain conditions are not considered income, so they are not taxed.
4. It may wish to increase the company's permanent capital by transferring an amount from retained earnings to contributed capital.

The total stockholders' equity is not affected by a stock dividend. The effect of a stock dividend is to transfer a dollar amount from retained earnings to contributed capital on the date of declaration. The amount transferred is the fair market value (usually, the market price) of the additional shares to be issued. The laws of most states specify the minimum value of each share transferred under a stock dividend, which is normally the minimum legal capital (par or stated value). However, generally accepted accounting principles state that market value reflects the economic effect of small stock distributions (less than 20 to 25 percent of a company's outstanding common stock) better than par or stated value does. For this reason, market price should be used to account for small stock dividends.[22]

To illustrate how to account for a stock dividend, let us assume that Caprock Corporation has the following stockholders' equity structure:

Contributed capital
 Common stock, $5 par value, 100,000 shares
  authorized, 30,000 shares issued and outstanding $ 150,000
 Paid-in capital in excess of par value, common   30,000
 Total contributed capital $ 180,000
Retained earnings   900,000
Total stockholders' equity $1,080,000

Suppose that the board of directors declares a 10 percent stock dividend on February 24, distributable on March 31 to stockholders of record on March 15, and that the market price of the stock on February 24 is $20 per share. The entries to record the declaration and distribution of the stock dividend are as follows:

Date of Declaration

A = L + OE   Feb. 24   Stock Dividends Declared   60,000
 −   Common Stock Distributable   15,000
 +   Paid-in Capital in Excess of Par
 +   Value, Common   45,000
                         Declared a 10 percent stock dividend
                         on common stock, distributable on
                         March 31 to stockholders of record
                         on March 15:
                         30,000 shares × .10 = 3,000 shares
                         3,000 shares × $20/share = $60,000
                         3,000 shares × $5/share = $15,000

KEY POINT: For a small stock dividend, the portion of retained earnings transferred is determined by multiplying the number of shares to be distributed by the stock's market price on the date of declaration.

Date of Record

Mar. 15   No entry required.

Date of Distribution

A = L + OE   Mar. 31   Common Stock Distributable   15,000
 −   Common Stock   15,000
 +   Distributed a stock dividend of
                         3,000 shares

The effect of this stock dividend is to permanently transfer the market value of the stock, $60,000, from retained earnings to contributed capital and to increase the

KEY POINT: The declaration of a stock dividend results in a reshuffling of stockholders' equity. That is, a portion of retained earnings is converted into contributed capital (by closing the Stock Dividends Declared account). Total stockholders' equity is not affected. Retained earnings are transferred at the time of the recording (date of declaration) and not at the closing of the Stock Dividends Declared account.

KEY POINT: Common Stock Distributable is a contributed capital (stockholders' equity) account, not a liability. When the shares are issued, this account is converted to the Common Stock account.

number of shares outstanding by 3,000. The Stock Dividends Declared account is used to record the total amount of the stock dividend. Retained Earnings is reduced by the amount of the stock dividend when the Stock Dividends Declared account is closed to Retained Earnings at the end of the accounting period. Common Stock Distributable is credited for the par value of the stock to be distributed (3,000 × $5 = $15,000).

In addition, when the market value is greater than the par value of the stock, Paid-in Capital in Excess of Par Value, Common must be credited for the amount by which the market value exceeds the par value. In this case, the total market value of the stock dividend ($60,000) exceeds the total par value ($15,000) by $45,000. No entry is required on the date of record. On the distribution date, the common stock is issued by debiting Common Stock Distributable and crediting Common Stock for the par value of the stock ($15,000).

Common Stock Distributable is not a liability account because there is no obligation to distribute cash or other assets. The obligation is to distribute additional shares of capital stock. If financial statements are prepared between the date of declaration and the date of distribution, Common Stock Distributable should be reported as part of contributed capital:

Contributed capital
Common stock, $5 par value, 100,000 shares
   authorized, 30,000 shares issued and outstanding $ 150,000
Common stock distributable, 3,000 shares   15,000
Paid-in capital in excess of par value, common   75,000
Total contributed capital $ 240,000
Retained earnings   840,000
Total stockholders' equity $1,080,000

● **STOP AND THINK!**
The receipt of additional shares of stock resulting from a stock dividend has no effect on a stockholder's income. Why not? *Although the stockholder receives additional shares of stock, that stockholder's share of ownership remains unchanged because all other stockholders receive the same proportionate increase in the number of shares owned. The company's net worth remains unchanged since net assets have not increased or decreased. Therefore, the stockholder still owns the same percentage of the company's unchanged net worth.* ∎

Three points can be made from this example. First, the total stockholders' equity is the same before and after the stock dividend. Second, the assets of the corporation are not reduced as they are with a cash dividend. Third, the proportionate ownership in the corporation of any individual stockholder is the same before and after the stock dividend. To illustrate these points, assume that a stockholder owns 1,000 shares before the stock dividend. After the 10 percent stock dividend is distributed, this stockholder would own 1,100 shares, as illustrated below.

Stockholders' Equity	Before Dividend	After Dividend
Common stock	$ 150,000	$ 165,000
Paid-in capital in excess of par value, common	30,000	75,000
Total contributed capital	$ 180,000	$ 240,000
Retained earnings	900,000	840,000
Total stockholders' equity	$1,080,000	$1,080,000
Shares outstanding	30,000	33,000
Stockholders' equity per share	$ 36.00	$ 32.73

Stockholders' Investment

Shares owned	1,000	1,100
Shares outstanding	30,000	33,000
Percentage of ownership	3⅓%	3⅓%
Proportionate investment ($1,080,000 × .03⅓)	$36,000	$36,000

Both before and after the stock dividend, the stockholders' equity totals $1,080,000 and the stockholder owns 3⅓ percent of the company. The proportionate investment (stockholders' equity times percentage ownership) remains at $36,000.

KEY POINT: When a large (greater than 20 to 25 percent) stock dividend is declared, the transfer from retained earnings is based on the stock's par or stated value, not on its market value.

All stock dividends have an effect on the market price of a company's stock. But some stock dividends are so large that they have a material effect. For example, a 50 percent stock dividend would cause the market price of the stock to drop about 33 percent because the increase is now one-third of shares outstanding. The AICPA has decided that large stock dividends, those greater than 20 to 25 percent, should be accounted for by transferring the par or stated value of the stock on the date of declaration from retained earnings to contributed capital.[23]

STOCK SPLITS

KEY POINT: Stock splits and stock dividends reduce earnings per share because they increase the number of shares issued and outstanding. Cash dividends have no effect on earnings per share.

www.gillette.com

A **stock split** occurs when a corporation increases the number of issued shares of stock and reduces the par or stated value proportionally. A company may plan a stock split when it wants to lower the stock's market value per share and increase the demand for the stock at this lower price. This action may be necessary if the market value per share has become so high that it hinders the trading of the stock or if the company wants to signal to the market its success in achieving its operating goals. The Gillette Company achieved these strategic objectives in a recent year by declaring a 2-for-1 stock split and raising its cash dividend. The market viewed these actions positively, pushing Gillette's share price from $77 to $106. After the stock split, the number of shares outstanding doubled, thereby cutting the share price in half and also the dividend per share. Most important, each stockholder's total wealth was unchanged as a result of the stock split.

To illustrate a stock split, suppose that Caprock Corporation has 30,000 shares of $5.00 par value stock outstanding. The market value is $70.00 per share. The corporation plans a 2-for-1 split. This split will lower the par value to $2.50 and increase the number of shares outstanding to 60,000. A stockholder who previously owned 400 shares of the $5.00 par value stock would own 800 shares of the $2.50 par value stock after the split. When a stock split occurs, the market value tends to fall in proportion to the increase in outstanding shares of stock. For example, a 2-for-1 stock split would cause the price of the stock to drop by approximately 50 percent, to about $35.00. It would also halve earnings per share and cash dividends per share (if the board does not increase the dividend). The lower price and the increase in shares tend to promote the buying and selling of shares.

ENRICHMENT NOTE: Stock splits greater than 2 for 1 are unusual. Splits such as 3 for 2 or 4 for 3 are far more common. On occasion, companies whose stock sells for a very low price will perform a reverse stock split, which reduces the number of shares and increases the market price.

A stock split does not increase the number of shares authorized. Nor does it change the balances in the stockholders' equity section of the balance sheet. It simply changes the par value and number of shares issued, both shares outstanding and treasury stock. Thus, an entry is unnecessary. However, it is appropriate to document the change with a memorandum entry in the general journal. For example:

July 15   The 30,000 shares of $5 par value common stock issued and outstanding were split 2 for 1, resulting in 60,000 shares of $2.50 par value common stock issued and outstanding.

FOCUS ON BUSINESS PRACTICE

Do Stock Splits Help Increase a Company's Market Price?

Stock splits tend to follow the market. When the market went up dramatically in 1998, 1999, and 2000, there were record numbers of stock splits—more than 1,000 per year. At the height of the market in early 2000, stock splitters included such diverse companies as Alcoa <www.alcoa.com>, Apple Computer <www.apple.com>, Chase Manhattan <www.chase.com>, Intel <www.intel.com>, Nvidia <www.nvidia.com>, Juniper Networks <www.juniper.net>, and Tiffany & Co. <www.tiffany.com>. Some analysts liken stock splits to the air a pastry chef whips into a mousse: it doesn't make it any sweeter, just frothier. There is no fundamental reason a stock should go up because of a stock split. When Rambus Inc. <www.rambus.com>, a developer of high-speed memory technology, announced a four-for-one split on March 10, 2000, its stock rose more than 50 percent, to $471 per share.[24] But when the market deflated in 2001, its stock dropped to less than $10 per share. Research shows that stock splits have no long-term effect on stock prices.

The change for the Caprock Corporation is as follows:

Before Stock Split

Contributed capital	
Common stock, $5 par value, 100,000 shares authorized, 30,000 shares issued and outstanding	$ 150,000
Paid-in capital in excess of par value, common	30,000
Total contributed capital	$ 180,000
Retained earnings	900,000
Total stockholders' equity	$1,080,000

After Stock Split

Contributed capital	
Common stock, $2.50 par value, 100,000 shares authorized, 60,000 shares issued and outstanding	$ 150,000
Paid-in capital in excess of par value, common	30,000
Total contributed capital	$ 180,000
Retained earnings	900,000
Total stockholders' equity	$1,080,000

KEY POINT: A stock split affects only the common stock calculation. In this case, there are twice as many shares after the split, but par value is now half of what it was.

KEY POINT: As long as the newly outstanding shares do not exceed the previously authorized shares, permission from the state is not needed for a stock split.

Although the amount of stockholders' equity per share is half as much, each stockholder's proportionate interest in the company remains the same.

If the number of split shares will exceed the number of authorized shares, the board of directors must secure state and stockholders' approval before it can issue additional shares.

✓ Check out ACE for a Review Quiz at http://accounting.college.hmco.com/students.

BOOK VALUE

LO7 Calculate book value per share.

RELATED TEXT ASSIGNMENTS
Q: 19
SE: 10
E: 12
P: 4, 5, 7, 8
SD: 4, 5
FRA: 5, 6

KEY POINT: Book value per share represents the equity of one share of stock in the net assets (assets minus liabilities) of a corporation. It can apply to both common and preferred stock.

The word *value* is associated with shares of stock in several ways. Par value or stated value is set when the stock is authorized and establishes the legal capital of a company. Neither par value nor stated value has any relationship to a stock's book value or market value. The **book value** of a company's stock represents the total assets of the company less its liabilities. It is simply the stockholders' equity of the company or, to look at it another way, the company's net assets. The **book value per share** therefore represents the equity of the owner of one share of stock in the net assets of the corporation. That value, of course, does not necessarily equal the amount the shareholder would receive if the company were sold or liquidated. It differs in most cases because assets are usually recorded at historical cost, not at the current value at which they could be sold.

When a company has only common stock outstanding, book value per share is calculated by dividing the total stockholders' equity by the total common shares outstanding. In computing the shares outstanding, common stock distributable is included. Treasury stock (shares previously issued and now held by the company), however, is not included. For example, suppose that Caprock Corporation has total stockholders' equity of $1,030,000 and 29,000 shares outstanding after recording the purchase of treasury shares. The book value per share of Caprock's common stock is $35.52 ($1,030,000 ÷ 29,000 shares).

If a company has both preferred and common stock, the determination of book value per share is not so simple. The general rule is that the call value (or par value, if a call value is not specified) of the preferred stock plus any dividends in arrears is subtracted from total stockholders' equity to determine the equity pertaining to common stock. As an illustration, refer to the stockholders' equity section of Tri-

● Stop and Think!

What is the effect of a stock dividend or a stock split on book value per share?

Both a stock dividend and a stock split reduce the book value per share because they increase the number of shares outstanding without changing the total of stockholders' equity. ■

State Corporation's balance sheet in Exhibit 3. Assuming that no dividends are in arrears and that the preferred stock is callable at $105, the equity pertaining to common stock is calculated as follows:

Total stockholders' equity	$2,014,400
Less equity allocated to preferred shareholders (3,000 shares × $105)	315,000
Equity pertaining to common shareholders	$1,699,400

There are 41,300 shares of common stock outstanding (41,800 shares issued less 500 shares of treasury stock). The book values per share are computed as follows:

> Preferred Stock: $315,000 ÷ 3,000 shares = $105 per share
> Common Stock: $1,699,400 ÷ 41,300 shares = $41.15 per share

If we assume the same facts except that the preferred stock is 8 percent cumulative and that one year of dividends is in arrears, the stockholders' equity would be allocated as follows:

Total stockholders' equity		$2,014,400
Less: Call value of outstanding preferred shares	$315,000	
Dividends in arrears ($300,000 × .08)	24,000	
Equity allocated to preferred shareholders		339,000
Equity pertaining to common shareholders		$1,675,400

The book values per share are then as follows:

> Preferred Stock: $339,000 ÷ 3,000 shares = $113 per share
> Common Stock: $1,675,400 ÷ 41,300 shares = $40.57 per share

Undeclared preferred dividends fall into arrears on the last day of the fiscal year (the date shown on the financial statements). Also, dividends in arrears do not apply to unissued preferred stock.

✓ Check out ACE for a Review Quiz at http://accounting.college.hmco.com/students.

Chapter Review

REVIEW OF LEARNING OBJECTIVES

LO1 Prepare a corporate income statement and identify the issues related to evaluating the quality of earnings.

The operating income section on the income statement of a corporation with both continuing and discontinued operations is called income from continuing operations. Income from continuing operations before income taxes is affected by choices of accounting methods and estimates and may contain such items as gains and losses, write-downs, and restructurings. The income taxes expense section of the statement is also subject to special accounting rules. The lower part of the statement may contain such nonoperating items as discontinued operations, extraordinary gains and losses, and effects of accounting changes. Earnings per share information appears at the bottom of the statement. The quality of a company's earnings refers to the substance of earnings and their sustainability into future accounting periods. The quality of earnings may be affected by the accounting methods and estimates the company's management chooses and by the gains and losses, the write-downs and restructurings, and the nature of the nonoperating items reported on the income statement. The reason for considering quality of earnings issues is to assess their effects on cash flows and performance measures. Generally speaking, except for possible income tax effects, none of the gains and losses, asset write-downs, restructurings, and nonoperating items has any effect on cash flows. Quality of earnings issues can affect key performance ratios like return on assets and return on equity.

LO2 Show the relationships among income taxes expense, deferred income taxes, and net of taxes.

Income taxes expense is the taxes applicable to income from operations on an accrual basis. Income tax allocation is necessary when differences between accrual-based accounting income and taxable income cause a material difference between income taxes expense as shown on the income statement and actual income tax liability. The difference between income taxes expense and income taxes payable is debited or credited to an account called Deferred Income Taxes. *Net of taxes* is a phrase used to indicate that the effect of income taxes has been considered when showing an item on the income statement.

LO3 Describe the disclosure on the income statement of discontinued operations, extraordinary items, and accounting changes.

Because of their unusual nature, a gain or loss on discontinued operations and on extraordinary items and the cumulative effect of accounting changes must be disclosed on the income statement separately from continuing operations and net of income taxes. Relevant information about any accounting change is shown in the notes to the financial statements.

LO4 Compute earnings per share.

Stockholders and other readers of financial statements use earnings per share data to evaluate a company's performance and to compare it with the performance of other companies. Therefore, earnings per share data are presented on the face of the income statement. The amounts are computed by dividing the income applicable to common stock by the number of common shares outstanding for the year. If the number of shares outstanding has varied during the year, then the weighted-average number of common shares outstanding should be used in the computation. When the company has a complex capital structure, both basic and diluted earnings per share must be disclosed on the face of the income statement.

LO5 Prepare a statement of stockholders' equity.

A statement of stockholders' equity shows changes over the period in each component of the stockholders' equity section of the balance sheet. This statement reveals much more about the transactions that affect stockholders' equity than does the statement of retained earnings.

LO6 Account for stock dividends and stock splits.

A stock dividend is a proportional distribution of shares among a corporation's stockholders. Here is a summary of the key dates and accounting treatment of stock dividends:

Key Date	Stock Dividend
Date of declaration	Debit Stock Dividends Declared for the market value of the stock to be distributed (if it is a small stock dividend), and credit Common Stock Distributable for the stock's par value and Paid-in Capital in Excess of Par Value, Common for the excess of the market value over the stock's par value.
Date of record	No entry.
Date of distribution	Debit Common Stock Distributable and credit Common Stock for the par value of the stock that has been distributed.

A stock split is usually undertaken to reduce the market value of a company's stock and improve the demand for the stock. Because there is normally a decrease in the par value of the stock in proportion to the number of additional shares issued, a stock split has no effect on the dollar amounts in the stockholders' equity accounts. The split should be recorded in the general journal by a memorandum entry only.

LO7 Calculate book value per share.

Book value per share is the stockholders' equity per share. It is calculated by dividing stockholders' equity by the number of common shares outstanding plus shares distributable. When a company has both preferred and common stock, the call or par value of the preferred stock plus any dividends in arrears is deducted from total stockholders' equity before dividing by the common shares outstanding.

REVIEW OF CONCEPTS AND TERMINOLOGY

The following concepts and terms were introduced in this chapter:

LO4 **Basic earnings per share:** The net income applicable to common stock divided by the weighted-average number of common shares outstanding.

LO7 **Book value:** The total assets of a company less its liabilities; stockholders' equity or net assets.

LO7 **Book value per share:** The equity of the owner of one share of stock in the net assets of the corporation.

LO4 **Complex capital structure:** A capital structure that includes exercisable stock options or convertible preferred stocks and bonds.

LO1 **Comprehensive income:** The change in a company's equity from sources other than owners during a period; it includes net income, changes in unrealized investment gains and losses, and other items affecting equity.

LO3 **Cumulative effect of an accounting change:** The effect that a different accounting principle would have had on the net income of prior periods if it had been used instead of the old principle.

LO2 **Deferred Income Taxes:** The account used to record the difference between the Income Taxes Expense and Income Taxes Payable accounts.

LO5 **Deficit:** A debit balance in the Retained Earnings account.

LO4 **Diluted earnings per share:** The net income applicable to common stock divided by the sum of the weighted-average number of common shares outstanding plus potentially dilutive securities.

LO3 **Discontinued operations:** Segments of a business that are no longer part of its on-going operations.

LO3 **Extraordinary items:** Events or transactions that are both unusual in nature and infrequent in occurrence.

LO1 **Income from continuing operations:** The operating income section of the income statement when a company has both continuing and discontinued operations.

LO2 **Income tax allocation:** An accounting method used to accrue income taxes expense on the basis of accounting income whenever there are differences between accounting and taxable income.

LO2 **Net of taxes:** A phrase indicating that the effect of applicable taxes (most often, income taxes) has been considered in determining the overall effect of an item on the financial statements.

LO4 **Potentially dilutive securities:** Stock options and convertible preferred stocks or bonds, which have the potential to dilute earnings per share.

LO1 **Quality of earnings:** The substance of earnings and their sustainability into future accounting periods.

LO5 **Restriction on retained earnings:** The required or voluntary identification of a portion of retained earnings that cannot be used to declare dividends.

LO1 **Restructuring:** The estimated cost associated with a change in a company's operations, usually involving the closing of facilities and the laying off of personnel.

LO5 **Retained earnings:** Stockholders' claims to assets arising from the earnings of the business; the accumulated earnings of a corporation from its inception, minus any losses, dividends, or transfers to contributed capital.

LO3 **Segments:** Distinct parts of business operations, such as a line of business or a class of customer.

LO4 **Simple capital structure:** A capital structure in which there are no stocks, bonds, or stock options that can be converted into common stock.

Chapter 13 The Corporate Income Statement and the Statement of Stockholders' Equity

LO5 **Statement of stockholders' equity:** A financial statement that summarizes changes in the components of the stockholders' equity section of the balance sheet. Also called *statement of changes in stockholders' equity*.

LO6 **Stock dividend:** A proportional distribution of shares among a corporation's stockholders.

LO6 **Stock split:** An increase in the number of outstanding shares of stock accompanied by a proportionate reduction in the par or stated value.

LO1 **Write-down:** The recording of a decrease in the value of an asset below the carrying value on the balance sheet and the reduction of income in the current period by the amount of the decrease. Also called *write-off*.

REVIEW PROBLEM

Comprehensive Stockholders' Equity Transactions

LO5 LO6 LO7 The stockholders' equity of Szatkowski Company on June 30, 20x4, was as follows:

Contributed capital		
Common stock, no par value, $6 stated value, 1,000,000 shares authorized, 250,000 shares issued and outstanding		$1,500,000
Paid-in capital in excess of stated value, common		820,000
Total contributed capital		$2,320,000
Retained earnings		970,000
Total stockholders' equity		$3,290,000

Stockholders' equity transactions for the next fiscal year were as follows:

a. The board of directors declared a 2-for-1 stock split.
b. The board of directors obtained authorization to issue 50,000 shares of $100 par value, 6 percent noncumulative preferred stock, callable at $104.
c. Issued 12,000 shares of common stock for a building appraised at $96,000.
d. Purchased 8,000 shares of the company's common stock for $64,000.
e. Issued 20,000 shares of preferred stock for $100 per share.
f. Sold 5,000 shares of treasury stock for $35,000.
g. Declared cash dividends of $6 per share on preferred stock and $.20 per share on common stock.
h. Declared a 10 percent stock dividend on common stock. The market value was $10 per share. The stock dividend is distributable after the end of the fiscal year.
i. Closed Net Income for the year, $340,000.
j. Closed the Cash Dividends Declared and Stock Dividends Declared accounts to Retained Earnings.

Because of a loan agreement, the company is not allowed to reduce retained earnings below $100,000. The board of directors determined that this restriction should be disclosed in the notes to the financial statements.

REQUIRED ▶
1. Record the stockholders' equity components of the preceding transactions in T accounts. Indicate when there is no entry.
2. Prepare the stockholders' equity section of the company's balance sheet on June 30, 20x5, including appropriate disclosure of the restriction on retained earnings.
3. Compute the book values per share of common stock on June 30, 20x4 and 20x5, and of preferred stock on June 30, 20x5, using end-of-year shares outstanding.

ANSWER TO REVIEW PROBLEM

1. Entries in T accounts:

   a. No entry: memorandum in journal
   b. No entry: memorandum in journal

Preferred Stock			Common Stock		
	e.	2,000,000		Beg. bal.	1,500,000
				c.	36,000
				End. Bal	1,536,000

Common Stock Distributable			Paid-in Capital in Excess of Stated Value, Common		
	h.	152,700		Beg. bal.	820,000
				c.	60,000
				h.	356,300
				End. Bal.	1,236,300

Retained Earnings				Treasury Stock, Common		
f.	5,000	Beg. bal.	970,000	d.	64,000	f.	40,000
j.	730,800	i.	340,000	End. Bal.	24,000		
		End. bal.	574,200				

Cash Dividends Declared				Stock Dividend Declared		
g.	221,800*	j.	221,800	h.	509,000**	j.	509,000

* 20,000 × $6 = $120,000
509,000 × $.20 = $101,800
Total = $221,800

**509,000 shares × .10 × $10 = $509,000

2. Stockholders' equity section of the balance sheet:

Szatkowski Company
Stockholders' Equity
June 30, 20x5

Contributed capital
  Preferred stock, $100 par value, 6 percent
  noncumulative, 50,000 shares authorized,
  20,000 shares issued and outstanding $2,000,000
  Common stock, no par value, $3 stated value,
  1,000,000 shares authorized, 512,000 shares
  issued, 509,000 shares outstanding $1,536,000
  Common stock distributable, 50,900 shares   152,700
  Paid-in capital in excess of stated value, common   1,236,300   2,925,000
Total contributed capital $4,925,000
Retained earnings (Note x)   574,200
Total contributed capital and retained earnings $5,499,200
Less treasury stock, common (3,000 shares, at cost)   24,000
Total stockholders' equity $5,475,200

Note x: The board of directors has restricted retained earnings available for dividends by the amount of $100,000 as required under a loan agreement.

3. Book values:
   June 30, 20x4
     Common Stock: $3,290,000 ÷ 250,000 shares = $13.16 per share

June 30, 20x5
Preferred Stock: Call price of $104 per share equals book value per share
Common Stock:
($5,475,200 − $2,080,000) ÷ (509,000 shares + 50,900 shares) =
$3,395,200 ÷ 559,900 shares = $6.06 per share

Chapter Assignments

BUILDING YOUR KNOWLEDGE FOUNDATION

QUESTIONS

1. What is comprehensive income? How does it differ from net income?
2. What is quality of earnings, and what are four ways in which quality of earnings may be affected?
3. Why would the reader of financial statements be interested in management's choice of accounting methods and estimates? Give an example.
4. What is the difference between a write-down and a restructuring, and where do they appear on the corporate income statement?
5. In the first quarter of 1994, AT&T, the giant telecommunications company, reported a net loss because it reduced its income by $1.3 billion, or $.96 per share, as a result of changing its method of accounting for disability and severance payments. Without this charge, the company would have earned $1.15 billion, or $.85 per share. Where on the corporate income statement do you find the effects of changes in accounting principles? As an analyst, how would you treat this accounting change?
6. "Accounting income should be geared to the concept of taxable income because the public understands that concept." Comment on this statement, and tell why income tax allocation is necessary.
7. Nabisco had about $1.3 billion of deferred income taxes in 1996, equal to about 11 percent of total liabilities. This percentage had risen or remained steady for many years. Given management's desire to put off the payment of taxes for as long as possible, the long-term growth of the economy and inflation, and the definition of a liability (probable future sacrifice of economic benefits arising from present obligations), make an argument for not accounting for deferred income taxes.
8. Why should a gain or loss on discontinued operations be disclosed separately on the income statement?
9. Explain the two major criteria for extraordinary items. How should extraordinary items be disclosed in the financial statements?
10. When an accounting change occurs, what disclosures must be made in the financial statements?
11. How are earnings per share disclosed in the financial statements?
12. When does a company have a simple capital structure? A complex capital structure?
13. What is the difference between basic and diluted earnings per share?
14. What is the difference between the statement of stockholders' equity and the stockholders' equity section of the balance sheet?
15. When does a company have a deficit in retained earnings?
16. What is the purpose of a restriction on retained earnings? Why might a company have restrictions on its retained earnings?
17. Explain how the accounting treatment of stock dividends differs from that of cash dividends.
18. What is the difference between a stock dividend and a stock split? What is the effect of each on the capital structure of the corporation?

19. Would you expect a corporation's book value per share to equal its market value per share? Why or why not?

SHORT EXERCISES

LO1 Quality of Earnings

SE 1. Each of the items listed below is a quality of earnings issue. Indicate whether the item is (a) an accounting method, (b) an accounting estimate, or (c) a nonoperating item. For any item for which the answer is (a) or (b), indicate which alternative is usually the more conservative choice.

1. LIFO versus FIFO
2. Extraordinary loss
3. 10-year useful life versus 15-year useful life
4. Effect of change in accounting principle
5. Straight-line versus accelerated method
6. Discontinued operations
7. Immediate write-off versus amortization
8. Increase versus decrease in percentage of uncollectible accounts

LO1 Corporate Income Statement

SE 2. Assume that Bedard Company's chief financial officer gave you the following information: Net Sales, $720,000; Cost of Goods Sold, $350,000; Loss from Discontinued Operations (net of income tax benefit of $70,000), $200,000; Loss on Disposal of Discontinued Operations (net of income tax benefit of $16,000), $50,000; Operating Expenses, $130,000; Income Taxes Expense on Continuing Operations, $80,000. From this information, prepare the company's income statement for the year ended June 30, 20xx. (Ignore earnings per share information.)

LO2 Corporate Income Tax Rate Schedule

SE 3. Using the corporate tax rate schedule in Table 1, compute the income tax liability for taxable income of (1) $400,000 and (2) $20,000,000.

LO4 Earnings per Share

SE 4. During 20x4, Halmut Corporation reported a net income of $669,200. On January 1, Halmut had 360,000 shares of common stock outstanding. The company issued an additional 240,000 shares of common stock on August 1. In 20x4, the company had a simple capital structure. During 20x5, there were no transactions involving common stock, and the company reported net income of $870,000. Determine the weighted-average number of common shares outstanding for 20x4 and 20x5. Also, compute earnings per share for 20x4 and 20x5.

LO5 Statement of Stockholders' Equity

SE 5. Refer to the statement of stockholders' equity for Tri-State Corporation in Exhibit 2 to answer the following questions: (1) At what price per share were the 5,000 shares of common stock sold? (2) What was the conversion price per share of the common stock? (3) At what price was the common stock selling on the date of the stock dividend? (4) At what price per share was the treasury stock purchased?

LO5 Effects of Stockholders'
LO6 Equity Actions

SE 6. Tell whether each of the following actions will increase, decrease, or have no effect on total assets, total liabilities, and total stockholders' equity:

1. Declaration of a stock dividend
2. Declaration of a cash dividend
3. Stock split
4. Restriction of retained earnings
5. Purchase of treasury stock

LO5 Restriction of Retained Earnings

SE 7. Jasmine Company has a lawsuit filed against it. The board took action to restrict retained earnings in the amount of $2,500,000 on May 31, 20x4, pending the outcome of the suit. On May 31, the company had retained earnings of $3,725,000. Show how the restriction on retained earnings would be disclosed as a note to the financial statements.

LO6 Stock Dividends

SE 8. On February 15, Purple Mountain Corporation's board of directors declared a 2 percent stock dividend applicable to the outstanding shares of its $10 par value common stock, of which 200,000 shares are authorized, 130,000 are issued, and 20,000 are held in the treasury. The stock dividend was distributable on March 15 to stockholders of record on March 1. On February 15, the market value of the common stock was $15 per share. On March 30, the board of directors declared a $.50 per share cash dividend. No other stock transactions have occurred. Record, as necessary, the transactions of February 15, March 1, March 15, and March 30.

LO6 Stock Split

SE 9. On August 10, the board of directors of Torrinni International declared a 3-for-1 stock split of its $9 par value common stock, of which 800,000 shares were authorized and 250,000 were issued and outstanding. The market value on that date was $60 per share. On the same date, the balance of paid-in capital in excess of par value, common was $6,000,000, and the balance of retained earnings was $6,500,000. Prepare the stockholders' equity section of the company's balance sheet after the stock split. What entry, if any, is needed to record the stock split?

LO7 Book Value for Preferred and Common Stock

SE 10. Using data from the stockholders' equity section of Gerhardt Corporation's balance sheet shown below, compute the book value per share for both the preferred and the common stock.

Contributed capital
Preferred stock, $100 par value, 8 percent cumulative, 10,000 shares authorized,
500 shares issued and outstanding* $ 50,000
Common stock, $10 par value, 100,000 shares authorized, 40,000 shares issued and
outstanding $400,000
Paid-in capital in excess of par value, common   516,000   916,000
Total contributed capital $ 966,000
Retained earnings   275,000
Total stockholders' equity $1,241,000

*The preferred stock is callable at $104 per share, and one year's dividends are in arrears.

EXERCISES

LO1 Effect of Alternative Accounting Methods

E 1. At the end of its first year of operations, a company calculated its ending merchandise inventory according to three different accounting methods, as follows: FIFO, $95,000; average-cost, $90,000; LIFO, $86,000. If the company used the average-cost method, its net income for the year would be $34,000.

1. Determine net income if the company used the FIFO method.
2. Determine net income if the company used the LIFO method.
3. Which method is more conservative?
4. Will the consistency convention be violated if the company chooses to use the LIFO method?
5. Does the full-disclosure convention require disclosure of the inventory method used in the financial statements?

LO1 Corporate Income Statement

E 2. Assume that the Sedgeway Furniture Company's chief financial officer gave you the following information: net sales, $1,900,000; cost of goods sold, $1,050,000; extraordinary gain (net of income taxes of $3,500), $12,500; loss from discontinued operations (net of income tax benefit of $30,000), $50,000; loss on disposal of discontinued operations (net of income tax benefit of $13,000), $35,000; selling expenses, $50,000; administrative expenses, $40,000; income taxes expense on continuing operations, $300,000. From this information, prepare the company's income statement for the year ended June 30, 20xx. (Ignore earnings per share information.)

LO1 LO2 LO3 LO4 Corporate Income Statement

E 3. The following items are components of Asheville Corporation's income statement for the year ended December 31, 20x4:

Sales	$555,000
Cost of goods sold	(275,000)
Operating expenses	(112,500)
Restructuring	(55,000)
Total income taxes expense for period	(82,350)
Income from operations of a discontinued segment	80,000
Gain on disposal of segment	70,000
Extraordinary gain	36,000
Cumulative effect of a change in accounting principle	(24,000)
Net income	$192,150
Earnings per share	$.96

Recast the income statement in proper multistep form, including allocating income taxes to appropriate items (assume a 30 percent income tax rate) and showing earnings per share figures (200,000 shares outstanding).

LO2 Corporate Income Tax Rate Schedule

E 4. Using the corporate tax rate schedule in Table 1, compute the income tax liability for the following situations:

Situation	Taxable Income
A	$ 70,000
B	85,000
C	320,000

LO2 Income Tax Allocation

E 5. Ft. Worth Corporation reported the following accounting income before income taxes, income taxes expense, and net income for 20x2 and 20x3:

	20x2	20x3
Income before income taxes	$280,000	$280,000
Income taxes expense	88,300	88,300
Net income	$191,700	$191,700

On the balance sheet, deferred income taxes liability increased by $38,400 in 20x2 and decreased by $18,800 in 20x3.

1. How much did Ft. Worth Corporation actually pay in income taxes for 20x2 and 20x3?
2. Prepare entries in journal form to record income taxes expense for 20x2 and 20x3.

LO4 Earnings per Share

E 6. During 20x3, Portland Corporation reported a net income of $1,529,500. On January 1, Portland had 700,000 shares of common stock outstanding. The company issued an additional 420,000 shares of common stock on October 1. In 20x3, the company had a simple capital structure. During 20x4, there were no transactions involving common stock, and the company reported net income of $2,016,000.

1. Determine the weighted-average number of common shares outstanding each year.
2. Compute earnings per share for each year.

LO5 Restriction of Retained Earnings

E 7. The board of directors of the Sunset Company has approved plans to acquire another company during the coming year. The acquisition should cost approximately $550,000. The board took action to restrict retained earnings of the company in the amount of $550,000 on July 17, 20x4. On July 31, the company had retained earnings of $975,000. Show how the restriction on retained earnings would be disclosed in a note to the financial statements.

LO5 Statement of Stockholders' Equity

E 8. The stockholders' equity section of Mallory Corporation's balance sheet on December 31, 20x4, appears as follows:

Contributed capital	
Common stock, $2 par value, 500,000 shares authorized, 400,000 shares issued and outstanding	$ 800,000
Paid-in capital in excess of par value, common	1,200,000
Total contributed capital	$2,000,000
Retained earnings	4,200,000
Total stockholders' equity	$6,200,000

Prepare a statement of stockholders' equity for the year ended December 31, 20x5, assuming the following transactions occurred in sequence during 20x5:

a. Issued 10,000 shares of $100 par value, 9 percent cumulative preferred stock at par after obtaining authorization from the state.
b. Issued 40,000 shares of common stock in connection with the conversion of bonds having a carrying value of $600,000.
c. Declared and issued a 2 percent common stock dividend. The market value on the date of declaration was $14 per share.
d. Purchased 10,000 shares of common stock for the treasury at a cost of $16 per share.
e. Earned net income of $460,000.
f. Declared and paid the full year's dividend on preferred stock and a dividend of $.40 per share on common stock outstanding at the end of the year.
g. Had foreign currency translation adjustment of minus $100,000.

Chapter 13 The Corporate Income Statement and the Statement of Stockholders' Equity

LO6 Journal Entries: Stock Dividends

E 9. Perfect Rest Company has 30,000 shares of its $1 par value common stock outstanding. Record in journal form the following transactions as they relate to the company's common stock:

July 17 Declared a 10 percent stock dividend on common stock to be distributed on August 10 to stockholders of record on July 31. Market value of the stock was $5 per share on this date.
31 Record date.
Aug. 10 Distributed the stock dividend declared on July 17.
Sept. 1 Declared a $.50 per share cash dividend on common stock to be paid on September 16 to stockholders of record on September 10.

LO6 Stock Split

E 10. Teuong Company currently has 500,000 shares of $1 par value common stock authorized with 200,000 shares outstanding. The board of directors declared a 2-for-1 split on May 15, when the market value of the common stock was $2.50 per share. The retained earnings balance on May 15 was $700,000. Paid-in capital in excess of par value, common on this date was $20,000. Prepare the stockholders' equity section of the company's balance sheet before and after the stock split. What entry, if any, would be necessary to record the stock split?

LO6 Stock Split

E 11. On January 15, the board of directors of Exavier International declared a 3-for-1 stock split of its $12 par value common stock, of which 800,000 shares were authorized and 200,000 were issued and outstanding. The market value on that date was $45 per share. On the same date, the balance of paid-in capital in excess of par value, common was $4,000,000, and the balance of retained earnings was $8,000,000. Prepare the stockholders' equity section of the company's balance sheet before and after the stock split. What entry, if any, is needed to record the stock split?

LO7 Book Value for Preferred and Common Stock

E 12. Below is the stockholders' equity section of Village Corporation's balance sheet. Determine the book value per share for both the preferred and the common stock.

Contributed capital
  Preferred stock, $100 per share, 6 percent
    cumulative, 10,000 shares authorized, 200
    shares issued and outstanding* $ 20,000
  Common stock, $5 par value, 100,000 shares
    authorized, 10,000 shares issued, 9,000 shares
    outstanding $50,000
  Paid-in capital in excess of par value, common 28,000 78,000
Total contributed capital $ 98,000
Retained earnings 95,000
Total contributed capital and retained earnings $193,000
Less treasury stock, common (1,000 shares at cost) 15,000
Total stockholders' equity $178,000

*The preferred stock is callable at $105 per share, and one year's dividends are in arrears.

Problems

LO1 Effect of Alternative Accounting Methods

P 1. Carsey Company began operations in 20xx. At the beginning of the year, the company purchased plant assets of $450,000, with an estimated useful life of ten years and no salvage value. During the year, the company had net sales of $650,000, salaries expense of $100,000, and other expenses of $40,000, excluding depreciation. In addition, Carsey Company purchased inventory as follows:

Jan. 15	400 units at $200	$ 80,000
Mar. 20	200 units at $204	40,800
June 15	800 units at $208	166,400
Sept. 18	600 units at $206	123,600
Dec. 9	300 units at $210	63,000
Total	2,300 units	$473,800

At the end of the year, a physical inventory disclosed 500 units still on hand. The managers of Carsey Company know they have a choice of accounting methods, but they are unsure how those methods will affect net income. They have heard of the FIFO and LIFO inventory methods and the straight-line and double-declining-balance depreciation methods.

REQUIRED ▶
1. Prepare two income statements for Carsey Company, one using the FIFO and straight-line methods and the other using the LIFO and double-declining-balance methods. Ignore income taxes.
2. Prepare a schedule accounting for the difference in the two net income figures obtained in **1**.
3. What effect does the choice of accounting method have on Carsey's inventory turnover? What conclusions can you draw?
4. How does the choice of accounting methods affect Carsey's return on assets? Assume the company's only assets are cash of $40,000, inventory, and plant assets. Use year-end balances to compute the ratios. Is your evaluation of Carsey's profitability affected by the choice of accounting methods?

P 2.
LO1 Corporate Income Statement
LO2
LO3
LO4

Income statement information for Dimsum Corporation during 20x3 is as follows:
a. Administrative expenses, $110,000.
b. Cost of goods sold, $440,000.
c. Restructuring charge, $125,000.
d. Cumulative effect of a change in inventory methods that decreased income (net of taxes, $28,000), $60,000.
e. Extraordinary loss from a storm (net of taxes, $10,000), $20,000.
f. Income taxes expense, continuing operations, $42,000.
g. Net sales, $1,015,000.
h. Selling expenses, $190,000.

REQUIRED ▶
1. Prepare Dimsum Corporation's income statement for 20x3, including earnings per share, assuming a weighted average of 200,000 shares of common stock outstanding for 20x3.
2. What is a restructuring charge, and why is it deducted before income from operations before income taxes?

P 3.
LO1 Corporate Income Statement
LO2 and Evaluation of Business
LO3 Operations
LO4

During 20x3, Burston Corporation engaged in a number of complex transactions to improve the business—selling off a division, retiring bonds, and changing accounting methods. The company has always issued a simple single-step income statement, and the accountant has accordingly prepared the December 31 year-end income statements for 20x2 and 20x3, as shown below.

Burston Corporation
Income Statements
For the Years Ended December 31, 20x3 and 20x2

	20x3	20x2
Net sales	$3,500,000	$4,200,000
Cost of goods sold	(1,925,000)	(2,100,000)
Operating expenses	(787,500)	(525,000)
Income taxes expense	(576,450)	(472,500)
Income from operations of a discontinued segment	560,000	
Gain on disposal of discontinued segment	490,000	
Extraordinary gain	252,000	
Cumulative effect of a change in accounting principle	(168,000)	
Net income	$1,345,050	$1,102,500
Earnings per share	$ 6.73	$ 5.51

Theodore Burston, the president of Burston Corporation, is pleased to see that both net income and earnings per share increased by 22 percent from 20x2 to 20x3 and intends to announce to the company's stockholders that the plan to improve the business has been successful.

REQUIRED
1. Recast the 20x3 and 20x2 income statements in proper multistep form, including allocating income taxes to appropriate items (assume a 30 percent income tax rate) and showing earnings per share figures (200,000 shares outstanding).
2. What is your assessment of Burston Corporation's plan and business operations in 20x3?

P 4.
LO5 LO6 LO7 Dividends, Stock Splits, and Stockholders' Equity

The stockholders' equity section of Montpelior Linen Mills, Inc., as of December 31, 20x2, was as follows:

Contributed capital	
Common stock, $6 par value, 500,000 shares authorized, 80,000 shares issued and outstanding	$ 480,000
Paid-in capital in excess of par value, common	150,000
Total contributed capital	$ 630,000
Retained earnings	480,000
Total stockholders' equity	$1,110,000

A review of the stockholders' equity records of Montpelior Linen Mills, Inc., disclosed the following transactions during 20x3:

Mar. 25 The board of directors declared a 5 percent stock dividend to stockholders of record on April 20 to be distributed on May 1. The market value of the common stock was $11 per share.
Apr. 20 Date of record for the stock dividend.
May 1 Distributed the stock dividend.
Sept. 10 Declared a 3-for-1 stock split.
Dec. 15 Declared a 10 percent stock dividend to stockholders of record on January 15 to be distributed on February 15. The market price on this date is $3.50 per share.

REQUIRED
1. Record the stockholders' equity components of the transactions for Montpelior Linen Mills, Inc., in T accounts.
2. Prepare the stockholders' equity section of the company's balance sheet as of December 31, 20x3. Assume net income for 20x3 is $47,000.
3. Calculate book value per share before and after the above transactions.

P 5.
LO5 LO6 LO7 Dividends, Stock Splits, and Stockholders' Equity

The balance sheet of O'Malley Woolen Company disclosed the following stockholders' equity as of September 30, 20x3:

Contributed capital	
Common stock, $2 par value, 1,000,000 shares authorized, 300,000 shares issued and outstanding	$ 600,000
Paid-in capital in excess of par value, common	370,000
Total contributed capital	$ 970,000
Retained earnings	350,000
Total stockholders' equity	$1,320,000

The following stockholders' equity transactions were completed during the next fiscal year in the order presented:

20x3
Dec. 17 Declared a 10 percent stock dividend to be distributed January 20 to stockholders of record on January 1. The market value per share on the date of declaration was $4.

20x4
Jan. 1 Date of record.
  20 Distributed the stock dividend.
Apr. 14 Declared a $.25 per share cash dividend. The cash dividend is payable May 15 to stockholders of record on May 1.

May 1 Date of record.
     15 Paid the cash dividend.
June 17 Split its stock 2 for 1.
Sept. 15 Declared a cash dividend of $.10 per share payable October 10 to stockholders of record on October 1.

On September 14, the board of directors restricted retained earnings for plant expansion in the amount of $175,000. The restriction should be shown in the notes to the financial statements.

REQUIRED ▶
1. Record the above transactions in journal form.
2. Prepare the stockholders' equity section of the company's balance sheet as of September 30, 20x4, with an appropriate disclosure of the restriction of retained earnings. Assume net income for the year is $150,000.
3. Calculate book value per share before and after the transactions.

ALTERNATE PROBLEMS

P 6.

LO1 **Corporate Income Statement**
LO2
LO3
LO4

Information concerning operations of MacFarland Weather Gear Corporation during 20xx is as follows:

a. Administrative expenses, $90,000.
b. Cost of goods sold, $420,000.
c. Write-down of assets, $75,000.
d. Cumulative effect of an accounting change in depreciation methods that increased income (net of taxes, $20,000), $42,000.
e. Extraordinary loss from an earthquake (net of taxes, $36,000), $60,000.
f. Sales (net), $975,000.
g. Selling expenses, $80,000.
h. Income taxes expense applicable to continuing operations, $105,000.

REQUIRED ▶
1. Prepare the corporation's income statement for the year ended December 31, 20xx, including earnings per share information. Assume a weighted average of 100,000 common shares outstanding during the year.
2. What is a write-down, and why is it deducted before income from operations?

P 7.

LO5 **Dividends, Stock Splits, and**
LO6 **Stockholders' Equity**
LO7

The stockholders' equity section of the balance sheet of Boysan Corporation as of December 31, 20x4, was as follows:

Contributed capital	
Common stock, $4 par value, 500,000 shares authorized, 200,000 shares issued and outstanding	$ 800,000
Paid-in capital in excess of par value, common	1,000,000
Total contributed capital	$1,800,000
Retained earnings	1,200,000
Total stockholders' equity	$3,000,000

The following transactions occurred in 20x5 for Boysan Corporation:

Feb. 28 The board of directors declared a 10 percent stock dividend to stockholders of record on March 25 to be distributed on April 5. The market value on this date is $16.
Mar. 25 Date of record for stock dividend.
Apr. 5   Distributed the stock dividend.
Aug. 3   Declared a 2-for-1 stock split.
Nov. 20 Purchased 18,000 shares of the company's common stock at $8 per share for the treasury.
Dec. 31 Declared a 5 percent stock dividend to stockholders of record on January 25 to be distributed on February 5. The market value per share was $9.

REQUIRED ▶
1. Record the stockholders' equity components of the transactions for Boysan Corporation in T accounts.
2. Prepare the stockholders' equity section of the company's balance sheet as of December 31, 20x5. Assume net income for 20x5 is $108,000.
3. Calculate book value per share before and after the above transactions.

LO5 **Dividends, Stock Splits, and**
LO6 **Stockholders' Equity**
LO7

P 8. The stockholders' equity section of Blue Ridge Furniture Restoration Company's balance sheet as of December 31, 20x2, was as follows:

Contributed capital	
Common stock, $1 par value, 3,000,000 shares authorized, 500,000 shares issued and outstanding	$ 500,000
Paid-in capital in excess of par value, common	200,000
Total contributed capital	$ 700,000
Retained earnings	540,000
Total stockholders' equity	$1,240,000

The company engaged in the following stockholders' equity transactions during 20x3:

Mar. 5 Declared a $.20 per share cash dividend to be paid on April 6 to stockholders of record on March 20.
     20 Date of record.
Apr. 6 Paid the cash dividend.
June 17 Declared a 10 percent stock dividend to be distributed August 17 to stockholders of record on August 5. The market value of the stock was $7 per share.
Aug. 5 Date of record.
     17 Distributed the stock dividend.
Oct. 2 Split its stock 3 for 1.
Dec. 27 Declared a cash dividend of $.05 payable January 27, 20x4, to stockholders of record on January 14, 20x4.

On December 9, the board of directors restricted retained earnings for a pending lawsuit in the amount of $100,000. The restriction should be shown in the notes to the firm's financial statements.

REQUIRED ▶
1. Record the 20x3 transactions in journal form.
2. Prepare the stockholders' equity section of the company's balance sheet as of December 31, 20x3, with an appropriate disclosure of the restriction on retained earnings. Assume net income for the year is $200,000.
3. Calculate book value per share before and after the above transactions.

SKILLS DEVELOPMENT CASES

Conceptual Analysis

SD 1.
LO1 **Interpretation of Earnings Reports**

In a recent year, analysts expected International Business Machines (IBM) <www.ibm.com> to earn $1.32 per share. The company actually earned $1.33. Microsoft Corporation <www.microsoft.com> was expected to earn $.43 per share, but it earned only $.41. The corporate income statements of these companies show that Microsoft had a special charge (with corresponding liability) of $660 million, or $.06 per share, based on settlement of a class-action law suit filed on behalf of consumers, whereas IBM had no such a charge.[25] Who did better, Microsoft or IBM? Use quality of earnings to support your answer. Also, what is the effect of Microsoft's special charge on current and future cash flows?

SD 2.
LO1 **Classic Quality of Earnings**
LO3

On Tuesday, January 19, 1988, IBM <www.ibm.com> reported greatly increased earnings for the fourth quarter of 1987. Despite this reported gain in earnings, the price of IBM's stock on the New York Stock Exchange declined by $6 per share to $111.75. In sympathy with this move, most other technology stocks also declined.[26]

IBM's fourth-quarter net earnings rose from $1.39 billion, or $2.28 a share, to $2.08 billion, or $3.47 a share, an increase of 49.6 percent and 52.2 percent over the same period a year earlier. Management declared that these results demonstrated the effectiveness of IBM's efforts to become more competitive and that, despite the economic uncertainties of 1988, the company was planning for growth.

The apparent cause of the stock price decline was that the huge increase in income could be traced to nonrecurring gains. Investment analysts pointed out that IBM's high earnings stemmed primarily from such factors as a lower tax rate. Despite most analysts' expectations of a tax rate between 40 and 42 percent, IBM's was a low 36.4 percent, down from the previous year's 45.3 percent. Analysts were also disappointed in IBM's revenue growth. Revenues within the United States were down, and much of the company's growth in revenues came through favorable currency translations, increases that might not be repeated. In fact, some estimates of IBM's fourth-quarter earnings attributed $.50 per share to currency translations and another $.25 to tax-rate changes.

Other factors contributing to IBM's rise in earnings were one-time transactions, such as the sale of Intel Corporation stock and bond redemptions, along with a corporate stock buyback program that reduced the amount of stock outstanding in the fourth quarter by 7.4 million shares.

The analysts were concerned about the quality of IBM's earnings. Identify four quality of earnings issues reported in the case and the analysts' concern about each. In percentage terms, what is the impact of the currency changes on fourth-quarter earnings? Comment on management's assessment of IBM's performance. Do you agree with management? (Optional question: What has IBM's subsequent performance been?) Be prepared to discuss your answers in class.

Ethical Dilemma

SD 3.

LO6 Ethics and Stock Dividends

For 20 years Bass Products Corporation, a public corporation, has followed the practice of paying a cash dividend every quarter and has promoted itself to investors as a stable, reliable company. Recent competition from Asian companies has negatively affected its earnings and cash flows. As a result, Sandra Bass, president of the company, is proposing that the board of directors declare a stock dividend of 5 percent this year instead of a cash dividend. She says, "This will maintain our consecutive dividend record and will not require any cash outflow." What is the difference between a cash dividend and a stock dividend? Why does a corporation usually distribute either kind of dividend, and how does each affect the financial statements? Is the action that Sandra Bass has proposed ethical?

Research Activity

SD 4.

LO1 Corporate Income Statement,
LO2 Statement of Stockholders'
LO3 Equity, and Book Value per
LO5 Share
LO6
LO7

Select the annual reports of three corporations, using one or more of the following sources: your library, the Internet, or the Needles Accounting Resource Center Web Site at http://accounting.college.hmco.com/students. You may choose companies from the same industry or at random, at the direction of your instructor. (If you completed the related research activity in the chapter on contributed capital, use the same three companies.) Prepare a table with a column for each corporation. Then, for any year covered by the balance sheet, the statement of stockholders' equity, and the income statement, answer the following questions: Does the company own treasury stock? Did it buy or retire any treasury stock? Did it declare a stock dividend or a stock split? What other transactions appear in the statement of stockholders' equity? Has the company deferred any income taxes? Were there any discontinued operations, extraordinary items, or accounting changes? Compute the book value per common share for the company. In *The Wall Street Journal* or the financial section of another daily newspaper, find the current market price of each company's common stock and compare it with the book value you computed. Should there be any relationship between the two values? Be prepared to discuss your answers in class.

Decision-Making Practice

SD 5.

LO5 Analyzing Effects of
LO6 Stockholders' Equity
LO7 Transactions

Metzger Steel Corporation (MSC) is a small specialty steel manufacturer located in northern Alabama. It has been owned by the Metzger family for several generations. Arnold Metzger is a major shareholder in MSC by virtue of his having inherited 200,000 shares of common stock in the company. Metzger has not shown much interest in the business because of his enthusiasm for archaeology, which takes him to far parts of the world. However, when he received the minutes of the last board of directors meeting, he questioned a number of transactions involving stockholders' equity. He asks you, as a person with a knowledge of accounting, to help him interpret the effect of these transactions on his interest in MSC.

You begin by examining the stockholders' equity section of MSC's December 31, 20x4, balance sheet:

Metzger Steel Corporation
Stockholders' Equity
December 31, 20x4

Contributed capital	
Common stock, $10 par value, 5,000,000 shares authorized, 1,000,000 shares issued and outstanding	$10,000,000
Paid-in capital in excess of par value, common	25,000,000
Total contributed capital	$35,000,000
Retained earnings	20,000,000
Total stockholders' equity	$55,000,000

Then you read the relevant parts of the minutes of the board of directors meeting on December 15, 20x5:

Item A The president reported the following transactions involving the company's stock during the last quarter:

October 15. Sold 500,000 shares of authorized common stock through the investment banking firm of T.R. Kendall at a net price of $50 per share.

November 1. Purchased 100,000 shares for the corporate treasury from Lucy Metzger at a price of $55 per share.

Item B The board declared a 2-for-1 stock split (accomplished by halving the par value and doubling each stockholder's shares), followed by a 10 percent stock dividend. The board then declared a cash dividend of $2 per share on the resulting shares. Cash dividends are declared on outstanding shares and shares distributable. All these transactions are applicable to stockholders of record on December 20 and are payable on January 10. The market value of MSC stock on the board meeting date after the stock split was estimated to be $30.

Item C The chief financial officer stated that he expected the company to report net income for the year of $4,000,000.

1. Prepare a stockholders' equity section of MSC's balance sheet as of December 31, 20x5, that reflects the above transactions. (**Hint:** Use T accounts to analyze the transactions. Also use a T account to keep track of the shares of common stock outstanding.)
2. Write a memorandum to Arnold Metzger that shows the book value per share and Metzger's percentage of ownership at the beginning and end of the year. Explain the difference and state whether Metzger's position has improved during the year. Tell why or why not and state how Metzger may be able to maintain his percentage of ownership.

FINANCIAL REPORTING AND ANALYSIS CASES

Interpreting Financial Reports

FRA 1.
LO1 Interpretation of Statement
LO5 of Stockholders' Equity

The consolidated statement of stockholders' equity for Jackson Electronics, Inc., a manufacturer of a broad line of electrical components, is presented at the top of the next page.

This statement has nine summary transactions. (1) Show that you understand it by preparing an entry in journal form with an explanation for each entry. In each case,

Jackson Electronics, Inc.
Consolidated Statement of Stockholders' Equity
(In thousands)

	Preferred Stock $100 Par Value	Common Stock $1 Par Value	Paid-in Capital in Excess of Par Value, Common	Retained Earnings	Treasury Stock, Common	Accumulated Other Comprehensive Income	Total
Balance at September 30, 20x4	$2,756	$3,902	$14,149	$119,312	($942)		$139,177
Net income	—	—	—	18,753	—		18,753
Unrealized gain on available for sale securities						$12,000	12,000
Redemption and retirement of preferred stock (27,560 shares)	(2,756)	—	—	—	—		(2,756)
Stock options exercised (89,000 shares)	—	89	847	—	—		936
Purchases of common stock for treasury (501,412 shares)	—	—	—	—	(12,552)		(12,552)
Issuance of common stock (148,000 shares) in exchange for convertible subordinated debentures	—	148	3,635	—	—		3,783
Issuance of common stock (715,000 shares) for cash	—	715	24,535	—	—		25,250
Issuance of 500,000 shares of common stock in exchange for investment in Electrix Company shares	—	500	17,263	—	—		17,763
Cash dividends—common stock ($.80 per share)				(3,086)	—		(3,086)
Balance at September 30, 20x5	$—	$5,354	$60,429	$134,979	($13,494)	$12,000	$199,268

if applicable, determine the average price per common share. At times, you will have to make assumptions about an offsetting part of the entry. For example, assume debentures (long-term bonds) are recorded at face value and that employees pay cash for stock purchased under company incentive plans. (2) Define comprehensive income and determine the amount for Jackson Electronics.

 Group Activity: Assign each transaction to a different group to develop the entry and present the explanation to the class.

FRA 2.
LO2 Analysis of Income Taxes from Annual Report

In its 2000 annual report, The Washington Post Company <www.washingtonpost.com>, a newspaper publishing and television broadcasting company based in Washington, D.C., provided the following data about its current and deferred income tax provisions (in millions):[27]

	2000	
	Current	Deferred
U.S. federal	$ 77.5	$ 4.9
Foreign	1.0	—
State	22.6	(12.7)
	$101.1	($7.8)

1. What was the 2000 income taxes expense? Record in journal form the overall income tax liability for 2000, using income tax allocation procedures.
2. In the long-term liability section of its balance sheet, The Washington Post Company shows deferred income taxes of $117.7 million in 2000 versus $114.0 million in 1999. This shows an increase in the amount of deferred income taxes. How do such deferred income taxes arise? What would cause deferred income taxes to increase? Give an example of this process. Given the definition of a liability, do you see a potential problem with the company's classifying deferred income taxes as a liability?

International Company

FRA 3.

LO5 Restriction of Retained Earnings

In some countries, including Japan, the availability of retained earnings for the payment of dividends is restricted. The following disclosure appeared in the annual report of Yamaha Motor Company, Ltd. <www.yamaha.com>, the Japanese motorcycle manufacturer:[28]

> The Commercial Code of Japan provides that an amount not less than 10 percent of the total of cash dividends and bonuses [paid] to directors and corporate auditors be appropriated as a legal reserve until such reserve equals 25 percent of stated capital. The legal reserve may be used to reduce a deficit or may be transferred to stated capital, but is not available as dividends.

"Stated capital" is equivalent to common stock. For Yamaha, this legal reserve amounted to ¥34.4 billion, or $290 million. How does this practice differ from that in the United States? Why do you think it is government policy in Japan? Do you think it is a good idea?

Toys "R" Us Annual Report

FRA 4.

LO1 Corporate Income Statement,
LO3 Statement of Stockholders'
LO5 Equity, and Book Value per Share

Refer to the Toys "R" Us <www.tru.com> annual report to answer the following questions:

1. Does Toys "R" Us have discontinued operations, extraordinary items, or cumulative effects from accounting changes? Would you say the income statement for Toys "R" Us is relatively simple or relatively complex?
2. What transactions most commonly affect the stockholders' equity section of the balance sheet of Toys "R" Us? Examine the statements of stockholders' equity.

Comparison Case: Toys "R" Us and Walgreen Co.

FRA 5.

LO7 Book Value and Market Value

Refer to the annual report for Toys "R" Us <www.tru.com> and the financial statements for Walgreens <www.walgreens.com> in the Supplement to Chapter 1. Compute the 2002 and 2001 book value per share for both companies and compare the results to the average stock price of each in the fourth quarter of 2002 as shown in the notes to the financial statements. How do you explain the differences in book value per share, and how do you interpret their relationship to market prices?

Fingraph® Financial Analyst™

FRA 6.

LO1 Stockholders' Equity Analysis
LO3
LO4
LO5
LO6
LO7

Choose any two companies in the same industry from the list of Fingraph companies on the Needles Accounting Resource Center Student Web Site at http://accounting.college.hmco.com/students. Access the Microsoft Excel spreadsheets for the companies you selected. Click on the URL at the top of each company's spreadsheet for a link to the company's web site and annual report.

1. In the annual reports of the companies you have selected, find the corporate income statement and summary of significant accounting policies (usually the first note to the financial statements). Did the companies report any discontinued operations, extraordinary items, or accounting changes? What percentage impact did these items have on earnings per share? Summarize the methods and estimates each company

uses in a table. If the company changed its accounting methods, was the change the result of a new accounting standard or a voluntary choice by management? Evaluate the quality of earnings for each company.
2. Did the companies provide a statement of stockholders' equity or summarize changes in stockholders' equity in the notes only? Did the companies declare any stock dividends or stock splits? Calculate book value per common share.
3. Find in the financial section of your local paper the current market prices of the companies' common stock. Discuss the difference between market price per share and book value per share.
4. Find and read references to earnings per share in management's discussion and analysis in each annual report.
5. Write a one-page executive summary that highlights the quality of earnings for these companies, the relationship of book value and market value, and the existence or absence of stock splits or dividends, including reference to management's assessment. Include your table with your report.

Internet Case

FRA 7.
LO1 **Comparison of Comprehensive**
LO4 **Income Disclosures**
LO5

When the FASB ruled that public companies should report comprehensive income, it did not issue specific guidelines for how this amount and its components should be disclosed. Choose two companies in the same industry from the Needles Accounting Resource Center Web Site at http://accounting.college.hmco.com/students. Using web links, go to the annual reports on the web sites of the two companies you have selected. In the latest annual report, look at the financial statements. How have your two companies reported comprehensive income—as a part of the income statement, a part of stockholders' equity, or a separate statement? What items create a difference between net income and comprehensive income? Is comprehensive income greater or less than net income? Is comprehensive income more volatile than net income? Which measure of income is used to compute basic earnings per share?

14

Chapter 14 presents the statement of cash flows and explains the changes in cash flows from operating, investing, and financing activities. The chapter also focuses on how to analyze the statement of cash flows to determine a company's cash-generating ability and its free cash flow.

The Statement of Cash Flows

LEARNING OBJECTIVES

LO1 State the principal purposes and uses of the statement of cash flows, and identify its components.
LO2 Analyze the statement of cash flows.
LO3 Use the indirect method to determine cash flows from operating activities.
LO4 Determine cash flows from investing activities.
LO5 Determine cash flows from financing activities.

DECISION POINT
A USER'S FOCUS

Marriott International, Inc. <www.marriott.com>
Marriott International, Inc., is a world leader in lodging and contract hotel services. The balance sheet, income statement, and statement of stockholders' equity presented in Marriott's annual report give an excellent picture of the company's philosophy and performance.

Although these three financial statements are essential to the evaluation of any company, they do not tell the entire story. A fourth statement, the statement of cash flows, contains some additional information, as shown in the Financial Highlights on page 616.[1] This statement shows how much cash the company's operations generated during the past three years and how much cash investing and financing activities used or provided.

Marriott feels that maintaining adequate cash flows is important to the future of the company. In fact, Marriott's emphasis on cash flows is reflected in its compensation plan for top executives. A review of the plan indicates that cash flows, at the firm or business group level, are the financial measure given the greatest weight in determining compensation. Why would Marriott emphasize cash flows to such an extent?

Strong cash flows are essential to management's key goal of liquidity. If cash flows exceed the amount needed for operations and expansion, the company will not have to borrow additional funds. The excess cash flows will be available to reduce the company's debt and improve its financial position by lowering its debt to equity ratio. Another reason for the emphasis

What does Marriott's statement of cash flows reveal about the company's success in providing top-notch lodging and hotel services?

on cash flows may be the belief that strong cash flows from operations generate shareholder value and increase the market value of the company's stock.

The statement of cash flows demonstrates management's commitments in ways that are not readily apparent in the other financial statements. For example, it can show whether management's focus is on the short term or the long term. This statement, which is required by the FASB,[2] satisfies the board's long-held position that a primary objective of financial statements is to provide investors and creditors with information about a company's cash flows.

Financial Highlights: Consolidated Statement of Cash Flows
Marriott International, Inc., and Subsidiaries
(In millions)

	2002	2001	2000
OPERATING ACTIVITIES			
Net income	$ 448	$ 236	$ 479
Adjustments to reconcile to cash provided by operations:			
Depreciation and amortization	187	222	195
Income taxes	(105)	9	133
Timeshare activity, net	(63)	(358)	(195)
Loss on discontinued operations	(171)	—	—
Other	223	278	54
Working capital changes:			
Accounts receivable	(31)	57	(53)
Other current assets	60	(20)	24
Accounts payable and accruals	(32)	(21)	219
Cash provided by operations	516	403	856
INVESTING ACTIVITIES			
Capital expenditures	(292)	(560)	(1,095)
Dispositions	729	554	742
Loan advances	(237)	(367)	(389)
Loan collections and sales	124	71	93
Other	(7)	(179)	(377)
Cash used in investing activities	317	(481)	(1,026)
FINANCING ACTIVITIES			
Commercial paper, net	102	(827)	46
Issuance of long-term debt	26	1,329	338
Repayment of long-term debt	(946)	(123)	(26)
Redemption of convertible subordinated debt	(347)	405	—
Issuance of Class A common stock	35	76	58
Dividends paid	(65)	(61)	(55)
Purchase of treasury stock	(252)	(235)	(340)
Cash provided by financing activities	(1,447)	564	21
(DECREASE) INCREASE IN CASH AND EQUIVALENTS	(614)	486	(149)
CASH AND EQUIVALENTS, beginning of year	812	326	475
CASH AND EQUIVALENTS, end of year	$ 198	$ 812	$ 326

VIDEO CASE

Goodyear Tire & Rubber Company
<www.goodyear.com>

OBJECTIVES

- To state the purposes of the statement of cash flows
- To identify the three components of the statement of cash flows
- To identify the reasons why cash flows from operating activities usually differ from net income
- To understand the importance of cash flows from investing and financing activities

BACKGROUND FOR THE CASE

Goodyear was founded in 1898 by Frank Seiberling, who borrowed $3,500 to start a bicycle tire factory and subsequently began making tires for horseless carriages. Today, Goodyear is the world's largest tire and rubber company, with factories in 28 countries and more than 100,000 employees. In a recent year, sales exceeded $14 billion. In addition to producing Goodyear tires, the company makes Dunlop, Kelly, Fulda, Lee, Sava, and Debica tires and rubber products for the automotive and industrial markets.

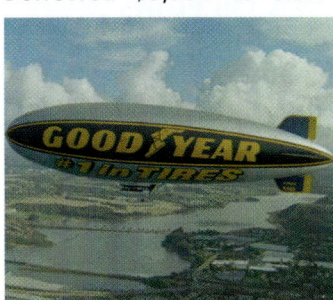

Goodyear's goal is to be ranked by all measures as the best tire and rubber company in the world. It intends to accomplish this by doing the following:

- having fast and profitable growth in all core businesses.
- achieving a number one or two market position.
- making strategic acquisitions and expansions.
- being the lowest cost producer.

To achieve these objectives, especially "fast and profitable growth" and "strategic acquisitions and expansions," Goodyear will need adequate funding. Management expects the funding to come from strong cash flows; divestiture of underperforming, nonstrategic assets; and debt issues. Within this framework, management must maintain the company's financial health and a strong balance sheet, with a debt to debt plus equity ratio of 25 to 30 percent.

Understanding Goodyear's performance in meeting the challenge of achieving adequate funding requires an ability to read and understand the statement of cash flows.

For more information about Goodyear Tire & Rubber Company, visit the company's web site through the Needles Accounting Resource Center Web Site at **http://accounting.college.hmco.com/students**.

REQUIRED

1. What are the purposes and three main components of the statement of cash flows?
2. What is the most important amount in the statement of cash flows? Why is it the most important?
3. What is the relationship of cash flows from operating activities to net income for Goodyear, and how do you account for the difference?
4. What are Goodyear's principal investing and financing activities?

OVERVIEW OF THE STATEMENT OF CASH FLOWS

LO1 State the principal purposes and uses of the statement of cash flows, and identify its components.

RELATED TEXT ASSIGNMENTS
Q: 1, 2, 3, 4, 5, 6
SE: 1, 8
E: 1
P: 1, 5
SD: 1, 2, 3
FRA: 3

The **statement of cash flows** shows how a company's operating, investing, and financing activities have affected cash during an accounting period. It explains the net increase (or decrease) in cash during the period. For purposes of preparing this statement, **cash** is defined as including both cash and cash equivalents. The FASB defines **cash equivalents** as short-term, highly liquid investments, including money market accounts, commercial paper, and U.S. Treasury bills. A company maintains cash equivalents to earn interest on cash that would otherwise remain unused temporarily. Suppose, for example, that a company has $1,000,000 that it will not need for 30 days. To earn a return on this amount, the company may place the cash in an account that earns interest (such as a money market account), it may lend the cash to another corporation by purchasing that corporation's short-term notes (commercial paper), or it may purchase a short-term obligation of the U.S. government (Treasury bills). In this context, short-term refers to original maturities of 90 days or less. Since cash and cash equivalents are considered the same, transfers between the Cash account and cash equivalents are not treated as cash receipts or cash payments. In effect, cash equivalents are combined with the Cash account on the statement of cash flows.

KEY POINT: Money market accounts, commercial paper (short-term notes), and U.S. Treasury bills are considered cash equivalents because they are highly liquid, temporary (90 days or less) holding places for cash not currently needed to operate the business. They can be quickly converted into cash if the need arises.

● **STOP AND THINK!**
Which statement is more useful—the income statement or the statement of cash flows?
The statements are equally useful. The income statement relates most directly to the goal of profitability, whereas the statement of cash flows is more closely tied to the goal of liquidity. ■

KEY POINT: Management uses the statement of cash flows to make various investing and financing decisions. Investors and creditors, on the other hand, use the statement primarily to assess cash flow prospects.

KEY POINT: Operating activities arise from the day-to-day sale of goods and services, investing activities involve long-term assets and investments, and financing activities deal with stockholders' equity accounts and debt (borrowing).

Cash equivalents should not be confused with short-term investments or marketable securities, which are not combined with the Cash account on the statement of cash flows. Purchases of marketable securities are treated as cash outflows and sales of marketable securities as cash inflows on the statement of cash flows. In this chapter, we assume that cash includes cash and cash equivalents.

PURPOSES OF THE STATEMENT OF CASH FLOWS

The primary purpose of the statement of cash flows is to provide information about a company's cash receipts and cash payments during an accounting period. A secondary purpose of the statement is to provide information about a company's operating, investing, and financing activities during the accounting period. Some information about those activities may be inferred from other financial statements, but it is on the statement of cash flows that all the transactions affecting cash are summarized.

INTERNAL AND EXTERNAL USES OF THE STATEMENT OF CASH FLOWS

The statement of cash flows is useful internally to management and externally to investors and creditors. Management uses the statement to assess liquidity, to determine dividend policy, and to evaluate the effects of major policy decisions involving investments and financing. In other words, management may use the statement to determine if short-term financing is needed to pay current liabilities, to decide whether to raise or lower dividends, and to plan for investing and financing needs.

Investors and creditors find the statement useful in assessing the company's ability to manage cash flows, to generate positive future cash flows, to pay its liabilities, to pay dividends and interest, and to anticipate its need for additional financing. Also, they may use the statement to explain the differences between net income on the income statement and the net cash flows generated from operations. In addition, the statement shows both the cash and the noncash effects of investing and financing activities during the accounting period.

CLASSIFICATION OF CASH FLOWS

The statement of cash flows classifies cash receipts and cash payments into the categories of operating, investing, and financing activities. The components of these activities are illustrated in Figure 1 and summarized below.

1. **Operating activities** include the cash effects of transactions and other events that enter into the determination of net income. Included in this category as cash inflows are cash receipts from customers for goods and services, interest and dividends received on loans and investments, and sales of trading securities. Included as cash outflows are cash payments for wages, inventory, expenses, interest, taxes, and purchases of trading securities. In effect, the income statement is changed from an accrual to a cash basis.

2. **Investing activities** include the acquisition and sale of long-term assets and marketable securities, other than trading securities or cash equivalents, and the making and collecting of loans. Cash inflows include the cash received from selling long-term assets and marketable securities and from collecting loans. Cash outflows include the cash expended for purchases of long-term assets and marketable securities and the cash lent to borrowers.

3. **Financing activities** include obtaining resources from stockholders and providing them with a return on their investments, and obtaining resources from creditors and repaying the amounts borrowed or otherwise settling the obligations. Cash inflows include the proceeds from issues of stocks and from short-term and long-term borrowing. Cash outflows include the repayments of loans (excluding interest) and payments to owners, including cash dividends. Treasury stock transactions are also considered financing activities. Repayments of

FIGURE 1
Classification of Cash Inflows and Cash Outflows

accounts payable or accrued liabilities are not considered repayments of loans under financing activities; they are classified as cash outflows under operating activities.

Companies occasionally engage in significant **noncash investing and financing transactions** involving only long-term assets, long-term liabilities, or stockholders' equity. For instance, a company might exchange a long-term asset for a long-term liability, settle a debt by issuing capital stock, or take out a long-term mortgage for the purchase of land and a building. Such transactions represent significant investing and financing activities, but they would not be reflected on the statement of cash flows because they do not involve either cash inflows or outflows. However, because such transactions will affect future cash flows, the FASB has determined

FOCUS ON INTERNATIONAL BUSINESS

How Universal Is the Statement of Cash Flows?

Despite the importance of the statement of cash flows in assessing the liquidity of companies in the United States, considerable variation in its use and format has existed in other countries. For example, the principal directives related to financial reporting for the European Union do not address the statement of cash flows. In many countries, the statement shows the change in working capital instead of the change in cash and cash equivalents. However, international accounting standards require the statement of cash flows, and international financial markets expect it to be presented. As a result, most multinational companies include the statement in their financial reports. Most European countries will adopt the statement of cash flows by 2006, when the European Union will require the use of international accounting standards.

that they should be disclosed in a separate schedule as part of the statement of cash flows. In this way, the reader of the statement can see the company's investing and financing activities more clearly.

FORMAT OF THE STATEMENT OF CASH FLOWS

As shown in the Financial Highlights at the beginning of this chapter, the statement of cash flows is divided into three sections. The first section, cash flows from operating activities, is presented using the indirect method. This is the most common method and is explained later in the chapter. The other two sections of the statement of cash flows are the cash flows from investing activities and the cash flows from financing activities. The individual cash inflows and outflows from investing and financing activities are shown separately in their respective categories. Normally, cash outflows for the purchase of plant assets are shown separately from cash inflows from the disposal of plant assets. However, because the inflows are not usually material, some companies follow the practice of combining these two lines in order to show the net amount of outflow.

A reconciliation of the beginning and ending balances of cash appears near the bottom of the statement. Again referring to the Financial Highlights, note that Marriott International had a net decrease in cash of $614 million in 2002, which together with the beginning balance of $812 million results in $198 million of cash and cash equivalents on hand at the end of the year.

www.marriott.com

 Check out ACE for a Review Quiz at http://accounting.college.hmco.com/students.

ANALYZING THE STATEMENT OF CASH FLOWS

LO2 Analyze the statement of cash flows.

RELATED TEXT ASSIGNMENTS
Q: 7, 8
SE: 2, 3
E: 2
P: 2, 3, 4, 6, 7
SD: 3, 4
FRA: 1, 2, 3, 4, 5, 6

www.marriott.com

Like the other financial statements, the statement of cash flows can be analyzed to reveal significant relationships. Two areas analysts examine when studying a company are cash-generating efficiency and free cash flow.

CASH-GENERATING EFFICIENCY

Cash-generating efficiency is the ability of a company to generate cash from its current or continuing operations. Three ratios are helpful in measuring cash-generating efficiency: cash flow yield, cash flows to sales, and cash flows to assets. We compute these ratios for Marriott International in 2002 using data from the Financial Highlights at the beginning of this chapter and those presented below.[3] All dollar amounts are stated in millions.

Financial Highlights for Marriott International
(In millions of dollars)

	2002	2001	2000
Net Sales	$8,441	$7,786	$7,911
Total Assets	8,296	9,107	8,237

ENRICHMENT NOTE: The cash flow yield enables users to assess whether sufficient cash flows underlie earnings. Serious questions would be raised if cash flow yield was less than 1.0. For example, receivables and inventories might be growing too fast, perhaps signaling a slowdown in sales growth or a problem in managing receivables collection or inventory levels.

Cash flow yield is the ratio of net cash flows from operating activities to net income, computed as follows:

$$\text{Cash Flow Yield} = \frac{\text{Net Cash Flows from Operating Activities}}{\text{Net Income}}$$

$$= \frac{\$516}{\$448}$$

$$= 1.2 \text{ times}$$

Marriott International has a good cash flow yield of 1.2 times; that is, the corporation's operating activities are generating about 20 percent more cash flow than net income. If special items, such as discontinued operations, appear on the income statement and are material, income from continuing operations should be used as the denominator.

Cash flows to sales is the ratio of net cash flows from operating activities to sales, computed as follows:

$$\text{Cash Flows to Sales} = \frac{\text{Net Cash Flows from Operating Activities}}{\text{Net Sales}}$$

$$= \frac{\$516}{\$8,441}$$

$$= 6.1\%$$

Marriott generates cash flows to sales of 6.1 percent. The company generated a positive but relatively small percentage of net cash from sales.

Cash flows to assets is the ratio of net cash flows from operating activities to average total assets, computed as follows:

$$\text{Cash Flows to Assets} = \frac{\text{Net Cash Flows from Operating Activities}}{\text{Average Total Assets}}$$

$$= \frac{\$516}{(\$8,296 + \$9,107) \div 2}$$

$$= 5.9\%$$

● **STOP AND THINK!**
If cash flow yield is less than 1.0, would cash flows to sales and cash flows to assets be greater or less than profit margin and return on assets, respectively?

Cash flows to sales and cash flows to assets would be less than profit margin and return on assets, respectively, because a cash flow yield of less than 1.0 means that cash flows from operations are less than net income. Both are numerators in ratios that have the same denominators. ■

The cash flows to assets ratio is slightly less than the cash flows to sales ratio because Marriott International has a good asset turnover ratio (sales ÷ average total assets) of approximately .97 times (5.9% ÷ 6.1%). Cash flows to sales and cash flows to assets are closely related to the profitability measures of profit margin and return on assets. They exceed those measures by the amount of the cash flow yield ratio because cash flow yield is the ratio of net cash flows from operating activities to net income.

Although Marriott's cash flow yield and cash flows to assets are relatively good, its efficiency at generating cash flows from operating activities, as measured by cash flows to sales, could be improved.

FREE CASH FLOW

www.marriott.com

In 2002, Marriott had a net cash outflow of $317 million for investing activities, which could indicate that the company was expanding. However, that figure mixes capital expenditures for plant assets, which reflect management's expansion of operations, with loan advances and collections. Cash flows from financing activities used $1,447 million, but that figure combines financing activities associated with long-term debt and stocks with dividends paid to stockholders. While something can be learned by looking at those broad categories, many analysts

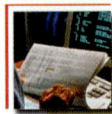

FOCUS ON BUSINESS PRACTICE

What Do You Mean, "Free Cash Flow"?

Because the statement of cash flows has been around for less than 20 years, no generally accepted analyses have yet been developed. For example, the term *free cash flow* is commonly used in the business press, but there is no agreement on its definition. An article in *Forbes* defines *free cash flow* as "cash available after paying out capital expenditures and dividends, *but before taxes and interest*"[4] [emphasis added]. An article in *The Wall Street Journal* defines it as "operating income less maintenance-level capital expenditures."[5] The definition with which we are most in agreement is the one used in *Business Week*: free cash flow is net cash flows from operating activities less net capital expenditures and dividends. This "measures truly discretionary funds—company money that an owner could pocket without harming the business."[6]

KEY POINT: Free cash flow should be interpreted in light of the company's overall need for cash. For instance, the purchase of treasury stock will reduce the amount of cash that is free for operating uses.

find it more informative to go beyond them to focus on a computation called free cash flow.

Free cash flow is the amount of cash that remains after deducting the funds a company must commit to continue operating at its planned level. The commitments must cover current or continuing operations, interest, income taxes, dividends, and net capital expenditures. Cash requirements for current or continuing operations, interest, and income taxes must be paid or the company's creditors and the government can take legal action. Although the payment of dividends is not strictly required, dividends normally represent a commitment to stockholders. If these payments are reduced or eliminated, stockholders will be unhappy and the price of the company's stock will fall. Net capital expenditures represent management's plans for the future.

If free cash flow is positive, it means that the company has met all its planned cash commitments and has cash available to reduce debt or to expand. A negative free cash flow means that the company will have to sell investments, borrow money, or issue stock in the short term to continue at its planned level. If free cash flow remains negative for several years, a company may not be able to raise cash by issuing stock or bonds.

Since cash commitments for current or continuing operations, interest, and income taxes are incorporated in cash flows from current operations, free cash flow for Marriott is computed as follows (in millions):

Free Cash Flow = Net Cash Flows from Operating Activities − Dividends − Purchases of Plant Assets + Sales of Plant Assets

= $516 − $65 − $292 + $729

= $888

FOCUS ON BUSINESS PRACTICE

Cash Flows Tell All.

In early 2001, the telecommunications industry began one of the biggest market crashes in history. Could it have been predicted? The telecommunications industry depends on heavy capital expenditures in equipment, such as cable lines and computers. When the cash flows from sales of 41 telecommunications companies are compared with their capital expenditures (a negative component of free cash flow) over the six years preceding the crash, an interesting pattern emerges. In the first three years, both cash flows from sales and capital expenditures were about 20 percent of sales. In other words, free cash flows were neutral, with operations generating enough cash flows to cover capital expenditures. In the next three years, these measures diverged. Cash flows to sales stayed at about 20 percent of sales, but the companies increased capital expenditures dramatically, to 35 percent of sales. Thus, free cash flows turned very negative, and almost half of capital expenditures had to be financed by debt instead of operations, making these companies more vulnerable to the downturn in the economy that occurred in 2001.[7]

Purchases and sales of plant assets appear in the investing activities section of the statement of cash flows; Marriott reported both capital expenditures and dispositions of property and equipment. Dividends are in the financing activities section. Marriott had positive free cash flow of $888 million due mainly to its strong operating cash flow of $516 million and $729 million cash received on disposal of property and equipment. The cash used by financing activities was the largest in three years, $1,447 million, because Marriott repaid long-term debt of $946 million and convertible subordinated debt of $347 million. Marriott also issued common stock in the amount of $35 million and purchased treasury stock for $252 million.

Cash flows can vary from year to year, so it is best to look at trends in cash flow measures over several years when analyzing a company's cash flows. Marriott's cash flow yield was less in 2002 than in 2001 and thus should be watched in 2003. Management summed this up in the company's annual report:

> **Liquidity and Capital Resources**
> We consider [our credit] resources, together with cash we expect to generate from operations, adequate to meet our short-term and long-term liquidity requirements.[8]

Check out ACE for a Review Quiz at http://accounting.college.hmco.com/students.

PREPARING THE STATEMENT OF CASH FLOWS: OPERATING ACTIVITIES

LO3 Use the indirect method to determine cash flows from operating activities.

RELATED TEXT ASSIGNMENTS
Q: 9, 10, 11, 12
SE: 4, 5, 8
E: 3, 4, 5, 9
P: 2, 3, 4, 6, 7
SD: 1, 4
FRA: 3, 5

KEY POINT: The direct and indirect methods relate only to the operating activities section of the statement of cash flows. They are both acceptable for financial reporting purposes.

To demonstrate the preparation of the statement of cash flows, we will work through an example step by step. The data for this example are presented in Exhibits 1 and 2, which show Ryan Corporation's balance sheets for December 31, 20x5 and 20x4, and its 20x5 income statement. Exhibit 1 shows the balance sheet accounts that we use for analysis and whether the change in each account is an increase or a decrease. Exhibit 2 contains data about transactions that affected noncurrent accounts. The company's accountants would identify those transactions from the records.

The first step in preparing the statement of cash flows is to determine cash flows from operating activities. The income statement indicates a business's success or failure in earning an income from its operating activities. However, because the income statement is prepared on an accrual basis, it does not reflect the inflow and outflow of cash from those activities. Revenues are recorded even though the cash for them may not have been received, and expenses are recorded even though the cash for them may not have been expended. Thus, to arrive at cash flows from operations, the figures on the income statement must be converted from an accrual basis to a cash basis. There are two methods of accomplishing this: the direct method and the indirect method. Under the **direct method**, each item on the income statement is adjusted from the accrual basis to the cash basis. The result is a statement that begins with cash receipts from sales and interest and deducts cash payments for purchases, operating expenses, interest payments, and income taxes to arrive at net cash flows from operating activities. The **indirect method** does not require the individual adjustment of each item on the income statement; it lists only the adjustments necessary to convert net income to cash flows from operations.

The direct and indirect methods always produce the same net figure. The direct method is more easily understood by the average reader because it results in a more straightforward presentation of operating cash flows than does the indirect method. However, the indirect method is the overwhelming choice of most companies and accountants. A survey of large companies shows that 99 percent use this method.[9] The indirect method is superior to the direct method from the analysts' perspective because its format begins with net income and derives cash flows from operations.

Exhibit 1
Comparative Balance Sheets with Changes in Accounts Indicated

Ryan Corporation
Comparative Balance Sheets
December 31, 20x5 and 20x4

	20x5	20x4	Change	Increase or Decrease
Assets				
Current assets				
Cash	$ 46,000	$ 15,000	$ 31,000	Increase
Accounts receivable (net)	47,000	55,000	(8,000)	Decrease
Inventory	144,000	110,000	34,000	Increase
Prepaid expenses	1,000	5,000	(4,000)	Decrease
Total current assets	$238,000	$185,000	$ 53,000	
Investments available for sale	$115,000	$127,000	($ 12,000)	Decrease
Plant assets				
Plant assets	$715,000	$505,000	$210,000	Increase
Accumulated depreciation	(103,000)	(68,000)	(35,000)	Increase
Total plant assets	$612,000	$437,000	$175,000	
Total assets	$965,000	$749,000	$216,000	
Liabilities				
Current liabilities				
Accounts payable	$ 50,000	$ 43,000	$ 7,000	Increase
Accrued liabilities	12,000	9,000	3,000	Increase
Income taxes payable	3,000	5,000	(2,000)	Decrease
Total current liabilities	$ 65,000	$ 57,000	$ 8,000	
Long-term liabilities				
Bonds payable	295,000	245,000	50,000	Increase
Total liabilities	$360,000	$302,000	$ 58,000	
Stockholders' Equity				
Common stock, $5 par value	$276,000	$200,000	$ 76,000	Increase
Paid-in capital in excess of par value, common	214,000	115,000	99,000	Increase
Retained earnings	140,000	132,000	8,000	Increase
Treasury stock	(25,000)	0	(25,000)	Increase
Total stockholders' equity	$605,000	$447,000	$158,000	
Total liabilities and stockholders' equity	$965,000	$749,000	$216,000	

KEY POINT: The indirect method begins with net income and adjusts up or down to produce net cash flows from operating activities.

The analyst can readily identify the factors that cause cash flows from operations. Further, from the company's standpoint, the indirect method is easier and less expensive to prepare. For these reasons, we use the indirect method in this book.

As illustrated in Figure 2, the indirect method focuses on items from the income statement that must be adjusted to reconcile net income to net cash flows

EXHIBIT 2
Income Statement and Other Information on Noncurrent Accounts

Ryan Corporation
Income Statement
For the Year Ended December 31, 20x5

Net sales		$698,000
Cost of goods sold		520,000
Gross margin		$178,000
Operating expenses (including depreciation expense of $37,000)		147,000
Operating income		$ 31,000
Other income (expenses)		
Interest expense	($23,000)	
Interest income	6,000	
Gain on sale of investments	12,000	
Loss on sale of plant assets	(3,000)	(8,000)
Income before income taxes		$ 23,000
Income taxes		7,000
Net income		$ 16,000

Other transactions affecting noncurrent accounts during 20x5:

1. Purchased investments in the amount of $78,000.
2. Sold investments that cost $90,000 for $102,000.
3. Purchased plant assets in the amount of $120,000.
4. Sold plant assets that cost $10,000 with accumulated depreciation of $2,000 for $5,000.
5. Issued $100,000 of bonds at face value in a noncash exchange for plant assets.
6. Repaid $50,000 of bonds at face value at maturity.
7. Issued 15,200 shares of $5 par value common stock for $175,000.
8. Purchased treasury stock in the amount of $25,000.
9. Paid cash dividends in the amount of $8,000.

from operating activities. The items that require adjustment are those that affect net income but not net cash flows from operating activities. They include depreciation and amortization, gains and losses, and changes in the balances of current asset and current liability accounts. The reconciliation of Ryan Corporation's net income to net cash flows from operating activities is shown in Exhibit 3. Each adjustment is discussed in the sections that follow.

FIGURE 2
Indirect Method of Determining Net Cash Flows from Operating Activities

EXHIBIT 3
Schedule of Cash Flows from Operating Activities: Indirect Method

Ryan Corporation
Schedule of Cash Flows from Operating Activities
For the Year Ended December 31, 20x5

Cash flows from operating activities		
Net income		$16,000
Adjustments to reconcile net income to net cash flows from operating activities		
Depreciation expense	$37,000	
Gain on sale of investments	(12,000)	
Loss on sale of plant assets	3,000	
Changes in current assets and current liabilities		
Decrease in accounts receivable	8,000	
Increase in inventory	(34,000)	
Decrease in prepaid expenses	4,000	
Increase in accounts payable	7,000	
Increase in accrued liabilities	3,000	
Decrease in income taxes payable	(2,000)	14,000
Net cash flows from operating activities		$30,000

● **STOP AND THINK!**
If a company has positive earnings, can cash flows from operating activities ever be negative?

If a company has large gains, large increases in current assets, or decreases in current liabilities, the results could overwhelm the earnings and create negative cash flows from operating activities. ■

DEPRECIATION

Cash payments for plant assets, intangibles, and natural resources occur when the assets are purchased and are reflected as investing activities on the statement of cash flows at that time. When depreciation expense, amortization expense, and depletion expense appear on the income statement, they simply indicate allocations of the costs of the original purchases to the current accounting period; they do not affect net cash flows in the current period. The amount of such expenses can usually be found by referring to the income statement or a note to the financial statements. For Ryan Corporation, the income statement reveals depreciation expense of $37,000, which would have been recorded as follows:

KEY POINT: Operating expenses on the income statement include depreciation expense, which does not require a cash outlay.

A = L + OE
−   −

Depreciation Expense	37,000	
Accumulated Depreciation		37,000
To record annual depreciation on plant assets		

The recording of depreciation involved no outlay of cash even though depreciation expense appears on the income statement. Thus, to derive cash flows from operations, an adjustment for depreciation is needed to increase net income by the amount of depreciation recorded.

GAINS AND LOSSES

STUDY NOTE: Gains and losses by themselves do not represent cash flows; they are merely bookkeeping adjustments. For example, when a long-term asset is sold, it is the *proceeds* (cash received), not the gain or loss, that constitute cash flow.

Gains and losses that appear on the income statement also do not affect cash flows from operating activities and need to be removed from this section of the statement of cash flows. The cash receipts generated by the disposal of the assets that resulted in the gains or losses are shown in the investing section of the statement of cash flows. Thus, gains and losses are removed from net income (preventing double counting) to reconcile net income to cash flows from operating activities. For example, on its income statement, Ryan Corporation showed a $12,000 gain on the sale of investments, and this is subtracted from net income to reconcile net income to net cash flows from operating activities. The reason for this is that the $12,000 is already included (added) in the investing activities section as part of the $102,000 cash from the sale of the investment. Because the gain is included in the calculation of net income, the $12,000 gain needs to be subtracted to prevent double counting. Also, Ryan Corporation showed a $3,000 loss on the sale of plant assets. Following the same logic, the $3,000 loss is already reflected in the $5,000 sale of plant assets in the investing activities section. Thus, the $3,000 is added to net income to reconcile net income to net cash flows from operating activities.

CHANGES IN CURRENT ASSETS

Decreases in current assets other than cash have positive effects on cash flows, and increases in current assets have negative effects on cash flows. A decrease in a current asset frees up invested cash, thereby increasing cash flow. An increase in a current asset consumes cash, thereby decreasing cash flow. For example, refer to the balance sheets and income statement for Ryan Corporation in Exhibits 1 and 2. Note that net sales in 20x5 were $698,000 and that Accounts Receivable decreased by $8,000. Thus, cash received from sales was $706,000, calculated as follows:

$$\$706,000 = \$698,000 + \$8,000$$

Collections were $8,000 more than sales recorded for the year. This relationship may be illustrated as follows:

	Accounts Receivable		
Sales to Customers →	Beg. Bal. 55,000	706,000 →	Cash Receipts from Customers
	698,000		
	End. Bal. 47,000		

Thus, to reconcile net income to net cash flows from operating activities, the $8,000 decrease in Accounts Receivable is added to net income.

Inventory may be analyzed in the same way. For example, Exhibit 1 shows that Inventory increased by $34,000 from 20x4 to 20x5. This means that Ryan Corporation expended $34,000 more in cash for purchases than was included in cost of goods sold on the income statement. As a result of this expenditure, net income is higher than the net cash flows from operating activities, so $34,000 must be deducted from net income. Using the same logic, the decrease of $4,000 in Prepaid Expenses is added to net income to reconcile net income to net cash flows from operating activities.

CHANGES IN CURRENT LIABILITIES

Changes in current liabilities have the opposite effects on cash flows from those of changes in current assets. Increases in current liabilities are added to net income, and decreases in current liabilities are deducted from net income to reconcile net income to net cash flows from operating activities. An increase in a current liability represents a postponement of a cash payment, which frees up cash and increases cash flow in the current period. A decrease in current liabilities consumes cash, thereby decreasing cash flow. For example, Exhibit 1 shows that Ryan Corporation had a $7,000 increase in accounts payable from 20x4 to 20x5. This means that Ryan Corporation paid $7,000 less to creditors than the amount of purchases indicates in cost of goods sold on the income statement. This relationship may be visualized as follows:

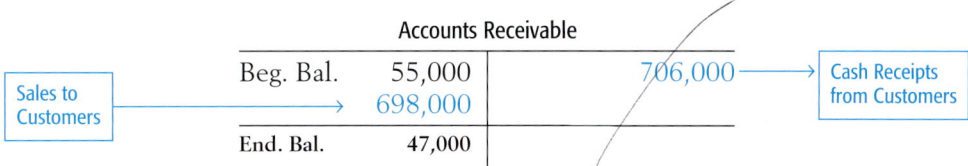

*Purchases = Cost of Goods Sold ($520,000) + Increase in Inventory ($34,000).

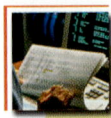

Focus on Business Practice

What's Your "Burn Rate"?
Why would a company have a total market value less than the amount of cash it has on hand? The answer is "burn rate." Burn rate is the pace at which companies use cash in their operations. A major contributor to the market crash of the stocks of dot-com companies was the difficulty these firms had in generating enough revenue to produce positive cash flows from operations. For example, when investors thought Webvan Group, Inc., the Internet grocer, would be the delivery service model of the future, the company was valued as high as $11.4 billion. However, as Webvan's burn rate reached $55 million a month, its market value dropped to a mere $132 million, even though the company had $212 million in cash.[10] The company was never able to generate sufficient revenues and soon declared bankruptcy.

As a result, $7,000 is added to net income to reconcile net income to net cash flows from operating activities. By the same logic, the increase of $3,000 in accrued liabilities is added to net income, and the decrease of $2,000 in income taxes payable is deducted from net income.

SCHEDULE OF CASH FLOWS FROM OPERATING ACTIVITIES

In summary, Exhibit 3 shows that by using the indirect method, net income of $16,000 has been adjusted by reconciling items totaling $14,000 to arrive at net cash flows from operating activities of $30,000. This means that although net income was $16,000, Ryan actually had net cash flows of $30,000 available from operating activities to use for purchasing assets, reducing debts, or paying dividends.

The effects of items on the income statement that do not affect cash flows may be summarized as follows:

	Add to or Deduct from Net Income
Depreciation expense	Add
Amortization expense	Add
Depletion expense	Add
Losses	Add
Gains	Deduct

The adjustments for increases and decreases in current assets and current liabilities may be summarized as follows:

	Add to Net Income	Deduct from Net Income
Current assets		
Accounts receivable (net)	Decrease	Increase
Inventory	Decrease	Increase
Prepaid expenses	Decrease	Increase
Current liabilities		
Accounts payable	Increase	Decrease
Accrued liabilities	Increase	Decrease
Income taxes payable	Increase	Decrease

✓ Check out ACE for a Review Quiz at http://accounting.college.hmco.com/students.

PREPARING THE STATEMENT OF CASH FLOWS: INVESTING ACTIVITIES

LO4 Determine cash flows from investing activities.

RELATED TEXT ASSIGNMENTS
Q: 13
SE: 6, 8
E: 6, 7, 8, 9
P: 2, 3, 4, 6, 7
SD: 4
FRA: 3, 5

To determine cash flows from investing activities, accounts involving cash receipts and cash payments from investing activities are examined individually. The objective is to explain the change in each account balance from one year to the next.

Investing activities center on the long-term assets shown on the balance sheet, but they also include transactions affecting short-term investments from the current assets section of the balance sheet and investment gains and losses from the income statement. The balance sheets in Exhibit 1 show that Ryan Corporation had long-term assets of investments and plant assets, but no short-term investments. The income statement in Exhibit 2 shows that Ryan had investment-related items in the form of a gain on the sale of investments and a loss on the sale of plant assets.

KEY POINT: Investing activities involve long-term assets and short- or long-term investments. Both inflows and outflows of cash are shown in the investing activities section of the statement of cash flows.

The schedule at the bottom of Exhibit 2 lists the following five items pertaining to investing activities in 20x5:

1. Purchased investments in the amount of $78,000. — CASH GOES ↓
2. Sold investments that cost $90,000 for $102,000.
3. Purchased plant assets in the amount of $120,000.
4. Sold plant assets that cost $10,000 with accumulated depreciation of $2,000 for $5,000.
5. Issued $100,000 of bonds at face value in a noncash exchange for plant assets.

The following sections analyze the accounts related to investing activities to determine their effects on Ryan Corporation's cash flows.

INVESTMENTS

The objective here is to explain Ryan Corporation's $12,000 decrease in investments, all of which are classified as available-for-sale securities. This is accomplished by analyzing the increases and decreases in the Investments account to determine the effects on the Cash account. Purchases increase investments, and sales decrease investments.

Item 1 in Ryan's list of investing activities shows purchases of $78,000 during 20x5. This transaction is recorded as follows:

A = L + OE
\+
−

Investments	78,000	
Cash		78,000
Purchase of investments		

The entry shows that the effect of this transaction is a $78,000 decrease in cash flows.

Item 2 in the list shows that Ryan sold investments that cost $90,000 for $102,000, resulting in a gain of $12,000. This transaction is recorded as follows:

A = L + OE
\+   +
−

Cash	102,000	
Investments		90,000
Gain on Sale of Investments		12,000
Sale of investments for a gain		

KEY POINT: The $102,000 price obtained, not the $12,000 gain, constitutes the cash flow here.

The effect of this transaction is a $102,000 increase in cash flows. Note that the gain on sale of investments is included in the $102,000. This is why we excluded it in computing cash flows from operations. If it had been included in that section, it would have been counted twice.

The $12,000 decrease in the Investments account (unrelated to the $12,000 gain above) during 20x5 has now been explained, as seen in the following T account:

Investments			
Beg. Bal.	127,000	Sales	90,000
Purchases	78,000		
End. Bal.	115,000		

● **STOP AND THINK!**
Which adjustments to net income in the operating activities section of the statement of cash flows are directly related to cash flows reported in other sections?

Gains and losses from operating activities are directly related to the cash flows from the sale of assets reported in the investing activities section. ■

The cash flow effects from these transactions are shown in the investing activities section on the statement of cash flows as follows:

Purchase of investments	($ 78,000)
Sale of investments	102,000

Notice that purchases and sales are listed separately as cash outflows and inflows to give readers of the statement a complete view of investing activity. Some companies prefer to combine them into a single net amount.

If Ryan Corporation had short-term investments or marketable securities, the analysis of cash flows would be the same.

PLANT ASSETS

In the case of plant assets, it is necessary to explain the changes in both the Plant Assets account and the related Accumulated Depreciation account. According to Exhibit 1, Ryan Corporation's plant assets increased by $210,000, and accumulated depreciation increased by $35,000. Purchases increase plant assets, and sales decrease plant assets. Accumulated depreciation is increased by the amount of depreciation expense and decreased by the removal of the accumulated depreciation associated with plant assets that are sold. Three items listed in Exhibit 2 affect plant assets. Item **3** in the list indicates that Ryan Corporation purchased plant assets totaling $120,000 during 20x5, as shown by the following entry:

A = L + OE
\+
\-

Plant Assets	120,000	
Cash		120,000
Purchase of plant assets		

This transaction results in a cash outflow of $120,000.

Item **4** states that Ryan Corporation sold for $5,000 plant assets that cost $10,000 and had accumulated depreciation of $2,000, which resulted in a loss of $3,000. The entry to record this transaction is as follows:

A = L + OE
\+
\+
\-

Cash	5,000	
Accumulated Depreciation	2,000	
Loss on Sale of Plant Assets	3,000	
Plant Assets		10,000
Sale of plant assets at a loss		

KEY POINT: Even though Ryan had a loss on the sale, it realized a positive cash flow of $5,000, which will be reported in the investing activities section of the statement of cash flows. When the indirect approach is used, the loss is eliminated with an "add-back" to net income.

Note that in this transaction the positive cash flow is equal to the amount of cash received, or $5,000. The loss on the sale of plant assets is included here, and excluded from the operating activities section (see page 627), by adjusting net income for the amount of the loss. The amount of a loss or gain on the sale of an asset is determined by the amount of cash received and does not represent a cash outflow or inflow.

The disclosure of these two transactions in the investing activities section of the statement of cash flows is as follows:

Purchase of plant assets	($120,000)
Sale of plant assets	5,000

Cash outflows and cash inflows are listed separately here, though companies sometimes combine them into a single net amount, as they do the purchase and sale of investments.

Item **5** in Exhibit 2 is a noncash exchange that affects two long-term accounts, Plant Assets and Bonds Payable. It is recorded as follows:

A = L + OE
\+ +

Plant Assets	100,000	
Bonds Payable		100,000
Issued bonds at face value for plant assets		

Although this transaction does not involve an inflow or outflow of cash, it is a significant transaction involving both an investing activity (the purchase of plant assets) and a financing activity (the issue of bonds payable). Because one purpose of the statement of cash flows is to show important investing and financing activities, the transaction is listed in a separate schedule, either at the bottom of the statement of cash flows or accompanying the statement, as follows:

Schedule of Noncash Investing and Financing Transactions

Issue of bonds payable for plant assets	$100,000

Through our analysis of the preceding transactions and the depreciation expense for plant assets, we have now accounted for all the changes in the Plant Assets accounts, as shown in the following T accounts:

Plant Assets

Beg. Bal.	505,000	Sale	10,000
Cash Purchase	120,000		
Noncash Purchase	100,000		
End. Bal.	715,000		

Accumulated Depreciation

Sale	2,000	Beg. Bal.	68,000
		Dep. Expense	37,000
		End. Bal.	103,000

Had the balance sheet included specific plant asset accounts (e.g., Buildings and Equipment and related accumulated depreciation accounts) or other long-term asset accounts (e.g., Intangibles), the analysis would have been the same.

✓ Check out ACE for a Review Quiz at http://accounting.college.hmco.com/students.

PREPARING THE STATEMENT OF CASH FLOWS: FINANCING ACTIVITIES

LO5 Determine cash flows from financing activities.

RELATED TEXT ASSIGNMENTS
Q: 14
SE: 7, 8
E: 8, 9
P: 2, 3, 4, 6, 7
SD: 4
FRA: 3, 5

KEY POINT: Financing activities involve stockholders' equity accounts and short- and long-term borrowings. Because dividends paid involve retained earnings, they are appropriately included in this category.

The procedure for determining cash flows from financing activities is like the analysis of investing activities, including treatment of related gains or losses, but the accounts analyzed are short-term borrowings, long-term liabilities, and stockholders' equity accounts. Cash dividends from the statement of stockholders' equity must also be considered. Since Ryan Corporation does not have short-term borrowings, we deal only with long-term liabilities and stockholders' equity accounts.

These items from Exhibit 2 pertain to Ryan's financing activities in 20x5:

5. Issued $100,000 of bonds at face value in a noncash exchange for plant assets. CASH ↓
6. Repaid $50,000 of bonds at face value at maturity.
7. Issued 15,200 shares of $5 par value common stock for $175,000.
8. Purchased treasury stock for $25,000. CASH ↓
9. Paid cash dividends in the amount of $8,000. CASH ↓

BONDS PAYABLE

Exhibit 1 shows that Bonds Payable increased by $50,000 in 20x5. This account is affected by items **5** and **6**. Item **5** was analyzed in connection with plant assets. As noted above, it is reported on the schedule of noncash investing and financing transactions, but it must be remembered here in preparing the T account for Bonds Payable. Item **6** results in a cash outflow, which is recorded as follows:

A = L + OE
    – –

Bonds Payable	50,000	
Cash		50,000
Repayment of bonds at face value at maturity		

This appears in the financing activities section of the statement of cash flows as:

Repayment of bonds   ($50,000)

The following T account explains the change in Bonds Payable:

Bonds Payable

Repayment	50,000	Beg. Bal.	245,000
		Noncash Issue	100,000
		End. Bal.	295,000

If Ryan Corporation had any notes payable, the analysis would be the same.

COMMON STOCK

Like the Plant Asset account and its related accounts, related stockholders' equity accounts should be analyzed together. For example, Paid-in Capital in Excess of Par Value, Common should be examined with Common Stock. In 20x5, Ryan Corporation's Common Stock account increased by $76,000, and Paid-in Capital in Excess of Par Value, Common increased by $99,000. Those increases are explained by item 7 in the list in Exhibit 2, which states that Ryan issued 15,200 shares of $5 par value common stock for $175,000. The entry to record the cash inflow is as follows:

A = L + OE
+   +
        +

Cash	175,000	
Common Stock		76,000
Paid-in Capital in Excess of Par Value, Common		99,000
Issued 15,200 shares of $5 par value common stock		

STUDY NOTE: The purchase of treasury stock would also qualify as a financing activity, but would appear as a cash outflow.

This appears in the financing activities section of the statement of cash flows as:

Issue of common stock $175,000

The following analysis of this transaction is all that is needed to explain the changes in the two accounts during 20x5:

Common Stock			Paid-in Capital in Excess of Par Value, Common		
	Beg. Bal.	200,000		Beg. Bal.	115,000
	Issue	76,000		Issue	99,000
	End. Bal.	276,000		End. Bal.	214,000

RETAINED EARNINGS

At this point, we have dealt with several items that affect retained earnings. For instance, we used Ryan's net income in the analysis of cash flows from operating activities. The only other item affecting Ryan's retained earnings is the payment of $8,000 in cash dividends (item 9 in Exhibit 2), which is recorded as follows:

A = L + OE
−   −

Retained Earnings	8,000	
Cash		8,000
Cash dividends for 20x5		

Ryan Corporation would have declared the dividend before paying it and therefore would have debited the Cash Dividends Declared account instead of Retained Earnings, but after paying the dividend and closing the Cash Dividends Declared account to Retained Earnings, the effect is as shown. Cash dividends are displayed in the financing activities section of the statement of cash flows as follows:

Payment of dividends   ($8,000)

KEY POINT: It is dividends paid, not dividends declared, that appear on the statement of cash flows.

The following T account shows the change in the Retained Earnings account:

Retained Earnings			
Dividends	8,000	Beg. Bal.	132,000
		Net Income	16,000
		End. Bal.	140,000

TREASURY STOCK

As noted in the chapter on contributed capital, many companies buy back their own stock on the open market. These buybacks use cash, as this entry shows:

A = L + OE
−   −

Treasury Stock	25,000	
Cash		25,000

This use of cash is classified in the statement of cash flows as a financing activity:

Stop and Think!
In computing free cash flow, what is an argument for treating purchases of treasury stock like dividend payments?

Both purchases of treasury stock and dividend payments represent payments to stockholders. Each diverts cash from productive use in the business (as assets), and thus each reduces free cash flow. ■

Exhibit 4
Statement of Cash Flows: Indirect Method

Purchase of treasury stock ($25,000)

The T account for this transaction is as follows:

Treasury Stock	
Purchase 25,000	

We have now analyzed all Ryan's income statement items, explained all balance sheet changes, and taken all additional data into account. The resulting information can now be assembled into the statement of cash flows shown in Exhibit 4.

Ryan Corporation
Statement of Cash Flows
For the Year Ended December 31, 20x5

Cash flows from operating activities		
Net income		$ 16,000
Adjustments to reconcile net income to net cash flows from operating activities		
Depreciation expense	$ 37,000	
Gain on sale of investments	(12,000)	
Loss on sale of plant assets	3,000	
Changes in current assets and current liabilities		
Decrease in accounts receivable	8,000	
Increase in inventory	(34,000)	
Decrease in prepaid expenses	4,000	
Increase in accounts payable	7,000	
Increase in accrued liabilities	3,000	
Decrease in income taxes payable	(2,000)	14,000
Net cash flows from operating activities		$ 30,000
Cash flows from investing activities		
Purchase of investments	($ 78,000)	
Sale of investments	102,000	
Purchase of plant assets	(120,000)	
Sale of plant assets	5,000	
Net cash flows from investing activities		(91,000)
Cash flows from financing activities		
Repayment of bonds	($ 50,000)	
Issue of common stock	175,000	
Payment of dividends	(8,000)	
Purchase of treasury stock	(25,000)	
Net cash flows from financing activities		92,000
Net increase (decrease) in cash		$ 31,000
Cash at beginning of year		15,000
Cash at end of year		$ 46,000
Schedule of Noncash Investing and Financing Transactions		
Issue of bonds payable for plant assets		$100,000

 Check out ACE for a Review Quiz at http://accounting.college.hmco.com/students.

Chapter Review

REVIEW OF LEARNING OBJECTIVES

LO1 State the principal purposes and uses of the statement of cash flows, and identify its components.

The statement of cash flows explains the changes in cash and cash equivalents from one accounting period to the next by showing cash inflows and outflows from the operating, investing, and financing activities of a company for an accounting period. For the statement of cash flows, *cash* is defined as including both cash and cash equivalents. The primary purpose of the statement is to provide information about a firm's cash receipts and cash payments during an accounting period. A secondary purpose is to provide information about a firm's operating, investing, and financing activities.

Cash flows may be classified as stemming from (1) operating activities, which include the cash effects of transactions and other events that enter into the determination of net income; (2) investing activities, which include the acquisition and sale of marketable securities and property, plant, and equipment, and the making and collecting of loans, excluding interest; or (3) financing activities, which include obtaining resources from stockholders and creditors and providing the former with a return on their investments and the latter with repayment. Noncash investing and financing transactions are also important because they affect future cash flows; these exchanges of long-term assets or liabilities are of interest to potential investors and creditors.

LO2 Analyze the statement of cash flows.

In analyzing a firm's statement of cash flows, analysts tend to focus on cash-generating efficiency and free cash flow. Cash-generating efficiency is a firm's ability to generate cash from its current or continuing operations. Three ratios used in measuring cash-generating efficiency are cash flow yield, cash flows to sales, and cash flows to assets. Free cash flow is the cash that remains after deducting the funds a firm must commit to continue operating at its planned level. Such commitments must cover current or continuing operations, interest, income taxes, dividends, and net capital expenditures.

LO3 Use the indirect method to determine cash flows from operating activities.

The indirect method adjusts net income for all noncash effects and for items that need to be converted from an accrual to a cash basis to arrive at a cash flow basis, as follows:

Cash flows from operating activities		
Net income		xxx
Adjustments to reconcile net income to net cash		
flows from operating activities		
(list of individual items)	xxx	xxx
Net cash flows from operating activities		xxx

LO4 Determine cash flows from investing activities.

Cash flows from investing activities are determined by identifying the cash flow effects of the transactions that affect each account relevant to investing activities. Such accounts include all long-term assets and short-term marketable securities.

LO5 Determine cash flows from financing activities.

The procedure for determining cash flows from financing activities is almost identical to that for investing activities. The difference is that the accounts involved are short-term borrowings, long-term liabilities, and stockholders' equity. The effects of gains and losses reported on the income statement must also be considered. After the changes in the balance sheet accounts from one accounting period to the next have been explained, all the cash flow effects should have been identified.

REVIEW OF CONCEPTS AND TERMINOLOGY

The following concepts and terms were introduced in this chapter:

LO1 **Cash:** For purposes of the statement of cash flows, both cash and cash equivalents.

LO1 **Cash equivalents:** Short-term (90 days or less), highly liquid investments, including money market accounts, commercial paper, and U.S. Treasury bills.

LO2 **Cash flows to assets:** The ratio of net cash flows from operating activities to average total assets.

LO2 **Cash flows to sales:** The ratio of net cash flows from operating activities to sales.

LO2 **Cash flow yield:** The ratio of net cash flows from operating activities to net income.

LO2 **Cash-generating efficiency:** The ability of a company to generate cash from its current or continuing operations.

LO3 **Direct method:** The procedure for converting the income statement from an accrual basis to a cash basis by separately adjusting each item on the income statement.

LO1 **Financing activities:** Business activities that involve obtaining resources from stockholders and creditors and providing the former with a return on their investments and the latter with repayment.

LO2 **Free cash flow:** The amount of cash that remains after deducting the funds a company must commit to continue operating at its planned level; net cash flows from operating activities minus dividends paid minus net capital expenditures.

LO3 **Indirect method:** The procedure for converting the income statement from an accrual basis to a cash basis by adjusting net income for items that do not affect cash flows, including depreciation, amortization, depletion, gains, losses, and changes in current assets and current liabilities.

LO1 **Investing activities:** Business activities that involve the acquisition and sale of long-term assets and marketable securities, other than trading securities or cash equivalents, and the making and collecting of loans.

LO1 **Noncash investing and financing transactions:** Significant investing and financing transactions involving only long-term assets, long-term liabilities, or stockholders' equity that do not affect current cash inflows or outflows.

LO1 **Operating activities:** Business activities that involve the cash effects of transactions and other events that enter into the determination of net income.

LO1 **Statement of cash flows:** A financial statement that shows how a company's operating, investing, and financing activities have affected cash during an accounting period.

REVIEW PROBLEM

The Statement of Cash Flows

LO2
LO3 Northwest Corporation's 20x5 income statement appears below. Its comparative balance sheets for 20x5 and 20x4 are presented on the next page.
LO4
LO5

Northwest Corporation
Income Statement
For the Year Ended December 31, 20x5

Net sales		$1,650,000
Cost of goods sold		920,000
Gross margin		$ 730,000
Operating expenses (including depreciation expense of $12,000 on buildings and $23,100 on equipment, and amortization expense of $4,800)		470,000
Operating income		$ 260,000
Other income (expenses)		
Interest expense	($ 55,000)	
Dividend income	3,400	
Gain on sale of investments	12,500	
Loss on disposal of equipment	(2,300)	(41,400)
Income before income taxes		$ 218,600
Income taxes		52,200
Net income		$ 166,400

Northwest Corporation
Comparative Balance Sheets
December 31, 20x5 and 20x4

	20x5	20x4	Change	Increase or Decrease
Assets				
Cash	$ 105,850	$ 121,850	($16,000)	Decrease
Accounts receivable (net)	296,000	314,500	(18,500)	Decrease
Inventory	322,000	301,000	21,000	Increase
Prepaid expenses	7,800	5,800	2,000	Increase
Long-term investments	36,000	86,000	(50,000)	Decrease
Land	150,000	125,000	25,000	Increase
Buildings	462,000	462,000	—	—
Accumulated depreciation, buildings	(91,000)	(79,000)	(12,000)	Increase
Equipment	159,730	167,230	(7,500)	Decrease
Accumulated depreciation, equipment	(43,400)	(45,600)	2,200	Decrease
Intangible assets	19,200	24,000	(4,800)	Decrease
Total assets	$1,424,180	$1,482,780	($58,600)	
Liabilities and Stockholders' Equity				
Accounts payable	$ 133,750	$ 233,750	($100,000)	Decrease
Notes payable (current)	75,700	145,700	(70,000)	Decrease
Accrued liabilities	5,000	—	5,000	Increase
Income taxes payable	20,000	—	20,000	Increase
Bonds payable	210,000	310,000	(100,000)	Decrease
Mortgage payable	330,000	350,000	(20,000)	Decrease
Common stock, $10 par value	400,000	340,000	60,000	Increase
Paid-in capital in excess of par value, common	90,000	50,000	40,000	Increase
Retained earnings	209,730	93,330	116,400	Increase
Treasury stock	(50,000)	(40,000)	(10,000)	Increase
Total liabilities and stockholders' equity	$1,424,180	$1,482,780	($ 58,600)	

The company's records for 20x5 provide the following additional information:

a. Long-term investments (available-for-sale securities) that cost $70,000 were sold at a gain of $12,500; additional long-term investments were made in the amount of $20,000.
b. Five acres of land to build a parking lot were purchased for $25,000.
c. Equipment that cost $37,500 with accumulated depreciation of $25,300 was sold at a loss of $2,300; new equipment costing $30,000 was purchased.
d. Notes payable in the amount of $100,000 were repaid; an additional $30,000 was borrowed by signing notes payable.
e. Bonds payable in the amount of $100,000 were converted into 6,000 shares of common stock.
f. The Mortgage Payable account was reduced by $20,000.
g. Cash dividends declared and paid were $50,000.
h. Treasury stock was purchased for $10,000.

REQUIRED
1. Prepare a statement of cash flows using the indirect method.
2. Compute cash flow yield, cash flows to sales, cash flows to assets, and free cash flow for 20x5.

ANSWER TO REVIEW PROBLEM

1. Statement of cash flows using the indirect method:

Northwest Corporation
Statement of Cash Flows
For the Year Ended December 31, 20x5

Cash flows from operating activities
Net income		$166,400
Adjustments to reconcile net income to net cash flows from operating activities		
Depreciation expense, buildings	$ 12,000	
Depreciation expense, equipment	23,100	
Amortization expense, intangible assets	4,800	
Gain on sale of investments	(12,500)	
Loss on disposal of equipment	2,300	
Changes in current assets and current liabilities		
Decrease in accounts receivable	18,500	
Increase in inventory	(21,000)	
Increase in prepaid expenses	(2,000)	
Decrease in accounts payable	(100,000)	
Increase in accrued liabilities	5,000	
Increase in income taxes payable	20,000	(49,800)
Net cash flows from operating activities		$116,600

Cash flows from investing activities
Sale of long-term investments	$ 82,500[a]	
Purchase of long-term investments	(20,000)	
Purchase of land	(25,000)	
Sale of equipment	9,900[b]	
Purchase of equipment	(30,000)	
Net cash flows from investing activities		17,400

Cash flows from financing activities
Repayment of notes payable	($100,000)	
Issuance of notes payable	30,000	
Reduction in mortgage	(20,000)	
Payment of dividends	(50,000)	
Purchase of treasury stock	(10,000)	
Net cash flows from financing activities		(150,000)

Net increase (decrease) in cash	($ 16,000)
Cash at beginning of year	121,850
Cash at end of year	$105,850

Schedule of Noncash Investing and Financing Transactions

Conversion of bonds payable into common stock	$100,000

[a] $70,000 + $12,500 (gain) = $82,500
[b] $37,500 − $25,300 = $12,200 (book value) − $2,300 (loss) = $9,900

2. Cash flow yield, cash flows to sales, cash flows to assets, and free cash flow for 20x5:

$$\text{Cash Flow Yield} = \frac{\$116,600}{\$166,400} = .7 \text{ times}$$

$$\text{Cash Flows to Sales} = \frac{\$116,600}{\$1,650,000} = 7.1\%$$

$$\text{Cash Flows to Assets} = \frac{\$116,600}{(\$1,424,180 + \$1,482,780) \div 2} = 8.0\%$$

$$\text{Free Cash Flow} = \$116,600 - \$50,000 - \$25,000 - \$30,000 + \$9,900$$
$$= \$21,500$$

Chapter Assignments

BUILDING YOUR KNOWLEDGE FOUNDATION

QUESTIONS

1. In the statement of cash flows, what does cash include?
2. To earn a return on cash on hand during 20x3, Sallas Corporation transferred $45,000 from its checking account to a money market account, purchased a $25,000 Treasury bill, and invested $35,000 in common stocks. How will each of these transactions affect the statement of cash flows?
3. What are the purposes of the statement of cash flows?
4. Why is the statement of cash flows needed when most of the information in it is available from a company's comparative balance sheets and income statement?
5. What are the three classifications of cash flows? Give some examples of each.
6. Why is it important to disclose certain noncash transactions? How should they be disclosed?
7. Define *cash-generating efficiency* and identify three ratios that measure it.
8. Define *free cash flow* and identify its components. What do *positive* and *negative* free cash flows mean?
9. What is the basic difference between the direct method and the indirect method of determining cash flows from operations?
10. In determining net cash flows from operating activities (assuming the indirect method is used), what are the effects on cash generated by the following items: (a) an increase in accounts receivable, (b) a decrease in inventory, (c) an increase in accounts payable, (d) a decrease in wages payable, (e) depreciation expense, and (f) amortization of patents?
11. In 20x1, Cell-Borne Corporation had a net loss of $12,000 but positive cash flows from operations of $9,000. What conditions might have caused this situation?
12. Glen Corporation has the following other income and expense items: interest expense, $12,000; interest income, $3,000; dividend income, $5,000; and loss on the retirement of bonds, $6,000. Where does each of these items appear on the statement of cash flows, or how does the item affect the statement?
13. What is the proper treatment on the statement of cash flows of a transaction in which a building that cost $50,000 with accumulated depreciation of $32,000 was sold at a loss of $5,000?
14. What is the proper treatment on the statement of cash flows of (a) a transaction in which buildings and land were purchased by the issuance of a mortgage for

$234,000 and (b) a conversion of $50,000 in bonds payable into 2,500 shares of $6 par value common stock?

Short Exercises

SE 1.
LO1 Classification of Cash Flow Transactions

Stahl Corporation engaged in the transactions listed below. Identify each as (a) an operating activity, (b) an investing activity, (c) a financing activity, (d) a noncash transaction, or (e) none of the above.

1. Sold land.
2. Declared and paid a cash dividend.
3. Paid interest.
4. Issued common stock for plant assets.
5. Issued preferred stock.
6. Borrowed cash on a bank loan.

SE 2.
LO2 Cash-Generating Efficiency Ratios and Free Cash Flow

In 20x5, Portillo Corporation had year-end assets of $550,000, net sales of $790,000, net income of $90,000, net cash flows from operating activities of $180,000, purchases of plant assets of $120,000, and sales of plant assets of $20,000, and it paid dividends of $40,000. In 20x4, year-end assets were $500,000. Calculate the cash-generating efficiency ratios of cash flow yield, cash flows to sales, and cash flows to assets. Also calculate free cash flow.

SE 3.
LO2 Cash-Generating Efficiency Ratios and Free Cash Flow

Examine the cash flow measures in part **2** of the review problem in this chapter. Discuss the meaning of these ratios.

SE 4.
LO3 Computing Cash Flows from Operating Activities: Indirect Method

Global Market Corporation had a net income of $33,000 during 20x4. During the year, the company had depreciation expense of $14,000. Accounts Receivable increased by $11,000, and Accounts Payable increased by $5,000. Those were the company's only current assets and current liabilities. Use the indirect method to determine net cash flows from operating activities.

SE 5.
LO3 Computing Cash Flows from Operating Activities: Indirect Method

During 20x4, Cheng Corporation had a net income of $72,000. Included on its income statement were depreciation expense of $8,000 and amortization expense of $900. During the year, Accounts Receivable decreased by $4,100, Inventories increased by $2,700, Prepaid Expenses decreased by $500, Accounts Payable decreased by $7,000, and Accrued Liabilities decreased by $850. Use the indirect method to determine net cash flows from operating activities.

SE 6.
LO4 Cash Flows from Investing Activities and Noncash Transactions

During 20x5, Okee Company purchased land for $750,000. It paid $250,000 in cash and signed a $500,000 mortgage for the rest. The company also sold a building that originally cost $180,000, on which it had $140,000 of accumulated depreciation, for $190,000 cash, making a gain of $150,000. Prepare the cash flows from investing activities and schedule of noncash investing and financing transactions sections of the statement of cash flows.

SE 7.
LO5 Cash Flows from Financing Activities

During 20x4, Dakota Company issued $1,000,000 in long-term bonds at 96, repaid $150,000 of bonds at face value, paid interest of $80,000, and paid dividends of $50,000. Prepare the cash flows from the financing activities section of the statement of cash flows.

SE 8.
LO1
LO3
LO4
LO5
Identifying Components of the Statement of Cash Flows

Assuming the indirect method is used to prepare the statement of cash flows, tell whether each of the following items would appear (a) in cash flows from operating activities, (b) in cash flows from investing activities, (c) in cash flows from financing activities, (d) in the schedule of noncash investing and financing transactions, or (e) not on the statement of cash flows at all:

1. Dividends paid
2. Cash receipts from sales
3. Decrease in accounts receivable
4. Sale of plant assets
5. Gain on sale of investment
6. Issue of stock for plant assets
7. Issue of common stock
8. Net income

EXERCISES

E 1.
LO1 Classification of Cash Flow Transactions

Trout Corporation engaged in the transactions listed below. Identify each transaction as (a) an operating activity, (b) an investing activity, (c) a financing activity, (d) a noncash transaction, or (e) not on the statement of cash flows. (Assume the indirect method is used.)

1. Declared and paid a cash dividend.
2. Purchased a long-term investment.
3. Increased accounts receivable.
4. Paid interest.
5. Sold equipment at a loss.
6. Issued long-term bonds for plant assets.
7. Increased dividends receivable on securities held.
8. Issued common stock.
9. Declared and issued a stock dividend.
10. Repaid notes payable.
11. Decreased wages payable.
12. Purchased a 60-day Treasury bill.
13. Purchased land.

E 2.
LO2 Cash-Generating Efficiency Ratios and Free Cash Flow

In 20x5, Ignatz Corporation had year-end assets of $4,800,000, net sales of $6,600,000, net income of $560,000, net cash flows from operating activities of $780,000, dividends of $240,000, and net capital expenditures of $820,000. In 20x4, year-end assets were $4,200,000.

Calculate the cash-generating efficiency ratios of cash flow yield, cash flows to sales, and cash flows to assets. Also calculate free cash flow.

E 3.
LO3 Cash Flows from Operating Activities: Indirect Method

The condensed single-step income statement for the year ended December 31, 20x4, of Gro-More Chem Company, a distributor of farm fertilizers and herbicides, appears as follows:

Sales		$6,500,000
Less: Cost of goods sold	$3,800,000	
Operating expenses (including depreciation of $410,000)	1,900,000	
Income taxes	200,000	5,900,000
Net income		$ 600,000

Selected accounts from Gro-More Chem Company's balance sheets for 20x4 and 20x3 are as follows:

	20x4	20x3
Accounts receivable, net	$1,200,000	$850,000
Inventory	420,000	510,000
Prepaid expenses	130,000	90,000
Accounts payable	480,000	360,000
Accrued liabilities	30,000	50,000
Income taxes payable	70,000	60,000

Present in good form a schedule of cash flows from operating activities using the indirect method.

E 4.
LO3 Computing Cash Flows from Operating Activities: Indirect Method

During 20x5, Germaine Corporation had net income of $41,000. Included on its income statement were depreciation expense of $2,300 and amortization expense of $300. During the year, Accounts Receivable increased by $3,400, Inventories decreased by $1,900, Prepaid Expenses decreased by $200, Accounts Payable increased by $5,000, and Accrued Liabilities decreased by $450. Determine net cash flows from operating activities using the indirect method.

E 5.
LO3 Preparing a Schedule of Cash Flows from Operating Activities: Indirect Method

For the year ended June 30, 20xx, net income for Pine Corporation was $7,400. Depreciation expense was $2,000. During the year, Accounts Receivable increased by $4,400, Inventories increased by $7,000, Prepaid Rent decreased by $1,400, Accounts Payable increased by $14,000, Salaries Payable increased by $1,000, and Income Taxes Payable decreased by $600. Use the indirect method to prepare a schedule of cash flows from operating activities.

LO4 **E 6.** FBR Company's T account for long-term available-for-sale investments at the end of 20x3 is as follows:

Computing Cash Flows from Investing Activities: Investments

Investments			
Beg. Bal.	38,000	Sales	39,000
Purchases	58,000		
End Bal.	57,000		

In addition, FBR's income statement shows a loss on the sale of investments of $6,500. Compute the amounts to be shown as cash flows from investing activities and show how they are to appear in the statement of cash flows.

LO4 **E 7.** The T accounts for plant assets and accumulated depreciation for FBR Company at the end of 20x3 are as follows:

Computing Cash Flows from Investing Activities: Plant Assets

Plant Assets				Accumulated Depreciation			
Beg. Bal.	65,000	Disposals	23,000	Disposals	14,700	Beg. Bal.	34,500
Purchases	33,600					Depreciation	10,200
End. Bal.	75,600					End. Bal.	30,000

In addition, FBR Company's income statement shows a gain on sale of plant assets of $4,400. Compute the amounts to be shown as cash flows from investing activities and show how they are to appear on the statement of cash flows.

LO4 **E 8.** All transactions involving Notes Payable and related accounts of Wix Company during 20x4 are as follows:

LO5 **Determining Cash Flows from Investing and Financing Activities**

Cash	18,000	
Notes Payable		18,000
Bank loan		
Patent	30,000	
Notes Payable		30,000
Purchase of patent by issuing note payable		
Notes Payable	5,000	
Interest Expense	500	
Cash		5,500
Repayment of note payable at maturity		

Determine the amounts of the transactions affecting financing activities and show how they are to appear on the statement of cash flows for 20x4.

LO3 **E 9.** Margol Corporation's 20x5 income statement appears below. Its comparative balance sheets for June 30, 20x5 and 20x4 are on the next page.

LO4 **Preparing the Statement of Cash Flows: Indirect Method**

LO5

Margol Corporation
Income Statement
For the Year Ended June 30, 20x5

Sales		$468,000
Cost of goods sold		312,000
Gross margin		$156,000
Operating expenses		90,000
Operating income		$ 66,000
Interest expense		5,600
Income before income taxes		$ 60,400
Income taxes		24,600
Net income		$ 35,800

Margol Corporation
Comparative Balance Sheets
June 30, 20x5 and 20x4

	20x5	20x4
Assets		
Cash	$139,800	$ 25,000
Accounts receivable (net)	42,000	52,000
Inventory	86,800	96,800
Prepaid expenses	6,400	5,200
Furniture	110,000	120,000
Accumulated depreciation, furniture	(18,000)	(10,000)
Total assets	$367,000	$289,000
Liabilities and Stockholders' Equity		
Accounts payable	$ 26,000	$ 28,000
Income taxes payable	2,400	3,600
Notes payable (long-term)	74,000	70,000
Common stock, $10 par value	230,000	180,000
Retained earnings	34,600	7,400
Total liabilities and stockholders' equity	$367,000	$289,000

The following information is also available: The company issued a $44,000 note payable for purchase of furniture; sold furniture that cost $54,000 with accumulated depreciation of $30,600 at carrying value; recorded depreciation on the furniture during the year, $38,600; repaid a note in the amount of $40,000; issued $50,000 of common stock at par value; and declared and paid dividends of $8,600.

Prepare Margol Corporation's statement of cash flows for the year 20x5 using the indirect method.

PROBLEMS

P 1.

LO1 Classification of Cash Flow Transactions

Analyze each transaction listed in the table that follows and place X's in the appropriate columns to indicate the transaction's classification and its effect on cash flows using the indirect method.

Transaction	Operating Activity	Investing Activity	Financing Activity	Noncash Transaction	Increase	Decrease	No Effect
	Cash Flow Classification				Effect on Cash Flows		
1. Incurred a net loss.							
2. Declared and issued a stock dividend.							
3. Paid a cash dividend.							
4. Decreased accounts receivable.							
5. Increased inventory.							
6. Retired long-term debt with cash.							
7. Sold available-for-sale securities at a loss.							
8. Issued stock for equipment.							
9. Decreased prepaid insurance.							
10. Purchased treasury stock with cash.							
11. Retired a fully depreciated truck (no gain or loss).							
12. Increased interest payable.							
13. Decreased dividends receivable on investment.							
14. Sold treasury stock.							
15. Increased income taxes payable.							
16. Transferred cash to money market account.							
17. Purchased land and building with a mortgage.							

P 2.

LO2 Statement of Cash Flows:
LO3 Indirect Method
LO4
LO5

Maron Corporation's comparative balance sheets as of December 31, 20x5 and 20x4 and its income statement for the year ended December 31, 20x5 are presented on the next page.

During 20x5, Maron Corporation sold furniture and fixtures that cost $35,600, on which it had accumulated depreciation of $28,800, at a gain of $7,000. The corporation also purchased furniture and fixtures in the amount of $39,600; paid a $20,000 note payable and borrowed $40,000 on a new note; converted bonds payable in the amount of $100,000 into 2,000 shares of common stock; and declared and paid $6,000 in cash dividends.

REQUIRED 1. Using the indirect method, prepare a statement of cash flows for Maron Corporation. Include a supporting schedule of noncash investing and financing transactions.

Maron Corporation
Comparative Balance Sheets
December 31, 20x5 and 20x4

	20x5	20x4
Assets		
Cash	$164,800	$ 50,000
Accounts receivable (net)	165,200	200,000
Merchandise inventory	350,000	450,000
Prepaid rent	2,000	3,000
Furniture and fixtures	148,000	144,000
Accumulated depreciation, furniture and fixtures	(42,000)	(24,000)
Total assets	$788,000	$823,000
Liabilities and Stockholders' Equity		
Accounts payable	$143,400	$200,400
Income taxes payable	1,400	4,400
Notes payable (long-term)	40,000	20,000
Bonds payable	100,000	200,000
Common stock, $20 par value	240,000	200,000
Paid-in capital in excess of par value, common	181,440	121,440
Retained earnings	81,760	76,760
Total liabilities and stockholders' equity	$788,000	$823,000

Maron Corporation
Income Statement
For the Year Ended December 31, 20x5

Net sales		$1,609,000
Cost of goods sold		1,127,800
Gross margin		$ 481,200
Operating expenses (including depreciation expense of $46,800)		449,400
Income from operations		$ 31,800
Other income (expenses)		
Gain on sale of furniture and fixtures	$ 7,000	
Interest expense	(23,200)	(16,200)
Income before income taxes		$ 15,600
Income taxes		4,600
Net income		$ 11,000

2. What are the primary reasons for Maron Corporation's large increase in cash from 20x4 to 20x5, despite its low net income?
3. Compute and assess cash flow yield and free cash flow for 20x5.

LO2 **Statement of Cash Flows:**
LO3 **Indirect Method**
LO4
LO5

P 3. The comparative balance sheets for Pierre Fabrics, Inc., for December 31, 20x5, and 20x4 appear below.

Pierre Fabrics, Inc.
Comparative Balance Sheets
December 31, 20x5 and 20x4

	20x5	20x4
Assets		
Cash	$ 38,560	$ 27,360
Accounts receivable (net)	102,430	75,430
Inventory	112,890	137,890
Prepaid expenses	—	20,000
Land	25,000	—
Building	137,000	—
Accumulated depreciation, building	(15,000)	—
Equipment	33,000	34,000
Accumulated depreciation, equipment	(14,500)	(24,000)
Patents	4,000	6,000
Total assets	$423,380	$276,680
Liabilities and Stockholders' Equity		
Accounts payable	$ 10,750	$ 36,750
Notes payable (current)	10,000	—
Accrued liabilities	—	12,300
Mortgage payable	162,000	—
Common stock, $10 par value	180,000	150,000
Paid-in capital in excess of par value, common	57,200	37,200
Retained earnings	3,430	40,430
Total liabilities and stockholders' equity	$423,380	$276,680

Additional information about Pierre Fabrics' operations during 20x5 is as follows: net loss, $28,000; building and equipment depreciation expense amounts, $15,000 and $3,000, respectively; equipment that cost $13,500 with accumulated depreciation of $12,500 sold for a gain of $5,300; equipment purchases, $12,500; patent amortization, $3,000; purchase of patent, $1,000; funds borrowed by issuing notes payable, $25,000; notes payable repaid, $15,000; land and building purchased for $162,000 by signing a mortgage for the total cost; 3,000 shares of $10 par value common stock issued for a total of $50,000; and cash dividend paid, $9,000.

REQUIRED
1. Using the indirect method, prepare a statement of cash flows for Pierre Fabrics, Inc.
2. Why did Pierre Fabrics have an increase in cash in a year in which it recorded a net loss of $28,000? Discuss and interpret.
3. Compute and assess cash flow yield and free cash flow for 20x5.

P 4.
LO2 **Statement of Cash Flows:**
LO3 **Indirect Method**
LO4
LO5

The comparative balance sheets for Maggio Masonry, Inc., for December 31, 20x5 and 20x4 are presented on the next page. During 20x5, the company had net income of $96,000 and building and equipment depreciation expenses of $80,000 and $60,000, respectively. It amortized intangible assets in the amount of $20,000; purchased

Maggio Masonry, Inc.
Comparative Balance Sheets
December 31, 20x5 and 20x4

	20x5	20x4
Assets		
Cash	$ 257,600	$ 305,600
Accounts receivable (net)	738,800	758,800
Inventory	960,000	800,000
Prepaid expenses	14,800	26,800
Long-term investments	440,000	440,000
Land	361,200	321,200
Building	1,200,000	920,000
Accumulated depreciation, building	(240,000)	(160,000)
Equipment	480,000	480,000
Accumulated depreciation, equipment	(116,000)	(56,000)
Intangible assets	20,000	40,000
Total assets	$4,116,400	$3,876,400
Liabilities and Stockholders' Equity		
Accounts payable	$ 470,800	$ 660,800
Notes payable (current)	40,000	160,000
Accrued liabilities	10,800	20,800
Mortgage payable	1,080,000	800,000
Bonds payable	1,000,000	760,000
Common stock	1,300,000	1,300,000
Paid-in capital in excess of par value, common	80,000	80,000
Retained earnings	254,800	194,800
Treasury stock	(120,000)	(100,000)
Total liabilities and stockholders' equity	$4,116,400	$3,876,400

investments for $116,000; sold investments for $150,000, on which it recorded a gain of $34,000; issued $240,000 of long-term bonds at face value; purchased a warehouse and land through a $320,000 mortgage; paid $40,000 to reduce the mortgage; borrowed $60,000 by issuing notes payable; repaid notes payable in the amount of $180,000; declared and paid cash dividends in the amount of $36,000; and purchased treasury stock in the amount of $20,000.

REQUIRED
1. Using the indirect method, prepare a statement of cash flows for Maggio Masonry, Inc.
2. Why did Maggio Masonry experience a decrease in cash in a year in which it had a net income of $96,000? Discuss and interpret.
3. Compute and assess cash flow yield and free cash flow for 20x5.

ALTERNATE PROBLEMS

P 5.

Analyze each transaction listed in the table that follows and place X's in the appropriate columns to indicate the transaction's classification and its effect on cash flows using the indirect method.

	Cash Flow Classification				Effect on Cash Flows		
Transaction	Operating Activity	Investing Activity	Financing Activity	Noncash Transaction	Increase	Decrease	No Effect
1. Earned a net income.							
2. Declared and paid a cash dividend.							
3. Issued stock for cash.							
4. Retired long-term debt by issuing stock.							
5. Increased accounts payable.							
6. Decreased inventory.							
7. Increased prepaid insurance.							
8. Purchased a long-term investment with cash.							
9. Sold trading securities at a gain.							
10. Sold a machine at a loss.							
11. Retired fully depreciated equipment.							
12. Decreased interest payable.							
13. Purchased available-for-sale securities (long-term).							
14. Decreased dividends receivable.							
15. Decreased accounts receivable.							
16. Converted bonds to common stock.							
17. Purchased 90-day Treasury bill.							

P 6. Sulyat Corporation's income statement for 20x7 appears below.

LO2 Statement of Cash Flows:
LO3 Indirect Method
LO4
LO5

Sulyat Corporation
Income Statement
For the Year Ended June 30, 20x7

Net sales		$1,040,900
Cost of goods sold		656,300
Gross margin		$ 384,600
Operating expenses (including depreciation expense of $60,000)		189,200
Income from operations		$ 195,400
Other income (expenses)		
Loss on sale of equipment	($ 4,000)	
Interest expense	(37,600)	(41,600)
Income before income taxes		$ 153,800
Income taxes		34,200
Net income		$ 119,600

Sulyat Corporation's comparative balance sheets as of June 30, 20x7 and 20x6 are as follows:

Sulyat Corporation
Comparative Balance Sheets
June 30, 20x7 and 20x6

	20x7	20x6
Assets		
Cash	$167,000	$ 20,000
Accounts receivable (net)	100,000	120,000
Inventory	180,000	220,000
Prepaid expenses	600	1,000
Property, plant, and equipment	628,000	552,000
Accumulated depreciation, property, plant, and equipment	(183,000)	(140,000)
Total assets	$892,600	$773,000
Liabilities and Stockholders' Equity		
Accounts payable	$ 64,000	$ 42,000
Notes payable (due in 90 days)	30,000	80,000
Income taxes payable	26,000	18,000
Mortgage payable	360,000	280,000
Common stock, $5 par value	200,000	200,000
Retained earnings	212,600	153,000
Total liabilities and stockholders' equity	$892,600	$773,000

During 20x7, Sulyat Corporation sold equipment that cost $24,000, on which it had accumulated depreciation of $17,000, at a loss of $4,000. The corporation also purchased land and a building for $100,000 through an increase of $100,000 in Mortgage Payable; made a $20,000 payment on the mortgage; repaid notes of $80,000 but borrowed an additional $30,000 through the issuance of a new note payable; and declared and paid a $60,000 cash dividend.

REQUIRED

1. Using the indirect method, prepare a statement of cash flows. Include a supporting schedule of noncash investing and financing transactions.
2. What are the primary reasons for Sulyat Corporation's large increase in cash from 20x6 to 20x7?
3. Compute and assess cash flow yield and free cash flow for 20x7.

P 7.

LO2 **Statement of Cash Flows:**
LO3 **Indirect Method**
LO4
LO5

The comparative balance sheets for Fernandez Fashions, Inc., for December 31, 20x6 and 20x5 appear on the next page. Additional information about Fernandez Fashions' operations during 20x6 is as follows: net income, $56,000; building and equipment depreciation expense amounts, $30,000 and $6,000, respectively; equipment that cost $27,000 with accumulated depreciation of $25,000 sold at a gain of $10,600; equipment purchases, $25,000; patent amortization, $6,000; purchase of patent, $2,000; funds borrowed by issuing notes payable, $50,000; notes payable repaid, $30,000; land and building purchased for $324,000 by signing a mortgage for the total cost; 3,000 shares of $20 par value common stock issued for a total of $100,000; cash dividend paid $18,000; and treasury stock purchased, $15,000.

Fernandez Fashions, Inc.
Comparative Balance Sheets
December 31, 20x6 and 20x5

	20x6	20x5
Assets		
Cash	$174,120	$ 54,720
Accounts receivable (net)	204,860	150,860
Inventory	225,780	275,780
Prepaid expenses	—	40,000
Land	50,000	—
Building	274,000	—
Accumulated depreciation, building	(30,000)	—
Equipment	66,000	68,000
Accumulated depreciation, equipment	(29,000)	(48,000)
Patents	8,000	12,000
Total assets	$943,760	$553,360
Liabilities and Stockholders' Equity		
Accounts payable	$ 21,500	$ 73,500
Notes payable	20,000	—
Accrued liabilities (current)	—	24,600
Mortgage payable	324,000	—
Common stock, $20 par value	370,000	310,000
Paid-in capital in excess of par value, common	114,400	74,400
Retained earnings	118,860	80,860
Treasury stock	(25,000)	(10,000)
Total liabilities and stockholders' equity	$943,760	$553,360

REQUIRED
1. Using the indirect method, prepare a statement of cash flows for Fernandez Fashions, Inc.
2. Why did Fernandez Fashions have an increase in cash of $119,400 when it recorded net income of $56,000? Discuss and interpret.
3. Compute and assess cash flow yield and free cash flow for 20x6.

SKILLS DEVELOPMENT CASES

Conceptual Analysis

SD 1.
LO1 **EBITDA and the Statement of**
LO3 **Cash Flows**

When Fleetwood Enterprises, Inc. <www.fleetwood.com>, a large producer of recreational vehicles and manufactured housing, warned that it might not be able to generate enough cash to satisfy debt requirements and avoid default of a loan agreement, its cash flow, defined in the financial press as "EBITDA" (earnings before interest, taxes, depreciation, and amortization), was a negative $2.7 million. The company would have had to generate $17.7 million in the next accounting period to comply with the loan terms.[11] To what section of the statement of cash flows does EBITDA most closely relate? Is EBITDA a good approximation for this section of the statement of cash flows?

Explain your answer, which should include an identification of the major differences between EBITDA and the section of the statement of cash flows you chose.

Ethical Dilemma

LO1 Ethics and Cash Flow Classifications

SD 2. Chemical Waste Treatment, Inc., a fast-growing company that disposes of chemical wastes, has an $800,000 line of credit at its bank. One section in the credit agreement says that the ratio of cash flows from operations to interest expense must exceed 3.0. If this ratio falls below 3.0, the company must reduce the balance outstanding on its line of credit to one-half the total line if the funds borrowed against the line of credit exceed one-half of the total line.

After the end of the fiscal year, the company's controller informs the president: "We will not meet the ratio requirements on our line of credit in 20x5 because interest expense was $1.2 million and cash flows from operations were $3.2 million. Also, we have borrowed 100 percent of our line of credit. We do not have the cash to reduce the credit line by $400,000." The president says, "This is a serious situation. To pay our ongoing bills, we need our bank to increase our line of credit, not decrease it. What can we do?" "Do you recall the $500,000 two-year note payable for equipment?" replied the controller. "It is now classified as 'Proceeds from Notes Payable' in cash flows provided from financing activities in the statement of cash flows. If we move it to cash flows from operations and call it 'Increase in Payables,' it would increase cash flows from operations to $3.7 million and put us over the limit." "Well, do it," ordered the president. "It surely doesn't make any difference where it is on the statement. It is an increase in both places. It would be much worse for our company in the long term if we failed to meet this ratio requirement."

What is your opinion of the president's reasoning? Is the president's order ethical? Who benefits and who is harmed if the controller follows the president's order? What are management's alternatives? What would you do?

 Group Activity. Assign in-class groups to develop a position in support of or against the president's reasoning and have them defend that position in a debate.

Research Activity

LO1 Basic Research Skills
LO2

SD 3. Find the statement of cash flows in the annual reports of three corporations, using sources in your library or the Fingraph® Financial Analyst™ CD-ROM software that accompanies this text. You may choose corporations from the same industry or at random, at the direction of your instructor. (If you did a Research Activity in a previous chapter, use the same three companies.)

For any year covered by these companies' statements of cash flows, answer the following questions: Does the company use the direct or the indirect method? Is its net income more or less than its net cash flows from operating activities? What are the major causes of differences between net income and net cash flows from operating activities? Compute cash flow efficiency ratios and free cash flow for each company. Does the dividend appear secure? Did the company make significant capital expenditures during the year? How did the company finance the expenditures? Do you notice anything unusual about the investing and financing activities of these three companies? Do the investing and financing activities provide any insights into management's plan for each company? If so, what are they?

Be prepared to discuss your findings in class.

Decision-Making Practice

LO2 Analysis of Cash Flow Difficulty
LO3
LO4
LO5

SD 4. Lou Klein, certified public accountant, has just given his employer May Hashimi, the president of Hashimi Print Gallery, Inc., the income statement that appears at the top of the next page.

Hashimi Print Gallery, Inc.
Income Statement
For the Year Ended December 31, 20x4

Net sales	$884,000
Cost of goods sold	508,000
Gross margin	$376,000
Operating expenses (including depreciation expense of $20,000)	204,000
Operating income	$172,000
Interest expense	24,000
Income before income taxes	$148,000
Income taxes	28,000
Net income	$120,000

After examining the statement, Hashimi said to Klein, "Lou, the statement seems to be well done, but what I need to know is why I don't have enough cash to pay my bills this month. You show that I earned $120,000 in 20x4, but I have only $24,000 in the bank. I know I bought a building on a mortgage and paid a cash dividend of $48,000, but what else is going on?" Klein replied, "To answer your question, we have to look at comparative balance sheets and prepare another type of statement. Take a look at these balance sheets." The statement handed to Hashimi follows.

Hashimi Print Gallery, Inc.
Comparative Balance Sheets
December 31, 20x4 and 20x3

	20x4	20x3
Assets		
Cash	$ 24,000	$ 40,000
Accounts receivable (net)	178,000	146,000
Inventory	240,000	180,000
Prepaid expenses	10,000	14,000
Building	400,000	—
Accumulated depreciation	(20,000)	—
Total assets	$832,000	$380,000
Liabilities and Stockholders' Equity		
Accounts payable	$ 74,000	$ 96,000
Income taxes payable	6,000	4,000
Mortgage payable	400,000	—
Common stock	200,000	200,000
Retained earnings	152,000	80,000
Total liabilities and stockholders' equity	$832,000	$380,000

1. To what statement is Klein referring? From the information given, prepare the additional statement using the indirect method.
2. Hashimi Print Gallery, Inc., has a cash problem despite profitable operations. Why is this the case?

FINANCIAL REPORTING AND ANALYSIS CASES

Interpreting Financial Reports

FRA 1.
LO2 Anatomy of a Disaster

On October 16, 2001, Kenneth Lay, chairman and CEO of Enron Corporation <www.enron.com>, announced the company's earnings for the first nine months of 2001 as follows:

> Our 26 percent increase in recurring earnings per diluted share shows the very strong results of our core wholesale and retail energy businesses and our natural gas pipelines. The continued excellent prospects in these businesses and Enron's leading market position make us very confident in our strong earnings outlook.[12]

Less than six months later, the company filed for the biggest bankruptcy in U.S. history. Its stock dropped to less than $1 per share, and a major financial scandal was underway. Presented on the opposite page is Enron's statement of cash flows for the first nine months of 2001 and 2000 (restated to correct the previous accounting errors). Assume you report to an investment analyst who has asked you to analyze this statement for clues as to why the company went under.

1. For the two time periods shown, compute the cash-generating efficiency ratios of cash flow yield, cash flows to sales (Enron's revenues were $133,762 million in 2001 and $55,494 million in 2000), and cash flows to assets (use total assets of $61,783 million for 2001 and $64,926 million for 2000). Also compute free cash flows for the two years.
2. Prepare a memorandum to the investment analyst that assesses Enron's cash-generating efficiency in light of the chairman's remarks and that evaluates its available free cash flow, taking into account its financing activities. Identify significant changes in operating items and any special operating items that should be considered. Include your computations as an attachment.

International Company

FRA 2.
LO2 Cash-Generating Efficiency Ratios and Free Cash Flow

The following data pertain to two of Japan's best-known and most successful companies, Sony Corporation <www.sony.com> and Canon, Inc. <www.canon.com>.[13] (Numbers are in billions of yen.)

	Sony Corporation		Canon, Inc.	
	2000	1999	2000	1999
Net sales	¥6,238	¥6,415	¥2,781	¥2,622
Net income	122	179	134	70
Average total assets	6,579	6,351	2,711	2,658
Net cash flows from operating activities	597	663	347	309
Dividends	21	25	15	15
Net capital expenditures	374	340	165	194

Calculate the ratios of cash flow yield, cash flows to sales, and cash flows to assets, as well as free cash flow, for the two years for both Sony Corporation and Canon, Inc.

Enron Corporation
Statement of Cash Flows
For the Nine Months Ending September 30, 2001 and 2002

	2001	2000
	(In millions)	
Cash Flows from Operating Activities		
Reconciliation of net income to net cash provided by operating activities		
Net income	$ 225	$ 797
Cumulative effect of accounting changes, net of tax	(19)	0
Depreciation, depletion and amortization	746	617
Deferred income taxes	(134)	8
Gains on sales of non-trading assets	(49)	(135)
Investment losses	768	0
Changes in components of working capital		
Receivables	987	(3,363)
Inventories	1	339
Payables	(1,764)	2,899
Other	464	(455)
Trading investments		
Net margin deposit activity	(2,349)	541
Other trading activities	173	(555)
Other, net	198	(566)
Net Cash Provided by (Used in) Operating Activities	$ (753)	$ 127
Cash Flows from Investing Activities		
Capital expenditures	(1,584)	(1,539)
Equity investments	(1,172)	(858)
Proceeds from sales of non-trading investments	1,711	222
Acquisition of subsidiary stock	0	(485)
Business acquisitions, net of cash acquired	(82)	(773)
Other investing activities	(239)	(147)
Net Cash Used in Investing Activities	$(1,366)	$(3,580)
Cash Flows from Financing Activities		
Issuance of long-term debt	4,060	2,725
Repayment of long-term debt	(3,903)	(579)
Net increase in short-term borrowings	2,365	1,694
Issuance of common stock	199	182
Net redemption of company-obligated preferred securities of subsidiaries	0	(95)
Dividends paid	(394)	(396)
Net (acquisition) disposition of treasury stock	(398)	354
Other financing activities	(49)	(12)
Net Cash Provided by Financing Activities	$ 1,880	$ 3,873
Increase (Decrease) in Cash and Cash Equivalents	$ (239)	$ 420
Cash and Cash Equivalents, Beginning of Period	1,240	333
Cash and Cash Equivalents, End of Period	$ 1,001	$ 753

Source: Adapted from Enron Corporation, SEC filings, 2001.

Toys "R" Us Annual Report

LO1 Analysis of the Statement of
LO2 Cash Flows
LO3
LO4
LO5

FRA 3. Refer to the statement of cash flows in the Toys "R" Us <www.tru.com> annual report to answer the following questions:

1. Does Toys "R" Us use the indirect method of reporting cash flows from operating activities? Other than net earnings, what are the most important factors affecting the company's cash flows from operating activities? Explain the trend of each of these factors.
2. Based on the cash flows from investing activities, would you say that Toys "R" Us is a contracting or an expanding company? Explain.
3. Has Toys "R" Us used external financing? If so, where did it come from?

Comparison Case: Toys "R" Us and Walgreen Co.

LO2 Cash Flows Analysis

FRA 4. Refer to the annual report of Toys "R" Us <www.tru.com> and the financial statements of Walgreens <www.walgreens.com> in the Supplement to Chapter 1. Calculate for two years each company's cash flow yield, cash flows to sales ratio, cash flows to assets ratio, and free cash flows. In 2000, Walgreens' total assets were $7,103,700,000. Discuss and compare the trends of the cash-generating ability of both Toys "R" Us and Walgreens. Comment on each company's change in cash and cash equivalents over the two-year period.

Fingraph® Financial Analyst™

LO2 Cash Flow Analysis
LO3
LO4
LO5

FRA 5. Choose any two companies in the same industry from the list of Fingraph companies on the Needles Accounting Resource Center Web Site at **http://accounting.college.hmco.com/students**. Access the Microsoft Excel spreadsheets for the companies you selected. Click on the URL at the top of each company's spreadsheet for a link to the company's web site and annual report.

1. In the annual reports of the companies you have selected, find the statement of cash flows. Do the companies use the direct or indirect method of preparing the statement?
2. Using the Fingraph CD-ROM software, display and print in tabular and graphic form the Statement of Cash Flows: Operating Activities Analysis page. Prepare a table that compares the cash flow yield, cash flows to sales, and cash flows to assets ratios for both companies for two years. Are the ratios moving in the same direction or opposite ones? Study the operating activities sections of the statements to determine the main causes of differences between the net income and cash flows from operations. How do the companies compare?
3. Using the Fingraph CD-ROM software, display and print in tabular and graphic form the Statement of Cash Flows: Investing and Financing Activities Analysis page. Prepare a table that compares the free cash flow for both companies for two years. How do the companies compare? Are the companies growing or contracting? Study the investing and financing activities sections of the statements to determine the main causes of differences between the companies.
4. Find and read references to cash flows in the liquidity analysis section of management's discussion and analysis in each annual report.
5. Write a one-page executive summary that reports your findings from parts **1–4**, including your assessment of the companies' comparative liquidity. Include the Fingraph pages and your tables with your report.

Internet Case

FRA 6.
LO2 Follow-up Analysis of Cash Flows

Go to Marriott International's web site <www.marriott.com> and find the statement of cash flows in the company's latest annual report. Compare it with the 2002 statement at the beginning of this chapter by (1) identifying major changes in operating, investing, and financing activities; (2) reading management's financial review of cash flows; and (3) calculating the cash flow ratios (cash flow yield, cash flows to sales, cash flows to assets) and free cash flow for the most recent year. How does Marriott's cash flow performance differ between these two years? Be prepared to discuss your conclusions in class.

15

Chapter 15 describes the approaches that businesses have developed to meet the challenges of today's changing business environment and the role that management accounting plays in meeting those challenges.

The Changing Business Environment: A Manager's Perspective

LEARNING OBJECTIVES

LO1 Distinguish management accounting from financial accounting and explain the role of management accounting in the management cycle.

LO2 Describe the value chain and its usefulness in analyzing a business.

LO3 Identify the management tools used for continuous improvement and describe how they work to meet the demands of global competition and how management accounting supports them.

LO4 Explain the balanced scorecard and its relationship to performance measures.

LO5 Prepare an analysis of nonfinancial data.

LO6 Identify the standards of ethical conduct for management accountants.

DECISION POINT

A MANAGER'S FOCUS

Honda Motor Company <www.honda.com> If organizations are to prosper, they must identify the factors that are critical to their success. Key success factors include satisfying customer needs, developing efficient manufacturing processes and advanced technologies, and being a leader in marketing innovative products. Honda Motor Company had all these factors in mind when it introduced a "green car" called the Insight to the U.S. market. Like other green cars, the Insight is a hybrid vehicle, running on both a gasoline engine and an electric motor. Priced at less than $20,000, it gets more than 60 miles to the gallon. The Insight thus meets regulators' demands for vehicles that emit fewer air-polluting fumes and consumers' demands for inexpensive, practical transportation.[1]

Using new technology and innovative design to address both customers' needs and environmental concerns is just part of Honda's strategy to stay agile, flexible, and ahead of its competitors. Equally important to Honda's success is the development of efficient manufacturing operations.[2] The company is standardizing manufacturing tools and eliminating the need to modify its assembly lines. Its model-specific subassembly lines will feed their products to a new and shorter assembly line.

All these innovations demonstrate Honda's resolve to remain an industry leader. What role does management accounting play in this endeavor?

Management accounting provides the information necessary for effective decision making. Honda's managers use management accounting information in

What managment accounting tools does Honda utilize to stay ahead of its competitors?

making decisions about everything from buying materials to developing and implementing new production processes to pricing, marketing, and distributing vehicles. Management accounting also provides Honda's managers with objective data by which they can measure the company's performance in terms of its key success factors. Among the tools of management accounting are budgets, which set daily operating goals for workers and provide targets for evaluating the workers' performance. Performance measures for the production process may include the time to complete one cycle of the process, the number of setups, and the time to rework errors in production. Performance measures of customer satisfaction may include number of customer complaints, number of service change notices, and number of customer referrals. As Honda strives to improve its products and maintain its record of success with vehicles like the Insight, it will continue to rely on the information that management accounting provides.

The Role of Management Accounting

LO1 Distinguish management accounting from financial accounting and explain the role of management accounting in the management cycle.

RELATED TEXT ASSIGNMENTS
Q: 1, 2, 3, 4, 5, 6, 7, 8
SE: 1, 2, 3, 4
E: 1, 2, 3, 4, 5
P: 1, 6
SD: 5
MRA: 1, 2

◆ **STOP AND THINK!**
A financial report often contains estimates and projections. How does the writer of such a report make sure the reader understands the uncertainties involved?

The writer should include a clear statement of the assumptions underlying the report and the conditions under which the estimates and projections were made. This will enable the reader to assess how valid the estimates and projections are. ■

To plan and control an organization's operations, to measure its performance, and to make decisions about pricing products or services and many other matters, managers need accurate and timely accounting information. To do their jobs efficiently, employees who handle daily operations, such as managing the flow of materials into a production system, also rely on accurate and timely accounting information. The role of management accounting is to provide an information system that enables persons throughout an organization to make informed decisions, to be more effective at their jobs, and to improve the organization's performance.

The need for management accounting information exists regardless of the type of organization—manufacturing, retail, service, or governmental—or its size. Although multidivisional corporations need more information and more complex accounting systems than small ones, even small businesses need certain types of management accounting information to ensure efficient operating conditions. The precise type of information needed depends on an organization's goals and the nature of its operations.

In 1982, the Institute of Management Accountants (IMA) defined **management accounting** as

> the process of identification, measurement, accumulation, analysis, preparation, interpretation, and communication of financial information used by management to plan, evaluate, and control within the organization and to assure appropriate use of and accountability for its resources.[3]

Since this definition was written, the importance of nonfinancial information has increased significantly. Today, management accounting information includes such nonfinancial data as the time needed to complete one cycle of the production process or to rework production errors, as well as nonfinancial data pertaining to customer satisfaction.

MANAGEMENT ACCOUNTING AND FINANCIAL ACCOUNTING: A COMPARISON

Both management accounting and financial accounting assist decision makers by identifying, measuring, and processing relevant information and communicating

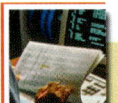

FOCUS ON BUSINESS PRACTICE

Why Is Management Accounting Vitally Important to Excellent Companies?

Futura Industries <www.futuraind.com> is not a famous company, but it is one of the best. Based in Utah, it is rated as that state's top privately owned employer. An international company with more than 50 years' experience in aluminum extruding, finishing, fabrication, machining, and design, Futura serves a high-end niche in such diverse markets as floor covering, electronics, transportation, and shower doors.

In achieving its success, Futura has used a management accounting technique called the balanced scorecard. The balanced scorecard focuses on four key dimensions of a company's operations: learning and growth among employees, internal business processes, satisfaction of customers, and financial goals. Using the balanced scorecard, Futura has developed measures of performance in each of these dimensions. For example, employee turnover is a measure of employee learning and growth. Percentage of sales from new products and total production cost per standard hour are measures of how well the company's internal processes are performing, and number of customers' complaints and percentage of materials returned are measures of customer satisfaction. Finally, income and gross margin are among the measures of financial performance. To be truly successful, Futura must excel in all four dimensions.[4]

Management accounting plays an important role in helping companies attain their goals, providing information for making operating decisions, developing budgets, determining costs of products, measuring performance, and evaluating results. Without the interplay of information, decisions, and performance measurement that management accounting facilitates, companies like Futura could not be so successful.

KEY POINT: Management accounting is *not* a subordinate activity to financial accounting. Rather, management accounting is a process that includes financial accounting, tax accounting, information analysis, and other accounting activities.

TABLE 1. Comparison of Management and Financial Accounting

Areas of Comparison	Management Accounting	Financial Accounting
Primary users	Managers, employees	Owners or stockholders, lenders, customers, governmental agencies
Report format	Flexible, driven by user's needs	Based on generally accepted accounting principles
Purpose of reports	Provide information for planning, control, performance measurement, and decision making	Report on past performance
Nature of information	Objective and verifiable for decision making; more subjective for planning (relies on estimates)	Objective and verifiable
Units of measure	Dollars at historical, market, or projected values; physical measures of time or number of objects	Dollars at historical and market values
Frequency of reports	Prepared as needed; may or may not be on a periodic basis	Prepared on a periodic basis

KEY POINT: Financial accounting requires consistency and comparability to ensure the usefulness of information to those outside the firm. Management accounting can use innovative analyses and presentation techniques to enhance information's usefulness to management within the firm.

this information through reports. Both provide managers with key measures of a company's performance and with cost information for valuing inventories on the balance sheet. Despite the overlap in their functions, management accounting and financial accounting differ in a number of ways. Table 1 summarizes these differences.

As we have indicated, management accounting provides managers and employees with the information they need to make informed decisions, to perform their jobs effectively, and to achieve their organization's goals. Thus, the primary users of management accounting information are people inside the organization. Financial accounting takes the actual results of management decisions about operating, investing, and financing activities and prepares financial statements for parties outside the organization—owners or stockholders, lenders, customers, and governmental agencies. Although these reports are prepared primarily for external use, managers also rely on them in evaluating an organization's performance.

Because management accounting reports are for internal use, their format can be flexible, driven by the user's needs. They may report either historical or future-oriented information without any formal guidelines or restrictions. In contrast, financial accounting reports, which focus on past performance, must follow standards and procedures specified by generally accepted accounting principles.

The information in management accounting reports may be objective and verifiable, expressed in terms of dollar amounts or physical measures of time or objects; if needed for planning purposes, the information may be based on estimates, and it will thus be more subjective. In contrast, the statements that financial accounting provides must be based on objective and verifiable information, which is generally historical in nature and measured in monetary terms. Management accounting reports are prepared as often as needed—annually, quarterly, monthly, and even daily if they are needed for special purposes. Financial statements, on the other hand, are prepared and distributed periodically, usually on a quarterly and annual basis.

Management Accounting and the Management Cycle

Management is expected to use resources wisely, operate profitably, pay debts, and abide by laws and regulations. To fulfill these expectations, managers establish the goals, objectives, and strategic plans of the organization and guide and control operating, investing, and financing activities accordingly. Although management actions differ from organization to organization, they generally follow a four-stage cycle. As illustrated in Figure 1, the four stages of the management cycle are (1) planning, (2) executing, (3) reviewing, and (4) reporting. Management accounting supports each stage of the cycle.

■ **Planning** Figure 2 shows the overall framework in which planning takes place. The overriding goal of a business is to increase the value of the owners' interest in the business. For corporations, this means increasing stockholders' value, or the value of the company as represented by the total market value of the shares of stock in the corporation. A company's mission is a statement of the fundamental way in which the company will achieve its goal of increasing the owners' value. The mission statement is essential to the planning process, which must consider both strate-

Figure 1
The Management Cycle

FIGURE 2
Overview of the Planning Framework

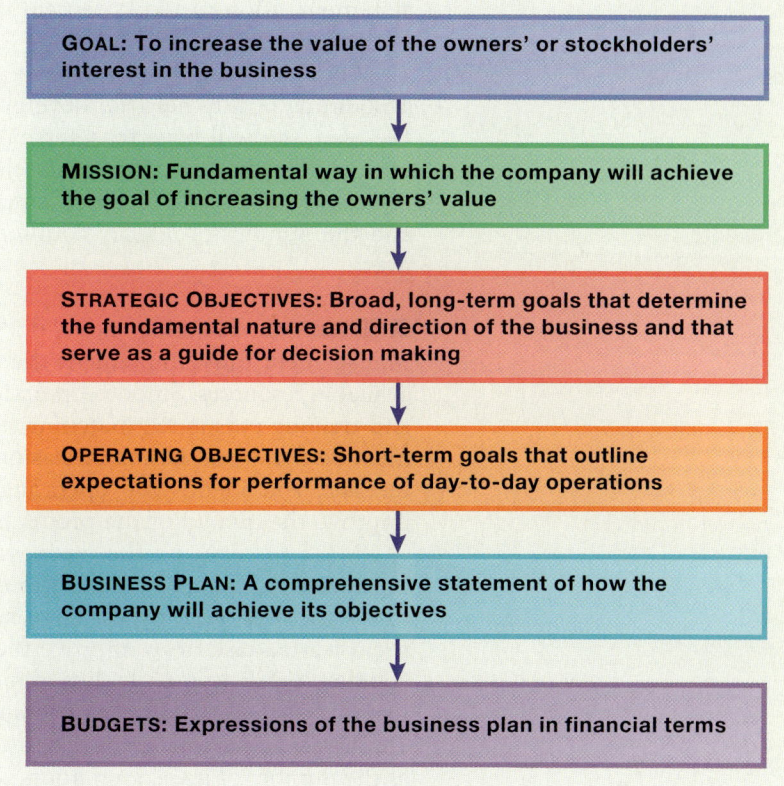

gic objectives and operating objectives. **Strategic objectives** are broad, long-term goals that determine the fundamental nature and direction of the business and that serve as a guide for decision making. Strategic objectives are established by top management and involve such basic issues as what the company's main products or services will be, who its primary customers will be, and where it will operate. **Operating objectives** are short-term goals that outline expectations for performance of day-to-day operations. The development of strategic and operating objectives requires managers to formulate a business plan, which involves making decisions concerning various alternatives. The **business plan** is a comprehensive statement of how the company will achieve its objectives. It is usually expressed in financial terms in the form of budgets, and it often includes performance goals for individuals, teams, products, or services. Management accounting supports the planning process by providing the information managers need to develop strategic and operating objectives and the comprehensive business plan.

To illustrate the role of management accounting in the planning process, let's suppose that Abbie Wang is about to open her own retail business called Sweet Treasures Candy Store. Wang's goal is to obtain an income from the business and to increase the value of her investment in it. The business's mission is to attract customers and retain them by selling satisfying sweets and providing excellent service. Wang's strategic objectives call for the purchase of high-quality confections from various candy distributors and the resale of these items to consumers. Her operating objectives call for courteous and efficient customer service; to measure performance in this area, she decides to keep a record of the number and type of complaints about poor customer service. Before Wang can open her store, she needs to apply to a local bank for a start-up loan. To do so, she must have a business plan that includes a full description of the business, as well as a complete operating budget for the first two years of operations. The budget must include a forecasted income statement, a forecasted statement of cash flows, and a forecasted balance sheet for both years.

Because Wang does not have a financial background, she will consult a local accounting firm to help her develop the business plan. To provide relevant input for the plan, she will have to determine the types of candy she wants to sell; the volume of sales she anticipates; the selling price for each product; the monthly costs of leasing or purchasing facilities, employing personnel, and maintaining the facilities; and the number of display counters, storage units, and cash registers that she will need.

■ **Executing** Planning alone does not guarantee satisfactory operating results. Management must implement the business plan in ways that make optimal use of available resources. Smooth operations require one or more of the following: hiring and training personnel, matching human and technical resources to the work that must be done, purchasing or leasing facilities, maintaining an inventory of products for sale, and identifying operating activities, or tasks, that minimize waste and improve the quality of the products or services.

Managers execute the business plan by overseeing the daily operations of the organization. In small organizations, managers generally have frequent direct contact with their employees. They supervise them and interact with them to help them learn a task or to improve their performance. In larger, more complex organizations, there is usually less direct contact between managers and employees. Instead of directly observing employees, managers in large companies monitor employees' performance by measuring the time taken to complete an activity (such as the number of inspection hours) or the frequency of an activity (such as the number of inspections).

To illustrate how management accounting provides information to support the executing stage of the management cycle, let's assume that Abbie Wang has obtained the bank loan, and Sweet Treasures Candy Store is now open for business. The budget prepared for the store's first two years of business provides the link between the business plan and executing the plan. Items that relate to the business plan appear in the budget and become authorizations for expenditures. They include such matters as spending on store fixtures, hiring employees, developing advertising campaigns, and pricing items for special sales.

Critical to managing any retail business is the supply chain. As Figure 3 shows, the **supply chain** (also called the *supply network*) is the path that leads from the suppliers of the materials from which a product is made to the final consumer. In the supply chain for candy, sugar and other ingredients flow from suppliers to manufacturers to distributors to retailers to consumers. Wang's business is toward the end of the supply chain. She buys from distributors and sells to consumers. She must coordinate deliveries from distributors so that she meets the demands of her customers without having too much inventory on hand, which would tie up cash, or being out of stock when a customer asks for a certain type of candy. Management

KEY POINT: The supply chain is primarily concerned with logistics and with shortening the cycle time of suppliers to customers.

Figure 3
The Supply Chain

accounting information about deliveries and sales will help her manage the supply chain.

■ **REVIEWING** In the reviewing stage of the management cycle, managers compare actual performance with the performance levels they established in the planning stage. They earmark any significant variations for further analysis so that they can correct the problems. If the problems result from a change in the organization's operating environment, they may revise the original objectives. Ideally, the adjustments made in the reviewing stage will improve the company's performance.

KEY POINT: Revenues and expenses accumulated in accounting systems for financial reporting purposes are also used in management accounting to support budgeting of next year's business activities.

To evaluate how well Sweet Treasures Candy Store is doing, Abbie Wang will compare the amounts estimated in the budget with information about actual results. If any differences occur, she will analyze why they have occurred. Reasons for these differences may lead Wang to change parts of her original business plan. In addition to reviewing employees' performance in regard to financial goals, such as avoiding waste, Wang will want to review how well her employees served customers. As noted earlier, she decided to monitor service quality by keeping a record of the number and type of complaints about poor customer service. Her review of this record may help her develop new and better business strategies.

■ **REPORTING** Whether accounting reports are prepared for internal or external use, it is essential that they provide accurate information and that they clearly communicate this information to the reader. Internal reports that provide inaccurate information or that present information in such a way that it is unclear to the employee or manager can have a negative effect on a company's operations and ultimately on its profitability. Full disclosure and transparency in financial statements issued to external parties is a fundamental of generally accepted accounting principles, and violation of this precept can now result in stiff penalties. After reporting violations by Enron, WorldCom, and other companies, Congress passed legislation that requires top management of companies that file financial statements with the Securities and Exchange Commission to certify that these statements are accurate; the penalty for issuing false public reports can be loss of compensation, fines, and jail time.

www.enron.com
www.worldcom.com

The key to producing a management accounting report that communicates accurate and useful information in such a way that the meaning is transparent to the reader is to apply the four *w*'s: why, who, what, and when.

- *Why?* Know the purpose of the report. Focus on it as you write.
- *Who?* Identify the audience for your report. Communicate at a level that matches your readers' understanding of the issue and their familiarity with accounting information. A detailed, informal report may be appropriate for your manager, but a more concise summary may be necessary for other audiences, such as the president or board of directors of your organization.
- *What?* What information is needed, and what method of presentation is best? Select relevant information from reliable sources. You may draw information from pertinent documents or from interviews with knowledgeable managers and employees. The information should be not only relevant, but also easy to read and understand. You may need to include visual aids, such as bar charts or graphs, to present the information clearly.
- *When?* Know the due date for the report. Strive to prepare an accurate report on a timely basis. If the report is urgently needed, you may have to sacrifice some accuracy in the interest of timeliness.

The four *w*'s are also applicable to financial accounting reports. Assume that Abbie Wang has hired Salvador Chavez to be her company's accountant. In the financial statements that he prepares, the purpose—or *why*—is to report on the financial health of Sweet Treasures Candy Store. In this case, Wang, her bank and

> **EXHIBIT 1**
> **A Management Accounting Report**
>
> Memorandum
>
> When: Today's Date
> Who: To: Abbie Wang, Sweet Treasures Candy Store
>   From: Salvador Chavez, Accountant
> Why: Re: Ordering and Shipping Costs—Analysis and Recommendations
>
> What: As you requested, I have analyzed the ordering and shipping costs of candy that we receive from our distributors. I found that during the past year, the ordering costs of receiving candy were 9 percent of sales, or $36,000.
>
> On average, we are placing about two orders per week, or eight orders per month. Placing each order requires about two and one-half hours of an employee's time. Further, the distributors charge a service fee for each order, and shippers charge high rates for orders as small as ours.
>
> My recommendations are (1) to reduce orders to four per month (the candy's freshness will not be affected if we order at least once a week) and (2) to begin placing orders through the distributors' web sites (our distributors do not charge a service fee for online orders). If we follow these recommendations, I project that the costs of receiving candy will be reduced to 4 percent of sales, or $16,000, annually—a savings of $20,000.

> ● **STOP AND THINK!**
> A financial report often contains estimates and projections. How does the writer of such a report make sure the reader understands the uncertainties involved?
>
> *The writer should include a clear statement of the assumptions underlying the report and the conditions under which the estimates and projections were made. This will enable the reader to assess how valid the estimates and projections are.* ■

other creditors, and potential investors are the *who*. The *what* consists of disclosures about assets, liabilities, product costs, and sales. The required reporting deadline for the accounting period answers the question of *when*.

Wang will also want periodic internal reports on various aspects of operations. For example, a monthly report may summarize the costs of ordering candy from distributors and the related shipping charges. If the costs in the monthly reports appear too high, she may ask Salvador Chavez to conduct a special study. The results of such a study might result in a memorandum report like the one shown in Exhibit 1.

In summary, management accounting can provide a constant stream of relevant information. Compare Wang's activities and information needs with the management cycle shown in Figure 1. She started with a business plan, executed the plan, and reviewed the results. Accounting information helped her develop her business plan, communicate that plan to her bank and employees, evaluate the performance of employees, and report the results of operations. As you can see, accounting plays a critical role in managing the operations of an organization.

 Check out ACE for a Review Quiz at http://accounting.college.hmco.com/students.

VALUE CHAIN ANALYSIS

LO2 Describe the value chain and its usefulness in analyzing a business.

RELATED TEXT ASSIGNMENTS
Q: 9, 10
SE: 4, 5
E: 6
P: 2
SD: 1

Each step in the manufacture of a product or the delivery of a service can be thought of as a link in a chain that adds value to the product or service. This concept of how a business fulfills its mission and objectives is known as the **value chain**. As shown in Figure 4, the steps that add value to a product or service—which range from research and development to customer service—are known as **primary processes**. The value chain also includes **support services**, such as legal services and management accounting. These services facilitate the primary processes but do not add value to the final product or service. Their roles are critical, however, to making the primary processes as efficient and effective as possible.

FIGURE 4
The Value Chain

Primary Processes and Support Services

Let's assume that Sweet Treasures Candy Store has had some success, and Abbie Wang now wants to determine the feasibility of making and selling her own brand of candy. The primary processes that will add value to the new candy are as follows:

Research and development: developing new and better products or services. Wang plans to add value by developing a candy that has less sugar content than similar confections.

Design: creating improved and distinctive shapes, labels, or packages for products. For example, a package that is attractive and that describes the desirable features of Wang's new candy will add value to the product.

Supply: purchasing materials for products or services. Wang will want to purchase high-quality sugar, chocolate, and other ingredients for the candy, as well as high-quality packaging.

Production: manufacturing the product or service. To add value to the new candy, Wang will want to implement efficient manufacturing and packaging processes.

Marketing: communicating information about the products or services and selling them. Attractive advertisements will facilitate sale of the new candy to customers.

Distribution: delivering the product or service to the customer. Courteous and efficient service for in-store customers will add value to the product; Wang may also want to accommodate Internet customers by providing shipping.

Customer service: following up with service after sales or providing warranty service. For example, Wang may offer free replacement of any candy that does not satisfy the customer. She could also use questionnaires to measure customer satisfaction.

● **Stop and Think!**
Is it better for a company to have a primary process or a support service as a core competency?

A company needs to be good at both. However, it is more important to have a primary process as a core competency because primary processes add value to the final product, and it is on the basis of primary processes that a company distinguishes itself from its competitors. ■

The services that support the primary processes are as follows:

Human resources: hiring and training employees to carry out all the functions of the business. Wang will need to hire and train personnel to make the new candy.

Legal services: maintaining and monitoring all contracts, agreements, obligations, and other relationships with outside parties. For example, Wang will want legal advice when applying for a trademark for the new candy's name and when signing contracts with suppliers.

Information systems: establishing and maintaining technological means of controlling and communicating within the organization. Wang will want a computerized accounting system that keeps not only financial records, but customer information as well.

Management accounting: provides essential information in any business.

ADVANTAGES OF VALUE CHAIN ANALYSIS

KEY POINT: A company cannot succeed by trying to do everything at the highest level. It has to focus on its core competencies to give customers the best value.

www.sony.com

An advantage of value chain analysis is that it allows a company to focus on its core competencies. A **core competency** is what a company does best. It is what gives a company an advantage over its competitors. For example, Sony Corporation, the company that invented the Walkman, has a reputation for making consumer electronic devices that are ever-smaller in size. Its core competencies are the design and manufacture of these devices.

www.nike.com

www.ibm.com

A common result of value chain analysis is outsourcing, which can also be of benefit to a business. **Outsourcing** is the engagement of other companies to perform a process or service of the value chain that is not among an organization's core competencies. For instance, Nike's core competencies are the design and marketing of athletic shoes. The company does not manufacture any shoes; it outsources manufacturing to companies that specialize in shoe manufacture. Many companies also outsource support services. A main source of IBM's growth in recent years, for instance, has been the operation and maintenance of information systems for other companies.

MANAGEMENT ACCOUNTING'S SUPPORT OF VALUE CHAIN ANALYSIS

www.gm.com
www.honda.com

In today's competitive business environment, analysis of the value chain is critical to most companies' survival. Managers must provide the highest value to customers at the lowest cost, and low cost often equates with the speed at which the primary processes of the value chain are executed. Time to market is very important. For example, General Motors can take up to five years to design and bring a new car to market, whereas Honda may take only three years. Some cars on the General Motors assembly line leave every 60 minutes, whereas Honda can produce a car every 40 minutes. When millions of dollars and thousands of cars are involved, these differences can result in significant competitive advantages for Honda.

FOCUS ON BUSINESS TECHNOLOGY

How Can the Internet Be Used to Support the Value Chain?

The Internet can be a very effective means of supporting the value chain, as Baxter International's use of this technology demonstrates. Baxter <www.baxter.com>, a large pharmaceutical concern, uses an integrated global information system and digital network to support and coordinate human resource management, research and development, supply chain management, manufacturing, and marketing and sales worldwide. Among the benefits the company has realized are savings of $75 million from the outsourcing of parts of the value chain, a reduction in the cost of customer orders from $4.00 to $.80, faster collection of accounts receivable, reduced transportation costs, increased employee productivity, improved customer service, and faster time to market.[5]

EXHIBIT 2
Value Chain Analysis

Sweet Treasures Candy Store
Projected Costs of New Candy
June 1, 20x5

Primary Process	Initial Costs per Pound	Revised Costs per Pound
Research and development	$ .25	$ .25
Design	.10	.10
Supply	1.10	.60
Production	4.50	3.50
Marketing	.50	.50
Distribution	.90	.90
Customer service	.65	.65
Total cost	$8.00	$6.50

Managers must also make the services that support the primary processes as efficient as possible. These services are essential and cannot be eliminated, but because they do not add value to the final product, they must be implemented as economically as possible. Businesses have been making progress in this area. For example, over the past ten years, the cost of the accounting function in many companies has declined as a percentage of total revenue from 6 percent to 2 percent. Technology has played a big role in making this economy possible.

As a support service, management accounting must be efficient and provide value to managers by developing information useful for decision making. For example, to determine whether manufacturing and selling her own brand of candy will be profitable, Abbie Wang will need accurate information about the cost of the candy. She knows that to be competitive with other candy manufacturers, she cannot sell the candy for more than $10 per pound. Further, she has an idea of how much candy she can sell in the first year. Based on this information, her accountant, Salvador Chavez, analyzes the value chain and projects the initial costs per pound shown in Exhibit 2. The total cost of $8 per pound worries Wang because with a selling price of $10, it leaves only $2, or 20 percent of revenue, to cover all the support services and leave a profit. Wang believes that if the enterprise is to be successful, this percentage, called the *margin*, must be at least 35 percent. Since the selling price is constrained by the competition, she must find a way to reduce costs.

Chavez tells her that the company could achieve a lower total cost per pound by selling a higher volume of candy, but that is not realistic for the new product. He also points out that the largest projected costs in the candy store's value chain are for supply and production. Because Wang plans to order ingredients from a number of suppliers, her orders would not be large enough to qualify for quantity discounts and to save on shipping. By using a single supplier, the supply cost could be reduced by $.50 per unit. A way of reducing the cost of production would be to outsource this process to a candy manufacturer whose high volume of products would allow it to produce the candy at a much lower cost than could be done at Sweet Treasures Candy Store. Outsourcing would reduce the production cost to $3.50 per unit. Thus, the total unit cost would be reduced to $6.50, as shown in Exhibit 2. This per unit cost would enable the company to sell the candy at a competitive $10 per pound and make the targeted margin of 35 percent ($3.50 ÷ $10).

This value chain analysis illustrates two important points. First, Sweet Treasures Candy Store's mission is as a retailer. The company has no experience in making candy. To manufacture candy would require a change in the company's mission and major changes in the way it does business. Second, it is often the best business policy to outsource portions of the value chain that are not part of a business's core competency. Since Sweet Treasures Candy Store does not have a core competency in manufacturing candy, it would not be competitive in this field. Abbie Wang would be better off having an experienced candy manufacturer produce the candy according to her specifications, which she could then sell under her store's label. As Wang's business grows, increased volume may allow her to reconsider undertaking the manufacture of candy.

✓ Check out ACE for a Review Quiz at http://accounting.college.hmco.com/students.

MEETING THE DEMANDS OF GLOBAL COMPETITION

LO3 Identify the management tools used for continuous improvement and describe how they work to meet the demands of global competition and how management accounting supports them.

RELATED TEXT ASSIGNMENTS
Q: 11, 12, 13, 14, 15, 16
SE: 6, 7
E: 7, 8
SD: 2

Today, managers in all parts of the world have ready access to international markets and to current information for informed decision making. As a result, global competition has increased significantly. One of the most valuable lessons gained from this increase in competition is that management cannot afford to become complacent. The concept of **continuous improvement** evolved to avoid such complacency. Organizations that adhere to continuous improvement are never satisfied with what is; they constantly seek improved efficiency and lower cost through better methods, products, services, processes, or resources. Their goal is perfection in everything they do. In response to this concept, several important management tools have emerged. These tools help companies remain competitive by focusing on continuous improvement of business methods.

MANAGEMENT TOOLS FOR CONTINUOUS IMPROVEMENT

Among the management tools that companies use to deal with expanding global competition are the just-in-time operating philosophy, total quality management, activity-based management, and the theory of constraints.

■ **JUST-IN-TIME OPERATING PHILOSOPHY** The **just-in-time (JIT) operating philosophy** requires that all resources—materials, personnel, and facilities—be acquired and used only as needed. Its objectives are to improve productivity and eliminate waste. In a JIT environment, production processes are consolidated, and workers are trained to be multiskilled so that they can operate several different machines. Raw materials and parts are scheduled for delivery just at the time they are needed in the production process, which significantly reduces inventories of materials. Goods are produced continuously, so work in process inventories are very small. They are usually put into production only when an order is received and are shipped when completed, which reduces the inventories of finished goods.

Adopting the JIT operating philosophy reduces production time and costs, investment in materials inventory, and materials waste, and it results in higher-quality goods. Funds that are no longer invested in inventory can be redirected according to the goals of the company's business plan. Management accounting responds to a JIT operating environment by providing an information system that is sensitive to changes in production processes. JIT methods help manufacturers like General Motors and Harley-Davidson assign more accurate costs to their products and identify the costs of waste and inefficient operations. JIT methods are also of benefit to service companies like AT&T and retailers like Sweet Treasures Candy Store and Wal-Mart. Wal-Mart, for example, requires vendors to restock inventory often and pays them only when the goods sell. This minimizes the funds invested in inventory and allows the retailer to focus on offering high-demand merchandise at attractive prices.

www.gm.com
www.harley-davidson.com
www.att.com
www.walmart.com

■ **TOTAL QUALITY MANAGEMENT** **Total quality management (TQM)** requires that all parts of a business work together to build quality into the business's product or service. Improved quality of both the product or service and the work environment is TQM's goal. Workers act as team members and are empowered to make operating decisions that improve quality in both areas.

TQM has many of the characteristics of the JIT operating philosophy. It focuses on improving product or service quality by identifying and reducing or eliminating the causes of waste. The emphasis is on examining current operations to spot possible causes of poor quality and on using resources efficiently and effectively to improve quality and reduce the time needed to complete a task or provide a service. Like JIT, TQM results in reduced waste of materials, higher-quality goods, and lower production costs in manufacturing environments, such as those of Hewlett-Packard and Kodak. It also helps service organizations like USAA and Federal Express realize time savings and provide higher-quality services.

www.hp.com
www.kodak.com
www.usaa.com
www.fedex.com

To determine the impact of poor quality on profits, TQM managers use accounting information about the costs of quality. The **costs of quality** include both the costs of achieving quality (such as training costs and inspection costs) and the costs of poor quality (such as the costs of rework and of handling customer complaints).

www.motorola.com
www.ge.com

Managers at companies like Motorola and General Electric use information about the costs of quality to relate their organization's business plan to daily operating activities, to stimulate improvement by sharing this information with all employees, to identify opportunities for reducing costs and customer dissatisfaction, and to determine the costs of quality relative to net income. For example, Motorola's managers use the information that management accounting supplies about defects per unit and cycle time to ensure that a job is done right the first time and in the shortest amount of time. Motorola uses this approach in everything it does. For retailers like Sweet Treasures Candy Store, TQM results in a quality customer experience before, during, and after the sale.

■ **ACTIVITY-BASED MANAGEMENT** **Activity-based management (ABM)** is an approach to managing an organization that identifies all major operating activities, determines the resources consumed by each of those activities and the cause of the resource usage, and categorizes the activities as either adding value to a product or service or not adding value. ABM includes a management accounting practice called activity-based costing. **Activity-based costing (ABC)** identifies all of an organization's major operating activities (both production and nonproduction), traces costs to those activities, and then assigns costs to the products or services that use the resources supplied by those activities.

Activities that add value to a product or service, as perceived by the customer, are known as **value-adding activities**. All other activities are called **nonvalue-adding activities**; they add cost to a product or service but do not increase its market value. ABM eliminates nonvalue-adding activities that do not support the organization; those that do support the organization are focal points for cost reduction. ABM results in reduced costs, reduced waste of resources, increased efficiency, and increased customer satisfaction. In addition, ABC produces more accurate costs than traditional cost allocation methods, which leads to improved decision making.

To illustrate the ABM approach, suppose you and three friends want to take a skiing trip. The travel agent quotes a flat fee of $400 per person, or a total of $1,600 for a package that includes skiing, food, lodging, and entertainment. But one of your friends does not plan to ski, another eats much more than the rest of you, and two people plan to stay for only two days. How would you allocate the costs? Should each person pay an equal share (i.e., $400)? Or should the costs be allocated according to activity? The issue is how to assign costs fairly if each person is involvd in different activites. According to ABM, each person should make a payment equal to his or her involvement in each activity.

■ **THEORY OF CONSTRAINTS** According to the **theory of constraints (TOC)**, limiting factors, or bottlenecks, occur during the production of any product or service, but once managers identify such a constraint, they can focus attention and resources on it and achieve significant improvements. TOC thus helps managers set priorities for how they spend their time and resources. In identifying constraints, managers rely on the information that management accounting provides.

To illustrate TOC, suppose a marketing manager wants to increase sales of doughnut-shaped chew toys for dogs. After reviewing management accounting reports, she concludes that potential sales are limited by the production capacity of her company's manufacturing plant. The problem lies in the plant's molding machine, which can shape only 1,000 toys per hour. To overcome this constraint, she persuades the vice president of manufacturing to purchase a second molding machine. The increase in production will enable her to increase sales.

TOC complements JIT, TQM, and ABM by focusing resources on efforts that will yield the most effective improvements.

ACHIEVING CONTINUOUS IMPROVEMENT

JIT, TQM, ABM, and TOC all have perfection by means of continuous improvement as their goal. Figure 5 shows how each approach tries to accomplish this goal. In the just-in-time operating environment, management wages war on wasted time, wasted resources, and wasted space. All employees are encouraged to look for ways of improving processes and saving time. Total quality management focuses on improving the quality of the product or service and the work environment. It pur-

FIGURE 5
The Continuous Improvement Environment

FOCUS ON INTERNATIONAL BUSINESS

How Has Ecommerce Changed the Nature of Business?

Global ecommerce has radically changed the way in which numerous goods and services, including plane tickets, books, automobiles, and even medical help, are sold. Many products and services are on sale 24 hours a day and can be delivered the day after purchase. These revolutionary changes in the way business is conducted have created a vast array of new opportunities. But they have also forced managers to recognize the important role that performance measures play in keeping a company competitive. Organizations now set performance targets for all areas of their operation—from new-product development to purchasing, marketing, sales, shipping, and customer satisfaction. Such measures are developed and tracked by management accountants. The Business and Industry Executive Committee (formerly the Management Accounting Executive Committee) of the American Institute of Certified Public Accountants has coined the term *new finance* to describe this revolution in management accounting.[6]

● **STOP AND THINK!**

How does a company know whether the quality of its products or services is improving?

Managers must first develop measures that reflect the quality they seek. They must then carefully monitor these measures and report the results on a regular basis. ■

sues continuous improvement by reducing the number of defective products and the time needed to complete a task or provide a service. Activity-based management seeks continuous improvement by emphasizing the ongoing reduction or elimination of nonvalue-adding activities. The theory of constraints helps managers focus resources on efforts that will produce the most effective improvements.

Each of these management tools can be used individually, or parts of them can be combined to create a new operating environment. They are applicable in service businesses, such as banking, as well as in manufacturing and retail businesses. By continuously trying to improve and fine-tune operations, they contribute to the same results in any organization: a reduction in product or service costs and delivery time, an improvement in the quality of the product or service, and an increase in customer satisfaction.

 Check out ACE for a Review Quiz at http://accounting.college.hmco.com/students.

PERFORMANCE MEASURES: A KEY TO ACHIEVING ORGANIZATIONAL OBJECTIVES

LO4 Explain the balanced scorecard and its relationship to performance measures.

RELATED TEXT ASSIGNMENTS
Q: 17, 18, 19
SE: 8
E: 9
P: 3
SD: 3
MRA: 5

ENRICHMENT NOTE:
Using nonfinancial measures in an international business environment often eliminates the problems associated with different currencies and different accounting standards.

Performance measures are quantitative tools that gauge an organization's performance in relation to a specific goal or an expected outcome. Performance measures may be financial or nonfinancial. Financial performance measures include return on investment, net income as a percentage of sales, and the costs of poor quality as a percentage of sales. Such measures use monetary information to gauge the performance of a profit-generating organization or its segments—its divisions, departments, product lines, sales territories, or operating activities.

Nonfinancial performance measures include the number of times an activity occurs or the time taken to perform a task. Examples are number of customer complaints, number of orders shipped the same day, hours of inspection, and the time taken to fill an order. Such performance measures are useful in reducing or eliminating waste and inefficiencies in operating activities.

USE OF PERFORMANCE MEASURES IN THE MANAGEMENT CYCLE

Managers use performance measures in all stages of the management cycle. In the planning stage, they establish performance measures that will support the organization's mission and the objectives of its business plan, such as reducing costs and increasing quality, efficiency, timeliness, and customer satisfaction. As you will recall from earlier in the chapter, Abbie Wang selected the number of customer complaints as a performance measure to monitor the quality of service at Sweet Treasures Candy Store.

During the executing stage, performance measures guide and motivate the performance of employees and assist in assigning costs to products, departments, or operating activities. Abbie Wang will record the number of customer complaints during the year. She can group the information by type of complaint or the employee involved in the service.

In the reviewing stage, managers use the information that performance measures have provided to analyze significant differences between actual and planned performance and to improvise ways of improving performance. By comparing the actual and planned number of customer complaints, Wang can identify problem areas and develop solutions.

In the reporting stage, performance measurement information is useful in communicating performance evaluations and developing new budgets. If Wang needed formal reports, she could have her accountant prepare performance evaluations based on this information.

THE BALANCED SCORECARD

KEY POINT: The balanced scorecard focuses all perspectives of the business on accomplishing the business's mission.

● **STOP AND THINK!**
In what sense is the balanced scorecard "balanced?"

The balanced scorecard is "balanced" in the sense that it weighs the needs of the four perspectives of an organization in a way that achieves the organization's mission. ■

If an organization is to achieve its mission and objectives, it must identify the areas in which it needs to excel and establish measures of performance in these critical areas. As we have indicated, effective performance measurement requires an approach that uses both financial and nonfinancial measures that are tied to a company's mission and objectives. One such approach that has gained wide acceptance is the balanced scorecard. The **balanced scorecard** is a framework that links the perspectives of an organization's four stakeholder groups with the organization's mission, objectives, resources, and performance measures. Stakeholders with a financial perspective (owners, investors, and creditors) value improvements in financial measures, such as net income and return on investment. Stakeholders with a learning and growth perspective (employees) value high wages, job satisfaction, and opportunities to fulfill their potential. Stakeholders who focus on the business's internal processes value the safe and cost-effective production of high-quality products. Holders of the customer perspective value high-quality, low-cost products. Although their perspectives differ, these stakeholder groups may be interested in the same measurable performance goals. For example, holders of both the customer and business processes perspectives are interested in performance that results in high-quality products.

Figure 6 applies the balanced scorecard to Sweet Treasures Candy Store. The company's mission is to be the candy store of choice in the community. It is at the center of the company's balanced scorecard. Surrounding it are the four interrelated perspectives.

At the base of the scorecard is the learning and growth perspective. Here, the objective, or performance goal, is to provide courteous service. Because training

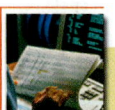

FOCUS ON BUSINESS PRACTICE

Do Many Companies Use the Balanced Scorecard?

Research shows that about 50 percent of large companies in the Unites States and about 45 percent of those in Europe use the balanced scorecard. And the number is growing.

One of the most successful companies of the last decade, Dell Computer Corporation <www.dell.com>, uses the balanced scorecard to measure its progress in meeting objectives in the two areas that are most critical to its success: operational efficiency and customer service. Dell's learning and growth measures focus on training, patents, innovations, and sharing of information. Its business process measures focus on defect rates, forecasting accuracy, cash cycle time, and the implementation of innovations. Customer measures focus on customer retention, customer perceptions, and delivery time. Financial measures include cash flows, gross margins, revenue growth, and economic returns.[7]

FIGURE 6
The Balanced Scorecard for Sweet Treasures Candy Store

Source: Adapted from Robert S. Kaplan and David P. Norton, "Using the Balanced Scorecard as a Strategic Management System," *Harvard Business Review,* January–February 1996.

employees in customer service should result in courteous service, performance related to this objective can be measured in terms of how many employees have received training. The number of customer complaints is another measure of courteous service.

From the perspective of internal business processes, the objective is to help achieve the company's mission by managing the supply chain efficiently, which should contribute to customer satisfaction. Efficiency in the ordering process can be measured by recording the number of orders placed with distributors each month and the number of times per month that customers ask for candy that is not in stock.

KEY POINT: The balanced scorecard presents a way of linking the management of employees, internal business processes, and customer needs to external financial results.

If the objectives of the learning and growth and business processes perspectives are met, they should result in attracting customers and retaining them, which is the objective of the customer perspective. Performance related to this objective is measured by tracking the number of new customers and the number of repeat customers. Satisfied customers should help achieve the objective of the financial perspective, which is profitable growth. Profitable growth is measured by growth in sales, profit margin, and return on assets.

BENCHMARKING

The balanced scorecard enables a company to determine whether it is making continuous improvement in its operations. But to ensure its success, a company must also compare its performance with that of similar companies in the same industry. **Benchmarking** is a technique for determining a company's competitive advantage by comparing its performance with that of its closest competitors. **Benchmarks** are measures of the best practices in an industry. To obtain information about benchmarks in the retail and candy industry, Abbie Wang might join a trade association for small retail shops or candy stores. Information about these benchmarks would be useful to her in setting targets for the performance measures in Sweet Treasures Candy Store's balanced scorecard.

> Check out ACE for a Review Quiz at http://accounting.college.hmco.com/students.

ANALYSIS OF NONFINANCIAL DATA IN A SERVICE ORGANIZATION

LO5 Prepare an analysis of nonfinancial data.

RELATED TEXT ASSIGNMENTS
Q: 20
SE: 9
E: 10, 11, 12
P: 4, 5, 7, 8
SD: 6
MRA: 3, 4

As we have noted throughout this chapter, managers use many kinds of nonfinancial measures to determine whether performance targets for internal business processes and customer satisfaction are being met. The following example illustrates how a manager in a service organization uses nonfinancial data in order to analyze changes in employee performance.

Lynda Babb supervises tellers at King's National Bank. The bank has three drive-up windows, each with a full-time teller. In the past, each teller served an average of 30 customers per hour. However, on November 1, 20x5, management implemented a new check-scanning procedure that has reduced the number of customers served per hour.

Data on the number of customers served for the three-month period ended December 31, 20x5, are shown in Part A of Exhibit 3. Each teller works an average of 170 hours per month. Window 1 is always the busiest. Windows 2 and 3 receive progressively less business. Babb is preparing a report for management on the effects of the new procedure. Part B of Exhibit 3 shows her analysis of the number of customers served over the three months at each teller window. She computed the number of customers served per hour by dividing the number of customers served by the monthly average hours worked per teller (170). By averaging the customer service rates for the three tellers, she got 28.43 customers per hour per window for November and 28.83 customers for December. As you can see, the service rate has decreased since October. But December's average is higher than November's, which means the tellers, as a group, are becoming more accustomed to the new procedure. Part C of Exhibit 3 is a graphic comparison of the number of customers served per hour.

Stop and Think!
Which is more important to running a company: financial data or nonfinancial data?
Both are important. Nonfinancial data are important for measuring the performance of business processes, but ultimately these data are translated into budgets and financial reports that reflect the financial objectives of the company.

> Check out ACE for a Review Quiz at http://accounting.college.hmco.com/students.

STANDARDS OF ETHICAL CONDUCT

LO6 Identify the standards of ethical conduct for management accountants.

RELATED TEXT ASSIGNMENTS
Q: 20, 21
SE: 10
E: 13, 14, 15
SD: 4

Managers are responsible to external parties (e.g., owners, creditors, governmental agencies, and the local community) for the proper use of organizational resources and the financial reporting of their actions. Conflicts may arise that require managers to balance the interests of all external parties, and management accountants have a responsibility to help them balance these interests. For example, the community wants a safe living environment, while owners seek to maximize profits. If management decides to purchase an expensive device to extract pollutants from the production process, it will protect the community, but profits will decline. The benefit will be greater for the community than for the owners. On the other hand,

EXHIBIT 3
Analysis of Nonfinancial Data

King's Beach National Bank
Summary of Number of Customers Served
For the Quarter Ended December 31, 20x5

Part A — Number of Customers Served

Window	October	November	December	Quarter Totals
1	5,428	5,186	5,162	15,776
2	5,280	4,820	4,960	15,060
3	4,593	4,494	4,580	13,667
Totals	15,301	14,500	14,702	44,503

Part B — Number of Customers Served per Hour

Window	October	November	December	Quarter Averages
1	31.93	30.51	30.36	30.93
2	31.06	28.35	29.18	29.53
3	27.02	26.44	26.94	26.80
Totals	90.01	85.30	86.48	87.26
Average per hour per window	30.00	28.43	28.83	26.09

Part C Graphic Comparison of the Number of Customers Served per Hour

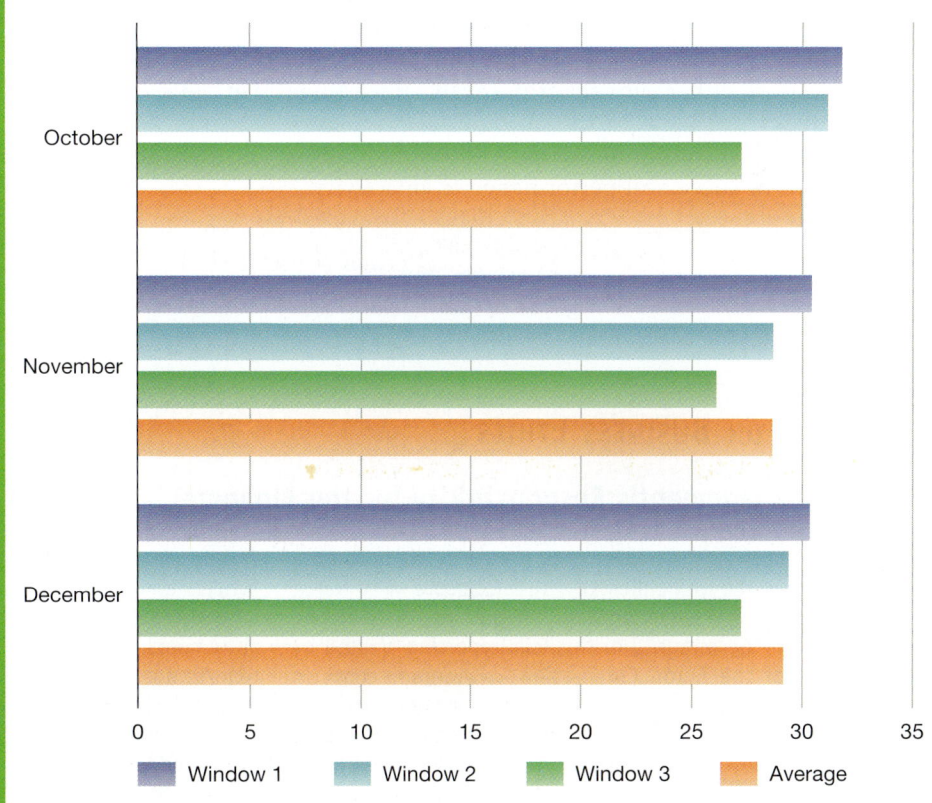

Exhibit 4
Standards of Ethical Conduct for Practitioners of Management Accounting and Financial Management

Practitioners of management accounting and financial management have an obligation to the public, their profession, the organization they serve, and themselves, to maintain the highest standards of ethical conduct. In recognition of this obligation, the Institute of Management Accountants has promulgated the following standards of ethical conduct for practitioners of management accounting and financial management. Adherence to these standards, both domestically and internationally, is integral to achieving the Objectives of Management Accounting. Practitioners of management accounting and financial management shall not commit acts contrary to these standards nor shall they condone the commission of such acts by others within their organizations.

Competence. Practitioners of management accounting and financial management have a responsibility to:

- Maintain an appropriate level of professional competence by ongoing development of their knowledge and skills.
- Perform their professional duties in accordance with relevant laws, regulations, and technical standards.
- Prepare complete and clear reports and recommendations after appropriate analysis of relevant and reliable information.

Confidentiality. Practitioners of management accounting and financial management have a responsibility to:

- Refrain from disclosing confidential information acquired in the course of their work except when authorized, unless legally obligated to do so.
- Inform subordinates as appropriate regarding the confidentiality of information acquired in the course of their work and monitor their activities to assure the maintenance of that confidentiality.
- Refrain from using or appearing to use confidential information acquired in the course of their work for unethical or illegal advantage either personally or through third parties.

Integrity. Practitioners of management accounting and financial management have a responsibility to:

- Avoid actual or apparent conflicts of interest and advise all appropriate parties of any potential conflict.
- Refrain from engaging in any activity that would prejudice their ability to carry out their duties ethically.
- Refuse any gift, favor, or hospitality that would influence or would appear to influence their actions.
- Refrain from either actively or passively subverting the attainment of the organization's legitimate and ethical objectives.
- Recognize and communicate professional limitations or other constraints that would preclude responsible judgment or successful performance of an activity.

Focus on Business Ethics

What Is Management's Responsibility for the Financial Statements?

Top-level managers have not only an ethical responsibility to ensure that the financial statements issued by their companies adhere to the principles of full disclosure and transparency; today, they have a legal responsibility as well. Strong concerns about the integrity of financial reporting created by the collapse of the Enron Corporation <www.enron.com> in 2001 fueled widespread support for accounting reform. An important outcome of the reform efforts was the passage of the Sarbanes-Oxley Act in 2002. Among the provisions of this law is one that directed the Securities and Exchange Commission (SEC) to adopt a rule requiring the chief executive officers and chief financial officers of companies filing reports with the SEC to certify that those reports contain no untrue statements and include all facts needed to ensure that the reports are not misleading. In addition to issuing this rule, the SEC adopted one requiring managers to ensure that the information in reports filed with the SEC "is recorded, processed, summarized and reported on a timely basis."[8]

- Communicate unfavorable as well as favorable information and professional judgments or opinions.
- Refrain from engaging in or supporting any activity that would discredit the profession.

Objectivity. Practitioners of management accounting and financial management have a responsibility to:

- Communicate information fairly and objectively.
- Disclose fully all relevant information that could reasonably be expected to influence an intended user's understanding of the reports, comments, and recommendations presented.

Resolution of Ethical Conflict. In applying the standards of ethical conduct, practitioners of management accounting and financial management may encounter problems in identifying unethical behavior or in resolving an ethical conflict. When faced with significant ethical issues, practitioners of management accounting and financial management should follow the established policies of the organization bearing on the resolution of such conflict. If these policies do not resolve the ethical conflict, such practitioner should consider the following courses of action:

- Discuss such problems with the immediate superior except when it appears that the superior is involved, in which case the problem should be presented initially to the next higher managerial level. If a satisfactory resolution cannot be achieved when the problem is initially presented, submit the issues to the next higher managerial level.
- If the immediate superior is the chief executive officer, or equivalent, the acceptable reviewing authority may be a group such as the audit committee, executive committee, board of directors, board of trustees, or owners. Contact with levels above the immediate superior should be initiated only with the superior's knowledge, assuming the superior is not involved. Except where legally prescribed, communication of such problems to authorities or individuals not employed or engaged by the organization is not considered appropriate.
- Clarify relevant ethical issues by confidential discussion with an objective advisor (e.g., IMA Ethics Counseling Service) to obtain a better understanding of possible courses of action.
- Consult your own attorney as to legal obligations and rights concerning the ethical conflict.
- If the ethical conflict still exists after exhausting all levels of internal review, there may be no other recourse on significant matters than to resign from the organization and to submit an informative memorandum to an appropriate representative of the organization. After resignation, depending on the nature of the ethical conflict, it may also be appropriate to notify other parties.

Source: From *Standards of Ethical Conduct for Practitioners of Management Accounting and Financial Management.* Institute of Management Accountants, July 1997. Reprinted by permission.

⬢ STOP AND THINK!

If you encounter financial irregularities in your company, what should your first step be? What is your last recourse?

Your first step should be to discuss the situation with your immediate superior unless he or she is involved, in which case you should discuss the situation with someone at at higher level. You may have to take the matter to the board of directors or to the authorities. If you cannot resolve it, your last resort is to resign. ∎

management could achieve higher profits for the owners by purchasing a less expensive, less effective antipollution device that would not protect the community as well. Such conflicts between external parties can create ethical dilemmas for management and for accountants.

To be viewed credibly by the various parties that rely on the information they provide, management accountants must adhere to the highest standards of performance. To provide guidance, the Institute of Management Accountants has issued standards of ethical conduct for practitioners of management accounting and financial management. Those standards, presented in Exhibit 4, emphasize that management accountants have responsibilities in the areas of competence, confidentiality, integrity, and objectivity.

✓ Check out ACE for a Review Quiz at http://accounting.college.hmco.com/students.

Chapter Review

REVIEW OF LEARNING OBJECTIVES

LO1 Distinguish management accounting from financial accounting and explain the role of management accounting in the management cycle.

Management accounting is the process of identifying, measuring, accumulating, analyzing, preparing, interpreting, and communicating information that management uses to plan, evaluate, and control an organization and to ensure that its resources are used and accounted for appropriately. Management accounting reports provide information for planning, control, performance measurement, and decision making to managers and employees when they need such information. These reports follow a flexible format and may present either historical or future-oriented information expressed in dollar amounts or physical measures. In contrast, financial accounting reports provide information about an organization's past performance to owners, lenders, customers, and government agencies on a periodic basis. Financial accounting reports follow strict guidelines defined by generally accepted accounting principles.

Management accounting supports each stage of the management cycle. In the planning stage, managers use the information that management accounting provides to establish strategic and operating objectives that reflect their company's mission and to formulate a comprehensive business plan for achieving those objectives. The plan is usually expressed in financial terms in the form of budgets. In the executing stage, managers use the information in the budgets to implement the plan. In the reviewing stage, they compare actual performance with planned performance and take steps to correct any problems. Reports reflect the results of planning, executing, and reviewing operations and may be prepared for external or internal use.

LO2 Describe the value chain and its usefulness in analyzing a business.

The value chain conceives of each step in the manufacture of a product or the delivery of a service as a link in a chain that adds value to the product or service. These value-adding steps—research and development, design, supply, production, marketing, distribution, and customer service—are known as primary processes. The value chain also includes support services—human resources, legal services, information services, and management accounting. Support services facilitate the primary processes but do not add value to the final product. Value chain analysis enables a company to focus on its core competencies. Parts of the value chain that are not core competencies are frequently outsourced.

LO3 Identify the management tools used for continuous improvement and describe how they work to meet the demands of global competition and how management accounting supports them.

Management tools for continuous improvement include the just-in-time (JIT) operating philosophy, total quality management (TQM), activity-based management (ABM), and the theory of constraints (TOC). These tools are designed to help businesses meet the demands of global competition by reducing resource waste and costs and improving product or service quality, thereby increasing customer satisfaction. Management accounting responds to a JIT operating environment by providing an information system that is sensitive to changes in production processes. In a TQM environment, management accounting provides information about the costs of quality. ABM's assignment of overhead costs to products or services relies on the accounting practice known as activity-based costing (ABC). In businesses that use TOC, management accounting identifies process or product constraints.

LO4 Explain the balanced scorecard and its relationship to performance measures.

The balanced scorecard links the perspectives of an organization's stakeholder groups—financial (investors and owners), learning and growth (employees), internal business processes, and customers—with the organization's mission, objectives, resources, and performance measures. Performance measures are used to assess whether the objectives of each of the four perspectives are being met. Benchmarking is a technique for determining a company's competitive advantage by comparing its performance with that of its industry peers.

LO5 Prepare an analysis of nonfinancial data.

Using management tools like TQM and ABM and comprehensive frameworks like the balanced scorecard requires analysis of both financial and nonfinancial data. In analyzing nonfinancial data, it is important to compare performance measures with the objectives that are to be achieved.

LO6 Identify the standards of ethical conduct for management accountants.

Standards of ethical conduct for management accountants emphasize practitioners' responsibilities in the areas of competence, confidentiality, integrity, and objectivity. These standards of conduct help management accountants recognize and avoid situations that could compromise their ability to supply management with accurate and relevant information.

REVIEW OF CONCEPTS AND TERMINOLOGY

The following concepts and terms were introduced in this chapter:

LO3 **Activity-based costing (ABC):** A management accounting practice that identifies all of an organization's major operating activities (both production and nonproduction), traces costs to those activities, and then assigns costs to the products or services that use the resources and services supplied by those activities.

LO3 **Activity-based management (ABM):** An approach to managing an organization that identifies all major operating activities, determines the resources consumed by each of those activities and the cause of the resource usage, categorizes the activities as either adding value to a product or service or not adding value, and seeks to eliminate or reduce nonvalue-adding activities.

LO4 **Balanced scorecard:** A framework that links the perspectives of an organization's stakeholder groups with the organization's mission, objectives, resources, and performance measures.

LO4 **Benchmarking:** A technique for determining a company's competitive advantage by comparing its performance with that of its best competitors.

LO4 **Benchmarks:** Measures of the best practices in an industry.

LO1 **Business plan:** A comprehensive statement of how a company will achieve its objectives.

LO3 **Continuous improvement:** The management concept that one should never be satisfied with what is but should instead constantly seek improved efficiency and lower cost through better methods, products, services, processes, or resources.

LO2 **Core competency:** What a company does best and what gives it an advantage over its competitors.

LO3 **Costs of quality:** Both the costs of achieving quality and the costs of poor quality in the manufacture of a product or the delivery of a service.

LO3 **Just-in-time (JIT) operating philosophy:** A management tool aimed at improving productivity and eliminating waste by requiring that all resources—materials, personnel, and facilities—be acquired and used only as needed.

LO1 **Management accounting:** The process of identifying, measuring, accumulating, analyzing, preparing, interpreting, and communicating information that management uses to plan, evaluate, and control an organization and to ensure that its resources are used and accounted for appropriately.

LO1 **Mission:** A statement of the fundamental way in which a business will achieve its goal of increasing the value of the owners' interest in the business.

LO3 **Nonvalue-adding activities:** Activities that add cost to a product or service but do not increase its market value.

LO1 **Operating objectives:** Short-term goals that outline expectations for the performance of day-to-day operations.

LO2 **Outsourcing:** The engagement of other companies to perform a process or service of the value chain that is not among an organization's core competencies.

LO4 Performance measures: Quantitative tools that gauge an organization's performance in relation to a specific goal or expected outcome.

LO2 Primary processes: Components of the value chain that add value to a product or service.

LO1 Strategic objectives: Broad, long-term goals that determine the fundamental nature and direction of a business and that serve as a guide for decision making.

LO1 Supply chain: The path that leads from the suppliers of the materials from which a product is made to the final consumer. Also called the *supply network*.

LO2 Support services: Components of the value chain that facilitate the primary processes but do not add value to a product or service.

LO3 Theory of constraints (TOC): A management theory that contends that limiting factors, or bottlenecks, occur during the production of any product or service, but that once managers identify such a constraint, they can focus attention and resources on it and thus achieve significant improvements.

LO3 Total quality management (TQM): A management tool that requires that all parts of a business work together to build quality into the business's product or service.

LO3 Value-adding activities: Activities that add value to a product or service as perceived by the customer.

LO2 Value chain: A way of defining a business as a set of primary processes and support services that link together to add value to a business's products or services, thus fulfilling the business's mission and objectives.

REVIEW PROBLEM

Analysis of Nonfinancial Data

LO5 Youngdale Painting, Inc., employs painters who specialize in interior walls and exterior trim. George Youngdale, the owner, recently assigned two interior painters and three exterior trim painters to jobs at Yakima High School and Jerome Elementary School. He prepared the following table estimating the number of hours that the painters would work during June:

	Estimated Hours to Be Worked				
	Week 1	Week 2	Week 3	Week 4	Totals
Interior	80	80	80	80	320
Exterior	120	120	120	120	480

On July 2, Youngdale assembled the following data on the actual number of hours worked:

	Actual Hours Worked				
	Week 1	Week 2	Week 3	Week 4	Totals
Interior	96	108	116	116	436
Exterior	104	108	116	108	436

Youngdale is concerned about the excess hours worked during June.

REQUIRED
1. For each group of painters (interior and exterior), prepare an analysis that shows the estimated hours, the actual hours worked, and the number of hours under or over the estimates for each week and in total.
2. Using the same information, prepare a line graph for the interior painters and another line graph for the exterior painters. Place the weeks on the X axis and the number of hours on the Y axis.

3. Using the information from 1 and 2, identify which group of painters worked more hours than George Youngdale planned and offer several reasons for the additional hours.

ANSWER TO REVIEW PROBLEM

1.

Interior Painters

Week	Estimated Hours	Actual Hours	Hours Under or (Over) Estimate
1	80	96	(16)
2	80	108	(28)
3	80	116	(36)
4	80	116	(36)
Total	320	436	(116)

Exterior Painters

Week	Projected Hours	Actual Hours	Hours Under or (Over) Estimate
1	120	104	16
2	120	108	12
3	120	116	4
4	120	108	12
Total	480	436	44

2.

3. The interior painters worked more hours than Youngdale had planned. The following are possible reasons for the additional hours:
   a. The quality of the paint or painting materials may have been poor, which would have required the painters to apply extra coats.
   b. One of the painters may have been recently hired and inexperienced. He would therefore have worked more slowly than anticipated, and the other painter may have taken extra time to train him.
   c. The customer may have requested a change in color or finish after the painting had started, in which case the painters would have had to repaint some areas.
   d. Youngdale may have underestimated the time required for the interior painting.

Chapter Assignments

BUILDING YOUR KNOWLEDGE FOUNDATION

QUESTIONS

1. What is management accounting, and how is it similar to financial accounting?
2. How do management accounting and financial accounting reports differ in terms of format, purpose, and primary users?
3. How do management accounting and financial accounting reports differ in terms of units of measure, nature of information, and frequency of preparation?
4. What are the four stages of the management cycle? Briefly explain each stage.
5. How is management accounting used in the management cycle?
6. What are the six components of the planning framework? Briefly describe each.
7. What is the supply chain?
8. What are the four *w*'s of report preparation? Explain the importance of each.
9. What is the value chain, and what are the primary processes and support services? How do primary processes and support services differ?
10. What are core competencies and outsourcing?
11. What management tools do companies use to deal with expanding global competition?
12. How does the just-in-time operating philosophy affect an organization's operating environment?
13. How does total quality management help managers do their jobs?
14. How does activity-based management affect an organization's operating environment?
15. How does the theory of constraints affect an organization's operating environment?
16. What is the goal of all the management approaches described in this chapter?
17. What are performance measures? Give examples of both financial and nonfinancial performance measures.
18. How does the balanced scorecard help managers evaluate performance?
19. What perspectives are included in the balanced scorecard?
20. Why do ethical standards for management accountants emphasize competence?
21. Why is it so important for management accountants to maintain their integrity?

SHORT EXERCISES

LO1 Management Accounting Versus Financial Accounting

SE 1. Management accounting differs from financial accounting in a number of ways. Indicate whether each of the following characteristics relates to management accounting (MA) or financial accounting (FA):

1. Focuses on various segments of the business entity
2. Demands objectivity
3. Relies on the criterion of usefulness rather than formal guidelines in reporting information
4. Measures units in historical dollars
5. Reports information on a regular basis
6. Uses only monetary measures for reports
7. Adheres to generally accepted accounting principles
8. Prepares reports whenever needed

LO1 The Management Cycle

SE 2. Indicate whether each of the following management activities in a department store is part of the planning stage (P), the executing stage (E), the reviewing stage (REV), or the reporting stage (REP) of the management cycle:

1. Completing a balance sheet and income statement at the end of the year
2. Training a clerk to complete a cash sale
3. Meeting with department managers to develop performance measures for sales personnel
4. Renting a local warehouse to store excess inventory of clothing
5. Evaluating the performance of the shoe department by examining the significant differences between its actual and planned expenses for the month
6. Preparing an annual budget of anticipated sales for each department and the entire store

LO1 Report Preparation

SE 3. Melissa Mertz, president of Mertz Industries, asked controller Rick Caputo to prepare a report on the use of electricity by each of the organization's five divisions. Increases in electricity costs in the divisions ranged from 20 to 35 percent over the past year. What questions should Rick ask before he begins his analysis?

LO1 The Supply Chain and the
LO2 Value Chain

SE 4. Indicate whether each of the following is part of the supply chain (SC), a primary process (PP) in the value chain, or a support service (SS) in the value chain:

1. Human resources
2. Research and development
3. Supplier
4. Management accounting
5. Customer service
6. Retailer

LO2 The Value Chain

SE 5. From the following unit costs, which were determined by dividing total costs of each cost component by the number of products produced, determine the total cost per unit of primary processes and the total cost per unit of support services:

Research and development	$1.25
Human resources	1.35
Design	.15
Supply	1.10
Legal services	.40
Production	4.00
Marketing	.80
Distribution	.90
Customer service	.65
Information systems	.75
Management accounting	.10
Total cost per unit	$11.45

LO3 JIT and Continuous Improvement

SE 6. The just-in-time operating environment focuses on reducing or eliminating the waste of resources. Resources include physical assets such as machinery and buildings, labor time, and materials and parts used in the production process. Choose one of those resources and tell how it could be wasted. How can an organization prevent the waste of that resource? How can the concept of continuous improvement be implemented to reduce the waste of that resource?

LO3 ABC and the Assignment of Cost

SE 7. Get Away Enterprises offers weeklong Florida vacation packages to student groups. The trip includes meals, lodging, a parasailing excursion, and transportation. The price is $1,400 per couple. Courtney and Chris sign up. What are some ways of assigning the cost of the trip to each of them? Support your answer.

LO4 The Balanced Scorecard: Stakeholder Values

SE 8. In the balanced scorecard approach, stakeholder groups with different perspectives value different performance goals. Sometimes, however, they may be interested in the same goal. Indicate which stakeholder groups—financial (F), learning and growth (L), internal business processes (P), and customers (C)—value the following performance goals:

1. High wages
2. Safe products

3. Low-priced products
4. Improved return on investment
5. Job security
6. Cost-effective production processes

LO5 Analysis of Nonfinancial Data

SE 9. Precision Technologies has been having a problem with the computerized welding operation in its extractor assembly line. The extractors are used to separate metal shavings into piles of individual metals for recycling and scrap sales. The time for each welding operation has been increasing at an erratic rate. Management has asked that the time intervals be analyzed to see if the cause of the problem can be determined. The number of parts welded per shift during the previous week is as follows:

	Machine Number	Monday	Tuesday	Wednesday	Thursday	Friday
First shift:						
Kovacs	1	642	636	625	617	602
Abington	2	732	736	735	729	738
Geisler	3	745	726	717	694	686
Second shift:						
Deragon	1	426	416	410	404	398
Berwager	2	654	656	661	664	670
Grass	3	526	524	510	504	502

What can you deduce from this information that may help management solve the welding operation problem?

LO6 Ethical Conduct

SE 10. Tyler Jones, a management accountant for Pegstone Cosmetics Company, has lunch every day with his friend Joe Blaik, a management accountant for Shepherd Cosmetics, Inc., a competitor of Pegstone. Last week, Jones couldn't decide how to treat some information in a report he was preparing, so he discussed it with Blaik. Is Jones adhering to the ethical standards of management accountants? Defend your answer.

EXERCISES

LO1 Management Accounting Versus Financial Accounting

E 1. Explain this statement: "It is impossible to distinguish the point at which financial accounting ends and management accounting begins."

LO1 The Management Cycle

E 2. Indicate whether each of the following management activities in a community hospital is part of the planning stage (P), the executing stage (E), the reviewing stage (REV), or the reporting stage (REP) of the management cycle:

1. Leasing five ambulances for the current year
2. Comparing the actual number with the planned number of patient days in the hospital for the year
3. Developing a strategic plan for a new pediatric wing
4. Preparing a report showing the past performance of the emergency room
5. Developing standards, or expectations, for performance in the hospital admittance area for next year
6. Preparing and distributing the hospital's balance sheet and income statement to the board of directors
7. Maintaining an inventory of bed linens and bath towels
8. Formulating a corporate policy for the treatment and final disposition of hazardous waste materials
9. Preparing a report of the types and amounts of hazardous waste materials removed from the hospital in the last three months
10. Recording the time taken to deliver food trays to patients

LO1 Report Preparation

E 3. Jeff Johnson is the sales manager for Sunny Days Greeting Cards, Inc. At the beginning of the year, the organization introduced a new line of humorous birthday cards to the U.S. market. Management will hold a strategic planning meeting on August 31 to discuss next year's operating activities. One item on the agenda is to review the success of the new line of cards and decide if there is a need to change the selling price or to stimulate sales volume in the five sales territories. Johnson has been asked to prepare a report addressing those issues and to present it at the meeting. His report is to include profits generated in each sales territory by the new card line only.

On August 31, Johnson arrived at the meeting late and immediately distributed his report to the strategic planning team. The report consisted of comments made by seven of Johnson's leading sales representatives. The comments were broad in scope and touched only lightly on the success of the new card line. Johnson was pleased that he had met the deadline for distributing the report, but the other team members were disappointed in the information he had provided.

Using the four *w*'s for report presentation, comment on Johnson's effectiveness in preparing his report.

LO1 The Planning Framework

E 4. Edward Ortez has just opened a company that imports fine ceramic gifts from Mexico and sells them over the Internet. In planning his business, Ortez did the following:
1. Listed his expected expenses and revenues for the first six months of operations
2. Decided that he wanted the company to provide him with income for a good lifestyle and funds for retirement
3. Determined that he would keep his expenses low and generate enough revenues during the first two months of operations so that he would have a positive cash flow by the third month
4. Decided to focus his business on providing customers with the finest Mexican ceramics at a favorable price
5. Developed a complete list of goals, objectives, procedures, and policies relating to how he would find, buy, store, sell, and ship goods and collect payment
6. Decided not to have a retail operation but to rely solely on the Internet to market the products

Match each of Ortez's actions to the components of the planning framework: goal, mission, strategic objectives, operating objectives, business plan, and budget.

LO1 The Supply Chain

E 5. In recent years, United Parcel Service (UPS) has been positioning itself as a solver of supply chain issues. Visit its web site at www.ups-scs.com and read one of the case studies related to its supply chain solutions. Explain how UPS helped improve the supply chain of the business featured in the case.

LO2 The Value Chain

E 6. As mentioned in **E4**, Edward Ortez recently opened his own company. He has been thinking of ways to improve the business. Here is a list of the actions that he will be undertaking:
1. Engaging an accountant to help analyze progress in meeting the objectives of the company
2. Hiring a company to handle payroll records and employee benefits
3. Developing a logo for labeling and packaging the ceramics
4. Making gift packages by placing gourmet food products in ceramic pots and wrapping them in plastic
5. Engaging an attorney to write contracts
6. Traveling to Mexico himself to arrange for purchase and shipment of products back to the company
7. Arranging new ways of taking orders over the Internet and shipping the products
8. Keeping track of the characteristics of customers and the number and types of products they buy
9. Following up with customers to see if they received the products and if they are happy with them
10. Arranging for an outside firm to keep the accounting records
11. Distributing brochures that display the ceramics and refer to the web site

Classify each of Ortez's actions as one of the value chain's primary processes—research and development, design, supply, production, marketing, distribution, or customer service—or as a support service—human resources, legal services, information systems, or management accounting. Of the eleven actions, which are the most likely candidates for outsourcing? Why?

LO3 Management Tools

E 7. Recently, you were dining with four chief financial officers who were attending a seminar on management tools and approaches to improving operations. During dinner, they shared information about their organizations' current operating environments. Excerpts from the dinner conversation appear on the following page. Indicate whether each excerpt describes activity-based management (ABM), the just-in-time (JIT) operating philosophy, total quality management (TQM), or the theory of constraints (TOC).

CFO 1: We think quality can be achieved through carefully designed production processes. We focus on minimizing the time needed to move, store, queue, and inspect our materials and products. We've reduced inventories by purchasing and using materials only when they're needed.

CFO 2: Your approach is good. But we're more concerned with our total operating environment, so we have a strategy that asks all employees to contribute to the quality of both our products and our work environment. We focus on eliminating poor product quality by reducing waste and inefficiencies in our current operating methods.

CFO 3: Our organization has adopted a strategy for producing high-quality products that incorporates many of your approaches. We also want to manage our resources effectively, but we do it by monitoring operating activities. We analyze all activities to eliminate or reduce the ones that don't add value to products.

CFO 4: All of your approaches are good, but how do you set priorities for your management efforts? We find that we achieve the greatest improvements by focusing our time and resources on the bottlenecks in our production processes.

LO3 TQM and Value

E 8. De Silva Dry Cleaners recently adopted total quality management. Jorge De Silva, the owner, has hired you as a consultant. Classify each of the following activities as either value-adding (V) or nonvalue-adding (NV):

1. Providing same-day service
2. Closing store on weekends
3. Providing free delivery service
4. Having seamstress on site
5. Making customers pay for parking

LO4 The Balanced Scorecard

E 9. Connie's Takeout caters to young professionals who want a good meal at home but do not have time to prepare it. Connie's has developed the following business objectives:

1. To provide fast, courteous service
2. To manage its inventory of food carefully
3. To have repeat customers
4. To be profitable and grow

Connie's has also developed the following performance measures:

5. Growth in revenues per quarter and net margin
6. Average unsold food at the end of the business day as a percentage of the total food purchased that day
7. Average customer time at counter before being waited on
8. Percentage of customers who have shopped in the store before

Match each of these objectives and performance measures with the four perspectives of the balanced scorecard: financial perspective, learning and growth perspective, internal business processes perspective, and customer perspective.

LO5 Nonfinancial Data Analysis

E 10. Bluegrass Landscaping specializes in lawn installations requiring California bluegrass sod. The sod comes in 1-yard squares. To evaluate performance in laying sod layers, Bluegrass Landscaping uses the guideline of 500 square yards per person per hour. The company collected the following data about its operations during the first week of March:

Employee	Hours Worked	Square Yards of Sod Planted
S. Elway	38	18,240
R. Mahoney	45	22,500
N. Fencereaux	40	19,800
O. Pfister	42	17,640
B. Onski	44	22,880
J. Mantero	45	21,500

Evaluate the performance of the six employees.

LO5 Nonfinancial Data Analysis

E 11. Mother's Cookie Company recently adopted total quality management. According to a quality performance measure set by Elián Gomez, the vice president in charge of production, no more than ten cookies should be rejected per day. Data gathered for a recent week showed that the actual number of rejected cookies per day was as follows.

Day	Actual Number of Rejected Cookies
Monday	5
Tuesday	6
Wednesday	7
Thursday	4
Friday	8
Total	30

Analyze the activity for the week by preparing a table showing each day's maximum number of rejected cookies allowed, actual number of rejected cookies, and variance from the maximum number allowed. Compute the daily average for each column. Based on the information in your table, how successful was Gomez in increasing the quality of the company's cookies?

LO5 Nonfinancial Data Analysis

E 12. Sara Fowler, who is in charge of information technology at Cergo Corporation, must decide whether to purchase additional memory for her department's three computers or to buy additional new computers to increase her department's productivity. Six weeks ago, Fowler installed additional memory on Computer CM. She is impressed with the processing improvement, but she has yet to decide between the two courses of action. Information on the number of bytes processed per nanosecond by each computer for the past ten weeks is as follows:

	Weeks									
Computer	One	Two	Three	Four	Five	Six	Seven	Eight	Nine	Ten
CM	51	52	53	50	80	82	84	87	88	89
CN	52	51	52	52	54	54	53	54	54	54
CP	50	49	50	48	50	52	51	50	52	50

Fowler has asked you to analyze the two courses of action based on the assumption that two memory upgrades can be purchased for the price of one new computer. Your analysis is to include the computation of the average weekly output per nanosecond for Computers CN and CP, a comparison of that average with the output of Computer CM, and the computation of the weekly difference between the average output and the output of Computer CM. What course of action do you recommend?

LO6 Ethical Conduct

E 13. Katrina Kim went to work for Billings Industries five years ago. She was recently promoted to cost accounting manager and now has a new boss, Vic Howard, the corporate controller. Last week, Kim and Howard went to a two-day professional development program on accounting changes in the manufacturing environment. During the first hour of the first day's program, Howard disappeared, and Kim didn't see him again until the cocktail hour. The same thing happened on the second day. During the trip home, Kim asked Howard if he had enjoyed the conference. He replied:

> Katrina, the golf course was excellent. You play golf. Why don't you join me during the next conference? I haven't sat in on one of those sessions in ten years. This is my R&R time. Those sessions are for the new people. My experience is enough to keep me current. Plus, I have excellent people to help me as we adjust our accounting system to the changes being implemented on the production floor.

Does Katrina Kim have an ethical dilemma? If so, what is it? What are her options? How would you solve her problem? Be prepared to defend your answer.

LO6 Ethical Responsibility

E 14. Rank in order of importance the management accountant's four areas of responsibility: competence, confidentiality, integrity, and objectivity. Explain the reasons for your ranking.

LO6 Corporate Ethics

E 15. To answer the following questions, conduct a search of several companies' web sites: (1) Does the company have an ethics statement? (2) Does it express a commitment to environmental or social issues? (3) In your opinion, is the company ethically responsible? Select one of the companies you researched and write a brief description of your findings.

Problems

LO1 Report Preparation

P 1. Classic Industries, Inc., is deciding whether to expand its line of women's clothing called Pants by Olene. Sales in units of this product were 22,500, 28,900, and 36,200 in 20x4, 20x5, and 20x6, respectively. The product has been very profitable, averaging 35 percent profit (above cost) over the three-year period. Classic has ten sales representatives covering seven states in the Northeast. Present production capacity is about 40,000 pants per year. There is adequate plant space for additional equipment, and the labor needed can be easily hired and trained.

The organization's management is made up of four vice presidents: the vice president of marketing, the vice president of production, the vice president of finance, and the vice president of management information systems. Each vice president is directly responsible to the president, Teresa Jefferson.

REQUIRED
1. What types of information will Jefferson need before she can decide whether to expand the Pants by Olene line?
2. Assume that one report needed to support Jefferson's decision is an analysis of sales, broken down by sales representatives, over the past three years. How would each of the four w's pertain to this report?
3. Design a format for the report described in **2**.

LO2 The Value Chain

P 2. Zeigler Electronics is a manufacturer of cell phones, a highly competitive business. Zeigler's phones carry a price of $99, but competition forces the company to offer significant discounts and rebates. As a result, the average price of Zeigler's cell phones has dropped to around $50, and the company is losing money. Management is applying value chain analysis to the company's operations in an effort to reduce costs and improve product quality. A study by the company's management accountant has determined the following per unit costs for primary processes:

Primary Process	Cost per Unit
Research and development	$ 2.50
Design	3.50
Supply	4.50
Production	6.70
Marketing	8.00
Distribution	1.90
Customer service	.50
Total cost	$27.60

To generate a gross margin large enough for the company to cover overhead costs and earn a profit, Zeigler must lower its total cost per unit for primary processes to at least $20. After analyzing operations, management reached the following conclusions with regard to primary processes:

- Research and development and design are critical functions because the market and competition require constant development of new features with "cool" designs at lower cost. Nevertheless, management feels that the cost per unit of these processes must be reduced by 10 percent.
- Six different suppliers currently provide the components for the cell phones. Ordering these components from just two suppliers and negotiating lower prices could result in a savings of 15 percent.
- The cell phones are currently manufactured in Mexico. By shifting production to China, the unit cost of production can be lowered by 20 percent.
- Most cell phones are sold through wireless communication companies that are trying to attract new customers with low-priced cell phones. Management believes these companies should bear more of the marketing costs and that it is feasible to renegotiate its marketing arrangements with them so that they will bear 35 percent of the current marketing costs.

- Distribution costs are already very low, but management will set a target of reducing the cost per unit by 10 percent.
- Customer service is a weakness of the company and has resulted in lost sales. Management therefore proposes increasing the cost per unit of customer service by 50 percent.

REQUIRED

1. Prepare a table showing the current cost per unit of primary processes and the projected cost per unit based on management's proposals for cost reduction.
2. Will management's proposals for cost reduction achieve the targeted total cost per unit? What further steps should management take to reduce costs? Which steps that management is proposing do you believe will be the most difficult to accomplish?
3. What are the company's support services? What role should these services play in the value chain analysis?

P 3.
LO4 The Balanced Scorecard and Benchmarking

Bychowski Associates is an independent insurance agency that sells business, automobile, home, and life insurance. Myra Bychowski, senior partner of the agency, recently attended a workshop at the local university in which the balanced scorecard was presented as a way of focusing all of a company's functions on its mission. After the workshop, she met with her managers in a weekend brainstorming session. The group determined that the agency's mission was to provide high-quality, innovative risk-protection services to individuals and businesses. To ensure that the agency would fulfill this mission, the group established the following objectives:

- To provide a sufficient return on investment by increasing sales and maintaining the liquidity needed to support operations
- To add value to the agency's services by training employees to be knowledgeable and competent
- To retain customers and attract new customers
- To operate an efficient and cost-effective office support system for customer agents

To determine the agency's progress in meeting these objectives, the group established the following performance measures:

- Number of new ideas for customer insurance
- Percentage of customers who rate services as excellent
- Average time for processing insurance applications
- Number of dollars spent on training
- Growth in revenues for each type of insurance
- Average time for processing claims
- Percentage of employees who complete 40 hours of training during the year
- Percentage of new customer leads that result in sales
- Cash flow
- Number of customer complaints
- Return on assets
- Percentage of customers who renew policies
- Percentage of revenue devoted to office support system (information systems, accounting, orders, and claims processing)

REQUIRED

1. Prepare a balanced scorecard for Bychowski Associates by stating the agency's mission and matching its four objectives to the four stakeholder perspectives: the financial, learning and growth, internal business processes, and customer perspectives. Indicate which of the agency's performance measures would be appropriate for each objective.
2. Bychowski Associates is a member of an association of independent insurance agents that provides industry statistics about many aspects of operating an insurance agency. What is benchmarking, and in what ways would the industry statistics assist Bychowski Associates in further developing its balanced scorecard?

P 4.
LO5 Nonfinancial Data Analysis

Action Skateboards, Inc., manufactures state-of-the-art skateboards and related equipment. Lindy Raymond is the manager of the California branch. The production process involves the following departments and tasks: the Molding Department, where the board's base is molded; the Sanding Department, where the base is sanded after being taken out of the mold; the Fiber-Ap Department, where a fiberglass coating is applied; and the Assembling Department, where the wheels are attached and the board is inspected. After the board is molded, all processes are performed by hand.

Raymond is concerned about the number of hours her employees are working. The plant has a two-shift labor force. The actual hours worked for the past four weeks are as follows:

Actual Hours Worked—First Shift

Department	Week 1	Week 2	Week 3	Week 4	Totals
Molding	420	432	476	494	1,822
Sanding	60	81	70	91	302
Fiber-Ap	504	540	588	572	2,204
Assembling	768	891	952	832	3,443

Actual Hours Worked—Second Shift

Department	Week 1	Week 2	Week 3	Week 4	Totals
Molding	360	357	437	462	1,616
Sanding	60	84	69	99	312
Fiber-Ap	440	462	529	506	1,937
Assembling	670	714	782	726	2,892

Expected labor hours per product for each operation are Molding, 3.4 hours; Sanding, .5 hour; Fiber-Ap, 4.0 hours; and Assembling, 6.5 hours. Actual units completed are as follows:

Week	First Shift	Second Shift
1	120	100
2	135	105
3	140	115
4	130	110

REQUIRED
1. Prepare an analysis of each week to determine the average actual labor hours worked per board for each phase of the production process and for each shift. Carry your solution to two decimal places.
2. Using the information from 1 and the expected labor hours per board for each department, prepare an analysis showing the differences in each phase of each shift. Identify possible reasons for the differences.

P 5.
LO5 Nonfinancial Data Analysis

The flow of passenger traffic is an important factor in airport management, and over the past year, heightened security measures at Winnebago County Airport in Rockford, Illinois, have slowed passenger flow significantly. The airport uses eight metal detectors to screen passengers for weapons. The facility is open from 6:00 A.M. to 10:00 P.M. daily, and present machinery allows a maximum of 45,000 passengers to be checked each day.

Management has selected four of the metal detectors for special analysis to determine if additional equipment is needed or if a passenger traffic director could solve the problem. The passenger traffic director would be responsible for guiding people to different machines and instructing them on the detection process. Because this solution would be less expensive than acquiring new machines, management decides to assign a suitable person to this function on a trial basis. Management hopes this procedure will speed up the flow of passenger traffic by at least 10 percent. Manufacturers of the machinery have stated that each machine can handle an average of 400 passengers per hour. Data on passenger traffic through the four machines for the past 10 days are shown at the top of the next page.

In the past, passenger flow has favored Machine 1 because of its location. Overflow traffic goes to Machine 2, Machine 3, and Machine 4, in that order.

The passenger traffic director, Lynn Hedlund, began her duties on March 13. If her work results in at least a 10 percent increase in the number of passengers handled, management plans to hire a second traffic director for the other four machines rather than purchasing additional metal detectors.

REQUIRED
1. Calculate the average daily traffic flow for the period March 6–12 and then calculate management's traffic flow goal.
2. Calculate the average traffic flow for the period March 13–15. Did the passenger traffic director's work result in the minimum increase in flow set by management, or should airport officials purchase additional metal directors?

	Passengers Checked by Metal Detectors				
Date	Machine 1	Machine 2	Machine 3	Machine 4	Totals
March 6	5,620	5,490	5,436	5,268	21,814
March 7	5,524	5,534	5,442	5,290	21,790
March 8	5,490	5,548	5,489	5,348	21,875
March 9	5,436	5,592	5,536	5,410	21,974
March 10	5,404	5,631	5,568	5,456	22,059
March 11	5,386	5,667	5,594	5,496	22,143
March 12	5,364	5,690	5,638	5,542	22,234
March 13	5,678	6,248	6,180	6,090	24,196
March 14	5,720	6,272	6,232	6,212	24,436
March 15	5,736	6,324	6,372	6,278	24,710

3. Is there anything unusual in the analysis of passenger traffic flow that management should look into? Explain your answer.

ALTERNATE PROBLEMS

LO1 Report Preparation

P 6. Sam Ratha recently purchased Yard & More, Inc., a wholesale distributor of equipment and supplies for lawn and garden care. The organization, headquartered in Baltimore, has four distribution centers that service 14 eastern states. The centers are located in Boston; Rye, New York; Reston, Virginia; and Lawrenceville, New Jersey. Company profits for 20x2, 20x3, and 20x4 were $225,400, $337,980, and $467,200, respectively.

Shortly after purchasing the organization, Ratha appointed people to the following positions: vice president, marketing; vice president, distribution; corporate controller; and vice president, research and development. Ratha has called a meeting of his management group. He wants to create a deluxe retail lawn and garden center that would include a large, fully landscaped plant and tree nursery. The purposes of the retail center would be (1) to test equipment and supplies before selecting them for sales and distribution and (2) to showcase the effects of using the company's products. The retail center must also make a profit on sales.

REQUIRED
1. What types of information will Ratha need before deciding whether to create the retail lawn and garden center?
2. To support his decision, Ratha will need a report from the vice president of research and development analyzing all possible plants and trees that could be planted and their ability to grow in the places where the new retail center might be located. How would each of the four *w*'s pertain to this report?
3. Design a format for the report in **2**.

LO5 Nonfinancial Data Analysis

P 7. Holiday Candy Company, which has recently developed a strategic plan based on total quality management, wants its candy canes to have the highest quality of color, texture, shape, and taste possible. To ensure that quality standards are met, management has chosen many quality performance measures, including the number of rejected candy canes. Working with Luisa Ortes, the production supervisor, management has decided that no more than 50 candy canes should be rejected each day.

Using data on rejections in Week 1 of 20x4, Luisa Ortes prepared the following summary and the graph that appears on the next page.

Week 1, 20x4	Maximum Number of Rejected Candy Canes Allowed	Actual Number of Rejected Candy Canes	Variance Under (Over) Allowed Maximum
Monday	50	60	(10)
Tuesday	50	63	(13)
Wednesday	50	58	(8)
Thursday	50	59	(9)
Friday	50	62	(12)
Total for the week	250	302	(52)
Daily average	50	60.4	

Because the variance was 20.8 percent (52 ÷ 250), Ortes decided to analyze the data further. She found that the rejected candy canes contained too little sugar (ingredients), were not circular in shape (shaping), or were undercooked (cooking time). The number of rejects in each category appears below.

Week 1, 20x4	Reasons for Rejects
Ingredients	40
Shaping	195
Cooking time	67
Total	302

The following week, Ortes reviewed the recipe with the cooks. She trained them to measure ingredients more precisely, to shape the candy more carefully, and to time the cooking process more accurately. Then, in Week 3 of 20x4, she gathered the following information on the actual number of rejected candy canes and reasons for the rejects:

Week 3, 20x4	Actual Number of Rejects	Week 3, 20x4	Reasons for Rejects
Monday	20	Ingredients	7
Tuesday	21	Shaping	63
Wednesday	22	Cooking time	30
Thursday	19	Total	100
Friday	18		
Total	100		

REQUIRED

1. Analyze the activity in Week 3 of 20x4 by preparing a table showing each day's maximum number of rejected candy canes allowed, actual number of rejected candy canes, and variance under (over) the maximum number allowed. In addition, prepare a graph comparing the maximum and actual numbers for each day of Week 3.
2. Analyze how the reasons for rejecting candy canes changed from Week 1 to Week 3 by preparing a table showing the number of times each reason occurred each week. In addition, prepare a graph comparing the reasons for rejects each week.
3. How successful was Ortes in increasing the quality of Holiday's candy canes? What recommendations, if any, would you make about monitoring candy production in the future?

LO5 Nonfinancial Data Analysis

P 8. Texas State Bank was founded in 1869. It has had a record of slow, steady growth since its inception. Management has always kept the processing of information as current as technology allows. Leslie Oistins, manager of the Brazas branch, is upgrading the check-sorting equipment in her office. There are ten check-sorting machines in operation. Information on the number of checks sorted by machine during the past eight weeks is as follows:

Machine	Weeks							
	One	Two	Three	Four	Five	Six	Seven	Eight
AA	89,260	89,439	89,394	90,288	90,739	90,658	90,676	90,630
AB	91,420	91,237	91,602	91,969	91,950	92,502	92,446	92,816
AC	94,830	95,020	94,972	95,922	96,401	96,315	96,334	96,286
AD	91,970	91,786	92,153	92,522	92,503	93,058	93,002	93,375
AE	87,270	87,445	87,401	88,275	88,716	88,636	88,654	88,610
BA	92,450	92,265	92,634	93,005	92,986	93,544	93,488	93,862
BB	91,910	92,094	92,048	92,968	93,433	93,349	93,368	93,321
BC	90,040	89,860	90,219	90,580	90,562	91,105	91,051	91,415
BD	87,110	87,190	87,210	130,815	132,320	133,560	134,290	135,770
BE	94,330	94,519	94,471	95,416	95,893	95,807	95,826	95,778

The Brazas branch has increased its checking business significantly over the past two years. Oistins must decide whether to purchase additional check-sorting machines or attachments for the existing machines to increase productivity. Five weeks ago the Colonnade Company convinced her to experiment with one such attachment, and it was placed on Machine BD. Oistins is impressed with the attachment but has yet to decide between the two courses of action. Labor costs are not a factor in her decision.

REQUIRED
1. Compute the average weekly output of all machines except BD.
2. Compare the weekly output of Machine BD with the average weekly output of the nine machines without the attachment. Compute the weekly difference in the number of checks and the percentage change (difference divided by the average weekly output of the nine machines).
3. Assume that Colonnade's attachment costs about the same as a new check-sorting machine. Which alternative would you recommend that Oistins choose?
4. Would you change your recommendation if two attachments could be purchased for the price of one check-sorting machine? Does this decision require more data?
5. Assume three attachments could be purchased for the price of one check-sorting machine. What action would you recommend?

SKILLS DEVELOPMENT CASES

Conceptual Analysis

LO2 The Value Chain and Core Competency

SD 1. Medical Products Company (MPC) is known for developing innovative and high-quality products for use in hospitals and medical and dental offices. Its latest product is a nonporous, tough, and very thin disposable glove that will not leak or split and molds tightly to the hand, making it ideal for use in medical and dental procedures. MPC buys the material it uses in making the gloves from another company, which manufactures it according to MPC'S exact specifications and quality standards. MPC makes two models of the glove—one white, and one transparent—in its own plant and sells them through independent agents who represent various manufacturers. When an agent informs MPC of a sale, MPC ships the order directly to the buyer. MPC advertises the gloves in professional journals and gives free samples to physicians and dentists. It provides a product warranty and periodically surveys users about the product's quality.

Briefly explain how MPC accomplishes each of the primary processes of the value chain. What is a core competency? Which one of the primary processes would you say is MPC's core competency? Explain your choice.

LO3 Continuous Improvement

SD 2. Achieving high quality requires high standards of performance. To maintain high standards of quality, individuals and organizations must continuously improve their performance. To illustrate this concept, select your favorite sport or hobby.

1. Answer the following questions:
    a. What standards do you have for assessing your performance?
    b. What processes have you designed for achieving high quality in your performance?
    c. How do you know when you have achieved high quality in your performance?
    d. Once you know you perform well, how easy will it be for you to maintain that level of expertise?
    e. What can you do to ensure that you are continuously improving your performance?
2. If you owned a business, which of the above questions would be important to answer?
3. Answer the questions in 1, assuming you own a business.

LO4 Performance Measures and the Balanced Scorecard

SD 3. General Motors Corporation <www.gm.com> had a plan to revamp the way it makes small cars. Called Project Yellowstone, the plan called for GM to build two U.S. plants that would use modular assembly systems. GM's suppliers would develop and send large chunks of cars, like dashboards, to the two new plants for final assembly. The amount of GM's investment and the number of employees needed to assemble the cars would be greatly reduced. The United Auto Workers union blasted the new approach as an attempt to eliminate union jobs, and GM retreated from the plan.[9]

1. What financial performance measures mentioned in the chapter would have prompted GM to try this new approach?
2. The balanced scorecard uses performance measures that are linked to the perspectives of all stakeholder groups. Who are GM's stakeholders, and what performance measures do they value?
3. Refer to the discussion of Honda Motor Company <www.honda.com> in the Decision Point at the beginning of this chapter. How does Honda's modular assembly plan differ from the one GM proposed?
4. In your opinion, what options does GM have if it wishes to pursue the use of modular assembly systems?

Ethical Dilemma

LO6 Professional Ethics

SD 4. Mark Taylor is the controller for Krohm Corporation. Taylor has been with the company for 17 years and is being considered for the job of chief financial officer (CFO). His boss, the current CFO and former company controller, will be Krohm Corporation's new president. Taylor has just discussed the year-end closing with his boss, who made the following statement during the conversation:

> Mark, why are you being so inflexible? I'm only asking you to postpone the $2,500,000 write-off of obsolete inventory for ten days so that it won't appear on this year's financial statements. Ten days! Do it. Your promotion is coming up, you know. Make sure you keep all the possible outcomes in mind as you complete your year-end work. Oh, and keep this conversation confidential—just between you and me. Okay?

Identify the ethical issue or issues involved and state the appropriate solution to the problem. Be prepared to defend your answer.

Research Activity

LO1 Report Preparation

SD 5. The registrar's office of Polk Community College is responsible for maintaining a record of each student's grades and credits for use by students, instructors, and administrators.

1. Assume you are a manager in the registrar's office and that you recently joined a team of managers to review the grade-reporting process. Explain how you would prepare a report of grades for students' use and the same report for instructors' use by answering the following questions:
    a. Who will read the grade report?
    b. Why is the grade report necessary?
    c. What information should the grade report contain?
    d. When is the grade report due?

2. Why does the information in a grade report for students' use and in a grade report for instructors' use differ?
3. Visit the registrar's office of your school in person or through your school's web site. Obtain a copy of your grade report and a copy of the form the registrar's office uses to report grades to instructors. Compare the information that these reports supply with the information you listed in **1**. Explain any differences.
4. What can the registrar's office do to make sure that its grade reports are effective in communicating all necessary information to readers?

Decision-Making Practice

SD 6.
LO5 Nonfinancial Data Analysis

Aviation Products Company is a subcontractor that specializes in producing housings for landing gears on jet airplanes. Its production process begins with Machine 1, which bends pieces of metal into cylinder-shaped housings and trims off the rough edges. Machine 2 welds the seam of the cylinder and pushes the entire piece into a large die to mold the housing into its final shape.

Joe Mee, the production supervisor, believes the current process creates too much scrap (i.e., wasted metal). To verify this, James Kincaid, the company's accountant, began comparing the amounts of scrap generated in the last four weeks with the amounts of scrap the company anticipated for that period. Because of a death in his family, Kincaid could not complete his analysis. His incomplete report appears below. Mee asks you to complete the report and submit a recommendation to him.

Aviation Products Company
Comparison of Actual Scrap and Expected Scrap
Four-Week Period

	Scrap in Pounds		Difference	
	Actual	Expected	Pounds	Percentage
Machine 1				
Week 1	36,720	36,720		
Week 2	54,288	36,288		
Week 3	71,856	35,856		
Week 4	82,440	35,640		
Machine 2				
Week 1	43,200	18,180		
Week 2	39,600	18,054		
Week 3	7,200	18,162		
Week 4	18,000	18,108		

1. Present the information in two ways:
   a. Prepare a table that shows the difference between the actual and the expected scrap in pounds per machine per week. Calculate the difference in pounds and as a percentage (divide the difference in pounds by the expected pounds of scrap for each week). If the actual poundage of scrap is less than the expected poundage, record the difference as a negative. (This means there is less scrap than expected.)
   b. Prepare a line graph for each machine showing the weeks on the X axis and the pounds of scrap on the Y axis.
2. Examine the differences for the four weeks for each machine and determine which machine operation is creating excessive scrap.
3. What could be causing this problem?
4. What could Mee do to encourage early identification of the specific cause of such problems?

MANAGERIAL REPORTING AND ANALYSIS CASES

Interpreting Management Reports

MRA 1.

LO1 **Management Information**

Obtain a copy of a recent annual report of a publicly held organization in which you have a particular interest. (Copies of annual reports are available at your campus library, at a local public library, on the Internet, or by direct request to an organization.) Assume that you have just been appointed to a middle-management position in a division of the organization you have chosen. You are interested in obtaining information that will help you better manage the activities of your division and have decided to study the contents of the annual report in an attempt to learn as much as possible. You particularly want to know about the following:

1. Size of inventory maintained
2. Ability to earn income
3. Reliance on debt financing
4. Types, volume, and prices of products or services sold
5. Type of production process used
6. Management's long-range strategies
7. Success (profitability) of the division's various product lines
8. Efficiency of operations
9. Operating details of your division

1. Write a brief description of the organization and its products or services and activities.
2. Based on a review of the financial statements and the accompanying disclosure notes, prepare a written summary of information pertaining to items 1 through 9 above.
3. Is any of the information in which you are interested in other sections of the annual report? If so, which information, and in which sections of the report is it?
4. The annual report also includes other types of information you may find helpful in your new position. In outline form, summarize this additional information.

Formulating Management Reports

MRA 2.

LO1 **Management Information Needs**

In **MRA 1**, you examined your new employer's annual report and found some useful information. However, you are interested in knowing whether your division's products or services are competitive, and you were unable to find the necessary information in the annual report.

1. What kinds of information about your competition do you want to find?
2. Why is this information relevant? (Link your response to a particular decision about your organization's products or services. For example, you might seek information to help you determine a new selling price.)
3. From what sources could you obtain the information you need?
4. When would you want to obtain this information?
5. Create a report that will communicate your findings to your superior.

International Company

MRA 3.

LO5 **Management Information Needs**

McDonald's <www.mcdonalds.com> is a leading competitor in the fast-food restaurant business. One component of McDonald's marketing strategy is to increase sales by expanding its foreign markets. At present, more than 40 percent of McDonald's restaurants are located outside the United States. In making decisions about opening restaurants in foreign markets, the company uses quantitative and qualitative financial and nonfinancial information. For example, the following types of information would be important to such a decision: the cost of a new building (quantitative financial information), the estimated number of hamburgers to be sold in the first year (quantitative nonfinancial information), and site desirability (qualitative information).

You are a member of a management team that must decide whether or not to open a new restaurant in England. Identify at least two examples each of the (a) quantitative financial, (b) quantitative nonfinancial, and (c) qualitative information you will need before you can make a decision.

 Group Activity: Divide the class into groups and ask them to discuss this case. Then debrief the entire class by asking one person from each group to summarize his or her group's discussion.

Excel Spreadsheet Analysis

MRA 4.
LO5 Nonfinancial Data Analysis

Refer to assignment **P 2** in this chapter. Lindy Raymond needs to analyze the work performed by each shift in each department during Weeks 1 through 4.

1. For each department, calculate the average labor hours worked per board for each shift during Weeks 1 through 4. Carry your solution to two decimal places. (Note: Hours worked per board = hours worked each week ÷ boards produced each week.)
2. Using the ChartWizard and the information from **1**, prepare a line graph for each department that compares the hours per board worked by the first and second shifts and the estimate for that department during Weeks 1 through 4. The following is the suggested format to use for the information table necessary to complete the line graph for the Molding Department:

	Molding Department			
	Week 1	Week 2	Week 3	Week 4
First shift	3.50	3.20	3.40	3.80
Second shift	3.60	3.40	3.80	4.20
Estimated	3.40	3.40	3.40	3.40

3. Examine the four graphs that you prepared in **2**. Which shift is more efficient in all four departments? List some reasons for the differences between the shifts.

Internet Case

MRA 5.
LO4 Comparison of Performance Measures

As noted in this chapter's Decision Point, Honda Motor Company <www.honda.com> makes a green car called the Insight. Toyota Motor Company <www.toyota.com> also makes a green car, which it calls the Prius. Search the web sites of both these companies for data concerning the success of their green cars. (**Hint:** Review annual reports and press releases, or use the company's search engine.)

1. List the financial and nonfinancial performance measures that Toyota uses. List the measures used by Honda.
2. Use the data you found to prepare a brief comparison of the two cars. Do the two companies use comparable performance measures? If so, use these measures to evaluate the performance of the Prius and the Insight. If the measures are not comparable, how do they differ?

16

Chapter 16 describes how managers use information about costs, classify costs, compile product unit costs, and allocate costs using the traditional method and the newer activity-based approach.

Cost Concepts and Cost Allocation

Learning Objectives

LO1 Describe how managers use information about costs in the management cycle.

LO2 Explain how managers classify costs and how they use these cost classifications.

LO3 Define and give examples of the three elements of product cost and compute the unit cost of a product.

LO4 Describe the flow of costs through a manufacturer's inventory accounts.

LO5 Compare how service, retail, and manufacturing organizations report costs on their financial statements and how they account for inventories.

LO6 Define *cost allocation* and explain how cost objects, cost pools, and cost drivers are used to assign manufacturing overhead costs.

LO7 Using the traditional method of allocating manufacturing overhead costs, calculate product unit cost.

LO8 Using activity-based costing to assign manufacturing overhead costs, calculate product unit cost.

LO9 Apply costing concepts to a service organization.

DECISION POINT

A MANAGER'S FOCUS

Southwest Airlines <www.southwest.com> With approximately 2,800 flights a day, an average trip length of 715 miles, and an average one-way fare of $82.84, Southwest Airlines is the nation's leading high-frequency, short-haul, low-fare carrier. It is also the only large domestic airline to have remained profitable for more than 30 years. In both 2001 and 2002, the Official Airline Guide <www.oag.com>, an independent provider of travel information, products, and services, named Southwest "Best Low-Cost Airline."

To have achieved such a status and to maintain it, Southwest managers must know the costs the airline is incurring, including the cost of selling tickets and of flight operations. For example, knowing that selling a ticket through a travel agent costs Southwest as much as $6 to $8 whereas selling a ticket through its web site costs the airline just $1 enables managers to offer lower fares to customers who buy tickets online. Online ticket sales at southwest.com generated approximately 46 percent, or $500 million, of the company's passenger revenues for the first quarter of 2002.[1]

Determining the cost of selling tickets online or the cost of operating a flight requires complex analyses of many costs. What are some of these costs, and how do they bear on Southwest's management decisions?

When determining the cost of online ticket sales, Southwest's managers analyze the costs of direct labor and materials (if a paper ticket is issued), as well

How does Southwest Airlines determine the cost of selling tickets or operating a flight?

as the costs of activities needed to support these sales, such as supervision, equipment maintenance, depreciation, and utilities. When determining the cost of operating a flight, they analyze the costs of the materials (e.g., peanuts, drinks, jet fuel) and labor used (e.g., flight attendants, pilot), as well as overhead costs, such as aircraft maintenance and depreciation. Southwest's managers also consider any other relevant selling, administrative, or general operating costs that the flight incurs.

To help managers make decisions that will sustain Southwest's profitability, all costs must be analyzed in terms of their traceability and behavior, whether they add value, and how they affect the financial statements. Because many costs cannot be directly traced to specific flights, activities, or departments, management must use a method of allocation to assign them. Possibilities include traditional allocation methods and a newer method called activity-based costing, which we introduce in this chapter.

Cost Information and the Management Cycle

LO1 Describe how managers use information about costs in the management cycle.

RELATED TEXT ASSIGNMENTS
Q: 1
E: 1
SD: 1

One of a company's primary goals is to be profitable. Because owners expect to earn profits, managers have a responsibility to use resources wisely and to generate revenues that will exceed the costs of the company's operating, investing, and financing activities. In this chapter, we focus on costs related to the operating activities of manufacturing, retail, and service organizations. We begin by looking at how managers in these different organizations use information about costs during the management cycle.

Use of Cost Information in the Management Cycle

During the management cycle, managers use information about operating costs to plan, execute, review, and report the results of operating activities. Figure 1 provides an overview of operating costs and the management cycle.

■ **Planning** In the planning stage, managers of manufacturing companies, such as John Deere, Motorola, and General Motors, use estimates of product costs to develop budgets for production, materials, labor, and overhead, as well as to determine the selling price or sales level required to cover all costs. In retail companies, such as Sears, Pep Boys, and Chico's, managers work with estimates of the cost of merchandise purchases to develop budgets for purchases and net income, as well as to determine the selling prices or sales units required to cover all costs. In service organizations, like Citibank, Humana, and USAA, managers use the estimated costs

www.johndeere.com
www.motorola.com
www.gm.com
www.sears.com
www.pepboys.com
www.chicos.com
www.citibank.com
www.humana.com
www.usaa.com

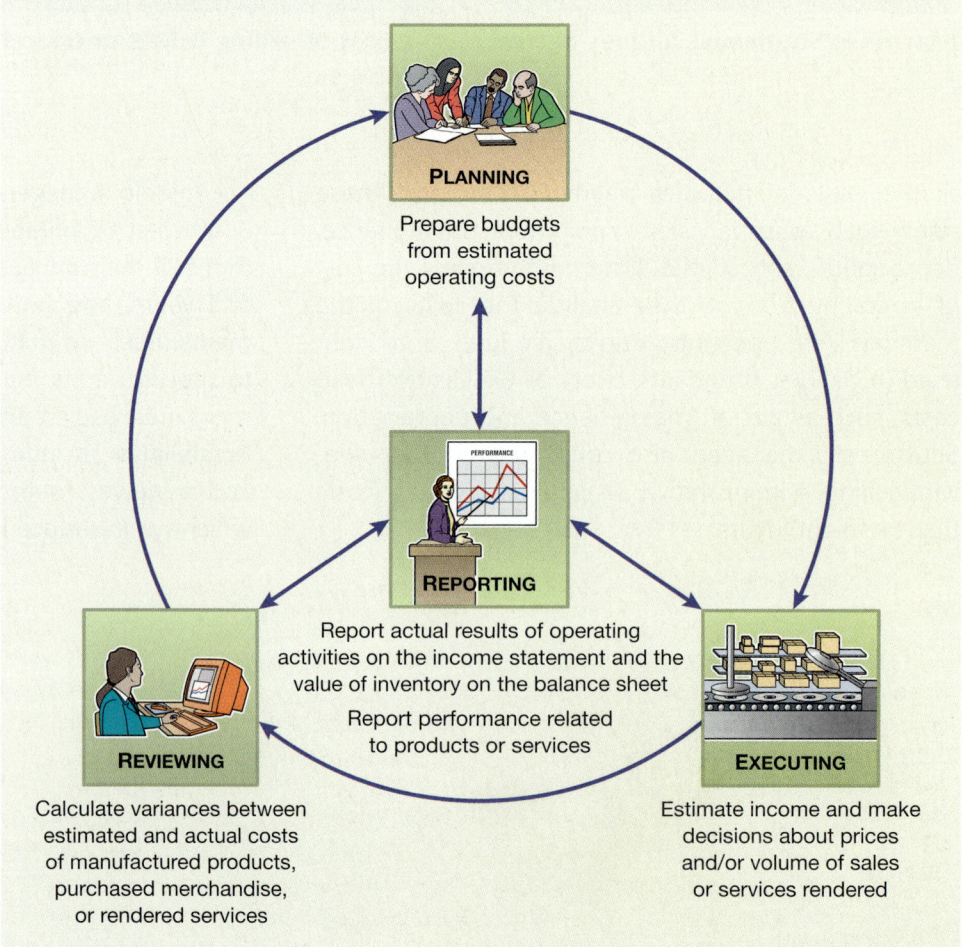

FIGURE 1
Operating Costs and the Management Cycle

of rendering services to develop budgets, estimate revenues, and manage the organization's work force.

■ **EXECUTING** In the executing stage, managers of manufacturing companies use estimated product costs to predict the gross margin and operating income on sales and to make decisions about such matters as dropping a product line, outsourcing the manufacture of a part to another company, bidding on a special order, or negotiating a selling price. In retail organizations, managers work with the estimated cost of merchandise purchases to predict gross margin, operating income, and value of merchandise sold and to make decisions about such matters as reducing selling prices for clearance sales, lowering selling prices for bulk sales, or dropping a product line. In service organizations, managers find the estimated cost of services helpful in estimating profitability and making decisions about such matters as bidding on future business, lowering or negotiating their fees, or dropping one of their services.

■ **REVIEWING** In the reviewing stage, managers want to know about significant differences between the estimated costs and actual costs of their products, merchandise purchases, or services. The identification of variances between estimated and actual costs helps them determine the causes of cost overruns, which may enable them to make decisions that will avoid such problems in the future.

■ **REPORTING** In the reporting stage, managers expect to see income statements that show the actual costs of operating activities and balance sheets that show the value of inventory. They also expect performance reports that summarize the variance analyses done in the reviewing stage.

COST INFORMATION AND ORGANIZATIONS

Although all organizations use cost information to determine profits and selling prices and to value inventories, different types of organizations have different types of costs. Manufacturing organizations need information about the costs of manufacturing products. Product costs include the costs of direct materials, direct labor, and manufacturing overhead. Retail organizations need information about the costs of purchasing products for resale. These costs include adjustments for freight-in costs, purchase returns and allowances, and purchase discounts. Service organizations need information about the costs of providing services, which include the costs of labor and related overhead. Among the other costs that these organizations incur are the costs of marketing, distributing, installing, and repairing a product or the costs of marketing and supporting the delivery of services. Ultimately, a company is profitable only when its revenues from sales or services rendered exceed all costs.

✓ Check out ACE for a Review Quiz at http://accounting.college.hmco.com/students.

● **STOP AND THINK!**
Do managers in all organizations need the same type of cost information?

The type of cost information managers need varies according to the type of organization. Managers in manufacturing organizations need information about the cost of manufacturing a product, those in retail organizations need information about the cost of purchasing a product, and those in service organizations need information about the cost of providing a service. ■

COST CLASSIFICATIONS AND THEIR USES

LO2 Explain how managers classify costs and how they use these cost classifications.
RELATED TEXT ASSIGNMENTS
Q: 2, 3, 4, 5
SE: 1
E: 2
SD: 1, 4
MRA: 2, 5

A single cost can be classified and used in several ways, depending on the purpose of the analysis. Figure 2 provides an overview of commonly used cost classifications. These classifications enable managers to (1) control costs by determining which are traceable to a particular cost object, such as a service or product; (2) calculate the number of units that must be sold to obtain a certain level of profit (cost behavior); (3) identify the costs of activities that do and do not add value to a product or service; and (4) classify costs for the preparation of financial statements. Cost classifications are important in all types of organizations. They help managers select and use relevant information to improve the efficiency of operations, provide quality products or services, and satisfy customer needs.

FIGURE 2
Overview of Cost Classifications

COST TRACEABILITY

Managers trace costs to cost objects, such as products or services, sales territories, departments, or operating activities, to develop a fairly accurate measurement of costs. They use both direct and indirect measures of costs to support pricing decisions or decisions to reallocate resources to other cost objects.

Direct costs are costs that can be conveniently and economically traced to a cost object. For example, the wages of a Southwest Airlines flight crew can be conveniently traced to a flight because the time worked and the hourly wages are shown on time cards and payroll records. Similarly, jet fuel costs for a flight can be easily traced.

www.southwest.com

In some cases, even though a material becomes part of a finished product, the expense of tracing its cost is too great. Some examples include the nails used in furniture, the salt used in cookies, and the rivets used in airplanes. Such costs are considered indirect costs of the product. **Indirect costs** are costs that cannot be conveniently and economically traced to a cost object. For the sake of accuracy, however, indirect costs must be included in the cost of a product or service. Because they are difficult to trace, management uses a formula to assign them. For example, Southwest Airlines' insurance costs cannot be conveniently traced to individual flights; management solves the problem by assigning a portion of the insurance costs to each flight flown.

The following examples illustrate cost objects and their direct and indirect costs in service, retail, and manufacturing organizations:

- In a service organization, such as an accounting firm, costs can be traced to a specific service, such as preparation of tax returns. Direct costs for such a service include the costs of government reporting forms, computer usage, and the accountant's labor. Indirect costs include the costs of supplies, office rental, utilities, secretarial labor, telephone usage, and depreciation of office furniture.

- In a retail organization, such as a department store, costs can be traced to a department. For example, the direct costs of the shoe department include the costs of shoes and the wages of employees working in that department. Indirect costs include the costs of utilities, insurance, property taxes, storage, and handling.

- In a manufacturing organization, costs can be traced to the product. Direct costs include the costs of the materials and labor needed to make the product. Indirect costs include the costs of utilities, depreciation of plant and equipment, insurance, property taxes, inspection, supervision, maintenance of machinery, storage, and handling.

■ STOP AND THINK!
Are the costs of a product always traceable as direct or indirect costs?
Because products are cost objects, their costs can always be classified as direct or indirect. ■

Focus on Business Practice

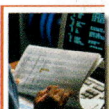

How Does an Airline Manage Its Fixed Costs?
One of Southwest Airlines' nonfinancial performance measures is a twenty-minute turnaround time on the ground. This standard helps Southwest <www.southwest.com> efficiently manage the many fixed costs of running an airline. If additional security measures or other circumstances forced Southwest to add even ten minutes to its ground turnaround time, it would result in higher fixed costs because the company would need additional planes to keep to its daily flight schedule. For an airline to be profitable, it needs to maximize its fleet's time in the air and minimize its time on the ground.[2]

Cost Behavior

Managers are also interested in the way costs respond to changes in volume or activity. By analyzing those patterns of behavior, they gain information about how changes in selling prices or operating costs affect the company's net income, and they can then make adjustments so that the company obtains a certain level of profit.

Costs can be separated into variable costs and fixed costs. A **variable cost** is a cost that changes in direct proportion to a change in productive output (or any other measure of volume). A **fixed cost** is a cost that remains constant within a defined range of activity or time period.

All types of organizations have variable and fixed costs. The following are a few examples:

- The variable costs of a landscaping service include the costs of landscaping materials and labor to plant the materials. Fixed costs include the costs of depreciation on trucks and equipment, rent, insurance, and property taxes.
- The variable costs of a used-car dealer include the cost of cars sold and sales commissions. Fixed costs include the costs of building and lot rental, depreciation on office equipment, and receptionist's and accountant's salaries.
- The variable costs of a lawn-mower manufacturer include the costs of direct materials, direct labor, indirect materials (e.g., bolts, nails, lubricants), and indirect labor (e.g., inspection and maintenance labor). Fixed costs include the costs of supervisors' salaries and depreciation on buildings.

As a landscaping service plants more trees, as a used-car dealer sells more cars, or as a lawn-mower manufacturer increases its output of products, its variable costs will increase proportionately. But its fixed costs will remain the same for a specified period; rent, for example, will not change over the term of the lease, and property taxes will remain the same until the next assessment.

Value-Adding Versus Nonvalue-Adding Costs

A **value-adding cost** is the cost of an activity that increases the market value of a product or service. A **nonvalue-adding cost** is the cost of an activity that adds cost to a product or service but does not increase its market value. For example, the depreciation of a machine that shapes a part used in the final product is a value-adding cost; the depreciation of a car used by the Sales Department is a nonvalue-adding cost. Managers examine the value-adding attributes of their company's operating activities and, wherever possible, reduce or eliminate those that do not directly add value to the company's products or services. Managers also identify which characteristics of their company's products or services customers value and are willing to pay for. This information influences the design of future products or services.

Costs incurred to improve the quality of a product are value-adding costs if the customer is willing to pay more for the higher-quality product; otherwise, they are nonvalue-adding costs because they do not increase the product's market value. The costs of administrative activities, such as accounting and human resource management, are nonvalue-adding costs; they are necessary for the operation of the business, but they do not add value to the product.

Cost Classifications for Financial Reporting

For purposes of preparing financial statements, managers classify costs as product costs or period costs. **Product costs**, or *inventoriable* costs, are costs assigned to inventory; they include direct materials, direct labor, and manufacturing overhead.

KEY POINT: Product costs remain assets until they are expensed and transferred from the Finished Goods Inventory account to Cost of Goods Sold.

BUSINESS WORLD EXAMPLE: The length of time costs remain in inventory is not a consideration in determining product cost. For example, fast-food operations maintain a direct materials inventory, have a rapid turnover in work in process inventory, and have virtually no finished goods inventory at any given time.

TABLE 1. Examples of Cost Classifications for a Candy Manufacturer

Cost Examples	Traceability to Product	Cost Behavior	Value Attribute	Financial Reporting
Sugar for candy	Direct	Variable	Value-adding	Product (direct materials)
Labor for mixing	Direct	Variable	Value-adding	Product (direct labor)
Labor for supervision	Indirect	Fixed	Nonvalue-adding	Product (manufacturing overhead)
Depreciation on mixing machine	Indirect	Fixed	Value-adding	Product (manufacturing overhead)
Sales commission	—*	Variable	Value-adding†	Period
Accountant's salary	—*	Fixed	Nonvalue-adding	Period

*Sales commissions and accountants' salaries cannot be directly or indirectly traced to a cost object; they are not product costs.
†Sales commissions can be value-adding because customers' perceptions of the salesperson and the selling experience can strongly affect their perceptions of the product's market value.

STUDY NOTE: Product costs and period costs can be explained using the matching rule. Product costs must be charged to the period in which the product generates revenue, and period costs are charged against the revenue of the current period.

Product costs appear on the income statement as cost of goods sold and on the balance sheet as finished goods inventory. **Period costs**, or *noninventoriable* costs, are costs of resources used during the accounting period and not assigned to products. They appear as operating expenses on the income statement. For example, selling and administrative expenses are period costs.

Table 1 shows how some costs of a candy manufacturer can be classified in terms of traceability, behavior, value attribute, and financial reporting.

 Check out ACE for a Review Quiz at http://accounting.college.hmco.com/students.

ELEMENTS OF PRODUCT COSTS

LO3 Define and give examples of the three elements of product cost and compute the unit cost of a product.

RELATED TEXT ASSIGNMENTS
Q: 6, 7, 8, 9
SE: 2, 3
E: 3
P: 1
MRA: 5

KEY POINT: Direct materials and direct labor are costs that can be conveniently and economically traced to the product. This is an application of cost-benefit analysis.

As noted above, product costs include all costs related to the manufacturing process. The three elements of product cost are direct materials costs, direct labor costs, and manufacturing overhead costs, which are indirect costs.

Direct materials costs are the costs of materials used in making a product that can be conveniently and economically traced to specific units of the product. Some examples of direct materials are the iron ore used in making steel, the sheet metal used in making automobiles, and the sugar used in making candy. Direct materials may also include parts purchased from another manufacturer.

Direct labor costs are the costs of the labor needed to make a product that can be conveniently and economically traced to specific units of the product. For example, the wages of production-line workers are direct labor costs.

Manufacturing overhead costs (also called *factory overhead, factory burden,* or *indirect manufacturing costs*) are production-related costs that cannot be practically or conveniently traced directly to an end product. They include **indirect materials costs**, such as the costs of nails, rivets, lubricants, and small tools, and **indirect labor costs**, such as the costs of labor for machinery and tool maintenance, inspection, engineering design, supervision, and materials handling. Other indirect manufacturing costs include the costs of building maintenance, property taxes, property insurance, depreciation on plant and equipment, rent, and utilities. As indirect costs, manufacturing overhead costs are allocated to a product's cost using traditional or activity-based costing methods, which we discuss later in the chapter.

To illustrate product costs and the manufacturing process, we'll refer throughout the chapter to Candy Company, Inc., a manufacturer of chocolate candy bars. Olga Santee, the company's founder and president, has identified the following elements of the product cost of one candy bar:

- *Direct materials costs:* costs of sugar, chocolate, and wrapper

FOCUS ON BUSINESS TECHNOLOGY

Has Technology Shifted the Elements of Product Costs?

New technology and manufacturing processes have produced new patterns of product costs. The three elements of product costs are still direct materials, direct labor, and manufacturing overhead, but the percentage that each contributes to the total cost of a product has changed. From the 1950s through the 1970s, direct labor was the dominant element, making up over 40 percent of total product cost, while direct materials contributed 35 percent and manufacturing overhead, around 25 percent. Thus, 75 percent of total product cost was a direct cost, traceable to the product. Improved production technology caused a dramatic shift in the three product cost elements. Machines replaced people, significantly reducing direct labor costs. Today, only 50 percent of the cost of a product is directly traceable to the product; the other 50 percent is manufacturing overhead, an indirect cost.

- *Direct labor costs:* costs of labor used in making the candy bar
- *Manufacturing overhead costs:* indirect materials costs, including the costs of salt and flavorings; indirect labor costs, including the costs of labor to move materials to the production area and to inspect the candy bars during production; other indirect overhead costs, including depreciation on the building and equipment, utilities, property taxes, and insurance

COMPUTING PRODUCT UNIT COST

Product unit cost is the cost of manufacturing a single unit of a product. It is made up of the costs of direct materials, direct labor, and manufacturing overhead. These three cost elements are accumulated as a batch of products is being produced. When the batch has been completed, the product unit cost is computed either by dividing the total cost of direct materials, direct labor, and manufacturing overhead by the total number of units produced, or by determining the cost per unit for each element of the product cost and summing those per-unit costs.

Unit cost information helps managers price products and calculate gross margin and net income. Managers and accountants can calculate product unit cost by using actual costing, normal costing, or standard costing methods. Table 2 summarizes how these three cost-measurement methods use actual and estimated costs.

■ **ACTUAL COSTING METHOD** The **actual costing** method uses the costs of direct materials, direct labor, and manufacturing overhead at the end of an accounting period or when actual costs become known to calculate the product unit cost. The actual product unit cost is assigned to the finished goods inventory on the balance sheet and to the cost of goods sold on the income statement. For example, assume

● STOP AND THINK!
How do the costing methods used to compute a product's cost per unit affect the three elements of product cost?

The three elements of product cost, direct materials, direct labor, and manufacturing overhead, may differ in amount depending on whether the actual, normal, or standard costing method is used. ■

TERMINOLOGY NOTE:
Estimated costs are also called *projected, standard, predetermined,* or *budgeted costs.*

TABLE 2. Use of Actual and Estimated Costs in Three Cost-Measurement Methods

Product Cost Elements	Actual Costing	Normal Costing	Standard Costing
Direct materials	Actual costs	Actual costs	Estimated costs
Direct labor	Actual costs	Actual costs	Estimated costs
Manufacturing overhead	Actual costs	Estimated costs	Estimated costs

KEY POINT: Many management decisions require estimates of future costs. Managers often use actual cost as a basis for estimating future cost.

that Candy Company, Inc., produced 3,000 candy bars on December 28, 20x6, for a corporate customer in Seattle. Maya Kee, the company's accountant, calculated that the actual costs for the Seattle order were direct materials, $540; direct labor, $420; and manufacturing overhead, $240. The actual product unit cost for the order was $.40, calculated as follows:

Direct materials ($540 ÷ 3,000 candy bars)	$.18
Direct labor ($420 ÷ 3,000 candy bars)	.14
Manufacturing overhead ($240 ÷ 3,000 candy bars)	.08
Product cost per candy bar ($1,200 ÷ 3,000 candy bars)	$.40

In this case, the product unit cost was computed after the job was completed and all cost information was known. Sometimes, however, a manufacturer needs to know product unit cost during production, when the actual direct materials costs and direct labor costs are known but the actual manufacturing overhead costs are uncertain. In that case, the computation of product unit cost will include an estimate of the manufacturing overhead, and the normal costing method will be helpful.

■ **NORMAL COSTING METHOD** The **normal costing** method combines actual direct costs of materials and labor with estimated manufacturing overhead costs to determine a product unit cost. The normal costing method is simple and allows a smoother, more even assignment of manufacturing overhead costs to production during an accounting period than is possible with the actual costing method. It also contributes to better pricing decisions and profitability estimates. However, at the end of the accounting period, any difference between the estimated and actual costs must be identified and removed so that the financial statements show only the actual product costs.

Assume that Maya Kee used normal costing to price the Seattle order for 3,000 candy bars and that manufacturing overhead was applied to the product's cost using an estimated rate of 60 percent of direct labor costs. In this case, the costs for the order would include the actual direct materials cost of $540, the actual direct labor cost of $420, and an estimated manufacturing overhead cost of $252 ($420.00 × 60%). The product unit cost would be $.404:

Direct materials ($540.00 ÷ 3,000 candy bars)	$.180
Direct labor ($420.00 ÷ 3,000 candy bars)	.140
Manufacturing overhead ($252.00 ÷ 3,000 candy bars)	.084
Product cost per candy bar ($1,212 ÷ 3,000 candy bars)	$.404

■ **STANDARD COSTING METHOD** Managers sometimes need product cost information before the accounting period begins so that they can control the cost of operating activities or price a proposed product for a customer. In such situations, product unit costs must be estimated, and the **standard costing** method can be helpful. This method uses estimated, or standard, costs of direct materials, direct labor, and manufacturing overhead to calculate the product unit cost.

Assume that Candy Company is placing a bid to manufacture 2,000 candy bars for a new customer. From standard cost information developed at the beginning of the period, Kee estimates the following costs: $.20 per unit for direct materials, $.15 per unit for direct labor, and $.09 per unit for manufacturing overhead (assuming a standard overhead rate of 60 percent of direct labor cost). The standard cost per unit would be $.44:

Direct materials	$.20
Direct labor	.15
Manufacturing overhead ($.15 × 60%)	.09
Product cost per candy bar	$.44

FIGURE 3
Relationships Among Product Cost Classifications

The $.44 product unit cost is useful in determining the cost of the bid, $880 ($.44 × 2,000 candy bars), estimating the gross margin for the job, and deciding the price to bid for the business. We cover standard costing in more detail in another chapter.

PRIME COSTS AND CONVERSION COSTS

The three elements of manufacturing costs can be grouped into prime costs and conversion costs. **Prime costs** are the primary costs of production; they are the sum of the direct materials costs and direct labor costs. **Conversion costs** are the costs of converting direct materials into a finished product; they are the sum of direct labor costs and manufacturing overhead costs. Using the figures for Candy Company's actual unit cost, the per-unit prime costs and conversion costs are as follows:

	Prime Costs	Conversion Costs
Direct materials	$.18	—
Direct labor	.14	$.14
Manufacturing overhead	—	.08
Totals	$.32	$.22

These classifications are important for understanding the costing methods discussed in later chapters. Figure 3 summarizes the relationships among the product cost classifications presented so far.

 Check out ACE for a Review Quiz at http://accounting.college.hmco.com/students.

INVENTORY ACCOUNTS IN MANUFACTURING ORGANIZATIONS

LO4 Describe the flow of costs through a manufacturer's inventory accounts.

RELATED TEXT ASSIGNMENTS
Q: 10, 11, 12
SE: 4, 5
E: 4, 5

Transforming materials into finished products ready for sale requires a number of production and production-related activities, including purchasing, receiving, inspecting, storing, and moving materials; converting them into finished products using labor, equipment, and other resources; and moving, storing, and shipping the finished products. A manufacturing organization's accounting system tracks these activities as product costs flowing through the Materials Inventory, Work in Process Inventory, and Finished Goods Inventory accounts. The **Materials Inventory** account shows the balance of the cost of unused materials, the **Work in Process Inventory account** shows the manufacturing costs that have been incurred and assigned to partially completed units of product, and the **Finished Goods Inventory account** shows the costs assigned to all completed products that have not been sold.

DOCUMENT FLOWS AND COST FLOWS THROUGH THE INVENTORY ACCOUNTS

In many companies, accountants accumulate and report manufacturing costs based on documents pertaining to production and production-related activities. Although paper documents are still used for this purpose, electronic documents have become increasingly common. Looking at how the documents for the three elements of product cost relate to the flow of costs through the three inventory accounts provides insight into when an activity must be recorded in the accounting records. Figure 4 summarizes the relationships among the production activities, the documents for each of the three cost elements, and the inventory accounts affected by the activities.

To illustrate the document flow and changes in inventory balances for production activities, we continue with our example of Candy Company, Inc.

■ **PURCHASE OF MATERIALS** The same process is used for purchasing both direct and indirect materials. The purchasing process starts with a *purchase request* for specific quantities of materials needed in the manufacturing process but not currently available in the materials storeroom. A qualified manager approves the request. Based on the information in the purchase request, the Purchasing Department sends a *purchase order* to a supplier. When the materials arrive, an employee on the receiving dock counts and examines them and prepares a *receiving report*. Later, an accounting clerk matches the information on the receiving report with the descriptions and quantities listed on the purchase order. A materials handler moves the newly arrived materials from the receiving area to the materials storeroom. Soon, Candy Company receives a *vendor's invoice* from the supplier requesting payment for the purchased materials. The cost of those materials increases the balance of the Materials Inventory account.

■ **PRODUCTION OF GOODS** When candy bars are scheduled for production, the storeroom clerk receives a *materials request form*. The materials request form is essential for controlling materials. In addition to showing the supervisor's signature of approval, it describes the types and quantities of materials the storeroom clerk is to send to the production area, and it authorizes the release of those materials from the materials inventory into production. If the appropriate manager has approved the materials request form, the storeroom clerk has the materials handler move the materials to the production floor. The cost of the direct materials transferred will increase the balance of the Work in Process Inventory account and decrease the balance of the Materials Inventory account. The cost of the indirect materials transferred will increase the balance of the Manufacturing Overhead account and decrease the balance of the Materials Inventory account. (We discuss overhead in more detail later in this chapter.)

Each of the production employees who make the candy bars prepares a *time card* to record the number of hours he or she has worked on this and other orders each day. The costs of the direct labor and manufacturing overhead used to manufacture the candy bars increase the balance of the Work in Process Inventory account. A *job order cost card* is used to record all costs incurred as the products move through production.

■ **PRODUCT COMPLETION AND SALE** Employees place completed candy bars in cartons and then move the cartons to the finished goods storeroom, where they are kept until shipped to customers. The cost of the completed candy bars increases the

---

● **STOP AND THINK!**
Are paper documents always used in accounting for manufacturing costs?

Although paper documents have traditionally been used, many companies today use electronic documents. ■

ENRICHMENT NOTE:
Some companies use sophisticated computer programs to match receiving reports to purchase orders.

FIGURE 4
Activities, Documents, and Cost Flows Through the Inventory Accounts of a Manufacturing Organization

FIGURE 5
Manufacturing Cost Flow: An Example Using Actual Costing for Candy Company, Inc.

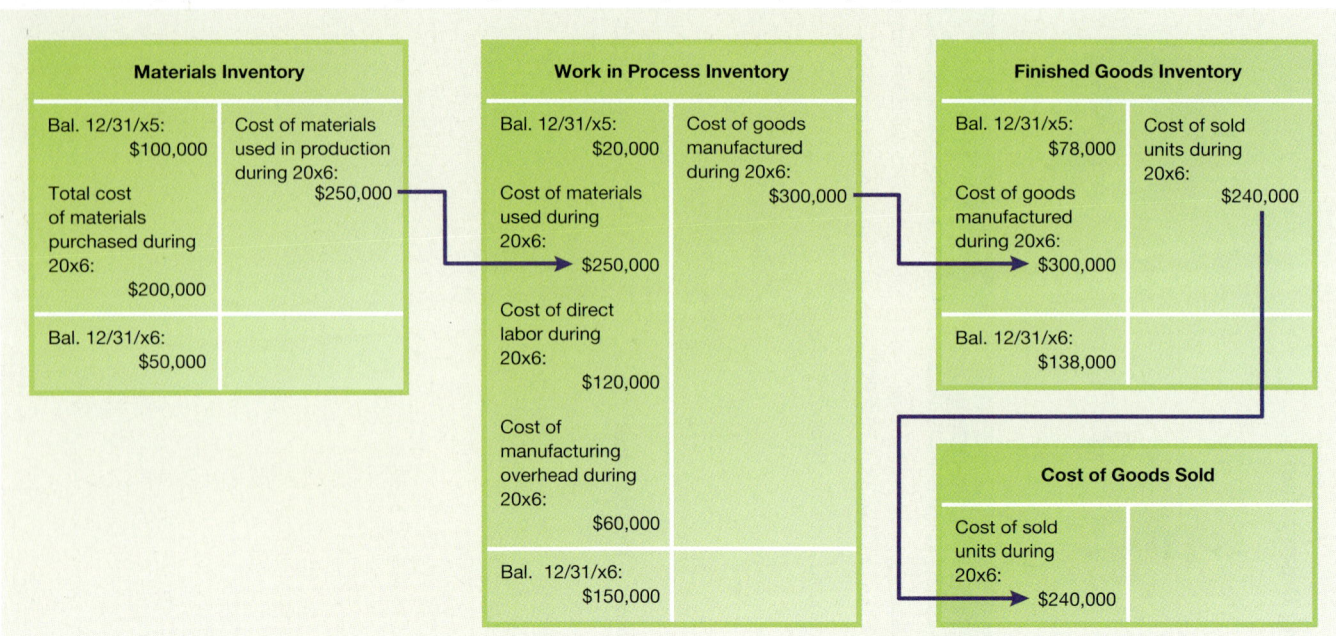

balance of the Finished Goods Inventory account and decreases the balance of the Work in Process Inventory account.

When candy bars are sold, a clerk prepares a *sales invoice*, and another employee fills the order by removing the candy bars from the storeroom, packaging them, and shipping them to the customer. A *shipping document* shows the quantity of the products that are shipped and gives a description of them. The cost of the candy bars sold, which is shown on the job order cost card, increases the Cost of Goods Sold account and decreases the balance of the Finished Goods Inventory account.

THE MANUFACTURING COST FLOW

Manufacturing cost flow is the flow of manufacturing costs (direct materials, direct labor, and manufacturing overhead) through the Materials Inventory, Work in Process Inventory, and Finished Goods Inventory accounts into the Cost of Goods Sold account. A defined, structured manufacturing cost flow is the foundation for product costing, inventory valuation, and financial reporting. Figure 5 summarizes the manufacturing cost flow as it relates to the inventory accounts and production activity of Candy Company for the year ended December 31, 20x6. To show the basic flows in this example, we assume that all materials can be traced directly to the candy bars. This means there are no indirect materials in the Materials Inventory account. We also work with the actual amount of manufacturing overhead, rather than an estimated amount.

Because there are no indirect materials in this case, the Materials Inventory account shows the balance of unused direct materials. The cost of direct materials purchased increases the balance of the Materials Inventory account, and the cost of direct materials used by the Production Department decreases it. The following formula may be used to summarize the activity of Candy Company's Materials Inventory account during the year:

Materials Inventory, Ending Balance	=	Materials Inventory, Beginning Balance	+	Cost of Materials Purchased	−	Cost of Materials Used
$50,000	=	$100,000	+	$200,000	−	$250,000

The Work in Process Inventory account records the balance of partially completed units of the product. As direct materials and direct labor are used, their costs are added to the Work in Process Inventory account. The cost of manufacturing overhead for the current period is also added. The total costs of direct materials, direct labor, and manufacturing overhead incurred and transferred to work in process inventory during an accounting period are called **total manufacturing costs** (also called *current manufacturing costs*). These costs increase the balance of the Work in Process Inventory account.

KEY POINT: When costs are transferred from one inventory account to another in a manufacturing company, they remain assets. They are inventoriable product costs and are not expensed until the finished goods are sold.

The cost of all units completed and moved to finished goods storage during an accounting period is the **cost of goods manufactured**. The cost of goods manufactured for the period decreases the balance of the Work in Process Inventory account. The following formulas show the activity in Candy Company's Work in Process Inventory account during the year:

Total Manufacturing Costs	=	Cost of Direct Materials Used	+	Direct Labor Costs	+	Manufacturing Overhead Costs
$430,000	=	$250,000	+	$120,000	+	$60,000
Work in Process Inventory, Ending Balance	=	Work in Process Inventory, Beginning Balance	+	Total Manufacturing Costs	−	Cost of Goods Manufactured
$150,000	=	$20,000	+	$430,000	−	$300,000

KEY POINT: Materials Inventory and Work in Process Inventory support the production process, while Finished Goods Inventory supports the sales and distribution functions.

The Finished Goods Inventory account holds the balance of costs assigned to all completed products that a manufacturing company has not yet sold. The cost of goods manufactured increases the balance, and the cost of goods sold decreases the balance. The following formula shows the activity in Candy Company's Finished Goods Inventory account during the year:

KEY POINT: When a credit sale occurs, Accounts Receivable and Sales are increased by the *revenue* amount. Cost of Goods Sold is increased and Finished Goods Inventory is decreased by the *cost* amount, or inventory carrying value.

Finished Goods Inventory, Ending Balance	=	Finished Goods Inventory, Beginning Balance	+	Cost of Goods Manufactured	−	Cost of Goods Sold
$138,000	=	$78,000	+	$300,000	−	$240,000

 Check out ACE for a Review Quiz at http://accounting.college.hmco.com/students.

FINANCIAL STATEMENTS AND THE REPORTING OF COSTS

LO5 Compare how service, retail, and manufacturing organizations report costs on their financial statements and how they account for inventories.

RELATED TEXT ASSIGNMENTS
Q: 13, 14
SE: 6, 7
E: 6, 7, 8, 9, 10
P: 2, 3
MRA: 1, 3

The key to preparing an income statement for a manufacturing organization is to determine the cost of goods manufactured. This dollar amount is calculated on the statement of cost of goods manufactured, a special report based on an analysis of the Work in Process Inventory account.

STATEMENT OF COST OF GOODS MANUFACTURED

At the end of an accounting period, the flow of all manufacturing costs incurred during the period is summarized in the **statement of cost of goods manufactured**. Exhibit 1 shows Candy Company's statement of cost of goods manufactured for the year ended December 31, 20x6. (The company's flow of manufacturing costs for the same period appears in Figure 5.) It is helpful to think of the statement of cost of goods manufactured as being developed in three steps, as described below.

■ **STEP 1** *Compute the cost of direct materials used during the accounting period.* To do so, add the beginning balance in the Materials Inventory account to the direct materials purchased ($100,000 + $200,000). The subtotal ($300,000) represents

EXHIBIT 1
Statement of Cost of Goods Manufactured and Partial Income Statement for a Manufacturing Organization

Candy Company, Inc.
Statement of Cost of Goods Manufactured
For the Year Ended December 31, 20x6

Direct materials used		
Materials inventory, December 31, 20x5	$100,000	
Direct materials purchased	200,000	
Cost of direct materials available for use	$300,000	
Less materials inventory, December 31, 20x6	50,000	
Cost of direct materials used		$250,000
Direct labor		120,000
Manufacturing overhead		60,000
Total manufacturing costs		$430,000
Add work in process inventory, December 31, 20x5		20,000
Total cost of work in process during the year		$450,000
Less work in process inventory, December 31, 20x6		150,000
Cost of goods manufactured		$300,000

Candy Company, Inc.
Income Statement
For the Year Ended December 31, 20x6

Sales		$500,000
Cost of goods sold		
Finished goods inventory, December 31, 20x5	$ 78,000	
Cost of goods manufactured	300,000	
Total cost of finished goods available for sale	$378,000	
Less finished goods inventory, December 31, 20x6	138,000	
Cost of goods sold		240,000
Gross margin		$260,000
Selling and administrative expenses		160,000
Operating income		$100,000

● **STOP AND THINK!**
What inventory accounts accumulate the cost information used in the statement of cost of goods manufactured?
The Materials Inventory and Work in Process Inventory accounts accumulate this information. ■

the cost of direct materials available for use during the accounting period. Next, subtract the ending balance of the Materials Inventory account from the cost of direct materials available for use. The difference is the cost of direct materials used during the period ($300,000 − $50,000 = $250,000).

■ **STEP 2** *Calculate total manufacturing costs for the period.* As shown in Exhibit 1, the costs of direct materials used ($250,000) and direct labor ($120,000) are added to total manufacturing overhead costs incurred during the period ($60,000) to arrive at total manufacturing costs ($430,000).

ENRICHMENT NOTE: An alternative to the cost of goods manufactured calculation uses the cost flow concept. Current manufacturing costs (direct materials, direct labor, and manufacturing overhead) become the cost of goods manufactured if the Work in Process Inventory balance remains unchanged in the accounting period. Similarly, the cost of goods manufactured becomes the cost of goods sold if the Finished Goods Inventory remains unchanged in the period.

■ **STEP 3** *Determine total cost of goods manufactured for the period.* To do so, add the beginning balance in the Work in Process Inventory account to total manufacturing costs to arrive at the total cost of work in process during the period. From this amount, subtract the ending balance in the Work in Process Inventory account to arrive at the cost of goods manufactured ($450,000 − $150,000 = $300,000).

Total manufacturing costs should not be confused with the cost of goods manufactured. To understand the difference between these two amounts, look again at the computations in Exhibit 1. Total manufacturing costs of $430,000 incurred during the period are added to the $20,000 beginning balance in the Work in Process Inventory account to arrive at the total cost of work in process during the period ($430,000 + $20,000 = $450,000). The costs of products still in process ($150,000) are then subtracted from the total cost of work in process during the year. The remainder, $300,000, is the cost of goods manufactured (completed) during the current year. Note that the costs attached to the ending balance of Work in Process Inventory come from the current period's total manufacturing costs; they will not become part of the cost of goods manufactured until the next period, when the products are completed.

COST OF GOODS SOLD AND A MANUFACTURING ORGANIZATION'S INCOME STATEMENT

STUDY NOTE: It is important not to confuse the cost of goods manufactured with the cost of goods sold.

Exhibit 1 demonstrates the relationship between Candy Company's income statement and its statement of cost of goods manufactured. The total amount of the cost of goods manufactured during the period is carried over to the income statement, where it is used to compute the cost of goods sold. The beginning balance of the Finished Goods Inventory account is added to the cost of goods manufactured to arrive at the total cost of finished goods available for sale during the period ($78,000 + $300,000 = $378,000). The cost of goods sold is then computed by subtracting the ending balance in Finished Goods Inventory (the cost of goods completed but not sold) from the total cost of finished goods available for sale ($378,000 − $138,000 = $240,000). The cost of goods sold is considered an expense in the period in which the goods are sold.

COST REPORTING AND ACCOUNTING FOR INVENTORIES IN SERVICE, RETAIL, AND MANUFACTURING ORGANIZATIONS

www.southwest.com
www.ups.com
www.enterprise.com

Because the operations of service and retail concerns differ from those of manufacturing organizations, the accounts presented in their financial statements differ as well. For example, because service organizations, such as Southwest Airlines, United Parcel Service (UPS), and Enterprise Rent-a-Car, sell services, not products, they maintain no inventories for sale or resale and thus, unlike manufacturing and retail organizations, have no inventory accounts on the balance sheet. When preparing income statements, they calculate the cost of sales rather than the cost of goods sold, using the following equation:

FOCUS ON BUSINESS PRACTICE

What Candy Company Has the Sweetest Share of the U.S. Market?
Among the top U.S. candy vendors are Hershey <www.hershey.com>, Mars <www.mars.com>, Wrigley's <www.wrigley.com>, Nestlé <www.nestle.com>, Philip Morris <www.altria.com>, and Russell Stover Candies <www.russellstover.com>. Hershey has the sweetest share of the market, leading with 30 percent. Mars is second with a 17.1 percent market share, and Wrigley's, Nestlé, and Phillip Morris vie for third place, with 6.7 percent, 6.5 percent, and 6.3 percent, respectively.[3]

Cost of Sales = Net Cost of Services Sold

Suppose, for instance, that Sweet Treasures Candy Store, the retail shop that we used as an example in the last chapter, employs UPS to deliver 50 boxes of candy. The cost of sales for UPS would include the wages and salaries of personnel plus the expense of trucks, planes, supplies, and anything else UPS used to deliver the packages for Sweet Treasures Candy Store.

Retail organizations, such as Wal-Mart, Toys "R" Us, and Sweet Treasures Candy Store, which purchase

FIGURE 6
Financial Statements of Service, Retail, and Manufacturing Organizations

	Service Company	Retail Company	Manufacturing Company

Income Statement	Sales
	− Cost of sales
	Gross margin
	− Operating expenses
	Net income
		Sales
		− Cost of goods sold*
		Gross margin
		− Operating expenses
		Net income
		
		*Cost of goods sold:
		  Beginning merchandise inventory
		+ Net cost of purchases
		  Cost of goods available for sale
		− Ending merchandise inventory
		  Cost of goods sold
			Sales
			− Cost of goods sold†
			Gross margin
			− Operating expenses
			Net income
			
			†Cost of goods sold:
			  Beginning finished goods inventory
			+ Cost of goods manufactured
			  Cost of goods available for sale
			− Ending finished goods inventory
			  Cost of goods sold

Balance Sheet (current assets section)	No inventory accounts	One inventory account:
		  Merchandise Inventory
		  (finished product ready for sale)
			Three inventory accounts:
			  Materials Inventory
			  (unused materials)
			  Work in Process Inventory
			  (unfinished product)
			  Finished Goods Inventory
			  (finished product ready for sale)

Example with numbers		Income Statement: Beg. merchandise inventory $3,000 Net cost of purchases 23,000 Cost of goods available for sale $26,000 End. merchandise inventory 4,500 Cost of goods sold $21,500 Balance Sheet: Merchandise inventory, ending $4,500	Income Statement: Beg. finished goods inventory $52,000 Cost of goods manufactured 144,000 Cost of goods available for sale $196,000 End. finished goods inventory 78,000 Cost of goods sold $118,000 Balance Sheet: Finished goods inventory, ending $78,000

www.walmart.com
www.tru.com

products ready for resale, maintain just one inventory account on the balance sheet. Called the Merchandise Inventory account, it reflects the costs of goods held for resale. Retail organizations include the cost of purchases in the calculation of cost of goods sold, as follows:

$$\text{Cost of Goods Sold} = \text{Beginning Merchandise Inventory} + \text{Net Cost of Purchases} - \text{Ending Merchandise Inventory}$$

Suppose that Sweet Treasures Candy Store had a balance of $3,000 in its Merchandise Inventory account on December 31, 20x4. During the next year, its purchases of candy products totaled $23,000 (adjusted for purchase discounts, returns and allowances, and freight-in). On December 31, 20x5, its Merchandise Inventory balance was $4,500. The cost of goods sold for 20x5 is thus $21,500:

$$\text{Cost of Goods Sold} = \$3,000 + \$23,000 - \$4,500 = \$21,500$$

www.motorola.com
www.sony.com

As we have seen, manufacturing organizations, such as Motorola, Sony, and Candy Company, which make products for sale, maintain three inventory accounts on the balance sheet: the Materials Inventory, Work in Process Inventory, and

Finished Goods Inventory accounts. The Materials Inventory account shows the balance of the cost of materials purchased but unused in the production process. During the production process, the costs of manufacturing the product are accumulated in the Work in Process Inventory account; the balance of this account represents the costs of the unfinished product. Once the product is complete and ready for sale, the cost of the goods manufactured is transferred to the Finished Goods Inventory account; the balance in this account is the cost of the unsold completed product. When the product is sold, the manufacturing organization uses the following equation to calculate the cost of goods sold:

$$\text{Cost of Goods Sold} = \text{Beginning Finished Goods Inventory} + \textbf{Cost of Goods Manufactured} - \text{Ending Finished Goods Inventory}$$

For example, suppose that Candy Company had a balance of $52,000 in its Finished Goods Inventory account on December 31, 20x4. During the next year, the cost of the products that Candy Company manufactured totaled $144,000. On December 31, 20x5, its Finished Goods Inventory balance was $78,000. The cost of goods sold for 20x5 is thus $118,000:

$$\text{Cost of Goods Sold} = \$52,000 + \$144,000 - \$78,000 = \$118,000$$

Remember that all organizations—service, retail, and manufacturing—use the following income statement format:

$$\text{Sales} - \genfrac{}{}{0pt}{}{\text{Cost of Sales}}{\text{or Cost of Goods Sold}} = \text{Gross Margin} - \text{Operating Expenses} = \text{Net Income}$$

Figure 6 compares the financial statements of service, retail, and manufacturing organizations. Note in particular the differences in inventory accounts and cost of goods sold. As pointed out earlier, product costs, or inventoriable costs, appear as finished goods inventory on the balance sheet and as cost of goods sold on the income statement; period costs, or noninventoriable costs, are reflected in the operating expenses on the income statement.

 Check out ACE for a Review Quiz at http://accounting.college.hmco.com/students.

Cost Allocation

LO6 Define *cost allocation* and explain how cost objects, cost pools, and cost drivers are used to assign manufacturing overhead costs.

RELATED TEXT ASSIGNMENTS
Q: 15, 16, 17
SE: 8, 9, 10
E: 11, 12, 13
P: 4, 6, 8
SD: 2
MRA: 4

ENRICHMENT NOTE: Because allocation by its very nature is a relatively arbitrary process, a rational allocation scheme is best. Rational allocation approaches help avoid behavior problems for management.

As noted earlier, the costs of direct materials and direct labor can be easily traced to a product, but manufacturing overhead costs are indirect costs that must be collected and allocated in some manner. **Cost allocation** is the process of assigning a collection of indirect costs to a specific **cost object**, such as a product or service, a department, or an operating activity, using an allocation base known as a **cost driver**. A cost driver might be direct labor hours, direct labor costs, units produced, or another activity base that is important to a business. As the cost driver increases in volume, it causes the **cost pool**—the collection of indirect costs assigned to a cost object—to increase in amount. For example, suppose Candy Company has a machine-maintenance cost pool. The cost pool consists of overhead costs for the supplies and labor needed to maintain the machines, the cost object is the product, and the cost driver is machine hours. As more machine hours are used, the amount of the cost pool increases, thus increasing the costs assigned to the product.

For purposes of product costing, cost allocation is defined as the assignment of manufacturing overhead costs to the product (cost object) during an accounting period. It requires (1) the pooling of manufacturing overhead costs that are affected by a common activity (e.g., machine maintenance) and (2) the selection of a cost driver whose activity level causes a change in the cost pool (e.g., machine hours).

> ◆ **STOP AND THINK!**
> What are the two main uses of a predetermined manufacturing overhead rate?
>
> *A predetermined, or estimated, manufacturing overhead rate enables managers to make timely decisions about pricing products and controlling costs. It also allows them to apply overhead costs to each unit produced in an equitable and timely manner.* ■

ALLOCATING THE COSTS OF MANUFACTURING OVERHEAD

Allocating manufacturing overhead costs is a four-step process that corresponds to the four stages of the management cycle. In the first step (the planning stage), managers estimate manufacturing overhead costs and calculate a rate at which they will assign those costs to products. In the second step (the executing stage), this rate is applied to products as manufacturing overhead costs are incurred and recorded during production. In the third step (the reviewing stage), actual manufacturing overhead costs are recorded as they are incurred, and managers calculate the difference between the estimated and actual costs. In the fourth step (the reporting stage), managers report on this difference. Figure 7 summarizes these four steps in terms of their timing, the procedures involved, and the journal entries they require. It also shows how the cost flows in the various steps affect the accounting records.

■ **PLANNING THE OVERHEAD RATE** Before an accounting period begins, managers determine cost pools and cost drivers and calculate a **predetermined overhead rate** by dividing the cost pool of total estimated overhead costs by the total estimated cost driver level. Grouping all estimated overhead costs into one cost pool and using direct labor hours or machine hours as the cost driver results in a single, plantwide overhead rate. By applying this predetermined rate in the same way to all units of production during the period, managers can better estimate product costs. This step requires no journal entry because no business activity has occurred.

■ **APPLYING THE OVERHEAD RATE** As units of the product are manufactured during the accounting period, the estimated manufacturing overhead costs are assigned to the product's costs at the predetermined overhead rate. The overhead rate for each cost pool is multiplied by that pool's actual cost driver level (e.g., the actual number of direct labor hours used to complete the product). The purpose of this calculation is to assign a consistent manufacturing overhead cost to each unit produced during the accounting period. A journal entry records the allocation of overhead to the product as an increase in the Work in Process Inventory account and a decrease in the Manufacturing Overhead account.

■ **RECORDING ACTUAL OVERHEAD COSTS** The actual manufacturing overhead costs are recorded as they are incurred during the accounting period. These costs, which include the costs of indirect materials, indirect labor, depreciation, property taxes, and other production costs, will be part of the actual product cost. The journal entry made for the actual manufacturing overhead costs records an increase in the Manufacturing Overhead account and a decrease in asset accounts or an increase in contra-asset or liability accounts.

■ **RECONCILING THE APPLIED AND ACTUAL OVERHEAD AMOUNTS** At the end of the accounting period, the difference between the applied and actual manufacturing overhead costs is calculated and reconciled. If the manufacturing overhead costs applied to production during the period are greater than the actual manufacturing overhead costs, the difference in the amounts represents **overapplied overhead costs**. If this difference is immaterial, the Manufacturing Overhead account is increased and the Cost of Goods Sold account is decreased by the difference. If the difference is material, adjustments are made to the accounts affected—that is, the Work in Process Inventory, Finished Goods Inventory, and Cost of Goods Sold accounts. If the manufacturing overhead costs applied to production during the period are less than the actual manufacturing overhead costs, the difference represents **underapplied overhead costs**. The Cost of Goods Sold account is increased and the Manufacturing Overhead account is decreased by this difference, assuming the difference is not material. The adjustment for overapplied or underapplied overhead costs, whether they are immaterial or material, is necessary to reflect the actual manufacturing overhead costs on the income statement.

Cost Allocation   717

FIGURE 7
Allocating Manufacturing Overhead Costs: A Four-Step Process

Year 20x5 |————————————————|————————— Year 20x6 ——————————————→
                          January 1   December 31

	Step 1: Planning the Overhead Rate	Step 2: Applying the Overhead Rate	Step 3: Recording Actual Overhead Costs	Step 4: Reconciling Applied and Actual Overhead Costs
Timing and Procedure	Before the accounting period begins, determine cost pools and cost drivers. Calculate the overhead rate by dividing the cost pool of total estimated overhead costs by the total estimated cost driver level.	During the accounting period, as units are produced, apply overhead costs to products by multiplying the predetermined overhead rate for each cost pool by the actual cost driver level for that pool. Record costs.	Record actual manufacturing overhead costs as they are incurred during the accounting period.	At the end of the accounting period, calculate and reconcile the difference between applied and actual manufacturing overhead costs.
Journal Entry	None	Increase Work in Process Inventory account and decrease Manufacturing Overhead account: Dr. Work in Process XX Cr. Manufacturing Overhead XX	Increase Manufacturing Overhead account and decrease asset accounts or increase contra-asset or liability accounts: Dr. Manufacturing Overhead XX Cr. Various Accounts XX	Entry will vary depending on how costs have been applied. If overapplied, increase Manufacturing Overhead and decrease Cost of Goods Sold. If underapplied, increase Cost of Goods Sold and decrease Manufacturing Overhead.
Cost Flow Through the Accounts		Manufacturing Overhead —	Overhead applied using predetermined rate Work in Process Inventory Overhead applied using predetermined rate	Manufacturing Overhead Actual overhead costs recorded Various Asset and Liability Accounts —	Actual costs recorded	**Overapplied:** Manufacturing Overhead Actual overhead costs recorded	Overhead applied using predetermined rate **Overapplied** Bal. $0 Cost of Goods Sold Bal.	Overapplied Actual bal. **Underapplied:** Manufacturing Overhead Actual overhead costs recorded	Overhead applied using predetermined rate **Underapplied** Bal. $0 Cost of Goods Sold Bal. **Underapplied** Actual bal.

The Importance of Good Estimates

A predetermined, or estimated, manufacturing overhead rate has two main uses. First, it enables managers to make decisions about pricing products and controlling costs before some of the actual costs are known. The product cost calculated at the end of a period, when all product costs are known, is, of course, more accurate. But when the overhead portion of product cost is estimated in advance, managers can compare actual and estimated costs throughout the year and more quickly correct any problems that may cause the under- or overallocation of overhead costs.

Second, an advance estimate allows managers to apply manufacturing overhead costs to each unit produced in an equitable and timely manner. Actual manufacturing overhead costs fluctuate from month to month as a result of the timing of the costs and the variability of the amounts. For example, some manufacturing overhead costs (such as supervisors' salaries and depreciation on equipment) may be expensed monthly. Others (like payroll taxes) may be paid quarterly, and still others (like property taxes and insurance) may be paid annually. In addition, indirect hourly labor costs (such as the costs of machine maintenance and materials handling) fluctuate with changes in production levels.

The successful allocation of manufacturing overhead costs depends on two factors. One is a careful estimate of the total manufacturing overhead costs. The other is a good forecast of the cost driver level.

An accurate estimate of total manufacturing overhead costs is crucial. If the estimate is wrong, the manufacturing overhead rate will be wrong. This will cause an overstatement or understatement of the product unit cost. If an organization relies on information that overstates product unit cost, it may fail to bid on profitable projects because the costs appear too high. If it relies on information that understates product unit cost, it may accept business that is not as profitable as expected. So, to provide managers with reliable product unit costs, the management accountant must be careful to include all manufacturing overhead items and to forecast the costs of those items accurately.

The budgeting process usually includes estimating manufacturing overhead costs. Managers who use production-related resources will provide cost estimates for direct and indirect production activities. For example, the managers for materials handling and inspection at Candy Company, Inc., estimate the costs related to their departments' activities, and Maya Kee, the accountant, includes their cost estimates in developing total manufacturing overhead costs.

Managers also need to provide accurate estimates of cost driver levels. An understated cost driver level will cause an overstatement of the predetermined manufacturing overhead rate (the cost is spread over a lesser level), and an overstated cost driver level will cause an understatement of the predetermined manufacturing overhead rate (the cost is spread over a greater level).

In the following sections, we present two approaches to allocating manufacturing overhead. We use the first two steps of the four-step overhead allocation process to demonstrate these approaches.

 Check out ACE for a Review Quiz at http://accounting.college.hmco.com/students.

Allocating Manufacturing Overhead: The Traditional Approach

LO7 Using the traditional method of allocating manufacturing overhead costs, calculate product unit cost.

RELATED TEXT ASSIGNMENTS
Q: 18
SE: 9, 10
E: 11, 12, 13, 14
P: 4, 6, 8
SD: 2
MRA: 4

The traditional approach to applying manufacturing overhead costs to a product cost is to use a single predetermined overhead rate. This approach is especially useful when companies manufacture only one product or a few very similar products that require the same production processes and production-related activities, such as setup, inspection, and materials handling. The total manufacturing overhead costs constitute one cost pool, and a traditional activity base—such as direct labor hours, direct labor costs, machine hours, or units of production—is the cost driver.

FIGURE 8
Using the Traditional Approach to Assign Manufacturing Overhead Costs to Production

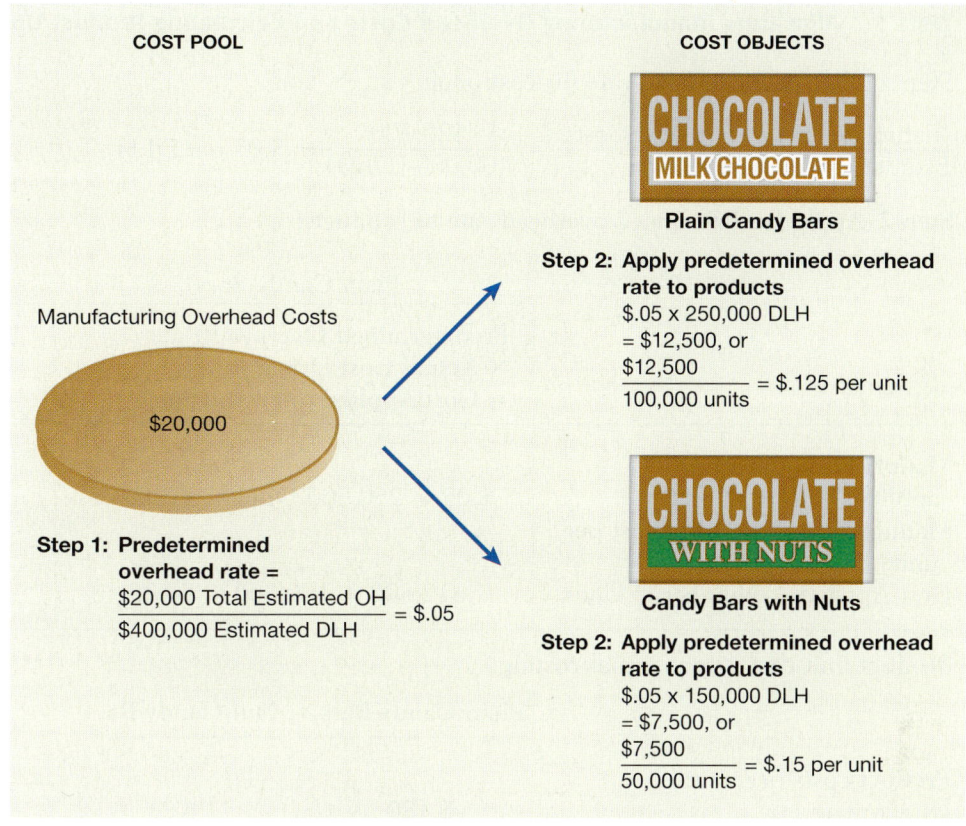

● **STOP AND THINK!**
How many overhead cost pools are used in the traditional approach to cost allocation?

In the traditional approach to cost allocation, total manufacturing overhead costs constitute one cost pool. ■

STUDY NOTE: Don't make the mistake of thinking that because a cost is not traced directly to a product it is not a product cost. All manufacturing costs, both direct and indirect, are product costs.

Figure 8 illustrates the application of one cost pool of manufacturing overhead costs to two product lines. As we continue with our example of Candy Company, Inc., let's assume that the company will be selling two product lines in 20x7—plain candy bars and candy bars with nuts—and that Maya Kee chooses direct labor hours as the cost driver. Kee estimates that total manufacturing overhead costs for the next year will be $20,000 and that total direct labor hours (DLH) worked will be 400,000 hours.

Table 3 summarizes the first two steps in the traditional approach to allocating manufacturing overhead costs. In the first step, Kee uses the following formula to compute the rate at which manufacturing overhead costs will be applied:

$$\text{Predetermined Overhead Rate} = \frac{\$20,000}{400,000 \text{ DLH}} = \$.05 \text{ per DLH}$$

In the second step, Kee applies the predetermined overhead rate to the products. During the year, Candy Company used 250,000 direct labor hours to produce 100,000 plain candy bars and 150,000 direct labor hours to produce 50,000 candy bars with nuts. When Kee applies the predetermined overhead rate, the portion of the manufacturing overhead cost applied to the plain candy bars totals $12,500 ($.05 × 250,000 DLH), or $.125 per unit ($12,500 ÷ 100,000 units), and the portion applied to the candy bars with nuts totals $7,500 ($.05 × 150,000 DLH), or $.15 per unit ($7,500 ÷ 50,000 units).

Kee also wanted to calculate the product unit cost for the accounting period using normal costing. She gathered the following data for the two product lines:

	Plain Candy Bars	Candy Bars with Nuts
Actual direct materials cost per unit	$.18	$.21
Actual direct labor cost per unit	.14	.16
Prime cost per unit	$.32	$.37

TABLE 3. Allocating Manufacturing Overhead Costs and Calculating Product Unit Cost: Traditional Approach

Step 1. Calculate overhead rate for cost pool:

$$\frac{\text{Estimated Total Overhead Costs}}{\text{Estimated Total Cost Driver Level}} = \frac{\$20,000}{400,000 \text{ (DLH)}} = \$.05 \text{ per DLH}$$

Step 2. Apply predetermined overhead rate to products:

	Plain Candy Bars	Candy Bars with Nuts
	Predetermined Overhead Rate × Actual Cost Driver Level = Cost Applied to Production	Predetermined Overhead Rate × Actual Cost Driver Level = Cost Applied to Production
Manufacturing overhead applied: $.05 per DLH	$.05 × 250,000 DLH = $12,500	$.05 × 150,000 DLH = $7,500
Manufacturing overhead cost per unit: Cost Applied ÷ Number of Units	$12,500 ÷ 100,000 = $.125	$7,500 ÷ 50,000 = $.15

Product unit cost using normal costing:

	Plain Candy Bars	Nut Candy Bars
Product costs per unit:		
Direct materials	$.180	$.21
Direct labor	.140	.16
Applied manufacturing overhead	.125	.15
Product unit cost	$.445	$.52

At the bottom of Table 3 is Kee's calculation of the normal product unit cost for each product line. The nut candy bar's product unit cost ($.52) is higher than the plain candy bar's ($.445) because producing the candy bar with nuts required more expensive materials and more labor time.

 Check out ACE for a Review Quiz at http://accounting.college.hmco.com/students.

ALLOCATING MANUFACTURING OVERHEAD: THE ABC APPROACH

LO8 Using activity-based costing to assign manufacturing overhead costs, calculate product unit cost.

RELATED TEXT ASSIGNMENTS
Q: 19
SE: 11
E: 14
P: 5, 7, 8
SD: 2
MRA: 4

Activity-based costing (ABC) is a more accurate method of assigning overhead costs to products than the traditional approach. It categorizes all indirect costs by activity, traces the indirect costs to those activities, and assigns activity costs to products using a cost driver related to the cause of the cost. A company that uses ABC identifies production-related activities and the events and circumstances that cause, or drive, those activities, such as number of inspections or maintenance hours. As a result, many smaller activity pools are created from the single manufacturing overhead cost pool used in the traditional method. This means that managers will calculate an overhead rate, or activity cost rate, for each activity pool and then use that rate and a cost driver amount to determine the portion of manufacturing overhead costs to assign to a product. Managers must select an appropriate number of activity pools for manufacturing overhead, and a system must be designed to capture the actual cost driver amounts. Because each activity pool requires a cost driver, the

● **STOP AND THINK!**

How many overhead cost pools are used in the ABC approach to cost allocation?

In the ABC approach to cost allocation, managers use as many cost pools as are needed for effective and efficient management of overhead costs. ■

www.tacobell.com

Focus on Business Ethics

What Can a Company Do to Be Resource-Responsible?

United Parcel Service <www.ups.com> has taken a proactive role in its commitment to efficient and responsible management of resources. UPS recycles computer paper, letter envelopes, and delivery notices, and it records delivery information electronically, which saves an estimated 30,000 trees annually. UPS also helps customers protect the environment by using packaging methods that prevent product damage and minimize waste and by operating a national recycling program for its customer's packaging materials. For example, Ethan Allen, Inc. <www.ethanallen.com>, a furniture maker and retailer, uses UPS's services to retrieve foam-sheet shipping material, which makes money for Ethan Allen in addition to reducing its disposal costs.[4]

benefit of grouping manufacturing overhead costs into several smaller pools to obtain more accurate estimates of product costs is offset by the additional costs of measuring many different cost drivers.

ABC will improve the accuracy of product cost estimates for organizations that sell many different types of products (product diversity) or that use varying, significant amounts of different production-related activities to complete the products (process complexity). To remain competitive in today's global marketplace, many organizations are selling a wider range of products or services than in the past. For example, 20 years ago, Taco Bell had only 6 food items on its menu; today, it has more than 25. This diversity of product lines requires more careful cost allocation, especially when it comes to making decisions about pricing products, outsourcing processes to other organizations, or choosing to keep a food item or drop it from the menu.

For other organizations, some products are more complicated to manufacture, store, move, package, or ship than others (process complexity). For example, an auto parts distributor receives, stores, selects, moves, consolidates, packs, and ships auto parts to auto dealers. The distributor's greatest costs are overhead costs, which under the traditional method are assigned based on what it costs to purchase a part for resale. With the traditional method, more expensive parts, such as car radios, receive a greater allocation of overhead costs than do less expensive parts, such as windshields. However, because a glass windshield is more delicate than a car radio, it costs the distributor more to move, store, pack, and ship. If ABC were used, the cost of the windshield would increase to reflect a fairer allocation of the distributor's overhead costs. Thus, by assigning overhead costs based on the relative use of overhead resources, ABC would provide managers with better information for making decisions, such as pricing car radios, windshields, and other auto parts; choosing to discontinue selling windshields; or reducing the amount of storage space.

Planning Overhead Rates

As discussed earlier, Maya Kee, the accountant for Candy Company, Inc., calculated product unit cost by computing one manufacturing overhead rate for one cost pool and applying that rate to the direct labor hours used to manufacture plain candy bars and candy bars with nuts. As we continue with our example, we find that Olga Santee, president of Candy Company, is concerned about the product cost for each type of candy bar. Santee believes that the difference in cost between the plain and nut candy bars should be more than $.075 ($.52 − $.445). She has asked Kee to review her estimate. Kee found no error when she rechecked the calculation of direct materials costs and direct labor costs. However, she believes the traditional approach to assigning manufacturing overhead cost could be misleading, so she wants to use activity-based costing to obtain a more accurate estimate of product cost. Figure 7 illustrates the use of ABC to assign manufacturing overhead costs to two product lines.

Kee analyzed the production-related activities and decided that the estimated $20,000 in manufacturing overhead cost could be grouped into four activity pools. The first activity, setup, includes estimated total costs of $7,000 for indirect labor and indirect materials used in preparing machines for each batch of production. The second activity, inspection, includes $6,000 for salaries and indirect materials costs, indirect labor, and depreciation on testing equipment. The third activity, packaging,

FIGURE 9
Using ABC to Assign Manufacturing Overhead Costs to Production

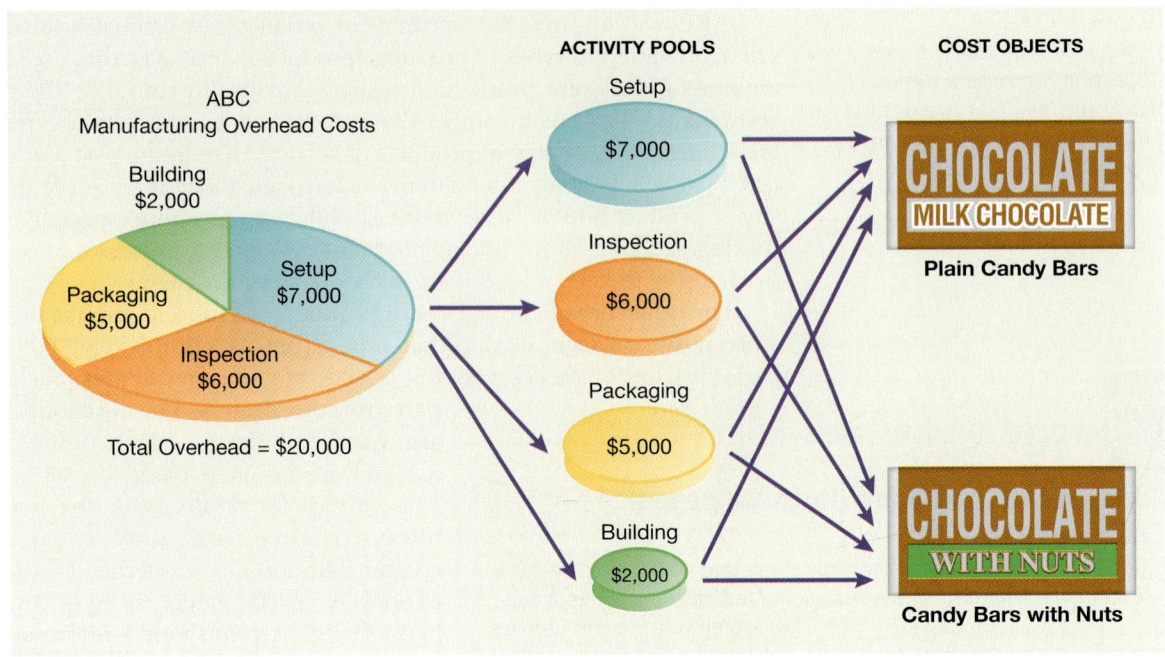

includes estimated total costs of $5,000 for indirect materials, indirect labor, and equipment depreciation. The last activity, building operations, includes estimated total overhead costs of $2,000 for building depreciation, maintenance, janitorial wages, property taxes, insurance, security, and all other costs not related to the first three activities.

After identifying the four activity pools, Kee selected a cost driver and estimated the cost driver level for each activity pool. The following schedule shows those amounts by product line and in total:

	Estimated Cost Driver Level		
Cost Driver	Plain	Nut	Total
Number of setups	300	400	700
Number of inspections	150	350	500
Packaging hours	600	1,400	2,000
Machine hours	4,000	6,000	10,000

KEY POINT: Under ABC, activity pools are allocated to cost objects using multiple cost drivers.

After identifying activity pools, estimated activity pool amounts, cost drivers, and estimated cost driver levels, Kee performed Step 1 of the overhead allocation process by calculating the activity cost rate for each activity pool. The activity cost rate is the estimated activity pool amount divided by the estimated cost driver level. Step 1 of Table 4 shows the activity cost rates to be $10 per setup, $12 per inspection, $2.50 per packaging hour, and $.20 per machine hour.

APPLYING THE OVERHEAD RATES

In Step 2, Kee applied manufacturing overhead to the two product lines using the cost driver level for each cost driver multiplied by the activity cost rate shown in the preceding schedule. Step 2 of Table 4 shows those calculations. For example, Kee applied $3,000 in setup costs ($10 × 300 setups) to the plain candy bar line and $4,000 ($10 × 400 setups) to the nut candy bar line. After applying the over-

TABLE 4. Allocating Manufacturing Overhead Costs and Calculating Product Unit Cost: ABC Approach

Step 1. Calculate activity cost rate for cost pool:

$$\frac{\text{Estimated Total Activity Costs}}{\text{Estimated Total Cost Driver Level}} = \text{Activity Cost Rate for Cost Pool}$$

Activity	Estimated Total Activity Costs	Estimated Total Cost Driver Level	Activity Cost Rate for Cost Pool
Setup	$ 7,000	700 setups	$7,000 ÷ 700 = $10 per setup
Inspection	6,000	500 inspections	$6,000 ÷ 500 = $12 per inspection
Packaging	5,000	2,000 packaging hours	$5,000 ÷ 2,000 = $2.50 per packaging hour
Building	2,000	10,000 machine hours	$2,000 ÷ 10,000 = $.20 per machine hour
	$20,000		

Step 2. Apply predetermined activity cost rates to products:

	Plain Candy Bars		Nut Candy Bars	
Activity Pool	Predetermined Overhead Rate × Actual Cost Driver Level = Cost Applied to Production		Predetermined Overhead Rate × Actual Cost Driver Level = Cost Applied to Production	
Setup	$10 × 300 =	$3,000	$10 × 400 =	$4,000
Inspection	$12 × 150 =	1,800	$12 × 350 =	4,200
Packaging	$2.50 × 600 =	1,500	$2.50 × 1,400 =	3,500
Building	$.20 × 4,000 =	800	$.20 × 6,000 =	1,200
Total overhead applied		$7,100		$12,900
Applied overhead cost per unit: Cost Applied ÷ Number of Units	$7,100 ÷ 100,000 =	$.071	$12,900 ÷ 50,000 =	$.258

Product unit cost using normal costing:

	Plain Candy Bars	Nut Candy Bars
Product costs per unit:		
Direct materials	$.180	$.210
Direct labor	.140	.160
Applied manufacturing overhead	.071	.258
Product unit cost	$.391	$.628

head costs from the four activity pools to the product lines, Kee estimated that total manufacturing overhead costs of $7,100, or $.071 per bar ($7,100 ÷ 100,000 units), should be applied to the plain candy bar line and that $12,900, or $.258 per bar ($12,900 ÷ 50,000 units), should be applied to the nut candy bar line.

Kee also wanted to calculate the unit cost for each product line using normal costing. Her calculations appear at the bottom of Table 4. The product unit cost is $.391 for the plain line and $.628 for the nut line.

Kee presented the following information to Olga Santee:

	Plain	Nut
Product unit cost: Traditional approach with one manufacturing overhead cost pool	$.445	$.520
Product unit cost: ABC with four activity pools	.391	.628
Difference: decrease (increase)	$.054	($.108)

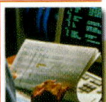

FOCUS ON BUSINESS PRACTICE

How Costly Is Television Talent?

If salary is measured per unit, your perspective on the cost of television talent may change. Compare the salaries and cost per viewer (salary divided by number of viewers per season) for the following television personalities in 2002. In your opinion, who is the highest paid talent?[5]

	2002 Salary	Season Viewers	Cost per Viewer
Larry King	$7 million	1.3 million	$5.39
Conan O'Brien	$8 million	2.55 million	$3.14
Katie Couric	$13 million	6.1 million	$2.13
David Letterman	$16 million	4.35 million	$3.68

Because ABC assigned more costs to the product line that used more resources, it provided a more accurate estimate of product unit cost. The increased information about the production requirements for the nut candy bar line that went into the ABC calculation of product unit cost also provided valuable insights. Santee found that the nut candy bars cost more to manufacture because the changes in the ingredients require more setups and machine hours and because more inspections are needed to test the candy quality. Because the nut candy bar line requires more production and production-related activities, its product unit cost is higher. Based on this analysis, Santee may want to reconsider some of her decisions about the manufacture and sale of these two product lines.

 Check out ACE for a Review Quiz at http://accounting.college.hmco.com/students.

COST ALLOCATION IN SERVICE ORGANIZATIONS

LO9 Apply costing concepts to a service organization.

RELATED TEXT ASSIGNMENTS
Q: 20
SE: 12
E: 15
SD: 3, 5
MRA: 2

🔴 **STOP AND THINK!**
How should a manager in a service organization handle materials costs?

Any materials costs in a service organization would be for supplies used in providing services. Because these are indirect materials costs, the manager should include them in service overhead. ■

Processing loans, representing people in courts of law, selling insurance policies, and computing people's income taxes are typical of the services performed by professionals in many service organizations. Like other services, these are labor-intensive processes supported by indirect labor and overhead costs.

Because no products are manufactured in the course of providing services, service organizations have no direct materials costs. As noted, however, they do have both labor and overhead costs, which must be included when computing the cost of providing a service. The most important cost in a service organization is the direct cost of professional labor, and the usual standard is applicable; that is, the direct labor cost must be traceable to the service rendered. The indirect costs incurred in performing a service are similar to those incurred in manufacturing a product. They are classified as service overhead and, along with professional labor costs, are considered service costs rather than period costs. Just as product costs appear on manufacturers' income statements as cost of goods sold, service costs appear on service organizations' income statements as cost of sales.

To illustrate how overhead costs are applied in service organizations, assume that the Loan Department of the Campus Bank wants to determine the total costs incurred in processing a typical loan application. Its policy for the past five years has been to charge a $150 fee for processing a home-loan application. Jerome Hill, the chief loan officer, thinks the fee is far too low. Because of the way operating costs have soared in the past five years, he proposes that the fee be doubled. The bank has asked you to compute the cost of processing a typical home-loan application and has given you the following information about its processing of loan applications:

Direct professional labor

Loan processors' monthly salaries:
    4 people at $3,000 each $12,000

Indirect monthly overhead costs

Chief loan officer's salary	$ 4,500
Telephone	750
Depreciation	5,750
Legal advice	2,460
Customer relations	640
Credit check function	1,980
Internal audit function	2,400
Utilities	1,690
Clerical personnel	3,880
Miscellaneous	1,050
Total overhead costs	$25,100

The Loan Department usually processes 100 home-loan applications each month.

The Loan Department performs several other functions in addition to processing home-loan applications. Roughly one-half of the department is involved in loan collection. After determining how many of the processed loans were not home loans, you conclude that only 25 percent of the overhead costs of the Loan Department were applicable to the processing of home-loan applications. The cost of processing one home-loan application can be computed as follows:

Direct professional labor cost:	
$12,000 ÷ 100	$120.00
Service overhead cost:	
$25,100 × 25% ÷ 100	62.75
Total processing cost per loan	$182.75

Finally, you conclude that the chief loan officer was correct; the present fee does not cover the current costs of processing a typical home-loan application. However, doubling the loan fee seems too extreme. To allow for a profit margin, the loan fee could be raised to $225 or $250.

 Check out ACE for a Review Quiz at http://accounting.college.hmco.com/students.

Chapter Review

REVIEW OF LEARNING OBJECTIVES

LO1 Describe how managers use information about costs in the management cycle.

During the management cycle, managers in manufacturing, retail, and service organizations use information about operating costs and product or service costs to prepare budgets, make pricing and other decisions, calculate variances between estimated and actual costs, and report results.

LO2 Explain how managers classify costs and how they use these cost classifications.

A single cost can be classified as a direct or indirect cost, a variable or fixed cost, a value-adding or nonvalue-adding cost, and a product or period cost. These cost classifications enable managers to control costs by tracing them to cost objects, to calculate the number of units that must be sold to obtain a certain level of profit, to identify the costs of activities that do and do not add value to a product or service, and to prepare financial statements for parties outside the organization.

LO3 Define and give examples of the three elements of product cost and compute the unit cost of a product.

Direct materials costs are the costs of materials used in making a product that can be conveniently and economically traced to specific product units. Direct labor costs include all labor costs needed to make a product that can be conveniently and economically traced to specific product units. All other production-related costs are classified and accounted for as manufacturing overhead costs. Such costs cannot be conveniently or economically traced to end products, so a cost allocation method is used to assign them to products.

When a batch of products has been completed, the product unit cost is computed by dividing the total cost of direct materials, direct labor, and manufacturing overhead by the total number of units produced. The product unit cost can be calculated using actual, normal, or standard costing methods. Under normal costing, the actual costs of direct materials and direct labor are combined with the estimated cost of manufacturing overhead to determine the product unit cost. Under standard costing, the estimated costs of direct materials, direct labor, and manufacturing overhead are used to calculate the product unit cost. The components of product cost may be classified as prime costs or conversion costs. Prime costs are the primary costs of production; they are the sum of direct materials costs and direct labor costs. Conversion costs are the costs of converting direct materials into finished product; they are the sum of direct labor costs and manufacturing overhead costs.

LO4 Describe the flow of costs through a manufacturer's inventory accounts.

The flow of costs through the inventory accounts begins when costs are incurred for direct materials, direct labor, and manufacturing overhead. Materials costs flow first into the Materials Inventory account, which is used to record the costs of materials when they are received and again when they are issued for use in a production process. All manufacturing-related costs—direct materials, direct labor, and manufacturing overhead—are recorded in the Work in Process Inventory account as the production process begins. When products are completed, their costs are transferred from the Work in Process Inventory account to the Finished Goods Inventory account. Costs remain in the Finished Goods Inventory account until the products are sold, at which time they are transferred to the Cost of Goods Sold account.

LO5 Compare how service, retail, and manufacturing organizations report costs on their financial statements and how they account for inventories.

Because the operations of service, retail, and manufacturing organizations differ, their financial statements differ as well. A service organization maintains no inventory accounts on its balance sheet. The cost of sales on its income statement reflects the net cost of the services sold. A retail organization, which purchases products ready for resale, maintains only a Merchandise Inventory account, which is used to record and account for items in inventory. The cost of goods sold is simply the difference between the cost of goods available for sale and the ending merchandise inventory. A manufacturing organization, because it creates a product, maintains three inventory accounts: Materials Inventory, Work in Process Inventory, and Finished Goods Inventory. Manufacturing costs flow through all three inventory accounts. During the accounting period, the cost of completed products is transferred to the Finished Goods Inventory account; the cost of units that have been manufactured and sold is transferred to the Cost of Goods Sold account.

LO6 Define *cost allocation* and explain how cost objects, cost pools, and cost drivers are used to assign manufacturing overhead costs.

Cost allocation is the process of assigning collected indirect costs to a specific cost object using an allocation base known as a cost driver. The allocation of manufacturing overhead costs requires the pooling of overhead costs that are affected by a common activity and the selection of a cost driver whose activity level causes a change in the cost pool. A cost pool is the collection of overhead costs assigned to a cost object. A cost driver is an activity base that causes the cost pool to increase in amount as the cost driver increases.

Allocating manufacturing overhead is a four-step process that involves planning a rate at which overhead costs will be assigned to products, assigning overheard costs at this predetermined rate to product costs during production, recording actual manufacturing overhead costs as they are incurred, and reconciling the difference between the actual and applied overhead costs. The Cost of Goods Sold account is corrected for an immaterial amount of over- or underapplied manufacturing overhead costs assigned to the products. If the difference is material, adjustments are made to the Work in Process Inventory, Finished Goods Inventory, and Cost of Goods Sold accounts.

LO7 Using the traditional method of allocating manufacturing overhead costs, calculate product unit cost.

The traditional method applies manufacturing overhead costs to a product's cost by estimating a predetermined overhead rate and multiplying that rate by the actual cost driver level. The product unit cost is computed either by dividing the total product cost (the sum of the total applied manufacturing overhead cost and the actual costs of direct materials and direct labor) by the total number of units produced or by determining the cost per unit for each element of the product cost and summing those per-unit costs.

Chapter Review

LO8 Using activity-based costing to assign manufacturing overhead costs, calculate product unit cost.

When ABC is used, manufacturing overhead costs are grouped into a number of cost pools related to specific activities. Cost drivers are identified, and cost driver levels are estimated for each activity pool. Each activity cost rate is calculated by dividing the estimated activity pool amount by the estimated cost driver level. Manufacturing overhead, which is divided into the activity pools, is applied to the product's cost by multiplying the various activity cost rates by their actual cost driver levels. The product unit cost is computed by dividing the total product cost (the sum of the total applied cost pools and the actual costs of direct materials and direct labor) by the total number of units produced.

LO9 Apply costing concepts to a service organization.

Because no products are manufactured in the course of providing services, service organizations have no materials costs. They do, however, have both direct labor costs and overhead costs, which are similar to those in manufacturing organizations. To determine the cost of performing a service, professional labor and service-related overhead costs are included in the analysis.

Review of Concepts and Terminology

The following concepts and terms were introduced in this chapter:

LO8 **Activity-based costing (ABC):** A method of assigning overhead costs that categorizes all indirect costs by activity, traces the indirect costs to those activities, and assigns activity costs to products using a cost driver related to the cause of the cost.

LO3 **Actual costing:** A method of cost measurement that uses the actual costs of direct materials, direct labor, and manufacturing overhead to calculate a product unit cost.

LO3 **Conversion costs:** The costs of converting direct materials into a finished product; the sum of direct labor costs and manufacturing overhead costs.

LO6 **Cost allocation:** The process of assigning a collection of indirect costs to a specific cost object using an allocation base known as a cost driver.

LO6 **Cost driver:** An activity base that causes a cost pool to increase in amount as the cost driver increases in volume.

LO6 **Cost object:** The destination of an assigned, or allocated, cost.

LO4 **Cost of goods manufactured:** The cost of all units completed and moved to finished goods storage during an accounting period.

LO6 **Cost pool:** The collection of overhead costs assigned to a cost object.

LO2 **Direct costs:** Costs that can be conveniently and economically traced to a cost object.

LO3 **Direct labor costs:** The costs of the labor needed to make a product that can be conveniently and economically traced to specific units of the product.

LO3 **Direct materials costs:** The costs of the materials used in making a product that can be conveniently and economically traced to specific units of the product.

LO4 **Finished Goods Inventory account:** An inventory account that shows the costs assigned to all completed products that have not been sold.

LO2 **Fixed cost:** A cost that remains constant within a defined range of activity or time period.

LO2 **Indirect costs:** Costs that cannot be conveniently or economically traced to a cost object.

LO3 **Indirect labor costs:** The costs of labor for production-related activities that cannot be conveniently or economically traced to a unit of the product.

LO3 **Indirect materials costs:** The costs of materials that cannot be conveniently and economically traced to a unit of the product.

LO4 **Manufacturing cost flow:** The flow of manufacturing costs (direct materials, direct labor, and overhead) through the Materials Inventory, Work in Process

LO3 **Manufacturing overhead costs:** Production-related costs that cannot be practically or conveniently traced to an end product. Also called *factory overhead*, *factory burden*, or *indirect manufacturing costs*.

LO4 **Materials Inventory account:** An inventory account that shows the balance of the cost of unused materials.

LO2 **Nonvalue-adding cost:** The cost of an activity that adds cost to a product or service but does not increase its market value.

LO3 **Normal costing:** A method of cost measurement that combines the actual direct costs of materials and labor with estimated manufacturing overhead costs to determine a product unit cost.

LO6 **Overapplied overhead costs:** The amount that overhead costs applied using the predetermined overhead rate exceed the actual overhead costs for the accounting period.

LO2 **Period costs:** The costs of resources used during an accounting period and not assigned to products. Also called *noninventoriable costs*.

LO6 **Predetermined overhead rate:** The rate calculated before an accounting period begins by dividing the cost pool of total estimated overhead costs by the total estimated cost driver for that pool.

LO3 **Prime costs:** The primary costs of production; the sum of direct materials costs and direct labor costs.

LO2 **Product costs:** The costs assigned to inventory, which include the costs of direct materials, direct labor, and manufacturing overhead. Also called *inventoriable costs*.

LO3 **Product unit cost:** The cost of manufacturing a single unit of a product, computed either by dividing the total cost of direct materials, direct labor, and manufacturing overhead by the total number of units produced, or by determining the cost per unit for each element of the product cost and summing those per-unit costs.

LO3 **Standard costing:** A method of cost measurement that uses the estimated costs of direct materials, direct labor, and manufacturing overhead to calculate a product unit cost.

LO5 **Statement of cost of goods manufactured:** A formal statement summarizing the flow of all manufacturing costs incurred during an accounting period.

LO4 **Total manufacturing costs:** The total costs of direct materials, direct labor, and manufacturing overhead incurred and transferred to Work in Process Inventory during an accounting period. Also called *current manufacturing costs*.

LO6 **Underapplied overhead costs:** The amount that actual overhead costs exceed the overhead costs applied using the predetermined overhead rate for the accounting period.

LO2 **Value-adding cost:** The cost of an activity that increases the market value of a product or service.

LO2 **Variable cost:** A cost that changes in direct proportion to a change in productive output (or any other measure of volume).

LO4 **Work in Process Inventory account:** An inventory account used to record the manufacturing costs incurred and assigned to partially completed units of product.

REVIEW PROBLEM

Calculating Cost of Goods Manufactured: Three Fundamental Steps

LO3
LO4
LO5 Nikita Company requires its controller to prepare not only a year-end balance sheet and income statement, but also a statement of cost of goods manufactured. During 20x6, Nikita purchased $361,920 of direct materials. The company's direct labor costs for the year were $99,085 (10,430 hours at $9.50 per hour); its indirect labor costs totaled $126,750 (20,280 hours at $6.25 per hour). Account balances for 20x6 were as follows:

Account	Balance
Plant Supervision	$ 42,500
Factory Insurance	8,100
Utilities, Factory	29,220
Depreciation, Factory Building	46,200
Depreciation, Factory Equipment	62,800
Factory Security	9,460
Factory Repair and Maintenance	14,980
Selling and Administrative Expenses	76,480
Materials Inventory, December 31, 20x5	26,490
Work in Process Inventory, December 31, 20x5	101,640
Finished Goods Inventory, December 31, 20x5	148,290
Materials Inventory, December 31, 20x6	24,910
Work in Process Inventory, December 31, 20x6	100,400
Finished Goods Inventory, December 31, 20x6	141,100

REQUIRED
1. Compute the cost of materials used during the year.
2. Given the cost of materials used, compute the total manufacturing costs for the year.
3. Given the total manufacturing costs for the year, compute the cost of goods manufactured during the year.
4. If 13,397 units were manufactured during the year, what was the actual product unit cost? (Round your answer to two decimal places.)

ANSWER TO REVIEW PROBLEM

1. Cost of materials used:

Materials inventory, December 31, 20x5		$ 26,490
Add direct materials purchased (net)		361,920
Cost of materials available for use		$388,410
Less materials inventory, December 31, 20x6		24,910
Cost of materials used		$363,500

2. Total manufacturing costs:

Cost of materials used		$363,500
Add direct labor costs		99,085
Add total manufacturing overhead costs		
Plant supervision	$ 42,500	
Indirect labor	126,750	
Factory insurance	8,100	
Utilities, factory	29,220	
Depreciation, factory building	46,200	
Depreciation, factory equipment	62,800	
Factory security	9,460	
Factory repair and maintenance	14,980	
Total manufacturing overhead costs		340,010
Total manufacturing costs		$802,595

3. Cost of goods manufactured:

Total manufacturing costs	$802,595
Add work in process inventory, December 31, 20x5	101,640
Total cost of work in process during the year	$904,235
Less work in process inventory, December 31, 20x6	100,400
Cost of goods manufactured	$803,835

4. Actual product unit cost:

$$\frac{\text{Cost of Goods Manufactured}}{\text{Number of Units Manufactured}} = \frac{\$803,835}{13,397} = \$60.00$$

Chapter Assignments

BUILDING YOUR KNOWLEDGE FOUNDATION

QUESTIONS

1. How do managers use information about costs?
2. Why do managers use different classifications of costs?
3. What is the difference between a direct cost and an indirect cost?
4. What is the difference between a value-adding cost and a nonvalue-adding cost?
5. What are product costs and period costs?
6. What three kinds of costs are included in a product's cost?
7. What characteristics identify a cost as part of manufacturing overhead?
8. What is the difference between actual costing and normal costing?
9. What is the difference between prime costs and conversion costs?
10. Identify and describe the inventory accounts used by a manufacturing company.
11. What does the term *manufacturing cost flow* mean?
12. How do total manufacturing costs differ from the cost of goods manufactured?
13. How do service, retail, and manufacturing organizations differ, and how do these differences affect accounting for inventories?
14. How is the cost of goods manufactured used in computing the cost of goods sold?
15. What is cost allocation?
16. Explain the relationship among cost objects, cost pools, and cost drivers. Give an example of each.
17. List the four steps involved in allocating manufacturing overhead costs. Briefly explain each step.
18. How does traditional overhead allocation differ from ABC overhead allocation?
19. What allocation measure does ABC use to relate an activity pool to a cost object? Explain.
20. "The concept of product costs is not applicable to service organizations." Is this statement correct? Defend your answer.

SHORT EXERCISES

LO2 Cost Classifications

SE 1. Indicate whether each of the following is a direct (D) or indirect (ID) cost and a variable (V) or fixed (F) cost. Also indicate whether each adds value (VA) or does not add value (NVA) to the product and whether each is a product cost (PD), period cost (PER), or neither (N).

1. Production supervisor's salary
2. Sales commission
3. Wages of a production-line worker

LO3 Elements of Manufacturing Costs

SE 2. Daisy Luna, the bookkeeper at Candlelight, Inc., must group the costs of manufacturing candles. Indicate whether each of the following items should be classified as direct materials (DM), direct labor (DL), manufacturing overhead (MO), or none of these (N). Also indicate whether each is a prime cost (PC), conversion cost (CC), or neither (N).

1. Depreciation of the cost of vats to hold melted wax
2. Cost of wax
3. Rent on the factory where candles are made
4. Cost of George's time to dip the wicks into the wax
5. Cost of coloring for candles
6. Cost of Ray's time to design candles for Halloween
7. Sam's commission to sell candles to Candles Plus

LO3 **SE 3. Computation of Product Unit Cost**

What is the product unit cost for Job 14, which consists of 300 units and has total manufacturing costs of direct materials, $4,500; direct labor, $7,500; and manufacturing overhead, $3,600? What are the prime costs and conversion costs per unit?

LO4 **SE 4. Cost Flow in a Manufacturing Organization**

Given the following information, compute the ending balances of the Materials Inventory, Work in Process Inventory, and Finished Goods Inventory accounts:

Materials Inventory, beginning balance	$ 23,000
Work in Process Inventory, beginning balance	25,750
Finished Goods Inventory, beginning balance	38,000
Direct materials purchased	85,000
Direct materials placed into production	74,000
Direct labor costs	97,000
Manufacturing overhead costs	35,000
Cost of goods completed	123,000
Cost of goods sold	93,375

LO4 **SE 5. Document Flows in a Manufacturing Organization**

Identify the document needed to support each of the following activities in a manufacturing organization:

1. Placing an order for direct materials with a supplier
2. Recording direct labor time at the beginning and end of each work shift
3. Receiving direct materials at the shipping dock
4. Recording the costs of a specific job requiring direct materials, direct labor, and overhead
5. Issuing direct materials into production
6. Billing the customer for a completed order
7. Fulfilling a request from the Production Scheduling Department for the purchase of direct materials

LO5 **SE 6. Income Statement for a Manufacturing Organization**

Using the following information from Hakim Company, prepare an income statement through operating income for 20x6:

Sales	$900,000
Finished goods inventory, December 31, 20x5	45,000
Cost of goods manufactured	585,000
Finished goods inventory, December 31, 20x6	60,000
Operating expenses	275,000

LO5 **SE 7. Comparison of Income Statement Formats**

Indicate whether each of these equations applies to a service organization (SER), retail organization (RET), or manufacturing organization (MANF):

1. Cost of Goods Sold = Beginning Merchandising Inventory + Net Cost of Purchases − Ending Merchandise Inventory
2. Cost of Sales = Net Cost of Services Sold
3. Cost of Goods Sold = Beginning Finished Goods Inventory + Cost of Goods Manufactured − Ending Finished Goods Inventory

LO6 **SE 8. Calculation of Underapplied or Overapplied Overhead**

At year end, records show that actual manufacturing overhead costs incurred were $25,870 and the amount of manufacturing overhead costs applied to production was $27,000. Identify the amount of under- or overapplied manufacturing overhead, and indicate whether the Cost of Goods Sold account should be increased or decreased to reflect actual manufacturing overhead costs.

LO6 LO7 **SE 9. Computation of Overhead Rate**

Compute the overhead rate per service request for the Maintenance Department if estimated overhead costs are $18,290 and the number of estimated service requests is 3,100.

LO6 LO7 **SE 10. Allocation of Manufacturing Overhead to Production**

Calculate the amount of manufacturing overhead costs applied to production if the predetermined overhead rate is $4 per direct labor hour and 1,200 direct labor hours were worked.

LO8 **SE 11. Activity-Based Costing and Cost Drivers**

Mazzola Clothiers Company relies on the information from its activity-based costing system when setting prices for its products. Compute ABC rates from the following estimated data for each of the activity centers:

Estimated Activity	Pool Amount	Cost Driver Level
Cutting/Stitching	$5,220,000	145,000 machine hours
Trimming/Packing	998,400	41,600 operator hours
Designing	1,187,500	62,500 designer hours

SE 12.
LO9 Unit Costs in a Service Business

Fickle Picking Services provides inexpensive, high-quality labor for farmers growing vegetable and fruit crops. In September, Fickle Picking Services paid laborers $4,000 to harvest 500 acres of apples. The company incurred overhead costs of $2,400 for apple-picking services in September. This amount included the costs of transporting the laborers to the orchards; of providing facilities, food, and beverages for the laborers; and of scheduling, billing, and collecting from the farmers. Of this amount, 50 percent was related to picking apples. Compute the cost per acre to pick apples.

Exercises

E 1.
LO1 The Management Cycle and Operating Costs

Indicate whether each of the following activities takes place during the planning (P), executing (E), reviewing (RV), or reporting (RP) stage of the management cycle:
1. Changing regular price to clearance price
2. Communicating results to appropriate personnel
3. Preparing budgets of operating costs
4. Comparing estimated and actual costs to determine variances

E 2.
LO2 Cost Classifications

Indicate whether each of the following costs for a bicycle manufacturer is a direct or indirect cost of the bicycle, a variable or fixed cost, a value-adding or nonvalue-adding cost, and a product or period cost:

	Cost Classification			
	Direct or Indirect	Variable or Fixed	Value-adding or Nonvalue-adding	Product or Period
Example: Bicycle tire	Direct	Variable	Value-adding	Product

1. Depreciation on office computer
2. Labor to assemble bicycle
3. Labor to inspect bicycle
4. Internal auditor's salary
5. Lubricant for wheels

E 3.
LO3 Unit Cost Determination

The Pattia Winery is one of the finest wineries in the country. One of its famous products is a red wine called Old Vines. Recently, management has become concerned about the increasing cost of making Old Vines and needs to determine if the current selling price of $10 per bottle is adequate. The winery wants to achieve a 25 percent gross profit on the sale of each bottle. The following information is given to you for analysis:

Batch size	10,550 bottles
Costs	
Direct materials	
Olen Millot grapes	$22,155
Chancellor grapes	9,495
Bottles	5,275
Total direct materials costs	$36,925
Direct labor	
Pickers/loaders	2,110
Crusher	422
Processors	8,440
Bottler	$13,293
Total direct labor costs	$24,265
Manufacturing overhead	
Depreciation, equipment	2,743
Depreciation, building	5,275
Utilities	1,055
Indirect labor	6,330
Supervision	7,385
Supplies	9,917
Repairs	1,477
Miscellaneous	633
Total manufacturing overhead costs	$34,815
Total production costs	$96,005

1. Compute the unit cost per bottle for materials, labor, and overhead.
2. How would you advise management regarding the price per bottle of wine?
3. Compute the prime costs per unit and the conversion costs per unit.

LO4 Documentation

E 4. Lisette Company manufactures music boxes. Seventy percent of its products are standard items produced in long production runs. The other 30 percent are special orders with specific requests for tunes. The latter cost from three to six times as much as the standard product because they require additional materials and labor.

Reza Seca, the controller, recently received a complaint memorandum from Iggy Paulo, the production supervisor, about the new network of source documents that was added to the existing cost accounting system. The new documents include a purchase request, a purchase order, a receiving report, and a materials request. Paulo claims that the forms create extra work and interrupt the normal flow of production.

Prepare a written memorandum from Reza Seca to Iggy Paulo that fully explains the purpose of each type of document.

LO4 Cost Flows and Inventory Accounts

E 5. For each of the following activities, identify the inventory account (Materials Inventory, Work in Process Inventory, Finished Goods Inventory), if any, that is affected. If an inventory account is affected, indicate whether the account balance will increase or decrease. (*Example:* Moved completed units to finished goods inventory. *Answer:* Increase Finished Goods Inventory; decrease Work in Process Inventory.) If no inventory account is affected, use "None of these" as your answer.

1. Moved materials requested by production
2. Sold units of product
3. Purchased and received direct materials for production
4. Used direct labor and manufacturing overhead in the production process
5. Received payment from customer
6. Purchased office supplies and paid cash
7. Paid monthly office rent

LO5 Statement of Cost of Goods Manufactured

E 6. During August 31, 20x5, Rao Company's purchases of direct materials totaled $139,000; direct labor for the month was 3,400 hours at $8.75 per hour. Rao also incurred the following manufacturing overhead costs: utilities, $5,870; supervision, $16,600; indirect materials, $6,750; depreciation, $6,200; insurance, $1,830; and miscellaneous, $1,100.

Inventory accounts on July 31 were as follows: Materials Inventory, $48,600; Work in Process Inventory, $54,250; and Finished Goods Inventory, $38,500. Inventory accounts on August 31 were as follows: Materials Inventory, $50,100; Work in Process Inventory, $48,400; and Finished Goods Inventory, $37,450.

From the information given, prepare a statement of cost of goods manufactured.

LO5 Statement of Cost of Goods Manufactured and Cost of Goods Sold

E 7. Treetec Corp. makes irrigation sprinkler systems for tree nurseries. Rama Shih, Treetec's new controller, can find only the following partial information for the past year:

	Oak Division	Loblolly Division	Maple Division	Spruce Division
Direct materials used	$3	$ 7	$ g	$ 8
Total manufacturing costs	6	d	h	14
Manufacturing overhead	1	3	2	j
Direct labor	a	6	4	4
Ending work in process inventory	b	3	2	5
Cost of goods manufactured	7	20	12	k
Beginning work in process inventory	2	e	3	l
Ending finished goods inventory	2	6	i	9
Beginning finished goods inventory	3	f	5	7
Cost of goods sold	c	18	13	9

Using the information given, compute the unknown values. List the accounts in the proper order and show subtotals and totals as appropriate.

LO5 Characteristics of Organizations

E 8. Indicate whether each of the following is typical of a service organization (SER), retail organization (RET), or manufacturing organization (MANF):

1. Maintains only one balance sheet inventory account
2. Maintains no balance sheet inventory accounts
3. Maintains three balance sheet inventory accounts
4. Purchases products ready for resale
5. Designs and makes products for sale

6. Sells services
7. Determines the cost of sales
8. Includes the cost of goods manufactured in calculating cost of goods sold
9. Includes the cost of purchases in calculating cost of goods sold

E 9. Presented below are incomplete inventory and income statement data for Trevor Corporation. Determine the missing amounts.

LO5 Missing Amounts— Manufacturing

	Cost of Goods Sold	Cost of Goods Manufactured	Beginning Finished Goods Inventory	Ending Finished Goods Inventory
1.	$ 10,000	$12,000	$ 1,000	?
2.	$140,000	?	$45,000	$60,000
3.	?	$89,000	$23,000	$20,000

E 10. The data presented below are for a retail organization and a manufacturing organization.

LO5 Inventories, Cost of Goods Sold, and Net Income

1. Fill in the missing data for the retail organization:

	First Quarter	Second Quarter	Third Quarter	Fourth Quarter
Sales	$9	$ e	$15	$ k
Gross margin	a	4	5	l
Ending merchandise inventory	5	f	5	m
Beginning merchandise inventory	4	g	h	5
Net cost of purchases	b	7	9	n
Operating income	3	2	i	2
Operating expenses	c	2	2	4
Cost of goods sold	5	6	j	11
Cost of goods available for sale	d	12	15	15

2. Fill in the missing data for the manufacturing organization:

	First Quarter	Second Quarter	Third Quarter	Fourth Quarter
Ending finished goods inventory	$a	$3	$h	$6
Cost of goods sold	6	3	5	l
Operating income	1	3	1	m
Cost of goods available for sale	8	d	10	13
Cost of goods manufactured	5	e	i	8
Gross margin	4	f	j	7
Operating expenses	3	g	5	6
Beginning finished goods inventory	b	2	3	n
Sales	c	10	k	14

E 11. The overhead costs that Lucca Industries, Inc., used to compute its overhead rate for 20x6 are as follows:

LO6 Computation of Overhead
LO7 Rate

Indirect materials and supplies	$ 79,200
Repairs and maintenance	14,900
Outside service contracts	17,300
Indirect labor	79,100
Factory supervision	42,900
Depreciation, machinery	85,000
Factory insurance	8,200
Property taxes	6,500
Heat, light, and power	7,700
Miscellaneous manufacturing overhead	5,760
	$346,560

The allocation base for 20x6 was 45,600 total machine hours. In 20x7, all overhead costs except depreciation, property taxes, and miscellaneous manufacturing overhead are expected to increase by 10 percent. Depreciation should increase by 12 percent, and property taxes and miscellaneous manufacturing overhead are expected to increase by 20 percent. Plant capacity in terms of machine hours used will increase by 4,400 hours.

1. Compute the 20x6 overhead rate. (Carry your answer to three decimal places.)
2. Compute the overhead rate for 20x7. (Carry your answer to three decimal places.)

LO6, LO7 Computation and Application of Overhead Rate

E 12. Compumatics specializes in the analysis and reporting of complex inventory costing projects. Materials costs are minimal, consisting entirely of operating supplies (DVDs, inventory sheets, and other recording tools). Labor is the highest single expense, totaling $693,000 for 75,000 hours of work in 20x8. Manufacturing overhead costs for 20x8 were $916,000 and were applied to specific jobs on the basis of labor hours worked. In 20x9, the company anticipates a 25 percent increase in manufacturing overhead costs. Labor costs will increase by $130,000, and the number of hours worked is expected to increase by 20 percent.

1. Determine the total amount of manufacturing overhead anticipated in 20x9.
2. Compute the manufacturing overhead rate for 20x9. (Round your answer to the nearest cent.)
3. During April 20x9, 11,980 labor hours were worked. Calculate the manufacturing overhead amount assigned to April production.

LO6, LO7 Disposition of Overapplied Overhead

E 13. At the end of 20x9, Compumatics had compiled a total of 89,920 labor hours worked. The actual manufacturing overhead incurred was $1,143,400.

1. Using the overhead rate computed in **E 12**, determine the total amount of manufacturing overhead applied to operations during 20x9.
2. Compute the amount of overapplied overhead for the year.
3. Will the Cost of Goods Sold account be increased or decreased to correct the overapplication of manufacturing overhead?

LO7, LO8 Activities and Activity-Based Costing

E 14. Zone Enterprises produces wireless components used in telecommunications equipment. One of the most important features of the company's new just-in-time production process is quality control. Initially, a traditional allocation method was used to assign the costs of quality control to products; all these costs were included in the plant's overhead cost pool and allocated to products based on direct labor dollars. Recently, the firm implemented an activity-based costing system. The activities, cost drivers, and rates for the quality control function are summarized below, along with cost allocation information from the traditional method. Also shown is information related to one order, Order HL14. Compute the quality control cost that would be assigned to the order under both the traditional method and the activity-based costing method.

Traditional costing method:
Quality control costs were assigned at a rate of 12 percent of direct labor dollars. Order HL14 was charged with $9,350 of direct labor costs.

Activity-based costing method:

Activity	Activity Cost Driver	Cost Rate	Activity Usage for Order HL14
Incoming materials inspection	Types of materials used	$17.50 per type of material used	17 types of materials
In-process inspection	Number of products	$.06 per product	2,400 products
Tool and gauge control	Number of processes per cell	$26.50 per process per cell	11 processes
Product certification	Per order	$94.00 per order	1 order

LO9 Unit Costs in a Service Business

E 15. Walden Green provides custom farming services to owners of five-acre wheat fields. In July, he earned $2,400 by cutting, turning, and baling 3,000 bales. In the same month, he incurred the following costs: gas, $150; tractor maintenance, $115; and labor, $600. His annual tractor depreciation was $1,500. What was Green's cost per bale? What was his revenue per bale? Should he increase the amount he charges for his services?

Problems

LO3 Computation of Unit Cost

P 1. Carola Industries, Inc., manufactures discs for several of the leading recording studios in the United States and Europe. Department 60 is responsible for the electronic circuitry within each disc. Department 61 applies the plastic-like surface to the discs and packages them for shipment. Carola recently produced 4,000 discs for the Milo Company. In fulfilling this order, the departments incurred the following costs:

	Department	
	60	61
Direct materials used	$29,440	$3,920
Direct labor	6,800	2,560
Manufacturing overhead	7,360	4,800

REQUIRED
1. Compute the unit cost for each department.
2. Compute the total unit cost for the Milo Company order.
3. The selling price for this order was $14 per unit. Was the selling price adequate? List the assumptions and/or computations upon which you based your answer. What suggestions would you make to Carola Industries' management about the pricing of future orders?
4. Compute the prime costs and conversion costs per unit for each department.

P 2.
LO5 Statement of Cost of Goods Manufactured

Dillo Vineyards, a large winery in Texas, produces a full line of varietal wines. The company, whose fiscal year begins on November 1, has just completed a record-breaking year. Its inventory account balances on October 31, 20x7, were Materials Inventory, $1,803,800; Work in Process Inventory, $2,764,500; and Finished Goods Inventory, $1,883,200. On October 31, 20x6, the inventory account balances were Materials Inventory, $2,156,200; Work in Process Inventory, $3,371,000; and Finished Goods Inventory, $1,596,400.

During the 20x6–20x7 fiscal year, the company's purchases of direct materials totaled $6,750,000. Direct labor hours totaled 142,500, and the average labor rate was $8.20 per hour. The following manufacturing overhead costs were incurred during the year: depreciation, plant and equipment, $685,600; indirect labor, $207,300; property tax, plant and equipment, $94,200; plant maintenance, $83,700; small tools, $42,400; utilities, $96,500; and employee benefits, $76,100.

REQUIRED Prepare a statement of cost of goods manufactured for the fiscal year ended October 31, 20x7.

P 3.
LO5 A Manufacturing Organization's Balance Sheet

The following information is from the balance sheet of Mills Manufacturing Company:

	Debit	Credit
Cash	$ 34,000	
Accounts receivable	27,000	
Materials inventory, 12/31/x6	31,000	
Work in process inventory, 12/31/x6	47,900	
Finished goods inventory, 12/31/x6	54,800	
Production supplies	5,700	
Small tools	9,330	
Land	160,000	
Factory building	575,000	
Accumulated depreciation, factory building		$ 199,000
Factory equipment	310,000	
Accumulated depreciation, factory equipment		137,000
Patents	33,500	
Accounts payable		26,900
Insurance premiums payable		6,700
Income taxes payable		41,500
Mortgage payable		343,000
Common stock		200,000
Retained earnings, 12/31/x6		334,130
	$1,288,230	$1,288,230

REQUIRED
1. Manufacturing organizations use asset accounts that are not needed by merchandising organizations.
   a. List the titles of the asset accounts that are specifically related to manufacturing organizations.
   b. List the titles of the asset, liability, and equity accounts that you would see on the balance sheets of both manufacturing and merchandising organizations.

2. Assuming that the following information reflects the results of operations for 20x6, calculate the (a) gross margin, (b) cost of goods sold, (c) cost of goods available for sale, and (d) cost of goods manufactured:

Operating income	$138,130
Operating expenses	53,670
Sales	500,000
Finished goods inventory, 12/31/x5	50,900

3. Does Mills Manufacturing use the periodic or perpetual inventory system?

P 4.
LO6 Allocation of Manufacturing
LO7 Overhead

Natural Cosmetics Company applies manufacturing overhead costs on the basis of machine hours. The overhead rate is computed by analyzing data from the previous two years and projecting figures for the current year, adjusted for expected changes. The controller prepared the overhead rate analysis for 20x7 using the following information:

	20x5	20x6
Machine hours	47,800	57,360
Manufacturing overhead costs		
Indirect labor	$ 18,100	$ 23,530
Employee benefits	22,000	28,600
Manufacturing supervision	16,800	18,480
Utilities	10,350	14,490
Factory insurance	6,500	7,800
Janitorial services	11,000	12,100
Depreciation, factory and machinery	17,750	21,300
Miscellaneous manufacturing overhead	5,750	7,475
Total manufacturing overhead	$108,250	$133,775

In 20x7, the cost of utilities is expected to increase by 40 percent over 20x6; the cost of indirect labor, employee benefits, and miscellaneous manufacturing overhead is expected to increase by 30 percent; the cost of insurance and depreciation is expected to increase by 20 percent; and the cost of supervision and janitorial services is expected to increase by 10 percent. Machine hours are expected to total 68,832.

REQUIRED

1. Compute the projected costs and the overhead rate for 20x7 using the information about expected cost increases. (Carry your answer to three decimal places.)
2. Jobs completed during 20x7 and the machine hours used were as follows:

Job No.	Machine Hours
2214	12,300
2215	14,200
2216	9,800
2217	13,600
2218	11,300
2219	8,100

Determine the amount of manufacturing overhead to be applied to each job and to total production during 20x7. (Round answers to whole dollars.)

3. Actual manufacturing overhead costs for 20x7 were $165,845. Was overhead underapplied or overapplied? By how much? Should the Cost of Goods Sold account be increased or decreased to reflect actual overhead costs?

P 5.
LO8 Activities and Activity-Based Costing

Byte Computer Company, a manufacturing organization, has been in operation for ten years. It has just completed an order that Grater, Ltd., placed for 80 computers. Byte recently shifted from a traditional system of allocating costs to an activity-based costing system. Simone Faure, Byte's controller, wants to know the impact that the ABC system had on the Grater order. Raw materials, purchased parts, and direct labor costs for the Grater order are as follows:

Cost of direct materials	$36,750.00	Direct labor hours	220
Cost of purchased parts	$21,300.00	Average direct labor pay rate	$15.25

Other operating costs are as follows:

Traditional costing data:
Manufacturing overhead costs were applied at a single, plant-wide overhead rate of 270 percent of direct labor dollars.

Activity-based costing data:

Activity	Cost Driver	Activity Cost Rate	Activity Usage for Grater Order
Electrical engineering design	Engineering hours	$19.50 per engineering hour	32 engineering hours
Setup	Number of setups	$29.40 per setup	11 setups
Parts production	Machine hours	$26.30 per machine hour	134 machine hours
Product testing	Product testing hours	$32.80 per product testing hour	52 product testing hours
Packaging	Packaging hours	$17.50 per packaging hour	22 packaging hours
Building occupancy	Machine hours	$9.80 per machine hour	134 machine hours

REQUIRED
1. Using the traditional costing method, compute the total cost of the Grater order.
2. Using the activity-based costing method, compute the total cost of the Grater order.
3. What difference in the amount of cost assigned to the Grater order resulted from the shift to activity-based costing? Was Byte Computer Company's shift to activity-based costing a good management decision?

ALTERNATE PROBLEMS

P 6.

LO6 Allocation of Manufacturing
LO7 Overhead

Lund Products, Inc., uses a predetermined manufacturing overhead rate in its production, assembly, and testing departments. One rate is used for the entire company; it is based on machine hours. The rate is determined by analyzing data from the previous two years and projecting figures for the current year, adjusted for expected changes. Lise Jensen is about to compute the rate for 20x6 using the following data:

	20x4	20x5
Machine hours	38,000	41,800
Manufacturing overhead costs		
Indirect materials	$ 44,500	$ 57,850
Indirect labor	21,200	25,440
Supervision	37,800	41,580
Utilities	9,400	11,280
Labor-related costs	8,200	9,020
Depreciation, factory	9,800	10,780
Depreciation, machinery	22,700	27,240
Property taxes	2,400	2,880
Insurance	1,600	1,920
Miscellaneous manufacturing overhead	4,400	4,840
Total manufacturing overhead	$162,000	$192,830

In 20x6, the cost of indirect materials is expected to increase by 30 percent over the previous year. The cost of indirect labor, utilities, machinery depreciation, property taxes, and insurance is expected to increase by 20 percent. All other expenses are expected to increase by 10 percent. Machine hours for 20x6 are estimated at 45,980.

REQUIRED
1. Compute the projected costs and the manufacturing overhead rate for 20x6 using the information about expected cost increases. (Round your answer to three decimal places.)
2. During 20x6, Lund Products completed the following jobs using the machine hours shown:

Job No.	Machine Hours	Job No.	Machine Hours
H–142	7,840	H–201	10,680
H–164	5,260	H–218	12,310
H–175	8,100	H–304	2,460

Determine the amount of manufacturing overhead applied to each job. What was the total manufacturing overhead applied during 20x6? (Round answers to the nearest dollar.)
3. Actual manufacturing overhead costs for 20x6 were $234,485. Was overhead underapplied or overapplied in 20x6? By how much? Should the Cost of Goods Sold account be increased or decreased to reflect actual overhead costs?

4. At what point during 20x6 was the manufacturing overhead rate computed? When was it applied? Finally, when was underapplied or overapplied overhead determined and the Cost of Goods Sold account adjusted to reflect actual costs?

P 7.

LO8 Activities and Activity-Based Costing

Fraser Products, Inc., which produces fax machines for wholesale distributors in the Pacific Northwest, has just completed packaging an order from Kent Company for 150 Model 14 fax machines. Fraser recently switched from a traditional system of allocating costs to an activity-based costing system. Before the Kent order is shipped, the controller wants a unit cost analysis comparing the amounts computed under the traditional costing system with those computed under the ABC system. Raw materials, purchased parts, and direct labor costs for the Kent order are as follows:

Cost of direct materials	$17,450.00	Direct labor hours	140
Cost of purchased parts	$14,800.00	Average direct labor pay rate	$16.50

Other operating costs are as follows:

Traditional costing data:
Manufacturing overhead costs were applied at a single, plant-wide overhead rate of 240 percent of direct labor dollars.

Activity-based costing data:

Activity	Cost Driver	Activity Cost Rate	Activity Usage for Kent Order
Engineering systems design	Engineering hours	$28.00 per engineering hour	18 engineering hours
Setup	Number of setups	$42.00 per setup	8 setups
Parts production	Machine hours	$37.50 per machine hour	84 machine hours
Assembly	Assembly hours	$44.00 per assembly hour	36 assembly hours
Packaging	Packaging hours	$28.50 per packaging hour	28 packaging hours
Building occupancy	Machine hours	$10.40 per machine hour	84 machine hours

REQUIRED ▶

1. Using the traditional costing approach, compute the total cost of the Kent order.
2. Using the activity-based costing approach, compute the total cost of the Kent order.
3. What difference in the amount of cost assigned to the Kent order resulted from the shift to activity-based costing? Does the use of activity-based costing guarantee cost reduction for every product?

P 8.

LO6 Allocation of Manufacturing
LO7 Overhead: Traditional and
LO8 Activity-Based Costing Methods

Sea Scout, Inc., manufactures two types of underwater vehicles. Oil companies use the vehicle called Rigger II to examine offshore oil rigs, and marine biology research foundations use the BioScout to study coastlines. The company's San Diego factory is not fully automated and requires some direct labor. Using estimated manufacturing overhead costs of $220,000 and an estimated 16,000 hours of direct labor, Oz Parson, the company's controller, calculated a traditional overhead rate of $13.75 per direct labor hour. He used normal costing to calculate the product unit cost for both product lines, as shown in the following summary:

	Rigger II	BioScout
Product costs per unit		
Direct materials	$ 10,000.00	$12,000.00
Direct labor	1,450.00	1,600.00
Applied manufacturing overhead	412.50*	550.00†
Product unit cost	$11,862.50	$14,150.00
Units of production	400	100
Direct labor hours	12,000	4,000

*$13.75 per Direct Labor Hour × 30 Direct Labor Hours per Unit = $412.50
†$13.75 per Direct Labor Hour × 40 Direct Labor Hours per Unit = $550

Parson believes the product unit cost for the BioScout is too low. After carefully observing the production process, he has concluded that the BioScout requires much more attention than the Rigger II. Because of BioScout's more intricate design, it requires more production activities, and fewer subassemblies by suppliers are possible. He has therefore created four overhead activity pools, estimated the manufacturing overhead costs of the activity pools, selected a cost driver for each pool, and estimated the cost driver levels for each product line, as shown in the following summary:

Activity Pool	Estimated Manufacturing Overhead Cost
Setup	$ 70,000
Inspection	20,000
Engineering	50,000
Assembly	80,000
Total	$220,000

Cost Driver	Rigger II Cost Driver Level	BioScout Cost Driver Level	Total Cost Driver Level
Number of setups	250	450	700
Number of inspections	150	350	500
Engineering hours	600	1,400	2,000
Machine hours	5,000	5,000	10,000

REQUIRED ▶

1. Use activity-based costing to do the following:
   a. Calculate the activity cost rate for each activity pool.
   b. Compute the overhead costs applied to each product line by activity pool and in total.
   c. Calculate the product unit cost for each product line.
2. What differences in the costs assigned to the two product lines resulted from the shift to activity-based costing?

SKILLS DEVELOPMENT CASES

Conceptual Analysis

SD 1.

LO1 **Comparison of Costs in**
LO2 **Different Types of Businesses**

H & R Block <www.hrblock.com> is a service company that prepares tax returns; Borders <www.bordersstores.com> is a retail company that sells books and CDs; Indian Motorcycle Corporation <www.indianmotorcycle.com> is a manufacturing company that makes motorcycles. Show that you understand how these companies differ by giving for each one an example of a direct and indirect cost, a variable and fixed cost, a value-adding and nonvalue-adding cost, and a product and period cost. Discuss the use of cost classifications in these three types of organizations.

SD 2.

LO6 **Comparison of Approaches to**
LO7 **Developing Overhead Rates**
LO8

Both Matos Company and Stubee Corporation use predetermined overhead rates for product costing, inventory valuation, and sales quotations. The two businesses are about the same size, and they compete in the corrugated box industry. Because the overhead rate is an estimated measure, Matos Company's management believes that the controller's department should spend little effort in developing it. The company computes the rate annually based on an analysis of the previous year's costs. No one monitors its accuracy during the year. Stubee Corporation takes a different approach. One person in the controller's office is responsible for developing overhead rates on a monthly basis. All cost estimates are checked carefully to make sure they are realistic. Accuracy checks are done routinely at the end of each month, and forecasts of changes in business activity are taken into account.

Assume that Cooke Corporation, an East Coast manufacturer of corrugated boxes, has hired you as a consultant. Asimina Hiona, Cooke's controller, wants you to recommend the best method of developing overhead rates. Based on your knowledge of Matos's and Stubee's practices, write a memo to Hiona that answers the following questions:

1. What are the advantages and disadvantages of Matos's and Stubee's approaches to developing overhead rates?
2. Which company has taken the more cost-effective approach to developing overhead rates? Defend your answer.
3. Is an accurate overhead rate most important for product costing, inventory valuation, or sales quotations? Why?
4. What is activity-based costing (ABC)? Would it be better than the two approaches discussed above? Explain.

Why would John H. Daniel Company use a job order costing system for the manufacture of its made-to-order suits?

The appropriateness of a product costing system depends on the nature of the production process. Because the manufacture of custom orders and the manufacture of large quantities of similar products involve different processes, they generally require different costing systems. When a product is custom-made, it is possible to collect the costs of each order. When a product is mass-produced, the costs of a specific unit cannot be collected because there is a continuous flow of similar products; in this case, costs are collected by process, department, or work cell. Thus, each of John H. Daniel Company's two divisions will probably need its own costing system to determine the cost of a suit.

Performance measures will also differ for John H. Daniel Company's two divisions. For the custom suit division, management can measure the profitability of each order by comparing the order's cost and price. For the retail suit division, management will measure performance by comparing the budgeted and actual costs for a process, department, or work cell.

Product Cost Information and the Management Cycle

LO1 Discuss the role information about costs plays in the management cycle and explain why unit cost is important.

RELATED TEXT ASSIGNMENTS
Q: 1, 2, 3, 4
SE: 1
SD: 1, 2
MRA: 1, 2, 3, 5

www.toyota.com
www.harley-davidson.com
www.levistrauss.com
www.century21.com
www.hrblock.com
www.orkin.com

Managers depend on relevant and reliable information about costs to manage their organizations. The role of the management accountant is to develop a management information system that provides managers with the cost information they need. Although companies vary in their approaches to gathering, analyzing, and reporting information about costs, managers share the same basic concerns as they move through the management cycle. Figure 1 summarizes the management cycle and the concerns managers address with relevant and timely information about costs.

Planning

During the planning stage, managers use information about costs to set performance expectations and estimate unit costs. In manufacturing companies, such as Toyota, Harley-Davidson, and Levi Strauss & Co., managers use cost information to develop budgets, establish product prices, and plan production volumes. In service organizations, such as Century 21, H&R Block, and Orkin Exterminating Company, managers use cost information to develop budgets, establish prices, set sales goals, and determine human resource needs. During the planning stage, knowledge of unit costs helps managers of both manufacturing and service companies set reasonable selling prices and estimate the cost of their products or services.

Executing

During the executing stage, managers make decisions about controlling costs, managing the company's activity volume, assuring quality, and negotiating prices. They use timely cost and volume information and actual unit costs to support their decision making. In manufacturing companies, managers use information about costs to decide whether to drop a product line, add a production shift, outsource the manufacture of a subassembly to another company, bid on a special order, or negotiate a selling price. In service organizations, managers use cost information to make decisions about bidding on jobs, dropping a current service, outsourcing a task to an independent contractor, adding staff, or negotiating a price. All these decisions can have far-reaching effects, including possible changes in unit cost or quality.

Reviewing

During the reviewing stage, managers watch for changes in cost and quality. They compare actual and targeted total and unit costs and monitor relevant price and volume information. They analyze the information to evaluate their performance, and on the basis of this evaluation, they adjust their planning and decision-making strategies. For example, if a product's quality is suffering, managers may study the design, materials purchasing, and manufacturing processes to determine the source of the problem so that they can make changes that will assure the product's quality. If operating costs in a service business have risen too high, managers may break a unit cost of service down into its many components to analyze where costs can be cut or how the service can be performed more efficiently.

Reporting

Finally, during the reporting stage, managers prepare financial statements. In manufacturing companies, managers use product unit costs to determine inventory balances for the organization's balance sheet and the cost of goods sold for its income statement. In service organizations, managers use unit costs of services to determine cost of sales for the income statement. During this stage, managers also prepare per-

▪ **Stop and Think!**
Why is unit cost important at every stage of the management cycle?
Unit cost is the primary measure of performance expectations, management control, performance evaluation, and financial reporting. ▪

FIGURE 1
Uses of Product Costing Information in the Management Cycle

formance evaluation reports for internal use. These reports compare actual unit costs and targeted costs, as well as actual and targeted nonfinancial measures of performance. Managers in both manufacturing and service organizations analyze the data in the performance evaluation reports to determine whether cost goals for products or services are being achieved.

 Check out ACE for a Review Quiz at http://accounting.college.hmco.com/students.

JOB ORDER VERSUS PROCESS COSTING

LO2 Distinguish between the two basic types of product costing systems and identify the information each provides.

RELATED TEXT ASSIGNMENTS
Q: 5, 6, 7, 8, 9
SE: 2, 3
E: 1, 2, 3
MRA: 2, 3

For an organization to succeed, its managers must sell its products or services at prices that exceed the costs of creating and delivering them, thus ensuring a profit. To do so, managers need extensive information about such product-related costs as setup, production, and distribution. To meet managers' needs for cost information, it is necessary to have a highly reliable product costing system specifically designed to record and report the organization's operations. A **product costing system** is a set of procedures used to account for an organization's product costs and to provide timely and accurate unit cost information for pricing, cost planning and control, inventory valuation, and financial statement preparation.

KEY POINT: In job order costing, costs are traced to jobs; in process costing, costs are traced to production processes.

TABLE 1. Characteristics of Job Order Costing and Process Costing Systems

Job Order Costing System	Process Costing System
Traces manufacturing costs to a specific job order	Traces manufacturing costs to processes, departments, or work cells and then assigns the costs to products manufactured
Measures the cost of each completed unit	Measures costs in terms of units completed during a specific period
Uses a single Work in Process Inventory account to summarize the cost of all job orders	Uses several Work in Process Inventory accounts, one for each process, department, or work cell
Typically used by companies that make large, unique, or special-order products, such as customized publications, built-in cabinets, or made-to-order draperies	Typically used by companies that make large amounts of similar products or liquid products or that have long, continuous production runs of identical products, as makers of paint, soft drinks, candy, bricks, and paper

The product costing system enables managers to track costs throughout the management cycle. It provides a structure for recording the revenue earned from sales and the costs incurred for direct materials, direct labor, and manufacturing overhead.

Two basic types of product costing systems have been developed: job order costing and process costing systems. A **job order costing system** is used by companies that make large, unique, or special-order products, such as customized publications, specially built cabinets, made-to-order draperies, or custom-tailored suits. Such a system uses a single Work in Process Inventory account to record the costs of all job orders. It traces the costs of direct materials, direct labor, and manufacturing overhead to a specific batch of products or a specific **job order** (i.e., a customer order for a specific number of specially designed, made-to-order products) by using a subsidiary ledger of job order cost cards. A **job order cost card** is the document on which all costs incurred in the production of a particular job order are recorded. The costs that a job order costing system gathers are used to measure the cost of each completed unit.

Companies that produce large amounts of similar products or liquid products or that have long, continuous production runs of identical products use a **process costing system**. Makers of paint, soft drinks, candy, bricks, and paper would use such a system, as would John H. Daniel Company's retail suit division. A process costing system first traces the costs of direct materials, direct labor, and manufacturing overhead to processes, departments, or work cells and then assigns the costs to the products manufactured by those processes, departments, or work cells during a specific period. A process costing system uses several Work in Process Inventory accounts, one for each process, department, or work cell. Table 1 summarizes the characteristics of job order costing and process costing systems.

KEY POINT: The product cost arrived at by both job order and process costing systems is an average cost. Process costing usually averages cost over a greater volume of product.

In reality, few production processes are a perfect match for either a job order costing system or a process costing system. The typical product costing system therefore combines parts of job order costing and process costing to create a hybrid

FOCUS ON INTERNATIONAL BUSINESS

Why Does Toyota Use a Hybrid Product Costing System?

Thanks to its virtual production line, Toyota <www.toyota.com> can now manufacture custom vehicles in five days. Computer software allows Toyota to calculate the exact number of parts needed at each precise point on its production line for a certain mix of cars. The mix can be modified up to five days in advance of actual production, allowing Toyota to modify a production run to include custom orders. When Toyota announced its hybrid approach, General Motors <www.gm.com> was taking 17 to 18 days to assemble a custom vehicle, and DaimlerChrysler <www.daimlerchrysler.com> needed an average of 10 to 12 days. Because most vehicles are mass-produced either in batches or on continuous flow assembly lines, manufacturers' process costing systems have not handled custom orders well. With its virtual production line and a hybrid product costing system, Toyota has gained a competitive advantage.[1]

www.toyota.com
www.gm.com

🔴 **Stop and Think!**
What kind of product costing system do most companies use?
Most companies use hybrid systems that combine features of both job order costing and process costing to meet the specific needs of the business. ■

system designed specifically for an organization's production process. For example, an automobile maker like Toyota or General Motors may use process costing to track the costs of manufacturing a standard car and job order costing to track the costs of customized features, such as a convertible top or a stick shift. Managers who know the terms and procedures related to both job order and process costing can help design product costing systems that fit their information needs in any operating environment.

In recent years, global competition, technology, and the shifting mix of materials, labor, and overhead in the manufacturing process have changed the way companies approach product costing. The use of multidisciplinary teams of managers has fostered the development of new management accounting practices that improve product costing. These new practices emphasize the elimination of waste, the importance of quality, products and services, value-added processing, and increased customer satisfaction. We discuss some of the new practices, including the value chain, process value analysis, activity-based management, and the just-in-time operating environment, elsewhere in the text. In the rest of this chapter, we focus on the job order costing system; we cover the process costing system in a separate chapter.

 Check out ACE for a Review Quiz at http://accounting.college.hmco.com/students

JOB ORDER COSTING IN A MANUFACTURING COMPANY

LO3 Explain the cost flow in a manufacturer's job order costing system.

RELATED TEXT ASSIGNMENTS
Q: 10, 11, 12, 13, 14, 15
SE: 4, 5, 6
E: 4, 5, 6, 7
P: 1, 2, 3, 6, 7
SD: 3, 4, 5

KEY POINT: In a job order costing system, the specific job or batch of product rather than a department or work cell is the focus of cost accumulation.

A job order costing system traces the costs of a specific order or batch of products to provide timely, accurate cost information and to facilitate the smooth and continuous flow of that information. Because such a system emphasizes cost flow, it is important to understand how costs are incurred, recorded, and transferred within the system. A basic part of a job order costing system is the set of procedures, documents, and accounts that a company uses when it incurs costs for materials, labor, and manufacturing overhead. Job order cost cards and subsidiary ledgers for materials and finished goods inventories form the core of a job order costing system.

To study the cost flows in a job order costing system, let's look at how Jon Lyman, the owner of Augusta, Inc., operates his business. For the past few years, Lyman has been building both customized and general-purpose golf carts. The direct materials costs for a golf cart include the costs of a cart frame, wheels, upholstered seats, a windshield, a motor, and a rechargeable battery. Direct labor costs include the wages of the two production workers who assemble the golf carts. Manufacturing overhead includes indirect materials costs for upholstery zippers, cloth straps to hold equipment in place, wheel lubricants, screws and fasteners, and

Exhibit 1
The Job Order Costing System—Augusta, Inc.

Materials Inventory

Beg. Bal.	1,230	Requests:	
(1) Purchases	912	Direct Materials 1,880 (3)	
(2) Purchases	82	Indirect Materials 96 (3)	
End. Bal.	248		

Work in Process Inventory

Beg. Bal.	400		
(3) Direct Materials Used	1,880	Completed	3,880 (9)
(5) Direct Labor	1,640		
(8) Overhead	1,394		
End. Bal.	1,434		

Factory Payroll

(4) Wages Earned	2,400	Direct Labor	1,640 (5)
		Indirect Labor	760 (5)

Manufacturing Overhead

(3) Indirect Materials Used	96	Applied	1,394 (8)
(5) Indirect Labor	760		
(6) Other	295		
(7) Adjustment	240		
	1,391		1,394
(11) To close	3		

Subsidiary Ledgers

Materials Ledger

Cart Frames

Beg. Bal.	830	Used	1,240 (3)
(1) Purchases	572		
End. Bal.	162		

Wheels

Beg. Bal.	370	Used	640 (3)
(1) Purchases	340		
End. Bal.	70		

Indirect Materials

Beg. Bal.	30	Used	96 (3)
(2) Purchases	82		
End. Bal.	16		

Job Order Cost Cards

Job CC

Costs from the Previous Period	400
Direct Materials	1,038
Direct Labor	1,320
Manufacturing Overhead	1,122
Completed Cost	3,880

Job JB

Direct Materials	842
Direct Labor	320
Manufacturing Overhead	272
Ending Balance	1,434

silicon to attach the windshield. It also includes indirect labor costs for moving materials to the production area and inspecting a golf cart during its construction; depreciation on the manufacturing plant and equipment used to make the golf carts; and utilities, insurance, and property taxes related to the manufacturing plant. Exhibit 1 shows the flow of each of these costs. Notice that all three inventory accounts have subsidiary ledgers backing up their totals. The beginning balance in

Finished Goods Inventory					Cost of Goods Sold			
Beg. Bal.	—				(10) Sold		Adjustment	3 (11)
(9) Completed During Period	3,880	Sold	1,940 (10)		During Period	1,940		
					End. Bal.	1,937		
End. Bal.	1,940							

Finished Goods Ledger

Job CC			
Beg. Bal.	—	Sold	1,940 (10)
(9) Completed	3,880		
End. Bal.	1,940		

STUDY NOTE: Companies use time cards for payroll purposes, whereas they use job order cost cards to distribute the cost of labor to the various job orders worked on during the period.

the Materials Inventory account means there are already direct and indirect materials in the materials storeroom. (The materials ledger contains cost information about individual materials.) The beginning balance in Work in Process Inventory means Job CC is in production (with specifics given in the job order cost card). The zero beginning balance in Finished Goods Inventory means all previously completed golf carts have been shipped.

MATERIALS

STUDY NOTE: An understanding of the purchasing process and the purpose of the documents related to it can be helpful in product costing.

When Augusta receives or expects to receive a sales order, the purchasing process begins with a request for specific quantities of direct and indirect materials needed for the order but not currently available in the materials storeroom. When the new materials arrive at Augusta, the Accounting Department records the materials purchased by making an entry that increases the balance of the Materials Inventory account.

During the month, Augusta made two purchases. In transaction **1**, the company purchased cart frames costing $572 and wheels costing $340 from one of its vendors. As shown in Exhibit 1, these purchases increase the balances in the Materials Inventory account and the corresponding accounts in the materials ledger. In transaction **2**, the company purchased indirect materials costing $82 from another vendor. This purchase also increases the balance in the Materials Inventory account, as well as the balance in the Indirect Materials account in the materials ledger.

When golf carts are scheduled for production, direct materials are sent to the production area. Transaction **3** shows the request for materials for the production of two jobs. Of the $1,880 of direct materials requested, the materials ledger shows that $1,240 was for cart frames and $640 was for wheels. Job CC, a batch run of two general-purpose golf carts already in production, required $1,038 of the additional direct materials. Job JB, a customized golf cart made to the specifications of an individual customer, required $842 of the direct materials. Notice that the $1,880 of direct materials requested appears as a debit in the Work in Process Inventory account because that account records the costs of partially completed units of product. The cost of direct materials requested is also recorded on the corresponding job order cost cards. In addition, transaction **3** accounts for the $96 of indirect materials requested for production. As you will see in our discussion of overhead, because the $96 was for indirect materials rather than direct materials, it flows to the Manufacturing Overhead account instead of to a specific job.

LABOR

STUDY NOTE: Parts of transaction 4 are not posted in Exhibit 1. Although transaction 4 is necessary for an accurate payroll, it does not deal directly with product costs. Exhibit 1 focuses only on the flow of product costs through the accounts.

As noted earlier, Augusta's two production employees assemble the golf carts. Several other employees support the production process by moving materials and inspecting the products. Transaction **4** shows the total cost of wages earned during the period by these employees as a $2,400 debit to the Factory Payroll account. (The corresponding credit, which is not shown, is to Augusta's Wages Payable account.) Factory Payroll is a clearing account—that is, it holds costs for only a short time, until they are distributed to the various production accounts. This distribution is shown in transaction **5**. Job CC required direct labor of $1,320, and Job JB required $320. The total direct labor cost of $1,640 ($1,320 + $320) is shown as a debit to the Work in Process Inventory account. The indirect labor cost of $760 shown in transaction **5** flows to the Manufacturing Overhead account instead of to a particular job.

MANUFACTURING OVERHEAD

Thus far, indirect materials and indirect labor have been the only costs debited to the Manufacturing Overhead account. Other indirect production costs, such as utilities, property taxes, insurance, and depreciation, are also charged to the Manufacturing Overhead account as they are incurred during the period. Transaction **6** shows that other indirect costs amounting to $295 were paid. Transaction **7** records the $240 adjustment for factory-related depreciation.

During the period, to recognize all product-related costs for a job, an overhead cost estimate is applied using a predetermined rate. Based on its budget and past

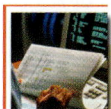

Focus on Business Practice

How Long Does Production Take?
As the following list shows, throughput time—the time it takes to manufacture products—varies according to the product:[2]

Product	Time
Yogurt	Up to eight hours
Beer	Two weeks or longer
Processed foods	Less than two hours
Paint	Less than an hour
Refined oil	Less than two hours
Cement	Less than three hours

experience, Augusta currently uses a predetermined overhead rate of 85 percent of direct labor costs. In transaction 8, total manufacturing overhead of $1,394 is applied, with $1,122 going to Job CC (85 percent of $1,320) and $272 to Job JB (85 percent of $320). Notice that the Work in Process Inventory account is debited for $1,394.

Completed Units

When a custom job or a batch of general-purpose golf carts is completed, the products are moved from the manufacturing area to the finished goods storeroom. As shown in transaction 9, when Job CC is completed and moved to the finished goods storeroom, its cost of $3,880 is transferred from the Work in Process Inventory account to the Finished Goods Inventory account. Its job order cost card is also completed and transferred to the finished goods file. Figure 2 shows the job order cost card for Job CC. Notice that the product unit cost for each of the two golf carts in the job is computed.

Sold Units

ENRICHMENT NOTE: In a periodic inventory system, the cost of goods sold is calculated at the end of the period.

When a company uses a perpetual inventory system, as Augusta does, two accounting entries are made when products are sold. One is prompted by the sales invoice and records the quantity and selling price of the products sold. This entry, which is

FIGURE 2
Job Order Cost Card—Manufacturing Company

ENRICHMENT NOTE:
A job order cost card can take the form of an actual card in a card file, a reporting form on a clipboard, a computer file, or a record in a database. Each form captures essentially the same information.

JOB ORDER COST CARD
Augusta, Inc.
Spring Hill, Florida

Job Order: __CC__

Customer: __Stock__ Batch: __X__ Custom: _____
Specifications: __Two general-purpose golf carts__
Date of Order: __2/26/x7__
Date of Completion: __3/6/x7__

Costs Charged to Job	Previous Months	Current Month	Cost Summary
Direct materials	$165	$1,038	$1,203
Direct labor	127	1,320	1,447
Manufacturing overhead (85% of direct labor cost)	108	1,122	1,230
Totals	$400	$3,480	$3,880
Units completed			2
Product unit cost			$1,940

not shown in Exhibit 1, is a debit to the Accounts Receivable or Cash account and a credit to the Sales account. The other entry, prompted by the delivery of products to a customer, records the quantity and cost of the products shipped. In transaction 10, the $1,940 cost of the one general-purpose golf cart that was sold during the period is transferred from the Finished Goods Inventory account to the Cost of Goods Sold account. The $1,940 cost of the unsold cart remains in the Finished Goods Inventory account.

RECONCILIATION OF MANUFACTURING OVERHEAD COSTS

◆ **STOP AND THINK!**
Why do financial statements require the reconciliation of manufacturing overhead costs?
Financial statements report actual cost information; therefore, estimated manufacturing overhead costs applied during the accounting period must be adjusted to reflect actual manufacturing overhead costs. ■

To prepare financial statements at the end of the accounting period, the actual manufacturing overhead cost for the period ($1,391) and the estimated manufacturing overhead that was applied during the period ($1,394) must be reconciled. In transaction 11, the Manufacturing Overhead account is closed by transferring its balance of $3 to the Cost of Goods Sold account. Because the applied overhead exceeded the actual overhead by $3, Cost of Goods Sold must be reduced by the amount of the overcharge. It will then reflect the actual overhead costs incurred. Given that the amount is minor, the company prefers to subtract it from the cost of the cart that was sold rather than tracing it back to the individual units worked on during the period. Thus, $3 is deducted from the Cost of Goods Sold account, making the ending balance of that account $1,937.

✓ Check out ACE for a Review Quiz at http://accounting.college.hmco.com/students.

A MANUFACTURER'S JOB ORDER COST CARD AND THE COMPUTATION OF PRODUCT UNIT COST

LO4 Prepare a job order cost card and compute a job order's product unit cost.
RELATED TEXT ASSIGNMENTS
Q: 16, 17
SE: 7, 8
E: 8, 9, 10, 11
P: 2, 3, 6, 7, 8
SD: 5

As is evident from the preceding discussion, job order cost cards play a key role in a job order costing system. Because all manufacturing costs are accumulated in one Work in Process Inventory account, a separate accounting procedure is needed to trace those costs to specific jobs. The solution is the subsidiary ledger made up of job order cost cards. Each job being worked on has a job order cost card. As costs are incurred, they are classified by job and recorded on the appropriate card.

As you can see in Figure 2, a manufacturer's job order cost card has space for direct materials, direct labor, and manufacturing overhead costs. It also includes the

FOCUS ON BUSINESS ETHICS

Does a Product Unit's Cost Tell the Whole Story?

In response to a tip from the fraud hotline maintained by the Department of Defense <www.defenselink.mil>, the office of the Inspector General, the watchdog agency for the Pentagon, conducted an audit of The Boeing Company <www.boeing.com>. The audit found several instances in which Boeing had evidently overcharged the government for parts. For example, it had charged $1.24 for each of 31,108 springs previously priced at $.05 and $403 each for 246 actuator sleeves priced earlier at $24.72.

Boeing spokesperson Dick Dalton said, "This is a story that looks a whole lot worse than it is." According to Boeing, the audit cited prices from 15 to 20 years ago, when the Pentagon bought and stored large quantities of products. Today, the Pentagon receives small deliveries of parts on short notice, as needed. The new system saves the Pentagon huge inventory storage costs, but the price per part is higher because of the higher cost of frequent deliveries and on-demand ordering. The Inspector General, Eleanor Hill, told a Senate Armed Services subcommittee, "We found considerable evidence that the Department of Defense had not yet learned how to be an astute buyer in the commercial marketplace."[3]

● **STOP AND THINK!**
What is the purpose of a job order cost card?

A job order cost card is used to list a job's specifications, to accumulate the job's costs, and to compute the job's product unit cost. It can also be used to compute a job's profit margin and price. ■

job order number, product specifications, the name of the customer, the date of the order, the projected completion date, and a cost summary. As a job incurs direct materials and direct labor costs, its job order cost card is updated. Manufacturing overhead is also posted to the job order cost card at the predetermined rate. Job order cost cards for incomplete jobs make up the subsidiary ledger for the Work in Process Inventory account. To ensure correctness, the ending balance in the Work in Process Inventory account is compared with the total of the costs shown on the job order cost cards.

A job order costing system simplifies the calculation of product unit costs. When a job is finished, the costs of direct materials, direct labor, and manufacturing overhead that have been recorded on its job order cost card are totaled. The product unit cost is computed by dividing the total costs for the job by the number of good (i.e., salable) units produced. The product unit cost is entered on the job order cost card and will be used to value items in inventory. The job order cost card in Figure 2 shows the costs for completed Job CC. Two golf carts were produced at a total cost of $3,880, so the product unit cost was $1,940.

 Check out ACE for a Review Quiz at http://accounting.college.hmco.com/students.

JOB ORDER COSTING IN A SERVICE ORGANIZATION

LO5 Apply job order costing to a service organization.

RELATED TEXT ASSIGNMENTS
Q: 18, 19
SE: 9, 10
E: 12, 13, 14, 15
P: 4, 5, 8
SD: 3
MRA: 4

● **STOP AND THINK!**
How do the job order cost cards of a manufacturing company and a service company differ?

The job order cost cards of a manufacturing company group product costs by direct materials, direct labor, and manufacturing overhead. Those of a service company group the costs of materials, supplies, labor, and overhead by the service activities that go into the job. ■

Many service organizations use a job order costing system to compute the cost of rendering services. As pointed out elsewhere in the text, the costs of service organizations differ from those of a manufacturing organization in that they are not associated with a physical product that can be assembled, stored, and valued as inventory. Because these organizations sell services rather than making products for sale, the costs that they incur for materials are usually negligible. The most important cost of service organizations is labor, which is carefully accounted for through the use of time cards.

The cost flow of services is similar to the cost flow of manufactured products. Job order cost cards are used to keep track of the costs incurred for each job. Job costs include labor, materials and supplies, and service overhead. To cover these costs and earn a profit, many service organizations base jobs on **cost-plus contracts**. Such contracts require the customer to pay all costs incurred in performing the job plus a predetermined amount of profit, which is based on the amount of costs incurred. When the job is complete, the costs on the completed job order cost card become the cost of services. The cost of services is adjusted at the end of the accounting period for the difference between the applied service overhead costs and the actual service overhead costs.

To illustrate how a service organization uses a job order costing system, let's assume that a company called Gartner Landscaping Services employs 15 people and serves the San Francisco Bay area. Gartner earns its revenue by designing and installing landscapes for homes and offices. Figure 3 shows Gartner's job order cost card for the landscaping of Rico Corporation's corporate headquarters. Costs have been categorized into three separate activities: landscape design, landscape installation, and job-site cleanup. Costs have been tracked to the Rico Corporation job throughout its duration, and now that the job is finished, it is time to complete the job order cost card. The service overhead cost for landscape design is 40 percent of design labor cost, and the service overhead cost for landscape installation is 50 percent of installation labor cost. Total costs incurred for this job were $5,400. Gartner's cost-plus contract with Rico has a 15 percent profit guarantee; therefore, $810 of profit margin is added to the total cost to arrive at the total contract revenue of $6,210, which is the amount billed to Rico.

FIGURE 3
Job Order Cost Card—Service Organization

JOB ORDER COST CARD
Gartner Landscaping Services

Customer: Rico Corporation
Job Order Number: _____
Contract Type: Cost-Plus
Type of Service: Landscape Corporate Headquarters
Date Completed: May 31, 20xx

Costs Charged to Job	Previous Months	Current Month	Total Cost
Landscape design			
Supplies	$ 100	$ —	$ 100
Design labor	850	—	850
Service overhead (40% of design labor)	340	—	340
Totals	$1,290	$ —	$1,290
Landscape installation			
Planting materials	$ 970	$1,200	$2,170
Installation labor	400	620	1,020
Service overhead (50% of installation labor)	200	310	510
Totals	$1,570	$2,130	$3,700
Job-site cleanup			
Janitorial service cost	$ 90	$ 320	$ 410
Totals	$2,950	$2,450	$5,400

Cost Summary to Date	Total Cost
Landscape design	$1,290
Landscape installation	3,700
Job-site cleanup	410
Totals	$5,400
Profit margin (15%)	810
Contract revenue	$6,210

KEY POINT: Job order cost cards for service businesses may record costs by activities done for the job. Notice that the activity cost includes supplies, labor, and overhead.

Check out ACE for a Review Quiz at http://accounting.college.hmco.com/students.

JOB ORDER COSTING VERSUS PROJECT COSTING

LO6 Distinguish between job order costing and project costing.
RELATED TEXT ASSIGNMENTS
Q: 20
SD: 2

Although the concept of a job order costing system that collects the costs of direct materials, direct labor, and overhead by specific job order for custom products or services remains valid, new approaches to costing are being developed. In today's business environment, many jobs take a long time to complete and require the talents of many departments, consultants, and subcontractors. These complex jobs have evolved into **projects**, jobs that are made up of many tasks and that take a broad, multidisciplinary approach to the production of goods or services. Examples of projects include the con-

Focus on Business Practice

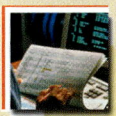

Who Uses Project Costing?
One company that uses project costing is Industrial Light & Magic <www.ilm.com>. Today, the special-effects company founded by George Lucas in 1975 works on over a dozen film projects and more than 50 commercial projects a year. One cost shared by all the company's projects is that of the company's Computer Graphics Weeklies. At the weeklies (now held every six weeks), a project team shows how it solved a special-effects problem or asks for help from other teams. These hour-long forums encourage group learning and cross-pollination between ILM's projects and artists and enable the company to collectively celebrate its new ways of creating digital illusions and expanding cinematic boundaries.[4]

● **STOP AND THINK!**
How do projects differ from jobs?
Projects are more complex than jobs; they are made up of many tasks and take a broad, multidisciplinary approach to the production of goods or services. ■

www.ilm.com

BUSINESS WORLD EXAMPLE: Managers at construction companies and software companies commonly manage projects.

struction of a skyscraper and the development of a computer software program. At companies like Industrial Light & Magic, discussed in the Focus on Business Practice box that appears above, effective project management requires a product costing system that accommodates today's environment of multidisciplinary work teams, networks of shared computer files, and integrated computer systems.

In the past, managers tended to focus on products or customer requests one at a time. Today, they often need to coordinate many jobs that are being performed at many different times in many different places. For that purpose, they may use project costing. In contrast to job order costing, which focuses on a specific job order, project costing links many different job orders and processes by transferring costs from one job or process to another, collecting and summarizing costs in a variety of ways, and providing appropriate internal controls to manage complicated projects. The detailed processes involved in project costing and project management are covered in more advanced accounting courses.

 Check out ACE for a Review Quiz at http://accounting.college.hmco.com/students.

Chapter Review

REVIEW OF LEARNING OBJECTIVES

LO1 Discuss the role information about costs plays in the management cycle and explain why unit cost is important.

During the planning stage of the management cycle, information about costs helps managers develop budgets, establish prices, set sales goals, plan production volumes, estimate product or service unit costs, and determine human resource needs. During the executing stage, managers use cost information to make decisions about controlling costs, managing the company's volume of activity, assuring quality, and negotiating prices. During the reviewing stage, they analyze actual and targeted information to evaluate performance and make any necessary adjustments to their planning and decision-making strategies. During the reporting stage, managers use unit costs to determine inventory balances and the cost of goods or services sold for the financial statements. They also analyze various internal reports that compare the organization's measures of actual and targeted performance to determine whether cost goals for products or services are being achieved.

LO2 Distinguish between the two basic types of product costing systems and identify the information each provides.

A job order costing system is a product costing system used by companies that make large, unique, or special-order products. Such a system traces the costs of direct materials, direct labor, and manufacturing overhead to a specific batch of products or to a specific job order. A job order costing system measures the cost of each complete unit and summarizes the cost of all jobs in a single Work in Process Inventory account that is supported by job order cost cards.

A process costing system is a product costing system used by companies that produce large amounts of similar products or liquid products or that have long, continuous production runs of identical products. Such a system first traces the costs of direct materials, direct labor, and manufacturing overhead to processes, departments, or work cells and then assigns the costs to the products manufactured by those processes, departments, or work cells. A process costing system uses several Work in Process Inventory accounts, one for each department, process, or work cell.

LO3 Explain the cost flow in a manufacturer's job order costing system.

In a manufacturer's job order costing system, the costs of materials are first charged to the Materials Inventory account and to the respective materials accounts in the subsidiary ledger. Labor costs are first accumulated in the Factory Payroll account. The various manufacturing overhead costs are charged to the Manufacturing Overhead account. As products are manufactured, the costs of direct materials and direct labor are transferred to the Work in Process Inventory account and are recorded on the job's job order cost card. Manufacturing overhead costs are applied and charged to the Work in Process Inventory account using a predetermined overhead rate. Those charges are used to reduce the balance in the Manufacturing Overhead account. They, too, are recorded on the job's job order cost card.

When products and jobs are completed, the costs assigned to them are transferred to the Finished Goods Inventory account. Then, when the products are sold and shipped, their costs are transferred to the Cost of Goods Sold account.

LO4 Prepare a job order cost card and compute a job order's product unit cost.

All costs of direct materials, direct labor, and manufacturing overhead for a particular job are accumulated on a job order cost card. When the job has been completed, those costs are totaled. The total is then divided by the number of good units produced to find the product unit cost for that order. The product unit cost is entered on the job order cost card and will be used to value items in inventory.

LO5 Apply job order costing to a service organization.

Many service organizations use a job order costing system to track the costs of labor, materials and supplies, and service overhead to specific customer jobs. Labor is an important cost for service organizations, but their materials costs are usually negligible. To cover their costs and earn a profit, service organizations often base jobs on cost-plus contracts, which require the customer to pay all costs incurred plus a predetermined amount of profit.

LO6 Distinguish between job order costing and project costing.

Projects are complex, time-consuming jobs that are made up of many tasks and that take a broad, multidisciplinary approach to the production of products or services. In contrast to job order costing, which focuses on a specific job order, project costing links many different job orders and processes by transferring costs from one job or process to another, collecting and summarizing costs in a variety of ways, and providing appropriate internal controls to manage complicated projects.

REVIEW OF CONCEPTS AND TERMINOLOGY

The following concepts and terms were introduced in this chapter:

LO5 **Cost-plus contracts:** Job contracts that require the customer to pay all costs incurred in performing the job plus a predetermined amount of profit.

LO2 **Job order:** A customer order for a specific number of specially designed, made-to-order products.

LO2 **Job order cost card:** A document on which all costs incurred in the production of a particular job order are recorded; part of the subsidiary ledger for the Work in Process Inventory account.

LO2 **Job order costing system:** A product costing system that traces the costs of direct materials, direct labor, and manufacturing overhead to a specific batch of products or a specific job order; used by companies that make large, unique, or special-order products.

LO2 **Process costing system:** A product costing system that traces the costs of direct materials, direct labor, and manufacturing overhead to processes, departments, or work cells and then assigns the costs to the products manufactured by those processes, departments, or work cells; used by companies that produce large amounts of similar products or liquid products or that have long, continuous production runs of identical products.

LO2 **Product costing system:** A set of procedures that is used to account for an organization's product costs and to provide timely and accurate unit cost information for pricing, cost planning and control, inventory valuation, and financial statement preparation.

LO6 **Projects:** Complex jobs that are made up of many tasks and that take a broad, multi-disciplinary approach to the production of products or services.

REVIEW PROBLEM

Job Order Costing in a Service Organization

LO3
LO4
LO5
Sanibel Plumbing Company employs 30 people and serves the metropolitan Fort Myers area. The company earns roughly half its revenue from installing plumbing in newly constructed houses and half from plumbing repairs and remodeling jobs in older houses. It uses job order cost cards to keep track of the costs incurred on each job. Job costs—direct materials and supplies, direct labor, and service overhead—are categorized under three activities: plumbing system design, system installation, and job-site cleanup. The service overhead charge for plumbing system design is 30 percent of engineering labor costs, and the service overhead charge for system installation is 50 percent of direct labor cost.

Sanibel has tracked all costs of the Clary job, and now that the work is finished, it is time to complete the job order cost card. Sanibel's cost-plus contract with Clary has a 25 percent profit guarantee. The costs for the Clary job are as follows:

Beginning Balances

Plumbing system design	$ 2,635
System installation	14,250
Job-site cleanup	75

Costs During October

Plumbing system design	
Supplies	0
Engineering labor	250
System installation	
Materials	2,150
Direct labor	6,400
Job-site cleanup	
Janitorial service cost	525

REQUIRED ▶
1. Create the job order cost card for the Clary job.
2. What amount will Sanibel Plumbing Company bill for the Clary job?
3. Using the format of the Work in Process Inventory account in Exhibit 1, reconstruct the beginning balance for the current month and the current month's costs.

Answer to Review Problem

1. Job order cost card for the Clary job

JOB ORDER COST CARD
Sanibel Plumbing Company

Customer: Clary
Job Order No.: 153
Contract Type: Cost-Plus
Type of Service: New Home Plumbing
Date of Completion: October 31, 20xx

Costs Charged to Job	Previous Months	Current Month	Total Cost
Plumbing system design			
Beginning balance	$ 2,635		$ 2,635
Current month's costs			
Supplies		$ 0	0
Engineering labor		250	250
Service overhead (30% of engineering labor)		75	75
Totals	$ 2,635	$ 325	$ 2,960
System installation			
Beginning balance	$14,250		$14,250
Current month's costs			
Materials		$ 2,150	2,150
Direct labor		6,400	6,400
Service overhead (50% of direct labor)		3,200	3,200
Totals	$14,250	$11,750	$26,000
Job-site cleanup			
Beginning balance	$ 75		75
Current month's costs		$ 525	525
Totals	$ 75	$ 525	$ 600

Cost Summary to Date	Total Cost
Plumbing system design	$ 2,960
System installation	26,000
Job-site cleanup	600
Total	$29,560
Profit margin (25% of total cost)	7,390
Contract revenue	$36,950

2. Sanibel Plumbing will bill Clary $36,950 for this job.

3. Beginning balance for the current month and the current month's costs:

Work in Process Inventory			
Beg. Bal.*	16,960	Completed	29,560
Plumbing System Design: Engineering Labor	250		
Plumbing System Design: Overhead	75		
Systems Installation: Materials	2,150		
Systems Installation: Direct Labor	6,400		
Systems Installation: Overhead	3,200		
Job-Site Cleanup	525		
End. Bal.	0		

*$2,635 + $14,250 + $75 = $16,960

Chapter Assignments

BUILDING YOUR KNOWLEDGE FOUNDATION

QUESTIONS

1. How do managers in manufacturing and service organizations use cost information during the planning stage of the management cycle?
2. Managers use cost information to support their decision making during the executing stage of the management cycle. What kinds of decisions do they make at this stage?
3. How do managers use cost information during the reviewing stage of the management cycle?
4. In manufacturing companies, how do managers use product unit costs in the preparation of financial statements?
5. What kind of information can managers gain from internal reports that compare targeted and actual costs and key nonfinancial performance measures?
6. What is a product costing system?
7. What is a job order costing system? Identify the kinds of companies that use such a system.
8. What is a job order?
9. What are the main similarities and differences between a job order costing system and a process costing system? (Focus on the characteristics of these two types of systems.)
10. Why does the Materials Inventory account have a subsidiary ledger?
11. When a company buys direct materials and indirect materials, does it record both purchases in the same way? Explain your answer.
12. What is the purpose of the Work in Process Inventory account?
13. Why is the Factory Payroll account a clearing account?
14. What kind of information is recorded in the Manufacturing Overhead account?
15. Why is the Manufacturing Overhead account reconciled at the end of an accounting period?
16. What is the purpose of a job order cost card? Identify the kinds of information recorded on that document.

17. Explain how to compute product unit cost in a job order costing system. How are the necessary data accumulated?
18. How do the costs of a service organization and a manufacturing organization differ? How do these differences affect the job order costing system of a service organization?
19. What is a cost-plus contract? How does this type of contract benefit a service organization?
20. How does a project differ from a job order?

Short Exercises

LO1 Uses of Product Costing Information

SE 1. Shelley's Kennel provides boarding for dogs and cats. Shelley, the owner of the kennel, must make several business decisions in the near future. Write *yes* or *no* to indicate whether knowing the cost to board one animal per day (i.e., the product unit cost) can help Shelley answer the following questions:

1. Is the boarding fee high enough to cover the kennel's costs?
2. How much profit will the kennel make if it boards an average of 10 dogs per day for 50 weeks?
3. What costs can be reduced to make the kennel's boarding fee competitive with that of its competitor?

LO2 Companies That Use Job Order Costing

SE 2. Write *yes* or *no* to indicate whether each of the following companies would typically use a job order costing system:

1. Soft drink producer
2. Jeans manufacturer
3. Submarine contractor
4. Office building contractor
5. Stuffed toy maker

LO2 Job Order Versus Process Costing Systems

SE 3. State whether a job order costing system or a process costing system would typically be used to account for the costs of the following:

1. Manufacturing cat collars   PROCESS
2. Manufacturing custom-designed fencing for outdoor breeding kennels   JO
3. Providing pet grooming   JO
4. Manufacturing one-gallon aquariums   PROC
5. Manufacturing dog food   PROCESS
6. Providing veterinary services   JO

LO3 Transactions in a Manufacturer's Job Order Costing System

SE 4. For each of the following transactions, state which account(s) would be affected in a job order costing system:

1. Purchased materials, $12,890
2. Charged direct labor to production, $3,790
3. Requested direct materials for production, $6,800
4. Applied manufacturing overhead to jobs in process, $3,570

LO3 Transactions in a Manufacturer's Job Order Costing System

SE 5. Enter the following transactions into T accounts:

1. Incurred $34,000 of direct labor and $18,000 of indirect labor
2. Applied manufacturing overhead based on 12,680 labor hours @ $6.50 per labor hour

LO3 Accounts for Job Order Costing

SE 6. Identify the accounts in which each of the following transactions for Dom's Furniture, a custom manufacturer of oak tables and chairs, would be recorded:

1. Issued oak materials into production for Job ABC
2. Recorded direct labor time for the first week in February for Job ABC
3. Received indirect materials from a vendor
4. Received a production-related electricity bill
5. Applied manufacturing overhead to Job ABC
6. Completed but did not yet sell Job ABC

LO4 Product Unit Cost

SE 7. Write *yes* or *no* to indicate whether each of the following costs is included in a product unit cost. Then explain your answers.

1. Direct materials costs
2. Fixed manufacturing overhead costs
3. Variable selling costs
4. Fixed administrative costs
5. Direct labor costs
6. Variable manufacturing overhead costs

LO4 Computation of Product Unit Cost

SE 8. Complete the following job order cost card for six custom-built computer systems:

Job Order __168__

JOB ORDER COST CARD
Keeper 3000
Apache City, North Dakota

Customer: __Brian Patcher__   Batch: _____   Custom: __X__
Specifications: __6 Custom Computer Systems__
Date of Order: __4/4/x7__   Date of Completion: __6/8/x7__

Costs Charged to Job	Previous Months	Current Month	Cost Summary
Direct materials	$3,540	$2,820	$ _____
Direct labor	2,340	1,620	_____
Manufacturing overhead applied	2,880	2,550	_____
Totals	$ _____	$ _____	$ _____
Units completed			_____
Product unit cost			$ _____

LO5 Job Order Costing in a Service Organization

SE 9. For each of the following transactions, state which account(s) would be affected in a job order costing system for a desert landscaping business:

1. Charged customer for landscape design
2. Purchased cactus plants and gravel on credit for one job
3. Paid three employees to prepare soil for gravel
4. Paid for rental equipment to move gravel to job site

LO5 Job Order Costing with Cost-Plus Contracts

SE 10. Complete the job order cost card for an annual individual tax return that appears at the top of the next page.

JOB ORDER COST CARD
Doremus Tax Service
Puyallup, Washington

Job Order 2008-A7

Customer: Arthur Farnsworth   Batch: _____   Custom: X
Specifications: Annual Individual Tax Return
Date of Order: 3/24/x8   Date of Completion: 4/8/x8

Costs Charged to Job	Previous Months	Current Month	Total Cost
Client interview			
Supplies	$ 10		$ _____
Labor	50	$ 60	_____
Overhead (40% of interview labor costs)	20	24	_____
Totals	$ _____	$ _____	$ _____
Preparation of return			
Supplies		$ 16	$ _____
Computer time		12	_____
Labor		240	_____
Overhead (50% of preparation labor costs)		120	_____
Totals		$ _____	$ _____
Delivery			
Postage		$ 12	$ _____
Totals		$ _____	$ _____

Cost Summary to Date   Total Cost
Client interview $ _____
Preparation of return   _____
Delivery   _____
  Total $ _____
Profit margin (25% of total cost)   _____
Job revenue $ _____

EXERCISES

E 1. Anniversary Printing Company specializes in wedding invitations. Anniversary needs information to budget next year's activities. Write *yes* or *no* to indicate whether each of the following costs is likely to be available in the company's product costing system:

1. Cost of paper and envelopes
2. Printing machine setup costs
3. Depreciation of printing machinery
4. Advertising costs
5. Repair costs for printing machinery
6. Costs to deliver stationery to customers

LO2 Product Costing

7. Office supplies costs
8. Costs to design a wedding invitation
9. Cost of ink
10. Sales commissions

LO2 Costing Systems: Industry Linkage

E 2. Which of the following products would typically be accounted for using a job order costing system? Which would typically be accounted for using a process costing system? (a) Paint, (b) jelly beans, (c) jet aircraft, (d) bricks, (e) large milling machines, (f) liquid detergent, (g) aluminum compressed-gas cylinders of standard size and capacity, and (h) aluminum compressed-gas cylinders with a special fiberglass wrap for a Mount Everest expedition.

LO2 Costing Systems: Industry Linkage

E 3. Which of the following products would typically be accounted for using a job order costing system? Which would typically be accounted for using a process costing system? (a) Standard nails, (b) television sets, (c) printed wedding invitations, (d) a limited edition of lithographs, (e) flea collars for pets, (f) high-speed lathes with special-order drill threads, (g) breakfast cereal, and (h) an original evening gown.

LO3 Job Order Cost Flow

E 4. The three product cost elements—direct materials, direct labor, and manufacturing overhead—flow through a job order costing system in a structured, orderly fashion. Specific accounts and subsidiary ledgers are used to verify and record cost information. Write a paragraph describing the cost flow in a job order costing system.

LO3 Work in Process Inventory: T Account Analysis

E 5. On June 30, Specialty Company's Work in Process Inventory account showed a beginning balance of $29,400. Production activity for July was as follows: Direct materials costing $238,820 were requested for production; total manufacturing payroll was $140,690, of which $52,490 was used to pay for indirect labor; indirect materials costing $28,400 were purchased and used; and manufacturing overhead was applied at a rate of 150 percent of direct labor costs.

1. Record Specialty's materials, labor, and manufacturing overhead costs for July in T accounts.
2. Compute the ending balance in the Work in Process Inventory account. Assume a transfer of $461,400 to the Finished Goods Inventory account during the period.

LO3 T Account Analysis with Unknowns

E 6. Partial operating data for Vue Picture Company are presented below. Management has set the predetermined overhead rate for the current year at 120 percent of direct labor costs.

Account/Transaction	June	July
Beginning Materials Inventory	$ a	$ e
Beginning Work in Process Inventory	89,605	f
Beginning Finished Goods Inventory	79,764	67,660
Direct materials requested	59,025	g
Materials purchased	57,100	60,216
Direct labor costs	48,760	54,540
Manufacturing overhead applied	b	h
Cost of units completed	c	231,861
Cost of goods sold	166,805	i
Ending Materials Inventory	32,014	27,628
Ending Work in Process Inventory	d	j
Ending Finished Goods Inventory	67,660	30,515

Using T accounts and the data provided, compute the unknown values. Show all your computations.

LO3 T Account Analysis with Unknowns

E 7. Partial operating data for Starke Company are presented at the top of the next page. Starke Company's management has set the predetermined overhead rate for the current year at 80 percent of direct labor costs.

Account/Transaction	December
Beginning Materials Inventory	$ 42,000
Beginning Work in Process Inventory	66,000
Beginning Finished Goods Inventory	29,000
Direct materials used	168,000
Direct materials purchased	a
Direct labor costs	382,000
Manufacturing overhead applied	b
Cost of units completed	c
Cost of goods sold	808,000
Ending Materials Inventory	38,000
Ending Work in Process Inventory	138,600
Ending Finished Goods Inventory	d

Using T accounts and the data provided, compute the unknown values. Show all your computations.

LO4 Job Order Cost Card and Computation of Product Unit Cost

E 8. During January, the Cabinet Company worked on six different job orders for specialty kitchen cabinets. It began Job A-62 for Thomas Cabinets, Inc., on January 10 and completed the job on January 24. Partial data for Job A-62 are as follows:

	Costs	Machine Hours Used
Direct materials		
Cedar	$7,900	
Pine	6,320	
Hardware	2,930	
Assembly supplies	988	
Direct labor		
Sawing	2,840	120
Shaping	2,200	220
Finishing	2,250	180
Assembly	2,890	50

The Cabinet Company produced a total of 34 cabinets for Job A-62. Its current predetermined manufacturing overhead rate is $21.60 per machine hour. From the information given, prepare a job order cost card and compute the job order's product unit cost. (Round to whole dollars.)

LO4 Computation of Product Unit Cost

E 9. Using job order costing, determine the product unit cost based on the following costs incurred during March: liability insurance, manufacturing, $2,500; rent, sales office, $2,900; depreciation, manufacturing equipment, $6,100; direct materials, $32,650; indirect labor, manufacturing, $3,480; indirect materials, $1,080; heat, light, and power, manufacturing, $1,910; fire insurance, manufacturing, $2,600; depreciation, sales equipment, $4,250; rent, manufacturing, $3,850; direct labor, $18,420; manager's salary, manufacturing, $3,100; president's salary, $5,800; sales commissions, $8,250; and advertising expenses, $2,975. The Inspection Department reported that 48,800 good units were produced during March. Carry your answer to two decimal places.

LO4 Computation of Product Unit Cost

E 10. Wild Things, Inc., manufactures custom-made stuffed animals. Last month the company produced 4,540 stuffed bears with stethoscopes for the local children's hospital to sell at a fundraising event. Using job order costing, determine the product unit cost of a stuffed bear based on the following costs incurred during the month: manufacturing utilities, $500; depreciation on manufacturing equipment, $450; indirect materials, $300; direct materials, $1,300; indirect labor, $800; direct labor, $2,400; sales commissions, $3,000; president's salary, $4,000; insurance on manufacturing plant, $600; advertising expense, $500; rent on manufacturing plant, $5,000; rent on sales office, $4,000; and legal expense, $250. Carry your answer to two decimal places.

LO4 Computation of Product Unit Cost

E 11. Style Corporation manufactures specialty lines of women's apparel. During February, the company worked on three special orders: A-25, A-27, and B-14. Cost and production data for each order are as follows:

	Job A-25	Job A-27	Job B-14
Direct materials			
Fabric Q	$10,840	$12,980	$17,660
Fabric Z	11,400	12,200	13,440
Fabric YB	5,260	6,920	10,900
Direct labor			
Garment maker	8,900	10,400	16,200
Layout	6,450	7,425	9,210
Packaging	3,950	4,875	6,090
Manufacturing overhead			
(120% of direct labor costs)	?	?	?
Number of units produced	700	775	1,482

1. Compute the total cost associated with each job. Show the subtotals for each cost category.
2. Compute the product unit cost for each job. (Round your computations to the nearest cent.)

LO5 Job Order Costing in a Service Organization

E 12. A job order cost card for Hal's Computer Services appears below. Complete the missing information. The profit factor in the organization's cost-plus contract is 30 percent of total cost.

JOB ORDER COST CARD
Hal's Computer Services

Customer: James Lowe
Job Order No.: 8-324
Contract Type: Cost-Plus
Type of Service: Software Installation and Internet Interfacing
Date of Completion: October 6, 20x8

Costs Charged to Job	Total Cost
Software installation services	
Installation labor	$300
Service overhead (?% of installation labor costs)	?
Total	$450
Internet services	
Internet labor	$200
Service overhead (20% of Internet labor costs)	40
Total	$?

Costs Summary to Date	Total Cost
Software installation services	$?
Internet services	?
Total	$?
Profit margin (30% of total cost)	?
Contract revenue	$?

LO5 Job Order Costing in a Service Organization

E 13. A job order cost card for Miniblinds by Jenny appears at the top of the next page. Complete the missing information. The profit factor in the company's cost-plus contract is 50 percent of total cost.

JOB ORDER COST CARD
Miniblinds by Jenny

Customer: Carmen Sawyer
Job Order No.: 8-482
Contract Type: Cost-Plus
Type of Service: Miniblind Installation and Design
Date of Completion: June 12, 20x8

Costs Charged to Job	Total Cost
Installation services	
Installation labor	$445
Service overhead (80% of installation labor costs)	?
Total	$?
Designer services	
Designer labor	$200
Service overhead (?% of designer labor costs)	?
Total	$400

Cost Summary to Date	Total Cost
Installation services	$?
Designer services	?
Total	$?
Profit margin (50% of total cost)	?
Contract revenue	$?

LO5 Job Order Costing in a Service Organization

E 14. Personal Shoppers, Inc., relieves busy women executives of the stress of shopping for clothes by taking an inventory of a client's current wardrobe and shopping for her needs for the next season or a special event. The company charges clients $30 per hour for the service plus the cost of the clothes purchased. It pays its employees various hourly wage rates.

During September, Personal Shoppers worked with three clients. It began Job 9-3, for Lucinda Mapley, on September 3 and completed the job on September 30. Using the partial data that follows, prepare the job order cost card. What amount of profit will Personal Shoppers make on this job?

Costs Charged to Job	Costs	Hours	Other
In-person consultation			
Supplies	$ 30		
Labor ($10 per hour)		4	
Overhead (10% of in-person labor costs)			
Shopping			
Purchases	$560		
Labor ($15 per hour)		8	
Overhead (25% of shopping labor costs)			
Telephone consultations			
Cell phone calls ($1 per call)			6 calls
Labor ($6 per hour)		2	
Overhead (50% of telephone labor costs)			

LO5 Job Order Costing in a Service Organization

E 15. A job order cost card for Personal Trainers, Inc., appears below. Compute the missing information.

Job Order **H.W.**

JOB ORDER COST CARD
Personal Trainers, Inc.

Customer: **Hillary White**   Batch: _____   Custom: **X**
Specifications: **Marathon Training**
Date of Order: **4/2/xx**   Date of Completion: **7/24/xx**

Costs Charged to Job	Previous Months	Current Month	Total Cost
In-person consultation			
Training logbook	$ 20.00	$ 0	$20.00
Labor ($10 per hour)	20.00	?	50.00
Overhead (10% of in-person labor costs)	?	3.00	5.00
Total	$?	$?	$?
Training			
Bike rental	$ 30.00	$?	$60.00
Labor ($5 per hour)	150.00	300.00	?
Overhead (25% of training labor costs)	37.50	?	?
Total	$?	$?	$?
Telephone consultations			
Cell phone calls ($1 per call)	$ 30.00	$ 10.00	$?
Labor ($10 per hour)	10.00	10.00	?
Overhead (50% of telephone labor costs)	?	?	?
Total	$?	$?	$?
Total cost			$?

Job Revenue and Profit

Logbook and bike rental	$?
Service fee: 97 hours* × $30	?
Job revenue	$2,990.00
Less total cost	?
Profit	$2,222.50

*5 + 90 + 2 = 97 hours

PROBLEMS

LO3 T Account Analysis with Unknowns

P 1. Flagstaff Enterprises makes peripheral equipment for computers. Dana Dona, the company's new controller, can find only the following partial information for the past two months:

Account/Transaction	May	June
Materials Inventory, Beginning	$ 36,240	$ e
Work in Process Inventory, Beginning	56,480	f
Finished Goods Inventory, Beginning	44,260	g
Materials purchased	a	96,120
Direct materials requested	82,320	h
Direct labor costs	b	72,250
Manufacturing overhead applied	53,200	i
Cost of units completed	c	221,400
Cost of units sold	209,050	j
Materials Inventory, Ending	38,910	41,950
Work in Process Inventory, Ending	d	k
Finished Goods Inventory, Ending	47,940	51,180

REQUIRED ▶ The current year's predetermined overhead rate is 80 percent of direct labor cost. Using the data provided and T accounts, compute the unknown values.

P 2.

LO3 Job Order Costing: T Account
LO4 Analysis

Par Carts, Inc., produces electric golf carts. The carts are special-order items, so Par Carts uses a job order costing system. Manufacturing overhead is applied at the rate of 90 percent of direct labor cost. The following is a list of transactions for January:

Jan. 1 Purchased direct materials on account, $215,400.
2 Purchased indirect materials on account, $49,500.
4 Requested direct materials costing $193,200 (all used on Job X) and indirect materials costing $38,100 for production.
10 Paid the following manufacturing overhead costs: utilities, $4,400; manufacturing rent, $3,800; and maintenance charges, $3,900.
15 Recorded the following gross wages and salaries for employees: direct labor, $120,000 (all for Job X); indirect labor, $60,620; sales commissions, $32,400; and administrative salaries, $38,000.
15 Applied manufacturing overhead to production.
19 Purchased indirect materials costing $27,550 and direct materials costing $190,450 on account.
21 Requested direct materials costing $214,750 (Job X, $178,170; Job Y, $18,170; and Job Z, $18,410) and indirect materials costing $31,400 for production.
31 Recorded the following gross wages and salaries for employees: direct labor, $132,000 (Job X, $118,500; Job Y, $7,000; Job Z, $6,500); indirect labor, $62,240; sales commissions, $31,200; and administrative salaries, $38,000.
31 Applied manufacturing overhead to production.
31 Completed and transferred Job X (375 carts) and Job Y (10 carts) to finished goods inventory; total cost was $855,990.
31 Shipped Job X to the customer; total production cost was $824,520 and sales price was $996,800.
31 Recorded these manufacturing overhead costs (adjusting entries): prepaid insurance expired, $3,700; property taxes (payable at year end), $3,400; and depreciation, machinery, $15,500.

REQUIRED ▶ 1. Record the entries for all transactions in January using T accounts for the following: Materials Inventory, Work in Process Inventory, Finished Goods Inventory, Manufacturing Overhead, Cash, Accounts Receivable, Prepaid Insurance, Accumulated Depreciation—Machinery, Accounts Payable, Factory Payroll, Property Taxes Payable, Sales, Cost of Goods Sold, and Selling and Administrative Expenses. Use job order cost cards for Job X, Job Y, and Job Z. Determine the partial account balances. Assume no beginning inventory balances. Also assume that when the payroll was recorded, entries were made to the Factory Payroll account.
2. Compute the amount of underapplied or overapplied overhead as of January 31 and transfer it to the Cost of Goods Sold account.
3. Why should the Manufacturing Overhead account's underapplied or overapplied overhead be transferred to the Cost of Goods Sold account?

P 3.

LO3 Job Order Cost Flow
LO4

On May 31, the inventory balances of Abbey Designs, a manufacturer of high-quality children's clothing, were as follows: Materials Inventory, $21,360; Work in Process Inventory, $15,112; and Finished Goods Inventory, $17,120. Job order cost cards for jobs in process as of June 30 had these totals:

Job No.	Direct Materials	Direct Labor	Manufacturing Overhead
24-A	$1,596	$1,290	$1,677
24-B	1,492	1,380	1,794
24-C	1,984	1,760	2,288
24-D	1,608	1,540	2,002

The predetermined overhead rate is 130 percent of direct labor cost. Materials purchased and received in June were as follows:

June 4	$33,120
June 16	28,600
June 22	31,920

Direct labor costs for June were as follows:

June 15 payroll	$23,680
June 29 payroll	25,960

Direct materials requested by production during June were as follows:

June 6	$37,240
June 23	38,960

During June, Abbey Designs sold finished goods with a 75 percent markup over cost for $320,000.

REQUIRED
1. Using T accounts for Materials Inventory, Work in Process Inventory, Finished Goods Inventory, Manufacturing Overhead, Accounts Receivable, Factory Payroll, Sales, and Cost of Goods Sold, reconstruct the transactions in June.
2. Compute the cost of units completed during the month.
3. What was the total cost of units sold during June?
4. Determine the ending inventory balances.
5. Jobs 24-A and 24-C were completed during the first week of July. No additional materials costs were incurred, but Job 24-A required $960 more of direct labor, and Job 24-C needed an additional $1,610 of direct labor. Job 24-A was composed of 1,200 pairs of trousers; Job 24-C, of 950 shirts. Compute the product unit cost for each job. (Round your answers to two decimal places.)

P 4.

LO5 Job Order Costing in a Service Organization

Riggs & Associates is a CPA firm located in Clinton, Kansas. The firm deals primarily in tax and audit work. For billing of major audit engagements, it uses cost-plus contracts, and its profit factor is 25 percent of total job cost. Costs are accumulated for three primary activities: preliminary analysis, field work, and report development. Current service overhead rates based on billable hours are preliminary analysis, $12 per hour; field work, $20 per hour; and report development, $16 per hour. Supplies are treated as direct materials, traceable to each engagement. Audits for three clients—Fulcrum, Inc., Rainy Day Bakeries, and Our Place Restaurants—are currently in process. During March 20x8, costs related to these projects were as follows:

	Fulcrum, Inc.	Rainy Day Bakeries	Our Place Restaurants
Beginning Balances			
Preliminary analysis	$1,160	$2,670	$2,150
Field work	710	1,980	3,460
Report development	0	1,020	420
Costs During March			
Preliminary analysis			
Supplies	$ 710	$ 430	$ 200
Labor: hours	60	10	12
dollars	$1,200	$ 200	$ 240
Field work			
Supplies	$ 450	$1,120	$ 890
Labor: hours	120	240	230
dollars	$4,800	$9,600	$9,200
Report development			
Supplies	$ 150	$ 430	$ 390
Labor: hours	30	160	140
dollars	$ 900	$4,800	$4,200

REQUIRED ▶
1. Using the format shown in this chapter's Review Problem, create the job order cost card for each of the three audit engagements.
2. Riggs & Associates will complete the audits of Rainy Day Bakeries and Our Place Restaurants by the end of March. What will the billing amount for each of those audit engagements be?
3. What is the March ending balance of Riggs & Associates' Audit in Process account for the three jobs?

P 5.
LO5 Job Order Costing in a Service Organization

Peruga Engineering Company specializes in designing automated characters and displays for theme parks. It uses cost-plus profit contracts, and its profit factor is 30 percent of total cost.

Peruga uses a job order costing system to track the costs of developing each job. Costs are accumulated for three primary activities: bid and proposal, design, and prototype development. Current service overhead rates based on engineering hours are as follows: bid and proposal, $18 per hour; design, $22 per hour; and prototype development, $20 per hour. Supplies are treated as direct materials, traceable to each job. Peruga worked on three jobs, P-12, P-15, and P-19, during January. The following table shows the costs for those jobs:

	P-12	P-15	P-19
Beginning Balances			
Bid and proposal	$2,460	$2,290	$ 940
Design	1,910	460	0
Prototype development	2,410	1,680	0
Costs During January			
Bid and proposal			
Supplies	0	$ 280	$2,300
Labor: hours	12	20	68
dollars	$ 192	$ 320	$1,088
Design			
Supplies	$ 400	$ 460	$ 290
Labor: hours	64	42	26
dollars	$1,280	$ 840	$ 520
Prototype development			
Special materials	$6,744	$7,216	$2,400
Labor: hours	120	130	25
dollars	$2,880	$3,120	$ 600

REQUIRED ▶
1. Using the format shown in this chapter's Review Problem, create the job order cost card for each of the three jobs.
2. Peruga completed Jobs P-12 and P-15, and the customers approved of the prototype products. Customer A plans to produce 12 special characters using the design and specifications created by Job P-12. Customer B plans to make 18 displays from the design developed by Job P-15. What dollar amount will each customer use as the cost of design for each of those products (i.e., what is the product unit cost for Jobs P-12 and P-15)? Round to the nearest dollar.
3. What is the January ending balance of Peruga's Contract in Process account for the three jobs?
4. Rank the jobs in order of most costly to least costly based on each job's total cost. From the rankings of cost, what observations can you make?
5. Speculate on the price Peruga should charge for such jobs.

ALTERNATE PROBLEMS

P 6.
LO3 Job Order Costing: T Account
LO4 Analysis

Rothi Industries, Inc., the finest name in parking attendants' apparel, has been in business for over 30 years. Its colorful and stylish uniforms are special-ordered by luxury hotels all over the world. During September, Rothi Industries completed the following transactions:

Sept. 1 Purchased direct materials on account, $59,400.
       3 Requested direct materials costing $26,850 for production (all for Job A).
       4 Purchased indirect materials for cash, $22,830.
       8 Issued checks for the following manufacturing overhead costs: utilities, $4,310; manufacturing insurance, $1,925; and repairs, $4,640.
      10 Requested direct materials costing $29,510 (all used on Job A) and indirect materials costing $6,480 for production.
      15 Recorded the following gross wages and salaries for employees: direct labor, $62,900 (all for Job A); indirect labor, $31,610; manufacturing supervision, $26,900; and sales commissions, $32,980.
      15 Applied overhead to production at a rate of 120 percent of direct labor cost.
      22 Paid the following manufacturing overhead costs: utilities, $4,270; maintenance, $3,380; and rent, $3,250.
      23 Recorded the purchase on account and receipt of $31,940 of direct materials and $9,260 of indirect materials.
      27 Requested $28,870 of direct materials (Job A, $2,660; Job B, $8,400; Job C, $17,810) and $7,640 of indirect materials for production.
      30 Recorded the following gross wages and salaries for employees: direct labor, $64,220 (Job A, $44,000; Job B, $9,000; Job C, $11,220); indirect labor, $30,290; manufacturing supervision, $28,520; and sales commissions, $36,200.
      30 Applied manufacturing overhead to production at a rate of 120 percent of direct labor cost.
      30 Completed and transferred Job A (58,840 units) and Job B (3,525 units) to finished goods inventory; total cost was $322,400.
      30 Shipped Job A to the customer; total production cost was $294,200, and sales price was $418,240.
      30 Recorded the following adjusting entries: $2,680 for depreciation, manufacturing equipment; and $1,230 for property taxes, manufacturing, payable at month end.

REQUIRED ▶ 1. Record the entries for all Rothi's transactions in September using T accounts for the following: Materials Inventory, Work in Process Inventory, Finished Goods Inventory, Manufacturing Overhead, Cash, Accounts Receivable, Accumulated Depreciation—Manufacturing Equipment, Accounts Payable, Factory Payroll, Property Taxes Payable, Sales, Cost of Goods Sold, and Selling and Administrative Expense. Use job order cost cards for Job A, Job B, and Job C. Determine the partial account balances. Assume no beginning inventory balances. Assume also that when payroll was recorded, entries were made to the Factory Payroll account. (Round your answers to the nearest whole dollar.)
2. Compute the amount of underapplied or overapplied overhead for September and transfer it to the Cost of Goods Sold account.
3. Why should the Manufacturing Overhead account's underapplied or overapplied overhead be transferred to the Cost of Goods Sold account?

LO3 **Job Order Cost Flow**
LO4

P 7. Dori Hatami is the chief financial officer of Gotham Industries, a company that makes special-order printers for personal computers. Her records for February revealed the following information:

Beginning inventory balances
   Materials Inventory $27,450
   Work in Process Inventory   22,900
   Finished Goods Inventory   19,200

Direct materials purchased and received
   February 6 $ 7,200
   February 12   8,110
   February 24   5,890

Direct labor costs
   February 14 $13,750
   February 28   13,230

Direct materials requested for production
February 4	$ 9,080
February 13	5,940
February 25	7,600

Job order cost cards for jobs in process on February 28 had the following totals:

Job No.	Direct Materials	Direct Labor	Manufacturing Overhead
AJ-10	$3,220	$1,810	$2,534
AJ-14	3,880	2,110	2,954
AJ-30	2,980	1,640	2,296
AJ-16	4,690	2,370	3,318

The predetermined manufacturing overhead rate for the month was 140 percent of direct labor costs. Sales for February totaled $152,400, which represented a 70 percent markup over the cost of production.

REQUIRED

1. Using T accounts for Materials Inventory, Work in Process Inventory, Finished Goods Inventory, Manufacturing Overhead, Accounts Receivable, Factory Payroll, Sales, and Cost of Goods Sold, reconstruct the transactions in February.
2. Compute the cost of units completed during the month.
3. What was the total cost of units sold during February?
4. Determine the ending balances in the inventory accounts.
5. During the first week of March, Jobs AJ-10 and AJ-14 were completed. No additional direct materials costs were incurred, but Job AJ-10 needed $720 more of direct labor, and Job AJ-14 needed an additional $1,140 of direct labor. Job AJ-10 was 40 units; Job AJ-14, 55 units. Compute the product unit cost for each completed job (round to two decimal places).

P 8.

LO4 Job Order Costing in a Service
LO5 Organization

Locust Lodge, a restored 1920s lodge located in Arizona, caters and serves special events for businesses and social occasions. The company earns 60 percent of its revenue from weekly luncheon meetings of local clubs like Kiwanis. The remainder of its business comes from bookings for weddings and receptions.

Locust Lodge uses job order cost cards to keep track of the costs incurred. Job costs are separated into three categories: food and beverage, labor, and facility overhead. The facility overhead cost for weekly events is 10 percent of food and beverage costs, the facility overhead cost for sit-down receptions is 40 percent of food and beverage costs, and the facility overhead cost for stand-up receptions is 20 percent of food and beverage costs. Accumulated costs for three Locust Lodge clients in the current quarter are as follows:

	Food and Beverage	Labor	Facility Overhead
Tuesday Club meetings	Last month: $2,000 This month: $2,500	Last month: $200 This month: $250	Last month: ? This month: ?
Doar-Turner engagement and wedding parties	Last month: $3,000 This month: $8,000 Both sit-down affairs	Last month: $1,000 This month: $2,000	Last month: ? This month: ?
Reception for the new president	This month: $5,000 A stand-up affair	This month: $1,000	This month: ?

The number of attendees served at Tuesday Club meetings is usually 200 per month. The Doar-Turner parties paid for 500 guests. The organizers of the reception for the new president paid for 1,000 invitees.

REQUIRED

1. Using the format shown in this chapter's Review Problem, create a job order cost card for each of the three clients.
2. Calculate the total cost of each of the three jobs on its job order cost card.
3. Calculate the cost per attendee for each job.
4. Rank the jobs in order of most costly to least costly based on each job's total cost and on the cost per attendee. From the rankings of cost, what observations are you able to make?
5. Speculate on the price Locust Lodge should charge for such jobs.

SKILLS DEVELOPMENT CASES

Conceptual Analysis

LO1 Business Plans

SD 1. In the past 20 years, Fortune 500 companies have eliminated over 5 million jobs; yet the U.S. economy has grown by almost 30 million jobs. New businesses have created most of the new employment. A key step in starting a new business is a realistic analysis of the people, opportunities, context, risks, and rewards of the venture and the formulation of a business plan. Note the similarities between the questions accountants answer in the management cycle and the questions every great business plan should answer:[5]

- Who is the new company's customer?
- How does the customer make decisions about buying this product or service?
- To what degree is the product or service a compelling purchase for the customer?
- How will the product or service be priced?
- How will the company reach all the identified customer segments?
- How much does it cost (in time and resources) to acquire a customer?
- How much does it cost to produce and deliver the product or service?
- How much does it cost to support a customer?
- How easy is it to retain a customer?

Assume a new business has hired you as a consultant because of your knowledge of the management cycle. Write a memo that discusses how the nine questions listed above fit into the management cycle.

LO1 Role of Cost Information in
LO6 Software Development

SD 2. Michael Cassidy of Teoma <www.teoma.com> has a problem: When is "good enough" good enough? As the creator of search technology that makes finding information on the Internet both quick and easy, Cassidy worries about how many developer hours should be devoted to a new product. His industry's rule of thumb is that developing and shipping new software takes six to nine months. Cassidy's company develops and ships products much more quickly, so by this measure, it is indeed "good enough."

Another performance measure that Michael Cassidy uses to answer his question is a "good enough" calculation based on the economic value (not cost) of what his company's developers create. Taking the estimated current market valuation of his firm and dividing it by the number of product developers in the firm, he arrives at the market value created per developer. Cassidy further refines this calculation to determine the value that each developer creates per workday. He estimates this value to be $10,000. Thus, the company's "good enough" measure focuses on whether a new product's potential justifies an investment of time by someone who is worth $10,000 per day.[6]

The salary cost of the company's developers is not used in the "good enough" calculation. Why is that cost not relevant?

Ethical Dilemma

LO3 Costing Procedures and Ethics
LO5

SD 3. Kevin Rogers, the production manager of Stitts Metal Products Company, entered the office of controller Ed Harris and asked, "Ed, what gives here? I was charged for 330 direct labor hours on Job AD22, and my records show that we spent only 290 hours on that job. That 40-hour difference caused the total cost of direct labor and manufacturing overhead for the job to increase by over $5,500. Are my records wrong, or was there an error in the direct labor assigned to the job?"

Harris replied, "Don't worry about it, Kevin. This job won't be used in your quarterly performance evaluation. Job AD22 was a federal government job, a cost-plus contract, so the more costs we assign to it, the more profit we make. We decided to add a few hours to the job in case there is some follow-up work to do. You know how fussy the feds are." What should Kevin Rogers do? Discuss Ed Harris's costing procedure.

Research Activity

LO3 Job Order Costing

SD 4. Many businesses accumulate costs for each job performed. Examples of businesses that use a job order costing system include print shops, car repair shops, health clinics, and kennels.

Visit a local business that uses job order costing, and interview the owner, manager, or accountant about the process and the documents the business uses to accumulate product costs. Write a paper that summarizes the information you obtained. Include the following in your summary:

1. The name of the business and the type of operations performed
2. The name and position of the individual you interviewed
3. A description of the process of starting and completing a job
4. A description of the accounting process and the documents used to track a job
5. Your responses to these questions:

    a. Did the person you interviewed know the actual amount of materials, labor, and overhead charged to a particular job? If the job includes some estimated costs, how are the estimates calculated? Do the costs affect the determination of the selling price of the product or service?
    b. Compare the documents discussed in this chapter with the documents used by the company you visited. How are they similar, and how are they different?
    c. In your opinion, does the business record and accumulate its product costs effectively? Explain.

 Group Activity: Group students according to the type of business they selected and ask them to discuss their responses to the questions in 5.

Decision-Making Practice

  LO3 Analysis of a Job Order
LO4 Costing System

SD 5. Zavala Manufacturing Company is a small family-owned business that makes specialty plastic products. Since it was started three years ago, the company has grown quickly and now employs ten production people. Because of the nature of its products, it uses a job order costing system. The company's manual accounting system is falling behind in processing transactions.

Two months ago, in May, Zavala's accountant quit. You have been called in to help management. The following information is available to you:

Beginning Inventory Balances (December 31)

Materials Inventory	$50,420
Work in Process Inventory (Job K-2)	59,100
Finished Goods Inventory (Job K-1)	76,480

Direct Materials Requested by Production During the Year

Job K-2	$33,850
Job K-4	53,380
Job K-5	82,400

Direct Labor for the Year

Job K-2	$25,300
Job K-4	33,480
Job K-5	45,600

The company purchased materials only once (in February), for $126,500. All jobs use the same materials. For the current year, the company has used an overhead application rate of 150 percent of direct labor costs. So far this year, it has completed two jobs, K-2 and K-4, and has shipped Jobs K-1 and K-2 to customers. Job K-1 contained 3,200 units; Job K-2, 5,500 units; and Job K-4, 4,600 units. The beginning balance of Work in Process Inventory for Job K-2 consisted of $16,975 of direct materials, $16,850 of direct labor, and $25,275 of manufacturing overhead.

1. Calculate the product unit costs for Jobs K-1, K-2, and K-4, and the costs so far for Job K-5.
2. From the information given, prepare job order cost cards for Jobs K-2, K-4, and K-5, and compute the current balances in the Materials Inventory, Work in Process Inventory, Finished Goods Inventory, and Cost of Goods Sold accounts.
3. Zavala's president has asked you to analyze the current job order costing system. Do you think the system should be changed? How? Why? Prepare an outline of your response to the president.

MANAGERIAL REPORTING AND ANALYSIS CASES

Interpreting Management Reports

MRA 1.
LO1 Interpreting Nonfinancial Data

Eagle Manufacturing supplies engine parts to Cherokee Cycle Company, a major U.S. manufacturer of motorcycles. Like all of Cherokee's suppliers, Eagle has always added a healthy profit margin to its cost when quoting selling prices to Cherokee. Recently, however, several companies have offered to supply engine parts to Cherokee for lower prices than Eagle has been charging.

Because Eagle Manufacturing wants to keep Cherokee Cycle Company's business, a team of Eagle's managers analyzed their company's product costs and decided to make minor changes in the company's manufacturing process. No new equipment was purchased, and no additional labor was required. Instead, the machines were rearranged, and some of the work was reassigned.

To monitor the effectiveness of the changes, Eagle introduced three new performance measures to its information system: inventory levels, lead time (total time required for a part to move through the production process), and productivity (number of parts manufactured per person per day). Eagle's goal was to reduce the quantities of the first two performance measures and to increase the quantity of the third.

A section of a recent management report, shown below, summarizes the quantities for each performance measure before and after the changes in the manufacturing process were made.

Measure	Before	After	Improvement
Inventory in dollars	$21,444	$10,772	50%
Lead time in minutes	17	11	35%
Productivity (parts per person per day)	515	1,152	124%

1. Do you believe Eagle improved the quality of its manufacturing process and the quality of its engine parts? Explain your answer.
2. Can Eagle lower its selling price to Cherokee? Explain your answer.
3. Did the introduction of the new measures affect the design of the product costing system? Explain your answer.
4. Do you believe that the new measures caused a change in Eagle's cost per engine part? If so, how did they cause the change?

Formulating Management Reports

MRA 2.
LO1 Product Costing Systems and
LO2 Nonfinancial Data

  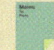

Refer to the information in **MRA 1**. Jordan Smith, the president of Eagle Manufacturing, wants to improve the quality of the company's operations and products. She believes waste exists in the design and manufacture of standard engine parts. To begin the improvement process, she has asked you to (1) identify the sources of such waste, (2) develop performance measures to account for the waste, and (3) estimate the current costs associated with the waste. She has asked you to submit a memo of your findings within two weeks so that she can begin strategic planning to revise the price at which Eagle sells engine parts to Cherokee.

You have identified two sources of costly waste. The Production Department is redoing work that was not done correctly the first time, and the Engineering Design Department is redesigning products that were not initially designed to customer specifications. Having improper designs has caused the company to buy parts that are not used in production. You have also obtained the following information from the product costing system:

Direct labor costs	$673,402
Engineering design costs	124,709
Indirect labor costs	67,200
Depreciation on production equipment	84,300
Supervisors' salaries	98,340
Direct materials costs	432,223
Indirect materials costs	44,332

1. In preparation for writing your memo, answer the following questions:
   a. For whom are you preparing the memo? What is the appropriate length of the memo?
   b. Why are you preparing the memo?
   c. What information is needed for the memo? Where can you get such information? What performance measure would you suggest for each activity? Is the accounting information sufficient for your memo?
   d. When is the memo due? What can be done to provide accurate and timely information?
2. Prepare an outline of the sections you would want to include in your memo.

International Company

MRA 3.
LO1 Design of a Product Costing
LO2 System

The Al Khali Corporation's copper mines contain 63 percent of the 23.2 million tons of copper in Saudi Arabia. The owners of the mining operation are willing to invest millions of dollars in the latest pyrometallurgical copper-extraction process. Production managers are currently examining both batch and continuous versions of the new process. The method they choose will replace the hydrometallurgical process now in use.

What impact will the method that the production managers select have on the design of the product costing system? What impact would changing from hydrometallurgical to pyrometallurgical processing have on the design of the product costing system if both processes use continuous methods of extraction?

Excel Spreadsheet Analysis

MRA 4.
LO5 Job Order Costing in a Service Organization

Refer to assignment **P 5** in this chapter. Peruga Engineering Company needs to analyze its jobs in process during the month of January.

1. Using the Chart Wizard and the job order cost cards that you created for Jobs P-12, P-15, and P-19, prepare a bar chart that compares the bid and proposal costs, design costs, and prototype development costs of the jobs. Below is the suggested format to use for the information table necessary to complete the bar chart.

	A	B	C	D
1		P-12	P-15	P-19
2	Bid and proposal			
3	Design			
4	Prototype development			
5	Total job cost			

2. Examine the chart you prepared in **1**. List some reasons for the differences between the costs of the various jobs.

Internet Case

MRA 5.
LO1 Evaluating Internet Shopping Sites

Do a key word online search for clothing manufacturers or retailers. Select two companies that make or sell similar clothes and access their web sites. Conduct an Internet shopping audit similar to the one P. Kelly Mooney does as the president and chief executive officer for Resource Marketing, Inc.<www.resource.com>, a technology marketing and communications company based in Columbus, Ohio. Mooney uses five principles to evaluate Internet shopping sites in such areas as prepurchase customer service, gift giving, special promotions, and postpurchase follow-through. She describes the five principles as follows:[7]

- *Don't just do it:* The web site should be more than the company's catalogue loaded online.

- *Don't let your seams show:* Shopping, whether online or in a retail store, should be a seamless experience that guides customers according to their needs.
- *Own the customer experience:* The web site should be intuitively easy to use and accessible. It should personalize service by asking customers about the types of information they want.
- *Avoid barriers to entry:* The web site should center on the customer. It should have clear connection paths, quick-loading graphics, well-organized pages, crisp self-help features, and personal email responses that state all details of the shopping transaction in plain language.
- *Trust is a must:* The web site should not follow a one-size-fits-all information-gathering approach. It should allow customers to personalize their approaches to browsing and buying so that they may come to view the company as a valued and trusted adviser.

Use Mooney's five principles to answer the following questions about the two companies you chose:

1. Identify the companies, their product lines, and their URLs. From a customer's perspective, what are your impressions of their web sites and their products?
2. Compare the companies' order forms. Do the companies request the same measurements and other information? Are their prices for like items comparable? How do the order forms differ?
3. Assume you are the manager of each company you chose. Did your product unit cost influence your pricing decisions? What other factors had a significant effect on the prices you set?
4. If the companies' financial statements are available on their web sites, review the figures for cost of goods sold and inventories. Describe your findings. Do the financial results agree with your previous impressions?

18

Chapter 18 describes process costing systems, including product flow patterns, equivalent production, and the preparation of process cost reports.

Costing Systems: Process Costing

Learning Objectives

LO1 Describe the process costing system, identify the reasons for its use, and discuss its role in the management cycle.

LO2 Relate the patterns of product flows to the cost flow methods in a process costing environment.

LO3 Explain the role of the Work in Process Inventory accounts in a process costing system.

LO4 Define *equivalent production* and compute equivalent units.

LO5 Prepare a process cost report using the FIFO costing method.

LO6 Prepare a process cost report using the average costing method.

LO7 Evaluate operating performance using information about product cost.

DECISION POINT
A MANAGER'S FOCUS

Intel Corporation <www.intel.com> Intel Corporation, which introduced the microprocessor to the marketplace in 1971, is the world's largest manufacturer of computer chips, as well as a leading manufacturer of networking and communications products. Because chips are becoming an off-the-shelf commodity, many of Intel's competitors have contracted to have their chips made by other companies. Intel, however, continues to manufacture chips. By using the latest manufacturing technology, the company is able to boost its operating performance and reduce production costs. Its costs per chip produced are some of the lowest among chipmakers.[1] What type of product costing system will provide Intel's management with the best information about chip production costs?

Because there is a continuous flow of similar products during most of the chip-making process, the most appropriate costing system for Intel is a process costing system. Such a system accumulates costs by process, department, or work cell and assigns them to the products as they pass through the production system. Use of the process costing system does not imply that every finished product is exactly the same. For instance, some computer chips are more complex than others and are therefore more difficult and costly to produce. Intel's management has created a system for tracking the activities involved in chip production. All costs connected with processing activities are assigned to a batch of chips based on the types of activities involved in production. This process costing system provides the information management needs

Why is a process costing system appropriate for Intel?

to make product decisions. In this chapter, we discuss the two most commonly used process costing systems.

THE PROCESS COSTING SYSTEM

LO1 Describe the process costing system, identify the reasons for its use, and discuss its role in the management cycle.

RELATED TEXT ASSIGNMENTS
Q: 1, 2, 3
SE: 1, 2
E: 1
SD: 1, 3, 4
MRA: 3, 5

● **STOP AND THINK!**
What types of businesses use process costing?

Process costing is appropriate for businesses that make large amounts of similar products or liquid products or that have long, continuous production runs of identical products. ■

A product costing system is expected to provide unit cost information, supply cost data to support management decisions, and furnish ending values for the Materials, Work in Process, and Finished Goods Inventory accounts. The job order costing system is one approach to satisfying those objectives. The process costing system is another approach.

As noted in the previous chapter, a **process costing system** is a product costing system used by companies that make large amounts of similar products or liquid products or that have long, continuous production runs of identical products. Companies that produce paint, beverages, bricks, canned foods, milk, and paper are typical users of a process costing system. Tracking costs to individual products in a continuous flow environment would be too difficult and too expensive and would not reveal significantly different product costs. One gallon of green paint is identical to the next gallon; one brick looks just like the next brick. Because the products are alike, they should cost the same amount to produce. A process costing system accumulates the costs of direct materials, direct labor, and manufacturing overhead for each process, department, or work cell and assigns those costs to the products as they are produced during a particular period.

In the last chapter, we described how managers use the cost information that both job order costing and process costing systems yield. Figure 1 reviews those uses. In the planning stage of the management cycle, managers use information

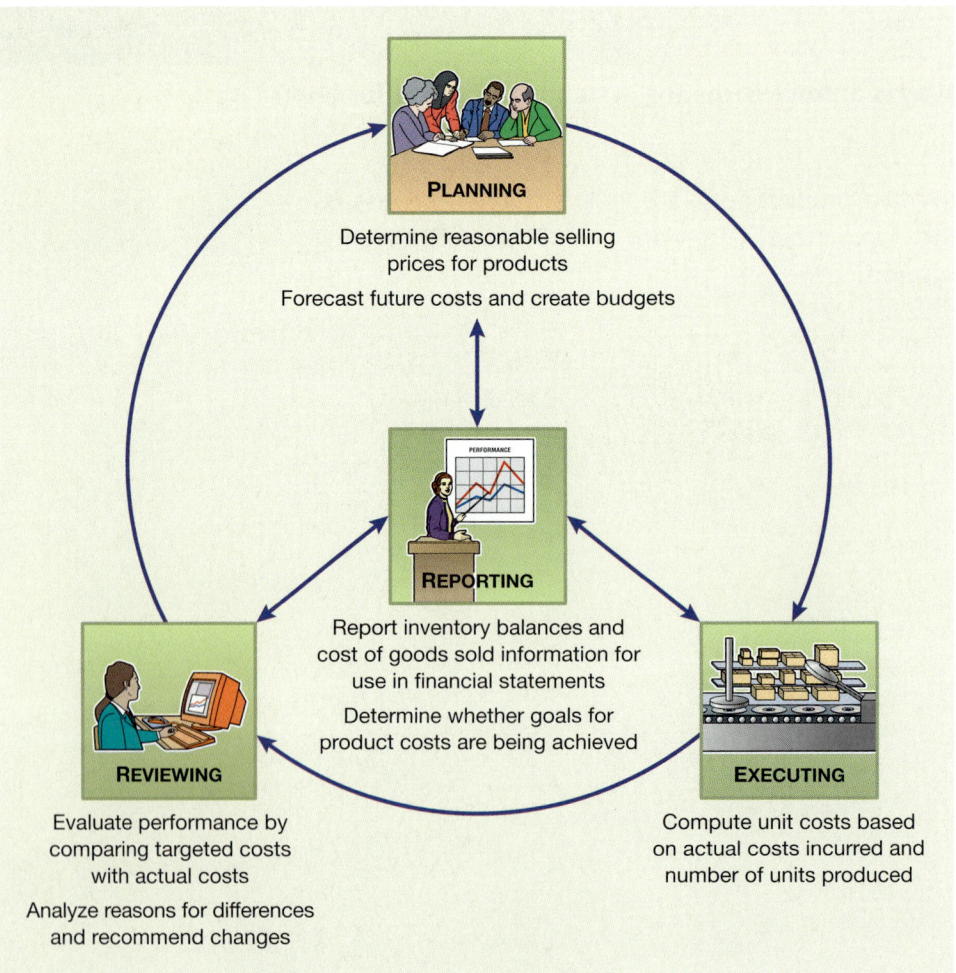

FIGURE 1
Uses of Product Costing Information in the Management Cycle

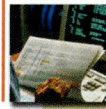

FOCUS ON BUSINESS PRACTICE

What Kinds of Companies Use Process Costing?

Process costing is appropriate for companies in many types of industries. The following list provides some examples:

Industry	Company	Industry	Company
Aluminum	Alcoa, Inc. <www.alcoa.com>	Foods	Kellogg Company <www.kelloggs.com>
Beverages	Coors <www.coors.com>	Machinery	Caterpillar Inc. <www.caterpillar.com>
Building materials	Owens Corning <www.owenscorning.com>	Manufacturing	Minnesota Mining & Manufacturing <www.3m.com>
Chemicals	Engelhard Corporation <www.engelhard.com>	Oil and gas	Exxon <www.exxon.com>
Computers	Apple Computer <www.apple.com>	Paper products	Boise Cascade <www.boisecascade.com>
Containers	Crown Cork & Seal <www.crowncork.com>	Photography	Eastman Kodak <www.eastmankodak.com>
Electrical equipment	Emerson Electric <www.emersonelectric.com>	Plastic products	Tupperware <www.tupperware.com>
		Soft drinks	Coca-Cola <www.cocacola.com>

KEY POINT: In process costing, costs are traced to production processes, whereas in job order costing, costs are traced to jobs.

about past and projected product costing and customer preferences to decide what a product should cost and if that amount is reasonable. After they have determined a target number of units to be sold, all product-related costs for that targeted number of units can be computed and used in the budget. During the executing stage, actual costs are incurred as units are produced, so actual unit costs can be computed. In the reviewing stage, managers evaluate performance by comparing targeted costs with actual costs. If costs have exceeded expectations, managers analyze why this has occurred and recommend changes. In the reporting stage, they use actual units produced and costs incurred to value inventory on the balance sheet and cost of goods sold on the income statement. Managers are also interested in whether goals for product costs are being achieved.

 Check out ACE for a Review Quiz at http://accounting.college.hmco.com/students.

PATTERNS OF PRODUCT FLOWS AND COST FLOW METHODS

LO2 Relate the patterns of product flows to the cost flow methods in a process costing environment.

RELATED TEXT ASSIGNMENTS
Q: 4, 5, 6, 7
E: 2
SD: 2, 3
MRA: 2

During production in a process costing environment, products flow in a first-in, first-out (FIFO) fashion through several processes, departments, or work cells and may undergo many different combinations of operations. At its simplest, product flow in a process costing environment follows a linear pattern. Because a linear approach illustrates all the concepts that would be applied in both simple and complex environments, we present only that approach in this chapter.

Although the manufacture of computer chips is a complex operation, it is possible to visualize its product flow as a simple linear pattern, as shown in Figure 2 and described below.

- *Producing the silicon wafer:* Silicon, which is extracted from sand and then purified, is the direct material from which computer chips are made. Through a process of crystallization, the refined, molten silicon is converted to a cylindrical ingot. The ingot is then sliced into wafers, and the wafers are polished to meet flatness and thickness specifications. The workers involved in these steps provide direct labor. Overhead includes the costs of the equipment the workers use and the resources necessary to operate and maintain the equipment.

- *Fabricating the chips:* Fabrication includes photolithography, etching, ion implantation, and all the other steps needed to create the electronic circuits that make up each chip on a wafer. Additional direct labor and overhead costs are incurred during fabrication.

Figure 2
Product Flows in a Process Costing System for Computer Chip Making

- *Final testing, assembly, and packaging of the chips:* Although the wafers are tested at each step in the fabrication process, each chip on a wafer is tested again when fabrication is complete. Those that pass this test are cut from the wafer, placed in metal or plastic packages, tested once again, and transferred to finished goods inventory in the warehouse. These steps incur additional direct labor, direct materials, and overhead costs.

Process costing environments can be considerably less complex than the one we have just described, but even in simple process costing environments, production generally involves a number of separate manufacturing processes, departments, or works cells. For example, the separate processes involved in manufacturing sofas include making the frames and cushions, upholstering the frames, and assembling the frames and cushions into finished products.

As products pass through each manufacturing process, department, or work cell, the process costing system accumulates their costs and passes them on to the next process, department, or work cell. At the end of every accounting period, the system generates a report that assigns the costs that have accumulated during the period to the units that have transferred out of the process, department, or work cell and to the units that are still work in process.

A process cost report may assign costs by using the FIFO costing method or the average costing method. In the **FIFO costing method**, the cost flow follows the logical physical flow of production—that is, the costs assigned to the first materials processed are the first costs transferred out when those materials flow to the next process, department, or work cell. Thus, in Figure 2, the costs assigned to the production of the silicon wafers would be the first costs transferred to the fabrication of the chips. In contrast, the **average costing method** assigns an average cost to all products made during an accounting period; this method thus uses total cost averages and does not try to match cost flow with the physical flow of production. We discuss process cost reports that use the FIFO and average costing methods later in this chapter.

✓ Check out ACE for a Review Quiz at http://accounting.college.hmco.com/students.

🔶 Stop and Think!
What are the two cost flow methods?
FIFO costing and average costing are the two methods used to account for cost flows. ■

COSTS FLOWS THROUGH THE WORK IN PROCESS INVENTORY ACCOUNTS

LO3 Explain the role of the Work in Process Inventory accounts in a process costing system.

RELATED TEXT ASSIGNMENTS
Q: 8
SE: 3
E: 3
SD: 2
MRA: 3

www.nabisco.com

● **STOP AND THINK!**
How many Work in Process Inventory accounts does a process costing system require?

A process costing system requires a Work in Process Inventory account for each process, department, or work cell in the production process. ■

As we pointed out in the last chapter, a job order costing system uses a single Work in Process Inventory account, whereas a process costing system has a separate Work in Process Inventory account for each process, department, or work cell. These accounts are the focal point of process costing. As products move from one process, department, or work cell to the next, the costs of the direct materials, direct labor, and manufacturing overhead associated with them flow to the Work in Process Inventory account of that process, department, or work cell. Once the products are completed, packaged, and ready for sale, their costs are transferred to the Finished Goods Inventory account.

To illustrate how costs flow through the Work in Process Inventory accounts in a process costing system, let's consider a company like Nabisco, which makes large quantities of identical cookies in a continuous flow. Such a company would have mixing, baking, and packaging departments. After its Mixing Department has prepared the cookie dough, the costs incurred for direct materials, direct labor, and manufacturing overhead are transferred from that department's Work in Process Inventory account to the Work in Process Inventory account of the Baking Department. When the cookies are baked, the costs of the cookie dough and the baking costs are transferred from the Baking Department's Work in Process Inventory account to the Work in Process Inventory account of the Packaging Department. After the cookies are packaged and ready for sale, all their costs—for dough, baking, and packaging—are transferred to the Finished Goods Inventory account. When the packages of cookies are sold, their costs transfer from the Finished Goods Inventory account to the Cost of Goods Sold account.

Because the production of homogeneous products like packaged cookies, paint, or paper clips is continuous, it would be impractical to try to assign their costs to a specific batch of products, as is done with a job order costing system. Instead, as we have noted, in a process costing system, a report prepared at the end of every accounting period assigns the costs that have accumulated in each Work in Process Inventory account to the units transferred out and to the units still in process. The process cost report uses a method like FIFO or average costing to compute the unit cost of all products worked on during the period. Thus, the product unit cost includes all costs from all processes, departments, or work cells.

FOCUS ON BUSINESS ETHICS

How Hard Is It to Detect Fraud?
Managers are finding fraud to be an increasingly common business problem. Fortunately, some types of fraud, including scams that involve product costs and expenses, are relatively easy to detect. In a study in which fraud examiners were asked to rate their difficulty in detecting fraud on a scale of 1 (most difficult to detect) to 7 (easiest to detect), the results showed that the most difficult scams to detect were extortion (2.5) and illegal gratuities (2.86). Cash larceny (5.04), check tampering (4.40), illegal disbursements (4.35), expense scams (4.34), financial statement irregularities (4.28), skimming (4.24), and payroll schemes (4.20) were much easier to find.[2]

✓ Check out ACE for a Review Quiz at http://accounting.college.hmco.com/students.

COMPUTING EQUIVALENT PRODUCTION

LO4 Define *equivalent production* and compute equivalent units.

RELATED TEXT ASSIGNMENTS
Q: 9, 10, 11, 12
SE: 4
E: 4, 5, 6
P: 1, 2, 3, 4, 6, 7
SD: 5
MRA: 1, 2

A process costing system makes no attempt to associate costs with particular job orders. Instead, it assigns the costs incurred in a process, department, or work cell to the units worked on during an accounting period by computing an average cost per unit. To compute the unit cost, the total cost of direct materials, direct labor, and manufacturing overhead is divided by the total number of units worked on during the period. Thus, a critical question is exactly how many units were worked on in the period. Do we count only units started and completed during the period? Or should we include partially completed units in the beginning work in process inventory? And what about incomplete products in the ending work in process inventory?

FIGURE 3
Computation of Equivalent Production

Note: Conversion costs (the cost of direct labor and manufacturing overhead) are incurred uniformly as each physical unit of drink moves through production. Equivalent production for Week 2 is 4.25 units for conversion costs. But direct materials costs are all added to production at the beginning of the process. Because four physical units of drinks entered production in Week 2, equivalent production for the week is 4.0 units of effort for direct materials costs.

● **STOP AND THINK!**
What is an education-based example of equivalent production?

Funding of state-supported universities and colleges is based on the number of full-time equivalents (FTEs) these institutions generate each funding period. One FTE is equal to 12 credit hours of course work—the equivalent whole unit of effort expended on the education process during a period. Since some students take more or less than 12 credit hours, their course loads must be converted into FTEs for funding purposes. ■

ENRICHMENT NOTE:
Direct materials are often added at stages of production other than the beginning (e.g., cans for packaging paint are added at the end).

The answers to these questions relate to the concept of equivalent production. **Equivalent production** (also called *equivalent units*) is a measure that applies a percentage-of-completion factor to partially completed units to calculate the equivalent number of whole units produced in an accounting period for each type of input (i.e., direct materials, direct labor, and manufacturing overhead). The number of equivalent units produced is the sum of (1) total units started and completed during the period and (2) an amount representing the work done on partially completed products in both the beginning and the ending work in process inventories.

Equivalent production must be computed separately for each type of input because of differences in the ways costs are incurred. Direct materials are usually added to production at the beginning of the process. The costs of direct labor and manufacturing overhead are often incurred uniformly throughout the production process. Thus, it is convenient to combine direct labor and manufacturing overhead when calculating equivalent units. These combined costs are called **conversion costs**.

We will explain the computation of equivalent production by using a simplified example. Soda Products Company makes bottled soft drinks. As illustrated in Figure 3, the company started Week 2 with one half-completed drink in process. During Week 2, it started and completed three drinks, and at the end of Week 2, it had one drink that was three-quarters completed.

EQUIVALENT PRODUCTION FOR DIRECT MATERIALS

At Soda Products, all direct materials, including the liquids and the bottles, are added at the beginning of production. Thus, the drink that was half-completed at the beginning of Week 2 had had all its direct materials added during the previous week. For this reason, no direct materials costs for this drink are included in the computation of Week 2's equivalent units.

STUDY NOTE: The number of units started and completed is not the same as the total number of units completed during the period. Total units completed include units in beginning work in process inventory and units started and completed.

KEY POINT: Work in the current period is applied to three distinct product groups: units in beginning Work in Process Inventory, which must be completed; goods started and completed during the period; and goods started but not completed by the end of the accounting period.

During Week 2, work began on four new drinks—the three drinks that were completed and the drink that was three-quarters completed at week's end. Because all direct materials are added at the beginning of the production process, all four drinks were 100 percent complete in regard to direct materials at the end of Week 2. Thus, for Week 2, the equivalent production for direct materials was 4.0 units. This figure includes direct materials for both the 3.0 units that were started and completed and the 1.0 unit that was three-quarters completed.

EQUIVALENT PRODUCTION FOR CONVERSION COSTS

Because conversion costs at Soda Products are incurred uniformly throughout the production process, the equivalent production for conversion costs during Week 2 consists of three components: the cost to finish the half-completed unit in beginning work in process inventory (0.5), the cost to begin and finish three completed units (3.0), and the cost to begin work on the three-quarters completed unit in ending work in process inventory (0.75). For Week 2, the total equivalent production for conversion costs was 4.25 (0.5 + 3.0 + 0.75) units.

In reality, Soda Products would make many more drinks during an accounting period and would have many more partially completed drinks in its beginning and ending work in process inventories. The number of partially completed drinks would be so great that it would be impractical to take a physical count of them. So, instead of taking a physical count, Soda Products would estimate an average percentage of completion for all drinks in process.

 Check out ACE for a Review Quiz at http://accounting.college.hmco.com/students.

PREPARING A PROCESS COST REPORT USING THE FIFO COSTING METHOD

LO5 Prepare a process cost report using the FIFO costing method.
RELATED TEXT ASSIGNMENTS
Q: 13, 14, 15, 16, 17
SE: 5, 6
E: 7, 8, 9
P: 1, 2, 3, 4, 6, 7
SD: 5
MRA: 1, 2

STUDY NOTE: The FIFO method focuses on the work done in the current period only.

KEY POINT: The process cost report is developed for the purpose of assigning a value to one transaction: the transfer of goods from one department to another or to finished goods inventory. The ending balance in the Work in Process Inventory account represents the costs that remain after this transfer.

A *process cost report*, shown in Exhibit 1, is a report that managers use to track and analyze costs for a process, department, or work cell in a process costing system. In a process cost report that uses the FIFO costing method, the cost flow follows the logical physical flow of production—that is, the costs assigned to the first materials processed are the first costs transferred out when those materials flow to the next process, department, or work cell.

The preparation of a process cost report involves five steps. The first two steps account for the units of product being processed, the next two steps account for the costs of the direct material, direct labor, and manufacturing overhead being incurred, and the final step assigns costs to products transferring out of the area and to those remaining behind in ending work in process inventory.

ACCOUNTING FOR UNITS

Managers must account for the physical flow of products through their areas (Step 1) before they can compute equivalent production for the accounting period (Step 2). To continue with the Soda Products example, assume the following facts for the accounting period of February 20x6:

- The beginning work in process inventory consists of 6,200 partially completed units (60 percent processed in the previous period).
- During the period, the 6,200 units in beginning inventory were completed, and 57,500 units were started into production.
- Of the 57,500 units started during the period, 52,500 units were completed. The other 5,000 units remain in ending work in process inventory and are 45 percent complete.

In Step 1 of Exhibit 1, Soda Products' department manager computes the total units to be accounted for by adding the 6,200 units in beginning inventory to the

EXHIBIT 1
Process Cost Report: FIFO Costing Method

Step 1: Account for physical units.						
	Beginning inventory (units started last period)	6,200				
	Units started this period	57,500				
	Units to be accounted for	63,700				

Step 2: Account for equivalent units.			Direct Materials Costs	% Incurred During Period	Conversion Costs	% Incurred During Period
	Beginning inventory (units completed this period)	6,200	0	0%	2,480	40%
	Units started and completed this period	52,500	52,500	100%	52,500	100%
	Ending inventory (units started but not completed this period)	5,000	5,000	100%	2,250	45%
	Units accounted for	63,700	57,500		57,230	

Step 3: Account for costs.		Total Costs				
	Beginning inventory	$ 41,540	=	$ 20,150	+	$ 21,390
	Current costs	510,238	=	189,750	+	320,488
	Total costs	$551,778				

Step 4: Compute cost per equivalent unit.					
	Current Costs		$189,750		$320,488
	Equivalent Units		57,500		57,230
	Cost per equivalent unit	$8.90	=	$3.30	+	$5.60

Step 5: Assign costs to cost of goods manufactured and ending inventory.						
	Cost of goods manufactured and transferred out:					
	From beginning inventory	$ 41,540				
	Current costs to complete	13,888	=	0	+	(2,480 × $5.60)
	Units started and completed this period	467,250	=	(52,500 × $3.30)	+	(52,500 × $5.60)
	Cost of goods manufactured	$522,678	(No rounding necessary)			
	Ending inventory	29,100	=	(5,000 × $3.30)	+	(2,250 × $5.60)
	Total costs	$551,778				

Work in Process Inventory Account: Cost Recap

Beg. Bal.	$ 41,540	$522,678 (Cost of goods manufactured and transferred out)
Direct Materials	$189,750	
Conversion Costs	$320,488	
End. Bal.	$29,100	

Work in Process Inventory Account: Unit Recap

Beg. Bal.	6,200	58,700 (FIFO units transferred out from the 6,200 in beginning inventory plus the 52,500 started and completed)
Direct Materials and Conversion Costs	57,500	
End. Bal.	5,000	

ENRICHMENT NOTE: The percentage of completion for beginning work in process inventory is the amount of work completed the prior period. Under FIFO, the amount of effort required to complete beginning work in process inventory is the relevant percentage.

KEY POINT: Units in beginning work in process inventory represent work accomplished in the previous accounting period that has already been assigned a certain portion of its total cost. Those units must be completed in the current period, incurring additional costs.

57,500 units started into production in this period. These 63,700 units are the actual physical units that the manager is responsible for during the period.

Step 2 continues accounting for physical units. As shown in the "Physical Units" column of Exhibit 1, the 6,200 units in beginning inventory that were completed during the period, the 52,500 units that were started and finished in the period, and the 5,000 units remaining in the department at the end of the period are summed, and the total is listed as "units accounted for." (Notice that the "units accounted for" in Step 2 must equal the "units to be accounted for" in Step 1.) These amounts are used to compute equivalent production for the department's direct materials and conversion costs for the month, as described below.

■ **BEGINNING INVENTORY** Because all direct materials are added at the beginning of the production process, the 6,200 partially completed units that began February as work in process were already 100 percent complete in regard to direct materials. They were 60 percent complete in regard to conversion costs on February 1. The remaining 40 percent of their conversion costs were incurred as they were completed during the month. Thus, as shown in the far right column of Exhibit 1, the equivalent production for their conversion costs is 2,480 units (40% × 6,200).

■ **UNITS STARTED AND COMPLETED DURING THE PERIOD** All the costs of the 52,500 units started and completed during February were incurred during this accounting period. Thus, the full amount of 52,500 is entered as the equivalent units for both direct materials costs and conversion costs.

■ **ENDING INVENTORY** Because the materials for the 5,000 drinks still in process at the end of February were added when the drinks went into production during the month, the full amount of 5,000 is entered as the equivalent units for their direct materials cost. However, these drinks are only 45 percent complete in terms of conversion costs. Thus, as shown in the far right column of Exhibit 1, the equivalent production for their conversion costs is 2,250 units (45% × 5,000).

■ **TOTALS** Step 2 is completed by summing all the physical units to be accounted for, all equivalent units for direct materials costs, and all equivalent units for conversion costs. Exhibit 1 shows that for February, Soda Products accounted for 63,700 units. Equivalent units for direct materials costs totaled 57,500, and equivalent units for conversion costs totaled 57,230. Once Soda Products knows February's equivalent unit amounts, it can complete the remaining three steps in the preparation of a process cost report.

ACCOUNTING FOR COSTS

Thus far, we have focused on accounting for units of productive output—in our example, bottled soft drinks. We now turn our focus to cost information. Step 3 in preparing a process cost report accumulates and analyzes all costs charged to the Work in Process Inventory account of each production process, department, or work cell. Step 4 computes the cost per equivalent unit for direct materials costs and conversion costs. The following information about Soda Products' manufacture of soft drinks during February 20x6 enables us to complete Steps 3 and 4:

Work in Process Inventory	
Costs from beginning inventory	
Direct materials costs	$ 20,150
Conversion costs	21,390
Current period costs	
Direct materials costs	189,750
Conversion costs	320,488

KEY POINT: The cost per equivalent unit using the FIFO method measures the current cost divided by current effort. Notice in Exhibit 1 that the cost of beginning work in process inventory is omitted.

As shown in Step 3 of Exhibit 1, all costs for the period are accumulated in the "Total Costs" column. Beginning inventory's direct material costs of $20,150 are added to the conversion costs of $21,390 to determine the total cost of beginning inventory ($41,540). Current period costs for direct materials ($189,750) are added to conversion costs ($320,488) to determine the total current manufacturing costs ($510,238). The grand total of $551,778 is the sum of beginning inventory costs ($41,540) and current period costs ($510,238). Notice that only the "Total Costs" column is totaled. Since only the current period costs for materials and conversion are used in Step 4, there is no need to find the total costs of the direct materials and conversion columns in Step 3.

In Step 4, the direct materials costs and conversion costs for the current period are divided by their respective units of equivalent production to arrive at the cost per equivalent unit. Prior period costs attached to units in beginning inventory are not included in these computations because the FIFO costing method uses separate costing analyses for each accounting period. (The FIFO method treats the costs of beginning inventory separately, in Step 5.) Exhibit 1 shows that the total current cost of $8.90 per equivalent unit consists of $3.30 per equivalent unit for direct materials costs ($189,750 ÷ 57,500 equivalent units) plus $5.60 per equivalent unit for conversion costs ($320,488 ÷ 57,230 equivalent units). (Note that the equivalent units are taken from Step 2 of Exhibit 1.)

Assigning Costs

KEY POINT: All costs must be accounted for, including costs from both beginning inventory and costs incurred during the current period. All costs must be assigned to either ending inventory or the goods transferred out.

Step 5 in the preparation of a process costing report uses information from Steps 2 and 4 to assigns costs, as shown in Exhibit 1. This final step determines the costs that are transferred out either to the next production process, department, or work cell or to the Finished Goods Inventory account (i.e., the cost of goods manufactured), as well as the costs that remain in the ending balance in the Work in Process Inventory account. The total costs assigned to units completed and transferred out and to ending inventory must equal the total costs in Step 3.

■ **COST OF GOODS MANUFACTURED AND TRANSFERRED OUT** Step 5 of Exhibit 1 shows that the costs transferred to the Finished Goods Inventory account include the $41,540 in direct materials and conversion costs for completing the 6,200 units in beginning inventory. Step 2 in the exhibit shows that 2,480 equivalent units of conversion costs were required to complete these 6,200 units. Because the equivalent unit conversion cost for February is $5.60, the cost to complete the units carried over from January is $13,888 (2,480 units × $5.60).

FOCUS ON INTERNATIONAL BUSINESS

How Do Businesses Today Handle the Costs of Scrap and Rework?

Traditional product costing approaches, which trace actual costs incurred to products produced, were developed at a time when businesses believed it was efficient to anticipate scrap and rework. The costs of machine and worker downtime were part of the product cost, and significant amounts of managerial time and dollars were spent tracking those costs and analyzing differences between actual and budgeted costs.

Businesses worldwide no longer tolerate defects in the production process, and the importance of scrap and rework in product costing has therefore diminished. To cost out their products, many managers now use "engineered" costs, which exclude the costs of scrap and rework. Engineered costs are computed by determining the resources needed to manufacture a product and assigning anticipated costs to those resources. All similar products are given the same product cost. Using engineered costs frees managers to focus on nonfinancial measures, such as product throughput time and costs of quality, rather than on traditional cost-based measures that tolerate scrap and rework.

Focus on Business Technology

Does Technology Make a Difference?
Managers at Intel Corporation <www.intel.com> know that one way of minimizing product cost is to improve the ways in which products are developed and manufactured. In order to promote efficiency and effectiveness in these areas and to provide a foundation for future product growth, Intel spends billions of dollars on technological research each year. When scientists in Intel's research and development division make advances in the areas of manufacturing and product development, Intel's managers are quick to apply them to the company's business infrastructure.[3]

Each of the 52,500 units started and completed in February cost $8.90 to produce. Their combined cost of $467,250 is added to the $41,540 and $13,888 of costs required to produce the 6,200 units from beginning inventory to arrive at the total of $522,678 that is transferred to the Finished Goods Inventory account.

■ **ENDING INVENTORY** All costs remaining in Soda Products Company's Work in Process Inventory account after the cost of goods manufactured has been transferred out represent the costs of the drinks still in production at the end of February. As shown in Step 5 of Exhibit 1, the balance of $29,100 in the ending Work in Process Inventory is made up of $16,500 of direct materials costs (5,000 units × $3.30 per unit) and $12,600 of conversion costs (5,000 × 45% × $5.60 per unit).

STUDY NOTE: Rounding product unit costs to even dollars may lead to a significant difference in total costs, giving the impression that costs have been miscalculated. Carry product unit costs to two decimal places where appropriate.

■ **ROUNDING DIFFERENCES** As you perform Step 5 in any process cost report, remember that the total costs in Steps 3 and 5 must always be the same number. In Exhibit 1, for example, they are both $551,778. If the numbers are not the same, first check for omission of any costs and for calculation errors. If that does not solve the problem, check whether any rounding was necessary in computing the costs per equivalent unit in Step 4. If rounding was done in Step 4, rounding differences will occur when assigning costs in Step 5. In that case, adjust the total costs transferred out for any rounding difference so that the total costs in Step 5 equal the total costs in Step 3.

■ **RECAP OF WORK IN PROCESS INVENTORY ACCOUNT** When the process cost report is complete, an account recap may be prepared to show the effects of the report on the Work in Process Inventory account for the period. Two recaps of Soda Products' Work in Process Inventory account for February—one for costs and one for units—appear at the end of Exhibit 1.

PROCESS COSTING FOR TWO OR MORE PRODUCTION DEPARTMENTS

● **Stop and Think!**
When a company has two or more production processes, departments, or work cells and uses the average costing method, how many Work in Process Inventory accounts must it have?

It must have one Work in Process Inventory account for every process, department, or work cell. ■

Because Soda Products Company has only one production department, it needs only one Work in Process Inventory account. However, a company that has more than one production department must have a Work in Process Inventory account for each department. For instance, a soft drink maker that has a production department for formulation, another for bottling, and another for packaging needs three Work in Process Inventory accounts. When products flow from the Formulation Department to the Bottling Department, their costs flow from the Formulation Department's Work in Process Inventory account to the Bottling Department's Work in Process Inventory account. The costs transferred into the Bottling Department's Work in Process Inventory account are treated in the same way as the cost of direct materials added at the beginning of the production process. When production flows to the Packaging Department, the accumulated costs (incurred in the two previous departments) are transferred to that department's Work in Process Inventory account. At the end of the accounting period, a separate process cost report is prepared for each department.

✓ Check out ACE for a Review Quiz at http://accounting.college.hmco.com/students.

Preparing a Process Cost Report Using the Average Costing Method

LO6 Prepare a process cost report using the average costing method.

RELATED TEXT ASSIGNMENTS
Q: 18
SE: 7, 8, 9
E: 10, 11, 12, 13, 14
P: 5, 6, 8
MRA: 4

When a process cost report uses the average costing method, cost flows do not follow the logical physical flow of production as they do when the FIFO method is used. Instead, the costs in beginning inventory are averaged with current period costs to compute the product unit costs. A process cost report that uses the average costing method includes the same five steps as the FIFO method, but the procedures for completing the steps differ. We now return to the example of Soda Products Company, but this time we assume that Soda Products uses the average costing method of process costing.

Accounting for Units

Step 1 of a process cost report, which accounts for the physical units in a production process, department, or work cell during an accounting period, is identical for the average costing and FIFO costing methods. The physical units in beginning inventory are added to the physical units started during the period to arrive at "units to be accounted for." In Step 1 of Exhibit 2, Soda Products' department manager computes the 63,700 total units to be accounted for by adding the 6,200 units in beginning inventory to the 57,500 units started into production in this period.

Step 2 also accounts for production during the period in terms of units. After the number of units completed and transferred to finished goods inventory and the number of units in ending inventory have been added to arrive at "units accounted for," the equivalent units in terms of direct materials and conversion costs are computed, as described below.

■ **Units Completed and Transferred Out** As you can see in Exhibit 2, the average costing method treats both the direct materials costs and conversion costs of the 58,700 units completed in February (6,200 units from beginning inventory + 52,500 started this period) as if they were incurred in the current period. Thus, the full amount of 58,700 is entered as the equivalent units for these costs. In contrast, as shown in Exhibit 1, the FIFO costing method disregards the previous period costs of units started in the last period and calculates only the equivalent units required to complete the units in beginning inventory in the current period.

■ **Ending Inventory** The average costing method treats ending inventory in exactly the same way as the FIFO costing method. Because all direct materials are added at the beginning of the production process, the full amount of 5,000 is entered as the equivalent units for direct materials cost. Because the 5,000 units in ending inventory are only 45 percent complete in terms of conversion costs, the amount of equivalent units is 2,250 (45% × 5,000).

■ **Totals** Whether the FIFO costing or average costing method is used, Step 2 in a process costing report is completed by summing all the physical units to be accounted for, all equivalent units for direct materials costs, and all equivalent units for conversion costs. Exhibit 2 shows that for the month of February, Soda Products accounted for 63,700 physical units. Equivalent units for direct materials costs totaled 63,700, and equivalent units for conversion costs totaled 60,950.

Accounting for Costs

As we noted in our discussion of process costs reports that use the FIFO method, Step 3 of the report accumulates and analyzes all costs in the Work in Process Inventory account, and Step 4 computes the cost per equivalent unit for direct

EXHIBIT 2
Process Cost Report: Average Costing Method

Step 1:
Account for physical units.

Beginning inventory (units started last period)	6,200
Units started this period	57,500
Units to be accounted for	63,700

Step 2:
Account for equivalent units.

		Direct Materials Costs	% Incurred During Period	Conversion Costs	% Incurred During Period
Units completed and transferred out	58,700	58,700	100%	58,700	100%
Ending inventory (units started but not completed this period)	5,000	5,000	100%	2,250	45%
Units accounted for	63,700	63,700		60,950	

Step 3:
Account for costs.

	Total Costs		Direct Materials		Conversion
Beginning inventory	$ 41,540	=	$ 20,150	+	$ 21,390
Current costs	510,238	=	189,750	+	$320,488
Total costs	$551,778		$209,900		341,878

Step 4:
Compute cost per equivalent unit.

Total Costs			$209,900		$341,878
Equivalent Units			63,700		60,950
Cost per equivalent unit	$8.91	=	$3.30*	+	$5.61*
			*Rounded to nearest cent		*Rounded to nearest cent

Step 5:
Assign costs to cost of goods manufactured and ending inventory.

Cost of goods manufactured and transferred out	$522,655	= (58,700 × $3.30) +	(58,700 × $5.61)	
		(Less rounding, $362)		
Ending inventory	29,123	= (5,000 × $3.30) +	(2,250 × $5.61)	
Total costs	$551,778*			

*Rounded.

Work in Process Inventory Account: Cost Recap

Beg. Bal.	$ 41,540	$522,655 (cost of goods manufactured and transferred out)
Direct Materials	$189,750	
Conversion Costs	$320,488	
End. Bal.	$ 29,123	

Work in Process Inventory Account: Cost Recap

Beg. Bal.	6,200	58,700 units goods transferred out
Direct Materials and Conversion Costs	57,500	
End. Bal.	5,000	

> **STOP AND THINK!**
> In Step 4, how do the average costing and FIFO costing methods differ in computing the cost per equivalent unit for direct materials costs and conversion costs?
>
> *While the FIFO costing method considers only current costs and effort in Step 4, the average costing method includes all costs and effort incurred both in the current period and from prior periods.* ∎

materials costs and conversion costs. You may recall from that discussion that the costs of Soda Products' beginning inventory were $20,150 for direct materials and $21,390 for conversion. Current period costs were $189,750 for direct materials and $320,488 for conversion.

If you compare Exhibit 2 with Exhibit 1, you will see that the average costing and FIFO costing methods deal with Step 3 in the same manner. All direct materials costs and conversion costs for beginning inventory and the current period are accumulated in the "Total Costs" column. The total of $551,778 consists of $209,900 in direct materials costs and $341,878 in conversion costs.

Step 4 computes the cost per equivalent unit for direct materials costs and conversion costs by dividing the total of these costs by their respective equivalent units. The $8.91 total cost per equivalent unit consists of $3.30 per equivalent unit for direct materials ($209,900 ÷ 63,700 equivalent units) plus $5.61 per equivalent unit for conversion ($341,878 ÷ 60,950 equivalent units). Notice that the cost per equivalent unit for both direct materials and conversion costs has been rounded to the nearest cent. In this text, any rounding differences are assigned to the units transferred out in Step 5. Notice also that the average costing and FIFO costing methods use different numerators and denominators in Step 4. Average costing divides *total* cost by *total* equivalent units, whereas FIFO divides *current* costs by *current* equivalent units.

ASSIGNING COSTS

Using information from Steps 2 and 4, Step 5 of a process cost report assigns direct materials and conversion costs to the units transferred out and to the units still in process at the end of the period. As noted above, any rounding issues that arise in completing Step 5 are included in units completed and transferred out. Soda Products completes Step 5 as described below.

■ **COST OF GOODS MANUFACTURED AND TRANSFERRED OUT** As shown in Exhibit 2, the costs of the units completed and transferred out are assigned by multiplying the equivalent units for direct materials and conversion (accounted for in Step 2) by their respective cost per equivalent unit (computed in Step 4) and then totaling these assigned values. Thus, the $522,655 assigned to cost of goods manufactured and transferred out includes $193,710 of direct materials costs (58,700 equivalent units × $3.30 cost per equivalent unit) plus $329,307 of conversion costs (58,700 equivalent units × $5.61 cost per equivalent unit). In this case, because the costs per equivalent unit were rounded in Step 4, a rounding difference of $362 has been deducted from the total cost. The $522,655 of transferred costs will go either to the next department's Work in Process Inventory account or to the Finished Goods Inventory account if the goods are ready for sale.

■ **ENDING INVENTORY** The costs of the units in ending work in process inventory are assigned in the same way as the costs of cost of goods manufactured and transferred out. As you can see in Exhibit 2, the total of $29,123 assigned to ending inventory includes $16,500 of direct materials costs (5,000 equivalent units × $3.30 cost per equivalent unit) plus $12,623 of conversion costs (2,250 equivalent units × $5.61 cost per equivalent unit). The $29,123 (rounded) will appear as the ending balance in this department's Work in Process Inventory account.

■ **ROUNDING DIFFERENCES** Because the costs per equivalent unit computed in Step 4 were rounded to the nearest cent, rounding differences occurred when costs were assigned in Step 5. Thus, in Step 5, a $362 deduction was made to cost of goods manufactured and transferred out so that total costs in Step 5 would equal the total costs in Step 3.

■ **RECAP OF WORK IN PROCESS ACCOUNT** As we noted earlier, when a process cost report is complete, an account recap may be prepared to show the effects of the report on the Work in Process Inventory account for the period. Exhibit 2 includes a cost recap and a unit recap of Soda Products' Work in Process Inventory account for February.

 Check out ACE for a Review Quiz at http://accounting.college.hmco.com/students.

USING INFORMATION ABOUT PRODUCT COST TO EVALUATE PERFORMANCE

LO7 Evaluate operating performance using information about product cost.

RELATED TEXT ASSIGNMENTS
Q: 19, 20
SE: 10
E: 15
SD: 5
MRA: 4

STUDY NOTE: Performance measures are quantitative tools that help managers assess the performance of a specific process or expected outcome.

● **STOP AND THINK!**
How can information about product costs help managers evaulate operating performance?
By analyzing the information from a job order or process costing system, managers can compare budgeted and actual costs for a process, department, or work cell. They can also track units produced per period and monitor labor and materials costs to evaluate operating performance. ■

A product costing system—whether it's a job order or a process costing system—provides managers with valuable information. As we have noted, managers use the information that such a system provides in determining a product's price and in computing the balances in the Materials Inventory, Work in Process Inventory, and Finished Goods Inventory accounts on the balance sheet and the Cost of Goods Sold account on the income statement. Managers also use product cost information to evaluate operating performance. Such an analysis may include consideration of the following:

- Cost trends of a product or product line
- Units produced per time period
- Materials usage per unit produced
- Labor cost per unit produced
- Special needs of customers
- Cost-effectiveness of changing to a more advanced production process

Cost trends can be developed from product cost data over several time periods. Such trends help managers identify areas of rising costs or areas in which cost-effectiveness has improved. Tracking units produced per time period, a figure easily pulled from a product cost analysis, can help managers evaluate operating efficiency.

Direct materials and labor costs are significant parts of a product's cost and should be monitored constantly. Trends in direct materials usage and labor costs per unit produced can help managers determine optimal resource usage.

Anticipating customers' needs is very important to managers. By tracking the size, cost, and type of products ordered by customers, managers can see which customers are increasing or reducing their orders and take action to improve customer relations.

Finally, decisions to purchase new machinery and equipment are often based on the savings that the change is expected to produce. Information from a product costing system helps managers make such decisions in that it enables them to estimate unit costs for the new equipment and to compare them with cost trends for the existing equipment.

Check out ACE for a Review Quiz at http://accounting.college.hmco.com/students.

Chapter Review

REVIEW OF LEARNING OBJECTIVES

LO1 Describe the process costing system, identify the reasons for its use, and discuss its role in the management cycle.

A process costing system is a product costing system used by companies that produce large amounts of similar products or liquid products or that have long, continuous production runs of identical products. Because these companies have a continuous production flow, it would be impractical for them to use a job order costing system, which tracks costs to a specific batch of products or a specific job order. In contrast to a job order costing system, a process costing system accumulates the costs of direct materials, direct labor, and manufacturing overhead for each process, department, or work cell and assigns those costs to the products as they are produced during a particular period.

The product costs provided by a process costing system play a key role in the management cycle. During the planning stage of the cycle, managers use past and projected information about product costs to set selling prices and prepare budgets. During the executing stage, actual costs are incurred as units are produced, so actual unit costs can be computed. In the reviewing stage, managers evaluate performance by comparing targeted costs with actual costs. In the reporting stage, they use actual units produced and costs incurred to value inventory on the balance sheet and cost of goods sold on the income statement.

LO2 Relate the patterns of product flows to the cost flow methods in a process costing environment.

During production in a process costing environment, products flow in a first-in, first-out (FIFO) fashion through several processes, departments, or work cells. As they do, the process costing system accumulates their costs, and passes them on to the next process, department, or work cell. At the end of every accounting period, the system generates a report that assigns the costs that have accumulated during the period to the units that have transferred out of the process, department, or work cell and to the units that are still work in process. The process cost report may assign costs by using the FIFO costing method—in which the costs assigned to the first materials processed are the first costs transferred out when those materials flow to the next process, department, work cell—or the average costing method, which assigns an average cost to all products made during an accounting period.

LO3 Explain the role of the Work in Process Inventory accounts in a process costing system.

The Work in Process Inventory accounts are the focal point of a process costing system. Each production process, department, or work cell has its own Work in Process Inventory account. All costs charged to that process, department, or work cell flow into its Work in Process Inventory account. A process cost report prepared at the end of every accounting period assigns the costs that have accumulated during the period to the units that have flowed out of the process, department, or work cell (the cost of goods transferred out) and to the units that are still in process (the cost of ending inventory).

LO4 Define *equivalent production* and compute equivalent units.

Equivalent production is a measure that applies a percentage-of-completion factor to partially completed units to compute the equivalent number of whole units produced in an accounting period for each type of input. Equivalent units are computed from (1) units in the beginning work in process inventory and their percentage of completion, (2) units started and completed during the period, and (3) units in the ending work in process inventory and their percentage of completion. The computation of equivalent units differs depending on whether the FIFO method or the average costing method is used.

LO5 Prepare a process cost report using the FIFO costing method.

In a process cost report that uses the FIFO costing method, the cost flow follows the logical physical flow of production—that is, the costs assigned to the first materials processed are the first costs transferred when those materials flow to the next process, department, or work cell. Preparation of a process cost report involves five steps. Steps 1 and 2 account for the physical flow of products and compute the equivalent units of production. Once equivalent production has been determined, the focus of the report shifts to accounting for costs. In Step 3, all direct materials and conversion costs for the current period are added to arrive at total costs. In Step 4, the cost per equivalent unit for both direct materials and conversion costs is found by dividing those costs by their respective equivalent units. In Step 5, costs are assigned to the units completed and transferred out during the period, as well as to the ending work in process inventory. The costs assigned to units completed and transferred out include the costs incurred in the preceding period and the conversion costs needed to complete those units during the current period. That amount is added to the total cost of producing all units started and completed during the period. The result is the total cost transferred out for the units completed during the period. Step 5 also assigns costs to units still in process at the end of the period by multiplying their direct materials and conversion costs by their respective equivalent units. The total equals the balance in the Work in Process Inventory account at the end of the period.

LO6 Prepare a process cost report using the average costing method.

The average costing method is an alternative method of accounting for production costs in a manufacturing environment characterized by a continuous production flow. The difference between a process costing report that uses the FIFO method and one that use the average costing method is that the latter does not differentiate about when work was done on inventory. When the average costing method is used, the costs in beginning inventory are averaged with current period costs to compute the product unit costs. These costs are used to value the ending balance in Work in Process Inventory and the goods completed and transferred out of the process, department, or work cell.

LO7 Evaluate operating performance using information about product cost.

Both the job order and process costing systems supply information that managers can use to evaluate operating performance. Such an analysis may include consideration of the cost trends of a product or product line, units produced per time period, materials usage per unit produced, labor cost per unit produced, special needs of customers, and the cost-effectiveness of changing to a more advanced production process.

REVIEW OF CONCEPTS AND TERMINOLOGY

The following concepts and terms were introduced in this chapter:

LO2 **Average costing method:** A process costing method that assigns an average cost to all products made during an accounting period.

LO4 **Conversion costs:** The combined costs of direct labor and manufacturing overhead.

LO4 **Equivalent production:** A measure that applies a percentage-of-completion factor to partially completed units to compute the equivalent number of whole units produced in an accounting period for each type of input. Also called *equivalent units*.

LO2 **FIFO costing method:** A process costing method in which the cost flow follows the actual flow of production, so that the costs assigned to the first materials processed are the first costs transferred out when those materials flow to the next process, department, or work cell.

LO1 **Process costing system:** A product costing system that traces the costs of direct materials, direct labor, and manufacturing overhead to processes, departments, or work cells and then assigns the costs to the products manufactured by them; used by companies that produce large amounts of similar products or liquid products or that have long, continuous production runs of identical products.

LO5 **Process cost report:** A report that managers use to track and analyze costs in a process costing system.

REVIEW PROBLEM

Process Costing Using the FIFO Costing and Average Costing Methods

LO4
LO5
LO6

Pop Chewing Gum Company produces several flavors of bubble gum. Two basic direct materials, gum base and flavored sweetener, are blended at the beginning of the manufacturing process. No materials are lost in the process, so one kilogram of materials input produces one kilogram of bubble gum. Direct labor and manufacturing overhead costs are incurred uniformly throughout the blending process. On June 30, 20x4, 16,000 units were in process. All direct materials had been added, but the units were only 70 percent complete in regard to conversion costs. Direct materials costs of $8,100 and conversion costs of $11,800 were attached to the beginning inventory. During July, 135,000 kilograms of gum base and 270,000 kilograms of flavored sweetener were used at costs of $122,500 and $80,000, respectively. Direct labor charges were $299,200, and manufacturing overhead costs applied during July were $284,000. The ending work in process inventory was 21,600 kilograms. All direct materials have been added to those units, and 25 percent of the conversion costs have been assigned. Output from the Blending Department is transferred to the Packaging Department.

REQUIRED
1. Prepare a process cost report using the FIFO costing method for the Blending Department for July.
2. Identify the amount that should be transferred out of the Work in Process Inventory account, and state where those dollars should be transferred.

3. Repeat **1** using the average costing method.
4. Repeat **2** using the average costing method.

ANSWER TO REVIEW PROBLEM

1. Process cost report using the FIFO costing method:

Pop Chewing Gum Company
Blending Department
Process Cost Report: FIFO Method
For the Month Ended July 31, 20x4

Step 1:
Account for physical units.

Beginning inventory (units started last period)	16,000	
Units started this period	405,000	
Units to be accounted for	421,000	

Step 2:
Account for equivalent units.

		Direct Materials Costs	% Incurred During Period	Conversion Costs	% Incurred During Period
Beginning inventory (units completed this period)	16,000	0	0%	4,800	30%
Units started and completed this period	383,400	383,400	100%	383,400	100%
Ending inventory (units started but not completed this period)	21,600	21,600	100%	5,400	25%
Units accounted for	421,000	405,000		393,600	

Step 3:
Account for costs.

	Total Costs		Direct Costs		
Beginning inventory	$ 19,900	=	$ 8,100	+	$ 11,800
Current costs	785,700	=	$202,500	+	$583,200
Total costs	$805,600				

Step 4:
Compute cost per equivalent unit.

Current Costs		$202,500		$583,200
Equivalent Units		405,000		393,600
Cost per equivalent unit	$1.98 =	$ .50	+	$ 1.48*

*Rounded to nearest cent

Step 5:
Assign costs to cost of goods manufactured and ending inventory.

Cost of goods manufactured and transferred out:

From beginning inventory	$19,900				
Current costs to complete	7,104	=	0	+	(4,800 × $1.48)
Units started and completed this period	759,132	=	(383,400 × $.50)	+	(383,400 × $1.48)
Cost of goods manufactured	$786,808				
			(Add rounding, $672)		
Ending inventory	18,792	=	(21,600 × $.50)	+	(5,400 × $1.48)
Total costs	$805,600				

(continued)

Work in Process Inventory Account: Cost Recap			Work in Process Inventory Account: Unit Recap		
Beg. Bal.	$ 19,900	$786,808 (cost of goods manufactured and transferred out)	Beg. Bal.	16,000	399,400 (FIFO units transferred out from the 16,000 in beginning inventory plus the 383,400 started and completed)
Direct Materials	$202,500		Direct Materials and Conversion Costs		
Conversion Costs	$583,200			405,000	
End. Bal.	$18,792		End. Bal.	21,600	

2. The amount of $786,808 should be transferred to the Work in Process Inventory account of the Packaging Department.
3. Process cost report using the average costing method:

Pop Chewing Gum Company
Blending Department
Process Cost Report: Average Costing Method
For the Month Ended July 31, 20x4

Step 1:
Account for physical units.

Beginning inventory:
  units started last period   16,000
Units started this period   405,000
Units to be accounted for   421,000

Step 2:
Account for equivalent units.

			Direct Materials Costs	% Incurred During Period	Conversion Costs	% Incurred During Period
Units completed and transferred out		399,400	399,400	100%	399,400	100%
Ending inventory: units started but not completed this period		21,600	21,600	100%	5,400	25%
Units accounted for		421,000	421,000		404,800	

Step 3:
Account for costs.

	Total Costs				
Beginning inventory	$ 19,900	=	$ 8,100	+	$ 11,800
Current costs	785,700	=	202,500	+	583,200
Total costs	$805,600		$210,600		$595,000

Step 4:
Compute cost per equivalent unit.

Total Costs		$210,600 ←		$595,000 ←
Equivalent Units		421,000 ←		404,800 ←
Cost per equivalent unit	$1.97 =	$.50*	+	$1.47*
		*Rounded to nearest cent		*Rounded to nearest cent

Step 5:
Assign costs to cost of goods manufactured and ending inventory.

Cost of goods manufactured and transferred out:	$786,862	= (399,400 × $.50) + (399,400 × $1.47)
		(Add rounding, $44)
Ending inventory	18,738	= (21,600 × $.50) + (5,400 × $1.47)
Total costs	$805,600	

(continued)

Work in Process Inventory Account: Cost Recap			Work in Process Inventory Account: Cost Recap		
Beg. Bal.	19,900	$786,862 (cost of goods manufactured and transferred out)	Beg. Bal.	16,000	399,400 units goods transferred out
Direct materials	202,500		Direct materials and		
Conversion costs	583,200		Conversion costs	405,000	
End. Bal.	18,738		End. Bal.	21,600	

4. The amount of $786,862 should be transferred to the Work in Process Inventory account of the Packaging Department.

Chapter Assignments

BUILDING YOUR KNOWLEDGE FOUNDATION

QUESTIONS

1. What is a process costing system?
2. What types of companies are likely to use a process costing system?
3. How is information about process costs used during the four stages of the management cycle?
4. What two methods are used to assign costs to products in a process costing system?
5. Explain the FIFO costing method of assigning costs to products in a process costing system.
6. Explain the similarity between the job order costing system and the process costing system in accounting for the costs of direct materials, direct labor, and manufacturing overhead.
7. Explain the difference between the job order costing system and the process costing system in assigning costs to products.
8. "In job order costing, only one Work in Process Inventory account is used for all jobs processed. In process costing, several Work in Process Inventory accounts are used." Explain these statements. Why does process costing require multiple Work in Process Inventory accounts?
9. Define *equivalent production* (also called *equivalent units*).
10. Why must actual unit data be changed to equivalent unit data to cost products in a process costing system?
11. Define *conversion costs*. Why does a process costing system compute conversion costs?
12. Why do you think it would be easier to compute equivalent units without units in beginning inventory than with units in beginning inventory?
13. What five steps does a process cost report entail?
14. What are the purposes of accounting for costs in a process cost report?
15. What two important dollar amounts come from the assignment of costs in Step 5 of a process cost report? How do they relate to the year-end financial statements?
16. Describe how to check the accuracy of the results of assigning costs in Step 5 of a process cost report.
17. Compare the process costing system of a company that has only one production department with the process costing system of a company that has two or more production departments.

18. Briefly describe the similarities and differences in process cost reports that use the FIFO and average costing methods.
19. Explain the average costing method of assigning costs to products in a process costing system.
20. What type of operating performance can be evaluated with the information that a product costing system provides about (a) units produced per time period, (b) labor cost per unit produced, and (c) special needs of customers?

SHORT EXERCISES

LO1 **Process Costing Versus Job Order Costing**

SE 1. Indicate whether the manufacturer of each of the following products should use a job order costing system or a process costing system to accumulate product costs:
1. Plastics
2. Ocean cruise ships
3. Cereal
4. Medical drugs for veterinary practices

LO1 **Process Costing Versus Job Order Costing**

SE 2. Indicate whether each of the following is a characteristic of job order costing or of process costing:
1. Several Work in Process Inventory accounts are used, one for each department or work cell in the process.
2. Costs are grouped by process, department, or work cell.
3. Costs are measured for each completed job.
4. Only one Work in Process Inventory account is used.
5. Costs are measured in terms of units completed in specific time periods.
6. Costs are assigned to specific jobs or batches of product.

LO3 **Process Costing and a Work In Process Inventory Account**

SE 3. Prue Chemical uses an automated mixing machine in its Mixing Department to combine three raw materials into a product called Triogo. On the average, each unit of Triogo contains $3 of Material X, $6 of Material Y, $9 of Material Z, $2 of direct labor, and $12 of manufacturing overhead. Total costs charged to the Mixing Department's Work in Process Inventory account during the month were $208,000. There were no units in beginning or ending work in process inventory. How many units were completed and transferred to Finished Goods Inventory during the month?

LO4 **Equivalent Production: FIFO Costing Method**

SE 4. Blue Blaze adds direct materials at the beginning of its production process and adds conversion costs uniformly throughout the process. Given the following information from Blue Blaze's records for July 20x7 and using Steps 1 and 2 of the FIFO costing method, compute the equivalent units of production:

Units in beginning inventory	3,000
Units started during the period	17,000
Units partially completed	2,500
Percentage of completion of ending work in process inventory	70%
Percentage of completion of beginning inventory	100% for direct materials; 40% for conversion costs

LO5 **Determining Unit Cost: FIFO Costing Method**

SE 5. Using the information from SE 4 and the following data, compute the total cost per equivalent unit:

	Costs for the Period	Beginning Work in Process
Direct materials costs	$20,400	$7,600
Conversion costs	32,490	2,545

LO5 **Assigning Costs: FIFO Costing Method**

SE 6. Using the data in SE 4 and SE 5, assign costs to the units transferred out and to the units in ending inventory for July 20x7.

LO6 **Equivalent Production: Average Costing Method**

SE 7. Using the same data as in SE 4 but Steps 1 and 2 of the average costing method, compute the equivalent units of production for the month.

LO6 **Determining Unit Cost: Average Costing Method**

SE 8. Using the average costing method and the information from SE 4 and SE 7, compute the total cost per equivalent unit.

LO6 Assigning Costs: Average Costing Method

SE 9. Using the data in **SE 4**, **SE 7**, and **SE 8** and assuming that Blue Blaze uses the average costing method, assign costs to the units completed and transferred out and to the units in ending inventory for July 20x7.

LO7 Measuring Performance with Product Costing Data

SE 10. The following table presents the weekly average of direct materials costs per unit for two products. How could the manager of the department that makes these products use this information?

Week	Product A	Product B
1	$45.20	$23.90
2	46.10	23.80
3	48.30	23.80
4	49.60	23.60

EXERCISES

LO1 Process Costing Versus Job Order Costing

E 1. Indicate whether the manufacturer of each of the following products should use a job order costing system or a process costing system to accumulate product costs:
1. Paint
2. Fruit juices
3. Tailor-made suits
4. Milk
5. Coffee cups printed with your school insignia
6. Paper
7. Roller coaster for a theme park
8. Posters for a fundraising event

LO2 Use of Process Costing Information

E 2. Tom's Bakery makes a variety of cakes, cookies, and pies for distribution to five major chains of grocery stores in the Quad-City area. The company uses a standard manufacturing process for all items except special-order cakes. It currently uses a process costing system. Tom, the owner of the company, has some urgent questions, which are listed below. Which of these questions can be answered using information from a process costing system? Which can be best answered using information from a job order costing system? Explain your answers.

1. How much does it cost to make one chocolate cheesecake?
2. Did the cost of making special-order cakes exceed the cost budgeted for this month?
3. What is the value of the pie inventory at the end of June?
4. What were the costs of the cookies sold during June?
5. At what price should Tom's Bakery sell its famous brownies to the grocery store chains?
6. Were the planned production costs of $3,000 for making pies in June exceeded?

LO3 Work in Process Inventory Accounts in Process Costing Systems

E 3. Gilbert, Inc., which uses a process costing system, makes a chemical used as a food preservative. The manufacturing process involves Departments A and B. The company had the following total costs and unit costs for completed production last month, when it manufactured 10,000 pounds of the chemical. Neither Department A nor Department B had any beginning or ending work in process inventories.

	Total Cost	Unit Cost
Department A		
Direct materials	$10,000	$1.00
Direct labor	2,600	.26
Manufacturing overhead	1,300	.13
Total costs	$13,900	$1.39
Department B		
Direct materials	$ 3,000	$ .30
Direct labor	700	.07
Manufacturing overhead	1,000	.10
Total costs	$ 4,700	$ .47
Totals	$18,600	$1.86

1. How many Work in Process Inventory accounts would Gilbert use?
2. What dollar amount of the chemical's production cost was transferred from Department A to Department B last month?
3. What dollar amount was transferred from Department B to the Finished Goods Inventory account?
4. What dollar amount is useful in determining a selling price for one pound of the chemical?

E 4.
LO4 Equivalent Production: FIFO Costing Method

McCabe Stone Company produces bricks. Though the company has been in operation for only twelve months, it already enjoys a good reputation. During its first year, it put 600,000 bricks into production and completed and transferred 586,000 bricks to finished goods inventory. The remaining bricks were still in process at the end of the year and were 60 percent complete. The company's process costing system adds all direct materials costs at the beginning of the process; conversion costs are incurred uniformly throughout the production process. From this information, compute the equivalent units of production for direct materials and conversion costs for the company's first year, which ended December 31, 20x7. Use the FIFO costing approach.

E 5.
LO4 Equivalent Production: FIFO Costing Method

Olivares Enterprises makes Rainberry Shampoo for professional hair stylists. On July 31, 20x5, it had 5,200 liters of shampoo in process, which were 80 percent complete in regard to conversion costs and 100 percent complete in regard to direct materials costs. During August, it put 212,500 liters of direct materials into production. Data for work in process inventory on August 31, 20x5, were as follows: shampoo, 4,500 liters; stage of completion, 60 percent for conversion costs and 100 percent for direct materials.

From this information, compute the equivalent units of production for direct materials and conversion costs for the month. Use the FIFO costing approach.

E 6.
LO4 Equivalent Production: FIFO Costing Method

Cunningham Paper Corporation produces wood pulp that is used in making paper. The following data pertain to the company's production of pulp during September:

		Percentage Complete	
	Tons	Direct Materials	Conversion Costs
Work in process, Aug. 31	40,000	100%	60%
Placed into production	250,000	—	—
Work in process, Sept. 30	80,000	100%	40%

Compute the equivalent units of production for direct materials and conversion costs for September using the FIFO costing method.

E 7.
LO5 Work in Process Inventory Accounts: Total Unit Cost

Scientists at Anschultz Laboratories, Inc., have just perfected Dentalite, a liquid substance that dissolves tooth decay. The substance, which is generated by a complex process involving five departments, is very expensive. Cost and equivalent unit data for the latest week are as follows (units are in ounces):

	Direct Materials Costs		Conversion Costs	
Dept.	Dollars	Equivalent Units	Dollars	Equivalent Units
A	$12,000	1,000	$33,825	2,050
B	21,835	1,985	13,065	1,005
C	23,896	1,030	20,972	2,140
D	—	—	22,086	2,045
E	—	—	15,171	1,945

From these data, compute the unit cost for each department and the total unit cost of producing one ounce of Dentalite.

E 8.
LO5 Determining Unit Cost: FIFO Costing Method

Turner's Pots, Inc., manufactures sets of heavy-duty cookware. It has just completed production for August 20x8. At the beginning of August, its Work in Process Inventory account showed direct materials costs of $31,700 and conversion costs of $29,400. The cost of direct materials used in August was $275,373; conversion costs were $175,068. During the month, the company started and completed 15,190 sets. For August, a total of 16,450 equivalent sets for direct materials and 16,210 equivalent sets for conversion costs have been computed.

From this information, determine the cost per equivalent set for August. Use the FIFO costing method.

E 9.
LO5 Assigning Costs: FIFO Costing Method

The Beach Bakery produces Healthnut coffee bread. It uses a process costing system. In March 20x9, its beginning inventory was 450 units, which were 100 percent complete for direct materials costs and 10 percent complete for conversion costs. The cost of beginning inventory was $655. Units started and completed during the month totaled 14,200. Ending inventory was 410 units, which were 100 percent complete for direct materials costs and 70 percent complete for conversion costs. Costs per equivalent unit for March were $1.40 for direct materials costs and $.80 for conversion costs.

From this information, compute the cost of goods transferred to the Finished Goods Inventory account, the cost remaining in the Work in Process Inventory account, and the total costs to be accounted for. Use the FIFO costing method.

E 10.
LO6 Equivalent Production: Average Costing Method

Using the data in **E 4** and assuming that the company uses the average costing method, compute the equivalent units of production for direct materials and conversion costs for the year ended December 31, 20x7.

E 11.
LO6 Equivalent Production: Average Costing Method

Using the data in **E 5** and assuming that the company uses the average costing method, compute the equivalent units of production for direct materials and conversion for August 20x5.

E 12.
LO6 Equivalent Production: Average Costing Method

Using the data in **E 6** and assuming that the company uses the average costing method, compute the equivalent units of production for direct materials and conversion for September.

E 13.
LO6 Determining Unit Cost: Average Costing Method

Using the data in **E 8** and the average costing method, determine the cost per equivalent set for August. Assume equivalent sets are 16,900 for direct materials and 17,039 for conversion.

E 14.
LO6 Process Cost Report: Average Costing Method

Toy Country Corporation produces children's toys using a liquid plastic formula and a continuous production process. In the company's work cell, the plastic is heated and fed into a molding machine. The molded toys are then cooled and trimmed and sent to the packaging work cell. All direct materials are added at the beginning of the process. In November, the beginning work in process inventory was 420 units, which were 40 percent complete; the ending balance was 400 units, which were 70 percent complete.

During November, 15,000 units were started into production. The Work in Process Inventory account had a beginning balance of $937 for direct materials costs and $370 for conversion costs. In the course of the month, $35,300 of direct materials were added to the process, and $31,760 of conversion costs were assigned to the work cell. Using the average costing method, prepare a process cost report that computes the equivalent units for November, the product unit cost for the toys, and the ending balance in the Work in Process Inventory account.

E 15.
LO7 Measuring Performance with Nonfinancial Product Data

During December, Carola Products Company conducted a study of the productivity of its metal-trimming operation, which requires the use of three machines. The data were condensed into product units per hour so that managers could analyze the productivity of the three workers who operate the machines. The target output established for the year was 125 units per hour. From the following data, analyze the productivity of the three machine operators:

Week	Operator 1	Operator 2	Operator 3
1	119 per hour	129 per hour	124 per hour
2	120 per hour	127 per hour	124 per hour
3	122 per hour	125 per hour	123 per hour
4	124 per hour	122 per hour	124 per hour

Problems

P 1.
LO4 Process Costing: FIFO Costing
LO5 Method

Lightning Industries specializes in making Flash, a high-moisture, low-alkaline wax used to protect and preserve skis. The company began producing a new, improved brand of Flash on January 1, 20x5. Materials A-14 and C-9 and a wax base are introduced at the beginning of the production process. During January, 640 pounds of A-14, 1,860 pounds of C-9, and 12,800 pounds of wax base were used at costs of $15,300, $29,070, and $2,295, respectively. Direct labor of $17,136 and manufacturing overhead costs of $25,704 were incurred uniformly throughout the month. By January 31, 13,600 pounds of Flash had been completed and transferred to the finished goods inventory (one pound of input equals one pound of output). Since no spoilage occurred, the leftover materials remained in production and were 40 percent complete on average.

REQUIRED ▶
1. Using the FIFO costing method, prepare a process cost report for January.
2. From the information in the process cost report, identify the amount that should be transferred out of the Work in Process Inventory account, and state where those dollars should be transferred.

P 2.
LO4 **Process Costing: FIFO Costing**
LO5 **Method**

Liquid Extracts Company produces a line of fruit extracts for home use in making wine, jams and jellies, pies, and meat sauces. Fruits enter the production process in pounds; the product emerges in quarts (one pound of input equals one quart of output). On May 31, 20x6, 4,250 units were in process. All direct materials had been added, and the units were 70 percent complete for conversion costs. Direct materials costs of $4,607 and conversion costs of $3,535 were attached to the units in beginning work in process inventory. During June, 61,300 pounds of fruit were added—23,500 pounds of apples costing $20,915, 22,600 pounds of grapes costing $28,153, and 15,200 pounds of bananas costing $22,040. Direct labor for the month totaled $19,760, and overhead costs applied were $31,375. On June 30, 20x6, 3,400 units remained in process. All direct materials for these units had been added, and 50 percent of conversion costs had been incurred.

REQUIRED ▶
1. Using the FIFO costing method, prepare a process cost report for June.
2. From the information in the process cost report, identify the amount that should be transferred out of the Work in Process Inventory account, and state where those dollars should be transferred.

P 3.
LO4 **Process Costing: FIFO Costing**
LO5 **Method**

Canned fruits and vegetables are the main products made by Good Foods, Inc. All direct materials are added at the beginning of the Mixing Department's process. When the ingredients have been mixed, they go to the Cooking Department. There the mixture is heated to 100° Celsius and simmered for 20 minutes. When cooled, the mixture goes to the Canning Department for final processing. Throughout the operations, direct labor and manufacturing overhead costs are incurred uniformly. No direct materials are added in the Cooking Department.

Cost data and other information for the Mixing Department for January 20x8 are as follows:

Production Cost Data	Direct Materials Costs	Conversion Costs
Mixing Department		
Beginning inventory	$ 28,560	$ 5,230
Current period costs	$450,000	$181,200
Work in process inventory		
Beginning inventory		
Mixing Department (40% complete)	5,000 liters	
Ending inventory		
Mixing Department (60% complete)	6,000 liters	
Unit production data		
Units started during January	90,000 liters	
Units transferred out during January	89,000 liters	

Assume that no spoilage or evaporation loss took place during January.

REQUIRED ▶
1. Using the FIFO costing method, prepare a process cost report for the Mixing Department for January.
2. Explain how the analysis for the Cooking Department will differ from the analysis for the Mixing Department.

P 4.
LO4 **Process Costing: One Process**
LO5 **and Two Time Periods—FIFO Costing Method**

Wash Clean Laboratories produces liquid detergents that leave no soap film. All elements are biodegradable. The production process has been automated, so that the product can now be produced in one operation instead of in a series of heating, mixing, and cooling operations. All direct materials are added at the beginning of the process, and conversion costs are incurred uniformly throughout the process. Operating data for July and August 20x8 are as follows:

	July	August
Beginning work in process inventory		
Units (pounds)	2,300	3,050
Direct materials costs	$4,699	?*
Conversion costs	$1,219	?*
Production during the period		
Units started (pounds)	31,500	32,800
Direct materials costs	$65,520	$66,912
Conversion costs	$54,213	$54,774
Ending work in process inventory		
Units (pounds)	3,050	3,600

*From calculations at end of July.

The beginning work in process inventory was 30 percent complete for conversion costs. The ending work in process inventory for July was 60 percent complete; for August, it was 50 percent complete. Assume that the loss from spoilage and evaporation was negligible.

REQUIRED

1. Using the FIFO costing method, prepare a process cost report for July.
2. From the information in the process cost report, identify the amount that should be transferred out of the Work in Process Inventory account, and state where those dollars should be transferred.
3. Repeat 1 and 2 for August.

P 5.
LO6 Process Costing: Average Costing Method

Hurricane Products, Inc., makes high-vitamin, calorie-packed wafers that are popular among professional athletes because they supply quick energy. The company produces the wafers in a continuous flow, and it uses a process costing system based on the average costing method. It recently purchased several automated machines so that the wafers can be produced in a single department. All direct materials are added at the beginning of the process. The costs for the machine operators' labor and production-related overhead are incurred uniformly throughout the process.

In February 20x7, the company put a total of 231,200 liters of direct materials into production at a cost of $294,780. Two liters of direct materials were used to produce one unit of output (one unit = 144 wafers). Direct labor costs for February were $60,530. Manufacturing overhead was $181,590. The beginning work in process inventory for February was 14,000 units, which were 100 percent complete for direct materials and 20 percent complete for conversion costs. The total cost of those units was $55,000, $48,660 of which was assigned to the cost of direct materials. The ending work in process inventory of 12,000 units was fully complete for direct materials but only 30 percent complete for conversion costs.

REQUIRED

1. Using the average costing method and assuming no loss due to spoilage, prepare a process cost report for February.
2. From the information in the process cost report, identify the amount that should be transferred out of the Work in Process Inventory account, and state where those dollars should be transferred.

ALTERNATE PROBLEMS

P 6.
LO4 Process Costing: FIFO Costing
LO5 and Average Costing Methods
LO6

Sunshine Soda Company manufactures and sells several different kinds of soft drinks. Direct materials (sugar syrup and artificial flavor) are added at the beginning of production in the Mixing Department. Direct labor and manufacturing overhead costs are applied to products throughout the process. For August 20x8, beginning inventory for the citrus flavor was 2,400 gallons, 80 percent complete. Ending inventory was 3,600 gallons, 50 percent complete. Production data show 240,000 gallons started during August. A total of 238,800 gallons was completed and transferred to the Bottling Department. Beginning inventory costs were $600 for direct materials and $676 for conversion costs. Current period costs were $57,600 for direct materials and $83,538 for conversion costs.

REQUIRED

1. Using the FIFO costing method, prepare a process cost report for the Mixing Department for August.
2. From the information in the process cost report, identify the amount that should be transferred out of the Work in Process Inventory account, and state where those dollars should be transferred.
3. Repeat 1 and 2 using the average costing method.

LO4 P 7. Process Costing: One Process
LO5 and Two Time Periods—FIFO Costing Method

The Honey Dews Company produces organic honey, which it sells to health food stores and restaurants. The company owns thousands of beehives. No direct materials other than honey are used. The production operation is a simple one. Impure honey is added at the beginning of the process and flows through a series of filterings, leading to a pure finished product. Costs of labor and manufacturing overhead are incurred uniformly throughout the filtering process. Production data for April and May 20x9 are as follows:

	April	May
Beginning work in process inventory		
Units (liters)	7,100	12,400
Direct materials costs	$2,480	?*
Conversion costs	$5,110	?*
Production during the period		
Units started (liters)	288,000	310,000
Direct materials costs	$100,800	$117,800
Conversion costs	$251,550	$277,281
Ending work in process inventory		
Units (liters)	12,400	16,900

*From calculations at end of April.

The beginning work in process inventory for April was 80 percent complete for conversion costs, and ending work in process inventory was 20 percent complete. The ending work in process inventory for May was 30 percent complete for conversion costs. Assume that there was no loss from spoilage or evaporation.

REQUIRED
1. Using the FIFO method, prepare a process cost report for April.
2. From the information in the process cost report, identify the amount that should be transferred out of the Work in Process Inventory account, and state where those dollars should be transferred.
3. Repeat **1** and **2** for May.

LO6 P 8. Process Costing: Average Costing Method

Many of the products made by Wireless Plastics Company are standard replacement parts for telephones that require long production runs and are produced continuously. A unit for Wireless Plastics is a box of parts. During April 20x8, direct materials for 25,250 units were put into production. Total cost of direct materials used during April was $2,273,000. Direct labor costs totaled $1,135,000, and manufacturing overhead was $2,043,000. The beginning work in process inventory contained 1,600 units, which were 100 percent complete for direct materials costs and 60 percent complete for conversion costs. Costs attached to the units in beginning inventory totaled $232,515, which included $143,500 of direct materials costs. At the end of the month, 1,250 units were in ending inventory; all direct materials had been added, and the units were 70 percent complete for conversion costs.

REQUIRED
1. Using the average costing method and assuming no loss due to spoilage, prepare a process cost report for April.
2. From the information in the process cost report, identify the amount that should be transferred out of the Work in Process Inventory account, and state where those dollars should be transferred.

SKILLS DEVELOPMENT CASES

Conceptual Analysis

LO1 SD 1. Concept of Process Costing Systems

For more than 60 years, Dow Chemical Company <www.dow.com> has made and sold a tasteless, odorless, and calorie-free substance called Methocel. When heated, this liquid plastic (methyl cellulose) has the unusual characteristic (for plastics) of becoming a gel that resembles cooked egg whites. It is used in over 400 food products, including gravies, soups, and puddings. It was also used as wampa drool in *The Empire Strikes Back* and dinosaur sneeze in *Jurassic Park*. What kind of costing system is most appropriate for the manufacture of Methocel? Why is that system most appropriate? Describe the system; include in the description a general explanation of how costs are determined.

LO2 Changing the Accounting
LO3 System

SD 2. Transnational Cablecom produces several types of communications cable for a worldwide market. Since the manufacturing process is continuous, the company uses a process costing system to develop product costs. Until recently, costs were accumulated monthly, and revised product costs were made available to management by the tenth of the following month. Because the company has installed a computer-integrated manufacturing (CIM) system, cost information is now available as soon as each production run is finished. The production superintendent has asked the controller to change the accounting system so that product unit costs are available the day after a production run ends.

Prepare a memorandum to the corporate vice president justifying the proposed change in the accounting system. Identify reasons that the controller can use to support the production superintendent's request. What benefits would be obtained from the proposed modification? Be prepared to share your ideas with your classmates.

Ethical Dilemma

LO1 Continuing Professional
LO2 Education

SD 3. Paula Woodward is the head of the Information Systems Department at Moreno Manufacturing Company. Roland Randolph, the company's controller, is meeting with her to discuss changes in data gathering that relate to the company's new flexible manufacturing system. Woodward opens the conversation by saying, "Roland, the old job order costing methods just will not work with the new flexible manufacturing system. The new system is based on continuous product flow, not batch processing. We need to change to a process costing system for both data gathering and product costing. Otherwise, our product costs will be way off, and it will affect our pricing decisions. I found out about the need for this change at a professional seminar I attended last month. You should have been there with me."

Randolph responds, "Paula, who is the accounting expert here? I know what product costing approach is best for this situation. Job order costing has provided accurate information for this product line for more than 15 years. Why should we change just because we've purchased a new machine? We've purchased several machines for this line over the years. And as for your seminar, I don't need to learn about costing methods. I was exposed to them all when I studied management accounting back in the late 1970s."

Is Randolph's behavior ethical? If not, what has he done wrong? What can Woodward do if Randolph continues to refuse to update the product costing system?

Group Activity: Divide the class into groups and direct the groups to develop a strategy for Woodward. Debrief the groups in class.

Research Activity

LO1 Process Costing Systems

SD 4. Locate an article about a company that you believe would use a process costing system. Conduct your search using an Internet search engine or a business periodical, such as *The Wall Street Journal*. Prepare a short report describing the product(s) the company makes, its production process, and why it would probably use a process costing system. Bring this information to class to share with your classmates. Be sure to include the company's name and identify the article's title, author(s), and publication date.

Decision-Making Practice

LO4 Setting a Selling Price
LO5
LO7

SD 5. For the past four years, three companies have dominated the soft drink industry, holding a combined 85 percent of market share. Wonder Cola, Inc., ranks second nationally in soft drink sales; it had gross revenues of $27,450,000 last year. Its management is thinking about introducing a new low-calorie drink called Zero Cola.

Wonder soft drinks are processed in a single department. All ingredients are added at the beginning of the process. At the end of the process, the beverage is poured into bottles that cost $.24 per case produced. Direct labor and manufacturing overhead costs are applied uniformly throughout the process.

Corporate controller Adam Daneen believes that costs for the new cola will be very much like those for the company's Cola Plus drink. Last year (20x8), he collected the following data about Cola Plus:

	Units*	Costs
Work in process inventory		
December 31, 20x7†	2,200	
Direct materials costs		$ 2,080
Conversion costs		620
December 31, 20x8‡	2,000	
Direct materials costs		1,880
Conversion costs		600
Units started during 20x8	458,500	
Costs for 20x8		
Liquid materials added		430,990
Direct labor and manufacturing overhead		229,400
Bottles		110,068

*Each unit is a 24-bottle case.
†50% complete.
‡60% complete.

The company's variable general administrative and selling costs are $1.10 per unit. Fixed administrative and selling costs are assigned to products at the rate of $.50 per unit. Each of Wonder Cola's two main competitors is already marketing a diet cola. Company A's product sells for $4.10 per unit; Company B's, for $4.05. All costs are expected to increase by 10 percent in the next three years. Wonder Cola tries to earn a profit of at least 15 percent on the total unit cost.

1. What factors should Wonder Cola, Inc., consider in setting a unit selling price for a case of Zero Cola?
2. Using the FIFO costing approach, compute (a) equivalent units for direct materials, cases of bottles, and conversion costs; (b) the total production cost per unit; and (c) the total cost per unit of Cola Plus for 20x8.
3. What is the expected unit cost of Zero Cola for 20x9?
4. Recommend a unit selling price range for Zero Cola for 20x9 and give the reason(s) for your choice.

MANAGERIAL REPORTING AND ANALYSIS CASES

Interpreting Management Reports

MRA 1.
LO4 **Analysis of Product Cost**
LO5

Ready Tire Corporation makes several lines of automobile and truck tires. The company operates in a competitive marketplace, so it relies heavily on cost data from its FIFO-based process costing system. It uses that information to set prices for its most competitive tires. The company's radial line has lost some of its market share during each of the past four years. Management believes that price breaks allowed by the company's three biggest competitors are the main reason for the decline in sales.

The company controller, Sara Birdsong, has been asked to review the product costing information that supports price decisions on the radial line. In preparing her report, she collected the following data for 20x8, the most recent full year of operations:

		Units	Dollars
Equivalent units:	Direct materials costs	84,200	
	Conversion costs	82,800	
Manufacturing costs:	Direct materials		$1,978,700
	Direct labor		800,400
	Manufacturing overhead applied		1,600,800
Unit cost data:	Direct materials costs		23.50
	Conversion costs		29.00
Work in process inventory:	Beginning (70% complete)	4,200	
	Ending (30% complete)	3,800	

Units started and completed during 20x8 totaled 80,400. Attached to the beginning Work in Process Inventory account were direct materials costs of $123,660 and conversion costs of $57,010. Birdsong found that little spoilage had occurred. The proper cost allowance for spoilage was included in the predetermined overhead rate of $2 per direct labor dollar. The review of direct labor cost revealed, however, that $90,500 had been charged twice to the production account, the second time in error. This resulted in overly high overhead costs being charged to the production account.

So far in 20x9, the radial has been selling for $92 per tire. This price was based on the 20x8 unit data plus a 75 percent markup to cover operating costs and profit. During 20x9, the company's three main competitors have charged about $87 for a tire of comparable quality. The company's process costing system adds all direct materials at the beginning of the process, and conversion costs are incurred uniformly throughout the process.

1. Identify what inaccuracies in costs, inventories, and selling prices result from the company's cost-charging error.
2. Prepare a revised process cost report for 20x8.
3. What should have been the minimum selling price per tire in 20x9?
4. Suggest ways of preventing such errors in the future.

Formulating Management Reports

MRA 2.
LO2 **Using the Process Costing**
LO4 **System**
LO5

  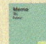

You are the production manager for Great Grain Corporation, a manufacturer of four cereal products. The company's best-selling product is Smackaroos, a sugar-coated puffed rice cereal. Yesterday, Clark Winslow, the controller, reported that the production cost for each box of Smackaroos has increased approximately 22 percent in the last four months. Because the company is unable to increase the selling price for a box of Smackaroos, the increased production costs will reduce profits significantly.

Today, you received a memo from Gilbert Rom, the company president, asking you to review your production process to identify inefficiencies or waste that can be eliminated. Once you have completed your analysis, you are to write a memo presenting your findings and suggesting ways to reduce or eliminate the problems. The president will use your information during a meeting with the top management team in ten days.

You are aware of previous problems in the Baking Department and the Packaging Department. At your request, Winslow has provided you with process cost reports for the two departments. He has also given you the following detailed summary of the cost per equivalent unit for a box of Smackaroos cereal:

	April	May	June	July
Baking Department				
Direct materials	$1.25	$1.26	$1.24	$1.25
Direct labor	.50	.61	.85	.90
Manufacturing overhead	.25	.31	.34	.40
Department totals	$2.00	$2.18	$2.43	$2.55
Packaging Department				
Direct materials	$ .35	$ .34	$ .33	$ .33
Direct labor	.05	.05	.04	.06
Manufacturing overhead	.10	.16	.15	.12
Department totals	$ .50	$ .55	$ .52	$ .51
Total cost per equivalent unit	$2.50	$2.73	$2.95	$3.06

1. In preparation for writing your memo, answer the following questions:
   a. For whom are you preparing the memo? Does this affect the length of the memo? Explain.
   b. Why are you preparing the memo?
   c. What actions should you take to gather information for the memo? What information is needed? Is the information that Winslow provided sufficient for analysis and reporting?
   d. When is the memo due? What can be done to provide accurate, reliable, and timely information?
2. Based on your analysis of the information that Winslow provided, where is the main problem in the production process?
3. Prepare an outline of the sections you would want in your memo.

International Company

MRA 3.
LO1 Process Costing and Work in
LO3 Process Inventory Accounts

SvenskStål, AB, is a steel-producing company located in Solentuna, Sweden. The company originally produced only specialty steel products that were made-to-order for customers. A job order product costing system is used for the made-to-order products. This year, after purchasing three continuous processing work cells, the company created a new division that produces three types of sheet steel in continuous rolls. Ingrid Bjorn, the company controller, has redesigned the management accounting system to accommodate these changes and has installed a process costing system for the new division.

At a recent meeting of the company's executive committee, Bjorn explained that the new product costing system uses three new Work in Process Inventory accounts, one for each of the three work cells. Lars Karlsson, the production superintendent, questioned the need to change product costing approaches and did not understand why so many new Work in Process Inventory accounts were necessary.

Why did Bjorn install a process costing system in the new division? Was a new division necessary, or could the three new work cells have been merged with the specialty production facilities? Why were three new Work in Process Inventory accounts required? Could the single Work in Process Inventory account used for the specialty orders have tracked and accumulated the costs incurred in the three new work cells?

Excel Spreadsheet Analysis

MRA 4.
LO6 Average Process Costing: Two
LO7 Time Periods

Lid Corporation produces a line of beverage lids in its plant in Old Town, Florida. The production process has been automated, so the product can now be produced in one operation rather than in the three operations that were needed before the company purchased the automated machinery. All direct materials are added at the beginning of the process, and conversion costs are incurred uniformly throughout the process. Operating data for May and June of 20x5 are as follows:

	May	June
Beginning work in process inventory		
Units (May: 40% complete)	220,000	?
Direct materials costs	$3,400	$400
Conversion costs	$6,480	$420
Production during the month		
Units started	24,000,000	31,000,000
Direct materials costs	$45,000	$93,200
Conversion costs	$66,000	$92,796
Ending work in process inventory		
Units (May: 70% complete; June: 60% complete)	200,000	320,000

1. Using the average costing method, prepare process cost reports for May and June. (Round unit costs to three decimal places; round all other costs to the nearest dollar.)
2. From the information in the process cost report for May, identify the amount that should be transferred out of the Work in Process Inventory account, and state where those dollars should be transferred.
3. Compare the product costing results for June with those for May. What is the most significant change? What are some possible causes of this change?

Internet Case

MRA 5.
LO1 Comparison of Companies
That Use Process Costing
Systems

The Focus on Business Practice box in this chapter lists many companies for which process costing systems are appropriate. Access the web sites of at least two of these companies. Find as much information as you can about the products the companies make and how they make them, including the manufacturing processes involved. For which products would process costing be most appropriate? For which products would it be inappropriate? Identify differences in the nature of the business conducted by the companies you chose. Do you think those differences have any bearing on the type of product costing system the company uses? Explain your reasoning. Do the companies make any products that might require a costing system other than process costing? Be prepared to present the results of your research in class.

19

Chapter 19 describes activity-based management and the just-in-time operating philosophy, demonstrating how these two activity-based systems help managers improve operating processes and make better pricing decisions.

Activity-Based Systems: ABM and JIT

LEARNING OBJECTIVES

LO1 Explain the role of activity-based systems in the management cycle.

LO2 Define *activity-based management (ABM)* and discuss its relationship to the supply chain and the value chain.

LO3 Distinguish between value-adding and nonvalue-adding activities, and describe process value analysis.

LO4 Define *activity-based costing* and explain how a cost hierarchy and a bill of activities are used.

LO5 Define the *just-in-time (JIT) operating philosophy* and identify the elements of a JIT operating environment.

LO6 Identify the changes in product costing that result when a firm adopts a JIT operating environment.

LO7 Define and apply *backflush costing*, and compare the cost flows in traditional and backflush costing.

LO8 Compare ABM and JIT as activity-based systems.

DECISION POINT
A MANAGER'S FOCUS

England, Inc. England, Inc., is a division of La-Z-Boy, Inc. <www.lazboy.com>. A critical factor in the success of this company is the speed of its value chain. England makes about 11,000 built-to-order sofas and chairs each week in its Tennessee plant, and it generally delivers them less than three weeks after customers have placed their orders with a retailer. This is quite a feat, especially since the company offers 85 styles of sofas and a choice of 550 fabrics. It also gives England, Inc., a competitive advantage. How does the company maintain this advantage?

England's managers use activity-based management (ABM) and a just-in-time (JIT) operating environment to identify and reduce or eliminate activities that do not add value to the company's products. These systems focus on minimizing waste, reducing costs, improving the allocation of resources, and ensuring that suppliers deliver materials just at the time a company needs them. They help managers make better decisions about costing and pricing products, adding or dropping product styles, changing production and delivery systems, and contracting with suppliers. The continuous flow of information that ABM and JIT provide has enabled England's managers to improve production processes; for example, they are able to adjust labor needs each week to meet order requirements. It has also enabled them to schedule timely deliveries from suppliers and thus maintain appropriate inventory levels, as well as to keep track of England's own fleet of delivery trucks.

England's disciplined monitoring of order, production, and delivery activities is the factor that gives it a

How have ABM and JIT helped England, Inc.'s managers to improve production processes and reduce delivery time?

competitive edge. By using ABM and JIT, England has achieved higher productivity than other furniture manufacturers, is able to offer more than 40,000 product variations, and over five years has cut its delivery time by one-half to one-third.[1]

ACTIVITY-BASED SYSTEMS AND MANAGEMENT

LO1 Explain the role of activity-based systems in the management cycle.

RELATED TEXT ASSIGNMENTS
Q: 1, 2, 3, 4, 5
SE: 1
E: 1

www.dell.com

Many companies operate in volatile business environments that are strongly influenced by customer demands. Managers know that customers buy value, usually in the form of quality products or services that are delivered on a timely basis for a reasonable price. Companies generate revenue when customers see value and buy their products or services. Thus, companies measure value as revenue (customer value = revenue generated).

Value exists when some characteristic of a product or service satisfies customers' wants or needs. For example, customers who appreciate convenience are an important market segment for Dell Computer Corporation. In response to their needs, Dell creates value and increases revenue by selling customized computer systems that include the latest microprocessor, monitor, graphics card, CD-ROM or DVD drive, sound card, modem, speakers, and preinstalled software products.

Creating value by satisfying customers' needs for quality, reasonable price, and timely delivery requires that managers do the following:

- Work with suppliers and customers.
- View the organization as a collection of value-adding activities.
- Use resources for value-adding activities.
- Reduce or eliminate nonvalue-adding activities.
- Know the total cost of creating value for a customer.

If an organization's business plan focuses on providing products or services that customers esteem, then managers will work with suppliers and customers to find ways of improving quality, reducing costs, and shortening delivery time. Managers will also focus their attention internally to find the best ways of using resources to create and maintain the value of their products or services. This requires matching resources to the operating activities that add value to a product or service. Managers will examine all business activities, including research and development, purchasing, production, storing, selling, shipping, and customer service, so that they can allocate resources effectively. In addition, managers need to know the **full product cost**, which includes not only the costs of direct materials and direct labor, but also the costs of all production and nonproduction activities required to satisfy the customer. For example, the full product cost of a Dell computer system includes the cost of the computer components and software, as well as the costs of taking the sales order, processing the order, packaging and shipping the system, and providing subsequent customer service for warranty work and software upgrades. If the activities are executed well and in agreement with the business plan, and if costs are assigned fairly, the company can improve product pricing and quality, increase productivity, and generate revenues (value) and profits.

ACTIVITY-BASED SYSTEMS

Organizations that focus on customers design their accounting information systems to provide customer-related, activity-based information. **Activity-based systems** are information systems that provide quantitative information about an organization's activities. They create opportunities to improve the cost information supplied to managers. They also help managers view their organization as a collection of activities. Activity-based cost information helps managers improve operating processes and make better pricing decisions.

Activity-based systems developed because traditional accounting systems failed to produce the types of information today's managers need for decision making. Traditional systems focused primarily on measurements needed for financial reporting and auditing, such as the measurement of cost of goods sold and the valuation

● **STOP AND THINK!**
What is the main focus of an activity-based system?
An activity-based system's main focus is on managing activities rather than costs. ∎

of inventory. Because they were not designed to capture data on activities or to trace the full cost of a product, these systems could not isolate the cost of unnecessary activities, penalize for overproduction, or quantify measures that improved quality or reduced throughput time.

In this chapter, we explore two types of activity-based systems—activity-based management (ABM) and the just-in-time (JIT) operating environment—and consider how they affect product costing. Both systems help organizations manage activities, not costs, but by managing activities, organizations can reduce or eliminate many nonvalue-adding activities, which leads to reduced costs and hence to increased income.

KEY POINT: ABM and JIT focus on value-adding activities—not costs—to increase income.

USING ACTIVITY-BASED COST INFORMATION IN THE MANAGEMENT CYCLE

In this section, we look at the ways in which managers use activity-based cost information to answer basic questions during the management cycle. Figure 1 summarizes those uses.

■ **PLANNING** In the planning stage, managers want answers to questions like "Which activities add value to a product or service?" "What resources are needed to perform those activities?" and "How much should the product or service cost?" By examining their company's value-adding activities and the related costs, managers

FIGURE 1
Activity-Based Systems and the Management Cycle

can ensure that the company is offering quality products or services at the lowest cost. With budgeted costs prepared for each activity, they can not only better allocate resources to cost objects (such as product or service lines, customer groups, or sales territories) and estimate product or service unit cost more accurately, but also measure operating performance. If managers assume that resource-consuming activities cause costs and that products and services incur costs by the activities they require, the estimated unit cost will be more accurate.

■ **Executing** In the executing stage, managers want an answer to the question "What is the actual cost of making our product or providing our service?" They want to know what activities are being performed, how well they are being performed, and what resources they are consuming. Although managers focus on the activities that create the most value for customers, they also monitor some nonvalue-adding activities that have been reduced but not completely eliminated. An activity-based accounting information system measures actual quantities of activity (a quantitative nonfinancial measure) and accumulates related activity costs (a quantitative financial measure). Gathering quantitative information at the activity level allows managers the flexibility to create cost pools for different types of cost objects. For example, the costs of the selling activity can be assigned to a customer, a sales territory, or a product or service line.

■ **Reviewing** In the reviewing stage, managers want answers to the questions "What actions will reduce the full product and service cost?" and "Did we meet our cost-reduction goals for nonvalue-adding activities?" Managers measure an activity's performance by reviewing the difference between its actual and budgeted costs. With this information, they can analyze the variances in activity levels, identify waste and inefficiencies, and take action to improve processes and activities. They can also continue to monitor the costs of nonvalue-adding activities to see if the company met its goals of reducing or eliminating those costs. Careful review and analysis will increase value for the customer by improving product quality and reducing costs and cycle time.

■ **Reporting** Finally, in the reporting stage of the management cycle, managers prepare reports about the company's performance for internal and external use. Internal reports show the application of the costs of activities to cost objects, which results in a better measurement of profitability, as we discuss later in the chapter. External reports summarize past performance and answer such questions as "Did the company earn a profit?"

✓ Check out ACE for a Review Quiz at http://accounting.college.hmco.com/students.

Activity-Based Management

LO2 Define *activity-based management (ABM)* and discuss its relationship to the supply chain and the value chain.

RELATED TEXT ASSIGNMENTS
Q: 6, 7
SE: 2, 3
E: 2, 3
P: 1
SD: 2

As you may recall from an earlier chapter, **activity-based management (ABM)** is an approach to managing an organization that identifies all major operating activities, determines the resources consumed by each activity and the cause of the resource usage, and categorizes the activities as either adding value to a product or service or not adding value. ABM focuses on reducing or eliminating nonvalue-adding activities. Because it provides financial and performance information at the activity level, ABM is useful both for strategic planning and for making operational decisions about business segments, such as product lines, market segments, and customer groups. It also helps managers eliminate waste and inefficiencies and redirect resources to activities that add value to the product or service. Activity-based cost-

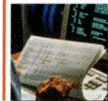

FOCUS ON BUSINESS PRACTICE

How Do Traditional and ABC Reports Differ?

Many companies are finding that ABC enhances managerial reporting and decision making because it reflects the cause-and-effect relationships between indirect costs and individual processes, products, services, or customers. ABC is not a replacement for traditional general ledger accounting, which collects costs by departments. Rather, it is a practical spreadsheet translation of general ledger data into a format aimed at estimating true cost. The table on the right compares the reports of a department in a health-related company. Identify the report that would be used for financial purposes and the one that would be used for decision making.[2]

Chart of Accounts View		Activity-Based Costing View	
Salaries	$621,400	Enter claims into system	$ 32,000
Equipment	161,200	Analyze claims	121,000
Travel Expenses	58,000	Suspend claims	32,500
Supplies	43,900	Receive provider inquiries	101,500
Use and Occupancy	30,000	Resolve member problems	83,400
Total	$914,500	Process batches	45,000
		Determine eligibility	119,000
		Make copies	145,000
		Write correspondence	77,100
		Attend training	158,000
		Total	$914,500

ENRICHMENT NOTE: Some activities or functions occur before production; their costs are sometimes called *upstream costs*. Other activities or functions occur after production; their costs are called *downstream costs*. In the new operating environment, both upstream and downstream costs are part of a product's total cost.

ing (ABC) is the tool used in an ABM environment to assign activity costs to cost objects. ABC helps managers make better pricing decisions, inventory valuations, and profitability decisions.

VALUE CHAINS AND SUPPLY CHAINS

As we noted earlier in the text, a **value chain** is a sequence of activities, or primary processes, that add value to a company's product or service; the value chain also includes support services, such as management accounting, that facilitate the primary processes. ABM enables managers to see their organization's value chain as part of a larger system that includes the value chains of suppliers and customers. This larger system is the **supply chain**—the path that leads from the suppliers of the materials from which a product is made to the final customer. The supply chain (also called the *supply network*) includes both suppliers and suppliers' suppliers, and customers and customers' customers.

As Figure 2 shows, in the supply chain for automobiles, a metal manufacturer supplies metal to an engine manufacturer, which supplies engines to the car manufacturer. The car manufacturer supplies cars to car dealerships, which supply cars to the final customers. Except for the metal manufacturer, each organization in this supply chain is a customer of an earlier supplier, and each, including the metal manufacturer, has its own value chain. The sequence of primary processes in the value chain varies from company to company depending on a number of factors, including the size of the company and the types of products or services it sells. Figure 2 shows the primary processes that add value for a car manufacturer—marketing, research and development, purchasing, production, sales, shipping, and customer service.

Value chains and supply chains give managers a better grasp of their company's internal and external operations. Managers who understand the supply

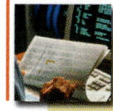

FOCUS ON BUSINESS PRACTICE

How Can a Changing Business Economy Cause Strategy Shifts in a Company's Value Chain?

Because of an economic downturn and overcapacity in the technology sector, high-tech companies like Oracle <www.oracle.com>, SAP <www.sap.com>, and PeopleSoft <www.peoplesoft.com> have shifted the emphasis of their value chain from marketing to customer service. Measures once used to gauge the performance of an aggressive sales force, such as sales volume, are no longer relevant and have been replaced by measures of customer satisfaction and retention.[3]

FIGURE 2
Supply Chain and Value Chain for a Manufacturing Company

> ● **STOP AND THINK!**
> How does the focus of a supply chain differ from that of a value chain?
>
> *A supply chain focuses on external relationships, whereas a value chain focuses on internal relationships.* ■
>
> www.ford.com

chain and how their company's value-adding activities fit into their suppliers' and customers' value chains can see their company's role in the overall process of creating and delivering products or services. Such an understanding can also make a company more profitable. By working with suppliers and customers across the entire supply chain, managers may be able to reduce the total cost of making a product, even though costs for one activity may increase. For example, assume that Ford Motor Company decided to place computers for online order entry in its car dealerships. The new computers would streamline the processing of orders and make the orders more accurate. In this case, even though Ford would incur the cost of the computers, the total cost of making and delivering a car would decrease because the cost of order processing would decrease. When organizations work cooperatively with others in their supply chain, they can develop new processes that reduce the total costs of their products or services.

ABM IN A SERVICE ORGANIZATION

To illustrate how a service organization can use ABM, let's assume that a firm called Western Data Services, Inc. (WDSI), offers database marketing strategies to help companies increase their sales. WDSI's basic package of services includes the design of a mailing piece (either a Classic Letter with or without inserts or a Self-Mailer),

FIGURE 3
Supply Chain and Value Chain for a Service Organization

www.pb.com

creation and maintenance of marketing databases containing information about the client's target group, and a production process that prints a promotional piece and prepares it for mailing. WDSI's primary customers are financial institutions throughout the western states, but the company also serves small businesses and nonprofit organizations.

In preparing WSDI's business plan, Carl Marcus, the owner and manager of WDSI, reviewed the company's supply chain. As Figure 3 shows, this supply chain includes one supplier (Pitney Bowes), WDSI as a service provider, one customer group (financial institutions), and the customer group's customers. WDSI had a number of suppliers, including office supply companies, printers, and computer stores, but Marcus chose to include only Pitney Bowes because of the significant cost savings from using this supplier's equipment to fold, insert, address, seal, and meter mailing pieces. Marcus chose financial institutions as the supply chain's primary customer group because they represent 75 percent of revenues. The customers of the financial institutions are included in the supply chain because those individuals and businesses receive the mailing pieces that WDSI prepares. Based on his review of the supply chain, Marcus concluded that WDSI's strategy to work with Pitney Bowes and the financial institutions to improve WDSI's services was sound.

Marcus also decided to use ABM to manage processes and activities. He developed a value chain of activities for the company so that he could identify all major operating activities, the resources each activity consumes, and the cause of the resource usage. As shown in Figure 3, the activities that add value to WDSI's services are marketing, preparing marketing databases, purchasing supplies, processing orders, mailing promotional pieces, and customer relations.

 Check out ACE for a Review Quiz at http://accounting.college.hmco.com/students.

VALUE-ADDING AND NONVALUE-ADDING ACTIVITIES AND PROCESS VALUE ANALYSIS

LO3 Distinguish between value-adding and nonvalue-adding activities, and describe process value analysis.

RELATED TEXT ASSIGNMENTS
Q: 8, 9
SE: 4
E: 4, 5
P: 1
SD: 2, 5
MRA: 1, 4, 5

KEY POINT: The customer's perspective is what governs whether an activity adds value to a product or service.

An important element of activity-based management is the identification of value-adding and nonvalue-adding activities. A **value-adding activity** adds value to a product or service as perceived by the customer. Examples include designing the components of a new car, assembling the car, painting it, and installing seats and airbags. A **nonvalue-adding activity** adds cost to a product or service but does not increase its market value. ABM focuses on eliminating nonvalue-adding activities that are not essential to an organization and on reducing the costs of those that are essential, such as legal services, management accounting, machine repair, materials handling, and building maintenance. The costs of both value-adding and nonvalue-adding activities are accumulated to measure performance and to determine whether the goal of reducing the cost of nonvalue-adding activities has been achieved.

To minimize costs, managers continuously seek to improve processes and activities. To manage the cost of an activity, they can reduce the activity's frequency or eliminate it. For example, inspection costs can be reduced if an inspector samples one of every three engines received from a supplier rather than inspecting every engine. If the supplier is a reliable source of high-quality engines, such a reduction in inspection activity is appropriate. Another way to reduce costs is to outsource an activity—that is, to have it done by another company that is more competent at the work and can perform it at a lower cost. Many companies outsource purchasing, accounting, and the maintenance of their information systems.

Some activities can be eliminated completely if business processes are changed. For example, when a company adopts a just-in-time operating philosophy, it can eliminate some recordkeeping activities. Because it purchases materials just in time for production and manufactures products just in time for customer delivery, it no longer needs to accumulate costs as the product is made.

VALUE-ADDING AND NONVALUE-ADDING ACTIVITIES IN A SERVICE ORGANIZATION

To illustrate how service organizations deal with value-adding and nonvalue-adding activities, let's suppose Carl Marcus, the owner and manager of WDSI, has examined the activities related to the design, processing, and mailing of his company's Classic Letters and drawn up the list of value-adding activities shown in Table 1. When Marcus's customers ask for database marketing services, these are the activities they pay for. Marcus also identified the following nonvalue-adding activities:

- Preparing a job order form and scheduling the job
- Ordering, receiving, inspecting, and storing paper, envelopes, and other supplies
- Setting up machines to process a specific letter size
- Logging the total number of items processed in a batch
- Billing the client and recording and depositing payments from the client

After reviewing the list of nonvalue-adding activities, Marcus arranged with his suppliers to have paper, envelopes, and other supplies delivered the day a job is performed. This helped reduce WDSI's storage costs. Marcus was also able to reduce the costs of some value-adding activities. For example, he reduced the cost of the labor involved in verifying the conformity of mailings with United States Postal Service (USPS) requirements by purchasing computer software that verifies addresses, determines postage, and automatically sorts the letters.

● STOP AND THINK!
Are customers willing to pay for nonvalue-adding activities?
Customers are not willing to pay for such activities, which is why businesses try to minimize or eliminate them. ■

Why does Kraft's management analyze cost behavior to project the profitability of it's core sectors?

pounds actually produced. To project the profitability of a particular year, Kraft's management must take into account both the selling price and the estimated production and sales mix of products and the effects those estimates have on a product's unit cost.

Cost Behavior and the Management Cycle

LO1 Define *cost behavior* and explain how managers use this concept in the management cycle.

RELATED TEXT ASSIGNMENTS
Q: 1, 2
SE: 1
SD: 1

Cost behavior—the way costs respond to changes in volume or activity—is a factor in almost every decision managers make. Managers commonly use it to analyze alternative courses of action so that they can select the course that will best generate income for an organization's owners and maintain liquidity for its creditors. Figure 1 shows how managers use cost behavior throughout the management cycle.

Planning

In the planning stage, managers use cost behavior to determine how many units of products or services must be sold to generate a targeted amount of profit and how changes in planned operating, investing, and financing activities will affect operating income. For example, when Kraft's managers launched a product called Boca, they used cost behavior to analyze how offering two flavors of this meatless soy-based burger would contribute to the organization's operating income.

www.kraft.com

www.daimlerchysler.com

Manufacturers of cars and trucks, such as DaimlerChrysler, use cost behavior to decide how to adjust output to meet changing sales demand. If increased demand for trucks suggests the need to increase truck production and decrease car production, management can use cost behavior analysis to estimate the changes in operating income for those product lines. Cost behavior analysis is also useful to service businesses. For example, Blockbuster's managers use cost behavior in the planning stage to determine the optimal mix of DVD or VCR movies to rent and whether to price rentals to subscribers on a per movie or flat monthly fee basis.

www.blockbuster.com

Executing

As we have noted, managers use information about cost behavior in almost every decision they make. Throughout the executing stage of the management cycle, managers at Kraft and at service businesses like Sprint and Verizon must understand and anticipate cost behavior to determine the impact of their decisions on operating income. For example, Kraft's managers must understand the changes in income that can result from a decision to buy new, more productive manufacturing equipment or to launch a Saturday morning advertising campaign to promote a new Post cereal.

www.sprint.com
www.verizon.com

Reviewing and Reporting

When reviewing operations and preparing reports for various product or service lines or geographic regions, managers in all types of organizations, including serv-

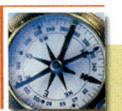

Focus on Business Ethics

Core Values Guide Kraft Foods.

Six core values—focus, innovation, passion, speed, trust, and teamwork—guide Kraft Foods <www.kraft.com> in its mission to be recognized as the undisputed leader of the global food industry. Kraft's *focus* is on what matters most to consumers and on what's most important for its employees, brands, and business. The company encourages *innovation* to create ideas that will satisfy consumers, contribute to better service, and improve management. It values individuals who set high goals and have an uncompromising drive, or *passion*, to achieve them. *Speed* is important to Kraft in that it expects its decision makers to move quickly, with appropriate discipline, to stay ahead of the competition. The company regards *trust* as the foundation of all relationships and emphasizes the importance of integrity, respect, and responsibility. Finally, Kraft values *teamwork* because it recognizes that the power of working together across functions and business units around the world is what will make all the difference in the world.[2]

FIGURE 1
The Use of Cost Behavior in the Management Cycle

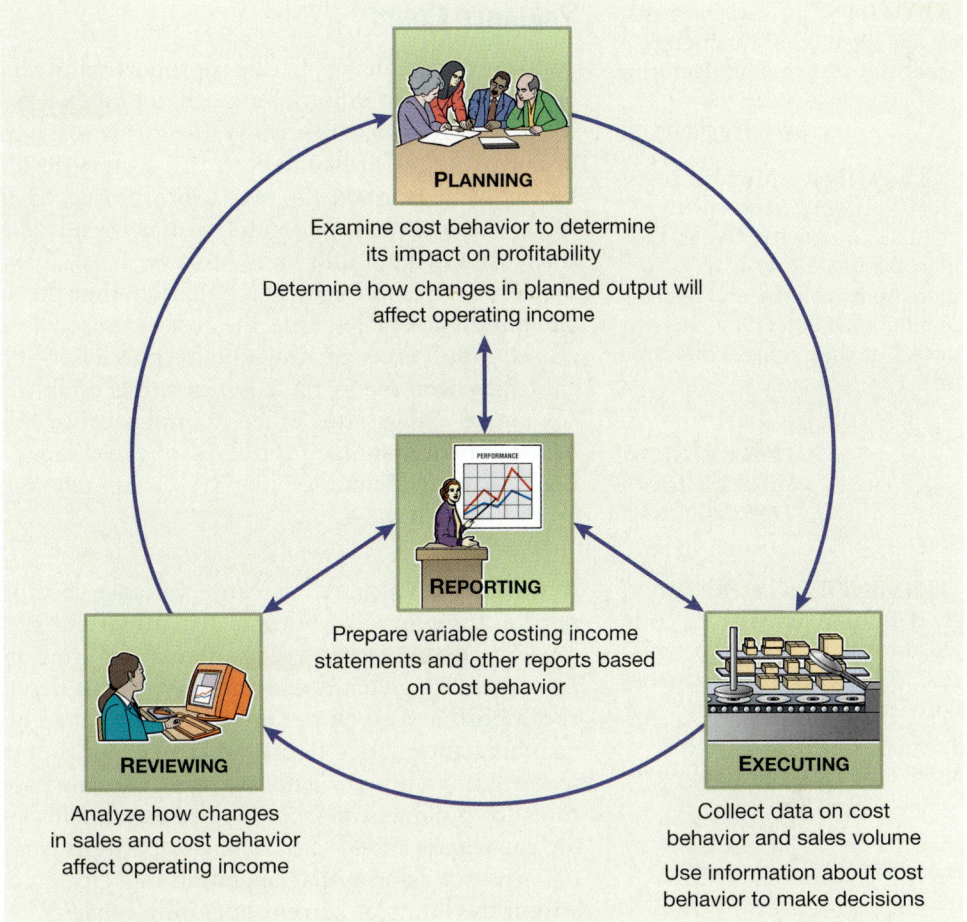

◆ **STOP AND THINK!**
Why do managers need to understand cost behavior?
Almost every decision managers make involves cost ramifications; to make good decisions, managers must understand the ways costs respond to changes in volume or activity. ■

www.fedex.com
www.ups.com

ice businesses like Federal Express and UPS, need to understand cost behavior. Variable costing income statements are commonly used to analyze how changes in cost and sales affect the profitability of product lines, sales territories, customers, departments, and other segments. Other reports based on cost behavior are used when deciding whether to eliminate a product line, accept a special order, or outsource services.

 Check out ACE for a Review Quiz at http://accounting.college.hmco.com/students.

THE BEHAVIOR OF COSTS

LO2 Identify variable, fixed, and mixed costs, and separate mixed costs into their variable and fixed components.

RELATED TEXT ASSIGNMENTS
Q: 3, 4, 5, 6, 7, 8, 9, 10, 11
SE: 2, 3
E: 1, 2, 3, 4
P: 1, 5
SD: 1, 4, 5

Although our focus in this chapter is on cost behavior as it relates to products and services, cost behavior can also be observed in selling, administrative, and general activities. For example, increases in the number of shipments affect shipping costs; the number of units sold or total sales revenue affects the cost of sales commissions; and the number of customers billed or the number of hours needed to bill affects total billing costs. If managers can predict how costs behave, then costs become manageable.

Some costs vary with volume or operating activity (variable costs). Others remain fixed as volume changes (fixed costs). Between those two extremes are costs that exhibit characteristics of each type (mixed costs).

KEY POINT: Variable costs are incurred in all functional areas, not just in manufacturing.

www.landrover.com

KEY POINT: Variable costs change in *direct proportion* to changes in activity; that is, they increase *in total* with an increase in volume and decrease *in total* with a decrease in volume, but they remain the same on a *per unit* basis.

www.goodyear.com
www.wellsfargo.com
www.walmart.com

TERMINOLOGY NOTE: By definition, no variable costs exist at the level of zero production, which is why variable costs are sometimes described as the direct costs of production, sales, and administration.

ENRICHMENT NOTE: In a just-in-time operating environment, theoretical (ideal) capacity is used as a benchmark, a relatively constant reference point against which to measure improvement.

TERMINOLOGY NOTE: Practical capacity is sometimes called *engineering capacity*.

◆ **STOP AND THINK!**
What is the most realistic measure of operating capacity?
Normal capacity is the most realistic measure of operating capacity because it measures what a company is likely to produce, not what it can produce. ■

VARIABLE COSTS

Total costs that change in direct proportion to changes in productive output (or any other measure of volume) are called **variable costs**. To explore how variable costs work, consider the tire costs of Land Rover, a maker of off-road vehicles. Each new vehicle has four tires, and each tire costs $48. The total cost of tires, then, is $192 for one vehicle, $384 for two, $960 for five, $1,920 for ten, $19,200 for one hundred, and so on. In the production of off-road vehicles, the total cost of tires is a variable cost. On a per unit basis, however, a variable cost remains constant. In this case, the cost of tires per vehicle is $192 whether the automaker produces one vehicle or one hundred vehicles. True, the cost of tires will vary depending on the number purchased if discounts are available for purchases of large quantities. But once the purchase has been made, the cost per tire is established.

Figure 2 illustrates other examples of variable costs. All those costs—whether incurred by a manufacturer like Goodyear Tires, a service business like Wells Fargo Bank, or a merchandiser like Wal-Mart—are variable based on either productive output or total sales.

■ **OPERATING CAPACITY** Because variable costs increase or decrease in direct proportion to volume or output, it is important to know an organization's operating capacity. **Operating capacity** is the upper limit of an organization's productive output capability, given its existing resources. It describes just what an organization can accomplish in a given period. Operating capacity can be expressed in several ways, including total labor hours, total machine hours, and total units of output. Any increase in volume or activity over operating capacity requires additional expenditures for buildings, machinery, personnel, and operations. When additional operating capacity is added, cost behavior patterns can change. In our discussion of those patterns, we assume that operating capacity is constant and that all activity occurs within the limits of current operating capacity.

There are **three common measures, or types, of operating capacity:** theoretical, or ideal, capacity; practical capacity; and normal capacity. **Theoretical (ideal) capacity** is the maximum productive output for a given period in which all machinery and equipment are operating at optimum speed, without interruption. In a just-in-time operating environment, the long-term goal is to approach theoretical capacity through continuous improvement; however, no company ever actually operates at such an ideal level. **Practical capacity** is theoretical capacity reduced by normal and expected work stoppages, such as machine breakdowns; downtime for retooling, repairs, and maintenance; and employees' breaks. Although theoretical capacity and practical capacity are useful when estimating maximum production levels, neither measure is realistic when planning operations.

When planning operations, managers use **normal capacity**, which is the average annual level of operating capacity needed to meet expected sales demand. The sales demand figure is adjusted for seasonal changes and industry and economic cycles. Normal capacity is therefore a realistic measure of what an organization is *likely* to produce, not what it *can* produce. Each variable cost should be related to an appropriate measure of normal capacity, but in many cases, more than one measure of normal capacity applies. Operating costs can be related to machine hours used or total units produced. Sales commissions, on the other hand, usually vary in direct proportion to total sales dollars.

The basis for measuring the activity of variable costs should be carefully selected for two reasons. First, an appropriate activity base simplifies cost planning and control. Second, the management accountant must combine (aggregate) many variable costs with the same activity base so that the costs can be analyzed in a reasonable way. Such aggregation also provides information that allows management to predict future costs.

FIGURE 2
Examples of Variable, Fixed, and Mixed Costs

Costs	Manufacturing Company—Tire Manufacturer	Merchandising Company—Department Store	Service Company—Bank
VARIABLE	Direct materials Direct labor (hourly) Indirect labor (hourly) Operating supplies Small tools	Merchandise to sell Sales commissions Shelf stockers (hourly)	Computer equipment leasing (based on usage) Computer operators (hourly) Operating supplies Data storage disks

FIXED	Depreciation, machinery
	  and building
	Insurance premiums
	Labor (salaried)
	Supervisory salaries
	Property taxes
		Depreciation, building
		Insurance premiums
		Buyers (salaried)
		Supervisory salaries
		Property taxes (on equipment
		  and building)
			Depreciation, furniture and fixtures
			Insurance premiums
			Salaries:
			  Programmers
			  Systems designers
			  Bank administrators
			Rent, buildings

MIXED	Electrical power Telephone Heat	Electrical power Telephone Heat	Electrical power Telephone Heat

TERMINOLOGY NOTE: An activity base is often called *denominator activity*; it is the activity for which relationships are established. The basic relationships should not change greatly if activity fluctuates around the level of denominator activity.

The general guide for selecting an activity base is to relate costs to their most logical or causal factor. For example, machinery setup costs should be considered variable in relation to the number of setups needed for a particular job. This will allow machinery setup costs to be budgeted and controlled more effectively.

■ **LINEAR RELATIONSHIPS AND THE RELEVANT RANGE** The traditional definition of a variable cost assumes that costs go up or down as volume increases or decreases, as demonstrated by the linear relationship in the tire example we cited earlier. Figure 3 shows a similar straight-line relationship. There, each unit of output requires $2.50 of labor cost. Total labor costs grow in direct proportion to the increase in units of output. For two units, total labor costs are $5.00; for six units, the organization incurs $15.00 in labor costs.

CLARIFICATION NOTE: Nonlinear costs can be roughly estimated by treating them as if they were linear (variable) costs within set limits of volume.

Many costs, however, vary with operating activity in a nonlinear fashion. Graph A in Figure 4 shows the behavior of power costs as usage increases and the unit cost of power consumption falls. Graph B shows the behavior of rental costs when each additional hour of computer usage costs more than the previous hour. Graph C shows how labor costs vary as efficiency increases and decreases. These three nonlinear cost patterns are variable in nature, but they differ from the linear variable cost pattern shown in Figure 3.

FIGURE 3
A Common Variable Cost Behavior Pattern: A Linear Relationship

TERMINOLOGY NOTE:
Relevant range is the range of activity in which costs are expected to behave as predicted.

Variable costs with linear relationships to a volume measure are easy to analyze and project for cost planning and control. Nonlinear variable costs are not easy to use. But all costs must be included in an analysis if the results are to be useful to management. To simplify cost analysis procedures and make variable costs easier to use, accountants have developed a method of converting nonlinear variable costs into linear variable costs. Called *linear approximation*, this method relies on the concept of relevant range. **Relevant range** is the span of activity in which a company expects to operate. Within the relevant range, it is assumed that both total fixed costs and per unit variable costs are constant. Under that assumption, many nonlinear costs can be estimated using the linear approximation approach illustrated in Figure 5. Those estimated costs can then be treated as part of the other variable costs.

A linear approximation of a nonlinear variable cost is not a precise measure, but it allows the inclusion of nonlinear variable costs in cost behavior analysis, and the loss of accuracy is usually not significant. The goal is to help management estimate costs and prepare budgets, and linear approximation helps accomplish that goal.

FIGURE 4
Other Variable Cost Behavior Patterns: Nonlinear Relationships

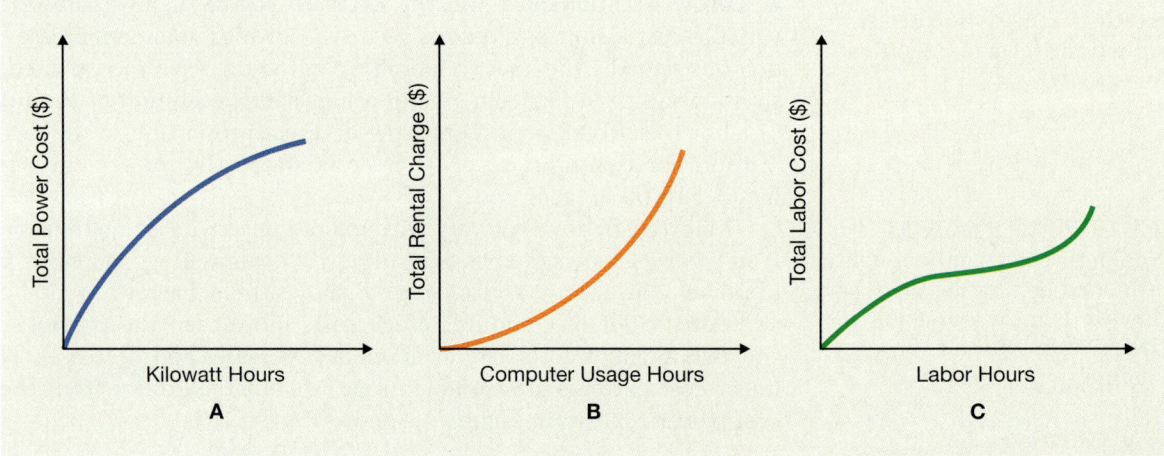

FIGURE 5
The Relevant Range and Linear Approximation

FIXED COSTS

TERMINOLOGY NOTE: Because fixed costs are expected to hold relatively constant over the entire relevant range of activity, they can be described as the costs of providing capacity.

KEY POINT: Cost behavior is closely linked to the concept of cost control. In the short run, it is generally easier to control variable costs than fixed costs.

Fixed costs behave very differently from variable costs. **Fixed costs** are total costs that remain constant within a relevant range of volume or activity—that is, the range in which actual operations are likely to occur. Look back at Figure 2 for examples of fixed costs. The manufacturer, the department store, and the bank all incur depreciation costs and fixed annual insurance premiums. In addition, all salaried personnel have fixed earnings for a particular period. The manufacturer and the department store own their buildings and pay annual property taxes, and the bank pays an annual fixed rental charge for the use of its building.

According to economic theory, all costs tend to be variable in the long run; thus, as the examples in Figure 2 suggest, a cost is fixed only within a limited period. A change in plant capacity, machinery, labor needs, or other production factors causes fixed costs to increase or decrease. For planning, management usually considers a one-year period, and fixed costs are expected to be constant within that period.

Of course, fixed costs change when activity exceeds the relevant range. For example, assume that a manufacturer of aluminum cans needs one supervisor for an eight-hour work shift. Production can range from zero to 500,000 units (cans) per month per shift. The relevant range, then, is from zero to 500,000 units. The supervisor's salary is $4,000 per month. The cost behavior analysis is as follows:

Units of Output per Month	Total Supervisory Salaries per Month
0–500,000	$4,000
Over 500,000–1,000,000	$8,000

If a maximum of 500,000 units can be produced per month per shift, output over 500,000 units would require another shift and another supervisor. Like all fixed costs, the new fixed cost remains constant in total within the new relevant range.

What about unit costs? Fixed unit costs vary inversely with activity or volume. On a per unit basis, fixed costs go down as volume goes up, as long as a firm is operating within the relevant range of activity. Look at how supervisory costs per unit fall as the volume of activity increases within the relevant range:

Volume of Activity	Cost per Unit
100,000 units	$4,000 ÷ 100,000 = $.0400
300,000 units	$4,000 ÷ 300,000 = $.0133
500,000 units	$4,000 ÷ 500,000 = $.0080
600,000 units	$8,000 ÷ 600,000 = $.0133

FIGURE 6
A Common Fixed Cost Behavior Pattern

At 600,000 units, the activity level is above the relevant range, which means another shift must be added and another supervisor must be hired; thus, the per unit cost increases to $.0133.

Figure 6 shows this behavior pattern. The fixed supervisory costs for the first 500,000 units of production are $4,000. Those costs hold steady at $4,000 for any level of output within the relevant range. But if output goes above 500,000 units, another supervisor must be hired, pushing fixed supervisory costs to $8,000.

MIXED COSTS

KEY POINT: A business's cost accounts often fall into the mixed-cost category.

Mixed costs have both variable and fixed cost components. Part of a mixed cost changes with volume or usage, and part is fixed over a particular period. Monthly electricity costs are an example. Such costs include charges per kilowatt-hour used plus a basic monthly service charge. The kilowatt-hour charges are variable because they depend on the amount of use; the monthly service charge is a fixed cost. Graph A in Figure 7 depicts an organization's total electricity cost. The monthly bill begins with a fixed charge for the service and increases as kilowatt-hours are consumed. Graph B illustrates a special contractual arrangement. Here, the annual cost of equipment maintenance provided by an outside company increases for each maintenance hour worked, up to a maximum amount per period. After the maximum is reached, additional maintenance is done at no cost.

FIGURE 7
Behavior Patterns of Mixed Costs

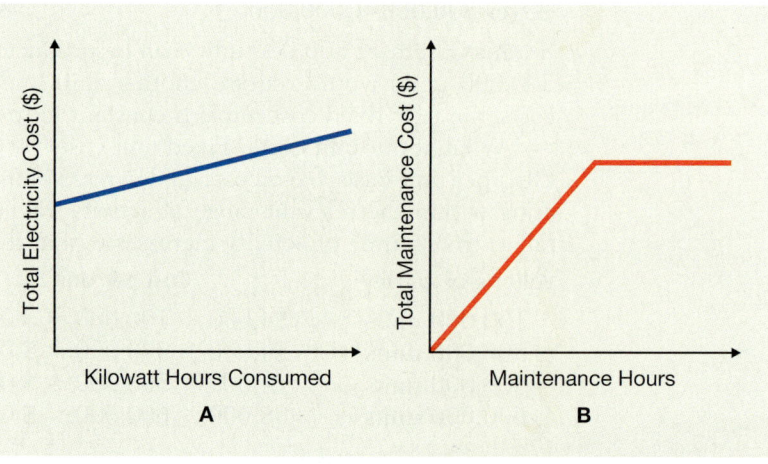

$$S - VC - FC = 0$$
$$\$90x - \$50x - \$20{,}000 = 0$$
$$\$40x = \$20{,}000$$
$$x = 500 \text{ Units}$$

We can also compute it in sales dollars:

$$\$90 \times 500 \text{ Units} = \$45{,}000$$

In addition, we can make a rough estimate of the breakeven point using a scatter graph. This method is less exact, but it does yield meaningful data. Figure 7 shows a breakeven graph for Valley Metal Products. As you can see there, the graph has five parts:

1. A horizontal axis for units of output
2. A vertical axis for dollars of revenue
3. A line running horizontally from the vertical axis at the level of fixed costs
4. A total cost line that begins at the point where the fixed cost line crosses the vertical axis and slopes upward to the right (The slope of the line depends on the variable cost per unit.)
5. A total revenue line that begins at the origin of the vertical and horizontal axes and slopes upward to the right (The slope depends on the selling price per unit.)

At the point at which the total revenue line crosses the total cost line, revenues equal total costs. The breakeven point, stated in either sales units or dollars of sales, is found by extending broken lines from this point to the axes. As Figure 7 shows, Valley Metal Products will break even when it has sold 500 plant stands for $45,000.

KEY POINT: Graphs can be powerful management tools because they visually depict relationships between revenues and expenses that otherwise might not be evident.

● **STOP AND THINK!**
Why does the total revenue line in a breakeven graph start at the origin (zero units, zero dollars) while the total cost line usually starts higher on the vertical axis?
At zero sales, there is zero revenue; at zero sales and production, there is no variable cost, yet fixed costs still exist. ■

FIGURE 7
Graphic Breakeven Analysis for Valley Metal Products, Inc.

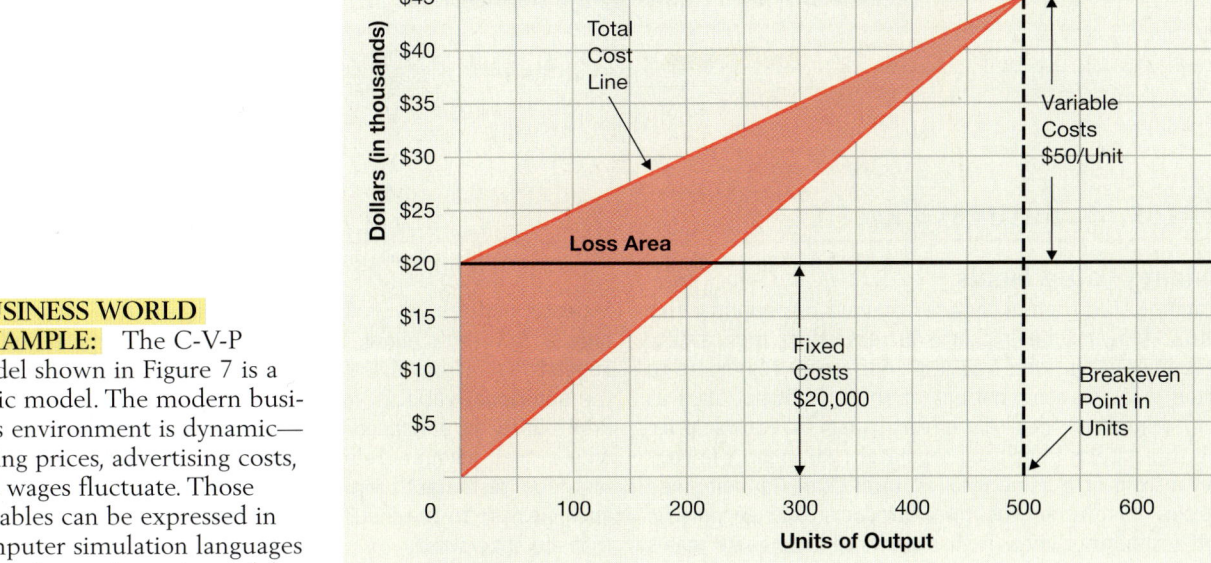

BUSINESS WORLD EXAMPLE: The C-V-P model shown in Figure 7 is a static model. The modern business environment is dynamic—selling prices, advertising costs, and wages fluctuate. Those variables can be expressed in computer simulation languages to produce a dynamic model.

Using Contribution Margin to Determine the Breakeven Point

KEY POINT: Contribution margin equals sales minus variable costs, whereas gross margin equals sales minus the cost of goods sold.

KEY POINT: The maximum contribution a unit of product can make is its selling price. After paying for itself (variable costs), a product provides a contribution margin to help pay total fixed costs and then earn a profit.

A simpler method of determining the breakeven point uses contribution margin. Contribution margin (CM) is the amount that remains after all variable costs are subtracted from sales:

$$S - VC = CM$$

A product line's contribution margin represents its net contribution to paying off fixed costs and earning a profit. Profit (P) is what remains after fixed costs are paid and subtracted from the contribution margin:

$$CM - FC = P$$

The example that follows uses contribution margin to determine the profitability of Valley Metal Products.

Symbols		Units Produced and Sold		
		250	500	750
S	Sales revenue ($90 per unit)	$22,500	$45,000	$67,500
VC	Less variable costs ($50 per unit)	12,500	25,000	37,500
CM	Contribution margin ($40 per unit)	$10,000	$20,000	$30,000
FC	Less fixed costs	20,000	20,000	20,000
P	Profit (loss)	($10,000)	$ 0	$10,000

The breakeven point (BE) can be expressed as the point at which contribution margin minus total fixed costs equals zero (or the point at which contribution margin equals total fixed costs). In terms of units of product, the equation for the breakeven point looks like this:

$$(CM\ per\ Unit \times BE\ Units) - FC = 0$$

It can also be expressed like this:

$$BE\ Units = \frac{FC}{CM\ per\ unit}$$

To show how the formula works, we use the data for Valley Metal Products:

$$BE\ Units = \frac{FC}{CM\ per\ unit} = \frac{\$20,000}{\$90 - \$50} = \frac{\$20,000}{\$40} = 500\ Units$$

The breakeven point in total sales dollars may be determined by multiplying the breakeven point in units by the selling price (SP) per unit:

$$BE\ Dollars = SP \times BE\ Units = \$90 \times 500\ Units = \$45,000$$

Focus on Business Practice

Supersizing Value Meals

Understanding their costs helps fast-food restaurants like McDonald's <www.mcdonalds.com> increase their profitability in at least two ways. One way is to encourage customers to buy "value meals"—combinations of three products, such as sandwich, drink, and fries—by offering them at a lower price than the three items purchased separately. Although the contribution margin of a value meal is lower than the combined contribution margins of the three products sold separately, fast-food restaurants know from experience that value meals lead to higher total sales. Another way fast-food restaurants increase profitability is by offering "supersized" orders for only a few cents more than the price of a regular order. Supersizing increases the total contribution margin because the additional variable cost of the larger size is very small. Profitability is enhanced even though revenue increases by only a small amount. Selling larger sizes is so important to a fast-food restaurant's profitability that a common performance measure in the industry is the percentage of value meals that are supersized.

FIGURE 8
Sales Mix for Valley Metal Products, Inc.

An alternative way of determining the breakeven point in total sales dollars is to divide the fixed costs by the contribution margin ratio. The contribution margin ratio is the contribution margin divided by the selling price:

$$\text{CM Ratio} = \frac{\text{CM}}{\text{SP}} = \frac{\$40}{\$90} = .444, \text{ or } 4/9$$

$$\text{BE Dollars} = \frac{\text{FC}}{\text{CM Ratio}} = \frac{\$20,000}{.444} = \$45,045*$$

*Difference due to rounding up.

THE BREAKEVEN POINT FOR MULTIPLE PRODUCTS

To satisfy the needs of different customers, many manufacturers sell a variety of products, which often have different variable and fixed costs and different selling prices. To calculate the breakeven point for each product, its unit contribution margin must be weighted by the sales mix. The **sales mix** is the proportion of each product's unit sales relative to the organization's total unit sales. Let's assume that Valley Metal Products sells two types of plant stands: a floor stand model and a smaller tabletop model. If the company sells 500 units, of which 300 units are floor stands and 200 are tabletops, the sales mix would be 3:2. For every three floor stands sold, two tabletops are sold. The sales mix can also be stated in percentages. Of the 500 units sold, 60 percent (300 ÷ 500) are floor stand sales, and 40 percent (200 ÷ 500) are tabletop sales (see Figure 8).

The breakeven point for multiple products can be computed in three steps. To illustrate, we will use Valley Metal Products' sales mix of 60 percent floor stands to 40 percent tabletops and total fixed costs of $32,000; the selling price, variable cost, and contribution margin per unit for each product line are shown in Step 1 below.

Step 1. *Compute the weighted-average contribution margin.* To do so, multiply the contribution margin for each product by its percentage of the sales mix, as follows:

	Selling Price		Variable Costs		Contribution Margin (CM)		Percentage of Sales Mix		Weighted-Average CM
Floor stand	$90	−	$50	=	$40	×	.60	=	$24
Tabletop	$40	−	$20	=	$20	×	.40	=	8
Weighted-average contribution margin									$32

KEY POINT: A company's sales mix can be very dynamic. If the mix is constantly changing, an assumption of stability may undermine the C-V-P analysis.

Step 2. *Calculate the weighted-average breakeven point.* Divide total fixed costs by the weighted-average contribution margin:

Weighted-Average Breakeven Point = Total Fixed Costs ÷ Weighted-Average Contribution Margin

= $32,000 ÷ $32

= 1,000 Units

Step 3. *Calculate the breakeven point for each product.* Multiply the weighted-average breakeven point by each product's percentage of the sales mix:

	Weighted-Average Breakeven Point		Sales Mix		Breakeven Point
Floor stand	1,000 units	×	.60	=	600 units
Tabletop	1,000 units	×	.40	=	400 units

To verify, determine the contribution margin of each product and subtract the total fixed costs:

Contribution margin
Floor stand	600 × $40 =	$24,000
Tabletop	400 × $20 =	8,000
Total contribution margin		$32,000
Less fixed costs		32,000
Profit		$ 0

✓ Check out ACE for a Review Quiz at http://accounting.college.hmco.com/students.

USING C-V-P ANALYSIS TO PLAN FUTURE SALES, COSTS, AND PROFITS

LO5 Use C-V-P analysis to project the profitability of products and services.

RELATED TEXT ASSIGNMENTS
Q: 17, 18, 19
SE: 9, 10
E: 6, 9, 12, 13, 14, 15
P: 1, 2, 3, 4, 5, 6, 7, 8
SD: 2
MRA: 2, 4, 5

The primary goal of a business venture is not to break even; it is to generate profits. C-V-P analysis adjusted for targeted profit can be used to estimate the profitability of a venture. This approach is excellent for "what-if" analysis, in which managers select several scenarios and compute the profit that may be anticipated from each. For instance, what if sales increase by 17,000 units? What effect will the increase have on profit? What if sales increase by only 6,000 units? What if fixed costs are reduced by $14,500? What if the variable unit cost increases by $1.40? Each scenario generates a different amount of profit or loss.

APPLYING C-V-P TO A MANUFACTURING BUSINESS

To illustrate how a manufacturing business can apply C-V-P analysis, assume that Van Bryce, the president of Valley Metal Products, Inc., has set $4,000 in profit as this year's goal for the plant stands. If all the data in our earlier example remain the same, how many plant stands must Valley Metal Products sell to reach the targeted profit? Again, x equals the number of units.

$$S = VC + FC + P$$
$$\$90x = \$50x + \$20,000 + \$4,000$$
$$\$40x = \$24,000$$
$$x = 600 \text{ Units}$$

To check the answer, insert all known data into the equation:

$$S - VC - FC = P$$
$$(600 \times \$90) - (600 \times \$50) - \$20,000 = \$4,000$$
$$\$54,000 - \$30,000 - \$20,000 = \$4,000$$

The contribution margin approach can also be used for profit planning. To do so, simply add the targeted profit to the numerator of the contribution margin breakeven equation:

$$\text{Targeted Sales Units} = \frac{FC + P}{CM \text{ per Unit}}$$

The number of sales units Valley Metal Products needs to generate $4,000 in profit is computed this way:

$$\text{Targeted Sales Units} = \frac{FC + P}{CM \text{ per Unit}} = \frac{\$20,000 + \$4,000}{\$40} = \frac{\$24,000}{\$40} = 600 \text{ Units}$$

Contribution income statements, which are prepared for internal use, are also useful to managers in planning and making decisions about their company's operations. As you can see in the contribution income statement for Valley Metal Products that appears below, the focus of such a statement is on cost behavior, not cost function. All variable costs related to production, selling, and administration are subtracted from sales to determine the total contribution margin. All fixed costs related to production, selling, and administration are subtracted from the total contribution margin to determine operating income. (As we noted earlier, in income statements involving an entire company, the term *operating income* is more appropriate than *profit*.)

Valley Metal Products, Inc.
Contribution Income Statement
For the Year Ended December 31, 20x8

	Per Unit	Total for 600 Units
Sales revenue	$90	$54,000
Less variable costs	50	30,000
Contribution margin	$40	$24,000
Less fixed costs		20,000
Operating income		$ 4,000

Van Bryce wants Valley Metal Products' planning team to consider three alternatives to the original plan shown in the contribution income statement. In the following sections, we examine each of these alternatives and its impact on operating income. In the summary, we review our work and analyze the different breakeven points.

■ **ALTERNATIVE 1: DECREASE VARIABLE COSTS, INCREASE SALES VOLUME** The planning team worked with production, purchasing, and sales employees to determine what operating income would be if the company purchased and used aluminum rather than iron to make the plant stands. If aluminum were used, the direct materials cost per unit would decrease by $3 to $47. If the company painted the aluminum to meet the needs of a new customer group, it would increase sales volume by 10 percent to 660 units. What is the estimated operating income for this alternative? How does this alternative affect operating income?

	Per Unit	Total for 660 units
Sales revenue	$90	$59,400
Less variable costs	47	31,020
Contribution margin	$43	$28,380
Less fixed costs		20,000
Operating income		$ 8,380
Increase in operating income ($8,380 − $4,000)		$ 4,380

A different way to determine the impact of changes in selling price, cost, or sales volume on operating income is to analyze only the data that change between the original plan and the proposed alternative. If Alternative 1 is used, variable costs will decrease by $3 (from $50 to $47), which will increase the contribution margin per unit by $3 (from $40 to $43). This will increase the total contribution margin and operating income by $1,800 ($3 × 600). In addition, a sales increase of 60 units (.10 × 600) will increase the total contribution margin and operating income by $2,580 ($43 × 60). The total increase in operating income due to the decrease in variable costs and the increase in sales volume will be $4,380.

Analysis of Changes Only

Increase in contribution margin from	
Planned sales [($43 − $40) × 600 units]	$1,800
Additional sales ($43 × 60 units)	2,580
Increase in operating income	$4,380

■ **ALTERNATIVE 2: INCREASE FIXED COSTS, INCREASE SALES VOLUME** Instead of changing the direct materials, the Marketing Department suggested that a $500 increase in advertising costs would increase sales volume by 5 percent. What is the estimated operating income for this alternative? How does this alternative affect operating income?

	Per Unit	Total for 630 units
Sales revenue	$90	$56,700
Less variable costs	50	31,500
Contribution margin	$40	$25,200
Less fixed costs		20,500
Operating income		$ 4,700
Increase in operating income ($4,700 − $4,000)		$ 700

Additional advertising costs will affect both sales volume and fixed costs. The sales volume will increase by 30 plant stands, from 600 units to 630 units (600 × 1.05), which increases the total contribution margin and operating income by $1,200 (from $24,000 to $25,200). Fixed costs will increase from $20,000 to $20,500, which decreases operating income by $500. The increase in operating income will be $700 ($1,200 − $500).

Analysis of Changes Only

Increase in contribution margin from	
additional units sold [($40 × (600 × .05)]	$1,200
Less increase in fixed costs	500
Increase in operating income	$ 700

■ **ALTERNATIVE 3: INCREASE SELLING PRICE, DECREASE SALES VOLUME** Van Bryce asked the planning team to evaluate the impact of a $10 increase in selling price on the company's operating income. If the selling price is increased, the team estimates that the sales volume will decrease by 15 percent to 510 units. What is the estimated operating income for this alternative? How does this alternative affect operating income?

	Per Unit	Total for 510 Units
Sales revenue	$100	$51,000
Less variable costs	50	25,500
Contribution margin	50	$25,500
Less fixed costs		20,000
Operating income		$ 5,500
Increase in operating income ($5,500 − $4,000)		$ 1,500

Analysis of Changes Only

Increase in contribution margin from increase in selling price ($10 increase in selling price × 510 units sold)	$5,100
Decrease in contribution margin from decrease in sales volume ($40 contribution margin per unit × 90 sales units lost)	(3,600)
Increase in operating income	$1,500

■ **COMPARATIVE SUMMARY** In preparation for a meeting with Van Bryce, the planning team at Valley Metal Products compiled the summary presented in Exhibit 1. It compares the three alternatives with the original plan and shows how changes in variable and fixed costs, selling price, and sales volume affect the breakeven point.

EXHIBIT 1
Comparative Summary of Alternatives at Valley Metal Products, Inc.

	Original Plan Totals for 600 Units	Alternative 1 Decrease Direct Materials Costs for 660 Units	Alternative 2 Increase Advertising Costs for 630 Units	Alternative 3 Increase Selling Price for 510 Units
Sales revenue	$54,000	$59,400	$56,700	$51,000
Less variable costs	30,000	31,020	31,500	25,500
Contribution margin	$24,000	$28,380	$25,200	$25,500
Less fixed costs	20,000	20,000	20,500	20,000
Operating income	$ 4,000	$ 8,380	$ 4,700	$ 5,500
Breakeven point in whole units				
$20,000 FC ÷ $40 CM	500			
$20,000 FC ÷ $43 CM		466*		
$20,500 FC ÷ $40 CM			513	
$20,000 FC ÷ $50 CM				400

*Rounded up to next whole unit.

> **STOP AND THINK!**
> Why is the breakeven point important?
> *The breakeven point is important because it is the point at which an organization can begin to earn a profit.* ∎

Note that the decrease in variable costs (direct materials) proposed in Alternative 1 increases the contribution margin per unit (from $40 to $43), which reduces the breakeven point. Because fewer sales dollars are required to cover variable costs, the breakeven point is reached sooner than in the original plan—at a sales volume of 466 units rather than at 500 units. In Alternative 2, the increase in fixed costs has no effect on the contribution margin per unit, but it does require the total contribution margin to cover more fixed costs before reaching the breakeven point. Thus, the breakeven point is higher than in the original plan—513 units as opposed to 500. The increase in selling price in Alternative 3 increases the contribution margin per unit, which reduces the breakeven point. Because more sales dollars are available to cover fixed costs, the breakeven point of 400 units is lower than the breakeven point in the original plan.

Which plan should Bryce choose? If he wants the highest operating income, he will choose Alternative 1. If, however, he wants the company to begin generating operating income more quickly, he will choose the plan with the lowest breakeven point, Alternative 3. Remember that the breakeven point provides a rough estimate of the number of units that must be sold to cover the total costs. Additional qualitative information may help Bryce make a better decision. Will customers perceive that the quality of the plant stands is lower if the company uses aluminum rather than iron, as proposed in Alternative 1? Will increased expenditures on advertising yield a 5 percent increase in sales volume, as Alternative 2 postulates? Will the increase in selling price suggested in Alternative 3 create more than a 15 percent decline in unit sales? Quantitative information is essential for planning, but managers must also be sensitive to qualitative factors, such as product quality, reliability and quality of suppliers, and availability of human and technical resources.

APPLYING C-V-P ANALYSIS TO A SERVICE BUSINESS

In this section, we look at how a service business can use C-V-P analysis in planning its operations. Assume that Glenda Haley, the manager of the Appraisal Department at Edmunds Mortgage Company, wants to plan the home appraisal activities that each mortgage loan application requires. She estimates that over the next year, her department will perform an average of 100 appraisals per month and service fee revenue will be $400 per appraisal. Other estimated data for the year are as follows:

Variable costs: direct professional labor, $160 per appraisal; county survey map fee, $99 per appraisal

Mixed costs (monthly service overhead):

Volume	Month	Activity Level	Cost
Highest	March	180 appraisals	$23,380
Lowest	February	98 appraisals	20,018

■ **ESTIMATING SERVICE OVERHEAD COSTS** Haley wants to estimate the total service overhead cost of appraisals for next year. She uses the high-low method to do so:

Step 1. *Calculate the variable service overhead cost per appraisal.*

$$\begin{aligned}\text{Variable Service Overhead Cost per Appraisal} &= (\text{Highest Cost} - \text{Lowest Cost}) \div (\text{Highest Volume} - \text{Lowest Volume}) \\ &= (\$23{,}380 - \$20{,}018) \div (180 - 98) \\ &= \$3{,}362 \div 82 \text{ Appraisals} = \$41\end{aligned}$$

Step 2. *Calculate the total fixed service overhead costs.*

$$\begin{aligned}\text{Total Fixed Service Overhead Costs} &= \text{Total Service Overhead Costs} - \text{Total Variable Service Overhead Costs}\\ \text{Total Fixed Service Overhead Costs for March} &= \$23{,}380 - (\$41 \times 180)\\ &= \$16{,}000\end{aligned}$$

Step 3. *Calculate the total service overhead costs for one month.*

Total Service Overhead Costs = Total Fixed Service Overhead Costs + (Variable Rate × Estimated Number of Appraisals)
= $16,000 + ($41 per Appraisal × Number of Appraisals)

Step 4. *Calculate the total service overhead costs for one month assuming that 100 appraisals will be made.*

Total Overhead Service Costs = $16,000 + ($41 × 100) = $20,100

■ **DETERMINING THE BREAKEVEN POINT** Glenda Haley also wants to know how many appraisals her department must perform each month to cover the fixed and variable appraisal costs. She calculates the breakeven point as follows:

Let x = Number of Appraisals per Month at Breakeven Point
S = VC + FC
$400x = $300x + $16,000
$100x = $16,000
x = 160 Appraisals per Month

The variable rate of $300 per appraisal includes the variable service overhead rate, the direct professional labor, and the county survey map fee ($41 + $160 + $99).

■ **DETERMINING THE EFFECT OF A CHANGE IN OPERATING COSTS** Haley is worried because her department can perform an average of only 100 appraisals each month, but the estimated breakeven point is 160 appraisals per month. Because of strong competition, increasing the appraisal fee is not an option; to make the appraisals profitable, the mortgage company has asked Haley to find ways of reducing costs. In reviewing the situation, Haley has determined that improved scheduling of appraisals will reduce appraisers' travel time. Travel time is included in the current professional labor cost of $160 per appraisal (four hours of an appraiser's time at $40 per hour). By scheduling the jobs according to location, Haley can reduce the appraisers' travel time enough to reduce the total time required by 50 percent, thus cutting the professional labor cost to $80 per appraisal [(.50 × 4 hours) × $40 per hour]. The new scheduling process will increase fixed costs by $200 per month. Given these circumstances, what will the breakeven point be?

Let x = Number of Appraisals per Month at Breakeven Point
S = VC + FC
$400x = $220x + $16,200
$180x = $16,200
x = 90 Appraisals per Month

Variable costs become $220 ($300 − $80) per appraisal due to the reduced labor costs. This change increases the contribution margin by $80 per appraisal. Fixed costs increase from $16,000 to $16,200. The increase in the contribution margin is greater than the increase in the fixed costs, so the breakeven point decreases from 160 appraisals per month to 90 appraisals per month.

■ **ACHIEVING A TARGETED PROFIT** How many appraisals would Glenda Haley's department have to perform each month to achieve a targeted profit of $18,000 per month?

Let x = Targeted Sales in Units
S = VC + FC + P
$400x = $220x + $16,200 + $18,000
$180x = $34,200
x = 190 Units

 Check out ACE for a Review Quiz at http://accounting.college.hmco.com/students.

Chapter Review

REVIEW OF LEARNING OBJECTIVES

LO1 Define *cost behavior* and explain how managers use this concept in the management cycle.

Cost behavior is the way costs respond to changes in volume or activity. In the planning stage of the management cycle, managers use cost behavior to determine how many units of products or services must be sold to generate a targeted amount of profit and how changes in planned activities will affect operating income. In the executing stage, managers must understand and anticipate cost behavior to determine the impact of their decisions on operating income. In the reviewing and reporting stages, managers analyze how changes in cost and sales affect the profitability of product lines, sales territories, customers, departments, and other business segments by preparing reports using variable costing.

LO2 Identify variable, fixed, and mixed costs, and separate mixed costs into their variable and fixed components.

Some costs vary in relation to volume or operating activity; other costs remain fixed as volume changes. Cost behavior depends on whether the focus is total costs or cost per unit. Total costs that change in direct proportion to changes in productive output (or any other volume measure) are called *variable costs*. They include hourly wages, the cost of operating supplies, direct materials costs, and the cost of merchandise. Total *fixed costs* remain constant within a relevant range of volume or activity. They change only when volume or activity exceeds the relevant range—for example, when new equipment or new buildings must be purchased, higher insurance premiums and property taxes must be paid, or additional supervisory personnel must be hired to accommodate increased activity. A *mixed cost*, such as the cost of electricity, has both variable and fixed cost components. For cost planning and control, mixed costs must be separated into their variable and fixed components. To separate them, managers use a variety of methods, including the engineering, scatter diagram, high-low, and statistical methods.

LO3 Define *cost-volume-profit (C-V-P) analysis* and discuss how managers use it as a tool for planning and control.

Cost-volume-profit analysis is an examination of the cost behavior patterns that underlie the relationships among cost, volume of output, and profit. It is a tool for both planning and control. The techniques and problem-solving procedures involved in C-V-P analysis express relationships among revenue, sales mix, cost, volume, and profit. Those relationships provide a general model of financial activity that management can use for short-range planning and for evaluating performance and analyzing alternatives.

LO4 Define *breakeven point* and use contribution margin to determine a company's breakeven point for multiple products.

The *breakeven point* is the point at which total revenues equal total costs—in other words, the point at which net sales equal variable costs plus fixed costs. Once the number of units needed to break even is known, the number can be multiplied by the product's selling price to determine the breakeven point in sales dollars. *Contribution margin* is the amount that remains after all variable costs have been subtracted from sales. A product's contribution margin represents its net contribution to paying off fixed costs and earning a profit. The breakeven point in units can be computed by using the following formula:

$$\text{BE Units} = \frac{\text{FC}}{\text{CM per Unit}}$$

A sales mix is used to calculate the breakeven point for each product when a company sells more than one product.

LO5 Use C-V-P analysis to project the profitability of products and services.

The addition of targeted profit to the breakeven equation makes it possible to plan levels of operation that yield the targeted profit. The formula in terms of contribution margin is

$$\text{Targeted Sales Units} = \frac{\text{FC} + \text{P}}{\text{CM per Unit}}$$

C-V-P analysis, whether used by a manufacturing company or a service organization, enables managers to select several "what if" scenarios and evaluate the outcome of each to determine which will generate the desired amount of profit.

REVIEW OF CONCEPTS AND TERMINOLOGY

The following concepts and terms were introduced in this chapter:

LO4 **Breakeven point:** The point at which total revenues equal total costs.

LO4 **Contribution margin:** The amount that remains after all variable costs are subtracted from sales.

LO1 **Cost behavior:** The way costs respond to changes in volume or activity.

LO3 **Cost-volume-profit (C-V-P) analysis:** An examination of the cost behavior patterns that underlie the relationships among cost, volume of output, and profit.

LO2 **Engineering method:** A method that separates costs into their fixed and variable components by performing a step-by-step analysis of the tasks, costs, and processes involved in completing an activity or product.

LO2 **Fixed costs:** Total costs that remain constant within a relevant range of volume or activity.

LO2 **High-low method:** A three-step approach to separating a mixed cost into its variable and fixed components.

LO4 **Margin of safety:** The number of sales units or amount of sales dollars by which actual sales can fall below planned sales without resulting in a loss.

LO2 **Mixed costs:** Costs that have both variable and fixed components.

LO2 **Normal capacity:** The average annual level of operating capacity needed to meet expected sales demand.

LO2 **Operating capacity:** The upper limit of an organization's productive output capability, given its existing resources.

LO2 **Practical capacity:** Theoretical capacity reduced by normal and expected work stoppages.

LO2 **Regression analysis:** A mathematical approach to separating a mixed cost into its variable and fixed components.

LO2 **Relevant range:** The span of activity in which a company expects to operate.

LO4 **Sales mix:** The proportion of each product's unit sales relative to the organization's total unit sales.

LO2 **Scatter diagram:** A chart of plotted points that helps determine whether a linear relationship exists between a cost item and its related activity measure.

LO2 **Theoretical (ideal) capacity:** The maximum productive output for a given period in which all machinery and equipment are operating at optimum speed, without interruption.

LO2 **Variable costs:** Total costs that change in direct proportion to changes in productive output or any other measure of volume.

REVIEW PROBLEM

Breakeven Analysis and Profitability Planning

LO4
LO5 Olympia, Inc., is a major producer of golf clubs. Its oversized putter has a large potential market. The following is a summary of data from the company's operations in 20x5:

Total fixed costs		
Manufacturing overhead	195,000	
Advertising	55,000	
Administrative expense	68,000	
Variable costs per unit		
Direct materials	$	23
Direct labor		8
Manufacturing overhead		6
Selling expense		5
Selling price per unit		95

REQUIRED
1. Compute the breakeven point in units for 20x5.
2. Olympia sold 6,500 putters in 20x5. How much profit did the company realize?
3. To improve profitability in 20x6, management is considering the four alternative courses of action indicated below. (In performing the required steps, use the figures from item **2** and treat each alternative independently.)
   a. Calculate the number of units Olympia must sell to generate a targeted profit of $95,400. Assume that costs and selling price remain constant.
   b. Calculate the operating income if the company increases the number of units sold by 20 percent and cuts the selling price by $5 per unit.
   c. Determine the number of units that must be sold to break even if advertising costs are increased by $47,700.
   d. Find the number of units that must be sold to generate a targeted profit of $120,000 if variable costs are cut by 10 percent.

ANSWER TO REVIEW PROBLEM

1. Breakeven point in units for 20x5:

$$\text{Breakeven Units} = \frac{FC}{CM \text{ per Unit}} = \frac{\$318{,}000}{\$95 - \$42} = \frac{\$318{,}000}{\$53} = 6{,}000 \text{ Units}$$

2. Profit from sale of 6,500 units:

Units sold	6,500
Units required to break even	6,000
Units over breakeven	500

20x5 profit = $53 per unit × 500 = $26,500

Contribution margin equals sales minus all variable costs. Contribution margin per unit equals the amount left to cover fixed costs and earn a profit after variable costs have been subtracted from sales dollars. If all fixed costs have been absorbed by the time breakeven is reached, the entire contribution margin of each unit sold in excess of breakeven represents profit.

3. a. Number of units that must be sold to generate a targeted profit of $95,400:

$$\text{Targeted Sales Units} = \frac{FC + P}{CM \text{ per Unit}}$$

$$\frac{\$318{,}000 + \$95{,}400}{\$53} = \frac{\$413{,}400}{\$53} = 7{,}800 \text{ Units}$$

b. Operating income if unit sales increase 20 percent and unit selling price decreases by $5:

Sales revenue [7,800 (6,500 × 1.20) units at $90 per unit]	$702,000
Less variable costs (7,800 units × $42)	327,600
Contribution margin	$374,400
Less fixed costs	318,000
Operating income	$ 56,400

c. Number of units needed to break even if advertising costs (fixed costs) increase by $47,700:

$$\text{BE Units} = \frac{FC}{CM \text{ per Unit}}$$

$$\frac{\$318{,}000 + \$47{,}700}{\$53} = \frac{\$365{,}700}{\$53} = 6{,}900 \text{ Units}$$

d. Number of units that must be sold to generate a targeted profit of $120,000 if variable costs decrease by 10 percent:

CM per Unit = $95.00 − ($42.00 × .9) = $95.00 − $37.80 = $57.20

$$\text{Targeted Sales Units} = \frac{FC + P}{CM \text{ per Unit}}$$

$$\frac{\$318{,}000 + \$120{,}000}{\$57.20} = \frac{\$438{,}000}{\$57.20} = 7{,}658 \text{ Units*}$$

*Note that the answer is rounded up to the next whole unit.

Chapter Assignments

BUILDING YOUR KNOWLEDGE FOUNDATION

QUESTIONS

1. Define *cost behavior*.
2. Why is an understanding of cost behavior useful to managers?
3. What is the difference between theoretical capacity and practical capacity?
4. Why does a company never operate at theoretical capacity?
5. What is normal capacity? Why is normal capacity considered more relevant and useful than either theoretical or practical capacity?
6. What does *relevant range of activity* mean?
7. What makes variable costs different from fixed costs?
8. "Fixed costs remain constant in total but decrease per unit as productive output increases." Explain this statement.
9. What is a mixed cost? Give an example.
10. What is a scatter diagram?
11. Describe the high-low method of separating mixed costs.
12. Define *cost-volume-profit analysis*.
13. Identify two uses of C-V-P analysis and explain their significance to management.
14. What conditions must be met for C-V-P computations to be accurate?
15. Define *breakeven point*. Why is information about the breakeven point important to managers?
16. Define *contribution margin* and describe its use in breakeven analysis.
17. State the equation that uses fixed costs, targeted profit, and contribution margin per unit to determine targeted sales units.
18. Give examples of the ways in which a service business can use C-V-P analysis.
19. Identify the differences and similarities in breakeven analysis for manufacturing organizations and service organizations.

SHORT EXERCISES

LO1 Concept of Cost Behavior

SE 1. Dapper Hat Makers is in the business of designing and producing specialty hats. The material used for derbies costs $4.50 per unit, and Dapper pays each of its two full-time employees $250 per week. If Employee A makes 15 derbies in one week, what is the variable cost per derby, and what is this worker's fixed cost per derby? If Employee B makes only 12 derbies in one week, what are this worker's variable and fixed costs per derby? (Round to two decimal places where necessary.)

LO2 Identification of Variable, Fixed, and Mixed Costs

SE 2. Identify the following as fixed costs, variable costs, or mixed costs:

1. Direct materials
2. Telephone expense
3. Operating supplies
4. Personnel manager's salary
5. Factory building rent payment

LO2 Mixed Costs: High-Low Method

SE 3. Using the high-low method and the information below, compute the monthly variable cost per telephone hour and total fixed costs for Sadiko Corporation.

Month	Telephone Hours Used	Telephone Expenses
April	96	$4,350
May	93	4,230
June	105	4,710

LO3 C-V-P Analysis

SE 4. DeLuca, Inc., wants to make a profit of $20,000. It has variable costs of $80 per unit and fixed costs of $12,000. How much must it charge per unit if 4,000 units are sold?

LO4	**SE 5.** Breakeven Analysis	How many units must Braxton Company sell to break even if the selling price per unit is $8.50, variable costs are $4.30 per unit, and fixed costs are $3,780? What is the breakeven point in total dollars of sales?
LO4	**SE 6.** Contribution Margin	Using the contribution margin approach, find the breakeven point in units for Norcia Consumer Products if the selling price per unit is $11, the variable cost per unit is $6, and the fixed costs are $5,500.
LO4	**SE 7.** Contribution Margin Ratio	Using the information in **SE 6**, compute the breakeven point in total sales dollars using the contribution margin ratio.
LO4	**SE 8.** Breakeven Analysis for Multiple Products	Using the contribution margin approach, find the breakeven point in units for Sardinia Company's two products. Product A's selling price per unit is $10, and its variable cost per unit is $4. Product B's selling price per unit is $8, and its variable cost per unit is $5. Fixed costs are $15,000, and the sales mix of Product A to Product B is 2:1.
LO4, LO5	**SE 9.** Contribution Margin and Projected Profit	If Oui Watches sells 300 watches at $48 per watch and has variable costs of $18 per watch and fixed costs of $4,000, what is the projected profit?

SE 10.

LO5 **Cost Behavior in a Service Business**

Guy Spy, a private investigation firm, has the following costs for December:

Direct labor: $190 per case
Service overhead

Salary for director of investigations	$ 4,800
Telephone	930
Depreciation	8,300
Legal advice	2,300
Supplies	590
Advertising	360
Utilities	1,560
Wages for clerical personnel	2,000
Total service overhead	$20,840

Service overhead for October was $21,150; for November, it was $21,350. The number of cases investigated during October, November, and December was 93, 97, and 91, respectively. Compute the variable and fixed cost components of service overhead. Then determine the variable and fixed costs per case for December. (Round to nearest dollar where necessary.)

EXERCISES

E 1.

LO2 **Identification of Variable and Fixed Costs**

Indicate whether each of the following costs of productive output is usually variable or fixed: (1) packing materials for stereo components, (2) real estate taxes, (3) gasoline for a delivery truck, (4) property insurance, (5) depreciation expense of buildings (calculated with the straight-line method), (6) supplies, (7) indirect materials, (8) bottles used to package liquids, (9) license fees for company cars, (10) wiring used in radios, (11) machine helper's wages, (12) wood used in bookcases, (13) city operating license, (14) machine depreciation based on machine hours used, (15) machine operator's hourly wages, and (16) cost of required outside inspection of each unit produced.

E 2.

LO2 **Variable Cost Analysis**

Zero Time Oil Change has been in business for six months. The company pays $.50 per quart for the oil it uses in servicing cars, and each job requires an average of four quarts of oil. The company estimates that in the next three months, it will service 240, 288, and 360 cars.

1. Compute the cost of oil for each of the three months and the total cost for all three months.

Month	Cars to Be Serviced	Required Quarts/Car	Cost/Quart	Total Cost/Month
1	240	4	$.50	_____
2	288	4	.50	_____
3	360	4	.50	_____
Three-month total	888			======

2. Complete the following sentences by choosing the words that best describe the cost behavior at Zero Time Oil Change:

Cost per unit (increased, decreased, remained constant).
Total variable cost per month (increased, decreased) as the quantity of oil used (increased, decreased).

LO2 Mixed Costs: High-Low Method

E 3. Whitehouse Company manufactures major appliances. Because of increased interest in its refrigerators, it has just had its most successful year. In preparing the budget for next year, Jackson Harper, the company's controller, compiled these data:

Month	Volume in Machine Hours	Electricity Costs
July	6,000	$60,000
August	5,000	53,000
September	4,500	49,500
October	4,000	46,000
November	3,500	42,500
December	3,000	39,000

Using the high-low method, determine (1) the variable electricity cost per machine hour, (2) the monthly fixed electricity cost, and (3) the total variable electricity costs and fixed electricity costs for the six-month period.

LO2 Mixed Costs: High-Low Method

E 4. When Jerome Company's monthly costs were $75,000, sales were $80,000; when its monthly costs were $60,000, sales were $50,000. Use the high-low method to develop a monthly cost formula for Jerome Company's coming year.

LO4 Contribution Margin

E 5. Senora Company manufactures a single product that sells for $110 per unit. The company projects sales of 500 units per month. Projected costs are as follows:

Type of Cost	Manufacturing	Nonmanufacturing
Variable	$10,000	$5,000
Nonvariable (FIXED)	$12,500	$7,500

TOTAL = 10,000 + 5,000 = 15,000
TOTAL = 12,500 + 7,500 = 20,000

1. What is the company's contribution margin per unit?
2. What is the contribution margin ratio?
3. What volume, in terms of units, must the company sell to break even?

LO4 Breakeven Point and C-V-P
LO5 Analysis

E 6. Using the data in the contribution income statement for Sedona, Inc., that appears below, calculate (1) selling price, (2) variable costs, and (3) breakeven point in sales.

Sedona, Inc.
Contribution Income Statement
For the Year Ended December 31, 20x7

Sales (10,000 units)		$16,000,000
Less variable costs		
Cost of goods sold	$8,000,000	
Selling, administrative, and general	4,000,000	
Total variable costs		12,000,000
Contribution margin		$ 4,000,000
Less fixed costs		
Overhead	$1,200,000	
Selling, administrative, and general	800,000	
Total fixed costs		2,000,000
Operating Income		$ 2,000,000

Chapter 20 Cost Behavior Analysis

LO4 Graphic Breakeven Analysis

E 7. Identify the letter of the point, line segment, or area of the breakeven graph shown below that correctly completes each of the following statements:

1. The maximum possible operating loss is
   - a. A.
   - b. D.
   - c. B.
   - d. F.

2. The breakeven point in sales dollars is
   - a. C.
   - b. D.
   - c. A.
   - d. G.

3. At volume F, total contribution margin is
   - a. C.
   - b. D.
   - c. E.
   - d. G.

4. Net income is represented by area
   - a. KDL.
   - b. KCJ.
   - c. BDC.
   - d. GCJ.

5. At volume J, total fixed costs are represented by
   - a. H.
   - b. G.
   - c. I.
   - d. J.

6. If volume increases from F to J, the change in total costs is
   - a. HI minus DE.
   - b. DF minus HJ.
   - c. BC minus DF.
   - d. AB minus DE.

LO4 Breakeven Analysis

E 8. Techno Designs Company produces head covers for golf clubs. The company expects to generate a profit next year. It anticipates fixed manufacturing costs of $126,500 and fixed general and administrative expenses of $82,030 for the year. Variable manufacturing and selling costs per set of head covers will be $4.65 and $2.75, respectively. Each set will sell for $13.40.

1. Compute the breakeven point in sales units.
2. Compute the breakeven point in sales dollars.
3. If the selling price is increased to $14 per unit and fixed general and administrative expenses are cut by $33,465, what will the new breakeven point be in units?
4. Prepare a graph to illustrate the breakeven point computed in **2**.

LO4 Breakeven Analysis and
LO5 Pricing

E 9. McLennon Company has a plant capacity of 100,000 units per year, but its budget for 20x6 indicates that only 60,000 units will be produced and sold. The entire budget for 20x6 is as follows:

Sales (60,000 units at $4)		$240,000
Less cost of goods produced (based on production of 60,000 units)		
Direct materials (variable)	$60,000	
Direct labor (variable)	30,000	
Variable manufacturing costs	45,000	
Fixed manufacturing costs	75,000	
Total cost of goods produced		210,000
Gross margin		$ 30,000
Less selling and administrative expenses		
Selling (fixed)	$24,000	
Administrative (fixed)	36,000	
Total selling and administrative expenses		60,000
Operating income (loss)		($ 30,000)

1. Given the budgeted selling price and cost data, how many units would McLennon have to sell to break even? (**Hint**: Be sure to consider selling and administrative expenses.)
2. Market research indicates that if McLennon were to drop its selling price to $3.80 per unit, it could sell 100,000 units in 20x6. Would you recommend the drop in price? What would the new operating income or loss be?

E 10.
LO4 Breakeven Point for Multiple Products

Saline Aquarium, Inc., manufactures and sells aquariums, water pumps, and air filters. The sales mix is 1:2:2 (i.e., for every one aquarium sold, two water pumps and air filters are sold). Using the contribution margin approach, find the breakeven point in units for each product. The company's fixed costs are $26,000. Other information is as follows:

	Selling Price per Unit	Variable Cost per Unit
Aquariums	$60	$25
Water pumps	20	12
Air filters	10	3

E 11.
LO4 Sales Mix Analysis

Ella Mae Simpson is the owner of a hairdressing salon in Palm Coast, Florida. Her salon provides three basic services: shampoo and set, permanents, and cut and blow dry. The following are its operating results from the past quarter:

Type of Service	Number of Customers	Total Sales	Contribution Margin Dollars
Shampoo and set	1,200	$24,000	$14,700
Permanents	420	21,000	15,120
Cut and blow dry	1,000	15,000	10,000
	2,620	$60,000	$39,820
Total fixed costs			30,000
Profit			$ 9,820

Compute the breakeven point in units based on the weighted average contribution margin for the sales mix.

E 12.
LO4 Contribution Margin and
LO5 Profit Planning

Target Systems, Inc., makes heat-seeking missiles. It has just been offered a government contract from which it may realize a profit. The contract purchase price is $130,000 per missile, but the number of units to be purchased has not yet been decided. The company's fixed costs are budgeted at $3,973,500, and variable costs are $68,500 per unit.

1. Compute the number of units the company should agree to make at the stated contract price to earn a profit of $1,500,000.
2. Using a lighter material, the variable unit cost can be reduced by $1,730, but total fixed overhead will increase by $27,500. How many units must be produced to make $1,500,000 in profit?
3. Given the figures in **2**, how many additional units must be produced to increase profit by $1,264,600?

LO5 Planning Future Sales

E 13. Short-term automobile rentals are the specialty of ASAP Auto Rentals, Inc. Average variable operating costs have been $12.50 per day per automobile. The company owns 60 cars. Fixed operating costs for the next year are expected to be $145,500. Average daily rental revenue per automobile is expected to be $34.50. Management would like to earn a profit of $47,000 during the year.

1. Calculate the total number of daily rentals the company must have during the year to earn the targeted profit.
2. On the basis of your answer to 1, determine the average number of days each automobile must be rented.
3. Determine the total revenue needed to achieve the targeted profit of $47,000.
4. What would the total rental revenue be if fixed operating costs could be lowered by $5,180 and the targeted profit increased to $70,000?

LO5 Cost Behavior in a Service Business

E 14. Luke Ricci, CPA, is the owner of a firm that provides tax services. The firm charges $50 per return for the direct professional labor involved in preparing standard short-form tax returns. In January, the firm prepared 850 such returns; in February, 1,000; and in March, 700. Service overhead (telephone and utilities, depreciation on equipment and building, tax forms, office supplies, and wages of clerical personnel) for January was $18,500; for February, $20,000; and for March, $17,000.

1. Determine the variable and fixed cost components of the firm's Service Overhead account.
2. What would the estimated total cost per tax return be if the firm prepares 825 standard short-form tax returns in April?

LO5 C-V-P Analysis in a Service Business

E 15. Flossmoor Inspection Service specializes in inspecting cars that have been returned to automobile leasing companies at the end of their leases. Flossmoor's charge for each inspection is $50; its average cost per inspection is $15. Tony Lomangeno, Flossmoor's owner, wants to expand his business by hiring another employee and purchasing an automobile. The fixed costs of the new employee and automobile would be $3,000 per month. How many inspections per month would the new employee have to perform to earn Lomangeno a profit of $1,200?

PROBLEMS

LO2, LO5 Cost Behavior and Projection

P 1. Luster Auto, Inc., specializes in "detailing" automobile exteriors—that is, revitalizing them so the cars look as if they had just rolled off the showroom floor. The company charges $100 for a full exterior detailing. It has just completed its first year of business and has asked its accountants to analyze the operating results. Management wants costs divided into variable, fixed, and mixed components and would like them projected for the coming year. Anticipated volume for next year is 1,100 jobs.

The process used to detail a car's exterior is as follows:

1. One $20-per-hour employee spends 20 minutes cleaning the car's exterior.
2. One can per car of Bugg-Off, a cleaning compound, is used on trouble spots.
3. A chemical compound called Buff Glow is used to remove oxidants from the paint surface and restore the natural oils to the paint.
4. Poly Wax is applied by hand, allowed to sit for 10 minutes, and then buffed off.
5. The final step is an inspection to see that all wax and debris have been removed.

On average, two hours are spent on each car, including cleaning time and drying time for the wax. Operating information for Luster Auto's first year is as follows:

Number of automobiles detailed	840
Labor per auto	2 hours at $20.00 per hour
Containers of Bugg-Off consumed	840 at $3.50 per can
Pounds of Buff Glow consumed	105 pounds at $32.00 per pound
Pounds of Poly Wax consumed	210 pounds at $8.00 per pound
Rent	$1,400.00 per month

During the year, utilities costs ranged from $800 for 40 jobs in March to $1,801 for 110 jobs in August.

REQUIRED

1. Classify the costs as variable, fixed, or mixed.
2. Using the high-low method, separate the mixed costs into their variable and fixed components. Use number of jobs as the basis.

3. Project the same costs for next year, assuming that the anticipated increase in activity will occur and that fixed costs will remain constant.
4. Compute the unit cost per job for next year.
5. Given your answer to 4, should the price remain at $100 per job?

P 2.
LO4 Breakeven Analysis
LO5

Luce & Morgan, a law firm in downtown Jefferson City, is considering opening a legal clinic for middle- and low-income clients. The clinic would bill at a rate of $18 per hour. It would employ law students as paraprofessional help and pay them $9 per hour. Other variable costs are anticipated to be $5.40 per hour, and annual fixed costs are expected to total $27,000.

REQUIRED ▶

1. Compute the breakeven point in billable hours.
2. Compute the breakeven point in total billings.
3. Find the new breakeven point in total billings if fixed costs should go up by $2,340.
4. Using the original figures, compute the breakeven point in total billings if the billing rate decreases by $1 per hour, variable costs decrease by $.40 per hour, and fixed costs go down by $3,600.

P 3.
LO4 Planning Future Sales:
LO5 Contribution Margin Approach

Icon Industries is considering a new product for its Trophy Division. The product, which would feature an alligator, is expected to have global market appeal and to become the mascot for many high school and university athletic teams. Expected variable unit costs are as follows: direct materials, $18.50; direct labor, $4.25; production supplies, $1.10; selling costs, $2.80; and other, $1.95. Annual fixed costs are depreciation, building and equipment, $36,000; advertising, $45,000; and other, $11,400. Icon Industries plans to sell the product for $55.00.

REQUIRED ▶

1. Using the contribution margin approach, compute the number of units the company must sell to (a) break even and (b) earn a profit of $70,224.
2. Using the same data, compute the number of units that must be sold to earn a profit of $139,520 if advertising costs rise by $40,000.
3. Using the original information and sales of 10,000 units, compute the selling price the company must use to make a profit of $131,600. (**Hint:** Calculate contribution margin per unit first.)
4. According to the vice president of marketing, Albert Flora, the most optimistic annual sales estimate for the product would be 15,000 units, and the highest competitive selling price the company can charge is $52 per unit. How much more can be spent on fixed advertising costs if the selling price is $52, if the variable costs cannot be reduced, and if the targeted profit for 15,000 unit sales is $251,000?

P 4.
LO4 Breakeven Analysis and
LO5 Planning Future Sales

Write Company has a maximum capacity of 200,000 units per year. Variable manufacturing costs are $12 per unit. Fixed manufacturing overhead is $600,000 per year. Variable selling and administrative costs are $5 per unit, and fixed selling and administrative costs are $300,000 per year. The current sales price is $23 per unit.

REQUIRED ▶

1. What is the breakeven point in (a) sales units and (b) sales dollars?
2. How many units must Write Company sell to earn a profit of $240,000 per year?
3. A strike at one of the company's major suppliers has caused a shortage of materials, so the current year's production and sales are limited to 160,000 units. To partially offset the effect of the reduced sales on profit, management is planning to reduce fixed costs to $841,000. Variable cost per unit is the same as last year. The company has already sold 30,000 units at the regular selling price of $23 per unit.
   a. What amount of fixed costs was covered by the total contribution margin of the first 30,000 units sold?
   b. What contribution margin per unit will be needed on the remaining 130,000 units to cover the remaining fixed costs and to earn a profit of $210,000 this year?

P 5.
LO2 Cost Behavior and Projection
LO5 for a Service Business

Power Brite Painting Company specializes in refurbishing exterior painted surfaces that have been hard hit by humidity and insect debris. It uses a special technique, called pressure cleaning, before priming and painting the surface. The refurbishing process involves the following steps:

1. Unskilled laborers trim all trees and bushes within two feet of the structure.
2. Skilled laborers clean the building with a high-pressure cleaning machine, using about six gallons of chlorine per job.

3. Unskilled laborers apply a coat of primer.
4. Skilled laborers apply oil-based exterior paint to the entire surface.

On average, skilled laborers work 12 hours per job, and unskilled laborers work 8 hours. The refurbishing process generated the following operating results during 20x5:

Skilled labor	$20.00 per hour
Unskilled labor	$8.00 per hour
Gallons of chlorine used	3,768 gallons at $5.50 per gallon
Paint primer	7,536 gallons at $15.50 per gallon
Paint	6,280 gallons at $16.00 per gallon
Paint spraying equipment	$600.00 per month depreciation
Two leased vans	$800.00 per month total
Rent for storage building	$450.00 per month

Data on utilities for the year are as follows:

Month	Number of Jobs	Cost	Hours Worked
January	42	$ 3,950	840
February	37	3,550	740
March	44	4,090	880
April	49	4,410	980
May	54	4,720	1,080
June	62	5,240	1,240
July	71	5,820	1,420
August	73	5,890	1,460
September	63	5,370	1,260
October	48	4,340	960
November	45	4,210	900
December	40	3,830	800
Totals	628	$55,420	12,560

REQUIRED

1. Classify the costs as variable, fixed, or mixed.
2. Using the high-low method, separate mixed costs into their variable and fixed components. Use total hours worked as the basis.
3. Compute the average cost per job for 20x5. (**Hint**: Divide the total of all costs for 20x5 by the number of jobs completed.)
4. Project the average cost per job in 20x6 if variable costs per job increase 20 percent.

Alternate Problems

P 6.
LO4 Breakeven Analysis
LO5

At the beginning of each year, the Accounting Department at Moon Glow Lighting, Ltd., must find the point at which projected sales revenue will equal total budgeted variable and fixed costs. The company produces custom-made, low-voltage outdoor lighting systems. Each system sells for an average of $435. Variable costs per unit are $210. Total fixed costs for the year are estimated to be $166,500.

REQUIRED

1. Compute the breakeven point in sales units.
2. Compute the breakeven point in sales dollars.
3. Find the new breakeven point in sales units if the fixed costs go up by $10,125.
4. Using the original figures, compute the breakeven point in sales units if the selling price decreases to $425 per unit, fixed costs go up by $15,200, and variable costs decrease by $15 per unit.

P 7.
LO4 Planning Future Sales:
LO5 Contribution Margin Approach

Garden Marbles manufactures birdbaths, statues, and other decorative items, which it sells to florists and retail home and garden centers. The company's Design Department has proposed a new product, a statue of a frog, that it believes will be popular with home gardeners. Expected variable unit costs are as follows: direct materials, $9.25; direct labor, $4.00; production supplies, $.55; selling costs, $2.40; and other, $3.05. The following are fixed costs: depreciation, building and equipment, $33,000; advertising, $40,000; and other, $6,000. Management plans to sell the product for $29.25.

REQUIRED

1. Using the contribution margin approach, compute the number of statues the company must sell to (a) break even and (b) earn a profit of $50,000.
2. Using the same data, compute the number of statues that must be sold to earn a profit of $70,000 if advertising costs rise by $20,000.

3. Using the original data and sales of 15,000 units, compute the selling price the company must charge to make a profit of $100,000.
4. According to the vice president of marketing, Yvonne Palmer, if the price of the statues is reduced and advertising is increased, the most optimistic annual sales estimate is 25,000 units. How much more can be spent on fixed advertising costs if the selling price is reduced to $28.00 per statue, if the variable costs cannot be reduced, and if the targeted profit for sales of 25,000 statues is $120,000?

P 8.
LO5 Planning Future Sales for a Service Business

Lending Hand Financial Corporation is a subsidiary of Gracey Enterprises. Its main business is processing loan applications. Last year, Bettina Brent, the manager of the corporation's Loan Department, established a policy of charging a $250 fee for every loan application processed. Next year's variable costs have been projected as follows: loan consultant's wages, $15.50 per hour (a loan application takes five hours to process); supplies, $2.40 per application; and other variable costs, $5.60 per application. Annual fixed costs include depreciation of equipment, $8,500; building rental, $14,000; promotional costs, $12,500; and other fixed costs, $8,099.

REQUIRED ▶
1. Using the contribution margin approach, compute the number of loan applications the company must process to (a) break even and (b) earn a profit of $14,476.
2. Using the same approach and assuming promotional costs increase by $5,662, compute the number of applications the company must process to earn a profit of $20,000.
3. Assuming the original information and the processing of 500 applications, compute the loan application fee the company must charge if the targeted profit is $41,651.
4. Brent's staff can handle a maximum of 750 loan applications. How much more can be spent on promotional costs if the highest fee tolerable to the customer is $280, if variable costs cannot be reduced, and if the targeted profit for the loan applications is $50,000?

SKILLS DEVELOPMENT CASES

Conceptual Analysis

SD 1.
LO1 Concept of Cost Behavior
LO2

Gulf Coast Shrimp Company is a small company. It owns an icehouse and processing building, a refrigerated van, and three shrimp boats. Bob Jones inherited the company from his father three months ago. The company employs three boat crews of four people each and five processing workers. Trey Goodfellow of Bayou Accountants, a local accounting firm, has kept the company's financial records for many years. In his last analysis of operations, Goodfellow stated that the company's fixed cost base of $100,000 is satisfactory for its type and size of business. However, variable costs have averaged 70 percent of sales over the last two years, which is too high for the volume of business. Last year, only 30 percent of the sales revenue of $300,000 contributed to covering fixed costs. As a result, the company reported a $10,000 operating loss.

Jones wants to improve the company's net income, but he is confused by Goodfellow's explanation of the fixed and variable costs. Prepare a response to Jones from Goodfellow in which you explain the concept of cost behavior as it relates to Gulf Coast's operations. Include ideas for improving the company's net income based on changes in fixed and variable costs.

SD 2.
LO5 Comparison of Cost Behavior

Allstate Insurance Co. <www.allstate.com> and USAA <www.usaa.com> are two well-known insurers of motorists. Allstate has agents and offices all over the country. USAA sells only through the mail and over the telephone or Internet. In addition to offering collision and liability coverage for automobiles, each company offers life insurance and homeowners' insurance. When a motorist buys auto insurance from Allstate, the agent generally offers life insurance and homeowners' insurance as well—a strategy that helps increase Allstate's profitability. Although USAA usually sells its policies at lower prices than Allstate does, it is a very profitable company.

Identify and discuss the role that fixed costs, sales mix, and contribution margin can play in increasing profitability. Suggest a performance measure that could be used to evaluate agents who sell auto insurance. What is the role of variable costs? What is it about the relationship of USAA's fixed and variable costs that allows the company to sell policies at lower prices than Allstate and yet remain profitable?

Group Activity: Divide the class into groups and have them discuss this case. Ask one student from each group to summarize his or her group's discussion, and use the presentations to review the material in LO5.

Ethical Dilemma

LO4 Breaking Even and Ethics

SD 3. Lesley Chomski is the supervisor of the New Product Division of MCO Corporation. Her annual bonus is based on the success of new products and is computed on the number of sales that exceed each new product's projected breakeven point. In reviewing the computations supporting her most recent bonus, Chomski found that although an order for 7,500 units of a new product called R56 had been refused by a customer and returned to the company, the order had been included in the calculations. She later discovered that the company's accountant had labeled the return an overhead expense and had charged the entire cost of the returned order to the plantwide Manufacturing Overhead account. The result was that R56 appeared to exceed breakeven by more than 5,000 units and Chomski's bonus from this product amounted to over $800. What actions should Chomski take? Be prepared to discuss your response in class.

Research Activity

LO2 Cost Behavior and
LO4 Contribution Margin

SD 4. Make a trip to a local fast-food restaurant. Observe all aspects of the operation and take notes on the entire process. Describe the procedures used to take, process, and fill an order and deliver the order to the customer. Based on your observations, make a list of the costs incurred by the operation. Identify at least three variable costs and three fixed costs. Can you identify any potential mixed costs? Why is the restaurant willing to sell a large drink for only a few cents more than a medium drink? How is the restaurant able to offer a "value meal" (e.g., sandwich, drink, and fries) for considerably less than those items would cost if they were bought separately? Bring your notes to class and be prepared to discuss your findings.

Decision-Making Practice

LO2 Mixed Costs

SD 5. Officials of the Hidden Hills Golf and Tennis Club are in the process of preparing a budget for the year ending December 31, 20x6. Because Ramon Saud, the club treasurer, has had difficulty with two expense items, the process has been delayed by more than four weeks. The two items are mixed costs—expenses for electricity and for repairs and maintenance—and Saud has been having trouble breaking them down into their variable and fixed components. An accountant friend and golfing partner has suggested that he use the high-low method to divide the costs into their variable and fixed parts. The spending patterns and activity measures related to each cost during the past year are as follows:

Month	Electricity Expense Amount	Kilowatt-Hours	Repairs and Maintenance Amount	Labor Hours
January	$ 7,500	210,000	$ 7,578	220
February	8,255	240,200	7,852	230
March	8,165	236,600	7,304	210
April	8,960	268,400	7,030	200
May	7,520	210,800	7,852	230
June	7,025	191,000	8,126	240
July	6,970	188,800	8,400	250
August	6,990	189,600	8,674	260
September	7,055	192,200	8,948	270
October	7,135	195,400	8,674	260
November	8,560	252,400	8,126	240
December	8,415	246,600	7,852	230
Totals	$92,550	2,622,000	$96,416	2,840

1. Using the high-low method, compute the variable cost rates used last year for each expense. What was the monthly fixed cost for electricity and for repairs and maintenance?
2. Compute the total variable cost and total fixed cost for each expense category for last year.
3. Saud believes that in the coming year, the electricity rate will increase by $.005 and the repairs rate, by $1.20. Usage of all items and their fixed cost amounts will remain constant. Compute the projected total cost for each category. How will those increases in costs affect the club's profits and cash flow?

MANAGERIAL REPORTING AND ANALYSIS CASES

Interpreting Management Reports

LO3 **C-V-P Analysis**
LO4

MRA 1. Established in 1963 in Datura, Italy, Datura, Ltd., is an international importer-exporter of pottery with distribution centers in the United States, Europe, and Australia. The company was very successful in its early years, but since then, its profitability has steadily declined. As a member of a management team selected to gather information for Datura's next strategic planning meeting, you have been asked to review its most recent contribution income statement, which appears below.

Datura, Ltd.
Contribution Income Statement
For the Year Ended December 31, 20x4

Sales revenue		€13,500,000
Less variable costs		
Purchases	€ 6,000,000	
Distribution	2,115,000	
Sales commissions	1,410,000	
Total variable costs		9,525,000
Contribution margin		€ 3,975,000
Less fixed costs		
Distribution	€ 985,000	
Selling	1,184,000	
General and administrative	871,875	
Total fixed costs		3,040,875
Operating income		€ 934,000

In 20x4, Datura sold 15,000 sets of pottery.

1. For each set of pottery sold in 20x4, calculate the (a) selling price, (b) variable purchases cost, (c) variable distribution cost, (d) variable sales commission, and (e) contribution margin.
2. Calculate the breakeven point in units and in sales euros.
3. Historically, Datura's variable costs have been about 60 percent of sales. What was the ratio of variable costs to sales in 20x4? List three actions Datura could take to correct the difference.
4. How would fixed costs have been affected if Datura had sold only 14,000 sets of pottery in 20x4?

Formulating Management Reports

MRA 2.
LO5 C-V-P Analysis Applied

Refer to the information in **MRA 1**. In January 20x5, Sophia Callas, the president and chief executive officer of Datura, Ltd., conducted a strategic planning meeting. During the meeting, Phillipe Mazzeo, vice president of distribution, noted that because of a new contract with an international shipping line, the company's fixed distribution costs for 20x5 would be reduced by 10 percent and its variable distribution costs by 4 percent. Gino Roma, vice president of sales, offered the following information:

> We plan to sell 15,000 sets of pottery again in 20x5, but based on review of the competition, we are going to lower the selling price to €890 per set. To encourage increased sales, we will raise sales commissions to 12 percent of the selling price.

Sophia Callas is concerned that the changes described by Roma and Mazzeo may not improve operating income sufficiently in 20x5. If operating income does not increase by at least 10 percent, she will want to find other ways to reduce the company's costs. She asks you to evaluate the situation in a written report. Because it is already January of 20x5 and changes need to be made quickly, she requests your report within five days.

1. Prepare a budgeted contribution income statement for 20x5. Your report should show the budgeted (estimated) operating income based on the information provided above and in **MRA 1**. Will the changes improve operating income sufficiently? Explain.
2. In preparation for writing your report, answer the following questions:
   a. Why are you preparing the report?
   b. Who needs the report?
   c. What sources of information will you use?
   d. When is the report due?

International Company

MRA 3.
LO3 C-V-P Analysis and Decision Making

The Goslar Corporation cuts granite, marble, and sandstone for use in the construction and restoration of cathedrals throughout Europe. The German-based company has operations in Italy and Switzerland. Gunder Shillar, the controller, recently determined that the breakeven point was €325,000 in sales. In preparation for a quarterly planning meeting, Shillar must provide information for the following six proposals, which will be discussed individually by the planning team:

1. Increase the selling price of marble slabs by 10 percent.
2. Change the sales mix to respond to an increased demand for marble slabs—that is, increase production and sales of marble slabs and decrease the production and sales of sandstone slabs, the least profitable product.
3. Increase fixed production costs by €40,000 annually to cover depreciation on new stone-cutting equipment.
4. Increase variable costs by 1 percent to cover higher export duties on foreign sales.
5. Decrease the sales volume of sandstone slabs because of a reduction in demand in Eastern Europe.
6. Decrease the number of days a customer can defer payment without being charged interest.

1. For each proposal, determine whether cost-volume-profit (C-V-P) analysis would provide useful financial information.
2. Indicate how each proposal that lends itself to C-V-P analysis would affect profit.

Excel Spreadsheet Analysis

MRA 4.
LO5 Planning Future Sales

As noted in **MRA 2**, Datura, Ltd., had targeted sales of 15,000 sets of pottery for 20x5 and was reducing the selling price to €890 per set. It was increasing sales commissions to 12 percent of the selling price and decreasing its fixed distribution costs by 10 percent and its variable distribution costs by 4 percent. Based on analysis of these changes, Sophia Callas has concluded that they would not increase Datura's 20x5 operating income by 10 percent over the previous year's income. Now, however, Gino Roma has reported that a new salesperson has just obtained a sales contract with an Australian distributor for 4,500 sets of pottery. The selling price, variable purchases cost per unit, sales commission, and total fixed costs will remain the same, but the variable distribution costs will be €160 per unit.

Using an Excel spreadsheet, complete the following:

1. Calculate the targeted operating income for 20x5.
2. Prepare a budgeted contribution income statement for 20x5 based on the information in **MRA 1** and the adjustments presented in **MRA 2**. Do you agree with Sophia Callas that Datura's projected operating income for 20x5 will be less than the operating income for 20x4? Explain.
3. Calculate the total contribution margin from the Australian sales.
4. Prepare a revised budgeted contribution income statement for 20x5 by combining the information from **2** and **3** above.
5. Does Datura need the Australian sales to achieve its targeted operating income for 20x5?

Internet Case

MRA 5.

LO4 Planning Future Sales and
LO5 Costs

Find a recent annual report on the Internet and read management's letter to the stockholders. This section of an annual report typically discusses initiatives or actions that the company implemented during the year as part of its strategic plan. (1) Identify at least three such initiatives or actions that you believe affected the company's annual sales or costs. (2) Also identify one initiative or action the company is planning for the coming year that you believe will affect revenue or expenses.

21

Chapter 21 describes the budgeting process, identifies the elements of a master budget, and demonstrates the preparation of operating budgets and financial budgets.

The Budgeting Process

LEARNING OBJECTIVES

LO1 Define *budgeting* and explain its role in the management cycle.

LO2 Identify the elements of a master budget in different types of organizations and the guidelines for preparing budgets.

LO3 Prepare the operating budgets that support the financial budgets.

LO4 Prepare a budgeted income statement, a cash budget, and a budgeted balance sheet.

LO5 Describe management's role in budget implementation.

DECISION POINT
A MANAGER'S FOCUS

Johnson & Johnson <www.jnj.com>   With products that range from baby powder, Band-Aids, Tylenol, and contact lenses to diagnostic and surgical devices, Johnson & Johnson is the largest and most diversified manufacturer of health care products in the world. It has had affiliated companies operating in Latin America, Europe, Africa, and Australia for more than fifty years. Today, it is a global family of over 200 decentralized companies. Unifying the strategic planning of these companies' management teams are the set of common values and ethical principles expressed in Johnson & Johnson's credo, or mission statement. The strategic direction and major developments of the various companies are discussed at board meetings throughout the year and at meetings between management and board members. This ongoing dialogue provides managers with insight into the activities and direction of the company's businesses and is the basis for Johnson & Johnson's budgeting decisions.[1]

How does Johnson & Johnson's budgeting process work? First, sales and marketing teams from the decentralized companies develop sales budgets by product, geographic territory, and distribution channel. Senior management and staff then review the sales budgets to see that they meet the goals of Johnson & Johnson's strategic plan. Second, scheduling teams prepare production and shipping schedules to coordinate activities at the different manufacturing plants. Third, the managers responsible for functional areas (such as research and development, production, marketing, distribution, and customer service)

How is Johnson & Johnson's budgeting process linked to the company's long-term goals and objectives?

prepare cost and expense budgets. Fourth, the company accounting group reviews all budgets from the decentralized companies and analyzes their contents to determine whether they are in accord with the overall strategic plan. Fifth, Johnson & Johnson's controller prepares a complete set of companywide budgeted financial statements.

The budgeting process can be a highly effective way of linking strategic planning to operations, especially when it is coupled with ongoing discussions about a company's activities and direction, as is the case at Johnson & Johnson. Because a budget sets forth a company's objectives in concrete terms, it enables managers and employees to act in ways that will attain those objectives; it also gives them a means of monitoring the results of their actions. At Johnson & Johnson, the budgeting process and ongoing dialogue about strategy foster rapid improvements in productivity and customer service, as well as innovation in product and market development.

THE BUDGETING PROCESS

LO1 Define *budgeting* and explain its role in the management cycle.

RELATED TEXT ASSIGNMENTS
Q: 1, 2, 3, 4, 5, 6, 7, 8
SE: 1, 2, 3, 4
E: 1, 2, 3, 4
SD: 1, 3, 5
MRA: 1, 2, 5

www.jnj.com
www.merck.com
www.national.unitedway.org
www.unitednations.org

TERMINOLOGY NOTE:
For-profit organizations often use the term *profit planning* rather than *budgeting*.

ENRICHMENT NOTE: Any budget, even a poorly prepared one, is probably better than no budget at all. As the budgeting process is refined, the benefits to the organization will increase.

Budgeting is the process of identifying, gathering, summarizing, and communicating financial and nonfinancial information about an organization's future activities. It is an essential part of the continuous planning an organization must do to accomplish its long-term goals. The budgeting process provides managers of all types of organizations—including for-profit organizations, such as Johnson & Johnson and Merck, and not-for-profit organizations, such as the United Way and the United Nations—the opportunity to match organizational goals with the resources necessary to accomplish those goals. As part of the ongoing budgeting process, managers evaluate operational, tactical, value chain, and capacity issues; assess how resources for operating, investing, and financial activities are currently being used and how they can be efficiently used in the future; and develop contingency budgets as business conditions change.

Budgets—plans of action based on forecasted transactions, activities, and events—are synonymous with managing an organization. They are essential to accomplishing the goals articulated in an organization's strategic plan. They are used to communicate information, coordinate activities and resource usage, motivate employees, and evaluate performance. For example, a board of directors may use budgets to determine managers' areas of responsibility and to measure managers' performance in those areas. Budgets are, of course, also used to manage and account for cash. Such budgets establish minimum or targeted levels of cash receipts and limits on the spending of cash for particular purposes.

Budgets come in many forms. For example, a cash budget focuses on financial information; it shows, among other things, how cash resources will be allotted to operating, investing, and financing activities over a future period. A production budget, on the other hand, focuses on nonfinancial information; it shows planned production in units and identifies the activities needed to meet certain requirements or standards established in the planning stage of the management cycle.

To compete successfully in today's fast-paced global market, an organization must ensure that its managers have continuously updated operating data against which to measure performance. Thus, an ongoing budgeting process is especially important in the current business environment.

BUDGETING AND GOALS

■ **LONG-TERM GOALS** **Strategic planning** is the process by which management establishes an organization's long-term goals. These goals define the strategic direction an organization will take over a five- to ten-year period and are the basis for making annual operating plans and preparing budgets. Long-term goals should take into consideration economic and industry forecasts, employee management relations, the structure and role of management, value chain considerations, organizational capacity, and any other operational and tactical issues facing the organization, such as the expected quality of products or services, growth rates, and desired market share.

Long-term goals cannot be vague; they must set specific targets and timetables and assign responsibility for achieving the goals to specific personnel. For example, a long-term goal for a company that currently holds only 4 percent of its product's market share might specify that the vice president of market-

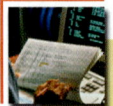

FOCUS ON BUSINESS PRACTICE

What Can Cause the Planning Process to Fail?
When chief financial officers were asked what caused their planning process to fail, the six factors they most commonly cited were as follows:[2]

- An inadequately defined strategy
- No clear link between strategy and the operational budget
- Lack of individual accountability for results
- Lack of meaningful performance measures
- Inadequate pay for performance
- Lack of appropriate data

Video Case

Enterprise Rent-A-Car
<www.enterprise.com>

Objectives

- To become familiar with the budgeting process and budgets
- To understand the relationship between strategic plans and operating budgets
- To describe the role of budgeting in the management cycle

Background for the Case

Because its core business is not the airport market, Enterprise Rent-A-Car does not have the high profile most of its competitors enjoy. However, with over $6.5 billion in annual revenues, more than 4,800 locations worldwide, and offices within 15 miles of 90 percent of the U.S. population, it is the largest car rental company in North America. Founded in 1947 in St. Louis, Missouri, where it operated out of the basement of a car dealership, Enterprise now employs more than 50,000 people. It focuses on two market segments: people who need a replacement vehicle when their own car is unavailable—for instance, when it is undergoing repairs—and people who want a car for a business or leisure trip or for a special occasion.

Enterprise prides itself on providing excellent customer service, including free customer pickup. To accomplish its goals, the company has an incentive plan for employees and a decentralized organization that allows great latitude in decision making. Enterprise's managers prepare budgets to integrate, coordinate, and communicate the operating plans necessary to achieve the company's strategic objectives. The budgeting system includes measurement of performance at each location and for each employee. Good systems and budgeting also facilitate the company's objective of expanding its business in Canada, the United Kingdom, Ireland, and Germany.[3]

Required

View the video on Enterprise Rent-A-Car that accompanies this book. As you are watching the video, take notes pertaining to the following:

1. In your own words, explain what a budget is and list all the reasons you believe a company like Enterprise would prepare a set of budgets.
2. What is the relationship between Enterprise's strategic plans and its operating budgets?
3. What is the role of budgeting in the management cycle?

ENRICHMENT NOTE: Long-term goals are often expressed in subjective terms, such as increasing market share, becoming the industry leader, or having the best product on the market.

KEY POINT: As plans are formulated for time periods closer to the current date, they become more specific and quantified. The annual budget is a very specific plan of action.

ing is to develop strategies to ensure that the company controls 10 percent of the market in five years and 15 percent by the end of ten years. An organization's strategic plan should include a range of long-term goals and give direction to its efforts to achieve those goals. It should include profit projections and describe new products or services in general terms.

■ **Short-Term Goals** Annual operating plans involve every part of an enterprise and are much more detailed than long-term strategic plans. To formulate an annual operating plan, an organization must restate its long-term goals in terms of what it needs to accomplish during the next year. The process entails making decisions about sales and profit targets, human resource needs, and the introduction of new products or services. The short-term goals identified in an annual operating plan are the basis of an organization's operating budgets for the year.

Once management has established short-term goals, the organization's controller takes charge of coordinating the budgeting process. This person designs a complete set of budget-development directions, including a timetable complete with deadlines for all parts of the year's operating plan, and assigns clearly defined responsibilities for carrying out each part of the budget's development to specific individuals or management teams.

Depending on organizational practice, a budget may be reviewed and revised during the year. As pointed out in the focus box that follows, there is a growing trend to more frequent budget revisions.

Focus on International Business

Budget Revision Practices in the United Kingdom

A recent survey of 1,000 leading U.K. companies has suggested that to keep pace in today's fast-changing business environment, managers would like more frequent budget revisions. The survey asked participants how often they revise their budgets and how often they believe budget revisions should be done. The survey results, summarized in the table to the right, show the trend to more frequent revisions.[4]

Frequency	Current Practice	Desired Practice
Daily	—	1%
Weekly	—	4%
Monthly	24%	44%
Quarterly	36%	33%
Twice a year	15%	17%
Once a year	15%	—
No revision	10%	1%

The Importance of Participation

Because an organization's main activities—such as production, sales, and employee training—take place at its lower levels, information necessary for establishing a budget flows from the supervisors of those activities through middle managers to senior executives. Each person in this chain of communication thus plays a role in developing a budget, as well as in implementing it. If these individuals feel they have a voice in setting the budget targets, they will feel personally motivated to ensure that their departments attain those targets and stay within the budget. If they do not feel they have a role in the budgeting process, motivation will suffer. The key to a successful budget is therefore **participative budgeting**, a process in which personnel at all levels of an organization actively engage in making decisions about the budget.

Because the controller is at the center of the budgeting process—collecting and distributing information and coordinating all budgeting activities—that person has considerable influence over the nature of the budgeting process. Participative budgeting depends on joint decision making, and to foster a climate in which that can take place, a controller must be able to communicate and negotiate effectively with people at all levels of an organization—from the senior executives who formulate the organization's long- and short-term goals to the middle managers and supervisors responsible for daily operations.

Senior executives also play a central role in determining the nature of the budgeting process. If they dictate targets instead of allowing middle managers and supervisors a voice in setting them, the budgeting process will be authoritative rather than participative. Without input from personnel at operational levels, the targets may be unrealistic and impossible to attain, which will further undermine the motivation of the managers and supervisors whose cooperation is essential for successful budget implementation. Problems may also arise if senior executives allow the controller to develop the budget without consulting other managers. In that case, managers may feel that budgeting is not a top priority and that budgets need not be taken seriously. Such difficulties can be avoided if senior executives recognize the importance of allowing personnel at all levels to play meaningful roles in the budgeting process.

Budgeting and the Management Cycle

As Figure 1 shows, budgeting is helpful to managers at each stage of the management cycle. To illustrate the relationship between budgeting and the management cycle, we will refer to the budgeting activities of Framecraft Company, a manufacturer that specializes in high-quality plastic picture frames. Framecraft's owner, Chase Vittel, believes the future growth of his company depends on a good budgeting process.

● **Stop and Think!**
Why are budgets important at every stage of the management cycle?
An organization's budgets constitute its master plan for profitable operations. ■

FIGURE 1
Budgeting and the Management Cycle

KEY POINT: Although we present the four stages of the management cycle linearly, organizations are dynamic and managers may move through one stage, such as the executing stage, more often than another, such as the planning stage. For example, as part of the reviewing stage, a manager may evaluate performance reports on a weekly basis. On the other hand, as part of the planning stage, a manager may prepare a capital expenditures budget for new equipment only once a year.

KEY POINT: Budgeting is not only an essential part of planning; it also helps in controlling operations.

■ **PLANNING** Budgets originate in the planning stage of the management cycle. They reflect an organization's long- and short-term plans for achieving key success factors, such as high-quality products, reasonable costs, and timely delivery. Chase Vittel believes that by carefully distributing workloads and allotting resources to specific products, departments, and sales territories, budgets help his managers orchestrate short-term activities to accomplish long-term goals. Because he recognizes the benefits of participative budgeting, Vittel includes personnel from all levels of the company in the budgeting process. To motivate employees to achieve the targets set forth in the budget, Framecraft Company awards bonuses for good performance. As measures of performance, managers have selected profits, number of units sold, number of defective units, and cycle time (the time to obtain, manufacture, and ship an order).

■ **EXECUTING** During the executing stage, managers use budget information for communication, performance measurement, and resource allocation. The managers of Framecraft Company use budget information daily, weekly, and monthly to communicate expectations about performance, to measure performance and motivate employees, and to coordinate activities and allot resources among various departments. For example, Geoff Vukovic, the production manager, uses the units of production specified in the budget as an operating target for his workers and the number of defective units as a performance measure to motivate them to manufacture quality products. Chase Vittel uses standard product costs, generated in the planning process, to submit bids and estimate profits.

- **REVIEWING** In the reviewing stage, managers evaluate performance, including its timeliness. They look for variances between planned and actual performance and create solutions for the variances they detect. As we have already indicated, Framecraft Company's managers use the targets established in the planning stage as targets for actual performance in the executing stage. During the reviewing stage, they compare planned performance with actual performance. If they identify variances, they focus on finding solutions to the problems, which promotes continuous improvement of the company's products and processes. Framecraft Company's managers review their budgets on a regular basis because doing so helps them evaluate past performance and chart the course of future operations.

- **REPORTING** Because budgets are plans of action based on forecasts of transactions, activities, and events, they serve as a reference point for many kinds of reports. For example, performance reports that support bonuses and promotions are based on budget information. Other budget-based reports support operating decisions. To provide continuous feedback about an organization's operating, investing, and financing activities, managers prepare and distribute reports based on budget information throughout the year.

Check out ACE for a Review Quiz at http://accounting.college.hmco.com/students.

THE MASTER BUDGET

LO2 Identify the elements of a master budget in different types of organizations and the guidelines for preparing budgets.

RELATED TEXT ASSIGNMENTS
Q: 9, 10, 11, 12
SE: 5
E: 5
SD: 1
MRA: 1, 2

TERMINOLOGY NOTE:
Budgeted financial statements often are referred to as *forecasted financial statements* or *pro forma statements*.

A **master budget** consists of a set of operating budgets and a set of financial budgets that detail an organization's financial plans for a specific accounting period, generally a year. When a master budget covers an entire year, some of the operating and financial budgets may show planned results by month or by quarter. As the term implies, **operating budgets** are plans used in daily operations. They are also the basis for preparing the **financial budgets**, which are projections of financial results for the accounting period. Financial budgets include a budgeted income statement, a capital expenditures budget, a cash budget, and a budgeted balance sheet.

The budgeted financial statements—that is, the budgeted income statement and budgeted balance sheet—are also called **pro forma statements**, meaning that they show projections rather than actual results. Pro forma statements are often used to communicate business plans to external parties. If, for example, you wanted to obtain a bank loan so you could start a new business, you would have to present the bank with a pro forma, or budgeted, income statement and balance sheet showing that you could repay the loan with cash generated by profitable operations.

Suppose you have started your own business. Whether it is a manufacturing, retail, or service organization, to manage it effectively, you would prepare a master budget each period. A master budget provides the information needed to match long-term goals to short-term activities and to plan the resources needed to ensure an organization's profitability and liquidity.

Figures 2, 3, and 4 display the elements of a master budget for a manufacturing organization, retail organization, and service organization, respectively. As these figures indicate, the process of preparing a master budget is similar in all three types of organizations in that each prepares a set of operating budgets that serve as the basis for preparing the financial budgets. The process differs mainly in the kinds of operating budgets that each type of organization prepares.

The operating budgets of manufacturing organizations like Intel and John Deere include budgets for

FOCUS ON BUSINESS TECHNOLOGY

Rolling Budgets Never End.
Many companies are shifting their budgeting focus from preparation and revision to an ever-changing budgeting process known as a rolling forecast. With computerized information systems that are able to capture accurate, up-to-the-minute financial and nonfinancial data, a rolling forecast can be refreshed continuously. The rolling forecast differs from a budget revision in that it includes only a few key performance indicators, such as orders, sales, costs, and capital expenditures; can be compiled quickly; has no fixed profit targets; and gives all authorized personnel in an organization immediate access to the same current information.[5]

FIGURE 2
Preparation of a Master Budget for a Manufacturing Organization

Operating Budgets:
- Sales Budget
  - Production Budget
    - Direct Materials Purchases Budget
    - Direct Labor Budget
    - Manufacturing Overhead Budget
  - Cost of Goods Manufactured Budget
  - Cost of Goods Sold Budget*
  - Selling and Administrative Expense Budget

Financial Budgets:
- Budgeted Income Statement
- Cash Budget
- Capital Expenditures Budget
- Budgeted Balance Sheet

*Some organizations choose to include the cost of goods sold budget in the budgeted income statement.

www.intel.com
www.johndeere.com
www.nordstrom.com
www.talbots.com
www.lowes.com
www.enterprise.com
www.ups.com
www.amtrak.com

sales, production, direct materials purchases, direct labor, manufacturing overhead, selling and administrative expenses, and cost of goods manufactured. Retail organizations, such as Nordstrom, Talbots, and Lowe's, prepare a sales budget, purchases budget, selling and administrative expense budget, and cost of goods sold budget. The operating budgets of service organizations, such as Enterprise Rent-A-Car, UPS, and Amtrak, include budgets for service revenue, labor, services overhead, and selling and administrative expenses.

FIGURE 3
Preparation of a Master Budget for a Retail Organization

● **STOP AND THINK!**
How is the process of preparing a master budget similar in manufacturing, retail, and service organizations? How does it differ?

All three types of organizations begin the process by developing a set of operating budgets, which provide the data needed to prepare the financial budgets. The process differs mainly in the kinds of operating budgets each type of organization prepares. ■

The sales budget (or in service organizations, the service revenue budget) is prepared first because it is used to estimate sales volume and revenues. Once managers know the quantity of products or services to be sold and how many sales dollars to expect, they can develop other budgets that will enable them to manage their organization's resources so that they generate profits on those sales. For example, in a retail organization, the purchases budget provides managers with information about the quantity of merchandise needed to meet the sales demand and maintain a minimum level of inventory. In a service organization, the labor budget provides information about the labor hours and labor rates needed to provide services and generate the revenues planned for each period; managers use this information in scheduling services and setting prices.

Because procedures for preparing budgets vary from organization to organization, no standard format for budget preparation exists. The only universal requirement is that budgets communicate the appropriate information to the reader in a clear and understandable manner. By keeping that in mind and using the following guidelines, managers can improve the quality of budgets in any type of organization:

1. Know the purpose of the budget.
2. Identify the user group and its information needs.
3. Identify sources of accurate, meaningful budget information. Such information may be gathered from documents or from interviews with employees, suppliers, or managers who work in the related areas.
4. Establish a clear format for the budget. A budget should begin with a clearly stated heading that includes the organization's name, the type of budget, and

FIGURE 4
Preparation of a Master Budget for a Service Organization

the accounting period under consideration. The budget's components should be clearly labeled, and the unit and financial data should be listed in an orderly manner.

5. Use suitable formulas and calculations to derive the quantitative information.
6. Revise the budget until it includes all planning decisions. Several revisions may be required before the final version is ready for distribution.

✓ Check out ACE for a Review Quiz at http://accounting.college.hmco.com/students.

OPERATING BUDGETS

LO3 Prepare the operating budgets that support the financial budgets.

RELATED TEXT ASSIGNMENTS
Q: 13, 14, 15, 16, 17
SE: 5, 6, 7
E: 5, 6, 7, 8, 9, 10, 11, 12
P: 1, 2
SD: 3, 4
MRA: 4

Although procedures for preparing operating budgets vary, the tools used in the process do not. They include cost behavior analysis, cost-volume-profit (C-V-P) analysis, and a product costing method. In this section, we use Framecraft Company to illustrate how a manufacturing organization prepares its operating budgets. Because Framecraft makes only one product—a plastic picture frame—it prepares only one of each type of operating budget. Organizations that manufacture a variety of products or provide many types of services may prepare either separate operating budgets or one comprehensive budget for each product or service.

THE SALES BUDGET

As we indicated earlier, the first step in preparing a master budget is to prepare a sales budget. A **sales budget** is a detailed plan, expressed in both units and dollars, that identifies the product (or service) sales expected in an accounting period. Sales managers use this information to plan sales- and marketing-related activities and to determine human, physical, and technical resource needs. Accountants use the information to determine estimated cash receipts for the cash budget.

The following equation is used to determine the total budgeted sales:

$$\begin{array}{c}\text{Total} \\ \text{Budgeted} \\ \text{Sales}\end{array} = \begin{array}{c}\text{Estimated} \\ \text{Selling Price} \\ \text{per Unit}\end{array} \times \begin{array}{c}\text{Estimated} \\ \text{Sales in} \\ \text{Units}\end{array}$$

Although the calculation is easy, selecting the best estimates for the selling price per unit and the sales demand in units can be difficult. An estimated selling price below the current selling price may be needed if competitors are currently selling the same product at lower prices or if the organization wants to increase its share of the market. On the other hand, if the organization has improved the product's quality by using more expensive materials or production processes, the estimated selling price may have to be higher than the current price.

> **KEY POINT:** The sales budget is the only budget subject to customer demand. Other budgets for the period depend on the numbers it provides.

The estimated sales volume is very important because it will affect the level of operating activities and the amount of resources needed for operations. Resources for production, packing, shipping, accounting, purchasing, selling, and administrative activities will increase in varying degrees with increases in the estimated sales volume. To help estimate sales volume, managers often use a **sales forecast**, which is a projection of sales demand (the estimated sales in units) based on an analysis of external and internal factors. The external factors include

1. The state of the local and national economies
2. The state of the industry's economy
3. The nature of the competition and its sales volume and selling price

Internal factors taken into consideration in a sales forecast include

1. The number of units sold in prior periods
2. The organization's credit policies
3. The organization's collection policies
4. The organization's pricing policies
5. Any new products the organization plans to introduce to the market
6. The capacity of the organization's manufacturing facilities

Exhibit 1 illustrates Framecraft Company's sales budget for 20x7. The budget shows the estimated number of unit sales and dollar revenue amounts for each quarter and for the entire year. Because a sales forecast indicated a highly competitive marketplace, Framecraft's managers have estimated a selling price of $5 per unit. The sales forecast also indicated highly seasonal sales activity; the estimated sales volume therefore varies from 10,000 to 40,000 per quarter.

THE PRODUCTION BUDGET

> **KEY POINT:** The production budget must provide for sufficient goods to meet current sales and must ensure that finished goods inventory levels are maintained according to company policy.

A **production budget** is a detailed plan showing the number of units a company must produce to meet budgeted sales and inventory needs. Production managers use this information to plan for the materials and human resources that production-related activities will require. To prepare a production budget, managers must know the budgeted number of unit sales (which is specified in the sales budget) and the desired level of ending finished goods inventory for each period in the budget year. That level is often stated as a percentage of the next period's budgeted unit sales. For example, Framecraft Company's desired level of ending finished goods inventory is 10 percent of the next quarter's budgeted unit sales. (Its desired level of beginning finished goods inventory is 10 percent of the current quarter's budgeted unit sales.)

EXHIBIT 1
Sales Budget

Framecraft Company
Sales Budget
For the Year Ended December 31, 20x7

	Quarter				
	1	2	3	4	Year
Sales in units	10,000	30,000	10,000	40,000	90,000
× Selling price per unit	× $5	× $5	× $5	× $5	× $5
Total sales	$50,000	$150,000	$50,000	$200,000	$450,000

The following formula identifies the production needs for each accounting period:

$$\text{Total Production Units} = \text{Budgeted Sales in Units} + \text{Desired Units of Ending Finished Goods Inventory} - \text{Desired Units of Beginning Finished Goods Inventory}$$

Exhibit 2 shows Framecraft Company's production budget for 20x7. Notice that each quarter's desired total units of ending finished goods inventory become the next quarter's desired total units of beginning finished goods inventory. Because 15,000 unit sales are budgeted for the first quarter of 20x8, the ending finished goods inventory for the fourth quarter of 20x7 is 1,500 units (.10 × 15,000 units), which is the same as the desired number of units of ending finished goods inventory for the entire year. Similarly, the number of desired units for the first quarter's beginning finished goods inventory—1,000—is the same as the desired number of units of beginning finished goods inventory for the entire year.

EXHIBIT 2
Production Budget

Framecraft Company
Production Budget
For the Year Ended December 31, 20x7

	Quarter				
	1	2	3	4	Year
Sales in units	10,000	30,000	10,000	40,000	90,000
Plus desired units of ending finished goods inventory	3,000	1,000	4,000	1,500	1,500
Desired total units	13,000	31,000	14,000	41,500	91,500
Less desired units of beginning finished goods inventory	1,000	3,000	1,000	4,000	1,000
Total production units	12,000	28,000	13,000	37,500	90,500

The Direct Materials Purchases Budget

KEY POINT: The direct materials purchases budget must reflect both quantities of materials to be acquired and purchase prices. Those quantities and prices will be used again in the preparation of the cash budget.

A **direct materials purchases budget** is a detailed plan that identifies the quantity of purchases required to meet budgeted production and inventory needs and the costs associated with those purchases. A purchasing department uses this information to plan purchases of direct materials. Accountants use the same information to estimate cash payments to suppliers.

To prepare a direct materials purchases budget, managers must know what production needs will be in each accounting period in the budget; this information is provided by the production budget. They must also know the desired level of the direct materials inventory for each period and the per unit cost of direct materials. The desired level of ending direct materials inventory is usually stated as a percentage of the next period's production needs. Framecraft Company's desired level of ending direct materials inventory is 20 percent of the next quarter's budgeted production needs. (Its desired level of beginning direct materials inventory is 20 percent of the current quarter's budgeted production needs.)

The first step in preparing a direct materials purchases budget is to calculate each period's total production needs in units of direct materials. Plastic is the only direct material used in Framecraft Company's picture frames; each frame requires 10 ounces of plastic. Framecraft's managers therefore calculate units of production needs in ounces; they multiply the number of frames budgeted for production in a quarter by the 10 ounces of plastic each frame requires.

In the second step, the following formula is used to determine the quantity of direct materials to be purchased during each accounting period in the budget:

$$\text{Total Units of Direct Materials to Be Purchased} = \text{Total Production Needs in Units of Direct Materials} + \text{Desired Units of Ending Direct Materials Inventory} - \text{Desired Units of Beginning Direct Materials Inventory}$$

The third step is to calculate the cost of the direct materials purchases by multiplying the total number of unit purchases by the direct materials cost. Framecraft's Purchasing Department has estimated the cost of the plastic used in the picture frames at $.05 per ounce.

Exhibit 3 shows Framecraft's direct materials purchases budget for 20x7. Notice that each quarter's desired units of ending direct materials inventory become the next quarter's desired units of beginning direct materials inventory. The company's budgeted number of units for the first quarter of 20x8 is 150,000 ounces; its ending direct materials inventory for the fourth quarter of 20x7 is therefore 30,000 ounces (.20 × 150,000 ounces), which is the same as the number of desired units of ending direct materials inventory for the entire year. Similarly, the number of desired units for the first quarter's beginning direct materials inventory—24,000 ounces—is the same as the beginning amount for the entire year.

The Direct Labor Budget

A **direct labor budget** is a detailed plan that estimates the direct labor hours needed in an accounting period and the associated costs. Production managers use estimated direct labor hours to plan how many employees will be required during the period and the hours each will work, and accountants use estimated direct labor costs to plan for cash payments to the workers. Managers of human resources use the information in a direct labor budget in deciding whether to hire new employees or reduce the existing work force, as well as a guide in training employees and preparing schedules of employee fringe benefits.

The first step in preparing a direct labor budget is to estimate the total direct labor hours by multiplying the estimated direct labor hours per unit by the anticipated units of production (see Exhibit 2). The second step in preparing such a budget is to calculate the total budgeted direct labor cost by multiplying the esti-

EXHIBIT 3
Direct Materials Purchases Budget

Framecraft Company
Direct Materials Purchases Budget
For the Year Ended December 31, 20x7

	Quarter 1	Quarter 2	Quarter 3	Quarter 4	Year
Total production units	12,000	28,000	13,000	37,500	90,500
× 10 ounces per unit	× 10	× 10	× 10	× 10	× 10
Total production needs in ounces	120,000	280,000	130,000	375,000	905,000
Plus desired ounces of ending direct materials inventory	56,000	26,000	75,000	30,000	30,000
	176,000	306,000	205,000	405,000	935,000
Less desired ounces of beginning direct materials inventory	24,000	56,000	26,000	75,000	24,000
Total ounces of direct materials to be purchased	152,000	250,000	179,000	330,000	911,000
× Cost per ounce	× $.05	× $.05	× $.05	× $.05	× $.05
Total cost of direct materials purchases	$ 7,600	$ 12,500	$ 8,950	$ 16,500	$ 45,550

mated total direct labor hours by the estimated direct labor cost per hour. A company's human resources department provides an estimate of the hourly labor wage.

$$\text{Total Budgeted Direct Labor Cost} = \text{Estimated Total Direct Labor Hours} \times \text{Estimated Direct Labor Cost per Hour}$$

Exhibit 4 shows how Framecraft Company uses these formulas to estimate the total direct labor cost. Framecraft's Production Department needs an estimated one-tenth (.10) of a direct labor hour to complete one unit. Its Human Resources Department estimates a direct labor cost of $6 per hour.

THE MANUFACTURING OVERHEAD BUDGET

A **manufacturing overhead budget** is a detailed plan of anticipated manufacturing costs, other than direct materials and direct labor costs, that must be incurred to meet budgeted production needs. A manufacturing overhead budget has two purposes: to integrate the overhead cost budgets developed by the managers of production and production-related departments, and to group information for the calculation of manufacturing overhead rates for the forthcoming accounting period.

The format for presenting information in a manufacturing overhead budget is flexible. Grouping information by activities is useful for organizations that use activity-based costing. This approach makes it easier for accountants to determine the application rates for each cost pool.

As Exhibit 5 shows, Framecraft Company prefers to group information into variable and fixed costs to facilitate C-V-P analysis during the executing stage of the management cycle. The manufacturing overhead rate is the estimated total

● **STOP AND THINK!**
Why are the direct materials purchases, direct labor, and manufacturing overhead budgets prepared after the production budget?

A production budget shows the number of units a company must produce to meet budgeted sales and inventory needs. Managers must have this information to estimate the direct materials, direct labor, and manufacturing overhead that production will require. ■

EXHIBIT 4
Direct Labor Budget

Framecraft Company
Direct Labor Budget
For the Year Ended December 31, 20x7

	Quarter 1	Quarter 2	Quarter 3	Quarter 4	Year
Total production units	12,000	28,000	13,000	37,500	90,500
× Direct labor hours per unit	× .1	× .1	× .1	× .1	× .1
Total direct labor hours	1,200	2,800	1,300	3,750	9,050
× Direct labor cost per hour	× $6	× $6	× $6	× $6	× $6
Total direct labor cost	$ 7,200	$16,800	$ 7,800	$22,500	$54,300

EXHIBIT 5
Manufacturing Overhead Budget

Framecraft Company
Manufacturing Overhead Budget
For the Year Ended December 31, 20x7

	Quarter 1	Quarter 2	Quarter 3	Quarter 4	Year
Variable overhead costs					
Factory supplies	$ 2,160	$ 5,040	$ 2,340	$ 6,750	$ 16,290
Employee benefits	2,880	6,720	3,120	9,000	21,720
Inspection	1,080	2,520	1,170	3,375	8,145
Maintenance and repair	1,920	4,480	2,080	6,000	14,480
Utilities	3,600	8,400	3,900	11,250	27,150
Total variable overhead costs	$11,640	$27,160	$12,610	$36,375	$ 87,785
Fixed overhead costs					
Depreciation, machinery	$ 2,810	$ 2,810	$ 2,810	$ 2,810	$ 11,240
Depreciation, building	3,225	3,225	3,225	3,225	12,900
Supervision	9,000	9,000	9,000	9,000	36,000
Maintenance and repair	2,150	2,150	2,150	2,150	8,600
Other overhead expenses	3,175	3,175	3,175	3,175	12,700
Total fixed overhead costs	$20,360	$20,360	$20,360	$20,360	$ 81,440
Total manufacturing overhead costs	$32,000	$47,520	$32,970	$56,735	$169,225

manufacturing costs divided by the estimated total direct labor hours. Framecraft's predetermined manufacturing overhead rate for 20x7 is $18.70 per direct labor hour ($169,225 ÷ 9,050 direct labor hours), or $1.87 per unit produced ($18.70 per direct labor hour × .10 direct labor hour per unit). The variable portion of the manufacturing overhead rate is $9.70 per direct labor hour ($87,785 ÷ 9,050 direct labor hours), which includes factory supplies, $1.80; employee benefits, $2.40; inspection, $.90; maintenance and repair, $1.60; and utilities, $3.00.

THE SELLING AND ADMINISTRATIVE EXPENSE BUDGET

KEY POINT: Remember that selling and administrative expenses are period costs, not product costs.

A **selling and administrative expense budget** is a detailed plan of operating expenses, other than those related to production, that are needed to support sales and overall operations in an accounting period. Accountants use this budget to estimate cash payments for products or services used in nonproduction-related activities. Framecraft Company's selling and administrative expense budget for 20x7 appears in Exhibit 6. The company groups its selling and administrative expenses into variable and fixed components for purposes of cost behavior analysis, C-V-P analysis, and profit planning. Framecraft Company's estimated variable selling and administrative expense rate for 20x7 is $.29 per unit sold, which includes delivery expenses, $.08; sales commissions, $.10; accounting, $.07; and other administrative expenses, $.04.

EXHIBIT 6
Selling and Administrative Expense Budget

Framecraft Company
Selling and Administrative Expense Budget
For the Year Ended December 31, 20x7

	Quarter 1	Quarter 2	Quarter 3	Quarter 4	Year
Variable selling and administrative expenses					
Delivery expenses	$ 800	$ 2,400	$ 800	$ 3,200	$ 7,200
Sales commissions	1,000	3,000	1,000	4,000	9,000
Accounting	700	2,100	700	2,800	6,300
Other administrative expenses	400	1,200	400	1,600	3,600
Total variable selling and administrative expenses	$ 2,900	$ 8,700	$ 2,900	$11,600	$ 26,100
Fixed selling and administrative expenses					
Sales salaries	$ 4,500	$ 4,500	$ 4,500	$ 4,500	$ 18,000
Executive salaries	12,750	12,750	12,750	12,750	51,000
Depreciation, office equipment	925	925	925	925	3,700
Taxes and insurance	1,700	1,700	1,700	1,700	6,800
Total fixed selling and administrative expenses	$19,875	$19,875	$19,875	$19,875	$ 79,500
Total selling and administrative expenses	$22,775	$28,575	$22,775	$31,475	$105,600

EXHIBIT 7
Cost of Goods Manufactured Budget

Framecraft Company
Cost of Goods Manufactured Budget
For the Year Ended December 31, 20x7

			Sources of Data
Direct materials used			
Direct materials inventory, December 31, 20x6	$ 1,200*		Exhibit 3
Purchases for 20x7	45,550		Exhibit 3
Cost of direct materials available for use	$46,750		
Less direct materials inventory, December 31, 20x7	1,500*		Exhibit 3
Cost of direct materials used		$ 45,250	
Direct labor costs		54,300	Exhibit 4
Manufacturing overhead costs		169,225	Exhibit 5
Total manufacturing costs		$268,775	
Work in process inventory, December 31, 20x6		—†	
Less work in process inventory, December 31, 20x7		—†	
Cost of goods manufactured		$268,775	

*The desired direct materials inventory balance at December 31, 20x6, is $1,200 (24,000 ounces × $.05 per ounce); at December 31, 20x7, it is $1,500 (30,000 ounces × $.05 per ounce).
†It is the company's policy to have no units in process at the beginning or end of the year.

THE COST OF GOODS MANUFACTURED BUDGET

A **cost of goods manufactured budget** is a detailed plan that summarizes the estimated costs of production in an accounting period. The sources of information for total manufacturing costs are the direct materials, direct labor, and manufacturing overhead budgets. Most manufacturing organizations anticipate some work in process at the beginning or end of the period covered by a budget. However, Framecraft Company has a policy of no work in process on December 31 of any year. Exhibit 7 summarizes the company's estimated costs of production in 20x7. (The column to the right of the exhibit shows the sources of key data.) The budgeted, or standard, product unit cost for one picture frame is rounded to $2.97 ($268,775 ÷ 90,500 units).

 Check out ACE for a Review Quiz at http://accounting.college.hmco.com/students.

FINANCIAL BUDGETS

LO4 Prepare a budgeted income statement, a cash budget, and a budgeted balance sheet.

RELATED TEXT ASSIGNMENTS
Q: 18, 19
SE: 7, 8, 9, 10
E: 5, 13, 14, 15
P: 2, 3, 4, 5, 6, 7, 8
SD: 2, 4, 5
MRA: 2, 3, 4

With revenues and expenses itemized in the operating budgets, an organization's controller is able to prepare the financial budgets, which, as we noted earlier, are projections of financial results for the accounting period. Financial budgets include a budgeted income statement, a capital expenditures budget, a cash budget, and a budgeted balance sheet.

THE BUDGETED INCOME STATEMENT

A **budgeted income statement** projects an organization's net income in an accounting period based on the revenues and expenses estimated for that period. Exhibit 8

EXHIBIT 8
Budgeted Income Statement

Framecraft Company
Budgeted Income Statement
For the Year Ended December 31, 20x7

			Sources of Data
Sales		$450,000	Exhibit 1
Cost of goods sold			
Finished goods inventory, December 31, 20x6	$ 2,970		
Cost of goods manufactured	268,775		Exhibit 7
Total cost of goods available for sale	$271,745		
Less finished goods inventory, December 31, 20x7	4,455		
Cost of goods sold		267,290	
Gross margin		$182,710	
Selling and administrative expenses		105,600	Exhibit 6
Income from operations		$ 77,110	
Interest expense (8% × $70,000)		5,600	
Income before income taxes		$ 71,510	
Income taxes expense (30%)		21,453	
Net income		$ 50,057	

Note: Finished goods inventory balances assume that product unit costs were the same in 20x6 and 20x7:

December 31, 20x6	December 31, 20x7
1,000 units	1,500 units (Exhibit 2)
× $ 2.97	× $ 2.97
$2,970	$4,455

shows Framecraft Company's budgeted income statement for 20x7. The company's expenses include 8 percent interest paid on a $70,000 note payable and income taxes paid at a rate of 30 percent.

Information about projected sales and costs comes from several operating budgets, as indicated by the column to the right of Exhibit 8, which identifies the sources of key data and makes it possible to trace how Framecraft's budgeted income statement was developed. At this point, you can review the overall preparation of the operating budgets and the budgeted income statement by comparing the preparation flow in Figure 2 with the budgets in Exhibits 1 through 8. You will notice that Framecraft Company has no budget for cost of goods sold; that information is included in its budgeted income statement.

THE CAPITAL EXPENDITURES BUDGET

A **capital expenditures budget** is a detailed plan outlining the anticipated amount and timing of capital outlays for long-term assets in an accounting period. Managers rely on the information in a capital expenditures budget when making decisions about such matters as buying equipment, building a new plant, purchasing and installing a materials handling system, or acquiring another business. Framecraft Company's capital expenditures budget for 20x7 includes $30,000 for the purchase of a new extrusion machine. The company plans to pay $15,000 in the first quarter of 20x7, when the order is placed, and $15,000 in the second quarter of 20x7, when it receives the extrusion machine. This information is necessary in preparing the company's cash budget. We discuss capital expenditures in more detail in another chapter.

THE CASH BUDGET

KEY POINT: The cash budget depends heavily on information from the operating budgets. Therefore, errors in those budgets could be compounded in the cash budget.

A **cash budget** is a projection of the cash an organization will receive and the cash it will pay out in an accounting period. It summarizes the cash flow prospects of all transactions considered in the master budget. The information that the cash budget provides enables managers to plan for short-term loans when the cash balance is low and for short-term investments when the cash balance is high. Table 1 shows how the elements of a cash budget relate to operating, investing, and financing activities.

A cash budget excludes planned noncash transactions, such as depreciation expense, amortization expense, issuance and receipt of stock dividends, uncollectible accounts expense, and gains and losses on sales of assets. Some organizations also exclude deferred taxes and accrued interest from the cash budget.

The following formula is useful in preparing a cash budget:

$$\text{Estimated Ending Cash Balance} = \text{Total Estimated Cash Receipts} - \text{Total Estimated Cash Payments} + \text{Estimated Beginning Cash Balance}$$

Estimates of cash receipts are based on information from several sources. Among these sources are the sales budget, the budgeted income statement, cash budgets from previous periods, cash collection records and analyses of collection trends, and records pertaining to notes, stocks, and bonds. Information used in estimating cash payments comes from the operating budgets, the budgeted income statement, the capital expenditures budget, the previous year's financial statements, and loan records.

TABLE 1. Elements of a Cash Budget

Activities	Cash Receipts From	Cash Payments For
Operating	Cash sales Cash collections on credit sales Interest income from investments Cash dividends from investments	Purchases of direct materials Purchases of indirect materials Direct labor Manufacturing overhead expenses Selling expenses Administrative expenses Interest expense Income taxes
Investing	Sale of investments Sale of long-term assets	Purchases of investments Purchases of long-term assets
Financing	Proceeds from loans Proceeds from issue of stock Proceeds from issue of bonds	Loan repayments Cash dividends to stockholders Purchases of treasury stock Retirement of bonds

Note: Classifications of cash receipts and cash payments correspond to those in a statement of cash flows.

LO4 **Capital expenditures budget:** A detailed plan outlining the anticipated amount and timing of capital outlays for long-term assets in an accounting period.

LO4 **Cash budget:** A projection of the cash an organization will receive and the cash it will pay out in an accounting period.

LO3 **Cost of goods manufactured budget:** A detailed plan that summarizes the estimated costs of production in an accounting period.

LO3 **Direct labor budget:** A detailed plan that estimates the direct labor hours needed in an accounting period and the associated costs.

LO3 **Direct materials purchases budget:** A detailed plan that identifies the quantity of purchases required to meet budgeted production and inventory needs and the costs associated with those purchases.

LO2 **Financial budgets:** Budget projections of the financial results for an accounting period.

LO3 **Manufacturing overhead budget:** A detailed plan of anticipated manufacturing costs, other than direct materials and direct labor costs, that must be incurred to meet budgeted production needs.

LO2 **Master budget:** A set of operating budgets and a set of financial budgets that detail an organization's financial plans for a specific accounting period.

LO2 **Operating budgets:** Budget plans used in daily operations.

LO1 **Participative budgeting:** A process in which personnel at all levels of an organization actively engage in making decisions about a budget.

LO3 **Production budget:** A detailed plan showing the number of units a company must produce to meet budgeted sales and inventory needs.

LO2 **Pro forma statements:** Financial statements that show projections rather than actual results and that are often used to communicate business plans to external parties.

LO3 **Sales budget:** A detailed plan, expressed in both units and dollars, that identifies the product (or service) sales expected in an accounting period.

LO3 **Sales forecast:** A projection of sales demand based on an analysis of external and internal factors.

LO3 **Selling and administrative expense budget:** A detailed plan of operating expenses, other than those related to production, that are needed to support sales and overall operations in an accounting period.

LO1 **Strategic planning:** The process by which management establishes an organization's long-term goals.

REVIEW PROBLEM

Preparing a Cash Budget

LO4 Info Processing Company provides database management services. It uses state-of-the-art equipment and employs five information specialists. Each specialist works an average of 160 hours a month. Info Processing's controller has compiled the following information:

	Actual Data for 20x6		Forecasted Data for 20x7		
	November	December	January	February	March
Client billings (sales)	$25,000	$35,000	$25,000	$20,000	$40,000
Selling and administrative expenses	12,000	13,000	12,000	11,000	12,500
Operating supplies	2,500	3,500	2,500	2,500	4,000
Processing overhead	3,200	3,500	3,000	2,500	3,500

Sixty percent of the client billings are cash sales collected during the month of sale; 30 percent are collected in the first month following the sale; and 10 percent are collected in the second month following the sale. Operating supplies are paid for in the month of purchase. Selling and administrative expenses and processing overhead are paid in the month following the cost's incurrence.

The company has a bank loan of $12,000 at a 12 percent annual interest rate. Interest is paid monthly, and $2,000 of the loan principal is due on February 28, 20x7. Income taxes of $4,550 for calendar year 20x6 are due and payable on March 15, 20x7. The information specialists earn $8.50 an hour, and all payroll-related employee benefit costs are included in processing overhead. The company anticipates no capital expenditures for the first quarter of the coming year. It expects its cash balance on December 31, 20x6, to be $13,840.

REQUIRED ▶ Prepare a monthly cash budget for Info Processing Company for the three-month period ended March 31, 20x7. Comment on whether the ending cash balances are adequate for Info Processing's cash needs.

Answer to Review Problem

Info Processing Company
Monthly Cash Budget
For the Three-Month Period Ended March 31, 20x7

	January	February	March	Totals
Cash receipts				
Client billings	$28,000	$23,000	$32,500	$83,500
Cash payments				
Operating supplies	$ 2,500	$ 2,500	$ 4,000	$ 9,000
Direct labor	6,800	6,800	6,800	20,400
Selling and administrative expenses	13,000	12,000	11,000	36,000
Processing overhead	3,500	3,000	2,500	9,000
Interest expense	120	120	100	340
Loan payment	—	2,000	—	2,000
Income tax payment	—	—	4,550	4,550
Total cash payments	$25,920	$26,420	$28,950	$81,290
Cash increase (decrease)	$ 2,080	($ 3,420)	$ 3,550	$ 2,210
Beginning cash balance	13,840	15,920	12,500	13,840
Ending cash balance	$15,920	$12,500	$16,050	$16,050

The details supporting the individual computations in this cash budget are as follows:

	January	February	March
Client billings			
November	$ 2,500	—	—
December	10,500	$ 3,500	—
January	15,000	7,500	$ 2,500
February	—	12,000	6,000
March	—	—	24,000
	$28,000	$23,000	$32,500

Operating supplies			
Paid for in the month purchased	$ 2,500	$ 2,500	$ 4,000
Direct labor			
5 employees × 160 hours a month × $8.50 an hour	6,800	6,800	6,800
Selling and administrative expenses			
Paid in the month following incurrence	13,000	12,000	11,000
Processing overhead			
Paid in the month following incurrence	3,500	3,000	2,500
Interest expense			
January and February = 1% of $12,000	120	120	
March = 1% of $10,000			100
Loan payment	—	2,000	—
Income tax payment		—	4,550

The ending cash balances of $15,920, $12,500, and $16,050 for January, February, and March 20x7, respectively, appear to be comfortable but not too large for Info Processing Company.

Chapter Assignments

BUILDING YOUR KNOWLEDGE FOUNDATION

QUESTIONS

1. Define budgeting.
2. What is a budget? What type of information may a budget include?
3. List three ways in which an organization can use budgets.
4. What is the difference between long-term strategic plans and annual operating plans?
5. What factors should be considered in establishing long-term goals?
6. Explain the purpose of the following budgeting practice: "Restate long-term plans in terms of short-term plans for products or services and in terms of a detailed profit plan."
7. Describe what happens in the budgeting process after management has set short-term goals.
8. Give examples of ways in which budgeting can help managers during the stages of the management cycle.
9. What is a master budget? What is its purpose?
10. In what ways are the master budgets of manufacturing, retail, and service organizations similar?
11. In what ways do the master budgets of a retail organization and a service organization differ?
12. List the guidelines for preparing a budget.
13. What is a sales forecast? What internal and external factors does a sales forecast take into consideration?
14. What are the three steps in preparing a direct materials purchases budget?
15. What are the two steps in preparing a direct labor budget?
16. Why is it useful to distinguish between variable and fixed expenses in a selling and administrative expense budget?
17. Why does a selling and administrative expense budget use units sold rather than units produced?

18. How is the cash budget related to the master budget? What are the purposes of preparing a cash budget?
19. What is the final step in developing a master budget?
20. Who are the people responsible for ensuring that budget implementation is successful? What are their responsibilities?

SHORT EXERCISES

LO1 **Budgeting and the Management Cycle**

SE 1. All the management activities listed below require the use of budget information. Indicate whether each activity is part of the planning stage (P), executing stage (E), reviewing stage (REV), or reporting stage (REP) of the management cycle.

1. Coordinating purchasing, production, sales, and shipping
2. Selecting performance measures to monitor the timeliness of shipping
3. Calculating variances between the planned direct materials and actual direct materials used in production
4. Developing a budget to distribute the organization's resources among its various departments
5. Preparing a report on the performance of the production department over the last three months

LO1 **Budgeting in a Retail Organization**

SE 2. Sam Zubac is the manager of the shoe department in a discount department store. During a recent meeting, Zubac and his supervisor agreed that Zubac's goal for the next year would be to increase the number of pairs of shoes sold by 20 percent. The department sold 8,000 pairs of shoes last year. Two salespersons currently work for Zubac. What types of budgets should Zubac use to help him achieve his sales goal? What kinds of information should those budgets provide?

LO1 **Budgetary Control**

SE 3. Toby Andres owns a tree nursery. She analyzes her business's results by comparing actual operating results with figures budgeted at the beginning of the year. When the business generates large profits, she often overlooks the differences between actual and budgeted data. But when profits are low, she spends many hours analyzing the differences. If you owned Andres's business, would you use her approach to budgetary control? If not, what changes would you make?

LO1 **Budgeting and Goals**

SE 4. The dashboard assembly team at Rockford Automobile Company is participating in the company's budgeting process for the first time. After the team participated in a discussion of the basic principles of budgeting, one team member asked the controller to explain how the company's long-term goals relate to its short-term plan. How should the controller respond?

LO2 **Components of a Master**
LO3 **Budget**

SE 5. A master budget is a compilation of forecasts for the coming year or operating cycle made by various departments or functions within an organization. What is the most basic forecast made in a master budget? List the reasons for your answer. Which budgets must managers prepare before they can prepare a direct materials purchases budget?

LO3 **Preparing an Operating Budget**

SE 6. Quester Company expects to sell 50,000 units of its product in the coming year. Each unit sells for $45. Sales brochures and supplies for the year are expected to cost $7,000. Three sales representatives cover the southeast region. Each one's base salary is $20,000, and each earns a sales commission of 5 percent of the selling price of the units he or she sells. The sales representatives supply their own transportation; they are reimbursed for travel at a rate of $.40 per mile. The company estimates that the sales representatives will drive a total of 75,000 miles next year.

From the information provided, calculate Quester Company's budgeted selling expenses for the coming year.

LO3 **Budgeted Gross Margin**
LO4

SE 7. Operating budgets for the DiPaolo Company reveal the following information: net sales, $450,000; beginning materials inventory, $23,000; materials purchased, $185,000; beginning work in process inventory, $64,700; beginning finished goods inventory, $21,600; direct labor costs, $34,000; manufacturing overhead applied, $67,000; ending work in process inventory, $61,200; ending materials inventory, $18,700; and ending finished goods inventory, $16,300.

Compute DiPaola Company's budgeted gross margin.

LO4 Estimating Cash Collections

SE 8. KD Insurance Company specializes in term life insurance contracts. Cash collection experience shows that 20 percent of billed premiums are collected in the month before they are due, 60 percent are paid in the month they are due, and 16 percent are paid in the month following their due date. Four percent of the billed premiums are paid late (in the second month following their due date) and include a 10 percent penalty payment. Total billing notices in January were $58,000; in February, $62,000; in March, $66,000; in April, $65,000; in May, $60,000; and in June, $62,000. How much cash does the company expect to collect in May?

LO4 Cash Budget

SE 9. The projections of direct materials purchases that follow are for the Stromboli Corporation.

	Purchases on Account	Cash Purchases
December 20x6	$40,000	$20,000
January 20x7	60,000	30,000
February 20x7	50,000	25,000
March 20x7	70,000	35,000

The company pays for 60 percent of purchases on account in the month of purchase and 40 percent in the month following the purchase. Prepare a monthly schedule of expected cash payments for direct materials for the first quarter of 20x7.

LO4 Budgeted Balance Sheet

SE 10. Wellman Corporation's budgeted balance sheet for the coming year shows total assets of $4,650,000 and total liabilities of $1,900,000. Common stock and retained earnings make up the entire stockholders' equity section of the balance sheet. Common stock remains at its beginning balance of $1,500,000. The projected net income for the year is $349,600. The company pays no cash dividends. What is the balance of retained earnings at the beginning of the budget period?

EXERCISES

LO1 Budgeting and the Management Cycle

E 1. All the activities described below require the use of budget information. Indicate whether each activity is part of the planning stage (P), executing stage (E), reviewing stage (REV), or reporting stage (REP) of the management cycle.

1. Vivian Gentry, manager of a golf and tennis resort, develops a budget to distribute limited resources to the resort's pro shop, maintenance department, golf and tennis operations, hotel operations, and restaurant operations.
2. Gentry challenges employees to increase the volume of customers eating in the restaurant by 10 percent, a goal set forth in the restaurant's budget.
3. Gentry selects the number of golf lessons given each month as a measure of performance for the golf operations.
4. The resort's accountant prepares a performance report for the restaurant.
5. Gentry analyzes the restaurant's performance report and finds that sales volume was 25 percent lower than planned.
6. Gentry meets with restaurant managers and employees to discuss the results from a survey of resort guests. Based on her findings, Gentry decides to expand the number of items offered on the menu, increase advertising for the restaurant, and replace the chef.
7. Edgar Thorn, the manager of golf operations, uses the budgeted number of golf lessons to motivate the golf pros to provide more lessons.
8. At the end of the month, Thorn calculates the variance between the actual number of golf lessons given and the budgeted number of golf lessons. He finds that the number of lessons given was fewer than planned.
9. Thorn prepares a variance report and gives it to the golf pros for review.
10. Thorn selects the number of hours of golf instruction as a new performance measure for the remainder of the year.

LO1 Characteristics of Budgets

E 2. You recently attended a workshop on budgeting and overheard the following comments as you walked to the refreshment table:

1. "Budgets are the same regardless of the size of an organization or management's role in the budgeting process."

2. "Budgets can include financial or nonfinancial data. In our organization, we plan the number of hours to be worked and the number of customer contacts we want our salespeople to make."
3. "All budgets are complicated. You have to be an expert to prepare one."
4. "Budgets don't need to be highly accurate. No one in our company stays within a budget anyway."

Do you agree or disagree with each comment? Explain.

LO1 Budgeting and Goals

E 3. Effective planning of long- and short-term goals has contributed to the success of Multitasker Calendars, Inc. Described below are the actions the company's management team took during a recent planning meeting. Indicate whether the goals related to those actions are short-term or long-term.

1. In forecasting the next ten-year period, the management team considered economic and industry forecasts, employee-management relationships, and the structure and role of management.
2. Based on the ten-year forecast, the team made decisions about next year's sales and profit targets.

LO1 Budgeting and Goals

E 4. Assume that you work in the accounting department of a small wholesale warehousing company. Inspired by a recent seminar on budgeting, the company's president wants to develop a budgeting system and has asked you to direct it. Identify the points about the initial steps in the budgeting process that you should communicate to the president. Concentrate on principles related to long-term goals and short-term goals.

LO2 Components of a Master
LO3 Budget
LO4

E 5. Identify the order in which the following budgets are prepared. Use the letter *a* to indicate the first budget to be prepared, *b* for the second, and so on.

1. Production budget
2. Direct labor budget
3. Direct materials purchases budget
4. Sales budget
5. Budgeted balance sheet
6. Cash budget
7. Budgeted income statement

LO3 Sales Budget

E 6. Quarterly and annual sales for 20x7 for Steen Manufacturing Company are shown below.

Steen Manufacturing Company
Actual Sales Revenue
For the Year Ended December 31, 20x7

Product Class	January–March	April–June	July–September	October–December	Annual Totals	Estimated 20x8 Percent Increases by Product Class
Marine products	$ 44,500	$ 45,500	$ 48,200	$ 47,900	$ 186,100	10%
Mountain products	36,900	32,600	34,100	37,200	140,800	5%
River products	29,800	29,700	29,100	27,500	116,100	30%
Hiking products	38,800	37,600	36,900	39,700	153,000	15%
Running products	47,700	48,200	49,400	49,900	195,200	25%
Biking products	65,400	65,900	66,600	67,300	265,200	20%
Totals	$263,100	$259,500	$264,300	$269,500	$1,056,400	

Prepare a sales budget for 20x8 for the company. Show both quarterly and annual totals for each product class.

Chapter Assignments

LO3 Production Budget

E 7. Isobel Law, the controller for Aberdeen Lock Company, is preparing a production budget for 20x7. The company's policy is to maintain a finished goods inventory equal to one-half of the following month's sales. Sales of 7,000 locks are budgeted for April. Complete the monthly production budget for the first quarter:

	January	February	March
Sales in units	5,000	4,000	6,000
Add desired units of ending finished goods inventory	2,000	?	?
Desired total units	7,000		
Less desired units of beginning finished goods inventory	2,500	?	?
Total production units	4,500	?	?

LO3 Production Budget

E 8. Santa Fe Corporation produces and sells a single product. Expected sales for September are 12,000 units; for October, 15,000 units; for November, 9,000 units; for December, 10,000 units; and for January, 14,000 units. The company's desired level of ending finished goods inventory at the end of a month is 10 percent of the following month's sales in units. At the end of August, 1,200 units were on hand. How many units need to be produced in the fourth quarter?

LO3 Direct Materials Purchases Budget

E 9. The U-Z Door Company manufactures garage door units. The units include hinges, door panels, and other hardware. Prepare a direct materials purchases budget for the first quarter of 20x7 based on budgeted production of 16,000 garage door units. Sandee Morton, the controller, has provided the following information:

Hinges	4 sets per door	$11.00 per set
Door panels	4 panels per door	$27.00 per panel
Other hardware	1 lock per door	$31.00 per lock
	1 handle per door	$22.50 per handle
	2 roller tracks per door	$16.00 per set of 2 roller tracks
	8 rollers per door	$ 4.00 per roller

Assume no beginning or ending quantities of direct materials inventory.

LO3 Direct Materials Purchases Budget

E 10. Hard Corporation projects sales of $230,000 in May, $250,000 in June, $260,000 in July, and $240,000 in August. The dollar value of the company's cost of goods sold is generally 65 percent of total sales. The dollar value of its desired ending inventory is 25 percent of the following month's cost of goods sold.

Compute the total purchases budgeted for June and the total purchases budgeted for July.

LO3 Direct Labor Budget

E 11. Paige Metals Company has two departments—Cutting and Grinding—and manufactures three products. Budgeted unit production in 20x7 is 21,000 of Product T, 36,000 of Product M, and 30,000 of Product B. The company is currently analyzing direct labor hour requirements for 20x7.

Data for each department are as follows:

	Cutting	Grinding
Estimated hours per unit		
Product T	1.1	.5
Product M	.6	2.9
Product B	3.2	1.0
Hourly labor rate	$9	$7

Prepare a direct labor budget for 20x7 that shows the budgeted direct labor costs for each department and for the company as a whole.

LO3 Manufacturing Overhead Budget

E 12. Carole Dahl is chief financial officer of the Phoenix Division of Dahl Corporation, a multinational company with three operating divisions. As part of the budgeting process, Dahl's staff is developing the manufacturing overhead budget for 20x7. The division estimates that it will manufacture 50,000 units during the year. The budgeted cost information is as follows:

	Variable Rate per Unit	Total Fixed Costs
Indirect materials	$1.00	
Indirect labor	4.00	
Supplies	.40	
Repairs and maintenance	3.00	$ 40,000
Electricity	.10	20,000
Factory supervision		180,000
Insurance		25,000
Property taxes		35,000
Depreciation, machinery		82,000
Depreciation, building		72,000

Using the data provided, prepare the division's manufacturing overhead budget for 20x7.

LO4 Cash Collections

E 13. Dacahr Bros., Inc., is an automobile maintenance and repair company with outlets throughout the western United States. Henley Turlington, the company controller, is starting to assemble the cash budget for the fourth quarter of 20x7. Projected sales for the quarter are as follows:

	On Account	Cash
October	$452,000	$196,800
November	590,000	214,000
December	720,500	218,400

Cash collection records pertaining to sales on account indicate the following collection pattern:

Month of sale	40%
First month following sale	30%
Second month following sale	28%
Uncollectible	2%

Sales on account during August were $346,000. During September, sales on account were $395,000.

Compute the amount of cash to be collected from customers during each month of the fourth quarter.

LO4 Cash Collections

E 14. XYZ Company collects payment on 50 percent of credit sales in the month of sale, 40 percent in the month following sale, and 5 percent in the second month following the sale. Its sales budget is as follows:

Month	Cash Sales	Credit Sales
May	$20,000	$ 40,000
June	40,000	60,000
July	60,000	80,000
August	80,000	100,000

Compute XYZ Company's total cash collections in July and its total cash collections in August.

LO4 Cash Budget

E 15. Alberta Limited needs a cash budget for the month of November. The following information is available:

a. The cash balance on November 1 is $6,000.
b. Sales for October and November are $80,000 and $60,000, respectively. Cash collections on sales are 30 percent in the month of sale and 65 percent in the month after the sale; 5 percent of sales are uncollectible.
c. General expenses budgeted for November are $25,000 (depreciation represents $2,000 of this amount).
d. Inventory purchases will total $30,000 in October and $40,000 in November. The company pays for half of its inventory purchases in the month of purchase and for the other half the month after purchase.
e. The company will pay $4,000 in cash for office furniture in November. Sales commissions for November are budgeted at $12,000.

f. The company maintains a minimum ending cash balance of $4,000 and can borrow from the bank in multiples of $100. All loans are repaid after 60 days.

Prepare a cash budget for Alberta Limited for the month of November.

PROBLEMS

P 1.
LO3 Preparing Operating Budgets

The principal product of Yangsoo Enterprises, Inc., is a multipurpose hammer that carries a lifetime guarantee. Listed below are cost and production data for the Yangsoo hammer.

Direct materials
  Anodized steel: 2 kilograms per hammer at $1.60 per kilogram
  Leather strapping for the handle: .5 square meter per hammer at $4.40 per square meter
Direct labor
  Forging operation: $12.50 per labor hour; 6 minutes per hammer
  Leather-wrapping operation: $12.00 per direct labor hour; 12 minutes per hammer
Manufacturing overhead
  Forging operation: rate equals 70 percent of department's direct labor dollars
  Leather-wrapping operation: rate equals 50 percent of department's direct labor dollars

In October, November, and December of 20x7, Yangsoo Enterprises expects to produce 108,000, 104,000, and 100,000 hammers, respectively. The company has no beginning or ending balances of direct materials inventory or work in process inventory for the year.

REQUIRED
1. For the three-month period ending December 31, 20x7, prepare monthly production cost information for the Yangsoo hammer. Classify the costs as direct materials, direct labor, or manufacturing overhead and show your computations.
2. Prepare a cost of goods manufactured budget for the hammer. Show monthly cost data and combined totals for the quarter for each cost category.

P 2.
LO3 Preparing a Comprehensive
LO4 Budget

Bertha's Bathworks began manufacturing hair and bath products in 20x7. Its biggest customer is a national retail chain that specializes in such products. Bertha Jackson, the owner of Bertha's Bathworks, would like to have an estimate of the company's net income in 20x8.

REQUIRED Calculate Bertha's Bathworks' net income in 20x8 by completing the operating budgets and budgeted income statement that follow.

1. Sales budget:

Bertha's Bathworks
Sales Budget
For the Year Ended December 31, 20x8

| | Quarter | | | | |
	1	2	3	4	Year
Sales in units	4,000	3,000	5,000	5,000	17,000
× Selling price per unit	× $5	× ?	× ?	× ?	× ?
Total sales	$20,000	?	?	?	?

2. Production budget:

Bertha's Bathworks
Production Budget
For the Year Ended December 31, 20x8

	Quarter 1	Quarter 2	Quarter 3	Quarter 4	Year
Sales in units	4,000	?	?	?	?
Plus desired units of ending finished goods inventory*	300	?	?	600	600
Desired total units	4,300				
Less desired units of beginning finished goods inventory†	400	?	?	?	400
Total production units	3,900	?	?	?	?

*Desired units of ending finished goods inventory = 10% of next quarter's budgeted sales.
†Desired units of beginning finished goods inventory = 10% of current quarter's budgeted sales.

3. Direct materials purchases budget:

Bertha's Bathworks
Direct Materials Purchases Budget
For the Year Ended December 31, 20x8

	Quarter 1	Quarter 2	Quarter 3	Quarter 4	Year
Total production units	3,900	3,200	5,000	5,100	17,200
× 3 ounces per unit	× 3	× ?	× ?	× ?	× ?
Total production needs in ounces	11,700	?	?	?	?
Plus desired ounces of ending direct materials inventory*	1,920	?	?	3,600	3,600
	13,620				
Less desired ounces of beginning direct materials inventory†	2,340	?	?	?	2,340
Total ounces of direct materials to be purchased	11,280	?	?	?	?
× Cost per ounce	× $.10	× ?	× ?	× ?	× ?
Total cost of direct materials purchases	$ 1,128	?	?	?	?

Note: Budgeted production needs in ounces for the first quarter of 20x9 = 18,000 ounces.
*Desired ounces of ending direct materials inventory = 20% of next quarter's budgeted production needs in ounces.
†Desired ounces of beginning direct materials inventory = 20% of current quarter's budgeted production needs in ounces.

4. Direct labor budget:

Bertha's Bathworks
Direct Labor Budget
For the Year Ended December 31, 20x8

	Quarter				
	1	2	3	4	Year
Total production units	3,900	?	?	?	?
× Direct labor hours per unit	× .1	× ?	× ?	× ?	× ?
Total direct labor hours	390	?	?	?	?
× Direct labor cost per hour	× $7	× ?	× ?	× ?	× ?
Total direct labor cost	$2,730	?	?	?	?

5. Manufacturing overhead budget:

Bertha's Bathworks
Manufacturing Overhead Budget
For the Year Ended December 31, 20x8

	Quarter				
	1	2	3	4	Year
Variable overhead costs					
Factory supplies ($.05)	$ 195	?	?	?	?
Employee benefits ($.25)	975	?	?	?	?
Inspection ($.10)	390	?	?	?	?
Maintenance and repair ($.15)	585	?	?	?	?
Utilities ($.05)	195	?	?	?	?
Total variable overhead costs	$2,340	?	?	?	?
Fixed overhead costs					
Depreciation, machinery	$ 500	?	?	?	?
Depreciation, building	700	?	?	?	?
Supervision	1,800	?	?	?	?
Maintenance and repair	400	?	?	?	?
Other overhead expenses	600	?	?	?	?
Total fixed overhead costs	$4,000	?	?	?	?
Total manufacturing overhead costs	$6,340	?	?	?	?

Note: The figures in parentheses are variable costs per unit.

6. Selling and administrative expense budget:

Bertha's Bathworks
Selling and Administrative Expense Budget
For the Year Ended December 31, 20x8

	Quarter				
	1	2	3	4	Year
Variable selling and administrative expenses					
Delivery expenses ($.10)	$ 400	?	?	?	?
Sales commissions ($.15)	600	?	?	?	?
Accounting ($.05)	200	?	?	?	?
Other administrative expenses ($.20)	800	?	?	?	?
Total variable selling and administrative expenses	$2,000	?	?	?	?
Fixed selling and administrative expenses					
Sales salaries	$5,000	?	?	?	?
Depreciation, office equipment	900	?	?	?	?
Taxes and insurance	1,700	?	?	?	?
Total fixed selling and administrative expenses	$7,600	?	?	?	?
Total selling and administrative expenses	$9,600	?	?	?	?

Note: The figures in parentheses are variable costs per unit.

7. Cost of goods manufactured budget:

Bertha's Bathworks
Cost of Goods Manufactured Budget
For the Year Ended December 31, 20x8

Direct materials used		
Direct materials inventory, December 31, 20x7	?	
Purchases for 20x8	?	
Cost of direct materials available for use	?	
Less direct materials inventory, December 31, 20x8	?	
Cost of direct materials used		?
Direct labor costs		?
Manufacturing overhead costs		?
Total manufacturing costs		?
Work in process inventory, December 31, 20x7*		?
Less work in process inventory, December 31, 20x8*		?
Cost of goods manufactured		?

*It is the company's policy to have no units in process at the end of the year.

8. Budgeted income statement:

Bertha's Bathworks
Budgeted Income Statement
For the Year Ended December 31, 20x8

Sales		?
Cost of goods sold		
Finished goods inventory, December 31, 20x7	?	
Cost of goods manufactured	?	
Cost of goods available for sale	?	
Less finished goods inventory, December 31, 20x8	?	
Cost of goods sold		?
Gross margin		?
Selling and administrative expenses		?
Income from operations		?
Income taxes expense (30%)*		?
Net income		?

*The figure in parentheses is the company's income tax rate.

P 3.
LO4 Basic Cash Budget

Tex Kinkaid's dream was to develop the biggest produce operation with the widest selection of fresh fruits and vegetables in northern Texas. Within three years of opening Minigarden Produce, Inc., Kincaid accomplished his objective. Kinkaid has asked you to prepare monthly cash budgets for Minigarden Produce for the quarter ended September 30, 20x7.

Credit sales to retailers in the area constitute 80 percent of Minigarden Produce's business; cash sales to customers at the company's retail outlet make up the other 20 percent. Collection records indicate that Minigarden Produce collects payment on 50 percent of all credit sales during the month of sale, 30 percent in the month after the sale, and 20 percent in the second month after the sale.

The company's total sales in May were $66,000; in June, they were $67,500. Anticipated sales in July are $69,500; in August, $76,250; and in September, $84,250. The company's purchases are expected to total $43,700 in July, $48,925 in August, and $55,725 in September. The company pays for all purchases in cash.

Projected monthly costs for the quarter include $1,040 for heat, light, and power; $375 for bank fees; $1,925 for rent; $1,120 for supplies; $1,705 for depreciation of equipment; $1,285 for equipment repairs; and $475 for miscellaneous expenses. Other projected costs for the quarter are salaries and wages of $18,370 in July, $19,200 in August, and $20,300 in September.

The company's cash balance at June 30, 20x7, was $2,745. It has a policy of maintaining a minimum monthly cash balance of $1,500.

REQUIRED
1. Prepare a monthly cash budget for Minigarden Produce, Inc., for the quarter ended September 30, 20x7.
2. Should Minigarden Produce anticipate taking out a loan during the quarter? If so, how much should it borrow, and when?

P 4.
LO4 Budgeted Income Statement and Budgeted Balance Sheet

Moontrust Bank has asked the president of Wishware Products, Inc., for a budgeted income statement and budgeted balance sheet for the quarter ended June 30, 20x7. These pro forma statements are needed to support Wishware Product's request for a loan.

Wishware Products routinely prepares a quarterly master budget. The operating budgets prepared for the quarter ending June 30, 20x7, have provided the following information: Projected sales for April are $220,400; for May, $164,220; and for June, $165,980. Direct materials purchases for the period are estimated at $96,840; direct materials usage, at $102,710; direct labor expenses, at $71,460; manufacturing overhead, at $79,940; selling and administrative expenses, at $143,740; capital expenditures, at $125,000 (to be spent on June 29); cost of goods manufactured, at $252,880; and cost of goods sold, at $251,700.

Balance sheet account balances at March 31, 20x7, were as follows: Accounts Receivable, $26,500; Materials Inventory, $23,910; Work in Process Inventory, $31,620; Finished Goods Inventory, $36,220; Prepaid Expenses, $7,200; Plant, Furniture, and Fixtures, $498,600; Accumulated Depreciation, Plant, Furniture, and Fixtures, $141,162; Patents, $90,600; Accounts Payable, $39,600; Notes Payable, $105,500; Common Stock, $250,000; and Retained Earnings, $207,158.

Projected monthly cash balances for the second quarter of 20x7 are as follows: April 30, $20,490; May 31, $35,610; and June 30, $45,400. During the quarter, accounts receivable are expected to increase by 30 percent, patents to go up by $6,500, prepaid expenses to remain constant, and accounts payable to go down by 10 percent (Wishware Products will make a $5,000 payment on a note payable, $4,100 of which is principal reduction).

The federal income tax rate is 34 percent, and the second quarter's tax is paid in July. Depreciation for the quarter will be $6,420, which is included in the manufacturing overhead budget. The company will pay no dividends.

REQUIRED
1. Prepare a budgeted income statement for the quarter ended June 30, 20x7. Round answers to the nearest dollar.
2. Prepare a budgeted balance sheet as of June 30, 20x7.

P 5.
LO4 Comprehensive Cash Budget

Located in Telluride, Colorado, Wellness Centers, Inc., emphasizes the benefits of regular workouts and the importance of physical examinations. The corporation operates three fully equipped fitness centers, as well as a medical center that specializes in preventive medicine. Wellness Center's controller has compiled the following data pertaining to the first quarter of 20x7:

Cash Receipts

Memberships: December 20x6, 870; January 20x7, 880; February, 910; March, 1,030
Membership dues: $90 per month, payable on the 10th of the month (80 percent collected on time; 20 percent collected one month late)
Medical examinations: January, $35,610; February, $41,840; March, $45,610
Special aerobics classes: January, $4,020; February, $5,130; March, $7,130
High-protein food sales: January, $4,890; February, $5,130; March, $6,280

Cash Payments

Salaries and wages:
  Corporate officers: 2 at $12,000 per month
  Physicians: 2 at $7,000 per month
  Nurses: 3 at $2,900 per month
  Clerical staff: 2 at $1,500 per month
  Aerobics instructors: 3 at $1,100 per month
  Clinic staff: 6 at $1,700 per month
  Maintenance staff: 3 at $900 per month
  Health-food servers: 3 at $750 per month
Purchases:
  Muscle-toning machines: January, $14,400; February, $13,800 (no purchases in March)
  Pool supplies: $520 per month
  Health food: January, $3,290; February, $3,460; March, $3,720
  Medical supplies: January, $10,400; February, $11,250; March, $12,640
  Medical uniforms and disposable garments: January, $7,410; February, $3,900; March, $3,450
  Medical equipment: January, $11,200; February, $3,400; March $5,900
Advertising: January, $2,250; February, $1,190; March, $2,450

Utilities expense: January, $5,450; February, $5,890; March, $6,090
Insurance:
   Fire: January, $3,470
   Liability: March, $3,980
Property taxes: $3,760 due in January
Federal income taxes: 20x6 taxes of $21,000 due in March 20x7
Miscellaneous: January, $2,625; February, $2,800; March, $1,150

Wellness Center's controller anticipates that the beginning cash balance for 20x7 will be $9,840.

REQUIRED ▶ Prepare a cash budget for Wellness Centers, Inc., for the first quarter of 20x7. Use the following column headings:

| January | February | March | Quarter |

ALTERNATE PROBLEMS

P 6.
LO4 Budgeted Income Statement
LO5

Delft House, Inc., a multinational company based in Amsterdam, organizes and coordinates art shows and auctions throughout the world. Its budgeted and actual costs for last year, 20x4, are as follows:

	Budgeted Cost	Actual Cost
Salaries expense, staging	€ 480,000	€ 512,800
Salaries expense, executive	380,000	447,200
Travel costs	640,000	652,020
Auctioneer services	540,000	449,820
Space rental costs	251,000	246,580
Printing costs	192,000	182,500
Advertising expense	169,000	183,280
Insurance, merchandise	84,800	77,300
Insurance, liability	64,000	67,100
Home office costs	209,200	219,880
Shipping costs	105,000	112,560
Miscellaneous	25,000	25,828
Total expenses	€3,140,000	€3,176,868
Net receipts	€6,200,000	€6,369,200

Delft House has budgeted the following fixed costs for the current year, 20x5: executive salaries, €440,000; advertising expense, €190,000; merchandise insurance, €80,000; and liability insurance, €68,000. Additional information pertaining to the organization's current operations is as follows:

a. Net receipts are estimated at €6,400,000.
b. Salaries expense for staging will increase 20 percent over the actual figures for the previous year.
c. Travel costs are expected to be 11 percent of net receipts.
d. Auctioneer services will be billed at 9.5 percent of net receipts.
e. Space rental costs will be 20 percent higher than the amount budgeted in the previous year.
f. Printing costs are expected to be €190,000.
g. Home office costs are budgeted for €230,000.
h. Shipping costs are expected to be 20 percent higher than the amount budgeted in the previous year.
i. Miscellaneous expenses for the current year will be budgeted at €28,000.

REQUIRED ▶
1. Prepare the company's budgeted income statement for the current year, 20x5. Since the company sells only services, assume it has expenses only and no cost of sales. (Net receipts equal gross margin.) Use a 34 percent income tax rate.
2. Should the budget committee be worried about the trend in the company's operations? Explain your answer.

LO4 **Basic Cash Budget**

P 7. Felasco Nurseries, Inc., has been in business for six years and has four divisions. Ethan Poulis, the corporation's controller, has been asked to prepare a cash budget for the Southern Division for the first quarter of 20x8.

Projected data supporting this budget are as follows:

Sales (60 percent on credit)		Purchases	
November 20x7	$160,000	December 20x7	$ 86,800
December 20x7	200,000	January 20x8	124,700
January 20x8	120,000	February 20x8	99,440
February 20x8	160,000	March 20x8	104,800
March 20x8	140,000		

Collection records of accounts receivable have shown that 30 percent of all credit sales are collected in the month of sale, 60 percent in the month following the sale, and 8 percent in the second month following the sale; 2 percent of the sales are uncollectible. All purchases are paid for in the month after the purchase. Salaries and wages are projected to be $25,200 in January, $33,200 in February, and $21,200 in March. Estimated monthly costs are utilities, $4,220; collection fees, $1,700; rent, $5,300; equipment depreciation, $5,440; supplies, $2,480; small tools, $3,140; and miscellaneous, $1,900.

Each of the corporation's divisions maintains a $6,000 minimum cash balance. As of December 31, 20x7, the Southern Division had a cash balance of $9,600.

REQUIRED
1. Prepare a monthly cash budget for Felasco Nurseries' Southern Division for the first quarter of 20x8.
2. Should Felasco Nurseries anticipate taking out a loan for the Southern Division during the quarter? If so, how much should it borrow, and when?

LO4 **Budgeted Income Statement and Budgeted Balance Sheet**

P 8. Whatever Video Company, Inc., produces and markets two popular video games, "High Range" and "Star Boundary." The closing account balances on the company's balance sheet for 20x6 are as follows: Cash, $18,735; Accounts Receivable, $19,900; Materials Inventory, $18,510; Work in Process Inventory, $24,680; Finished Goods Inventory, $21,940; Prepaid Expenses, $3,420; Plant and Equipment, $262,800; Accumulated Depreciation, Plant and Equipment, $55,845; Other Assets, $9,480; Accounts Payable, $52,640; Mortgage Payable, $70,000; Common Stock, $90,000; and Retained Earnings, $110,980.

Operating budgets for the first quarter of 20x7 show the following estimated costs: direct materials purchases, $58,100; direct materials usage, $62,400; direct labor expense, $42,880; manufacturing overhead, $51,910; selling expenses, $35,820; general and administrative expenses, $60,240; cost of goods manufactured, $163,990; and cost of goods sold, $165,440. Estimated ending cash balances are as follows: January, $34,610; February, $60,190; and March, $54,802. The company will have no capital expenditures during the quarter.

Sales are projected to be $125,200 in January, $105,100 in February, and $112,600 in March. Accounts receivable are expected to double during the quarter and accounts payable to decrease by 20 percent. Mortgage payments for the quarter will total $6,000, of which $2,000 will be interest expense. Prepaid expenses are expected to go up by $20,000, and other assets are projected to increase 50 percent over the budget period. Depreciation for plant and equipment (already included in the manufacturing overhead budget) averages 5 percent of total plant and equipment per year. Federal income taxes (34 percent of profits) are payable in April. The company pays no dividends.

REQUIRED
1. Prepare a budgeted income statement for the quarter ended March 31, 20x7.
2. Prepare a budgeted balance sheet as of March 31, 20x7.

SKILLS DEVELOPMENT CASES

Conceptual Analysis

LO1 **The Budgeting Process**
LO2

SD 1. Many people believe the budgeting process is wasteful and ineffective. They maintain that managers spend too much time focusing on budgeting mechanics and not enough on strategic issues. They believe that emphasis on the budgeting process causes managers to neglect more important matters, such as eliminating nonvalue-adding activities that waste resources. Critics of the budgeting process also maintain that the information and formats that managers use in budgets fail to communicate the short-term business activities needed to achieve long-term goals.

Place yourself in the role of a company's controller and search the Internet for articles on budgeting. Based on your research, prepare a memorandum to your company's owner justifying the need for budgeting. Also suggest ways to make the budgeting process, the budget information, and the budgets themselves efficient, effective, and meaningful.

 Group Activity: Ask students to complete the assignment individually. Then have them work in groups to prepare (1) an argument justifying the use of budgeting and (2) a list of ways to make the budgeting process, the budget information, and the budgets efficient, effective, and meaningful. Select one person from each group to report the group's findings to the class.

SD 2.

LO4 Budgeting for Cash Flows

The nature of a company's business affects its need to budget for cash flows. H&R Block <www.hrblock.com> is a service company whose main business is preparing tax returns. Most tax returns are prepared after January 31 and before April 15. For a fee and interest, the company will advance cash to clients who are due refunds. The clients are then expected to repay the cash advances when they receive their refunds. Although H&R Block has some revenues throughout the year, it devotes most of the nontax season to training potential employees in tax preparation procedures and to laying the groundwork for the next tax season.

Toys "R" Us <www.tru.com> is a toy retailer whose sales are concentrated in October, November, and December of one year and January of the next year. Sales continue at a steady but low level during the rest of the year. The company sells very few products on credit. Its purchases of inventory are concentrated in the period from July to September.

Mitsubishi <www.mitsubishi.com> manufactures large-screen TVs and other electronic products. Its sales tend to be concentrated in the last six months of the year. The company sells its products to retailers, and the retailers sell them to the final customer. Mitsubishi offers retailers credit terms of 60 to 90 days. In addition, when a retailer makes a sale to a buyer who has a good credit rating, Mitsubishi offers the buyer a very generous credit deal that features no payments or interest for one year after the date of the sale.

Discuss the nature of cash receipts and cash disbursements over a calendar year in the three companies we have just described. What are some key estimates that the management of these companies must make when preparing a cash budget?

Ethical Dilemma

SD 3.

LO1 Ethical Considerations in
LO3 Budgeting
LO5

Javier Gonzales is the manager of the Repairs and Maintenance Department of JG Industries. He is responsible for preparing his department's annual budget. Most managers in the company inflate their budget numbers by at least 10 percent because their bonuses depend upon how much below budget their departments operate. Gonzales turned in the following information for his department's 20x8 budget to the company's budget committee:

	Budget 20x7	Actual 20x7	Budget 20x8
Supplies	$ 20,000	$ 16,000	$ 24,000
Labor	80,000	82,000	96,000
Utilities	8,500	8,000	10,200
Tools	12,500	9,000	15,000
Hand-carried equipment	25,000	16,400	30,000
Cleaning materials	4,600	4,200	5,520
Miscellaneous	2,000	2,100	2,400
Totals	$152,600	$137,700	$183,120

Because the figures for 20x8 are 20 percent above those in the 20x7 budget, the budget committee questioned them. Gonzales defended them by saying that he expects a significant increase in activity in his department in 20x8.

What do you think are the real reasons for the increase in the budgeted amounts? What ethical considerations enter into this situation?

Research Activity

LO3 Developing a Budget
LO4

SD 4. Suppose a fundraising club at your school has asked you to manage its bake sales, which are held each weekend in the fall that the football team has a home game. This year, there will be five home games. The club sells only chocolate chip cookies in packages of two dozen; the selling price per package is $5.00. The packaging material costs $.75 per package. Baking utensils and supplies for the entire season will cost $500. Before each game, the cookies are prepared in a school kitchen for a fixed fee of $300 per session; workers are paid a total of $150 to help with the cleanup after each baking session. You estimate that 500 packages of cookies will be baked for each sale and that 96 percent of them will be sold. Alumni volunteers, who receive no compensation, sell half of the packages; students, who receive a commission of $.50 per package, sell the other half. You plan to run an advertisement in the school newspaper before all five games; each advertisement costs $200. The ingredients for four dozen cookies are as follows:

2 1/4 cups all-purpose flour	3/4 cup granulated sugar	2 cups semisweet
1 teaspoon baking soda	3/4 cup brown sugar	chocolate chips
1 teaspoon salt	1 teaspoon vanilla extract	1 cup walnuts
2 sticks butter	2 eggs	

Research the prices of the cookie ingredients at a local supermarket. Then develop a budget for the five bake sales. What is your assessment of the club's fundraising effort?

Decision-Making Practice

LO1 Budgeting Procedures
LO4
LO5

SD 5. Since Rxanne Enterprises inaugurated participative budgeting ten years ago, everyone in the organization—from maintenance personnel to the president's staff—has had a voice in the budgeting process. Until recently, participative budgeting has worked in the best interests of the company as a whole. Now, however, it is becoming evident that some managers are using the practice solely to benefit their own divisions. The budget committee has therefore asked you, the company's controller, to analyze this year's divisional budgets carefully before incorporating them into the company's master budget.

The Motor Division was the first of the company's six divisions to submit its budget request for 20x6. The division's budgeted income statement appears on the opposite page.

1. Recast the Motor Division's budgeted income statement into the following format (round percentages to two places):

	Budget for 12/31/x5		Budget for 12/31/x6	
Account	Amount	Percentage of Sales	Amount	Percentage of Sales

2. Actual results for 20x5 revealed the following information about revenues and cost of goods sold:

	Amount	Percentage of Sales
Net sales		
Radios	$ 780,000	43.94
Appliances	640,000	36.06
Telephones	280,000	15.77
Miscellaneous	75,000	4.23
Net sales	$1,775,000	100.00
Less cost of goods sold	763,425	43.01
Gross margin	$1,011,575	56.99

On the basis of this information and your analysis in **1**, what do you think the budget committee should say to the managers of the Motor Division? Identify any specific areas of the budget that may need to be revised and explain why the revision is needed.

Rxanne Enterprises
Motor Division
Budgeted Income Statement
For the Years Ended December 31, 20x5 and 20x6

	Budget 12/31/x5	Budget 12/31/x6	Increase (Decrease)
Net sales			
Radios	$ 850,000	$ 910,000	$ 60,000
Appliances	680,000	740,000	60,000
Telephones	270,000	305,000	35,000
Miscellaneous	84,400	90,000	5,600
Net sales	$1,884,400	$2,045,000	$160,600
Less cost of goods sold	750,960	717,500*	(33,460)
Gross margin	$1,133,440	$1,327,500	$194,060
Operating expenses			
Wages			
Warehouse	$ 94,500	$ 102,250	$ 7,750
Purchasing	77,800	84,000	6,200
Delivery/shipping	69,400	74,780	5,380
Maintenance	42,650	45,670	3,020
Salaries			
Supervisory	60,000	92,250	32,250
Executive	130,000	164,000	34,000
Purchases, supplies	17,400	20,500	3,100
Merchandise moving equipment			
Maintenance	72,400	82,000	9,600
Depreciation	62,000	74,750†	12,750
Building rent	96,000	102,500	6,500
Sales commissions	188,440	204,500	16,060
Insurance			
Fire	12,670	20,500	7,830
Liability	18,200	20,500	2,300
Utilities	14,100	15,375	1,275
Taxes			
Property	16,600	18,450	1,850
Payroll	26,520	41,000	14,480
Miscellaneous	4,610	10,250	5,640
Total operating expenses	$1,003,290	$1,173,275	$169,985
Income from operations	$ 130,150	$ 154,225	$ 24,075

*Less expensive merchandise will be purchased in 20x6 to boost profits.
†Depreciation is increased because additional equipment must be bought to handle increased sales.

MANAGERIAL REPORTING AND ANALYSIS CASES

Interpreting Management Reports

LO1 **Policies for Budget**
LO2 **Development**
LO5

MRA 1. Hector Corporation is a manufacturing company with annual sales of $25 million. Its budget committee created a policy that the company uses each year in developing its master budget for the following calendar year. The policy is as follows:

May   The company's controller and corporate officers of the budget committee meet to discuss plans and objectives for next year. The controller conveys all relevant information from this meeting to division managers and department heads.

June   Division managers, department heads, and the controller meet to discuss the corporate plans and objectives for next year. They develop a timetable for developing next year's budget data.

July   Division managers and department heads develop budget data. The vice president of sales provides them with final sales estimates, and they complete monthly sales estimates for each product line.

August   Estimates of next year's monthly production activity and inventory levels are completed. Division managers and department heads communicate these estimates to the controller, who distributes them to other operating areas.

September All operating areas submit their revised budget data. The controller integrates their labor requirements, direct materials requirements, unit cost estimates, cash requirements, and profit estimates in a preliminary master budget for next year.

October   The budget committee meets to discuss the preliminary master budget and to make any necessary corrections, additions, or deletions. The controller incorporates all authorized changes into a final draft of the master budget.

November The controller submits the final draft to the corporate officers of the budget committee for approval. If they approve it, it is distributed to all corporate officers, division managers, and department heads.

Comment on this policy. What changes would you recommend?

Formulating Management Reports

LO1 **Financial Budgets**
LO2
LO4

MRA 2. Suppose you have just signed a partnership agreement with your cousin Eddie to open a bookstore near your college. You believe the store will be able to provide excellent service and undersell the local competition. To fund operations, you and Eddie have applied for a loan from the Small Business Administration. The loan application requires you to submit two financial budgets—a pro forma income statement and a pro forma balance sheet—within six weeks. Because of your expertise in accounting and business, Eddie has asked you to prepare the financial budgets.

1. How do the four *w*'s of preparing an accounting report apply in this situation—that is, *why* are you preparing these financial budgets, *who* needs them, *what* information do you need to prepare for them, and *when* are they due?
2. If you obtain the loan and open the bookstore, how can you and Eddie use the pro forma statements that you prepared?

International Company

LO4 **Goals and the Cash Budget**

MRA 3. The products of Minnesota Mining and Manufacturing Company (3M) <www.3m.com> range from office supplies, duct tape, and road reflectors to laser imagers for CAT scanners. One of the company's goals is to accelerate sales and product development. Toward that end, it spends over $1 billion a year on research and development and related investment activities. It has also redesigned many of its products to satisfy the needs of its three international operations groups (Asia-Pacific; Europe and Middle East; and Latin American, Africa, and Canada).[7]

Suppose the manager of 3M's Asia-Pacific group is preparing the cash budget for next year's operations. Explain how research and development expenses would affect the cash receipts and cash payments in that cash budget.

Excel Spreadsheet Analysis

MRA 4.

LO3 The Budgeting Process
LO4

Refer to our development of Framecraft Company's master budget for 20x7 in this chapter. Suppose that because of a new customer in Canada, Chase Vittel has decided to increase budgeted sales in the first quarter of 20x7 by 5,000 units. The expenses for this sale will include direct materials, direct labor, variable manufacturing overhead, and variable selling and administrative expenses. The delivery expense for the Canadian customer will be $.18 per unit rather than the regular $.08 per unit. The desired units of beginning finished goods inventory will remain at 1,000 units.

1. Using an Excel spreadsheet, revise Framecraft Company's budgeted income statement and the operating budgets that support it to reflect the changes described above. (Round manufactured cost per unit to three decimals.)
2. What was the change in income from operations? Would you recommend accepting the order from the Canadian customer? If so, why?

Internet Case

MRA 5.

LO1 The Budgeting Process

Some corporate web sites include areas specifically designed for student needs. Search the student area of Johnson & Johnson's web site (www.jnj.com/student resources/index.htm). What kinds of information does it provide? How does the information apply to the material discussed in this chapter?

22

Chapter 22 describes how standard costs are computed and how managers use the variances between standard and actual costs to evaluate performance and control costs.

Standard Costing and Variance Analysis

LEARNING OBJECTIVES

LO1 Define *standard costs* and describe how managers use standard costs in the management cycle.

LO2 Explain how standard costs are developed and compute a standard unit cost.

LO3 Prepare a flexible budget and describe how variance analysis is used to control costs.

LO4 Compute and analyze direct materials variances.

LO5 Compute and analyze direct labor variances.

LO6 Compute and analyze manufacturing overhead variances.

LO7 Explain how variances are used to evaluate managers' performance.

DECISION POINT

A MANAGER'S FOCUS

Coach, Inc. <www.coach.com> The durability of a well-crafted baseball glove was the inspiration for the high-quality leather goods that Coach began making more than fifty years ago. Now sold worldwide, the company's products include not only leather goods, such as handbags and luggage, but also jewelry, shoes, hats, eyewear, scarves, and home furnishings.

Coach's managers value a by-the-numbers approach to business. They keep Coach highly profitable by using design specifications to set standard costs for the company's product lines.[1] How does setting standard costs help control costs?

Managers base standard costs on realistic estimates of operating costs. They use these figures as performance targets and as benchmarks against which to measure actual spending trends. To keep standard costs realistic, they continuously monitor changes in market prices and operating costs and update the estimated figures as conditions warrant. By analyzing variances between standard and actual costs, they gain insight into the causes of those differences. Once they have identified an operating problem that is causing a cost variance, they can devise a solution to the problem.

How do Coach managers control costs by setting performance standards?

Standard Costing

 LO1 Define *standard costs* and describe how managers use standard costs in the management cycle.

RELATED TEXT ASSIGNMENTS
Q: 1, 2, 3
SE: 1, 2
E: 1
SD: 2, 3
MRA: 5

Standard costs are realistic estimates of costs based on analyses of both past and projected operating costs and conditions. They are usually stated in terms of cost per unit. They provide a standard, or predetermined, performance level for use in **standard costing**, a method of cost control that also includes a measure of actual performance and a measure of the difference, or **variance**, between standard and actual performance. This method of measuring and controlling costs differs from the actual and normal costing methods in that it uses estimated costs exclusively to compute all three elements of product cost—direct materials, direct labor, and manufacturing overhead.

Using standard costing can be expensive because the estimated costs are based not just on past costs, but also on engineering estimates, forecasted demand, worker input, time and motion studies, and type and quality of direct materials. However, this method can be used in any type of business. Both manufacturers and service businesses use standard costing in conjunction with a job order costing, process costing, or activity-based costing system.

Standard Costs and the Management Cycle

As shown in Figure 1, standard costs are useful tools throughout the management cycle. Managers use them to develop budgets in the planning stage, to control costs as they occur during the executing stage, and to prepare reports. Because of their usefulness in comparing planned and actual costs, standard costs have usually been most closely associated with the performance evaluation that takes place in the reviewing stage.

KEY POINT: Standard costs are necessary for planning and control. Budgets are developed from standard costs, and performance is measured against them.

■ **PLANNING** During the planning stage, after managers have projected sales and production targets for the next accounting period, standard costs can be used in developing budgets for direct materials, direct labor, and variable manufacturing overhead. These estimated operating costs not only serve as targets for product costing; they are also useful in making decisions about product distribution and pricing.

■ **EXECUTING** During the executing stage, as actual costs are incurred and recorded, managers apply standard costs to the work in process. By using these standards as yardsticks for measuring expenditures, they can control costs as they occur. For example, when the price a vendor offers is higher than the standard cost, a manager may decide to take the company's business elsewhere.

Focus on Business Practice

Why Go on a Factory Tour?
If you've had some manufacturing experience, you probably understand the importance of standard costing and variance analysis. If you haven't had any manufacturing experience, gain some insight into the importance of cost planning and control by visiting a factory. Consult your local chamber of commerce for factory tours near you. You can also tour factories online. Check out the production of jellybeans at <www.jellybelly.com> or see how crayons are made at <www.crayola.com>.

■ **REVIEWING** At the end of an accounting period—whether it is a day, a week, a month, or a quarter—managers compare the actual costs incurred with standard costs and compute the variances. Variances provide measures of performance that can be used to control costs. In reviewing a variance, managers compute its amount, and if the amount is significant, they analyze what is causing it. Their analysis of significant unfavorable variances may reveal operating problems, such as inefficient functions within a department or work cell, which they can then act to correct. Managers also investigate significant favorable variances to determine why and how the positive performance

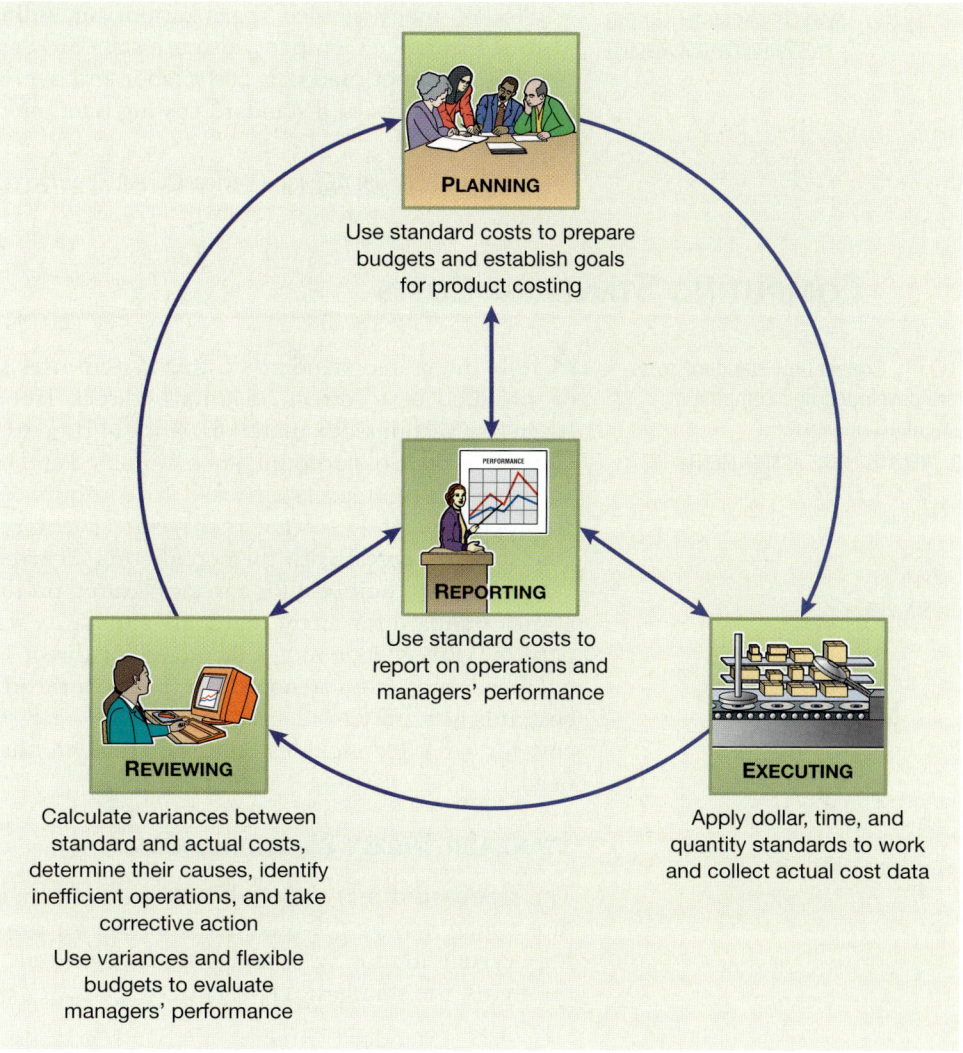

FIGURE 1
Standard Costing, Variance Analysis, and the Management Cycle

● **STOP AND THINK!**
Why should managers be interested in changes in the cost of materials?

Information about changes in the cost of materials enables managers to adjust the prices of goods to reflect those changes. ■

www.coach.com
www.kraft.com
www.boeing.com

occurred. Favorable variances may indicate desirable practices that should be implemented elsewhere or a need to revise the existing standards. Both favorable and unfavorable variances from standard costs can be used to evaluate an individual manager's performance.

■ **REPORTING** During the reporting stage, managers use standard costs to report on operations and managerial performance. A variance report tailored to a manager's specific responsibilities provides useful information about how well operations are proceeding and how well the manager is controlling them.

THE RELEVANCE OF STANDARD COSTING IN TODAY'S BUSINESS ENVIRONMENT

In recent years, the increasing automation of manufacturing processes has caused a significant decrease in direct labor costs and a corresponding decline in the importance of labor-related standard costs and variances. As a result, Coach, Kraft Foods, Boeing, and many other manufacturers that once used standard costing for all three elements of product cost now apply this method only to direct materials and manufacturing overhead.

www.bankofamerica.com
www.libertymutual.com

Today, many service organizations, including Bank of America and Liberty Mutual Insurance Company, also use standard costing. Although a service organization has no direct materials costs, labor and overhead costs are very much a part of providing services, and standard costing is an effective way of planning and controlling them.

 Check out ACE for a Review Quiz at http://accounting.college.hmco.com/students.

COMPUTING STANDARD COSTS

LO2 Explain how standard costs are developed and compute a standard unit cost.

RELATED TEXT ASSIGNMENTS
Q: 4, 5, 6, 7, 8
SE: 3
E: 2, 3
P: 1, 6
SD: 2, 3, 4

A fully integrated standard costing system uses standard costs for all the elements of product cost: direct materials, direct labor, and manufacturing overhead. Inventory accounts for materials, work in process, and finished goods, as well as the Cost of Goods Sold account, are maintained and reported in terms of standard costs, and standard unit costs are used to compute account balances. Actual costs are recorded separately so that managers can compare what should have been spent (the standard costs) with the actual costs incurred.

A standard unit cost for a manufactured product has the following six elements: a price standard for direct materials, a quantity standard for direct materials, a standard for direct labor rate, a standard for direct labor time, a standard for variable overhead rate, and a standard for fixed overhead rate. To compute a standard unit cost, it is necessary to identify and analyze each of these elements. (A standard unit cost for a service includes only the elements that relate to direct labor and overhead.)

STANDARD DIRECT MATERIALS COST

The **standard direct materials cost** is found by multiplying the price standard for direct materials by the quantity standard for direct materials. If the price standard for a certain item is $2.75 and a specific job calls for a quantity standard of eight of the items, the standard direct materials cost for that job is computed as follows:

$$\begin{array}{c}\text{Standard Direct} \\ \text{Materials Cost}\end{array} = \begin{array}{c}\text{Direct Materials} \\ \text{Price Standard}\end{array} \times \begin{array}{c}\text{Direct Materials} \\ \text{Quantity Standard}\end{array}$$

$$\$22.00 = \$2.75 \times 8$$

● **STOP AND THINK!**
Why would a purchasing agent or department not always buy the least costly direct materials available?
The quality of the direct materials used in production must remain consistent. Introducing an inexpensive material of an inferior grade can result in excess spoilage and waste and cause unfavorable quantity variances. ■

The **direct materials price standard** is a careful estimate of the cost of a specific direct material in the next accounting period. An organization's purchasing agent or its purchasing department is responsible for developing price standards for all direct materials and for making the actual purchases. When estimating a direct materials price standard, the purchasing agent or department must take into account all possible price increases, changes in available quantities, and new sources of supply.

The **direct materials quantity standard** is an estimate of the amount of direct materials, including scrap and waste, that will be used in an accounting period. It is influenced by product engineering specifications, the quality of direct materials, the age and productivity of machinery, and the quality and experience of the work force. Production managers or management accountants usually establish and monitor standards for direct materials quantity, but engineers, purchasing agents, and machine operators may also contribute to the development of these standards.

STANDARD DIRECT LABOR COST

The **standard direct labor cost** for a product, task, or job order is calculated by multiplying the standard wage for direct labor by the standard hours of direct labor. If the standard direct labor rate is $8.40 per hour and a product takes 1.5 standard direct labor hours to produce, the product's standard direct labor cost is computed as follows:

$$\begin{array}{c} \text{Standard Direct} \\ \text{Labor Cost} \end{array} = \begin{array}{c} \text{Direct Labor} \\ \text{Rate Standard} \end{array} \times \begin{array}{c} \text{Direct Labor} \\ \text{Time Standard} \end{array}$$

$$\$12.60 = \$8.40 \times 1.5 \text{ hours}$$

KEY POINT: Both the direct labor rate standard and the direct labor time standard are based on an average of the different levels of skilled workers, and both are related to the production of one unit or batch.

KEY POINT: Updating time and dollar standards for valid reasons produces more meaningful standards. However, if the updates are too frequent, the standards may lose credibility and be perceived as moving targets by managers.

The **direct labor rate standard** is the hourly direct labor rate expected to prevail during the next accounting period for each function or job classification. Although rate ranges are established for each type of worker and rates vary within those ranges according to each worker's experience and length of service, an average standard rate is developed for each task. Even if the person making the product is paid more or less than the standard rate, the standard rate is used to calculate the standard direct labor cost. Standard labor rates are fairly easy to develop because labor rates are either set by a labor union contract or defined by the company.

The **direct labor time standard** is the expected labor time required for each department, machine, or process to complete the production of one unit or one batch of output. In many cases, standard time per unit is a small fraction of an hour. Current time and motion studies of workers and machines, as well as records of their past performance, provide the data for developing this standard. The direct labor time standard should be revised whenever a machine is replaced or the quality of the labor force changes.

STANDARD MANUFACTURING OVERHEAD COST

The **standard manufacturing overhead cost** is the sum of the estimates of variable and fixed overhead costs in the next accounting period. It is based on standard overhead rates that are computed in much the same way as the predetermined overhead rate that we discussed in an earlier chapter. Unlike that rate, however, the standard manufacturing overhead rate has two parts, one for variable costs and one for fixed costs. The reason for computing the standard variable and fixed overhead rates separately is that their cost behavior differs.

[handwritten: BASED ON VOLUME]

The **standard variable overhead rate** is computed by dividing the total budgeted variable overhead costs by an expression of capacity, such as the number of standard machine hours or standard direct labor hours. (Other bases may be used if machine hours or direct labor hours are not good predictors, or drivers, of variable overhead costs.) Using standard machine hours as the base, the formula is as follows:

$$\begin{array}{c} \text{Standard Variable} \\ \text{Overhead Rate} \end{array} = \frac{\text{Total Budgeted Variable Overhead Costs}}{\text{Expected Number of Standard Machine Hours}}$$

[handwritten: WILL NOT CHANGE]

The **standard fixed overhead rate** is computed by dividing the total budgeted fixed overhead costs by an expression of capacity, usually normal capacity in terms of standard hours or units. The denominator is expressed in the same terms as the variable overhead rate. Using normal capacity in terms of standard machine hours as the denominator, the formula is as follows:

$$\begin{array}{c} \text{Standard Fixed} \\ \text{Overhead Rate} \end{array} = \frac{\text{Total Budgeted Fixed Overhead Costs}}{\text{Normal Capacity in Terms of Standard Machine Hours}}$$

KEY POINT: Normal capacity is the average annual level of operating capacity needed to meet expected sales demand; it is the level of activity at which a company expects to operate.

Recall that normal capacity is the level of operating capacity needed to meet expected sales demand. Using it as the application base ensures that all fixed overhead costs have been applied to units produced by the time normal capacity is reached.

TOTAL STANDARD UNIT COST

Using standard costs eliminates the need to calculate unit costs from actual cost data every week or month or for each batch of goods produced. Once standard costs for direct materials, direct labor, and variable and fixed overhead have been developed, a total standard unit cost can be computed at any time.

To illustrate how standard costs are used to compute total unit cost, let's suppose that a company called Remember When, Inc., recently updated the standards for its line of watches. Direct materials price standards are now $9.20 per square foot for casing materials and $2.17 for each movement mechanism. Direct materials quantity standards are .025 square foot of casing materials per watch and one movement mechanism per watch. Direct labor time standards are .01 hour per watch for the Case Stamping Department and .05 hour per watch for the Watch Assembly Department. Direct labor rate standards are $8.00 per hour for the Case Stamping Department and $10.20 per hour for the Watch Assembly Department. Standard manufacturing overhead rates are $12.00 per direct labor hour for the standard variable overhead rate and $9.00 per direct labor hour for the standard fixed overhead rate. The standard cost of making one watch would be computed in the following manner:

Direct materials costs:	
Casing ($9.20 per sq. ft. × .025 sq. ft.)	$ .23
One movement mechanism	2.17
Direct labor costs:	
Case Stamping Department ($8.00 per hour × .01 hour per watch)	.08
Watch Assembly Department ($10.20 per hour × .05 hour per watch)	.51
Variable overhead ($12.00 per hour × .06 hour per watch)	.72
Total standard variable cost of one watch	$3.71
Fixed overhead ($9.00 per hour × .06 hour per watch)	.54
Total standard cost of one watch	$4.25

KEY POINT: The total standard cost of $4.25 represents the *desired* cost of producing one watch.

 Check out ACE for a Review Quiz at http://accounting.college.hmco.com/students.

VARIANCE ANALYSIS

LO3 Prepare a flexible budget and describe how variance analysis is used to control costs.

RELATED TEXT ASSIGNMENTS
Q: 9, 10, 11, 12, 13
SE: 4, 5
E: 4
P: 2
SD: 1, 4
MRA: 1, 2, 3, 4

Managers in all types of organizations—manufacturing, retail, and service—constantly compare the costs of what was expected to happen with the costs of what did happen. By examining the **differences**, or variances, between standard and actual costs, they can gather much valuable information. **Variance analysis** is the process of computing the differences between standard costs and actual costs and identifying the causes of those differences. In this section, we look at how managers use flexible budgets to improve the accuracy of variance analysis and at how they use variance analysis to control costs.

THE ROLE OF FLEXIBLE BUDGETS IN VARIANCE ANALYSIS

The accuracy of variance analysis depends to a large extent on the type of budget managers use when comparing variances. *Static*, or fixed, budgets forecast revenues and expenses for just one level of sales and just one level of output. The budgets that constitute a master budget are usually based on a single level of output, but many things can happen over an accounting period that will cause actual output to differ from the estimated output. If a company produces more products than predicted, total production costs will almost always be greater than predicted. When that is the case, a comparison of actual production costs with fixed budgeted costs will inevitably show variances.

The performance report in Exhibit 1 compares data from Remember When's static master budget with the actual costs of its Watch Division for the year ended December 31, 20x5. As you can see, actual costs exceeded budgeted costs by $5,539, or 7.4 percent. On the face of it, most managers would consider such a cost

EXHIBIT 1
Performance Report Using Data from a Static Budget

Remember When, Inc.
Performance Report—Watch Division
For the Year Ended December 31, 20x5

Cost Category	Budgeted Costs*	Actual Costs†	Difference Under (Over) Budget
Direct materials	$42,000	$46,000	($4,000)
Direct labor	10,325	11,779	(1,454)
Manufacturing overhead			
Variable			
Indirect materials	3,500	3,600	(100)
Indirect labor	5,250	5,375	(125)
Utilities	1,750	1,810	(60)
Other	2,100	2,200	(100)
Fixed			
Supervisory salaries	4,000	3,500	500
Depreciation	2,000	2,000	—
Utilities	450	450	—
Other	3,000	3,200	(200)
Totals	$74,375	$79,914	($5,539)

*Budgeted costs are based on an output of 17,500 units.
†Actual output was 19,100 units.

● **STOP AND THINK!**
When is a flexible budget prepared?
A flexible budget is prepared at the end of an accounting period to evaluate performance; it may then also be used in planning for the next period. ■

FOCUS ON BUSINESS TECHNOLOGY

Why Complicate the Flexible Budget?
Because of the database capabilities of enterprise resource management (ERM) systems and the principles of resource consumption accounting (RCA), what we refer to as the *flexible budget* has become more complicated. This new and more complex version of a flexible budget is called *authorized reporting*. Authorized reporting is like a flexible budget in that it restates an accounting period's costs in terms of different levels of output, but it enhances cost restatement by taking into account all the factors that can influence a cost's behavior. With its more sophisticated cost analyses, authorized reporting is a more relevant yardstick for cost comparison and control than the traditional flexible budget.[3]

overrun significant. But was there really a cost overrun? The budgeted amounts are based on an output of 17,500 units; the actual output was, however, 19,100 units. To judge the division's performance accurately, the company's managers must change the budgeted data to reflect an output of 19,100 units. They can do this by using a flexible budget. A **flexible budget** (also called a *variable budget*) is a summary of expected costs for a range of activity levels. Unlike a static budget, a flexible budget provides forecasted data that can be adjusted for changes in the level of output. The flexible budget is used primarily as a cost control tool in evaluating performance at the end of a period.

A flexible budget for Remember When's Watch Division appears in Exhibit 2. It shows the estimated costs for 15,000, 17,500, and 20,000 units of output. The total cost of a variable cost item is found by multiplying the number of units produced by the item's per unit cost. For example, if the Watch Division produces 15,000 units, direct materials will cost $36,000 (15,000 units × $2.40). An important element in this exhibit is the **flexible budget formula,** an equation that determines the expected, or budgeted, cost for any level of output. Its components include a per unit amount for variable costs and a total amount for fixed costs. (In Exhibit 2, the $3.71 variable cost per unit is computed in the far right column, and the $9,450 is found in the section on fixed manufacturing overhead costs.) Using the flexible budget formula, you can

EXHIBIT 2
Flexible Budget for Evaluation of Overall Performance

Remember When, Inc.
Flexible Budget—Watch Division
For the Year Ended December 31, 20x5

Cost Category	Units Produced* 15,000	17,500	20,000	Variable Cost per Unit†
Direct materials	$36,000	$42,000	$48,000	$2.40
Direct labor	8,850	10,325	11,800	.59
Variable manufacturing overhead				
Indirect materials	3,000	3,500	4,000	.20
Indirect labor	4,500	5,250	6,000	.30
Utilities	1,500	1,750	2,000	.10
Other	1,800	2,100	2,400	.12
Total variable costs	$55,650	$64,925	$74,200	$3.71
Fixed manufacturing overhead				
Supervisory salaries	$ 4,000	$ 4,000	$ 4,000	
Depreciation	2,000	2,000	2,000	
Utilities	450	450	450	
Other	3,000	3,000	3,000	
Total fixed manufacturing overhead costs	$ 9,450	$ 9,450	$ 9,450	
Total costs	$65,100	$74,375	$83,650	

Flexible budget formula:
Total Budgeted Costs = (Variable Cost per Unit × Number of Units Produced)
 + Budgeted Fixed Costs
 = ($3.71 × Units Produced) + $9,450

*Flexible budgets are commonly used only for overhead costs; when they are, machine hours or direct labor hours are used in place of units produced.
†Computed by dividing the dollar amount in any column by the respective level of output.

KEY POINT: Flexible budgets allow managers to compare budgeted and actual costs at the same level of output.

create a budget for the Watch Division at any level of output in the range of levels given.

The performance report in Exhibit 3 is based on data from the flexible budget shown in Exhibit 2. Variable unit costs have been multiplied by 19,100 units actually produced to arrive at the total budgeted costs, and fixed overhead information has been carried over from Exhibit 2. In this performance report, actual costs are $397 less than the amount budgeted. In other words, when we use a flexible budget, we find that the performance of the Watch Division in this period actually exceeded budget targets by $397.

USING VARIANCE ANALYSIS TO CONTROL COSTS

As Figure 2 shows, using variance analysis to control costs is a four-step process. First, managers compute the amount of the variance. If the amount is insignificant—meaning actual operating results are close to those anticipated—no corrective action

EXHIBIT 3
Performance Report Using Data from a Flexible Budget

Remember When, Inc.
Performance Report—Watch Division
For the Year Ended December 31, 20x5

Cost Category (Variable Unit Cost)	Budgeted Costs*	Actual Costs	Difference Under (Over) Budget
Direct materials ($2.40)	$45,840	$46,000	($160)
Direct labor ($.59)	11,269	11,779	(510)
Manufacturing overhead			
Variable			
Indirect materials ($.20)	3,820	3,600	220
Indirect labor ($.30)	5,730	5,375	355
Utilities ($.10)	1,910	1,810	100
Other ($.12)	2,292	2,200	92
Fixed			
Supervisory salaries	4,000	3,500	500
Depreciation	2,000	2,000	—
Utilities	450	450	—
Other	3,000	3,200	(200)
Totals	$80,311	$79,914	$397

*Budgeted costs are based on an output of 19,100 units.

FIGURE 2
Variance Analysis: A Four-Step Approach to Controlling Costs

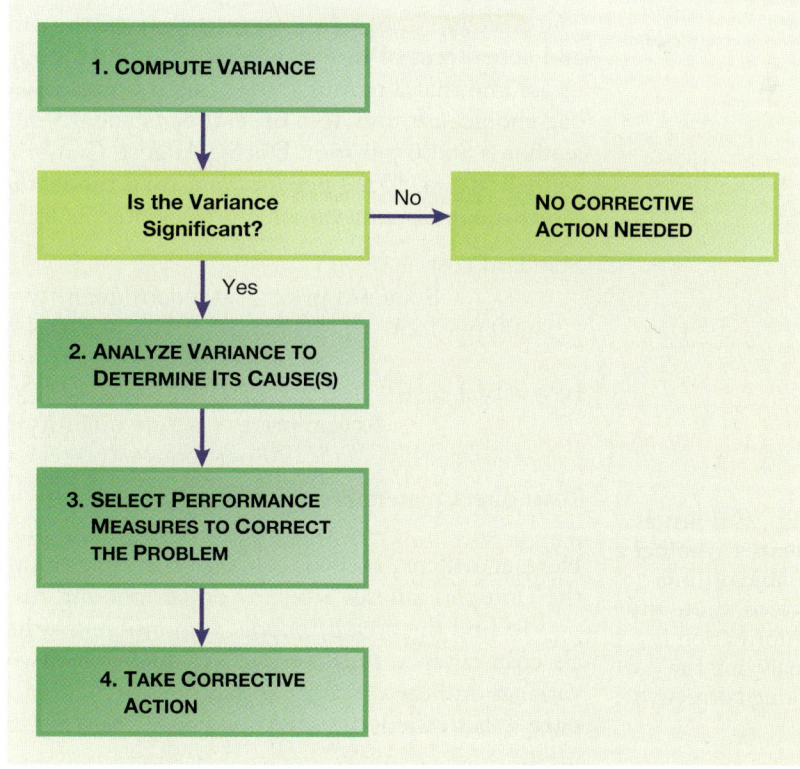

KEY POINT: Many companies use a percentage, such as plus or minus 3 percent of standard, to determine if the dollar amount of a variance is significant.

KEY POINT: Computing variances is only the first step in cost control. Managers must also identify the problem areas causing the variances and take appropriate corrective action.

is needed. If the amount is significant, then managers analyze the variance to identify its cause. In identifying the cause, they are usually able to pinpoint the activities that need to be monitored. They then select performance measures that will enable them to track those activities, analyze the results, and determine the action needed to correct the problem. Their final step is to take the appropriate corrective action.

While computing the amount of a variance is important, it is also important to remember that this computation does nothing to prevent the variance from reoccurring. To control costs, managers must determine the cause of the variance and select performance measures that will help them track the problem and find the best solution for it.

As we focus on the computation and analysis of variances in the next sections, we follow the steps outlined in Figure 2. We limit our analysis to eight variances, two for each of the cost categories of direct materials, direct labor, variable manufacturing overhead, and fixed manufacturing overhead. We give examples of operating problems that might cause each of these variances to occur. We also identify some financial and nonfinancial performance measures that can be used to track the cause of a variance and that can be helpful in correcting it.

 Check out ACE for a Review Quiz at http://accounting.college.hmco.com/students.

COMPUTING AND ANALYZING DIRECT MATERIALS VARIANCES

LO4 Compute and analyze direct materials variances.

RELATED TEXT ASSIGNMENTS
Q: 14, 15, 16
SE: 6
E: 5, 6
P: 3, 4, 7, 8
MRA: 3

To control operations, managers compute and analyze variances for whole cost categories, such as total direct materials costs, as well as variances for elements of those categories, such as the price and quantity of each direct material. The more detailed their analysis of direct materials variances is, the more effective they will be in controlling costs.

COMPUTING DIRECT MATERIALS VARIANCES

The **total direct materials cost variance** is the difference between the standard cost and actual cost of direct materials. To illustrate how this variance is computed, let us assume that a manufacturer called Cambria Company makes leather bags. Each bag should use four feet of leather (standard quantity), and the standard price of leather is $6.00 per foot. During August, Cambria Company purchased 760 feet of leather costing $5.90 per foot and used the leather to produce 180 bags. The total direct materials cost variance is calculated as follows:

Standard cost
    Standard price × standard quantity =
    $6.00 per foot × (180 bags × 4 feet per bag) =
        $6.00 per foot × 720 feet = $4,320

Less actual cost
    Actual price × actual quantity =
    $5.90 per foot × 760 feet =   4,484

Total direct materials cost variance $ 164 (U)

EXAMPLE

STUDY NOTE: It is just as important to identify whether a variance is favorable or unfavorable as it is to compute the variance. This information is necessary for analyzing the variance and taking corrective action.

Here, actual cost exceeds standard cost. The situation is unfavorable, as indicated by the U in parentheses after the dollar amount. An F means a favorable situation.

To find the area or people responsible for the variance, the total direct materials cost variance must be broken down into two parts: the direct materials price variance and the direct materials quantity variance. The **direct materials price variance** (also called the *direct material spending or rate variance*) is the difference

> **STOP AND THINK!**
> What can cause a direct materials price variance?
> *Causes of this variance include a change in the quality of materials being used, a change in the price of materials, and a change in vendors.* ■
>
> **KEY POINT:** The direct materials price variance relates to the difference between the standard cost and actual cost of purchased materials. It does not relate to the quantity of materials used in the production process.

between the standard price and the actual price per unit multiplied by the actual quantity purchased. For Cambria Company, the direct materials price variance is computed as follows:

Standard price (EXPECTED) $6.00
Less actual price   5.90
Difference per foot $ .10 (F)

$$\begin{aligned}\text{Direct Materials Price Variance} &= (\text{Standard Price} - \text{Actual Price}) \\ &\quad \times \text{Actual Quantity} \\ &= \$.10 \times 760 \text{ feet} \\ &= \$76 \text{ (F)}\end{aligned}$$

Because the price the company paid for the direct materials was less than the standard price it expected to pay, the variance is favorable.

The **direct materials quantity variance** (also called the *direct material efficiency* or *usage variance*) is the difference between the standard quantity allowed and the actual quantity used multiplied by the standard price. It is computed as follows:

Standard quantity allowed (180 bags × 4 feet per bag)   720 feet
Less actual quantity   760 feet
Difference   40 feet (U)

$$\begin{aligned}\text{Direct Materials Quantity Variance} &= \text{Standard Price} \times (\text{Standard Quantity Allowed} \\ &\quad - \text{Actual Quantity}) \\ &= \$6 \times 40 \text{ feet} \\ &= \$240 \text{ (U)}\end{aligned}$$

Because more leather than the standard quantity was used in the production process, the direct materials quantity variance is unfavorable.

If the calculations are correct, the net of the direct materials price variance and the direct materials quantity variance should equal the total direct materials cost variance. The following check shows that the variances were computed correctly:

Direct materials price variance $ 76 (F)
Direct materials quantity variance   240 (U)
Total direct materials cost variance $164 (U)

Variance analyses are sometimes easier to interpret in diagram form. Figure 3 illustrates our analysis of Cambria Company's direct materials variances. Notice that although direct materials are purchased at actual cost, they are entered in the Materials Inventory account at standard price; thus, the direct materials price variance of $76 (F) is obvious when the costs are recorded. As Figure 3 shows, the standard price times the standard quantity is the amount entered in the Work in Process Inventory account.

ANALYZING AND CORRECTING DIRECT MATERIALS VARIANCES

Cambria Company's managers were concerned because the company had been experiencing direct materials price variances and quantity variances for some time; moreover, as our analysis shows, the price variances were always favorable, and the quantity variances were always unfavorable. By tracking the purchasing activity for three months, the managers discovered that the company's purchasing agent, without any authorization, had been purchasing a lower grade of leather at a reduced price. After careful analysis, the engineering manager determined that the substitute

FIGURE 3
Diagram of Direct Materials Variance Analysis

leather was not appropriate and that the company should resume purchasing the grade of leather originally specified. In addition, an analysis of scrap and rework revealed that the inferior quality of the substitute leather was causing the unfavorable quantity variance. By tracking the purchasing activity, Cambria's managers were able to solve the problems the company had been having with direct materials variances.

 Check out ACE for a Review Quiz at http://accounting.college.hmco.com/students.

COMPUTING AND ANALYZING DIRECT LABOR VARIANCES

LO5 Compute and analyze direct labor variances.

RELATED TEXT ASSIGNMENTS
Q: 17
SE: 7
E: 7, 8
P: 3, 4, 7, 8
SD: 5
MRA: 2, 3

The procedure for computing and analyzing direct labor cost variances parallels the procedure for finding direct material variances. Again, the more detailed the analysis is, the more effective managers will be in controlling costs.

COMPUTING DIRECT LABOR VARIANCES

The total direct labor cost variance is the difference between the standard direct labor cost for good units produced and actual direct labor costs. (*Good units* are the total units produced less units that are scrapped or need to be reworked.) At Cambria Company, each leather bag requires 2.4 standard direct labor hours, and the standard direct labor rate is $8.50 per hour. During August, 450 direct labor hours were used to make 180 bags at an average pay rate of $9.20 per hour. The total direct labor cost variance is computed as follows:

Standard cost
  Standard rate × standard hours allowed =
  $8.50 × (180 bags × 2.4 hours per bag) =
  $8.50 × 432 hours = $3,672
Less actual cost
  Actual rate × actual hours = $9.20 × 450 hours = 4,140
Total direct labor cost variance $ 468 (U)

Both the actual direct labor hours per bag and the actual direct labor rate varied from the standard. For effective performance evaluation, management must know how much of the total cost arose from different direct labor rates and how much from different numbers of direct labor hours. This information is found by computing the direct labor rate variance and the direct labor efficiency variance.

The **direct labor rate variance** (also called the *direct labor spending variance*) is the difference between the standard direct labor rate and the actual direct labor rate multiplied by the actual direct labor hours worked. It is computed as follows:

Standard rate $8.50
Less actual rate   9.20
Difference per hour $0.70 (U)

Direct Labor Rate Variance = (Standard Rate − Actual Rate) × Actual Hours
                           = $.70 × 450 hours
                           = $315 (U)

STUDY NOTE: The computation of the direct labor rate variance is very similar to the computation of the direct materials price variance. Computations of the direct labor efficiency variance and the direct materials quantity variance are also similar.

The **direct labor efficiency variance** (also called the *direct labor quantity* or *usage variance*) is the difference between the standard direct labor hours allowed for good units produced and the actual direct labor hours worked multiplied by the standard direct labor rate. It is computed this way:

Standard hours allowed (180 bags × 2.4 hours per bag)   432 hours
Less actual hours   450 hours
Difference   18 hours (U)

Direct Labor Efficiency Variance = Standard Rate × (Standard Hours Allowed − Actual Hours)
                                 = $8.50 × 18 hours
                                 = $153 (U)

● **STOP AND THINK!**
What can cause a direct labor efficiency variance?
Inadequate labor skills and the condition of equipment are among the factors than can contribute to a direct labor efficiency variance. ■

If the calculations are correct, the net of the direct labor rate variance and the direct labor efficiency variance should equal the total direct labor cost variance. The following check shows that the variances were computed correctly:

Direct labor rate variance $315 (U)
Direct labor efficiency variance   153 (U)
Total direct labor cost variance $468 (U)

Figure 4 summarizes our analysis of Cambria Company's direct labor variances. Unlike direct materials variances, the direct labor rate and efficiency variances are usually computed and recorded at the same time.

ANALYZING AND CORRECTING DIRECT LABOR VARIANCES

Because Cambria Company's direct labor rate variance and direct labor efficiency variance were unfavorable, its managers investigated the causes of these variances. An analysis of employee time cards revealed that the Bag Assembly Department had replaced an assembly worker who was ill with a machine operator from another department. The machine operator made $9.20 per hour, whereas the assembly

FIGURE 4
Diagram of Direct Labor Variance Analysis

worker earned the standard $8.50 per hour rate. When questioned about the unfavorable efficiency variance, the assembly supervisor identified two causes. First, the machine operator had to learn assembly skills on the job, so his assembly time was longer than the standard time per bag. Second, the materials handling people were partially responsible because they delivered parts late on five different occasions. Because the machine operator was a temporary replacement, Cambria's managers took no corrective action, but they decided to keep a close eye on the materials handling function by tracking delivery times and number of delays for the next three months. Once they have collected and analyzed the new data, they will take whatever action is needed to correct the scheduling problem.

✓ Check out ACE for a Review Quiz at http://accounting.college.hmco.com/students.

COMPUTING AND ANALYZING MANUFACTURING OVERHEAD VARIANCES

LO6 Compute and analyze manufacturing overhead variances.

RELATED TEXT ASSIGNMENTS
Q: 18, 19
SE: 8, 9
E: 9, 10, 11, 12, 13, 14
P: 4, 5, 8
SD: 5
MRA: 2, 4

Many types of variable and fixed overhead costs may contribute to variances from standard costs. Controlling these costs is more difficult than controlling direct materials and labor costs because the responsibility for overhead costs is hard to assign. Fixed overhead costs are unavoidable past costs, such as depreciation and lease expenses; they are therefore not under the control of any department manager. If variable overhead costs can be related to departments or activities, however, some control is possible.

EXHIBIT 4
Flexible Budget for Evaluation of Manufacturing Overhead Costs

Cambria Company
Flexible Budget—Manufacturing Overhead
Bag Assembly Department
For an Average One-Month Period

Cost Category	Direct Labor Hours (DLH) 400	432	500	Variable Cost per DLH
Budgeted variable overhead				
Indirect materials	$ 600	$ 648	$ 750	$1.50
Indirect labor	800	864	1,000	2.00
Supplies	300	324	375	.75
Utilities	400	432	500	1.00
Other	200	216	250	.50
Total budgeted variable overhead costs	$2,300	$2,484	$2,875	$5.75
Budgeted fixed overhead				
Supervisory salaries	$ 600	$ 600	$ 600	
Depreciation	400	400	400	
Other	300	300	300	
Total budgeted fixed overhead costs	$1,300	$1,300	$1,300	
Total budgeted overhead costs	$3,600	$3,784	$4,175	

Flexible budget formula (based on a normal capacity of 400 direct labor hours):
Total Budgeted Overhead Costs = (Variable Costs per Direct Labor Hour × Number of DLH) + Budgeted Fixed Overhead Costs
= ($5.75 × number of DLH) + $1,300

USING A FLEXIBLE BUDGET TO ANALYZE MANUFACTURING OVERHEAD VARIANCES

Earlier in the chapter, we described the flexible budget that the managers of Remember When, Inc., use to evaluate overall performance. That budget, shown in Exhibit 2, is based on units of output. Cambria Company's managers also use a flexible budget but to analyze manufacturing overhead costs only. As you can see in Exhibit 4, Cambria's flexible budget uses direct labor hours as the expression of activity. Thus, variable costs vary with the number of direct labor hours worked. Total fixed overhead costs remain constant. The flexible budget formula in such cases is as follows:

Total Budgeted Overhead Costs = (Variable Costs per Direct Labor Hour × Number of Direct Labor Hours) + Budgeted Fixed Overhead Costs

When applied to Cambria Company's data, the flexible budget formula is as follows:

Total Budgeted Overhead Costs = ($5.75 × Number of Direct Labor Hours) + $1,300

Cambria's flexible budget shows monthly overhead costs for 400, 432, and 500 direct labor hours. To find the total monthly budgeted overhead costs, you simply insert the direct labor hours in the flexible budget formula—for example, ($5.75 × 432 direct labor hours) + $1,300 = $3,784.

COMPUTING MANUFACTURING OVERHEAD VARIANCES

Analyses of overhead variances differ in degree of detail. The basic approach is to compute the **total manufacturing overhead variance**, which is the difference between actual overhead costs and standard overhead costs. The latter costs are applied to production by using a standard overhead rate.

A standard overhead rate has two parts: a variable rate and a fixed one. For Cambria Company, the standard variable rate is $5.75 per direct labor hour (from the flexible budget). The standard fixed overhead rate is found by dividing total budgeted fixed overhead ($1,300) by normal capacity (Cambria's normal capacity is 400 direct labor hours). The result is a fixed overhead rate of $3.25 per direct labor hour ($1,300 ÷ 400 hours). So, Cambria's total standard overhead rate is $9.00 per direct labor hour ($5.75 + $3.25).

Cambria Company's total manufacturing overhead variance would be computed as follows:

Standard overhead costs applied to good units produced	
$9.00 per direct labor hour × (180 bags × 2.4 hr. per bag)	$3,888
Less actual overhead costs	4,100
Total manufacturing overhead variance	$ 212 (U)

This amount can be divided into variable overhead variances and fixed overhead variances.

■ **VARIABLE OVERHEAD VARIANCES** The **total variable overhead variance** is the difference between actual variable overhead costs and the standard variable overhead costs that are applied to good units produced using the standard variable rate. The procedure for finding this variance is similar to the procedure for finding direct materials and labor variances.

Figure 5 shows an analysis of Cambria Company's variable overhead variances. At Cambria, each leather bag requires 2.4 standard direct labor hours, and the standard variable overhead rate is $5.75 per direct labor hour. During August, the company incurred $2,500 of variable overhead costs. The total variable overhead cost variance is computed as follows:

Overhead applied to good units produced	
Standard variable rate × standard direct labor hours allowed =	
$5.75 per hour × (180 bags × 2.4 hours per bag) =	
$5.75 × 432 hours =	$2,484
Less actual cost	2,500
Total variable overhead cost variance	$ 16 (U)

Both the actual variable overhead and the direct labor hours per bag may vary from the standard. For effective performance evaluation, managers must know how

FIGURE 5
Diagram of Variable Overhead Variance Analysis

much of the total cost arose from variable overhead spending deviations and how much from variable overhead application deviations (i.e., applied and actual direct labor hours). This information is found by computing the variable overhead spending variance and the variable overhead efficiency variance.

The **variable overhead spending variance** (also called the *variable overhead rate variance*) is computed by multiplying the actual hours worked by the difference between actual variable overhead costs and the standard variable overhead rate, as follows:

Variable Overhead Spending Variance = Budgeted Variable Costs at Actual Hours − Actual Variable Overhead
= (Standard Variable Rate × Actual Hours Worked) − Actual Variable Overhead
= ($5.75 × 450 hours) − $2,500
= $2,587.50 − $2,500
= $87.50 (F)

The **variable overhead efficiency variance** is the difference between the standard direct labor hours allowed for good units produced and the actual hours worked multiplied by the standard variable overhead rate per hour. It is computed as follows:

> **STOP AND THINK!**
> Can the variable overhead efficiency variance have the same causes as the direct labor efficiency variance?
> *The efficiency variances for direct labor and variable overhead are generally based on the same quantity—that is, direct labor hours—and thus are caused by the same factors.* ∎

Standard direct labor hours allowed (180 bags × 2.4 hours per bag) 432 hours
Less actual hours 450 hours
Difference 18 hours (U)

$$\text{Variable Overhead Efficiency Variance} = \text{Standard Variable Rate} \times (\text{Standard Hours Allowed} - \text{Actual Hours})$$
$$= \$5.75 \times 18 \text{ hours}$$
$$= \$103.50 \text{ (U)}$$

If the calculations are correct, the net of the variable overhead spending variance and the variable overhead efficiency variance should equal the total variable overhead cost variance. The following check shows that these variances have been computed correctly:

Variable overhead spending variance $87.50 (F)
Variable overhead efficiency variance 103.50 (U)
Total variable overhead cost variance $16.00 (U)

■ **FIXED OVERHEAD VARIANCES** The **total fixed overhead variance** is the difference between actual fixed overhead costs and the standard fixed overhead costs that are applied to good units produced using the standard fixed overhead rate. The procedure for finding this variance differs from the procedure used for finding direct materials, direct labor, and variable overhead variances.

Figure 6 shows an analysis of fixed overhead variances for Cambria Company. At Cambria, each bag requires 2.4 standard direct labor hours, and the standard fixed overhead rate is $3.25 per direct labor hour. As we noted earlier, the standard fixed overhead rate is found by dividing budgeted fixed overhead ($1,300) by normal capacity. In this case, because normal capacity is 400 direct labor hours, the fixed overhead rate is $3.25 per direct labor hour ($1,300 ÷ 400 hours). During August, Cambria incurred $1,600 of actual fixed overhead costs. The total fixed overhead cost variance is computed as follows:

Overhead applied to the good units produced
  Standard fixed rate × standard direct labor hours allowed =
    $3.25 × (180 bags × 2.4 hours per bag) =
      $3.25 × 432 hours = $1,404
Less actual cost 1,600
Total fixed overhead cost variance $196 (U)

For effective performance evaluation, managers break down the total fixed overhead cost variance into two additional variances: the fixed overhead budget variance and the fixed overhead volume variance.

The **fixed overhead budget variance** (also called the *budgeted fixed overhead variance*) is the difference between budgeted and actual fixed overhead costs, computed as follows:

$$\text{Fixed Overhead Budget Variance} = \text{Budgeted Fixed Overhead} - \text{Actual Fixed Overhead}$$
$$= \$1,300 - \$1,600$$
$$= \$300 \text{ (U)}$$

The **fixed overhead volume variance** is the difference between budgeted fixed overhead costs and the manufacturing overhead costs that are applied to produc-

FIGURE 6
Diagram of Fixed Overhead Variance Analysis

tion using the standard fixed overhead rate. The fixed overhead volume variance is computed as follows:

Standard fixed overhead applied to good units produced	
$3.25 per direct labor hour × (180 bags × 2.4 hr. per bag)	$1,404
Less total budgeted fixed overhead	1,300
Fixed overhead volume variance	$ 104 (F)

Because the fixed overhead volume variance measures the use of existing facilities and capacity, a volume variance will occur if more or less than normal capacity is used. At Cambria Company, 400 direct labor hours are considered normal use of facilities. Because fixed overhead costs are applied on the basis of standard hours allowed, Cambria Company's manufacturing overhead was applied on the basis of 432 hours, even though the fixed overhead rate was computed using 400 hours. Thus, more fixed costs would be applied to products than were budgeted. When capacity exceeds the expected amount, the result is a favorable overhead volume variance.

When a company operates at a level below the normal capacity in units, the result is an unfavorable volume variance. Not all of the fixed overhead costs will be applied to units produced, and it then becomes necessary to add the amount of underapplied fixed overhead to the cost of good units produced, thereby increasing their unit cost.

In some cases, an unfavorable volume variance is in a company's best interest. For example, in a period of slow sales, an unfavorable volume variance would mean the company was not building up excessive inventory that might be subject to obsolescence, weathering, and storage costs. For this reason, a favorable volume variance does not always indicate that a manager has performed well.

■ **SUMMARY OF MANUFACTURING OVERHEAD VARIANCES** If our calculations of variable and fixed overhead variances are correct, the net of these variances should equal the total manufacturing overhead variance. Checking the computations, we find that the variable and fixed overhead variances do equal the total manufacturing overhead variance:

Variable overhead spending variance	$ 87.50 (F)
Variable overhead efficiency variance	103.50 (U)
Fixed overhead budget variance	300.00 (U)
Fixed overhead volume variance	104.00 (F)
Total manufacturing overhead variance	$212.00 (U)

Figures 5 and 6 summarize our analysis of manufacturing overhead variances. The total manufacturing overhead variance is also the amount of overapplied or underapplied overhead. You may recall from an earlier chapter that actual variable and fixed overhead costs are recorded as they occur, that variable and fixed overhead are applied to products as they are produced, and that the overapplied or underapplied overhead is computed and reconciled at the end of each accounting period. By breaking down the total manufacturing overhead variance into variable and fixed variances, managers can more accurately control costs and reconcile their causes. An analysis of these two overhead variances will help explain why the amount of overhead applied to units produced is different from the actual overhead costs incurred.

ANALYZING AND CORRECTING MANUFACTURING OVERHEAD VARIANCES

In analyzing the unfavorable total manufacturing overhead variance of $212, the manager of Cambria Company's Bag Assembly Department found causes for the variances that contributed to it. Although the variable overhead spending variance was favorable ($87.50 less than expected because of savings on purchases), the inefficiency of the machine operator who substituted for an assembly worker created unfavorable variances for both direct labor efficiency and variable overhead efficiency. As a result, the manager is going to consider the feasibility of implementing a program for cross-training employees.

After reviewing the fixed overhead costs, the manager of the Bag Assembly Department concluded that higher than anticipated factory insurance premiums were the reason for the unfavorable fixed overhead budget variance and were the result of an increase in the number of insurance claims filed by employees. To obtain more specific information, the manager will study the insurance claims filed over a three-month period.

Finally, since the 432 standard hours were well above the normal capacity of 400 direct labor hours, fixed overhead was overapplied, and it resulted in a

FOCUS ON INTERNATIONAL BUSINESS

Have You Bought Gold Medal Sneakers Yet?
Founded by Li-Ning, winner of the 1984 Olympic Gold medal for gymnastics, Beijing Li-Ning Sports Goods Company is aiming to become a dominant force in the global market by 2008, when the Olympic games will be held in Beijing. The company's products include athletic shoes and sportswear. Currently, its sneakers are the best-selling ones in China, a market soon to be the second largest in the world. Controlling costs through the use of standard costing is a key to the company's success. Because its prices are up to two-thirds lower than those of its international competitors and because it controls its costs well, Beijing Li-Ning Sports Goods Company is an up-and-coming global contender.[4]

$104 (F) volume variance. The overutilization of capacity was traced to high seasonal demand that pressed the company to use almost all its capacity. Management decided not to do anything about the fixed overhead volume variance because it fell within an anticipated seasonal range.

 Check out ACE for a Review Quiz at http://accounting.college.hmco.com/students.

USING COST VARIANCES TO EVALUATE MANAGERS' PERFORMANCE

LO7 Explain how variances are used to evaluate managers' performance.

RELATED TEXT ASSIGNMENTS
Q: 20
SE: 10
E: 15

How effectively and fairly a manager's performance is evaluated depends on human factors—the people doing the evaluating—as well as on company policies. The evaluation process becomes more accurate when managerial performance reports include variances from standard costs.

To ensure that the evaluation of a manager's performance is effective and fair, a company's policies should be based on input from managers and employees and should specify the procedures that managers are to use for

- Preparing operational plans
- Assigning responsibility for carrying out the operational plans
- Communicating the operational plans to key personnel
- Evaluating performance in each area of responsibility
- Identifying the causes of significant variances from the operational plan
- Taking corrective action to eliminate problems

Because variance analysis provides detailed data about differences between standard and actual costs and thus helps identify the causes of those differences, it is usually more effective at pinpointing efficient and inefficient operating areas than are basic comparisons of budgeted and actual data. A managerial performance report based on standard costs and related variances should identify the causes of each significant variance, as well as the personnel involved and the corrective actions taken. It should be tailored to the manager's specific areas of responsibility, explaining clearly and accurately in what way the manager's department met or did not meet operating expectations. Managers should be held accountable only for cost areas under their control.

● **STOP AND THINK!**
Why should evaluations of managers' performance not follow a set pattern?
Because managers have different responsibilities, evaluations of their performance should be tailored to those responsibilities. ■

Exhibit 5 shows a performance report for the manager of Cambria Company's Bag Assembly Department. The report summarizes all cost data and variances for direct materials, direct labor, and manufacturing overhead. In addition, it identifies the causes of the variances and the corrective actions taken. Such a report would enable a supervisor to review a manager's actions and evaluate his or her performance.

A point to remember is that the mere occurrence of a variance does not indicate that a manager has performed poorly. However, if a variance consistently occurs and no cause is identified and no corrective action is taken, it may well indicate poor managerial performance.

The report in Exhibit 5 shows that the causes of the variances have been identified and corrective actions have been taken, indicating that the manager of the Cambria Company's Bag Assembly Department has the operation under control.

FOCUS ON BUSINESS ETHICS

Ethics = Profits
According to a recent five-year study, companies that demonstrate a commitment to ethical practices are more profitable than companies that do not demonstrate such a commitment. Conducted by researchers in the United Kingdom and the United States, the study used financial performance measures, including economic value added and return on capital, and nonfinancial performance measures, such as whether a company was on a list of most admired companies. The study found that in the long run, ethical companies outperformed their less ethical peers.[5]

EXHIBIT 5
Managerial Performance Report Using Variance Analysis

Cambria Company
Managerial Performance Report
Bag Assembly Department
For the Month Ended August 31, 20x6

Productivity Summary:

Normal capacity in units	167 bags
Normal capacity in direct labor hours (DLH)	400 DLH
Good units produced	180 bags
Performance level (standard hours allowed for good units produced)	432 DLH

Cost and Variance Analysis:

	Standard Costs	Actual Costs	Total Variance	Variance Breakdown Amount	Variance Breakdown Type
Direct materials	$ 4,320	$ 4,484	$164 (U)	$ 76.00 (F)	Direct materials price variance
				240.00 (U)	Direct materials quantity variance
Direct labor	3,672	4,140	468 (U)	315.00 (U)	Direct labor rate variance
				153.00 (U)	Direct labor efficiency variance
Overhead					
Variable	2,484	2,500	16 (U)	87.50 (F)	Variable overhead spending variance
				103.50 (U)	Variable overhead efficiency variance
Fixed	1,404	1,600	196 (U)	300.00 (U)	Fixed overhead budget variance
				104.00 (F)	Fixed overhead volume variance
Totals	$11,880	$12,724	$844 (U)	$844.00 (U)	

Causes of Variances

Direct materials price variance:
  New direct material purchased at reduced price

Direct materials quantity variance:
  Poor quality of new direct material

Direct labor rate variance:
  Machine operator who had to learn assembly skills
Direct labor efficiency variance:
  Machine operator who had to learn assembly skills
  Late delivery of parts to assembly floor

Variable overhead spending variance:
  Cost savings on purchases
Variable overhead efficiency variance:
  Machine operator who had to learn assembly skills on the job
Fixed overhead budget variance:
  Large number of factory insurance claims
Fixed overhead volume variance:
  High number of orders caused by seasonal demand

Actions Taken

New direct material deemed inappropriate; resumed purchasing material originally specified

New direct material deemed inappropriate; resumed using direct material originally specified

Temporary replacement; no action taken on the job

Temporary replacement; no action taken on the job
Material delivery times and number of delays being tracked

No action necessary

A cross-training program for employees now under consideration

Study of insurance claims being conducted

No action necessary

Check out ACE for a Review Quiz at http://accounting.college.hmco.com/students.

Chapter Review

REVIEW OF LEARNING OBJECTIVES

LO1 Define *standard costs* and describe how managers use standard costs in the management cycle.

Standard costs are realistic estimates of costs based on analyses of both past and projected operating costs and conditions. They provide a standard, or predetermined, performance level for use in standard costing, a method of cost control that also includes a measure of actual performance and a measure of the variance between standard and actual performance. In the planning stage of the management cycle, managers use standard costs to develop budgets for direct materials, direct labor, and variable overhead. These estimated costs not only serve as targets for product costing; they are also useful in making decisions about product distribution and pricing. During the executing stage, managers use standard costs to measure expenditures and to control costs as they occur. At the end of an accounting period, they compare actual costs with standard costs and compute the variances. The variances provide measures of performance that can be used to control costs. Managers also use standard costs to report on operations and managerial performance.

LO2 Explain how standard costs are developed and compute a standard unit cost.

A standard unit cost has six elements. The direct materials price standard is based on a careful estimate of all possible price increases, changes in available quantities, and new sources of supply in the next accounting period. The direct materials quantity standard is based on product engineering specifications, the quality of direct materials, the age and productivity of the machines, and the quality and experience of the work force. Labor union contracts or company policies define the direct labor rate standard. Current time and motion studies of workers and machines and records of their past performance provide the data for developing the direct labor time standard. Standard variable and fixed overhead rates are found by dividing total budgeted variable and fixed overhead costs by an appropriate application base.

A total standard unit cost is computed by adding the following costs: direct materials costs (direct materials price standard times direct materials quantity standard), direct labor costs (direct labor rate standard times direct labor time standard), and manufacturing overhead costs (standard variable and standard fixed overhead rate times standard direct labor hours allowed per unit).

LO3 Prepare a flexible budget and describe how variance analysis is used to control costs.

A flexible budget is a summary of anticipated costs for a range of activity levels. It provides forecasted cost data that can be adjusted for changes in level of output. The variable cost per unit and total fixed costs presented in a flexible budget are components of the flexible budget formula, an equation that determines the budgeted cost for any level of output. A flexible budget improves the accuracy of variance analysis, which is a four-step approach to controlling costs. First, managers compute the amount of the variance. If the amount is insignificant, no corrective action is needed. If the amount is significant, managers then analyze the variance to identify its cause. In identifying the cause, they are usually able to pinpoint the activities that need to be monitored. They then select performance measures that will enable them to track those activities, analyze the results, and determine the action needed to correct the problem. Their final step is to take the appropriate corrective action.

LO4 Compute and analyze direct materials variances.

The direct materials price variance is computed by finding the difference between the standard price and the actual price per unit and multiplying it by the actual quantity purchased. The direct materials quantity variance is the difference between the standard quantity that should have been used and the actual quantity used, multiplied by the standard price. An analysis of these variances enables managers to identify what is causing them and to formulate plans for correcting related operating problems.

LO5 Compute and analyze direct labor variances.

The direct labor rate variance is computed by determining the difference between the standard direct labor rate and the actual rate and multiplying it by the actual direct labor hours worked. The direct labor efficiency variance is the difference between the standard hours allowed for the number of good units produced and the actual hours worked multiplied by the standard direct labor rate. Managers analyze these variances to find the causes of differences between standard direct labor costs and actual direct labor costs.

LO6 Compute and analyze manufacturing overhead variances.

The total manufacturing overhead variance is equal to the amount of under- or overapplied overhead costs for an accounting period. An analysis of the variable and fixed overhead variances will help explain why the amount of overhead applied to units produced differs from the actual overhead costs incurred. The total overhead variance can be broken down into a variable overhead spending variance, a variable overhead efficiency variance, a fixed overhead budget variance, and a fixed overhead volume variance.

LO7 Explain how variances are used to evaluate managers' performance.

How effectively and fairly a manager's performance is evaluated depends on human factors—the people doing the evaluating—as well as on company policies. To ensure that performance evaluation is effective and fair, a company's evaluation policies should be based on input from managers and employees and should be specific about the procedures managers are to follow. The evaluation process becomes more accurate when managerial performance reports include variances from standard costs. A managerial performance report based on standard costs and related variances should identify the causes of each significant variance, as well as the personnel involved, and the corrective actions taken. It should be tailored to the manager's specific areas of responsibility.

REVIEW OF CONCEPTS AND TERMINOLOGY

The following concepts and terms were introduced in this chapter:

LO5 **Direct labor efficiency variance:** The difference between the standard direct labor hours allowed for good units produced and the actual direct labor hours worked multiplied by the standard direct labor rate. Also called *direct labor quantity* or *usage variance*.

LO2 **Direct labor rate standard:** The hourly direct labor rate expected to prevail during the next accounting period for each function or job classification.

LO5 **Direct labor rate variance:** The difference between the standard direct labor rate and the actual direct labor rate multiplied by the actual direct labor hours worked. Also called *direct labor spending variance*.

LO2 **Direct labor time standard:** The expected labor time required for each department, machine, or process to complete the production of one unit or one batch of output.

LO2 **Direct materials price standard:** A careful estimate of the cost of a specific direct material in the next accounting period.

LO4 **Direct materials price variance:** The difference between the standard price and the actual price per unit multiplied by the actual quantity purchased. Also called *direct material spending* or *rate variance*.

LO2 **Direct materials quantity standard:** An estimate of the amount of direct materials, including scrap and waste, that will be used in an accounting period.

LO4 **Direct materials quantity variance:** The difference between the standard quantity allowed and the actual quantity used multiplied by the standard price. Also called *direct material efficiency* or *usage variance*.

LO6 **Fixed overhead budget variance:** The difference between budgeted and actual fixed overhead costs. Also called *budgeted fixed overhead variance*.

LO6 **Fixed overhead volume variance:** The difference between budgeted fixed overhead costs and the overhead costs that are applied to production using the standard fixed overhead rate.

LO3 **Flexible budget:** A summary of expected costs for a range of activity levels. Also called *variable budget*.

LO3 **Flexible budget formula:** An equation that determines the expected, or budgeted, cost for any level of productive output.

- **LO1** **Standard costing:** A method of cost control with three components: a standard, or predetermined, performance level; a measure of actual performance; and a measure of the difference, or variance, between standard and actual performance.
- **LO1** **Standard costs:** Realistic estimates of costs based on analyses of both past and projected operating costs and conditions.
- **LO2** **Standard direct labor cost:** The standard wage for direct labor multiplied by the standard hours of direct labor.
- **LO2** **Standard direct materials cost:** The standard price for direct materials multiplied by the standard quantity for direct materials.
- **LO2** **Standard fixed overhead rate:** Total budgeted fixed overhead costs divided by an expression of capacity, usually normal capacity in terms of standard hours or units.
- **LO2** **Standard manufacturing overhead cost:** The sum of the estimates of variable and fixed overhead costs in the next accounting period.
- **LO2** **Standard variable overhead rate:** Total budgeted variable overhead costs divided by an expression of capacity, such as the expected number of standard machine hours or standard direct labor hours.
- **LO5** **Total direct labor cost variance:** The difference between the standard direct labor cost for good units produced and actual direct labor costs.
- **LO4** **Total direct materials cost variance:** The difference between the standard cost and actual cost of direct materials.
- **LO6** **Total fixed overhead variance:** The difference between actual fixed overhead costs and the standard fixed overhead costs that are applied to good units produced using the standard fixed overhead rate.
- **LO6** **Total manufacturing overhead variance:** The difference between actual manufacturing overhead costs and standard manufacturing overhead costs.
- **LO6** **Total variable overhead variance:** The difference between actual variable overhead costs and the standard variable overhead costs that are applied to good units produced using the standard variable overhead rate.
- **LO6** **Variable overhead efficiency variance:** The difference between the standard direct labor hours allowed for good units produced and the actual hours worked multiplied by the standard variable overhead rate per hour.
- **LO6** **Variable overhead spending variance:** The difference between actual variable overhead costs and the standard variable overhead rate multiplied by the actual hours used. Also called the *variable overhead rate variance*.
- **LO1** **Variance:** The difference between a standard cost and an actual cost.
- **LO3** **Variance analysis:** The process of computing the differences between standard costs and actual costs and identifying the causes of those differences.

REVIEW PROBLEM

Variance Analysis

LO2 LO4 LO5 LO6 Alexa Manufacturing Company has a standard costing system and keeps all its cost standards up to date. The company's main product is copper water pipe, which is made in a single department. The standard variable costs for one unit of finished pipe are as follows:

Direct materials (3 sq. meters @ $12.50 per sq. meter)	$37.50
Direct labor (1.2 hours @ $9.00 per hour)	10.80
Variable overhead (1.2 hours @ $5.00 per direct labor hour)	6.00
Standard variable cost per unit	$54.30

The company's normal capacity is 15,000 direct labor hours. Its budgeted fixed overhead costs for the year were $54,000. During the year, it produced and sold 12,200 units, and it purchased and used 37,500 square meters of direct materials; the purchase cost was $12.40 per square meter. The average labor rate was $9.20 per hour, and 15,250 direct labor hours were worked. The company's actual variable overhead costs for the year were $73,200, and its fixed overhead costs were $55,000.

REQUIRED ▶ Using the data given, compute the following using formulas or diagram form:

1. Standard hours allowed for good output
2. Standard fixed overhead rate
3. Direct materials cost variances:
   a. Direct materials price variance
   b. Direct materials quantity variance
   c. Total direct materials cost variance
4. Direct labor cost variances:
   a. Direct labor rate variance
   b. Direct labor efficiency variance
   c. Total direct labor cost variance
5. Variable overhead cost variances:
   a. Variable overhead spending variance
   b. Variable overhead efficiency variance
   c. Total variable overhead cost variance
6. Fixed overhead cost variances:
   a. Fixed overhead budget variance
   b. Fixed overhead volume variance
   c. Total fixed overhead cost variance

ANSWER TO REVIEW PROBLEM

1. Standard Hours Allowed = Good Units Produced × Standard Direct Labor Hours per Unit
   = 12,200 units × 1.2 direct labor hours per unit
   = **14,640 hours**

2. Standard Fixed Overhead Rate = $\frac{\text{Budgeted Fixed Overhead Cost}}{\text{Normal Capacity}}$

   = $\frac{\$54,000}{15,000 \text{ direct labor hours}}$

   = **$3.60 per direct labor hour**

3. Direct materials cost variances:
   a. Direct materials price variance

   Price difference: Standard price $12.50
                 Less actual price   12.40
                 Difference $ .10 (F)

   Direct Materials Price Variance = (Standard Price − Actual Price) × Actual Quantity
   = $.10 × 37,500 sq. meters
   = **$3,750 (F)**

   b. Direct materials quantity variance

   Quantity difference: Standard quantity
       (12,200 units × 3 sq. meters) 36,600 sq. meters
       Less actual quantity   37,500 sq. meters
       Difference   900 sq. meters (U)

   Direct Materials Quantity Variance = Standard Price × (Standard Quantity − Actual Quantity)
   = $12.50 per sq. meter × 900 sq. meters
   = **$11,250 (U)**

c. Total Direct Materials Cost Variance:

$$\begin{aligned}\text{Total Direct Materials Cost Variance} &= \text{Net of Direct Materials Price Variance} \\ &\quad \text{and Direct Materials Quantity Variance} \\ &= \$3{,}750 \text{ (F)} - \$11{,}250 \text{ (U)} \\ &= \underline{\underline{\$7{,}500 \text{ (U)}}}\end{aligned}$$

Diagram Form:

	Actual Price × Actual Quantity		Standard Price × Actual Quantity		Standard Price × Standard Quantity
Direct Materials	$12.40 × 37,500 = $465,000	Price Variance	$12.50 × 37,500 = $468,750	Quantity Variance	$12.50 × (12,200 × 3) = $457,500
		$3,750 (F)	Total Direct Materials Cost Variance	$11,250 (U)	
			$7,500 (U)		

4. Direct labor cost variances:
   a. Direct labor rate variance:

   Rate difference: Standard labor rate $9.00
   Less actual labor rate 9.20
   Difference $ .20 (U)

   $$\begin{aligned}\text{Direct Labor Rate Variance} &= (\text{Standard Rate} - \text{Actual Rate}) \times \text{Actual Hours} \\ &= \$.20 \times 15{,}250 \text{ hours} \\ &= \underline{\underline{\$3{,}050 \text{ (U)}}}\end{aligned}$$

   b. Direct labor efficiency variance:

   Difference in hours: Standard hours allowed 14,640 hours*
   Less actual hours 15,250 hours
   Difference 610 hours (U)

   $$\begin{aligned}\text{Direct Labor Efficiency Variance} &= \text{Standard Rate} \times (\text{Standard Hours Allowed} - \text{Actual Hours}) \\ &= \$9.00 \text{ per hour} \times 610 \text{ hours (U)} \\ &= \underline{\underline{\$5{,}490 \text{ (U)}}}\end{aligned}$$

   *12,200 units produced × 1.2 hours per unit = 14,640 hours.

   c. Total direct labor cost variance:

   $$\begin{aligned}\text{Total Direct Labor Cost Variance} &= \text{Net of Direct Labor Rate Variance and} \\ &\quad \text{Direct Labor Efficiency Variance} \\ &= \$3{,}050 \text{ (U)} + \$5{,}490 \text{ (U)} \\ &= \underline{\underline{\$8{,}540 \text{ (U)}}}\end{aligned}$$

Diagram Form:

	Actual Rate × Actual Hours		Standard Rate × Actual Hours		Standard Rate × Standard Hours
Direct Labor	$9.20 × 15,250 = $140,300	Rate Variance	$9.00 × 15,250 = $137,250	Efficiency Variance	$9.00 × (12,200 × 1.2) = $131,760
		$3,050 (U)	Total Direct Labor Cost Variance	$5,490 (U)	
			$8,540 (U)		

5. Variable overhead cost variances:
    a. Variable overhead spending variance:

Budgeted variable overhead for actual hours Variable overhead cost		
($5.00 per hour × 15,250 labor hours)	$76,250	
Less actual variable overhead costs incurred	73,200	
Variable overhead spending variance	$ 3,050 (F)	

    b. Variable overhead efficiency variance:

Variable overhead applied to good units produced		
(14,640 hours* × $5.00 per hour)	$73,200	
Less budgeted variable overhead for actual hours		
(15,250 hours × $5.00 per hour)	76,250	
Variable overhead efficiency variance	$ 3,050 (U)	

    *12,200 units produced × 1.2 hours per unit = 14,640 hours.

    c. Total variable overhead cost variance:

    Total Variable Overhead Cost Variance = Net of Variable Overhead Spending Variance and Variable Overhead Efficiency Variance
    = $3,050 (F) − $3,050 (U)
    = $0

Diagram Form:

	Actual Variable Overhead Costs		Standard Rate × Actual Hours		Standard Rate × Standard Hours
Variable Overhead	$73,200	Spending Variance	$5.00 × 15,250 = $76,250	Efficiency Variance	$5.00 × (12,200 × 1.2) = $73,200
		$3,050 (F)	Total Variable Overhead Cost Variance	$3,050 (U)	
			$0		

6. Fixed overhead cost variances:
    a. Fixed overhead budget variance:

Budgeted fixed overhead	$54,000	
Less actual fixed overhead	55,000	
Fixed overhead budget variance	$ 1,000 (U)	

    b. Fixed overhead volume variance:

Standard fixed overhead applied		
(14,640 labor hours × $3.60 per hour)	$52,704	
Less total budgeted fixed overhead	54,000	
Fixed overhead volume variance	$ 1,296 (U)	

    c. Total fixed overhead cost variance:

    Total Fixed Overhead Cost Variance = Net of Fixed Overhead Budget Variance and Fixed Overhead Volume Variance
    = $1,000 (U) + $1,296 (U)
    = $2,296 (U)

Diagram Form:

	Actual Fixed Overhead Costs		Budgeted Fixed Overhead Costs		Standard Rate × Standard Hours
Fixed Overhead	$55,000	Budget Variance	$54,000	Volume Variance	$3.60 × (12,200 × 1.2) = $52,704
		$1,000 (U)	Total Fixed Overhead Variance	$1,296 (U)	
			$2,296 (U)		

Chapter Assignments

BUILDING YOUR KNOWLEDGE FOUNDATION

QUESTIONS

1. What are standard costs?
2. What is a variance?
3. Can a service organization use standard costing? Explain your answer.
4. Explain the following statement: "Standard costing is a total unit cost concept in that standard unit costs are determined for direct materials, direct labor, and manufacturing overhead."
5. What general ledger accounts are affected by a standard costing system?
6. What do a standard overhead manufacturing rate and a predetermined overhead rate have in common? How do they differ?
7. Name the six elements used to compute a standard unit cost.
8. Identify three factors that could affect a direct materials price standard.
9. "Performance is evaluated by comparing what did happen with what should have happened." What does this statement mean? How does it relate to cost control?
10. What is variance analysis?
11. What is a flexible budget? What is its purpose?
12. What are the components of the flexible budget formula? How are they related?
13. How can variances help managers control costs?
14. What is the formula for computing a direct materials price variance?
15. How would you interpret an unfavorable direct materials price variance?
16. Can an unfavorable direct materials quantity variance be caused, at least in part, by a favorable direct materials price variance? Explain your answer.
17. Identify two possible causes of a direct labor rate variance and describe the measures used to track performance in those areas. Then do the same for a direct labor efficiency variance.
18. Distinguish between the fixed overhead budget variance and the fixed overhead volume variance.
19. If standard hours allowed exceed normal hours, will the period's fixed manufacturing overhead volume variance be favorable or unfavorable? Explain your answer.

20. What should a managerial performance report based on standard costs and related variances include? How should it be prepared?

Short Exercises

SE 1. (LO1 Uses of Standard Costs) Lago Corporation is considering adopting the standard costing method. Dan Sarkis, the manager of the Ohio Division, attended a corporate meeting at which Leah Rohr, the controller, discussed the proposal. Sarkis asked, "Leah, how will this new method benefit me? How will I use it?" Prepare Rohr's response to Sarkis.

SE 2. (LO1 Purposes of Standard Costs) Suppose you are a management consultant and a client asks you why companies include standard costs in their cost accounting systems. Prepare your response, listing several purposes for using standard costs in a cost accounting system.

SE 3. (LO2 Computing a Standard Unit Cost) Using the following information, compute the standard unit cost of Product JLT:

Direct materials quantity standard	5 pounds per unit
Direct materials price standard	$10.20 per pound
Direct labor time standard	.4 hour per unit
Direct labor rate standard	$10.75 per hour
Variable overhead rate standard	$7.00 per machine hour
Fixed overhead rate standard	$11.00 per machine hour
Machine hour standard	2 hours per unit

SE 4. (LO3 Analyzing Cost Variances) Garden Metal Works produces lawn sculptures. The company analyzes only variances that differ by more than 5 percent from the standard cost. The controller computed the following direct labor efficiency variances for March:

	Direct Labor Efficiency Variance	Standard Direct Labor Cost
Product 4	$1,240 (U)	$26,200
Product 6	3,290 (F)	41,700
Product 7	2,030 (U)	34,300
Product 9	1,620 (F)	32,560
Product 12	2,810 (U)	59,740

For each product, determine the percentage of the variance to the standard cost (round to one decimal place). Then identify the products whose variances should be analyzed and suggest possible causes for the variances..

SE 5. (LO3 Preparing a Flexible Budget) Prepare a flexible budget for 10,000, 12,000, and 14,000 units of output, using the following information:

Variable costs	
Direct materials	$8.00 per unit
Direct labor	$2.50 per unit
Variable overhead	$6.00 per unit
Total budgeted fixed overhead	$81,200

SE 6. (LO4 Direct Materials Variances) Using the standard costs in **SE 3** and the following actual cost and usage data, compute the direct materials price and direct materials quantity variances:

Direct materials purchased and used	55,000 pounds
Price paid for direct materials	$10.00 per pound
Number of good units produced	11,000 units

SE 7. (LO5 Direct Labor Variances) Using the standard costs in **SE 3** and the following actual cost and usage data, compute the direct labor rate and direct labor efficiency variances:

Direct labor hours used	4,950 hours
Total cost of direct labor	$53,460
Number of good units produced	11,000 units

SE 8. (LO6 Manufacturing Overhead Variances) Sutherland Products uses standard costing. The following information about manufacturing overhead was generated during August:

Standard variable overhead rate	$2 per machine hour
Standard fixed overhead rate	$3 per machine hour
Actual variable overhead costs	$443,200
Actual fixed overhead costs	$698,800

		Budgeted fixed overhead costs	$700,000
		Standard machine hours per unit produced	12
		Good units produced	18,940
		Actual machine hours	228,400

Compute the variable overhead spending and efficiency variances and the fixed overhead budget and volume variances.

LO6 Fixed Overhead Rate and Variances

SE 9. To the Point Manufacturing Company uses the standard costing method. The company's main product is a fine quality fountain pen that normally takes 2.5 hours to produce. Normal annual capacity is 30,000 direct labor hours, and budgeted fixed overhead costs for the year were $15,000. During the year, the company produced and sold 14,000 units. Actual fixed overhead costs were $19,000. Compute the fixed overhead rate per direct labor hour and determine the fixed overhead budget and volume variances.

LO7 Evaluating Managerial Performance

SE 10. Gina Rolando, the controller at WAWA Industries, gave Jason Ponds, the production manager, a report containing the following information:

	Actual Cost	Standard Cost	Variance
Direct materials	$38,200	$36,600	$1,600 (U)
Direct labor	19,450	19,000	450 (U)
Variable overhead	62,890	60,000	2,890 (U)

Rolando asked for a response. If you were Ponds, how would you respond? What additional information might you need to prepare your response?

Exercises

LO1 Uses of Standard Costs

E 1. Summer Diaz has just assumed the duties of controller for Market Research Company. She is concerned that the company's methods of cost planning and control do not accurately track the operations of the business. She plans to suggest to the company's president, Sydney Tyson, that the company start using standard costing for budgeting and cost control. The new method could be incorporated into the existing accounting system. The anticipated cost of adopting it and training managers is around $7,500. Prepare a memo from Summer Diaz to Sydney Tyson that defines standard costing and outlines its uses and benefits.

LO2 Computing Standard Costs

E 2. Normal Corporation uses standard costing and is in the process of updating its direct materials and direct labor standards for Product 20B. The following data have been accumulated:

Direct materials

In the previous period, 20,500 units were produced, and 32,800 square yards of direct materials at a cost of $122,344 were used to produce them.

Direct labor

During the previous period, 57,400 direct labor hours were worked—34,850 hours on machine H and 22,550 hours on machine K. Machine H operators earned $9.40 per hour, and machine K operators earned $9.20 per hour last period. A new labor union contract calls for a 10 percent increase in labor rates for the coming period.

Using this information as the basis for the new standards, compute the direct materials quantity and price standards and the direct labor time and rate standards for each machine for the coming accounting period.

LO2 Computing a Standard Unit Cost

E 3. Weather Aerodynamics, Inc., makes electronically equipped weather-detecting balloons for university meteorology departments. Because of recent nationwide inflation, the company's management has ordered that standard costs be recomputed. New direct materials price standards are $600 per set for electronic components and $13.50 per square meter for heavy-duty canvas. Direct materials quantity standards include one set of electronic components and 100 square meters of heavy-duty canvas per balloon. Direct labor time standards are 26 hours per balloon for the Electronics Department and 19 hours per balloon for the Assembly Department. Direct labor rate standards are $11 per hour for the Electronics Department and $10 per hour for the Assembly Department. Standard manufacturing overhead rates are $16 per direct labor hour for the standard variable overhead rate and $12 per direct labor hour for the standard fixed overhead rate. Using these production standards, compute the standard unit cost of one weather balloon.

LO3 Preparing a Flexible Budget

E 4. Keel Company's fixed overhead costs for 20x5 are expected to be as follows: depreciation, $72,000; supervisory salaries, $92,000; property taxes and insurance, $26,000; and other fixed overhead, $14,500. Total fixed overhead is thus expected to be $204,500. Variable costs per unit are expected to be as follows: direct materials, $16.50; direct labor, $8.50; operating supplies, $2.60; indirect labor, $4.10; and other variable overhead costs, $3.20. Prepare a flexible budget for the following levels of production: 18,000 units, 20,000 units, and 22,000 units. What is the flexible budget formula for 20x5?

LO4 Direct Materials Price and Quantity Variances

E 5. SITO Elevator Company manufactures small hydroelectric elevators with a maximum capacity of ten passengers. One of the direct materials used is heavy-duty carpeting for the floor of the elevator. The direct materials quantity standard for April was 8 square yards per elevator. During April, the purchasing agent purchased this carpeting at $11 per square yard; the standard price for the period was $12. Ninety elevators were completed and sold during the month; the Production Department used an average of 8.5 square yards of carpet per elevator. Calculate the company's direct materials price and quantity variances for carpeting for April.

LO4 Direct Materials Variances

E 6. Diekow Productions manufactured and sold 1,000 products at $11,000 each during the past year. At the beginning of the year, production had been set at 1,200 products; direct materials standards had been set at 100 pounds of direct materials at $2 per pound for each product produced. During the year, the company purchased and used 98,000 pounds of direct materials; the cost was $2.04 per pound. Calculate Diekow Production's direct materials price and quantity variances for the year.

LO5 Direct Labor Variances

E 7. At the beginning of last year, Diekow Productions set direct labor standards of 20 hours at $15 per hour for each product produced. During the year, 20,500 direct labor hours were actually worked at an average cost of $16 per hour. Using this information and the applicable information in **E 6,** calculate Diekow Production's direct labor rate and efficiency variances for the year.

LO5 Direct Labor Rate and Efficiency Variances

E 8. NEO Foundry, Inc., manufactures castings that other companies use in the production of machinery. For the past two years, NEO's best-selling product has been a casting for an eight-cylinder engine block. Standard direct labor hours per engine block are 1.8 hours. A labor union contract requires that the company pay all direct labor employees $14 per hour. During June, NEO produced 16,500 engine blocks. Actual direct labor hours and costs for the month were 29,900 hours and $433,550, respectively.

1. Compute the direct labor rate variance for eight-cylinder engine blocks during June.
2. Using the same data, compute the direct labor efficiency variance for eight-cylinder engine blocks during June. Check your answer, assuming that the total direct labor cost variance is $17,750 (U).

LO6 Variable Overhead Variances

E 9. At the beginning of last year, Diekow Productions set standards of 10 machine hours at a variable rate of $10 per hour for each product produced. During the year, 10,800 machine hours were used at a cost of $10.20 per hour. Using this information and the applicable information in **E 6,** calculate Diekow Production's variable overhead spending and efficiency variances for the year.

LO6 Fixed Overhead Variances

E 10. At the beginning of last year, Diekow Productions set budgeted fixed overhead costs at $456,000. During the year, actual fixed overhead costs were $500,000. Using this information and the applicable information in **E 6,** calculate Diekow Production's fixed overhead budget and volume variances for the year.

LO6 Variable Overhead Variances for a Service Business

E 11. Design Architects, LLP, billed clients for 6,000 hours of design work for the month. Actual variable overhead costs for the month were $315,000, and 6,250 hours were worked. At the beginning of the year, a variable overhead standard of $50 per design hour had been developed based on a budget of 5,000 design hours each month. Calculate Design Architect's variable overhead spending and efficiency variances for the month.

LO6 Fixed Overhead Variances for a Service Business

E 12. Engineering Associates billed clients for 11,000 hours of engineering work for the month. Actual fixed overhead costs for the month were $435,000, and 11,850 hours were worked. At the beginning of the year, a fixed overhead standard of $40 per design hour had been developed based on a budget of 10,000 engineering hours each month. Calculate Engineering Associates' fixed overhead budget and volume variances for the month.

E 13. **LO6 Manufacturing Overhead Variances**

Cedar Key Company produces handmade clamming buckets and sells them to distributors along the Gulf Coast of Florida. The company incurred $9,400 of actual manufacturing overhead costs ($8,000 variable; $1,400 fixed) in May. Budgeted standard overhead costs for May were $4 of variable overhead costs per direct labor hour and $1,500 of fixed overhead costs. Normal capacity was set at 2,000 direct labor hours per month. In May, the company produced 10,100 clamming buckets by working 1,900 direct labor hours. The time standard is .2 direct labor hour per clamming bucket. Compute (1) the variable overhead spending and efficiency variances and (2) the fixed overhead budget and volume variances for May.

E 14. **LO6 Manufacturing Overhead Variances**

Suncoast Industries uses standard costing and a flexible budget for cost planning and control. Its monthly budget for overhead costs is $200,000 of fixed costs plus $5.20 per machine hour. Monthly normal capacity of 100,000 machine hours is used to compute the standard fixed overhead rate. During December, employees worked 105,000 machine hours. Only 98,500 standard machine hours were allowed for good units produced during the month. Actual overhead costs incurred during December totaled $441,000 of variable costs and $204,500 of fixed costs. Compute (1) the under- or overapplied overhead during December and (2) the variable overhead spending and efficiency variances and the fixed overhead budget and volume variances.

E 15. **LO7 Evaluating Managerial Performance**

Ron LaTulip oversees projects for ACE Construction Company. Recently, the company's controller sent him a performance report regarding the construction of the Campus Highlands Apartment Complex, a project that LaTulip supervised. Included in the report was an unfavorable direct labor efficiency variance of $1,900 for roof structures. What types of information does LaTulip need to analyze before he can respond to this report?

PROBLEMS

P 1. **LO2 Computing and Using Standard Costs**

Prefabricated houses are the specialty of Affordable Homes, Inc., of Corsicana, Texas. Although Affordable Homes produces many models, and customers can even place special orders, the company's best-selling model is the Welcome Home, a three-bedroom, 1,400-square-foot house with an impressive front entrance. In 20x5, the standard costs for the six basic direct materials used in manufacturing the entrance were as follows: wood framing materials, $2,140; deluxe front door, $480; door hardware, $260; exterior siding, $710; electrical materials, $580; and interior finishing materials, $1,520. Three types of direct labor are used to build the entrance: carpenter, 30 hours at $12 per hour; door specialist, 4 hours at $14 per hour; and electrician, 8 hours at $16 per hour. In 20x5, the company used a manufacturing overhead rate of 40 percent of total direct materials cost.

During 20x6, the cost of wood framing materials is expected to increase by 20 percent, and a deluxe front door will cost $496. The cost of the door hardware will increase by 10 percent, and the cost of electrical materials will increase by 20 percent. Exterior siding cost should decrease by $16 per unit. The cost of interior finishing materials is expected to remain the same. The carpenter's wages will increase by $1 per hour, and the door specialist's wages should remain the same. The electrician's wages will increase by $.50 per hour. Finally, the manufacturing overhead rate will decrease to 25 percent of total direct materials cost.

REQUIRED ▶

1. Compute the total standard cost of direct materials per entrance for 20x5.
2. Using your answer to item 1, compute the total standard unit cost per entrance for 20x5.
3. Compute the total standard unit cost per entrance for 20x6.

P 2. **LO3 Preparing a Flexible Budget and Evaluating Performance**

Home Products Company manufactures a complete line of kitchen glassware. The Beverage Division specializes in 12-ounce drinking glasses. Erin Fisher, the superintendent of the Beverage Division, asked the controller to prepare a report of her division's performance in April 20x4. The following report was handed to her a few days later:

Cost Category (Variable Unit Cost)	Budgeted Costs*	Actual Costs	Difference Under (Over) Budget
Direct materials ($.10)	$ 5,000	$ 4,975	$ 25
Direct labor ($.12)	6,000	5,850	150
Manufacturing overhead			
Variable			
Indirect labor ($.03)	1,500	1,290	210
Supplies ($.02)	1,000	960	40
Heat and power ($.03)	1,500	1,325	175
Other ($.05)	2,500	2,340	160
Fixed			
Heat and power	3,500	3,500	—
Depreciation	4,200	4,200	—
Insurance and taxes	1,200	1,200	—
Other	1,600	1,600	—
Totals	$28,000	$27,240	$760

*Based on normal capacity of 50,000 units.

In discussing the report with the controller, Fisher stated, "Profits have been decreasing in recent months, but this report indicates that our production process is operating efficiently."

REQUIRED

1. Prepare a flexible budget for the Beverage Division using production levels of 45,000 units, 50,000 units, and 55,000 units.
2. What is the flexible budget formula?
3. Assume that the Beverage Division produced 46,560 units in April and that all fixed costs remained constant. Prepare a revised performance report similar to the one above, using actual production in units as a basis for the budget column.
4. Which report is more meaningful for performance evaluation, the original one above or the revised one? Why?

P 3.

LO4 Direct Materials and Direct
LO5 Labor Variances

Winners Trophy Company produces a variety of athletic awards, most of them in the form of trophies. Its deluxe trophy stands three feet tall above the base. The company's direct materials standards for the deluxe trophy include one pound of metal and eight ounces of wood for the base. Standard prices for 20x6 were $3.30 per pound of metal and $.45 per ounce of wood. Direct labor standards for the deluxe trophy specify .2 hour of direct labor in the Molding Department and .4 hour in the Trimming/Finishing Department. Standard direct labor rates are $10.75 per hour in the Molding Department and $12.00 per hour in the Trimming/Finishing Department.

During January 20x6, the company made 16,400 deluxe trophies. Actual production data are as follows:

Direct materials
  Metal   16,640 pounds @ $3.25 per pound
  Wood   131,400 ounces @ $.48 per ounce
Direct labor
  Molding   3,400 hours @ $10.60 per hour
  Trimming/Finishing 6,540 hours @ $12.10 per hour

REQUIRED

1. Compute the direct materials price and quantity variances for metal and wood.
2. Compute the direct labor rate and efficiency variances for the Molding and the Trimming/Finishing Departments.

P 4.

LO4 Direct Materials, Direct Labor,
LO5 and Manufacturing Overhead
LO6 Variances

The Doormat Division of Clean Sweep Company produces all-vinyl mats. Each doormat calls for .4 meter of vinyl material; the material should cost $3.10 per meter. Standard direct labor hours and labor cost per doormat are .2 hour and $1.84 (.2 hour × $9.20 per hour), respectively. Currently, the division's standard variable overhead rate is $1.50 per direct labor hour, and its standard fixed overhead rate is $.80 per direct labor hour.

In August 20x5, the division manufactured and sold 60,000 doormats. During the month, it used 25,200 meters of vinyl material; the total cost of the material was $73,080. The total actual manufacturing overhead costs for August were $28,200, of which $18,200 was variable. The total number of direct labor hours worked was 10,800, and the factory payroll for direct labor for the month was $95,040. Budgeted fixed overhead for August was $9,280. Normal monthly capacity for the year was set at 58,000 doormats.

REQUIRED ▶
1. Compute for August 20x5 the (a) direct materials price variance, (b) direct materials quantity variance, (c) direct labor rate variance, (d) direct labor efficiency variance, (e) variable overhead spending variance, (f) variable overhead efficiency variance, (g) fixed overhead budget variance, and (h) fixed overhead volume variance.
2. Prepare a performance report based on your variance analysis and suggest possible causes for each variance.

P 5.

LO6 Overhead Variances

Celine Corporation's accountant left for vacation before completing the monthly cost variance report. George Celine, the corporation's president, has asked you to complete the report. The following data are available to you (capacities are expressed in machine hours):

Actual machine hours	17,100
Standard machine hours allowed	17,500
Actual variable overhead	a
Standard variable overhead rate	$2.50
Variable overhead spending variance	$ 250 (F)
Variable overhead efficiency variance	b
Actual fixed overhead	c
Budgeted fixed overhead	$153,000
Fixed overhead cost variance	$1,300 (U)
Fixed overhead volume variance	$4,500 (F)
Normal capacity in machine hours	d
Standard fixed overhead rate	e
Fixed overhead applied	f

REQUIRED ▶ Analyze the data and fill in the missing amounts. (**Hint:** Use the structure of Figures 5 and 6 in this chapter to guide your analysis.)

ALTERNATE PROBLEMS

P 6.

LO2 Computing Standard Costs for Direct Materials

TickTock, Ltd., assembles clock movements for grandfather clocks. Each movement has four components: the clock facing, the clock hands, the time movement, and the spring assembly. For the current year, 20x5, the company used the following standard costs: clock facing, $15.90; clock hands, $12.70; time movement, $66.10; and spring assembly, $52.50.

Prices of materials are expected to change in 20x6. TickTock will purchase 60 percent of the facings from Company A at $18.50 each and the other 40 percent from Company B at $18.80 each. The clock hands, which are produced for TickTock by Hardware, Inc., will cost $15.50 per set in 20x6. TickTock will purchase 30 percent of the time movements from Company Q at $68.50 each, 20 percent from Company R at $69.50 each, and 50 percent from Company S at $71.90 each. The manufacturer that supplies TickTock with spring assemblies has announced that it will increase its prices by 20 percent in 20x6.

REQUIRED ▶
1. Determine the total standard direct materials cost per unit for 20x6.
2. Suppose that because TickTock has guaranteed Hardware, Inc., that it would purchase 2,500 sets of clock hands in 20x6, the cost of a set of clock hands has been reduced by 20 percent. Find the standard direct materials cost per clock.
3. Suppose that to avoid the increase in the cost of spring assemblies, TickTock purchased substandard ones from a different manufacturer at $50 each; 20 percent of them turned out to be unusable and cannot be returned. Assuming that all other data remain the same, compute the standard direct materials unit cost. Spread the cost of the defective materials over good units produced.

P 7.

LO4 Direct Materials and Direct
LO5 Labor Variances

Fruit Packaging Company makes plastic baskets for food wholesalers. Each basket requires .8 gram of liquid plastic and .6 gram of an additive that includes color and hardening agents. The standard prices are $.15 per gram of liquid plastic and $.09 per gram of additive. Two kinds of direct labor—molding and trimming/packing—are required to make the baskets. The direct labor time and rate standards for a batch of 100 baskets are as follows: molding, 1.0 hour per batch at an hourly rate of $12; and trimming/packing, 1.2 hours per batch at $10 per hour.

During 20x9, the company produced 48,000 baskets. It used 38,600 grams of liquid plastic at a total cost of $5,404 and 28,950 grams of additive at $2,895. Actual direct labor included 480 hours for molding at a total cost of $5,664 and 560 hours for trimming/packing at $5,656.

REQUIRED
1. Compute the direct materials price and quantity variances for both the liquid plastic and the additive.
2. Compute the direct labor rate and efficiency variances for the molding and trimming/packing processes.

P 8.

LO4 Computing Variances and
LO5 Evaluating Performance
LO6

During 20x6, Biomed Laboratories, Inc., researched and perfected a cure for the common cold. Called Cold-Gone, the product sells for $28.00 per package, each of which contains five tablets. Standard unit costs for this product were developed in late 20x6 for use in 20x7. Per package, the standard unit costs were as follows: chemical ingredients, 6 ounces at $1.00 per ounce; packaging, $1.20; direct labor, .8 hour at $14.00 per hour; standard variable overhead, $4.00 per direct labor hour; and standard fixed overhead, $6.40 per direct labor hour. Normal capacity is 46,875 units per week.

In the first quarter of 20x7, demand for the new product rose well beyond the expectations of management. During those three months, the peak season for colds, the company produced and sold over 500,000 packages of Cold-Gone. During the first week in April, it produced 50,000 packages but used materials for 50,200 packages costing $60,240. It also used 305,000 ounces of chemical ingredients costing $292,800. The total cost of direct labor for the week was $579,600; direct labor hours totaled 40,250. Total variable overhead was $161,100, and total fixed overhead was $242,000. Budgeted fixed overhead for the week was $240,000.

REQUIRED
1. Compute for the first week of April 20x7 (a) all direct materials price variances, (b) all direct materials quantity variances, (c) the direct labor rate variance, (d) the direct labor efficiency variance, (e) the variable overhead spending variance, (f) the variable overhead efficiency variance, (g) the fixed overhead budget variance, and (h) the fixed overhead volume variance.
2. Prepare a performance report based on your variance analysis and suggest possible causes for each significant variance.

SKILLS DEVELOPMENT CASES

Conceptual Analysis

SD 1.

LO3 Using Variance Analysis to Control Costs

Holding down operating costs is an ongoing challenge for managers. The lower the costs a company incurs, the higher its profit will be. But two factors can make a target profit difficult to achieve. First, human error and unexpected machine breakdowns may cause dozens of operating inefficiencies, and each inefficiency will cause costs to rise. Second, a company may control its costs so strictly that it will use cheaper materials or labor, which may cause a decline in the quality of its product or service and in its sales. To control costs and still produce high-quality goods or services, managers must continually assess operating activities by analyzing both financial and nonfinancial data.

Write a one-page paper on how variance analysis helps managers control costs. Focus on both the financial and the nonfinancial data used in standard costing.

SD 2.

LO1 Cost Standards for Service
LO2 Companies: A Comparison

Both ChemLawn <www.chemlawn.com> and United Parcel Service (UPS) <www.ups.com> use truck drivers to deliver services to clients. ChemLawn's drivers use a hose connected to the tanks on their trucks to spray liquid fertilizers and weed killers on clients' lawns. Drivers of UPS trucks deliver packages to residences and businesses. If you were setting cost standards for ChemLawn and UPS, what standards would you set that apply to the drivers, and what cost components would you use? What measures would you use to evaluate the drivers' performance? How would cost standards for these two service companies be similar, and how would they differ? How do cost standards for service companies differ from those of manufacturing companies?

Ethical Dilemma

LO1 **An Ethical Question Involving**
LO2 **Standard Costs**

SD 3. Taylor Industries, Inc., develops standard costs for all its direct materials, direct labor, and manufacturing overhead costs. It uses these costs for pricing products, costing inventories, and evaluating the performance of purchasing and production managers. It updates standard costs whenever costs, prices, or rates change by 3 percent or more. It also reviews and updates all standard costs each December; this practice provides current standards appropriate for use in valuing year-end inventories on the company's financial statements.

Jody Elgar is in charge of standard costing at Taylor Industries. On November 30, 20x6, she received a memo from the chief financial officer informing her that Taylor Industries was considering purchasing another company and that she and her staff were to postpone adjusting standard costs until late February; they were instead to concentrate on analyzing the proposed purchase.

In the third week of November, prices on over 20 of Taylor Industries' direct materials had been reduced by 10 percent or more, and a new labor union contract had reduced several categories of labor rates. A revision of standard costs in December would have resulted in lower valuations of inventories, higher cost of goods sold due to inventory write-downs, and lower net income for the year. Elgar believed the company was facing an operating loss and that the assignment to evaluate the proposed purchase was designed primarily to keep her staff from revising and lowering standard costs. She questioned the chief financial officer about the assignment and reiterated the need for updating the standard costs but was again told to ignore the update and concentrate on the proposed purchase. Elgar and her staff were relieved of the assignment in early February. The purchase never materialized.

Assess Jody Elgar's actions in this situation. Did this manager follow all ethical paths to solving the problem? What are the consequences of failing to adjust the standard costs?

Research Activity

LO2 **Standard Costs and Variance**
LO3 **Analysis**

SD 4. Domino's Pizza <www.dominos.com> is a major purveyor of home-delivered pizzas. Although customers can pick up their orders at the shops where Domino's makes its pizzas, employees deliver most orders to customers' homes, and they use their own cars to do it.

Specify what standard costing for a Domino's pizza shop would entail. Where would you obtain the information for determining the cost standards? In what ways would the standards help in managing a pizza shop? If necessary to gain a better understanding of the operation, visit a pizzeria. (It does not have to be a Domino's.)

Group Activity: Have students work in groups to complete **SD 4.** Select one person from each group to report the group's findings to the class.

Decision-Making Practice

LO5 **Standard Costing in a Service**
LO6 **Company**

SD 5. Annuity Life Insurance Company (ALIC) markets several types of life insurance policies, but P20A—a permanent, 20-year life annuity policy—is its most popular. This policy sells in $10,000 increments and features variable percentages of whole life insurance and single-payment annuities, depending on the policyholder's needs and age. ALIC devotes an entire department to supporting and marketing the P20A policy. Because both the support staff and salespersons contribute to each P20A policy, ALIC categorizes them as direct labor for purposes of variance analysis, cost control, and performance evaluation. For unit costing, each $10,000 increment is considered one unit; thus, a $90,000 policy is counted as nine units. Standard unit cost information for January is as follows:

Direct labor
    Policy support staff
        3 hours at $12.00 per hour $ 36.00
    Policy salesperson
        8.5 hours at $14.20 per hour   120.70
Operating overhead
    Variable operating overhead
        11.5 hours at $26.00 per hour   299.00
    Fixed operating overhead
        11.5 hours at $18.00 per hour   207.00
Standard unit cost $662.70

Actual costs incurred for the 265 units sold during January were as follows:

Direct labor
    Policy support staff
        848 hours at $12.50 per hour $10,600.00
    Policy salespersons
        2,252.5 hours at $14.00 per hour   31,535.00
Operating overhead
    Variable operating overhead   78,440.00
    Fixed operating overhead   53,400.00

Normal monthly capacity is 260 units, and the budgeted fixed operating overhead for January was $53,820.

1. Compute the standard hours allowed in January for policy support staff and policy salespersons.
2. What should the total standard costs for January have been? What were the total actual costs that the company incurred in January? Compute the total cost variance for the month.
3. Compute the direct labor rate and efficiency variances for policy support staff and policy salespersons.
4. Compute the variable and fixed operating overhead variances for January.
5. Identify possible causes for each variance and suggest possible solutions.

MANAGERIAL REPORTING AND ANALYSIS CASES

Interpreting Management Reports

MRA 1.
LO3 Flexible Budgets and Performance Evaluation

Cassen Realtors, Inc., specializes in the sale of residential properties. It earns its revenue by charging a percentage of the sales price. Commissions for salespersons, listing agents, and listing companies are its main costs. Business has improved steadily over the last ten years. Bonnie Cassen, the managing partner of Cassen Realtors, receives a report summarizing the company's performance each year. The report for the most recent year appears at the top of the facing page.

1. Analyze the performance report. What does it say about the company's performance? Is the performance report reliable? Explain your answer.
2. Calculate the budgeted selling fee and budgeted variable costs per sale.
3. Prepare a performance report using a flexible budget based on the actual number of sales.
4. Analyze the report you prepared in 3. What does it say about the company's performance? Is the performance report reliable? Explain your answer.
5. What recommendations would you make to improve the company's performance next year?

Cassen Realtors, Inc.
Performance Report
For the Year Ended December 31, 20x5

	Budgeted*	Actual†	Difference Under (Over) Budget
Total selling fees	$2,052,000	$2,242,200	($190,200)
Less variable costs			
Sales commissions	$1,102,950	$1,205,183	($102,233)
Automobile	36,000	39,560	(3,560)
Advertising	93,600	103,450	(9,850)
Home repairs	77,400	89,240	(11,840)
General overhead	656,100	716,970	(60,870)
	$1,966,050	$2,154,403	($188,353)
Less fixed costs			
general overhead	60,000	62,300	(2,300)
Total costs	$2,026,050	$2,216,703	($190,653)
Operating income	$ 25,950	$ 25,497	$ 453

*Budgeted data are based on 180 units sold.
†Actual data of 200 units sold.

Formulating Management Reports

MRA 2.
LO3 Preparing Performance
LO5 Reports
LO6

Troy Corrente, the president of Forest Valley Spa, is concerned about the spa's operating performance during March 20x6. He budgeted his costs carefully so that he could reduce the 20x6 membership fees. He now needs to evaluate those costs to make sure the spa's profits are at the level he expected.

He has asked you, the spa's controller, to prepare a performance report on labor and overhead costs for March 20x6. He also wants you to analyze the report and suggest possible causes for any problems you find. He wants to attend to any problems quickly, so he has asked you to submit your report as soon as possible. The following information for the month is available to you:

	Budgeted Costs	Actual Costs
Variable costs		
Operating labor	$10,880	$12,150
Utilities	2,880	3,360
Repairs and maintenance	5,760	7,140
Fixed costs		
Depreciation, equipment	2,600	2,680
Rent	3,280	3,280
Other	1,704	1,860
Totals	$27,104	$30,470

Corrente's budget allows for eight employees to work 160 hours each per month. During March, nine employees worked an average of 150 hours each.

1. Answer the following questions:
   a. Why are you preparing this performance report?
   b. Who will use the report?
   c. What information do you need to develop the report? How will you obtain that information?
   d. When are the performance report and the analysis needed?
2. With the limited information available to you, compute the labor rate variance, the labor efficiency variance, and the variable and fixed overhead variances.
3. Prepare a performance report for the spa for March 20x6. Analyze the report and suggest causes for any problems that you find.

International Company

MRA 3.

LO3 Variance Analysis
LO4
LO5

Ying Zsoa recently became the controller of a joint venture in Hong Kong. He has been using standard costing to plan and control the company's activities. In a meeting with the budget team, which includes managers and employees from purchasing, engineering, and production, Zsoa asked the team members to share any operating problems they had encountered during the last quarter. He explained that his staff would use this information in analyzing the causes of significant cost variances that had occurred in the quarter.

For each of the following situations, identify the direct materials and/or direct labor variance(s) that could be affected and indicate the whether the variances are favorable or unfavorable:

1. The production department used highly skilled, higher-paid workers.
2. Machines were improperly adjusted.
3. Direct labor personnel worked more carefully to manufacture the product.
4. The product design engineer substituted a direct material that was less expensive and of lower quality.
5. The Purchasing Department bought higher-quality materials at a higher price.
6. A major supplier used a less-expensive mode of transportation to deliver the raw materials.
7. Work was halted for two hours because of a power disruption.

Excel Spreadsheet Analysis

MRA 4.

LO3 Developing a Flexible Budget
LO6 and Analyzing Overhead Variances

Ezelda Marva is the controller at FH Industries. She has asked you, her new assistant, to analyze the following data related to projected and actual overhead costs for October 20x8:

	Standard Variable Costs per Machine Hour (MH)	Actual Variable Costs in October
Indirect materials and supplies	$1.10	$ 2,380
Indirect machine setup labor	2.50	5,090
Materials handling	1.40	3,950
Maintenance and repair	1.50	2,980
Utilities	.80	1,490
Miscellaneous	.10	200
Totals	$7.40	$16,090

	Budgeted Fixed Overhead	Actual Fixed Overhead in October
Supervisory salaries	$ 3,630	$ 3,630
Machine depreciation	8,360	8,580
Other	1,210	1,220
Totals	$13,200	$13,430

For October, the number of good units produced was used to compute the 2,100 standard machine hours allowed.

1. Prepare a monthly flexible budget for operating activity at 2,000 machine hours, 2,200 machine hours, and 2,500 machine hours.
2. Develop a flexible budget formula.
3. The company's normal operating capacity is 2,200 machine hours per month. Compute the fixed overhead rate at this level of activity. Then break the rate down into individual rates for each element of fixed overhead.
4. Prepare a detailed comparative cost analysis for October. Include all variable and fixed overhead costs. Format your analysis by using columns for the following five elements: cost category, cost per machine hour, costs applied, actual costs incurred, and variance.
5. Develop a manufacturing overhead variance analysis for October that identifies the variable overhead spending and efficiency variances and the fixed overhead budget and volume variances.
6. Prepare an analysis of the variances. Could a manager control some of the fixed costs? Defend your answer.

Internet Case

MRA 5.
LO1 Resources for Developing Cost Standards

Suppose you have recently taken a job at a company that manufactures parts for automobiles. You have been assigned the task of developing manufacturing cost standards. You want to gather as much background information as you can about these standards. Using a standard search engine, such as Google, search the Internet for web sites that provide information about cost standards, manufacturing, and automobile manufacturers. Visit the sites that look most interesting. List the five sites you think are most useful. Bring your list to class and compare your findings with those of your classmates.

23

Chapter 23 discusses performance measurement and describes the role of the balanced scorecard, responsibility accounting, and economic value added as they relate to performance management and evaluation.

Performance Management and Evaluation

Learning Objectives

LO1 Describe how the balanced scorecard aligns performance with organizational goals, and explain the role of the balanced scorecard in the management cycle.

LO2 Discuss performance measurement, and state the issues that affect management's ability to measure performance.

LO3 Define *responsibility accounting,* and describe the role that responsibility centers play in performance management and evaluation.

LO4 Prepare performance reports for cost centers using flexible budgets and for profit centers using variable costing.

LO5 Prepare performance reports for investment centers using traditional measures of return on investment and residual income and the newer measure of economic value added.

LO6 Explain how properly linked performance incentives and measures add value for all stakeholders in performance management and evaluation.

DECISION POINT
A MANAGER'S FOCUS

Vail Resorts <www.vailresorts.com> Vail Resorts PEAKS is an all-in-one card for guests of four Colorado vacation spots: Vail, Breckenridge, Keystone, and Beaver Creek. Guests at all resorts in these areas can use the PEAKS card to pay for lift tickets, skiing and snowboarding lessons, equipment rentals, dining, and more. They like its convenience and its program for earning points toward free or reduced-rate lift tickets, dining, and lodging. They enroll in the PEAKS system by filling out a one-page form that asks for their name, street address, email address, phone number, date of birth, credit card number, and a signed charge privilege authorization. Data for up to eight family members may be linked into one membership account. Each family member receives a bar-coded picture identification card, usually worn on a souvenir cord around the guest's neck, that is scanned each time he or she rides the ski lifts, attends ski school, or charges purchases, dining, or lodging.[1] How can the managers of the Vail Resorts Management Company use the PEAKS card and its integrated database to manage and evaluate the performance of their resorts better?

Managers like PEAKS because it enables them to collect huge amounts of information in a simple way and because the data have so many uses. New data are entered in the system each time a guest's card is scanned. Those data then become part of an integrated management information system that allows managers to measure and control costs, quality, and performance in all four resort areas. The system's abil-

How do managers at Vail Resorts evaluate for peak performance?

ity to store both financial and nonfinancial data about all aspects of the resorts enables managers to learn about and balance the interests of all the company's stakeholders: financial (investors), learning and growth (employees), internal business processes, and customers. The managers can then use the information to answer traditional financial questions about measuring cost of sales and valuing inventory (such as food ingredients in its restaurants and merchandise in its shops) and to obtain performance information about the resorts' activities, products, services, and customers. In addition, managers and employees receive timely feedback about their performance measures so that they can continuously improve.

Organizational Goals and the Balanced Scorecard

LO1 Describe how the balanced scorecard aligns performance with organizational goals, and explain the role of the balanced scorecard in the management cycle.

RELATED TEXT ASSIGNMENTS
Q: 1, 2, 3, 4
SE: 1
E: 1, 2
SD: 1
MRA: 1

The **balanced scorecard**, developed by Robert S. Kaplan and David P. Norton, is a framework that links the perspectives of an organization's four basic stakeholder groups—financial (investors), learning and growth (employees), internal business processes, and customers—with the organization's mission and vision, performance measures, strategic plan, and resources. To succeed, an organization must add value for all groups in both the short and the long terms. Thus, an organization will determine each group's objectives and translate them into performance measures that have specific, quantifiable performance targets. Ideally, managers should be able to see how their actions contribute to the achievement of organizational goals and understand how their compensation is related to their actions. The balanced scorecard assumes that an organization will get only what it measures.

The Balanced Scorecard and the Management Cycle

We will use the Decision Point about the PEAKS card to illustrate the use of the balanced scorecard in the management cycle.

■ **Planning** During the planning stage, the balanced scorecard provides a framework that enables managers to translate their organization's vision and strategy into operational terms. Managers evaluate the company vision from the perspective of each stakeholder group and seek to answer one key question for each group:

- **Financial (investors):** To achieve our organization's vision, how should we appear to our shareholders?
- **Learning and growth (employees):** To achieve our organization's vision, how should we sustain our ability to improve and change?
- **Internal business processes:** To succeed, at what business processes must our organization excel?
- **Customers:** To achieve our organization's vision, how should we appear to our customers?

These key questions align the organization's strategy from all perspectives. The answers to the questions result in performance objectives that are mutually beneficial to all stakeholders. Once the organization's objectives are set, managers can select performance measures and set performance targets to translate objectives into an action plan.

For example, if Vail Resorts' collective vision and strategy is customer satisfaction, its managers might establish the following overall objectives:

Perspective	Objective
Financial (investors)	Customer satisfaction means revenue growth.
Learning and growth (employees)	Customer satisfaction means cross-trained, customer service–oriented employees.
Internal business processes	Customer satisfaction means reliable products and short delivery cycles.
Customers	Customer satisfaction means keeping customer loyalty through repeat visits and redeemed PEAKS points.

These overall objectives are then translated into specific performance objectives and measures for managers. For example, a ski lift manager's performance objectives might be measured in terms of the following:

● **Stop and Think!**
On which perspective do most businesses focus?
Most businesses focus on the financial perspective. ■

www.vailresorts.com

KEY POINT: The alignment of an organization's strategy with all the perspectives of the balanced scorecard results in performance objectives that benefit all stakeholders.

VIDEO CASE

Harley-Davidson, Inc.
<www.harley-davidson.com>

OBJECTIVES

- To describe the role a performance measurement and evaluation system plays in business today.
- To become familiar with how the balanced scorecard provides a framework for performance management and accountability.
- To show how responsibility accounting is useful in performance evaluation.
- To understand the value of linking organizational goals, objectives, measures, targets, and performance-based pay.

BACKGROUND FOR THE CASE

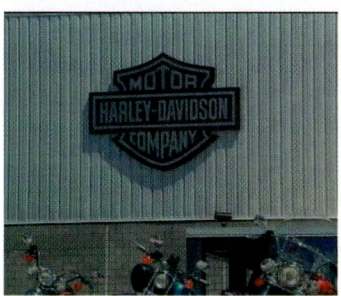

Harley-Davidson continues to excel at providing motorcyclists and the general public an expanding line of motorcycles and branded products and services. Strong sales of motorcycles, apparel, parts, insurance, product licensing, and financial services have enabled the company to sustain and improve on its success. Harley's journey to success can be charted through its performance management and evaluation system. Performance measures like market share, units shipped, revenue, operating profit, and number of employees illustrate its remarkable turnaround. In the 1980s, Harley rose above near bankruptcy to emerge today as the internationally recognized company that "fulfills dreams through the experience of motorcycling." Like many other companies, Harley-Davidson uses a performance management and evaluation system to identify how well it is doing, where it is going, and what improvements will make it more profitable.

For more information about Harley-Davidson, Inc., visit the company's web site directly or access it through the Needles Accounting Resource Center Web Site at http://accounting.college.hmco.com/students.

REQUIRED

View the video on Harley-Davidson that accompanies this book. As you are watching the video, take notes related to the following questions:

1. What role does performance measurement and evaluation play in business today?
2. In your own words, describe the balanced scorecard. Who are its stakeholders?
3. Define responsibility accounting. Why is it useful in performance evaluation?
4. Explain how Harley uses Performance Effectiveness Process (PEP) to link performance goals, objectives, measures, and targets. Why does this linking process improve the effectiveness of its performance management and evaluation system?

- **Financial (investors):** hourly lift cost, lift ticket sales in dollars and in units
- **Learning and growth (employees):** number of cross-trained tasks per employee, employee turnover
- **Internal business processes:** number of accident-free days, number and cost of mechanical breakdowns, average lift cycle time (that is, the time between getting in line to ride the ski lift and completing the ski run)
- **Customers:** average number of ski runs per daily lift ticket, number of repeat customers, number of PEAKS points redeemed

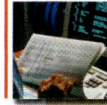

FOCUS ON BUSINESS PRACTICE

How Many Stakeholder Groups Has Harley Identified?

Harley-Davidson, Inc., <www.harley-davidson.com> has identified not four but six stakeholder groups. In addition to balancing the needs of investors, employees, business processes, and customers, Harley managers also consider the interests of the community at large and government. Taking a broader perspective enables the company to sustain its competitive advantage and implement effective employee reward programs.[2]

Figure 1 summarizes the planning stage of the management cycle: Vail Resorts' managers link their organization's vision and strategy to objectives, then link the objectives to logical performance measures, and, finally, set performance targets. As a result, a ski lift manager will have a variety of performance measures that balance the perspectives and needs of all stakeholders.

■ **EXECUTING** Managers use the mutually agreed-on strategic objectives for the entire organization as the basis for decision making within their individual areas

FIGURE 1
Sample Balanced Scorecard of Linked Objectives, Performance Measures, and Targets

Financial (Investors') Perspective

Objective	Performance Measure	Target
Sustain revenue growth	Annual percentage growth in lift-ticket sales	Increase number of lift tickets sold by at least 10% per year

Customer Perspective

Objective	Performance Measure	Target
Customer retention	PEAKS points earned	Increase PEAKS points earned by at least 10% per year

CUSTOMER SATISFACTION

Internal Business Processes Perspective

Objective	Performance Measure	Target
Shorten cycle times	Ski-lift cycle time	Decrease average ski-lift cycle time by 10% per year

Learning and Growth (Employees') Perspective

Objective	Performance Measure	Target
Multitasked employees	Number of tasks in which employees are cross-trained	Each employee cross-trained in at least five tasks

Source: Adapted from Robert S. Kaplan and David P. Norton, "Using the Balanced Scorecard as a Strategic Management System," *Harvard Business Review*, January–February 1996.

ENRICHMENT NOTE: If managers want results, they must understand the causal relationship between their actions and the organization's overall performance. If the relationship can be measured and tracked, it can be improved.

of responsibility. This practice ensures that they consider the needs of all stakeholder groups and how measuring and managing performance for some stakeholder groups can lead to improved performance for another stakeholder group. Specifically, improving performance of internal business processes and learning and growth will lead to improvements for customers, which in turn will result in improved financial performance. For example, when making decisions about available ski lift capacity, the ski lift manager at Vail Resorts will balance such factors as lift ticket sales, snow conditions, equipment reliability, trained staff availability, and length of wait for ski lifts.

When managers understand the causal and linked relationship between their actions and their company's overall performance, they can see new ways to be more effective. For example, a ski lift manager may hypothesize that short waiting lines for the ski lifts would improve customer satisfaction and lead to more visits to the ski lift. The manager could test this possible cause-and-effect relationship by measuring and tracking the length of ski lift waiting lines and the number of visits to the ski lift. If a causal relationship exists, the manager can improve the performance of the ski lift operation by doing everything possible to ensure that waiting lines are short because a quicker ride to the top will result in improved results for the operation and for other perspectives as well.

■ **REVIEWING** Managers will review financial and nonfinancial results frequently during the year, at year end, and over longer periods to evaluate their strategies in

FIGURE 2
The Balanced Scorecard and the Management Cycle

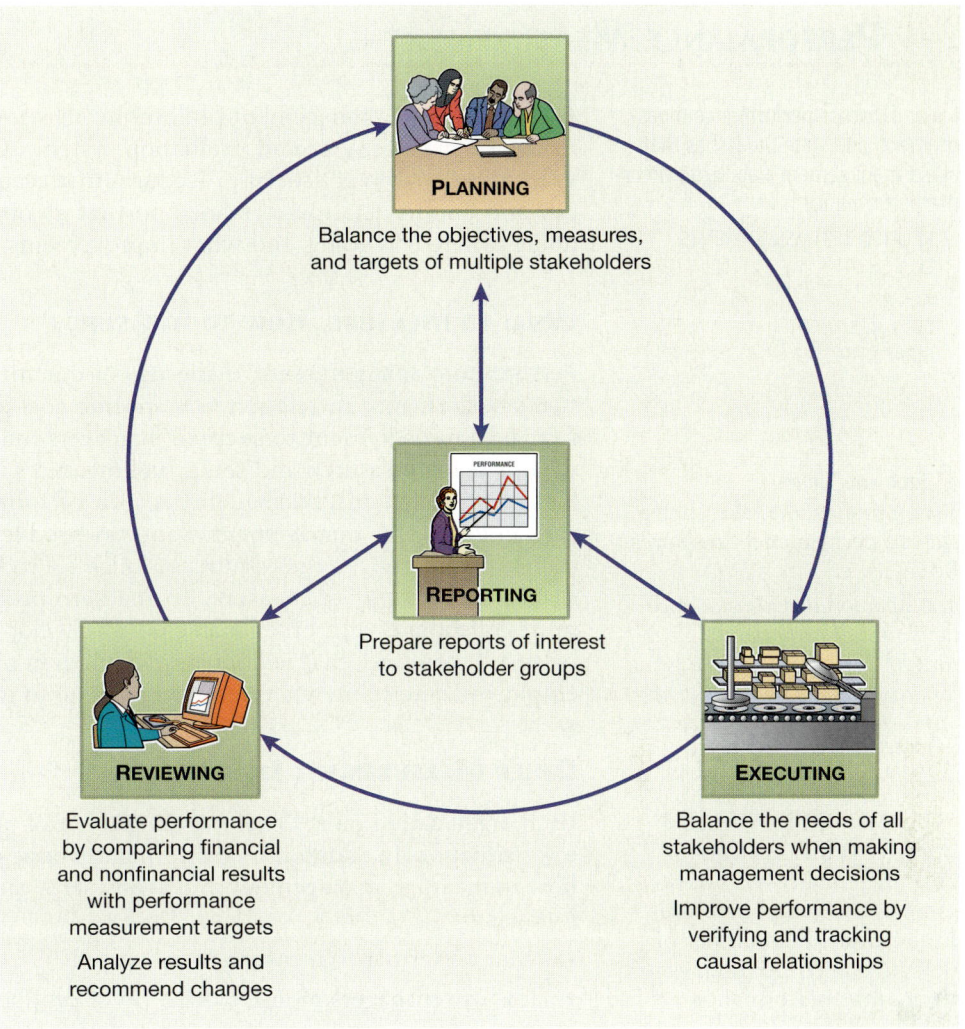

meeting the objectives and performance targets set during the planning stage. They will compare performance objectives and targets with actual results to determine if the targets were met, what measures need to be changed, and what strategies or objectives need revision. For example, the ski lift manager at Vail Resorts would analyze the reasons for performance gaps and make recommendations to improve the performance for the ski lift area.

■ **REPORTING** Finally, during the reporting stage of the management cycle, a variety of reports are prepared. For example, the database makes it possible to prepare financial performance reports, customer PEAKS statements, internal business process reports for targeted performance measures and results, and performance appraisals of individual employees. Such reports enable managers to monitor and evaluate performance measures that add value for stakeholder groups.

As you can see in Figure 2, the balanced scorecard adds dimension to the management cycle. Managers plan, execute, review, and report on the organization's performance from multiple perspectives. By balancing the needs of all stakeholders, managers are more likely to achieve their objectives in both the short and the long terms.

Check out ACE for a Review Quiz at http://accounting.college.hmco.com/students.

PERFORMANCE MEASUREMENT

LO2 Discuss performance measurement, and state the issues that affect management's ability to measure performance.

RELATED TEXT ASSIGNMENTS
Q: 5
E: 3, 4
SD: 1, 4, 5
MRA: 2, 3

As a company's management philosophy changes, so must the measures in its performance management and evaluation system. A **performance management and evaluation system** is a set of procedures that account for and report on both financial and nonfinancial performance, so that a company can identify how well it is doing, where it is going, and what improvements will make it more profitable.

WHAT TO MEASURE, HOW TO MEASURE

Performance measurement is the use of quantitative tools to gauge an organization's performance in relation to a specific goal or an expected outcome. For performance measurement to succeed, managers must be able to distinguish between what is being measured and the actual measures used to monitor performance. For instance, product or service quality is *not* a performance measure. It is part of a management strategy: management wants to produce the highest-quality product or service possible, given the resources available. Product or service quality thus is what management *wants* to measure. To measure product or service quality, managers must collaborate with other managers to develop a group of measures, such as the balanced scorecard, that will identify changes in product or service quality and help employees determine what needs to be done to improve quality.

● **STOP AND THINK!**
When managers make changes, should performance measures be reviewed?
Yes. Appropriate financial and nonfinancial performance measures are key to yielding the performance results managers want. ■

OTHER MEASUREMENT ISSUES

Each organization must develop a unique set of performance measures appropriate to its situation. In addition to answering the basic questions of what to measure and how to measure, management must consider a variety of other issues, including the following:

- What performance measures can be used?
- How can managers monitor the level of product or service quality?
- How can managers monitor production and other business processes to identify areas that need improvement?
- How can managers measure customer satisfaction?
- How can managers monitor financial performance?
- Are there other stakeholders to whom a manager is accountable?
- What performance measures do government entities impose on the company?
- How can a manager measure the company's effect on the environment?

STUDY NOTE: What a manager is measuring—for example, quality—is not the same as the actual measures—for example, the number of defective units per hour—used to monitor performance.

FOCUS ON INTERNATIONAL BUSINESS

"Old" Doesn't Mean "Out-of-Date."

The *tableau de bord*, or "dashboard," was developed by French process engineers around 1900 as a concise performance measurement system that helped managers understand the cause-and-effect relationships between business actions and performance. The indicators, both financial and nonfinancial, allowed managers at any level to monitor their progress in terms of the mission and objectives of their unit and their company overall.

Like a set of nested Russian dolls, each unit's key success factors and key performance indicators were integrated with those of other units with which it was interdependent and needed to collaborate. The dashboard continues to encourage a performance measurement system that focuses on and supports an organization's strategic plan.[3]

 Check out ACE for a Review Quiz at http://accounting.college.hmco.com/students.

Responsibility Accounting

LO3 Define *responsibility accounting,* and describe the role that responsibility centers play in performance management and evaluation.

RELATED TEXT ASSIGNMENTS
Q: 6, 7, 8, 9, 10, 11, 12
SE: 2, 3
E: 5, 6, 7
P: 1, 3, 7
SD: 2, 5
MRA: 2

🔴 **STOP AND THINK!**
How should managers' performance be evaluated?
Evaluation should be based on how managers perform their assigned responsibilities. ■

As part of their performance management systems, many organizations assign resources to specific areas of responsibility and track how the managers of those areas use those resources. For example, DaimlerChrysler Corp. assigns resources to its Jeep, Eagle, and Mercedes automotive divisions and holds the managers of those divisions responsible for generating revenue and managing costs. In addition, the company may give the managers resources to invest in assets that will support the growth of their divisions. Within each division, other managers are assigned responsibility for such tasks as manufacturing subassemblies or assembling automobiles. All managers at all levels are then evaluated in terms of their ability to manage their areas of responsibility in keeping with organizational goals.

To assist in performance management and evaluation, many organizations use responsibility accounting. **Responsibility accounting** is an information system that classifies data according to areas of responsibility and reports each area's activities by including only the revenue, cost, and resource categories that the assigned manager can control. A **responsibility center** is an organizational unit whose manager has been assigned the responsibility of managing a portion of the organization's resources. The activity of a responsibility center dictates the extent of a manager's responsibility.

TYPES OF RESPONSIBILITY CENTERS

There are five types of responsibility centers: (1) cost centers, (2) discretionary cost centers, (3) revenue centers, (4) profit centers, and (5) investment centers.

www.daimlerchrysler.com
www.apple.com
www.kraft.com

■ **COST CENTERS** A responsibility center whose manager is accountable only for controllable costs that have well-defined relationships between the center's resources and products or services is called a **cost center**. Manufacturing companies such as DaimlerChrysler, Apple Computer, and Kraft use cost centers to manage assembly plants, where the relationship between the costs of resources (direct material, direct labor) and the resulting products is well defined.

Nonmanufacturing organizations use cost centers to manage activities in which resources are clearly linked with a service provided at no additional charge. For example, in nursing homes and hospitals, there is a clear relationship between the costs of food and direct labor and the number of inpatient meals served.

The performance of a cost center is usually evaluated by comparing an activity's actual cost with its budgeted cost and analyzing the resulting variances. You may recall this performance evaluation process from the chapter on standard costing.

■ **DISCRETIONARY COST CENTERS** A responsibility center whose manager is accountable for costs only and in which the relationship between resources and products or services produced is not well defined is called a **discretionary cost center**. Units that perform administrative activities, such as accounting, human resources, and legal services, are typical examples of discretionary cost centers. These centers, like cost centers, have approved budgets that set spending limits.

www.monsanto.com
www.intel.com

Because the spending and use of resources in discretionary cost centers are not clearly linked to the production of a product or service, cost-based measures cannot usually be used to evaluate performance (although such centers are penalized if they exceed their approved budgets). For example, among the performance measures used to evaluate the research and development activities at manufacturing companies such as DaimlerChrysler, Monsanto, and Intel are the number of patents obtained and the number of cost-saving innovations that are developed. At service

national.unitedway.org

organizations, such as the United Way, a common measure of administrative activities is how low their costs are as a percentage of total contributions.

■ **REVENUE CENTERS** A responsibility center whose manager is accountable primarily for revenue and whose success is based on its ability to generate revenue is called a **revenue center**. Examples of revenue centers are Hertz's national car reservation center and the clothing retailer Nordstrom's ecommerce order department. A revenue center's performance is usually evaluated by comparing its actual revenue with its budgeted revenue and analyzing the resulting variances. Performance measures at both manufacturing and service organizations may include sales dollars, number of customer sales, or sales revenue per minute.

www.hertz.com
www.nordstrom.com

■ **PROFIT CENTERS** A responsibility center whose manager is accountable for both revenue and costs and for the resulting operating income is called a **profit center**. A good example is the local store of a national chain such as Wal-Mart, Kinko's, or Jiffy Lube. The performance of a profit center is usually evaluated by comparing the figures in its actual income statement with the figures in its master or flexible budget income statement. You may recall this type of comparison from our discussion in previous chapters.

www.walmart.com
www.kinkos.com
www.jiffylube.com

■ **INVESTMENT CENTERS** A responsibility center whose manager is accountable for profit generation and can also make significant decisions about the resources the center uses is called an **investment center**. For example, the president of DaimlerChrysler's Jeep Division, the president of Harley-Davidson's Buell subsidiary, and the president of Brinker International's Chili's Grill and Bar Concept can control revenues, costs, and the investment of assets to achieve organizational goals. The performance of these centers is evaluated using such measures as return on investment, residual income, and economic value added. These measures are used in all types of organizations, both manufacturing and nonmanufacturing, and are discussed later in this chapter.

www.harley-davidson.com
www.brinker.com

The key characteristics of the five types of responsibility centers are summarized in Table 1.

ORGANIZATIONAL STRUCTURE AND PERFORMANCE MANAGEMENT

Much can be learned about an organization by examining how its managers organize activities and resources. A company's organizational structure formalizes its lines of managerial authority and control. An **organization chart** is a visual representation of an organization's hierarchy of responsibility for the purposes of management control. Within an organization chart, the five types of responsibility centers are arranged by level of management authority and control.

A responsibility accounting system establishes a communications network within an organization that is ideal for gathering and reporting information about the operations of each area of responsibility. The system is used to prepare budgets by responsibility area and to report the actual results of each responsibility center. The report for a responsibility center should contain only the costs, revenues, and resources that the manager of the center can control. Such costs and revenues are called **controllable costs and revenues** because they result from a manager's actions, influence, or decisions. A responsibility accounting system ensures that managers will not be held responsible for items they cannot change.

FOCUS ON BUSINESS TECHNOLOGY

Keep It Simple!

There is a new profession: information architect. An information architect develops meaningful ways to report information in print and on the web. In *Understanding USA*, Richard Saul Wurman and a team of twelve information architects have created a graph-rich book (downloadable at www.understandingusa.com and for sale in bookstores) that is the result of a $1 million project backed by many blue-chip organizations. The team's message to managers: Keep it simple. If you define what is important and what you can omit and if you stay honest, reporting information becomes simple.[4]

Figure 4
Factors That Affect the Return on Investment Calculation

```
                                    ROI =
                              Operating Income
                              ────────────────
                               Assets Invested
                        ┌───────────┴───────────┐
              Profit Margin =              Asset Turnover =
              Operating Income                   Sales
              ────────────────              ────────────────
                   Sales                     Assets Invested
           ┌─────────┴─────────┐         ┌─────────┴─────────┐
    Operating Income =       Sales =                      Assets =
         Sales               Price        Sales            Fixed
           −                   X                             +
    Controllable costs       Volume                       Current
     ┌─────┴─────┐              │                       ┌─────┴─────┐
                                                                    Cash
                Controllable   Unit Selling                      + Receivables
    Sales          Costs         Prices      Fixed Assets        + Inventory
                                                                 + Prepaids
                     │             │
                 Selling and
    Cost of      Administrative   Product
  Goods Sold      Expenses        Volume
                                    │
                                 Product
                                Sales Mix
```

based on residual income for Consuelo Jorges, the president of the Café Cubano Restaurant Division, is shown in Exhibit 5. Assume that the president's residual income performance target is to exceed a 20 percent return on assets invested in the division. Note that the division's residual income is $450, which was lower than the $690 projected in the master budget.

Comparisons with other residual income figures will strengthen the analysis. To add context to the analysis of the division and its manager, questions such as the following need to be answered: How did the division's residual income for this year compare to those of previous years? Did the actual residual income exceed the budgeted residual income? How did this division's residual income compare with amounts generated by other investment centers of the company?

Caution is called for when using residual income to compare investment centers within a company. For their residual income figures to be comparable, all investment centers must have equal access to resources and similar asset investment bases. Some managers may be able to produce larger residual incomes simply because their investment centers are larger rather than because their performance is better. Like ROI, RI has some flaws.

EXHIBIT 5
Performance Report Based on Residual Income for the Café Cubano Restaurant Division

	Actual Results	Variance	Master Budget
Operating income	$610	$280 (U)	$ 890
Assets invested	$800	$200 (F)	$1,000
Desired ROI			20%
Performance measures			
ROI	76%	13% (U)	89%
Residual income	$450	$240 (U)	$ 690

Residual Income = Operating Income − (Desired ROI × Assets Invested)
$890 − 20%($1,000) = $690
$610 − 20%($800) = $450

ECONOMIC VALUE ADDED

More and more businesses are using the shareholder wealth created by an investment center, or the **economic value added (EVA)**, as an indicator of performance. The calculation of EVA, a registered trademark of the consulting firm Stern Stewart & Company, can be quite complex because it makes various cost of capital and accounting principles adjustments. You will learn more about the cost of capital in the chapter that discusses capital investment decisions. However, for the purposes of computing EVA, the **cost of capital** is the minimum desired rate of return on an investment, such as assets invested in an investment center.

Basically, the computation of EVA is similar to the computation of residual income, except that after-tax operating income is used instead of pretax operating income, and a cost of capital percentage is multiplied by the center's invested assets less current liabilities instead of a desired ROI percentage being multiplied by invested assets. Also, like residual income, the economic value added is expressed in dollars. The formula is:

EVA = After-Tax Operating Income − Cost of Capital in Dollars

or

EVA = After-Tax Operating Income − [Cost of Capital × (Total Assets − Current Liabilities)]

A very basic computation of economic value added for Consuelo Jorges, the president of the Café Cubano Restaurant Division, is shown in Exhibit 6. The report

> **STOP AND THINK!**
> When is the EVA a complex measure?
> *EVA is complex because it is a composite index drawn from many causal relationships and independent financial elements.*

EXHIBIT 6
Performance Report Based on Economic Value Added for the Café Cubano Restaurant Division

	Actual Results	Variance	Master Budget
Performance measures			
ROI	76%	13% (U)	89%
Residual income	$450	$240 (U)	$690
Economic value added	$334		

Economic Value Added = After-Tax Operating Income − [Cost of Capital × (Total Assets − Current Liabilities)]
$400 − 12% ($800 − $250) = $334

FIGURE 5
Factors Affecting the Computation of Economic Value Added

```
Net Operating Income After Taxes
 − Cost of Capital in Dollars
 = Economic Value Added
```

- Net Operating Income After Taxes = Net Operating Income Before Taxes − Taxes
  - Taxes
  - Net Operating Income Before Taxes = Net Sales − Operating Costs
    - Operating Costs
      - Cost of Goods Sold
      - Selling and Administrative Expenses
    - Net Sales = Selling Price × Volume
      - Selling Price
      - Volume
- Cost of Capital in Dollars = Percentage Cost of Capital × (Total Assets − Current Liabilities)
  - Percentage Cost of Capital
  - Total Assets − Current Liabilities
    - Total Assets = Current Assets + Fixed Assets + Other Assets
    - Current Liabilities

assumes that the division's after-tax operating income is $400, its cost of capital is 12 percent, its total assets are $800, and its current liabilities are $250.

The report shows that the division has added $334 to its economic value after taxes and cost of capital. In other words, the division produced after-tax profits of $334 in excess of the cost of capital required to generate those profits.

Because many factors affect the economic value of an investment center, management should be cautious when drawing conclusions about performance. The evaluation will be more meaningful if the current economic value added is compared to EVAs from previous periods, target EVAs, and EVAs from other investment centers.

The factors that affect the computation of economic value added are illustrated in Figure 5. An investment center's economic value is affected by managers' decisions on pricing, product sales volume, taxes, cost of capital, capital investments, and other financial decisions. In essence, the EVA number is a composite index drawn from many cause-and-effect relationships and interdependent financial elements. A manager can improve the economic value of an investment center by increasing sales, decreasing costs, decreasing assets, or lowering the cost of capital.

The Importance of Multiple Performance Measures

In summary, to be effective, a performance management system must consider both operating results and multiple performance measures, such as return on investment, residual income, and economic value added. Comparing actual results to budgeted figures adds meaning to the evaluation. Performance measures such as ROI, RI, and EVA indicate whether an investment center is effective in coordinating its own goals with companywide goals because those measures take into account both operating income and the assets used to produce that income. However, all three measures are limited by their focus on short-term financial performance. To obtain a fuller picture, management needs to break these three measures down into their components, analyze such information as responsibility center income over time, and compare current results to the targeted amounts in the flexible or master budgets. In addition, the analysis of such nonfinancial performance indicators as average throughput time, employee turnover, and number of orders processed will ensure a more balanced view of a business's well-being and how to improve it.

 Check out ACE for a Review Quiz at http://accounting.college.hmco.com/students.

KEY POINT: Using multiple measures of both financial and nonfinancial performance over time presents a more balanced view of a business's health and how to improve it.

Performance Incentives and Goals

LO6 Explain how properly linked performance incentives and measures add value for all stakeholders in performance management and evaluation.

RELATED TEXT ASSIGNMENTS
Q: 20
SE: 10
E: 14, 15
SD: 4, 5
MRA: 3, 5

The effectiveness of a performance management and evaluation system depends on how well it coordinates the goals of responsibility centers, managers, and the entire company. Two factors are key to the successful coordination of goals: the logical linking of goals to measurable objectives and targets and the tying of appropriate compensation incentives to the achievement of the targets, that is, performance-based pay.

Linking Goals, Performance Objectives, Measures, and Performance Targets

The causal links between an organization's goals, performance objectives, measures, and targets must be apparent. For example, if a company seeks to be a friend of the environment, as do Bristol-Myers Squibb and Royal Dutch/Shell,[6] it may choose the following linked goal, objective, measure, and performance target:

www.bms.com
www.shell.com

Goal	Objective	Measure	Performance Target
To be a friend of the environment	To reduce the company's environmental risk	Number of products recycled	To recycle at least 10 percent of products sold

You may recall that the balanced scorecard also links objectives, measures, and targets, as shown in Figure 1 earlier in this chapter.

KEY POINT: The causal links between an organization's goals, objectives, measures, performance targets, and compensation incentives must be easy to understand.

Performance-Based Pay

The tying of appropriate compensation incentives to performance targets increases the likelihood that the goals of responsibility centers, managers, and the entire organization will be well coordinated. Unfortunately, this linkage does not always happen. A 1999 survey by AnswerThink reported that only 58 percent of companies link bonuses, merit pay increases, and profit sharing to the measurable performance of strategic and tactical plans.[7] Responsibility center managers are more likely to achieve their performance targets if their compensation depends on it. **Performance-based pay** is the linking of employee compensation to the achievement of measurable business targets. For example, at DaimlerChrysler, all 132,000

www.daimlerchrysler.com

German factory employees are eligible for some type of performance-based pay, such as cash bonuses, profit sharing, or stock options.[8]

Cash bonuses, awards, profit-sharing plans, and stock option programs are common types of incentive compensation. Cash bonuses are usually given to reward an individual's short-term performance. A bonus may be stated as a fixed dollar amount or as a percentage of a target figure, such as 5 percent of operating income or 10 percent of the dollar increase in operating income. An award may be a trip or some other form of recognition for desirable individual or group performance. For example, many companies sponsor a trip for all managers who have met their performance targets during a specified period. Other companies award incentive points that employees may redeem for goods or services. (Notice that awards can be used to encourage both short-term and long-term performance.) Profit-sharing plans reward employees with a share of the company's profits. Employees often receive company stock as recognition of their contribution to a profitable period. Using stock as a reward encourages employees to think and act as investors as well as employees and encourages a stable work force. In terms of the balanced scorecard, they assume two stakeholder perspectives and take both a short- and a long-term viewpoint. Stock options give individual employees the right to purchase a certain number of shares at a specific price within a certain period. Companies use stock options to motivate employees to achieve financial targets that increase the company's stock price. Managers like stock options because the options enable them to realize a profit if the actual stock price rises above their granted option price. Stock options usually have specific performance requirements attached to them. Because many of the variables that affect stock price are beyond a manager's control, stock options may not be the best way to promote the coordination of goals.

THE COORDINATION OF GOALS

KEY POINT: Not all businesses have comparable approaches to performance-based pay. Rather, each business will design a compensation program specific to the achievement of its organizational goals.

What performance incentives and measures should a company use to manage and evaluate performance? What actions and behaviors should an organization reward? Which incentive compensation plans work best? The answers to such questions depend on the facts and circumstances of each organization. What promotes the coordination of goals for one organization may not do so for another. To be effective, incentive plans must be developed with input from all employees. All must understand the causal links between goals, objectives, measures, and performance targets. To determine the right performance incentives for their organization, employees and managers must answer several questions:

- When should the reward occur: now or sometime in the future?
- Whose performance should be rewarded: that of responsibility centers, individual managers, or the entire company?
- How should the reward be computed?
- On what should the reward be based?
- What performance criteria should be used?
- Does our performance incentive plan address the interests of all stakeholders?

STOP AND THINK!
Which performance incentives work best?
Which incentives work best depends on the facts and circumstances of each organization. ■

The effectiveness of a performance management and evaluation system relies on the coordination of responsibility center, managerial, and company goals. Performance can be optimized by linking goals to measurable objectives and targets and by tying appropriate compensation incentives to the achievement of the targets. Common types of incentive compensation are cash bonuses, awards, profit-sharing plans, and stock option programs. Each organization's unique circumstances will determine its correct mix of measures and compensation incentives. If management values the perspectives of all of its stakeholder groups, its performance management and evaluation system will balance and benefit all interests.

 Check out ACE for a Review Quiz at http://accounting.college.hmco.com/students.

Chapter Review

REVIEW OF LEARNING OBJECTIVES

LO1 Describe how the balanced scorecard aligns performance with organizational goals, and explain the role of the balanced scorecard in the management cycle.

The balanced scorecard is a framework that links the perspectives of an organization's four basic stakeholder groups—financial, learning and growth, internal business processes, and customers—with its mission and vision, performance measures, strategic plan, and resources. Ideally, managers should see how their actions help to achieve organizational goals and understand how their compensation is linked to their actions. The balanced scorecard assumes that an organization will get what it measures.

LO2 Discuss performance measurement, and state the issues that affect management's ability to measure performance.

An effective performance measurement system accounts for and reports on both financial and nonfinancial performance so an organization can ascertain how well it is doing, where it is going, and what improvements will make it more profitable. Each organization must develop a unique set of performance measures appropriate to its specific situation. Besides answering basic questions about what to measure and how to measure, management must consider a variety of other issues. Managers must collaborate to develop a group of measures, such as the balanced scorecard, that will help them determine how to improve performance.

LO3 Define *responsibility accounting*, and describe the role that responsibility centers play in performance management and evaluation.

Responsibility accounting classifies data according to areas of responsibility and reports each area's activities by including only the revenue, cost, and resource categories that the assigned manager can control. There are five types of responsibility centers: cost, discretionary cost, revenue, profit, and investment. Performance reporting by responsibility center allows the source of a cost, revenue, or resource to be traced to the manager who controls it and thus makes it easier to evaluate a manager's performance.

LO4 Prepare performance reports for cost centers using flexible budgets and for profit centers using variable costing.

Performance reports contain information about costs, revenues, and resources that individual managers can control. The content and format of a performance report depend on the nature of the responsibility center. The performance of a cost center may be evaluated by comparing its actual costs with the corresponding amounts in the flexible and master budgets. A flexible budget is derived by multiplying actual unit output by predetermined standard unit costs for each cost item in the report. The resulting variances between actual costs and the flexible budget can be examined further by using standard costing to compute specific variances for direct materials, direct labor, and overhead. A profit center's performance is usually evaluated by comparing its actual income statement results to its budgeted income statement. When variable costing is used, the profit center manager's controllable costs are classified as variable or fixed. The resulting performance report takes the form of a contribution income statement instead of a traditional income statement. The variable costing income statement is useful because it focuses on cost variability and the profit center's contribution to operating income.

LO5 Prepare performance reports for investment centers using traditional measures of return on investment and residual income and the newer measure of economic value added.

Traditionally, the most common performance measure is return on investment (ROI). Its basic formula is ROI = Operating Income ÷ Assets Invested. Return on investment may also be examined in terms of profit margin and asset turnover. In that case, ROI = Profit Margin × Asset Turnover, where Profit Margin = Operating Income ÷ Sales and Asset Turnover = Sales ÷ Assets Invested. Residual income (RI) is the operating income that an investment center earns above a minimum desired return on invested assets. It is expressed as a dollar amount: Residual Income = Operating Income − (Desired ROI × Assets Invested). It is the amount of profit left after subtracting a predetermined desired income target for an investment. Today, businesses are increasingly using the shareholder wealth created by an investment center, or economic value added (EVA), as a performance measure. The calculation of economic value added can be quite complex because it is a composite of many cause-and-effect relationships and interdependent financial elements. Basically, the concept of economic value added is similar to residual income. EVA = After-Tax Operating Income − Cost of Capital (expressed in dollars). A manager can improve the economic value of an investment center by increasing sales, decreasing costs, decreasing assets, or lowering the cost of capital.

LO6 Explain how properly linked performance incentives and measures add value for all stakeholders in performance management and evaluation.

The effectiveness of a performance management and evaluation system depends on how well it coordinates the goals of responsibility centers, managers, and the entire company. Performance can be optimized by linking goals to measurable objectives and targets and tying appropriate compensation incentives to the achievement of those targets. Common types of incentive compensation are cash bonuses, awards, profit-sharing plans, and stock option programs. Each organization's unique circumstances will determine its correct mix of measures and compensation incentives. If management values the perspectives of all of its stakeholder groups, its performance management and evaluation system will balance and benefit all interests.

REVIEW OF CONCEPTS AND TERMINOLOGY

The following concepts and terms were introduced in this chapter:

LO5 **Asset turnover:** The productivity of assets, or the number of sales dollars generated by each dollar invested in assets; Sales ÷ Assets Invested.

LO1 **Balanced scorecard:** A framework that links the perspectives of an organization's four basic stakeholder groups—financial (investors), learning and growth (employees), internal business processes, and customers—with the organization's mission and vision, performance measures, strategic plan, and resources.

LO3 **Controllable costs and revenues:** Costs and revenues that result from a manager's actions, influence, or decisions.

LO3 **Cost center:** A responsibility center whose manager is accountable only for controllable costs that have well-defined relationships between the center's resources and products or services.

LO5 **Cost of capital:** The minimum desired rate of return on an investment, such as assets invested in an investment center.

LO3 **Discretionary cost center:** A responsibility center whose manager is accountable for costs only and in which the relationship between resources and products or services produced is not well defined.

LO5 **Economic value added (EVA):** The shareholder wealth created by an investment center; Economic Value Added = After-Tax Operating Income − Cost of Capital in Dollars.

LO3 **Investment center:** A responsibility center whose manager is accountable for profit generation and can also make significant decisions about the resources the center uses.

LO3 **Organization chart:** A visual representation of an organization's hierarchy of responsibility for the purposes of management control.

LO6 **Performance-based pay:** The linking of employee compensation to the achievement of measurable business targets.

LO2 **Performance management and evaluation system:** A set of procedures that account for and report on both financial and nonfinancial performance, so that a company can identify how well it is doing, where it is going, and what improvements will make it more profitable.

LO2 **Performance measurement:** The use of quantitative tools to gauge an organization's performance in relation to a specific goal or an expected outcome.

LO3 **Profit center:** A responsibility center whose manager is accountable for both revenue and costs and for the resulting operating income.

LO5 **Profit margin:** The percentage of each sales dollar that results in profit; Operating Income ÷ Sales.

LO5 **Residual income (RI):** The operating income that an investment center earns above a minimum desired return on invested assets; Residual Income = Investment Center's Operating Income − (Desired ROI × Assets Invested).

LO3 **Responsibility accounting:** An information system that classifies data according to areas of responsibility and reports each area's activities by including only the revenue, cost, and resource categories that the assigned manager can control.

LO3 **Responsibility center:** An organizational unit whose manager has been assigned the responsibility of managing a portion of the organization's resources. The five most common forms of responsibility center are cost centers, discretionary cost centers, revenue centers, profit centers, and investment centers.

LO5 **Return on investment (ROI):** A traditional performance measure that takes into account both operating income and the assets invested to produce that income; ROI = Operating Income ÷ Assets Invested. ROI can also be expressed as Profit Margin × Asset Turnover.

LO3 **Revenue center:** A responsibility center whose manager is accountable primarily for revenue and whose success is based on its ability to generate revenue.

LO4 **Variable costing:** A method of preparing profit center performance reports that classifies a manager's controllable costs as either fixed or variable and produces a contribution income statement.

REVIEW PROBLEM

Evaluating Profit Center and Investment Center Performance

LO3
LO4
LO5
Winter Wonderland is a full-service resort and spa. Mary Fortenberry, the resort's general manager, is responsible for guest activities, administration, and food and lodging. In addition, she is solely responsible for the resort's capital investments. The organization chart below shows the resort's various activities and the levels of authority that Fortenberry has established:

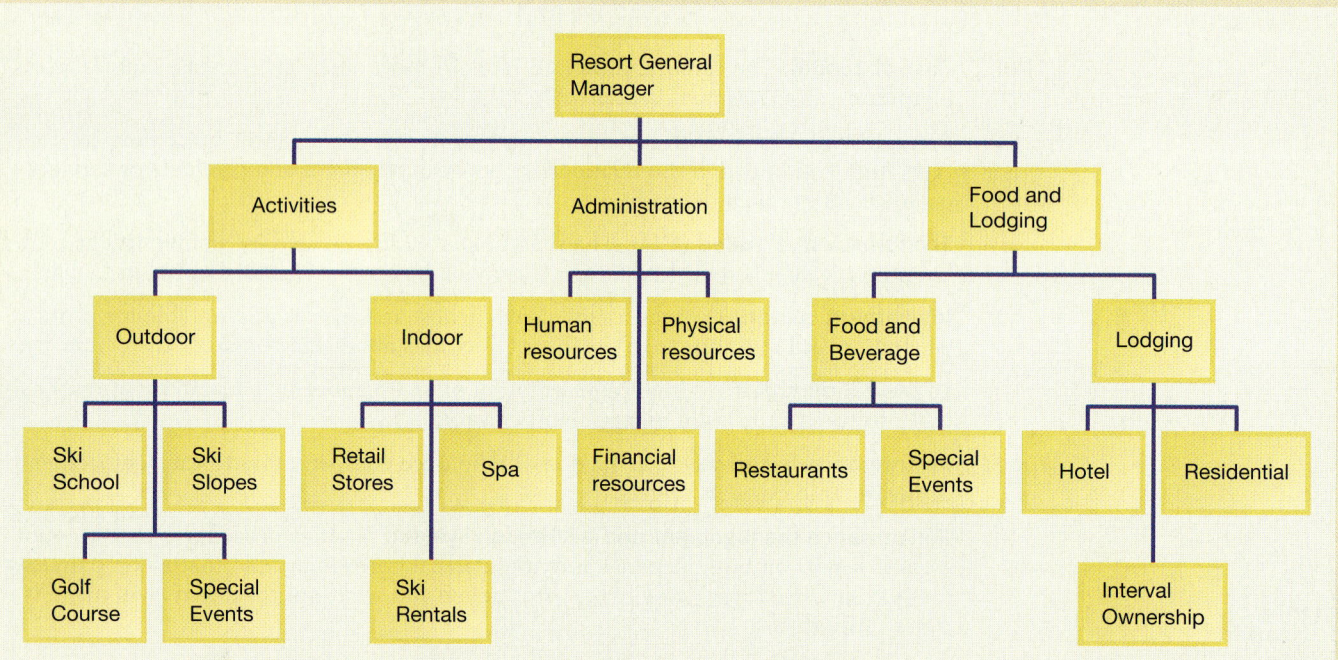

Three divisional managers receive compensation based on their division's performance and have authority to make employee compensation decisions for their division. Alexandra Patel manages the Food and Lodging Division. That division's master budget and actual results for the year ended June 30, 20x8, appear at the top of the opposite page.

REQUIRED ▶
1. What types of responsibility centers are Administration, Food and Lodging, and Resort General Manager?
2. Assume Food and Lodging is a profit center. Prepare a performance report using variable costing and flexible budgeting. Determine the variances between actual results and the corresponding figures in the flexible budget and the master budget.
3. Assume that the divisional managers have been assigned responsibility for capital expenditures and that their divisions are thus investment centers. Food and Lodging

Winter Wonderland
Food and Lodging Division
For the Year Ended June 30, 20x8
(Dollar amounts in thousands)

	Master Budget	Actual Results
Guest days	4,000	4,100
Sales	$38,000	$40,000
Variable cost of sales	24,000	25,000
Variable selling and administrative expenses	4,000	4,250
Fixed cost of sales	2,000	1,800
Fixed selling and administrative expenses	2,500	2,500

is expected to generate a desired ROI of at least 30 percent on average assets invested of $10,000,000.

a. Compute the division's return on investment and residual income using the average assets invested in both the actual and the budget calculations.

b. Using the ROI and residual income, evaluate Alexandra Patel's performance as divisional manager.

4. Compute the division's actual economic value added if the division's assets are $12,000,000, current liabilities are $3,000,000, after-tax operating income is $4,500,000, and the cost of capital is 20 percent.

Answer to Review Problem

1. Administration: discretionary cost center; Food and Lodging: profit center; Resort General Manager: investment center.
2. Performance report:

Winter Wonderland
Food and Lodging Division
For the Year Ended June 30, 20x8
(Dollar amounts in thousands)

	Actual Results	Variance	Flexible Budget	Variance	Master Budget
Guest days	4,100	0	4,100	100 (F)	4,000
Sales	$40,000	$1,050 (F)	$38,950	$950 (F)	$38,000
Controllable variable costs					
Variable cost of sales	25,000	400 (U)	24,600	600 (U)	24,000
Variable selling and administrative expenses	4,250	150 (U)	4,100	100 (U)	4,000
Contribution margin	$10,750	$ 500 (F)	$10,250	$250 (F)	$10,000
Controllable fixed costs					
Fixed cost of sales	1,800	200 (F)	2,000	0	2,000
Fixed selling and administrative expenses	2,500	0	2,500	0	2,500
Division operating income	$ 6,450	$ 700 (F)	$ 5,750	$250 (F)	$ 5,500

3. a. **Return on investment**
      Actual results: $6,450,000 \div \$10,000,000 = 64.50\%$
      Flexible budget: $\$5,750,000 \div \$10,000,000 = 57.50\%$
      Master budget: $\$5,500,000 \div \$10,000,000 = 55.00\%$
   Residual income
      Actual results: $\$6,450,000 - 30\%(\$10,000,000) = \$3,450,000$
      Flexible budget: $\$5,750,000 - 30\%(\$10,000,000) = \$2,750,000$
      Master budget: $\$5,500,000 - 30\%(\$10,000,000) = \$2,500,000$
   b. Alexandra Patel's performance as the divisional manager of Food and Lodging exceeds company performance expectations. Actual ROI was 64.5 percent, whereas the company expected an ROI of 30 percent and the flexible budget and the master budget showed projections of 57.5 percent and 55.0 percent, respectively. Residual income also exceeded expectations. The Food and Lodging Division generated $3,450,000 in residual income when the flexible budget and master budget had projected RIs of $2,750,000 and $2,500,000, respectively. The performance report for the division shows 100 more guest days than had been anticipated and a favorable controllable fixed cost variance. As a manager, Patel will investigate the unfavorable variances associated with her controllable variable costs.
4. Economic value added:
   $\$4,500,000 - 20\%(\$12,000,000 - \$3,000,000) = \$2,700,000$

Chapter Assignments

BUILDING YOUR KNOWLEDGE FOUNDATION

QUESTIONS

1. What four basic stakeholder groups are included in the balanced scorecard?
2. Once performance objectives are set in the planning stage of the management cycle, what do managers do?
3. Why is it important for managers to see the causal relationships between their actions and the company's overall performance?
4. How does the balanced scorecard add dimension to the management cycle?
5. What is a performance management and evaluation system?
6. Define responsibility accounting.
7. Describe a responsibility center.
8. Explain the difference between a cost center and a discretionary cost center.
9. What is a revenue center?
10. Compare and contrast a cost center, a profit center, and an investment center.
11. What is the role of a responsibility accounting system in an organization?
12. How does a company's organizational structure affect its responsibility accounting system?
13. What types of information are contained in performance reports?
14. What types of comparisons are contained in a performance report for a cost center?
15. Why is a contribution income statement useful in performance management and evaluation?
16. What are some similarities between the performance reports for the various kinds of responsibility centers?
17. Why is return on investment more than a ratio of two numbers?
18. How does residual income differ from return on investment?
19. What are the similarities and differences between residual income and EVA?
20. Why do incentive plans use performance-based pay?

Short Exercises

LO1 Balanced Scorecard

SE 1. One of your college's overall goals is customer satisfaction. In the light of that goal, match each of these stakeholders' perspectives with the appropriate objective:

Perspective	Objective
1. Financial (investors)	a. Customer satisfaction means that the faculty engages in cutting-edge research.
2. Learning and growth (employees)	b. Customer satisfaction means that students receive their degrees in four years.
3. Internal business processes	c. Customer satisfaction means that the college has a winning athletics program.
4. Customers	d. Customer satisfaction means that fund-raising campaigns are successful.

LO3 Responsibility Centers

SE 2. Identify each of the following as a cost center, a discretionary cost center, a revenue center, a profit center, or an investment center:

1. The manager of center A is responsible for generating cash inflows and incurring costs with the goal of making money for the company. The manager has no responsibility for assets.
2. Center B produces a product that is not sold to an external party.
3. The manager of center C is responsible for the telephone order operations of a large retailer.
4. Center D designs, produces, and sells products to external parties. The manager makes both long-term and short-term decisions.
5. Center E provides human resource support for the other centers in the company.

LO3 Controllable Costs

SE 3. Adana Kim is the manager of the Paper Cutting Department in the Northwest Division of Williams Paper Products. Identify each of the following costs as either controllable or not controllable by Kim:

1. Salaries of cutting machine workers
2. Cost of cutting machine parts
3. Cost of electricity for the Northwest Division
4. Lumber Department hauling costs
5. Vice president's salary

LO4 Cost Center Performance Report

SE 4. Complete the following performance report for cost center C for the month ended December 31, 20x8:

	Actual Results	Variance	Flexible Budget	Variance	Master Budget
Units produced	80	0	?	20 (U)	100
Center costs					
Direct materials	$ 84	$?	$ 80	$?	$100
Direct labor	150	?	?	40 (F)	200
Variable overhead	?	20 (U)	240	?	300
Fixed overhead	280	?	250	?	250
Total cost	$?	$44 (U)	$?	$120 (F)	$850
Performance measures					
Defect-free units to total produced	75%	?	N/A	N/A	90%
Average throughput time per unit	12 minutes	?	N/A	N/A	10 minutes

LO4 Profit Center Performance Report

SE 5. Complete the following performance report for profit center P for the month ended December 31, 20x8:

	Actual Results	Variance	Master Budget
Sales	$?	$20 (F)	$120
Controllable variable costs			
Variable cost of goods sold	25	10 (U)	?
Variable selling and administrative expenses	15	?	5
Contribution margin	$100	$?	$100
Controllable fixed costs	?	10 (F)	60
Profit center income	$ 50	$10 (F)	$?
Performance measures			
Number of orders processed	50	20 (F)	?
Average daily sales	$?	.66 (F)	$4.00
Number of units sold	100	40 (F)	?

LO5 Return on Investment

SE 6. Complete the return on investment, profit margin, and asset turnover calculations for investment centers D and V:

	Subsidiary D	Subsidiary V
Total sales	$1,650	$2,840
Operating income	$ 180	$ 210
Average assets invested	$ 940	$1,250
Profit margin	?	7.39%
Asset turnover	1.76 times	?
ROI	?	?

LO5 Return on Investment

SE 7. Complete the return on investment, profit margin, asset turnover, and average assets invested calculations for investment centers J and K:

	Subsidiary J	Subsidiary K
Total sales	$2,000	$2,000
Operating income	$ 500	$ 800
Beginning assets invested	$4,000	$ 500
Ending assets invested	$6,000	$1,500
Average assets invested	$?	$?
Profit margin	25%	?
Asset turnover	?	2 times
ROI	?	?

LO5 Residual Income

SE 8. Complete the operating income, ending assets invested, residual income, and average assets invested calculations for investment centers H and F:

	Subsidiary H	Subsidiary F
Total sales	$20,000	$25,000
Operating income	$ 1,500	$?
Beginning assets invested	$ 4,000	$ 500
Ending assets invested	$ 6,000	$?
Average assets invested	$?	$ 1,000
Desired ROI	20%	20%
Residual income	$?	$ 600

LO5 Economic Value Added

SE 9. Complete the current liabilities, total assets − current liabilities, and economic value added calculations for investment centers M and N:

	Subsidiary M	Subsidiary N
Total sales	$15,000	$18,000
After-tax operating income	$ 1,000	$ 1,100
Total assets	$ 4,000	$ 5,000
Current liabilities	$ 1,000	$?
Total assets − current liabilities	$?	$ 3,500

Cost of capital		15%	15%
Economic value added		$?	$?

LO6 Coordination of Goals

SE 10. One of your college's goals is customer satisfaction. In view of that goal, identify each of the following as a linked objective, a measure, or a performance target.

To have successful fund-raising campaigns
Number of publications per year per tenure-track faculty
To increase the average donation by 10 percent
Average number of dollars raised per donor
To have faculty engage in cutting-edge research
To increase the number of publications per faculty member by at least one per year

Exercises

LO1 Balanced Scorecard

E 1. Biggs Industries is considering adopting the balanced scorecard and has compiled the following list of possible performance measures. Select the balanced scorecard perspective that best matches each performance measure.

Performance Measure	Balanced Scorecard Perspective
1. Residual income	a. Financial (investors)
2. Customer satisfaction rating	b. Learning and growth (employees)
3. Employee absentee rate	c. Internal business processes
4. Growth in profits	d. Customers
5. On-time deliveries	
6. Manufacturing process time	

LO1 Balanced Scorecard

E 2. Virtual Online Products is considering adopting the balanced scorecard and has compiled the following list of possible performance measures. Select the balanced scorecard perspective that best matches each performance measure.

Performance Measure	Balanced Scorecard Perspective
1. Economic value added	a. Financial (investors)
2. Employee turnover	b. Learning and growth (employees)
3. Average daily sales	c. Internal business processes
4. Defect-free units	d. Customers
5. Number of repeat customer visits	
6. Employee training hours	

LO2 Performance Measures

E 3. Eva Washington wants to measure her division's product quality. Link an appropriate performance measure with each balanced scorecard perspective:

Product Quality	Possible Performance Measures
1. Financial (investors)	a. Number of defective products returned
2. Learning and growth (employees)	b. Number of products failing inspection
3. Internal business processes	c. Increased market share
4. Customers	d. Savings from employee suggestions

LO2 Performance Measures

E 4. Monty Sams wants to measure customer satisfaction within his region. Link an appropriate performance measure with each balanced scorecard perspective:

Customer Satisfaction	Possible Performance Measures
1. Financial (investors)	a. Number of cross-trained staff
2. Learning and growth (employees)	b. Customer satisfaction rating
3. Internal business processes	c. Time lapse from order to delivery
4. Customers	d. Dollar sales to repeat customers

LO3 Responsibility Centers

E 5. Identify the most appropriate type of responsibility center for each of the following organizational units:

1. A pizza store in a pizza chain
2. The ticket sales center of a major airline
3. The South American segment of a multinational company
4. A subsidiary of a business conglomerate
5. The information technology area of a company
6. A manufacturing department of a large corporation
7. An eye clinic in a community hospital
8. The food service function at a nursing home

9. The food preparation plant of a large restaurant chain
10. The catalog order department of a retailer

LO3 Controllable Costs

E 6. Angel Sweets produces pies. The company has the following three-tiered manufacturing structure:

Vice President–Production
↑
Plant Manager
↑
Production Supervisors

Identify the manager responsible for each of the following costs.

1. Repair and maintenance costs
2. Materials handling costs
3. Direct labor
4. Supervisors' salaries
5. Maintenance of plant grounds
6. Depreciation, equipment
7. Plant manager's salary
8. Cost of materials used
9. Storage of finished goods
10. Property taxes, plant
11. Depreciation, plant

LO3 Organization Chart

E 7. Hooper Industries wants to formalize its management structure by designing an organization chart. The company has a president, a board of directors, and two vice presidents. Four discretionary cost centers—Financial Resources, Human Resources, Information Resources, and Physical Resources—report to one of the vice presidents. The other vice president has one manufacturing plant with three subassembly areas reporting to her. Draw the company's organization chart.

LO4 Performance Reports

E 8. Jackie Jefferson, a new employee at Handown, Inc., is learning about the various types of performance reports. Describe the typical contents of a performance report for each type of responsibility center.

LO4 Variable Costing Income Statement

E 9. Vegan, LLC, owns a chain of gourmet vegetarian take-out markets. Last month, Store P generated the following information: sales, $890,000; direct materials, $220,000; direct labor, $97,000; variable overhead, $150,000; fixed overhead, $130,000; variable selling and administrative expenses, $44,500; and fixed selling expenses, $82,300. There were no beginning or ending inventories. Average daily sales (25 business days) were $35,600. Customer orders processed totaled 15,000. Vegan had budgeted monthly sales of $900,000; direct materials, $210,000; direct labor, $100,000; variable overhead, $140,000; fixed overhead, $140,000; variable selling and administrative expenses, $45,000; and fixed selling expenses, $85,000. Store P had been projected to do $36,000 in daily sales and process 16,000 customer orders. Using this information, prepare a performance report for Store P.

LO4 Variable Costing Income Statement

E 10. The income statement in the traditional reporting format for Green Products, Inc., for the year ended December 31, 20x7, is as follows:

Green Products, Inc.
Income Statement
For the Year Ended December 31, 20x7

Sales	$296,400
Less Cost of goods sold	112,750
Gross margin	$183,650
Less Operating expenses	
Selling expenses	
Variable	69,820
Fixed	36,980
Administrative expenses	27,410
Operating income	$ 49,440

Total fixed manufacturing costs for 20x7 were $16,750. All administrative expenses are considered to be fixed.

Using this information, prepare an income statement for Green Products, Inc., for the year ended December 31, 20x7, using the variable costing format.

LO4 Performance Report for a Cost Center

E 11. Archer, LLC, owns a blueberry processing plant. Last month, the plant generated the following information: blueberries processed, 50,000 pounds; direct materials, $50,000; direct labor, $10,000; variable overhead, $12,000; and fixed overhead, $13,000. There were no beginning or ending inventories. Average daily pounds processed (25 business days) were 2,000. Average rate of processing was 250 pounds per hour. At the beginning of the month, Archer had budgeted costs of blueberries, $45,000; direct labor, $10,000; variable overhead, $14,000; and fixed overhead, $14,000. The plant had been projected to process 2,000 pounds daily at the rate of 240 pounds per hour.

Using this information, prepare a performance report for the month for the blueberry processing plant. Include a flexible budget and a computation of variances in your report. Indicate whether the variances are favorable (F) or unfavorable (U) to the performance of the plant.

LO5 Investment Center Performance

E 12. Momence Associates is evaluating the performance of three divisions: Maple, Oaks, and Juniper.

Using the following data, compute the return on investment and residual income for each division, compare the divisions' performance, and comment on the factors that influenced performance:

	Maple	Oaks	Juniper
Sales	$100,000	$100,000	$100,000
Operating income	$ 10,000	$ 10,000	$ 20,000
Assets invested	$ 25,000	$ 12,500	$ 25,000
Desired ROI	40%	40%	40%

LO5 Economic Value Added

E 13. Leesburg, LLP, is evaluating the performance of three divisions: Lake, Sumpter, and Poe. Using the following data, compute the economic value added by each division, and comment on each division's performance:

	Lake	Sumpter	Poe
Sales	$100,000	$100,000	$100,000
After-tax operating income	$ 10,000	$ 10,000	$ 20,000
Total assets	$ 25,000	$ 12,500	$ 25,000
Current liabilities	$ 5,000	$ 5,000	$ 5,000
Cost of capital	15%	15%	15%

LO6 Performance Incentives

E 14. Dynamic Consulting is advising Solid Industries on the short-term and long-term effectiveness of cash bonuses, awards, profit sharing, and stock options as performance incentives. Prepare a chart identifying the effectiveness of each incentive as either long-term or short-term or both.

LO6 Goal Congruence

E 15. Necessary Toys, Inc., has adopted the balanced scorecard to motivate its managers to work toward the companywide goal of leading its industry in innovation. Identify the four stakeholder perspectives that would link to the following objectives, measures, and targets:

Perspective	Objective	Measure	Target
	Profitable new products	New product ROI	New product ROI of at least 75%
	Work force with cutting-edge skills	Percentage of employees cross-trained on work-group tasks	100% of work group cross-trained on new tasks within 30 days
	Agile product design and production processes	Time to market (the time between a product idea and its first sales)	Time to market less than one year for 80% of product introductions
	Successful product introductions	New product market share	Capture 80% of new product market within one year

PROBLEMS

P 1.
LO3 Evaluating Cost Center
LO4 Performance

Beverage Products, LLC, manufactures metal beverage containers. The division that manufactures soft drink beverage cans for the North American market has two plants that operate 24 hours a day, 365 days a year. The plants are evaluated as cost centers. Small tools and plant supplies are considered variable overhead. Depreciation and rent are considered fixed overhead. The master budget for a plant and the operating results of the two North American plants, East Coast and West Coast, are as follows:

	Master Budget	East Coast	West Coast
Center costs			
Rolled aluminum ($.01)	$4,000,000	$3,492,000	$5,040,000
Lids ($.005)	2,000,000	1,980,000	2,016,000
Direct labor ($.0025)	1,000,000	864,000	1,260,000
Small tools and supplies ($.0013)	520,000	432,000	588,000
Depreciation and rent	480,000	480,000	480,000
Total cost	$8,000,000	$7,248,000	$9,384,000
Performance measures			
Cans processed per hour	45,662	41,096	47,945
Average daily pounds of scrap metal	5	6	7
Cans processed (in millions)	400	360	420

REQUIRED
1. Prepare a performance report for the East Coast plant. Include a flexible budget and variance analysis.
2. Prepare a performance report for the West Coast plant. Include a flexible budget and variance analysis.
3. Compare the two plants, and comment on their performance.
4. Explain why a flexible budget should be prepared.

P 2.
LO4 Traditional and Variable Costing Income Statements

Roofing tile is the major product of the Tops Corporation. The company had a particularly good year in 20x8, as shown by its operating data. It sold 88,400 cases of tile. Variable cost of goods sold was $848,640; variable selling expenses were $132,600; fixed manufacturing overhead was $166,680; fixed selling expenses were $152,048; and fixed administrative expenses were $96,450. Selling price was $18 per case. There were no partially completed jobs in process at the beginning or the end of the year. Finished goods inventory had been used up at the end of the previous year.

REQUIRED
1. Prepare the year-end income statement for the Tops Corporation using the traditional reporting format.
2. Prepare the year-end income statement for the Tops Corporation using the variable costing format.

P 3.
LO3 Evaluating Profit and
LO4 Investment Center
LO5 Performance

Bobbie Howell, the managing partner of the law firm Howell, Bagan, and Clark, LLP, makes asset acquisition and disposal decisions for the firm. As managing partner, she supervises the partners in charge of the firm's three branch offices. Those partners have authority to make employee compensation decisions. The partners' compensation depends on the profitability of their branch office. Victoria Smith manages the City Branch, which has the following master budget and actual results for 20x8:

	Master Budget	Actual Results
Billed hours	5,000	4,900
Revenue	$250,000	$254,800
Controllable variable costs		
Direct labor	120,000	137,200
Variable overhead	40,000	34,300
Contribution margin	$ 90,000	$ 83,300
Controllable fixed costs		
Rent	30,000	30,000
Other administrative expenses	45,000	42,000
Branch operating income	$ 15,000	$ 11,300

REQUIRED
1. Assume that the City Branch is a profit center. Prepare a performance report that includes a flexible budget. Determine the variances between actual results, the flexible budget, and the master budget.

2. Evaluate Victoria Smith's performance as manager of the City Branch.
3. Assume that the branch managers are assigned responsibility for capital expenditures and that the branches are thus investment centers. City Branch is expected to generate a desired ROI of at least 30 percent on average invested assets of $40,000.
    a. Compute the branch's return on investment and residual income.
    b. Using the ROI and residual income, evaluate Victoria Smith's performance as branch manager.

LO5 Return on Investment and Residual Income

P 4. The financial results for the past two years for Ornamental Iron, a division of the Iron Foundry Company, follow.

Iron Foundry Company
Ornamental Iron Division
Balance Sheet
December 31, 20x7 and 20x8

	20x8	20x7
Assets		
Cash	$ 5,000	$ 3,000
Accounts receivable	10,000	8,000
Inventory	30,000	32,000
Other current assets	600	600
Fixed assets	128,300	120,300
Total assets	$173,900	$163,900
Liabilities and Stockholders' Equity		
Current liabilities	$ 13,900	$ 10,000
Long-term liabilities	90,000	93,900
Stockholders' equity	70,000	60,000
Total liabilities and stockholders' equity	$173,900	$163,900

Iron Foundry Company
Ornamental Iron Division
Income Statement
For the Years Ended December 31, 20x7 and 20x8

	20x8	20x7
Sales	$180,000	$160,000
Cost of goods sold	100,000	90,000
Selling and administrative expenses	27,500	26,500
Operating income	$ 52,500	$ 43,500
Income taxes	17,850	14,790
After-tax operating income	$ 34,650	$ 28,710

REQUIRED ▶
1. Compute the division's profit margin, asset turnover, and return on investment for 20x8 and 20x7. Beginning total assets for 20x7 were $157,900. Round to two decimal places.
2. The desired return on investment for the division has been set at 12 percent. Compute Ornamental Iron's residual income for 20x8 and 20x7.
3. The cost of capital for the division is 8 percent. Compute the division's economic value added for 20x8 and 20x7.
4. Before drawing conclusions on this division's performance, what additional information would you want?

P 5.

LO5 Return on Investment and Economic Value Added

The balance sheet for the New Products Division of NuBone Corporation showed invested assets of $200,000 at the beginning of the year and $300,000 at the end of the year. During the year, the division's operating income was $12,500 on sales of $500,000.

REQUIRED ▶
1. Compute the division's residual income if the desired ROI is 6 percent.
2. Compute the following performance measures for the division: (a) profit margin, (b) asset turnover, and (c) return on investment
3. Recompute the division's ROI under each of the following independent assumptions:
   a. Sales increase from $500,000 to $600,000, causing operating income to rise from $12,500 to $30,000.
   b. Invested assets at the beginning of the year are reduced from $200,000 to $100,000.
   c. Operating expenses are reduced, causing operating income to rise from $12,500 to $20,000.
4. Compute NuBone's EVA if total corporate assets are $500,000, current liabilities are $80,000, after-tax operating income is $50,000, and the cost of capital is 8 percent.

ALTERNATE PROBLEMS

P 6.

LO4 Traditional and Variable Costing Income Statements

Interior designers often use the deluxe carpet products of Lux Mills, Inc. The Maricopa blend is the company's top product line. In March 20x9, Lux produced and sold 174,900 square yards of Maricopa blend. Factory operating data for the month included variable cost of goods sold of $2,623,500 and fixed manufacturing overhead of $346,875. Other expenses were variable selling expenses, $166,155; fixed selling expenses, $148,665; and fixed general and administrative expenses, $231,500. Total sales revenue equaled $3,935,250. All production took place in March, and there was no work in process at month end. Goods are usually shipped when completed.

REQUIRED ▶
1. Prepare the March 20x9 income statement for Lux Mills, Inc., using the traditional reporting format.
2. Prepare the March 20x9 income statement for Lux Mills, Inc., using the variable costing format.

P 7.

LO3 Return on Investment and
LO4 Residual Income
LO5

Portia Carter is the president of a company that owns six multiplex movie theaters. Carter has delegated decision-making authority to the theater managers for all decisions except those relating to capital expenditures and film selection. The theater managers' compensation depends on the profitability of their theaters. Max Burgman, the manager of the Park Theater, had the following master budget and actual results for the month:

	Master Budget	Actual Results
Tickets sold	120,000	110,000
Revenue–tickets	$840,000	$880,000
Revenue–concessions	480,000	330,000
Controllable variable costs		
Concessions	120,000	99,000
Direct labor	420,000	330,000
Variable overhead	540,000	550,000
Contribution margin	$240,000	$231,000
Controllable fixed costs		
Rent	55,000	55,000
Other administrative expenses	45,000	50,000
Theater operating income	$140,000	$126,000

REQUIRED ▶
1. Assuming that the theaters are profit centers, prepare a performance report for the Park Theater. Include a flexible budget. Determine the variances between actual results, the flexible budget, and the master budget.
2. Evaluate Burgman's performance as manager of the Park Theater.
3. Assume that the managers are assigned responsibility for capital expenditures and that the theaters are thus investment centers. Park Theater is expected to generate a desired ROI of at least 6 percent on average invested assets of $2,000,000.
   a. Compute the theater's return on investment and residual income.
   b. Using the ROI and residual income, evaluate Burgman's performance as manager.

P 8.
LO5 Return on Investment and Economic Value Added

Micanopy Company makes replicas of Indian artifacts. The balance sheet for the Arrowhead Division showed that the company had invested assets of $300,000 at the beginning of the year and $500,000 at the end of the year. During the year, the Arrowhead Division's operating income was $80,000 on sales of $1,200,000.

REQUIRED ▶
1. Compute the Arrowhead Division's residual income if the desired ROI is 20 percent.
2. Compute the following performance measures for the division:
   a. Profit margin
   b. Asset turnover
   c. Return on investment
3. Compute Micanopy Company's economic value added if total corporate assets are $6,000,000, current liabilities are $800,000, after-tax operating income is $750,000, and the cost of capital is 12 percent.

SKILLS DEVELOPMENT CASES

Conceptual Analysis

SD 1.
LO1 Performance Measures and
LO2 the Balanced Scorecard

Identify several performance measures for a business located near you, and link each measure with a specific stakeholder's perspective from the balanced scorecard. Be sure to select at least one performance measure for each perspective. If you were the manager of the business, how would you set performance targets for each measure? Prepare an email-style report stating the business's name, location, and activities and your linked performance measures and perspectives. Be prepared to discuss your business and performance measures in class.

Group Activity: Have students complete this assignment by working in groups of four to six, with each group member assuming a different stakeholder perspective (add government and community if you want more than four perspectives). The group should become familiar with the background of the business, and interview the business's manager or accountant. Ask the group to discuss all perspectives and to prepare a report summarizing their findings.

SD 2.
LO3 Comparison of Business Types Using Responsibility Accounting

The structure of an organization affects its responsibility accounting system. Accenture <www.accenture.com>, a major management consulting firm, organizes its consultants by industry and location. Target <www.target.com>, formerly Dayton-Hudson Corporation, has a division for each major retail department store chain it owns: Target, Mervyn's, Marshall Field's, Dayton's, and Hudson's. Monsanto <www.monsanto.com>, a manufacturer, structures its organization by products: agricultural, pharmaceutical, and nutritional (the last includes NutraSweet).

What is a responsibility accounting system, what is it based on, and what is the criterion for including an item in a manager's operating report? Discuss the general effects that organizational structure has on the creation of a responsibility reporting system and give an example of a cost center, a profit center, and an investment center at Accenture, Target, and Monsanto.

Ethical Dilemma

SD 3.
LO5 Effects of Manager's Decisions on ROI

Cooper Huntington is the manager of the upstate store of a large farm products retailer. His company is a stable, consistently profitable member of the farming industry. The upstate store is doing fine despite severe drought conditions in the area. At the first of the year, corporate headquarters set a targeted return on investment for the store of 20 percent. The upstate store currently averages $140,000 in invested assets (beginning invested assets, $130,000; ending invested assets, $150,000) and is projected to have an operating income of $30,800. Huntington is considering whether to take one or both of the following actions before year end:

- Hold off paying $5,000 in bills owed until the start of the next fiscal year.
- Write down $3,000 in store inventory (nonperishable emergency flood supplies) to zero value because Huntington was unable to sell the items all year.

Currently, Huntington's bonus is based on store profits. Next year, corporate headquarters is changing its performance incentive program so that bonuses will be based on a store's actual return on investment.

1. What effect would each of Huntington's possible actions have on the store's operating income this year? (**Hint:** Use Figure 4 to trace the effects.) In your opinion, is either action unethical?
2. Independent of question 1, if corporate headquarters changes its performance incentive plan for store managers, how will the inventory writedown affect next year's income and return on investment if the items are sold for $4,000 next year? In your opinion, does Huntington have an ethical dilemma?

Research Activity

SD 4. Earnings Management
LO2
LO4
LO6

Many large multinational companies have recently taken large one-time write-offs or applied other downsizing or reengineering accounting practices that have affected the measurement of the company's performance in only one year. Conduct a search for the financial statements of a company that has recently taken a sizable reduction in income in just one year. Conduct a keyword search using an Internet search engine. Prepare a one-page description of your findings. Include the name of the company, the reason for the large decrease in income, and the probable effect on the company's ROI. Be prepared to present your findings to your classmates.

Decision-Making Practice

SD 5. Types of Responsibility Centers
LO2
LO3
LO4
LO6

Yuma Foods acquired Aldo's Tortillas several years ago. Aldo's has continued to operate as an independent company, except that Yuma Foods has exclusive authority over capital investments, production quantity, and pricing decisions because Yuma has been Aldo's only customer since the acquisition. Yuma uses return on investment to evaluate the performance of Aldo's manager. The most recent performance report is as follows:

Yuma Foods
Performance Report for Aldo's Tortillas
For the Year Ended June 30, 20x8

Sales	$6,000
Variable cost of goods sold	3,000
Variable administrative expenses	1,000
Variable corporate expenses (% of sales)	600
Contribution margin	$1,400
Fixed overhead (includes depreciation of $100)	400
Fixed administrative expenses	500
Operating income	$ 500
Average assets invested	$5,500
Return on investment	9.09%

1. Analyze the items listed in the performance report and identify the items Aldo controls and those Yuma controls. In your opinion, what type of responsibility center is Aldo's Tortillas? Explain your response.
2. Prepare a revised performance report for Aldo's Tortillas and an accompanying memo to the president of Yuma Foods that explains why it is important to change the content of the report. Cite some basic principles of responsibility accounting to support your recommendation.

MANAGERIAL REPORTING AND ANALYSIS CASES

Interpreting Management Reports

MRA 1.
LO1 Balanced Scorecard Results

IT, Inc., has adopted the balanced scorecard approach to motivate the managers of its product divisions to work toward the companywide goal of leading its industry in innovation. The corporation's selected performance measures and scorecard results are as follows:

	Division			Performance
Measure	A	B	C	Target
New product ROI	80%	75%	70%	75%
Employees cross-trained in new tasks within 30 days	95	96	94	100
New product's time to market less than one year	85	90	86	80
New product's market share one year after introduction	50	100	80	80

Can you effectively compare the performance of three divisions against the targets? What other measures mentioned in this chapter are needed to evaluate performance effectively?

Formulating Management Reports

MRA 2.
LO2 Responsibility Centers
LO3

Wood4Fun makes wooden playground equipment for the institutional and consumer markets. The company strives for low-cost, high-quality production because it operates in a highly competitive market in which product price is set by the marketplace and is not based on production costs. The company is organized into responsibility centers. The vice president of manufacturing is responsible for three manufacturing plants. The vice president of sales is responsible for four sales regions. Recently, these two vice presidents began to disagree about whether the manufacturing plants are cost centers or profit centers. The vice president of manufacturing views the plants as cost centers because the managers of the plants control only product-related costs. The vice president of sales believes the plants are profit centers because product quality and product cost strongly affect company profits.

1. Identify the controllable performance that Wood4Fun values and wants to measure. Give at least three examples of performance measures that Wood4Fun could use to monitor such performance.
2. For the manufacturing plants, what type of responsibility center is most consistent with the controllable performance Wood4Fun wants to measure?
3. For the sales regions, what type of responsibility center is most appropriate?

International Company

MRA 3.
LO2 Economic Value Added and
LO5 Performance
LO6

Sevilla Consulting offers environmental consulting services worldwide. The managers of branch offices are rewarded for superior performance with bonuses based on the economic value the office adds to the company. Last year's operating results for the entire company and for its three offices, expressed in millions of U.S. dollars, follow.

	Worldwide	Europe	Americas	Asia
Cost of capital	9%	10%	8%	12%
Total assets	$210	$70	$70	$70
Current liabilities	80	10	40	30
After-tax operating income	15	5	5	5

1. Compute economic value added for each office and worldwide. What factors affect each office's economic value added? How can an office improve its economic value added?
2. If managers' bonuses are based on economic value added to office performance, what specific actions will managers be motivated to take?
3. Is economic value added the only performance measure needed to evaluate investment centers adequately? Explain your response.

Excel Spreadsheet Analysis

MRA 4. *LO5 Return on Investment and Residual Income*

Tina Patel, the manager of the Food and Lodging Division at Winter Wonderland, has hired you as a consultant to help her examine her division's performance under several different circumstances.

1. Type the following format into a spreadsheet to compute the Food and Lodging Division's actual return on investment and residual income. Match your data entry to the rows and columns shown below. Data are from parts **3** and **4** of this chapter's Review Problem. (**Hint:** When entering the formulas, type = in front of the formula in the cell. Then the spreadsheet will know to compute the answer. Remember to format each cell for the type of numbers it holds, such as percentage, currency, or general.)

	A	B	C	D	E	F
1						
2	Investment Center		Food and Lodging Division			
3			Actual Results			
4	Sales		$40,000,000			
5	Operating income		$ 6,450,000			
6	Average assets invested		$10,000,000			
7	Desired ROI		30%			
8						
9	Return on Investment		C5/C6			
10						
11	Profit Margin		C5/C4			
12						
13	Asset Turnover		C4/C6			
14						
15	Residual Income		C5-(C7*C6)			
16						

2. Patel would like to know how the figures would change if Food and Lodging had a desired ROI of 40 percent and average assets invested of $10,000,000. Revise your spreadsheet from **1** to compute the division's return on investment and residual income under those conditions.
3. Patel also wants to know how the figures would change if Food and Lodging had a desired ROI of 30 percent and average assets invested of $12,000,000. Revise your spreadsheet from **1** to compute the division's return on investment and residual income under those conditions.
4. Does the use of formatted spreadsheets simplify the computation of ROI and residual income? Do such spreadsheets make it easier to do "what-if" analyses?

Internet Case

MRA 5.
LO6 Top Executive Compensation

Are top executives paid too much? Do the companies run by the most highly paid executives perform better than other companies? Do U.S. executives make more money than their foreign counterparts? These are some of the questions asked routinely in articles and surveys about executive compensation. Use the Internet to locate the top executive salary rankings compiled annually by business publications and other sources. Study the rankings and select several U.S. and foreign companies in the same industry for comparison.

Hint: There are several ways to access this type of information on the Internet. One approach is to do key word searches using search terms like *executive compensation* or *executive salary survey*. Another approach is to access a business publication web site such as <www.forbes.com> and do key word searches of articles. It is also possible to access corporate web sites to view their annual reports. Some corporate web sites are even searchable by key word.

1. In your review of top executive compensation, what types of incentives did you find included in annual compensation?
2. Are the companies with the highest-paid executives the best performers in their industry?
3. Do U.S. executives receive higher pay than their foreign counterparts? If so, do the U.S. companies perform better than their foreign counterparts?

24

Chapter 24 describes how managers perform incremental analyses to make the kind of decisions that will affect their organization's activities in the short run.

Short-Run Decision Analysis

LEARNING OBJECTIVES

LO1 Explain how managers make short-run decisions during the management cycle.

LO2 Define *incremental analysis* and describe how it applies to short-run decision analysis.

LO3 Perform incremental analysis for outsourcing decisions.

LO4 Perform incremental analysis for special order decisions.

LO5 Perform incremental analysis for segment profitability decisions.

LO6 Perform incremental analysis for sales mix decisions involving constrained resources.

LO7 Perform incremental analysis for sell or process-further decisions.

DECISION POINT
A MANAGER'S FOCUS

Bank of America <www.bankofamerica.com> Bank of America serves banking clients in over 150 countries worldwide. In its quest to find new ways to meet the needs of its commercial, consumer, global corporate, and investment banking customers, it is conducting more and more of its business over the Internet. At the end of 2002, the bank had more than 4.7 million active online customers. Expectations are that by 2006, nearly half of its 15 million active checking account customers will do their banking over the Internet.

Bank management believes this trend is good for business. In a survey of its account holders, Bank of America found that its online users were more likely to stay with the bank and maintain higher account balances and were less likely to make customer service calls. John Rosenfeld, senior vice president for ecommerce, believes that besides making money for the bank, online banking "deepens the relationship" and increases customer satisfaction.[1]

As customers become increasingly familiar with handling their finances online, banks will offer more product and service choices over the Internet. As bank managers make decisions about which business alternatives to pursue, they will ask questions like, When should bank products and services be outsourced? When should a special order for service be accepted? When is a bank segment profitable? What is the best sales mix when resource constraints exist? When should bank products be sold as is or processed fur-

How does Bank of America analyze short-run business opportunities offered by banking online?

ther into different products? To analyze these types of questions and make informed decisions, bank managers need useful information and analytic methods that will enable them to determine what could happen under various alternative courses of action.

SHORT-RUN DECISION ANALYSIS AND THE MANAGEMENT CYCLE

LO1 Explain how managers make short-run decisions during the management cycle.

RELATED TEXT ASSIGNMENTS
Q: 1, 2, 3
SE: 1
SD: 1

Readers of financial reports are interested in knowing what happened to produce the results that are presented in these reports. The historical information that the reports contain helps answer that question. For plannning and control purposes, managers want to know why things happened and what will happen. Many of the decisions they make will affect their organization's activities in the short run. Those decisions are the focus of this chapter. In making short-run decisions, managers need historical and estimated quantitative information that is both financial and nonfinancial in nature. Such information should be relevant, timely, and presented in a format that is easy to use in decision making.

As illustrated in Figure 1, **short-run decision analysis** is the systematic examination of any decision whose effects will be felt over the course of the next year. Although many business problems are unique and cannot be solved by following strict rules, managers frequently take five predictable actions when deciding what to do. The first four actions are taken during the planning stage of the management cycle, and the fifth and final action is taken during the reviewing stage.

PLANNING

In the planning stage of the management cycle, managers take the following four actions when performing short-run decision analysis:

1. Discover a problem or need.
2. Identify all reasonable courses of action that can solve the problem or meet the need.
3. Prepare a thorough analysis of each possible solution, identifying its total costs, savings, and other financial effects.
4. Select the best course of action.

www.bankofamerica.com

As a general rule, the managers of companies like Bank of America will make decisions that support the company's strategic plan. For example, the managers of a bank may have to make a decision about keeping or eliminating one of the bank's branch locations. Both quantitative and qualitative factors will influence the decision. The quantitative information includes the costs of operating the branch location and the fee revenues that the branch generates. Management may also want to know the number of customers serviced each year, the types of services offered, and the number and dollar amount of the branch's accounts.

The following qualitative factors will influence the managers' decision to keep or eliminate the branch:

- Competition (Do our competitors have a branch office located here?)
- Economic conditions (Is the community growing?)
- Social issues (Will keeping this branch benefit the community we serve?)
- Product or service quality (Can we attract more business because of the service quality of this branch?)
- Timeliness (Does the branch promote customer service?)

Managers must identify and assess the importance of all such qualitative and quantitative factors when they make short-run decisions.

● **STOP AND THINK!**
Are qualitative factors important in short-run decision making?
Yes, because qualitative factors such as competition, economic conditions, social issues, quality, and timeliness influence decision making. ■

EXECUTING

In this chapter, we focus on the executing stage of the management cycle—the stage in which managers must adapt to changing environments and take advantage of opportunities that will improve their organization's profitability and liquidity in the short run. During the year, managers may have an opportunity to accept a special order, examine the profitability of a segment, select the appropriate product mix

FIGURE 1
Short-Run Decisions in the Management Cycle

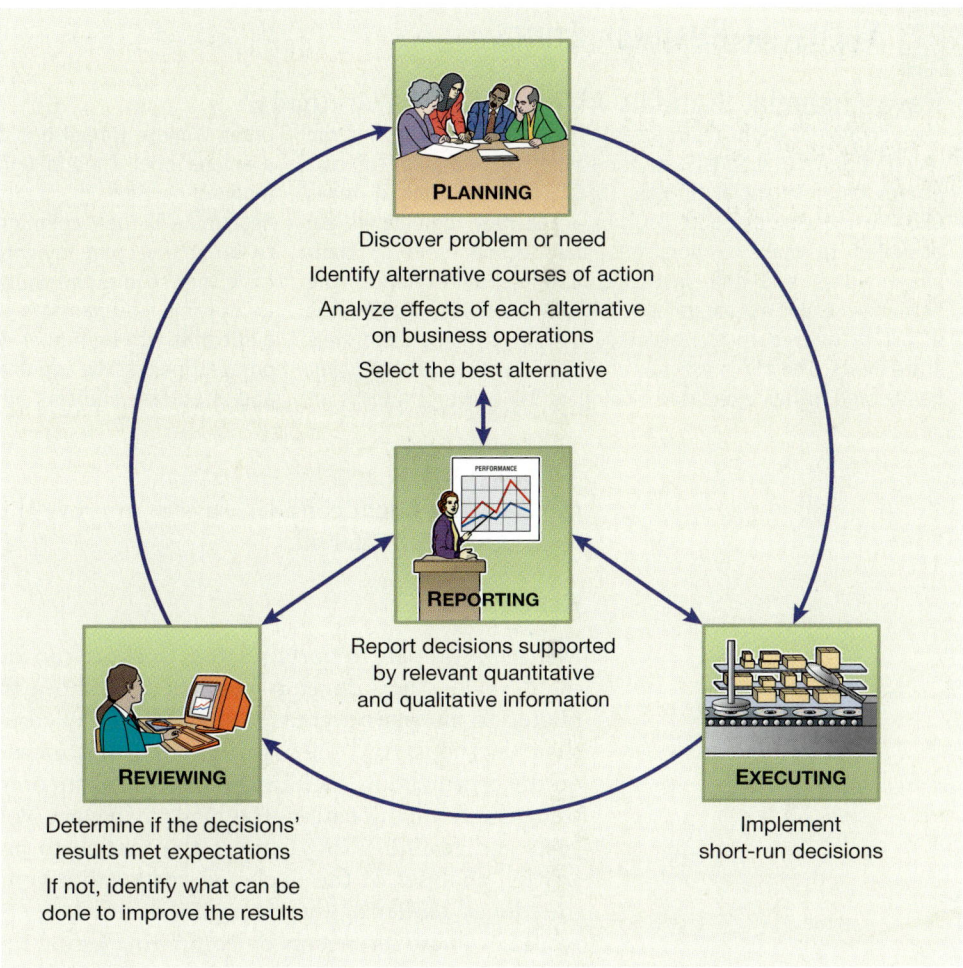

given a resource constraint, contract with outside suppliers of goods and services, or sell a product as is or process it further. All of those decisions affect operations in the current operating period.

In the executing stage, a bank's management might eliminate a branch if the costs of the branch exceed the revenues generated by it. However, management may choose to keep the branch because the community expects the organization to provide this service.

REVIEWING

In the reviewing stage of the management cycle, managers take the fifth predictable action when performing short-run decision analysis: they evaluate each decision to determine whether it produced the forecast results. They examine how each decision was carried out and how it affected the organization. If results fell short, the managers identify and prescribe corrective action. This post-decision audit supplies feedback about the results of the short-run decision. If the solution is not completely satisfactory or if the problem remains, the management cycle begins again. For example, if the bank decided to keep the branch location, the managers would evaluate the results of their decision in many ways. They would probably consider how successful the branch has been, how many people have benefited from the branch, and how well the branch fits in with the other kinds of services the bank offers. They would be interested in knowing how much operating income the branch has produced and in what other ways the branch has benefited the bank and the people the bank serves. Depending on what they discover during their review,

FOCUS ON BUSINESS ETHICS

Have Financial Scandals Affected CFOs' Workloads?

The documentation requirements that have resulted from recent financial scandals are increasing the workload of corporate chief financial officers (CFOs) and the time it takes CFOs to make and report decisions. The new regulations are designed to make corporations more accountable to their shareholders and the investing public. For example, the Sarbanes-Oxley Act requires that top corporate executives attest in writing to the accuracy of the company's earnings statements. The CFO must now confirm in writing with division heads and other executive managers that everything is in order, a more formal and time-consuming procedure than the previous one. In addition, CFOs are spending a significant amount of time thoroughly analyzing each rule and law to determine if their company is in compliance and, if not, how to bring the company into compliance. Although many CFOs have not computed how much adapting to all the new accounting standards is going to cost, they do know their audit bills will be higher due to the increased scrutiny of corporate finances by regulators and investors and the detailed audits outside auditors now require.[2]

the managers might consider ways to improve the branch, or they might decide to close the branch after all.

REPORTING

Managers prepare reports related to short-run decisions throughout the management cycle. They develop budgets that show the estimated costs and revenues related to alternative courses of action. They compile analyses of data that support their decisions. And they issue reports that measure the effect their decisions had on the organization, including its operating income. When deciding whether to continue the branch location, the bank managers would develop budgets showing the costs and revenues they expect the branch to generate. They would also prepare written analyses of the expected costs and revenues and of the qualitative factors mentioned earlier. If the managers decided to continue the branch location, they would evaluate its success by comparing actual financial and nonfinancial results to the results predicted in the budget and initial analyses. They would create reports showing how much operating income the branch has produced and how else the branch has benefited the bank and the people whom the bank serves.

 Check out ACE for a Review Quiz at http://accounting.college.hmco.com/students.

INCREMENTAL ANALYSIS FOR SHORT-RUN DECISIONS

LO2 Define *incremental analysis* and describe how it applies to short-run decision analysis.

RELATED TEXT ASSIGNMENTS
Q: 4, 5, 6
SE: 2
E: 1, 2
SD: 2, 4
MRA: 3

ENRICHMENT NOTE:
Incremental analysis is a technique used not only by businesses but also by individuals to solve daily problems.

Once managers have determined that a problem or need is worthy of consideration and have identified alternative courses of action, they must evaluate the effect that each alternative will have on their organization. The method of comparing alternatives by focusing on the differences in their projected revenues and costs is called **incremental analysis**. Incremental analysis is also called *differential analysis* if it ignores revenues or costs that stay the same or do not differ among the alternatives.

IRRELEVANT COSTS AND REVENUES

A cost that changes between alternatives is known as a **differential cost** (also referred to as an *incremental cost*). For example, assume that Home State Bank managers are deciding which of two ATM machines—C or W—to buy. The ATMs have the same purchase price but different revenues and cost characteristics. The company currently owns ATM B, which it bought three years ago for $15,000 and which has accumulated depreciation of $9,000 and a book value of $6,000. ATM B is now obsolete as a result of advances in technology and cannot be sold or traded in.

The accountant has collected the following annual revenue and operating cost estimates for the two new machines:

	ATM C	ATM W
Increase in revenue	$16,200	$19,800
Increase in annual operating costs		
Direct materials	4,800	4,800
Direct labor	2,200	4,100
Variable overhead	2,100	3,050
Fixed overhead (depreciation included)	5,000	5,000

The first step in the incremental analysis is to eliminate any irrelevant revenues and costs. *Irrelevant revenues* are those that will not differ between the alternatives. *Irrelevant costs* include sunk costs and costs that will not differ between the alternatives. A **sunk cost** is a cost that was incurred because of a previous decision and cannot be recovered through the current decision. An example of a sunk cost is the book value of ATM B. A manager might be tempted to say that the ATM should not be junked because the company still has $6,000 invested in it. However, the manager would be incorrect because the book value of the old ATM represents money that was spent in the past and so does not affect the decision about whether to replace the old ATM with a new one. The old ATM would be of interest only if it could be sold or traded in, and the amount received for it would be different, depending on which new ATM was chosen. In that case, the amount of the sale or trade-in value would be relevant to the decision because it would affect the future cash flows of the alternatives.

Another look at the financial data for ATMs C and W reveals two other irrelevant costs. The costs of direct materials and fixed overhead (depreciation included) can also be eliminated from the analysis because they are the same under both alternatives.

Once the irrelevant revenues and costs have been identified, the incremental analysis may be prepared using only the differential revenues and costs that will change between the alternative ATMs, as shown in Exhibit 1. The analysis shows that ATM W would produce $750 more in operating income than ATM C. Because the costs of buying the two ATMs are the same, this report would favor the purchase of ATM W.

KEY POINT: Sunk costs cannot be recovered and are irrelevant in short-run decision making.

EXHIBIT 1
Incremental Analysis

Home State Bank
Incremental Analysis

	ATM C	ATM W	Difference in Favor of ATM W
Increase in revenue	$16,200	$19,800	$3,600
Increase in operating costs that differ between alternatives			
Direct labor	$ 2,200	$ 4,100	($1,900)
Variable overhead	2,100	3,050	(950)
Total relevant operating costs	$ 4,300	$ 7,150	($2,850)
Resulting change in operating income	$11,900	$12,650	$ 750

● **STOP AND THINK!**
Should Home State Bank purchase ATM C or ATM W?
The bank should purchase ATM W. ■

Chapter 24 Short-Run Decision Analysis

FOCUS ON BUSINESS TECHNOLOGY

How Much Does It Cost to Process a Check?
Banks today have options for processing checks. They can outsource the processing of paper checks, use the quasi-paperless system of ATMs, or process transactions over the Internet. Bank managers have found that online banking substantially reduces transaction-processing costs. According to a study by an international consulting firm, the cost of processing a transaction is 1 cent if completed over the Internet, 27 cents using an ATM, or $1.07 if processed by a teller.[3]

KEY POINT: Opportunity costs arise when the choice of one course of action eliminates the possibility of another course of action.

OPPORTUNITY COSTS

Because incremental analysis focuses on only the quantitative differences among the alternatives, it simplifies management's evaluation of a decision and reduces the time needed to choose the best course of action. However, incremental analysis is only one input to the final decision. Management needs to consider other issues. For instance, the manufacturer of ATM C might have a reputation for better quality or service than the manufacturer of ATM W. **Opportunity costs** are the benefits that are forfeited or lost when one alternative is chosen over another.

Consider a plant nursery that has been in business for many years at the intersection of two highways. Suburbs have grown up around the nursery, and a bank has offered the nursery owner a high price for the land. The interest that could be earned from investing the proceeds of the sale is an opportunity cost for the nursery owner. It is revenue that the nursery owner has chosen to forgo to continue operating the nursery in that location.

A bank teller who is deciding whether to go back to school full time to earn a degree in finance also needs to consider opportunity costs. In this case, the opportunity cost is the salary the teller would lose by returning to school. The total cost of the degree includes not only tuition, books, supplies, and living expenses, but also the amount of salary forgone while the teller is a full-time student. This opportunity cost is one reason that many people choose to work full time and attend college part time.

Opportunity costs often come into play when a company is operating at or near capacity and must choose what products or services to offer. For example, assume that the Debit Card Company, which currently services 20,000 cards, has the option of offering 15,000 premium debit cards, a higher-priced product, but it cannot do both. The amount of income from the 20,000 debit cards is an opportunity cost of the premium debit cards.

 Check out ACE for a Review Quiz at http://accounting.college.hmco.com/students.

INCREMENTAL ANALYSIS FOR OUTSOURCING DECISIONS

LO3 Perform incremental analysis for outsourcing decisions.
RELATED TEXT ASSIGNMENTS
Q: 7, 8
SE: 3, 4
E: 3, 4
P: 1
SD: 3

BUSINESS WORLD EXAMPLE: Super Bakery, supplier of doughnuts and other baked goods to institutional markets, outsources its selling activities to a network of brokers, its production activities to independent bakeries, and its warehousing and shipping activities to trucking companies.

Outsourcing is the use of suppliers outside the organization to perform services or produce goods that could be performed or produced internally. **Make-or-buy decisions**, which are decisions about whether to make a part internally or buy it from an external supplier, may lead to outsourcing. Or a company may decide to outsource entire operating activities, such as warehousing and distribution, that it has traditionally performed in-house.

To improve operating income and compete effectively in global markets, many companies are focusing their resources on their core competencies, that is, the activities they perform best. One way to obtain the financial, physical, human, and technological resources needed to emphasize those competencies is to outsource expensive nonvalue-adding activities. Strong candidates for outsourcing include payroll processing, training, managing fleets of vehicles, sales and marketing, custodial services, and information management. Many such areas involve either relatively low skill levels (such as payroll processing or custodial services) or highly specialized knowledge (such as information management) that could be better acquired from experts outside the company.

Outsourcing production or operating activities can reduce a company's investment in physical assets and human resources, which can improve cash flow. It can also help a company reduce operating costs and improve operating income. Many companies like Bank of America and Amazon.com benefit from outsourcing. For example, Amazon.com outsources the distribution of most of its products and has been able to reduce its storage and distribution costs enough to offer product discounts of up to 40 percent off the list price. Outsourcing also enables it to provide additional value-adding services, such as online reviews by customers, personalized recommendations, and discussions and interviews about current products. Banks too are outsourcing to increase their online capabilities, especially in the areas of financial management software and analysis.

www.bankofamerica.com
www.amazon.com

In manufacturing companies, a common decision facing managers is whether to make or to buy some or all of the parts used in product assembly. The goal is to select the more profitable choice by identifying the costs of each alternative and their effects on revenues and existing costs. Managers need the following information for this analysis:

Information About Making	Information About Outsourcing
Need for additional machinery	Purchase price of item
Variable costs of making the item	Rent or net cash flow to be generated from vacated space in the factory
Incremental fixed costs	Salvage value of unused machinery

The case of Box Company illustrates an outsourcing decision. For the past five years, the firm has purchased packing cartons from an outside supplier at a cost of $1.25 per carton. The supplier has just informed Box Company that it is raising the price 20 percent, to $1.50 per carton, effective immediately. Box Company has idle machinery that could be adjusted to produce the cartons. Annual production and usage would be 20,000 cartons. The company estimates the cost of direct materials at $.84 per carton. Workers, who will be paid $8.00 per hour, can process 20 cartons per hour ($.40 per carton). The cost of variable manufacturing overhead will be $4 per direct labor hour, and 1,000 direct labor hours will be required. Fixed manufacturing overhead includes $4,000 of depreciation per year and $6,000 of other fixed costs. The company has space and machinery to produce the cartons; the machines are currently idle and will continue to be idle if the part is purchased. Should Box Company continue to outsource the cartons?

STUDY NOTE: When performing an incremental analysis for an outsourcing decision, do not incorporate irrelevant information, such as depreciation and other fixed costs. Include only costs that change between the alternatives.

Exhibit 2 presents an incremental analysis of the two alternatives. All relevant costs are listed. Because the machinery has already been purchased and neither the

EXHIBIT 2
Incremental Analysis: Outsourcing Decision

Box Company
Outsourcing Decision
Incremental Analysis

	Make	Outsource	Difference in Favor of Make
Direct materials (20,000 × $.84)	$16,800	—	($16,800)
Direct labor (20,000 × $.40)	8,000	—	(8,000)
Variable manufacturing overhead (1,000 hours × $4)	4,000	—	(4,000)
To purchase completed cartons (20,000 × $1.50)	—	$30,000	30,000
Totals	$28,800	$30,000	$ 1,200

● **STOP AND THINK!**
Should the company make or outsource the cartons?
The company should make the cartons. ■

machinery nor the required factory space has any other use, the depreciation costs and other fixed manufacturing overhead costs are the same for both alternatives; therefore, they are not relevant to the decision. The cost of making the needed cartons is $28,800. The cost of buying 20,000 cartons at the increased purchase price will be $30,000. Since the company would save $1,200 by making the cartons, management will decide to make the cartons.

 Check out ACE for a Review Quiz at http://accounting.college.hmco.com/students.

INCREMENTAL ANALYSIS FOR SPECIAL ORDER DECISIONS

LO4 Perform incremental analysis for special order decisions.

RELATED TEXT ASSIGNMENTS
Q: 9, 10, 11, 12
SE: 5, 6
E: 5, 6, 7
P: 2, 8
MRA: 1

KEY POINT: Special order decisions assume that excess capacity exists to accept the order and that the order, if accepted, will not have an impact on regular sales orders.

Managers are often faced with **special order decisions**, which are decisions about whether to accept or reject special orders at prices below the normal market prices. Special orders usually involve large numbers of similar products that are sold in bulk. Because these orders are not expected, they are not included in annual cost or sales estimates. And because they are one-time events, they should not be included in revenue or cost estimates for subsequent years. Before a firm accepts a special product order, it must be sure that the products involved are sufficiently different from its regular product line to avoid violating federal price discrimination laws and to avoid reducing unit sales from its full-priced regular product line.

The objective of a special order decision is to determine whether a special order should be accepted. A special order should be accepted only if it maximizes operating income, based on the organization's strategic plan and objectives, the relevant costs of the special order, and qualitative factors. One approach to such a decision is to compare the special order price to the relevant costs to produce, package, and ship the order. The relevant costs include the variable costs, variable selling costs, if any, and other costs directly associated with the special order (for example, freight, insurance, packaging, and labeling the product). Another approach is to prepare a special order bid price by calculating a minimum selling price for the special order. The bid price equals the relevant costs plus an estimated profit.

In many situations, sales commission expenses are excluded from a special order decision analysis because the customer approached the company directly. In addition, the fixed costs of existing facilities usually do not change if a company accepts a special order, and therefore they are usually irrelevant to the decision. If additional fixed costs must be incurred to fill the special order, they would be relevant to the decision. Examples of relevant fixed costs are the purchase of additional machinery, an increase in supervisory help, and an increase in insurance premiums required by a specific order.

For example, Home State Bank has been approved to provide and service four ATMs at a special event. The event sponsors want the fee per ATM transaction reduced to $.50 for these machines. At past special events, ATM use has averaged 2,000 transactions per machine. Home State Bank has located four idle ATMs and determined the following additional information:

ATM Cost Data for 400,000 Transactions (Annual Use for One Machine)

Direct materials	$ .10
Direct labor	.05
Overhead	
Variable	.20
Fixed ($100,000 ÷ 400,000)	.25
Advertising ($60,000 ÷ 400,000)	.15
Other fixed selling and administrative	
expenses ($120,000 ÷ 400,000)	.30
Cost per transaction	$1.05
Fee per transaction	$1.50

EXHIBIT 3
Incremental Analysis: Special Order Decision

Home State Bank
Special Order Decision
Incremental Analysis

	Without Order	With Order	Difference in Favor of Accepting Order
Sales	$2,400,000	$2,404,000	$4,000
Less variable costs			
Direct materials	$ 160,000	$ 160,800	($ 800)
Direct labor	80,000	80,400	(400)
Variable overhead	320,000	321,600	(1,600)
Total variable costs	$ 560,000	$ 562,800	($2,800)
Contribution margin	$1,840,000	$1,841,200	$1,200

● **STOP AND THINK!**
Should Home State Bank accept the special order?
Yes, the bank should accept the order. ■

Should Home State Bank accept the special event offer? An incremental analysis of the decision in the contribution-margin reporting format appears in Exhibit 3. The report shows the contribution margin for Home State Bank operations both with and without the special order. Fixed costs are not included because the only costs affected by the order are direct materials, direct labor, and variable overhead. The net result of accepting the special order is a $1,200 increase in contribution margin (and, correspondingly, in operating income). This amount is verified by the following incremental analysis:

Sales (2,000 transactions × 4) × $.50		$4,000
Less variable costs		
Direct materials (8,000 transactions × $.10)	$ 800	
Direct labor (8,000 transactions × $.05)	400	
Variable overhead (8,000 transactions × $.20)	1,600	
Total variable costs		2,800
Contribution margin		$1,200

The analysis reveals that Home State Bank should accept the special order.

Now let us assume that the event sponsor asks Home State Bank what its minimum special order price is. If the incremental costs for the special order are $2,800, the relevant cost per transaction is $.35 ($2,800 ÷ 8,000). The special order price should cover this cost and generate a profit. If Home State Bank would like to earn $800 from the special order, the special order price should be $.45 ($.35 cost per transaction plus $.10 profit per transaction [$800 ÷ 8,000 transactions]).

Of course, the decision that Home State Bank management makes must be consistent with the bank's strategic plan. Qualitative factors that might influence the decision are (1) the impact of the special order on regular customers, (2) the potential of the special order to lead into new sales areas, and (3) the customer's ability to maintain an ongoing relationship that includes good ordering and paying practices. Notice in Exhibit 3 that Home State Bank's sales of $2,400,000 without the special order absorbed all of the fixed costs of overhead, advertising, and selling and administration.

 Check out ACE for a Review Quiz at http://accounting.college.hmco.com/students.

INCREMENTAL ANALYSIS FOR SEGMENT PROFITABILITY DECISIONS

LO5 Perform incremental analysis for segment profitability decisions.
RELATED TEXT ASSIGNMENTS
Q: 13, 14
SE: 7
E: 8, 9
P: 3, 7
SD: 5
MRA: 2, 5

BUSINESS WORLD EXAMPLE Unilever, an English-Dutch incorporated company, is one of the largest consumer goods companies in the world. The company uses incremental analysis to evaluate more than 1,400 of its brands.

Another type of operating decision management must face is whether to keep or drop unprofitable segments, such as product lines, services, sales territories, divisions, departments, stores, or outlets. Management must select the alternative that maximizes operating income, based on the organization's strategic plan and objectives, the relevant revenues and costs, and qualitative factors. The objective of this analysis is to identify the segments that have a negative segment margin.

A **segment margin** is a segment's sales revenue minus its direct costs (direct variable costs and direct fixed costs traceable to the segment). Such costs are assumed to be **avoidable costs.** An avoidable cost could be eliminated if management were to drop the segment. If a segment has a positive segment margin (that is, if the segment's revenue is greater than its direct costs), management should keep the segment. The segment is able to cover its own direct costs and contribute a portion of its revenue to cover common costs and add to operating income. If a segment has a negative segment margin (the segment's revenue is less than its direct costs), management should eliminate the segment. However, certain common costs will be incurred regardless of the decision. Those are unavoidable costs, and the remaining segments must have sufficient contribution margin to cover their own direct costs and the common costs.

An analysis of segment profitability includes the preparation of a segmented income statement using variable costing to identify variable and fixed costs. The fixed costs that are traceable to the segments are called *direct fixed costs*. The remaining fixed costs are *common costs* and are not assigned to segments.

Assume that Home State Bank wants to determine if it should eliminate its Safe Deposit Division. Managers prepare a segmented income statement, separating variable and fixed costs to calculate the contribution margin. They separate the total fixed costs of $84,000 further by directly tracing $55,500 to Bank Operations and $16,500 to Safe Deposit; the remaining $12,000 are common fixed costs. The following segmented income statement shows the segment margins for Bank Operations and Safe Deposit and the operating income for the total company:

Home State Bank
Segmented Income Statement
For the Year Ended December 31, 20xx

	Bank Operations	Safe Deposit	Total Company
Sales	$135,000	$15,000	$150,000
Less variable costs	52,500	7,500	60,000
Contribution margin	$ 82,500	$ 7,500	$ 90,000
Less direct fixed costs	55,500	16,500	72,000
Segment margin	$ 27,000	($ 9,000)	$ 18,000
Less common fixed costs			12,000
Operating income			$ 6,000

The analysis of Situation 1 in Exhibit 4 shows that dropping Safe Deposit will increase operating income by $9,000. Unless the bank can increase Safe Deposit's segment margin by increasing sales revenue or reducing direct costs, management

EXHIBIT 4
Incremental Analysis: Segment Profitability Decision

Home State Bank
Segment Profitability Decision
Incremental Analysis—Situation 1

	Keep Safe Deposit	Drop Safe Deposit	Difference in Favor of Dropping Safe Deposit
Sales	$150,000	$135,000	($15,000)
Less variable costs	60,000	52,500	7,500
Contribution margin	$ 90,000	$ 82,500	($ 7,500)
Less direct fixed costs	72,000	55,500	16,500
Segment margin	$ 18,000	$ 27,000	$ 9,000
Less common fixed costs	12,000	12,000	0
Operating income	$ 6,000	$ 15,000	$ 9,000

🔴 **STOP AND THINK!**
Should Home State Bank keep or drop the Safe Deposit Division if there is no change in the activity of Bank Operations?
The bank should drop Safe Deposit. ■

Home State Bank
Segment Profitability Decision
Incremental Analysis—Situation 2

	Keep Safe Deposit	Drop Safe Deposit	Difference in Opposition to Dropping Safe Deposit
Sales	$150,000	$108,000	($42,000)
Less variable costs	60,000	42,000	18,000
Contribution margin	$ 90,000	$ 66,000	($24,000)
Less direct fixed costs	72,000	55,500	16,500
Segment margin	$ 18,000	$ 10,500	($ 7,500)
Less common fixed costs	12,000	12,000	0
Operating income	$ 6,000	($ 1,500)	($ 7,500)

FOCUS ON BUSINESS PRACTICE

To Drop or Not to Drop a Segment?

When Steve Bennett arrived at Intuit Corporation <www.intuit.com> in January 2000, he knew the company should have been doing much better than was indicated by its $1 billion in annual revenues from such popular software products as Quicken, QuickBooks, and Turbo Tax. Building on the reliable demand for its tax and accounting software, Bennett has guided Intuit in making acquisitions and building one of the industry's leading online subscription services. At the same time, Bennett began examining parts of Intuit that either weren't producing an adequate return or did not fit well with Intuit's core competencies. Since Bennett's arrival, Intuit has sold its mortgage loan division and eliminated its online insurance business.[4]

FOCUS ON INTERNATIONAL BUSINESS

Why Banks Prefer Ebanking

After performing segment analysis of online banking and face-to-face banking, bank managers worldwide are encouraging customers to do their banking over the Internet. Banks have found that linking worldwide Internet access with customer relationship management (CRM), customer-friendly financial software, and online bill payment in a secure banking environment will reduce costs, increase service and product availability, and boost earnings.[5]

should drop the segment. The incremental approach to analyzing this decision isolates the segment and focuses on its segment margin, as shown in the last column of the exhibit.

The decision to drop a segment also requires a careful review of the other segments to see if they will be affected. Let's extend the illustration by assuming that Bank Operation's sales volume and variable costs will decrease 20 percent if management eliminates Safe Deposit Division. The reduction in sales volume stems from the loss of customers who purchase products from both divisions. The analysis of Situation 2 in Exhibit 4 shows that dropping Safe Deposit would reduce both the segment margin and the bank's operating income by $7,500. In this situation, Home State Bank would want to keep Safe Deposit.

 Check out ACE for a Review Quiz at http://accounting.college.hmco.com/students.

INCREMENTAL ANALYSIS FOR SALES MIX DECISIONS

LO6 Perform incremental analysis for sales mix decisions involving constrained resources.

RELATED TEXT ASSIGNMENTS
Q: 15, 16
SE: 8
E: 10, 11, 12
P: 4, 5

KEY POINT: When resources such as direct materials, direct labor, or time are scarce, the goal is to maximize the contribution margin per unit of scarce resource.

KEY POINT: Selecting an alternative based on contribution margin per unit does not necessarily mean it is the best choice.

A company may not be able to provide the full variety of products or services that customers demand in a given time period. Limits on resources such as machine time or available labor may restrict the types or quantities of products or services. Resource constraints can also be associated with other activities, such as inspection and equipment setup. The question is, Which products or services contribute the most to company profitability in relation to the amount of capital assets or other constrained resources needed to offer those items? To satisfy customers' demands and maximize operating income, management will choose to offer the most profitable product or service first. To identify such products or services, the managers calculate the contribution margin per constrained resource (such as labor hours or machine hours) for each product or service.

The objective of a **sales mix decision** is to select the alternative that maximizes the contribution margin per constrained resource based on the organization's strategic plan and objectives, the relevant revenues and costs, and qualitative factors. The decision analysis, which uses incremental analysis to identify the relevant costs and revenues, consists of two steps. First, calculate the contribution margin per unit for each product or service affected by the constrained resource. The contribution margin per unit equals the selling price per unit less the variable costs per unit. Second, calculate the contribution margin per unit of the constrained resource. The contribution margin per unit of the constrained resource equals the contribution margin per unit divided by the quantity of the constrained resource required per unit.

Assume that Home State Bank offers three types of loans: commercial loans, auto loans and home loans. The product line data are as follows:

	Commercial Loans	Auto Loans	Home Loans
Current loan application demand	20,000	30,000	18,000
Processing hours per loan application	2	1	2.5
Loan origination fee	$24.00	$18.00	$32.00
Variable processing costs	$12.50	$10.00	$18.75
Variable selling costs	$ 6.50	$ 5.00	$ 6.25

The current loan application capacity is 100,000 processing hours.

Question 1: *Which loan type should be advertised and promoted initially because it is the most profitable for the bank? Which should be second? Which last?*

EXHIBIT 5
Incremental Analysis: Sales Mix Decision Involving Constrained Resources

Home State Bank
Sales Mix Decision: Ranking the Order of Loans
Incremental Analysis

	Commercial Loans	Auto Loans	Home Loans
Loan origination fee per loan	$24.00	$18.00	$32.00
Less variable costs			
Processing	$12.50	$10.00	$18.75
Selling	6.50	5.00	6.25
Total variable costs	$19.00	$15.00	$25.00
Contribution margin per loan (A)	$ 5.00	$ 3.00	$ 7.00
Processing hours per loan (B)	2	1	2.5
Contribution margin per processing hour (A ÷ B)	$ 2.50	$ 3.00	$ 2.80

Home State Bank
Sales Mix Decision: Number of Units to Make
Incremental Analysis

	Processing Hours
Total processing hours available	100,000
Less processing hours to produce auto loans (30,000 loans × 1 processing hour)	30,000
Balance of processing hours available	70,000
Less processing hours to produce home loans (18,000 loans × 2.5 processing hours per loan)	45,000
Balance of processing hours available	25,000
Less processing hours to produce commercial loans (12,500 loans × 2 processing hours per loan)	25,000
Balance of processing hours available	0

● **STOP AND THINK!**
In what order should Home State Bank sell the loans?
The bank should sell auto loans first, followed by home loans and commercial loans. ■

● **STOP AND THINK!**
Given the processing available, what quantity of each loan type should Home State Bank sell?
The bank should sell 30,000 auto loans, 18,000 home loans, and 12,500 commercial loans. ■

The sales mix analysis is shown in Exhibit 5. It indicates that the auto loans should be promoted first because they provide the highest contribution margin per processing hour. Home loans would be second, and commercial loans would be last.

Question 2: *How many of each type of loan should the bank sell to maximize its contribution margin based on the current loan application activity of 100,000 processing hours? What is the total contribution margin for that combination?*

To begin the analysis, compare the current loan application activity to the required loan activity to meet the current loan demand. The company needs 115,000 processing hours to meet the current loan demand: 40,000 processing hours for commercial loans (20,000 loans × 2 processing hours), 30,000 processing hours for auto loans (30,000 loans × 1 processing hour per loan), and 45,000 processing hours for home loans (18,000 loans × 2.5 processing hours per loan). Because that amount exceeds the current capacity of 100,000 processing hours, management must determine the sales mix that maximizes the company's contribution margin, which will also maximize its operating income. The calculations in the second part of Exhibit 5 show that Home State Bank should sell 30,000 auto loans, 18,000 home loans, and 12,500 commercial loans. The total contribution margin is as follows:

Auto loans (30,000 loans × $3.00 per loan)	$ 90,000
Home loans (18,000 loans × $7.00 per loan)	126,000
Commercial loans (12,500 loans × $5.00 per loan)	62,500
Total contribution margin	$278,500

As mentioned earlier, bank management makes the final decision based on the company's strategic plan and objectives, all relevant revenues and costs, and qualitative factors.

 Check out ACE for a Review Quiz at http://accounting.college.hmco.com/students.

INCREMENTAL ANALYSIS FOR SELL OR PROCESS-FURTHER DECISIONS

LO7 Perform incremental analysis for sell or process-further decisions.

RELATED TEXT ASSIGNMENTS
Q: 17, 18, 19, 20
SE: 9, 10
E: 13, 14
P: 6
MRA: 4

KEY POINT: Products are made by combining materials or by dividing materials, such as in oil refining or ore extraction.

TERMINOLOGY NOTE: The common cost shared by two or more products before they are split off are called *joint costs*. Joint costs are irrelevant in a sell or process-further decision.

Some companies offer products or services that can either be sold in a basic form or be processed further and sold as a more refined product or service to a different market. For example, a meatpacking company processes cattle into meat and meat-related products, such as bones and hides. The company may choose to sell sides of beef and pounds of bones and hides to other companies for further processing. Alternatively, it could choose to cut and package the meat for immediate sale in grocery stores, process bone into fertilizer for gardeners, or tan hides into refined leather for purses.

A **sell or process-further decision** is a decision about whether to sell a joint product at the split-off point or sell it after further processing. **Joint products** are two or more products made from a common material or process that cannot be identified as separate products or services during some or all of the processing. Only at a specific point, called the **split-off point**, do joint products or services become separate and identifiable. At that point, a company may choose to sell the product or service as is or to process it into another form for sale to a different market.

The objective of a sell or process-further decision is to select the alternative that maximizes operating income, based on the organization's strategic plan and objectives, the relevant revenues and costs, and qualitative factors. To complete the analysis, calculate the incremental revenue, which is the difference between the total revenue if the product or service is sold at the split-off point and the total revenue if the product or service is sold after further processing. Compare the incremental revenue to the incremental costs of processing further. Choose to process a product or service further if the incremental revenue is greater than the incremental costs of processing further. If the incremental costs are greater than the incremental revenue, choose to sell the product or service at the split-off point. Be sure to ignore joint costs (or common costs) in your analysis, because they are incurred *before* the split-off point and do not change if further processing occurs. Although accountants assign joint costs to products or services when valuing inventories and calculating cost of goods sold, joint costs are not relevant to a sell or process-further decision and are omitted from the decision analysis.

For example, as part of the company's strategic plan, Home State Bank's management is looking for new markets for banking services, and management is con-

EXHIBIT 6
Incremental Analysis: Sell or Process-Further Decision

Home State Bank
Sell or Process-Further Decision
Incremental Analysis

	Premier Checking	Personal Banker
Incremental revenue per account if processed further:		
Process further	$50	$250
Split-off — Basic Checking	25	25
Incremental revenue	$25	$225
Less incremental costs	30	200
Operating income (loss) from processing further	($ 5)	$ 25

● **STOP AND THINK!**
Should Home State Bank bundle services or offer Basic Checking accounts?
The bank should offer both Basic Checking and Personal Banker services to its customers. ■

sidering whether it would be profitable to bundle banking services. Home State Bank is considering adding two levels of service, Premier Checking and Personal Banker, beyond its current Basic Checking account services. The three levels have the following features:

- Basic Checking: online checking account, debit card, and online bill payment with a required minimum average balance of $500.
- Premier Checking: paper and online checking, a debit card, a credit card, and a small life insurance policy equal to the maximum credit limit on the credit card for customers who maintain a minimum average balance of $1,000.
- Personal Banker: all of the features of Premier Checking plus a safe deposit box, $5,000 personal line of credit at prime, financial investment advice, and a toaster upon opening the account for customers who maintain a minimum average balance of $5,000.

Assume the bank can earn sales revenue of 5 percent on its checking account balances and that the total cost of basic checking is currently $50,000. The bank's accountant provided these data for each level of service:

Product	Sales Revenue	Additional Costs
Basic Checking	$ 25	$ 0
Premier Checking	50	30
Personal Banker	250	200

The decision analysis in Exhibit 6 indicates that the bank should offer Personal Banking services in addition to Basic Checking accounts. Notice that the $50,000 joint costs of Basic Checking were ignored because they are sunk costs that will not influence the decision.

As mentioned earlier, management makes the final decision based on the bank's strategic plan and objectives, the relevant revenues and costs, and qualitative factors. A decision to process further must agree with the bank's strategic plan to expand into new markets. In addition, management must consider the bank's ability to obtain favorable returns on its bank deposit investments.

 Check out ACE for a Review Quiz at http://accounting.college.hmco.com/students.

Chapter Review

REVIEW OF LEARNING OBJECTIVES

LO1 Explain how managers make short-run decisions during the management cycle.

Both quantitative information and qualitative information are important for short-run decision analysis. Such information should be relevant, timely, and presented in a format that is easy to use in decision making. In the planning stage of the management cycle, managers discover a problem or need, identify alternative courses of action to solve the problem or meet the need, perform a complete analysis to determine the effects of each alternative on business operations, and choose the best alternative. Managers during the executing stage accept or reject a special order, examine the profitability of a segment, select the appropriate product mix given a resource constraint, contract with outside suppliers of goods and services, or sell a product as is or process it further. In the reviewing stage, each decision is evaluated to determine if the forecast results were obtained. Reporting occurs throughout the cycle to evaluate the information selected, the decision made, and the impact of that decision on the organization.

LO2 Define *incremental analysis* and describe how it applies to short-run decision analysis.

Incremental analysis helps managers compare alternatives by focusing on the differences in their projected revenues and costs. Any data that relate to future costs, revenues, or uses of resources and that will differ among alternative courses of action are considered relevant decision information. Projected sales or estimated costs, such as direct materials or direct labor, which differ for each decision alternative, are examples of relevant information. The accountant organizes relevant information to determine which alternative contributes the most to profits or incurs the lowest costs. Only data that differ for each alternative appear in the report. Differential or incremental costs are costs that vary among alternatives and thus are relevant to the decision. Sunk costs are past costs that cannot be recovered; they are irrelevant to the decision process. Opportunity costs are revenue or income forgone as a result of choosing an alternative.

LO3 Perform incremental analysis for outsourcing decisions.

Outsourcing (including make-or-buy) decision analysis helps managers decide whether to use suppliers from outside the organization to perform services or provide goods that could be performed or produced internally. An incremental analysis of the expected costs and revenues for each alternative is used to identify the best alternative.

LO4 Perform incremental analysis for special order decisions.

A special order decision is a decision about whether to accept or reject a special order at a price below the normal market price. One approach is to compare the special order price to the relevant costs to see if a profit can be generated. Another approach is to prepare a special order bid price by calculating a minimum selling price for the special order. Generally, fixed costs are irrelevant to a special order decision because such costs are covered by regular sales activity and do not differ among alternatives.

LO5 Perform incremental analysis for segment profitability decisions.

Segment profitability decisions involve the review of segments of an organization, such as product lines, services, sales territories, divisions, or departments. Often managers must decide whether to add or drop a segment. A segment with a negative segment margin may be dropped. A segment margin is a segment's sales revenue minus its direct costs, which include variable costs and avoidable fixed costs. Avoidable costs are costs traceable to a specific segment. If the segment is eliminated, the avoidable costs will also be eliminated.

LO6 Perform incremental analysis for sales mix decisions involving constrained resources.

Sales mix decisions require the selection of the most profitable combination of sales items when a company makes more than one product or service using a common constrained resource. The product or service generating the highest contribution margin per constrained resource is offered and sold first.

LO7 Perform incremental analysis for sell or process-further decisions.

Sell or process-further decisions require managers to choose between selling a joint product at its split-off point or processing it into a more refined product. The managers compare the incremental revenues and costs of the two alternatives. Joint processing costs are irrelevant to the decision because they are identical for both alternatives. A product should be processed further only if the incremental revenues generated exceed the incremental costs incurred.

REVIEW OF CONCEPTS AND TERMINOLOGY

The following concepts and terms were introduced in this chapter:

LO5 **Avoidable costs:** Costs that can be eliminated by dropping a segment.

LO2 **Differential cost:** A cost that changes among alternatives. Also known as *incremental cost*.

LO2 **Incremental analysis:** A technique used in decision analysis that compares alternatives by focusing on the differences in their projected revenues and costs. Also called *differential analysis*.

LO7 **Joint products:** Two or more products made from a common material or process that cannot be identified as separate products during some or all of the production process.

LO3 **Make-or-buy decisions:** Decisions about whether to make a part internally or buy it from an external supplier.

LO2 **Opportunity costs:** The benefits forfeited or lost when one alternative is chosen over another.

LO3 **Outsourcing:** The use of suppliers outside the organization to perform services or produce goods that could be performed or produced internally.

LO6 **Sales mix decision:** A decision to select the alternative that maximizes the contribution margin per constrained resource.

LO5 **Segment margin:** A segment's sales revenue minus its direct costs (direct variable costs and direct fixed costs traceable to the segment).

LO7 **Sell or process-further decision:** A decision about whether to sell a joint product at the split-off point or sell it after further processing.

LO1 **Short-run decision analysis:** The systematic examination of any decision whose effects will be most felt over the next year or less.

LO4 **Special order decisions:** Decisions about whether to accept or reject special orders at prices below normal market prices.

LO7 **Split-off point:** A specific point in the production process at which two or more joint products become separate and identifiable. At that point, a company may choose to sell the product as is or process it into another form for sale to a different market.

LO2 **Sunk cost:** A cost that was incurred because of a previous decision and cannot be recovered through the current decision.

REVIEW PROBLEM

Short-Run Operating Decision Analysis

LO5 Ten years ago, Dale Bandy formed Home Services, Inc., a company specializing in repair and maintenance services for the home and its surroundings. At present, Home Services has offices in six major cities across the country that offer repair and maintenance services to homeowners. During the past two years, the company's profitability has decreased, and Bandy wants to determine which service lines are not meeting the company's profit targets. Once the unprofitable service lines have been identified, he will either eliminate them or set higher prices. If higher prices are set, all variable and fixed operating, selling, and general administration costs will be covered by the price structure. Four service lines are under serious review. The following data from the most recent year-end closing were available for analysis:

Home Services, Inc.
Segmented Income Statement
For the Year Ended December 31, 20x8

	Auto Repair Service	Boat Repair Service	Tile Floor Repair Service	Tree Trimming Service	Total Company Impact
Sales	$297,500	$114,300	$126,400	$97,600	$635,800
Less variable costs					
Direct labor	$119,000	$ 40,005	$ 44,240	$34,160	$237,405
Operating supplies	14,875	5,715	6,320	4,880	31,790
Small tools	11,900	4,572	5,056	7,808	29,336
Replacement parts	59,500	22,860	25,280	—	107,640
Truck costs	—	11,430	12,640	14,640	38,710
Selling costs	44,625	17,145	18,960	9,760	90,490
Other variable costs	5,950	2,286	2,528	1,952	12,716
Total	$255,850	$104,013	$115,024	$73,200	$548,087
Contribution margin	$ 41,650	$ 10,287	$ 11,376	$24,400	$ 87,713
Less direct fixed costs	35,800	16,300	24,100	5,200	81,400
Segment margin	$ 5,850	($ 6,013)	($ 12,724)	$19,200	$ 6,313
Less common fixed costs					32,100
Operating income (loss)					($ 25,787)

REQUIRED
1. Analyze the performance of the four service lines being reviewed. Should Dale Bandy eliminate any of the service lines? Explain your answer.
2. Why might Bandy want to continue providing unprofitable service lines?
3. Even though some of the unprofitable services can be eliminated, the company still has an operating loss. Identify some possible causes for poor performance by the services. What actions do you recommend?

Answer to Review Problem

1. When deciding whether to eliminate any of the four service lines, Dale Bandy should concentrate on the service lines that have a negative segment margin. If the revenues from a service line are less than the sum of its variable and direct fixed costs, then other service lines must cover some of the losing line's costs while carrying the burden of the common fixed costs.

    By looking at the segmented income statement, Dale Bandy can see that the company will improve its operating income by $18,737 ($6,013 + $12,724) by eliminating the Boat Repair Service and the Tile Floor Repair Service, both of which have a negative segment margin. Bandy's decision can also be supported by the analysis at the top of the opposite page.

2. Bandy may want to continue offering the unprofitable service lines if their elimination would have a negative effect on the sale of the auto repair service or tree trimming service. Bandy may also want to diversify into new markets by offering new services. If Bandy does decide to enter new markets, he should be prepared to suffer some initial losses.

Bob's Burgers has hired you as a consultant and has given you an income statement comparing the operating incomes of its five restaurants in Eastern Europe. You have noticed that the Prague location is operating at a loss (including unallocated fixed costs) and must decide whether to recommend closing that restaurant.

Review the information used in making the decision to open the restaurant. Identify the types of information that would also be relevant in deciding whether to close the restaurant. What period or periods of time should be reviewed in making your decision? What additional information would be relevant in making your decision?

Excel Spreadsheet Analysis

MRA 4.

LO7 Sell or Process-Further Decision

Marketeers, Inc., has developed a promotional program for a large shopping center in Sunset Living, Arizona. After investing $360,000 in developing the original promotion campaign, the firm is ready to present its client with an add-on contract offer that includes the original promotion areas of (1) TV advertising campaign, (2) a series of brochures for mass mailing, and (3) a special rotating BIG SALE schedule for 10 of the 28 tenants in the shopping center. Following are the revenue terms from the original contract with the shopping center and the offer for an add-on contract, which extends the original contract terms.

	Contract Terms	
	Original Contract Terms	Extended Contract Including Add-On Terms
TV advertising campaign	$520,000	$ 580,000
Brochure series	210,000	230,000
Rotating BIG SALE schedule	170,000	190,000
Totals	$900,000	$1,000,000

Marketeers, Inc., estimates that the following additional costs will be incurred by extending the contract:

	TV Campaign	Brochures	BIG SALE Schedule
Direct labor	$30,000	$ 9,000	$7,000
Variable overhead costs	22,000	14,000	6,000
Fixed overhead costs*	12,000	4,000	2,000

*80 percent are direct fixed costs applied to this contract.

1. Using an Excel spreadsheet, compute the costs that will be incurred for each part of the add-on portion of the contract.
2. Should Marketeers, Inc., offer the add-on contract, or should it ask for a final settlement check based on the original contract only? Defend your answer.
3. If management of the shopping center indicated that the terms of the add-on contract were negotiable, how should Marketeers, Inc., respond?

Internet Case

MRA 5.

LO5 Comparison of Segment Performance

Public companies that operate in different businesses or segments are required to report operating results for those segments. This requirement makes it possible to evaluate the performance of comparable segments of different companies even though the rest of the companies' operations are not in comparable segments. Access the web sites for AOL Time Warner Inc. <www.aoltw.com> and Walt Disney Company <disney.go.com>. Both are diversified entertainment companies, but they operate in different segments. In the notes to each company's financial statements, find the note about segments and identify the segments that are comparable between the companies. Based on segment revenues, which company has the larger of the comparable segments? Based on segment operating income in relation to sales, which company has the more profitable segments?

25

Chapter 25 examines the various price-setting approaches managers use to establish prices of goods and services.

Pricing Decisions, Including Target Costing and Transfer Pricing

LEARNING OBJECTIVES

LO1 Identify the objectives and rules used to establish prices of goods and services, and relate pricing issues to the management cycle.

LO2 Describe economic pricing concepts including the auction-based pricing method used on the Internet.

LO3 Use cost-based pricing methods to develop prices.

LO4 Describe target costing and use that concept to analyze pricing decisions and evaluate a new product opportunity.

LO5 Describe how transfer pricing is used for transferring goods and services and evaluating performance within a division or segment.

DECISION POINT
A MANAGER'S FOCUS

Palm, Inc. <www.palm.com> Palm, Inc., invented and dominates the personal digital assistant (PDA) market. Its products range from simple two-button PDAs like the Zire to high-priced innovative models that combine the features of a cell phone and digital organizer with wireless Internet access. Competition between Palm, Handspring <www.handspring.com>, and other PDA and Pocket PC companies is very keen, and there is constant pressure to offer more technology-rich features to meet competition.

Historically, new PDA models have been expensive, priced to recover a product's cost plus some desired profit. As models age and are replaced with newer technology, their prices drop. In a recent market move, however, Palm began to use a different price approach for its lowest-priced products. Instead of offering its older technology at bargain prices, Palm decided to create a new product, the Zire, specifically targeted at the "under $100 market."[1] Palm's managers could not use a cost-based pricing strategy since the price was set at less than $100 before the new product's cost was computed. Instead, they used target costing. They subtracted their desired target profit for the Zire from the proposed $99 price to arrive at the maximum target cost for the Zire. A team of engineering, accounting, and sales managers then analyzed each proposed product feature to verify that the product could be designed and manufactured at or below the target cost. What resulted is a lightweight, simple, and easy-to-use organizer. Is determining the Zire's maximum cost from its market price a good

Why did Palm managers use target costing to establish a price for the Zire?

business practice? How should Palm's managers set the prices of their products and services?

Successful managers, like those at Palm, generally use several pricing approaches. No one pricing method is superior since each business and market segment differs.

THE PRICING DECISION AND THE MANAGER

LO1 Identify the objectives and rules used to establish prices of goods and services, and relate pricing issues to the management cycle.

RELATED TEXT ASSIGNMENTS
Q: 1, 2, 3, 4, 5, 6, 7
SE: 1, 2
E: 1, 2
SD: 1, 3

As you will learn in this chapter, there are many approaches to setting prices. However, each of these approaches may very well produce a different price for the same product or service. The process of establishing a correct price is, in fact, more an art than a science. The art of price setting depends on a manager's ability to analyze the marketplace and anticipate customers' reactions to a product or service and its price. Factors that managers consider when analyzing the market include competitors' price strategies, the economic environment, and legal, political, and niche issues. In today's global marketplace, managers perfect the art of price setting through experience in dealing with customers and products within their company's industry.

THE OBJECTIVES OF A PRICING POLICY

Setting appropriate prices is one of a manager's most difficult day-to-day decisions. Because such decisions affect the long-term survival of any profit-oriented enterprise, the long-run objectives of a company should include a pricing policy. A pricing policy is one way in which companies diffferentiate themselves from their competitors. Compare, for example, the pricing policies of Mercedes-Benz and Toyota or the pricing policies of the upscale retailer Nordstrom and the discount retailer Wal-Mart. Consider also how prices are set on eBay and Priceline.com. Although all these companies are successful, their pricing policies differ significantly because each company has different pricing objectives.

www.mercedes-benz.com
www.toyota.com
www.nordstrom.com
www.walmart.com
www.ebay.com
www.priceline.com
www.palm.com
www.handspring.com
www.gm.com

In addition, companies may use pricing policies to differentiate among their own brands. For example, companies like Palm, Handspring, and General Motors use price to differentiate their various product brands and the market segments that each brand targets. Thus, for each product brand, the company has identified the market segment it intends to serve and has developed pricing objectives to meet the needs of that market.

Possible objectives of a pricing policy include the following:

1. Identifying and adhering to both short-run and long-run pricing strategies
2. Maximizing profits
3. Maintaining or gaining market share
4. Setting socially responsible prices
5. Maintaining a minimum rate of return on investment
6. Being customer focused

 STOP AND THINK!
On what basis do companies compete if they sell basically identical commodities like paper clips and plastic bags rather than customized products?

Such companies differentiate themselves from their competitors primarily by price. ∎

Pricing strategies depend on many factors and conditions. Companies that produce standard items or commodities for a competitive marketplace will have different pricing strategies from firms that make custom-designed items. In a competitive market, companies can reduce prices to win sales away from competing companies. They can also continuously add value-enhancing features and upgrades to their products and services to create the impression that customers are receiving more for their money. In contrast, a company that makes custom-designed items can be more conservative in its pricing strategy.

Maximizing profits has traditionally been the underlying objective of any pricing policy. One key lead indicator of profit potential is increasing market share. Maintaining or gaining market share is closely related to pricing strategies. However, market share is important only if sales are profitable. To increase market share by reducing prices below cost can be economically disastrous unless such a move is accompanied by strategies that compensate for the lost revenues.

VIDEO CASE

Nokia Corporation <www.nokia.com>

OBJECTIVES

- Identify the objectives of pricing of goods and services.
- Identify and describe cost-based methods of developing prices of goods and services.
- Define target costing, and explain how it applies to a company like Nokia.

BACKGROUND FOR THE CASE

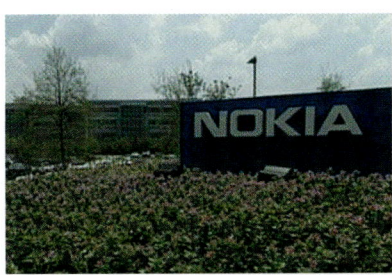

Nokia Corporation, one of the world's leaders in global telecommunications, is a Finnish company that was established in 1865 as a paper manufacturer. It entered the field of telecommunications in the 1960s and has since become the leading supplier of cell phones and other mobile phones. It is also a leading supplier of mobile, fixed broadband, and Internet protocol networks. Today Nokia has nearly 52,000 employees worldwide. Its phones are sold in more than 130 countries. In recent years Nokia has grown at astonishing rates as the overall global market for mobile phones has increased to 1,125 million users in 2002. Nokia projects that the mobile subscriber market will exceed 1.5 billion users by 2005 as more individuals realize the benefits of mobile connectivity and existing regional networks move to the next generation of secure, high-speed, high-capacity global networks. How are Nokia's managers preparing for future growth?

Competition in the cell phone market is intense. Nokia's two top competitors are Motorola <www.motorola.com>, a U.S. company, and Ericsson <www.ericsson.com>, a Swedish company. To maintain market share, Nokia must not only be innovative by producing smaller phones that have new multimedia features and advanced mobile services, such as Internet access, but it must also have competitive pricing. Many consumers view one cell phone as being much like another. They want the phone that costs them the least. Thus, the price of the phone becomes a very important competitive feature. Phones with similar features must be priced equal to or less than the competition, or sales will suffer. The issues of pricing cell phones are critical to Nokia's success.[2]

For more information about Nokia Corporation, visit the company's web site through the Needles Accounting Resource Center Web Site at **http://accounting.college.hmco.com/students.**

REQUIRED

View the video on Nokia Corporation that accompanies this book. As you are watching the video, take notes related to the following questions:

1. What are some common objectives of pricing goods and services, and how do they apply to Nokia in the pricing of cell phones?
2. What cost-based methods are available to Nokia for pricing cell phones?
3. What is target costing? Why is it applicable in today's competitive cell phone market?
4. What role do cooperative marketing agreements play in the pricing of Nokia cell phones?

Maximizing profits remains a dominant factor in price setting. However, to enhance their standing with the public and thus ensure their long-term survival, companies today also consider whether their prices are socially responsible. The pricing policies of many companies now take into consideration a variety of social concerns, including environmental factors, the influence of an aging population, legal constraints, and ethical issues.

Other pricing policy objectives include maintaining a minimum return on investment and enhancing value to customers. Organizations view each product or service as an investment. They will not invest in making a product or providing a service unless it will provide a minimum return. To maintain a minimum return on investment, an organization, when setting prices, adds a markup percentage to each product's costs of production. The markup percentage is closely related to the objective of profit maximization. Taking customers' needs into consideration when setting prices or increasing a product's value to customers is important for several reasons. First, sensitivity to customers is necessary to sustain sales growth. Second, customers' acceptance is crucial to success in a competitive market. Third, prices should reflect the enhanced value the company adds, which is another way of saying that prices are customer driven.

FIGURE 1
Pricing and the Management Cycle

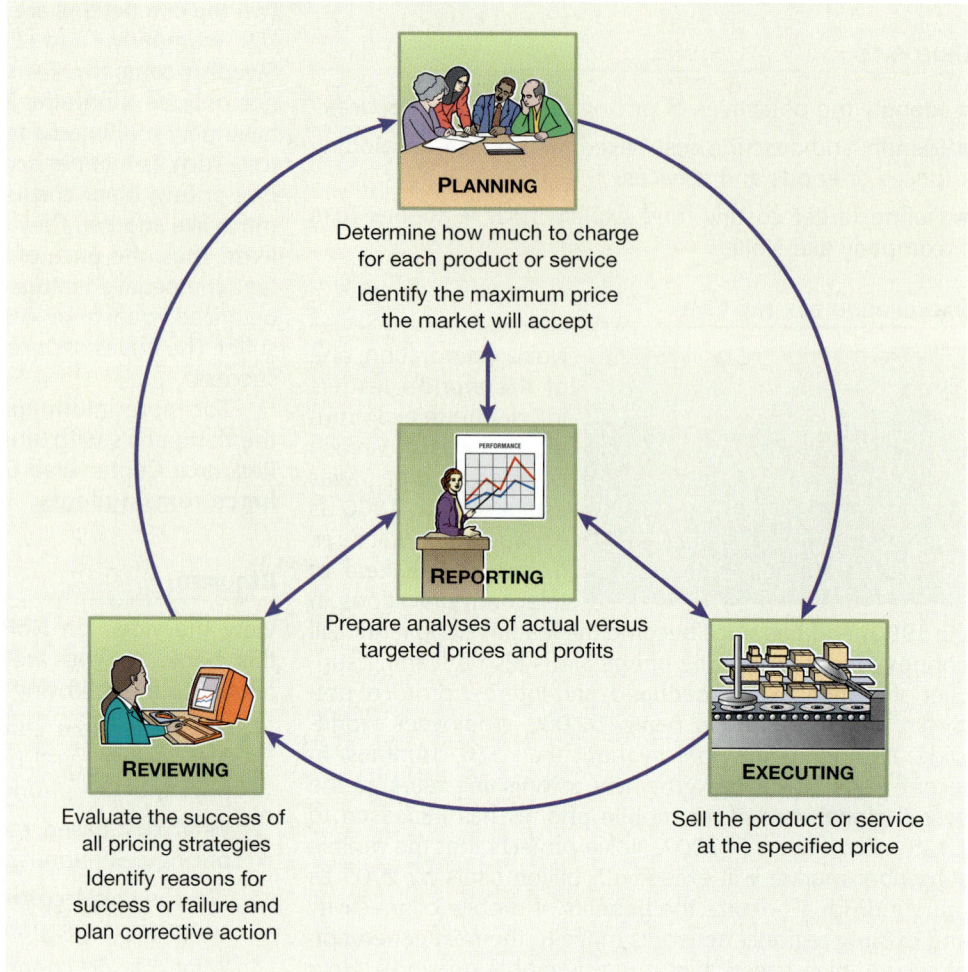

PRICING AND THE MANAGEMENT CYCLE

For an organization to stay in business, its selling price must (1) be competitive with the competition's price, (2) be acceptable to customers, (3) recover all costs incurred in bringing the product or service to market, and (4) return a profit. If a manager deviates from any of those four pricing rules, there must be a specific short-run objective that accounts for the change. Breaking those pricing rules for a long period will force a company into bankruptcy. Making sure that pricing issues are addressed at each stage of the management cycle, as illustrated in Figure 1, helps prevent this from happening.

■ **PLANNING** During the planning stage, managers must consider how much to charge for each product or service and identify the maximum price the market will accept and the minimum price the company can sustain. Those prices form the foundation for budgets as well as for projections of profitability.

■ **EXECUTING** During the executing stage, the products' or services' pricing strategies are followed. and products or services are sold either at the specified prices or on the auction market.

■ **REVIEWING** During the reviewing stage, managers evaluate sales to determine which pricing strategies were successful and which failed. At this stage, it is

FIGURE 2
External and Internal Factors Affecting Pricing Decisions

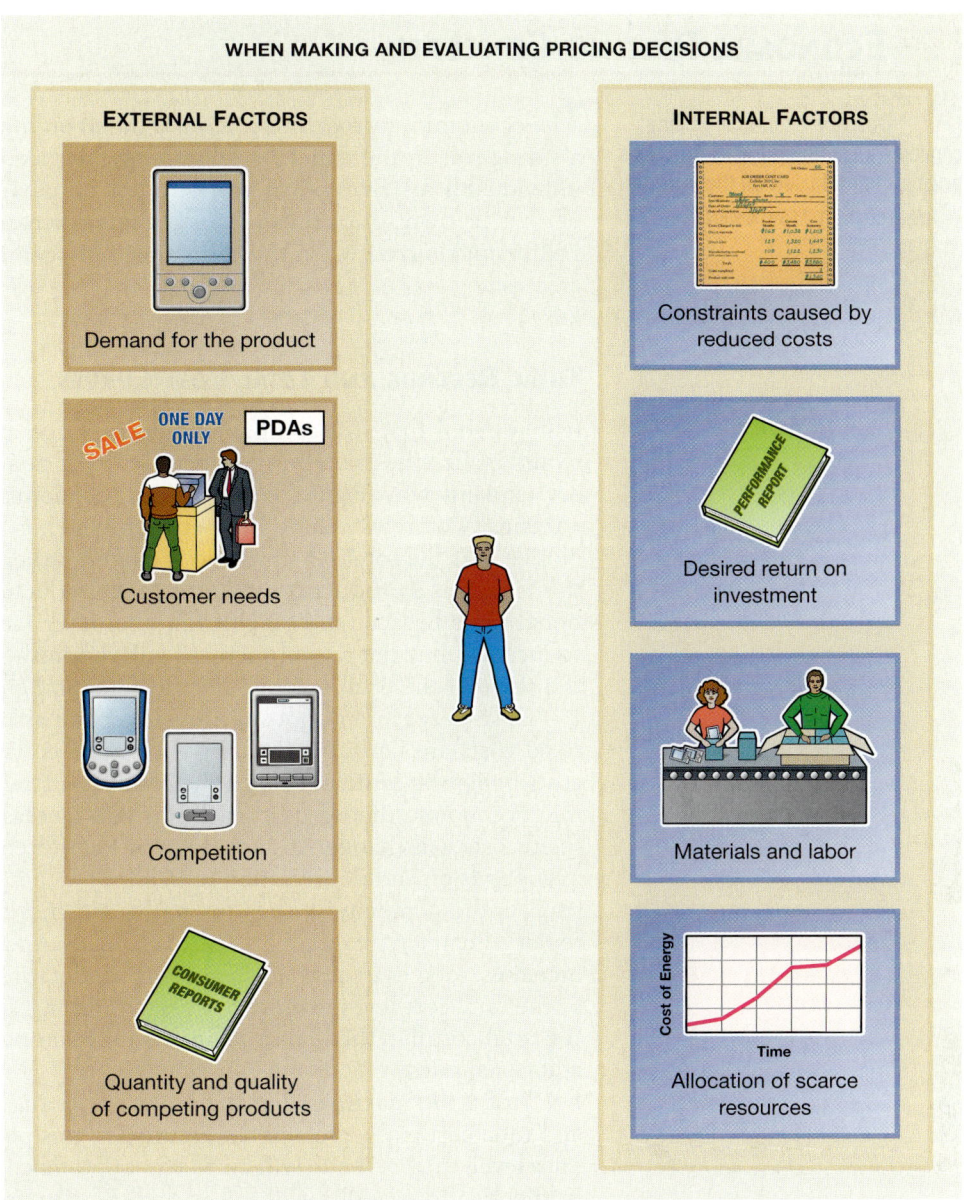

especially important to identify reasons for success or failure and plan any necessary corrective action.

■ **REPORTING** During the reporting stage, analyses of actual prices and profits versus targeted ones are prepared for use inside the organization. Those reports are used to assess past pricing strategies and plan future strategies.

When making and evaluating pricing decisions, managers must consider many factors. As shown in Figure 2, some of those factors relate to the external market, and others relate to internal constraints. The external factors focus on demand for the product, customer needs, competition, and quantity and quality of competing products or services. The internal factors focus on constraints caused by costs, desired return on investment, quality and quantity of materials and labor, and allocation of scarce resources.

✓ Check out ACE for a Review Quiz at http://accounting.college.hmco.com/students.

Economic Pricing Concepts

LO2 Describe economic pricing concepts including the auction-based pricing method used on the Internet.

RELATED TEXT ASSIGNMENTS
Q: 8, 9, 10
SE: 3
E: 3, 4
SD: 1, 2, 3

The economic approach to pricing is based on microeconomic theory. Pricing plays a strong role in the concepts underlying microeconomic theory as it is practiced at individual firms. Every firm is in business to maximize profits. Although each product has its own set of revenues and costs, microeconomic theory states that profit will be maximized when the difference between total revenue and total cost is the greatest.

Total Revenue and Total Cost Curves

It may seem that if a company could produce an infinite number of products, it would realize the maximum profit. But this is not the case, and microeconomic theory explains why. Figure 3A shows the economist's view of a breakeven chart. It contains two breakeven points, between which is a large space labeled "profit area." Notice that the total revenue line is curved rather than straight. The theory behind this is that as a product is marketed, price reductions will be necessary to sell additional units because of competition and other factors. Total revenue will continue to increase, but the rate of increase will diminish as more units are sold. Therefore, the slope of the total revenue line declines and curves toward the right.

Costs react in an opposite way. Over the assumed relevant range, variable and fixed costs are fairly predictable, with fixed costs remaining constant and variable costs being the same per unit. The result is a straight line for total costs. Following microeconomic theory, costs per unit will increase as more units are sold because fixed costs will change. As cost moves into different relevant ranges, such fixed costs as supervision and depreciation increase, and competition causes marketing costs to rise. As the company pushes for more and more products from limited facilities, repair and maintenance costs also increase. And as the push from management increases, total costs per unit rise at an accelerating rate. The result is that the slope of the total cost line in Figure 3A begins curving upward. The total revenue line and the total cost line then cross again; beyond that point the company suffers a loss on additional sales.

Profits are maximized at the point where the difference between total revenue and total cost is the greatest. In Figure 3A, this point is 6,000 units of sales. At that sales level, total revenue will be $195,000; total cost, $100,000; and profit, $95,000. In theory, if one additional unit is sold, profit per unit will drop because total cost is rising at a faster rate than total revenues. As you can see, if the company sells 11,000 units, total profits will be almost entirely depleted by the rising costs. Therefore, 6,000 sales units is the optimal operating level, and the price charged at that level is the optimal price.

Marginal Revenue and Marginal Cost Curves

Economists use marginal revenue and marginal cost to help determine the optimal price for a good or service. **Marginal revenue** is the change in total revenue caused by a one-unit change in output. **Marginal cost** is the change in total cost caused by a one-unit change in output. Graphic curves for marginal revenue and marginal cost are created by measuring and plotting the rate of change in total revenue and total cost at various activity levels. If you computed marginal revenue and marginal cost for each unit sold in our example and plotted them on a graph, the lines would resemble those in Figure 3B. Notice that the marginal cost line crosses the marginal revenue line at 6,000 units. After that point, profit per unit will decrease as additional units are sold. Marginal cost will exceed marginal revenue for each unit sold

FIGURE 3
Microeconomic Pricing Theory

FOCUS ON BUSINESS TECHNOLOGY

What's It Worth to Shop Online?

The Internet makes it possible to price efficiently at the level of marginal costs. For instance, the company Priceline.com <www.priceline.com> is a bargain hunter's dream. At Priceline's web site, travelers pick a destination and a price they are willing to pay for air or hotel reservations. The price must be guaranteed by credit card. An airline or hotel has one hour to accept or reject the bid. If the bid is accepted, the buyer is obligated to pay for the air or hotel reservation. The company claims that customers save 54 to 76 percent off the regular prices. The hotels and airlines are often willing to accept the low bid prices because the marginal cost of filling an additional seat on an airplane or an extra room in a hotel is very low. Even the low marginal revenue from the low bid prices is greater than the marginal cost.[3]

over 6,000. Profit will be maximized when the marginal revenue and marginal cost lines intersect. By projecting this point onto the product's demand curve, you can locate the optimal price, which is $32.50 per unit.

If all the information used in microeconomic theory were certain, picking the optimal price would be fairly easy. But most information used in such an analysis relies on projected amounts for unit sales, product costs, and revenues. Nevertheless, developing such an analysis usually highlights cost patterns and the unanticipated influences of demand. For this reason, it is important for managers to consider the microeconomic approach to pricing when setting product prices. However, the results of this type of analysis should not be the only data relied on.

● **STOP AND THINK!**

Why is auction-based pricing popular?

Buyers and sellers can obtain current knowledge of the market's supply and demand forces before making their selection. ■

www.ebay.com
www.yahoo.com
www.priceline.com

www.intel.com
www.sun.com

AUCTION-BASED PRICING

In recent years due to the Internet and companies that host auction markets such as eBay, Yahoo, and Priceline.com, auction-based pricing has skyrocketed in popularity. **Auction-based pricing** occurs two ways: Either sellers post what they have to sell, ask for price bids, and accept a buyer's offer to purchase at a certain price, or buyers interested in buying something post what they want, ask for prices, and accept a seller's offer to sell at a certain price.

To illustrate the seller auction-based price, consider a corporation such as Intel or Sun Microsystems that has excess silicon wafers from computer chip production. The company posts a message on the Internet asking for the quantity and price that prospective buyers are willing to pay for the excess silicon wafers. After the offers are received, a demand curve of all the offers is prepared, and the company selects the offer or bid that best fits the quantity of silicon wafers it has available for sale.

FOCUS ON BUSINESS ETHICS

How Big a Problem Is Fraud on the Internet?

A breakdown of the Internet Fraud Complaint Center's 2001 complaints reported the following most prevalent scams: auction fraud (42.8 percent), nondelivery of merchandise and payment (20.3 percent), the Nigerian letter fraud (15.5 percent), and credit/debit card fraud (9.4 percent). The Federal Bureau of Investigation and the National White Collar Crime Center formed the Internet Fraud Complaint Center in the spring of 2000. eBay <www.ebay.com>, the dominant player in Internet auction sites, battles against fraud by using a customer rating system or "feedback forum" to rate the reputation of all eBay members. The ratings of both buyers and sellers are prominently displayed on the site. According to eBay, less than 0.001 percent of the millions of transactions it handles a year are fraudulent.[4]

To illustrate the buyer's auction-based price, consider an individual who wants to fly roundtrip to Europe on certain dates and posts his or her needs on one of the hosted auction markets. After receiving the offers to sell roundtrip tickets to Europe, the individual will accept the offer that best suits his or her needs.

Auction-based pricing will continue to grow in importance due to the escalating amount of business that is conducted over the Internet by both organizations and individuals. Just about anything can be bought or sold via the Internet.

 Check out ACE for a Review Quiz at http://accounting.college.hmco.com/students.

Cost-Based Pricing Methods

LO3 Use cost-based pricing methods to develop prices.

RELATED TEXT ASSIGNMENTS
Q: 11, 12, 13
SE: 4, 5
E: 5, 6, 7, 8, 9
P: 1, 2, 3, 6
SD: 5
MRA: 3

Managers may use a variety of pricing methods. A good starting point for developing a price is to base it on the cost of producing a good or service. Two pricing methods based on cost are gross margin pricing and return on assets pricing. Remember that in a competitive environment, market prices and conditions also influence price; however, if prices do not cover a company's costs, the company will eventually fail.

To illustrate the two methods of cost-based pricing, we will consider the Energeez Company. This company buys parts from outside vendors and assembles them into portable solar panels. In the previous accounting period, the Energeez Company produced 14,750 solar panels. Total costs and unit costs incurred were as follows:

	Total Costs	Unit Costs
Variable production costs		
Direct materials and parts	$ 88,500	$ 6.00
Direct labor	66,375	4.50
Variable manufacturing overhead	44,250	3.00
Total variable production costs	$199,125	$13.50
Fixed manufacturing overhead	154,875	10.50
Total production costs	$354,000	$24.00
Selling, general, and administrative expenses		
Selling expenses	$ 73,750	$ 5.00
General expenses	36,875	2.50
Administrative expenses	22,125	1.50
Total selling, general, and administrative expenses	$132,750	$ 9.00
Total costs and expenses	$486,750	$33.00

No changes in unit costs are expected this period. The desired profit for the period is $110,625. The company uses assets totaling $921,875 in producing the solar panels and expects a 14 percent return on those assets.

Gross Margin Pricing

One cost-based approach emphasizes income statement information to determine a selling price and is called the gross margin pricing method. Gross margin is the difference between sales and the total production costs of those sales. **Gross margin pricing** is a cost-based pricing approach in which the price is computed using a markup percentage based on a product's total production costs. The markup percentage is designed to include all costs other than those used in the computation of gross margin. Therefore, the gross margin markup percentage is composed of selling, general, and administrative expenses and the desired profit. Because an accounting system often provides management with unit production cost data, both variable and fixed, this method of determining selling price can be easily applied. The formulas used are as follows:

TERMINOLOGY NOTE:
The gross margin pricing method is also known as the *income statement method*.

$$\text{Markup Percentage} = \frac{\text{Desired Profit} + \text{Total Selling, General, and Administrative Expenses}}{\text{Total Units Produced}}$$

$$\text{Gross Margin–Based Price} = \text{Total Production Costs per Unit} + (\text{Markup Percentage} \times \text{Total Production Costs per Unit})$$

For the Energeez Company, the markup percentage and selling price are computed as follows:

$$\text{Markup Percentage} = \frac{\$110{,}625 + \$132{,}750}{\$354{,}000}$$

$$= 68.75\%$$

$$\text{Gross Margin–Based Price} = \$24.00 + (68.75\% \times \$24.00)$$

$$= \underline{\underline{\$40.50}}$$

The numerator in the markup percentage formula is the sum of the desired profit ($110,625) and the total selling, general, and administrative expenses ($132,750). The denominator contains all production costs: variable costs of $199,125 and fixed production costs of $154,875. The gross margin markup is 68.75 percent of total production costs, or $16.50. Adding $16.50 to the total production costs per unit yields a selling price of $40.50.

An alternative way to express the gross margin–based price is to state the formula in terms of a company's desire to recover all of its costs and make a profit. This approach ignores the computation of the markup percentage, achieves the same gross margin–based price, and is stated as follows:

$$\text{Gross Margin–Based Price} = \frac{\text{Total Production Costs} + \text{Total Selling, General, and Administrative Expenses} + \text{Desired Profit}}{\text{Total Units Produced}}$$

Using this formula, the gross margin–based price for the Energeez Company is computed as follows:

$$\text{Gross Margin–Based Price} = \frac{\$88{,}500 + \$66{,}375 + \$44{,}250 + \$154{,}875 + \$73{,}750 + \$36{,}875 + \$22{,}125 + \$110{,}625}{14{,}750}$$

$$= \$597{,}375 \div 14{,}750$$

$$= \underline{\underline{\$40.50}}$$

KEY POINT: Gross margin–based price per unit equals total production, selling, general and administrative costs per unit plus a desired profit per unit.

Gross margin–based price can also be detailed on a per unit basis:

Gross Margin–Based Price = Direct Materials + Direct Labor + Variable Manufacturing Overhead + Fixed Manufacturing Overhead + Selling, General, and Administrative Expenses + Desired Profit per Unit

Applying this formula to the Energeez Company's data, the computations are:

Gross Margin–Based Price = $6.00 + $4.50 + $3.00 + $10.50 + $5.00 + $2.50 + $1.50 + ($110,625 ÷ 14,750)

= $\underline{\underline{\$40.50}}$

RETURN ON ASSETS PRICING

Return on assets pricing changes the objective of the price determination process. Earning a profit margin on total costs is replaced by earning a profit equal to a specified rate of return on assets employed in the operation. Because this approach focuses on a desired minimum rate of return on assets, it is known as the *balance sheet approach to pricing.*

TERMINOLOGY NOTE: The return on assets pricing method is also known as the *balance sheet method.*

The following formula is used to calculate the return on assets–based price:

Return on Assets–Based Price = Total Costs and Expenses per Unit + (Desired Rate of Return × Cost of Assets Employed per Unit)

The formula may also be expressed as follows:

Return on Assets–Based Price = [(Total Production Costs + Total Selling, General, and Administrative Expenses) ÷ Units to be Produced] + [Desired Rate of Return × (Total Cost of Assets Employed ÷ Units to be Produced)]

KEY POINT: Return on assets–based price per unit equals total production, selling, general and administrative costs per unit plus a per unit desired return on assets employed.

To compute the return on assets–based price, the total cost of the assets employed is divided by the projected number of units to be produced. The result is then multiplied by the rate of return to obtain desired earnings per unit. Desired earnings per unit plus total costs and expenses per unit yields the unit selling price.

Recall that the Energeez Company has an asset base of $921,875. It plans to produce 14,750 units and would like to earn a 14 percent return on assets. If the company uses return on assets pricing, the selling price per unit would be calculated as follows:

Return on Assets–Based Price = $24.00 + $9.00
   + [14% × ($921,875 ÷ 14,750)]
 = $41.75

or as:

Return on Assets–Based Price = [($354,000 + $132,750) ÷ 14,750]
   + [14% × ($921,875 ÷ 14,750)]
 = $33.00 + $8.75
 = $41.75

Notice that the desired profit that is used in gross margin pricing is replaced by an overall company rate of return on assets. By dividing cost of assets employed by projected units of output and multiplying the result by the desired minimum rate of return, a unit profit factor of $8.75 [14% × ($921,875 ÷ 14,750)] is obtained. Adding this profit factor to the total unit costs and expenses gives the selling price of $41.75.

SUMMARY OF COST-BASED PRICING METHODS

The two cost-based pricing methods are summarized in Figure 4. In this case, if Energeez Company uses return on assets pricing and has a desired rate of return of 14 percent, it will need to set a higher selling price ($41.75) than it would under the gross margin method ($40.50). Companies select their pricing methods based on their degree of trust in a cost base. The cost bases from which they can choose are (1) total product costs per unit or (2) total costs and expenses per unit. Often, total product costs per unit are readily available, which makes gross margin pricing a good way to compute selling prices. However, gross margin pricing depends on an accurate forecast of units because the fixed cost per unit portion of total production costs will vary if the actual number of units produced differs from the estimated number of units. Return on assets pricing is also a good pricing method if the assets used to manufacture a product can be identified and their cost determined. If this is not the case, the method yields inaccurate results.

PRICING SERVICES

TERMINOLOGY NOTE: Time and materials pricing is also known as *parts and labor pricing*.

Service businesses take a different approach to pricing. Although a service has no physical substance, it must still be priced and billed to the customer. Most service organizations use a form of **time and materials pricing** (also known as *parts and labor pricing*) to arrive at the price of a service. Service companies, such as appliance repair shops, home-remodeling specialists, pool cleaners, and automobile repair

FIGURE 4
Cost-Based Pricing Methods: Energeez Company

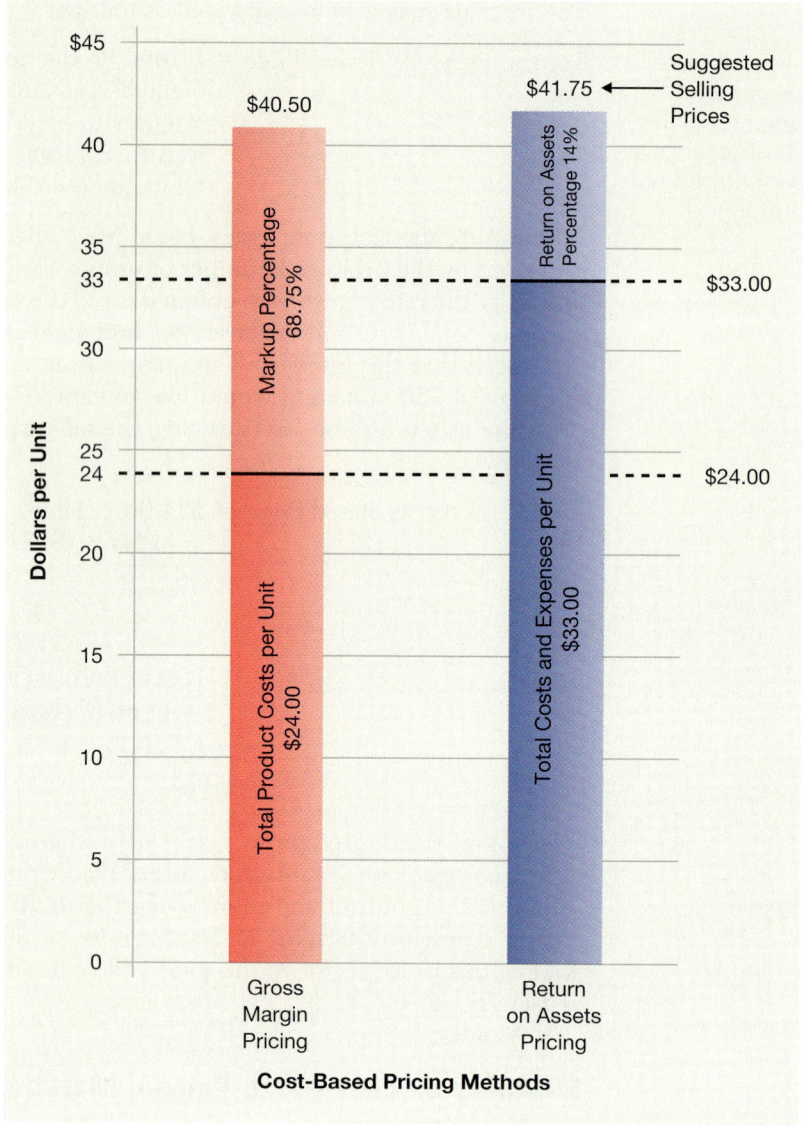

BUSINESS WORLD EXAMPLE: Time and materials pricing is commonly used by plumbing and auto repair businesses.

FOCUS ON BUSINESS PRACTICE

Pricing a Six-Pack
The average cost of a six-pack of Budweiser rose from $4.20 in 1997 to $4.80 in 2002. That's because Anheuser-Busch Company <www.anheuser-busch.com>, the world's largest brewer, dominates nearly half the U.S. beer market, and its competitors traditionally follow its price leads. For many years, Anheuser-Busch has tracked the U.S. beer market by brand, market, package, and channel. The company knows that although beer consumption in the U.S. market appears recession proof, there is little overall growth. Thus, Anheuser-Busch generally raises prices to keep pace with the consumer price index.[5]

businesses, arrive at prices by using two computations: one for direct labor and one for materials and parts. Markup percentages are added to the costs of materials and labor to cover the cost of overhead and provide a profit factor. If the service does not require materials and parts, then only direct labor costs are used in developing the price. Professionals, such as attorneys, accountants, and consultants, apply a factor representing all overhead costs to the base labor costs to establish a price for their services.

Gil Marquis just completed working on Lucinda Lowe's Mercedes. The parts used to repair the vehicle cost $840. The company's 40 percent markup rate on parts covers parts-related overhead costs and profit. The repairs required four hours of labor by a certified Mercedes specialist, whose wages are $35 per hour. The company's overhead markup rate on labor is 80 percent. Marquis will compute Lucinda Lowe's bill as follows:

Repair parts used	$840	
Overhead charges		
$840 × 40%	336	
Total parts charges		$1,176
Labor charges		
4 hours @ $35 per hour	$140	
Overhead charges		
$140 × 80%	112	
Total labor charges		252
Total billing		$1,428

Final Notes on Cost-Based Pricing Methods

> **Stop and Think!**
> What types of companies use cost-based methods?
> *Companies that do government contract work or that produce customized goods and services tend to use cost-based methods because those markets focus on cost recovery.* ■

In some areas of the economy, such as government contracts, cost-based pricing is widely used. Although a variety of cost-based methods may be used to mechanically compute a price, many factors external to the product or service still require a manager's attention. Once a cost-based price has been determined, the decision maker must consider such factors as competitors' prices, customers' expectations, and the cost of substitute products and services. Pricing is a risky part of operating a business, and care must be taken when establishing that all-important selling price.

✓ Check out ACE for a Review Quiz at http://accounting.college.hmco.com/students.

Pricing Based on Target Costing

LO4 Describe target costing and use that concept to analyze pricing decisions and evaluate a new product opportunity.
RELATED TEXT ASSIGNMENTS
Q: 14, 15
SE: 6, 7
E: 10, 11, 12, 13
P: 4, 7
MRA: 3, 4, 5

www.palm.com

TERMINOLOGY NOTE:
Target costing is sometimes referred to as *target pricing*.

> **Stop and Think!**
> What types of companies use target costing?
> *Companies entering established product markets, developing new products, or producing commodity-type products tend to use target costing because those markets focus on competitive pricing.* ■

Target costing is designed to enhance a company's ability to compete, especially in new or emerging product markets. The Decision Point at the start of this chapter focused on Palm, which used target costing to price a new product, the Zire. You may remember that this approach to pricing differs significantly from the cost-based methods just described, which Palm used to price its other products. Instead of first determining the cost of a product or service and then adding a profit factor to arrive at its price, target costing reverses the procedure. **Target costing** is a pricing method that (1) identifies the price at which a product will be competitive in the marketplace, (2) defines the desired profit to be made on the product, and (3) computes the target cost for the product by subtracting the desired profit from the competitive market price. The formula is

Target Price − Desired Profit = Target Cost

The target cost is then given to the engineers and product designers, who use it as the maximum cost to be incurred for the materials and other resources needed to design and manufacture the product. It is their responsibility to create the product at or below its target cost.

Pricing based on target costing may not seem revolutionary, but a detailed look at its underlying principles reveals its strategic superiority. Target costing gives managers the ability to control or dictate the costs of a new product beginning at the planning stage of the product's life cycle. In a competitive environment, the use of target costing enables managers to analyze a product's potential before they commit resources to its production. Figure 5 compares the timing of a pricing decision using a traditional approach and using target costing. The stages of the product life cycle, from the generation of the product idea to its final disposition, are identified at the base of the figure. When traditional cost-based pricing practices are used, prices cannot be set until production has taken place and costs have been incurred

FIGURE 5
Price Decision Timing Comparison

ENRICHMENT NOTE: Target costing is used by companies that have adopted the just-in-time philosophy, where goods are pulled by demand, not pushed.

STUDY NOTE: If desired profit is defined as a percentage of target cost, remember that target price is equal to 100 percent of target cost *plus* the percentage of target cost desired as profit.

and analyzed. At that point, a profit factor is added to the product's cost, and the product is ready to be offered to customers. In contrast, under target costing, the pricing decision takes place immediately after the market research for a new product. The market research not only reveals the potential demand for the product, but also identifies the maximum price a customer would be willing to pay for the product. Once the price is determined, target costing enables the company's engineers to design the product with a fixed maximum target cost on which to base the product's features.

An example will help to show how cost-based pricing differs from pricing based on target costing. Cost First Company and Price First Company are about to enter the market with a new product, the Starbeam. Both companies have conducted market research and know that demand exists for the product. Cost First Company's strategy is to jump right into the planning phase, design the product, and get into production as soon as possible. The product's prototype model will be tested during the production phase. The company assumes that flaws will be found, so engineering change orders will be necessary and the production process will have to be redesigned to fit the changes. Cost control will not be a part of this process. Only after the product has been produced successfully can a total unit cost be computed and a price determined.

The cost patterns associated with Cost First Company's new product are illustrated in Figure 6. Once the company makes the decision to produce a new product, new costs are incurred at each stage in the product's life cycle. The patterns of two kinds of cost are shown. **Committed costs** are the costs of design, development, engineering, testing, and production that are engineered into a product or service at the design stage of development. They should occur if all design specifications are followed during production. **Incurred costs** are the actual costs to make the product. When cost-based pricing is used, it is very difficult to control costs from the planning phase through the production phase. Management has a hard time setting realistic targets because the product is being made for the first time. Because customers are expected to pay whatever amount cost-based pricing identifies, the focus is on sales, not on the design and manufacture of the product. Cost control efforts will focus on incurred costs after the product has been introduced to the marketplace. In this example, Cost First Company's new product will cost around $70, so to earn a profit of 20 percent of target cost, the company will need to price the product at around $84.

LO3 Return on assets pricing: A pricing method in which the objective is to earn a profit equal to a specific rate of return on assets employed in the operation. Also called the *balance sheet approach to pricing*.

LO4 Target costing: A pricing method that (1) identifies the price at which a product will be competitive in the marketplace, (2) defines the desired profit to be made on the product, and (3) computes the target cost for the product by subtracting the desired profit from the competitive market price.

LO3 Time and materials pricing: An approach to pricing used by service businesses in which the total billing is composed of actual materials and parts costs and actual direct labor cost plus a percentage markup of each to cover overhead costs and a profit factor. Also called *parts and labor pricing*.

LO5 Transfer price: The price at which goods and services are charged and exchanged between a company's divisions or segments. Also called *artificial* or *created prices*.

REVIEW PROBLEM

Gross Margin Pricing

LO3 The Enforcer Toy Company makes a complete line of toy vehicles, including three types of vehicles: a fire truck, a police cruiser, and an ambulance transport. The toys are produced on an assembly line, beginning with the Stamping Department and continuing through the Welding, Painting, and Detailing departments. The projected costs of each toy and the percentages for assigning unavoidable fixed and common costs are as follows:

Cost Categories	Total Projected Costs	Toy Fire Truck	Toy Police Cruiser	Toy Ambulance Transport
Direct materials				
Metal	$137,000	$62,500	$29,000	$45,500
Axles	5,250	2,500	1,000	1,750
Wheels	9,250	3,750	2,000	3,500
Paint	70,500	30,000	16,000	24,500
Direct labor				
Stamping	53,750	22,500	12,000	19,250
Welding	94,000	42,500	20,000	31,500
Painting	107,500	45,000	24,000	38,500
Detailing	44,250	17,500	11,000	15,750
Indirect labor	173,000	77,500	36,000	59,500
Operating supplies	30,000	12,500	7,000	10,500
Variable manufacturing overhead	90,500	40,000	19,000	31,500
Fixed manufacturing overhead	120,000	45%	25%	30%
Distribution expenses	105,000	40%	20%	40%
Variable marketing expenses	123,000	$55,000	$26,000	$42,000
Fixed marketing expenses	85,400	40%	25%	35%
General and administrative expenses	47,600	40%	25%	35%

Enforcer Toy's policy is to earn a minimum of 30 percent over total cost on each type of toy produced. Expected sales for 20x6 are: fire truck, 50,000 units; police cruiser, 20,000 units; and ambulance transport, 35,000 units. Assume no change in inventory levels, and round all answers to two decimal places.

REQUIRED
1. Using the gross margin pricing method, compute the selling price for each kind of toy.
2. The competition is selling a similar fire truck for around $14. Should this influence Enforcer Toy's pricing decision? Give reasons for your answer.

ANSWER TO REVIEW PROBLEM

Before the selling prices are computed, the cost analysis must be completed and restructured to supply the information needed for the pricing computations.

Cost Categories	Total Projected Costs	Toy Fire Truck	Toy Police Cruiser	Toy Ambulance Transport
Total direct materials	$ 222,000	$ 98,750	$ 48,000	$ 75,250
Total direct labor	299,500	127,500	67,000	105,000
Indirect labor	173,000	77,500	36,000	59,500
Operating supplies	30,000	12,500	7,000	10,500
Variable manufacturing overhead	90,500	40,000	19,000	31,500
Fixed manufacturing overhead	120,000	54,000	30,000	36,000
Total production costs	$ 935,000	$410,250	$207,000	$317,750
Distribution expenses	$ 105,000	$ 42,000	$ 21,000	$ 42,000
Variable marketing expenses	123,000	55,000	26,000	42,000
Fixed marketing expenses	85,400	34,160	21,350	29,890
General and administrative expenses	47,600	19,040	11,900	16,660
Total selling, general, and administrative expenses	$ 361,000	$150,200	$80,250	$130,550
Total costs	$1,296,000	$560,450	$287,250	$448,300
Desired profit	$ 388,800	$168,135	$ 86,175	$134,490

1. Pricing using the gross margin approach.

   Markup percentage formula:

   $$\text{Markup Percentage} = \frac{\text{Desired Profit} + \text{Total Selling, General, and Administrative Expenses}}{\text{Total Production Costs}}$$

   Gross margin pricing formula:

   Gross Margin–Based Price = Total Production Costs per Unit + (Markup Percentage × Total Production Costs per Unit)

   Fire truck:

   $$\text{Markup Percentage} = \frac{\$168,135 + \$150,200}{\$410,250} = 77.60\%$$

   Gross Margin–Based Price = ($410,250 ÷ 50,000) + [77.6% × ($410,250 ÷ 50,000)] = $14.57

   Police cruiser:

   $$\text{Markup Percentage} = \frac{\$86,175 + \$80,250}{\$207,000} = 80.40\%$$

   Gross Margin–Based Price = ($207,000 ÷ 20,000) + [80.4% × ($207,000 ÷ 20,000)] = $18.67

   Ambulance transport:

   $$\text{Markup Percentage} = \frac{\$134,490 + \$130,550}{\$317,750} = 83.41\%$$

   Gross Margin–Based Price = ($317,750 ÷ 35,000) + [83.41% × ($317,750 ÷ 35,000)] = $16.65

2. Competition's influence on price: If the competition's toy fire truck is similar in quality and design, Enforcer Toy's management should consider reducing the price of its truck to the $14.00 range. At $14.57, Enforcer has a 30 percent profit built into its price. The fire truck's breakeven is at $11.21 ($14.57 ÷ 1.3). Therefore, the company could reduce its price below the competitor's price and still make a significant profit.

Chapter Assignments

Questions

1. Identify five possible pricing policy objectives. Discuss each one briefly.
2. If a manager's strategy is to price products so that total market share will increase, what considerations should go into selecting a price?
3. Do prices have a social effect? In what way?
4. For an organization to stay in business, what four rules must its selling price follow?
5. How are pricing issues addressed at each stage of the management cycle?
6. List four external factors to consider when establishing the price of a product or service.
7. Identify four internal factors that affect the price of a good or service.
8. In traditional economic theory, what role does total revenue play in maximizing profit?
9. Why is profit maximized at the point at which marginal revenue equals marginal cost?
10. What is auction-based pricing?
11. What is gross margin pricing? How is the markup percentage calculated under this method?
12. How does return on assets pricing differ from gross margin pricing?
13. In the pricing of services, what is time and materials pricing?
14. Describe pricing based on target costing, and state the formula used to compute a target cost.
15. Why is the target costing approach to pricing more useful in a competitive marketplace than the cost-based pricing methods are?
16. What is a transfer price? Why are transfer prices usually associated with decentralized companies?
17. Describe the cost-plus approach to setting transfer prices.
18. How are market prices used to develop a transfer price? Under what circumstances are market prices relevant to the setting of a transfer price?
19. "Most transfer prices are negotiated prices." Explain this statement.
20. How may transfer pricing be used to evaluate a division's performance?

Short Exercises

SE 1.
LO1 Rules for Establishing Prices
Jason Kellam is planning to open a pizza restaurant next month in Flora, Alabama. He plans to sell his large pizzas for a base price of $18 plus $2 for each topping selected. When asked how he arrived at the base price, he said that his cousin developed that price for his pizza restaurant in New York City. What pricing rules has Jason Kellam not followed?

SE 2.
LO1 External Factors That Influence Prices
Your client is about to introduce a very high-quality product that will remove Brazilian pepper bushes in the southern United States. The Marketing Department has established a price of $37 per gallon, and the company controller has projected total production, selling, and distribution costs of $26 per gallon. What other factors should your client consider before introducing the product into the marketplace?

SE 3.
LO2 Traditional Economic Pricing Concept
You are to decide the total demand for a particular product. Assume that the product you are evaluating has the total cost and total revenue curves pictured in Figure 3A in this chapter. Also assume that the difference between total revenue and total cost is the same at the 4,000 and 9,000 unit levels. If you had to choose between those two levels of activity as goals for total sales over the life of the product, which would you prefer? Why?

Chapter 25 Pricing Decisions, Including Target Costing and Transfer Pricing

LO3 Cost-Based Price Setting

SE 4. The Windwalker Company has collected the following data for one of its product lines: total production costs, $300,000; total selling, general, and administrative expenses, $112,600; desired profit, $67,400; and production costs per unit, $50. Using the gross margin pricing method, compute a suggested selling price for this product that would yield the desired profit.

LO3 Pricing a Service

SE 5. Evan Nathan runs a home repair business. Recently he gathered the following cost information about the repair of a client's pool deck: replacement wood, $650; deck screws and supplies, $112; and labor, 12 hours at $14 per hour. Nathan applies a 40 percent overhead rate to all direct costs of a job. Compute the total billing price for the repair of the pool deck.

LO4 Committed Costs and Target Costing

SE 6. Nanci Osborne is a design engineer for Dash Enterprises. In a discussion about a proposed new product, Osborne stated that the product's projected target cost was $6.50 below the committed costs identified by design estimates. Given this information, should the company proceed with the new product? Explain your answer, and include a definition of committed cost in your analysis.

LO4 Pricing Using Target Costing

SE 7. JTZ Furniture is considering a new product and must make a go or no-go decision before tomorrow's planning team meeting. Market research shows that the unit selling price agreeable to potential customers is $1,600, and the company's desired profit is 22 percent of target cost. The design engineer's preliminary estimate of the product's design, production, and distribution costs is $1,380 per unit. Using target costing, determine whether the company should market the new product.

LO5 Decision to Use Transfer Prices

SE 8. The production process at Premier Castings includes eight processes, each of which is currently treated as a cost center with a specific set of operations to perform on each casting produced. Following the fourth process's operations, the rough castings have an external market. The fourth process must also supply the fifth process with its direct materials. The management of Premier Castings wants to develop a new approach to measuring process performance. Is Premier a candidate for using transfer prices? Explain your answer.

LO5 Cost-Based Versus Market-Based Transfer Prices

SE 9. Refer to the information in **SE 8**. Should Premier Castings use economic-based, cost-based, market-based, or negotiated transfer prices?

LO5 Developing a Negotiated Transfer Price

SE 10. The Molding Process at Trophy Products has been treated as a cost center since the company was founded in 1968. Recently, management decided to change the performance evaluation approach and treat its processes as profit centers. Each process is expected to earn a 20 percent profit on its total production costs. One of Trophy's products is a plastic base for a display chest. The Molding Process supplies this base to the Cabinet Process, and it also sells the base to another company. Molding's total production cost for the base is $27.40. It sells the base to the other company for $38.00. What should the transfer price for the plastic base be?

EXERCISES

LO1 Pricing Policy Objectives

E 1. Old Denim, Ltd., is an international clothing company that retails medium-priced goods. Its retail outlets are located throughout the United States, France, Germany, and Great Britain. Management wants to maintain the company's image of providing the highest possible quality at the lowest possible prices. Selling prices are developed to draw customers away from competitors' stores. First-of-the-month sales are regularly held at all stores, and customers are accustomed to this practice. Company buyers are carefully trained to seek out quality goods at inexpensive prices. Sales are targeted to increase a minimum of 5 percent per year. All sales should yield a 15 percent return on assets. Sales personnel are expected to wear Old Denim clothing while working, and all personnel can purchase clothing at 10 percent above cost. All stores are required to be clean and well organized. Competitors' prices are checked daily.

Identify the pricing policy objectives of Old Denim, Ltd.

LO1 External and Internal Pricing Factors

E 2. Towne's Tire Outlet features more than a dozen brands of tires in many sizes. Two of the brands are Gripper and Roadster, both imports. The tire size 205/70-VR15 is available in both brands. The following information about the two brands was obtained:

	Gripper	Roadster
Selling price		
Single tire, installed	$125	$110
Set of four tires, installed	460	400
Cost per tire	90	60

As shown, selling prices include installation costs. Each Gripper or Roadster tire costs $20 to mount and balance.

1. Compute each brand's net unit selling price after installation for both a single tire and a set of four.
2. Was cost the main consideration in setting those prices?
3. What other factors could have influenced those prices?

LO2 Traditional Economic Pricing Theory

E 3. Texaza, a product design firm, has just completed a contract to develop a wireless phone/keychain. The phone/keychain needs to be recharged only once a week and can be used worldwide. Initial fixed costs for this product are $4,000. The designers estimate that the product will break even at the $5,000/100-unit mark. Total revenues will again equal total costs at the $25,000/900-unit point. Marginal cost is expected to equal marginal revenue when 550 units are sold.

1. Sketch total revenue and total cost curves for this product. Mark the vertical axis at each $5,000 increment and the horizontal axis at each 100-unit increment.
2. Based on your total revenue and total cost curves in **1**, at what unit selling price will profits be maximized?

LO2 Ebusiness

E 4. Conduct a web search of Priceline.com and eBay.com web sites. Write a brief comparison of each web site's features. Which web site do you prefer, and why?

LO3 Price Determination

E 5. Gillson Industries has just patented a new product called Gleam, an automobile wax for lasting protection against the elements. The company's controller has developed the following annual information for use in price determination meetings:

Variable production costs	$1,110,000
Fixed manufacturing overhead	540,000
Selling expenses	225,000
General and administrative expenses	350,000
Desired profit	250,000
Cost of assets employed	1,000,000

Annual demand for the product is expected to be 250,000 cans. On average, the company now earns a 10% return on assets.

1. Compute the projected unit cost for one can of Gleam.
2. Using gross margin pricing, compute the markup percentage and selling price for one can.
3. Using return on assets pricing, compute the unit price for one can.

LO3 Pricing a Service

E 6. Texas has just passed a law making it mandatory to have every head of cattle inspected at least once a year for a variety of communicable diseases. Big Springs Enterprises is considering entering this inspection business. After extensive studies, Tex Autry, the owner of Big Springs Enterprises, has developed the following annual projections:

Direct service labor	$525,000
Variable service overhead costs	250,000
Fixed service overhead costs	225,000
Selling expenses	142,500
General and administrative expenses	157,500
Minimum desired profit	120,000
Cost of assets employed	750,000

Autry believes his company could inspect 250,000 head of cattle per year. On average, the company now earns a 16 percent return on assets.

1. Compute the projected cost of inspecting each head of cattle.
2. Determine the price to charge for inspecting each head of cattle. Use gross margin pricing.
3. Using return on assets pricing, compute the unit price to charge for this inspection service.

LO3 Cost-based Pricing

E 7. Hometown Bank is determining the price for its newest mini debit card. The card can be used at any retail outlet with a swipe reader and is small enough to attach to a key chain—no PIN number or signature is required. Sigrid Olmo has developed the following annual information for use in upcoming price determination meetings.

Variable processing costs	$50 million
Fixed processing costs	36 million
Selling expenses (fixed)	10 million
General and administrative expenses (fixed)	4 million
Desired profit	3 billion
Cost of assets employed	10 billion

Annual usage is expected to be 10 billion transactions. On average, the company now earns a 6 percent return on assets.

1. Compute the projected cost of one transaction.
2. Using gross margin pricing, compute the price to charge per transaction.
3. Using return on assets pricing, compute the price to charge per transaction.

LO3 Pricing Services

E 8. Gator Car Repair specializes in repairing rental cars. The company uses a 50 percent markup rate on parts to cover parts-related overhead costs and profit margin. It uses a 100 percent markup rate on labor to cover labor-related overhead costs and profit margin. Compute the bill for a recent job that used the following parts and labor:

Material and repair parts used	$600
Labor used	5 hours at $40 per hour

LO3 Time and Materials Pricing

E 9. Cruz's Home Remodeling Service specializes in refurbishing older homes. Last week Cruz was asked to bid on a remodeling job for the town's mayor. His list of materials and labor needed to complete the job is as follows:

Materials		Labor	
Lumber	$ 6,500	Carpenter	$2,000
Nails/bolts	160	Floor specialist	1,300
Paint	1,420	Painter	1,500
Glass	2,890	Supervisor	1,420
Doors	730	Helpers	1,680
Hardware	600	Total	$7,900
Supplies	400		
Total	$12,700		

The company uses an overhead markup percentage for both materials (60 percent) and labor (40 percent). Those markups cover all operating costs of the business. In addition, Cruz expects to make at least a 25 percent profit on all jobs. Compute the price that Cruz should quote for the mayor's job.

LO4 Target Costing and Pricing

E 10. Environ Company has determined that its new fireplace screen would gain widespread customer acceptance if the company could price it at or under $90. Anticipated labor hours and costs for each unit of the new product are:

Direct materials cost	$15
Direct labor cost	
Manufacturing labor	
Hours	1.2
Hourly labor rate	$12
Assembly labor	
Hours	1.5
Hourly labor rate	$10
Machine hours	2

The company currently uses the following three activity-based cost rates:

Materials handling	$1.30 per dollar of direct materials
Production	$3.00 per machine hour
Product delivery	$5.50 per unit

The company's minimum desired profit is 25 percent over total production and delivery cost. Compute the target cost for the new fireplace screen, and determine if the company should market it.

LO4 Target Costing

E 11. Assume the same facts in **E 10** except the company's minimum desired profit has been revised to 10 percent over production and delivery costs due to a recent economic downturn. Compute the revised target cost for the new fireplace screen, and determine if the company should market it.

LO4 Target Costing

E 12. Ikea <www.ikea.com>, the Swedish furniture retailer, is developing a new chair targeted to sell for less than $100 and is considering the following two production alternatives. Rank the alternatives assuming the company's minimum desired profit is 30 percent over total production costs.

	Alternative A	Alternative B
Direct material costs	$35	$20
Direct labor cost	1 hour at $12 per hour	2 hours at $8 per hour
Manufacturing overhead costs	200 percent of direct labor costs	$2 per dollar of direct materials

LO4 Target Costing

E 13. Management at Fox Valley Machine Tool Co. is considering the development of a new automated drill press called the AutoDrill. After conferring with the design engineers, the controller's staff assembled the following data about this product:

Target selling price	$7,500 per unit
Desired profit percentage	25% of total unit cost
Projected unit demand	4,500 units
Activity-based cost rates	
Materials handling	5% of direct materials and purchased parts cost
Engineering	$300 per unit for AutoDrill
Production and assembly	$50 per machine hour
Delivery	$570 per unit for AutoDrill
Marketing	$400 per unit for AutoDrill
Per-unit data	
Direct materials cost	$1,620
Purchased parts cost	$840
Manufacturing labor	
Hours	6 hours
Hourly labor rate	$14
Assembly labor	
Hours	10 hours
Hourly labor rate	$15
Machine hours	30 hours

1. Compute the product's target cost.
2. Compute the product's projected unit cost based on the design engineers' estimates.
3. Should management produce and market the AutoDrill? Defend your answer.

LO5 Transfer Price Comparison

E 14. Mary Janus is developing a transfer price for the housing section of an automatic pool-cleaning device. The housing for the device is made in Department A. It is then passed on to Department D, where final assembly occurs. Unit costs for the housing are:

Cost Categories	Unit Costs
Direct materials	$5.20
Direct labor	2.30
Variable manufacturing overhead	1.30
Fixed manufacturing overhead	2.60
Profit markup, 20% of cost	?

An outside vendor can supply the housing for $13.00 per unit

1. Develop a cost-plus transfer price for the housing.
2. What should the transfer price be? Support your answer.

LO5 Transfer Pricing

E 15. Patch Watch Company's Seconds Store offers refurbished or factory seconds time-keeping products to the public at substantially reduced prices. The factory controller is developing transfer price alternatives to present to management to determine the best price to transfer products from the factory to the store from the following information:

Unit price if sold to outside retailers	$25
Variable product cost per unit	10
Fixed product cost per unit	5
Seconds store profit markup	40%

1. What is the market-based transfer price alternative?
2. What is the minimum transfer price alternative?
3. Compute the cost-plus transfer price alternative assuming cost includes variable costs only.

PROBLEMS

LO3 Pricing Decision

P 1. Ed Vetz & Company specializes in the assembly of home appliances. One division focuses most of its efforts on assembling a standard toaster oven. Projected costs of this product for 20x4 are as follows:

Cost Description	Budgeted Costs
Toaster casings	$ 960,000
Electrical components	2,244,000
Direct labor	3,648,000
Variable indirect assembly costs	780,000
Fixed indirect assembly costs	1,740,000
Selling expenses	1,536,000
General operating expenses	840,000
Administrative expenses	816,000

The projected costs are based on an estimated demand of 600,000 toaster ovens per year. The company wants to make a $1,260,000 profit.

Competitors have just published their wholesale prices for the coming year. They range from $21.60 to $22.64 per oven. The Vetz toaster oven is known for its high quality and modern look. It competes with products at the top end of the price range. Even with its reputation, however, every $.20 increase above the top competitor's price causes a drop in demand of 60,000 units below the original estimate. Assume that all price changes are in $.20 increments.

REQUIRED

1. Prepare a schedule of total projected costs and unit costs.
2. Use gross margin pricing to compute the anticipated selling price.
3. Based on competitors' prices, what should the Vetz toaster sell for in 20x4 (assume a constant unit cost)? Defend your answer. (**Hint:** Determine the total profit at various sales levels.)
4. Would your pricing structure in **2** change if the company had only limited competition at its quality level? If so, in what direction? Explain why.

LO3 Cost-Based Pricing

P 2. Centered Publishing Company specializes in health awareness books. Because the field of health awareness is very competitive, Jay Rosenbek, the company's president, maintains a strict policy about selecting manuscripts to publish. Rosenbek wants to publish only books whose projected earnings are 20 percent above total projected costs. Three titles were accepted for publication during 20x5. The authors of those books are Tone, Tyme, and Klay.

Projected costs for each book and allocation percentages for common costs are shown below.

Cost Categories	Total Projected Costs	Tone Book	Tyme Book	Klay Book
Direct labor	$487,500	$146,250	$243,750	$97,500
Royalty costs	120,000	36,000	60,000	24,000
Printing costs	248,600	74,580	124,300	49,720
Supplies	34,200	10,260	17,100	6,840
Variable production costs	142,000	42,600	71,000	28,400
Fixed production costs	168,000	35%	40%	25%
Distribution costs	194,000	30%	50%	20%
Marketing costs	194,000	$61,670	$90,060	$42,270
General and administrative costs	52,400	35%	40%	25%

Expected sales for 20x5 are as follows: Tone, 26,000 copies; Tyme, 32,000 copies; and Klay, 20,000 copies.

REQUIRED ▶
1. Prepare a cost analysis that computes the desired profit for each of the three books and in total.
2. Use gross margin pricing to compute the selling price for each book. (**Hint:** Treat royalty costs as production costs.)
3. If the competition's average selling price for a book on the same subject as Klay's is $22, should this influence Rosenbek's pricing decision? Explain.

P 3.
LO3 Time and Materials Pricing in a Service Business

Ace Maintenance, Inc., repairs heavy construction equipment and vehicles. Recently, the Shanti Construction Company had one of its giant earthmovers overhauled and its tires replaced. Repair work for a vehicle of that size usually takes from one week to ten days. The vehicle must be lifted up so that maintenance workers can gain access to the engine. Parts are normally so large that a crane must be used to put them into place.

Ace follows the time and materials pricing system and uses data from the previous year to compute markup percentages for parts- and materials-related and direct labor–related overhead. The company adds markups of 130% to the cost of materials and parts and 140% to the cost of direct labor to cover overhead and profit. The following materials, parts, and direct labor are needed to repair the giant earthmover.

Quantity		Unit Price	Hours		Hourly Rate
Materials and parts			Direct labor		
24	Spark plugs	$ 3.40	42	Mechanic	$18.20
20	Oil, quarts	2.90	54	Assistant mechanic	12.00
12	Hoses	11.60			
1	Water pump	764.00			
30	Coolant, quarts	6.50			
18	Clamps	5.90			
1	Distributor cap	128.40			
1	Carburetor	214.10			
4	Tires	820.00			

REQUIRED ▶ Prepare a complete billing for this job. Include itemized amounts for each type of materials, parts, and direct labor. Follow the time and materials pricing approach, and show the total price for the job.

P 4.
LO4 Pricing Using Target Costing

Young Joon Corp. is considering marketing two new graphing calculators, named Speed-Calc 4 and Speed-Calc 5. According to recent market research, the two products will surpass current competition in both speed and quality and would be welcomed into the market. Customers would be willing to pay $98 for Speed-Calc 4 and $110 for Speed-Calc 5, based on their projected design capabilities. Both products have many uses, but the primary market interest comes from college students. Current production capacity exists for the manufacture and assembly of the two products. The company has a minimum desired profit of 25 percent above all costs for all of its products. Current activity-based cost rates are:

Materials/parts handling	$1.20	per dollar of direct materials and purchased parts cost
Production	$8.00	per machine hour
Marketing/delivery	$4.40	per unit of Speed-Calc 4
	$6.20	per unit of Speed-Calc 5

Design engineering and accounting estimates to produce the two new products are:

	Speed-Calc 4	Speed-Calc 5
Projected unit demand	100,000	80,000
Per-unit data		
Direct materials cost	$ 5.50	$ 7.50
Computer chip cost	$10.60	$11.70
Production labor		
Hours	1.2	1.3
Hourly labor rate	$16.00	$16.00
Assembly labor		
Hours	.6	.5
Hourly labor rate	$12.00	$12.00
Machine hours	1	1.2

REQUIRED
1. Compute the target costs for each product.
2. Compute the projected total unit cost of production and delivery.
3. Using the target costing approach, decide whether the products should be produced.

P 5.
LO5 Developing Transfer Prices

Cylinder Company has two divisions, Glass Division and Instrument Division. For several years, Glass Division has manufactured a special glass container, which it sells to the Instrument Division at the prevailing market price of $20. Glass Division produces the glass containers only for the Instrument Division and does not sell the product to outside customers. Annual production and sales volume is 20,000 containers. A unit cost analysis for Glass Division showed the following.

Cost Categories	Costs per Container
Direct materials	$ 3.50
Direct labor, 1 1/4 hour	2.30
Variable manufacturing overhead	7.50
Avoidable fixed costs $30,000 ÷ 20,000	1.50
Corporate overhead, $18 per direct labor hour	4.50
Variable shipping costs	1.20
Unit cost	$20.50

Corporate overhead represents such allocated joint fixed costs of production as building depreciation, property taxes, fire insurance, and salaries of production executives. A profit markup of 20 percent is used in determining transfer prices.

REQUIRED
1. What would be the appropriate transfer price for Glass Division to use in billing its transactions with the Instrument Division?
2. If Glass Division decided to sell some containers to outside customers, would your answer to 1 change? Defend your response.
3. What factors concerning transfer price should management consider when transferring products between divisions?

ALTERNATE PROBLEMS

P 6.
LO3 Pricing Decision

Sumac & Oak, Ltd., designs and assembles low-priced portable Internet devices. Sumac & Oak estimates that there will be 235,000 requests for its most popular model in 20x5. Estimated costs related to this product for 20x5 areas follows:

Description	Budgeted Costs
Casing	$ 432,400
Battery chamber	545,200
Electronics	1,151,500
Direct labor	1,598,000
Variable indirect assembly costs	789,600
Fixed indirect assembly costs	338,400
Selling expenses	493,500
General operating expenses	183,300
Administrative expenses	126,900

The budget is based on the demand previously stated. The company wants to earn operating income of $846,000 in 20x5.

Last week four competitors released their wholesale prices for the next year, as shown below:

Competitor A	$25.68
Competitor B	24.58
Competitor C	23.96
Competitor D	25.30

Sumac & Oak portable devices are known for their high quality. However, every $1 price increase above the top competitor's price causes a 55,000-unit drop in demand from the original estimate. (Assume all price changes occur in $1 increments.)

REQUIRED
1. Prepare a schedule of total projected costs and unit costs.
2. Use gross margin pricing to compute the anticipated selling price.

3. Based on competitors' prices, what should Sumac & Oak's portable device sell for in 20x5 (assume a constant unit cost)? Defend your answer. (**Hint:** Determine the total operating income at various sales levels.)
4. Would your pricing structure in **2** change if the company had only limited competition at this quality level? If so, in what direction? Explain why.

P 7.
LO4 Pricing Using Target Costing

Clevenger Machine Tool Company designs and produces a line of high-quality machine tools and markets them throughout the world. The company's main competition comes from companies in France, Great Britain, and Korea. Two highly specialized machine tools, Y14 and Z33, have recently been introduced by five competing firms. The prices charged for Y14 range from $625 to $675 per tool, and the price range for Z33 is from $800 to $840 per tool. The company is contemplating entering the market for these two products. Market research has indicated that if Clevenger can sell Y14 for $650 per tool and Z33 for $750 per tool, the company will be successful in marketing the products worldwide. The company's profit markup is 25 percent over all costs to produce and deliver a product. Current activity-based cost rates are as follows:

Materials handling	$1.30 per dollar of direct materials and purchased parts cost
Production	$4.40 per machine hour
Product delivery	$34.00 per unit of Y14
	$40.00 per unit of Z33

Design engineering and accounting estimates for the production of the two new products are as follows:

	Product Y14	Product Z33
Projected unit demand	75,000	95,000
Per-unit data		
Direct materials cost	$50.00	$60.00
Purchased parts cost	$65.00	$70.00
Manufacturing labor		
Hours	6.2	7.4
Hourly labor rate	$14.00	$14.00
Assembly labor		
Hours	4.6	9.2
Hourly labor rate	$12.00	$12.00
Machine hours	14	16

REQUIRED ▶
1. Compute the target cost for each product.
2. Compute the total projected unit cost of producing and delivering each product.
3. Using target costing, decide whether the products should be produced.

P 8.
LO5 Developing Transfer Prices

Seven years ago, Hadley Sims formed the Sims Corporation and began producing sound equipment for home use. Because of the highly technical and competitive nature of the industry, Sims established the Research and Development Division (R & D), which is responsible for continually evaluating and updating critical electronic parts used in the corporation's products. The R & D staff has been very successful and has greatly contributed to the corporation's ranking as America's leader in the industry.

Two years ago, R & D took on the added responsibility of producing all microchip circuit boards for the company's sound equipment. One of Sims's specialties is a sound dissemination board (SDB) that greatly enhances the sound quality of Sims's speakers.

Demand for the SDB has increased significantly in the past year. As a result, R & D has increased its production and assembly labor force. Three outside customers want to purchase the SDB for their sound products. To date, R & D has been producing SDBs for internal use only.

The R & D controller wants to create a transfer price for the SDBs that will apply to all intracompany transfers. Estimated demand over the next six months is 235,000 SDBs for internal use and 165,000 SDBs for external customers, for a total of 400,000 units. The following data show cost projections for the next six months:

Materials and parts	$2,600,000
Direct labor	1,920,000
Supplies	100,000
Indirect labor	580,000
Other variable overhead costs	200,000

Fixed overhead, SDBs	$1,840,000
Other fixed overhead, corporate	560,000
Variable selling expenses, SDBs	1,480,000
Fixed selling expenses, corporate	520,000
General corporate operating expenses	880,000
Corporate administrative expenses	680,000

A profit markup of at least 20 percent must be added to total unit cost for internal transfer purposes. Outside customers are willing to pay $35 for each SDB. All categories of fixed costs are assumed to be entirely unavoidable.

REQUIRED ▶
1. Prepare a table that shows the total budgeted costs and the cost per unit for each component of the budget. Also show the profit markup and the cost-plus transfer price.
2. Should R & D use the computed transfer price? Explain the factors that influenced your decision.

SKILLS DEVELOPMENT CASES

Conceptual Analysis

LO1 **Product Differentiation and**
LO2 **Pricing**

SD 1. Maytag Corporation <www.maytag.com> can price its products higher than any other company in the home appliance industry and still maintain and even increase market share. How can it do this? Are its costs higher, resulting in higher prices than those of its competitors? No. Will customers shop around for products with lower price tags? No. Will competitors single out Maytag products in comparative ad campaigns and try to exploit the higher prices? No. Think about the Maytag repairman television commercials that you have seen over the past ten years. They feature a very lonely person who never gets a call to repair a Maytag product. The ads say nothing about price. They do not attack competitors' products. But the commercials do inspire customers to purchase Maytag products through what is known in the marketing field as product differentiation. Prepare a one-page memo to your teacher explaining how Maytag Corporation has differentiated its products from the competition. Is product cost a factor in Maytag's pricing strategy?

LO2 **Comparison of Pricing Policies**

SD 2. E*Trade <www.etrade.com> and Ameritrade <www.ameritrade.com> offer Internet stock-trading services at a very low price compared to traditional brokers. E*Trade has offered trades as low as $9.95 each and Ameritrade as low as $10.99 per trade. Future prices may be even lower. Traditional brokers, which offer more personal service, may charge $50 to $100 for the same trades. Both companies have been growing very rapidly in recent years. What internal and external factors influence the setting of prices? Why would the prices of online brokerage firms differ so greatly from the prices of traditional brokerage firms? Include in your answer a discussion of the role of marginal cost and marginal revenue as it may apply to such companies.

Ethical Dilemma

LO1 **Ethics in Pricing**
LO2

SD 3. Barnes Company has been doing business with mainland China for the past three years. The company produces leather handbags that are in great demand in the cities of China. On a recent trip to Hong Kong, Kwan Cho, the purchasing agent for Shen Enterprises, approached Barnes salesperson Harriet Makay to arrange for a purchase of 2,500 handbags. Barnes's usual price is $75 per bag. Kwan Cho wanted to purchase the handbags at $65 per bag. After an hour of haggling, they agreed to a final price of $68 per item. When Makay returned to her hotel room after dinner, she found an envelope containing five new $100 bills and a note that said, "Thank you for agreeing to our order of 2,500 handbags at $68 per bag. My company's president wants you to have the enclosed gift for your fine service." Makay later learned that Kwan Cho was following her company's normal business practice. What should Harriet Makay do? Is the gift hers to keep? Be prepared to justify your opinion.

Group Activity: Divide the class into small groups, and ask each group to decide what Makay should do. Assemble a panel consisting of one spokesperson from each group and debate Makay's position.

Research Activity

LO5 Transfer Pricing

SD 4. One reason that companies use transfer prices is to allow cost centers to function and be evaluated as profit centers. Transfer prices are artificial prices charged to one department by another for internally manufactured parts and products that are used by the "purchasing" department. Transfer pricing policies and methods have generated much controversy in recent years. Use an Internet search engine like Google or Ask Jeeves to locate an article about transfer prices. Prepare a one-page summary of the article, and use it as the basis for a classroom presentation. Include in your summary the name and web site of the publication, the article's title and author(s), a list of the issues being discussed, and a brief statement about the conclusions reached by the author(s).

Decision-Making Practice

LO3 Pricing Decisions

SD 5. The Fastener Company manufactures office equipment for retail stores. Carol Watson, the vice president of marketing, has proposed that Fastener introduce two new products: an electric stapler and an electric pencil sharpener.

Watson has requested that the Profit Planning Department develop preliminary selling prices for the two new products for her review. Profit Planning is to follow the company's standard policy for developing potential selling prices. It is to use all data available for each product. The data accumulated by Profit Planning are as follows:

	Electric Stapler	Electric Pencil Sharpener
Estimated annual demand in units	16,000	12,000
Estimated unit manufacturing costs	$14.00	$15.00
Estimated unit selling and administrative expenses	$3.00	Not available
Assets employed in manufacturing	$160,000	Not available

Fastener plans to use an average of $1,200,000 in assets to support operations in the current year. The condensed budgeted income statement that follows reflects the planned return on assets of 20 percent ($240,000 ÷ $1,200,000) for the entire company for all products.

Fastener Company
Budgeted Income Statement
For the Year Ended May 31, 20x7
($000 omitted)

Revenue	$2,400
Cost of goods sold	1,440
Gross profit	$ 960
Selling and administrative expenses	720
Operating income	$ 240

1. Calculate a potential selling price for the:
    a. electric stapler, using return on assets pricing
    b. electric pencil sharpener, using gross margin pricing

2. Could a selling price for the electric pencil sharpener be calculated using return on assets pricing? Explain your answer.
3. Which of the two pricing methods—return on assets pricing or gross margin pricing—is more appropriate for decision analysis? Explain your answer.
4. Discuss the additional steps Carol Watson is likely to take after she receives the potential selling prices for the two new products (as calculated in 1) to set an actual selling price for each of the two products. (CMA adapted)

MANAGERIAL REPORTING AND ANALYSIS CASES

Interpreting Management Reports

LO5 Transfer Pricing

MRA 1. Two major operating divisions, the Cabinet Division and the Electronics Division, make up Cirrus Industries, Inc. The company's main product is a deluxe console television set. The TV cabinets are manufactured by the Cabinet Division, and the Electronics Division produces all electronic components and assembles the sets. The company uses a decentralized organizational structure.

The Cabinet Division not only supplies cabinets to the Electronics Division but also sells cabinets to other TV manufacturers. Based on a typical sales order of 40 cabinets, the following unit cost breakdown for a deluxe television cabinet was developed:

Direct materials	$ 32.00
Direct labor	15.00
Variable manufacturing overhead	12.00
Fixed manufacturing overhead	18.00
Variable selling expenses	9.00
Fixed selling expenses	6.00
Fixed general and administrative expenses	8.00
Total unit cost	$100.00

The Cabinet Division's usual profit margin is 20 percent, and the regular selling price of a deluxe cabinet is $120. The division's managers recently decided that $120 will also be the transfer price for all intracompany transactions.

Managers at the Electronics Division are unhappy with that decision. They claim that the Cabinet Division will show superior performance at the expense of the Electronics Division. Competition recently forced the company to lower its prices. Because of the newly established transfer price for the cabinet, the Electronics Division's portion of the profit margin on deluxe television sets was lowered to 18 percent. To counteract the new intracompany transfer price, the managers of the Electronics Division announced that effective immediately, all cabinets will be purchased from an outside supplier, in lots of 200 cabinets at a unit price of $110 per cabinet. The company president, Joe Springer, has called a meeting of both divisions to negotiate a fair intracompany transfer price. The following prices were listed as possible alternatives:

Current market price	$120 per cabinet
Current outside purchase price (This price is based on a large-quantity purchase discount. It will cause increased storage costs for the Electronics Division.)	$110 per cabinet
Total unit manufacturing costs plus a 20 percent profit margin: $77.00 + $15.40	$92.40 per cabinet
Total unit costs excluding variable selling expenses plus a 20 percent profit margin: $91.00 + $18.20	$109.20 per cabinet

1. What price should be established for intracompany transactions? Defend your answer by showing the shortcomings of each alternative.
2. If there were an outside market for all units produced by the Cabinet Division at the $120 price, would you change your answer to 1? Why?

Formulating Management Reports

MRA 2.

LO5 Transfer Prices and Performance Evaluation

"That Champions Division is robbing us blind!" This statement by the director of the Tournament Division was heard during the meeting of the board of directors at Golf-Brell Company. The company produces golf umbrellas in a two-step process. The Champions Division prepares the fabric tops and transfers them to the Tournament Division, which produces the ribs and handles, secures the tops, and packs all finished umbrellas for shipment.

Because of the directors' concern, the company controller gathered data for the past year, as shown in the following table:

	Champions Division	Tournament Division
Sales		
Regular	$700,000	$1,720,000
Deluxe	900,000	3,300,000
Direct materials		
Fabric tops (from Champions Division)	—	1,600,000
Cloth	360,000	—
Aluminum	—	660,000
Closing mechanisms	—	1,560,000
Direct labor	480,000	540,000
Variable manufacturing overhead	90,000	240,000
Fixed divisional overhead—avoidable	150,000	210,000
Selling and general operating expenses	132,000	372,000
Company administrative expenses	84,000	108,000

During the year, 200,000 regular umbrellas and 150,000 deluxe umbrellas were completed and transferred or shipped by the two divisions. Transfer prices used by the Champions Division were:

Regular $3.50
Deluxe 6.00

The regular umbrella wholesales for $8.60 and the deluxe model for $22.00. Company administrative costs are allocated to divisions by a predetermined formula.

Management has indicated that the transfer price should include a 20 percent profit factor on total division costs.

1. Prepare a performance report on the Champions Division.
2. Prepare a performance report on the Tournament Division.
3. Compute each division's rate of return on controllable costs and on total division costs.
4. Do you agree with the statement made by the director of the Tournament Division? Explain your response.
5. What procedures would you recommend to the board of directors?

International Company

MRA 3.

LO3 Product Pricing in a Foreign
LO4 Market

Borner, Inc., is an international corporation that manufactures and sells home care products. Today, a meeting is being held at corporate headquarters in New York City. The purpose of the meeting is to discuss changing the price of the laundry detergent the company manufactures and sells in Brazil. During the meeting, a conflict develops between Carl Dickson, the corporate sales manager, and José Cabral, the Brazilian Division's sales manager.

Dickson insists that the selling price of the laundry detergent should be increased to the equivalent of U.S.$3. This increase is necessary because the Brazilian Division's costs are higher than those of other international divisions. The Brazilian Division is paying high interest rates on notes payable for the acquisition of the new manufacturing plant. In addition, a stronger, more expensive ingredient has been introduced into the laundry detergent, which has caused the product cost to increase by $.20.

Cabral believes that the laundry detergent's selling price should remain at $2.50 for several reasons. Cabral argues that the market for laundry detergent in Brazil is highly competitive. Labor costs are low, and the costs of distribution are small because the target market is limited to the Rio de Janeiro metropolitan area. Inflation is extremely high in Brazil, and the Brazilian government continues to impose policies to control inflation. Because of these controls, Cabral insists, the buyers will resist any price hikes.

1. What selling price do you believe Borner, Inc., should set for the laundry detergent? Explain your answer. Do you believe Borner, Inc., should let the Brazilian Division set the selling price for laundry detergent in the future? When should corporate headquarters set prices?
2. Based on the information given above, should cost-based pricing or target costing be used to set the selling price for laundry detergent in Brazil? Explain your answer.

Excel Spreadsheet Analysis

LO4 Target Costing

MRA 4. Every Electronics, Inc., produces circuit boards for electronic devices that are made by more than a dozen customers. Competition among the producers of circuit boards is keen, with over 30 companies bidding on every job request from those customers. The circuit boards can vary widely in their complexity, and their unit prices can range from $250 to more than $500.

Every's controller is concerned about the analysis just completed by the Engineering Design Department. The cost planning projection for a new complex circuit board, the CX35, was almost 6 percent above its target cost. The controller has asked the design engineers to review their design and projections and come up with alternatives that will reduce the proposed product's costs to equal to or below the target cost.

The following information was used to develop the initial cost projections:

Target selling price	$590.00 per unit
Desired profit percentage	25% of total unit cost
Projected unit demand	13,600 units
Per-unit data	
Direct materials cost	$56.00
Purchased parts cost	$37.00
Manufacturing labor	
Hours	4.5 hours
Hourly labor rate	$14.00
Assembly labor	
Hours	5.2 hours
Hourly labor rate	$15.00
Machine hours	26 hours
Activity-based cost rates	
Materials handling	10% of direct materials and purchased parts cost
Engineering	$13.50 per unit for CX35
Production	$8.20 per machine hour
Product delivery	$24.00 per unit for CX35
Marketing	$6.00 per unit for CX35

1. Compute the product's target cost.
2. Compute the product cost of the original estimate to verify that the controller's calculations were correct.
3. Rework the product cost calculations for each of the following alternatives recommended by the design engineers:
   a. Cut product quality, which will reduce direct materials cost by 20 percent and purchased parts cost by 15 percent.
   b. Increase the quality of direct materials, which will increase direct materials cost by 20 percent but will reduce machine hours by 10 percent, manufacturing labor hours by 16 percent, and assembly labor hours by 20 percent.
4. What decision should the management of Every Electronics, Inc., make about the new product? Defend your answer.

LO4 **Target Costing and the Internet**

Internet Case

MRA 5. Assume that you work for a company that wants to develop a product to compete with Palm's <www.palm.com> Zire. You have been assigned the task of using target costing to help in its development. Do a search for Zire product reviews and product specifications and get price quotes. Why would your company's management want to use target costing to help in its development of a competitive PDA? What retail price would you suggest be used as a basis for target costing? Assuming a desired profit of 25 percent of selling price, what is the resulting target cost? What actions should the company take now?

26

Chapter 26 presents an overview of the capital investment process and examines the most common methods used to evaluate whether a capital investment proposal meets the minimum rate of return to receive funding.

Capital Investment Analysis

LEARNING OBJECTIVES

LO1 Define *capital investment analysis* and describe its relation to the management cycle.

LO2 State the purpose of the minimum rate of return and identify the methods used to arrive at that rate.

LO3 Identify the types of projected costs and revenues used to evaluate alternatives for capital investment.

LO4 Apply the concept of the time value of money.

LO5 Analyze capital investment proposals using the net present value method.

LO6 Analyze capital investment proposals using the payback period method and the accounting rate-of-return method.

DECISION POINT

A MANAGER'S FOCUS

Air Products and Chemicals Inc. <www.airproducts.com> As an industrial producer of gases that are piped directly into steel mills and other factories, Air Products and Chemicals Inc. has many small gas plants located near its customers. What makes Air Products and Chemicals competitive is its use of a "lights-out" system, or, as the company describes it, "unattended operations with remote access." The system minimizes on-site labor by having regional operators remotely monitor several gas plants from a computer at their homes. If a problem occurs with a machine, an operator can repair it remotely or visit the plant.

Air Products and Chemicals is not alone in turning on-site labor's lights off. Linking machines to the Internet so that managers can monitor operations at any time and from anywhere is common in industries that produce identical products in high volume, such as gears and dental-floss containers.[1]

Companies have many equipment and factory needs, and completely automated factories are costly. Thus, when deciding whether to invest their company's capital in an expensive project like an automated plant, managers must focus on making the best decisions possible. How should they evaluate the capital investment alternatives and make wise allocations of limited resources? How can they minimize the risks involved?

Capital investments require decisions about long-term projects that may have positive or negative consequences for a company for many years. It is therefore essential to take a systematic approach to evaluating the projects. Air Products and Chemicals'

Why are capital investment decisions critical for a company like Air Products and Chemicals, Inc.?

management typically evaluates each proposed investment by determining whether it will generate an adequate return for the company.

THE CAPITAL INVESTMENT PROCESS

LO1 Define *capital investment analysis* and describe its relation to the management cycle.

RELATED TEXT ASSIGNMENTS
Q: 1, 2, 3, 4, 5
SE: 1
E: 1   www.airproducts.com
SD: 1, 4
MRA: 3, 5

KEY POINT: Capital investment analysis is a decision process for the purchase of capital facilities, such as buildings and equipment.

 STOP AND THINK!
How is capital investment analysis a part of both the long-term planning and annual budgeting processes?
Capital investment decisions will affect a company for many years—first as broad estimates used for planning purposes and finally, in the year of the expenditure, as specific investment analyses. ■

Among the most significant decisions that management must make are **capital investment decisions**, which are decisions about when and how much to spend on capital facilities and other long-term projects. Capital facilities and projects may include machinery, systems, or processes; new buildings or additions or renovations to existing buildings; entire new divisions or product lines; and distribution and software systems. For example, Air Products and Chemicals Inc. will make decisions about installing new equipment, replacing old equipment, expanding production by renovating or adding to a building, buying or building a new factory, or acquiring another company.

Capital facilities and projects are expensive. A new factory or production system may cost millions of dollars and require several years to complete. Managers must make capital investment decisions carefully to select the alternatives that will contribute the most to future profits.

CAPITAL INVESTMENT ANALYSIS

Capital investment analysis, or *capital budgeting*, is the process of making decisions about capital investments. It consists of identifying the need for a capital investment, analyzing courses of action to meet that need, preparing reports for managers, choosing the best alternative, and allocating funds among competing needs. Every part of the organization participates in this process. Financial analysts supply a target cost of capital or desired rate of return and an estimate of how much money can be spent annually on capital facilities. Marketing specialists predict sales trends and new product demands, which help in determining which operations need expansion or new equipment. Managers at all levels help identify facility needs and often prepare preliminary cost estimates for the desired capital investment. Then all work together to implement the project selected and to keep the results within revenue and cost estimates.

The capital investment process involves the evaluation of alternative proposals for large capital investments, including considerations for financing the projects. Capital investment analyses affect both short-term and long-term planning. Figure 1 illustrates the time span of the capital expenditure planning process. Most companies have a long-term plan, that is, a projection of operations for the next five or ten years. Large capital investments should be an integral part of that plan. Anticipated additions or changes to product lines, replacements of equipment, and acquisitions of other companies are examples of items to be included in long-term capital investment plans.

One element of budgeting is a capital investment budget. The capital investment budget fits into both the long-term planning process and the capital investment process. Long-term plans are not very specific; they are expressed in broad, goal-oriented terms. Each annual budget must help accomplish the organization's long-term goals. Look again at Figure 1. In 2007, the company plans to purchase a large, special-purpose machine. When the ten-year plan was developed, it included only a broad statement about a plan to purchase the machine. Nothing was specified about the cost of the machine or the anticipated operating details and costs. Those details are contained in the annual master budget for 2007, and it is in 2007 that the capital investment analysis will occur. So although capital investment decisions that will affect the company for many years are discussed and estimates of future revenues and expenditures are made when the long-term plan is first developed, the capital investment analysis is performed in the period when the expenditure will be made. This point is important to the understanding of capital investment analysis.

FIGURE 1
Time Span of the Capital Investment Planning Process

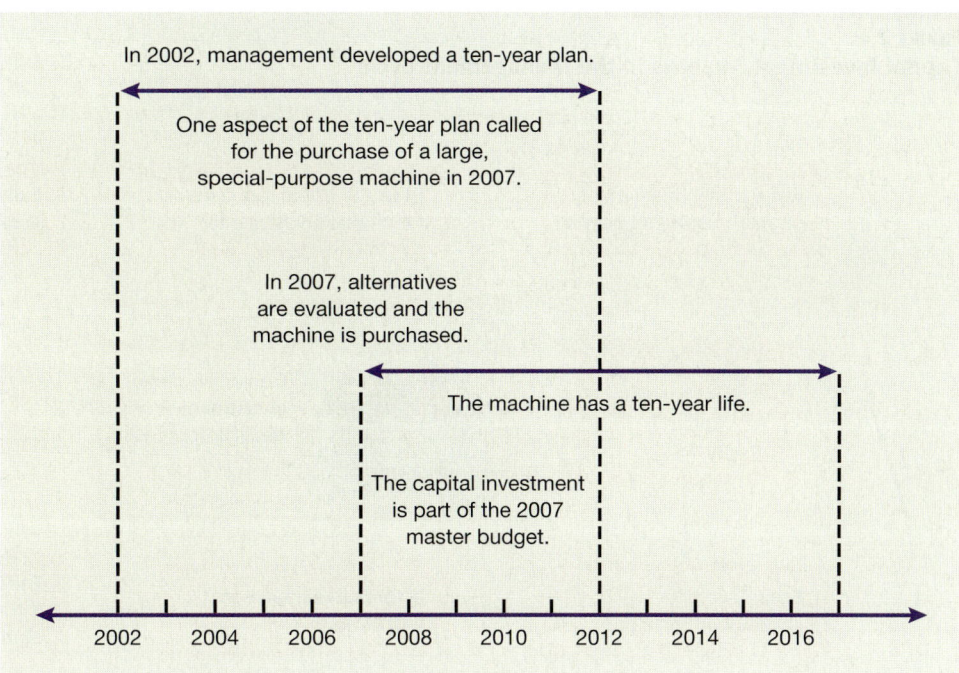

CAPITAL INVESTMENT ANALYSIS IN THE MANAGEMENT CYCLE

Managers pay close attention to capital investments throughout the management cycle, as shown in Figure 2. However, the greatest portion of capital investment analysis takes place during the planning phase.

■ **PLANNING** Each decision made about a capital investment is vitally important because it involves a large amount of money and commits a company to a course of action for years to come. For example, Air Products and Chemicals Inc., IBM, and Intel must make capital investment decisions that fit into their strategic plans. A series of poor decisions about capital investments can cause a company to fail. To ensure high-quality capital investment decisions, managers follow six key steps during the planning phase of the management cycle.

www.airproducts.com
www.ibm.com
www.intel.com

KEY POINT: The six steps of capital investment analysis are performed for both long-term and short-term planning purposes.

Step 1: Identification of Capital Investment Needs Identifying the need for a new capital investment is the starting point of capital investment analysis. Managers identify capital investment opportunities from past sales experience, changes in sources and quality of materials, employees' suggestions, production bottlenecks caused by obsolete equipment, new production or distribution methods, or customer complaints. In addition, capital investment needs are identified through proposals to:

1. Add new products to the product line.
2. Expand capacity in existing product lines.
3. Reduce production costs of existing products without altering operating levels.
4. Automate existing production processes.

Step 2: Formal Requests for Capital Investments To enhance control over capital investments, managers prepare formal requests for new capital investments. Each request includes a complete description of the investment under review, the reasons a new investment is needed, the alternative means of satisfying the need, the timing and estimated costs and related cost savings for each alternative, and the investment's engineering specifications, if necessary.

FIGURE 2
Capital Investment Analysis in the Management Cycle

Step 3: Preliminary Screening Organizations that have several branches and a highly developed system for capital investment analysis require that all proposals go through preliminary screening. The purpose of preliminary screening is to ensure that the only proposals to receive serious review are those that both meet company strategic goals and produce the minimum rate of return set by management.

Step 4: Establishment of the Acceptance-Rejection Standard To attract and maintain funding for capital investments, an organization establishes an acceptance-rejection standard. Such a standard may be expressed as a minimum rate of return or a minimum cash-flow payback period. If the number of acceptable requests for capital investments exceeds the limited funds available for such investments, the proposals must next be ranked according to their rates of return. Acceptance-rejection standards are used to identify projects that are expected to yield inadequate or marginal returns. They also identify proposed projects for which high product demand and high financial returns are expected. Cost of capital information is often used to establish minimum rates of return on investments. The development of such rates is discussed later in this chapter.

Step 5: Evaluation of Proposals Proposals are evaluated by verifying decision variables and applying established proposal evaluation methods. The key decision variables are (1) expected life, (2) estimated cash flow, and (3) investment cost. Each variable in a proposal should be checked for accuracy. Three commonly used methods of evaluating proposed capital investments are the net present value method, the payback period method, and the accounting rate-of-return method. Using one or more evaluation methods and the minimum acceptance-rejection standard, management evaluates all proposals. In addition to this quantitative analysis, management will also consider qualitative factors, such as availability and training of employees, competition, anticipated future technological improvements, and the proposal's impact on other company operations.

Step 6: Capital Investment Decisions The proposals that meet the standards of the evaluation process are given to the appropriate manager for final review. When deciding which requests to implement, the manager must consider the funds available for capital investments. The acceptable proposals are ranked in order of net present value, payback period, or rate of return, and the highest-ranking proposals are funded first. Often there will not be enough money to fund all proposals. The final capital investment budget is then prepared by allocating funds to the selected proposals.

■ **EXECUTING** In the executing phase, capital investment decisions are implemented. This involves scheduling projects and overseeing their development, construction, or purchase. Managers must establish controls to make sure projects are completed on time, within budget, and at the desired level of quality.

■ **REVIEWING** In the reviewing phase, each project undergoes a postcompletion audit to determine if it is meeting the goals and targets set forth in the planning phase. Many projects can be modified in midprocess if changes are advisable. The postdecision audit may also identify weaknesses in the original planning process that can be corrected to avoid similar problems in the future.

The postcompletion audit is a difficult step in the management cycle. To isolate how a decision affects a company's overall operating results requires extensive analysis. The main problems are that (1) long-term projects must be evaluated by concentrating on cash flows over the project's life, (2) a particular decision may influence the operations of existing facilities, and (3) profitability resulting from a decision may be difficult to isolate and identify.

■ **REPORTING** During the reporting phase, reports on the results of capital investment decisions are prepared and distributed within the organization. They include comparisons of budgeted expenditures and actual expenditures for each project. Once projects are in operation, reports should include comparisons of projected net cash flows or cost savings with actual results. Based on such reports, managers may decide to modify or curtail projects that are failing to meet expectations or to go forward with new projects. Such reports are critical to the postcompletion audit that occurs during the review phase.

✓ Check out ACE for a Review Quiz at http://accounting.college.hmco.com/students.

THE MINIMUM RATE OF RETURN ON INVESTMENT

LO2 State the purpose of the minimum rate of return and identify the methods used to arrive at that rate.

RELATED TEXT ASSIGNMENTS
Q: 6
SE: 2, 3
E: 2, 3
P: 1
SD: 2
MRA: 5

Most companies set a minimum rate of return, and any capital expenditure proposal that fails to produce that rate of return is automatically refused. The minimum rate of return is often referred to as a *hurdle rate* because it is the rate that must be exceeded, or hurdled. If none of the capital investment requests is expected to meet or exceed the minimum rate of return, or hurdle rate, all requests will be turned down.

Organizations set a minimum rate of return to guard their profitability. If the return from a capital investment falls below the minimum rate of return, the funds can be used more profitably in another part of the organization. Projects that produce poor returns will ultimately lower the organization's profitability.

Choosing a minimum rate of return is not a simple task. Each measure that can be used to set a cutoff point has certain advantages. The most commonly used measures are (1) cost of capital, (2) corporate return on investment, (3) industry average return on investment, and (4) bank interest rates.

COST OF CAPITAL

 STOP AND THINK!
Do all industries have the same cost of capital?
No. Due to industry differences, industry segments may not have the same cost of capital. ■

Of all the possible measures of minimum rates of return, cost of capital is the most widely used. The **cost of capital** is the weighted-average rate of return a company must pay to its long-term creditors and shareholders for the use of their funds. The components of cost of capital are the cost of debt, the cost of preferred stock, the cost of common stock, and the cost of retained earnings. Sophisticated methods may be used to determine these costs. However, in this discussion, we use a simplified definition of each cost. The cost of debt is the after-tax interest on the debt (interest times one minus the tax rate). The after-tax amount is used because the interest is tax deductible. In contrast, the cost of preferred stock is the full dividend rate because dividends are not tax deductible. The cost of equity capital (common stock and retained earnings) is the return required by investors in the company.

The cost of capital is computed in four steps:

ENRICHMENT NOTE:
Depending on the mixture of sources of capital, a company's cost of capital will vary.

1. Identify the cost of each source of capital.
2. Compute the proportion (percentage) of the organization's total amount of debt and equity that each source of capital represents.
3. Multiply each source's cost by its proportion of the capital.
4. Total the weighted costs computed in Step **3**.

For example, assume that the Wilson Company's financing structure is as follows:

Cost (Percentage)	Source of Capital	Amount	Proportion of Capital (Percentage)
6	Debt financing	$150,000	30
8	Preferred stock	50,000	10
12	Common stock	200,000	40
12	Retained earnings	100,000	20
	Totals	$500,000	100

The cost of capital of 9.8 percent would be computed as follows:

Source of Capital	Cost	×	Proportion of Capital	=	Weighted Cost
Debt financing	.06		.30		.018
Preferred stock	.08		.10		.008
Common stock	.12		.40		.048
Retained earnings	.12		.20		.024
Cost of capital					.098

FOCUS ON INTERNATIONAL BUSINESS

Why Look Beyond the Cost of a Capital Investment?

Because capital investments are made in long-term facilities and projects that require commitments of large amounts of money to be spent in anticipation of profitable future returns, many things in addition to costs should be evaluated. International trade and logistics can also be part of the capital investment decision. A case in point is Koss Corp. <www.koss.com>, located in Milwaukee, Wisconsin, and maker of high-fidelity headphones used for Walkmans, speakerphones, and other audio equipment. Company managers moved much of the production to China, where costs are low. However, that caused a problem with making timely deliveries to customers.[2] The just-in-time inventory philosophy had to be abandoned and inventories were tripled from $2 million to $6 million to avoid customer backorders and dissatisfaction. Now finished products are stacked in the Milwaukee factory to insure against dock worker strikes and missed deliveries. Looking beyond the numbers becomes an important consideration in capital investment decisions.

OTHER CUTOFF MEASURES

If cost of capital information is unavailable, management can use one of three less accurate but still useful amounts as the minimum rate of return. The first is the average total corporate return on investment. This measure is based on the notion that any capital investment that produces a lower return than the amount the company has earned historically will negatively affect investors' perception of the firm's future market value. A second method is to use the industry's average cost of capital. Most sizable industry associations supply such information. As a last resort, a company might use the current bank lending rate. But because most companies are financed by both debt and equity, the bank lending rate seldom reflects an accurate rate of return.

RANKING CAPITAL INVESTMENT PROPOSALS

The requests that a company receives for capital investments usually exceed the funds available for capital investments. Even after management evaluates and selects proposals under the minimum acceptance-rejection standard, there are often too many proposals to fund adequately. At that point, managers must rank the proposals according to their rates of return, or profitability, and begin a second selection process.

Assume that Queens Enterprises has $4,500,000 to spend this year for capital improvements and that five acceptable proposals are competing for those funds. The company's current minimum rate of return is 18 percent, and it is considering the following proposals:

Project	Rate of Return (Percentage)	Capital Investment	Cumulative Investment
A	32	$1,460,000	$1,460,000
B	30	1,890,000	3,350,000
C	28	460,000	3,810,000
D	24	840,000	4,650,000
E	22	580,000	5,230,000
Total		$5,230,000	

The proposals are listed in the order of their rates of return. Projects A, B, and C have the highest rates of return and together will cost a total of $3,810,000. That leaves $690,000 in capital funds for other projects. Project D should be examined first to see if it could be implemented for $150,000 less. If not, then Project E should be selected. The selection of projects A, B, C, and E means that $110,000 in capital funds will be uncommitted for the year.

 Check out ACE for a Review Quiz at http://accounting.college.hmco.com/students.

Measures Used in Capital Investment Analysis

LO3 Identify the types of projected costs and revenues used to evaluate alternatives for capital investment.

RELATED TEXT ASSIGNMENTS
Q: 7, 8, 9, 10, 11, 12
SE: 4
E: 4
P: 1
MRA: 2

When evaluating a proposed capital investment, managers must predict how the new asset will perform and how it will benefit the company. Various measures are used to estimate the benefits to be derived from a capital investment.

Net Income and Net Cash Inflows

Each capital investment analysis must include a measure of the expected benefit from the investment project. The measure of expected benefit depends on the method of analyzing capital investment alternatives. One possible measure is net income, calculated in the usual way. Managers determine increases in net income resulting from the capital investment for each alternative.

A more widely used measure of expected benefit is projected cash flows. **Net cash inflows** are the balance of increases in projected cash receipts over increases in projected cash payments resulting from a capital investment. In some cases, equipment replacement decisions involve alternatives when revenues are the same among alternatives. In such cases, **cost savings** measure the benefits, such as reduced costs, from proposed capital investments. Either net cash inflows or cost savings can be used as the basis for an evaluation, but one measure should not be confused with the other. If the analysis involves cash receipts, net cash inflows are used. If the analysis involves only cash outlays, cost savings are used. Managers must measure and evaluate all the investment alternatives consistently.

Stop and Think!
Why are operating expenses and cash expenses different?
Operating expenses include depreciation and other noncash expenses. ∎

Equal Versus Unequal Cash Flows

Projected cash flows may be the same for each year of an asset's life, or they may vary from year to year. Unequal cash flows are common and must be analyzed for each year of an asset's life. Proposed projects with equal annual cash flows require less detailed analysis. Both a project with equal cash flows and one with unequal cash flows are illustrated and explained later in this chapter.

Carrying Value of Assets

Carrying value is the undepreciated portion of the original cost of a fixed asset, that is, the asset's cost less its accumulated depreciation. When a decision to replace an asset is being evaluated, the carrying value of the old asset is irrelevant because it is a past, or historical, cost and will not be altered by the decision. Net proceeds from the asset's sale or disposal are relevant, however, because the proceeds affect cash flows and may differ for each alternative.

Focus on Business Technology

Counting Your Pennies the High-Tech Way
As noted in this chapter's Decision Point, "lights-out" machines are replacing human labor in factories. They are also replacing human labor in the counting of loose change. Coinstar <www.coinstar.com>, located in Bellevue Washington, manufactures and sells high-tech coin counters. Over 10,000 of these machines can be found in supermarkets in the United States, Canada, and Great Britain. They are 99.99 percent accurate and can count 600 coins per minute. They are considered high-tech because each one is connected to a central data processing center that monitors and maintains it.[3]

Depreciation Expense and Income Taxes

The techniques of capital investment analysis in this chapter compare the relative benefits of proposed capital investments by measuring the cash receipts and payments for a facility or project. Income taxes alter the amount and timing of cash flows of projects under consideration by for-profit companies. To assess the benefits of a capital project, a company must include the effects of taxes in its capital investment analyses. Depreciation expense is deductible when determining income taxes. (You may recall that the annual depreciation expense computation using the straight-line method is the asset's cost less its residual value, divided by the asset's useful life.) Thus, depreciation expense strongly influences the amount of income taxes a company pays and can lead to significant tax savings.

Corporate income tax rates vary and can change yearly. To examine how taxes affect capital investment analysis, assume that a company has a tax rate of 30 percent on taxable income. It is considering a capital project that will make the following annual contribution to operating income:

Cash revenues	$ 400,000
Cash expenses	(200,000)
Depreciation	(100,000)
Operating income before income taxes	$ 100,000
Income taxes at 30%	(30,000)
Operating income	$ 70,000

The net cash inflows for this project can be determined in two ways:

1. Net cash inflows—receipts and disbursements

Revenues (cash inflows)	$400,000
Cash expenses (outflows)	(200,000)
Income taxes (outflows)	(30,000)
Net cash inflows	$170,000

2. Net cash inflows—income adjustment procedure

Income after income taxes	$ 70,000
Add back noncash expenses (depreciation)	100,000
Less noncash revenues	—
Net cash inflows	$170,000

In both computations, the net cash inflows are $170,000, and the total effect of income taxes is to lower the net cash inflows by $30,000.

DISPOSAL OR RESIDUAL VALUES

Proceeds from the sale of an old asset are current cash inflows and are relevant to evaluating a proposed capital investment. Projected disposal or residual values of replacement equipment are also relevant because they represent future cash inflows and usually differ among alternatives. Remember that the residual value, sometimes called the *disposal* or *salvage value*, of an asset will be received at the end of the asset's estimated life.

STUDY NOTE: When using the net present value method, remember to consider the present value of the residual or disposal value.

 Check out ACE for a Review Quiz at http://accounting.college.hmco.com/students.

THE TIME VALUE OF MONEY

LO4 Apply the concept of the time value of money.

RELATED TEXT ASSIGNMENTS
Q: 13, 14
SE: 5
E: 5, 6, 7
P: 2, 3, 5, 6, 7, 8
SD: 5
MRA: 2

An organization has many options for investing capital besides buying fixed assets. Consequently, management expects a fixed asset to yield a reasonable return during its useful life. A key question in capital investment analysis is how to measure the return on a fixed asset. One way is to look at the cash flows the asset will generate during its useful life. When an asset has a long useful life, management will usually analyze those cash flows in terms of the time value of money. The **time value of money** is the concept that cash flows of equal dollar amounts separated by an interval of time have different present values because of the effect of compound interest. The notions of interest, present value, future value, and present value of an ordinary annuity are all related to the time value of money.

Interest

KEY POINT: Interest is a cost associated with the passage of time, whether or not there is a stated interest rate.

Interest is the cost associated with the use of money for a specific period of time. Because interest is a cost associated with time and "time is money," interest is an important consideration in any business decision. **Simple interest** is the interest cost for one or more periods when the amount on which the interest is computed stays the same from period to period. **Compound interest** is the interest cost for two or more periods when the amount on which interest is computed changes in each period to include all interest paid in previous periods. In other words, compound interest is interest earned on a principal sum that is increased at the end of each period by the interest for that period.

■ **EXAMPLE: SIMPLE INTEREST** Jo Sanka accepts an 8 percent, $30,000 note due in 90 days. How much will she receive in total when the note comes due? The formula for calculating simple interest is:

$$\text{Interest Expense} = \text{Principal} \times \text{Rate} \times \text{Time}$$
$$= \$30,000 \times 8/100 \times 90/360 = \$600$$

The total that Sanka will receive is computed as follows:

$$\text{Total} = \text{Principal} + \text{Interest}$$
$$= \$30,000 + \$600 = \$30,600$$

If the interest is paid and the note is renewed for an additional 90 days, the interest calculation will remain the same.

■ **EXAMPLE: COMPOUND INTEREST** Andy Clayburn makes a deposit of $5,000 in a savings account that pays 6 percent interest. He expects to leave the principal and accumulated interest in the account for three years. What will be his account total at the end of three years? Assume that the interest is paid at the end of the year, that the interest is added to the principal at that time, and that this total in turn earns interest.

The amount at the end of three years is computed as follows:

(1) Year	(2) Principal Amount at Beginning of Year	(3) Annual Amount of Interest (col. 2 × .06)	(4) Accumulated Amount at End of Year (col. 2 + col. 3)
1	$5,000.00	$300.00	$5,300.00
2	5,300.00	318.00	5,618.00
3	5,618.00	337.08	5,955.08

At the end of three years, Clayburn will have $5,955.08 in his savings account. Note that the annual amount of interest increases each year by the interest rate times the interest of the previous year. For example, between year 1 and year 2, the interest increased by $18 ($318 − $300), which exactly equals 6 percent times $300.

Present Value

Suppose that you had the choice of receiving $100 today or one year from today. Intuitively, you would choose to receive the $100 today. Why? You know that if you have the $100 today, you can put it in a savings account to earn interest, so that you will have more than $100 a year from today. Therefore, we can say that an amount to be received in the future (future value) is not worth as much today as the same amount to be received today (present value) because of the cost associated with the passage of time.

> **STOP AND THINK!**
> How do present value and future value differ?
>
> *Present value looks back to determine value in the present; future value looks forward to determine value at a future time.* ∎

Future value and present value are closely related. **Future value** is the amount an investment will be worth at a future date if invested today at compound interest. **Present value** is the amount that must be invested today at a given rate of compound interest to produce a given future value.

For example, assume that Daschel Company needs $1,000 one year from now. How much should the company invest today to achieve that goal if the interest rate is 5 percent? The following equation may be used:

$$\text{Present Value} \times (1.0 + \text{Interest Rate}) = \text{Future Value}$$
$$\text{Present Value} \times 1.05 = \$1,000.00$$
$$\text{Present Value} = \$1,000.00 \div 1.05$$
$$\text{Present Value} = \$952.38$$

Thus, to achieve a future value of $1,000.00, a present value of $952.38 must be invested. Interest of 5 percent on $952.38 for one year equals $47.62, and the two amounts added together equal $1,000.00.

PRESENT VALUE OF A SINGLE SUM DUE IN THE FUTURE

When more than one time period is involved, the calculation of present value is more complicated. For example, Reza Company wants to be sure of having $4,000 at the end of three years. How much must the company invest today in a 5 percent savings account to achieve that goal? By adapting the preceding equation, the present value of $4,000 at compound interest of 5 percent for three years in the future may be computed as follows:

Year	Amount at End of Year		Divide by		Present Value at Beginning of Year
3	$4,000.00	÷	1.05	=	$3,809.52
2	3,809.52	÷	1.05	=	3,628.11
1	3,628.11	÷	1.05	=	3,455.34

Reza Company must invest a present value of $3,455.34 to achieve a future value of $4,000 in three years. This calculation is made easier by using the appropriate table from the appendix on future value and present value tables. In Table 3, we look down the 5 percent column until we reach period 3. There we find the factor .864. Multiplied by $1, this factor gives the present value of $1 to be received three years from now at 5 percent interest. Thus, we solve the problem as follows:

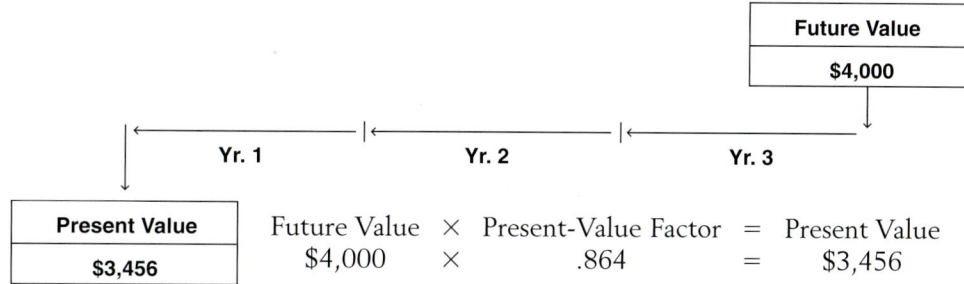

Except for a rounding difference of $.66, this gives the same result as the previous calculation.

PRESENT VALUE OF AN ORDINARY ANNUITY

It is often necessary to compute the present value of a series of receipts or payments. When we calculate the present value of equal amounts equally spaced over

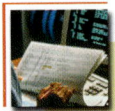

FOCUS ON BUSINESS PRACTICE

How Would You Decide Whether to Buy Rare Dinosaur Bones?

Not-for-profit organizations can also use the techniques of capital investment analysis. For example, the officers of the Field Museum <www.fmnh.org> in Chicago applied these techniques when they decided to bid at auction on the most complete skeleton of a *Tyrannosaurus rex* ever found. The museum bought the bones for $8.2 million and spent another $9 million to restore and install the dinosaur, named Sue. The museum projected that Sue would attract 1 million new visitors, who would produce $5 million in admissions and spend several more million dollars on food, gifts, and the like. After deducting operating costs, museum officials used discounted present values to calculate a return on investment of 10.5 percent. Given that the museum's cost of capital was 8.5 percent, Sue's purchase was considered a financial success. Sue has been extremely popular with the public and more than met the museum's attendance goals in the first year after installation.[4]

STUDY NOTE: The first payment of an ordinary annuity is always made at the end of the first year.

a period of time, we are computing the present value of an ordinary annuity. An **ordinary annuity** is a series of equal payments or receipts that will begin one time period from the current date.

For example, assume that Fodor Company has sold a piece of property and is to receive $15,000 in three equal annual cash payments of $5,000, beginning one year from today. What is the present value of this sale, assuming a current interest rate of 5 percent?

This present value may be determined by calculating a separate present value for each of the three payments (using Table 3 in the appendix on future value and present value tables) and summing the results, as follows:

Future Cash Receipts (Annuity)				Present-Value Factor at 5 Percent (from Table 3)		Present Value
Year 1	Year 2	Year 3				
$5,000			×	.952	=	$ 4,760
	$5,000		×	.907	=	4,535
		$5,000	×	.864	=	4,320
Total Present Value						$13,615

The present value of this sale is $13,615. Thus, there is an implied interest cost (given the 5 percent rate) of $1,385 associated with the payment plan that allows the purchaser to pay in three installments.

We can calculate this present value more easily by using Table 4 in the appendix on future value and present value tables. We look down the 5 percent column until we reach period 3. There we find the factor 2.723. That factor when multiplied by $1 gives the present value of a series of three $1 payments, spaced one year apart, at compound interest of 5 percent. Thus, we solve the problem as follows:

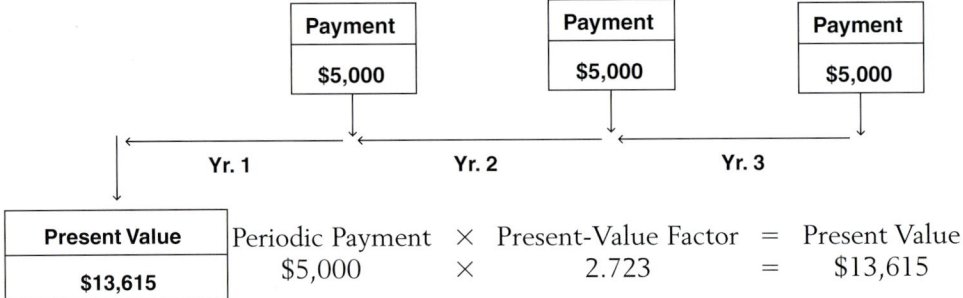

This result is the same as the one computed earlier. If Fodor Company is willing to accept a 5 percent rate of return, management will be equally satisfied to receive a single cash payment of $13,615 today or three equal annual cash payments of $5,000 spread over the next three years.

 Check out ACE for a Review Quiz at http://accounting.college.hmco.com/students.

THE NET PRESENT VALUE METHOD

LO5 Analyze capital investment proposals using the net present value method.

RELATED TEXT ASSIGNMENTS
Q: 15
SE: 6, 7
E: 8, 9, 10
P: 2, 3, 5, 6, 7, 8
SD: 3, 5
MRA: 1, 2, 4

◆ **STOP AND THINK!**
How do cost savings differ from cash inflows?
Cash inflows measure the cash received whereas cost savings measure the cash saved. ■

KEY POINT: If the net present value is zero, the investment will earn the minimum rate of return.

The **net present value method** evaluates a capital investment by discounting its future cash flows to their present values and subtracting the amount of the initial investment from their sum. All proposed capital investments are evaluated in the same way, and the projects with the highest net present value—the amount that exceeds the initial investment—are selected for implementation.

ADVANTAGES OF THE NET PRESENT VALUE METHOD

A significant advantage of the net present value method is that it incorporates the time value of money into the analysis of proposed capital investments. Future cash inflows and outflows are discounted by the company's minimum rate of return to determine their present values. The minimum rate of return should at least equal the company's average cost of capital.

When dealing with the time value of money, use discounting to find the present value of an amount to be received in the future. To determine the present values of future amounts of money, use Tables 3 and 4 in the appendix on future value and present value tables. Remember that Table 3 deals with a single payment or amount, whereas Table 4 is used for a series of equal periodic amounts.

Tables 3 and 4 are used to discount each future cash inflow and cash outflow over the life of the asset to the present. If the net present value is positive (the total of the discounted net cash inflows exceeds the cash investment at the beginning), the rate of return on the investment will exceed the company's minimum rate of return, or hurdle rate, and the project can be accepted. Assuming the project is accepted, investors will be pleased that the company earned a higher rate of return than they expected or required. Conversely, if the net present value is negative (the cash investment at the beginning exceeds the discounted net cash inflows), the return on the investment is less than the minimum rate of return and the project should be rejected. If the net present value is zero (if discounted cash inflows equal discounted cash outflows), the project meets the minimum rate of return and can be accepted.

THE NET PRESENT VALUE METHOD ILLUSTRATED

Assume that Open Imaging Company is considering the purchase of a magnetic resonance imaging (MRI) machine that will improve efficiency in its Radiology Department. Management must decide between two models of the machine.

Model M costs $17,500 and will have an estimated residual value of $2,000 after five years. It is projected to produce cash inflows of $6,000, $5,500, $5,000, $4,500, and $4,000 during its five-year life.

Model N costs $21,000 and will have an estimated residual value of $2,000. It is projected to produce cash inflows of $6,000 per year for five years.

The company's minimum rate of return is 16 percent.

Because Model M is expected to produce unequal cash inflows, Table 3 in the appendix on future value and present value tables is used to determine the present value of each cash inflow from each year of the machine's life. The net present value of Model M is determined as follows:

STUDY NOTE: Because it is based on cash flow, the net present value method is widely used not only in business but also by individuals.

Model M

Year	Net Cash Inflows	16% Factor	Present Value
1	$6,000	.862	$ 5,172.00
2	5,500	.743	4,086.50
3	5,000	.641	3,205.00
4	4,500	.552	2,484.00
5	4,000	.476	1,904.00
Residual value	2,000	.476	952.00
Total present value of cash inflows			$17,803.50
Less purchase price of Model M			17,500.00
Net present value			$ 303.50

BUSINESS WORLD EXAMPLE: State lotteries use the net present value method to compute the lump sum amount of the grand prize.

All the factors for this analysis can be found in the column for 16 percent in Table 3. The factors discount the individual cash flows, including the expected residual value, to the present. The amount of the investment in Model M is deducted from the total present value of the cash inflows to arrive at the net present value of $303.50. Since the entire investment of $17,500 in Model M is a cash outflow at the beginning, that is, time zero, no discounting of the $17,500 purchase price is necessary. Because the net present value is positive, the proposed investment in Model M will achieve at least the minimum rate of return.

Because Model N is expected to produce equal cash receipts in each year of its useful life, Table 4 in the appendix on future value and present value tables is used to determine the combined present value of those future cash inflows. However, Table 3 is used to determine the present value of the machine's residual value because it represents a single payment, not an annuity. The net present value of Model N is calculated as follows:

Model N

Year	Net Cash Inflows	16% Factor	Present Value
1–5	$6,000	3.274	$19,644.00
Residual value	2,000	.476	952.00
Total present value of cash inflows			$20,596.00
Less purchase price of Model N			21,000.00
Net present value			($ 404.00)

Table 4 is used to determine the factor of 3.274, which is found in the column for 16 percent and the row for five periods. Because the residual value is a single inflow in the fifth year, the factor of .476 must be taken from Table 3 (the column for 16 percent and the row for five periods). The result is a net present value of ($404). Because the net present value is negative, the proposed investment in Model N will not achieve the minimum rate of return and should be rejected.

The two analyses show that Model M should be chosen because it has a positive net present value and would exceed the company's minimum rate of return. Model N should be rejected because it does not achieve the minimum rate of return. Model M is the better choice because it is expected to produce cash inflows sooner and will thus produce a proportionately greater present value.

FOCUS ON BUSINESS PRACTICE

Why Are Luxury-Car Makers Interested in Used Cars?

Subsidized loan programs and other dealer incentives are being offered to prop up the prices of used luxury cars since the new-car market is driven by the used-car market. New-car makers know that if used luxury-car prices fall, it will undercut the demand for new cars.[5] So by supporting a higher capital investment cost of a used car, the demand for new cars will remain strong.

 Check out ACE for a Review Quiz at http://accounting.college.hmco.com/students.

OTHER METHODS OF CAPITAL INVESTMENT ANALYSIS

LO6 Analyze capital investment proposals using the payback period method and the accounting rate-of-return method.

RELATED TEXT ASSIGNMENTS
Q: 16, 17, 18, 19, 20
SE: 8, 9, 10
E: 11, 12, 13, 14, 15
P: 4, 5, 8
MRA: 2

The net present value method is the best method for capital investment analysis. However, two other commonly used methods provide rough guides to evaluating capital investment proposals. These methods are the payback period method and the accounting rate-of-return method.

THE PAYBACK PERIOD METHOD

Because cash is an essential measure of a business's health, many managers estimate the cash flow that the investment will generate. Their goal is to determine the minimum time it will take to recover the initial investment. If two investment alternatives are being studied, management should choose the investment that pays back its initial cost in the shorter time. That period of time is known as the payback period, and the method of evaluation is called the **payback period method**. Although the payback period method is simple to use, its use has declined because it does not consider the time value of money. The payback period is computed as follows:

KEY POINT: The payback period method measures the estimated length of time necessary to recover in cash the cost of an investment.

$$\text{Payback Period} = \frac{\text{Cost of Investment}}{\text{Annual Net Cash Inflows}}$$

To apply the payback period method assume the Gordon Company is interested in purchasing a new bottling machine that costs $51,000 and has a residual value of $3,000. To evaluate the proposed capital investment of the Gordon Company, begin by determining the net cash inflows. First find and eliminate the effects of all noncash revenue and expense items included in the analysis of net income. Assume that estimates for the proposal include revenue increases of $17,900 a year and operating cost increases of $11,696 a year (including depreciation and taxes). In this case, the only noncash expense or revenue is machine depreciation. To calculate this amount, you must know the asset's life and the depreciation method. Suppose the Gordon Company uses the straight-line method of depreciation, and the new bottling machine will have a ten-year service life. The annual depreciation is computed using this information and the facts given earlier, as follows:

$$\text{Annual Depreciation} = \frac{\text{Cost} - \text{Residual Value}}{10 \text{ (years)}}$$

$$= \frac{\$51,000 - \$3,000}{10} = \$4,800 \text{ per year}$$

STUDY NOTE: In computing the payback period, depreciation from cash expenses is omitted because depreciation is a noncash expense.

After removing the noncash annual depreciation amount from the operating costs, the payback period is computed as follows:

$$\text{Payback Period} = \frac{\text{Cost of Machine}}{\text{Cash Revenue} - \text{Cash Expenses}}$$

$$= \frac{\$51,000}{\$17,900 - (\$11,696 - \$4,800)}$$

$$= \frac{\$51,000}{\$11,004} = 4.6 \text{ years}$$

If the company's desired payback period is five years or less, this proposal would be approved.

If a proposed capital investment has unequal annual net cash inflows, the payback period is determined by subtracting each annual amount (in chronological order) from the cost of the capital facility. When a zero balance is reached, the payback period has been determined. This will often occur in the middle of a year. The portion of the final year is computed by dividing the amount needed to reach zero (the unrecovered portion of the investment) by the entire year's estimated cash inflow. The Review Problem in this chapter illustrates that process.

The payback period method is widely used because it is easy to compute and understand. It is especially useful in areas in which technology changes rapidly, such as in Internet companies, and when risk is high, such as when investing in emerging countries. However, the disadvantages of this approach far outweigh its advantages. First, the payback period method does not measure profitability. Second, it ignores differences in the present values of cash flows from different periods; thus, it does not adjust cash flows for the time value of money. Finally, the payback period method emphasizes the time it takes to recover the investment rather than the long-term return on the investment. It ignores all future cash flows after the payback period is reached.

THE ACCOUNTING RATE-OF-RETURN METHOD

> **Stop and Think!**
> Why are the payback period and accounting rate-of-return methods rough estimates?
> *These methods do not consider the time value of money.* ■

The **accounting rate-of-return method** is an imprecise but easy way to measure the estimated performance of a capital investment since it uses financial statement information. This method does not use an investment's cash flows but considers the financial reporting effects of the investment instead. The accounting rate-of-return method measures expected performance using two variables: (1) estimated annual net income from the project and (2) average investment cost. The basic equation is

$$\text{Accounting Rate of Return} = \frac{\text{Project's Average Annual Net Income}}{\text{Average Investment Cost}}$$

To compute average annual net income, use the cost and revenue data prepared for evaluating the project. Average investment in a proposed capital facility is calculated as follows:

$$\text{Average Investment Cost} = \left(\frac{\text{Total Investment} - \text{Residual Value}}{2}\right) + \text{Residual Value}$$

To see how this equation is used in evaluating a proposed capital investment, assume the same facts as before for the Gordon Company in its interest in purchasing a new bottling machine. Also assume the company's management will consider only projects that promise to yield more than a 16 percent return. To determine if the company should invest in the machine, compute the accounting rate of return as follows:

$$\text{Accounting Rate of Return} = \frac{\$17{,}900 - \$11{,}696}{\left(\frac{\$51{,}000 - \$3{,}000}{2}\right) + \$3{,}000}$$

$$= \frac{\$6{,}204}{\$27{,}000}$$

$$= 23\%$$

> **TERMINOLOGY NOTE:**
> Payback period is expressed in time, net present value is expressed in money, and accounting rate of return is expressed as a percentage.

The projected rate of return is higher than the 16 percent minimum, so management should think seriously about making the investment.

> **KEY POINT:** The accounting rate-of-return method is appealing because it is easy to understand. It has flaws, however, such as the failure to consider the time value of money.

The accounting rate-of-return method has been widely used because it is easy to understand and apply. It does have several disadvantages, however. First, because net income is averaged over the life of the investment, it is not a reliable figure. Actual net income may vary considerably from the estimates. Second, the method is unreliable if estimated annual net incomes differ from year to year. Third, cash flows are ignored. Fourth, the time value of money is not considered in the analysis. Thus, future and present dollars are treated as equal.

✓ Check out ACE for a Review Quiz at http://accounting.college.hmco.com/students.

Chapter Review

REVIEW OF LEARNING OBJECTIVES

LO1 Define *capital investment analysis* and describe its relation to the management cycle.

Capital investment decisions focus on when and how much to spend on capital facilities and other long-term projects. Capital investment analysis, often referred to as capital budgeting, consists of identifying the need for a capital investment, analyzing courses of action to meet that need, preparing reports for management, choosing the best alternative, and dividing funds among competing resource needs.

Capital investment analysis spans all stages of the management cycle, although most of the analysis occurs during the planning stage. The screening, evaluation, funding, and decision making that take place before a capital investment decision is made are all part of the planning stage. Implementation of the decisions takes place during the executing stage of the management cycle. Postcompletion audits are conducted as part of the reviewing stage. Reports on the results of capital investment decisions are prepared and distributed within the organization during the reporting stage. Based on such reports, managers may decide to modify or curtail projects that are failing to meet expectations or to go forward with new projects.

LO2 State the purpose of the minimum rate of return and identify the methods used to arrive at that rate.

The minimum rate of return, or hurdle rate, is used as a screening mechanism to eliminate from further consideration capital investment requests with anticipated inadequate returns. It saves executives' time by quickly identifying substandard requests. The most commonly used measures for determining minimum rates of return are (1) cost of capital, (2) corporate return on investment, (3) industry average return on investment, and (4) bank interest rates. The weighted-average cost of capital and the average return on investment are the most widely used measures.

LO3 Identify the types of projected costs and revenues used to evaluate alternatives for capital investment.

The accounting rate-of-return method requires measures of net income. Other methods of evaluating capital investments evaluate net cash inflows or cost savings. The analysis process must take into consideration whether each period's cash flows will be equal or unequal. Unless the after-income-tax effects on cash flows are being considered, carrying values and depreciation expense of assets awaiting replacement are irrelevant. Net proceeds from the sale of an old asset and estimated residual value of a new facility represent future cash flows and must be part of the estimated benefit of a project. Depreciation expense on replacement equipment is relevant to evaluations based on after-tax cash flows.

LO4 Apply the concept of the time value of money.

Cash flows of equal dollar amounts at different times have different values because of the effect of compound interest. This phenomenon is known as the time value of money. Of the evaluation methods discussed in this chapter, only the net present value method takes into account the time value of money.

LO5 Analyze capital investment proposals using the net present value method.

The net present value method incorporates the time value of money into the analysis of a proposed capital investment. A minimum required rate of return, usually the average cost of capital, is used to discount an investment's expected future cash flows to their present values. The present values are added together, and the amount of the initial investment is subtracted from their total. If the resulting amount, called the net present value, is positive, the rate of return on the investment will exceed the required rate of return, and the investment should be accepted. If the net present value is negative, the return on the investment will be less than the minimum rate of return, and the investment should be rejected.

LO6 Analyze capital investment proposals using the payback period method and the accounting rate-of-return method.

The payback period method of evaluating a capital investment focuses on the minimum length of time needed to get the amount of the initial investment back in cash. With the accounting rate-of-return method, managers evaluate two or more capital investment proposals and then select the alternative that yields the highest ratio of average annual net income to average cost of investment. Both methods are easy to use, but they are very rough measures that do not consider the time value of money. As a result, the net present value method is preferred.

Review of Concepts and Terminology

The following concepts and terms were introduced in this chapter:

LO6 **Accounting rate-of-return method:** A method of evaluating capital investments designed to measure the estimated performance of a potential capital project. It is calculated by dividing the project's average annual net income by the average cost of the investment.

LO1 **Capital investment analysis:** The process of making decisions about capital investments. It includes identifying the need for a capital investment, analyzing courses of action to meet that need, preparing reports for managers, choosing the best alternative, and dividing funds among competing needs. Also called *capital budgeting*.

LO1 **Capital investment decisions:** Management decisions about when and how much to spend on capital facilities and other long-term projects.

LO3 **Carrying value:** The undepreciated portion of the original cost of a fixed asset.

LO4 **Compound interest:** The interest cost for two or more periods when the amount on which interest is computed changes in each period to include all interest paid in previous periods.

LO2 **Cost of capital:** The weighted-average rate of return a company must pay to its long-term creditors and shareholders for the use of their funds.

LO3 **Cost savings:** Benefits, such as reduced costs, from a proposed capital investment.

LO4 **Future value:** The amount an investment will be worth at a future date if invested at compound interest.

LO4 **Interest:** The cost associated with the use of money for a specific period of time.

LO3 **Net cash inflows:** The balance of increases in projected cash receipts over increases in projected cash payments resulting from a proposed capital investment.

LO5 **Net present value method:** A method of evaluating capital investments in which all future cash flows for each proposed project are discounted to their present values and the amount of the initial investment is subtracted from their sum. The projects with the highest positive net present value—the amount that exceeds the initial investment—are selected for implementation.

LO4 **Ordinary annuity:** A series of equal payments or receipts that will begin one time period from the current date.

LO6 **Payback period method:** A method of evaluating capital investments that bases the decision to invest in a capital project on the minimum length of time it will take to get back the amount of the initial investment in cash.

LO4 **Present value:** The amount that must be invested today at a given rate of compound interest to produce a given future value.

LO4 **Simple interest:** The interest cost for one or more periods when the amount on which the interest is computed stays the same from period to period.

LO4 **Time value of money:** The concept that cash flows of equal amounts separated by an interval of time have different present values due to the effect of compound interest.

Review Problem

Capital Investment Analysis

LO3
LO4
LO5
LO6

The Rolla Construction Company specializes in developing large shopping centers. The company is considering the purchase of a new earth-moving machine and has gathered the following information:

Purchase price	$600,000			
Residual value	$100,000			
Desired payback period	3 years			
Minimum rate of return	15%			

The cash flow estimates are as follows:

Year	Cash Inflows	Cash Outflows	Net Cash Inflows	Projected Net Income
1	$ 500,000	$260,000	$240,000	$115,000
2	450,000	240,000	210,000	85,000
3	400,000	220,000	180,000	55,000
4	350,000	200,000	150,000	25,000
Totals	$1,700,000	$920,000	$780,000	$280,000

REQUIRED
1. Analyze the Rolla Construction Company's investment in the new earth-moving machine. In your analysis, use (a) the net present value method, (b) the accounting rate-of-return method, and (c) the payback period method.
2. Summarize your findings from 1, and recommend a course of action.

Answer to Review Problem

1a. Net present value method (factors are from Table 3 in the appendix on future value and present value tables):

Year	Net Cash Inflows	Present-Value Factor	Present Value
1	$240,000	.870	$208,800
2	210,000	.756	158,760
3	180,000	.658	118,440
4	150,000	.572	85,800
4	100,000 (residual value)	.572	57,200
Total present value			$629,000
Less cost of original investment			600,000
Net present value			$ 29,000

1b. Accounting rate-of-return method

$$\text{Accounting Rate of Return} = \frac{\text{Average Annual Net Income}}{\text{Average Investment Cost}}$$

$$= \frac{\$280,000 \div 4}{\left(\frac{\$600,000 - \$100,000}{2}\right) + \$100,000}$$

$$= \frac{\$70,000}{\$350,000} = 20\%$$

1c. Payback period method

Total cash investment		$600,000
Less cash-flow recovery		
Year 1	$240,000	
Year 2	210,000	
Year 3 (⅚ of $180,000)	150,000	(600,000)
Unrecovered investment		0

Payback period: 2.833 (2⅚) years, or 2 years 10 months

2. Rolla Construction Company: summary of decision analysis

	Decision Measures	
	Desired	Predicted
Net present value	—	$29,000
Accounting rate of return	15%	20%
Payback period	3 years	2.833 years

Based on the calculations in **1**, the proposed investment in the earth-moving machine meets all company criteria for such investments. Given these results, the company should invest in the machine.

Chapter Assignments

BUILDING YOUR KNOWLEDGE FOUNDATION

QUESTIONS

1. What are capital investments? Give examples of some capital investments.
2. Define *capital investment analysis*.
3. Identify the connections between the management cycle and capital investment analysis.
4. Arrange the following steps in the planning phase of the management cycle in their proper order:
   a. Preliminary screening
   b. Capital investment decisions, including determination of dollars available for capital investments
   c. Establishment of the acceptance-rejection standards, including determination of the cost of capital
   d. Identification of capital investment needs
   e. Evaluation of proposals
   f. Formal requests for capital investments
5. What difficulties may be encountered during the postcompletion audit step of the reviewing phase of the management cycle?
6. Identify some measures that companies use to determine a minimum rate of return for capital investment proposals.
7. If several investment projects all exceed the required rate of return, how do managers choose which projects to implement if funds available for capital investment are limited?
8. Distinguish between cost savings and net cash inflows.
9. Why is it important to know whether a capital investment will produce equal cash flows or unequal cash flows?
10. "In capital investment analysis, the carrying value of an asset is irrelevant, whereas current and future residual values are relevant." Is this statement valid? Why or why not?
11. In the evaluation of equipment replacement proposals, why is depreciation of the old equipment ignored?
12. How does the relationship between depreciation and income taxes affect capital investment analysis?
13. Discuss the statement, "To treat all future cash flows alike ignores the time value of money."
14. Which table in the appendix on future value and present value tables is used to determine the present value of a single sum to be received in the future? Which table is used to determine the present value of a series of payments (ordinary annuity) to be received in the future? How is each table used in the net present value method?
15. What is the role of the average cost of capital when the net present value method is used to evaluate capital investment proposals?
16. What formula is used to determine payback period?
17. Is the payback period method accurate? Defend your answer.

18. What formula is used to determine the accounting rate-of-return?
19. How would you characterize the accounting rate-of-return method of capital investment analysis?
20. List the advantages and disadvantages of the accounting rate-of-return method.

SHORT EXERCISES

SE 1.
LO1 Manager's Role in Capital Investment Decisions
Joe Pharr, the supervisor of the Logistics Department, has suggested to Nina Sadam, the plant manager, that a new machine costing $185,000 be purchased to improve material handling operations for the plant's newest product line. How should the plant manager proceed with this request?

SE 2.
LO2 Average Cost of Capital
Orley Industries is considering a $1 million plant expansion. Management needs to know the average cost of capital to use in evaluating this capital investment decision. The company's capital structure consists of $2,000,000 of debt at 8 percent interest and $3,000,000 of stockholders' equity at 12 percent. What is Orley Industries' average cost of capital?

SE 3.
LO2 Ranking Capital Investment Proposals
Zuni Corp. has the following capital investment requests pending from its three divisions: Request 1, $60,000, 11 percent projected return; Request 2, $110,000, 14 percent projected return; Request 3, $130,000, 16 percent projected return; Request 4, $160,000, 13 percent projected return; Request 5, $175,000, 12 percent projected return; and Request 6, $230,000, 15 percent projected return. Zuni's minimum rate of return is 13 percent, and $500,000 is available for capital investment this year. Which requests will be honored, and in what order?

SE 4.
LO3 Capital Investment Analysis and Revenue Measures
Maize Corp. is analyzing a proposal to switch its factory over to a lights-out operation similar to what was discussed in the opening Decision Point. To do so, it must acquire a fully automated machine. The machine will be able to produce an entire product line in a single operation. Projected annual net cash inflows from the machine are $180,000, and projected net income is $120,000. Why is projected net income lower than projected net cash inflows? Identify possible causes for the $60,000 difference.

SE 5.
LO4 Time Value of Money
Heidi Layne recently inherited a trust fund from a distant relative. On January 2, the bank managing the trust fund notified Layne that she has the option of receiving a lump-sum check for $175,500 or leaving the money in the trust fund and receiving an annual year-end check for $20,000 for each of the next 20 years. Layne likes to earn at least an 8 percent return on her investments. What should she do?

SE 6.
LO5 Residual Value and Present Value
Anna Joiner is developing a capital investment analysis for her supervisor. The proposed capital investment has an estimated residual value of $5,500 at the end of its five-year life. The company uses a 16 percent minimum rate of return. What is the present value of the residual value? Use Table 3 in the appendix on future value and present value tables.

SE 7.
LO5 Capital Investment Decision: Net Present Value Method
Noway Jose Communications, Inc., is considering the purchase of a new piece of computerized data transmission equipment. Estimated annual net cash inflows for the new equipment are $575,000. The equipment costs $2 million, it has a five-year life, and it will have no residual value at the end of the five years. The company has a minimum rate of return of 12 percent. Compute the net present value of the piece of equipment. Should the company purchase it? Use Table 4 in the appendix on future and present value tables.

SE 8.
LO6 Capital Investment Decision: Payback Period Method
Using the information about Noway Jose Communications, Inc., in **SE 7**, compute the payback period for the piece of equipment. Does this method yield a positive or negative response to the proposal to buy the equipment, assuming the company sets a maximum payback period of four years?

SE 9.
LO6 Capital Investment Decision: Payback Period Method
East-West Cable, Inc., is considering the purchase of new data transmission equipment. Estimated annual cash revenues for the new equipment are $1 million, and operating costs (including depreciation of $400,000) are $825,000. The equipment costs $2 million, it has a five-year life, and it will have no residual value at the end of the five years. Compute the payback period for the piece of equipment. Does this method yield a positive or a negative response to the proposal to buy the equipment, assuming the company sets a maximum payback period of four years?

SE 10.
LO6 Capital Investment Decision: Accounting Rate-of-Return Method

Best Cleaners is considering whether to purchase a delivery truck that will cost $29,000, last six years, and have an estimated residual value of $5,000. Average annual net income from the delivery service is estimated to be $4,000. Best Cleaners' owners seek to earn an accounting rate of return of 20 percent. Compute the average investment cost and the accounting rate of return. Should the investment be made?

Exercises

E 1.
LO1 Capital Investment Analysis

Genette Henderson was just promoted to supervisor of building maintenance for the Ford Valley Theater complex. The complex consists of seventeen buildings. Allpoints Entertainment, Inc., Henderson's employer, uses a companywide system for evaluating capital investment requests from its 22 supervisors. Henderson has approached you, the corporate controller, for advice on preparing her first proposal. She would also like to become familiar with the entire decision-making process.

1. What advice would you give Henderson before she prepares her first capital investment proposal?
2. Explain the role of capital investment analysis in the management cycle, including the six key steps taken during the planning phase.

E 2.
LO2 Minimum Rate of Return

The controller of Olaf Corporation wants to establish a minimum rate of return and would like to use a weighted-average cost of capital. Current data about the corporation's financing structure are as follows: debt financing, 40 percent; preferred stock, 30 percent; common stock, 20 percent; and retained earnings, 10 percent. The cost of debt is 9½ percent. The dividend rate on the preferred stock issue is 7½ percent. The cost of common stock and retained earnings is 12 percent.

Compute the average cost of capital.

E 3.
LO2 Ranking Capital Investment Proposals

Managers of the Emerald Bay Furniture Company have gathered all of the capital investment proposals for the year, and they are ready to make their final selections. The following proposals and related rate-of-return amounts were received during the period:

Project	Amount of Investment	Rate of Return (Percentage)
AB	$ 450,000	19
CD	500,000	28
EF	654,000	12
GH	800,000	32
IJ	320,000	23
KL	240,000	18
MN	180,000	16
OP	400,000	26
QR	560,000	14
ST	1,200,000	22
UV	1,600,000	20

Assume the company's minimum rate of return is 15 percent, and $5,000,000 is available for capital investments during the year.

1. List the acceptable capital investment proposals in order of profitability.
2. Which proposals should be selected for this year?

E 4.
LO3 Income Taxes and Net Cash Flow

San Falesco Company has a tax rate of 25 percent on taxable income. It is considering a capital project that will make the following annual contribution to operating income:

Cash revenues	$ 500,000
Cash expenses	(300,000)
Depreciation	(150,000)
Operating income before income taxes	$ 50,000
Income taxes at 25%	(12,500)
Operating income	$ 37,500

1. Determine the net cash inflows for this project in two different ways. Are net cash flows the same under either approach?
2. What is the impact of income taxes on net cash flows?

3. Compute the payback period for each machine.
4. From the information generated in **1**, **2**, and **3**, decide which machine should be purchased. Why?

SKILLS DEVELOPMENT CASES

Conceptual Analysis

LO1 **Factors in Capital Investment Decisions**

SD 1. PPG Industries <www.ppg.com>, founded in 1883, was the first commercially successful plate glass manufacturer in the United States. Today it is a global supplier of coatings, chemicals, and glass. Annually, management approves capital spending for modernization and productivity improvements, expansion of existing businesses, and environmental control projects. Management will receive many proposals for projects to use this money, and it must set an appropriate acceptance-rejection standard. What factors should be considered in setting this standard? If more proposed projects meet the minimum standard than can be funded, what other factors should management consider, and what should management do?

LO2 **Weighted-Average Cost of Capital**

SD 2. DaimlerChrysler <www.daimlerchrysler.com> is a multinational company that must evaluate many proposed capital investments. The company's investment policy is based on a weighted-average cost of capital. What is a weighted-average cost of capital? Briefly describe how DaimlerChrysler would go about calculating it.

Ethical Dilemma

LO5 **Ethics, Capital Investment Decisions, and the New Globally Competitive Business Environment**

SD 3. Marika Jonssen is the controller of Bramer Corporation, a globally competitive producer of standard and custom-designed window units for the housing industry. As part of the corporation's move to become automated, Jonssen was asked to prepare a capital investment analysis for a robot-guided aluminum extruding and stamping machine. This machine would automate the entire window-casing manufacturing line. She has just returned from an international seminar on the subject of qualitative inputs into the capital investment decision process and is eager to incorporate those new ideas into the analysis. In addition to the normal net present value analysis (which produced a significant negative result), Jonssen factored in figures for customer satisfaction, scrap reduction, reduced inventory needs, and reputation for quality. With the additional information included, the analysis produced a positive response to the decision question.

When the chief financial officer finished reviewing Jonssen's work, he threw the papers on the floor and said, "What kind of garbage is this! You know it's impossible to quantify such things as customer satisfaction and reputation for quality. How do you expect me to go to the board of directors and explain your work? I want you to redo the entire analysis and follow only the traditional approach to net present value. Get it back to me in two hours!"

What is Jonssen's dilemma? What ethical courses of action are available to her?

Research Activity

LO1 **Capital Investment Analysis**

SD 4. Computers are essential in today's business world. Every business benefits from computers' capabilities, which include rapid data processing, timely report generation, automated accounting systems, and the use of specialized software packages for such areas as payroll, accounts receivable, accounts payable, and tax return preparation. Make a trip to a local computer retailer. Inquire about the various types of computers available, and identify one that would be useful to a local nursery selling landscape plants and gardening supplies and equipment. Find out the cost of this computer. Make notes of its model name, its special features and capabilities, and its cost. After gathering the data, identify the benefits that the nursery's controller would include in an analysis to justify the purchase of the computer. Describe the effect of each benefit on cash flow and profitability. Be prepared to discuss your findings in class.

Group Activity: Assign teams to carry out the above assignments. Ask each team to present its findings to the rest of the class.

Decision-Making Practice

SD 5. The McCall Syndicate owns four resort hotels in Europe. Because the Paris operation (Hotel 1) has been booming over the past five years, management has decided to build an addition to the hotel. This addition will increase the hotel's capacity by 20 percent. A construction company has bid to build the addition at a cost of $30,000,000. The building will have an increased residual value of $3,000,000.

Da Van Dyke, the controller, has started an analysis of the net present value for the project. She has calculated the annual net cash inflows by subtracting the increase in cash operating expenses from the increase in cash inflows from room rentals. Her partially completed schedule follows.

Year	Net Cash Inflows
1–20 (each year)	$ 3,900,000

Capital investment projects must generate a 12 percent minimum rate of return to qualify for consideration.

Using net present value analysis, evaluate the proposal and make a recommendation to management. Explain how your recommendation would change if management were willing to accept a 10 percent minimum rate of return. Use Tables 3 and 4 in the appendix on future value and present value tables.

MANAGERIAL REPORTING AND ANALYSIS CASES

Interpreting Management Reports

MRA 1. Automated teller machines (ATMs) have become common in the banking industry. San Angelo Federal Bank is planning to replace some old teller machines and has decided to use the York Machine. Nola Chavez, the controller, has prepared the analysis shown below. She has recommended the purchase of the machine based on the positive net present value shown in the analysis.

San Angelo Federal Bank
Capital Investment Analysis
Net Present Value Method
March 2, 20x7

Year	Net Cash Inflows	Present-Value Factors	Present Value
1	$ 85,000	.909	$ 77,265
2	80,000	.826	66,080
3	85,000	.751	63,835
4	90,000	.683	61,470
5	95,000	.621	58,995
5 (residual value)	35,000	.621	21,735
Total present value			$349,380
Initial investment	$385,000		
Less proceeds from the sale of existing teller machines	50,000		
Net capital investment			(335,000)
Net present value			$ 14,380

The York Machine has an estimated useful life of five years and an expected residual value of $35,000. Its purchase price is $385,000. Two existing ATMs, each having a carrying value of $25,000, can be sold to a neighboring bank for a total of $50,000. Annual operating cash inflows are expected to increase in the following manner:

Year 1	$79,900
Year 2	76,600
Year 3	79,900
Year 4	83,200
Year 5	86,500

The bank uses straight-line depreciation. The minimum rate of return is 12 percent.

1. Analyze Ms. Chavez's work. What changes need to be made in her capital investment analysis?
2. What would be your recommendation to bank management about the purchase of the York Machine?

Formulating Management Reports

MRA 2.

LO3 **Evaluating a Capital**
LO4 **Investment Proposal**
LO5
LO6

Quality work and timely output are the distinguishing characteristics of Smile Photo, Inc. Smile Photo is a nationally franchised company with over 50 outlets located in the southern states. Part of the franchise agreement promises a centralized photo developing process with overnight delivery to the outlets.

Because of the tremendous increase in demand for its photo processing, Emma DuBarry, the corporation's president, is considering the purchase of a new, deluxe photo processing machine by the end of this month. DuBarry wants you to formulate a memo showing your evaluation of this purchase. Your memo will be presented at the board of directors' meeting next week.

According to your research, the new machine will cost $320,000. It will function for an estimated five years and should have a $32,000 residual value. All capital investments are expected to produce a 20 percent minimum rate of return, and the investment should be recovered in three years or less. All fixed assets are depreciated using the straight-line method. The forecast increases in operating results for the new machine are as follows:

	Cash Flow Estimates	
Year	Cash Inflows	Cash Outflows
1	$310,000	$210,000
2	325,000	220,000
3	340,000	230,000
4	300,000	210,000
5	260,000	180,000

1. In preparation for writing your memo, answer the following questions:
   a. What kinds of information do you need to prepare this memo?
   b. Why is the information relevant?
   c. Where would you find the information?
   d. When would you want to obtain the information?
2. Analyze the purchase of the machine and decide if the company should purchase it. Use (a) the net present value method, (b) the accounting rate-of-return method, and (c) the payback period method.

International Company

MRA 3.

LO1 **Evaluation of Proposed**
Capital Investments

The board of directors of the Tanashi Corporation met to review a number of proposed capital investments that would improve the quality of company products. One production line manager requested the purchase of new computer-integrated machines to replace the older machines in one of the ten production departments at the Tokyo plant. Although the manager had presented quantitative information to support the purchase of the new machines, the board members asked the following important questions:

1. Why do we want to replace the old machines? Have they deteriorated? Are they obsolete?
2. Will the new machines require less cycle time?
3. Can we reduce inventory levels or save floor space by replacing the old machines?
4. How expensive is the software used with the new machines?
5. Will we be able to find highly skilled employees to maintain the new machines? Or can we find workers who are trainable? What would it cost to train those workers? Would the training disrupt the staff by causing relocations?
6. Would the implementation of the machines be delayed because of the time required to recruit and train new workers?
7. How would the new machines affect the other parts of the manufacturing systems? Would the company lose some of the flexibility in its manufacturing systems if it introduced the new machines?

The board members believe that the qualitative information needed to answer their questions could lead to the rejection of the project, even though it would have been accepted based on the quantitative information.

1. Identify the questions that can be answered with quantitative information. Give an example of the quantitative information that could be used.
2. Identify the questions that can be answered with qualitative information. Explain why this information could negatively influence the capital investment decision even though the quantitative information suggests a positive outcome.

Excel Spreadsheet Analysis

MRA 4.
LO5 Net Present Value of Cash Flows

CPC Corporation is an international plumbing equipment and supply company located in southern California. The manager of the Pipe Division is considering the purchase of a computerized copper pipe machine that costs $120,000. The machine has a six-year life, and its expected residual value after six years of use will be 10 percent of its original cost. Cash revenue generated by the new machine is projected to be $50,000 in year 1 and will increase by $10,000 each year for the next five years. Variable cash operating costs will be materials and parts, 25 percent of revenue; machine labor, 5 percent of revenue; and manufacturing overhead, 15 percent of revenue. First-year sales and marketing cash outflows are expected to be $10,500 and will decrease by 10 percent each year over the life of the new machine. Anticipated cash administrative expenses will be $2,500 per year. The company uses a 15 percent minimum rate of return for all capital investment analyses.

1. Prepare an Excel spreadsheet to compute the net present value of the anticipated cash flows for the life of the proposed new machine. Use the following format:

Future Time Period	Projected Cash Revenue	Projected Cash Outflows					Projected Net Cash Inflows	15% Factor	Present Value
		Materials and Parts	Machine Labor	Manufacturing Overhead	Sales and Marketing	Administrative Expenses			

Should the company invest in the new machine?

2. After careful analysis, the controller has determined that the variable rate for materials and parts can be reduced to 22 percent of revenue. Will this reduction in cash outflow change the decision about investing in the new machine? Explain your answer.
3. The marketing manager has determined that the initial estimate of sales and marketing cash expenses was too high and has reduced that estimate by $1,000. The 10 percent annual reductions are still expected to occur. Together with the change in **2**, will this reduction affect the initial investment decision? Explain your answer.

Internet Case

MRA 5.
LO1 Comparison of Capital
LO2 Investment Disclosures by Two Large Companies

Companies vary in the amount of information they disclose about their criteria for selecting capital investments. Access the web sites for two companies—for example, Coca Cola <www.coca-cola.com> and International Paper <www.internationalpaper.com>. Find management's discussion and analysis (also called the financial review), which precedes the presentation of the financial statements. In that section, find the discussion of capital investments. Which company provides the more in-depth discussion? Does either disclose its criteria for making capital investment decisions? Also, look at the investing activities listed in the statement of cash flows for each company. What is the extent of capital expenditures for each company? Compare each company's capital investments with the amount of total assets on the balance sheet. Which company is more of a growth company? Explain your answer.

27

Chapter 27 describes financial and nonfinancial measures of quality and how they are used to evaluate operating performance.

Quality Management and Measurement

Learning Objectives

LO1 Describe a management information system and explain how it enhances the management cycle.

LO2 Define *total quality management (TQM)* and identify financial and nonfinancial measures of quality.

LO3 Use measures of quality to evaluate operating performance.

LO4 Discuss the evolving concept of quality.

LO5 Recognize the awards and organizations that promote quality.

DECISION POINT

A MANAGER'S FOCUS

Amazon.com <www.amazon.com> Through its innovative approach to selling books and other merchandise online, Amazon.com has changed the rules of successful book selling. To achieve a competitive advantage, Amazon's managers needed an information system that produced more than just financial data. Amazon.com managers demanded an extensive information infrastructure that would capture all kinds of information and produce huge, secure databases. Those databases contain over 1 trillion bytes of information that Amazon.com can privately mine and access in multiple applications. For example, Amazon has integrated its supply-chain software with its data mining and warehousing applications to ensure timely and efficient deliveries to its warehouses and its customers. In addition, Amazon's managers use their information system's highly evolved infrastructure to measure and meet the changing expectations of their diverse customer base. The quality of each customer's experience with Amazon.com is enhanced because the information system creates a personal profile based on the customer's previous visits and purchases. Return customers who sign on are greeted by name as they view their personalized Amazon.com web page.

So what is next for the managers of Amazon.com? Doing business over the Internet adds a rich dimension to quality. Customers expect innovative new features as well as excellent product reliability and customer service. To meet such high-quality expectations, Amazon's managers will need detailed, real-time

How has Amazon.com used an ERP system to merge its operating, financial, and management systems?

information, both financial and nonfinancial, about every aspect of their company's operation and the highly competitive environment of ecommerce. For such information, they must depend on their company's management information system. Amazon.com can continue to challenge and experiment with the ever-evolving ecommerce business model only if its management information system remains on the cutting edge of database technology and produces pertinent information of the highest quality.[1]

THE ROLE OF MANAGEMENT INFORMATION SYSTEMS IN QUALITY MANAGEMENT

LO1 Describe a management information system and explain how it enhances the management cycle.

RELATED TEXT ASSIGNMENTS
Q: 1, 2
SE: 1, 2
E: 1
SD: 3

◆ **STOP AND THINK!**

Why is a management information system so important to managers?

A management information system provides ready access to multiple sources of financial and nonfinancial information about a business. ■

Many traditional management information systems contain only financial data and do not produce the sort of information necessary for today's competitive business environment. To compete successfully, managers need information that enables them to determine accurate product, service, and customer costs; improve processes; and provide timely feedback to all their stakeholders about their organization. Such information can be produced only by a management information system that captures both financial and nonfinancial information. This kind of **management information system (MIS)** is a reporting system that identifies, monitors, and maintains continuous, detailed analyses of a company's activities and provides managers with timely measures of operating results. It is designed to support management philosophies such as just-in-time (JIT) operations, activity-based costing (ABC) and activity-based management (ABM), and total quality management (TQM).

The primary focus of an MIS is on the management of activities, not costs. By focusing on activities, an MIS provides managers with improved knowledge of the processes for which they are responsible. Activity-related information needed to speed responsiveness to customers and reduce processing time is readily available. More accurate product and service costs lead to improved pricing decisions. Nonvalue-adding activities are highlighted, and managers can work to reduce or eliminate them. In addition to providing information about product profitability, an MIS can analyze the profitability of individual customers and look at all aspects of serving customers. Overall, the MIS identifies resource usage and cost for each activity and fosters managerial decisions that lead to continuous improvement throughout the organization.

ENTERPRISE RESOURCE PLANNING SYSTEMS

An MIS may be designed as a customized, informally linked series of systems for specific purposes, such as financial reporting, product costing, and business process measurement, or as a fully integrated database system known as an **enterprise resource planning (ERP) system.** An ERP system combines the management of all major business activities, such as purchasing, manufacturing, marketing, sales, logistics, and order fulfillment, with support activities, such as accounting and human resources, to form one easy-to-access, centralized data warehouse. The Decision Point at the beginning of this chapter presents an example of an ERP system that has merged Amazon.com's operating, financial, and management systems. Because of its ability to access a variety of data types from multiple sources both inside and outside the company, Amazon has developed a competitive advantage in achieving

TERMINOLOGY NOTE:
The term *enterprise resource management (ERM)* can be used in place of *ERP*.

www.amazon.com

FOCUS ON BUSINESS TECHNOLOGY

Use Prepackaged Software or Build Your Own?

Three well-known suppliers of enterprise resource planning systems are SAP <www.sap.com>, Baan <www.baan.com>, and Oracle <www.oracle.com>. Such prepackaged software systems can improve the consistency of an organization's data and standardize its business processes. However, to use these packages, a company may have to change its business processes and data collection to fit the way the software works, and this may hinder the organization's ability to adapt to changing business conditions and to innovate. Companies such as Dell Computer <www.dell.com>, Holman Cement, and Allied Waste <www.alliedwaste.com>, whose business models do not fit the standard packages, are keeping their competitive edge by building their own custom systems.[2]

FIGURE 1
The Management Cycle and a Management Information System

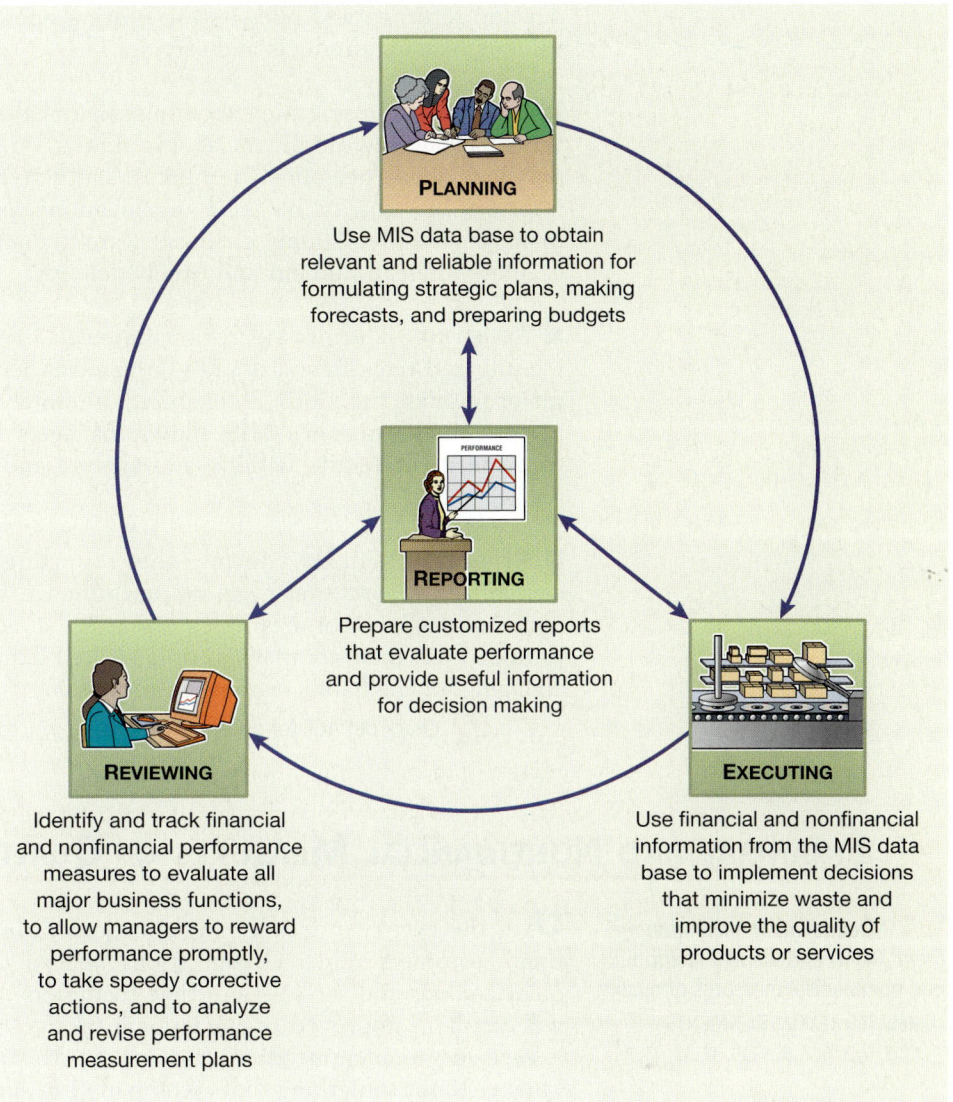

financial targets and quality results. Using improved knowledge of the activities and processes for which they are responsible, Amazon's managers have pinpointed resource usage and fostered managerial decisions that have led to continuous improvement throughout the organization.

USING MIS IN THE MANAGEMENT CYCLE

Like the managers at Amazon, today's business managers use their management information systems' detailed, real-time financial and nonfinancial information about customers, inventory, resources, and the supply chain to manage quality at every stage of the management cycle. Without the flexibility and power of database management information systems like ERP, today's managers would be at a disadvantage in a rapidly changing and highly competitive business environment. Figure 1 and the following sections illustrate how a management information system is used throughout the management cycle.

■ **PLANNING** During the planning stage, managers use the MIS database to obtain relevant and reliable information for formulating strategic plans, making forecasts, and preparing budgets. For example, managers at Amazon.com use their MIS to develop forecasts and budgets for existing operations and to create plans for new value-enhancing products and services.

■ **EXECUTING** During the executing stage of the management cycle, managers use the financial and nonfinancial information in the MIS database to implement decisions about personnel, resources, and activities that will minimize waste and improve the quality of their organization's products or services. At Amazon, managers use their supply-chain software to manage operations in ways that ensure accurate order fulfillment and timely delivery.

■ **REVIEWING** During the reviewing stage of the management cycle, managers identify and track financial and nonfinancial performance measures to evaluate all major business functions. By enabling the timely comparison of actual to expected performance, Amazon's MIS allows managers to reward performance promptly, take speedy corrective actions, and analyze and revise performance measurement plans.

■ **REPORTING** Finally, during the reporting stage, managers can generate customized reports that evaluate performance and provide useful information for decision making. For example, managers at Amazon can consolidate customer profiles from their company's sophisticated database to prepare reports about the changing buying habits of their customers.

✓ Check out ACE for a Review Quiz at http://accounting.college.hmco.com/students.

FINANCIAL AND NONFINANCIAL MEASURES OF QUALITY

LO2 Define *total quality management (TQM)* and identify financial and nonfinancial measures of quality.

RELATED TEXT ASSIGNMENTS
Q: 3, 4, 5, 6, 7, 8, 9, 10, 11, 12, 13, 14, 15, 16
SE: 3, 4, 5, 6, 7
E: 2, 3, 4, 5, 6, 7, 8, 9, 10, 11, 12
P: 1, 2, 3, 4, 5, 6, 7
SD: 2, 4, 5
MRA: 1, 2, 4

Over the past two decades, organizations have defined quality in terms of what their customers value. Organizations believe that customers want the highest-quality goods and services and that customers' willingness to pay for high quality will result in improved organizational profits. As a result, organizations strive to exceed customer expectations and improve the quality of their products or services. Quality is not something that a company can simply add at some point in the production process or assume will happen automatically. Inspections can detect bad products, but they do not ensure quality. Managers need reliable measures of quality to help them meet the goal of producing high-quality, reasonably priced products or services. They need to create a total quality management environment.

Total quality management (TQM) is an organizational environment in which all business functions work together to build quality into the firm's products or services. The first step toward creating a TQM environment is to identify and manage the financial measures of quality, or the costs of quality. The second step is to analyze operating performance using nonfinancial measures and to require that all business processes and products or services be improved continuously.

FINANCIAL MEASURES OF QUALITY

ETHICAL CONSIDERATION: Poor quality in products like tires, baby cribs, and bunk beds has caused accidents and deaths. Poor quality in audit work of publicly traded companies (e.g., Enron and WorldCom) has resulted in large lawsuits.

To the average person, *quality* means that one product or service is better than another—possibly because of design, durability, or some other attribute. In a business setting, however, **quality** is the result of an operating environment in which a product or service meets or conforms to a customer's specifications the first time it is produced or delivered. The **costs of quality** are the costs specifically associated with the achievement or nonachievement of product or service quality. Total costs of quality include (1) costs of good quality incurred to ensure the successful development of a product or service and (2) costs of poor quality incurred to transform a faulty product or service into one that is acceptable to the customer.

Table 1. Financial Measures of Quality

Costs of Conformance to Customer Standards

Prevention Costs
- Technical support for vendors
- Integrated system development
- Quality improvement projects
- Quality training of employees
- Design review of products and processes
- Quality-certified suppliers
- Quality circles
- Preventive maintenance
- Statistical process control
- Process engineering

Appraisal Costs
- Inspection of materials, processes, and machines
- End-of-process sampling and testing
- Vendor audits and sample testing
- Maintenance of test equipment
- Quality audits of products and processes
- Field testing

Costs of Nonconformance to Customer Standards

Internal Failure Costs
- Scrap and rework
- Reinspection and retesting of rework
- Quality-related downtime
- Scrap disposal losses
- Failure analysis
- Inventory control and scheduling
- Downgrading because of defects

External Failure Costs
- Lost sales
- Restoration of reputation
- Warranty claims and adjustments
- Customer complaint processing
- Returned goods and replacements
- Investigation of defects
- Product recalls
- Product-liability settlements

Measures of Quality

Total costs of quality as a percentage of net sales
Ratio of costs of conformance to total costs of quality
Ratio of costs of nonconformance to total costs of quality
Costs of nonconformance as a percentage of net sales

The costs of quality may make up a significant portion of a product's or service's total cost. Therefore, controlling the costs of quality strongly affects profitability. Today's managers should be able to identify the activities associated with improving quality and should be aware of the cost of resources used to achieve high quality.

The costs of quality have two components: the **costs of conformance**, which are the costs incurred to produce a quality product or service, and the **costs of nonconformance**, which are the costs incurred to correct defects in a product or service. Costs of conformance are made up of prevention costs and appraisal costs. **Prevention costs** are the costs associated with the prevention of defects and failures in products and services. **Appraisal costs** are the costs of activities that measure, evaluate, or audit products, processes, or services to ensure conformance to quality standards and performance requirements.

The costs of nonconformance include internal failure costs and external failure costs. **Internal failure costs** are the costs incurred when defects are discovered before a product or service is delivered to a customer. Costs incurred after the delivery of a defective product or service are called **external failure costs**. Examples of each cost category are shown in Table 1. Note that there is an inverse relationship

> **KEY POINT:** Costs of conformance include the costs of building quality into products and services by doing it right the first time.

> **KEY POINT:** Internal failure costs are costs incurred to correct mistakes found by the company. External failure costs are costs incurred to correct mistakes discovered by customers.

Focus on Business Practice

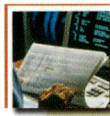

SDWT Managers Have to "Walk the Walk"

Self-directed work teams (SDWTs) are an important element of today's work environment. "A SDWT is a group of employees who have day-to-day responsibilities for managing themselves and a whole work process that delivers a service or a product."[3] Managing such a group of people requires a radical switch from traditional autocratic methods. A successful SDWT manager must play the following roles:

Leader—Holds an inspiring and motivating vision, one to which team members can make personal commitments

Role model—"Walks the walk," demonstrating the desired behaviors

Coach—Teaches and helps team members to realize their potential, ensures accountability, and maintains authority

Business analyzer—Brings the big picture perspective to the team and translates changes in the business environment into opportunities for the team

Advocate—Opens doors for the team, manages senior management support, and challenges the status quo and artificial barriers that limit team performance

Facilitator—Brings together resources, information, and technologies and does whatever it takes to allow the team to be successful

Customer advocate—Keeps close to the customers, understands customers' needs, and brings the customer perspective to the team

---

🔴 **Stop and Think!**
Why are internal failure costs less likely to harm future business than external failure costs?

External failure costs are mistakes discovered by customers, who as a result might be less likely to buy in the future. Internal failure costs are mistakes discovered before customer purchase and may be corrected before the product goes on sale. ∎

ENRICHMENT NOTE:
Nonfinancial measures gauge quality and the value created throughout the supply chain.

between the costs of conformance and the costs of nonconformance: If a company spends money on the costs of conformance, the costs of nonconformance should be reduced. However, if little attention is paid to the costs of conformance, the costs of nonconformance may escalate.

An organization's overall goal is to avoid costs of nonconformance because internal and external failures affect customers' satisfaction as well as the organization's profitability. High initial costs of conformance are justified when they minimize the total costs of quality over the life of a product or service. The cost-based measures of quality listed at the bottom of Table 1 are used and explained in the illustrative problem that follows in a few pages.

Nonfinancial Measures of Quality

By measuring the costs of quality, a company learns how much it has spent in its efforts to improve product or service quality. But critics say that tracking historical data to account for quality performance does little to enhance quality. What managers need is a measurement and evaluation system that signals poor quality early enough to allow problems to be corrected before a defective product or service reaches the customer. Implementing a policy of continuous improvement satisfies this need and is the second stage of total quality management.

Nonfinancial measures of performance, identified and reported to managers in a timely manner, are used to supplement cost-based measures. Although cost control is still an important consideration, a commitment to ongoing improvement encourages activities that enhance quality at every stage, from design to delivery. As explained earlier, those activities, or cost drivers, cause costs. By controlling the nonfinancial performance measures of activities, managers can ultimately maximize the financial return from operations. Some categories of nonfinancial measures of quality are discussed in the following sections.

■ **Product Design** Problems with quality often are the result of poor design. Most automated production operations use **computer-aided design (CAD)**, a computer-based engineering system with a built-in program to detect product design flaws. Such computer programs automatically identify poorly designed parts or manufacturing processes, which means that engineers can correct them before production begins. Managers monitor the CAD reports on design flaws to ensure that products are properly designed and free of defects. Among the measures they consider are number and types of design defects detected, average time between defect detection and correction, and number of unresolved design defects at the time of product introduction.

■ **VENDOR PERFORMANCE** Companies have recently changed how they do business with suppliers of materials. Instead of dealing with dozens of suppliers in the quest for the lowest cost, companies now analyze their vendors to determine which ones are most reliable, furnish high-quality goods, have a record of timely deliveries, and charge competitive prices. Once a company has identified such vendors, they become an integral part of the production team to ensure a continuing supply of high-quality materials. Vendors may even contribute to product design to ensure that the correct materials are being used. Managers monitor each vendor's performance using measures of quality (such as defect-free materials as a percentage of total materials received) and measures of delivery (such as timely deliveries as a percentage of total deliveries). Such measures enable managers to identify and monitor reliable vendors so that high-quality, reasonably priced materials are available when they are needed.

■ **PRODUCTION PERFORMANCE** Management must always be concerned about the wasted time and money that can be traced to defective products, scrapped parts, machine maintenance, and downtime. To minimize such concerns, more and more companies have adopted **computer-integrated manufacturing (CIM) systems**, in which production and its support operations are coordinated by computers. Within a CIM system, computer-aided manufacturing (CAM) may be used to coordinate and control production activities, or a flexible manufacturing system (FMS) may be used to link together automated equipment into a computerized flexible production network.

In CIM systems, most direct labor hours are replaced by machine hours, and very little direct labor cost is incurred. In addition, a significant part of variable product cost is replaced by the cost of expensive machinery, a fixed cost. Today, the largest item on a company's balance sheet is often automated machinery and equipment. Each piece of equipment has a specific capacity, above which continuous operation is threatened. When managers evaluate such machines, their measures have two objectives:

1. To evaluate the performance of each piece of equipment in relation to its capacity
2. To evaluate the performance of maintenance personnel in following a prescribed maintenance program

Measures of production quality, parts scrapped, equipment utilization, machine downtime, and machine maintenance time help managers monitor production performance.

■ **DELIVERY CYCLE TIME** Today's companies are extremely interested in the amount of time they take to respond to customers. To evaluate their responsiveness to customers, companies examine **delivery cycle time**, which is the time period between the acceptance of an order and the final delivery of the product or service. When a customer places an order, it is important for a salesperson to be able to promise an accurate delivery date. A company's goal is to fill its orders 100 percent of the time and to deliver its products 100 percent on time. To meet this goal, a company must establish and maintain consistency and reliability within its manufacturing process and be highly aware of its delivery cycle time.

Companies pay careful attention to delivery cycle time not only because timely delivery is important to customers, but also because a decrease in delivery cycle

KEY POINT: Delivery Cycle Time = Purchase Order Lead Time + Production Cycle Time + Delivery Time.

> **STOP AND THINK!**
> What is the difference between delivery cycle time and delivery time?
>
> *Delivery cycle time spans the time from order acceptance to order delivery and includes purchasing, production, and delivery times, whereas delivery time is the period between completion of a product and its receipt by the customer.*

time can lead to a significant increase in income from operations. Delivery cycle time consists of **purchase order lead time** (the time it takes for materials to be ordered and received so that production can begin), **production cycle time** (the time it takes to make a product), and **delivery time** (the time between the completion of a product and its receipt by the customer).

Management should establish measures that emphasize the importance of minimizing the actual purchase order lead time, production cycle time, and delivery time of each order. Management should also track the average purchase order lead time, production cycle time, and delivery time of all orders. Trends should be highlighted, and reports should be made available daily or weekly. Other measures designed to monitor delivery cycle time include waste time, order backlogs, on-time delivery performance, and percentage of orders filled.

■ **CUSTOMER SATISFACTION** The sale and shipment of a product no longer marks the end of performance measurement. Customer follow-up helps in evaluating total customer satisfaction. Measures used to determine the degree of customer satisfaction include (1) the number and types of customer complaints, (2) the number and causes of warranty claims, and (3) the percentage of shipments returned by customers (or the percentage of shipments accepted by customers). Several companies have developed their own customer satisfaction indexes from these measures so they can compare different product lines over different time periods.

Table 2 lists specific examples of the many nonfinancial measures used to monitor quality. These measures help a company continuously produce higher-quality products, improve production processes, and reduce throughput time and costs.

MEASURING SERVICE QUALITY

The quality of services rendered can be measured and analyzed. Many of the costs of product conformance and nonconformance also apply to the development and delivery of a service. Flaws in service design lead to poor-quality services. Timely service delivery is as important as timely product shipments. Customer satisfaction in a service business can be measured by services accepted or rejected, the number of complaints, and the number of returning customers. Poor service development leads to internal and external failure costs.

Many of the costs-of-quality categories and several of the nonfinancial measures of quality can be applied directly to services and can be adopted by any type of service company. For example, the service departments of Mercedes-Benz dealers ask customers to complete a short three-question form when they pay their bills. Chubb Insurance Company sends a brief questionnaire to customers after every claim. PBS offers phone, fax, and e-mail addresses where viewers can record their comments about programming.

www.mercedes-benz.com
www.chubb.com
www.pbs.org

FOCUS ON INTERNATIONAL BUSINESS

"Don't Judge Me on a Good Speech"

In the 1990s, Nissan, <www.nissan-global.com>, the Japanese automaker, had only one profitable year and was close to bankruptcy. In 1999, Renault <www.renault.com>, the French automaker, bought a controlling interest in Nissan and mapped out a revival plan with specific performance goals. The goals included a return to profitability, a reduction in purchasing cost by 20 percent, an increase in operating margins to 4.5 percent, and a cut in company debt by 50 percent. Nissan met its goals a year ahead of schedule. When asked about Nissan's turnaround, Carlos Ghosn, Nissan's CEO and a former Renault executive, responded: "Don't judge me on a good speech. Judge me on my results. Be very cynical. Be very cold. Look at the profits, the debt, the market share, the appeal of the cars. Then judge me."[4]

disney.go.com

Service businesses also recognize the importance of quality and seek to maximize customers' satisfaction with their services. For example, Disney theme parks minimize customers' impatience as they wait in long lines by having Disney characters interact and play with the crowd. A potential customer problem becomes another opportunity to deliver Disney magic.

The opening Decision Point showed not only how an ecommerce company like Amazon.com can manage the quality of a customer's shopping experience through customer-specific web pages, but also how it can continuously experiment to improve that experience. The need to create fresh features and innovative uses for web sites challenges managers to think of quality in new ways as their organizations adapt to Internet-based business models.

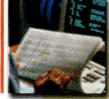

Focus on Business Practice

TQM Does Make a Difference

A five-year study compared a portfolio of award-winning TQM companies with various benchmark portfolios based, for example, on Standard & Poor's 500, industry, and size. In terms of financial measures, the portfolio of TQM companies outperformed the benchmark portfolios. The TQM award winners showed higher growth, improved profitability, and higher efficiency measures. The study also noted that it takes several years before financial measures start to reflect the benefits of TQM. Thus, managers must be patient with TQM if they hope to reap its long-term financial benefits.[7]

In summary, a manager's concept of quality must continuously evolve to fulfill customers' needs and expectations and to meet the demands of the changing business environment. Quality has many dimensions. Not only must a product or service be defect-free and dependable, but it must also embody such intangibles as prestige and good taste. Managers must meet or exceed a variety of expectations about customer service and create innovative new products and services that anticipate the opportunities to be offered by an ever-changing marketplace. The concept of quality means more than having zero defects in a product or service; it means doing everything possible to have zero defections of customers.

 Check out ACE for a Review Quiz at http://accounting.college.hmco.com/students.

RECOGNITION OF QUALITY

LO5 Recognize the awards and organizations that promote quality.

RELATED TEXT ASSIGNMENTS
Q: 20
SE: 10
E: 15
MRA: 5

Many awards and organizations have been established to recognize and promote the importance of quality. Two of the most prestigious awards are the Deming Application Prize and the Malcolm Baldrige Quality Award. In addition, the International Organization for Standardization works to promote quality standards worldwide.

In 1951, the Japanese Union of Scientists and Engineers established the Deming Prize to honor individuals or groups who have contributed to the development and dissemination of total quality control. The organization also awards the **Deming Application Prize** to companies that achieve distinctive results by carrying out total quality control. Consideration for the application prize was originally limited to Japanese companies, but interest in the prize was so great that the rules were revised to allow the participation of companies outside Japan. Recent winners of the Deming Application Prize include Lucent Technologies and Fuji Photo Optical Company.[8]

www.lucent.com
www.fujinon.com

In 1987, the U.S. Congress created the **Malcolm Baldrige Quality Award** to recognize U.S. organizations for their achievements in quality and business performance and to raise awareness of the importance of quality and performance excellence. Organizations are evaluated on the basis of the Baldrige performance excellence criteria, a set of standards divided into seven categories: leadership, strategic planning, customer and market focus, information and analysis, human resource focus, process management, and business results. Thousands of organizations throughout the world accept the Baldrige criteria as the standards for performance excellence and use them for training and self-assessment, whether they plan to compete for the award or not. Winners of the Baldrige Award include

www.ritzcarlton.com
www.3m.com
www.xerox.com

🔴 **STOP AND THINK!**
Why is ISO certification advantageous for a company?
ISO certification facilitates international trade opportunities and confirms a company's quality worldwide. ∎

ENRICHMENT NOTE: ISO standards may vary between countries. For example, the standard size of computer paper in the United States is different from the standard size in European countries.

the Ritz-Carlton Hotel Co., 3M Dental Products Division, and Xerox Business Services.[9] Award winners are showcased and encouraged to share their best practices with others.

The International Organization for Standardization (ISO) is a worldwide federation of national standards bodies from over 130 countries. It promotes standardization with a view to facilitating the international exchange of goods and services. For example, by developing a standard format for credit cards, standard film speed codes, and standard paper sizes, the ISO has saved time and money for both individuals and businesses worldwide. To standardize quality management and quality assurance, the ISO has developed **ISO 9000**, a set of guidelines for businesses covering the design, development, production, final inspection and testing, installation, and servicing of products, processes, and services. Because many organizations do business only with ISO-certified companies, these guidelines have been adopted worldwide. To become ISO certified, an organization must pass a rigorous third-party audit of its manufacturing and service processes. As a result, certified companies have detailed documentation of their operations. The ISO 14000 series provides a similar framework for environmental management.[10]

🔴 Check out ACE for a Review Quiz at http://accounting.college.hmco.com/students.

Chapter Review

REVIEW OF LEARNING OBJECTIVES

LO1 Describe a management information system and explain how it enhances the management cycle.

In a management information system (MIS), the primary focus is on the management of activities, not costs. By focusing on activities, an MIS provides managers with improved knowledge of the processes for which they are responsible. The MIS pinpoints resource usage for each activity and fosters managerial decisions that lead to continuous improvement throughout the organization.

During the planning stage, managers use the MIS database to obtain relevant and reliable information for formulating strategic plans, making forecasts, and preparing budgets. During the executing stage, managers use the financial and nonfinancial information in the MIS database to implement decisions about personnel, resources, and activities that will minimize waste and improve the quality of their organization's products or services. During the reviewing stage, managers identify and track financial and nonfinancial performance measures to evaluate all major business functions. By enabling the timely comparison of actual to expected performance, the MIS allows managers to reward performance promptly, take speedy corrective actions, and analyze and revise performance measurement plans. Finally, during the reporting stage, managers are able to generate customized reports that evaluate performance and provide useful information for decision making.

LO2 Define *total quality management (TQM)* and identify financial and nonfinancial measures of quality.

Total quality management is an organizational environment in which all business functions work together to build quality into a firm's products or services. The costs of quality are measures of costs specifically related to the achievement or nonachievement of product or service quality. The costs of quality have two components. One is the cost of conforming to a customer's product or service standards by preventing defects and failures and by appraising quality and performance. The other is the cost of nonconformance—the costs incurred when defects are discovered before a product is shipped and the costs incurred after a defective product or faulty service is delivered.

The objective of TQM is to reduce or eliminate the costs of nonconformance, the internal and external failure costs that are associated with customer dissatisfaction. To this end, managers can justify high initial costs of conformance if they minimize the total costs of quality over the product's or service's life cycle.

LO3 Use measures of quality to evaluate operating performance.	Nonfinancial measures of quality are related to product design quality, vendor performance, production performance, delivery cycle time, and customer satisfaction. Those measures, together with the costs of quality, help a firm meet its goal of continuously improving product or service quality and the production process.
LO4 Discuss the evolving concept of quality.	A manager's concept of quality must continuously evolve to fulfill customers' needs and expectations and meet the demands of the changing business environment. Quality has many dimensions that extend beyond the mere creation and delivery of a product or service. Managers must satisfy customers today and create innovative products and services for tomorrow. The evolving concept of quality means more than having zero defects in a product or service; it means doing everything possible to have zero defections of customers.
LO5 Recognize the awards and organizations that promote quality.	The importance of quality has been acknowledged worldwide through the granting of numerous awards, certificates, and prizes for quality. Two of the most prestigious awards are the Deming Application Prize and the Malcolm Baldrige Quality Award. In addition, the International Organization for Standardization promotes quality management through ISO 9000.

REVIEW OF CONCEPTS AND TERMINOLOGY

The following concepts and terms were introduced in this chapter:

LO2 **Appraisal costs:** The costs of activities that measure, evaluate, or audit products, processes, or services to ensure conformance to quality standards and performance requirements; a cost of conformance.

LO4 **Benchmarking:** The measurement of the gap between the quality of a company's process and the quality of a parallel process at the best-in-class company.

LO2 **Computer-aided design (CAD):** A computer-based engineering system with a built-in program to detect product design flaws.

LO2 **Computer-integrated manufacturing (CIM) systems:** Systems in which manufacturing and its support operations are coordinated by computer.

LO2 **Costs of conformance:** The costs of producing a quality product or service.

LO2 **Costs of nonconformance:** The costs of correcting defects in a product or service.

LO2 **Costs of quality:** The costs specifically associated with the achievement or nonachievement of product or service quality.

LO2 **Delivery cycle time:** The time period between acceptance of an order and final delivery of the product or service.

LO2 **Delivery time:** The time period between completion of a product and its receipt by the customer.

LO5 **Deming Application Prize:** A prize awarded by the Japanese Union of Scientists and Engineers to companies that achieve distinctive results by carrying out total quality control.

LO1 **Enterprise resource planning system (ERP) system:** An integrated information system that manages all major business functions of an organization through an easy-to-access, centralized data warehouse.

LO2 **External failure costs:** The costs incurred after the delivery of a defective product or service; a cost of nonconformance.

LO2 **Internal failure costs:** The costs incurred when a defect is discovered before a product or service is delivered to a customer: a cost of nonconformance.

LO5 **ISO 9000:** A set of quality management guidelines established by the International Organization for Standardization.

LO4 Kaizen: The continual or ongoing improvement of quality and cost reduction in a business.

LO5 Malcolm Baldrige Quality Award: An award established by the U.S. Congress to recognize U.S. organizations for their achievements in quality and business performance and to raise awareness about the importance of quality and performance excellence.

LO1 Management information system (MIS): A management reporting system that identifies, monitors, and maintains continuous, detailed analyses of a company's activities and provides managers with timely measures of operating results.

LO2 Prevention costs: The costs associated with the prevention of defects and failures in products and services; a cost of conformance.

LO4 Process mapping: A method of diagramming process inputs, outputs, constraints, and flows to help managers identify unnecessary efforts and inefficiencies in a business process.

LO2 Production cycle time: The time it takes for production personnel to make the product available for shipment to the customer.

LO2 Purchase order lead time: The time it takes for materials to be ordered and received so that production can begin.

LO2 Quality: The result of an operating environment in which a product or service meets or conforms to a customer's specifications the first time it is produced or delivered.

LO4 Return on quality (ROQ): The earnings that result when the marginal revenues possible from a higher-quality good or service exceed the marginal costs of providing that higher quality.

LO2 Total quality management (TQM): An organizational environment in which all business functions work together to build quality into the firm's products or services.

REVIEW PROBLEM

Analysis of Nonfinancial Data—Cruz Products, Inc.

LO2 LO3 Three months ago, the Cooper Motor Division of Cruz Products, Inc., installed a new manufacturing system in its Small Motors Department. A just-in-time approach is followed for everything from ordering materials and parts to product shipment and delivery. The division's superintendent is very interested in the initial results of the venture. The following data have been collected for your analysis:

	\multicolumn{8}{c}{Weeks}
	1	2	3	4	5	6	7	8
Warranty claims	2	4	1	1	0	5	7	11
Average setup time (hours)	.30	.25	.25	.30	.25	.20	.20	.15
Purchase order lead time (hours)	2.4	2.3	2.2	2.3	2.4	2.4	2.4	2.5
Production cycle time (hours)	2.7	2.6	2.5	2.6	2.6	2.6	2.6	2.7
Average process time (hours)	1.90	1.90	1.85	1.80	1.90	1.95	1.95	1.9
Customer complaints	12	12	10	8	9	7	6	4
Production backlog (units)	9,210	9,350	9,370	9,420	9,410	8,730	8,310	7,950
Machine downtime (hours)	86.5	83.1	76.5	80.1	90.4	100.6	120.2	124.9
Equipment utilization rate (%)	98.2	98.6	98.9	98.5	98.1	97.3	96.6	95.7
On-time deliveries (%)	93.2	94.1	96.5	95.4	92.1	90.5	88.4	89.3
Machine maintenance time (hours)	34.6	32.2	28.5	22.1	18.5	12.6	19.7	26.4

REQUIRED ▶
1. Analyze the nonfinancial measures of quality of the Cooper Motor Division for the eight-week period. Focus on the following areas of performance:
   a. Production performance
   b. Delivery cycle time
   c. Customer satisfaction
2. Summarize your findings in a report to the division's superintendent.

Answer to Review Problem

The data given were reorganized in the following manner, and one additional piece of information, average waste time, was calculated from the provided information.

1. Analysis of nonfinancial measures of performance:

	Week 1	Week 2	Week 3	Week 4	Week 5	Week 6	Week 7	Week 8	Weekly Average
a. Production Performance									
Machine downtime (hours)	86.5	83.1	76.5	80.1	90.4	100.6	120.2	124.9	95.3
Equipment utilization rate (%)	98.2	98.6	98.9	98.5	98.1	97.3	96.6	95.7	97.7
Machine maintenance time (hours)	34.6	32.2	28.5	22.1	18.5	12.6	19.7	26.4	24.3
b. Delivery Cycle Time									
On-time deliveries (%)	93.2	94.1	96.5	95.4	92.1	90.5	88.4	89.3	92.4
Average setup time (hours)	.30	.25	.25	.30	.25	.20	.20	.15	.24
Purchase order lead time (hours)	2.4	2.3	2.2	2.3	2.4	2.4	2.4	2.5	2.4
Production cycle time (hours)	2.7	2.6	2.5	2.6	2.6	2.6	2.6	2.7	2.6
Average process time (hours)	1.90	1.90	1.85	1.80	1.90	1.95	1.95	1.90	1.9
Production backlog (units)	9,210	9,350	9,370	9,420	9,410	8,730	8,310	7,950	8,969
Average waste time (hours)	.50	.45	.40	.50	.45	.45	.45	.65	.48
c. Customer Satisfaction									
Customer complaints	12	12	10	8	9	7	6	4	8.5
Warranty claims	2	4	1	1	0	5	7	11	3.9

2. Memorandum to the division superintendent:

My analysis of the operating data for the Cooper Motor Division for the last eight weeks revealed the following:

Production Performance
Machine downtime is increasing. Also, the equipment utilization rate is down. Machine maintenance time had also decreased, but has increased in the past two weeks. Department managers should be aware of these potential problem areas.

Delivery Cycle Time
We are having trouble maintaining the averages for delivery cycle time established eight weeks ago. On-time deliveries percentages are slipping. Waste time is increasing, which is contrary to our goals. Backlogged orders are decreasing, which is a good sign from a JIT viewpoint but could spell problems in the future. On the positive side, setup time seems to be under control. Emphasis needs to be placed on reducing lead time, cycle time, and process time.

Customer Satisfaction
Customer satisfaction seems to be improving, with the number of complaints decreasing rapidly. However, warranty claims have risen significantly in the past three weeks, which may be a signal of quality problems.

Overall, we can see good signs from the new equipment, but we need to pay special attention to all potential problem areas.

Chapter Assignments

BUILDING YOUR KNOWLEDGE FOUNDATION

QUESTIONS

1. Describe a management information system.
2. How does an enterprise resource planning system (ERP system) differ from other management information systems?
3. What is total quality management?
4. How can managers help a company move toward a TQM environment?
5. How is *quality* defined in business? What are the costs of quality?
6. Identify and describe the categories of costs of quality.
7. What is the relationship between the costs of conformance and the costs of nonconformance?
8. Why is it better to incur internal failure costs than external failure costs?
9. What does a company learn by measuring the costs of quality? Why is such knowledge insufficient? What else does a company need to do to achieve total quality management?
10. How do managers use computer-aided design (CAD) to measure product design quality?
11. What qualities do companies analyze when selecting suppliers of materials for use in manufacturing?
12. Explain why companies are adopting computer-integrated manufacturing (CIM) systems.
13. What nonfinancial performance measures can managers use to analyze production performance?
14. Why do companies pay careful attention to delivery cycle time?
15. What are some measures used to determine customer satisfaction? Do such measures focus on internal or external failure costs?
16. Discuss how the five categories of nonfinancial measures of quality apply to services as well as products.
17. What is return on quality (ROQ)? How does ROQ affect managers' thoughts and decisions about quality?
18. What is the Six Sigma quality standard?
19. What is process mapping, and how is it used to improve quality?
20. Identify two awards for quality, and explain the purpose of each.

SHORT EXERCISES

LO1 Traits of a Management Information System

SE 1. What kinds of information are captured by a management information system? How do managers use such information?

LO1 Continuous Improvement

SE 2. Maxine Lavon is the controller for Prater Industries. She has been asked to develop a plan for installing a management information system in her company. The president has already approved the concept and has given Lavon the go-ahead. What kind of information will Lavon need to provide to help managers at each stage of the management cycle?

LO2 Costs of Quality in a Service Business

SE 3. McGriff-Elam Insurance Agency incurred the following activity costs related to service quality. Identify those that are costs of conformance (CC) and those that are costs of nonconformance (CN):

Policy processing improvements	$76,400
Customer complaints response	34,100
Policy writer training	12,300
Policy error losses	82,700
Policy proofing	39,500

LO2 Measures of Quality

SE 4. Internal reports on quality at the Lakeside Publishing Company generated the following information for the School Division for the first three months of the year:

Total sales	$60,000,000
Costs of quality:	
Prevention	523,000
Appraisal	477,000
Internal failure	1,360,000
External failure	640,000

Compute:

a. Total costs of quality as a percentage of sales
b. Ratio of costs of conformance to total costs of quality
c. Ratio of costs of nonconformance to total costs of quality
d. Costs of nonconformance as a percentage of total sales

LO2 Nonfinancial Measures of Quality

SE 5. For a fast-food restaurant that specializes in deluxe cheeseburgers, identify two nonfinancial measures of good product quality and two nonfinancial measures of poor product quality.

LO2 Vendor Quality

SE 6. Cite some specific measures of vendor quality that Nick Michael could use when he installs a quality-certification program for the vendors that supply his company, Stamp It, Inc., with direct materials.

LO2 Measures of Delivery Cycle
LO3 Time

SE 7. Quality Cosmetics, Inc., has developed a set of nonfinancial measures to evaluate on-time product delivery performance for one of its best-selling cosmetics. The following data have been generated for the past four weeks.

Week	Purchase Order Lead Time	Production Cycle Time	Delivery Time
1	2.4 days	3.5 days	4.0 days
2	2.3 days	3.5 days	3.5 days
3	2.4 days	3.3 days	3.4 days
4	2.5 days	3.2 days	3.3 days

Compute total delivery cycle time for each week. Evaluate the product delivery performance. Is there an area that needs management's attention?

LO4 Return on Quality

SE 8. For many years June Pirolohas used return on quality (ROQ) to evaluate quality. What assumptions about quality did she make?

LO4 Quality and Cycle Time

SE 9. Motorola's <www.motorola.com> Finance Department has adapted the concept of delivery cycle time to include the measurement of cycle times for processing customer credit memos, invoices, and orders. Why would such performance measures contribute to Motorola's quest for Six Sigma quality?

LO5 Quality Award Recipients

SE 10. Review some of the recent recipients of the Malcolm Baldrige Award by consulting the web site at www.quality.nist.gov. What types of organizations are represented?

EXERCISES

LO1 Adapting to Changing Information Needs

E 1. "What's all the fuss about managers' needing to focus on activities instead of costs?" demanded Sam Edwards, the controller of Tyme Flies. "The bottom line is all that matters, and our company's current management information system is just fine for figuring that out. I know that our system is ten years old, but if it isn't broken, why should we fix it?"

How would you respond to Sam Edwards?

LO2 Costs of Conformance in a Service Business

E 2. Home Health Care, LLP incurred the following service-related activity costs for the month. Prepare an analysis of the costs of conformance by identifying the prevention costs and appraisal costs, and compute the percentage of sales represented by prevention costs, appraisal costs, and total costs of conformance.

Total sales	$22,000
Quality training of employees	500
Vendor audits	400
Quality-certified vendors	100
Preventive maintenance	300
Quality sampling of services	200
Field testing of new services	250
Quality circles	50
Quality improvement projects	150
Technical service support	75
Inspection of services rendered	175

LO2 Costs of Nonconformance in a Service Business

E 3. Home Health Care, LLP incurred the following service-related activity costs for the month. Prepare an analysis of the costs of nonconformance by identifying the internal failure costs and external failure costs, and compute the percentage of sales represented by internal failure costs, external failure costs, and total costs of nonconformance.

Total sales	$22,000
Reinspection of rework	50
Investigation of service defects	300
Lawsuits	0
Quality-related downtime	75
Failure analysis	50
Customer complaint processing	500
Retesting of service scheduling	25
Restoration of reputation	0
Lost sales	100
Replacement services	1,000

LO2 Measures of Quality in a Service Business

E 4. Rehab Health Care, LLC, incurred the service-related activity costs for the month that appear below. Prepare an analysis of the costs of quality for Rehab Health Care, LLC. Categorize the costs as (a) costs of conformance, with subsets of prevention costs and appraisal costs, or (b) costs of nonconformance, with subsets of internal failure costs and external failure costs. Compute the percentage of sales represented by prevention costs, appraisal costs, total costs of conformance, internal failure costs, external failure costs, total costs of nonconformance, and total costs of quality. Also compute the ratio of costs of conformance to total costs of quality and the ratio of costs of nonconformance to total costs of quality.

Total sales	$42,000
Customer complaint processing	1,200
Employee training	400
Reinspection and retesting	500
Design review of service procedures	300
Technical support	200
Investigation of service defects	800
Sample testing of vendors	100
Inspection of supplies	150
Quality audits	250
Quality-related downtime	300

LO2 LO3 Costs of Quality

E 5. Hauschlager Corp. produces and supplies automotive manufacturers with the mechanisms used to adjust the seat positions of front seating units. Several new competitors have recently entered the marketplace, and management is concerned that the quality of the company's current products may be surpassed by those of the new competitors. The controller was asked to conduct an analysis of the current efforts to improve product quality. His analysis generated the following costs of quality for January 20x8:

Training of employees	$22,400
Customer service	13,600
Reinspection of rework	28,000
Quality audits	31,300
Design review	27,500

Warranty claims	$67,100
Sample testing of materials	27,400
Returned goods	98,700
Preventive maintenance	26,500
Quality engineering	18,700
Setup for testing new products	42,100
Scrap and rework	76,500
Losses caused by vendor scrap	65,800
Product simulation	28,400

1. Prepare a detailed analysis of the costs of quality.
2. Comment on the company's current efforts to improve product quality.

E 6. **LO2 Measuring Costs of Quality** **LO3**

A corporation has two departments that produce two separate product lines. The company has been implementing total quality management over the past year. Revenue and costs of quality for that year are presented below.

	Dept. C	Dept. D	Totals
Annual Sales	$9,200,000	$11,000,000	$20,200,000
Costs of Quality			
Prevention costs	$ 186,000	$ 124,500	$ 310,500
Appraisal costs	136,000	68,000	204,000
Internal failure costs	94,000	197,500	291,500
External failure costs	44,000	160,000	204,000
Totals	$ 460,000	$ 550,000	$ 1,010,000

Which department is taking a more serious approach to implementing TQM? Base your answer on the following computations:
a. Total costs of quality as a percentage of sales
b. Ratio of costs of conformance to total costs of quality
c. Ratio of costs of nonconformance to total costs of quality
d. Costs of nonconformance as a percentage of sales

E 7. **LO2 Measures of Product Design Quality**

Being first to market with their newest product, the pocket e-book, was the goal of the managers at Read It, Inc. Comment on their measures of product design quality as compared to industry benchmarks:

Measures of Product Design Quality	Read It, Inc.	Industry Benchmark
Number of design defects detected	50	50
Unresolved design defects at time of product introduction	10	5
Average time between defect detection and correction (hours)	4	8
Time to market (time from design idea to market) (days)	60	100

E 8. **LO2 Measures of Vendor Performance**

Hal Justin, the manager of a hotel that caters to traveling businesspeople, is reviewing the nonfinancial measures of quality for the hotel's dry cleaning service. Six months ago, he contracted with a local dry cleaning company to provide the service to hotel guests. The cleaner promised a four-hour turnaround on all dry cleaning orders. Comment on the following measures for the past six months.

	January	February	March	April	May	June
Percentage of complaints	1%	2%	1%	2%	2%	1%
Percentage of on-time deliveries	100%	75%	100%	80%	85%	100%
Number of orders	300	400	400	500	600	600

E 9. **LO2 Measures of Production Performance**

Analyze the following nonfinancial measures of quality for Holiday Express, Inc., a supplier of mistletoe, for a recent four-week period. Focus specifically on measures of production performance.

Measures of Quality	Week 1	Week 2	Week 3	Week 4
Percentage of defective products per million produced	1%	.8%	.6%	.5%
Equipment utilization rate	90%	91%	89%	90%
Machine downtime (hours)	12	10	13	12
Machine maintenance time (hours)	8	8	8	8
Machine setup time (hours)	4	2	5	4

E 10. Compute the missing numbers for a, b, c, and d for the delivery cycle time for Companies M, N, Q, and P.

Company	Purchase Order Lead Time	Production Cycle Time	Delivery Time	Total Delivery Cycle Time
M	a	2	1	4
N	2	4	b	9
Q	10	c	15	30
P	2	7	1	d

E 11. Calculate the missing numbers for a, b, c, and d to analyze the waste time for the following orders. Comment on your findings.

Name of Order	Production Cycle Time	Average Process Time	Average Setup Time	Waste Time
Howe	6	a	1	1
Smith	b	9	4	2
Gomez	9	5	c	3
Patel	8	3	1	d

E 12. "A satisfied customer is the most important goal of this company!" was the opening remark of the corporate president, Alice Nunes, at the monthly executive committee meeting of Santiago Company. The company manufactures tube products for customers in sixteen western states. It has four divisions, each producing a different type of tubing material. Nunes, a proponent of total quality management, was reacting to the latest measures of quality from the four divisions. The data are as follows:

	Brass Division	Plastics Division	Aluminum Division	Copper Division	Company Averages
Vendor on-time delivery	97.20%	91.40%	98.10%	88.20%	93.73%
Production quality rates (defective parts per million)	1,440	2,720	1,370	4,470	2,500
On-time shipments	89.20%	78.40%	91.80%	75.60%	83.75%
Returned orders	1.10%	4.60%	.80%	6.90%	3.35%
Number of customer complaints	24	56	10	62	38
Number of warranty claims	7	12	4	14	9.3*

*Rounded.

Why was Nunes upset? Which division or divisions do not appear to have satisfied customers? What criteria did you use to make your decision?

E 13. Takada Company makes racing bicycles. Its Lightning model is considered the top of the line in the industry. Three months ago, to improve quality and reduce production time, Takada purchased and installed a computer-integrated manufacturing system for the Lightning. Management is interested in cutting time in all phases of the delivery cycle. The controller's office gathered these data for the past four-week period:

	Weeks			
	1	2	3	4
Average process time (hours)	24.6	24.4	23.8	23.2
Average setup time (hours)	1.4	1.3	1.2	1.1
Customer complaints	7	6	8	9
Delivery time (hours)	34.8	35.2	36.4	38.2
On-time deliveries (%)	98.1	97.7	97.2	96.3
Production backlog (units)	8,230	8,340	8,320	8,430
Production cycle time (hours)	28.5	27.9	27.2	26.4
Purchase order lead time (hours)	38.5	36.2	35.5	34.1
Warranty claims	2	3	3	2

Analyze the performance of the Lightning model for the four-week period, focusing specifically on product delivery cycle time and customer satisfaction.

E 14. Ecommerce has changed how goods and services are obtained. How do companies like Amazon.com continue to anticipate customer needs? Consult Amazon.com's web site at www.amazon.com.

LO5 Quality Awards

E 15. How do the Malcolm Baldrige Quality Award and ISO 9000 differ? Consult the web sites at www.quality.nist.gov and www.iso.ch.

PROBLEMS

LO2 Costs of Quality

P 1. Karen Setten, regional manager of Heavenly Pies, is evaluating the performance of four pie kitchens in her region. In accordance with the company's costs of quality standards of performance, the four locations provided these data for the past six months:

	Aspen	Basalt	Frisco	Dillon
Sales	$1,800,000	$1,500,000	$1,400,000	$1,200,000
Prevention costs	$ 32,000	$ 48,000	$ 16,000	$ 20,000
Appraisal costs	42,000	32,000	18,000	25,000
Internal failure costs	24,000	21,000	42,000	30,000
External failure costs	33,000	16,000	45,000	25,000
Total costs of quality	$ 131,000	$ 117,000	$ 121,000	$ 100,000

REQUIRED

1. For each location, compute the percentages of sales represented by prevention costs, appraisal costs, total costs of conformance, internal failure costs, external failure costs, total costs of nonconformance, and total costs of quality. Carry your answers to two decimal places.
2. For each location, calculate the ratio of costs of conformance to costs of quality and the ratio of costs of nonconformance to costs of quality.
3. Interpret the cost of quality data for each location. Rank the locations in terms of quality.

LO2 Costs and Nonfinancial Measures of Quality

P 2. Minturn Enterprises, Inc., operates as three autonomous companies, each with a chief executive officer who oversees its operations. At a recent corporate meeting, the company CEOs agreed to adopt total quality management and to track, record, and analyze their costs and nonfinancial measures of quality. All three companies are operating in highly competitive markets. Sales and quality-related data for September follow:

	Carbondale Company	Wolcott Company	Silverthorne Company
Annual Sales	$11,600,000	$13,300,000	$10,800,000
Costs of Quality			
Vendor audits	$ 69,000	$ 184,800	$ 130,800
Quality audits	58,900	115,550	141,700
Failure analysis	188,500	92,400	16,350
Design review of products	80,500	176,700	218,000
Scrap and rework	207,000	160,800	21,200
Quality-certified suppliers	49,200	105,600	231,600
Preventive maintenance	92,000	158,400	163,500
Warranty adjustments	149,550	105,600	49,050
Product recalls	201,250	198,000	80,050
Quality training of employees	149,500	237,600	272,500
End-of process sampling and testing	34,500	145,200	202,700
Reinspection of rework	126,500	66,000	27,250
Returned goods	212,750	72,600	16,350
Customer complaint processing	109,250	162,450	38,150
Total costs of quality	$ 1,728,400	$ 1,981,700	$ 1,609,200
Nonfinancial Measures of Quality			
Number of warranty claims	61	36	12
Customer complaints	107	52	18
Defective parts per million	4,610	2,190	1,012
Returned orders	9.20%	4.10%	.90%

REQUIRED

1. Prepare an analysis of the costs of quality for the three companies. Categorize the costs as (a) costs of conformance, with subsets of prevention costs and appraisal costs, or (b) costs of nonconformance, with subsets of internal failure costs and external failure costs. Compute the total costs in each category for each company.

2. For each company, compute the percentage of sales represented by prevention costs, appraisal costs, total costs of conformance, internal failure costs, external failure costs, total costs of nonconformance, and total costs of quality.
3. Interpret the cost-of-quality data for each company. Is its product of high or low quality? Why? Is each company headed in the right direction to be competitive?
4. Evaluate the nonfinancial measures of quality in terms of customer satisfaction. Are the results consistent with your analysis in 3? Explain your answer.

LO2 Interpreting Measures of
LO3 Quality

P 3. Watts Corporation supplies electronic circuitry to major appliance manufacturers in all parts of the world. Producing a high-quality product in each of the company's four divisions is the mission of management. Each division is required to record and report its efforts to achieve quality in all of its primary product lines. The following information was submitted to the chief financial officer for the most recent three-month period:

	Glenwood Division		Lakes Division		Springs Division		Gilman Division	
	Amount	% of Revenue	Amount	% of Revenue	Amount	% of Revenue	Amount	% of Revenue
Costs of Quality								
Costs of Conformance								
Prevention costs:								
Quality training of employees	$ 4,400		$ 15,600		$ 23,600		$ 8,900	
Process engineering	3,100		19,700		45,900		9,400	
Preventive maintenance	5,800		14,400		13,800		11,100	
Total prevention costs	$ 13,300	0.95%	$ 49,700	3.11%	$ 83,300	5.55%	$ 29,400	1.73%
Appraisal costs:								
End-of-process sampling and testing	$ 3,500		$ 19,500		$ 21,400		$ 6,900	
Quality audits of products	6,100		11,900		17,600		8,700	
Vendor audits	4,100		10,100		9,800		7,300	
Total appraisal costs	$ 13,700	0.98%	$ 41,500	2.59%	$ 48,800	3.25%	$ 22,900	1.35%
Total costs of conformance	$ 27,000	1.93%	$ 91,200	5.70%	$132,100	8.80%	$ 52,300	3.08%
Costs of Nonconformance								
Internal failure costs:								
Quality-related downtime	$ 26,800		$ 8,300		$ 6,500		$ 22,600	
Scrap and rework	17,500		9,100		7,800		16,200	
Scrap disposal losses	31,200		7,200		3,600		19,900	
Total internal failure costs	$ 75,500	5.39%	$ 24,600	1.54%	$ 17,900	1.19%	$ 58,700	3.45%
External failure costs:								
Warranty claims	$ 22,600		$ 4,400		$ 2,500		$ 17,100	
Customer complaint processing	31,600		8,100		6,400		22,300	
Returned goods	29,900		5,600		3,100		19,800	
Total external failure costs	$ 84,100	6.01%	$ 18,100	1.13%	$ 12,000	0.80%	$ 59,200	3.48%
Total costs of nonconformance	$159,600	11.40%	$ 42,700	2.67%	$ 29,900	1.99%	$117,900	6.93%
Total costs of quality	$186,600	13.33%	$133,900	8.37%	$162,000	10.79%	$170,200	10.01%
Ratios of Nonfinancial Measures:								
Number of sales to number of warranty claims	168 to 1		372 to 1		996 to 1		225 to 1	
Number of products produced to number of products reworked	1,420 to 1		3,257 to 1		6,430 to 1		2,140 to 1	
Change in throughput time (positive amount means time reduction)	−4.615%		2.163%		5.600%		−1.241%	
Total number of deliveries to number of late deliveries	86 to 1		168 to 1		290 to 1		128 to 1	

REQUIRED
1. Rank the divisions in order of their apparent product quality.
2. What three measures were most important in your rankings in 1? Why?

3. Which division is most successful in its bid to improve quality? What measures illustrate its high-quality rating?
4. Consider the two divisions producing the lowest-quality products. What actions would you recommend to the management of each division? Where should their quality dollars be spent?

P 4. Enterprises, Inc., manufactures several lines of small machinery. Before the company installed automated equipment, the total delivery cycle time for its Coin machine models averaged about three weeks. Last year, management decided to purchase a new computer-integrated manufacturing system for the Coin line. The following is a summary of operating data for the past eight weeks for the Coin line:

LO2 Analysis of Nonfinancial Data
LO3

	Weeks							
	1	2	3	4	5	6	7	8
Average process time (hours)	7.20	7.20	7.10	7.40	7.60	7.20	6.80	6.60
Average setup time (hours)	2.20	2.20	2.10	1.90	1.90	1.80	2.0	1.90
Customer complaints	5	6	4	7	6	8	9	9
Delivery time (hours)	36.20	37.40	37.20	36.40	35.90	35.80	34.80	34.20
Equipment utilization rate (%)	98.10	98.20	98.40	98.10	97.80	97.60	97.80	97.80
Machine downtime (hours)	82.30	84.20	85.90	84.30	83.40	82.20	82.80	80.40
Machine maintenance time (hours)	50.40	52.80	49.50	46.40	47.20	45.80	44.80	42.90
On-time deliveries (%)	92.40	92.50	93.20	94.20	94.40	94.10	95.80	94.60
Production backlog (units)	15,230	15,440	15,200	16,100	14,890	13,560	13,980	13,440
Production cycle time (hours)	12.20	12.60	11.90	11.80	12.20	11.60	11.20	10.60
Purchase order lead time (hours)	26.20	26.80	26.50	25.90	25.70	25.30	24.80	24.20
Warranty claims	2	2	3	2	3	4	3	3

REQUIRED 1. Analyze the performance of the Coin machine line for the eight-week period. Focus on performance in the following areas:
a. Production performance
b. Delivery cycle time
c. Customer satisfaction
Carry your answers to two decimal places.
2. Summarize your findings in a report to the company's president, Wilhem Devore.

ALTERNATE PROBLEMS

P 5. Creed Napier, the regional manager of E-Taxes, Inc., is evaluating the performance of four ecommerce tax preparation sites in her region. The following data for the past six months were presented to her by each site in accordance with the company's costs-of-quality standards of performance:

LO2 Costs of Quality

	Small Business Portal	Big Business Portal	Self-Employed Portal	Partnership Portal
Sales	$5,000,000	$10,000,000	$8,000,000	$6,000,000
Prevention costs	$ 62,000	$ 58,000	$ 16,000	$ 20,000
Appraisal costs	32,000	42,000	28,000	15,000
Internal failure costs	54,000	31,000	32,000	40,000
External failure costs	23,000	26,000	55,000	35,000
Total costs of quality	$ 171,000	$ 157,000	$ 131,000	$ 110,000

REQUIRED 1. For each site, compute the percentages of sales represented by prevention costs, appraisal costs, total costs of conformance, internal failure costs, external failure costs, total costs of nonconformance, and total costs of quality.
2. For each site, calculate the ratio of costs of conformance to costs of quality and the ratio of costs of nonconformance to costs of quality.
3. Interpret the cost-of-quality data for each site. Rank the sites in terms of quality.

P 6. The Janelle Company operates as three autonomous divisions. Each division has a general manager in charge of product development, production, and distribution. Management recently adopted total quality management, and the divisions now track, record, and analyze their costs and nonfinancial measures of quality. All three divisions

LO2 Costs and Nonfinancial Measures of Quality

are operating in highly competitive marketplaces. Sales and quality-related data for April are summarized below.

	East Division	Central Division	West Division
Annual Sales	$8,500,000	$9,500,000	$13,000,000
Costs of Quality			
Field testing	$ 51,600	$ 112,800	$ 183,950
Quality audits	17,200	79,100	109,650
Failure analysis	103,100	14,700	92,700
Quality training of employees	60,200	188,000	167,700
Scrap and rework	151,000	18,800	154,800
Quality-certified suppliers	34,400	94,000	108,200
Preventive maintenance	65,800	148,000	141,900
Warranty claims	107,500	42,300	106,050
Customer complaint processing	151,500	108,100	154,800
Process engineering	94,600	235,000	232,200
End-of-process sampling and testing	24,700	178,600	141,900
Scrap disposal losses	77,400	23,500	64,500
Returned goods	152,500	16,200	45,150
Product recalls	64,500	32,900	64,500
Total costs of quality	$1,156,000	$1,292,000	$ 1,768,000
Nonfinancial Measures of Quality			
Defective parts per million	3,410	1,104	1,940
Returned orders	7.40%	1.10%	3.20%
Customer complaints	62	12	30
Number of warranty claims	74	16	52

REQUIRED

1. Prepare an analysis of the costs of quality of the three divisions. Categorize the costs as (a) costs of conformance, with subsets of prevention costs and appraisal costs, or (b) costs of nonconformance, with subsets of internal failure costs and external failure costs. Compute the total costs for each category for each division.
2. For each division, compute the percentage of sales represented by prevention costs, appraisal costs, total costs of conformance, internal failure costs, external failure costs, total costs of nonconformance, and total costs of quality.
3. Interpret the cost-of-quality data for each division. Is each division's product of high or low quality? Explain your answers. Are the divisions headed in the right direction to be competitive?
4. Evaluate the nonfinancial measures of quality in terms of customer satisfaction. Are the results consistent with your analysis in 3? Explain your answers.

P 7.
LO2 Analysis of Nonfinancial Data
LO3

Park Electronics Company is known for its high-quality products and on-time deliveries. Six months ago, it installed a computer-integrated manufacturing system in its Sensitive Components Department. The new equipment produces the entire component so the finished product is ready to be shipped when needed. The controller's staff gathered the following data during the past eight-week period:

	Weeks							
	1	2	3	4	5	6	7	8
Average process time (hours)	10.90	11.10	10.60	10.80	11.20	11.80	12.20	13.60
Average setup time (hours)	2.50	2.60	2.60	2.80	2.70	2.40	2.20	2.20
Customer complaints	11	10	23	15	9	7	5	6
Delivery time (hours)	26.20	26.40	26.10	25.90	26.20	26.60	27.10	26.40
Equipment utilization rate (%)	96.20	96.10	96.30	97.20	97.40	96.20	96.40	95.30
Machine downtime (hours)	106.40	108.10	120.20	110.40	112.80	102.20	124.60	136.20
Machine maintenance time (hours)	64.80	66.70	72.60	74.20	76.80	66.60	80.40	88.20
On-time deliveries (%)	97.20	97.50	97.60	98.20	98.40	96.40	94.80	92.60
Production backlog (units)	10,246	10,288	10,450	10,680	10,880	11,280	11,350	12,100
Production cycle time (hours)	16.50	16.40	16.30	16.10	16.30	17.60	19.80	21.80
Purchase order lead time (hours)	15.20	15.10	14.90	14.60	14.60	13.20	12.40	12.60
Warranty claims	4	8	2	1	6	4	2	3

REQUIRED ▶
1. Analyze the performance of the Sensitive Components Department for the eight-week period. Focus on performance in the following areas:
   a. Production performance
   b. Delivery cycle time
   c. Customer satisfaction

   Carry your answers to two decimal places.
2. Summarize your findings in a report to the department's superintendent, André Park.

Skills Development Cases

Conceptual Analysis

LO4 Comparison of Ecommerce Quality

SD 1. Airlines, real estate agencies, retailers, and most other businesses have developed an Internet presence to sell their goods and services. Select two automobile companies, and evaluate their web sites to determine the quality of their ecommerce efforts. What features does each site offer its customers? What features are missing? Do the sites offer both pre- and postsale assistance? In your opinion, how have these web sites affected the way cars are sold?

LO2 Total Quality Management and Employee Attitudes

SD 2. For the total quality management philosophy to work, everyone in an organization must buy into the concept. Lane Lordon has just been told that he needs to attend four two-hour training sessions about his company's new "Quality or Else" approach to operations. Lordon has been with Boyer Industries for twenty-five years and is managing one of its JIT work cells. His response to the training program was, "Who needs it? I know this operation better than anyone else in the organization. My work cell outproduces all other work cells in this division. Give the training to the new people, especially those new M.B.A.s in middle management who are still wet behind the ears."

You are Lordon's supervisor. Write a memo to him explaining why every employee of Boyer Industries needs to go through a special training program to learn about TQM.

Ethical Dilemma

LO1 MIS and Ethics

SD 3. Three months ago, Maxwell Enterprises hired a consultant, Stacy Slone, to assist in the design and installation of a new management information system for the company. Mike Carns, one of Maxwell's systems design engineers, was assigned to work with Slone on the project. During the three-month period, Slone and Carns met six times and developed a tentative design and installation plan for the MIS. Before the plan was to be unveiled to top management, Carns asked his supervisor, Todd Bowman, to look it over and comment on the design.

Included in the plan was the consolidation of three engineering functions into one. Both of the supervisors of the other two functions had seniority over Bowman, so he believed that the design would lead to his losing his management position. He communicated this to Carns and ended his comments with the following statement: "If you don't redesign the system to accommodate all three of the existing engineering functions, I will give you an unsatisfactory performance evaluation for this year!"

How should Carns respond to Bowman's assertion? Should he handle the problem alone, keeping it inside the company, or communicate the comment to Slone? Outline Carns's options, and be prepared to discuss them in class.

Group Activity: Divide the class into groups, and ask them to discuss this case. Have one member from each group present his or her group's recommended course of action. Encourage debate when groups' recommendations differ.

Research Activity

LO2 Just-in-Time Production and
LO3 Quality

SD 4. Many large multinational companies have installed automated just-in-time production processes to improve product quality and compete for new domestic and foreign business. Locate an article about a company that has installed a JIT system to help improve product quality. Conduct your search using the company annual reports in your campus library, the business section of your local newspaper, or *The Wall Street Journal*, or use a web search engine such as Google.

Choose a source that describes the changes the company made within its plant to increase product quality and compete as a world-class manufacturer. Prepare a one-page description of those changes. Include in your report the name of the company, its geographic location, the name of the chief executive officer and/or president, and the dollar amount of the company's total sales for the most recent year, if stated. Be prepared to present your findings to your classmates.

Decision-Making Practice

LO2 Evaluating Performance
LO3 Measures

SD 5. Ahern Company and Siedle Company compete in the same industry. Each company is located in a large midwestern city, and each employs between 300 and 350 people. Both companies have adopted a total quality management approach, and both want to improve their ability to compete in the marketplace. They have installed common performance measures to help track their quest for quality and a competitive advantage. The following data were generated by the companies during the most recent three-month period:

Performance Measures	Ahern Company Financial	Ahern Company Nonfinancial	Siedle Company Financial	Siedle Company Nonfinancial
Production performance				
Equipment utilization rate		89.4%		92.1%
Machine downtime (in machine hours)		720		490
Delivery cycle time				
On-time deliveries		92.1%		96.5%
Purchase order lead time (hours)		17		18
Production cycle time (hours)		14		16
Waste time (hours)		3		2
Customer satisfaction				
Customer complaints		28		24
Scrap and rework costs	$14,390		$13,680	
Field service costs	9,240		7,700	

1. For each measure, indicate which company has the better performance.
2. Which company is more successful in achieving a total quality environment and an improved competitive position? Explain your answer.

MANAGERIAL REPORTING AND ANALYSIS CASES

Interpreting Management Reports

LO2 Costs of Quality

MRA 1. Pete Malarek was recently appointed chief accountant for Gary Industries. The business has three divisions that manufacture oil-well depth gauges. The business is very competitive, and Gary Industries has lost market share in each of the previous four years. Three years ago, management announced a companywide restructuring and the adoption of total quality management. Since that time, each of the divisions has been allowed to chart its own path toward TQM.

Being new to the company, Malarek asked to see a summary of the costs of quality for each of the divisions over the past six months. The report that he received appears at the top of the facing page.

Evaluate the three divisions' quality control programs by first computing the costs of conformance and the costs of nonconformance for each division. Also compute quality costs as a percentage of sales for each division. Identify the division that is developing

Gary Industries
Costs of Quality Report
For the Six Months Ended June 30, 20x3

	Illinois Division	Indiana Division	Ohio Division	Company Totals
Sales	$1,849,400	$1,773,450	$1,757,400	$5,380,250
Prevention costs	$ 32,680	$ 48,120	$ 15,880	$ 96,680
Appraisal costs	42,340	32,210	17,980	92,530
Internal failure costs	24,100	21,450	41,780	87,330
External failure costs	32,980	16,450	45,560	94,990
Total costs of quality	$ 132,100	$ 118,230	$ 121,200	$ 371,530

the strongest quality program. What division has been the slowest to react to the management directive? Be prepared to explain your answers.

Formulating Management Reports

MRA 2.
LO2 Reporting Quality Data
LO3

Jim Macklin is chief executive officer of Red Cliff Machinery, Inc. The company adopted a JIT operating environment about five years ago. Since then, each segment of the company has been converted, and a complete computer-integrated manufacturing system operates in all parts of the company's five plants. Processing of Red Cliff Machinery's products now averages less than four days once the materials have been placed into production.

Macklin is worried about customer satisfaction and has asked you, as the controller, for some advice and help. He also asked the Marketing Department to perform a quick survey of customers to determine weak areas in customer relations. Here is a summary of four customers' replies:

Customer A
Customer for five years; waits an average of six weeks for delivery; located 1,200 miles from plant; returns an average of 3 percent of products; receives 90 percent on-time deliveries; never hears from salesperson after placing order; likes quality or would go with competitor.

Customer B
Customer for seven years; waits an average of five weeks for delivery; orders usually sit in backlog for at least three weeks; located 50 miles from plant; returns about 5 percent of products; receives 95 percent on-time deliveries; has great rapport with salesperson; salesperson is why this customer is loyal.

Customer C
Customer for twelve years; waits an average of seven weeks for delivery; located 1,500 miles from plant; returns about 4 percent of products; receives 92 percent on-time deliveries; salesperson is available but of little help in getting faster delivery; customer is thinking about dealing with another source for its product needs.

Customer D
Customer for fifteen years; very pleased with company's product; waits almost five weeks for delivery; located 120 miles from plant; returns only 2 percent of goods received; rapport with salesperson is very good; follow-up service of salesperson is excellent; would like delivery cycle time reduced to equal that of competitors; usually deals with three-week backlog.

1. Identify the areas of concern, and give at least three examples of reports that will help managers improve the company's response to customer needs.
2. Assume you are asked to write a report that will provide information about customer satisfaction. In preparation, answer the following questions:
   a. What kinds of information do you need to prepare this report?
   b. Why is this information relevant?
   c. Where would you find this information (that is, what sources would you use)?
   d. When would you want to obtain this information?

International Company

MRA 3.   Motorola's <www.motorola.com> Total Customer Satisfaction (TCS) Teams are cross-functional teams that use customer-focused problem-solving methodology to solve quality and process problems. One TCS Team success story involved an international supplier with quality and delivery problems that required additional order expediting and rework that were causing customer dissatisfaction. The TCS Team's report to management disclosed the following results:

LO4 Quality Measures and Techniques

- By evaluating and revising the product's design, the team created a more robust finished product.
- The adoption of process capability studies with continuous monitoring resulted in improved quality.
- When sourcing was moved to a local supplier, inventory turnover improved from 26 to 52 turns annually.
- Over the three-year life of the product, the team's changes resulted in $831,438 in cost savings.[11]

1. From the TCS Team's report, identify the key issues in improving the international supplier's quality and process problems.
2. How could the team have applied the process-based techniques of benchmarking and process mapping to improve quality?

Excel Spreadsheet Analysis

MRA 4. Travis Corporation has five divisions, each manufacturing a product line that competes in the global marketplace. The company is planning to compete for the Malcolm Baldrige Award, so management requires that each division record and report its efforts to achieve quality in its product line. The information below was submitted to the company's controller for the most recent six-month period:

LO2 Interpreting Measures of
LO3 Quality

	Division A	Division B	Division C	Division D	Division E
Total Revenue	$886,000	$1,040,000	$956,000	$1,225,000	$1,540,000
Costs of Quality					
Customer complaint processing	$ 10,400	$ 12,600	$ 12,300	$ 10,100	$ 15,600
Scrap and rework	26,800	13,500	38,700	11,900	34,800
Quality audits of products	13,600	28,400	6,300	25,600	11,700
Returned goods	18,700	11,400	38,400	11,300	36,000
Warranty claims	21,100	6,400	36,200	6,500	42,600
Quality training of employees	8,900	12,600	4,600	11,400	4,200
Preventive maintenance	11,300	18,700	8,300	13,600	6,300
Failure analysis	34,800	9,800	46,900	10,200	56,900
Inspection of materials	12,500	18,700	7,800	17,500	5,600
Nonfinancial Measures of Quality					
Number of warranty claims versus	22	12	46	12	62
number of sales	6,500	8,900	7,200	9,800	9,600
Number of products reworked versus	150	140	870	70	900
number of products manufactured	325,000	456,000	365,000	450,000	315,600
Throughput time in hours versus	6.20	8.50	6.80	9.20	11.60
throughput time at beginning of period	6.20	8.60	6.50	9.80	10.80
Number of late deliveries versus	450	260	760	80	1,500
total number of deliveries	8,600	12,400	9,200	12,600	12,800

1. Prepare an analysis of the costs of quality for each division. Categorize the costs as costs of conformance or costs of nonconformance. Carry your answers to two decimal places.
2. For each division, compute the percentage of total revenue for each of the four cost-of-quality categories and the ratios for the nonfinancial data.
3. Rank the divisions in order of their apparent product quality.
4. What three measures were most important in your rankings in 3**? Why?**
5. Which division is most successful in its bid to improve quality? What measures illustrate its high-quality rating?
6. Consider the two divisions producing the lowest-quality products. What actions would you recommend to the management of each division? Where should their quality dollars be spent?

Internet Case

LO5 ISO Standards

MRA 5. Visit ISO's electronic information service, ISO Online, at www.iso.ch to learn more about ISO 9000 and ISO 14000. "News," "User Feedback," and "The Magical Demystifying Tour of ISO 9000 and ISO 14000" are pages where it's possible to learn more about these worldwide standards. Share your findings in a brief email message to your instructor.

28 Financial Performance Evaluation

Chapter 28 focuses on financial performance evaluation by internal and external users. The chapter describes the tools and techniques of financial analysis and ratio analysis.

Learning Objectives

LO1 Describe and discuss financial performance evaluation by internal and external users.

LO2 Describe and discuss the standards for financial performance evaluation.

LO3 Identify the sources of information for financial performance evaluation.

LO4 Apply horizontal analysis, trend analysis, vertical analysis, and ratio analysis to financial statements.

LO5 Apply ratio analysis to financial statements in a comprehensive evaluation of a company's financial performance.

DECISION POINT A USER'S FOCUS

Sun Microsystems <www.sun.com> Sun Microsystems is a global leader in providing products and services for computer networking. A committee of its board of directors has developed a compensation package for top management that is linked to, among other things, financial performance measures, some of which are presented in the Financial Highlights. These measures are, in turn, linked to creating shareholder value. How does Sun Microsystems make these links?

The company's executive compensation package consists primarily of the following three components:

- Base salary
- Long-term incentives
- Annual incentive bonus

Executives' base salaries are competitive within the industry, and long-term incentives are tied to stock options that will become more valuable if the stock price goes up, thereby creating shareholder value. Of the three components, the annual incentive bonus is most closely linked to financial performance in any given year. Although the company was profitable and its revenues increased in 2001, no annual incentive bonuses were awarded because growth in revenues and in earnings per share was below the company's plan. These results contrast sharply with those in 2000, when financial performance was outstanding and several executives received bonuses in excess of $1 million.[1]

Thus, at Sun Microsystems, as at many other companies that demand outstanding results, financial

How is financial performance tied to the annual incentive bonuses that executives at Sun hope to receive?

performance is an important factor in management compensation. Managers who work in such an environment must understand the comprehensive framework that internal and external users of financial statements commonly employ to evaluate a company's results. This chapter presents that framework.

Financial Highlights
(In millions except earnings per share)

	2001	2000	1999
Net revenues	$18,250	$15,721	$11,806
Net income	927	1,854	1,030
Earnings per share—basic	0.28	0.59	0.33

Financial Performance Evaluation by Internal and External Users

LO1 Describe and discuss financial performance evaluation by internal and external users.

RELATED TEXT ASSIGNMENTS
Q: 1, 2, 3, 4, 5
SE: 1
E: 1

Financial performance evaluation, also called *financial statement analysis*, comprises all the techniques users of financial statements employ to show important relationships in a firm's financial statements and to relate them to important financial objectives. Users of financial statements who evaluate financial performance fall into two categories: internal users and external users. Both groups have a strong interest in financial performance. Internal users include top managers, who set and strive to achieve financial performance objectives; middle-level managers of business processes; and employee stockholders. External users are creditors and investors who want to assess management's accomplishment of financial objectives, as well as customers who have cooperative agreements with the company.

Financial Performance Evaluation and the Management Cycle

Financial performance evaluation plays a key role in all phases of the management cycle, as shown in Figure 1.

■ **PLANNING** During the planning phase of the management cycle, managers set the financial performance objectives that will enable them to achieve the company's goals. All strategic and operating plans must eventually be stated in terms of financial objectives. One of the primary objectives of management is to increase the wealth of the company's stockholders, but this broad objective must be divided into more specific performance objectives. The Decision Point showed how Sun Microsystems' executive compensation is tied to certain measures of financial performance. A complete financial plan should have balanced financial performance objectives in all of the following categories:

www.sun.com

 Stop and Think!
Why is it essential that management compensation, including bonuses, be linked to financial goals and strategies that achieve shareholder value?

If the overall financial plan is expected to increase the owners' wealth, then aligning managers' compensation and bonuses with achieving or exceeding these financial targets encourages managers to act in their own and the owners' best interests. ■

Business Objectives	Links to Financial Performance
Liquidity	Ability to pay bills when due and to meet unexpected needs for cash
Profitability	Ability to earn a satisfactory net income
Long-term solvency	Ability to survive for many years
Cash flow adequacy	Ability to generate sufficient cash through operating, investing, and financing activities
Market strength	Ability to increase the wealth of stockholders

■ **EXECUTING** During the executing phase, management's main responsibility is to carry out the plans for achieving the financial performance objectives. For example, Sun's management will need to focus on growing revenues and improving profitability by expanding the business, investing in technology, managing assets, and controlling costs.

■ **REVIEWING** Management must constantly monitor key financial performance measures, determine causes for any deviations in the measures, and propose corrective actions. Annual measures provide data for long-term trend analysis. For Sun Microsystems, a key performance measure is growth in revenues and earnings per share, but other measures related to asset management and cost control will be important as well.

■ **REPORTING** Management develops monthly, quarterly, and annual reports that compare actual performance with planned performance in achieving the key

FIGURE 1
Financial Performance Evaluation in the Management Cycle

business objectives of liquidity, profitability, long-term solvency, cash flow adequacy, and market strength. Reports at Sun will focus on financial performance measures that relate to the company's specific long-term strategies, such as cash flow and return on assets.

FINANCIAL PERFORMANCE EVALUATION BY EXTERNAL USERS

Creditors make loans in the form of trade accounts, notes, or bonds. They expect them to be repaid according to specified terms and to receive interest on the notes and bonds payable. Investors buy capital stock, from which they hope to receive dividends and an increase in value. Both groups face risks. The creditor faces the risk that the debtor will fail to pay back the loan. The investor faces the risks that dividends will be reduced or not paid and that the market price of the stock will drop. For both groups, the goal is to achieve a return that makes up for the risk. In general, the greater the risk taken, the greater the return required as compensation.

Any one loan or any one investment can turn out badly. As a result, most creditors and investors put their funds into a **portfolio**, which is a group of loans or investments. The portfolio is designed to average the returns and the risks. Nevertheless, individual decisions about the loans or stock in the portfolio must still be made. It is in making those individual decisions that financial performance evaluation is most useful. Creditors and investors use financial performance evaluation in two general ways: to judge past performance and current position, and to judge future potential and the risk connected with that potential.

KEY POINT: Past performance is a measure of certainty, whereas trends and projections entail varying degrees of risk and uncertainty.

■ **ASSESSMENT OF PAST PERFORMANCE AND CURRENT POSITION** Past performance is often a good indicator of future performance. Therefore, an investor or creditor looks at the trends of past sales, expenses, net income, cash flow, and return on investment not only as means of judging management's past performance but also as possible indicators of future performance. In addition, an evaluation of current position will tell, for example, what assets the business owns and what liabilities it must pay. It will also tell what the company's cash position is, how much debt it has in relation to equity, and what levels of inventories and receivables exist. Knowing a company's past performance and current position is often important in judging future potential and the related risk.

■ **ASSESSMENT OF FUTURE POTENTIAL AND RELATED RISK** Information about the past and present is useful only insofar as it bears on decisions about the future. An investor evaluates a company's potential earning ability because that ability will affect the market price of the company's stock and the amount of dividends the company will pay. A creditor evaluates the company's potential debt-paying ability.

The riskiness of an investment or loan depends on how easy it is to predict future profitability or liquidity. If an investor can predict with confidence that a company's earnings per share will be between $2.50 and $2.60 in the next year, the investment is less risky than if the earnings per share are expected to fall between $2.00 and $3.00. For example, the potential associated with an investment in an established and stable electric utility, or a loan to it, is relatively easy to predict on the basis of the company's past performance and current position. The potential associated with investment in a small Internet firm, on the other hand, may be much harder to predict. For this reason, the investment in or loan to the electric utility carries less risk than the investment in or loan to the small Internet company.

Often, in return for taking a greater risk, an investor in the small Internet company will demand a higher expected return (increase in market price plus dividends) than will an investor in the established utility company. Also, a creditor of the Internet company will demand a higher interest rate and possibly more assurance of repayment (a secured loan, for instance) than a creditor of the utility company. The higher interest rate reimburses the creditor for assuming a higher risk.

FINANCIAL REPORTING UNDER THE SARBANES-OXLEY ACT

www.enron.com
www.worldcom.com

In response to the financial reporting issues raised by the cases of Enron, WorldCom, and others, the U.S. Congress passed broad legislation, referred to as the **Sarbanes-Oxley Act**, in an attempt to rectify the problems. This act includes numerous provisions designed to improve investor confidence in the financial reporting system as it applies to publicly traded companies, including the following:

- Establishes a Public Oversight Board for the accounting profession, which will establish auditing standards and oversee other regulations involving auditors.
- Requires the chief executor officer and chief financial officer to take responsibility for the accuracy of annual and quarterly financial statements under criminal penalties.
- Requires the audit committee of public corporations to be made up of independent (nonofficer) board members, some of whom must have financial expertise.
- Requires that the audit committee appoint the company's auditor and that the auditor not be allowed to do any consulting for the company.

The Sarbanes-Oxley Act does not apply to private (nonpublic) companies.

 Check out ACE for a Review Quiz at http://accounting.college.hmco.com/students.

STANDARDS FOR FINANCIAL STATEMENT ANALYSIS

LO2 Describe and discuss the standards for financial performance evaluation.

RELATED TEXT ASSIGNMENTS
Q: 6, 7
E: 1
SD: 1
FRA: 6

www.dunandbradstreet.com

ENRICHMENT NOTE:
Rules of thumb evolve and change as the environment changes. Not long ago, an acceptable current ratio was higher than today's 2:1.

When analyzing financial statements, decision makers must judge whether the relationships they find are favorable or unfavorable. Three commonly used standards of comparison are rule-of-thumb measures, past performance of the company, and industry norms.

RULE-OF-THUMB MEASURES

Many financial analysts, investors, and lenders employ general standards, or rule-of-thumb measures, for key financial ratios. For example, most analysts today agree that a current ratio (current assets divided by current liabilities) of 2:1 is acceptable. The credit-rating firm of Dun & Bradstreet, in its *Industry Norms and Key Business Ratios*, offers such rules of thumb as the following:

Current debt to tangible net worth Ordinarily, a business begins to pile up trouble when this relationship exceeds 80 percent.

Inventory to net working capital Ordinarily, this relationship should not exceed 80 percent.

  Although such measures may suggest areas that need further investigation, there is no proof that the specified levels are applicable to all companies. A company with a current ratio higher than 2:1 may have a poor credit policy (resulting in accounts receivable being too large), too much inventory, or poor cash management. Another company may have a ratio lower than 2:1 but still have excellent management in all three of those areas. Thus, rule-of-thumb measures must be used with great care.

PAST PERFORMANCE OF THE COMPANY

An improvement over rule-of-thumb measures is the comparison of financial measures or ratios of the same company over time. Such a comparison gives the analyst some basis for judging whether the measure or ratio is getting better or worse. It may also be helpful in showing possible future trends. However, trends reverse at times, so such projections must be made with care. Another problem with trend analysis is that past performance may not be enough to meet present needs. For example, even if a company has improved its return on total investment from 3 percent one year to 4 percent the next, the 4 percent return may, in fact, not be adequate for the company's needs.

INDUSTRY NORMS

◆ **STOP AND THINK!**
How are past performance and industry norms useful in evaluating a company's performance?
A company's past performance indicates whether performance is improving. Industry norms tell how well a company is performing in relation to its peer group. ■

One way of making up for the limitations of using past performance as a standard is to use industry norms. Such norms show how a company compares with others in the same industry. For example, if companies in the same industry have an average rate of return on total investment of 8 percent, returns on investment of 3 and 4 percent are probably not adequate. Industry norms can also be used to judge trends. Suppose a company's profit margin dropped from 12 to 10 percent because of a downward turn in the economy. If the average drop in profit margin of other companies in the same industry was from 12 to 4 percent, this norm would indicate that the company had done relatively well. Sometimes, instead of industry averages, data for the industry leader or a specific competitor are analyzed.

  Using industry norms as standards has three limitations. First, companies in the same industry may not be strictly comparable. Consider two companies in the oil industry. One purchases oil products and markets them through service stations. The other, an international company, discovers, produces, refines, and markets its

EXHIBIT 1
Selected Segment Information for Goodyear Tire & Rubber Co.

(In millions)	2002	2001	2000
Sales			
North American Tire	$ 6,703.3	$ 7,152.3	$ 7,111.3
European Union Tire	3,314.9	3,128.0	3,198.1
Eastern Europe, Africa, and Middle East Tire	807.1	703.1	793.0
Latin American Tire	947.6	1,012.6	1,047.9
Asia Tire	531.7	493.9	524.6
Total Tires	12,304.6	12,489.9	12,674.9
Engineered Products	1,126.5	1,122.3	1,174.2
Chemical Products	937.9	1,037.3	1,129.7
Total Segment Sales	14,369.0	14,649.5	14,978.8
Income			
North American Tire	$ (35.5)	$ 107.8	$ 260.7
European Union Tire	102.6	57.2	88.7
Eastern Europe, Africa, and Middle East Tire	91.9	20.2	54.6
Latin American Tire	102.4	89.8	69.8
Asia Tire	43.9	19.9	17.9
Total Tires	305.3	294.9	491.7
Engineered Products	45.6	11.6	43.1
Chemical Products	69.4	60.2	64.2
Total Segment Income	420.3	366.7	599.0
Assets			
North American Tire	$ 4,594.8	$ 4,856.7	$ 5,268.5
European Union Tire	3,124.4	2,836.9	3,088.1
Eastern Europe, Africa, and Middle East Tire	899.4	747.7	903.6
Latin American Tire	642.8	753.9	796.5
Asia Tire	604.0	600.9	668.5
Total Tires	9,865.4	9,796.1	10,725.2
Engineered Products	678.2	681.3	736.8
Chemical Products	636.9	601.6	742.9
Total Segment Assets	11,180.5	11,079.0	12,204.9

Source: Goodyear Tire & Rubber Co., *Annual Report,* 2002.

KEY POINT: Each segment represents an investment that the home office or parent company evaluates and reviews frequently. The segment can remain an active investment or be replaced by a more attractive one.

own oil products. Because of their different operations, these two companies cannot be compared.

Second, many large companies today operate in more than one industry or segment. Some of these **diversified companies**, or *conglomerates,* operate in many unrelated industries. The individual segments of a diversified company generally have different rates of profitability and different degrees of risk. In analyzing the consolidated financial statements of such companies, it is often impossible to use industry norms as standards. There are simply no comparable companies. A requirement of

FOCUS ON BUSINESS ETHICS

Take the Numbers with a Grain of Salt.

Traditionally, pro-forma statements presented financial statements as they would appear after certain agreed-upon transactions, such as mergers or acquisitions, took place. In recent years, pro-forma statements have become more widely used as a way for companies to present a better picture of their operations than would be the case under GAAP. According to a survey by the National Investor Relations Institute, 57 percent of companies across a range of industries use pro-forma reporting.[2] In one quarter, Amazon.com <www.amazon.com> reported a "pro-forma operating" loss of $49 million and a "pro-forma net" loss of $76 million; had the company used GAAP, it would have reported a net loss of $234 million. Among many other examples, JDS Uniphase <www.jdsu.com> reported a "pro-forma" gain of $.14 per share, when, in fact, its net loss using GAAP was $1.13 per share. Pro-forma statements, which are unaudited, have come to mean whatever a company's management wants them to mean. Thus, the analyst should rely exclusively on financial statements that are prepared using GAAP and that are audited by an independent CPA.[3]

www.goodyear.com

the Financial Accounting Standards Board, presented in *Statement No. 131*, provides a partial solution to this problem. It states that diversified companies must report profit or loss, certain revenue and expense items, and assets for each of their segments. Depending on how the company is organized for assessing performance, segment information may be reported for operations in different industries or different geographical areas, or for major customers.[4]

Exhibit 1 shows an example of segment reporting. Goodyear Tire & Rubber Co., well known as a tire manufacturer, also has significant engineered and chemical products divisions. The data on sales, income, and assets for these segments, shown in Exhibit 1, allow the analyst to compute important profitability performance measures, such as profit margin, asset turnover, and return on assets, for each segment and to compare them with the appropriate industry norms.

The third limitation of industry norms is that companies in the same industry with similar operations may use different acceptable accounting procedures. That is, they may use different methods to value inventories and different methods to depreciate assets. Even so, if little information about a company's past performance is available, industry norms probably offer the best available standards for judging current performance—as long as they are used with care.

 Check out ACE for a Review Quiz at http://accounting.college.hmco.com/students.

SOURCES OF INFORMATION

LO3 Identify the sources of information for financial performance evaluation.

RELATED TEXT ASSIGNMENTS
Q: 8
SE: 2
E: 1
SD: 2, 3, 4, 5
FRA: 6

The external analyst is often limited to using publicly available information about a company. The major sources of information about publicly held corporations are reports published by the company, SEC reports, business periodicals, and credit and investment advisory services.

REPORTS PUBLISHED BY THE COMPANY

A publicly held corporation's annual report is an important source of financial information. From a financial analyst's perspective, its main parts are management's analysis of the past year's operations; the financial statements; the notes to the financial statements, which include a summary of significant accounting policies; the auditors' report; and financial highlights for a five- or ten-year period.

Most publicly held companies also publish **interim financial statements** each quarter. Those reports present limited information in the form of condensed financial statements, which need not be subjected to a full audit by the independent auditor. The financial community watches the interim statements closely for early signs of important changes in a company's earnings trend.

Focus on Business Technology

Find It on the Internet.
Performance reports and other financial information, including stock quotes, reference data, and news about companies and markets, are available instantaneously through such Internet services as CompuServe <www.compuserve.com>, America Online, <www.aol.com>, Yahoo <www.yahoo.com>, and Wall Street Journal Interactive Edition <http://online.wsj.com>. With access to these online services and those of brokers like Charles Schwab & Co., Inc. <www.schwab.com>, which allow customers to use their own computers to buy and sell stock and other securities, individuals today can avail themselves of resources equivalent to those used by many professional analysts.

SEC Reports

Publicly held corporations in the United States must file annual reports, quarterly reports, and current reports with the Securities and Exchange Commission (SEC). If they have more than $10 million in assets and more than 500 shareholders, they must file these reports electronically at www.sec.gov/edgar.shtml, where anyone can access them free of charge.

The Securities and Exchange Commission requires companies to use a standard form, called Form 10-K, for the annual report. Form 10-K contains more information than the annual reports published by companies. For that reason, it is a valuable source of information.

Companies file their quarterly reports with the SEC on Form 10-Q. This report presents important facts about interim financial performance. The current report, filed on Form 8-K must be submitted to the SEC within a few days of the date of certain significant events, such as the sale or purchase of a division of the company or a change in the company's auditors. The current report is often the first indicator of important changes that may affect a company's financial performance in the future.

Business Periodicals and Credit and Investment Advisory Services

Financial analysts must keep up with current events in the financial world. Probably the best source of financial news is *The Wall Street Journal*, which is published every business day and is the most complete financial newspaper in the United States. Some helpful magazines, published every week or every two weeks, are *Forbes*, *Barron's*, *Fortune*, and the *Financial Times*.

For further details about the financial history of companies, the publications of such services as Moody's Investors Service, Inc., and Standard & Poor's are useful. Data on industry norms, average ratios and relationships, and credit ratings are available from such agencies as The Dun & Bradstreet Corp. In its publication entitled *Industry Norms and Key Business Ratios*, Dun & Bradstreet offers an annual analysis of 14 ratios for each of 125 industry groups, classified as retailing, wholesaling, manufacturing, and construction. *Annual Statement Studies*, published by the Risk Management Association (formerly Robert Morris Associates), presents many facts and ratios for 223 different industries. A number of private services are also available for a yearly fee.

An example of specialized financial reporting readily available to the public is Mergent's *Handbook of Dividend Achievers*, which profiles companies that have increased their dividends consistently over the past ten years. A listing from that publication—for PepsiCo Inc.—is shown in Exhibit 2. A wealth of information about the company is summarized on one page, including the market action of its stock; its business operations, recent developments, and prospects; earnings and dividend data; and annual financial data for the past ten years. The kind of data in these profiles is used in many of the analyses and ratios explained in this chapter.

● **Stop and Think!**

Why would ratios that include one balance sheet account and one income statement or statement of cash flows account, such as receivable turnover or return on assets, be questionable if they came from quarterly or other interim financial reports?

On quarterly financial statements, all numbers on the income statement and statement of cash flows are for less than one year, whereas the balance sheet figures are full values similar to those at year end. Thus, any ratios that use data from the income statement or statement of cash flows as their basis will be less than they might be on a full-year basis. ■

www.moodys.com
www.standardpoor.com
www.dunandbradstreet.com

www.rmahq.com

www.pepsi.com

EXHIBIT 2
Listing from Mergent's *Handbook of Dividend Achievers*

Source: Sample listing from *Handbook of Dividend Achievers, 2002.* Reprinted by permission of Mergent, Inc.

 Check out ACE for a Review Quiz at http://accounting.college.hmco.com/students.

TOOLS AND TECHNIQUES OF FINANCIAL ANALYSIS

LO4 Apply horizontal analysis, trend analysis, vertical analysis, and ratio analysis to financial statements.

RELATED TEXT ASSIGNMENTS
Q: 9, 10, 11, 12
SE: 3, 4, 5
E: 2, 3, 4
P: 1
SD: 6
FRA: 1

www.sun.com

Few numbers are very significant when looked at individually. It is their relationship to other numbers or their change from one period to another that is important. The tools of financial analysis are intended to show relationships and changes. Among the more widely used tools are horizontal analysis, trend analysis, vertical analysis, and ratio analysis. To illustrate how these tools are used, we devote the rest of this chapter to a comprehensive financial analysis of Sun Microsystems, Inc. Sun Microsystems was formed in 1982 and, as noted in this chapter's Decision Point, it has emerged as a global leader in network computing. It developed many of the networking technologies that are the basis of the Internet and corporate intranets, including the widely adopted Java technology.

HORIZONTAL ANALYSIS

Generally accepted accounting principles require the presentation of comparative financial statements that give financial information for the current year and the previous year. A common starting point for studying such statements is **horizontal analysis**, which computes changes from the previous year to the current year in both dollar amounts and percentages. The percentage change relates the size of the change to the size of the dollar amounts involved.

Exhibits 3 and 4 present the comparative balance sheets and income statements of Sun Microsystems and show both the dollar and percentage changes. The percentage change is computed as follows:

$$\text{Percentage Change} = 100 \times \left(\frac{\text{Amount of Change}}{\text{Base Year Amount}}\right)$$

The **base year** in any set of data is always the first year to be considered. For example, when studying data from 2000 and 2001, 2000 is the base year. As the balance sheets in Exhibit 3 show, between 2000 and 2001, Sun Microsystems' total current assets increased by $1,057 million, from $6,877 million to $7,934 million, or by 15.4 percent. This is computed as follows:

$$\text{Percentage Change} = 100 \times \left(\frac{\$1{,}057 \text{ million}}{\$6{,}877 \text{ million}}\right) = 15.4\%$$

The company's total current liabilities also increased—by $600 million, or 13.2 percent—in this two-year period. When examining such changes, it is important to consider both the dollar amount of the change as well as the percentage change in each component. For example, the difference between the percentage increase in warranty reserve (48.8 percent) and deferred revenues and customer deposits (41.7 percent) is not great. However, the dollar increase in deferred revenues and customer deposits is more than five times the dollar increase in warranty reserve ($538 million versus $103 million).

Sun Microsystems' balance sheets for this period also show an increase in total assets of $4,029 million, or 28.5 percent, which included an increase of $602 million, or 28.7 percent, in property, plant, and equipment, net. In addition, they show that stockholders' equity increased by $3,277 million, or 44.8 percent. All of this indicates that Sun Microsystems is a rapidly growing company.

The most important findings from the income statements in Exhibit 4 are that net revenues increased by $2,529 million, or 16.1 percent; operating income decreased by $1,082 million, or 45.2 percent; and net income decreased by $927 million, or 50.0 percent. These extremely negative results occurred in part because net revenues grew at a slower rate (16.1 percent) than cost of sales (33.0 percent) and operating expenses (19.4 percent).

ENRICHMENT NOTE:
Traditional horizontal analysis presents trends in terms of nominal dollars. Advanced analysis might adjust data over several time periods to remove any inflation effect or price-level changes.

EXHIBIT 3
Comparative Balance Sheets with Horizontal Analysis

Sun Microsystems, Inc.
Consolidated Balance Sheets
June 30, 2001 and 2000

			Increase (Decrease)	
(Dollar amounts in millions)	2001	2000	Amount	Percentage
Assets				
Current assets:				
Cash and cash equivalents	$ 1,472	$ 1,849	($377)	(20.4)
Short-term investments	387	626	(239)	(38.2)
Accounts receivable, net of allowances of $410 in 2001 and $534 in 2000	2,955	2,690	265	9.9
Inventories	1,049	557	492	88.3
Deferred tax assets	1,102	673	429	63.7
Prepaids and other current assets	969	482	487	101.0
Total current assets	$ 7,934	$ 6,877	$1,057	15.4
Property, plant and equipment, net	2,697	2,095	602	28.7
Long-term investments	4,677	4,496	181	4.0
Goodwill, net of accumulated amortization of $349 in 2001 and $88 in 2000	2,041	163	1,878	1,152.1
Other assets, net	832	521	311	59.7
Total assets	$18,181	$14,152	$4,029	28.5
Liabilities and Stockholders' Equity				
Current liabilities:				
Short-term borrowings	$ 3	$ 7	$ (4)	(57.1)
Accounts payable	1,050	924	126	13.6
Accrued payroll-related liabilities	488	751	(263)	(35.0)
Accrued liabilities and other	1,374	1,155	219	19.0
Deferred revenues and customer deposits	1,827	1,289	538	41.7
Warranty reserve	314	211	103	48.8
Income taxes payable	90	209	(119)	(56.9)
Total current liabilities	$ 5,146	$ 4,546	$ 600	13.2
Deferred income taxes	744	577	167	28.9
Long-term debt and other obligations	1,705	1,720	(15)	(0.9)
Stockholders' equity	10,586	7,309	3,277	44.8
Total liabilities and stockholders' equity	$18,181	$14,152	$4,029	28.5

Source: Sun Microsystems, Inc., *Annual Report,* 2001.

TREND ANALYSIS

A variation of horizontal analysis is **trend analysis**, in which percentage changes are calculated for several successive years instead of for two years. Trend analysis, with its long-run view, is important because it may point to basic changes in the nature of a business. In addition to presenting comparative financial statements, most companies present a summary of key data for five or more years. Exhibit 5 shows

EXHIBIT 4
Comparative Income Statements with Horizontal Analysis

Sun Microsystems, Inc.
Consolidated Income Statements
For the Years Ended June 30, 2001 and 2000

(Dollar amounts in millions, except per share amounts)	2001	2000	Increase (Decrease) Amount	Percentage
Net revenues	$18,250	$15,721	$ 2,529	16.1
Cost of sales	10,041	7,549	2,492	33.0
Gross margin	$ 8,209	$ 8,172	37	0.5
Operating expenses				
Research and development	$ 2,016	$ 1,630	$ 386	23.7
Selling, general and administrative	4,544	4,072	472	11.6
Goodwill amortization	261	65	196	301.5
Purchased in-process R&D	77	12	65	541.7
Total operating expenses	$ 6,898	$ 5,779	$ 1,119	19.4
Operating income	$ 1,311	$ 2,393	($ 1,082)	(45.2)
Gain (loss) on investments	(90)	208	(298)	(143.3)
Interest income	463	254	209	82.3
Interest expense	(100)	(84)	(16)	19.0
Income before income taxes	$ 1,584	$ 2,771	($ 1,187)	(42.8)
Provision for income taxes	603	917	(314)	(34.2)
Income before cumulative effect of change in accounting principle	$ 981	$ 1,854	($ 873)	(47.1)
Cumulative effect of change in accounting principle	(54)	—	(54)	NA
Net income	$ 927	$ 1,854	($ 927)	(50.0)
Net income per common share—basic	$0.28	$0.59	($0.31)	(52.2)
Net income per common share—diluted	$0.27	$0.55	($0.28)	(50.9)
Shares used in calculation of net income per common share—basic	3,234	3,151	83	2.6
Shares used in calculation of net income per common share—diluted	3,417	3,379	38	1.1

Source: Sun Microsystems, Inc., *Annual Report,* 2001

a trend analysis of Sun Microsystems' five-year summary of net revenues and operating income.

Trend analysis uses an **index number** to show changes in related items over time. For index numbers, the base year is equal to 100 percent. Other years are measured in relation to that amount. For example, the 2001 index for Sun Microsystems' net revenues is figured as follows (dollar amounts in millions):

$$\text{Index} = 100 \times \left(\frac{\text{Index Year Amount}}{\text{Base Year Amount}}\right)$$

$$= 100 \times \left(\frac{\$18,250}{\$8,661}\right) = 210.7\%$$

Exhibit 5
Trend Analysis

ENRICHMENT NOTE:
Trend analysis is usually done for a five-year period to reflect the general five-year economic cycle that affects the U.S. economy. Cycles of other lengths exist and are tracked by the National Bureau of Economic Research. Trend analysis needs to use the appropriate cycle time to cover the complete cycle's impact on the business being studied.

Sun Microsystems, Inc.
Net Revenues and Operating Income
Trend Analysis

	2001	2000	1999	1998	1997
Dollar values (in millions)					
Net revenues	$18,250	$15,721	$11,806	$9,862	$8,661
Operating income	1,311	2,393	1,520	1,114	1,033
Trend analysis (in percentages)					
Net revenues	210.7	181.5	136.3	113.9	100.0
Operating income	126.9	231.7	147.1	107.8	100.0

Source: Sun Microsystems, Inc., *Annual Report,* 2001.

The trend analysis in Exhibit 5 shows that net revenues at Sun Microsystems increased over the five-year period, as did operating income in every year except 2001, when it declined dramatically. Figure 2 illustrates these trends.

VERTICAL ANALYSIS

In **vertical analysis**, percentages are used to show the relationship of the different parts to a total in a single statement. The analyst sets a total figure in the statement equal to 100 percent and computes each component's percentage of that total. (The figure would be total assets or total liabilities and stockholders' equity on the balance sheet, and net revenues or net sales on the income statement.) The resulting statement of percentages is called a **common-size statement**. Common-size balance sheets and common-size income statements for Sun Microsystems are shown in pie-chart form in Figures 3 and 4, and in financial statement form in Exhibits 6 and 7.

Vertical analysis is useful for comparing the importance of specific components in the operation of a business. Also, comparative common-size statements can be used to identify important changes in the components from one year to the next. As shown in Figure 3 and Exhibit 6, from 2000 to 2001 the composition of Sun

Figure 2
Graph of Trend Analysis Shown in Exhibit 5

🛑 **STOP AND THINK!**
In a five-year trend analysis, why do the dollar values remain the same for their respective years while the percentages usually change when a new five-year period is chosen?

In a five-year trend analysis for a new five-year period, the base year changes. Unless two successive base years have exactly the same dollar values, the trend analysis percentages will be different each year. ■

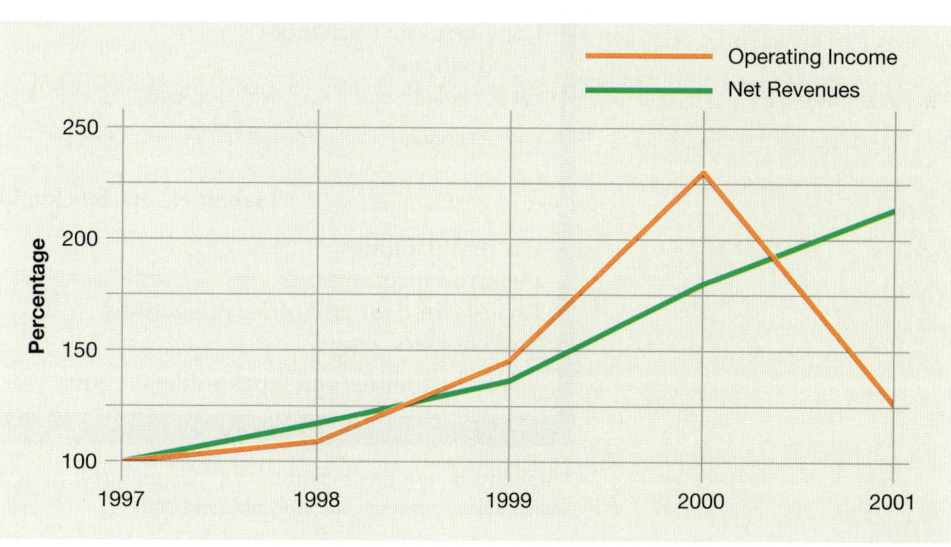

FIGURE 3
Common-Size Balance Sheets
Presented Graphically

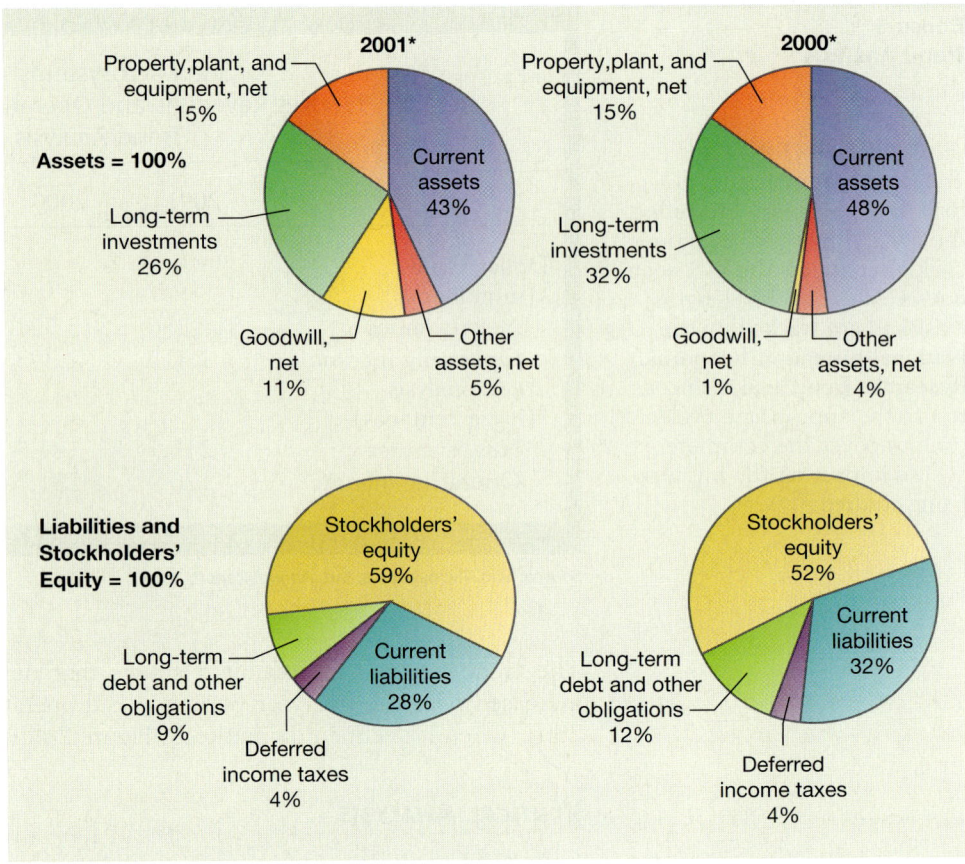

* Rounding causes some additions not to total precisely.

EXHIBIT 6
Common-Size Balance Sheets

Sun Microsystems, Inc.
Common-Size Balance Sheets
June 30, 2001 and 2000

	2001*	2000*
Assets		
Current assets	43.6%	48.6%
Property, plant and equipment, net	14.8	14.8
Long-term investments	25.7	31.8
Goodwill, net	11.2	1.2
Other assets, net	4.6	3.7
Total assets	100.0%	100.0%
Liabilities and Stockholders' Equity		
Current liabilities	28.3%	32.1%
Deferred income taxes	4.1	4.1
Long-term debt and other obligations	9.4	12.2
Stockholders' equity	58.2	51.6
Total liabilities and stockholders' equity	100.0%	100.0%

*Amounts do not precisely total 100 percent in all cases due to rounding.
Source: Sun Microsystems, Inc., *Annual Report,* 2001.

FIGURE 4
Common-Size Income Statements Presented Graphically

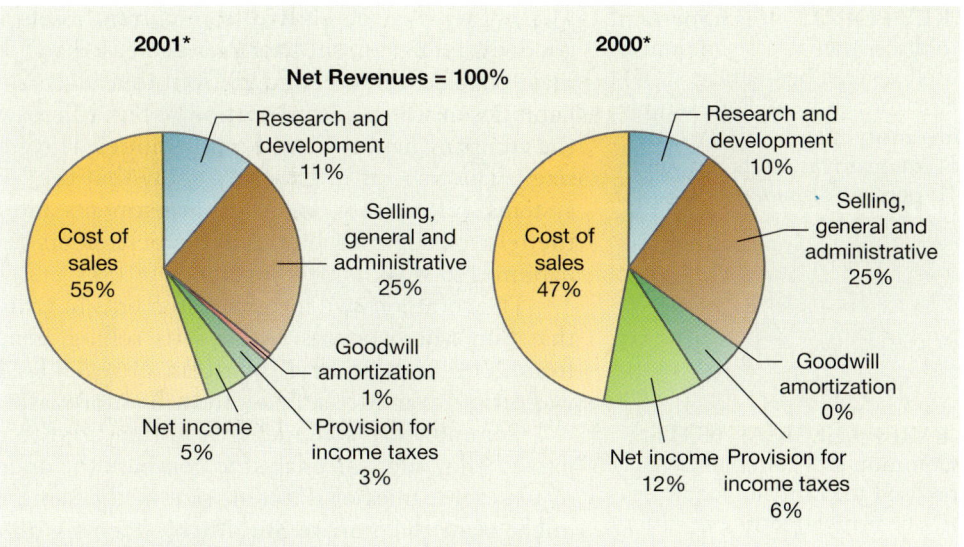

* Rounding causes some additions not to total precisely.
Note: Not all items are presented.

EXHIBIT 7
Common-Size Income Statements

Sun Microsystems, Inc.
Common-Size Income Statements
For the Years Ended June 30, 2001 and 2000

	2001*	2000*
Net revenues	100.0%	100.0%
Cost of sales	55.0	48.0
Gross margin	45.0%	52.0%
Operating expenses:		
Research and development	11.0%	10.4%
Selling, general, and administrative	24.9	25.9
Goodwill amortization	1.4	0.4
Purchased in-process R&D	0.4	0.1
Total operating expenses	37.8%	36.8%
Operating income	7.2%	15.2%
Other income (expense)	1.5	2.4
Income before income taxes	8.7%	17.6%
Provision for income taxes	3.3	5.8
Income before cumulative effect of change in accounting principle	5.4%	11.8%
Cumulative effect of change in accounting principle	(0.3)	—
Net income	5.1%	11.8%

*Rounding causes some additions and subtractions not to total precisely.
Source: Sun Microsystems, Inc., *Annual Report,* 2001.

KEY POINT: It is important to discern what base amount is used when a percentage describes an item. For example, inventory may be 50 percent of *total current assets* but only 10 percent of *total assets*.

PARENTHETICAL NOTE: Common-size statements can be used to compare characteristics of firms reporting in different currencies.

Microsystems' assets shifted from current assets and long-term investments toward goodwill, while current liabilities decreased and stockholders' equity increased. The main conclusions to be drawn from this analysis are that current assets and current liabilities make up a large portion of Sun Microsystems' financial structure and that the company has few long-term liabilities. The graphs in Figure 3 and the common-size balance sheets in Exhibit 6 show that the composition of assets at Sun Microsystems shifted from long-term investments and current assets toward goodwill. In the relationship of liabilities and stockholders' equity, there was a shift from total liabilities to stockholders' equity.

The common-size income statements in Exhibit 7, illustrated in Figure 4, show that Sun Microsystems reduced its selling, general, and administrative expenses from 2000 to 2001 by 1.0 percent of revenues (25.9% − 24.9%). This reduction was offset by an increase in goodwill amortization of 1.0 percent (1.4% − 0.4%).

Common-size statements are often used to make comparisons between companies. They allow an analyst to compare the operating and financing characteristics of two companies of different size in the same industry. For example, the analyst might want to compare Sun Microsystems with other companies in terms of percentage of total assets financed by debt or in terms of selling, general, and administrative expenses as a percentage of net revenues. Common-size statements would show those and other relationships.

RATIO ANALYSIS

Ratio analysis is a technique of financial performance evaluation that identifies meaningful relationships between the components of the financial statements. To be most meaningful, the interpretation of ratios must include a study of the underlying data. Ratios are useful guides or shortcuts in evaluating a company's financial position and operations and in comparing financial data for several years or for several companies. The primary purpose of ratios is to point out areas needing further investigation. To interpret ratios correctly, an analyst must have a general understanding of the company and its environment. Ratios may be expressed in several ways. For example, a ratio of net income of $100,000 to sales of $1,000,000 may be stated as:

1. Net income is 1/10 or 10 percent of sales.
2. The ratio of sales to net income is 10 to 1 (10:1), or sales are 10 times net income.
3. For every dollar of sales, the company has an average net income of 10 cents.

 Check out ACE for a Review Quiz at http://accounting.college.hmco.com/students.

COMPREHENSIVE ILLUSTRATION OF RATIO ANALYSIS

LO5 Apply ratio analysis to financial statements in a comprehensive evaluation of a company's financial performance.

RELATED TEXT ASSIGNMENTS
Q: 13, 14, 15, 16, 17, 18, 19
SE: 6, 7, 8, 9, 10
E: 5, 6, 7, 8, 9
P: 2, 3, 4, 5, 6
SD: 1, 6
FRA: 2, 3, 4, 5

www.sun.com

To illustrate how analysts apply ratio analysis to a company's financial statements in order to evaluate the company's financial situation, we will perform a comprehensive ratio analysis of Sun Microsystems' financial performance for 2000 and 2001. In the discussion and analysis section in Sun Microsystems' annual report, management states: "While we reported significant growth in our products net revenues on a year-over-year basis, all of this growth occurred in the first half of fiscal 2001. . . . If the current macro economic conditions persist, we expect demand, and therefore products net revenue in the first half of fiscal 2002, will be less than the comparable period in fiscal 2001."[5] These statements provide the context for evaluating Sun Microsystems' liquidity, profitability, long-term solvency, cash flow adequacy, and market strength. Most data for the analyses come from the financial statements presented in Exhibits 3 and 4. Other data are presented as needed.

EVALUATING LIQUIDITY

Liquidity is a company's ability to pay bills when they are due and to meet unexpected needs for cash. All the ratios that relate to liquidity involve working capital or some part of it, because it is out of working capital that debts are paid. The objective of liquidity is also closely related to the cash flow ratios.

KEY POINT: When examining ratios in published sources, be aware that publishers often redefine the content of the ratios provided by companies. While the general content is similar, variations occur. Be sure to evaluate exactly what information a published source says it uses to calculate its ratios.

The liquidity ratios from 2000 to 2001 for Sun Microsystems are presented in Exhibit 8. The **current ratio** and the **quick ratio** are measures of short-term debt-paying ability. The principal difference between the two is that the numerator of the current ratio includes inventories and prepaid expenses. Inventories take longer to convert to cash than do the current assets included in the numerator of the quick ratio. The quick ratio was 1.1 times in 2000 and 0.9 times in 2001. The current ratio was 1.5 times in both years primarily because current assets and current liabilities grew at similar rates. However, the composition of current assets shows a decline in quick ratio assets offset by increases in the remaining current assets.

Two major components of current assets, receivables and inventories, show improving trends. The relative size of the accounts receivable and the effectiveness of credit policies are measured by the **receivable turnover**, which rose from 6.3 times in 2000 to 6.5 times in 2001. The related ratio of **average days' sales uncollected** decreased by about one day, from 57.9 days in 2000 to 56.2 days in 2001. The major change in this category of ratios is in the inventory turnover. The **inventory turnover**, which measures the relative size of inventories, worsened. Inventory turnover decreased from 17.4 times in 2000 to 12.5 times in 2001. This results in an unfavorable increase in **average days' inventory on hand**, from 21.0 days in 2000 to 29.2 days in 2001. When taken together this means that Sun Microsystems' **operating cycle**, or the time it takes to sell products and collect for them, increased from 78.9 days in 2000 (57.9 days + 21.0 days or the average days' sales uncollected plus the average days' inventory on hand) to 85.4 days in 2001 (56.2 days + 29.2 days). Related to the operating cycle is the number of days the company takes to pay its accounts payable. The **payables turnover** increased from 9.3 times in 2000 to 10.7 times in 2001. This results in average days' payable of 39.2 days in 2000 and 34.1 days in 2001. Thus, if the **average days' payable** is subtracted from the operating cycle, the financing period, or days of financing required, are 39.7 days in 2000 and 51.3 days in 2001, a significant decline (see Figure 5). Overall, Sun Microsystems' liquidity declined.

● STOP AND THINK!
Why does a decrease in receivable turnover or inventory turnover create the need for cash from operating activities?
When receivable turnover or inventory turnover decreases, it means that the company has more average days' sales uncollected or more average days' inventory on hand to finance. Consequently, the company needs more cash to pay for the increase in receivables or inventory. ■

FIGURE 5
Financing Period for Sun Microsystems, 2001

EXHIBIT 8
Liquidity Ratios of Sun Microsystems, Inc.

(Dollar amounts in millions)	2001	2000

Current ratio: Measure of short-term debt-paying ability

$$\frac{\text{Current Assets}}{\text{Current Liabilities}} \qquad \frac{\$7,934}{\$5,146} = 1.5 \text{ times} \qquad \frac{\$6,877}{\$4,546} = 1.5 \text{ times}$$

Quick ratio: Measure of short-term debt-paying ability

$$\frac{\text{Cash + Marketable Securities + Receivables}}{\text{Current Liabilities}} \qquad \frac{\$1,472 + \$387 + \$2,955}{\$5,146} \qquad \frac{\$1,849 + \$626 + \$2,690}{\$4,546}$$

$$= \frac{\$4,814}{\$5,146} = .9 \text{ times} \qquad = \frac{\$5,165}{\$4,546} = 1.1 \text{ times}$$

Receivable turnover: Measure of relative size of accounts receivable and effectiveness of credit policies

$$\frac{\text{Net Sales}}{\text{Average Accounts Receivable}} \qquad \frac{\$18,250}{(\$2,955 + \$2,690) \div 2} \qquad \frac{\$15,721}{\$2,690 + \$2,287^* \div 2}$$

$$= \frac{\$18,250}{\$2,823} = 6.5 \text{ times} \qquad = \frac{\$15,721}{\$2,489} = 6.3 \text{ times}$$

Average days' sales uncollected: Measure of average days taken to collect receivables

$$\frac{\text{Days in Year}}{\text{Receivable Turnover}} \qquad \frac{365 \text{ days}}{6.5 \text{ times}} = 56.2 \text{ days} \qquad = \frac{365 \text{ days}}{6.3 \text{ times}} = 57.9 \text{ days}$$

Inventory turnover: Measure of relative size of inventory

$$\frac{\text{Costs of Goods Sold}}{\text{Average Inventory}} \qquad \frac{\$10,041}{(\$1,049 + \$557) \div 2} \qquad \frac{\$7,549}{\$557 + \$308^* \div 2}$$

$$= \frac{\$10,041}{\$803} = 12.5 \text{ times} \qquad = \frac{\$7,549}{\$433} = 17.4 \text{ times}$$

Average days' inventory on hand: Measure of average days taken to sell inventory

$$\frac{\text{Days in Year}}{\text{Inventory Turnover}} \qquad \frac{365 \text{ days}}{12.5 \text{ times}} = 29.2 \text{ days} \qquad = \frac{365 \text{ days}}{17.4 \text{ times}} = 21.0 \text{ days}$$

Payables turnover: Measure of relative size of accounts payable

$$\frac{\text{Costs of Goods Sold +/- Change in Inventory}}{\text{Average Accounts Payable}} \qquad \frac{\$10,041 + \$492}{(\$1,050 + \$924) \div 2} \qquad \frac{\$7,549 + \$249^*}{(\$924 + \$754^*) \div 2}$$

$$= \frac{\$10,533}{\$987} = 10.7 \text{ times} \qquad = \frac{\$7,798}{\$839} = 9.3 \text{ times}$$

Average days' payable: Measure of average days taken to pay accounts payable

$$\frac{\text{Days in Year}}{\text{Payables Turnover}} \qquad = \frac{365 \text{ days}}{10.7 \text{ times}} = 34.1 \text{ days} \qquad = \frac{365 \text{ days}}{9.3 \text{ times}} = 39.2 \text{ days}$$

*1999 figures are derived from the statement of cash flows in Sun Microsystems' annual report.
Source: Sun Microsystems, Inc., *Annual Report,* 2001.

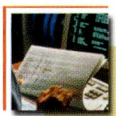

FOCUS ON BUSINESS PRACTICE

There's More Than One Way to Measure Profitability.

Efforts to link management compensation to the company's performance measures and to the creation of shareholder wealth are increasing. One such measure compares the company's return on assets with the cost of debt and equity capital. If the return on assets exceeds the cost of financing the assets with debt and equity, then management is indeed creating value for the shareholders. This measure is referred to in various ways. The originators refer to it as *Economic Value Added*, or *EVA*®. Coca-Cola <www.coca-cola.com>, which uses this measure to evaluate management performance, calls it by its more generic name, *economic profit*. In its annual report, Coca-Cola reports economic profit along with other key financial measures, such as free cash flow and return on equity.

EVALUATING PROFITABILITY

Profitability relates to a company's ability to earn a satisfactory income so that investors and stockholders will continue to provide capital to the company. Profitability is also closely linked to liquidity because earnings ultimately produce cash flow. For this reason, evaluating profitability is important to both investors and creditors. The profitability ratios of Sun Microsystems, Inc., are shown in Exhibit 9.

Profit margin, which measures the net income produced by each dollar of sales, decreased from 11.8 to 5.1 percent. **Asset turnover**, which measures how efficiently

EXHIBIT 9
Profitability Ratios of Sun Microsystems, Inc.

(Dollar amounts in millions)	2001	2000

Profit margin: Measure of net income produced by each dollar of sales

$$\frac{\text{Net Income}}{\text{Net Sales}} \qquad \frac{\$927}{\$18,250} = 5.1\% \qquad \frac{\$1,854}{\$15,721} = 11.8\%$$

Asset turnover: Measure of how efficiently assets are used to produce sales

$$\frac{\text{Net Sales}}{\text{Average Total Assets}} \qquad \frac{\$18,250}{(\$18,181+\$14,152) \div 2} \qquad \frac{\$15,721}{(\$14,152+\$8,499^*) \div 2}$$

$$= \frac{\$18,250}{\$16,167} = 1.1 \text{ times} \qquad = \frac{\$15,721}{\$11,326} = 1.4 \text{ times}$$

Return on assets: Measure of overall earning power or profitability

$$\frac{\text{Net Income}}{\text{Average Total Assets}} \qquad \frac{\$927}{\$16,167} = 5.7\% \qquad \frac{\$1,854}{\$11,326} = 16.4\%$$

Return on equity: Measure of the profitability of stockholders' investments

$$\frac{\text{Net Income}}{\text{Average Stockholders' Equity}} \qquad \frac{\$927}{(\$10,586 + \$7,309) \div 2} \qquad \frac{\$1,854}{(\$7,309 + \$4,867^*) \div 2}$$

$$= \frac{\$927}{\$8,948} = 10.4\% \qquad = \frac{\$1,854}{\$6,088} = 30.5\%$$

*1999 figures are from the 11-year financial history and the statement of stockholders' equity in Sun Microsystems' annual report.
Source: Sun Microsystems, Inc., *Annual Report,* 2001.

ENRICHMENT NOTE: In both asset turnover and return on assets, the analysis is improved if only productive assets are used in the calculations. For example, unfinished new plant construction or investments in obsolete or nonoperating plants could be removed from the asset base to give a better picture of the productivity of assets.

KEY POINT: Profit often is expressed in different ways in accounting literature. Examples are income before income taxes, income after income taxes, and net operating income. Being aware of the content of net income data in profitability ratios enables analysts to draw appropriate conclusions about the results of ratio computations.

assets are used to produce sales, decreased from 1.4 to 1.1 times. The result is a decrease in the company's earning power, or **return on assets**, from 16.4 percent in 2000 to 5.7 percent in 2001. These computations show the relationships:

Profit Margin		Asset Turnover		Return on Assets
$\dfrac{\text{Net Income}}{\text{Net Sales}}$	×	$\dfrac{\text{Net Sales}}{\text{Average Total Assets}}$	=	$\dfrac{\text{Net Income}}{\text{Average Total Assets}}$
2000 11.8%	×	1.4	=	16.5%
2001 5.1%	×	1.1	=	5.6%

(The small difference in the two sets of return on assets figures results from the rounding of the ratios.) The profitability of stockholders' investments, or **return on equity**, also declined, from 30.5 percent in 2000 to 10.4 percent in 2001.

Although we have used net income in computing profitability ratios for Sun Microsystems, net income is not always a good indicator of a company's sustainable earnings. For instance, if a company has discontinued operations, then income from continuing operations may be a better measure of sustainable earnings. For a company that has one-time items on the income statement, such as restructurings, gains, or losses, income from operations before these items may be a better measure. Some analysts like to use earnings before interest and taxes, or EBIT, for the earnings measure because it excludes the effects of the company's borrowings and the tax rates from the analysis. Whatever figure one uses for earnings, it is important to try to determine the effects of various components on future operations.

EVALUATING LONG-TERM SOLVENCY

Long-term solvency has to do with a company's ability to survive for many years. The aim of long-term solvency analysis is to detect early signs that a company is headed for financial difficulty. Studies have indicated that accounting ratios can show as much as five years in advance that a company may fail.[6] Declining profitability and liquidity ratios are key indicators of possible business failure. Two other ratios that analysts often consider when assessing long-term solvency are debt to equity and interest coverage, which are shown in Exhibit 10.

Increasing amounts of debt in a company's capital structure mean the company is becoming more heavily leveraged. Because of increasing legal obligations to pay

EXHIBIT 10
Long-Term Solvency Ratios of Sun Microsystems, Inc.

(Dollar amounts in millions)	2001	2000
Debt to equity ratio: Measure of capital structure and leverage		
$\dfrac{\text{Total Liabilities}}{\text{Stockholders' Equity}}$	$\dfrac{\$7{,}595}{\$10{,}586}$ = .7 times	$\dfrac{\$6{,}843}{\$7{,}309}$ = .9 times
Interest coverage ratio: Measure of creditors' protection from default on interest payments		
$\dfrac{\text{Income Before Income Taxes + Interest Expense}}{\text{Interest Expense}}$	$\dfrac{\$1{,}584 + \$100}{\$100}$ = 16.8 times	$\dfrac{\$2{,}771 + \$84}{\$84}$ = 34.0 times

Source: Sun Microsystems, Inc., *Annual Report*, 2001.

KEY POINT: Liquidity is a firm's ability to meet its current obligations, whereas solvency is a firm's ability to meet its maturing obligations as they come due, without losing the ability to continue operations.

interest periodically and the principal at maturity, this condition negatively affects long-term solvency. Failure to make those payments can result in bankruptcy. The **debt to equity ratio** measures capital structure and leverage by showing the amount of assets provided by creditors in relation to the amount provided by stockholders. Sun Microsystems' debt to equity ratio was only .9 times in 2000 and .7 times in 2001. Recall from Exhibit 3 that the company has primarily short-term debt and little long-term debt. It also has ample current assets, as reflected by the current ratio. All these are positive indications of Sun Microsystem's long-term solvency. Management sums up the company's position as follows: "We believe our level of financial resources is a significant competitive factor in our industry and we may choose at any time to raise additional capital through debt or equity financing to strengthen our financial position, facilitate growth, and provide us with additional flexibility to take advantage of business opportunities that may arise."[7]

If debt is risky, why have any? The answer is that the level of debt is a matter of balance. Despite its riskiness, debt is a flexible means of financing certain business operations. Sun Microsystems is using debt to finance a temporary increase in inventory. The interest paid on that debt is deductible for income tax purposes, whereas dividends on stock are not. Because debt usually carries a fixed interest charge, the cost of financing can be limited, and leverage can be used to advantage. If the company is able to earn a return on assets greater than the cost of interest, it makes an overall profit. In addition, there are advantages to being a debtor in periods of inflation because the debt, which is a fixed dollar amount, can be repaid with cheaper dollars. However, the company runs the risk of not earning a return on assets equal to the cost of financing those assets, thereby incurring a loss.

ENRICHMENT NOTE: Because of innovative financing plans and other means of acquiring assets, a beneficial modern-day ratio is the fixed charges ratio. This ratio includes interest, lease payments, and all other fixed obligations that must be met through earnings.

The **interest coverage ratio** measures the degree of protection creditors have from a default on interest payments. Because of its small amount of long-term debt, Sun Microsystems had interest coverage ratios of 34.0 times in 2000 and 16.8 times in 2001. Interest coverage, though declining, is not a problem for the company.

EVALUATING CASH FLOW ADEQUACY

Because cash flows are needed to pay debts when they are due, cash flow measures are closely related to liquidity and long-term solvency. Sun Microsystems' cash flow adequacy ratios are presented in Exhibit 11. By most measures, the company's ability to generate positive operating cash flows declined from 2000 to 2001. Key to those decreases is that net cash flows from operating activities had a large decrease, from $3,754 million in 2000 to $2,089 million in 2001, while net sales and average total assets increased. **Cash flow yield**, or the relationship of cash flows from operating activities to net income, increased from 2.0 to 2.3 because net income declined faster than net cash flows from operating activities. **Cash flows to sales**, or the ability of sales to generate operating cash flows, decreased from 23.9 to 11.4 percent. **Cash flows to assets**, or the ability of assets to generate operating cash flows, decreased from 33.1 to 12.9 percent.

Free cash flow, the cash generated after providing for commitments, also decreased but remains positive even though capital expenditures increased while net cash flows from operating activities decreased. Another factor is that the company pays no dividends. Management's comment with regard to cash flows in the future is, "We believe that the liquidity provided by existing cash, cash equivalents, and non-strategic investments, along with our borrowing arrangements and cash generated from operations, will provide sufficient capital to meet our requirements for at least the next 12 months."[8]

EVALUATING MARKET STRENGTH

The market price of a company's stock is of interest to the analyst because it represents what investors as a whole think of the company at a point in time. Market price is the price at which the stock is bought and sold. It provides information

Exhibit 11
Cash Flow Adequacy Ratios of Sun Microsystems, Inc.

(Dollar amounts in millions)	2001	2000

Cash flow yield: Measure of the ability to generate operating cash flows in relation to net income

$$\frac{\text{Net Cash Flows from Operating Activities}}{\text{Net Income}} \qquad \frac{\$2{,}089^*}{\$927} = 2.3 \text{ times} \qquad \frac{\$3{,}754^*}{\$1{,}854} = 2.0 \text{ times}$$

Cash flows to sales: Measure of the ability of sales to generate operating cash flows

$$\frac{\text{Net Cash Flows from Operating Activities}}{\text{Net Sales}} \qquad \frac{\$2{,}089^*}{\$18{,}250} = 11.4\% \qquad \frac{\$3{,}754^*}{\$15{,}721} = 23.9\%$$

Cash flows to assets: Measure of the ability of assets to generate operating cash flows

$$\frac{\text{Net Cash Flows from Operating Activities}}{\text{Average Total Assets}} \qquad \frac{\$2{,}089^*}{(\$18{,}181 + \$14{,}152) \div 2} \qquad \frac{\$3{,}754^*}{(\$14{,}152 + \$8{,}499^\dagger) \div 2}$$

$$= \frac{\$2{,}089}{\$16{,}167} = 12.9\% \qquad = \frac{\$3{,}754}{\$11{,}326} = 33.1\%$$

Free cash flow: Measure of cash generated or cash deficiency after providing for commitments

Net Cash Flows from Operating Activities − Dividends − Net Capital Expenditures

$$\$2{,}089^* - \$0 - \$1{,}292^* = \$797 \qquad \$3{,}754^* - \$0 - \$982^* = \$2{,}772$$

*These figures are from the statements of cash flows in Sun Microsystems' annual report.
†The 1999 figure is from the 11-year financial history in Sun Microsystems' annual report.
Source: Sun Microsystems, Inc., *Annual Report,* 2001.

Exhibit 12
Market Strength Ratios of Sun Microsystems, Inc.

	2001	2000

Price/earnings (P/E) ratio: Measure of investor confidence in a company

$$\frac{\text{Market Price per Share}}{\text{Earnings per Share}} \qquad \frac{\$18.21^*}{\$.28} = 65.0 \text{ times} \qquad \frac{\$43.47^*}{\$.59} = 73.7 \text{ times}$$

Dividends yield: Measure of a stock's current return to an investor

$$\frac{\text{Dividends per Share}}{\text{Market Price per Share}} \qquad \text{Sun Microsystems does not pay a dividend.}$$

*Market price is from Sun Microsystems' annual report.
Source: Sun Microsystems, Inc., *Annual Report,* 2001.

about how investors view the potential return and risk connected with owning the company's stock. Market price by itself is not very informative for this purpose, however. Companies differ in number of outstanding shares and amount of underlying earnings and dividends. Thus, market price must be related to earnings by considering the price/earnings ratio and the dividends yield. Those ratios for Sun Microsystems appear in Exhibit 12 and have been computed using the market prices for Sun Microsystems' stock at the end of 2000 and 2001.

The **price/earnings (P/E) ratio**, which measures investor confidence in a company, is the ratio of the market price per share to earnings per share. The P/E ratio is useful in comparing the relative values placed on the earnings of different companies and in comparing the value placed on a company's shares in relation to the overall market. With a lower P/E ratio, the investor obtains more underlying earnings per dollar invested.

Sun Microsystems' P/E ratio decreased from 73.7 times in 2000 to 65.0 times in 2001, which signals that investors have less confidence in the company. The **dividends yield** measures a stock's current return to an investor in the form of dividends. Because Sun Microsystems pays no dividend, it may be concluded that investors expect their return to come from increases in the stock's market value.

SUMMARY OF THE FINANCIAL ANALYSIS OF SUN MICROSYSTEMS, INC.

Our analysis clearly shows that Sun Microsystems' financial condition declined from 2000 to 2001, as measured by its liquidity, profitability, long-term solvency, and cash flow adequacy ratios. This performance resulted in a lower market price per share.

Check out ACE for a Review Quiz at http://accounting.college.hmco.com/students.

Chapter Review

REVIEW OF LEARNING OBJECTIVES

LO1 Describe and discuss financial performance evaluation by internal and external users.

Managers set objectives for their company's financial performance, carry out plans to achieve those objectives, and review and report the results by comparing the objectives with actual performance. Creditors and investors, as well as managers, use financial performance evaluation to judge the past performance and current position of a company, and also to judge its future potential and the risk associated with it. Creditors use the information gained from their evaluation to make reliable loans that will be repaid with interest. Investors use the information to make investments that will provide a return that is worth the risk. The Sarbanes-Oxley Act is intended to improve investor confidence in the financial reporting system.

LO2 Describe and discuss the standards for financial performance evaluation.

Three commonly used standards for financial performance evaluation are rule-of-thumb measures, the company's past performance, and industry norms. Rule-of-thumb measures are weak because of the lack of evidence that they can be widely applied. The past performance of a company can offer a guideline for measuring improvement but is not helpful in judging performance relative to other companies. Although the use of industry norms overcomes this last problem, its disadvantage is that firms are not always comparable, even in the same industry.

LO3 Identify the sources of information for financial performance evaluation.

The main sources of information about publicly held corporations are company-published reports, such as annual reports and interim financial statements; SEC reports; business periodicals; and credit and investment advisory services.

LO4 Apply horizontal analysis, trend analysis, vertical analysis, and ratio analysis to financial statements.

Horizontal analysis involves the computation of changes in both dollar amounts and percentages from year to year. Trend analysis is an extension of horizontal analysis in that it calculates percentage changes for several years. The changes are computed by setting a base year equal to 100 and calculating the results for subsequent years as percentages of that base year. Vertical analysis uses percentages to show the relationship of the component parts to a total in a single statement. The resulting financial statements, which are expressed entirely in percentages, are called common-size statements. Ratio analysis is a technique of financial performance evaluation that identifies meaningful relationships between the components of the financial statements.

LO5 Apply ratio analysis to financial statements in a comprehensive evaluation of a company's financial performance.

A comprehensive ratio analysis includes the evaluation of a company's liquidity, profitability, long-term solvency, cash flow adequacy, and market strength. The ratios for measuring these characteristics are shown in Exhibits 8 to 12.

REVIEW OF CONCEPTS AND TERMINOLOGY

The following concepts and terms were introduced in this chapter:

LO5 **Asset turnover:** Net sales divided by average total assets; a measure of how efficiently assets are used to produce sales.

LO5 **Average days' inventory on hand:** Days in the year divided by inventory turnover; a measure that shows the average number of days taken to sell inventory.

LO5 **Average days' payable:** Days in the year divided by payables turnover; a measure that shows the average number of days taken to pay accounts payable.

LO5 **Average days' sales uncollected:** Days in the year divided by receivable turnover; a measure that shows the number of days, on average, that a company must wait to receive payment for credit sales.

LO4 **Base year:** In financial analysis, the first year to be considered in any set of data.

LO5 **Cash flows to assets:** Net cash flows from operating activities divided by average total assets; a measure of the ability of assets to generate operating cash flows.

LO5 **Cash flows to sales:** Net cash flows from operating activities divided by net sales; a measure of the ability of sales to generate operating cash flows.

LO5 **Cash flow yield:** Net cash flows from operating activities divided by net income; a measure of a company's ability to generate operating cash flows in relation to net income.

LO4 **Common-size statement:** A financial statement in which the components of a total figure are stated in terms of percentages of that total.

LO5 **Current ratio:** Current assets divided by current liabilities; a measure of short-term debt-paying ability.

LO5 **Debt to equity ratio:** Total liabilities divided by stockholders' equity; a measure that shows the relationship of debt financing to equity financing, or the extent to which a company is leveraged.

LO2 **Diversified companies:** Companies that operate in more than one industry. Also called *conglomerates*.

LO5 **Dividends yield:** Dividends per share divided by market price per share; a measure of a stock's current return to an investor.

LO1 **Financial performance evaluation:** All the techniques used to show important relationships in financial statements and to relate them to important financial objectives. Also called *financial statement analysis*.

LO5 **Free cash flow:** Net cash flows from operating activities minus dividends minus net capital expenditures; a measure of cash generated or cash deficiency after providing for commitments.

LO4 **Horizontal analysis:** A technique for analyzing financial statements that involves the computation of changes from the previous to the current year in both dollar amounts and percentages.

LO4	**Index number:**	In trend analysis, a number that shows changes in related items over time, which is calculated by setting the base year equal to 100 percent.
LO5	**Interest coverage ratio:**	Income before income taxes plus interest expense divided by interest expense; a measure of the degree of protection creditors have from default on interest payments.
LO3	**Interim financial statements:**	Financial statements issued for a period of less than one year, usually a quarter or a month.
LO5	**Inventory turnover:**	The cost of goods sold divided by average inventory; a measure of the relative size of inventory.
LO5	**Operating cycle:**	Average days' inventory on hand plus average days' sales uncollected; the time it takes to sell products and collect for them.
LO5	**Payables turnover:**	Cost of goods sold plus or minus change in inventory divided by average accounts payable; a measure of the relative size of accounts payable.
LO1	**Portfolio:**	A group of loans or investments designed to average the returns and risks of a creditor or investor.
LO5	**Price/earnings (P/E) ratio:**	Market price per share divided by earnings per share; a measure of investor confidence in a company and a means of comparing stock values.
LO5	**Profit margin:**	Net income divided by net sales; a measure that shows the percentage of each revenue dollar that contributes to net income.
LO5	**Quick ratio:**	The more liquid current assets—cash, marketable securities or short-term investments, and receivables—divided by current liabilities; a measure of short-term debt-paying ability.
LO4	**Ratio analysis:**	A technique of financial performance evaluation that identifies meaningful relationships between the components of the financial statements.
LO5	**Receivable turnover:**	Net sales divided by average accounts receivable; a measure of the relative size of accounts receivable and the effectiveness of credit policies.
LO5	**Return on assets:**	Net income divided by average total assets; a measure of overall earning power, or profitability, that shows the amount earned on each dollar of assets invested.
LO5	**Return on equity:**	Net income divided by average stockholders' equity; a measure of how much income was earned on each dollar invested by stockholders.
LO1	**Sarbanes-Oxley Act:**	Legislation passed by the U.S. Congress to improve the financial reporting system.
LO4	**Trend analysis:**	A type of horizontal analysis in which percentage changes are calculated for several successive years instead of for two years.
LO4	**Vertical analysis:**	A technique for analyzing financial statements that uses percentages to show the relationships of the different parts to a total in a single statement.

REVIEW PROBLEM

Comparative Analysis of Two Companies

LO5

Maggie Washington is considering an investment in one of two fast-food restaurant chains because she believes the trend toward eating out more often will continue. She has narrowed her choices to Quik Burger and Big Steak, whose balance sheets and income statements are presented on the next page.

The statements of cash flows show that net cash flows from operating activities were $2,200,000 for Quik Burger and $3,000,000 for Big Steak. Net capital expenditures were $2,100,000 for Quik Burger and $1,800,000 for Big Steak. Dividends of $500,000 were paid by Quik Burger and $600,000 by Big Steak. The market prices of the stocks of Quik Burger and Big Steak were $30 and $20, respectively. Financial information pertaining to prior years is not readily available to Maggie Washington. Assume that all

Balance Sheets
December 31, 20xx
(in thousands)

	Quik Burger	Big Steak
Assets		
Cash	$ 2,000	$ 4,500
Accounts receivable (net)	2,000	6,500
Inventory	2,000	5,000
Property, plant, and equipment (net)	20,000	35,000
Other assets	4,000	5,000
Total assets	$30,000	$56,000
Liabilities and Stockholders' Equity		
Accounts payable	$ 2,500	$ 3,000
Notes payable	1,500	4,000
Bonds payable	10,000	30,000
Common stock, $1 par value	1,000	3,000
Paid-in capital in excess of par value, common	9,000	9,000
Retained earnings	6,000	7,000
Total liabilities and stockholders' equity	$30,000	$56,000

Income Statements
For the Year Ended December 31, 20xx
(in thousands, except per share amounts)

	Quik Burger	Big Steak
Net sales	$53,000	$86,000
Costs and expenses		
Cost of goods sold	$37,000	$61,000
Selling expenses	7,000	10,000
Administrative expenses	4,000	5,000
Total costs and expenses	$48,000	$76,000
Income from operations	$ 5,000	$10,000
Interest expense	1,400	3,200
Income before income taxes	$ 3,600	$ 6,800
Income taxes	1,800	3,400
Net income	$ 1,800	$ 3,400
Earnings per share	$ 1.80	$ 1.13

notes payable of these two companies are current liabilities and that all their bonds payable are long-term liabilities.

REQUIRED ▶ Conduct a comprehensive ratio analysis of Quik Burger and Big Steak and compare the results. Perform the analysis by following the steps outlined below. Use end-of-year balances for averages, assume no change in inventory, and round all ratios and percentages to one decimal place.

1. Prepare an analysis of liquidity.
2. Prepare an analysis of profitability.
3. Prepare an analysis of long-term solvency.
4. Prepare an analysis of cash flow adequacy.
5. Prepare an analysis of market strength.
6. Indicate in each analysis the company that apparently had the more favorable ratio. (Consider differences of .1 or less to be neutral.)
7. In what ways would having access to prior years' information aid this analysis?

ANSWER TO REVIEW PROBLEM

Ratio Name	Quik Burger	Big Steak	6. Company with More Favorable Ratio*
1. Liquidity analysis			
a. Current ratio	$\frac{\$2,000 + \$2,000 + \$2,000}{\$2,500 + \$1,500}$ $= \frac{\$6,000}{\$4,000} = 1.5$ times	$\frac{\$4,500 + \$6,500 + \$5,000}{\$3,000 + \$4,000}$ $= \frac{\$16,000}{\$7,000} = 2.3$ times	Big Steak
b. Quick ratio	$\frac{\$2,000 + \$2,000}{\$2,500 + \$1,500}$ $= \frac{\$4,000}{\$4,000} = 1.0$ times	$\frac{\$4,500 + \$6,500}{\$3,000 + \$4,000}$ $= \frac{\$11,000}{\$7,000} = 1.6$ times	Big Steak
c. Receivable turnover	$\frac{\$53,000}{\$2,000} = 26.5$ times	$\frac{\$86,000}{\$6,500} = 13.2$ times	Quik Burger
d. Average days' sales uncollected	$\frac{365}{26.5} = 13.8$ days	$\frac{365}{13.2} = 27.7$ days	Quik Burger
e. Inventory turnover	$\frac{\$37,000}{\$2,000} = 18.5$ times	$\frac{\$61,000}{\$5,000} = 12.2$ times	Quik Burger
f. Average days' inventory on hand	$\frac{365}{18.5} = 19.7$ days	$\frac{365}{12.2} = 29.9$ days	Quik Burger
g. Payables turnover	$\frac{\$37,000 + \$0}{\$2,500} = 14.8$ times	$\frac{\$61,000 + \$0}{\$3,000} = 20.3$ times	Quik Burger
h. Average days' payable	$\frac{365}{14.8} = 24.7$ days	$\frac{365}{20.3} = 18.0$ days	Quik Burger
2. Profitability analysis			
a. Profit margin	$\frac{\$1,800}{\$53,000} = 3.4\%$	$\frac{\$3,400}{\$86,000} = 4.0\%$	Big Steak

*This analysis indicates the company with the apparently more favorable ratio. Class discussion may focus on conditions under which different conclusions may be drawn.

Ratio Name	Quik Burger	Big Steak	6. Company with More Favorable Ratio
b. Asset turnover	$\dfrac{\$53{,}000}{\$30{,}000} = 1.8$ times	$\dfrac{\$86{,}000}{\$56{,}000} = 1.5$ times	Quik Burger
c. Return on assets	$\dfrac{\$1{,}800}{\$30{,}000} = 6.0\%$	$\dfrac{\$3{,}400}{\$56{,}000} = 6.1\%$	Neutral
d. Return on equity	$\dfrac{\$1{,}800}{\$1{,}000 + \$9{,}000 + \$6{,}000}$ $= \dfrac{\$1{,}800}{\$16{,}000} = 11.3\%$	$\dfrac{\$3{,}400}{\$3{,}000 + \$9{,}000 + \$7{,}000}$ $= \dfrac{\$3{,}400}{\$19{,}000} = 17.9\%$	Big Steak

3. **Long-term solvency analysis**

a. Debt to equity ratio	$\dfrac{\$2{,}500 + \$1{,}500 + \$10{,}000}{\$1{,}000 + \$9{,}000 + \$6{,}000}$ $= \dfrac{\$14{,}000}{\$16{,}000} = .9$ times	$\dfrac{\$3{,}000 + \$4{,}000 + \$30{,}000}{\$3{,}000 + \$9{,}000 + \$7{,}000}$ $= \dfrac{\$37{,}000}{\$19{,}000} = 1.9$ times	Quik Burger
b. Interest coverage ratio	$\dfrac{\$3{,}600 + \$1{,}400}{\$1{,}400}$ $= \dfrac{\$5{,}000}{\$1{,}400} = 3.6$ times	$\dfrac{\$6{,}800 + \$3{,}200}{\$3{,}200}$ $= \dfrac{\$10{,}000}{\$3{,}200} = 3.1$ times	Quik Burger

4. **Cash flow adequacy analysis**

a. Cash flow yield	$\dfrac{\$2{,}200}{\$1{,}800} = 1.2$ times	$\dfrac{\$3{,}000}{\$3{,}400} = .9$ times	Quik Burger
b. Cash flows to sales	$\dfrac{\$2{,}200}{\$53{,}000} = 4.2\%$	$\dfrac{\$3{,}000}{\$86{,}000} = 3.5\%$	Quik Burger
c. Cash flows to assets	$\dfrac{\$2{,}200}{\$30{,}000} = 7.3\%$	$\dfrac{\$3{,}000}{\$56{,}000} = 5.4\%$	Quik Burger
d. Free cash flow	$\$2{,}200 - \$500 - \$2{,}100$ $= (\$400)$	$\$3{,}000 - \$600 - \$1{,}800$ $= \$600$	Big Steak

5. **Market strength analysis**

a. Price/earnings ratio	$\dfrac{\$30}{\$1.80} = 16.7$ times	$\dfrac{\$20}{\$1.13} = 17.7$ times	Big Steak
b. Dividends yield	$\dfrac{\$500{,}000/1{,}000{,}000}{\$30} = 1.7\%$	$\dfrac{\$600{,}000/3{,}000{,}000}{\$20} = 1.0\%$	Quik Burger

7. **Usefulness of prior years' information**

Prior years' information would be helpful in two ways. First, turnover, return, and cash flows to assets ratios could be based on average amounts. Second, a trend analysis could be performed for each company.

Chapter Assignments

BUILDING YOUR KNOWLEDGE FOUNDATION

QUESTIONS

1. What actions related to financial performance evaluation does management take at each stage of the management cycle?
2. What are the five categories of business objectives included in a financial plan, and how does each relate to financial performance?
3. What are the differences and similarities in the ways investors and creditors use financial performance evaluation?
4. What is the purpose of the Sarbanes-Oxley Act, and what are its main provisions?
5. What determines the riskiness of a loan or investment?
6. What standards of comparison are commonly used to evaluate financial performance, and what are their relative merits?
7. Why would a financial analyst compare the ratios of Steelco, a steel company, with the ratios of other companies in the steel industry? What factors might invalidate such a comparison?
8. Where may an investor look for information about a publicly held company in which he or she is thinking of investing?
9. Why would an investor want to see both horizontal and trend analyses of a company's financial statements?
10. What does the following sentence mean: "Based on 1990 equaling 100, net income increased from 240 in 1997 to 260 in 1998"?
11. What is the difference between horizontal analysis and vertical analysis?
12. What information does ratio analysis provide? How can the information provided by ratio analysis be used?
13. Under what circumstances would a current ratio of 3:1 be good? Under what circumstances would it be bad?
14. In a period of high interest rates, why are receivable turnover and inventory turnover especially important?
15. The following statements were made on page 35 of the November 6, 1978, issue of *Fortune* magazine: "Supermarket executives are beginning to look back with some nostalgia on the days when the standard profit margin was 1 percent of sales. Last year the industry overall margin came to a thin 0.72 percent. "How could a supermarket earn a satisfactory return on assets with such a small profit margin?
16. Company A and Company B both have net incomes of $1,000,000. Is it possible to say that these companies are equally successful? Why or why not?
17. Circo Company has a return on assets of 12 percent and a debt to equity ratio of .5. Would you expect return on equity to be more or less than 12 percent?
18. What amount is common to all cash flow adequacy ratios? To what other groups of ratios are the cash flow adequacy ratios most closely related?
19. The market price of Company J's stock is the same as that of Company Q's. How might you determine whether investors are equally confident about the future of these companies?

SHORT EXERCISES

LO1 Management Cycle and Financial Performance Evaluation

SE 1. Match the activities below with the appropriate stage in the management cycle: planning (P), executing (E), reviewing (RV), or reporting (RP).

1. Monitor key financial performance measures.
2. Carry out plans to achieve financial performance objectives.

3. Set financial performance objectives.
4. Report in a form that compares actual performance with objectives.
5. Determine causes of any deviations and propose corrective actions.

LO3 Sources of Information

SE 2. For each piece of information listed below, indicate whether the *best* source would be (a) reports published by the company, (b) SEC reports, (c) business periodicals, or (d) credit and investment advisory services.

1. Current market value of a company's stock
2. Management's analysis of the past year's operations
3. Objective assessment of a company's financial performance
4. Most complete body of financial disclosures
5. Current events affecting the company

LO4 Trend Analysis

SE 3. Using 20x4 as the base year, prepare a trend analysis for the following data, and tell whether the results suggest a favorable or unfavorable trend. (Round your answers to one decimal place.)

	20x6	20x5	20x4
Net sales	$158,000	$136,000	$112,000
Accounts receivable (net)	43,000	32,000	21,000

LO4 Horizontal Analysis

SE 4. The comparative income statements and balance sheets of SiteWorks, Inc., appear on the opposite page. Compute the amount and percentage changes for the income statements, and comment on the changes from 20x4 to 20x5. (Round the percentage changes to one decimal place.)

LO4 Vertical Analysis

SE 5. Express the comparative balance sheets of SiteWorks, Inc., as common-size statements, and comment on the changes from 20x4 to 20x5. (Round computations to one decimal place.)

LO5 Liquidity Analysis

SE 6. Using the information for SiteWorks, Inc., in **SE 4** and **SE 5,** compute the current ratio, quick ratio, receivable turnover, average days' sales uncollected, inventory turnover, average days' inventory on hand, payables turnover, and average days' payable for 20x4 and 20x5. Inventories were $4,000 in 20x3, $5,000 in 20x4, and $7,000 in 20x5. Accounts Receivable were $6,000 in 20x3, $8,000 in 20x4, and $10,000 in 20x5. Accounts Payable were $9,000 in 20x3, $10,000 in 20x4, and $12,000 in 20x5. The company had no marketable securities or prepaid assets. Comment on the results. (Round computations to one decimal place.)

LO5 Profitability Analysis

SE 7. Using the information for SiteWorks, Inc., in **SE 4** and **SE 5,** compute the profit margin, asset turnover, return on assets, and return on equity for 20x4 and 20x5. In 20x3, total assets were $100,000 and total stockholders' equity was $30,000. Comment on the results. (Round computations to one decimal place.)

LO5 Long-Term Solvency Analysis

SE 8. Using the information for SiteWorks, Inc., in **SE 4** and **SE 5,** compute the debt to equity ratio and the interest coverage ratio for 20x4 and 20x5. Comment on the results. (Round computations to one decimal place.)

LO5 Cash Flow Adequacy Analysis

SE 9. Using the information for SiteWorks, Inc., in **SE 4, SE 5,** and **SE 7,** compute the cash flow yield, cash flows to sales, cash flows to assets, and free cash flow for 20x4 and 20x5. Net cash flows from operating activities were $21,000 in 20x4 and $16,000 in 20x5. Net capital expenditures were $30,000 in 20x4 and $40,000 in 20x5. Cash dividends were $6,000 in both years. Comment on the results. (Round computations to one decimal place.)

LO5 Market Strength Analysis

SE 10. Using the information for SiteWorks, Inc., in **SE 4, SE 5,** and **SE 9,** compute the price/earnings ratio and dividends yield for 20x4 and 20x5. The company had 10,000 shares of common stock outstanding in both years. The price of SiteWorks' common stock was $30 in 20x4 and $20 in 20x5. Comment on the results. (Round computations to one decimal place.)

SiteWorks, Inc.
Comparative Income Statements
For the Years Ended December 31, 20x5 and 20x4

	20x5	20x4
Net sales	$180,000	$145,000
Cost of goods sold	112,000	88,000
Gross margin	$ 68,000	$ 57,000
Operating expenses	40,000	30,000
Operating income	$ 28,000	$ 27,000
Interest expense	7,000	5,000
Income before income taxes	$ 21,000	$ 22,000
Income taxes	7,000	8,000
Net income	$ 14,000	$ 14,000
Earnings per share	$ 1.40	$ 1.40

SiteWorks, Inc.
Comparative Balance Sheets
December 31, 20x5 and 20x4

	20x5	20x4
Assets		
Current assets	$ 24,000	$ 20,000
Property, plant, and equipment (net)	130,000	100,000
Total assets	$154,000	$120,000
Liabilities and Stockholders' Equity		
Current liabilities	$ 18,000	$ 22,000
Long-term liabilities	90,000	60,000
Stockholders' equity	46,000	38,000
Total liabilities and stockholders' equity	$154,000	$120,000

EXERCISES

E 1.
LO1 Objectives, Standards, and
LO2 Sources of Information for
LO3 Financial Performance Evaluation

Identify each of the following as (a) an objective of financial statement analysis, (b) a standard for financial statement analysis, or (c) a source of information for financial statement analysis:

1. Average ratios of other companies in the same industry
2. Assessment of the future potential of an investment
3. Interim financial statements
4. Past ratios of the company
5. SEC Form 10-K
6. Assessment of risk
7. A company's annual report

Chapter 28 Financial Performance Evaluation

LO4 Horizontal Analysis

E 2. Compute the amount and percentage changes for the following balance sheets, and comment on the changes from 20x3 to 20x4. (Round the percentage changes to one decimal place.)

Trumpet Company
Comparative Balance Sheets
December 31, 20x4 and 20x3

	20x4	20x3
Assets		
Current assets	$ 37,200	$ 25,600
Property, plant, and equipment (net)	218,928	194,400
Total assets	$256,128	$220,000
Liabilities and Stockholders' Equity		
Current liabilities	$ 22,400	$ 6,400
Long-term liabilities	70,000	80,000
Stockholders' equity	163,728	133,600
Total liabilities and stockholders' equity	$256,128	$220,000

LO4 Trend Analysis

E 3. Using 20x3 as the base year, prepare a trend analysis of the following data, and tell whether the situation shown by the trends is favorable or unfavorable. (Round your answers to one decimal place.)

	20x7	20x6	20x5	20x4	20x3
Net sales	$25,520	$23,980	$24,200	$22,880	$22,000
Cost of goods sold	17,220	15,400	15,540	14,700	14,000
General and administrative expenses	5,280	5,184	5,088	4,896	4,800
Operating income	3,020	3,396	3,572	3,284	3,200

LO4 Vertical Analysis

E 4. Express the comparative income statements that follow as common-size statements, and comment on the changes from 20x5 to 20x6. (Round computations to one decimal place.)

Trumpet Company
Comparative Income Statements
For the Years Ended December 31, 20x6 and 20x5

	20x6	20x5
Net sales	$424,000	$368,000
Cost of goods sold	254,400	239,200
Gross margin	$169,600	$128,800
Selling expenses	$106,000	$ 73,600
General expenses	50,880	36,800
Total operating expenses	$156,880	$110,400
Operating income	$ 12,720	$ 18,400

LO5 Liquidity Analysis

E 5. Partial comparative balance sheet and income statement information for Helig Company is as follows:

	20x4	20x3
Cash	$ 6,800	$ 5,200
Marketable securities	3,600	8,600
Accounts receivable (net)	22,400	17,800
Inventory	27,200	24,800
Total current assets	$ 60,000	$ 56,400
Accounts payable	$ 20,000	$ 14,100
Net sales	$161,280	$110,360
Cost of goods sold	108,800	101,680
Gross margin	$ 52,480	$ 8,680

In 20x2, the year-end balances for Accounts Receivable and Inventory were $16,200 and $25,600, respectively. Accounts Payable was $15,300 in 20x2 and is the only current liability. Compute the current ratio, quick ratio, receivable turnover, average days' sales uncollected, inventory turnover, average days' inventory on hand, payables turnover, and average days' payable for each year. (Round computations to one decimal place.) Comment on the change in the company's liquidity position, including its operating cycle and required days of financing from 20x3 to 20x4.

LO5 Turnover Analysis

E 6. Main Tuxedo Shop has been in business for four years. Because the company has recently had a cash flow problem, management wonders whether there is a problem with receivables or inventories. Here are selected figures from the company's financial statements (in thousands):

	20x4	20x3	20x2	20x1
Net sales	$288	$224	$192	$160
Cost of goods sold	180	144	120	96
Accounts receivable (net)	48	40	32	24
Merchandise inventory	56	44	32	20
Accounts payable	25	20	15	10

Compute the receivable turnover, inventory turnover, and payables turnover for each of the four years, and comment on the results relative to the cash flow problem that Main Tuxedo Shop has been experiencing. Merchandise inventory was $22,000, accounts receivable was $22,000, and accounts payable was $8,000 in 20x0. (Round computations to one decimal place.)

LO5 Profitability Analysis

E 7. D.J. Company had total assets of $640,000 in 20x3, $680,000 in 20x4, and $760,000 in 20x5. Its debt to equity ratio was .67 times in all three years. In 20x4, the company had net income of $77,112 on revenues of $1,224,000. In 20x5, the company had net income of $98,952 on revenues of $1,596,000. Compute the profit margin, asset turnover, return on assets, and return on equity for 20x4 and 20x5. Comment on the apparent cause of the increase or decrease in profitability. (Round the percentages and other ratios to one decimal place.)

LO5 Long-Term Solvency and Market Strength Ratios

E 8. An investor is considering investing in the long-term bonds and common stock of Companies M and N. Both companies operate in the same industry. In addition, both companies pay a dividend per share of $4 and have a yield of 10 percent on their long-term bonds.

Other data for the two companies are as follows:

	Company M	Company N
Total assets	$2,400,000	$1,080,000
Total liabilities	1,080,000	594,000
Income before income taxes	288,000	129,600
Interest expense	97,200	53,460
Earnings per share	3.20	5.00
Market price of common stock	40	47.50

Compute the debt to equity, interest coverage, price/earnings (P/E), and dividends yield ratios for each company, and comment on the results. (Round computations to one decimal place.)

E 9.
LO5 Cash Flow Adequacy Analysis

Using the data below from the financial statements of Cheng, Inc., compute the company's cash flow yield, cash flows to sales, cash flows to assets, and free cash flow. (Round computations to one decimal place.)

Net sales	$6,400,000
Net income	704,000
Net cash flows from operating activities	912,000
Total assets, beginning of year	5,780,000
Total assets, end of year	6,240,000
Cash dividends	240,000
Net capital expenditures	596,000

PROBLEMS

P 1.
LO4 Horizontal and Vertical Analyses

The condensed comparative income statements and balance sheets for Rochelle Corporation appear below and at the top of the facing page.

Rochelle Corporation
Comparative Income Statements
For the Years Ended December 31, 20x5 and 20x4

	20x5	20x4
Net sales	$1,600,800	$1,485,200
Costs and expenses		
Cost of goods sold	$ 908,200	$ 792,400
Selling expenses	260,200	209,200
Administrative expenses	280,600	231,000
Total costs and expenses	$1,449,000	$1,232,600
Income from operations	$ 151,800	$ 252,600
Interest expense	50,000	40,000
Income before income taxes	$ 101,800	$ 212,600
Income taxes	28,000	70,000
Net income	$ 73,800	$ 142,600
Earnings per share	$ 1.23	$ 2.38

REQUIRED ▶ Perform the following analyses. (Round all ratios and percentages to one decimal place.)
1. Prepare schedules showing the amount and percentage changes from 20x4 to 20x5 for the comparative income statements and the balance sheets.
2. Prepare common-size income statements and common-size balance sheets for 20x4 and 20x5.
3. Comment on the results in **1** and **2** by identifying favorable and unfavorable changes in the components and composition of the statements.

Rochelle Corporation
Comparative Balance Sheets
December 31, 20x5 and 20x4

	20x5	20x4
Assets		
Cash	$ 62,200	$ 54,400
Accounts receivable (net)	145,000	85,400
Inventory	245,200	215,600
Property, plant, and equipment (net)	1,155,400	1,015,000
Total assets	$1,607,800	$1,370,400
Liabilities and Stockholders' Equity		
Accounts payable	$ 209,400	$ 144,600
Notes payable	100,000	100,000
Bonds payable	400,000	220,000
Common stock, $10 par value	600,000	600,000
Retained earnings	298,400	305,800
Total liabilities and stockholders' equity	$1,607,800	$1,370,400

P 2.

LO5 Effects of Transactions on Ratios

Jamal Corporation, a clothing retailer, engaged in the transactions listed in the first column of the table below. Opposite each transaction is a ratio and space to mark the effect of each transaction on the ratio.

		Effect		
Transaction	Ratio	Increase	Decrease	None
a. Issued common stock for cash.	Asset turnover			
b. Declared cash dividend.	Current ratio			
c. Sold treasury stock.	Return on equity			
d. Borrowed cash by issuing note payable.	Debt to equity ratio			
e. Paid salaries expense.	Inventory turnover			
f. Purchased merchandise for cash.	Current ratio			
g. Sold equipment for cash.	Receivable turnover			
h. Sold merchandise on account.	Quick ratio			
i. Paid current portion of long-term debt.	Return on assets			
j. Gave sales discount.	Profit margin			
k. Purchased marketable securities for cash.	Quick ratio			
l. Declared 5% stock dividend.	Current ratio			
m. Purchased a building.	Free cash flow			

REQUIRED ▶ Place an X in the appropriate column to show whether the transaction increased, decreased, or had no effect on the indicated ratio.

LO5 Ratio Analysis

P 3. Data for Rochelle Corporation in 20x5 and 20x4 follow. These data should be used in conjunction with the data in **P 1.**

	20x5	20x4
Net cash flows from operating activities	$128,000	$198,000
Net capital expenditures	$238,000	$76,000
Dividends paid	$62,800	$70,000
Number of common shares	60,000	60,000
Market price per share	$40	$60

Selected balances at the end of 20x3 were accounts receivable (net), $105,400; inventory, $198,800; total assets, $1,295,600; accounts payable, $134,400; and stockholders' equity, $753,200. All Rochelle's notes payable were current liabilities; all its bonds payable were long-term liabilities.

REQUIRED ▶ Perform a ratio analysis following the steps outlined below. Round all answers to one decimal place, and consider changes of .1 or less to be neutral. After making the calculations, indicate whether each ratio improved or deteriorated from 20x4 to 20x5 (use F for favorable and U for unfavorable).

1. Prepare a liquidity analysis by calculating for each year the (a) current ratio, (b) quick ratio, (c) receivable turnover, (d) average days' sales uncollected, (e) inventory turnover, (f) average days' inventory on hand, (g) payables turnover, and (h) average days' payable.
2. Prepare a profitability analysis by calculating for each year the (a) profit margin, (b) asset turnover, (c) return on assets, and (d) return on equity.
3. Prepare a long-term solvency analysis by calculating for each year the (a) debt to equity ratio and (b) interest coverage ratio.
4. Prepare a cash flow adequacy analysis by calculating for each year the (a) cash flow yield, (b) cash flows to sales, (c) cash flows to assets, and (d) free cash flow.
5. Prepare a market strength analysis by calculating for each year the (a) price/earnings ratio and (b) dividends yield.
6. Based on your analysis, assess Rochelle's performance in each of the following areas: liquidity, profitability, long-term solvency, and cash flow adequacy. Explain your evaluations.

LO5 Comprehensive Ratio Analysis of Two Companies

P 4. Juanita Maxwell has decided to invest some of her savings in common stock. She feels that the chemical industry has good growth prospects, and she has narrowed her choice to two companies in that industry. As a final step in making the choice, she has decided to perform a comprehensive ratio analysis of the two companies, Reynard and Bouche. Income statement and balance sheet data for these two companies follow.

	Reynard	Bouche
Net sales	$9,486,200	$27,287,300
Costs and expenses		
Cost of goods sold	$5,812,200	$18,372,400
Selling expenses	1,194,000	1,955,700
Administrative expenses	1,217,400	4,126,000
Total costs and expenses	$8,223,600	$24,454,100
Income from operations	$1,262,600	$ 2,833,200
Interest expense	270,000	1,360,000
Income before income taxes	$ 992,600	$ 1,473,200
Income taxes	450,000	600,000
Net income	$ 542,600	$ 873,200
Earnings per share	$ 1.55	$ .87

	Reynard	Bouche
Assets		
Cash	$ 126,100	$ 514,300
Marketable securities (at cost)	117,500	1,200,000
Accounts receivable (net)	456,700	2,600,000
Inventories	1,880,000	4,956,000
Prepaid expenses	72,600	156,600
Property, plant, and equipment (net)	5,342,200	19,356,000
Intangibles and other assets	217,000	580,000
Total assets	$8,212,100	$29,362,900
Liabilities and Stockholders' Equity		
Accounts payable	$ 517,400	$ 2,342,000
Notes payable	1,000,000	2,000,000
Income taxes payable	85,200	117,900
Bonds payable	2,000,000	15,000,000
Common stock, $1 par value	350,000	1,000,000
Paid-in capital in excess of par value, common	1,747,300	5,433,300
Retained earnings	2,512,200	3,469,700
Total liabilities and stockholders' equity	$8,212,100	$29,362,900

During the year, Reynard paid a total of $140,000 in dividends, and its current price per share is $20. Bouche paid a total of $600,000 in dividends during the year, and its current market price per share is $9. Reynard had net cash flows from operating activities of $771,500 and net capital expenditures of $450,000. Bouche had net cash flows from operating activities of $843,000 and net capital expenditures of $1,550,000.

Information pertaining to these companies' prior years is not readily available. Assume that all their notes payable are current liabilities and that all their bonds payable are long-term liabilities.

REQUIRED ▶ Conduct a comprehensive ratio analysis of Reynard and of Bouche following the steps outlined below. (Round all ratios and percentages except earnings per share to one decimal place.)

1. Prepare a liquidity analysis by calculating for each company the (a) current ratio, (b) quick ratio, (c) receivable turnover, (d) average days' sales uncollected, (e) inventory turnover, (f) average days' inventory on hand, (g) payables turnover, and (h) averages days' payables.
2. Prepare a profitability analysis by calculating for each company the (a) profit margin, (b) asset turnover, (c) return on assets, and (d) return on equity.
3. Prepare a long-term solvency analysis by calculating for each company the (a) debt to equity ratio and (b) interest coverage ratio.
4. Prepare a cash flow adequacy analysis by calculating for each company the (a) cash flow yield, (b) cash flows to sales, (c) cash flows to assets, and (d) free cash flow.
5. Prepare an analysis of market strength by calculating for each company the (a) price/earnings ratio and (b) dividends yield.
6. Compare the two companies by inserting the ratio calculations from 1 through 5 in a table with the following column headings: Ratio Name, Reynard, Bouche, and Company with More Favorable Ratio. Indicate in the last column which company had the more favorable ratio in each case.
7. How could the analysis be improved if information about these companies' prior years were available?

ALTERNATE PROBLEMS

LO5 Effects of Transactions on Ratios

P 5. Mankato Corporation engaged in the transactions listed in the first column of the following table. Opposite each transaction is a ratio and space to indicate the effect of each transaction on the ratio.

		Effect		
Transaction	Ratio	Increase	Decrease	None
a. Sold merchandise on account.	Current ratio			
b. Sold merchandise on account.	Inventory turnover			
c. Collected on accounts receivable.	Quick ratio			
d. Wrote off an uncollectible account.	Receivable turnover			
e. Paid on accounts payable.	Current ratio			
f. Declared cash dividend.	Return on equity			
g. Incurred advertising expense.	Profit margin			
h. Issued stock dividend.	Debt to equity ratio			
i. Issued bonds payable.	Asset turnover			
j. Accrued interest expense.	Current ratio			
k. Paid previously declared cash dividend.	Dividends yield			
l. Purchased treasury stock.	Return on assets			
m. Recorded depreciation expense.	Cash flow yield			

REQUIRED ▶ Place an X in the appropriate column to show whether the transaction increased, decreased, or had no effect on the indicated ratio.

LO5 Ratio Analysis

P 6. The condensed comparative income statements and balance sheets of Lisle Corporation follow. All figures are in thousands of dollars, except earnings per share.

Lisle Corporation
Comparative Income Statements
For the Years Ended December 31, 20x6 and 20x5

	20x6	20x5
Net sales	$1,638,400	$1,573,200
Costs and expenses		
Cost of goods sold	$1,044,400	$1,004,200
Selling expenses	238,400	259,000
Administrative expenses	223,600	211,600
Total costs and expenses	$1,506,400	$1,474,800
Income from operations	$ 132,000	$ 98,400
Interest expense	32,800	19,600
Income before income taxes	$ 99,200	$ 78,800
Income taxes	31,200	28,400
Net income	$ 68,000	$ 50,400
Earnings per share	$ 1.70	$ 1.26

Lisle Corporation
Comparative Balance Sheets
December 31, 20x6 and 20x5

	20x6	20x5
Assets		
Cash	$ 40,600	$ 20,400
Accounts receivable (net)	117,800	114,600
Inventory	287,400	297,400
Property, plant, and equipment (net)	375,000	360,000
Total assets	$820,800	$792,400
Liabilities and Stockholders' Equity		
Accounts payable	$133,800	$238,600
Notes payable	100,000	200,000
Bonds payable	200,000	—
Common stock, $5 par value	200,000	200,000
Retained earnings	187,000	153,800
Total liabilities and stockholders' equity	$820,800	$792,400

Additional data for Lisle Corporation in 20x6 and 20x5 are as follows:

	20x6	20x5
Net cash flows from operating activities	$106,500,000	$86,250,000
Net capital expenditures	$22,500,000	$16,000,000
Dividends paid	$22,000,000	$17,200,000
Number of common shares	40,000,000	40,000,000
Market price per share	$9	$15

Selected balances (in thousands) at the end of 20x4 were accounts receivable (net), $103,400; inventory, $273,600; total assets, $732,800; accounts payable $193,300; and stockholders' equity, $320,600. All Lisle Corporation's notes payable were current liabilities. All its bonds payable were long-term liabilities.

REQUIRED ▶ Perform a ratio analysis following the steps outlined below. Round percentages and ratios to one decimal place, and consider changes of .1 or less to be neutral. After making the calculations, indicate whether each ratio had a favorable (F) or unfavorable (U) change from 20x5 to 20x6.

1. Conduct a liquidity analysis by calculating for each year the (a) current ratio, (b) quick ratio, (c) receivable turnover, (d) average days' sales uncollected, (e) inventory turnover, (f) average days' inventory on hand, (g) payables turnover, and (h) average days' payable.
2. Conduct a profitability analysis by calculating for each year the (a) profit margin, (b) asset turnover, (c) return on assets, and (d) return on equity.
3. Conduct a long-term solvency analysis by calculating for each year the (a) debt to equity ratio and (b) interest coverage ratio.
4. Conduct a cash flow adequacy analysis by calculating for each year the (a) cash flow yield, (b) cash flows to sales, (c) cash flows to assets, and (d) free cash flow.
5. Conduct a market strength analysis by calculating for each year the (a) price/earnings ratio and (b) dividends yield.
6. Based on your analysis, assess Lisle's performance in each of the following areas: liquidity, profitability, long-term solvency, and cash flow adequacy. Explain your evaluations.

Skills Development Cases

Conceptual Analysis

LO2 **Standards for Financial**
LO5 **Performance Evaluation**

SD 1. Helene Curtis, a well-known, publicly owned corporation, became a take-over candidate and sold out in the 1990s after years of poor profit performance. As early as 1978, *Forbes* observed, "By almost any standard, Chicago-based Helene Curtis rates as one of America's worst-managed personal care companies. In recent years its return on equity has hovered between 10% and 13%, well below the industry average of 18% to 19%. Net profit margins of 2% to 3% are half that of competitors. . . . As a result, while leading names like Revlon <www.revlon.com> and Avon <www.avon.com> are trading at three and four times book value, Curtis trades at less than two-thirds book value."[9] Considering that many companies in other industries were happy with a return on equity of 10 percent to 13 percent, why is this analysis so critical of Curtis's performance? Assuming that Curtis could have doubled its profit margin, what other information would be necessary to project the resulting return on stockholders' investment? Why did Revlon's and Avon's stocks trade for more than Curtis's? Be prepared to discuss your answers in class.

LO3 **Using Segment Information**

SD 2. Refer to Exhibit 1, which shows the segment information of Goodyear Tire & Rubber Company <www.goodyear.com>. In what business segments does Goodyear operate? What is the relative size of its business segments in terms of sales and income in the most recent year shown? Which segment is most profitable in terms of return on assets? In which region of the world is the tires segment largest, and which tire segment is most profitable in terms of return on assets?

LO3 **Using Investors' Services**

SD 3. Refer to Exhibit 2, which contains the PepsiCo Inc. <www.pepsi.com> listing from Mergent's *Handbook of Dividend Achievers*. Assume that an investor has asked you to assess PepsiCo's recent history and prospects. Write a memorandum to the investor that addresses the following points:

1. PepsiCo's earnings history. (What has been the general relationship between PepsiCo's return on assets and its return on equity over the last seven years? What does this tell you about the way the company is financed? What figures back up your conclusion?)
2. The trend of PepsiCo's stock price and price/earnings ratio for the seven years shown.
3. PepsiCo's prospects, including developments likely to affect the company's future.

Ethical Dilemma

LO3 **Management of Earnings**

SD 4. Management of most companies is very sensitive to the fact that analysts watch key performance measures, such as whether a firm is meeting earnings targets. A slight weakening of analysts' confidence can severely affect the price of a company's stock. The SEC has been cracking down on companies that manipulate earnings to achieve financial goals. For instance, some time ago, the SEC filed a complaint against W. R. Grace & Co. <www.grace.com> for releasing $1.5 million from reserves into earnings in order to meet earnings targets. Grace officials claimed the amount was immaterial and that the company was in accord with accounting rules for booking an immaterial item. (The amount was about 1.5 percent of net income.) The SEC argued that it was a matter of principle: "Does anyone think that it's acceptable to intentionally book an error [false transaction] for the purpose of making earnings targets?" But some think such action on the part of the SEC will harm confidence in business.[10] Do you think it is unethical for a company's management to increase earnings periodically through the use of one-time transactions, such as adjustments of reserves or sale of assets, on which it has a profit?

Research Activity

LO3 **Using Investors' Services**

SD 5. Find *Moody's Investors Service* or *Standard & Poor's Industry Guide* in your library. Locate reports on three corporations. You may choose the corporations at random or from the same industry, as directed by your instructor. (If you did a related research activity in a previous chapter, use the same three companies.) Write a summary of what you learned about each company's financial performance, including the performance measures that it uses and its prospects for the future. Be prepared to discuss your findings in class.

Decision-Making Practice

SD 6.

LO4 **Effect of a One-Time Item on**
LO5 **a Loan Decision**

Apple a Day, Inc., and Unforgettable Edibles, Inc., are food catering businesses that operate in the same metropolitan area. Their customers include *Fortune* 500 companies, regional firms, and individuals. The two firms reported similar profit margins for the current year, and both base bonuses for managers on the achievement of a target profit margin and return on equity. Each firm has submitted a loan request to you, a loan officer for City National Bank. They have provided you with the following information:

	Apple a Day	Unforgettable Edibles
Net sales	$625,348	$717,900
Cost of goods sold	225,125	287,080
Gross margin	$400,223	$430,820
Operating expenses	281,300	371,565
Operating income	$118,923	$ 59,255
Gain on sale of real estate	—	81,923
Interest expense	(9,333)	(15,338)
Income before income taxes	$109,590	$125,840
Income taxes	25,990	29,525
Net income	$83,600	$96,315
Average stockholders' equity	$312,700	$390,560

1. Perform a vertical analysis and prepare a common-size income statement for each firm. Compute profit margin and return on equity.
2. Discuss these results, the bonus plan for management, and loan considerations. Identify the company that is the better loan risk.

MANAGERIAL REPORTING AND ANALYSIS CASES

Interpreting Financial Reports

MRA 1.

LO4 **Trend Analysis**

H. J. Heinz Company <www.heinz.com> is a global company engaged in several lines of business, including food service, infant foods, condiments, pet foods, and weight control food products. Below is a five-year summary of operations and other related data for Heinz.[11] (Dollars are expressed in thousands.)

Five-Year Summary of Operations and Other Related Data
H. J. Heinz Company and Subsidiaries

	2001	2000	1999	1998	1997
Summary of operations					
Sales	$9,430,422	$9,407,949	$9,299,610	$9,209,284	$9,397,007
Cost of products sold	5,883,618	5,788,565	5,944,867	5,711,213	6,385,091
Interest expense	552,957	269,748	258,815	258,616	274,746
Provision for income taxes	178,140	573,123	360,790	453,415	177,193
Net income (before special items)	494,918	890,553	474,341	801,566	301,871
Other related data					
Dividends paid: Common	537,290	513,756	484,817	452,966	416,923
Total assets	9,035,150	8,850,697	8,053,634	8,023,421	8,437,787
Total debt	4,885,687	4,112,401	3,376,413	5,806,905	5,997,366
Shareholders' equity	1,373,727	1,595,856	1,803,004	2,216,516	2,440,921

Prepare a trend analysis for Heinz with 1997 as the base year and discuss the results. Identify important trends and state whether the trends are favorable or unfavorable. Discuss significant relationships among the trends.

International Company

MRA 2.

LO5 Comparison of International Companies' Operating Cycles

Ratio analysis enables one to compare the performance of companies whose financial statements are presented in different currencies. Selected data from 2000 for two large pharmaceutical companies—one American, Pfizer, Inc. <www.pfizer.com>, and one Swiss, Roche <www.roche.com>—are presented below (in millions).[12]

	Pfizer, Inc. (U.S.)	Roche (Swiss)
Net Sales	$29,574	SF28,672
Cost of Goods Sold	4,907	9,163
Accounts Receivable	5,489	5,519
Inventories	2,702	5,754
Accounts Payable	1,719	2,215

Accounts receivable in 1999 were $5,368 for Pfizer and SF6,178 for Roche. Inventories in 1999 were $2,588 for Pfizer and SF6,546 for Roche. Accounts payable in 1999 were $1,889 for Pfizer and SF2,378 for Roche.

For each company, calculate the receivable, inventory, and payables turnovers and the respective days associated with each. Then determine the operating cycle for each company and the days of financing required for current operations. Compare the results.

Group Activity: Divide the class into groups to make the calculations. Assign the analysis of Pfizer to half of the groups, and the analysis of Roche to the other half. Have the groups compare results and discuss as a class.

Toys "R" Us Annual Report

MRA 3.

LO5 Comprehensive Ratio Analysis

Using data from the Toys "R" Us <www.tru.com> annual report, conduct a comprehensive ratio analysis that compares the company's performance in 2002 and 2001. If you have computed ratios for Toys "R" Us in previous chapters, you may prepare a table that summarizes the ratios for 2002 and 2001 and show calculations only for the ratios not previously calculated. If this is the first ratio analysis you have done for Toys "R" Us, show all your computations. In either case, after each group of ratios, comment on the performance of Toys "R" Us. Round your calculations to one decimal place. Prepare and comment on the following categories of ratios:

Liquidity analysis: current ratio, quick ratio, receivable turnover, average days' sales uncollected, inventory turnover, average days' inventory on hand, payables turnover, and average days' payable. (Accounts Receivable, Inventory, and Accounts Payable were [in millions] $225, $2,307, and $1,152, respectively, in 2000.)

Profitability analysis: profit margin, asset turnover, return on assets, and return on equity. (Comment on the effect of the restructuring in 2002 on the company's profitability.)

Long-term solvency analysis: debt to equity ratio and interest coverage ratio.

Cash flow adequacy analysis: cash flow yield, cash flows to sales, cash flows to assets, and free cash flow.

Market strength analysis: price/earnings ratio and dividends yield.

Comparison Case: Toys "R" Us and Walgreen Co.

MRA 4.

LO5 Comparison of Key Financial Performance Measures

Refer to the annual report of Toys "R" Us <www.tru.com> and the financial statements for Walgreens <www.walgreens.com> in the Supplement to Chapter 1. Calculate the following key financial performance measures for the two most recent years:

Liquidity: operating cycle
days of financing needed

Profitability: profit margin
asset turnover
return on assets

Long-term solvency: debt to equity ratio
Cash flow adequacy: cash flow yield
free cash flow

Evaluate and comment on the relative performance of the two companies with respect to each of the above categories. (**Note:** Accounts Receivable, Inventory, and Accounts Payable for Walgreens in 2000 were, in millions, $614.5, $2,830.8, and $1,364.0, respectively. Total assets for Walgreens in 2000 were $7,103.7 million.)

Fingraph® Financial Analyst™

MRA 5.

LO5 Comprehensive Financial Performance Evaluation

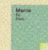

Choose any company from the list of Fingraph companies on the Needles Accounting Resource Center Web Site at http://accounting.college.hmco.com/students. Access the Microsoft Excel spreadsheets for the company you selected.

1. Using the Fingraph CD-ROM software, display and print the following pages for the company you have selected:
   a. Balance Sheet Analysis
   b. Current Assets and Current Liabilities Analysis
   c. Liquidity and Asset Utilization Analysis
   d. Income from Operations Analysis
   e. Statement of Cash Flows: Operating Activities Analysis
   f. Statement of Cash Flows: Investing and Financing Activities Analysis
   g. Market Strength Analysis

2. Prepare an executive summary that describes the company's financial condition and performance over the past two years. Attach the pages you printed in support of your analysis.

Internet Case

MRA 6.

LO2 Using Investors' Services
LO3

Go to the web site for Moody's Investors Service <www.moodys.com>. Click on "ratings," which will show revisions of debt ratings issued by Moody's in the past few days. Choose a rating that has been upgraded or downgraded and read the short press announcement related to it. What reasons does Moody's give for the change in rating? What is Moody's assessment of the future of the company or institution? What financial performance measures are mentioned in the article? Summarize your findings and be prepared to share them in class.

Appendix A

The Merchandising Work Sheet and Closing Entries

This appendix shows how to prepare the work sheet and closing entries for merchandising companies. The work sheet for a merchandising company is basically the same as for a service business (for an example, see the work sheet for Joan Miller Advertising Agency in the chapter on accounting information systems). However, it includes the additional accounts needed to handle merchandising transactions. The treatment of these accounts differs depending on whether a company uses the periodic or the perpetual inventory system.

THE PERIODIC INVENTORY SYSTEM

When a merchandising company uses the periodic inventory system, the accounts generally include Sales, Sales Returns and Allowances, Sales Discounts, Purchases, Purchases Returns and Allowances, Purchases Discounts, Freight In, and Merchandise Inventory. Except for Merchandise Inventory, these accounts are treated in much the same way as revenue and expense accounts for a service company. They are transferred to the Income Summary account in the closing process. On the work sheet, they are extended to the Income Statement columns.

Merchandise Inventory requires special treatment under the periodic inventory system because purchases of merchandise are accumulated in the Purchases account. No entries are made to the Merchandise Inventory account during the accounting period. Its balance at the end of the period, before adjusting and closing entries, is the same as it was at the beginning of the period. Thus, its balance at this point represents beginning merchandise inventory. Remember also that the cost of goods sold is determined by adding beginning merchandise inventory to net cost of purchases and then subtracting ending merchandise inventory. The objectives of handling merchandise inventory in the closing entries at the end of the period are to (1) remove the beginning balance from the Merchandise Inventory account, (2) enter the ending balance into the Merchandise Inventory account, and (3) enter the beginning inventory as a debit and the ending inventory as a credit to the Income Summary account to calculate net income. The following T accounts, which use figures for Fenwick Fashions Corporation from the chapter on merchandising operations, show how these objectives can be met:

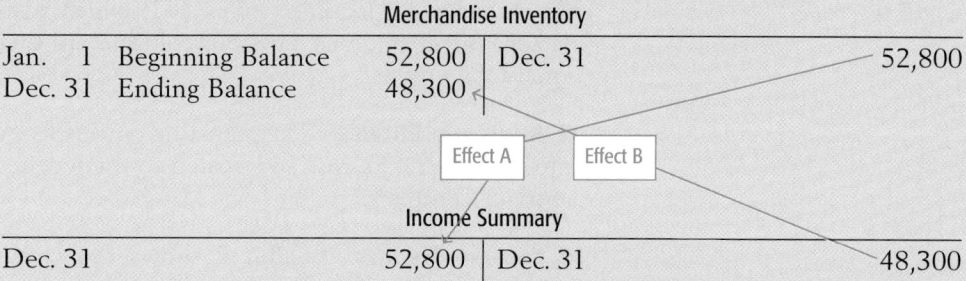

In this example, merchandise inventory was $52,800 at the beginning of the year and $48,300 at the end of the year. Effect A removes the $52,800 from Merchandise Inventory, leaving a zero balance, and transfers it to Income Summary. In Income Summary, the $52,800 is, in effect, added to net purchases because, like expenses, the balance of the Purchases account is debited to Income Summary in a closing entry. Effect B establishes the ending balance of Merchandise Inventory, $48,300, and enters it as a credit in the Income Summary account. The credit entry in Income Summary deducts the ending inventory from goods available for sale because both purchases and beginning inventory are debit entries. In other words, beginning merchandise inventory and purchases are debits to Income Summary, and ending merchandise inventory is a credit to Income Summary. The work sheet for Fenwick Fashions Corporation is shown in Exhibit 1 and is discussed below.

■ **TRIAL BALANCE COLUMNS** The first step in the preparation of the work sheet is to enter the balances from the ledger accounts into the Trial Balance columns.

■ **ADJUSTMENTS COLUMNS** The adjusting entries are entered in the Adjustments columns just as they are for service companies. No adjusting entry is made for merchandise inventory. After the adjusting entries are entered on the work sheet, the columns are totaled to prove that total debits equal total credits.

■ **OMISSION OF ADJUSTED TRIAL BALANCE COLUMNS** These two columns, which appear in the work sheet for a service company, can be omitted. They are optional and are used when there are many adjusting entries to record. When only a few adjusting entries are required, as is the case for Fenwick Fashions, these columns are not necessary and may be omitted to save time.

■ **INCOME STATEMENT AND BALANCE SHEET COLUMNS** After the Trial Balance columns have been totaled, the adjustments entered, and the equality of the columns proved, the balances are extended to the Income Statement and Balance Sheet columns. As on the work sheet for a service company, you begin with the Cash account at the top of the sheet and move sequentially down, one account at a time, entering each account balance in the correct Income Statement or Balance Sheet column.

The "problem" extension here is in the Merchandise Inventory row. The beginning inventory balance of $52,800 (which is already in the trial balance) is extended to the debit column of the Income Statement columns, as shown in Exhibit 1. This procedure has the effect of adding beginning inventory to net purchases because the Purchases account is also in the debit column of the Income Statement columns. The ending inventory balance of $48,300 (which is determined by the physical inventory and is not in the trial balance) is then inserted in the credit column of the Income Statement columns. This procedure has the effect of subtracting the ending inventory from goods available for sale in order to calculate the cost of goods sold. Finally, the ending merchandise inventory ($48,300) is inserted in the debit side of the Balance Sheet columns because it will appear on the balance sheet.

After all the items have been extended into the correct columns, the four columns are totaled. The net income or net loss is the difference between the debit and credit Income Statement columns. In this case, Fenwick Fashions Corporation has earned a net income of $24,481, which is extended to the credit side of the Balance Sheet columns. The four columns are then added to prove that total debits equal total credits.

■ **ADJUSTING ENTRIES** The adjusting entries from the work sheet are now entered into the general journal and posted to the ledger. The procedure is the same as for a service company.

■ **CLOSING ENTRIES** Exhibit 2 shows the closing entries for Fenwick Fashions. Notice that Merchandise Inventory is credited for the amount of beginning inventory ($52,800) in the first entry and debited for the amount of the ending inventory ($48,300) in the second entry. Otherwise, these closing entries are similar to those for a service company except that the merchandising accounts also must be closed to Income Summary. All income statement accounts with debit balances, including the merchandising accounts of Sales Returns and Allowances, Sales Discounts, Purchases, and Freight In, and beginning Merchandise Inventory are

Exhibit 1
Work Sheet for Fenwick Fashions Corporation: Periodic Inventory System

Fenwick Fashions Corporation
Work Sheet
For the Year Ended December 31, 20xx

Account Name	Trial Balance Debit	Trial Balance Credit	Adjustments Debit	Adjustments Credit	Income Statement Debit	Income Statement Credit	Balance Sheet Debit	Balance Sheet Credit
Cash	29,410						29,410	
Accounts Receivable	42,400						42,400	
Merchandise Inventory	52,800				52,800	48,300	48,300	
Prepaid Insurance	17,400			(a) 5,800			11,600	
Store Supplies	2,600			(b) 1,540			1,060	
Office Supplies	1,840			(c) 1,204			636	
Land	4,500						4,500	
Building	20,260						20,260	
Accumulated Depreciation, Building		5,650		(d) 2,600				8,250
Office Equipment	8,600						8,600	
Accumulated Depreciation, Office Equipment		2,800		(e) 2,200				5,000
Accounts Payable		25,683						25,683
Common Stock		50,000						50,000
Retained Earnings		68,352						68,352
Dividends	20,000						20,000	
Sales		246,350				246,350		
Sales Returns and Allowances	2,750				2,750			
Sales Discounts	4,275				4,275			
Purchases	126,400				126,400			
Purchases Returns and Allowances		5,640				5,640		
Purchases Discounts		2,136				2,136		
Freight In	8,236				8,236			
Sales Salaries Expense	22,500				22,500			
Freight Out Expense	5,740				5,740			
Advertising Expense	10,000				10,000			
Office Salaries Expense	26,900				26,900			
	406,611	406,611						
Insurance Expense, Selling			(a) 1,600		1,600			
Insurance Expense, General			(a) 4,200		4,200			
Store Supplies Expense			(b) 1,540		1,540			
Office Supplies Expense			(c) 1,204		1,204			
Depreciation Expense, Building			(d) 2,600		2,600			
Depreciation Expense, Office Equipment			(e) 2,200		2,200			
Income Taxes Expense			(f) 5,000		5,000			
Income Taxes Payable				(f) 5,000				5,000
			18,344	18,344	277,945	302,426	186,766	162,285
Net Income					24,481			24,481
					302,426	302,426	186,766	186,766

EXHIBIT 2
Closing Entries for a Merchandising Concern: Periodic Inventory System

			General Journal			Page 10
Date		Description		Post. Ref.	Debit	Credit
20xx Dec.	31	*Closing entries:* Income Summary			277,945	
		Merchandise Inventory				52,800
		Sales Returns and Allowances				2,750
		Sales Discounts				4,275
		Purchases				126,400
		Freight In				8,236
		Sales Salaries Expense				22,500
		Freight Out Expense				5,740
		Advertising Expense				10,000
		Office Salaries Expense				26,900
		Insurance Expense, Selling				1,600
		Insurance Expense, General				4,200
		Store Supplies Expense				1,540
		Office Supplies Expense				1,204
		Depreciation Expense, Building				2,600
		Depreciation Expense, Office Equipment				2,200
		Income Taxes Expense				5,000
		To close temporary expense and revenue accounts with debit balances and to remove the beginning inventory				
	31	Merchandise Inventory			48,300	
		Sales			246,350	
		Purchases Returns and Allowances			5,640	
		Purchases Discounts			2,136	
		Income Summary				302,426
		To close temporary expense and revenue accounts with credit balances and to establish the ending inventory				
	31	Income Summary			24,481	
		Retained Earnings				24,481
		To close the Income Summary account				
	31	Retained Earnings			20,000	
		Dividends				20,000
		To close the Dividends account				

credited in the first entry. The total of these accounts ($277,945) equals the total of the debit column in the Income Statement columns of the work sheet. All income statement accounts with credit balances—Sales, Purchases Returns and Allowances, and Purchases Discounts—and ending Merchandise Inventory are debited in the second entry. The total of these accounts ($302,426) equals the total of the Income Statement credit column in the work sheet. The third entry closes the Income Summary account and transfers net income to Retained Earnings. The fourth entry closes the Dividends account to Retained Earnings.

The Perpetual Inventory System

Exhibit 3 shows the work sheet for Fenwick Fashions Corporation, assuming the company uses the perpetual inventory system. Under this system, purchases of

EXHIBIT 3
Work Sheet for Fenwick Fashions Corporation: Perpetual Inventory System

Fenwick Fashions Corporation
Work Sheet
For the Year Ended December 31, 20xx

Account Name	Trial Balance Debit	Trial Balance Credit	Adjustments Debit	Adjustments Credit	Income Statement Debit	Income Statement Credit	Balance Sheet Debit	Balance Sheet Credit
Cash	29,410						29,410	
Accounts Receivable	42,400						42,400	
Merchandise Inventory	48,300						48,300	
Prepaid Insurance	17,400			(a) 5,800			11,600	
Store Supplies	2,600			(b) 1,540			1,060	
Office Supplies	1,840			(c) 1,204			636	
Land	4,500						4,500	
Building	20,260						20,260	
Accumulated Depreciation, Building		5,650		(d) 2,600				8,250
Office Equipment	8,600						8,600	
Accumulated Depreciation, Office Equipment		2,800		(e) 2,200				5,000
Accounts Payable		25,683						25,683
Common Stock		50,000						50,000
Retained Earnings		68,352						68,352
Dividends	20,000						20,000	
Sales		246,350				246,350		
Sales Returns and Allowances	2,750				2,750			
Sales Discounts	4,275				4,275			
Cost of Goods Sold	123,124				123,124			
Freight In	8,236				8,236			
Sales Salaries Expense	22,500				22,500			
Freight Out Expense	5,740				5,740			
Advertising Expense	10,000				10,000			
Office Salaries Expense	26,900				26,900			
	398,835	398,835						
Insurance Expense, Selling			(a) 1,600		1,600			
Insurance Expense, General			(a) 4,200		4,200			
Store Supplies Expense			(b) 1,540		1,540			
Office Supplies Expense			(c) 1,204		1,204			
Depreciation Expense, Building			(d) 2,600		2,600			
Depreciation Expense, Office Equipment			(e) 2,200		2,200			
Income Taxes Expense			(f) 5,000		5,000			
Income Taxes Payable				(f) 5,000				5,000
			18,344	18,344	221,869	246,350	186,766	162,285
Net Income					24,481			24,481
					246,350	246,350	186,766	186,766

EXHIBIT 4
Closing Entries for a Merchandising Concern: Perpetual Inventory System

		General Journal			Page 10
Date		Description	Post. Ref.	Debit	Credit
20xx Dec.	31	Closing entries: Income Summary		221,869	
		Sales Returns and Allowances			2,750
		Sales Discounts			4,275
		Cost of Goods Sold			123,124
		Freight In			8,236
		Sales Salaries Expense			22,500
		Freight Out Expense			5,740
		Advertising Expense			10,000
		Office Salaries Expense			26,900
		Insurance Expense, Selling			1,600
		Insurance Expense, General			4,200
		Store Supplies Expense			1,540
		Office Supplies Expense			1,204
		Depreciation Expense, Building			2,600
		Depreciation Expense, Office Equipment			2,200
		Income Taxes Expense			5,000
		To close temporary expense and revenue accounts with debit balances			
	31	Sales		246,350	
		Income Summary			246,350
		To close temporary revenue account with credit balance			
	31	Income Summary		24,481	
		Retained Earnings			24,481
		To close the Income Summary account			
	31	Retained Earnings		20,000	
		Dividends			20,000
		To close the Dividends account			

merchandise are recorded directly in the Merchandise Inventory account and costs are transferred from the Merchandise Inventory account to the Cost of Goods Sold account as merchandise is sold. Thus, the Merchandise Inventory account is up to date at the end of the accounting period and is not involved in the closing process. Note that the ending merchandise inventory in Exhibit 3 is $48,300 in both the Trial Balance and the Balance Sheet columns.

Exhibit 4 shows the closing entries for Fenwick Fashions under the perpetual inventory system. The Cost of Goods Sold account is closed to Income Summary along with the expense accounts because it has a debit balance. There are no entries to the Merchandise Inventory account. Also, there is no Purchases Returns and Allowances account under the perpetual inventory system, and Freight In is accounted for separately but is combined with Cost of Goods Sold on the income statement.

PROBLEMS

P 1.
Work Sheet, Financial Statements, and Closing Entries for a Merchandising Company: Periodic Inventory System

The following trial balance is from the ledger of David's Music Store, Inc., at the end of its annual accounting period:

David's Music Store, Inc.
Trial Balance
November 30, 20x5

Cash	$ 18,075	
Accounts Receivable	27,840	
Merchandise Inventory	88,350	
Store Supplies	5,733	
Prepaid Insurance	4,800	
Store Equipment	111,600	
Accumulated Depreciation, Store Equipment		$ 46,800
Accounts Payable		36,900
Common Stock		30,000
Retained Earnings		95,982
Dividends	36,000	
Sales		306,750
Sales Returns and Allowances	2,961	
Purchases	189,600	
Purchases Returns and Allowances		58,965
Purchases Discounts		4,068
Freight In	6,783	
Sales Salaries Expense	64,050	
Rent Expense	10,800	
Other Selling Expenses	7,842	
Utilities Expense	5,031	
	$579,465	$579,465

REQUIRED

1. Enter the trial balance on a work sheet and complete the work sheet using the following information: ending merchandise inventory, $99,681; ending store supplies inventory, $912; unexpired prepaid insurance, $600; estimated depreciation on store equipment, $12,900; sales salaries payable, $240; accrued utilities expense, $450; and estimated income taxes expense, $15,000.
2. Prepare an income statement, a statement of retained earnings, and a balance sheet. Sales salaries expense; other selling expenses; store supplies expense; and depreciation expense, store equipment are selling expenses.
3. From the work sheet, prepare the closing entries.

P 2.
Work Sheet, Financial Statements, and Closing Entries for a Merchandising Company: Perpetual Inventory System

The trial balance on the next page is from the ledger of Marjie's Party Costumes Corporation at the end of its annual accounting period.

REQUIRED

1. Enter the trial balance for Marjie's Party Costumes on a work sheet and complete the work sheet using the following information: ending store supplies inventory, $550; expired insurance, $2,400; estimated depreciation on store equipment, $5,000; sales salaries payable, $650; accrued utilities expense, $100; and estimated income taxes expense, $20,000.

Marjie's Party Costumes Corporation
Trial Balance
June 30, 20x5

Cash	$ 7,050	
Accounts Receivable	24,830	
Merchandise Inventory	88,900	
Store Supplies	3,800	
Prepaid Insurance	4,800	
Store Equipment	151,300	
Accumulated Depreciation, Store Equipment		$ 25,500
Accounts Payable		38,950
Common Stock		50,000
Retained Earnings		111,350
Dividends	24,000	
Sales		475,250
Sales Returns and Allowances	4,690	
Cost of Goods Sold	231,840	
Freight In	10,400	
Sales Salaries Expense	64,600	
Rent Expense	48,000	
Other Selling Expenses	32,910	
Utilities Expense	3,930	
	$701,050	$701,050

2. Prepare an income statement, a statement of retained earnings, and a balance sheet. Sales salaries expense; other selling expenses; store supplies expense; and depreciation expense, store equipment are selling expenses.
3. From the work sheet, prepare closing entries.

Appendix B
Special-Purpose Journals

Most business transactions—90 to 95 percent—fall into one of four categories. Each kind of transaction can be recorded in a special-purpose journal:

Transaction	Special-Purpose Journal	Posting Abbreviation
Sale of merchandise on credit	Sales journal	S
Purchase on credit	Purchases journal	P
Receipt of cash	Cash receipts journal	CR
Disbursement of cash	Cash payments journal	CP

The general journal is used to record transactions that do not fall into any of these special categories. (The posting abbreviation is J.)

Using special-purpose journals greatly reduces the work involved in entering and posting transactions in the general ledger. For example, in most cases, instead of posting every debit and credit for each transaction, only the total amounts of the transactions are posted. In addition, labor can be divided by assigning each journal to a different employee. This division of labor is important in establishing good internal control. Special-purpose journals thus promote efficiency, economy, and control. The concepts that underly these journals also underlie the programs that drive computerized general ledger accounting systems.

SALES JOURNAL

The *sales journal* is designed to handle all credit sales. Cash sales are recorded in the cash receipts journal. Exhibit 1 illustrates a page from a typical sales journal and related ledger accounts. The page records six sales transactions involving five customers. Notice how the sales journal saves time:

1. Only one line is needed to record each transaction. Each entry consists of a debit to a customer in Accounts Receivable. The corresponding credit to Sales is understood.

2. The account names do not have to be written out because each entry automatically is debited to Accounts Receivable and credited to Sales.

3. No explanations are necessary because the function of the sales journal is to record credit sales only.

4. Only one amount—the total credit sales for the month—has to be posted. It is posted twice: once as a debit to Accounts Receivable and once as a credit to Sales. You can see the time this saves for the six transactions listed in Exhibit 1. Imagine the time saved when there are hundreds of sales transactions.

■ **CONTROLLING ACCOUNTS AND SUBSIDIARY LEDGERS** Every entry in the sales journal represents a debit to a customer's account in Accounts Receivable. Throughout the book, we've posted all such transactions to Accounts Receivable. However, a single entry in Accounts Receivable does not tell us how much each customer has bought and how much each customer has paid or still owes. In practice, almost all companies that sell to customers on credit keep an individual accounts receivable record for each customer. If the company has 6,000 credit customers, there are 6,000 accounts receivable. To include all these accounts in the general ledger with the other asset, liability, and stockholders' equity accounts would make it very bulky. Consequently, most companies place individual customers' accounts in a separate ledger, called a *subsidiary ledger*. In the accounts receivable subsidiary

EXHIBIT 1
Sales Journal and Related Ledger Accounts

ledger, customers' accounts are filed either alphabetically or numerically (if account numbers are used).

When a company puts its individual customers' accounts in an accounts receivable subsidiary ledger, it still must maintain an Accounts Receivable account in the general ledger. This account is called a *controlling account* or *control account*, and it "controls" the subsidiary ledger in that its balance must equal the total of the individual account balances in the subsidiary ledger. The balance of the controlling account on the balance sheet date appears as Accounts Receivable on the balance sheet. For transactions that involve accounts receivable, entries must be posted to the individual customers' accounts daily. Amounts are posted to the controlling account at least once a month. If a wrong amount has been posted, the sum of customers' account balances in the subsidiary accounts receivable ledger will not equal the balance of the corresponding controlling account in the general ledger. When these amounts do not match, the accountant must find and correct the error.

Exhibit 2 shows how controlling accounts work. The single controlling account in the general ledger summarizes all the individual accounts in the subsidiary ledger. Most companies use an accounts payable subsidiary ledger as well.

■ **SUMMARY OF THE SALES JOURNAL PROCEDURE** Exhibit 2 illustrates the procedure for using a sales journal:

1. Enter each sales invoice in the sales journal on a single line. Record the date, the customer's name, the invoice number, and the amount. No column is needed for the terms if the terms on all sales are the same.

2. At the end of each day, post each individual sale to the customer's account in the accounts receivable subsidiary ledger. As each sale is posted, place a check-

EXHIBIT 2
Relationship of Sales Journal, General Ledger, and Accounts Receivable Subsidiary Ledger and the Posting Procedure

mark (or customer account number, if used) in the Post. Ref. (posting reference) column of the sales journal to indicate that it has been posted. In the Post. Ref. column of each customer's account, place an S and the sales journal page number (S1 means Sales Journal—Page 1) to indicate the source of the entry.

3. At the end of the month, sum the Amount column in the sales journal to determine the total credit sales, and post the total to the general ledger accounts (debit Accounts Receivable and credit Sales). Place the numbers of the accounts debited and credited beneath the total in the sales journal to indicate that this step has been completed. In the general ledger, indicate the source of the entry in the Post. Ref. column of each account.

4. Verify the accuracy of the posting by adding the account balances of the accounts receivable subsidiary ledger and comparing the total with the balance

Exhibit 3
Schedule of Accounts Receivable

Mitchell's Used Car Sales
Schedule of Accounts Receivable
July 31, 20xx

Peter Clark	$1,975
Eugene Cumberland	335
Maxwell Gertz	1,165
Georgetta Jones	500
Michael Powers	975
Total Accounts Receivable	$4,950

of the Accounts Receivable controlling account in the general ledger. You can do this by listing the accounts in a schedule of accounts receivable, like the one in Exhibit 3, in the order in which the accounts are maintained. This step is performed after posting collections on account in the cash receipts journal.

■ **SALES TAXES** Other columns can be added to the sales journal. Many cities and states require retailers to collect a sales tax from their customers and periodically remit the total collected to the city or state. In this case, an additional column is needed in the sales journal to record the credit to Sales Taxes Payable on credit sales. The form of the entry is shown in Exhibit 4.

PURCHASES JOURNAL

The *purchases journal* is used to record purchases on credit. It can take the form of either a single-column journal or a multicolumn journal. In the single-column journal shown in Exhibit 5, only credit purchases of merchandise for resale to customers are recorded. This kind of transaction is recorded with a debit to Purchases and a credit to Accounts Payable. When the single-column purchases journal is used, credit purchases of items other than merchandise are recorded in the general journal. Cash purchases are never recorded in the purchases journal; they are recorded in the cash payments journal, which we explain later.

Like the Accounts Receivable account, the Accounts Payable account in the general ledger is generally used as a controlling account. So that the company knows how much it owes each supplier, it keeps a separate account for each supplier in an accounts payable subsidiary ledger.

The procedure for using the purchases journal is much like that for using the sales journal:

1. Enter each purchase invoice in the purchases journal on a single line. Record the date, the supplier's name, the invoice date, the terms (if given), and the amount. It is not necessary to record the shipping terms in the terms column because they do not affect the payment date.

2. At the end of each day, post each individual purchase to the supplier's account in the accounts payable subsidiary ledger. As each purchase is posted, place a checkmark in the Post. Ref. column of the purchases journal to show that it has been posted. Also place a *P* and the page number of the purchases journal (*P1* stands for Purchases Journal—Page 1) in the Post. Ref. column of each supplier's account to show the source of the entry.

3. At the end of the month, sum the Amount column in the purchases journal, and post the total to the general ledger accounts (a debit to Purchases and a credit to Accounts Payable). Place the numbers of the accounts debited and credited beneath the totals in the purchases journal to show that this step has

EXHIBIT 4
Section of a Sales Journal with a Column for Sales Taxes

Sales Journal — Page 2

Date	Account Debited	Invoice Number	Post. Ref.	Debit Accounts Receivable	Credits Sales Taxes Payable	Sales
Aug. 1	Ralph P. Hake	727	✓	206	6	200

EXHIBIT 5
Relationship of Single-Column Purchases Journal to the General Ledger and the Accounts Payable Subsidiary Ledger

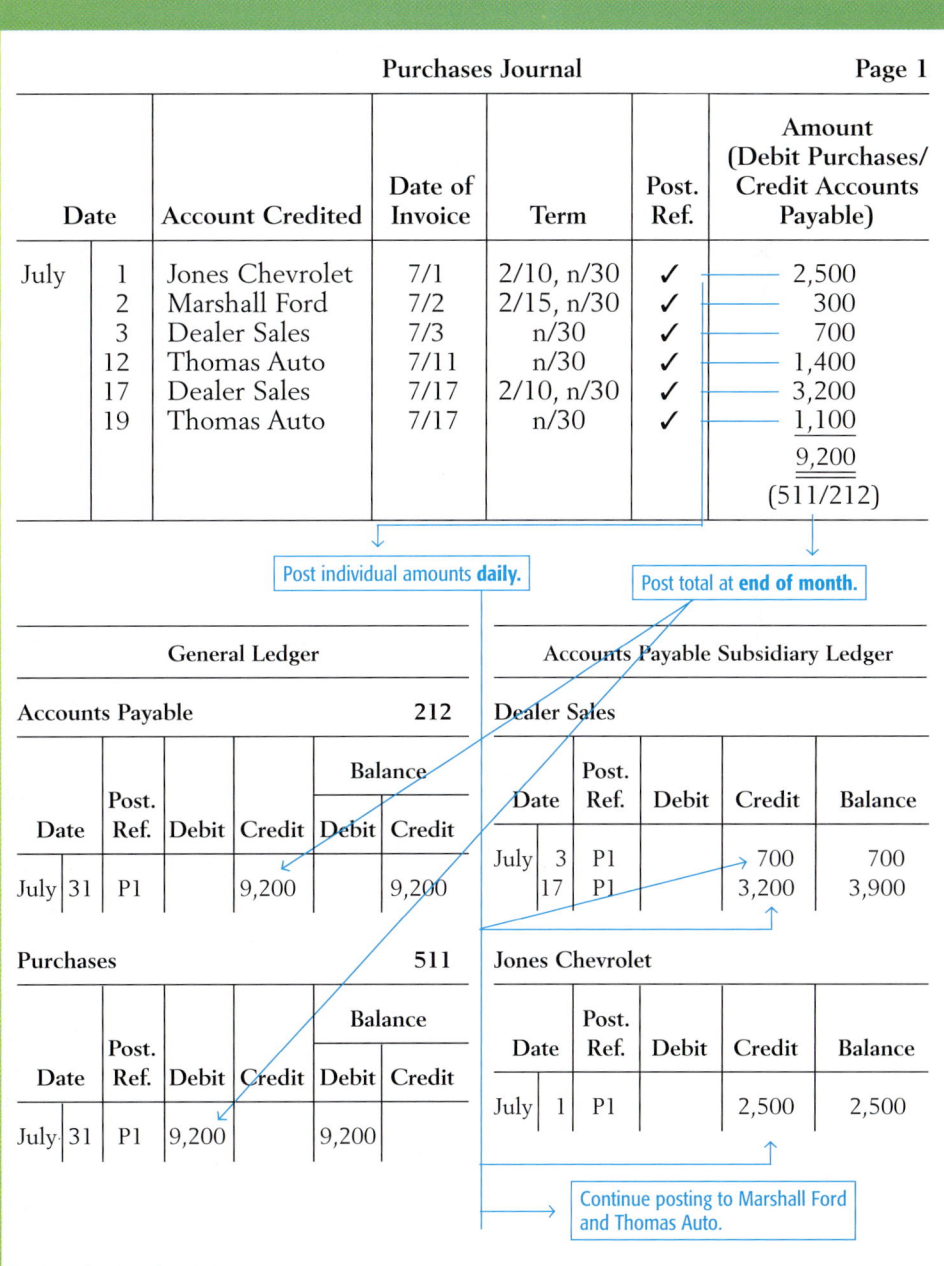

EXHIBIT 6
A Multicolumn Purchases Journal

Purchases Journal   Page 1

Date		Account Credited	Date of Invoice	Terms	Post. Ref.	Credit — Accounts Payable	Debits — Purchases	Freight In	Store Supplies	Office Supplies	Other Accounts — Account	Post. Ref.	Amount
July	1	Jones Chevrolet	7/1	2/10, n/30	✓	2,500	2,500						
	2	Marshall Ford	7/2	2/15, n/30	✓	300	300						
	2	Shelby Car Delivery	7/2	n/30	✓	50		50					
	3	Dealer Sales	7/3	n/30	✓	700	700						
	12	Thomas Auto	7/11	n/30	✓	1,400	1,400						
	17	Dealer Sales	7/17	2/10, n/30	✓	3,200	3,200						
	19	Thomas Auto	7/17	n/30	✓	1,100	1,100						
	25	Osborne Supply	7/21	n/10	✓	187			145	42			
	28	Auto Supply	7/28	n/10	✓	200					Parts	120	200
						9,637	9,200	50	145	42			200
						(212)	(511)	(514)	(132)	(133)			(✓)

been carried out. In the general ledger, indicate the source of the entry in the Post. Ref. column of each account.

4. Check the accuracy of the posting by adding the account balances of the accounts payable subsidiary ledger and comparing the total with the balance of the Accounts Payable controlling account in the general ledger. This step can be done by preparing a schedule of accounts payable from the subsidiary ledger.

The single-column purchases journal can be expanded to record credit purchases of items other than merchandise by adding separate debit columns for other accounts that are used often. For example, the multicolumn purchases journal in Exhibit 6 has columns for Freight In, Store Supplies, Office Supplies, and Other Accounts. Here, the total credits to Accounts Payable ($9,637) equal the total debits to the individual accounts listed ($9,200 + $50 + $145 + $42 + $200). Again, the individual transactions in the Accounts Payable column are posted daily to the accounts payable subsidiary ledger, and the totals of each column in the purchases journal are posted monthly to the corresponding general ledger accounts.

CASH RECEIPTS JOURNAL

All transactions involving receipts of cash are recorded in the *cash receipts journal*. Examples of these transactions are cash from cash sales and cash from credit customers in payment of their accounts. Although all cash receipts are alike in that they require a debit to Cash, they differ in that they require a variety of credit entries. Thus, the cash receipts journal must have several columns. The account numbers are entered in the Post. Ref. column, and the amounts are posted daily to the appropriate account in the general ledger.

The cash receipts journal shown in Exhibit 7 has three debit columns and three credit columns. The three debit columns are as follows:

1. *Cash*   Each entry must have an amount in this column because each transaction involves a receipt of cash.

EXHIBIT 7
Relationship of the Cash Receipts Journal to the General Ledger and the Accounts Receivable Subsidiary Ledger

2. *Sales Discounts* This company allows a 2 percent discount for prompt payment. Therefore, it is useful to have a column for sales discounts. Notice that in the transactions of July 8 and 28, the debits to Cash and Sales Discounts equal the credits to Accounts Receivable.
3. *Other Accounts* The Other Accounts column (sometimes called *Sundry Accounts*) is used for transactions that involve both a debit to Cash and a debit to some account other than Sales Discounts.

These are the credit columns:

1. *Accounts Receivable* This column is used to record collections on account from customers. The name of the customer is written in the Account Debited/Credited column so that the payment can be entered in the corresponding account in the accounts receivable subsidiary ledger. Posting to the individual accounts receivable accounts is usually done daily so that each customer's balance is up to date.
2. *Sales* This column is used to record all cash sales during the month. Retail firms that use cash registers would make an entry at the end of each day for the total sales from each cash register for that day. The debit, of course, is in the Cash debit column.
3. *Other Accounts* This column is used for the credit portion of any entry that is neither a cash collection from accounts receivable nor a cash sale. The name of the account to be credited is indicated in the Account Debited/Credited column. For example, the transactions of July 1, 20, and 24 involve credits to accounts other than Accounts Receivable or Sales. These individual postings should be done daily (or weekly if there are just a few of them). If a company finds that it consistently is crediting a certain account in the Other Accounts column, it can add another credit column to the cash receipts journal for that particular account.

The procedure for posting the cash receipts journal, as shown in Exhibit 7, is as follows:

1. Post the transactions in the Accounts Receivable column daily to the individual accounts in the accounts receivable subsidiary ledger. The amount credited to the customer's account is the same as that credited to Accounts Receivable. A checkmark in the Post. Ref. column of the cash receipts journal indicates that the amount has been posted, and a *CR1* (Cash Receipts Journal—Page 1) in the Post. Ref. column of each subsidiary ledger account indicates the source of the entry.
2. Post the debits/credits in the Other Accounts columns daily, or at convenient short intervals during the month, to the general ledger accounts. Write the account number in the Post. Ref. column of the cash receipts journal as the individual items are posted to indicate that the posting has been done, and write *CR1* in the Post. Ref. column of the general ledger account to indicate the source of the entry.
3. At the end of the month, total the columns in the cash receipts journal. The sum of the Debits column totals must equal the sum of the Credits column totals:

Debits Column Totals		Credits Column Totals	
Cash	$32,528	Accounts Receivable	$ 1,850
Sales Discounts	22	Sales	5,200
Other Accounts	0	Other Accounts	25,500
Total Debits	$32,550	Total Credits	$32,550

This step is called *crossfooting*.
4. Post the Debits column totals as follows:
   a. *Cash* Posted as a debit to the Cash account.
   b. *Sales Discounts* Posted as a debit to the Sales Discounts account.

5. Post the Credits column totals as follows:
   a. *Accounts Receivable* Posted as a credit to the Accounts Receivable controlling account.
   b. *Sales* Posted as a credit to the Sales account.
6. Write the account numbers below each column in the cash receipts journal as they are posted to indicate that these steps have been completed. *CR1* is written in the Post. Ref. column of each account in the general ledger to indicate the source of the entry.
7. Notice that the total of the Other Accounts column is not posted because each entry was posted separately when the transaction occurred. The individual accounts were posted in step **2**. Place a checkmark at the bottom of the column to show that postings in that column have been made and that the total is not posted.

CASH PAYMENTS JOURNAL

All transactions involving payments of cash are recorded in the *cash payments journal* (also called the *cash disbursements journal*). Examples of these transactions are cash purchases and payments of obligations resulting from earlier purchases on credit. The form of the cash payments journal is much like that of the cash receipts journal.

The cash payments journal shown in Exhibit 8 has three credit columns and two debit columns.

The credit columns for the cash payments journal are as follows:

1. *Cash* Each entry must have an amount in this column because each transaction involves a payment of cash.
2. *Purchases Discounts* When purchases discounts are taken, they are recorded in this column.
3. *Other Accounts* This column is used to record credits to accounts other than Cash or Purchases Discounts. Notice that the July 31 transaction shows a purchase of Land for $15,000, with a check for $5,000 and a note payable for $10,000.

The debit columns are as follows:

1. *Accounts Payable* This column is used to record payments to suppliers that have extended credit to the company. Each supplier's name is written in the Payee column so that the payment can be entered in the supplier's account in the accounts payable subsidiary ledger.
2. *Other Accounts* Cash can be expended for many reasons. Therefore, an Other Accounts or Sundry Accounts column is needed in the cash payments journal. The title of the account to be debited is written in the Account Credited/Debited column, and the amount is entered in the Other Accounts debit column. If a company finds that a particular account appears often in the Other Accounts column, it can add another debit column to the cash payments journal.

The procedure for posting the cash payments journal, shown in Exhibit 8, is as follows:

1. Post the transactions in the Accounts Payable column daily to the individual accounts in the accounts payable subsidiary ledger. Place a checkmark in the Post. Ref. column of the cash payments journal to indicate that the posting has been made.
2. Post the debits/credits in the Other Accounts debit/credit columns to the general ledger daily or at convenient short intervals during the month. Write the account number in the Post. Ref. column of the cash payments journal as the individual items are posted to indicate that the posting has been completed and

Exhibit 8
Relationship of the Cash Payments Journal to the General Ledger and the Accounts Payable Subsidiary Ledger

Cash Payments Journal — Page 1

Date	Ck. No.	Payee	Account Credited/Debited	Post. Ref.	Cash (Cr)	Purchases Discounts (Cr)	Other Accounts (Cr)	Accounts Payable (Dr)	Other Accounts (Dr)
July 2	101	Sondra Tidmore	Purchases	511	400				400
6	102	Daily Journal	Advertising Expense	612	200				200
8	103	Siviglia Agency	Rent Expense	631	250				250
11	104	Jones Chevrolet		✓	2,450	50		2,500	
16	105	Charles Kuntz	Salaries Expense	611	600				600
17	106	Marshall Ford		✓	294	6		300	
24	107	Grabow & Co.	Prepaid Insurance	119	480				480
27	108	Dealer Sales		✓	3,136	64		3,200	
30	109	A&B Equipment Company	Office Equipment / Service Equipment	144 / 146	900				400 / 500
31	110	Burns Real Estate	Notes Payable / Land	213 / 141	5,000		10,000		15,000
					13,710	120	10,000	6,000	17,830
					(111)	(512)	(✓)	(212)	(✓)

- Post individual amounts in Other Accounts column **daily**.
- Post individual amounts in Accounts Payable Subsidiary Ledger column **daily**.
- Post totals at **end of month**.
- Totals not posted.

General Ledger

Cash — 111

Date	Post. Ref.	Debit	Credit	Balance Debit	Balance Credit
July 31	CR1	32,528		32,528	
31	CP1		13,710	18,818	

Prepaid Insurance — 119

Date	Post. Ref.	Debit	Credit	Balance Debit	Balance Credit
July 24	CP1	480		480	

Continue posting to Land, Office Equipment, Service Equipment, Notes Payable, Purchases, Salaries Expense, Advertising Expense, and Rent Expense.

Continue posting to Purchases Discounts and Accounts Payable.

Accounts Payable Subsidiary Ledger

Dealer Sales

Date	Post. Ref.	Debit	Credit	Balance
July 3	P1		700	700
17	P1		3,200	3,900
27	CP1	3,200		700

Jones Chevrolet

Date	Post. Ref.	Debit	Credit	Balance
July 1	P1		2,500	2,500
11	CP1	2,500		—

Marshall Ford

Date	Post. Ref.	Debit	Credit	Balance
July 2	P1		300	300
17	CP1	300		—

CP1 (Cash Payments Journal—Page 1) in the Post. Ref. column of each general ledger account.

3. At the end of the month, the columns are footed and crossfooted. That is, the sum of the Credits column totals must equal the sum of the Debits column totals, as follows:

Credits Column Totals		Debits Column Totals	
Cash	$13,710	Accounts Payable	$ 6,000
Purchases Discounts	120	Other Accounts	17,830
Other Accounts	10,000		
Total Credits	$23,830	Total Debits	$23,830

4. At the end of the month, post the column totals for Cash, Purchases Discounts, and Accounts Payable to their respective accounts in the general ledger. Write the account number below each column in the cash payments journal as it is posted to indicate that this step has been completed and CP1 in the Post. Ref. column of each general ledger account. Place a checkmark under the total of each Other Accounts column in the cash payments journal to indicate that the postings in the column have been made and that the total is not posted.

GENERAL JOURNAL

Adjusting and closing entries are recorded in the general journal. Transactions that do not involve sales, purchases, cash receipts, or cash payments should also be recorded in the general journal. Usually, there are only a few of these transactions. Two examples of entries that do not fit in a special-purpose journal are a return of merchandise bought on account and an allowance from a supplier for credit.

These entries are shown in Exhibit 9. Notice that the entries include a debit or a credit to a controlling account (Accounts Payable or Accounts Receivable). The name of the customer or supplier also is given here. When this kind of debit or credit is made to a controlling account in the general ledger, the entry must be posted twice: once to the controlling account and once to the individual account in the subsidiary ledger. This procedure keeps the subsidiary ledger equal to the controlling account. Notice that the July 26 transaction is posted by a debit to Sales Returns and Allowances in the general ledger (shown by the account number 413), a credit to the Accounts Receivable controlling account in the general ledger (account number 114), and a credit to the Maxwell Gertz account in the accounts receivable subsidiary ledger (checkmark).

EXHIBIT 9
Transactions Recorded in the General Journal

General Journal — Page 1

Date		Description	Post. Ref.	Debit	Credit
July	25	Accounts Payable, Thomas Auto	212/✓	1,400	
		Purchases Returns and Allowances	513		1,400
		Returned used car for credit; invoice date: 7/11			
	26	Sales Returns and Allowances	413	35	
		Accounts Receivable, Maxwell Gertz	114/✓		35
		Allowance for faulty tire			

PROBLEMS

P 1.
Cash Receipts and Cash Payments Journals

The items below detail all cash transactions by O'Shea Company for the month of October. The company uses multicolumn cash receipts and cash payments journals similar to those illustrated in this appendix.

Oct. 1 The owner, Michael O'Shea, invested $50,000 cash and $24,000 in equipment in the business in exchange for common stock.
  2 Paid rent to Bell Agency, $600, with check no. 75.
  3 Cash sales, $2,200.
  6 Purchased store equipment for $5,000 from Quadrangle Company, with check no. 76.
  7 Purchased merchandise for cash, $6,500, from Fillet Company, with check no. 77.
  8 Paid Said Company invoice, $1,800, less 2 percent discount, with check no. 78 (assume that a payable has already been recorded).
  9 Paid advertising bill, $350, to WKBD, with check no. 79.
  10 Cash sales, $3,910.
  12 Received $800 on account from R. Sol.
  13 Purchased used truck for cash, $3,520, from Linexx Company, with check no. 80.
  19 Received $4,180 from Silber Company, in settlement of a $4,000 note plus interest.
  20 Received $1,078 ($1,100 less $22 cash discount) from Yi Li.
  21 Declared and paid O'Shea a dividend, $2,000, by issuing check no. 81.
  23 Paid Rolod Company invoice, $2,500, less 2 percent discount, with check no. 82.
  26 Paid Dusk Company for freight on merchandise received, $60, with check no. 83.
  27 Cash sales, $4,800.
  28 Paid B. Ricardo monthly salary, $1,400, with check no. 84.
  31 Purchased land from M. Lon for $20,000, paying $5,000 with check no. 85 and signing a note payable for $15,000.

REQUIRED
1. Enter the preceding transactions in the cash receipts and cash payments journals.
2. Foot and crossfoot the journals.

P 2.
Purchases and General Journals

The following items represent the credit transactions for Maglotz Company during the month of August. The company uses a multicolumn purchases journal and a general journal similar to those illustrated in this appendix.

Aug. 2 Purchased merchandise from Lemon Company, $1,400.
  5 Purchased truck to be used in the business from Correa Company, $8,000.
  8 Purchased office supplies from Rulers Company, $400.
  12 Purchased filing cabinets from Rulers Company, $550.
  14 Purchased merchandise, $1,400, and store supplies, $200, from Kessin Company.
  17 Purchased store supplies from Lemon Company, $100, and office supplies from Tuvail Company, $50.
  20 Purchased merchandise from Kessin Company, $1,472.
  24 Purchased merchandise from Lemon Company, $2,452; the $2,452 invoice total included shipping charges, $232.
  26 Purchased office supplies from Rulers Company, $150.
  29 Purchased merchandise from Kessin Company, $290.
  30 Returned defective merchandise purchased from Kessin Company on August 20 for full credit, $432.

REQUIRED
1. Enter the preceding transactions in the purchases journal and the general journal.

   Assume that all terms are n/30 and that invoice dates are the same as the transaction dates. Use Page 1 for all references.
2. Foot and crossfoot the purchases journal.

Margaret, Capital	Tracy, Capital	Lou, Capital
45,000	15,000	30,000

Each partner has agreed to admit Vonice to the partnership.

REQUIRED ▶ Prepare the entries to record Vonice's admission to or Margaret's withdrawal from the partnership under each of the following conditions: (a) Vonice pays Margaret $12,500 for 20 percent of Margaret's interest in the partnership. (b) Vonice invests $20,000 cash in the partnership and receives an interest equal to her investment. (c) Vonice invests $30,000 cash in the partnership for a 20 percent interest in the business. A bonus is to be recorded for the original partners on the basis of their capital balances. (d) Vonice invests $30,000 cash in the partnership for a 40 percent interest in the business. The original partners give Vonice a bonus according to the ratio of their capital balances on July 31, 20x5. (e) Margaret withdraws from the partnership, taking $52,500. The excess of withdrawn assets over Margaret's partnership interest is distributed according to the balances of the Capital accounts. (f) Margaret withdraws by selling her interest directly to Vonice for $60,000.

Appendix D

International Accounting

As businesses grow, they naturally look for new sources of supply and new markets in other countries. Today, it is common for businesses to operate in more than one country, and many of these so-called *multinational* or *transnational corporations* operate throughout the world.

The extent of a company's international operations can be found in its annual report in the segment information note to the financial statements. The annual report will also contain a description of the company's international operations.

www.pepsico.com

For example, the Frito Lay segment of PepsiCo, Inc., obtains more than one-third of its $13 billion in revenues from countries outside the United States. PepsiCo's annual report contains the following description of this division's international operations:

> Frito-Lay International manufactures, markets, sells and distributes salty and sweet snacks. Products include Walkers brand snack foods in the United Kingdom, Smith's brand snack foods in Australia, Sabritas brand snack foods and Alegro and Gamesa brand sweet snacks in Mexico. Many of our U.S. brands have been introduced internationally such as Lay's and Ruffles brand potato chips, Doritos and Tostitos brand tortilla chips, Fritos brand corn chips and Cheetos brand cheese-flavored snacks. Principal international snack markets include Mexico, the United Kingdom, Brazil, Spain, the Netherlands, Australia and South Africa.[1]

www.ibm.com

www.nestle.com

www.michelin.com
www.unilever.com
www.sony.com

Table 1 shows the extent of the foreign revenues of five large U.S. corporations. IBM, for example, has operations in 80 countries and receives almost 60 percent of its sales from outside the United States. Other industrial countries, such as Switzerland, France, Germany, Great Britain, the Netherlands, and Japan, have also given rise to numerous worldwide corporations. Nestlé, the large Swiss food company, makes 98 percent of its sales outside Switzerland. Other companies that make more than half their sales outside their home countries include Michelin, the French tire maker; Unilever, the British/Netherlands consumer products company; and Sony, the Japanese electronics company. More than five hundred companies are listed on at least one stock exchange outside their home countries.

Sophisticated investors no longer restrict their investment activities to domestic securities markets. Many Americans invest in foreign securities markets, and

TABLE 1. Extent of Foreign Revenues for Selected U.S. Companies

Company	Foreign Revenues (millions)	Total Revenues (millions)	Foreign Revenues (percentage)
Exxon Mobil <www.exxonmobil.com>	$158,403	$228,439	69.3
IBM <www.ibm.com>	50,377	87,548	57.5
Ford <www.ford.com>	51,691	170,064	30.4
General Motors <www.gm.com>	48,233	184,632	26.1
PepsiCo <www.pepsico.com>	7,259	20,438	35.5

Source: Form 10-K of each company.

FIGURE 1
Value of Securities Traded on the World's Stock Markets

Source: International Finance Corporation, *Emerging Stock Markets Factbook,* © 2000.

non-Americans invest heavily in the stock market in the United States. Figure 1 shows that from 1980 to 1999, the total value of securities traded on the world's stock markets increased over twentyfold, with the U.S. share of the pie declining from 55 to 51 percent.

EFFECTS OF FOREIGN BUSINESS TRANSACTIONS

Foreign business transactions have two major effects on accounting. First, most sales or purchases of goods and services in other countries involve different currencies. Thus, one currency needs to be translated into another, using exchange rates.* An *exchange rate* is the value of one currency stated in terms of another. For example, an English company purchasing goods from a U.S. company and paying in U.S. dollars must exchange British pounds for U.S. dollars before making payment. In effect, currencies are goods that can be bought and sold. Table 2 lists the exchange rates of several currencies in terms of dollars. It shows the exchange rate for the British pound as $1.61. Like the price of any good or service, these prices change daily according to supply and demand. Accounting for these price changes in recording foreign transactions and preparing financial statements for foreign subsidiaries are discussed in the next two sections.

The second major effect of international business on accounting is that financial standards differ from country to country, which makes it difficult to compare companies from different countries. The obstacles to achieving comparability and some of the progress in solving the problem are discussed later in this appendix.

TABLE 2. Partial Listing of Foreign Exchange Rates

Country	Price in $ U.S.	Country	Price in $ U.S.
Britain (pound)	1.61	Hong Kong (dollar)	0.128
Canada (dollar)	0.704	Japan (yen)	0.008
Europe (euro)	1.12	Mexico (peso)	0.10

Source: *The Wall Street Journal,* May 5, 2003.

*At the time this chapter was written, exchange rates were fluctuating rapidly. The examples, exercises, and probems in this book use exchange rates in the general range for the countries involved.

ACCOUNTING FOR TRANSACTIONS IN FOREIGN CURRENCIES

A U.S. manufacturer may expand by selling its product to foreign customers, or it may lower its product cost by buying a less expensive part from a source in another country. In previous chapters of the text, all purchases and sales were recorded in dollars, and it was assumed that the dollar is a uniform measure in the same way that the inch and the centimeter are. But in the international marketplace, a transaction may take place in Japanese yen, British pounds, or some other currency. The values of these currencies in relation to the dollar rise and fall daily. Thus, if there is a delay between the date of sale or purchase and the date of receipt or payment, the amount of cash involved may differ from that originally agreed upon.

■ **FOREIGN SALES** When a domestic company sells merchandise abroad, it may bill either in its own country's currency or in the foreign currency. If the billing and payment are both in the domestic currency, no accounting problem arises. For example, assume that a U.S. maker of precision tools sells $160,000 worth of its products to a British company and bills the British company in dollars. The entry to record the sale and receipt of payment is familiar:

Date of Sale

A = L + OE   Accounts Receivable, British company   160,000
+   +   Sales   160,000

Date of Receipt

A = L + OE   Cash   160,000
+   Accounts Receivable, British company   160,000
−

However, if the U.S. company bills the British company in British pounds and accepts payment in pounds, the U.S. company may incur an *exchange gain or loss*. A gain or loss will occur if the exchange rate between dollars and pounds changes between the date of sale and the date of receipt. Since gains and losses tend to offset one another, a single account is used during the year to accumulate the activity. The net exchange gain or loss is reported on the income statement. For example, assume that the sale of $160,000 above was billed at £100,000, reflecting an exchange rate of 1.60 (that is, $1.60 per pound) on the sale date. Now assume that by the date of receipt, the exchange rate has fallen to 1.50. The entries to record the transactions follow:

Date of Sale

A = L + OE   Accounts Receivable, British company   160,000
+   +   Sales   160,000
                    £100,000 × $1.60 = $160,000

Date of Receipt

A = L + OE   Cash   150,000
+   −   Exchange Gain or Loss   10,000
−   Accounts Receivable, British company   160,000
                    £100,000 × $1.50 = $150,000

The U.S. company has incurred an exchange loss of $10,000 because it agreed to accept a fixed number of British pounds in payment for its products, and the value of each pound dropped before the payment was made. Had the value of the pound in relation to the dollar increased, the U.S. company would have made an exchange gain.

FOREIGN PURCHASES The same logic applies to purchases as to sales, except that the relationship of exchange gains and losses to changes in exchange rates is reversed. For example, assume that the U.S. toolmaker purchases parts from a Japanese supplier for $15,000. If the purchase and payment are made in U.S. dollars, no accounting problem arises.

Date of Purchase

A = L + OE + −	Purchases Accounts Payable, Japanese company	15,000 15,000

Date of Payment

A = L + OE − −	Accounts Payable, Japanese company Cash	15,000 15,000

However, the Japanese company may bill the U.S. company in yen and be paid in yen. If so, the U.S. company will incur an exchange gain or loss if the exchange rate changes between the date of purchase and the date of payment. For example, assume that the transaction is for ¥2,500,000 and that the exchange rates on the dates of purchase and payment are $.0090 and $.0085 per yen, respectively. The entries are as follows:

Date of Purchase

A = L + OE
+   −
	Purchases
	    Accounts Payable, Japanese company
	    ¥2,500,000 × $.0090 = $22,500
		22,500
		22,500

Date of Payment

A = L + OE
−   −   +
	Accounts Payable, Japanese company
	    Exchange Gain or Loss
	    Cash
	    ¥2,500,000 × $.0085 = $21,250
		22,500
		1,250
		21,250

In this case, the U.S. company received an exchange gain of $1,250 because it agreed to pay a fixed ¥2,500,000, and between the dates of purchase and payment, the exchange value of the yen decreased in relation to the dollar.

REALIZED VERSUS UNREALIZED EXCHANGE GAIN OR LOSS The preceding illustrations dealt with completed transactions (in the sense that payment was made). In each case, the exchange gain or loss was recognized on the date of receipt or payment. If financial statements are prepared between the sale or purchase and the receipt or payment and exchange rates have changed, there will be unrealized gains or losses. The Financial Accounting Standards Board's *Statement No. 52* requires that exchange gains and losses "be included in determining net income for the period in which the exchange rate changes."[2] The requirement includes interim (quarterly) statements and applies whether or not a transaction is complete.

This ruling has caused much debate. Critics charge that it gives too much weight to fleeting changes in exchange rates, causing random changes in earnings that hide long-run trends. Others believe that the use of current exchange rates to value receivables and payables as of the balance sheet date is a major step toward economic reality (current values). To illustrate, we use the preceding case, in which a U.S. company buys parts from a Japanese supplier. We assume that the transaction has not been completed by the balance sheet date, when the exchange rate is $.0080 per yen:

	Date	Exchange Rate ($ per Yen)
Date of purchase	Dec. 1	.0090
Balance sheet date	Dec. 31	.0080
Date of payment	Feb. 1	.0085

The accounting effects of the unrealized gain are as follows:

	Dec. 1	Dec. 31	Feb. 1
Purchase recorded in U.S. dollars (billed as ¥2,500,000)	$22,500	$22,500	$22,500
Dollars to be paid to equal ¥2,500,000 (¥2,500,000 × exchange rate)	22,500	20,000	21,250
Unrealized gain (or loss)	—	$ 2,500	
Realized gain (or loss)			$ 1,250

A = L + OE + −	Dec. 1	Purchases Accounts Payable, Japanese company	22,500	22,500
A = L + OE − +	Dec. 31	Accounts Payable, Japanese company Exchange Gain or Loss	2,500	2,500
A = L + OE − − −	Feb. 1	Accounts Payable, Japanese company Exchange Gain or Loss Cash	20,000 1,250	21,250

In this case, the original sale was billed in yen by the Japanese company. Following the rules of *Statement No. 52*, an exchange gain of $2,500 is recorded on December 31, and an exchange loss of $1,250 is recorded on February 1. Even though these large fluctuations do not affect the net exchange gain of $1,250 for the whole transaction, the effect on each year's income statements may be important.

RESTATEMENT OF FOREIGN SUBSIDIARY FINANCIAL STATEMENTS

Companies often expand by establishing or buying foreign subsidiaries. If a company owns more than 50 percent of a foreign subsidiary and thus exercises control, then the foreign subsidiary should be included in the consolidated financial statements. The reporting of foreign subsidiaries is covered by FASB *Statement No. 52*. The consolidation procedure is the same as the one we described for domestic subsidiaries, except that the statements of the foreign subsidiary must be restated in the reporting currency before consolidation takes place. The *reporting currency* is the currency in which the consolidated financial statements are presented, which for U.S. companies is usually the U.S. dollar. Clearly, it makes no sense to combine the assets of a Mexican subsidiary stated in pesos with the assets of the U.S. parent company stated in dollars. Thus, *restatement* in the currency of the parent company is necessary.

The method of restatement depends on the foreign subsidiary's *functional currency*, which is the currency of the place where the subsidiary carries on most of its business. Generally, it is the currency in which a company earns and spends its cash. The functional currency used depends on the kind of foreign operation in which the subsidiary takes part.

There are two broad types of foreign operation. Type I includes those that are fairly self-contained and integrated within a certain country or economy. Type II includes those that are mainly a direct and integral part or extension of the parent company's operations. As a rule, Type I subsidiaries use the currency of the country in which they are located, and Type II subsidiaries use the currency of the parent company. If the parent is a U.S. company, the functional currency of a Type I subsidiary will be the currency of the country where the subsidiary carries on its business, and the functional currency of a Type II subsidiary will be the U.S. dollar. *Statement No. 52* makes an exception when a Type I subsidiary operates in a country where there is hyperinflation (as a rule of thumb, more than 100 percent cumulative inflation over three years), such as Brazil or Argentina. In such a case, the subsidiary is treated as a Type II subsidiary, with the functional currency being the U.S. dollar. Restatements in these situations do not affect cash flows because they are done simply for the convenience of preparing consolidated statements.

INTERNATIONAL ACCOUNTING STANDARDS

International investors need to compare the financial position and results of operations of companies from different countries. At present, however, few standards of accounting are recognized worldwide.[3] For example, LIFO is the most popular method of valuing inventory in the United States, but it is not acceptable in most European countries. Historical cost is strictly followed in Germany, replacement cost is used by some companies in the Netherlands, and a mixed system, allowing lower of cost or market in some cases, is used in the United States and Britain. Even the formats of financial statements differ from country to country. In Britain and France, for example, the order of the balance sheets is almost the reverse of that in the United States. In those countries, property, plant, and equipment is the first listing in the assets section.

A number of major problems stand in the way of setting international standards. One is that accountants and users of accounting information have not been able to agree on the goals of financial statements. Differences in the way the accounting profession has developed in various countries, in the laws regulating companies, and in governmental and other requirements present other hurdles. Further difficulties are created by differences among countries in the basic economic factors affecting financial reporting, inconsistencies in practices recommended by the accounting profession in different countries, and the influence of tax laws on financial reporting.

Probably the best hopes for finding areas of agreement among different countries are the International Accounting Standards Board (IASB) and the International Federation of Accountants (IFAC).

The role of the IASB is to contribute to the development and adoption of accounting principles that are relevant, balanced, and comparable throughout the world by formulating and publicizing accounting standards and encouraging their observance in the presentation of financial statements.[4] The standards issued by the IASB are generally followed by large multinational companies that are clients of international accounting firms. The IASB has been especially helpful to companies in developing economies that do not have the financial history or resources to develop accounting standards. The IASB is currently engaged in a major project to improve financial reporting worldwide by introducing a set of international accounting standards that will be acceptable to the world's securities regulators, such as the SEC in the United States. If successful, the effort should make it easier for companies to raise equity capital and list their stocks in other countries.

The IFAC, formed in 1977, also includes most of the world's accountancy organizations. It fully supports the work of the IASB and recognizes the IASB as the sole body with responsibility and authority to issue pronouncements on international accounting standards. The IFAC's principal role is to assure quality audits and financial statements prepared in accordance with international accounting standards. It attempts to accomplish this objective by issuing international auditing standards and monitoring the practice of international firms.

The European Community is also attempting to harmonize accounting standards. One of its directives requires certain minimum, uniform reporting and disclosure standards for financial statements. Other directives deal with uniform rules for preparing consolidated financial statements and qualifications of auditors. More importantly, the European Community has agreed to require international accounting standards beginning in 2005 for all companies that seek financing across borders. This is an important step for recognition of international accounting standards and for the goal of a single European market. It will leave the United States as the only major market that does not accept international accounting standards.

The road to international harmony is not easy. However, there is reason for optimism because an increasing number of countries are recognizing the appropriateness of uniform accounting standards in international trade and commerce.

PROBLEMS

P 1.
Recording International Transactions: Fluctuating Exchange Rate

Part A: Wooster Corporation purchased a special-purpose machine from Konigsberg Corporation on credit for E 50,000. At the date of purchase, the exchange rate was $.90 per euro. On the date of the payment, which was made in euros, the value of the euro was $.95. Prepare entries in journal form to record the purchase and payment in Wooster Corporation's accounting records.

Part B: U.S. Corporation made a sale on account to U.K. Company on November 15 in the amount of £300,000. Payment was to be made in British pounds on February 15. U.S. Corporation's fiscal year is the same as the calendar year. The British pound was worth $1.70 on November 15, $1.58 on December 31, and $1.78 on February 15. Prepare entries in journal form to record the sale, year-end adjustment, and collection on U.S. Corporation's books.

P 2.
International Transactions

Dolfsky Import/Export Company, whose year end is October 31, engaged in the following transactions (exchange rates in parentheses):

Aug. 12   Sold goods to a Mexican firm for $20,000; terms n/30 in U.S. dollars (peso = $.131).
     24   Purchased goods from a Japanese firm for $40,000; terms n/20 in yen (yen = $.0080).
Sept. 2   Sold goods to a British firm for $48,000; terms n/30 in pounds (pound = $1.60).
     11   Received payment in full for August 12 sale (peso = $.128).
     13   Paid for the goods purchased on August 24 (yen = $.0088).
     21   Purchased goods from an Italian firm for $28,000; terms n/10 in U.S. dollars (euro = $.90).
     30   Purchased goods from a Japanese firm for $35,200; terms n/60 in yen (yen = $.0088).
Oct. 2   Paid for the goods purchased on September 21 (euro = $.85).
      3   Received payment in full for the goods sold on September 2 (pound = $1.50).
      8   Sold goods to a French firm for $66,000; terms n/30 in euros (euro = $.88).
     19   Purchased goods from a Mexican firm for $37,000; terms n/30 in U.S. dollars (peso = $.135).
     31   Made year-end adjusting entries for incomplete foreign exchange transactions (euro = $.85; peso = $.130; pound = $1.40; yen = $.0100).
Nov. 9   Received payment for the goods sold on October 8 (euro = $.87).
     18   Paid for the goods purchased on October 19 (peso = $.132).
     28   Paid for the goods purchased on September 30 (yen = $.0090).

REQUIRED ▶ Prepare entries in journal form for these transactions.

Appendix E

Long-Term Investments

www.pepsico.com

Companies make long-term investments for a variety of reasons. For instance, PepsiCo makes investments in operations critical to the distribution of its products, such as its investments in PepsiCo Bottling Company. It also makes investments to expand its markets, as in its purchases of Tropicana, South Beach Beverage, and Quaker Oats. These are stock investments, but a company can also make long-term investments in bonds. Investments in bonds can be a way of ensuring that an affiliate company has sufficient long-term capital, or it can simply be a way of making a relatively secure investment. The following sections discuss the classifications of bonds and stocks and the methods used to account for such investments.

LONG-TERM INVESTMENTS IN BONDS

Like all investments, investments in bonds are recorded at cost, which, in this case, is the price of the bonds plus the broker's commission. When bonds are purchased between interest payment dates, the purchaser must also pay an amount equal to the interest that has accrued on the bonds since the last interest payment date. Then, on the next interest payment date, the purchaser receives an interest payment for the whole period. The payment for accrued interest should be recorded as a debit to Interest Income, which will be offset by a credit to Interest Income when the semiannual interest is received.

Subsequent accounting for a corporation's long-term bond investments depends on the classification of the bonds. If the company plans at some point to sell the bonds, they are classified as *available-for-sale securities*. If the company plans to hold the bonds until they are paid off on their maturity date, they are considered *held-to-maturity securities*. Except in industries like insurance and banking, it is unusual for companies to buy the bonds of other companies with the express purpose of holding them until they mature, which can be in 10 to 30 years. Thus, most long-term bond investments are available-for-sale securities. Such bonds are accounted for at fair value, much as equity or stock investments are; fair value is usually the market value. When bonds are intended to be held to maturity, they are accounted for not at fair value but at cost, adjusted for the amortization of their discount or premium. The procedure is similar to accounting for long-term bond liabilities, except that separate accounts for discounts and premiums are not used.

KEY POINT: The fair value of bonds is closely related to interest rates. An increase in interest rates lowers the fair value of bonds, and vice versa.

LONG-TERM INVESTMENTS IN STOCKS

All long-term investments in stocks are recorded at cost, in accordance with generally accepted accounting principles. The treatment of the investment in the accounting records after the initial purchase depends on the extent to which the investing company can exercise *significant influence* or *control* over the operating and financial policies of the other company. The Accounting Principles Board (APB) defined these important terms in its *Opinion No. 18*.

Significant influence is an investing firm's ability to affect the operating and financial policies of the company whose shares it owns, even though it holds 50 percent or less of the voting stock. Indications of significant influence include representation on the board of directors, participation in policymaking, and material

KEY POINT: Influence and control are related specifically to equity holdings, not debt holdings.

TABLE 1. Accounting Treatments of Long-Term Investments in Stocks

Level of Ownership	Percentage of Ownership	Accounting Treatment
Noninfluential and noncontrolling	Less than 20%	Cost initially; investment adjusted subsequent to purchase for changes in market value
Influential but noncontrolling	Between 20% and 50%	Equity method; investment valued subsequently at cost plus investor's share of income (or minus investor's share of loss) minus dividends received
Controlling	More than 50%	Financial statements consolidated

transactions, exchange of managerial personnel, and technological dependency between the two companies. For the sake of uniformity, the APB decided that without proof to the contrary, ownership of 20 percent or more of the voting stock should be presumed to confer significant influence.* Ownership of less than 20 percent of the voting stock does not confer significant influence.

Control is an investing firm's ability to decide the operating and financial policies of the other company. Control exists when the investor owns more than 50 percent of the voting stock of the company in which it has invested.

Thus, in the absence of information to the contrary, a noninfluential and noncontrolling investment would be less than 20 percent ownership. An influential but noncontrolling investment would be 20 to 50 percent ownership. And a controlling investment would be more than 50 percent ownership. The accounting treatment differs for each kind of investment. Table 1 summarizes these treatments.

■ **NONINFLUENTIAL AND NONCONTROLLING INVESTMENT** Available-for-sale securities are debt or equity securities that are not classified as trading or held-to-maturity securities. When equity securities are involved, a further criterion is that they be noninfluential and noncontrolling investments of less than 20 percent of the voting stock. The Financial Accounting Standards Board requires a *cost-adjusted-to market method* for accounting for available-for-sale securities. Under this method, available-for-sale securities must be recorded initially at cost and thereafter adjusted periodically through the use of an allowance account to reflect changes in the market value.[1]

Available-for-sale securities are classified as long term if management intends to hold them for more than one year. When accounting for long-term available-for-sale

---

*The Financial Accounting Standards Board pointed out in its *Interpretation No. 35* (May 1981) that this rule is not a rigid one. All relevant facts and circumstances should be examined to determine whether significant influence exists. The FASB noted five circumstances that may negate significant influence: (1) The company files a lawsuit against the investor or a complaint with a government agency; (2) the investor tries but fails to become a director; (3) the investor agrees not to increase its holdings; (4) the company is operated by a small group that ignores the investor's wishes; (5) the investor tries but fails to obtain company information that is not available to other stockholders.

securities, the unrealized gain or loss resulting from the adjustment is not reported on the income statement. Instead, the gain or loss is reported as a special item in the stockholders' equity section of the balance sheet and in comprehensive income disclosure.

At the end of each accounting period, the total cost and the total market value of these long-term stock investments must be determined. If the total market value is less than the total cost, the difference must be credited to a contra-asset account called Allowance to Adjust Long-Term Investments to Market. Because of the long-term nature of the investment, the debit part of the entry, which represents a decrease in value below cost, is treated as a temporary decrease and does not appear as a loss on the income statement. It is shown in a contra-stockholders' equity account called Unrealized Loss on Long-Term Investments.* Thus, both of these accounts are balance sheet accounts. If the market value exceeds the cost, the allowance account is added to Long-Term Investments, and the unrealized gain appears as an addition to stockholders' equity.

When long-term investments in stock are sold, the difference between the sale price and the cost of the stock is recorded and reported as a realized gain or loss on the income statement. Dividend income from such investments is recorded by a debit to Cash and a credit to Dividend Income. For example, assume the following facts about the long-term stock investments of Coleman Corporation:

June 1, 20x3 Paid cash for the following long-term investments: 10,000 shares of Durbin Corporation common stock (representing 2 percent of outstanding stock) at $25 per share; 5,000 shares of Kotes Corporation common stock (representing 3 percent of outstanding stock) at $15 per share.

Dec. 31, 20x3 Quoted market prices at year end: Durbin common stock, $21; Kotes common stock, $17.

Apr. 1, 20x4 Change in policy required sale of 2,000 shares of Durbin common stock at $23.

July 1, 20x4 Received cash dividend from Kotes equal to $.20 per share.

Dec. 31, 20x4 Quoted market prices at year end: Durbin common stock, $24; Kotes common stock, $13.

KEY POINT: On April 1, 20x4, a *change in policy* requires the sale. This points out that intent is often the only difference between long-term investments and short-term investments.

Entries to record these transactions are as follows:

Investment

20x3

A = L + OE June 1 Long-Term Investments 325,000
+   Cash 325,000
−   Investments in Durbin common stock (10,000 shares × $25 = $250,000) and Kotes common stock (5,000 shares × $15 = $75,000)

Year-End Adjustment

20x3

A = L + OE Dec. 31 Unrealized Loss on Long-Term Investments 30,000
−   −   Allowance to Adjust Long-Term Investments to Market 30,000
                        To record reduction of long-term investment to market

---

*If the decrease in market value of the long-term investment is deemed permanent, a different procedure is followed to record the decline. A loss account on the income statement is debited instead of the Unrealized Loss account.

Company	Shares	Market Price	Total Market	Total Cost
Durbin	10,000	$21	$210,000	$250,000
Kotes	5,000	17	85,000	75,000
			$295,000	$325,000

Total Cost − Total Market Value = $325,000 − $295,000 = $30,000

Sale

		20x4			
A = L + OE	Apr. 1	Cash		46,000	
+		Loss on Sale of Investments		4,000	
−		Long-Term Investments			50,000
		Sale of 2,000 shares of Durbin common stock			
		2,000 × $23 = $46,000			
		2,000 × $25 = 50,000			
		Loss $ 4,000			

Dividend Received

		20x4			
A = L + OE	July 1	Cash		1,000	
+		Dividend Income			1,000
+		Receipt of cash dividend from Kotes stock			
		5,000 × $.20 = $1,000			

Year-End Adjustment

		20x4			
A = L + OE	Dec. 31	Allowance to Adjust Long-Term Investments to Market		12,000	
+		Unrealized Loss on Long-Term Investments			12,000
+		To record the adjustment in long-term investment so it is reported at market			

The adjustment equals the previous balance ($30,000 from the December 31, 20x3, entry) minus the new balance ($18,000), or $12,000. The new balance of $18,000 is the difference at the present time between the total market value and the total cost of all investments. It is figured as follows:

Company	Shares	Market Price	Total Market	Total Cost
Durbin	8,000	$24	$192,000	$200,000
Kotes	5,000	13	65,000	75,000
			$257,000	$275,000

Total Cost − Total Market Value = $275,000 − $257,000 = $18,000

The Allowance to Adjust Long-Term Investments to Market and the Unrealized Loss on Long-Term Investments are reciprocal contra accounts, each with the same dollar balance, as shown by the effects of these transactions on the T accounts:

Contra-Asset Account

Allowance to Adjust Long-Term Investments to Market

20x4	12,000	20x3	30,000
		Bal. 20x4	18,000

Contra-Stockholders' Equity Account

Unrealized Loss on Long-Term Investment

20x3	30,000	20x4	12,000
Bal. 20x4	18,000		

The Allowance account reduces long-term investments by the amount by which the cost of the investments exceeds market; the Unrealized Loss account reduces stockholders' equity by a similar amount. The opposite effects will exist if market value exceeds cost, resulting in an unrealized gain.

■ **INFLUENTIAL BUT NONCONTROLLING INVESTMENT** As we have noted, ownership of 20 percent or more of a company's voting stock is considered sufficient to influence the company's operations. When this is the case, the stock investment should be accounted for using the *equity method*. The equity method presumes that an investment of 20 percent or more is not a passive investment and that the investor should therefore share proportionately in the success or failure of the company. The three main features of this method are as follows:

1. The investor records the original purchase of the stock at cost.
2. The investor records its share of the company's periodic net income as an increase in the Investment account, with a corresponding credit to an income account. Similarly, it records its share of a periodic loss as a decrease in the Investment account, with a corresponding debit to a loss account.
3. When the investor receives a cash dividend, the asset account Cash is increased, and the Investment account is decreased.

To illustrate the equity method of accounting, we assume the following facts about an investment by Vassor Corporation: On January 1 of the current year, Vassor acquired 40 percent of the voting common stock of Block Corporation for $180,000. With this share of ownership, Vassor can exert significant influence over Block's operations. During the year, Block reported net income of $80,000 and paid cash dividends of $20,000. Vassor recorded these transactions as follows:

Investment

A = L + OE
+
−

Investment in Block Corporation	180,000	
Cash		180,000
Investment in Block Corporation common stock		

Recognition of Income

A = L + OE
+   +

Investment in Block Corporation	32,000	
Income, Block Corporation Investment		32,000
Recognition of 40% of income reported by Block Corporation		
40% × $80,000 = $32,000		

Receipt of Cash Dividend

A = L + OE
+
−

Cash	8,000	
Investment in Block Corporation		8,000
Cash dividend from Block Corporation		
40% × $20,000 = $8,000		

STUDY POINT: Under the equity method, dividends received are credited to the Investment account because the dividends represent a return from or a decrease in the investment in Block Corporation.

The balance of the Investment in Block Corporation account after these transactions is $204,000, as shown here:

Investment in Block Corporation

Investment	180,000	Dividend received	8,000
Share of Income	32,000		
Balance	204,000		

ENRICHMENT NOTE:
Parents and subsidiaries are separate legal entities even though they combine their financial reports at year end.

■ **CONTROLLING INVESTMENT** Some investing firms that own less than 50 percent of the voting stock of a company exercise such powerful influence that for all practical purposes, they control the policies of the other company. Nevertheless, ownership of more than 50 percent of the voting stock is required for accounting recognition of control. When a firm has a controlling interest, a parent-subsidiary relationship is said to exist. The investing company is known as the *parent company*; the other company is a *subsidiary*. Because the two corporations are separate legal entities, each prepares separate financial statements. However, owing to their special relationship, they are viewed for public financial reporting purposes as a single economic entity. For this reason, they must combine their financial statements into a single set of statements called *consolidated financial statements*.

Accounting for consolidated financial statements is complex and is usually the subject of an advanced accounting course. However, most large public corporations have subsidiaries and must prepare consolidated financial statements. It is therefore important to have some understanding of accounting for consolidations.

PROBLEMS

Methods of Accounting for Long-Term Investments

P 1. Diversified Corporation has the following long-term investments:

1. 60 percent of the common stock of Down Corporation
2. 13 percent of the common stock of West Lake, Inc.
3. 50 percent of the nonvoting preferred stock of Invole Corporation
4. 100 percent of the common stock of its financing subsidiary, DCF, Inc.
5. 35 percent of the common stock of the French company Maison de Boutaine
6. 70 percent of the common stock of the Canadian company Alberta Mining Company

For each of these investments, tell which of the following methods should be used for external financial reporting, and why.

a. Cost adjusted to market method
b. Equity method
c. Consolidation of parent and subsidiary financial statements

Long-Term Investment Transactions

P 2. Red Bud Corporation made the following transactions in its Long-Term Investments account over a two-year period:

20x4
Apr. 1 Purchased with cash 20,000 shares of Season Company stock for $152 per share.
June 1 Purchased with cash 15,000 shares of Abbado Corporation stock for $72 per share.
Sept. 1 Received a $1 per share dividend from Season Company.
Nov. 1 Purchased with cash 25,000 shares of Frankel Corporation stock for $110 per share.
Dec. 31 Market values per share of shares held in the Long-Term Investments account were as follows: Season Company, $140; Abbado Corporation, $32; and Frankel Corporation, $122.

20x4
Feb. 1 Because of unfavorable prospects for Abbado Corporation, Abbado stock was sold for cash at $40 per share.
May 1 Purchased with cash 10,000 shares of Schulian Corporation for $224 per share.
Sept. 1 Received $2 per share dividend from Season Company.
Dec. 31 Market values per share of shares held in the Long-Term Investments account were as follows: Season Company, $160; Frankel Corporation, $140; and Schulian Corporation, $200.

REQUIRED ▶ Prepare entries to record these transactions in the Red Bud Corporation records. Assume that all investments represent less than 20 percent of the voting stock of the company whose stock was acquired.

Long-Term Investments: Equity Method

P 3. The Modi Company owns 40 percent of the voting stock of the Vivanco Company. The Investment account for this company on the Modi Company's balance sheet had a balance of $600,000 on January 1, 20xx. During 20xx, the Vivanco Company reported the following quarterly earnings and dividends paid:

Quarter	Earnings	Dividends Paid
1	$ 80,000	$ 40,000
2	60,000	40,000
3	160,000	40,000
4	(40,000)	40,000
	$260,000	$160,000

The Modi Company exercises a significant influence over the operations of the Vivanco Company and therefore uses the equity method to account for its investment.

REQUIRED ▶ 1. Prepare the entries in journal form that the Modi Company must make each quarter in accounting for its investment in the Vivanco Company.

2. Prepare a T account for the investment in common stock of the Vivanco Company. Enter the beginning balance, relevant portions of the entries made in **1**, and the ending balance.

Appendix F

The Time Value of Money

SIMPLE INTEREST AND COMPOUND INTEREST

Interest is the cost associated with the use of money for a specific period of time. Because interest is a cost associated with time, and "time is money," it is also an important consideration in any business decision. *Simple interest* is the interest cost for one or more periods, under the assumption that the amount on which the interest is computed stays the same from period to period. *Compound interest* is the interest cost for two or more periods, under the assumption that after each period the interest of that period is added to the amount on which interest is computed in future periods. In other words, compound interest is interest earned on a principal sum that is increased at the end of each period by the interest for that period.

■ **EXAMPLE—SIMPLE INTEREST** Joe Sanchez accepts an 8 percent, $30,000 note due in ninety days. How much will he receive in total at that time? Remember that the formula for calculating simple interest is as follows:

$$\begin{aligned} \text{Interest} &= \text{Principal} \times \text{Rate} \times \text{Time} \\ &= \$30{,}000 \times 8/100 \times 90/360 \\ &= \$600 \end{aligned}$$

Therefore, the total that Sanchez will receive is calculated as follows:

$$\begin{aligned} \text{Total} &= \text{Principal} + \text{Interest} \\ &= \$30{,}000 + \$600 \\ &= \$30{,}600 \end{aligned}$$

■ **EXAMPLE—COMPOUND INTEREST** Ann Clary deposits $5,000 in a savings account that pays 6 percent interest. She expects to leave the principal and accumulated interest in the account for three years. How much will her account total at the end of three years? Assume that the interest is paid at the end of the year and is added to the principal at that time, and that this total in turn earns interest. The amount at the end of three years is computed as follows:

(1) Year	(2) Principal Amount at Beginning of Year	(3) Annual Amount of Interest (Col. 2 × 6%)	(4) Accumulated Amount at End of Year (Col. 2 + Col. 3)
1	$5,000.00	$300.00	$5,300.00
2	5,300.00	318.00	5,618.00
3	5,618.00	337.08	5,955.08

At the end of three years, Clary will have $5,955.08 in her savings account. Note that the annual amount of interest increases each year by the interest rate times the interest of the previous year. For example, between year 1 and year 2, the interest increased by $18 ($318 − $300), which exactly equals 6 percent times $300.

FUTURE VALUE OF A SINGLE INVESTED SUM AT COMPOUND INTEREST

Another way to ask the question in the example of compound interest above is, What is the future value of a single sum ($5,000) at compound interest (6 percent) for three years? *Future value* is the amount that an investment will be worth at a future date if invested at compound interest. A businessperson often wants to know future value, but the method of computing the future value illustrated above is too time-consuming in practice. Imagine how tedious the calculation would be if the example were ten years instead of three. Fortunately, there are tables that simplify solving problems involving compound interest. Table 1, showing the future value of $1 after a given number of time periods, is an example. It is actually part of a larger table, Table 1 in the appendix on future value and present value tables. Suppose that we want to solve the problem of Clary's savings account above. We simply look down the 6 percent column in Table 1 until we reach the line for three periods and find the factor 1.191. This factor, when multiplied by $1, gives the future value of that $1 at compound interest of 6 percent for three periods (years in this case). Thus, we solve the problem as follows:

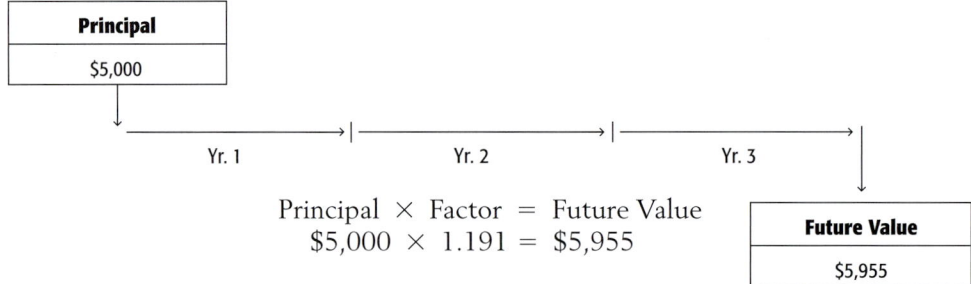

Except for a rounding difference of $.08, the answer is exactly the same as that calculated earlier.

TABLE 1. Future Value of $1 after a Given Number of Time Periods

Periods	1%	2%	3%	4%	5%	6%	7%	8%	9%	10%	12%	14%	15%
1	1.010	1.020	1.030	1.040	1.050	1.060	1.070	1.080	1.090	1.100	1.120	1.140	1.150
2	1.020	1.040	1.061	1.082	1.103	1.124	1.145	1.166	1.188	1.210	1.254	1.300	1.323
3	1.030	1.061	1.093	1.125	1.158	1.191	1.225	1.260	1.295	1.331	1.405	1.482	1.521
4	1.041	1.082	1.126	1.170	1.216	1.262	1.311	1.360	1.412	1.464	1.574	1.689	1.749
5	1.051	1.104	1.159	1.217	1.276	1.338	1.403	1.469	1.539	1.611	1.762	1.925	2.011
6	1.062	1.126	1.194	1.265	1.340	1.419	1.501	1.587	1.677	1.772	1.974	2.195	2.313
7	1.072	1.149	1.230	1.316	1.407	1.504	1.606	1.714	1.828	1.949	2.211	2.502	2.660
8	1.083	1.172	1.267	1.369	1.477	1.594	1.718	1.851	1.993	2.144	2.476	2.853	3.059
9	1.094	1.195	1.305	1.423	1.551	1.689	1.838	1.999	2.172	2.358	2.773	3.252	3.518
10	1.105	1.219	1.344	1.480	1.629	1.791	1.967	2.159	2.367	2.594	3.106	3.707	4.046

Source: Excerpt from Table 1 in the appendix on future value and present value tables.

FUTURE VALUE OF AN ORDINARY ANNUITY

Another common problem involves an *ordinary annuity*, which is a series of equal payments made at the end of equal intervals of time, with compound interest on these payments.

The following example shows how to find the future value of an ordinary annuity. Assume that Ben Katz makes a $200 payment at the end of each of the next three years into a savings account that pays 5 percent interest. How much money will he have in his account at the end of the three years? One way of computing the amount is shown in the following table.

(1) Year	(2) Beginning Balance	(3) Interest Earned (5% × Col. 2)	(4) Periodic Payment	(5) Accumulated at End of Period (Col. 2 + Col. 3 + Col. 4)
1	—	—	$200	$200.00
2	$200.00	$10.00	200	410.00
3	410.00	20.50	200	630.50

Katz would have $630.50 in his account at the end of three years, consisting of $600.00 in periodic payments and $30.50 in interest.

This calculation can also be simplified by using Table 2. We look down the 5 percent column until we reach three periods and find the factor 3.153. This factor, when multiplied by $1, gives the future value of a series of three $1 payments at compound interest of 5 percent. Thus, we solve the problem as follows:

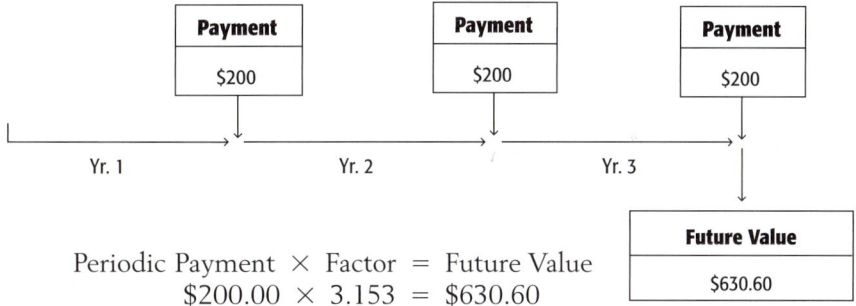

Periodic Payment × Factor = Future Value
$200.00 × 3.153 = $630.60

Except for a rounding difference of $.10, this result is the same as our earlier one.

PRESENT VALUE

Suppose that you had the choice of receiving $100 today or one year from today. Intuitively, you would choose to receive the $100 today. Why? You know that if you have the $100 today, you can put it in a savings account to earn interest, so that you will have more than $100 a year from today. Therefore, we can say that an amount to be received in the future (future value) is not worth as much today as an amount to be received today (present value) because of the cost associated with the passage of time. In fact, present value and future value are closely related. *Present value* is the amount that must be invested now at a given rate of interest to produce a given future value. For example, assume that Sue Dapper needs $1,000 one year from now. How much should she invest today to achieve that goal if the interest rate is 5 percent? From earlier examples, the following equation may be established.

$$\text{Present Value} \times (1.0 + \text{Interest Rate}) = \text{Future Value}$$
$$\text{Present Value} \times 1.05 = \$1,000.00$$
$$\text{Present Value} = \$1,000.00 \div 1.05$$
$$\text{Present Value} = \$952.38$$

Thus, to achieve a future value of $1,000.00, a present value of $952.38 must be invested. Interest of 5 percent on $952.38 for one year equals $47.62, and these two amounts added together equal $1,000.00.

■ **PRESENT VALUE OF A SINGLE SUM DUE IN THE FUTURE** When more than one time period is involved, the calculation of present value is more complicated. Consider the following example. Don Riley wants to be sure of having $4,000 at the end of three years. How much must he invest today in a 5 percent savings account to achieve this goal? Adapting the above equation, we compute the present value of $4,000 at compound interest of 5 percent for three years in the future.

Year	Amount at End of Year	Divide by		Present Value at Beginning of Year
3	$4,000.00	÷ 1.05	=	$3,809.52
2	3,809.52	÷ 1.05	=	3,628.11
1	3,628.11	÷ 1.05	=	3,455.34

Riley must invest a present value of $3,455.34 to achieve a future value of $4,000.00 in three years.

This calculation is again made much easier by using the appropriate table. In Table 3, we look down the 5 percent column until we reach three periods and find the factor .864. This factor, when multiplied by $1, gives the present value of $1 to be received three years from now at 5 percent interest. Thus, we solve the problem as shown on the next page.

TABLE 2. Future Value of an Ordinary Annuity of $1 Paid in Each Period for a Given Number of Time Periods

Periods	1%	2%	3%	4%	5%	6%	7%	8%	9%	10%	12%	14%	15%
1	1.000	1.000	1.000	1.000	1.000	1.000	1.000	1.000	1.000	1.000	1.000	1.000	1.000
2	2.010	2.020	2.030	2.040	2.050	2.060	2.070	2.080	2.090	2.100	2.120	2.140	2.150
3	3.030	3.060	3.091	3.122	3.153	3.184	3.215	3.246	3.278	3.310	3.374	3.440	3.473
4	4.060	4.122	4.184	4.246	4.310	4.375	4.440	4.506	4.573	4.641	4.779	4.921	4.993
5	5.101	5.204	5.309	5.416	5.526	5.637	5.751	5.867	5.985	6.105	6.353	6.610	6.742
6	6.152	6.308	6.468	6.633	6.802	6.975	7.153	7.336	7.523	7.716	8.115	8.536	8.754
7	7.214	7.434	7.662	7.898	8.142	8.394	8.654	8.923	9.200	9.487	10.09	10.73	11.07
8	8.286	8.583	8.892	9.214	9.549	9.897	10.26	10.64	11.03	11.44	12.30	13.23	13.73
9	9.369	9.755	10.16	10.58	11.03	11.49	11.98	12.49	13.02	13.58	14.78	16.09	16.79
10	10.46	10.95	11.46	12.01	12.58	13.18	13.82	14.49	15.19	15.94	17.55	19.34	20.30

Source: Excerpt from Table 2 in the appendix on future value and present value tables.

TABLE 3. Present Value of $1 to Be Received at the End of a Given Number of Time Periods

Periods	1%	2%	3%	4%	5%	6%	7%	8%	9%	10%
1	0.990	0.980	0.971	0.962	0.952	0.943	0.935	0.926	0.917	0.909
2	0.980	0.961	0.943	0.925	0.907	0.890	0.873	0.857	0.842	0.826
3	0.971	0.942	0.915	0.889	0.864	0.840	0.816	0.794	0.772	0.751
4	0.961	0.924	0.888	0.855	0.823	0.792	0.763	0.735	0.708	0.683
5	0.951	0.906	0.863	0.822	0.784	0.747	0.713	0.681	0.650	0.621
6	0.942	0.888	0.837	0.790	0.746	0.705	0.666	0.630	0.596	0.564
7	0.933	0.871	0.813	0.760	0.711	0.665	0.623	0.583	0.547	0.513
8	0.923	0.853	0.789	0.731	0.677	0.627	0.582	0.540	0.502	0.467
9	0.914	0.837	0.766	0.703	0.645	0.592	0.544	0.500	0.460	0.424
10	0.905	0.820	0.744	0.676	0.614	0.558	0.508	0.463	0.422	0.386

Source: Excerpt from Table 3 in the appendix on future value and present value tables.

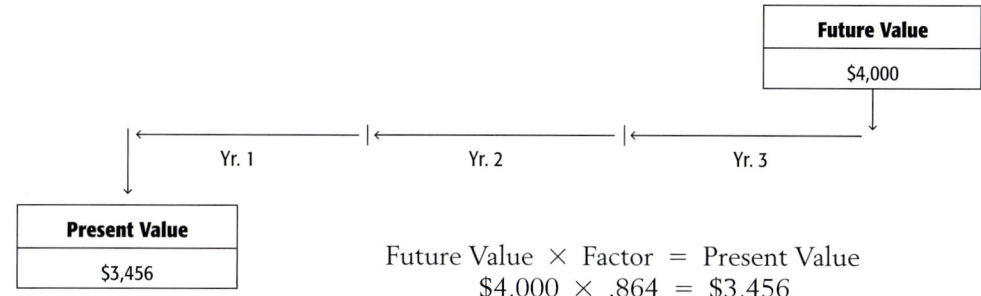

Future Value × Factor = Present Value
$4,000 × .864 = $3,456

Except for a rounding difference of $.66, this result is the same as the one above.

■ **PRESENT VALUE OF AN ORDINARY ANNUITY** It is often necessary to compute the present value of a series of receipts or payments. When we calculate the present value of equal amounts equally spaced over a period of time, we are computing the present value of an ordinary annuity.

For example, assume that Kathy Foster has sold a piece of property and is to receive $15,000 in three equal annual payments of $5,000, beginning one year from today. What is the present value of this sale, assuming a current interest rate of 5 percent? This present value may be computed by calculating a separate present value for each of the three payments (using Table 3) and summing the results, as shown in the table below.

Future Receipts (Annuity)				Present Value Factor at 5 Percent (from Table 3)		Present Value
Year 1	Year 2	Year 3				
$5,000			×	.952	=	$ 4,760
	$5,000		×	.907	=	4,535
		$5,000	×	.864	=	4,320
Total Present Value						$13,615

The present value of this sale is $13,615. Thus, there is an implied interest cost (given the 5 percent rate) of $1,385 associated with the payment plan that allows the purchaser to pay in three installments.

We can make this calculation more easily by using Table 4. We look down the 5 percent column until we reach three periods and find the factor 2.723. This factor, when multiplied by $1, gives the present value of a series of three $1 payments (spaced one year apart) at compound interest of 5 percent. Thus, we solve the problem as shown below.

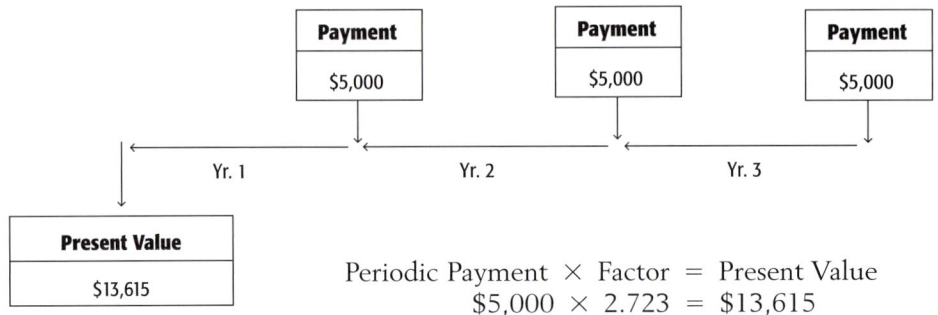

Periodic Payment × Factor = Present Value
$5,000 × 2.723 = $13,615

This result is the same as the one computed earlier.

TIME PERIODS

In all of the previous examples, and in most other cases, the compounding period is one year, and the interest rate is stated on an annual basis. However, in each of the four tables, the left-hand column refers not to years but to periods. This wording is intended to accommodate compounding periods of less than one year. Savings accounts that record interest quarterly and bonds that pay interest semiannually are cases in which the compounding period is less than one year. To use the tables in such cases, it is necessary to (1) divide the annual interest rate by the number of periods in the year, and (2) multiply the number of periods in one year by the number of years.

For example, assume that a $6,000 note is to be paid in two years and carries an annual interest rate of 8 percent. Compute the maturity (future) value of the note, assuming that the compounding period is semiannual. Before using the table, it is

TABLE 4. Present Value of an Ordinary Annuity of $1 Received Each Period for a Given Number of Time Periods

Periods	1%	2%	3%	4%	5%	6%	7%	8%	9%	10%
1	0.990	0.980	0.971	0.962	0.952	0.943	0.935	0.926	0.917	0.909
2	1.970	1.942	1.913	1.886	1.859	1.833	1.808	1.783	1.759	1.736
3	2.941	2.884	2.829	2.775	2.723	2.673	2.624	2.577	2.531	2.487
4	3.902	3.808	3.717	3.630	3.546	3.465	3.387	3.312	3.240	3.170
5	4.853	4.713	4.580	4.452	4.329	4.212	4.100	3.993	3.890	3.791
6	5.795	5.601	5.417	5.242	5.076	4.917	4.767	4.623	4.486	4.355
7	6.728	6.472	6.230	6.002	5.786	5.582	5.389	5.206	5.033	4.868
8	7.652	7.325	7.020	6.733	6.463	6.210	5.971	5.747	5.535	5.335
9	8.566	8.162	7.786	7.435	7.108	6.802	6.515	6.247	5.995	5.759
10	9.471	8.983	8.530	8.111	7.722	7.360	7.024	6.710	6.418	6.145

Source: Excerpt from Table 4 in the appendix on future value and present value tables.

necessary to compute the interest rate that applies to each compounding period and the total number of compounding periods. First, the interest rate to use is 4 percent (8% annual rate ÷ 2 periods per year). Second, the total number of compounding periods is 4 (2 periods per year × 2 years). From Table 1, therefore, the maturity value of the note is computed as follows:

$$\text{Principal} \times \text{Factor} = \text{Future Value}$$
$$\$6,000 \times 1.170 = \$7,020$$

The note will be worth $7,020 in two years.

This procedure for determining the interest rate and the number of periods when the compounding period is less than one year may be used with all four tables.

APPLICATIONS OF PRESENT VALUE TO ACCOUNTING

The concept of present value is widely applicable in the discipline of accounting. Here, the purpose is to demonstrate its usefulness in some simple applications. In-depth study of present value is deferred to more advanced courses.

■ IMPUTING INTEREST ON NON-INTEREST-BEARING NOTES

Clearly there is no such thing as an interest-free debt, regardless of whether the interest rate is explicitly stated. The Accounting Principles Board has declared that when a long-term note does not explicitly state an interest rate (or if the interest rate is unreasonably low), a rate based on the normal interest cost of the company in question should be assigned, or imputed.[1]

The following example applies this principle. On January 1, 20x0, Gato purchased merchandise from Haines by issuing an $8,000 non-interest-bearing note due in two years. Gato can borrow money from the bank at 9 percent interest. Gato paid the note in full after two years.

Note that the $8,000 note represents partly a payment for merchandise and partly a payment of interest for two years. In recording the purchase and sale, it is necessary to use Table 3 to determine the present value of the note. The calculation follows.

$$\text{Future Payment} \times \text{Present Value Factor (9\%, 2 years)} = \text{Present Value}$$
$$\$8,000 \times .842 = \$6,736$$

The imputed interest cost is $1,264 ($8,000 − $6,736) and is recorded as a discount on notes payable in Gato's records and as a discount on notes receivable in Haines's records.

The entries necessary to record the purchase in the Gato records and the sale in the Haines records are as follows:

	Gato Journal			Haines Journal		

A = L + OE
− −
+
	Purchases
	  Discount on
	    Notes Payable
	    Notes Payable
		6,736
		
		1,264
			
			8,000
				Notes Receivable
				  Discount on
				    Notes Receivable
				  Sales
					8,000
					
						1,264
						6,736
							A = L + OE
							+ +
							−

On December 31, 20x0, the adjustments to recognize the interest expense and interest income are as follows:

	Gato Journal			Haines Journal		

A = L + OE
+   −
	Interest Expense
	  Discount on
	    Notes Payable
		606.24
		
			606.24
				Discount on
				  Notes Receivable
				  Interest Income
					
					606.24
					
						606.24
							A = L + OE
							+ +

The interest is calculated by multiplying the amount of the original purchase by the interest rate for one year ($6,736.00 × .09 = $606.24). When payment is made on December 31, 20x0, the following entries are made in the respective journals.

	Gato Journal			Haines Journal		

A = L + OE
− + −
−
	Interest Expense
	Notes Payable
	Discount on
	   Notes Payable
	   Cash
		657.76
		8,000.00
			657.76
			8,000.00
				Discount on
				   Notes Receivable
				Cash
				Interest Income
				Notes Receivable
					657.76
					8,000.00
						657.76
						8,000.00

(Haines Journal: A = L + OE, + +, +, −)

The interest entries represent the remaining interest to be expensed or realized ($1,264 − $606.24 = $657.76). This amount approximates (because of rounding differences in the table) the interest for one year on the purchase plus last year's interest [($6,736 + $606.24) × .09 = $660.80].

■ **VALUING AN ASSET** An asset is recorded because it will provide future benefits to the company that owns it. These future benefits are the basis for the definition of an asset. Usually, the purchase price of the asset represents the present value of these future benefits. It is possible to evaluate a proposed purchase price for an asset by comparing that price with the present value of the asset to the company.

For example, Sam Hurst is thinking of buying a new machine that will reduce his annual labor cost by $700 per year. The machine will last eight years. The interest rate that Hurst assumes for making managerial decisions is 10 percent. What is the maximum amount (present value) that Hurst should pay for the machine?

The present value of the machine to Hurst is equal to the present value of an ordinary annuity of $700 per year for eight years at compound interest of 10 percent. Using the factor from Table 4, we compute the value as follows:

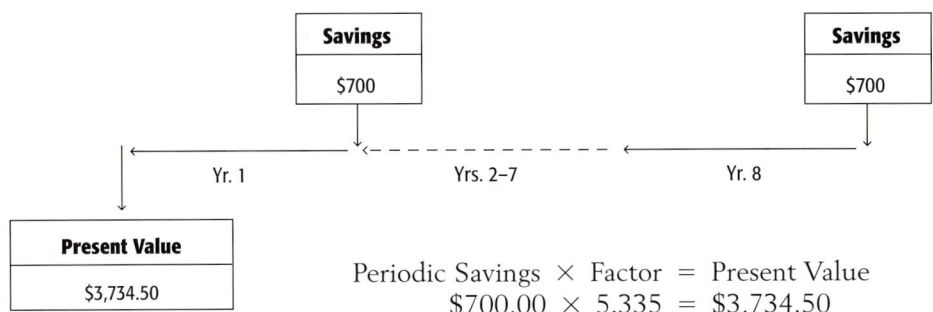

Periodic Savings × Factor = Present Value
$700.00 × 5.335 = $3,734.50

Hurst should not pay more than $3,734.50 for the new machine because this amount equals the present value of the benefits that will be received from owning the machine.

■ **DEFERRED PAYMENT** A seller will sometimes agree to defer payment for a sale in order to encourage the buyer to make the purchase. This practice is common, for example, in the farm implement industry, where the farmer needs the equipment in the spring but cannot pay for it until the fall crop is in. Assume that Plains Implement Corporation sells a tractor to Dana Washington for $50,000 on February 1, agreeing to take payment ten months later, on December 1. When this type of agreement is made, the future payment includes not only the sales price of the tractor but also an implied (imputed) interest cost. If the prevailing annual interest rate for such transactions is 12 percent compounded monthly, the actual sale (purchase) price of the tractor would be the present value of the future payment, computed using the factor from Table 3 (10 periods, 1 percent), as follows:

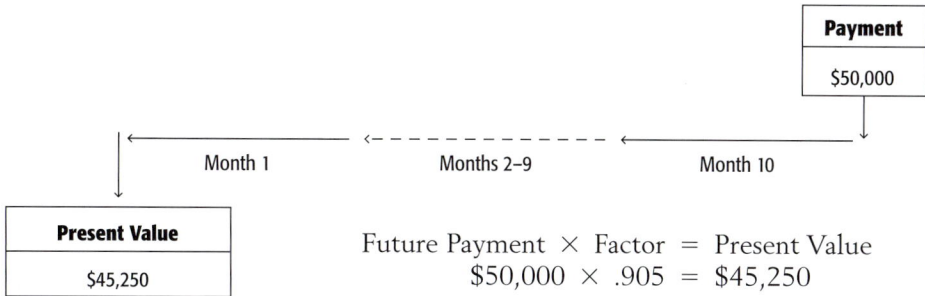

$$\text{Future Payment} \times \text{Factor} = \text{Present Value}$$
$$\$50{,}000 \times .905 = \$45{,}250$$

The present value, $45,250, is recorded in Washington's purchase records and in Plains's sale records. The balance consists of interest income. Washington records the purchase and Plains records the sale using the following entries:

	Washington Journal			Plains Journal		

A = L + OE
+ +
	Feb. 1 Tractor
	  Accounts Payable
	  Purchased tractor
		45,250	45,250	Accounts Receivable
				  Sales
				  Sold tractor
					45,250	45,250	A = L + OE
							+ +

When Washington pays for the tractor, the entries are as follows:

	Washington Journal			Plains Journal		

A = L + OE
− − −
	Dec. 1 Accounts Payable
	  Interest Expense
	  Cash
	  Paid on account,
	  including imputed
	  interest expense
		45,250
		4,750
			50,000	Cash
				  Accounts Receivable
				  Interest Income
				  Received on account
				  from Washington,
				  including imputed
				  interest earned
					50,000	45,250
						4,750
							A = L + OE
							− +
							+

■ **INVESTMENT OF IDLE CASH** Childware Corporation, a toy manufacturer, has just completed a successful selling season and has $10,000,000 in cash to invest for six months. The company places the cash in a money market account expected to pay 12 percent annual interest. Interest is compounded and credited to the company's account monthly. How much cash will the company have at the end of six months, and what entries will be made to record the investment and the monthly interest? The future value factor from Table 1 is based on six monthly periods of 1 percent (12 percent divided by 12 months), and the future value is computed as follows:

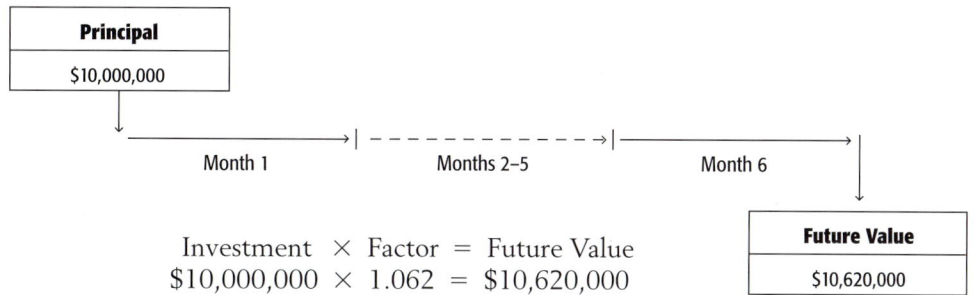

$$\text{Investment} \times \text{Factor} = \text{Future Value}$$
$$\$10{,}000{,}000 \times 1.062 = \$10{,}620{,}000$$

When the investment is made, the following entry is made:

A = L + OE
\+
−

Short-Term Investments	10,000,000	
Cash		10,000,000
Made investment of cash		

After the first month, the interest is recorded by increasing the Short-Term Investments account.

A = L + OE
\+   +

Short-Term Investments	100,000	
Interest Income		100,000
Earned one month's interest income		
$10,000,000 × .01 = $100,000		

After the second month, the interest is earned on the new balance of the Short-Term Investments account.

A = L + OE
\+   +

Short-Term Investments	101,000	
Interest Income		101,000
Earned one month's interest income		
$10,100,000 × .01 = $101,000		

Entries would continue in a similar manner for four more months, at which time the balance of Short-Term Investments would be about $10,620,000. The actual amount accumulated may vary from this total because the interest rate paid on money market accounts can vary over time as a result of changes in market conditions.

■ **ACCUMULATION OF A FUND** When a company owes a large fixed amount due in several years, management would be wise to accumulate a fund with which to pay off the debt at maturity. Sometimes creditors, when they agree to provide a loan, require that such a fund be established. In establishing the fund, management must determine how much cash to set aside each period in order to pay the debt. The amount will depend on the estimated rate of interest the investments will earn. Assume that Vason Corporation agrees with a creditor to set aside cash at the end of each year to accumulate enough to pay off a $100,000 note due in five years. Since the first contribution to the fund will be made in one year, five annual contributions will be made by the time the note is due. Assume also that the fund is projected to earn 8 percent, compounded annually. The amount of each annual payment is calculated using Table 2 (5 periods, 8 percent), as follows:

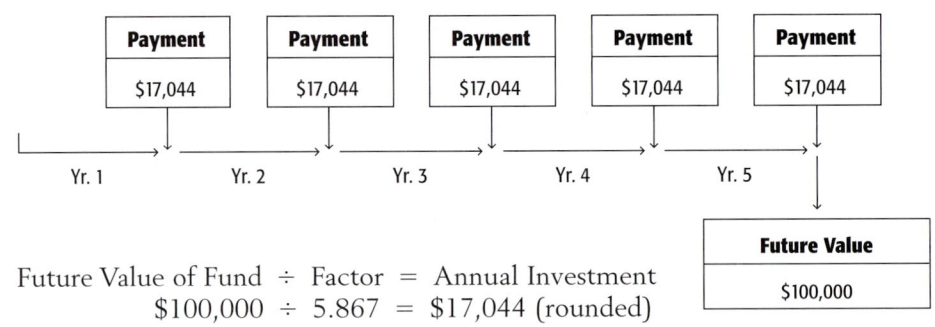

Future Value of Fund ÷ Factor = Annual Investment
$100,000 ÷ 5.867 = $17,044 (rounded)

Each year's contribution to the fund is $17,044, which is recorded as follows:

A = L + OE
\+
−

Loan Repayment Fund	17,044	
Cash		17,044
Recorded annual contribution to loan repayment fund		

■ **OTHER ACCOUNTING APPLICATIONS** There are many other applications of present value in accounting, including accounting for installment notes, valuing a bond, and recording lease obligations. Present value is also applied in such areas as pension obligations; premium and discount on debt; depreciation of property, plant, and equipment; capital expenditure decisions; and generally any problem in which time is a factor.

EXERCISES

Tables 1 to 4 in the appendix on future value and present value tables may be used where appropriate to solve these exercises.

Future Value Calculations

E 1. Wieland receives a one-year note for $3,000 that carries a 12 percent annual interest rate for the sale of a used car.

Compute the maturity value under each of the following assumptions: (1) The interest is simple interest. (2) The interest is compounded semiannually. (3) The interest is compounded quarterly. (4) The interest is compounded monthly.

Future Value Calculations

E 2. Find the future value of (1) a single payment of $20,000 at 7 percent for ten years, (2) ten annual payments of $2,000 at 7 percent, (3) a single payment of $6,000 at 9 percent for seven years, and (4) seven annual payments of $6,000 at 9 percent.

Future Value Calculations

E 3. Assume that $40,000 is invested today. Compute the amount that would accumulate at the end of seven years when the interest rate is (1) 8 percent compounded annually, (2) 8 percent compounded semiannually, and (3) 8 percent compounded quarterly.

Future Value Calculations

E 4. Calculate the accumulation of periodic payments of $1,000 made at the end of each of four years, assuming (1) 10 percent annual interest compounded annually, (2) 10 percent annual interest compounded semiannually, (3) 4 percent annual interest compounded annually, and (4) 16 percent annual interest compounded quarterly.

Future Value Applications

E 5. a. Two parents have $20,000 to invest for their child's college tuition, which they estimate will cost $40,000 when the child enters college twelve years from now.

Calculate the approximate rate of annual interest that the investment must earn to reach the $40,000 goal in twelve years. (**Hint:** Make a calculation; then use Table 1 in the appendix on future value and present value tables.)

b. Ted Pruitt is saving to purchase a summer home that will cost about $64,000. He has $40,000 now, on which he can earn 7 percent annual interest.

Calculate the approximate length of time he will have to wait to purchase the summer home. (**Hint:** Make a calculation; then use Table 1 in the appendix on future value and present value tables.)

Working Backward from a Future Value

E 6. Gloria Faraquez has a debt of $90,000 due in four years. She wants to save enough money to pay it off by making annual deposits in an investment account that earns 8 percent annual interest.

Calculate the amount she must deposit each year to reach her goal. (**Hint:** Use Table 2 in the appendix on future value and present value tables; then make a calculation.)

Determining an Advance Payment

E 7. Ellen Saber is contemplating paying five years' rent in advance. Her annual rent is $9,600.

Calculate the single sum that would have to be paid now for the advance rent, if we assume compound interest of 8 percent.

Present Value Calculations

E 8. Find the present value of (1) a single payment of $24,000 at 6 percent for twelve years, (2) twelve annual payments of $2,000 at 6 percent, (3) a single payment of $5,000 at 9 percent for five years, and (4) five annual payments of $5,000 at 9 percent.

Present Value of a Lump-Sum Contract

E 9. A contract calls for a lump-sum payment of $60,000. Find the present value of the contract, assuming that (1) the payment is due in five years, and the current interest rate is 9 percent; (2) the payment is due in ten years, and the current interest rate is 9 percent; (3) the payment is due in five years, and the current interest rate is 5 percent; and (4) the payment is due in ten years, and the current interest rate is 5 percent.

Present Value of an Annuity Contract

E 10. A contract calls for annual payments of $1,200. Find the present value of the contract, assuming that (1) the number of payments is seven, and the current interest rate is 6 percent; (2) the number of payments is fourteen, and the current interest rate is 6 percent; (3) the number of payments is seven, and the current interest rate is 8 percent; and (4) the number of payments is fourteen, and the current interest rate is 8 percent.

Non-Interest-Bearing Note

E 11. On January 1, 20x0, Pendleton purchased a machine from Leyland by signing a two-year, non-interest-bearing $32,000 note. Pendleton currently pays 12 percent interest to borrow money at the bank.

Prepare entries in Pendleton's and Leyland's journals to (1) record the purchase and the note, (2) adjust the accounts after one year, and (3) record payment of the note after two years (on December 31, 20x2).

Valuing an Asset for the Purpose of Making a Purchasing Decision

E 12. Oscaro owns a service station and has the opportunity to purchase a car wash machine for $30,000. After carefully studying projected costs and revenues, Oscaro estimates that the car wash machine will produce a net cash flow of $5,200 annually and will last for eight years. Oscaro believes that an interest rate of 14 percent is adequate for his business.

Calculate the present value of the machine to Oscaro. Does the purchase appear to be a correct business decision?

Deferred Payment

E 13. Johnson Equipment Corporation sold a precision tool machine with computer controls to Borst Corporation for $800,000 on January 1, agreeing to take payment nine months later, on October 1. Assuming that the prevailing annual interest rate for such a transaction is 16 percent compounded quarterly, what is the actual sale (purchase) price of the machine tool, and what journal entries will be made at the time of the purchase (sale) and at the time of the payment (receipt) on the records of both Borst and Johnson?

Investment of Idle Cash

E 14. Scientific Publishing Company, a publisher of college books, has just completed a successful fall selling season and has $5,000,000 in cash to invest for nine months, beginning on January 1. The company placed the cash in a money market account that is expected to pay 12 percent annual interest compounded monthly. Interest is credited to the company's account each month. How much cash will the company have at the end of nine months, and what entries are made to record the investment and the first two monthly (February 1 and March 1) interest amounts?

Accumulation of a Fund

E 15. Laferia Corporation borrowed $3,000,000 from an insurance company on a five-year note. Management agreed to set aside enough cash at the end of each year to accumulate the amount needed to pay off the note at maturity. Since the first contribution to the fund will be made in one year, four annual contributions are needed. Assuming that the fund will earn 10 percent compounded annually, how much will the annual contribution to the fund be (round to nearest dollar), and what will be the journal entry for the first contribution?

14%	15%	16%	18%	20%	25%	30%	35%	40%	45%	50%	Periods
0.877	0.870	0.862	0.847	0.833	0.800	0.769	0.741	0.714	0.690	0.667	1
1.647	1.626	1.605	1.566	1.528	1.440	1.361	1.289	1.224	1.165	1.111	2
2.322	2.283	2.246	2.174	2.106	1.952	1.816	1.696	1.589	1.493	1.407	3
2.914	2.855	2.798	2.690	2.589	2.362	2.166	1.997	1.849	1.720	1.605	4
3.433	3.352	3.274	3.127	2.991	2.689	2.436	2.220	2.035	1.876	1.737	5
3.889	3.784	3.685	3.498	3.326	2.951	2.643	2.385	2.168	1.983	1.824	6
4.288	4.160	4.039	3.812	3.605	3.161	2.802	2.508	2.263	2.057	1.883	7
4.639	4.487	4.344	4.078	3.837	3.329	2.925	2.598	2.331	2.109	1.922	8
4.946	4.772	4.607	4.303	4.031	3.463	3.019	2.665	2.379	2.144	1.948	9
5.216	5.019	4.833	4.494	4.192	3.571	3.092	2.715	2.414	2.168	1.965	10
5.453	5.234	5.029	4.656	4.327	3.656	3.147	2.752	2.438	2.185	1.977	11
5.660	5.421	5.197	4.793	4.439	3.725	3.190	2.779	2.456	2.197	1.985	12
5.842	5.583	5.342	4.910	4.533	3.780	3.223	2.799	2.469	2.204	1.990	13
6.002	5.724	5.468	5.008	4.611	3.824	3.249	2.814	2.478	2.210	1.993	14
6.142	5.847	5.575	5.092	4.675	3.859	3.268	2.825	2.484	2.214	1.995	15
6.265	5.954	5.669	5.162	4.730	3.887	3.283	2.834	2.489	2.216	1.997	16
6.373	6.047	5.749	5.222	4.775	3.910	3.295	2.840	2.492	2.218	1.998	17
6.467	6.128	5.818	5.273	4.812	3.928	3.304	2.844	2.494	2.219	1.999	18
6.550	6.198	5.877	5.316	4.844	3.942	3.311	2.848	2.496	2.220	1.999	19
6.623	6.259	5.929	5.353	4.870	3.954	3.316	2.850	2.497	2.221	1.999	20
6.687	6.312	5.973	5.384	4.891	3.963	3.320	2.852	2.498	2.221	2.000	21
6.743	6.359	6.011	5.410	4.909	3.970	3.323	2.853	2.498	2.222	2.000	22
6.792	6.399	6.044	5.432	4.925	3.976	3.325	2.854	2.499	2.222	2.000	23
6.835	6.434	6.073	5.451	4.937	3.981	3.327	2.855	2.499	2.222	2.000	24
6.873	6.464	6.097	5.467	4.948	3.985	3.329	2.856	2.499	2.222	2.000	25
6.906	6.491	6.118	5.480	4.956	3.988	3.330	2.856	2.500	2.222	2.000	26
6.935	6.514	6.136	5.492	4.964	3.990	3.331	2.856	2.500	2.222	2.000	27
6.961	6.534	6.152	5.502	4.970	3.992	3.331	2.857	2.500	2.222	2.000	28
6.983	6.551	6.166	5.510	4.975	3.994	3.332	2.857	2.500	2.222	2.000	29
7.003	6.566	6.177	5.517	4.979	3.995	3.332	2.857	2.500	2.222	2.000	30
7.105	6.642	6.234	5.548	4.997	3.999	3.333	2.857	2.500	2.222	2.000	40
7.133	6.661	6.246	5.554	4.999	4.000	3.333	2.857	2.500	2.222	2.000	50

An *annuity due* is a series of equal cash flows for N time periods, but the first payment occurs immediately. The present value of the first payment equals the face value of the cash flow; Table 4 then is used to measure the present value of $N - 1$ remaining cash flows.

■ **Example—Table 4** Determine the present value on January 1, 2002, of 20 lease payments; each payment of $10,000 is due on January 1, beginning in 2002. Assume an interest rate of 8 percent.

$$\text{Present Value} = \text{Immediate Payment} + \begin{cases} \text{Present Value of 19 Subsequent} \\ \text{Payments at 8\%} \end{cases}$$

$$= \$10{,}000 + (\$10{,}000 \times 9.604) = \$106{,}040$$

Endnotes

Chapter 1
1. Walgreen Co., *Annual Report*, 2002.
2. *Statement of Financial Accounting Concepts No. 1*, "Objectives of Financial Reporting by Business Enterprises" (Norwalk, Conn.: Financial Accounting Standards Board, 1978), par. 9.
3. Ibid.
4. Christopher D. Ittner, David F. Larcker, and Madhav V. Rajan, "The Choice of Performance Measures in Annual Bonus Contracts," *The Accounting Review*, April 1997.
5. Walgreen Co., *Annual Report*, 2002.
6. Kathy Williams and James Hart, "Microsoft: Tooling the Information Age," *Management Accounting*, May 1996, p. 42.
7. *Statement of the Accounting Principles Board No. 4*, "Basic Concepts and Accounting Principles Underlying Financial Statements of Business Enterprises" (New York: American Institute of Certified Public Accountants, 1970), par. 138.
8. Touche Ross & Co., "Ethics in American Business" (New York: Touche Ross & Co., 1988), p. 7.
9. "Global Ethics Codes Gain Importance as a Tool to Avoid Litigation and Fines," *The Wall Street Journal*, August 19, 1999.
10. *Statement Number IC*, "Standards of Ethical Conduct for Management Accountants" (Montvale, N.J.: Institute of Management Accountants, 1983, revised 1997).
11. J.C. Penney Company, Inc., *Annual Report*, 1995.
12. Nikhil Deogun, "Coca-Cola Reports 27% Drop in Profits Hurt by Weakness in Foreign Markets," *The Wall Street Journal*, January 27, 1999.
13. Southwest Airlines Co., *Annual Report*, 1996.
14. Queen Sook Kim, "Lechters Inc. Files for Chapter 11, Arranges Financing," *The Wall Street Journal*, May 22, 2001.
15. Charles Schwab Corporation, *Annual Report*, 2001.
16. Robert Frank, "Facing a Loss, Lego Narrates a Sad Toy Story," *The Wall Street Journal*, January 22, 1999.

Chapter 2
1. "Boeing Scores a Deal to Sell 15 Planes for Long-Haul Routes," *The Wall Street Journal*, October 5, 2000.
2. The Boeing Co., *Annual Report*, 1994.
3. Craig S. Smith, "China Halts New Purchases of Jets," *The Wall Street Journal*, February 9, 1999.
4. The Boeing Co., *Annual Report*, 2000.
5. Patricia Kranz, "Rubles? Who Needs Rubles?" *BusinessWeek*, April 13, 1998; Andrew Higgins, "Lacking Money to Pay, Russian Firms Survive on Deft Barter System," *The Wall Street Journal*, August 27, 1998.
6. Intel Corp., *Annual Report*, 2002.
7. Shawn Young, "Lucent Revises Its Revenue Downward," *The Wall Street Journal*, December 22, 2000.
8. Nike, Inc., *Annual Report*, 2002.
9. Mellon Bank, *Annual Report*, 2000.
10. Ajinomoto Company, *Annual Report*, 2000.

Chapter 3
1. Kelly Services, *Annual Report*, 2002.
2. *Statement of Financial Accounting Concepts No. 1*, "Objectives of Financial Reporting by Business Enterprises" (Norwalk, Conn.: Financial Accounting Standards Board, 1978), par. 44.
3. "Revenue Recognition in Financial Statements," *Staff Accounting Bulletin No. 10* (Securities and Exchange Commission, 1999).
4. Thomas J. Phillips Jr., Michael S. Luehlfing, and Cynthia M. Daily, "The Right Way to Recognize Revenue," *Journal of Accountancy*, June 2001.
5. Michael Schroeder and Elizabeth MacDonald, "SEC Expects More Big Cases on Accounting," *The Wall Street Journal*, December 24, 1998.
6. PricewaterhouseCoopers presentation, 1999.
7. Lyric Opera of Chicago, *Annual Report*, 2001.
8. The Walt Disney Company, *Annual Report*, 2001.
9. H. J. Heinz Company, *Annual Report*, 2001.
10. Takashimaya Company, Limited, *Annual Report*, 2000.

Chapter 4
1. Hershey Foods Corp., Form 10-Q, September 28, 2003.
2. News item, *Crain's Chicago Business*, October 2001.
3. News item, *The Wall Street Journal*, July 29, 1999.
4. Michael Totty, "The Next Phase," *The Wall Street Journal*, May 21, 2001.
5. Frank Potter, "Event-to-Knowledge: A New Metric for Finance Department Efficiency," *Strategic Finance*, July 2001.
6. Adapted from H & R Block, Inc., *Annual Report*, 2001.
7. Nestlé S.A., *Annual Report*, 2000.

Chapter 5
1. General Mills, Inc., *Annual Report*, 2001.
2. "Objectives of Financial Reporting by Business Enterprises," *Statement of Financial Accounting Concepts No. 1* (Norwalk, Conn.: Financial Accounting Standards Board, 1978), pars. 32–54.
3. "Qualitative Characteristics of Accounting Information," *Statement of Financial Accounting Concepts No. 1* (Norwalk, Conn.: Financial Accounting Standards Board, 1980), par. 20.
4. Accounting Principles Board, "Accounting Changes," *Opinion No. 20* (New York: American Institute of Certified Public Accountants, 1971), par. 17.
5. Securities and Exchange Commission, *Staff Accounting Bulletin No. 99*, 1999.
6. Ray J. Groves, "Here's the Annual Report. Got a Few Hours?" *The Wall Street Journal Europe*, August 26–27, 1994.
7. Roger Lowenstein, "Investors Will Fish for Footnotes in 'Abbreviated' Annual Reports," *The Wall Street Journal*, September 14, 1995.
8. General Mills, *Annual Report*, 2001.
9. Ibid.
10. National Commission on Fraudulent Financial Reporting, *Report of the National Commission on Fraudulent Financial Reporting* (Washington, D.C., 1987), p. 2.
11. Arthur Levitt, "The Numbers Game," NYU Center for Law and Business, September 28, 1998.
12. "Ex-chairman of Cendant Is Indicted," *The Wall Street Journal*, March 1, 2001; "SEC Sues Former Sunbeam Executive," *Chicago Tribune*, May 16, 2001; "Enron: A Wake-up Call," *The Wall Street Journal*, December 4, 2001; "SEC List of Accounting-Fraud Probes Grows," *The Wall Street Journal*, July 6, 2001.
13. *Accounting Research and Terminology Bulletin*, final edition (New York: American Institute of Certified Public Accountants, 1961), p. 20.
14. "Debt vs. Equity: Whose Call Counts," *BusinessWeek*, July 19, 1999.
15. Roger Lowenstein, "The '20% Club' No Longer Is Exclusive," *The Wall Street Journal*, May 4, 1995.
16. "SEC Probes Lucent Accounting Practices," *The Wall Street Journal*, February 9, 2001.
17. Albertson's Inc., *Annual Report*, 2001; Great Atlantic & Pacific Tea Company, *Annual Report*, 2001.
18. GlaxoSmithKline PLC, *Annual Report*, 2000.
19. Toys "R" Us, *Annual Report*, 1987.

Chapter 6
1. Target, *Annual Report*, 2002.
2. Ibid.
3. "Shop Online—Pickup at the Store," *BusinessWeek*, June 12, 2000; Nick Wingfield, "As Web Sales Grow Mail-Order Sellers Are Benefiting the Most," *The Wall Street Journal*, May 2, 2001.
4. Joel Millman, "Here's What Happens to Many Lovely Gifts After Santa Rides Off," *The Wall Street Journal*, December 26, 2001.
5. Matthew Rose, "Magazine Revenue at Newsstands Falls in Worst Year Ever," *The Wall Street Journal*, May 15, 2001.
6. Circuit City Stores, *Annual Report*, 2001.
7. *Professional Standards*, vol. 1 (New York: American Institute of Certified Public Accountants, June 1, 1999), Sec. AU 322.07.
8. "1998 Fraud Survey," KPMG Peat Marwick, 1998.
9. *Professional Standards*, vol. 1, Sec. AU 325.16.
10. Matthew Schifrin, "The Big Squeeze," *Forbes*, March 11, 1996.
11. Wal-Mart Stores, Inc., *Annual Report*, 2000; Kmart Corp., *Annual Report*, 2000.
12. Amy Merrick, "Starbucks Accuses Employee, Husband of Embezzling $3.7 Million from Firm," *The Wall Street Journal*, November 20, 2000.

Chapter 7
1. Pioneer Corporation, *Annual Report*, 2001.
2. "So Much for Detroit's Cash Cushion," *BusinessWeek*, November 5, 2001.
3. Michael Selz, "Big Customers' Late Bills Choke Small Suppliers," *The Wall Street Journal*, June 22, 1994.
4. Pioneer Corporation, *Annual Report*, 2001.
5. Circuit City Stores, Inc., *Annual Report*, 2001.
6. Pioneer Corporation, *Annual Report*, 2001.
7. *Accounting Trends & Techniques* (New York: American Institute of CPAs, 2000), p. 130.
8. *Statement of Financial Accounting Standards No. 115*, "Accounting for Certain Investments in Debt and Equity Securities" (Norwalk, Conn.: Financial Accounting Standards Board, 1993).
9. Pioneer Corporation, *Annual Report*, 2001.
10. "Bad Loans Rattle Telecom Vendors," *BusinessWeek*, February 19, 2001.
11. Craig S. Smith, "Chinese Companies Writing Off Old Debt," *The Wall Street Journal*, December 28, 1995.
12. Information based on promotional brochures of Mitsubishi Electric Corp.
13. Elizabeth McDonald, "Unhatched Chickens," *Forbes*, February 19, 2001.
14. Philips Electronics N.V., *Annual Report*, 2001; Heineken N.V., *Annual Report*, 2001.

Chapter 8
1. J.C. Penney Company, Inc., *Annual Report*, 2002.
2. Illinois Tool Works, Inc., *Annual Report*, 2002.
3. American Institute of Certified Public Accountants, *Accounting Research Bulletin No. 43* (New York: AICPA, 1953), ch. 4.
4. Gary McWilliams, "Whirlwind on the Web," *BusinessWeek*, April 7, 1997.
5. Karen Lundebaard, "Bumpy Ride," *The Wall Street Journal*, May 21, 2001.
6. American Institute of Certified Public Accountants, *Accounting Research Bulletin No. 43* (New York: AICPA, 1953), ch. 4.
7. Micah Frankel and Robert Trezevant, "The Year-End LIFO Inventory Purchasing Decision: An Empirical Test," *The Accounting Review*, April 1994.
8. American Institute of Certified Public Accountants, *Accounting Trends & Techniques* (New York: AICPA, 2002).
9. "As Rite Aid Grew, CEO Seemed Unable to Manage His Empire," *The Wall Street Journal*, October 20, 1999; "RentWay Details Improper Bookkeeping," *The Wall Street Journal*, June 8, 2001.
10. International Paper Company, *Annual Report*, 2001.
11. American Institute of Certified Public Accountants, *Accounting Trends & Techniques* (New York: AICPA, 2002).
12. "Cisco's Numbers Confound Some," *International Herald Tribune*, April 19, 2001; "Kmart Posts $67 Million Loss Due to Markdowns," *The Wall Street Journal*, November 10, 2000.
13. American Institute of Certified Public Accountants, *Accounting Trends & Techniques* (New York: AICPA, 2002).
14. Exxon Mobil, *Annual Report*, 2000.
15. Adapted from Hershey Foods Corp., *Annual Report*, 2000.
16. "SEC Case Judge Rules Crazy Eddie Principals Must Pay $72.7 Million," *The Wall Street Journal*, May 11, 2000.
17. Crane Company, *Annual Report*, 2000.
18. Pioneer Corporation, *Annual Report*, 2001; Yamaha Motor Co., Ltd., *Annual Report*, 2001.

Chapter 9
1. US Airways, Inc., *Annual Report*, 2001.
2. RadioShack Corporation, *Annual Report*, 2002.
3. Pamela L. Moore, "How Xerox Ran Short of Black Ink," *BusinessWeek*, October 30, 2000.
4. Goodyear Tire & Rubber Company, *Annual Report*, 2002.
5. US Airways, Inc., *Annual Report*, 2002.
6. Andersen Enterprise Group, cited in *Crain's Chicago Business*, July 5, 1999.
7. Raju Narisetti, "P&G Ad Chief Plots Demise of the Coupon," *The Wall Street Journal*, April 17, 1996; Renae Merle, "Slowdown Is Business Boon for Coupon Seller Valassis," *The Wall Street Journal*, May 1, 2001.
8. Scott McCartney, "Free Airline Miles Become a Potent Tool for Selling Everything," *The Wall Street Journal*, April 16, 1996; "You've Got Miles," *BusinessWeek*, March 6, 2000.
9. *Statement of Financial Accounting Standards No. 5*, "Accounting for Contingencies" (Norwalk, Conn.: Financial Accounting Standards Board, 1975).
10. American Institute of Certified Public Accountants, *Accounting Trends & Techniques*, 2002.
11. General Motors Corp., *Annual Report*, 2000.
12. American Institute of Certified Public Accountants, *Accounting Trends & Techniques*, 2002.
13. US Airways, Inc., *Annual Report*, 2000.
14. General Motors Corp., *Annual Report*, 2002.
15. Sun Micosystems Inc., *Annual Report*, 2001; Cisco Systems, *Annual Report*, 2001.
16. Texaco, Inc., *Annual Report*, 1986.
17. Man Nutzfahrzeuge Aktiengesellschaft, *Annual Report*, 1997.

Chapter 10
1. H. J. Heinz Company, *Annual Report*, 2002.
2. *Statement of Financial Accounting Standards No. 144*, "Accounting for the Impairment or Disposal of Long-Lived Assets" (Norwalk, Conn.: Financial Accounting Standards Board, 2001).
3. David Henry, "The Numbers Game," *BusinessWeek*, May 14, 2001.
4. H. J. Heinz Company, *Annual Report*, 2002.
5. Ford Motor Company, *Annual Report*, 2002.
6. *Statement of Position No. 98-1*, "Accounting for the Costs of Computer Software Developed or Planned for Internal Use" (New York: American Institute of Certified Public Accountants, 1996).
7. *Statement of Financial Accounting Standards No. 34*, "Capitalization of Interest Cost" (Norwalk, Conn.: Financial Accounting Standards Board, 1979), par. 9–11.
8. Jared Sandberg, Deborah Solomon, and Rebecca Blumenstein, "Inside WorldCom's Unearthing of a Vast Accounting Scandal," *The Wall Street Journal*, June 27, 2002.
9. *Financial Accounting Standards: Original Pronouncements as of July 1, 1977* (Norwalk, Conn.: Financial Accounting Standards Board, 1977), ARB No. 43, Ch. 9, Sec. C, par. 5.

10. Accounting Principles Board, *Opinion No. 29*, "Accounting for Nonmonetary Transactions" (New York: American Institute of Certified Public Accountants, 1973); Emerging Issues Task Force, *EITF Issue Summary 86-29*, "Nonmonetary Transactions: Magnitude of Boot and the Exceptions to the Use of Fair Value" (Norwalk, Conn.: Financial Accounting Standards Board, 1986).
11. *Statement of Financial Accounting Standards No. 25*, "Suspension of Certain Accounting Requirements for Oil and Gas Producing Companies" (Norwalk, Conn.: Financial Accounting Standards Board, 1979).
12. Adapted from Accounting Principles Board, *Opinion No. 17*, "Intangible Assets" (New York: American Institute of Certified Public Accountants, 1970), par. 2.
13. "What's in a Name?" *Time*, May 3, 1993.
14. General Motors, *Annual Report*, 2000.
15. Abbott Laboratories, *Annual Report*, 2000; Roche Group, *Annual Report*, 2000.
16. Allan B. Afterman, *International Accounting, Financial Reporting and Analysis* (New York: Warren, Gorham & Lamont, 1995).
17. *Statement of Financial Accounting Standards No. 2*, "Accounting for Research and Development Costs" (Norwalk, Conn.: Financial Accounting Standards Board, 1974), par. 12.
18. *Statement of Financial Accounting Standards No. 86*, "Accounting for the Costs of Computer Software to be Sold, Leased, or Otherwise Marketed" (Norwalk, Conn.: Financial Accounting Standards Board, 1985).
19. *Accounting Trends & Techniques*, 2002.
20. General Mills, *Annual Report*, 2002; Sara Lee Corporation, *Annual Report*, 2002; Tribune Company, *Annual Report*, 2002.
21. *Statement of Financial Accounting Standards No. 144*, "Accounting for the Impairment or Disposal of Long-Lived Assets" (Norwalk, Conn.: Financial Accounting Standards Board, 2001).
22. Edward P. McTague, "Accounting for Trade-Ins of Operational Assets," *National Public Accountant* (January 1986), p. 39.
23. General Motors Corp., *Annual Report*, 1987.
24. Polaroid Corporation, *Annual Report*, 1997.
25. Hilton Hotels Corporation, *Annual Report*, 2000; Marriott International, *Annual Report*, 2000.
26. "Stock Gives Case the Funds He Needs to Buy New Technology," *BusinessWeek*, April 15, 1996.
27. Roche Group, *Annual Report*, 2000; Baxter International, Inc., *Annual Report*, 2000.

Chapter 11
1. AT&T Corporation, *Annual Report*, 2002.
2. "Canadian Airline's Demise Adds to Industry Woes," *The Washington Post*, November 16, 2001; "A Striking End for Air Afrique," British Broadcasting Company, November 26, 2001; "Small Airlines Adapting Quicker," Associated Press, November 22, 2001; "Swiss Air Rescue Hopes Brighten," British Broadcasting Company, November 21, 2001.
3. AT&T Corporation, *Annual Report*, 2002.
4. Ibid.
5. Quentin Hardy, "Japanese Companies Need to Raise Cash, but First a Bond Market Must Be Built," *The Wall Street Journal*, October 20, 1992.
6. Bill Barnhart, "Bond Bellwether," *Chicago Tribune*, December 4, 1996.
7. Accounting Principles Board, *Opinion No. 21*, "Interest on Receivables and Payables" (New York: American Institute of Certified Public Accountants, 1971), par. 15.
8. *Statement of Financial Accounting Standards No. 13*, "Accounting for Leases" (Norwalk, Conn.: Financial Accounting Standards Board, 1976), par. 10.
9. Philip Morris Companies, Inc., *Annual Report*, 2000.
10. *Statement of Financial Accounting Standards No. 87*, "Employers' Accounting for Pensions" (Norwalk, Conn.: Financial Accounting Standards Board, 1985).
11. *Statement of Financial Accounting Standards No. 106*, "Employers' Accounting for Postretirement Benefits Other than Pensions" (Norwalk, Conn.: Financial Accounting Standards Board, 1990).
12. Stanley Ziemba, "TWA, American Revise O'Hare Gate Agreement," *The Wall Street Journal*, May 13, 1992.
13. FedEx Corporation, *Annual Report*, 2001.
14. "More Hotels Won't Be Able to Pay Debt from Operations, Study Says," *The Wall Street Journal*, October 30, 2001.
15. Amazon.com, Press Release, January 28, 1999.
16. NEC Corporation, *Annual Report*, 2001; Sanyo Electric Co., *Annual Report*, 2001.

Chapter 12
1. Cisco Systems, Inc., *Annual Report*, 2002.
2. Copyright © 2000 by Houghton Mifflin Company. Reproduced by permission from *The American Heritage Dictionary of the English Language, Fourth Edition*.
3. *Statement of Position No. 98-5*, "Report on the Costs of Start up Activities" (New York: American Institute of Certified Public Accountants, 1998).
4. Deborah Solomon, "AT&T Slashes Dividends 83%, Cuts Forecasts," *The Wall Street Journal*, December 21, 2002.
5. Abbott Laboratories, *Annual Report*, 2002.
6. Ibid.
7. American Institute of Certified Public Accountants, *Accounting Trends & Techniques* (New York: AICPA, 2001).
8. *Statement of Accounting Standards No. 123*, "Accounting for Stock-Based Compensation" (Norwalk, Conn.: Financial Accounting Standards Board, 1995).
9. Ruth Simon and Ianthe Jeanne Dugan, "Options Overdose," *The Wall Street Journal*, June 4, 2001.
10. Suzanne McGee, "Europe's New Markets for IPOs of Growth Start-Ups Fly High," *The Wall Street Journal*, February 22, 1999.
11. Microsoft Corporation, Inc., *Annual Report*, 1997.
12. G. Christian Hill, "Microsoft Plans Preferred Issue of $750 Million," *The Wall Street Journal*, December 3, 1996.
13. American Institute of Certified Public Accountants, *Accounting Trends & Techniques* (New York: AICPA, 2001).
14. Robert McGough, Suzanne McGee, and Cassell Bryan-Low, "Buyback Binge Now Creates Big Hangover," *The Wall Street Journal*, December 18, 2000.
15. "Avaya Prices Public Offering of Common Stock" and "Avaya Completes Sale of Approximately $200 Million Common Stock," *The Wall Street Journal Online*, March 22, 2002.
16. Tom Herman, "Preferreds' Rich Yields Blind Some Investors to Risks," *The Wall Street Journal*, March 24, 1992.
17. Stanley Ziemba, "USAir Defers Dividends on Preferred Stock," *Chicago Tribune*, September 30, 1994.
18. Susan Carey, "US Airways to Redeem Preferred Owned by Berkshire Hathaway," *The Wall Street Journal*, February 4, 1998.
19. Roche Group, *Annual Report*, 2001.

Chapter 13
1. AMR Corporation, *Annual Report*, 2002.
2. *Statement of Financial Accounting Standards No. 130*, "Reporting Comprehensive Income" (Norwalk, Conn.: Financial Accounting Standards Board, 1997).
3. American Institute of Certified Public Accountants, *Accounting Trends & Techniques* (New York: American Institute of Certified Public Accountants, 2002).
4. Cited in *The Week in Review* (Deloitte Haskins & Sells), February 28, 1985.
5. "Up to the Minute, Down to the Wire," *Twentieth Century Mutual Funds Newsletter*, 1996.

6. American Institute of Certified Public Accountants, *Accounting Trends & Techniques* (New York: American Institute of Certified Public Accountants, 2001).
7. Robert Manor and Melita Marie Garza, "Company's Accounting May Prove Hard to Criminalize," *Chicago Tribune*, January 11, 2002.
8. Sears, Roebuck and Co., *Annual Report*, 1997.
9. *Statement of Financial Accounting Standards No. 109*, "Accounting for Income Taxes" (Norwalk, Conn.: Financial Accounting Standards Board, 1992).
10. American Institute of Certified Public Accountants, *Accounting Trends & Techniques* (New York: American Institute of Certified Public Accountants, 2002).
11. Accounting Principles Board, *Opinion No. 30*, "Reporting the Results of Operations" (New York: American Institute of Certified Public Accountants, 1973), par. 20.
12. Ibid.
13. American Institute of Certified Public Accountants, *Accounting Trends & Techniques* (New York: American Institute of Certified Public Accountants, 2002).
14. Accounting Principles Board, *Opinion No. 20*, "Accounting Changes" (New York: American Institute of Certified Public Accountants, 1971), par. 20.
15. David Cairns International, *IAS Survey Update*, July 2001.
16. American Institute of Certified Public Accountants, *Accounting Trends & Techniques* (New York: American Institute of Certified Public Accountants, 2002).
17. Accounting Principles Board, *Opinion No. 15*, "Earnings per Share" (New York: American Institute of Certified Public Accountants, 1969), par. 12.
18. Minnesota Mining and Manufacturing Company, *Annual Report*, 2000.
19. *Statement of Financial Accounting Standards No. 128*, "Earnings per Share and the Disclosure of Information About Capital Structure" (Norwalk, Conn.: Financial Accounting Standards Board, 1997).
20. Tribune Company, *Annual Report*, 2002.
21. Skandia Group, *Annual Report*, 2000.
22. *Accounting Research Bulletin No. 43* (New York: American Institute of Certified Public Accountants, 1953), chap. 7, sec. B, par. 10.
23. Ibid., par. 13.
24. Robert O'Brien, "Techs' Chill Fails to Stem Stock Splits," *The Wall Street Journal*, June 8, 2000.
25. Rebecca Buckman, "Microsoft Posts Hefty 18% Revenue Rise," *The Wall Street Journal*, January 18, 2002; William M. Bulkeley, "IBM Reports 13% Decline in Net Income," *The Wall Street Journal*, January 18, 2002.
26. "Technology Firms Post Strong Earnings but Stock Prices Decline Sharply," *The Wall Street Journal*, January 21, 1988; Donald R. Seace, "Industrials Plunge 57.2 Points—Technology Stocks' Woes Cited," *The Wall Street Journal*, January 21, 1988.
27. The Washington Post Company, *Annual Report*, 2000.
28. Yamaha Motor Company, Ltd., *Annual Report*, 2001.

Chapter 14

1. Marriott International, Inc., *Annual Report*, 2002, adapted.
2. *Statement of Financial Accounting Standards No. 95*, "Statement of Cash Flows" (Norwalk, Conn.: Financial Accounting Standards Board, 1987); *Statement of Financial Accounting Concepts No. 1*, "Objectives of Financial Reporting for Business Enterprises" (Norwalk, Conn.: Financial Accounting Standards Board, 1978), par. 37–39.
3. Marriott International, Inc., *Annual Report*, 2002.
4. Gary Slutsker, "Look at the Birdie and Say: 'Cash Flow,'" *Forbes*, October 25, 1993.
5. Jonathan Clements, "Yacktman Fund Is Bloodied but Unbowed," *The Wall Street Journal*, November 8, 1993.
6. Jeffrey Laderman, "Earnings, Schmearnings—Look at the Cash," *BusinessWeek*, July 24, 1989.
7. "Deadweight on the Markets," *BusinessWeek*, February 19, 2001.
8. Marriott International, Inc., *Annual Report*, 2002.
9. American Institute of Certified Public Accountants, *Accounting Trends & Techniques* (New York: AICPA, 2001).
10. Pallavi Gogoi, "Cash-Rich, So?" *BusinessWeek*, March 19, 2001.
11. "Cash Flow Shortfall in Quarter May Lead to Default on Loan," *The Wall Street Journal*, September 4, 2001.
12. Enron Corporation, *Press Release*, October 16, 2001.
13. Sony Corporation, *Annual Report*, 2000; Canon, Inc., *Annual Report*, 2000.

Chapter 15

1. Frederic M. Biddle, "A Little Gas Fuels Hope for a New Type of Electric Car," *The Wall Street Journal*, July 9, 1999.
2. Northiko Shirouzu, "Honda Bucks Industry Wisdom, Aiming to Be Small and Efficient," *The Wall Street Journal*, July 9, 1999.
3. *Statement No. 1A* (New York: Institute of Management Accountants, 1982).
4. Andra Gumbus and Susan D. Johnson, "The Balanced Scorecard at Futura Industries," *Strategic Finance*, July 2003.
5. Presentation by management of Baxter International, October 2001.
6. American Institute of Certified Public Accountants, "The New Finance," www.aicpa.org.
7. Peter Brewer, "Putting Strategy into the Balanced Scorecard," *Strategic Finance*, January 2002.
8. American Institute of Certified Public Accountants, "Summary of Sarbanes-Oxley Act of 2002," www.aicpa.org/info/sarbanes_oxley_summary.htm; Securities and Exchange Commission, "Final Rule: Certification of Disclosure in Companies' Quarterly and Annual Reports," August 28, 2002, www.sec.gov/rules/final/33-8124.htm.
9. Gregory L. White, "GM Appears to Step Back from Proposal," *The Wall Street Journal*, March 30, 1999.

Chapter 16

1. Southwest Airlines, "Fact Sheet," www.southwest.com.
2. Melanie Trottman, "Vaunted Southwest Slips in On-Time Performance," *The Wall Street Journal*, September 25, 2002.
3. Robert Frank and Sarah Ellison, "Meltdown in Chocolatetown," *The Wall Street Journal*, September 19, 2002.
4. United Parcel Service, "About UPS," www.ups.com.
5. Lisa de Moraes, "Conan the Cost: NBC's Thrifty Numbers Game," *The Washington Post*, February 8, 2002.

Chapter 17

1. Robert L. Simison, "Toyota Finds Way to Make Custom Car in 5 Days," *The Wall Street Journal*, August 6, 1999.
2. John M. Parkinson, "Equivalent Units in Process Costing" (paper presented at the meeting of the American Accounting Association, August 2002).
3. Associated Press, "$75 Screws? The Pentagon Pays It," *The Gainesville Sun*, March 19, 1998.
4. Cheryl Dahle, "Sneak Previews Make Good Project Reviews," *Fast Company*, July–August 1999.
5. William A. Sahlman, "How to Write a Great Business Plan," *Harvard Business Review*, July–August 1997.
6. Gina Imperato, "When Is 'Good Enough' Good Enough?" *Fast Company*, July–August 1999.
7. P. Kelly Mooney, "The Experienced Customer," *Fast Company*, Fall 1999, pp. 25–9. Reprinted by permission of Gruner & Jahr USA Publishing.

Chapter 18

1. Don Clark, "Intel, Shaking Off Downturn, to Unveil New Chip Technology," *The Wall Street Journal*, August 13, 2002.
2. "Fraud Examiners Rate the Scams," *Journal of Accountancy*, June 2002.
3. Intel Corporation, "Corporate Overview," www.intel.com.

Chapter 19
1. Dan Morse, "Tennessee Producer Tries New Tactic in Sofas: Speed," *The Wall Street Journal*, November 19, 2002.
2. Gary Cokins, "Learning to Love ABC," *Journal of Accountancy*, August 1999.
3. Mylene Mangalindan, "Oracle Puts Priority on Customer Service," *The Wall Street Journal*, January 21, 2003.
4. Lance Thompson, "Examining Methods of VBM," *Strategic Finance*, December 2002.
5. Paulette Thomas, "Electronics Firm Ends Practice Just in Time," *The Wall Street Journal*, October 29, 2002.
6. Gina Imperato, "Time for Zero Time," *Net Company*, Fall 1999.
7. Sally Beatty, "Levi's Strive to Keep a Hip Image," *The Wall Street Journal*, January 23, 2003.

Chapter 20
1. Kraft Foods, "Profile," www.kraft.com.
2. Kraft Foods, "Inside Kraft: A Company Overview," http://164.109.16.145/investors/overview.html.

Chapter 21
1. Johnson & Johnson, "Our Company," www.jnj.com.
2. Omar Aguilar, "How Strategic Performance Management Is Helping Companies Create Business Value," *Strategic Finance*, January 2003.
3. Enterprise Rent-a-Car, "Overview," "Facts," "History," www.enterprise.com.
4. Richard Barrett, "From Fast Close to Fast Forward," *Strategic Finance*, January 2003.
5. Jeremy Hope and Robin Fraser, "Who Needs Budgets?" *Harvard Business Review*, February 2003.
6. Ibid.
7. Minnesota Mining and Manufacturing Company, "About 3M," www.3m.com.

Chapter 22
1. Erin White, "How Stogy Turned Stylish," *The Wall Street Journal*, May 3, 2002.
2. Katy McLaughlin, "Factory Tours," *The Wall Street Journal*, October 29, 2002.
3. David E. Keys and Anton Van Der Merwe, "Gaining Effective Organizational Control with RCA," *Strategic Finance*, May 2002.
4. Gabriel Kahn, "Still Going for Gold," *The Wall Street Journal*, January 28, 2003.
5. Curtis C. Verschoor, "Ethical Corporations Are Still More Profitable," *Strategic Finance*, June 2003.

Chapter 23
1. PEAKS Resorts, www.peakscard.com or 1-800-842-8062.
2. Rich Teerlink, "Harley's Leadership U-Turn," *Harvard Business Review*, July–August 2000.
3. Marc J. Epstein and Jean-François Manzoni, "The Balanced Scorecard and Tableau de Bord: Translating Strategy into Action," *Management Accounting*, August 1997.
4. Jill Rosenfeld, "Information as if Understanding Mattered," *Fast Company*, March 2000.
5. "Blue Jeans to Help Keep Cars Quiet: Who Thinks This Stuff Up?" *Fast Company*, May 2000.
6. Ans Kolk, "Green Reporting," *Harvard Business Review*, January–February 2000.
7. Russ Banham, "Better Budgets," *Journal of Accountancy*, February 2000.
8. Julia Flynn, "Use of Performance-Based Pay Spreads Across Continental Europe, Survey Says," *The Wall Street Journal*, November 17, 1999.

Chapter 24
1. Stephanie Miles, "What's a Check?" *The Wall Street Journal*, October 21, 2002.
2. Jonathan Eig, "One CFO Finds His Orderly World Upset After Enron," *The Wall Street Journal*, November 14, 2002.
3. Miles, "What's a Check?".
4. Michael Liedtke, "Keeping the Books," *The Gainesville Sun*, August 22, 2002.
5. Alan Fuhrman, "Your E-Banking Future," *Strategic Finance*, April 2002.
6. "The Ball and Chain," *Wireless Week*, June 21, 1999; "Iridium to Be Reborn Relatively Debt-Free?" *Newsbytes News Network*, August 19, 1999, www.iridium.com.

Chapter 25
1. Walter S. Mossberg, "An Affordable Palm Even Paper Lovers Might Use," *The Wall Street Journal*, October 16, 2002. Palm, Inc., "About Palm, Inc.," www.palm.com.
2. Nokia, "About Nokia," www.nokia.com.
3. Kathy Williams, "Tom D'Angelo, Priceline.com's Mr. Inside," *Strategic Finance*, July, 2002.
4. Nick Wingfield, "Are You Satisfied?" *The Wall Street Journal*, September 16, 2002.
5. Christopher Lawton, "Anheuser-Busch Rolls Out the Price Jump," *The Wall Street Journal*, October 23, 2002.

Chapter 26
1. Timothy Aeppel, "Workers Not Included," *The Wall Street Journal*, November 19, 2002.
2. Paulette Thomas, "Case Study: Electronics Firm Ends Practice Just in Time," *The Wall Street Journal*, October 29, 2002.
3. Kristina Shevory, "Heads or Tails?" *The Seattle Times*, September 5, 2002.
4. From a speech by Jim Croft, vice president of finance and administration of the Field Museum, Chicago, November 14, 2000.
5. Sholnn Freeman, "Discounting's Final Frontier: The Luxury-Car Lot," *The Wall Street Journal*, November 19, 2002.
6. DaimlerChrysler, "Investor Relations," www.daimlerchrisyselr.com

Chapter 27
1. Nick Wingfield, "Amazon Takes Page from Wal-Mart to Prosper on Web," *The Wall Street Journal*, November 22, 2002.
2. C. K. Prahalad and M. S. Krishna, "The New Meaning of Quality in the Information Age," *Harvard Business Review*, September–October 1999.
3. Don Irwin and Victor Rocine, "Self-Directed Work Teams," *CMA Magazine*, September 1994. Used by permission of The Society of Management Accountants of Canada.
4. Lisa Tischler, "Nissan Motor Co. Directions for a Turnaround," *Fast Company*, July 2002.
5. Julia Winn, "Quality Is Doing It Right the First Time," *Insight*, October 1993.
6. Nick Wingfield, "Amazon Takes Page from Wal-Mart to Prosper on Web," *The Wall Street Journal*, November 22, 2002.
7. Vinod R. Singhal, "Total Quality Management (TQM) Significantly Boosts Bottom Line," *CPA Letter/Business and Industry*, September 1999.
8. www.juse.or.jp/e-renmai/main-frame.htm.
9. National Institute of Standards and Technology, "Award Recipients," www.quality.nist.gov.
10. International Organization for Standardization, "ISO 9000/ISO 14000," www.iso.ch.
11. Motorola Internet and Networking Group, "Why Motorola?" www.motorola.com/MIMS/ISG/ING/quality.

Chapter 28

1. Sun Microsystems, *Proxy Statement*, 2001.
2. Phyllis Plitch, "Firms Embrace Pro Forma Way on Earnings," *The Wall Street Journal*, January 22, 2002.
3. David Henry, "The Numbers Game," *BusinessWeek*, May 14, 2001.
4. *Statement of Financial Accounting Standards No. 131*, "Segment Disclosures" (Norwalk, Conn.: Financial Accounting Standards Board, 1997).
5. Sun Microsystems, Inc. *Annual Report*, 2001.
6. William H. Beaver, "Alternative Accounting Measures as Indicators of Failure," *Accounting Review*, January 1968; Edward Altman, "Financial Ratios, Discriminant Analysis and the Prediction of Corporate Bankruptcy," *Journal of Finance*, September 1968.
7. Sun Microsystems, Inc., "Management's Discussion and Analysis," *Annual Report*, 2001.
8. Ibid.
9. *Forbes*, November 13, 1978, p. 154.
10. Elizabeth MacDonald, "Firms Say SEC Earnings Scrutiny Goes Too Far," *The Wall Street Journal*, February 1, 1999.
11. H. J. Heinz Company, *Annual Report*, 2001.
12. Pfizer, Inc., *Annual Report*, 2000; Roche Group, *Annual Report*, 2000.

Appendix D

1. PepsiCo., Inc., *Annual Report*, 2000.
2. *Statement of Financial Accounting Standards No. 52*, "Foreign Currency Translation" (Norwalk, Conn.: Financial Accounting Standards Board, 1981), par. 15.
3. *Financial Reporting: An International Survey* (New York: Price Waterhouse, May 1995).
4. "International Accounting Standards Committee Objectives and Procedures," *Professional Standards* (New York: American Institute of Certified Public Accountants, 1988), vol. B, sec. 9000, par. 24–27.

Appendix E

1. *Statement of Financial Accounting Standards No. 115*, "Accounting for Certain Investments in Debt and Equity Securities" (Norwalk, Conn.: Financial Accounting Standards Board, 1993).

Appendix F

1. Accounting Principles Board, *Opinion No. 21*, "Interest on Receivables and Payables" (New York: American Institute of Certified Public Accountants, 1971), par. 13.

Company Name Index

Abbott Laboratories, 474, 544, 545–546
Accenture, 1013
Ace Hardware, 11
Air Afrique, 501
Air Products and Chemicals, Inc., 1094–1095, 1096, 1097
Ajinomoto Company, 154
Albertson's Inc., 289
Alcoa Inc., 593, 785
Allied Waste, 1128
Allstate Insurance Co., 887
Amazon.com, 152, 172, 455, 535–536, 547, 573, 1126–1127, 1128–1129, 1140, 1141, 1150, 1167
American Airlines, Inc., 433, 534, 574–575
American Century Services Corp., 576
American Express, 578
America Online (AOL), 161, 433, 493, 571, 573, 1168
Ameritech Corp., 343
Ameritrade, 1088
AMR Corporation, 574–575, 584
Amtrak, 899
Anheuser-Busch Company, 1064, 1070
AOL (America Online), 161, 433, 493, 571, 573, 1168
AOL Time Warner Inc., 305, 433, 493, 571, 573, 1051
A&P (Great Atlantic & Pacific Tea Company), 289
Apple Computer, Inc., 544, 593, 785, 987
Association for Investment Management and Research, 576
AT&T Corporation, 498–499, 501–502, 504, 505, 544–545, 557, 600, 668
AutoLiv, Inc., 388
Avaya, Inc., 569
Avon, 1200

Baan, 1128
Babies "R" Us, 49
Bank of America, 347, 578, 942, 1018–1019, 1020, 1140
BankOne, 347
Barnes & Noble, 339, 392
Baxter International, 244, 495, 666

Beijing Li-Ning Sports Goods Company, 958
Bell South, 507
Berkshire Hathaway, 572
Blockbuster Entertainment Corporation, 392, 856
The Boeing Company, 114–115, 116, 462, 756, 941
Boise Cascade, 785
Borders, 740
BP Corporation, 349–350
Brinker International, Inc., 988, 989(table)
Bristol-Myers Squibb, 213, 998

Caesars World Inc., 159
Canon, Inc., 652, 654
Caterpillar Inc., 213, 785
Century 21, 748
Charles Schwab & Co., Inc., 46–47, 1168
Chase Manhattan, 569, 593
ChemLawn, 974–975
Chico's, 700
Chili's Grill and Bar, 988, 989(table)
Circuit City Stores, Inc., 301, 309, 345–346
Cisco Systems, Inc., 205, 353, 400, 450, 455, 538–539, 543, 545, 547
Citibank, 347, 569, 700–701
Claire's Stores, Inc., 297
Coach, Inc., 938–939, 941
Coca-Cola Company, 29(table), 44–45, 271, 507, 785, 994, 1124
Coinstar, 1102
Coleman, 335
Columbia HCA Healthcare, 507
CompuCredit, 380
CompuServe, 1168
Continental Airlines, Inc., 114–115, 116, 500, 863
Coors, 785
Costco Wholesale Corporation, 262
Crane Company, 418
Crazy Eddie, Inc., 418
Crown Cork & Seal, 785

DaimlerChrysler Corp., 343, 751, 856, 987, 988, 998–999, 1121
Dayton-Hudson Corporation, 1013
Daytons Stores, 1013

Defense Department, U.S., 756
Dell Computer Corporation, 258(exh.), 258–259, 259(fig.), 263–264, 264(exh.), 265(fig.), 272(fig.), 272–273, 290, 292, 386, 415, 672, 745, 816, 1128
Deloitte & Touche, 29(table)
Delta Airlines, 462, 863
Department of Defense, 756
Department of Energy, U.S., 455
Dillard Dept. Stores, Inc., 297, 344
Domino's Pizza, 975
Dow Chemical Company, 213, 809
Dun & Bradstreet Corp., 432, 1165, 1168
Du Pont, 29(table)

Eagle Brand, 1070
Eastman Kodak, 669, 785
eBay Inc., 573, 1054, 1060
Eclipsys, 161
Emerson Electric, 785
Energy, U.S. Department of, 455
Engelhard Corporation, 785
England, Inc., 814–815
Enron Corporation, 30, 253, 254, 580, 652, 653, 663, 676, 1130, 1164
Enterprise Rent-A-Car, 713, 895, 899
Ericcson, 1055
Ernst & Young, 29(table), 54, 252
Ethan Allen, Inc., 721
e*Trade, 1088
Exxon, 785
ExxonMobil, 14, 29(table), 348–350, 415, 1237(table)

Federal Express Corporation (FedEx), 534, 669, 857
Fermi National Accelerator Laboratory (Fermilab), 455
Field Museum of Chicago, 1106
Financial Executives Research Foundation, 523
Fleetwood Enterprises, Inc., 159, 649–650
FMCC (Ford Motor Credit Co.), 345
Forbes, 1017
Ford Motor Company, 29(table), 343, 345, 375, 457, 496, 819, 993, 1237(table)

Company Name Index

Ford Motor Credit Co. (FMCC), 345
Fruit of the Loom, 335
Fuji Photo Optical Company, 1141

The Gap, 7
Gateway, Inc., 745
General Electric, 29(table), 669, 994, 1140
General Mills, Inc., 5, 246–247, 253, 476
General Motors Acceptance Corp. (GMAC), 345
General Motors Corporation, 29(table), 343, 345, 434, 448–449, 474, 492, 545, 666, 668, 694, 700, 751, 994, 1054, 1237(table)
Getty Oil, 450
Gillette Company, 213, 593
GlaxoSmithKline PLC, 290–292
GMAC (General Motors Acceptance Corp.), 345
Goldman, Sachs & Co., 544
Goodyear Tire & Rubber Company, 250, 425, 617, 858, 1166(exh.), 1167, 1200
Great Atlantic & Pacific Tea Company (A&P), 289

Handspring, 1054
Harley-Davidson, Inc., 668, 748, 983, 988
Harrods, 338
Heineken N.V., 380
Helene Curtis Corp., 1200°
Hershey Foods Corp., 196–197, 206, 245, 417–418, 713
Hertz, 988
Hewlett-Packard, 557, 669
Hilton Hotels Corp., 5, 492–493
H.J. Heinz Company, 159, 194, 452–453, 472, 1201–1202
Holman Cement, 1128
The Home Depot, Inc., 342–343, 392, 1140
Honda Motor Company, 656–657, 666, 697
H&R Block, Inc., 243–244, 740, 748, 933
HSBC Bank USA, 569
Hudsons Stores, 1013
Humana, 700–701

IBM (International Business Machines), 29(table), 375, 399, 507, 569, 608–609, 666, 1097, 1237, 1237(table)
Ikea, 1068, 1083

Illinois Tool Works, Inc., 384
Indian Motorcycle Corporation, 740
Industrial Light and Magic, 759
Intel Corporation, 5, 48, 118, 557, 593, 609, 782–783, 793, 898–899, 987, 1060, 1097
International Business Machines (IBM), 29(table), 375, 507, 569, 608–609, 666, 1097, 1237, 1237(table)
International Paper Co., 395, 1124
Intuit Corporation, 1029

J.C. Penney Company, Inc., 44, 205, 351, 381, 382–383, 384, 385, 386–387, 415
JDS Uniphase, 1167
Jiffy Lube, 988, 989(table)
John Deere, 700, 898–899
John H. Daniel Company, 746–747, 750
Johnson & Johnson, 892–893, 894
J.P. Morgan Investment Management Inc., 46
JP MorganChase, 1140
Juniper Networks, 593

Kellogg Company, 785
Kelly Services, 156–157, 159, 170
Kentucky Fried Chicken (KFC), 1070
Kids "R" Us, 49
Kinko's, 988, 989(table)
Kmart, 337, 339, 400
KnowledgeWare, 161
Kodak, 669
Koss Corporation, 830, 1101
KPMG LLP, 29(table)
Kraft Foods, 854–855, 856, 865, 941, 987

Land O'Lakes, 823
Land Rover, 858
Lands' End, 301, 339, 1140
La-Z-Boy, Inc., 814
Lego Group, 47
Lehman Brothers Inc., 268
Levi Strauss & Co., 748, 853
Liberty Mutual Insurance COmpany, 942
The Limited, 381
L.L. Bean, 301
Lowe's, 899
Lucent Technologies, Inc., 126, 161, 287–288, 353, 455, 1141
Lyric Opera of Chicago, 192

Macy's, 344, 381

Man Nutzfahrzeuge Aktiengesellschaft, 450–451
Marriott International, Inc., 492–493, 614–616, 620–623, 655
Mars, 713
Marshall Field's, 344, 1013
May SWS Securities, 359
Maytag Corporation, 419, 1088
McDonald's, 29(table), 375, 696–697, 868
Medtronic, 1140
Mellon Bank, 153
Mercedes-Benz, 1054
Merck, 894
Mergent, Inc., 1168, 1169(exh.), 1200
Mervyn's, 1013
MGM-UA Communications Co., 159
Michelin, 1237
Microsoft Corporation, 10, 48, 550, 557, 608
Midway Airlines, 500, 501
Minnesota Mining and Manufacturing Company (3M), 586, 785, 936–937, 1142
Mitsubishi Corp., 378, 933
Monsanto, 987, 1013
Montgomery Ward, 199
Moody's Investor Services, Inc., 1168, 1200, 1203
Motorola, 353, 669, 700, 714–715, 1055, 1140, 1147, 1158

Nabisco, 600, 787
NCH Promotional Services, 432
NEC Corporation, 536
Neiman Marcus, 262
Nestlé S.A., 244, 713, 1237
Netscape Communications Corporation, 571–572
Neuer Markt, 547
Newark Morning Ledger Co., 474
Nike, Inc., 152, 264, 266, 266(exh.), 666
Nissan, 1134
Nokia, 1055
Nordstrom, 344, 899, 988, 1054
Nortel Networks, 353
Nouveau Marche, 547
Nvidia, 593

Office Depot, 301
Official Airline Guide, 698
Oracle Corporation, 155, 198, 245, 819, 1128
Orkin Exterminating Company, 748
Owens Corning, 785

Palm, Inc., 1052–1053, 1054, 1093
Peachtree Software, 202(fig.), 203
Pennzoil Company, 450
PeopleSoft, 198, 245, 819
Pep Boys, 700
PepsiCo Bottling Company, 1070, 1244
PepsiCo Inc., 1168, 1169(exh.), 1200, 1237, 1237(table), 1244
Pepsi Cola North America, 823
Pfizer, Inc., 1202
Philip Morris Companies, Inc., 451, 522, 713
Philips Electronics N.V., 380
Phillips Petroleum, 213
Piedmont Airlines, 462
Pillsbury, 246
Pioneer Corporation, 340–341, 344, 346, 350, 418–419
Pitney Bowes, 821
Polaroid Corporation, 492
PPG Industries, 1121
Preussag, 585
Priceline.com, 1054, 1060
PricewaterhouseCoopers, 29(table)
Procter & Gamble, 29(table)

Quaker Oats, 1244
Qualcomm, 353

RadioShack Corporation, 422–423
Rambus Inc., 593
Real Networks Inc., 547
Reebok International Ltd., 5
Renault, 1134
RentWay, Inc., 398
Resource Marketing, Inc., 780
Revlon, 1200
Risk Management Association, 1168
Rite Aid Corp., 398
Ritz-Carlton Hotel Co., 1142
RJR Nabisco, 451
Robert Morris Associates, 1168
Roche Group, 474, 495, 572, 1202
Royal Dutch/Shell, 998
Rubbermaid, 335
Russell Stover Candies, 713

Safeway Inc., 205, 534, 1070
Sam's Clubs, 262
Sanyo Electric Co., 536
SAP, 198, 245, 819, 1128
Sara Lee Corporation, 476
Sears, Roebuck and Co., 29(table), 345, 351, 381, 385, 580, 700, 1140

Sears Roebuck Acceptance Corp. (SRAC), 345
Sea World, 1070
Shanghai Industrial Sewing Machine, 354
Shanghai Steel Tube, 354
Simon & Schuster, 305
Skandia Group, 590
Sony Corporation, 5, 652, 654, 666, 714–715, 865, 1068, 1237
South Beach Beverage, 1244
Southwest Airlines Co., 5, 45, 698–699, 702, 703, 713, 863
Sprint Corp., 547, 856
SRAC (Sears Roebuck Acceptance Corp.), 345
Standard & Poor's, 536, 1168, 1200
Starbucks Corporation, 337–338
Sunbeam Corporation, 253, 335
Sun Microsystems, Inc., 155, 450, 1060, 1160–1161, 1162, 1170–1183, 1171(exh.)–1175(exh.), 1174(fig.), 1177(fig.), 1178(exh.)–1180(exh.), 1182(exh.)
Super Bakery, 1024
Swiss Air, 500, 501

Taco Bell, 721, 1070
Takashimaya Company, Ltd., 194
Talbots, 899
Target, 205, 294–295, 297–298, 381, 1013
Texaco Inc., 348–350, 450, 451
3M (Minnesota Mining and Manufacturing Company), 586, 785, 936–937, 1142
Tiffany & Co., 262, 593
Toyota Motor Company, 5, 697, 748, 751, 1054
Toys "R" Us, 16, 16(fig.), 26, 47–48, 49–56, 154, 159, 194, 244, 245, 292, 338, 339, 380–381, 384, 385, 392, 419, 451, 495, 496, 536, 573, 578, 612, 654, 713–714, 933, 1202–1203
Trans World Airlines (TWA), 500, 501, 534
Travelocity.com, 172
Tribune Company, 476, 587–588
Tropicana, 1244
Tupperware, 785
TWA (Trans World Airlines), 500, 501, 534
Twentieth Century Mutual Funds, 576

Unilever, 1028, 1237
United Nations, 894
United Parcel Service (UPS), 386, 659, 713, 721, 857, 899, 974–975, 994
U.S. Department of Defense, 756
U.S. Department of Energy, 455
U.S. Postal Service (USPS), 822, 863
United Way, 894, 988
UPS (United Parcel Service), 382, 659, 713, 721, 857, 899, 974–975, 994
USAA, 669, 700–701, 887
US Airways, Inc., 420–421, 422, 424, 425–426, 433, 434, 462, 501, 572
USPS (U.S. Postal Service), 822, 863

Vail Resorts, 980–981, 982–985, 984(fig.), 985(fig.)
Vanguard Airlines, 462
Verizon, 856
Vicorp Restaurants, 989

Walgreen Co., 2–3, 7, 24(exh.)–27(exh.), 25–28, 48, 49, 56, 154, 194, 245, 292, 338, 381, 419, 451, 496, 536, 573, 612, 654, 1202–1203
Wall Street Journal, 1168
Wal-Mart Stores, Inc., 271, 335–336, 337, 339, 347, 392, 668, 713–714, 853, 858, 988, 989(table), 1054, 1070
The Walt Disney Company, 159, 193, 271, 507, 1051, 1141
Washington Post Company, 611–612
Waste Management, Inc., 451
Webvan Group, Inc., 628
Wells Fargo, 569, 858
Wendy's International Inc., 5
Western Airlines, 462
Westinghouse Electric, 823
WorldCom, 253, 254, 461, 663, 912, 1130, 1164
W.R. Grace & Co., 1200
Wrigley's, 713

Xerox Corporation, 29(table), 424, 1142

Yahoo!, 573, 1060, 1168
Yamaha Motor Company, Ltd., 418–419, 612

Subject Index

Note: **Boldface** type indicates key terms.

ABC, see Activity-based costing (ABC)
ABM, see Activity-based management (ABM)
Absorption costing income statement, profit center performance evaluation using, 991–993, 992(exh.)
Accelerated methods, 464, 464–465, 466, 466(fig.)
Account(s), 17
   adjusting, see Adjusting entries; Adjustments
   chart of, 118, 119–120(exh.)
   after closing, 210, 211–212(exh.), 212
   contra, see Contra accounts
   controlling (control), 1214
   permanent (real), 205
   temporary (nominal), 205
   uncollectible, see Uncollectible accounts
   see also specific accounts
Account balance, 122
Accounting, 4
   financial, 7
   as information system, 4(fig.), 4–8
   management, 7
Accounting cycle, 199, 200(fig.), 201
Accounting equation, 15, 15–20
Accounting information
   processing, 7–8
   users of, 8(fig.), 8–10
   see also Financial statement(s); Report(s); specific financial statements
Accounting information systems, 196–229, 198
   accounting cycle and, 199, 200(fig.), 201
   closing entries and, see Closing entries
   compatibility principle and, 199
   computerized accounting systems and, see Computerized accounting systems
   control principle and, 198
   cost-benefit principle and, 198
   flexibility principle and, 199
   Internet and, 204–205

   post-closing trial balance and, 213, 213(exh.)
   reversing entries and, 214–215
   special-purpose journals in, see Special-purpose journals; specific journals
   work sheet and, see Work sheet
Accounting period issue, 159
Accounting policies, 116
Accounting practices
   adoption in emerging economies, 354
   changes in, cumulative effect of, 585
   operating decisions and, 397
   organizations influencing, 29–30
   quality of earnings and, 577–579
Accounting Principles Board (APB)
   on amortization of bond discount, 510
   on depreciation, 477
   on earnings per share, 586
   on extraordinary items, 584–585
   on imputing interest on noninterest-bearing notes, 1257
   on influence and control, 1244
   on intangible assets, 472, 474
   Opinion No. 9 of, 477
   Opinion No. 10 of, 1244
   Opinion No. 17 of, 472
   Opinion No. 20 of, 477
   Opinion No. 30 of, 584–585
Accounting rate-of-return method, 1110
Accounting standards
   international accounting and, 1238, 1242–1243
   international comparability of, 474
Accounts payable, 425
Accounts receivable, 351, 351(fig.), 351–358
   collection of, 19
   installment, 351
   uncollectible, see Uncollectible accounts
Accounts receivable aging method, 354, 354–357, 355(exh.), 356(fig.)
Account titles, 120–121
Accrual(s), 163
   year-end, of bond interest expense, 516–518

Accrual accounting, 160, 160–162
   adjustments and, see Adjusting entries; Adjustments
   cash flows and, 175–176
   performance measures and, 162
   recognition of revenues and expenses and, 160–161
Accrued expenses, 168
   adjustments for, 168–170, 169(fig.)
Accrued liabilities, 427
Accrued revenues, 171
   adjustments for, 171(fig.), 171–172
Accumulated Depreciation account, 167, 167(fig.), 167–168, 168(exh.), 630
Activity-based costing (ABC), 669, 720, 720–724, **824,** 824–828
   cost hierarchy and bill of activities and, 824–827
   reports and, 819
   for selling and administrative activities, 827–828, 828(exh.)
Activity-based management (ABM), 669, 818, 818–828
   just-in-time operating philosophy compared with, 835–836, 836(table)
   in service organizations, 820–821, 821(fig.)
Activity-based systems, 816, 816–817
   management cycle and, 817(fig.), 817–818
   see also Activity-based management (ABM); Just-in-time (JIT) entries
Actual costing, 705, 705–706
Additions, 478
Adjusted trial balance, 172, 172–173, 173(exh.), 174(exh.)
Adjusting entries, 163, 163, 361
   for promissory notes, 361
   recording using work sheet, 222, 223(exh.)
Adjustments, 161–162, 162(exh.), 163(fig.), 163–172
   for accrued expenses, 168–170, 169(fig.)
   for accrued revenues, 171(fig.), 171–172
   for deferred expenses, 163–168
   for deferred revenues, 170(fig.), 170–171

Subject Index

Advisers, as users of accounting information, 10
Aging of accounts receivable, 354
AICPA, *see* American Institute of Certified Public Accountants (AICPA)
Airline industry
  bankruptcies in, 501
  debt financing in, 500–501
  fixed costs in, 703
  frequent-flier miles and, 433
  pricing in, 863
Allowance for Doubtful Accounts account, 353
Allowance for Uncollectible Accounts account, 352, 352–353, 355, 358
Allowance method, 352, 352–353
Allowance to Adjust Long-Term Investments to Market account, 1246, 1247–1248
American Institute of Certified Public Accountants (AICPA), 29
  on depreciation, 461
  on inventory cost, 388
Amortization, 456(fig.)
  of bond discounts, 508–512
  of bond premium, 512–515
Annual reports, 49
  components of, 49–55
Annual Statement Studies, 1168
Annuities, ordinary, 1253, 1254(table)
Annuities due, 1269
APB, *see* Accounting Principles Board (APB)
Appraisal costs, 131, 131(table)
Articles of incorporation, 14, 540
Artificial prices, 1073
Asset(s), 15
  cash flows to, 621
  current, 254, 256, 627
  depreciation of, *see* Depreciation
  intangible, 256, 472, 472(fig.), 473(table), 474–476
  investing in partnerships, 1232
  long-term, *see* Long-term assets; Plant assets
  noncash, issuance of stock for, 554–555
  "other," 254
  plant (fixed; long-lived; operating; tangible), *see* Plant assets
  preference as to, 551
  purchase by incurring liabilities, 18
  purchase with cash, 17–18
  return on, 268–270, 269(fig.), 270(fig.)
  short-term, *see* Short-term financial assets
  valuing, 1258

Asset impairment, 454
Asset turnover, 268, 994, 1179, 1179(exh.), 1179–1180
ATMs (automated teller machines), 347
Auction-based pricing, 1060
Audit(s), 29
Audit committees, 14, 14–15, **540**
Authorized stock, 543
Automated teller machines (ATMs), 347
Available-for-sale securities, 350, 1244, 1245
Average costing method, 786
  process cost report using, 794–797, 795(exh.)
Average-cost method, 390, 390–391
Average days' inventory on hand, 387, 1177, 1178(exh.)
Average days' payable, 422, 423, 423(fig.), **1177,** 1178(exh.)
Average days' sales uncollected, 343, 344, **1177,** 1178(exh.)
Avoidable costs, 1028

Backflush costing, 832, 832–835, 833(fig.), 834(fig.)
Bad debts, *see* Uncollectible accounts
Bad Debts Expense account, 353
Balance(s), 122
  compensating, 346
  normal, 131, 132(table)
  trial, *see* Trial balance
Balanced scorecard, 672, 672–673, 673(fig.), **982,** 982–985
  management cycle and, 982–985
Balance sheet, 22, 23(exh.), 24
  budgeted, 912, 914(exh.)
  classified, 254, 255(exh.), 256–259
  disclosure of bonds on, 504
  reading and graphing, 258(exh.), 258–259, 259(fig.)
Bank loans, 425–426
Bar codes, 299
Barron's magazine, 1168
Base year, 1170
Basic earnings per share, 586, 586–588
Batch-level activities, 824, 824–825
Batch posting, 4
Benchmarking, 673–674, **674**
Betterments, 478
"Big baths," 579
Bill of activities, 825, 826(exh.), 827
Boards of directors, 14–15, 540
Bond(s), 503, 503–519, 1244
  balance sheet disclosure of, 504
  callable, 518
  convertible, 519
  costs of issuing, 507

  coupon, 504
  interest rates on, 505–506
  issued at discount, 506
  issued at face value, 504–505
  issued at premium, 506–507
  100-year, 507
  prices of, 505
  registered, 503–504
  retirement of, 518–519
  sale between interest dates, 515–516, 517(fig.)
  secured, 503
  serial, 503
  statement of cash flows and, 631
  term, 503
  unsecured, 503
  year-end accrual of interest expense for, 516–518
  zero coupon, 509
Bond certificates, 503
Bond discounts, amortizing, 508–512
Bond indentures, 503
Bonding, 311
Bond issues, 503
Bond premium, amortization of, 512–515
Bonds Payable account, bonds issued at discount and, 506
Bonuses to partners, 1233
Bookkeeping, 8
  double-entry, 121–124
Book of original entry, *see* Journal(s); Journal *entries*
Book value, 168, 454, **594,** 594–595
  in capital investment analysis, 1102
Book value per share, 594
Brand names, 473(table)
Breakeven analysis, 866–870, 867(fig.)
Breakeven point, 866
  contribution margin to determine, 868–869
  for multiple products, 869(fig.), 869–870
Budget(s), 894
  capital expenditures, 909–910
  cash, 910(table), 910–912, 911–913(exh.)
  cost of goods manufactured, 908, 908(exh.)
  direct labor, 904–905, 906(exh.)
  direct materials purchases, 904, 905(exh.)
  financial, 898, 908–912
  implementation of, 915
  manufacturing overhead, 905, 906(exh.), 907
  master, *see* Master budget
  operating, 898, 901–908

production, 902–903, 903(exh.)
sales, 901–902, 903(exh.)
selling and administrative expense, 907, 907(exh.)
Budget committee, **915**
Budgeted balance sheet, **912**, 914(exh.)
Budgeted income statement, **908**, 908–909, 909(exh.)
Budgeting, 892–917, **894**
goals and, 894–895
management cycle and, 896–898, 897(fig.)
participative, 896
Buildings
acquisition cost of, 460
see also Plant assets
Business(es), **4**
goals, activities, and performance measures for, 4–7, 6(fig.)
international, *see* International business
Business plans, **661**
Business transactions, **11**
analysis of, illustration of, 17–20, 548
analyzing and processing, 122–131, 123(fig.), 130(exh.)
document-less, 205
in foreign currencies, 1239–1241
see also International accounting
measurement of, *see* Measurement
Buyers, big, power of, 343

CAD (computer-aided design), 132–133
Callable bonds, **518**
Callable preferred stock, **552**
Call price, **518**, **552**
Candy industry, market share in, 713
Capital
contributed, 16
cost of, 996–997, 1100
legal, 543
working, 267
see also Owner's equity
Capital balance ratios, 1230
Capital budgeting, *See* Capital investment analysis
Capital expenditures, **459**
Capital expenditures budget, **909**, 909–910
Capital investment analysis, 1094–1114, **1096**, 1097(fig.)
accounting rate-of-return method for, 1110
in management cycle, 1097–1099, 1098(fig.)
measures used in, 1102–1103
minimum rate of return on investment and, 1100–1101

net present value method for, 1107–1108
for not-for-profit firms, 1106
payback period method for, 1109–1110
time value of money and, 1103–1107
Capital investment proposals, ranking, 1101
Capital leases, **521**
Capital Stock account, 553
Capital structure, **587**
Carrying value, **168**, **454**, 594–595
in capital investment analysis, 1102
Cash, **346**, 346–347, **617**
"burn rate" for, 628
idle, investment of, 1259–1260
plant assets sold for, 467–468
purchase of assets with, 17–18
see also Petty cash *entries*
Cash account, 617, 618
bonds issued at discount and, 506
Cash basis of accounting, **160**
Cash budget, **910**, 910(table), 910–912, 911–913(exh.)
Cash equivalents, **346**, **617**
Cash flow(s), **24**
accrual accounting and, 175–176
adequacy of, evaluation of, 1181, 1182(exh.)
classification of, 618–620, 619(fig.)
equal versus unequal, in capital investment analysis, 1102
free, 621–623
inventory measurement and, 399
liquidity and, 422–423, 423(fig.)
quality of earnings and, 580–581
Cash flow management, **296**
Cash flows to assets, **621**, 1181, 1182(exh.)
Cash flows to sales, **621**, 1181, 1182(exh.)
Cash flow yield, **621**
adequacy of, evaluation of, 1181, 1182(exh.)
Cash-generating efficiency, **620**, 620–621
Cash inflows, net, in capital investment analysis, 1102
Cash payments (disbursements) journal, 1221, 1222(exh.), 1223
Cash receipts, control of, 313
Cash receipts journal, 1218, 1219(exh.), 1220–1221
Cash reserves, 343
Category killers, 392
Certified public accountants (CPAs), **28**, 28–29, 29(table)
CFOs, *see* Chief financial officers (CFOs)

Chart of accounts, **118**, 119–120(exh.)
Check(s), **315**, 316(fig.), 317(fig.)
Check authorizations, **315**, 316(fig.), 317(fig.)
Chief financial officers (CFOs), 10
workloads of, financial scandals and, 1022
CIM (computer-integrated manufacturing) systems, 133
Classification, **118**
Classified balance sheet, **254**, 255(exh.), 256–259
Classified financial statements, **254**, 255(exh.), 256–259
Closely held corporations, 49
Closing entries, **205**, 205–212, 206(fig.)
accounts after closing and, 210, 211–212(exh.), 212
for merchandising business, 1205–1210
recording using work sheet, 222
required, 206–210, 207(exh.)
CM (contribution margin), 868–869
Commas, in financial statements, 136
Commercial paper, **426**
Commitments, **434**
Committed costs, **1066**
Common costs, 1028
Common-size statements, **1173**
Common stock, **548**
statement of cash flows and, 632
Common Stock account, 553, 554, 592
Common Stock Distributable account, 592
Company description, in annual reports, 50
Comparability, **250**
Compatibility principle, **199**
Compensating balances, **346**
Completed units, in job order costing system, 755, 755(fig.)
Complex capital structure, **587**
Compound entries, **133**, 134(exh.)
Compound interest, **1104**, 1251–1252, 1252(table)
Comprehensive income, **576**
Computer(s), **8**
software costs and, 475
Computer-aided design (CAD), **132**, 132–133
Computer-integrated manufacturing (CIM) systems, **133**
Computerized accounting systems
adjusting entries and, 175
interest and amortization tables and, 514
trial balances and, 132
value of, 199

Conformance, costs of, 131, 131(table)
Conservatism, 251
Consignments, 389
Consistency, 250
Consolidated financial statements, 1249
Consumers, as users of accounting information, 10
Contingent liabilities, 345, 434
Continuing operations, income from, 576
Continuity issue, 159, 159–160
Continuous improvement, 668, 668–671
   achieving, 670(fig.), 670–671
   activity-based management and, 669
   just-in-time operating philosophy and, 668
   theory of constraints and, 670
   total quality management and, 669
Contra accounts, 167
   Accumulated Depreciation account, 167–168
   Allowance to Adjust Long-Term Investments to Market account, 1246, 1247–1248
   Purchases Returns and Allowances, 308
   Unamortized Bond Discount account, 506
   Unrealized Loss on Long-Term Investments account, 1246, 1247–1248
Contributed capital, 16
Contribution margin (CM), 868, 868–869
Control
   internal, *see* Internal control(s)
   long-term investment in stock and, 1244, 1245
   over merchandising operations, 300–301
Control activities, 310
Control environment, 310
Controllable costs and revenues, 988
Controlling (control) accounts, 1214
Controlling interest, 1245, 1245(table), 1249
Control principle, 198
Conventions, 250
   for interpreting financial information, 250–253
Conversion costs, 707, 707(fig.), **788, 831**
   equivalent production for, 789
Conversion Costs account, backflush costing and, 835

Convertible bonds, 519
Convertible preferred stock, 551, 551–552
Copyrights, 473(table)
Core competencies, 666
Core values, 856
Corporations, 13, 540, 540–560
   advantages of, 542
   disadvantages of, 542–543
   dividends and, *see* Dividend(s)
   equity financing and, 543–544
   formation of, 14, 540–541, 541(fig.)
   management of, 540–543, 541(fig.)
   organization of, 14(fig.), 14–15
   private (closely held), 49
   as separate entities, 12–15
   stockholders' equity and, 547–548, 548(fig.)
   stock of, *see* Common stock; Dividend(s); Preferred stock; Stock *entries*
   stock options and, 546, 547
Cost(s), 117
   accounting for, process cost report and, 791–792, 794, 796
   of acquisition of plant assets, 459–461
   appraisal, 131, 131(table)
   assigning, in new manufacturing environment, 831–832, 832(table)
   assigning, process cost report and, 792–793, 796–797
   avoidable, 1028
   behavior of, 703
   classifications of, 701–704, 702(fig.)
   committed, 1066
   common, 1028
   of computer software, 475
   controllable, 988
   controlling using variance analysis, 946, 947(fig.), 948
   conversion, 707, 707(fig.), 831
   depreciable, 462
   development and exploration, in oil and gas industry, 471–472
   differential (incremental), 1022–1023
   direct, 702
   of doing business, *see* Expenses
   external failure, 131, 131(table)
   fixed, 703, 861–862, 862(fig.), 1028
   incurred, 1066
   indirect, 702
   irrelevant, 1023
   mixed, 862(fig.), 862–865

   in new manufacturing environment, classification of, 831
   opportunity, 1024
   overhead, *see* Manufacturing overhead costs
   period (noninventoriable), 704
   prevention, 131, 131(table)
   prime, 707, 707(fig.)
   of processing checks, 1024
   product (inventoriable), *see* Product cost(s)
   of quality, 135–137, 136–138(exh.), 139
   research and development, 474–475
   of sales, 262
   standard, 940–941
   start-up and organization, 544
   sunk, 1023
   of television talent, 724
   traceability of, 702
   value-adding and nonvalue-adding, 703
   variable, 858–860, 859(fig.)
Cost allocation, 715, 715–725
   ABC approach for, 720–724
   estimates and, 718
   of manufacturing overhead costs, 716, 717(fig.), 718–724, 719(fig.)
   for service organizations, 724–725
   traditional approach for, 718–720, 719(fig.), 720(table)
Cost-based pricing methods, 1061–1065
Cost behavior, 854–877, 856
   breakeven analysis and, 866–870, 867(fig.)
   cost-volume-profit analysis and, *see* Cost-volume-profit (CVP) analysis
   of fixed costs, 861–862, 862(fig.)
   management cycle and, 856–857, 857(fig.)
   of mixed costs, 862(fig.), 862–865
   of variable costs, 858–860, 859(fig.)
Cost-benefit convention, 252, 252–253
Cost-benefit principle, 198
Cost centers, 987, 987–988, 989(table)
   discretionary, 987–988, 989(table)
   evaluating performance using flexible budgeting, 990–991, 991(exh.)
Cost drivers, 715
Cost flows, 385
   of manufacturing costs, 710(fig.), 710–711

Subject Index

Cost hierarchy, **824**, 824–825, 825(table)
Cost information
  management cycle and, 700(fig.), 700–701
  organizations and, 701
Costing
  activity-based, *see* Activity-based costing (ABC)
  backflush, 832–835, 833(fig.), 834(fig.)
  hybrid systems for, 751
  job order, *see* Job order costing systems
  process, *see* Process costing systems
  product, *see* Job order costing systems; Process costing systems; Product costing systems
  standard, 940–942
  see also Variance analysis
  target, pricing based on, 1065–1070, 1066–1068(fig.)
  variable (full), profit center performance evaluation using, 991–993, 992(exh.)
Cost objects, 715
Cost of capital, **996**, 996–997, **1100**
Cost of goods manufactured, **711**
Cost of goods manufactured budget, 908, 908(exh.)
Cost of goods sold, 262
  income statement and, 713
Cost of Goods Sold account, 710, 716
  backflush costing and, 833, 835
  under periodic inventory system, 308
  under perpetual inventory system, 299
  process costing and, 787
Cost-plus transfer prices, 1071
Cost pools, **715**
Cost principle, **117**, 118
Costs of conformance, 131, 131(table)
Costs of nonconformance, 131, 131(table)
Costs of quality, 669
Cost-volume-profit (CVP) analysis, 865, 865–866
  for manufacturing businesses, 870–874, 873(exh.)
  for service businesses, 874–875
Coupon(s), 432
Coupon bonds, 504
Couric, Katie, 724
Created prices, 1073
Credit, 122
Credit cards, 823–824

Creditors
  statement of cash flows and, 618
  as users of accounting information, 9–10
Credit policies, 343–344, 344(fig.), 345(fig.)
Credit worthiness, profitability versus, 268
Crossfooting, 218, 1220
Cumulative effect of accounting changes, 585
Cumulative preferred stock, 550
Current assets, 254, 256
  changes in, statement of cash flows and, 627
Current liabilities, 256, 256–257, **424**, 424–441
  changes in, statement of cash flows and, 627–628
  contingent, 434
  definitely determinable, 425–431
  estimated, 431–433
  payroll accounting and, *see* Payroll accounting
Current manufacturing costs, 711
Current position, assessment of, 1164
Current ratio, 267, 267(fig.), **1177**, 1178(exh.)
Customer lists, 473(table)
Customer satisfaction, quality and, 134, 135(table)
CVP, *see* Cost-volume-profit (CVP) analysis

Dashboard system, 986
Data processing, 198
  electronic, *see* Computerized accounting systems; Technology
Date(s)
  for bonds, 549
  for promissory notes, 358–359
Date of declaration, 549
Date of payment, 549
Date of record, 549
Death of partners, 1234
Debentures, 502
Debit, 122
Debit cards, 347
Debt(s)
  bad, *see* Uncollectible accounts
  early extinguishment of, 518
  long-term, *see* Bond *entries;* Long-term liabilities
Debt to equity ratio, 270, 270–271, 271(fig.), 1180(exh.), **1181**
Decentralized organizations, 1070
Decision making
  capital investment decisions and, *see* Capital investment analysis

  incremental analysis for, *see* Incremental analysis
  short-run decision analysis and, *see* Short-run decision analysis
  users of accounting information and, 8(fig.), 8–10
Declining-balance method, 464, 464–465
Deferrals, 163
Deferred expenses, adjustments for, 163–168
Deferred Income Taxes account, 582, 582–583
Deferred payment, 1258–1259
Deferred revenues, adjustments for, 170(fig.), 170–171
Deficit, 588
Defined benefit plans, 522
Defined contribution plans, 522
Definitely determinable liabilities, 425, 425–431
Delivery cycle time, quality and, 133–134
Deming Application Prize, 141
Depletion, 456(fig.), 470–471
Depreciable cost, 462
Depreciation, 166, 166–167, 456(fig.), 461–465, 476–479
  accumulated, 167(fig.), 167–168, 168(exh.)
  in capital investment analysis, 1102–1103
  of closely related plant assets, 471
  comparison of methods for computing, 465, 465(fig.)
  cost recovery for income tax purposes and, 479
  declining-balance method for computing, 464–465
  disposal of depreciable assets and, 466–470
  factors affecting computation of, 462–463
  group, 478
  for partial years, 476–477
  of plant assets, 166–167
  production method for computing, 463–464
  revision of depreciation rates and, 477
  of special types of capital expenditures, 478–479
  statement of cash flows and, 626
  straight-line method for computing, 463
Development costs, in oil and gas industry, 471–472
Differential analysis, *see* Incremental analysis
Differential cost, 1022, 1022–1023

Subject Index

Diluted earnings per share, **587**, 587–588
Direct charge-off method, 351–352, **352**
Direct costs, **702**
Direct fixed costs, 1028
Direct labor budget, **904**, 904–905, 906(exh.)
Direct labor costs, **704**
  standard costs for, 942–943
Direct labor efficiency variance, **951**
Direct labor rate standard, **943**
Direct labor rate variance, **951**
Direct labor time standard, **943**
Direct labor variances, 950–952
Direct materials costs, **704**
  standard costs for, 942
Direct materials price standard, **942**
Direct materials price variance, **948**, 948–949
Direct materials purchases budget, **904**, 905(exh.)
Direct materials quantity standard, **942**
Direct materials quantity variance, **949**
Direct materials variances, 948–950, 950(fig.)
Direct method, **623**
Disclosure
  of bonds on balance sheet, 504
  full, 252
  of liabilities, 425
Discontinued operations, **584**
Discount(s), **505**
  on bonds, 505–506
  purchases, 318–319
  sales, 301, 318
  trade, 301
Discounting, **346**
Discount on Common Stock account, 554
Discretionary cost centers, **987**, 987–988, 989(table)
Dishonored notes, **361**
Disposal, of depreciable assets, 466–470
Disposal value, 462
Dissolution of partnerships, 1232–1234
Diversified companies, **1166**, 1166–1167
Dividend(s), **17**, 20
  liquidating, 548
  policies for, 544
  preference as to, 549–551
  stock, 590–593
Dividend income, **350**
Dividends account, closing to Retained Earnings account, 210, 210(exh.)

Dividends in arrears, **550**
Dividends payable, 427
Dividends yield, **544**, 1182(exh.), **1183**
Document-less transactions, 205
Dollar signs, in financial statements, 136
Double-declining-balance method, **464**
Double-entry system, **121**, 121–124
  analyzing and processing transactions and, 122–124, 123(fig.)
  T account and, 121–122
Double taxation, **542**, 542–543
Duality, principle of, 121
Due care, **31**
Dun & Bradstreet Corp., 1165, 1168
Duration of note, **359**, 359–360

Early extinguishment of debt, **518**
Earnings per share, **263**, 586–588
Ebbers, Bernard, 912
Economic approach to pricing, 1058, 1058(fig.)
Economic value added (EVA), **996**, 996(exh.), 996–997, 997(fig.)
Economy, value chains and, 819
EDI (electronic data interchange), 204
Effective interest method, **510**
  for amortization of bond discount, 510–512, 511(table), 512(fig.)
  for amortization of bond premium, 513–514, 514(table), 515(fig.)
Effective interest rate, 505, 509
EFT (electronic funds transfer), 347
E2K (event-to-knowledge) management, 205
Electronic commerce (ecommerce), 172, **204**
  global, 671
Electronic data interchange (EDI), **204**
Electronic funds transfer (EFT), 347
Emerging economies, accounting practices in, 354
Employee earnings record, **437–438**
Employee's Withholding Exemption Certificate, 435
Engineering method, **863**
Enterprise resource planning (ERP) systems, **128**, 128–129, **198**
Equipment
  acquisition cost of, 460
  depreciation of, 166–167
  see also Plant assets
Equity
  owners,' (fig.)**16**, 16(fig.), 16–17, 17(fig.)

  partners,' 1228–1229
  ratio of debt to, 270–271, 271(fig.)
  residual, 548
  return on, 271–272, 272(fig.), 545–546
  stockholders,' see Statement of stockholders' equity; Stockholders' equity
  trading on, 500
Equity financing, 543–544
Equity method, for accounting for stock investments, 1248
Equivalent production, 787–789, **788**, 788(fig.)
  for conversion costs, 789
  for direct materials, 788–789
ERP (enterprise resource planning) systems, 128–129, 198
Estimated liabilities, **431**, 431–637
Estimated useful life, **462**, 462–463
Estimation
  inventory valuation by, 401–402
  of overhead rate, 718
  quality of earnings and, 577–579
  of uncollectible accounts expense, 353
Ethics, **30**
  accounting practices and, 161
  budgeting and, 912
  core values and, 856
  of decision between long-term assets and expenses, 461
  of electronic funds transfer, 347
  financial scandals' effects on CFOs' workloads, 1022
  fraud and, 311, 787
  fraudulent financial reporting and, 253–254
  Internet fraud and, 1060
  inventory overstatement and, 398
  management's responsibility for ethical reporting and, 253–254, 676
  product unit cost and, 756
  professional, 30
  profits and, 959
  pro-forma statements and, 1167
  recycling and, 993
  standards of ethical conduct and, 674, 676–677(exh.), 677
  truthfulness of financial statements and, 126
  whistle-blowing and, 580
European Community, accounting standards and, 1243
EVA (economic value added), 996(exh.), 996–997, 997(fig.)
Event-to-knowledge (E2K) management, 205
Exchange, of plant assets, 468–470

Exchange gains/losses, 1239
  realized versus unrealized, 1240–1241
Exchange rates, 12, 1238, 1238(table)
Ex-dividend stock, 549
Executing stage of management cycle
  activity-based cost information and, 818
  balanced scorecard and, 983–984
  budgeting and, 897
  capital investment analysis and, 1099
  cost behavior and, 856
  cost information and, 701
  financial performance evaluation and, 1162
  management accounting and, 662(fig.), 662–663
  management information systems and, 130
  pricing and, 1056
  product cost information and, 748
  short-run decision analysis and, 1020–1021
  standard costs and, 940
Expenditure(s), 459
Expenses, 17, 19–20, **158,** 158–159
  accrued, adjustments for, 168–170, 169(fig.)
  deferred, adjustments for, 163–168
  depreciation, *see* Depreciation
  freight out, 262
  income taxes, 581(table), 581–584
  long-term assets versus, 461
  nonoperating, 262–263
  operating, 262
  prepaid, 164(fig.), 164–166
  recognition of, 161
Explanatory notes, in annual reports, 52–53
Exploration costs, in oil and gas industry, 471–472
Extensible Business Reporting Language (XBRL), 204
External failure costs, 131, 131(table)
Extraordinary items, 584, 584–585
Extraordinary repairs, 478

Face interest rate, 505
Face value, bonds issued at, 504–505
Facility-level activities, 825
Factor(s), 345
Factoring, 345
Factory burden, 704
Factory overhead, 704
  see also Manufacturing overhead costs

Factory tours, 940
FASB, *see* Financial Accounting Standards Board (FASB)
Fast-food restaurants, supersizing meals in, 868
Federal Unemployment Insurance tax, 430
FICA tax, 430
FIFO costing method, 786
  process cost report using, 789, 790(exh.), 791–793
FIFO (first-in, first-out) method, 391
Financial accounting, 7
  management accounting compared with, 658, 659(table), 660
Financial Accounting Standards Board (FASB), 29
  on available-for-sale securities accounting, 1245
  on comprehensive income, 576
  on exchange gains and losses, 1240, 1241
  on goodwill, 475–476
  on long-term leases, 521
  on noncash investing and financing transactions, 619–620
  on other postretirement benefits, **523**
  on pension expense, 523
  on reporting of foreign subsidiaries, 1241, 1242
  on short-term investments, 347
  Statement No. 13 of, 521
  Statement No. 52 of, 1240, 1241, 1242
  Statement No. 87 of, 523
Financial budgets, 898, 908–912
Financial highlights, in annual reports, 50
Financial information
  conventions for interpreting, 250–253
  objectives of, 248
  qualitative characteristics of, 248–250, 249(fig.)
Financial leverage, 500
Financial performance evaluation, 1160–1188, 1162
  by external users, 1162–1164
  horizontal analysis for, 1170, 1171x, 1172x
  information sources for, 1167–1169
  management cycle and, 1162–1163, 1163(fig.)
  ratio analysis for, *see* Ratio analysis
  reporting under Sarbanes-Oxley Act and, 1164
  standards for, 1165–1167

  trend analysis for, 1171–1173, 1173(exh.), 1173(fig.)
  vertical analysis for, 1173, 1174(exh.), 1174(fig.), 1175(exh.), 1175(fig.), 1176
Financial position, 15
Financial statement(s), 7, 22–28
  in annual reports, 50–52
  classified, 266–273
  common-size, 1173
  consolidated, 1249
  cost classifications for, 703–704, 704(table)
  of foreign subsidiaries, restatement of, 1241–1242
  inventory systems and, 396, 396(fig.)
  management's responsibility for ethical reporting and, 253–254
  preparing using work sheet, 223–224, 224(exh.), 225(exh.)
  presentation of, 136
  pro forma, 898
  under Sarbanes-Oxley Act, 1164
  truthfulness of, 126
  see also specific statements
Financial statement analysis, *see* Financial performance evaluation
Financial Times, 1168
Financing
  equity, 543–544
  of long-term assets, 457
Financing activities, 6, 618, 618–619
  statement of cash flows preparation and, 631–633
Financing period, 296, 296–297, 297(fig.)
Finished Goods Inventory account, 708, 710, 711, 715, 716
  backflush costing and, 833, 835
  process costing and, 787
First-in, first-out (FIFO) method, 391
Fiscal year, 159
Fixed assets, *see* Long-term assets; Plant assets
Fixed costs, 703, 861, 861–862, 862(fig.)
  in airline industry, 703
  direct, 1028
Fixed overhead budget variance, 956
Fixed overhead volume variance, 956, 956–958
Flexibility principle, 199
Flexible budget(s), 945
  analyzing manufacturing overhead variances using, 953(exh.), 953–954

Subject Index **1287**

cost center performance evaluation using, 990–991, 991(exh.)
in variance analysis, 944–946, 945–947(exh.)
Flexible budget formula, 945, 945–946
FOB destination, 302
FOB shipping point, 302
Folio column, *see* Post. Ref. column
Footings, 122
Forbes magazine, 1168
Form 8-K, 1168
Form 10-K, 49, 1168
Form 10-Q, 1168
Form W-4, 435
Fortune magazine, 1168
Franchises, 473(table)
Fraud
 detection of, 787
 on Internet, 1060
 payroll, 438
Fraudulent financial reporting, 253, 253–254
Free cash flow, 621–623, 1181, 1182(exh.)
Freight in, 303
Freight out expense, 262
Freight Out Expense account, 305
Frequent-flier miles, 433
Full-costing method, 471, 471–472
 profit center performance evaluation using, 991–993, 992(exh.)
Full disclosure, 252
Full product cost, 816
Functional currency, 1241
Fund accumulation, 1260
FUTA tax, 430
Future potential, assessment of, 1164
Future value, 1105, 1252–1253
 of ordinary annuity, 1253, 1254(table)
 of single sum at compound interest, 1252, 1252(table)
 tables of, 1264, 1264(table)–1265(table)

GAAP, *see* Generally accepted accounting principles (GAAP)
Gains
 exchange, 1239, 1240–1241
 on exchange of assets, 469–470
 from extraordinary items, 585
 quality of earnings and, 579
 statement of cash flows and, 626–627
GASB (Governmental Accounting Standards Board), 29
Gas industry, development and exploration costs in, 471–472

General journal, 133, 1223, 1223(exh.)
General ledger, 118, 134–136
 posting to, 135(exh.), 135–136
General Ledger Software, 203
General ledger systems, 201, 202(fig.), 203
 structure of, 203(fig.), 203–304
Generally accepted accounting principles (GAAP), 28, 28–30
Global business, *see* International business
Goals
 budgeting and, 894–895
 coordination of, 999
 linking to objectives and targets, 998
 management, internal control and, 312–313
Going concern, 159
Goods available for sale, 306
Goods flow, 389
Good units, 950
Goodwill, 473(table), 475–476
Government, as user of accounting information, 10
Governmental Accounting Standards Board (GASB), 29
Graphical user interface (GUI), 201
Gross margin, 262
Gross margin method, 402, 402(table)
Gross margin pricing, 1061, 1061–1062
Gross profit, 262
Gross profit method, 402, 402(table)
Gross sales, 261
Group depreciation, 478
Group purchases, 461
GUI (graphical user interface), 201

Handbook of Dividend Achievers, 1168
Held-to-maturity securities, 348, 1244
High-low method, 864, 864–865
Horizontal analysis, 1170, 1171(exh.), 1172(exh.)
Hurdle rate, 1100
Hybrid costing systems, 751

IASB (International Accounting Standards Board), 29, 1242
Icons, 201
Ideal capacity, 858
IFAC (International Federation of Accountants), 1242
IMA, *see* Institute of Management Accountants (IMA)

IMA (Institute of Management Accountants), 31
Impairment reviews, 475–476
Income
 comprehensive, 576
 dividend, 350
 interest, 350
 measurement issues and, 159–160
 net, *see* Net income
 operating, 262, 865
 partnership, 1228, 1229–1231
 residual, 994–995, 996(exh.)
 taxable, 581
Income before income taxes, 263
Income from continuing operations, 576
Income from operations, 262
Income statement, 22, 260–266
 absorption costing, profit center performance evaluation using, 991–993, 992(exh.)
 budgeted, 908–909, 909(exh.)
 cost of goods sold and, 713
 multistep, 260(fig.), 260–263, 261(exh.)
 quality of earnings and, 576–577, 577(exh.)
 reading and graphing, 263–264, 264–265(exh.)
 single-step, 264, 265(exh.), 266, 266(exh.)
Income statement accounts
 closing credit balances to Income Summary account, 208, 208(exh.)
 closing debit balances to Income Summary account, 208–209, 209(exh.)
Income Summary account, 206
 closing balance to Retained Earnings account, 209–210, 210(exh.)
 closing credit balances from income statement accounts to, 208, 208(exh.)
 closing debit balances from income account statements to, 208–209, 209(exh.)
Income tax(es), 263, 431–638, 581(table)
 in capital investment analysis, 1102–1103
 of corporations, 542–543
 cost recovery and, 479
 deferred, 582–583
 income before, 263
 inventory systems and, 396–397
 net of taxes and, 583–584
 payroll accounting and, 430
Income tax allocation, 582
Income taxes payable, 427–428

Incremental analysis, 1022,
  1022–1033
  irrelevant costs and revenues and,
    1022–1023, 1023(exh.)
  opportunity costs and, 1024
  for outsourcing decisions,
    1024–1026, 1025(exh.)
  for sales mix decisions,
    1030–1032, 1031(exh.)
  for segment profitability decisions,
    1028, 1029(exh.), 1030
  for sell or process-further decisions,
    1032–1033, 1033(exh.)
  for special order decisions,
    1026–1027, 1027(exh.)
Incremental cost, 1022–1023
Incurred costs, 1066
Independence, 30
Independent auditors' report, in
  annual reports, 53–54
Index numbers, 1172
Indirect costs, 702
Indirect labor costs, 704
Indirect manufacturing costs, 704
Indirect material costs, 704
Indirect method, 623
  for preparing statement of cash
    flows, 623–624, 623–626, 625f,
    626(exh.)
Industry norms, for financial
  statement analysis, 1165–1167,
  1166(exh.)
*Industry Norms and Key Business
  Ratios*, 1165, 1168
Influential but noncontrolling
  interest, 1244–1245,
  1245(table), 1248
**Information and communication,
  310**
Initial public offerings (IPOs), 543,
  543–544
Inspection time, 831
Installment accounts receivable, 351
Institute of Management
  Accountants (IMA), 31
  Code of Professional Conduct for
    Management Accountants of,
    676–677(exh.)
  definition of management
    accounting, 658
Intangible assets, 256, 472,
  472(fig.), 473(table), 474–476
Intangible resources, 456(fig.)
Integrity, 30
Interest, 360, 1104, 1251–1252
  imputing on noninterest-bearing
    notes, 1257–1258
  on promissory notes, 360
Interest (in company)
  controlling, 1245, 1245(table),
    1249

influential but noncontrolling,
  1244–1245, 1245(table), 1248
noninfluential and noncontrolling,
  1244–1245, 1245(table)
Interest (in partnership), 1230–1231
Interest coverage ratio, 501,
  1180(exh.), **1181**
Interest expense, for bonds, year-end
  accrual of, 516–518
Interest income, 350
Interest on partners' capital, 1229
Interest rates
  on bonds, 505–506
  on promissory notes, 360
Internal control(s), 309, 309–315
  of cash sales receipts, 313
  components of, 310
  computers in, 314
  control activities and, 310–311
  limitations of, 311–312
  management goals and, 312–313
  management's responsibility for,
    309
  of purchases and cash
    disbursements, 314(fig.),
    314–315, 316–317(fig.)
Internal controls, 300–301
Internal Revenue Service (IRS), 30
International accounting,
  1237(table), 1237–1243,
  1238(fig.)
  accounting standards for, 474,
    1238, 1242–1243
  exchange rates and, 1238,
    1238(table)
  foreign purchases and, 1240
  foreign sales and, 1239
  realized versus unrealized
    exchange gain or loss and,
    1240–1241
  restatement of foreign subsidiary
    financial statements and,
    1241–1242
International Accounting Standards
  (IASs), 474
**International Accounting Standards
  Board (IASB), 29,** 1242
International business
  accounting changes and, 585
  accounting practices in emerging
    economies and, 354
  airline bankruptcies and, 501
  budgeting and, 896
  capital investment decisions and,
    1101
  closing records and, 213
  comparability of accounting
    standards and, 474
  continuous improvement to
    address global competition and,
    see Continuous improvement

  cost-volume-profit analysis and,
    866
  dashboard system and, 986
  ebanking and, 1030
  ecommerce and, 671
  European stock markets and,
    547
  hybrid product costing systems
    and, 751
  just-in-time operating philosophy
    and, 830
  kaizen costing and, 1070
  need for accounting knowledge in
    former Soviet Union and
    Eastern Europe and, 167
  performance and, 134
  reserves and, 590
  standard costing and, 958
  statement of cash flows and, 620
  valuation and, 117
International Federation of
  Accountants (IFAC), 1242
International Organization for
  Standardization (ISO), 142
Internet, 204, 204–205
  support of value chain, 666
Inventoriable costs, *see* Product
  cost(s)
Inventory
  under just-in-time operating
    philosophy, 829
  in manufacturing businesses,
    accounts for, 707–711
  in merchandising businesses, *see*
    Merchandise inventory
  physical, 300
  see also Merchandise inventory;
    specific inventory accounts
Inventory cost, 388, 388–389
  goods flow versus cost flow and,
    389
  merchandise in transit and,
    388(fig.), 388–389
  merchandise on hand not included
    in inventory and, 389
Inventory systems, 298–300
  financial statements and, 396,
    396(fig.)
  income taxes and, 396–397
  see also Periodic inventory system;
    Perpetual inventory system
Inventory turnover, 386, 386–388,
  387(fig.), **1177,** 1178(exh.)
Inventory valuation
  by estimation, 401–402
  at lower of cost or market,
    399–400
  under periodic inventory system,
    389–392
  under perpetual inventory system,
    393–395, 395(fig.)

Subject Index

Investing activities, 6, 618
  statement of cash flows preparation and, 628–631
Investment(s), 256
  of assets in partnerships, 1232
  capital, *see* Capital investment *entries*
  of idle cash, 1259–1260
  long-term, 347, 1244–1249
  by owners, 17
  short-term, *see* Short-term investments
  statement of cash flows and, 629
Investment centers, 988, 989(table), 993–998
  economic value added and, 996(exh.), 996–997, 997(fig.)
  multiple performance measures for, 998
  residual income and, 994–995, 996(exh.)
  return on investment and, 993(exh.), 993–994, 995(fig.)
Investors
  statement of cash flows and, 618
  as users of accounting information, 9
Invoices, 315, 316(fig.), 317(fig.)
IPOs (initial public offerings), 543–544
Irrelevant costs, 1023
Irrelevant revenues, 1023
IRS (Internal Revenue Service), 30
ISO (International Organization for Standardization), 142
Issued stock, 548
Item-by-item method, 400

JIT, *see* Just-in-time (JIT) *entries*
Job order(s), 750
Job order cost cards, 708, 750
  product unit cost computation and, 756–757
Job order costing systems, 746–763, **750,** 750(table)
  in manufacturing companies, 751–757, 752–753(exh.)
  process costing versus, 749–751, 750(table)
  product cost information and management cycle and, 748–749, 749(fig.)
  project costing versus, 758–759
  in service organizations, 757, 758(fig.)
Joint products, 1032
Journal(s), 133, 1223, 1223(exh.)
  special-purpose, 1213–1223
Journal entries, 133, 172
  adjusting, *see* Adjusting entries
  closing, *See* Closing entries

  compound, 133, 134(exh.)
  reversing, 214, **214–215**
Journal form, 124
Journalizing, 133
Just-in-time (JIT) operating environment, 388
Just-in-time (JIT) operating philosophy, 668, 828, 828–836
  activity-based management compared with, 835–836, 836(table)
  backflush costing and, 832–835, 833(fig.), 834(fig.)
  continuous improvement of work environment and, 831
  minimum inventory levels and, 829
  multiskilled work force and, 830
  preventive maintenance and, 830
  product costs in, 831–832
  product quality and, 830
  pull-through production and, 829
  quick setup and flexible work cells and, 829–830

Kaizen costing, 1070
Kaplan, Robert S., 982
King, Larry, 724

Labor, in job order costing system, 754
Labor unions, as users of accounting information, 10
Land, acquisition cost of, 460
Land improvements, acquisition cost of, 460
Last-in, first-out (LIFO) method, 391, 391–392, 392(fig.), 394
LCM (lower-of-cost-or-market) rule, 399–400
Lease(s)
  capital, 521
  long-term, 520–522, 521(table)
  operating, 520
Leasehold(s), 473(table)
Leasehold improvements, 473(table), 475
Ledger(s), 118, 134–136
Ledger account form, 134, 134(exh.), 134–135
Legal capital, 543
Letterman, David, 724
Letter to the stockholders, 49–50
Liabilities, 15, 420–441
  accrued, 427
  classification of, 424
  contingent, 345, 434
  current, *see* Current liabilities
  disclosure of, 425
  estimated, 431–433
  long-term, 257, 424

  managing liquidity and cash flows and, 422–423, 423(fig.)
  payment of, 18
  payroll, 428, 429(fig.), 430–431
  purchase of assets by incurring, 18
  recognition of, 424
  valuation of, 424
Licenses, 473(table)
Life, useful, estimated, 462–463
LIFO liquidation, 397
LIFO method, *see* Last-in, first-out (LIFO) method
Limited life, of partnerships, 1228
Linear approximation, 860
Lines of credit, 425, 425–426
Li-Ning, 958
Liquidating dividends, 548
Liquidation of partnerships, 1234
Liquidity, 5, 5–6, **267,** 422–423, 423(fig.), 424
  evaluation of, 267, 1177, 1177(fig.), 1178(exh.)
Loans, from banks, 425–426
Long-lived assets, *see* Plant assets
Long-term assets, 452–483, **454**
  decision to acquire, 455–457
  depreciation of, *see* Depreciation
  expenses versus, 461
  financing, 457
  intangible, 472, 472(fig.), 473(table), 474–476
  matching rule applied to, 458, 458(fig.)
  natural resources, 470–472
  see also Plant assets
Long-term debt, current portions of, 428
Long-term investments, 347, 1244–1249
  in bonds, 1244
  in stocks, 1244–1249, 1245(table)
Long-term leases, 520–522, 521(table)
Long-term liabilities, 257, 424, 498–526
  amount of debt to carry and, 501(fig.), 501–502
  bonds, *see* Bond *entries*
  decision to issue long-term debt and, 500
  leases, 520–522, 521(table)
  mortgages payable, 520
  other postretirement benefits, 523
  pensions, 522–523
  types of debt and, 502
Losses
  exchange, 1239, 1240–1241
  on exchange of assets, 469
  from extraordinary items, 585
  net, 158

partnership, 1229–1231
quality of earnings and, 579
statement of cash flows and, 626–627
Lower-of-cost-or-market (LCM) rule, 399, 399–400
LP column, *see* Post. Ref. column

MACRS (modified accelerated cost recovery system), 479
Major category method, 400, 401(table)
Make-or-buy decisions, 1024
Malcolm Baldridge Quality Award, 1141, 1141–1142
Management, 9
　of corporations, 15
　goals of. internal control and, 312–313
　responsibility for ethical reporting, 253–254
　responsibility for financial statements, 676
　statement of cash flows and, 618
　as user of accounting information, 9
Management accounting, 7, 658, 658–664
　financial accounting compared with, 658, 659(table), 660
　management cycle and, 660(fig.), 660–664
　support of value chain analysis, 666–668, 667(exh.)
Management information systems (MISs), 8, 1128
　in management cycle, 1129(fig.), 1129–1130
　quality management and, 1128–1130
Management's discussion and analysis, in annual reports, 50
Managers, cost variances for evaluating performance of, 959, 960(exh.)
Manufacturing companies, 261
　cost reporting and inventory accounting in, 713, 714(fig.), 714–715
　cost-volume-profit analysis for, 870–874, 873(exh.)
　job order costing in, 751–757, 752–753(exh.)
　tours of, 940
Manufacturing cost flow, 710, 710(fig.), 710–711
Manufacturing Overhead account, 708, 716
Manufacturing overhead budget, 905, 906(exh.), 907

Manufacturing overhead costs, 704
　allocating, 716, 717(fig.), 718–724, 719(fig.)
　in job order costing system, 754–755
　over- and underapplied, 716
Manufacturing overhead variances, 952–959
　analyzing using flexible budgets, 953(exh.), 953–954
Margin(s), 667
　gross, 262
Marginal cost curve, pricing and, 1058, 1059(fig.), 1060
Marginal revenue curve, pricing and, 1058, 1059(fig.), 1060
Margin of safety, 866
Marketable securities, 347
　see also Short-term investments
Market interest rate, 505, 509
Market price, of companies, stock splits and, 593
Market share, in candy industry, 713
Market strength, evaluation of, 1181, 1182(exh.), 1183
Market transfer prices, 1071
Market value, 400
Master budget, 898, 898–901, 899–901(fig.)
Matching issue, 160
Matching rule, 160
　applying to inventories, 384–385
　long-term assets and, 458, 458(fig.)
Materiality, 251
Materials Inventory account, 707–708, 710, 714–715
　backflush costing and, 832
Materials Inventory account, in job order costing system, 754
Materials request form, 708
Maturity date, 358, 358–359
Maturity value, 360
　of promissory notes, 360
Measurement, 11–12, 114–140, 156–181
　accounting period issue and, 159
　accounts and, 118, 119–120(exh.), 120–121
　accrual accounting and, 160–162
　adjustments and, *See* Adjusting entries
　classification issue and, 118
　continuity issue and, 159–160
　double-entry system and, 121–124
　of income, *see* Income
　of inventory, *see* Inventory cost; Inventory systems; Inventory valuation
　matching issue and, 160

　money measure and, 11–12, 12(table)
　object of, 11
　of profitability, 158–159
　recognition issue and, 116–117
　recording and posting transactions and, 133–136
　separate entity concept and, 12
　transaction analysis illustration and, 124–131, 130(exh.)
　trial balance and, 131–133, 132(table), 131(exh.)
　valuation issue and, 117–118
Medical insurance, payroll accounting and, 430
Medicare tax, 430
Merchandise in transit, cost of, 388(fig.), 388–389
Merchandise inventory, 296, 382–408, **384**
　cost of, *see* Inventory cost
　evaluating level of, 386–388, 387(fig.)
　impact of inventory decisions and, 385, 386(fig.)
　loss of, 400
　matching rule applied to, 384–385
　overstatement of, 398
　valuation of, *see* Inventory valuation
　see also Inventory systems; *specific inventory systems*
Merchandise Inventory account, 714
　under periodic inventory system, 307
　under perpetual inventory system, 298–299
Merchandising businesses (companies), 261, 294–323, **296**
　cash flow management in, 296(fig.), 296–298, 297(fig.)
　control of, 300–301
　internal control of, *see* Internal control(s)
　inventory systems for *see* Inventory systems; *specific inventory systems*
　profitability management in, 298, 299(exh.)
　terms of sale and, 301–302
　work sheet and closing entries for, 1205–1210
Mergent, 1168
MISs, *see* Management information systems (MISs)
Mission, 660, 660–661
Misstatements, inventory measurement and, 397–399

Mixed costs, 862, 862(fig.), 862–865
  engineering method of separating, 863
  high-low method for, 864–865
  scatter diagram method for, 863–864, 864(fig.)
  statistical methods for, 865
Modified accelerated cost recovery system (MACRS), 479
Money, time value of, *see* Time value of money
Money measure, 11, 12(table), 11–12
Monitoring, 310
Moody's Investors Service, Inc., 1168
Mortgages(s), 520
Moving time, 831
Multistep income statement, 260, 260(fig.), 260–263, 261(exh.)
Mutual agency, partnerships and, 1228

Natural resources, 456(fig.), 470–472
  depletion of, 470–471
  depreciation of closely related plant assets and, 471
  development and exploration costs in oil and gas industry and, 471–472
Negotiated transfer prices, 1071
Net cash inflows, in capital investment analysis, 1102
Net cost of purchases, 306
Net income, 17, 158, **158, 263**
  in capital investment analysis, 1102
Net income per share, 263
Net losses, 17, 158
Net of taxes, 583, 583–584
Net present value method, 1107, 1107–1108
Net purchases, 306, 306–307
Net sales, 261
Networking, 201
Net worth, *see* Owner's equity
Neuer Markt, 547
New manufacturing environment, *see* Just-in-time (JIT) operating philosophy
Nominal accounts, 205
Noncash investing and financing transactions, 619, 619–620
Noncompete covenants, 473(table)
Nonconformance, costs of, 131, 131(table)
Noncumulative preferred stock, 550
Nonfinancial measures, in service organizations, 674, 675(exh.)
Noninfluential and noncontrolling interest, 1244–1245, 1245(table)
Noninventoriable costs, 704
Nonoperating items, 584–586
  accounting changes, 585–586
  discontinued operations, 584
  extraordinary items, 584–585
  quality of earnings and, 579–580
Nonoperating revenues and expenses, 262–263
Nonvalue-adding activities, 669, 822
  process value analysis and, 823–824
  in service organizations, 822
Nonvalue-adding costs, 703
No-par stock, 552, 554
Normal balance, 131, 132(table)
Normal capacity, 858
Normal costing, 706
Norton, David P., 982
Notes payable, 358, 426(fig.), 426–427
Notes receivable, 358
  see also Promissory notes
Notes to financial statements, in annual reports, 52–53
Not-for-profit organizations
  capital investment analysis for, 1106
  as users of accounting information, 10
Nouveau Marche, 547

Objectives, linking of goals to, 998
Objectivity, 30
O'Brien, Conan, 724
Obsolescence, 462
Oil industry, development and exploration costs in, 471–472
100-year bonds, 507
Operating activities, 6, 618
  statement of cash flows preparation and, 623–628, 624–626(exh.), 625(fig.)
Operating budgets, 298, 299(exh.), 898
Operating capacity, 858, 858–859
Operating cycle, 296, 296(fig.)
Operating decisions, accounting methods and, 397
Operating expenses, 262
Operating income, 262, 865
Operating leases, 520
Operating objectives, 661
Operations
  discontinued, 584
  income from, 262
Opinion section, of independent auditors' report, 54
Opportunity costs, 1024

Ordinary annuities, 1106
  present value of, 1105–1107
Ordinary repairs, 478
Organization charts, 988, 988–990, 990(fig.)
"Other assets," 254
Other postretirement benefits, 523
Other revenues and expenses, 262, 262–263
Outsourcing, 666, 1024
  incremental analysis for decisions involving, 1024–1026, 1025(exh.)
Outstanding stock, 548
Overapplied overhead costs, 716
Overhead rates
  applying, 722–724
  estimation of, 718
  planning, 721–722, 722(fig.), 723(table)
  predetermined, 716
Owners' equity, (fig.)**16,** 16(fig.), 16–17, 17(fig.)
Owners' investments, 17

Paid-in Capital in Excess of Par Value account, 592
Paid-in Capital in Excess of Stated Value account, 553, 554
Paid-in Capital, Retirement of Stock account, 557
Paid-in Capital, Treasury Stock account, 556–557
Parent company, 1249
Participative budgeting, 896
Partners' equity, 1228–1229
Partnership(s), 13, 1227–1228
  balance sheet for, 257
  dissolution of, 1232–1234
Partnership agreement, 1228
Parts and labor pricing, 1063–1065
Par value, 543
Par value stock, 553–554
Past performance
  assessment of, 1164
  for financial statement analysis, 1165
Patents, 473(table)
Payables turnover, 422, 423, 423(fig.), **1177,** 1178(exh.)
Payback period method, 1109, 1109–1110
Payment
  deferred, 1258–1259
  of liabilities, 18
  of long-term debt, timing of, 502
  of payroll and payroll taxes, 438–439
Payroll accounting, 434–439
  computation of take-home pay and, 434–435, 436(fig.)

employee earnings record and, 437–438
fraud and, 438
payment of payroll and payroll taxes and, 438–439
payroll register and, 436(exh.), 436–437, 437(exh.)
recording payroll and, 437
recording payroll taxes and, 438
Payroll Bank Account account, 438
Payroll liabilities, 428, 429(fig.), 430–431
Payroll register, 436, 436(exh.), 436–437, 437(exh.)
Payroll taxes
payment of, 438–439
recording, 438
Peachtree Complete Accounting, 202(fig.), 203
Pension(s), 522–523
Pension contributions, payroll accounting and, 430
Pension funds, 522
Pension plans, 522
P/E (price/earnings) ratio, 544, 1182(exh.), 1183
Percentage of net sales method, 353, 353–354, 356(fig.), 356–357
Performance-based pay, 998, 998–999
Performance evaluation, for managers, cost variances for, 959, 960(exh.)
Performance management and evaluation systems, 986
Performance measure(s), 671, 671–674
balanced scorecard and, 672–673, 673(fig.)
benchmarking and, 673–674
in management cycle, 671–672
Performance measurement, 980–1002, **986**
incentives and goals and, 998–999
multiple measures for, 998
object of, 986
quality of earnings and, 580–581
responsibility accounting for, *see* Investment centers; Responsibility accounting
transfer pricing for, 1073, 1074(exh.)
Performance measures, 6, 6–7
accrual accounting and, 162
Period costs, 704
Periodic inventory system, 299, 299–300, 306(exh.), 306–309, 307(fig.)
pricing inventory under, 389–392

purchases of merchandise under, 307–308
sales of merchandise under, 308–309
work sheet and closing entries under, 1205–1206, 1207(exh.), 1208
Periodicity, 159
Permanent accounts, 205
Perpetual inventory system, 298, 298–299, 302–305, 303(exh.)
pricing inventory under, 393–395, 395(fig.)
purchases of merchandise and, 302–304
sales of merchandise and, 304–305
work sheet and closing entries under, 1209(exh.), 1209–1210, 1210(exh.)
Physical deterioration, 462
Physical inventory, 300
Planning
activity-based cost information and, 817–818
balanced scorecard and, 982–983, 984(fig.)
budgeting and, 897
capital investment analysis and, 1097–1099
cost behavior and, 856
cost information and, 700–701
financial performance evaluation and, 1162
management accounting and, 660–662, 661(fig.)
management information systems and, 129–130
pricing and, 1056
product cost information and, 748
short-run decision analysis and, 1020
standard costs and, 940
strategic, 894
Plant assets
acquisition cost of, 459–461
closely related to natural resources, depreciation of, 471
depreciation of, *see* Depreciation
discarding, 466–467
exchanges of, 468–470
sale of, 466–468
statement of cash flows and, 630–631
Plant Assets account, 630
Portfolios, 1163
Post. Ref. column
in cash payments journal, 1221
in cash receipts journal, 1218, 1220

in purchases journal, 1216
in sales journal, 1215
Post-closing trial balance, 213, 213(exh.)
Posting, 135, 135(exh.), 135–136
batch, 204
real-time, 204
Potentially dilutive securities, 587
Practical capacity, 858
Predetermined overhead rate, 716
Preferred stock, 548, 549–552
callable, 552
convertible, 551–552
cumulative, 550
noncumulative, 550
preference as to assets, 551
preference as to dividends, 549–551
Preferred Stock account, 553
Premiums, 506
on bonds, 506–507
Prepaid expenses, 164, 164(fig.), 164–166
Present value, 1104–1107, **1105,** 1253–1256
of ordinary annuity, 1105–1107, 1255–1256, 1256(table)
of single sum due in future, 1105, 1254–1255, 1255(table)
tables of, 1265(table)–1269(table), 1265–1269
valuing bonds using, 507–508
Prevention costs, 131, 131(table)
Preventive maintenance, in just-in-time operating philosophy, 830
Price(s)
artificial (created), 1073
of bonds, 505
call (redemption), 518, 552
transfer, 1070–1075
Price/earnings (P/E) ratio, 544, 1182(exh.), **1183**
Pricing, 1052–1078
auction-based, 1060
cost-based methods for, 1061–1065
economic approach to, 1058–1060
gross margin, 1061–1062
management cycle and, 1056(fig.), 1056–1057
managers' involvement in, 1054–1057
return on assets, 1062–1063
of services, 1063–1065
target costing as basis, 1065–1070, 1066–1068(fig.)
transfer, 1070–1075
Pricing policies, objectives of, 1054–1055

Primary processes, 664
　in value chain analysis, 665–666
Prime costs, 707, 707(fig.)
Principle of duality, 121
Private corporations, 49
Process costing systems, 750, 750(table), 782–802, 784, 784(fig.)
　average costing method for, 786, 794–797, 795(exh.)
　cost flows through Work in process Inventory accounts, 787
　equivalent production computations and, 787–789, 788(fig.)
　FIFO costing method for, 786, 789, 790(exh.), 791–793
　patterns of product flows and cost flow methods and, 785–786, 786(fig.)
　for two or more production units, 793
Process cost reports, 789
　average costing method and, 794–797, 795(exh.)
　FIFO costing method and, 789, 790(exh.), 791–793
Processing time, 831
Process value analysis (PVA), 823, 823–824
Procurement cards, 823–824
Product(s)
　joint, 1032
　quality of, *see* Continuous improvement; Quality
Product cost(s), 703, 703–704, 704(table), 704–707
　computation of product unit cost and, 705(table), 705–707
　prime cost and conversion cost and, 707, 707(fig.)
　shifting patterns of, 705
Product costing systems, 749, 749–751
　job order, *see* Job order costing systems
　process, *see* Process costing systems
Product design, quality and, 132–133
Product flows, patterns of, 785–786, 786(fig.)
Production, quality and, 133
Production budget, 902, 902–903, 903(exh.)
Production method, 463, 463–464
Product-level activities, 825
Product quality, in just-in-time operating philosophy, 830
Product unit cost, 705, 705(table), 705–707

Product warranty liability, 432–433
Professional ethics, 30
Profit, 865
　defined, 158
　ethics and, 959
　gross, 262
　see also Cost-volume-profit (CVP) analysis
Profitability, 5, 268
　credit worthiness versus, 268
　desired level of, 271
　evaluation of, 268–273, 1179(exh.), 1179–1180
　in fast-food industry, 868
　measurement of, 158–159
Profitability management, 298, 299(exh.)
Profit centers, 988, 989(table)
　evaluating performance using flexible budgeting, 991–993, 992(exh.)
Profit margin, 268, 994, 1179, 1179(exh.)
Pro forma statements, 898
Project costing, job order costing versus, 758–759
Promissory notes, 358
　accounting entries for, 360–361
　computations for, 358–360
　dishonored, 361
Property, plant, and equipment, 256
　see also Plant assets
Property taxes, 432
Proprietorship, *see* Owner's equity
Public companies, 49
Pull-through production, 829
Purchase(s)
　of assets by incurring liabilities, 18
　of assets with cash, 17–18
　control of, 314(fig.), 314–315, 316–317(fig.)
　foreign, 1240
　group, 461
　of interest from a partner, 1232
　of materials, 708
　under periodic inventory system, 307–308
　under perpetual inventory system, 302–304
　of treasury stock, 556
Purchase order(s), 315, 316(fig.), 317(fig.), 708
Purchase order lead time, 134
Purchase request, 708
Purchase requisitions, 315, 316(fig.), 317(fig.)
Purchases account, 307
Purchases discounts, 318–319
Purchases journal, 1216, 1217(exh.), 1218, 1218(exh.)

Purchases Returns and Allowances account, 308
Push-through method, 829
PVA (process value analysis), 823–824

Qualitative characteristics, 249
　of accounting information, 248–250, 249(fig.)
Quality
　costs of, 669
　evolution of concept, 1140–1141
　in just-in-time operating philosophy, 830
　measurement of, *see* Quality measurement
　recognition of, 1141–1142
　return on, 1140
　see also Continuous improvement
Quality management, 1126–1130
　management information systems in, 1128–1130
Quality measurement
　evaluating costs of quality and, 1135–1137, 1136–1138(exh.), 1139
　financial measures for, 1130–1132, 1131(table)
　nonfinancial measures for, 1132–1134, 1135(table), 1139(fig.), 1139–1140
　for services, 1134
Quality of earnings, 576, 576–581
　accounting method and estimate choices and, 631–633
　corporate income statement and, 576–577, 577(exh.)
　effect on cash flows and performance measures, 580–581
　gains and losses and, 579
　nonoperating items and, 579–580
　reasons to study, 576
　write-downs and restructurings and, 579
Queue time, 831
Quickbooks General Ledger Software, 203
Quick ratio, 340, 1177, 1178(exh.)

Rate of return on investment, minimum, in capital investment analysis, 1100–1101
Ratio analysis, 1176, 1176–1183
　for cash flow adequacy evaluation, 1181, 1182(exh.)
　of cash-generating efficiency, 620–621
　graphing, 272(fig.), 272–273
　of liquidity, 267

for liquidity evaluation, 1177, 1177(fig.), 1178(exh.)
for long-term solvency evaluation, 1180–1181, 1180(exh.)
for market strength evaluation, 1181, 1182(exh.), 1183
of profitability, 268–273
for profitability evaluation, 1179(exh.), 1179–1180
Real accounts, 205
Realizable value, 400
Real-time posting, 204
Receivable turnover, 343, 344, **1177,** 1178(exh.)
Receiving reports, 315, 316(fig.), 317(fig.), 708
Recognition, 116, 116–117
of liabilities, 424
Recognition point, 116
Recourse, factoring and, 345
Redemption price, 518, 552
Registered bonds, 503, 503–504
Regression analysis, 865
Regulatory agencies, as users of accounting information, 10
Relevance, 249, 249–250
Relevant range, 860
Reliability, 250
Report(s)
activity-based costing, 819
for financial performance evaluation, 1167
see also Financial statement(s); specific financial statements
Reporting currency, 1241
Reporting stage of management cycle
activity-based cost information and, 818
balanced scorecard and, 985, 985(fig.)
budgeting and, 898
capital investment analysis and, 1099
cost behavior and, 856–857
cost information and, 701
financial performance evaluation and, 1162–1163
management accounting and, 663–664, 664(exh.)
management information systems and, 130
pricing and, 1057
product cost information and, 748–749
short-run decision analysis and, 1022
standard costs and, 941
Report of management's responsibilities, in annual reports, 53

Research and development costs, 474–475
Reserve(s)
cash, 343
international business and, 590
Reserve for Bad Debts account, 353
Residual equity, 548
Residual income (RI), 994, 994–995, 996(exh.)
Residual value, 462
Responsibility accounting, 987, 987–998
responsibility centers and, 987–988
see also Cost centers; Investment centers; Profit centers; Revenue centers
Responsibility centers, 987, 987–988
see also Cost centers; Investment centers; Profit centers; Revenue centers
Restatement, of foreign subsidiary financial statements, 1241–1242
Restriction on retained earnings, 590
Restructurings, 579
Retail businesses
cost reporting and inventory accounting in, 713–714, 714(fig.)
transfer pricing in, 1073, 1074(fig.), 1075
Retail method, 401, 401–402, 402(table)
Retained earnings, 16, 16–17, **588,** 590
restrictions on, 590
statement of cash flows and, 632
Retained Earnings account, 557
closing Dividends account balance to, 210, 210(exh.)
closing Income Summary account balance to, 209–210, 210(exh.)
Retirement
of bonds, 518–519
of treasury stock, 557–558
Return on assets, 268, 268–270, 269(fig.), 270(fig.), 1179(exh.), **1180**
Return on assets pricing, 1062, 1062–1063
Return on equity, 271, 271–272, 272(fig.), **545,** 545–546, 1179(exh.), **1180**
Return on investment (ROI), 993, 993(exh.), 993–994, 995(fig.)
Return on quality (ROQ), 140
Revenue(s), 17, 18–19, **158**
accrued, adjustments for, 171(fig.), 171–172

controllable, 988
deferred, adjustments for, 170(fig.), 170–171
irrelevant, 1023
nonoperating, 262–263
recognition of, 160–161
unearned, 170(fig.), 170–171, 431
Revenue centers, 988, 989(table)
Revenue expenditures, 459
Revenue recognition, 160, 160–161
Reversing entries, 214, 214–215
Reviewing stage of management cycle
activity-based cost information and, 818
balanced scorecard and, 984–985
budgeting and, 898
capital investment analysis and, 1099
cost behavior and, 856–857
cost information and, 701
financial performance evaluation and, 1162
management accounting and, 663
management information systems and, 130
pricing and, 1056–1057
product cost information and, 748
short-run decision analysis and, 1021–1022
standard costs and, 940–941
RI (residual income), 994–995, 996(exh.)
Risk assessment, 310
Risk Management Association, 1168
Robert Morris Associates, 1168
ROI (return on investment), 993(exh.), 993–994, 995(fig.)
Rolling forecasts, 898
ROQ (return on quality), 140
Ruled lines, in financial reports, 136
Rule-of-thumb measures, 1165

Salaries, 428
partnerships and, 1230–1231
Sales
of bonds between interest dates, 515–516, 517(fig.)
cash flows to, 621
collecting on, 353
cost of, 262
foreign, 1239
gross, 261
net, 261
under periodic inventory system, 308–309
under perpetual inventory system, 304–305
of plant assets, 466–468
terms of, 301–302
of treasury stock, 556–557

Sales budget, **901**, 901–902, 903(exh.)
Sales discounts, **301**, 318
Sales forecasts, **902**
Sales invoices, 710
Sales journal, 1213–1216, 1215(exh.)
Sales mix, **869**, 869(fig.)
Sales mix decisions, **1030**
  incremental analysis for, 1030–1032, 1031(exh.)
Sales returns, 305
Sales Returns and Allowances account, **305**
Sales taxes, in sales journal, 1216, 1217(exh.)
Sales taxes payable, 427–428
Salvage value, 462
Sarbanes-Oxley Act, 254, 676, **1164**
  financial reporting under, 1164
Scatter diagrams, **863**, 863–864, 864(fig.)
SDWTs (self-directed work teams), 132
Seasonal cycle, managing cash needs during, 342(fig.), 342–343
Secured bonds, **503**
Securities and Exchange Commission (SEC), **10**, 49
  reports required by, 663, 676, 1168
Securitization, **345**, 345–346
Segment(s), **584**
Segment margins, **1028**
Segment profitability decisions, incremental analysis for, 1028, 1029(exh.), 1030
Seiberling, Frank, 617
Self-directed work teams (SDWTs), 132
Selling and administrative activities, activity-based costing for, 827–828, 828(exh.)
Selling and administrative expense budget, **907**, 907(exh.)
Sell or process-further decisions, **1032**
  incremental analysis for, 1032–1033, 1033(exh.)
Separate entity, **12**
  corporation as, 12–15
Service(s)
  measuring quality of, 134
  pricing, 1063–1065
Service businesses
  activity-based management in, 820–821, 821(fig.)
  cost allocation in, 724–725
  cost reporting in, 713, 714(fig.)
  cost-volume-profit analysis for, 874–875
  job order costing in, 757, 758(fig.)
  nonfinancial data in, 674, 675(exh.)
  transfer pricing in, 1073, 1074(fig.), 1075
  value-adding and nonvalue-adding activities in, 822, 823(table)
Share buybacks, 557
Shares of stock, **540**
Shipping documents, 710
Short-run decision(s), incremental analysis for, *see* Incremental analysis
Short-run decision analysis, 1018–1037, **1020**, 1021(fig.)
  incremental analysis for, *see* Incremental analysis
  management cycle and, 1020–1022, 1022(fig.)
Short-term financial assets, **340**, 340–365
  accounts receivable and, *see* Accounts receivable
  cash and cash equivalents and, 346–347
  credit policies and, 343–344, 344(fig.), 345(fig.)
  financing receivables and, 345–346
  investments as, 347–350
  managing cash needs during seasonal cycles and, 342(fig.), 342–343
  notes receivable, *see* Promissory notes
Short-term investments, **347**, 347–512
  available-for-sale securities, 350
  dividend and interest income and, 350
  held-to-maturity securities, 348
  trading securities, 348–350
Significant influence, 1244–1245
Simple capital structure, **587**
Simple interest, **1104**, 1251
Single-step income statement, **264**, 265(exh.), 266, 266(exh.)
Six Sigma quality standard, 1140
Social security tax, 430
Software costs, 475
Sold units, in job order costing system, 755–756
Sole proprietorships, **12**, 12–13, 1227
  balance sheet for, 257
Solvency, long-term, evaluation of, 1180(exh.), 1180–1181
Source documents, **124**, 203–204, **204**
Special order decisions, **1026**
  incremental analysis for, 1026–1027, 1027(exh.)
Special-purpose journals, 1213–1223
Specific identification method, **390**
Split-off point, **1032**
Spreadsheets, **201**
Stakeholders, **983**
Standard cost(s), **940**, 940–941
  computing, 942–944
  management cycle and, 940–941, 941(fig.)
  total standard unit cost, 943–944
Standard costing, **706**, 706–707, **940**, 940–942
  relevance in today's business environment, 941–942
  see also Variance analysis
Standard direct labor cost, **942**, 942–943
Standard direct materials cost, **942**
Standard fixed overhead rate, **943**
Standard manufacturing overhead cost, **943**
Standard & Poor's, 1168
Standard variable overhead rate, **943**
Start-up and organization costs, **544**
Stated ratios, 1229–1231
Stated value, **553**
Statement of cash flows, **24**, 24–25, 614–635, **617**
  cash-generating efficiency and, 620–621
  classification of cash flows and, 618–620, 619(fig.)
  financing activities and, 631–633
  format of, 620
  free cash flow and, 621–623
  international use of, 620
  investing activities and, 628–631
  operating activities and, 623–628, 624–626(exh.), 625(fig.)
  purposes of, 618
  uses of, 618
Statement of changes in stockholders' equity, *see* Statement of stockholders' equity
Statement of cost of goods manufactured, **711**, 711–713, 712(exh.)
Statement of financial position, *See* Balance sheet
Statement of retained earnings, **22**
Statement of stockholders' equity, **22**, **588**, 589(exh.), 590
State unemployment insurance tax, 430
Stock
  authorized, 543
  book value of, 594–595
  common, *see* Common stock

earnings per share and, 263, 586–588
ex-dividend, 549
Initial public offerings of, 543–544
issued, 548
long-term investments in, 1244–1249, 1245(table)
outstanding, 548
par value, 543
preferred, *see* Preferred stock
share buybacks and, 557
shares of, 540
treasury, *see* Treasury stock
Stock certificates, 543
Stock dividends, 590, 590–593
Stock Dividends Declared account, 592
Stockholders, 14, 540
Stockholders' equity, 16, 257
components of, 547–548, 548(fig.)
Stockholders' equity accounts, 120, 121(fig.)
Stock issuance, 552–555
for noncash assets, 554–555
of no-par stock, 554
of par value stock, 553–554
Stock markets, European, 547
Stock option plans, 546, 547
Stock splits, 593, 593–594
Storage time, 831
Straight-line method, 463, 509
for amortization of bond discount, 509–510
for amortization of bond premium, 513
for depreciation, 463
Strategic objectives, 661
Strategic planning, 894
Subscriber lists, 474
Subsidiaries, 1249
Subsidiary ledgers, 1213–1214
Successful efforts method, 471
Summary of Significant Accounting Policies, in annual reports, 52
Sunk costs, 1023
Supplementary information notes, in annual reports, 54–55
Supply chain (network), 662, 662–663, **819,** 819–820, 820(fig.)
Supply-chain management, 204, 388
Support services, 664
in value chain analysis, 665–666

T account, 121–122, **122**
Tangible assets, 456(fig.)
see also Plant assets
Target(s), linking of goals to, 998
Target costing, 1065, 1065–1070, 1066–1068(fig.)

Taxable income, 581
Tax authorities, as users of accounting information, 10
Technology, 473(table)
airline industry pricing and, 863
bar codes and, 299
cost of processing checks and, 1024
for counting coins, 1102
ecommerce and, 172
enterprise resource planning systems and, 128
event-to-knowledge management and, 205
financial information available on Internet and, 1168
flexible budget and, 945
interest and amortization tables and, 514
internal controls and, 314
inventory turnover and, 386
LIFO inventory valuation and, 394
networking and, 201
online shopping, 1060
product costs and, 705
project costing and, 759
rolling forecasts and, 898
simplicity and, 988
Web sales and, 301
see also Computerized accounting systems; Internet
Telecommunications industry, cash flows in, 622
Television talent, cost of, 724
Temporary accounts, 205
Theoretical capacity, 858
Theory of constraints (TOC), 670
Throughput time, 831
Time, in new manufacturing environment, 831
Time and materials pricing, 1063, 1063–1065
Time and motion studies, 863
Time cards, 708
Time periods, for compounding interest, 1256–1257
Time value of money, 1103–1107, 1251–1261
accounting applications of, 1257–1261
future value and, 1252(table), 1252–1253, 1254(table)
interest and, 1104, 1251–1252
present value and, 1104–1107, 1253–1256, 1255(table), 1256(table)
time periods and, 1256–1257
TOC (theory of constraints), 670
Total cost curve, pricing and, 1058, 1059(fig.)

Total direct labor cost variance, 950, 950–951, 952(fig.)
Total direct materials cost variance, 948
Total fixed overhead variance, 956
Total manufacturing costs, 711
Total manufacturing overhead variance, 954
Total quality management (TQM), 669, 1130, 1141
Total revenue curve, pricing and, 1058, 1059(fig.)
Total variable overhead variance, 954, 954–955, 955(fig.)
TQM (total quality management), 669, **1130,** 1141
Trade credit, 351
Trade discount, 301
Trademarks, 473(table)
Trading on the equity, 500
Trading securities, 348, 348–350
Transactions, *see* Business transactions
Transfer prices, 1070, 1070–1075
cost-plus, 1071
developing, 1071(fig.), 1071–1073, 1072(exh.)
market, 1071
measuring performance using, 1073, 1074(exh.)
negotiated, 1071
in retail companies, 1073, 1074(fig.), 1075
in service organizations, 1073, 1074(fig.), 1075
Transportation in, 303
Treasury stock, 546, **555,** 555–558
purchase of, 556
retirement of, 557–558
sale of, 556–557
statement of cash flows and, 632–633, 633(exh.)
Trend analysis, 1171, 1171–1173, 1173(exh.), 1173(fig.)
Trial balance, 121(exh.), **131,** 131–133, 132(table)
adjusted, 172–173, 173(exh.), 174(exh.)
post-closing, 213, 213(exh.)

Unamortized Bond Discount account, 506
Uncollectible accounts, 351, 351–358
allowance method for, 352–353
direct charge-off method for, 351–352
estimating expense of, 353–357
recovery of written off accounts receivable and, 357–358
writing off, 357

Uncollectible Accounts Expense account, 352
Underapplied overhead costs, 716
Understandability, 249
Underwriters, 543
Unearned revenues, 170, 170(fig.), 170–171, **431**
Unemployment insurance tax, 430
Unincorporated businesses, 1227–1234
Unions, as users of accounting information, 10
Unit(s), accounting for, process cost report and, 789, 791, 794, 795(exh.)
Unit-level activities, 824
Unlimited liability, of partnerships, 1228
Unrealized Loss on Long-Term Investments account, 1246, 1247–1248
Unsecured bonds, 503
Useful life, estimated, 462–463
Usefulness, 249

Vacation pay liability, 433
Valuation, 117, 117–118
   of assets, 1258
   of bonds, using present value, 507–508
   of liabilities, 424
Value
   carrying (book), 168, 454, 594–595
   face, bonds issued at, 504–505
   future, *see* Future value
   market, 400
   maturity, of promissory notes, 360
   par, 543
   present, *see* Present value
   realizable, 400
   residual (disposal; salvage), 462
   stated, 553
   time, of money, *see* Time value of money
Value added, economic, 996(exh.), 996–997, 997(fig.)
Value-adding activities, 669, 822
   process value analysis and, 823–824
   in service organizations, 822, 823(table)
Value-adding costs, 703
Value-based management (VBM), 823
Value chain(s), 664, 819, 819–820
   Internet support of, 666
Value chain analysis, 664–668, 665(fig.)
   advantages of, 666
   management's support of, 666–668, 667(exh.)
   primary processes and support services and, 665–666
Values, core, 856
Variable budgets, in variance analysis, 944–946, 945–947(exh.)
Variable cost(s), 703, 858, 858–860, 859(fig.)
   linear relationships and relevant range and, 859–860, 860(fig.), 861(fig.)
   operating capacity and, 858–859
Variable costing, 991
   profit center performance evaluation using, 991–993, 992(exh.)
Variable overhead efficiency variance, 955, 955–956
Variable overhead spending variance, 955
Variance(s), 940
Variance analysis, 944, 944–959
   controlling costs using, 946, 947(fig.), 948
   direct labor variances and, 950–952
   direct materials variances and, 948–950
   evaluating managers' performances using cost variances and, 959, 960(exh.)
   flexible budgets in, 944–946, 945–947(exh.)
   manufacturing overhead variances and, 952–959
VBM (value-based management), 823
Vendors, quality and, 1133
Vendor's invoice, 708

Vertical analysis, (fig.)1075(exh.), **1173,** 1174(exh.), 1174(fig.), 1175(fig.), 1176
Voluntary association, partnerships as, 1228
Vouchers Payable account, 438

Wages, 428
Wall Street Journal, 1168
Whistle-blowing, 580
Withdrawal of partners, 1233–1234
Work cells, 830
Work environment, in just-in-time operating philosophy, 831
Work force, in just-in-time operating philosophy, 830
Working capital, 267
Working papers, 215
Work in Process Inventory account, 708, 710, 711, 714–715, 716
   backflush costing and, 832–833
   process costing and, 787
Work sheet, 215, 215–224
   for merchandising business, 1205–1210
   preparing, 216(exh.), 216–218, 217(exh.), 218, 219–221(exh.), 222
   preparing financial statements and, 223–224, 224(exh.), 225(exh.)
   recording adjusting entries and, 222, 223(exh.)
   recording closing entries and, 222
Write-downs, 579
Write-offs, 579
Writing off uncollectible accounts, 357–358
Wurman, Richard Saul, 988

XBRL (extensible Business Reporting Language), 204

Years
   base, 1170
   fiscal, 159
   partial, depreciation for, 476–477
Yield, cash flow, 621

Zero coupon bonds, 509